HOOVER'S GUIDE TO THE TOP NEW YORK COMPANIES

The Reference Press
Austin, Texas

The Reference Press, Inc.

10   9   8   7   6   5   4   3   2   1

Publisher Cataloging-In-Publication Data

Hoover's Guide to the Top New York Companies.

   Includes indexes.
   1. Business enterprises — Directories. 2. Corporations — Directories.
HF3010   338.7

Profiles from *Hoover's Handbooks* are also available on America Online, Bloomberg Financial Network, CompuServe, Dow Jones News Retrieval, eWorld, LEXIS-NEXIS, Microsoft Network, Reuters NewMedia, SandPoint Hoover, and on the Internet at Hoover's Online (http://www.hoovers.com), Pathfinder (http://pathfinder.com), InfoSeek (http://www.infoseek.com), PAWWS Financial Network (http://www.pawws.secapl.com), and infoMarket (http://www.infomkt.ibm.com).

ISBN 1-878753-59-2 trade paper

This book was produced by The Reference Press on Apple Macintosh computers using Adobe's PageMaker software and fonts from its Clearface and Futura families, Claris Corporation's FileMaker Pro, Em Software, Inc.'s Xdata, and Quark, Inc.'s QuarkXPress software. Cover design is by Daniel Pelavin. Electronic prepress and printing were done by Victor Graphics, Inc. in Baltimore, Maryland. Text paper is Postmark White 60# (manufactured by Union Camp). Cover stock is 10 point, coated one side, film laminated.

US AND WORLD DIRECT SALES
The Reference Press, Inc.
6448 Highway 290 E., Suite E-104
Austin, TX 78723
Phone: 512-454-7778
Fax: 512-454-9401
e-mail: refpress6@aol.com

US WHOLESALER ORDERS
Warner Publisher Services
Book Division
9210 King Palm Drive
Tampa, FL 33619
Phone: 800-873-BOOK
Fax: 813-664-8193

US BOOKSELLERS AND JOBBERS
Little, Brown and Co.
200 West Street
Waltham, MA 02154
Phone: 800-759-0190
Fax: 617-890-0875

EUROPE
William Snyder Publishing
5, Five Mile Drive
Oxford OX2 8HT
England
Phone & fax: +44-(01)86-551-3186
e-mail: 100072.2511@compuserve.com

THE REFERENCE PRESS

Founder: Gary Hoover
Chairman, President, CEO, and Publisher: Patrick J. Spain

Senior Managing Editor - Editorial: James R. Talbot
Managing Editor - Production: George Sutton
Senior Contributing Editors: Alta M. Campbell, Alan Chai
Senior Editor of Online Publishing: Matt Manning
Senior Editor: Thomas Trotter
Editors: Wilson Allen, Chris Barton, Patrice Sarath
Research Manager: Sherri M. Hale
Desktop Publishing Manager: Holly Hans Jackson
Researchers: Erin Carson, Chuck Green, Sarah Hallman, Jim Harris, Jenni Maiberger, Peter T. Nelson, Brian Pedder, Anouk Zijlma
Research Assistants: Melonie Hosea, Chelsea Kelly, Erica Taylor
Senior Writers: Joy Aiken, Stuart Hampton, Barbara M. Spain, Jeffrey A. Twining
Writers: Rebecca W. Chastenet de Géry, Michael Daecher, Margaret Dornbusch, Dean Folias, Joshua Hinsdale, Terry Hudson, Lesley Kees, Paul Mitchell, Lisa C. Norman, Alice Wightman
Financial Editors: Sam Gammon, Jenny Hill, Dixie Peterson, Dennis L. Sutton
Style Editors: Calvin Cahan, Jeanne Minnich, Anthony Shuga, John Willis
Senior Proofreader: Dawn Albright
Fact Checkers/Proofreaders: Casey Barton, Hank Bass, Yvonne A. Cullinan, Allan Gill, Melanie Hall, Diane Lee, Nancy Nowlin, Carole Sage
Database Editors: Stacey Chambers, Tweed Chouinard, J. Kirkland Greer III, Karen Hill
Desktop Publishers: Michelle de Ybarrondo, Kevin Dodds, Stephanie Dodds, JoAnn Estrada, Brenda Forsythe, Gregory Gosdin, Louanne Jones
Senior Brand Manager: Leslie A. Wolke
Brand Manager: Richard Finley
Online Production: Kyna Horton, Jeffrey Sandt, Aries Solis
Systems Manager: John Padwick

Senior Vice President, Sales and Marketing: Dana L. Smith
Vice President, Electronic Publishing: Tom Linehan
Treasurer and Controller: Deborah L. Dunlap
Fulfillment Manager: Beth DeVore
Publicity Manager: Jani Spede
Office Manager: Tammy Fisher
Sales and Marketing Analyst: William Cargill
Customer Service Manager: Rhonda T. Mitchell
Advertising Coordinator: Michelle Swann
Marketing and Publicity Coordinator: Angela Young
Administrative Assistants: Denise Mansfield, Kristie Wehe
Shipping Clerk: Michael Febonio

The Reference Press Mission Statement

1. To produce business information products and services of the highest quality, accuracy, and readability.

2. To make that information available whenever, wherever, and however our customers want it through mass distribution at affordable prices.

3. To continually expand our range of products and services and our markets for those products and services.

4. To reward our employees, suppliers, and shareholders based on their contributions to the success of our enterprise.

5. To hold to the highest ethical business standards, erring on the side of generosity when in doubt.

ABBREVIATIONS

AFL-CIO – American Federation of Labor and Congress of Industrial Organizations

AMA – American Medical Association

AMEX – American Stock Exchange

ARM – adjustable rate mortgage

ASIC – application-specific integrated circuit

ATM – asynchronous transfer mode

CAD/CAM – computer-aided design/computer-aided manufacturing

CASE – computer-aided software engineering

CD-ROM – compact disc – read-only memory

CEO – chief executive officer

CFO – chief financial officer

CISC – complex instruction set computer

CMOS – complementary metal oxide silicon

COO – chief operating officer

DAT – digital audio tape

DOD – Department of Defense

DOE – Department of Energy

DOS – disk operating system

DOT – Department of Transportation

DRAM – dynamic random-access memory

EPA – Environmental Protection Agency

EPROM – erasable programmable read-only memory

EPS – earnings per share

ESOP – employee stock ownership plan

EU – European Union

EVP – executive vice president

FCC – Federal Communications Commission

FDA – Food and Drug Administration

FDIC – Federal Deposit Insurance Corporation

FPGA – field programmable gate array

FSLIC – Federal Savings and Loan Insurance Corporation

FTC – Federal Trade Commission

FTP – file transfer protocol

GUI – graphical user interface

HMO – health maintenance organization

HR – human resources

HTML – hypertext markup language

IC – integrated circuit

ICC – Interstate Commerce Commission

IPO – initial public offering

IRS – Internal Revenue Service

ISDN – Integrated Services Digital Network

LAN – local-area network

LBO – leveraged buyout

LCD – liquid crystal display

LNG – liquefied natural gas

LP – limited partnership

Ltd. – limited

MIPS – million instructions per second

NAFTA – North American Free Trade Agreement

NASA – National Aeronautics and Space Administration

Nasdaq – National Association of Securities Dealers Automated Quotations

NATO – North Atlantic Treaty Organization

NYSE – New York Stock Exchange

OCR – optical character recognition

OEM – original equipment manufacturer

OPEC – Organization of Petroleum Exporting Countries

OS – operating system

OSHA – Occupational Safety and Health Administration

OTC – over-the-counter

PBX – private branch exchange

PCMCIA – Personal Computer Memory Card International Association

P/E – price-to-earnings ratio

PPO – preferred provider organization

RAM – random-access memory

R&D – research and development

RBOC – Regional Bell Operating Company

REIT – real estate investment trust

RISC – reduced instruction set computer

ROA – return on assets

ROE – return on equity

ROI – return on investment

ROM – read-only memory

S&L – savings and loan

SEC – Securities and Exchange Commission

SEVP – senior executive vice president

SIC – Standard Industrial Classification

SPARC – scalable processor architecture

SVP – senior vice president

VAR – value-added remarketer

VAT – value-added tax

VC – vice chairman

VP – vice president

WAN – wide-area network

www – world wide web

CONTENTS

ABOUT *HOOVER'S GUIDE TO THE TOP NEW YORK COMPANIES*

Brash, impatient, and quick to capitalize, New York City is the heart of the world's most powerful economy and culture. From the time of its establishment as a Dutch fur trading post in the 17th century, the Big Apple has always traded on its unique position as the New World's commercial emporium. Flush with cash from successful shipping interests, enterprising New Yorkers made the city an important banking and manufacturing center in the early 1800s, helping to wrest America away from its dependence on England. Infamous robber barons transformed the country from their New York City boardrooms as they built empires of railroads, steel, and oil in the late 19th century. Now, just a few years from the dawn of the next millennium, New York City businesses are poised to take advantage of being at the crossroads of a new, truly global economy.

Hoover's Guide to the Top New York Companies is just one of a series of regional guides produced by The Reference Press. Guides to the top Chicago, San Francisco Bay Area, and Texas companies have already been published, and a guide to Southern California companies will follow shortly. These books complement our other publications, which include *Hoover's Handbook of American Companies*, *Hoover's Handbook of World Business*, *Hoover's Handbook of Emerging Companies*, *Hoover's Guide to Private Companies*, *Hoover's Guide to Computer Companies*, and *Hoover's MasterList of America's Top 2,500 Employers*, among others. Our company profiles and other information are also available electronically on diskette and CD-ROM and on online services (e.g., America Online, CompuServe, and the Microsoft Network) and the Internet (e.g., Hoover's Online at http://www.hoovers.com).

This book is the product of extensive research. Our first step was to identify the region that we would be examining. For the purposes of this book, we consider the New York area to include, besides New York City, all municipalities in the following metropolitan statistical areas (MSAs): Danbury, New Haven-Meriden, and Stamford, Connecticut; Bergen-Passaic, Jersey City, Middlesex-Somerset-Hunterdon, Monmouth-Ocean, and Newark, New Jersey; and Nassau-Suffolk, New York. We realize that everyone will have a different concept of what makes up the "New York area," but this definition seemed the fairest that we could come up with.

Next, we consulted our extensive database of company information to identify public and private businesses headquartered in the region. We then turned to other sources to look for companies we may have missed, such as *Crain's New York Business* list of leading private companies and other trade publication lists. We contacted all of the companies that were candidates for inclusion in the book to obtain or update our information. Most companies were helpful and cooperative; some were not. For those companies that did not cooperate, we obtained the most reliable information we could find and in some cases made estimates regarding revenue. In all such cases, the revenue figures are marked as estimates.

Hoover's Guide to the Top New York Companies covers all public companies in the region, all private companies with revenues greater than $200 million, and all private companies with revenues of less than $200 million for whom we could compile accurate information. In addition to traditional for-profit companies, we have included partnerships (e.g., KKR and Ernst & Young), nonprofit organizations (e.g., Teachers Insurance), universities (e.g., Columbia and CUNY), and government-owned agencies (e.g., MTA New York City

Transit). We have included these enterprises because we believe they are as important to driving the region's economy and creating jobs as the for-profit sector.

After determining our universe of New York–area businesses, we selected 150 of them for in-depth profiles. These companies range from telecommunications behemoth AT&T Corp. (1994 revenues of $75.1 billion) to tiny hot-dog chain Nathan's Famous (1995 revenues of $26.2 million). We profiled 106 of the largest companies in our two-page format, each with up to 10 years of financial data and a separate section on its history. We also included long profiles of a few unique New York enterprises with colorful histories (e.g., auctioneer Sotheby's Holdings and ethnic food manufacturer Goya Foods). The remainder of the profiles (mostly of interesting or fast-growing companies under $1 billion in sales) are in our one-page format, with up to 6 years of financial data and a shorter history integrated into the overview of the company. In choosing these companies, we have tried to represent the full spectrum of New York–area businesses. All 150 of the companies in the book have capsule profiles.

This book consists of 6 components:

1. The first section, "Using the Profiles," describes the contents of the profiles and explains the ways in which we gathered and compiled our data.

2. The second section is an overview of the New York area that discusses the economic life of the area.

3. Next we have included "A List-Lover's Compendium," which contains lists of the largest and fastest-growing companies in the book as well as selected lists from other sources to provide different viewpoints.

4. The fourth section of the book contains the 150 in-depth profiles of New York–area businesses. The first 106 profiles are in our long, two-page format. The next 44 are in our medium-length, one-page format. The profiles are arranged alphabetically within each section.

5. The next section provides capsule profiles of 1,390 companies. If an in-depth profile also exists for a company, the page number of that profile is included in the entry for easier reference.

6. The book concludes with three indexes: (1) the companies organized by industry group-ings, (2) the companies organized by headquarters location, and (3) the main index of the book, containing all the names of brands, companies, and people mentioned in the in-depth profiles.

As always, we hope you find our books useful and informative. We invite your comments via phone (512-454-7778), fax (512-454-9401), mail (P.O. Box 140375, Austin, TX 78714-0375), or e-mail (comments@hoovers.com).

The Editors
Austin, Texas
January 1996

Using the Profiles

Organization of the Profiles

The company profiles are presented in either a one-page or two-page format. The two-page profiles contain extensive historical information, in addition to up to 10 years of financial data. The one-page profiles offer a shorter history and up to 6 years of financial data. In both formats the profiles are presented in alphabetical order. This alphabetization is word by word. We have shown the full legal name of the enterprise at the top of the page, unless it is too long, in which case you will find it above the address in the Where section of the profile. If a company name is also a person's name, like Estée Lauder, it will be alphabetized under the first name; if a company name starts with initials, like J.P. Morgan, look for it under the initials (here, JP). All company names (past and present) used in the profiles are indexed in the last index in the book.

Each profile lists the exchange where the company's stock is traded if it is public, the ticker symbol used by the stock exchange, and the company's fiscal year-end. This data can be found at the top left of the second page for two-page profiles and in the upper left corner of the How Much chart for one-page profiles.

The annual financial information contained in most profiles is current through fiscal year-ends occurring as late as September 1995. For certain nonpublic entities, such up-to-date information was not available. In those cases, we have used the most current data we could find. We have included nonfinancial developments, such as officer changes, through December 1995.

Overview

In this section we have tried to give a thumbnail description of the company and what it does. The description will usually include information on the company's strategy, reputation, and ownership. In the one-page profiles we also provide a brief history of the company, including the year of founding and the names of the founders where possible. We recommend that you read this section first.

When

This section, which appears only in the two-page profiles, reflects our belief that every enterprise is the sum of its history, and that you have to know where you came from in order to know where you are going. While some companies have very little historical awareness and were unable to help us much, and other companies are just plain boring, we think the vast majority of the enterprises in the book have colorful backgrounds. When we could find information, we tried to focus on the people who made the enterprise what it is today. We have found these histories to be full of twists and ironies; they can make for some fascinating, quick reading.

Who

Here we list the names of the people who run the company, insofar as space allows. In the case of public companies, we have shown the ages and pay levels of key officers. In some cases the published data are for last year although the company has announced promotions or retirements since year-end. We have tried to show current officers, with their pay for the latest year available. The pay represents cash compensation, including bonuses, but excludes stock option programs. Our best advice is that officers' pay levels are clear indicators of who the board of directors thinks are the most important on the management team.

While companies are free to structure their management titles any way they please, most modern corporations follow standard practices. The ultimate power in any corporation lies with the shareholders, who elect a board of directors, usually including officers or "insiders" as well as individuals from outside the company. The chief officer, the person on whose desk the buck stops, is usually called the chief executive officer (CEO). Normally, he or she is also the chairman of the board. As corporate management has become more complex, it is common for the CEO to have a "right-hand person" who oversees the day-to-day operations of the company, allowing the

CEO plenty of time to focus on strategy and long-term issues. This right-hand person is usually designated the chief operating officer (COO) and is often the president of the company. In other cases one person is both chairman and president.

A multitude of other titles exists, including chief financial officer (CFO), chief administrative officer, and vice chairman (VC). We have always tried to include the CFO, the chief legal officer, and the chief personnel or human resources officer. The people named in the profiles are indexed at the back of the book.

Where

Here we include the company's headquarters street address and phone and fax numbers as available. The back of the book includes an index of companies by headquarters locations.

We have also included as much information as we could gather and fit on the geographical distribution of the company's business, including sales and profit data. Note that these profit numbers, like those in the What section (described below), are usually operating or pretax profits rather than net profits. Operating profits are generally those before financing costs (interest income and payments) and before taxes, which are considered costs attributable to the whole company rather than to one division or part of the world. For this reason the net income figures (in the How Much section) are usually much lower, since they are after interest and taxes. Pretax profits are after interest but before taxes. When sales and operating profits by region were not available or were not appropriate, we have published other measures of geographic diversity. For example, for regional retailers we have listed the number of stores by state.

What

This section lists as many of the company's products, services, brand names, divisions, subsidiaries, and joint ventures as we could fit. We have tried to include all its major lines and all familiar brand names. The nature of this section varies by industry, company, and the amount of information available. If the company publishes sales and profit information by type of business, we have included it. The brand, division, and subsidiary names are listed in the last index in the book.

Key Competitors

In this section we have listed those other companies that compete with the profiled company. This feature is included as a quick way to locate similar companies and compare them. The universe of key competitors includes all public companies and all private companies with sales in excess of $500 million. In a few instances we have identified smaller private companies as key competitors. All the companies in the book are listed by broad industry groups in the first index at the back of the book.

How Much

Here we have tried to present as much data about each enterprise's financial performance as we could compile in the allocated space. While the information varies somewhat from industry to industry and is less complete in the case of private companies that do not release these data (though we have tried always to provide annual sales and employment), the following information is generally present:

A 10-year table (6 years for the one-page profiles), with relevant annualized compound growth rates, covering:

• Fiscal year sales (year-end assets for most financial companies)

• Fiscal year net income (before accounting changes)

• Fiscal year net income as a percent of sales (as a percent of assets for most financial firms)

• Fiscal year earnings per share (EPS, fully diluted)

• Stock price high, low, and close (for the calendar year unless otherwise noted)

• High and low price/earnings ratio (P/E, for the calendar year unless otherwise noted)

• Fiscal year dividends per share

• Fiscal year-end book value (shareholders' equity per share)

• Fiscal year-end or average number of employees

All revenue numbers are as reported by the company in its annual report.

The 10-year information on the number of employees (6 years on the one-page profiles) is intended to aid the reader interested in knowing whether a company has a long-term trend of increasing or decreasing employment. As far as we know, we are the only company that publishes this information in print format.

The year at the top of each column in the How Much section is the year in which the company's fiscal year actually ends. Thus, data for a company with a February 28, 1995 year-end are shown in the 1995 column. Stock prices for companies with fiscal year-ends between January and April are for the prior calendar year and are so footnoted on the chart. For companies with fiscal years in May or June, the 1995 stock data are for the 5 or 6 months preceding the fiscal year-end. This fact is also footnoted on the chart.

Key year-end statistics in this section generally show the financial strength of the enterprise, including:

• Debt ratio (total debt as a percent of combined total debt and shareholders' equity)

• Return on equity (net income divided by the average of beginning and ending common shareholders' equity)

• Cash and marketable securities

• Current ratio (ratio of current assets to current liabilities)

• Total long-term debt, including capital lease obligations

• Number of shares of common stock outstanding (less treasury shares)

• Dividend yield (fiscal year dividends per share divided by the calendar year-end closing stock price)

• Dividend payout (fiscal year dividends divided by fiscal year EPS)

• Market value at calendar year-end (calendar year-end closing stock price multiplied by fiscal year-end number of shares outstanding)

• Research and development as a percent of sales, when available (one-page profiles only)

• Advertising as a percent of sales, when available (one-page profiles only)

For financial institutions and insurance companies, we have also included annual sales, equity as a percent of assets, and return on assets in this section.

Per share data have been adjusted for stock splits.

The data for some public companies (and private companies with public debt) have been provided to us by Media General Financial Services, Inc. Other public company information was compiled by The Reference Press, which takes full responsibility for the content of this section.

In the case of private companies that do not publicly disclose financial information, we usually did not have access to such standardized data. We have gathered estimates of sales and other statistics from numerous sources; among the most helpful were trade publications such as *Crain's New York Business*, *Advertising Age*, and *Forbes*'s list of the largest private companies. ▲

New York–Area Economic Outlook

OVERVIEW OF THE NEW YORK–AREA ECONOMY AND BUSINESS ENVIRONMENT

By Mark Henricks

The stock market may have recovered within two years of its 1987 crash, but the world's financial center is taking a little longer. Only in the last two years have New York City and its environs begun shaking off the economic slump that began with Black Monday. In 1995 stocks posted stunning gains; a year earlier the Big Apple's securities, insurance, banking, and real estate firms had seen their first job increase in six years. These are key developments because approximately 10 percent of the total workforce in the region is employed at the likes of Wall Street's Merrill Lynch and Newark-based Prudential Insurance.

Good news for the financial services industry has long been seen as good news for the economy of the entire Tri-State area. True to form, 1994 (the latest year for which figures are available) was the strongest year for most major indicators since the bottom fell out. Employment was up across nearly the entire region. Retail sales, tourism, and office vacancies turned in their best improvements in years. Meanwhile, trends toward lower taxes, reduced crime, and improved quality of life bode well for the economic future.

The New York City area hosts over 10 million jobs, accounting for 8 percent of the nation's employment. This number has shown healthy growth lately. A one percent rise in regional employment in 1994 was followed by a projected 0.7 percent increase in 1995 — fairly sluggish but still twice the 1993 rate. That moderate employment growth is expected to continue. In an important reversal, private employment has grown faster than public employment in recent years. That is a promising trend for a region with one in six jobs in the public sector and, correspondingly, the highest business tax burden in the country.

One trend that shows no sign of changing is the decline in manufacturing. In the 1950s nearly a third of all jobs in the Tri-State region were in a broad range of manufacturing companies. But many of the Manhattan garment makers have fled to other countries, and the Long Island defense contractors have shriveled with the passing of the cold war. Today, fewer than one in eight regional workers labor in any kind of manufacturing.

Finance is still king in New York City, which handles more than half of all global

New York City Regional Employment
(thousand)

Area	1970	1980	1990	1995*	2000*	Percentage Change 1970–80	Percentage Change 1990–2000
New York metro	5,621.1	5,532.7	6,279.0	6,063.0	6,290.4	(1.6)	0.1
New York City	4,066.5	3,614.1	3,957.4	3,786.5	3,914.0	(11.1)	(1.1)
New Jersey	2,447.7	2,828.1	3,377.5	3,419.4	3,568.3	15.5	5.6
Connecticut	727.4	869.3	1,016.9	1,000.2	1,038.6	19.5	2.1
Total region	8,796.2	9,230.1	10,673.4	10,462.6	10,897.3	4.9	2.1

* Projected
Source: New York Metropolitan Transportation Council

securities trades. In fact, financial transactions account for a third of New York City's contribution to US gross domestic product. Currently, this industry is undergoing major changes. Widespread corporate restructuring at Citicorp and other large banks based in New York has cost thousands of employees their jobs. Mergers such as the Chemical Banking–Chase Manhattan marriage are creating bigger players, but it's worth noting that they remain far smaller than their counterparts in Japan and Europe.

Different and, perhaps, tougher obstacles face New York's role as world fashion center. Manufacturing's flight to lower-cost areas is the main reason apparel industry employment fell 26 percent in the region in the last decade. But, although leading apparel industry firms such as Liz Claiborne, Polo/Ralph Lauren, and Donna Karan and centers of design excellence like the Fashion Institute of Technology continue to call New York their home, the region accounted for just 11.7 percent of US fashion output in 1992, down from 15.8 percent in 1982.

New York has long been known as a publishing and entertainment center. Media behemoths Time Warner and Viacom base their companies in the city, as do all four of the major television networks. The nation's largest book publishers, such as McGraw-Hill and Bertelsmann's Bantam Doubleday Dell unit, can be found in midtown, and the New York Times Company publishes the "paper of record" from its home on 43rd Street. More than 565,000 New York–area jobs are in information and media services,

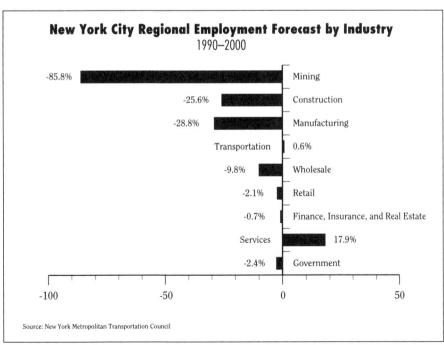

New York City Regional Employment Forecast by Industry
1990–2000

-85.8%	Mining
-25.6%	Construction
-28.8%	Manufacturing
Transportation	0.6%
-9.8%	Wholesale
-2.1%	Retail
-0.7%	Finance, Insurance, and Real Estate
Services	17.9%
-2.4%	Government

-100   -50   0   50

Source: New York Metropolitan Transportation Council

including education, printing, and publishing as well as broadcasting, film, music, and multimedia.

Despite high-profile debacles like the bankruptcy of Rockefeller Center, home of Radio City Music Hall and NBC, New York's real estate market has actually strengthened in recent years. Vacancy rates in midtown Manhattan fell to 13.4 percent in 1994, while leasing activity rose and rents firmed. The office rebound did not immediately spur much new construction. Commercial permits remained at or near historic lows. Residential real estate building activity, however, rose to the highest level in several years, and infrastructure spending registered double-digit percentage gains.

New York was founded as a trading center and, while the docks ringing Manhattan have mostly rotted away, modern container ships by the score unload today in nearby Elizabeth, New Jersey. Ocean cargo through the Port Authority of New York and New Jersey increased 7 percent in 1994, passenger travel at the region's three airports rose at a similar pace, and air cargo shipments vaulted 11 percent.

Macy's and Bloomingdale's may now be owned by Cincinnati-based Federated Department Stores, but these stores and other New York emporiums like Tiffany & Co. still have magical appeal for shoppers the world over. As a result, regional retail and wholesale trade employment grew 1.4 percent in 1994 and retail sales activity topped $145 billion per year.

World-class shopping is just one of the reasons 43 million visitors pump over $20 billion into the region annually. A revived

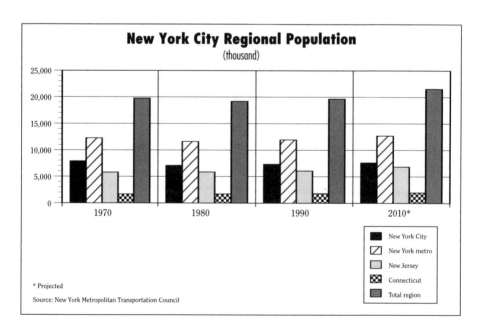

New York City Regional Population
(thousand)

* Projected

Source: New York Metropolitan Transportation Council

Legend:
- New York City
- New York metro
- New Jersey
- Connecticut
- Total region

Broadway has opened new shows at record rates, including high-priced blockbusters such as *Beauty and the Beast* and *Sunset Boulevard,* whose appeal has allowed producers to raise the average ticket price to nearly $45 while still increasing attendance. Perennial New York favorites such as the Statue of Liberty and the Empire State Building continue to draw tourists, as do new attractions such as Planet Hollywood, the Motown Cafe, and other thematic restaurants on 57th Street. All these visitors helped hotel occupancy rates top 75 percent in 1994, up from less than 70 percent the year before, while room rates hit $144 a night, up 5 percent.

The New York region is more than New York City. Connecticut is known as a center for large corporate headquarters, including General Electric Company in Fairfield, GTE and Xerox in Stamford, and UST Inc. and American Brands in Greenwich. New Jersey, building on the long tradition of excellence in Princeton University's chemistry department, is home to most of the nation's biggest pharmaceutical companies, including Merck & Co., Warner-Lambert, Eli Lilly, and Johnson & Johnson.

All told, with 20 million people and nearly half a billion dollars in personal income, the New York region remains firmly atop the heap of American metropolitan economies. Its globally dominant positions in such industries as financial services, fashion, and communications remain, for the most part, undisputed. And even if there is another Black Monday waiting for it, the region's unmatched diversity ensures that it will — perhaps with brief pauses for recovery — stay lively long into the future.

Mark Henricks is a New York–based business writer.

A List-Lover's Compendium

The 50 Largest Companies by Sales in the New York Area

Rank	Company	City	Sales ($ mil.)
1	AT&T Corp.	New York	75,094
2	Philip Morris Companies Inc.	New York	65,125
3	International Business Machines Corporation	Armonk	64,052
4	General Electric Company	Fairfield	60,109
5	The Prudential Insurance Company of America	Newark	43,557
6	Texaco Inc.	White Plains	33,353
7	Citicorp	New York	31,650
8	Metropolitan Life Insurance Company	New York	29,983
9	PepsiCo, Inc.	Purchase	28,472
10	American International Group, Inc.	New York	22,442
11	AT&T Systems & Technology	New York	21,161
12	GTE Corporation	Stamford	19,944
13	The Travelers Inc.	New York	18,465
14	Merrill Lynch & Co., Inc.	New York	18,233
15	Xerox Corporation	Stamford	17,837
16	New York Life Insurance Company	New York	15,807
17	Johnson & Johnson	New Brunswick	15,734
18	RJR Nabisco Holdings Corp.	New York	15,366
19	Merck & Co., Inc.	Whitehouse Station	14,970
20	International Paper Company	Purchase	14,966
21	The Goldman Sachs Group, L.P.	New York	14,470
22	American Express Company	New York	14,282
23	Continental Grain Company	New York	14,000
24	Loews Corporation	New York	13,515
25	NYNEX Corporation	New York	13,307
26	American Brands, Inc.	Old Greenwich	13,147
27	AlliedSignal Inc.	Morristown	12,817
28	Chemical Banking Corporation	New York	12,685
29	Bristol-Myers Squibb Company	New York	11,984
30	J.P. Morgan & Co. Incorporated	New York	11,915
31	Melville Corporation	Rye	11,286
32	Chase Manhattan Corp.	New York	11,187
33	Teachers Insurance and Annuity Association- College Retirement Equities Fund	New York	10,413
34	The Great Atlantic & Pacific Tea Company, Inc.	Montvale	10,332
35	Morgan Stanley Group Inc.	New York	9,376
36	Lehman Brothers Holdings Inc.	New York	9,190
37	American Home Products Corporation	Madison	8,966
38	Toys "R" Us, Inc.	Paramus	8,746
39	Woolworth Corporation	New York	8,293
40	Pfizer Inc.	New York	8,281
41	ITT Industries, Inc.	White Plains	7,758
42	Nabisco Holdings Corp.	Parsippany	7,699
43	Colgate-Palmolive Company	New York	7,588
44	Bankers Trust New York Corporation	New York	7,503
45	CPC International Inc.	Englewood Cliffs	7,425
46	Time Warner Inc.	New York	7,396
47	Viacom Inc.	New York	7,363
48	Federal Reserve Bank of New York	New York	7,133
49	Amerada Hess Corporation	New York	6,699
50	Schlumberger N.V.	New York	6,697

The 50 Largest Employers in the New York Area

Rank	Company	City	Employees
1	The Olsten Corporation	Melville	557,900
2	PepsiCo, Inc.	Purchase	471,000
3	AT&T Corp.	New York	304,500
4	General Electric Company	Fairfield	221,000
5	International Business Machines Corporation	Armonk	219,839
6	Career Horizons, Inc.	Woodbury	174,573
7	Philip Morris Companies Inc.	New York	165,000
8	Woolworth Corporation	New York	119,000
9	Melville Corporation	Rye	117,000
10	GTE Corporation	Stamford	111,000
11	The Prudential Insurance Company of America	Newark	99,386
12	The Great Atlantic & Pacific Tea Company, Inc.	Montvale	92,000
13	Xerox Corporation	Stamford	87,600
14	AlliedSignal Inc.	Morristown	87,500
15	Citicorp	New York	82,600
16	Johnson & Johnson	New Brunswick	81,500
17	AT&T Systems & Technology	New York	76,125
18	American Home Products Corporation	Madison	74,009
19	American Express Company	New York	72,412
20	KPMG Peat Marwick LLP	New York	72,000
21	RJR Nabisco Holdings Corp.	New York	70,600
22	International Paper Company	Purchase	70,000
23	Viacom Inc.	New York	70,000
24	Coopers & Lybrand L.L.P.	New York	67,000
25	NYNEX Corporation	New York	65,400
26	Ernst & Young LLP	New York	65,000
27	Deloitte Touche Tohmatsu International	Wilton	59,000
28	ITT Industries, Inc.	White Plains	58,400
29	Toys "R" Us, Inc.	Paramus	58,000
30	Metropolitan Life Insurance Company	New York	53,000
31	Price Waterhouse LLP	New York	53,000
32	Time Warner Inc.	New York	53,000
33	The Travelers Inc.	New York	52,000
34	Schlumberger N.V.	New York	48,000
35	Bristol-Myers Squibb Company	New York	47,700
36	Merck & Co., Inc.	Whitehouse Station	47,500
37	The Dun & Bradstreet Corporation	Wilton	47,000
38	Nabisco Holdings Corp.	Parsippany	45,000
39	Ogden Corporation	New York	45,000
40	Merrill Lynch & Co., Inc.	New York	44,000
41	Metropolitan Transportation Authority New York Transit	New York	44,000
42	Chemical Banking Corporation	New York	42,130
43	CPC International Inc.	Englewood Cliffs	41,900
44	New York City Health & Hospitals Corporation	New York	41,711
45	Pfizer Inc.	New York	40,800
46	American Standard Companies Inc.	Piscataway	38,500
47	Warner-Lambert Company	Morris Plains	36,000
48	Ingersoll-Rand Company	Woodcliff Lake	35,932
49	Chase Manhattan Corp.	New York	35,774
50	ITT Corporation	New York	35,000

The 50 Fastest-Growing Companies by Sales in the New York Area

Rank	Company	City	Annual % Change	Sales ($ mil.)
1	Transnational Re Corporation	Edison	5,007	72
2	White River Corporation	White Plains	3,372	63
3	Aristotle Corporation	New Haven	2,650	6
4	Savoy Pictures Entertainment, Inc.	New York	1,108	86
5	AGP and Company Inc.	New York	1,009	12
6	ERD Waste Corporation	Commack	857	7
7	Novadigm, Inc.	Mahwah	745	9
8	Unapix Entertainment, Inc.	New York	595	13
9	Corniche Group, Inc.	Wayne	500	21
10	Pudgie's Chicken, Inc.	Uniondale	450	8
11	CPT Holdings, Inc.	New York	438	31
12	AmeriData Technologies, Inc.	Stamford	364	1,019
13	Bradley Pharmaceuticals Inc.	Fairfield	357	20
14	Consolidated Technology Group Ltd.	New York	313	16
15	The Hain Food Group	Uniondale	287	58
16	Viacom Inc.	New York	267	7,363
17	Physician Computer Network, Inc.	Morris Plains	236	21
18	Steven Madden, Ltd.	Long Island City	223	8
19	Multi-Market Radio, Inc.	New York	223	7
20	Glasgal Communications, Inc.	Northvale	214	35
21	The Alpine Group, Inc.	New York	189	198
22	Professional Sports Care Management, Inc.	Harrison	188	16
23	Chef's International, Inc.	Point Pleasant Beach	182	32
24	Hauppauge Digital, Inc.	Hauppauge	176	12
25	HMG Worldwide Corporation	New York	173	56
26	The Travelers Inc.	New York	172	18,465
27	Alliance Entertainment Corp.	New York	167	535
28	Sonic Environmental Systems, Inc.	Parsippany	161	7
29	Robotic Vision Systems, Inc.	Hauppauge	159	64
30	Digital Solutions, Inc.	South Plainfield	159	38
31	Biomatrix, Inc.	Ridgefield	157	9
32	Inteplast Corporation	Livingston	150	250
33	Modern Medical Modalities Corporation	Morristown	144	8
34	Beechwood Data Systems	Clark	143	17
35	Family Golf Centers, Inc.	Melville	142	6
36	Comprehensive Environmental Systems, Inc.	West Babylon	137	8
37	Cygne Designs, Inc.	New York	134	516
38	Oxford Health Plans, Inc.	Norwalk	131	721
39	Ferolito, Vultaggio & Sons	Success	131	300
40	Cellular Communications of Puerto Rico, Inc.	New York	131	67
41	Esquire Communications Ltd.	New York	129	13
42	Dataflex Corporation	Edison	124	274
43	DualStar Technologies Corporation	New York	123	65
44	Harold Levinson Associates, Inc.	Hicksville	122	390
45	Regeneron Pharmaceuticals, Inc.	Tarrytown	119	23
46	People's Choice TV Corp.	Shelton	117	13
47	Rush Communications	New York	110	65
48	Alexander's, Inc.	Saddle Brook	107	12
49	Sid Tool Company	Plainview	107	248
50	Koo Koo Roo, Inc.	Iselin	106	13

Note: To be included on this list, companies must have sales greater than $5 million. These rates may have resulted from acquisitions or internal growth.

The 50 Fastest-Growing Employers in the New York Area

Rank	Company	City	Annual % Change	Employees
1	White River Corporation	White Plains	5,275	860
2	The Alpine Group, Inc.	New York	448	2,380
3	Viacom Inc.	New York	300	70,000
4	International Vitamin Corporation	Freehold	215	315
5	People's Choice TV Corp.	Shelton	206	521
6	Cygne Designs, Inc.	New York	203	5,000
7	Bradley Pharmaceuticals Inc.	Fairfield	201	208
8	Acclaim Entertainment, Inc.	Glen Cove	171	800
9	Oxford Health Plans, Inc.	Norwalk	146	1,770
10	SBM Industries, Inc.	Larchmont	145	125
11	Convergent Solutions, Inc.	Laurence Harbor	143	182
12	Robotic Vision Systems, Inc.	Hauppauge	136	128
13	Multi-Market Radio, Inc.	New York	135	200
14	Transworld Home HealthCare, Inc.	Hawthorne	131	375
15	Beechwood Data Systems	Clark	127	184
16	Allied Digital Technologies Corporation	Hauppauge	121	1,500
17	Marvel Entertainment Group, Inc.	New York	121	1,600
18	Health Management, Inc.	Holbrook	113	413
19	Home State Holdings, Inc.	Shrewsbury	112	138
20	Nextel Communications, Inc.	Rutherford	107	1,600
21	Benson Eyecare Corporation	Rye	101	2,300
22	MovieFone, Inc.	New York	97	59
23	Tridex Corporation	Westport	95	422
24	Lynch Corporation	Greenwich	93	1,173
25	Cheyenne Software, Inc.	Roslyn Heights	88	430
26	Hooper Holmes, Inc.	Basking Ridge	88	21,850
27	Shorewood Packaging Corporation	Farmingdale	83	2,200
28	United Water Resources Inc.	Harrington Park	82	1,282
29	Semiconductor Packaging Materials Co., Inc.	Mamaroneck	80	223
30	Professional Sports Care Management, Inc.	Harrison	77	323
31	Whitman Medical Corp.	Iselin	71	479
32	Cambrex Corporation	East Rutherford	69	1,336
33	Ampal-American Israel Corporation	New York	66	3,294
34	HFS Inc.	Parsippany	65	2,100
35	Infinity Broadcasting Corporation	New York	65	1,114
36	Creative Technologies Corp.	New York	63	130
37	Barnes & Noble, Inc.	New York	60	23,500
38	Centennial Cellular Corp.	New Canaan	60	540
39	Environmental Services of America, Inc.	Rahway	60	345
40	Graff Pay-Per-View Inc.	New York	59	100
41	Kenneth Cole Productions, Inc.	New York	59	285
42	Micro Warehouse, Inc.	Norwalk	54	2,300
43	Specialty Retail Group, Inc.	Westport	53	87
44	Advanced Technology Materials, Inc.	Danbury	51	109
45	Sigma Plastics Group	Lyndhurst	50	1,800
46	Young Broadcasting Inc.	New York	49	820
47	The Money Store Inc.	Union	48	2,035
48	Universal Holding Corp.	Brewster	47	250
49	Hyperion Software Corporation	Stamford	46	580
50	The Multicare Companies Inc.	Hackensack	46	7,000

Note: To be included on this list, companies must have 50 or more employees. These rates may have resulted from acquisitions or internal growth.

The 50 Largest Job Creators in the New York Area

Rank	Company	City	Jobs Added	Employees
1	The Olsten Corporation	Melville	114,300	557,900
2	Viacom Inc.	New York	52,500	70,000
3	PepsiCo, Inc.	Purchase	48,000	471,000
4	American Home Products Corporation	Madison	22,610	74,009
5	Hooper Holmes, Inc.	Basking Ridge	10,250	21,850
6	Barnes & Noble, Inc.	New York	8,800	23,500
7	American Express Company	New York	7,758	72,412
8	Melville Corporation	Rye	5,918	117,000
9	Colgate-Palmolive Company	New York	4,800	32,800
10	RJR Nabisco Holdings Corp.	New York	4,100	70,600
11	Trump Organization	New York	4,000	19,000
12	Ernst & Young LLP	New York	3,713	65,000
13	Cygne Designs, Inc.	New York	3,350	5,000
14	Ogden Corporation	New York	3,200	45,000
15	Volt Information Sciences, Inc.	New York	3,200	23,000
16	Automatic Data Processing, Inc.	Roseland	3,000	25,000
17	The Caldor Corporation	Norwalk	3,000	24,000
18	Maidenform, Inc.	New York	3,000	10,000
19	Time Warner Inc.	New York	3,000	53,000
20	Toys "R" Us, Inc.	Paramus	3,000	58,000
21	CPC International Inc.	Englewood Cliffs	2,900	41,900
22	Echlin Inc.	Branford	2,800	23,400
23	First Data Corporation	Hackensack	2,700	22,000
24	Dover Corporation	New York	2,547	22,992
25	American Standard Companies Inc.	Piscataway	2,500	38,500
26	Deloitte Touche Tohmatsu International	Wilton	2,400	59,000
27	The Multicare Companies, Inc.	Hackensack	2,200	7,000
28	Merrill Lynch & Co., Inc.	New York	2,100	44,000
29	Crane Co.	Stamford	2,000	10,700
30	Petrie Retail, Inc.	Secaucus	2,000	19,500
31	The Alpine Group, Inc.	New York	1,946	2,380
32	Dean Witter, Discover & Co.	New York	1,911	28,475
33	Arrow Electronics, Inc.	Melville	1,900	6,500
34	Paine Webber Group Inc.	New York	1,900	16,300
35	J.P. Morgan & Co. Incorporated	New York	1,862	17,055
36	"21" International Holdings, Inc.	New York	1,800	8,500
37	Foster Wheeler Corporation	Clinton	1,705	11,685
38	Omnicom Group Inc.	New York	1,700	16,100
39	Lechters, Inc.	Harrison	1,551	6,911
40	Hubbell Inc.	Orange	1,520	7,405
41	Colin Service Systems, Inc.	White Plains	1,500	8,500
42	CUC International Inc.	Stamford	1,500	8,000
43	Noel Group, Inc.	New York	1,455	6,025
44	Morgan Stanley Group Inc.	New York	1,412	9,685
45	Butler International, Inc.	Montvale	1,400	8,000
46	Pittston Services Group	Stamford	1,400	15,100
47	Citizens Utilities Company	Stamford	1,327	4,294
48	Ampal-American Israel Corporation	New York	1,312	3,294
49	Benson Eyecare Corporation	Rye	1,155	2,300
50	AlliedSignal Inc.	Morristown	1,100	87,500

Note: These rates may have resulted from acquisitions or internal growth.

The New York 500: Largest Companies by Sales in *Hoover's Guide to the Top New York Companies*

Rank	Company	Sales ($ mil.)	Rank	Company	Sales ($ mil.)
1	AT&T Corp.	75,094	51	Dean Witter, Discover & Co.	6,603
2	Philip Morris Companies Inc.	65,125	52	The Equitable Companies Inc.	6,447
3	IBM Corporation	64,052	53	Ernst & Young LLP	6,424
4	General Electric Company	60,109	54	Warner-Lambert Company	6,417
5	The Prudential Insurance		55	KPMG Peat Marwick LLP	6,405
	Company of America	43,557	56	Capital Cities/ABC, Inc.	6,379
6	Texaco Inc.	33,353	57	Consolidated Edison Company	6,373
7	Citicorp	31,650	58	Tosco Corporation	6,366
8	Metropolitan Life Insurance Co.	29,983	59	Salomon Inc	6,278
9	PepsiCo, Inc.	28,472	60	The Guardian Life Insurance	
10	American International Group	22,442		Company of America	6,091
11	AT&T Systems & Technology	21,161	61	Coopers & Lybrand L.L.P.	5,981
12	GTE Corporation	19,944	62	Deloitte Touche Tohmatsu Intl.	5,950
13	The Travelers Inc.	18,465	63	Public Service Enterprise Group	
14	Merrill Lynch & Co., Inc.	18,233		Incorporated	5,916
15	Xerox Corporation	17,837	64	The Chubb Corporation	5,710
16	New York Life Insurance Co.	15,807	65	Loral Corporation	5,484
17	Johnson & Johnson	15,734	66	MTA New York Transit	5,323
18	RJR Nabisco Holdings Corp.	15,366	67	Champion International Corp.	5,318
19	Merck & Co., Inc.	14,970	68	The Dun & Bradstreet Corp.	4,896
20	International Paper Company	14,966	69	Union Carbide Corporation	4,865
21	The Goldman Sachs Group, L.P.	14,470	70	Empire Blue Cross and Blue Shield	4,798
22	American Express Company	14,282	71	ITT Corporation	4,760
23	Continental Grain Company	14,000	72	Advance Publications, Inc.	4,690
24	Loews Corporation	13,515	73	Schering-Plough Corporation	4,657
25	NYNEX Corporation	13,307	74	Arrow Electronics, Inc.	4,649
26	American Brands, Inc.	13,147	75	Ingersoll-Rand Company	4,508
27	AlliedSignal Inc.	12,817	76	Price Waterhouse LLP	4,460
28	Chemical Banking Corporation	12,685	77	American Standard Companies	4,457
29	Bristol-Myers Squibb Company	11,984	78	Avnet, Inc.	4,300
30	J.P. Morgan & Co. Incorporated	11,915	79	Avon Products, Inc.	4,267
31	Melville Corporation	11,286	80	The Bank of New York Company	4,251
32	Chase Manhattan Corp.	11,187	81	Pathmark Stores, Inc.	4,182
33	Teachers Ins. and Annuity Assoc.	10,413	82	New York City Health & Hospitals	4,134
34	The Great Atlantic & Pacific Tea		83	Paine Webber Group Inc.	3,964
	Company, Inc.	10,332	84	General Re Corporation	3,837
35	Morgan Stanley Group Inc.	9,376	85	The Bear Stearns Companies Inc.	3,754
36	Lehman Brothers Holdings Inc.	9,190	86	Wakefern Food Corporation	3,740
37	American Home Products Corp.	8,966	87	CBS Inc.	3,712
38	Toys "R" Us, Inc.	8,746	88	General Public Utilities Corp.	3,650
39	Woolworth Corporation	8,293	89	AIOC Corporation	3,500
40	Pfizer Inc.	8,281	90	Marsh & McLennan Companies	3,435
41	ITT Industries, Inc.	7,758	91	Union Camp Corporation	3,396
42	Nabisco Holdings Corp.	7,699	92	Lefrak Organization Inc.	3,300
43	Colgate-Palmolive Company	7,588	93	Westvaco Corporation	3,272
44	Bankers Trust New York Corp.	7,503	94	Pitney Bowes Inc.	3,271
45	CPC International Inc.	7,425	95	Dover Corporation	3,085
46	Time Warner Inc.	7,396	96	The Reader's Digest Association	3,069
47	Viacom Inc.	7,363	97	Long Island Lighting Company	3,067
48	Federal Reserve Bank of New York	7,133	98	Reliance Group Holdings, Inc.	3,047
49	Amerada Hess Corporation	6,699	99	MacAndrews & Forbes Holdings	3,030
50	Schlumberger N.V.	6,697	100	U.S. Industries, Inc.	2,994

The New York 500: Largest Companies by Sales
in *Hoover's Guide to the Top New York Companies* (continued)

Rank	Company	Sales ($ mil.)	Rank	Company	Sales ($ mil.)
101	The Estée Lauder Companies Inc.	2,899	151	Metromedia Company	1,700
102	Automatic Data Processing, Inc.	2,894	152	Helmsley Enterprises, Inc.	1,698
103	The Mutual Life Insurance Co.	2,839	153	Crane Co.	1,654
104	The McGraw-Hill Companies, Inc.	2,761	154	First Data Corporation	1,652
105	The Caldor Corporation	2,749	155	USLIFE Corporation	1,651
106	Echlin Inc.	2,718	156	Renco Group Inc.	1,650
107	Becton, Dickinson and Company	2,713	157	Barnes & Noble, Inc.	1,623
108	Praxair, Inc.	2,711	158	Saks Holdings, Inc.	1,600
109	Subway Sandwich Shops, Inc.	2,700	159	Federal Paper Board Company	1,570
110	Olin Corporation	2,658	160	General Signal Corporation	1,528
111	The Turner Corporation	2,639	161	Entex Information Services	1,500
112	Computer Associates Intl.	2,623	162	McKinsey & Company	1,500
113	Republic New York Corporation	2,560	163	Petrie Retail, Inc.	1,480
114	First Fidelity Bancorporation	2,553	164	New York Power Authority	1,460
115	Ultramar Corporation	2,475	165	Trump Organization	1,450
116	Allegheny Power System, Inc.	2,452	166	Sequa Corporation	1,420
117	"21" International Holdings, Inc.	2,400	167	New York University	1,409
118	The Grand Union Company	2,392	168	Potamkin Manhattan Corp.	1,400
119	Engelhard Corporation	2,386	169	Leucadia National Corporation	1,384
120	The New York Times Company	2,358	170	AT&T Capital Corporation	1,384
121	Transammonia, Inc.	2,320	171	The Dyson-Kissner-Moran Corporation	1,370
122	The Hearst Corporation	2,299	172	Coltec Industries Inc.	1,327
123	Donaldson, Lufkin & Jenrette, Inc.	2,290	173	J. M. Huber Corporation	1,325
124	Foster Wheeler Corporation	2,271	174	Alexander & Alexander Services	1,324
125	The Olsten Corporation	2,260	175	International Flavors & Fragrances Inc.	1,315
126	Red Apple Group	2,250	176	World Color	1,300
127	Witco Corporation	2,235	177	National Basketball Association	1,259
128	The City University of New York	2,169	178	Phillips-Van Heusen Corporation	1,256
129	Liz Claiborne, Inc.	2,163	179	The Golodetz Group	1,250
120	American Retail Group, Inc.	2,120	180	UST Inc.	1,223
131	Ogden Corporation	2,110	181	The Brooklyn Union Gas Company	1,216
132	Dow Jones & Company, Inc.	2,091	182	Twin County Grocers Inc.	1,200
133	Duracell International Inc.	2,079	183	United Auto Group, Inc.	1,200
134	ASARCO Incorporated	2,032	184	WHX Corporation	1,194
135	Central National-Gottesman, Inc.	2,000	185	Parsons & Whittemore, Inc.	1,181
136	Century Business Credit Corp.	2,000	186	GAF Corporation	1,156
137	Polo/Ralph Lauren Corporation	2,000	187	Major League Baseball	1,134
138	The Interpublic Group of Cos.	1,984	188	Cytec Industries Inc.	1,101
139	The Port Authority of New York and New Jersey	1,980	189	The Connell Company	1,100
140	Pittston Services Group	1,872	190	Midlantic Corporation	1,084
141	Lexmark International Group, Inc.	1,852	191	Rayonier Inc.	1,070
142	Alleghany Corporation	1,827	192	Perkin-Elmer Corporation	1,064
143	TLC Beatrice International	1,822	193	Triarc Companies, Inc.	1,063
144	TIG Holdings, Inc.	1,778	194	Young & Rubicam Inc.	1,060
145	EMCOR Group, Inc.	1,764	195	Bell Communications Research Inc.	1,053
146	Omnicom Group Inc.	1,756	196	ICC Industries Inc.	1,050
147	National Football League	1,730	197	Johnson & Higgins	1,050
148	Southern New England Telecommunications	1,717	198	Neuman Distributors, Inc.	1,050
149	Health Insurance Plan of Greater New York	1,714	199	CUC International Inc.	1,045
150	Avis, Inc.	1,700	200	First Brands Corporation	1,037

The New York 500: Largest Companies by Sales
in *Hoover's Guide to the Top New York Companies* (continued)

Rank	Company	Sales ($ mil.)
201	Columbia University in the City of New York	1,032
202	AmeriData Technologies, Inc.	1,019
203	C. R. Bard, Inc.	1,018
204	Orange and Rockland Utilities	1,017
205	Hubbell Inc.	1,014
206	Transatlantic Holdings, Inc.	1,005
207	GoodTimes Entertainment Worldwide	1,000
208	Securitas Lock Group, Inc.	1,000
209	Air Express International Corp.	997
210	Prudential Reinsurance Holdings	997
211	Landstar Systems, Inc.	984
212	K-III Communications Corporation	965
213	Franciscan Sisters of the Poor Health System, Inc.	963
214	Nobody beats the Wiz	950
215	Wellman, Inc.	936
216	Di Giorgio Corp.	934
217	United States Surgical Corporation	919
218	Citizens Utilities Company	916
219	Big Flower Press Holdings, Inc.	897
220	Silgan Holdings Inc.	861
221	Catholic Healthcare Network	861
222	CARQUEST Corp.	860
223	Yale University	852
224	Ziff-Davis Publishing Company	852
225	Coca-Cola Bottling Co. of New York	850
226	Quality King Distributors Inc.	850
227	McCrory Corporation	840
228	Cablevision Systems Corporation	837
229	W. R. Berkley Corporation	831
230	Gould Paper Corporation	830
231	UIS, Inc.	830
232	Pall Corporation	829
233	Stone & Webster, Incorporated	818
234	National Hockey League	817
235	Associated Merchandising Corp.	800
236	Hartz Group Inc	800
237	PLY GEM Industries, Inc.	796
238	Pittston Minerals Group	795
239	The Warnaco Group, Inc.	789
240	Terex Corporation	787
241	Baker & Taylor Inc.	785
242	Getty Petroleum Corp.	785
243	Handy & Harman	781
244	Orion Capital Corporation	781
245	Micro Warehouse, Inc.	776
246	Hanover Direct, Inc.	769
247	Towers Perrin	767
248	UCAR International Inc.	758
249	Big V Supermarkets Inc.	754
250	Scholastic Corporation	750

Rank	Company	Sales ($ mil.)
251	Volt Information Sciences, Inc.	735
252	J. Crew Group Inc.	725
253	Oxford Health Plans, Inc.	721
254	King Kullen Grocery Company	706
255	Hovnanian Enterprises, Inc.	704
256	Warren Equities Inc.	701
257	Montefiore Medical Center	700
258	Metallurg, Inc.	700
259	The Newark Group, Inc.	700
260	Amphenol Corporation	693
261	Block Drug Company, Inc.	693
262	Tiffany & Co.	683
263	Watchtower Bible & Tract Society of New York Inc.	680
264	Village Super Market, Inc.	677
265	Carter-Wallace, Inc.	670
266	MasterCard International Inc.	665
267	AnnTaylor Stores Corporation	659
268	The United Illuminating Company	657
269	Emerson Radio Corp.	655
270	Dime Bancorp, Inc.	654
271	Nine West Group Inc.	652
272	Czarnikow-Rionda	650
273	Francosteel Corporation	650
274	M Fabrikant & Sons	650
275	Tambrands Inc.	645
276	Standard Motor Products, Inc.	641
277	Memorial Sloan-Kettering Cancer Center	637
278	D'Arcy Masius Benton & Bowles	626
279	Slim-Fast Nutritional Foods Intl.	625
280	Air & Water Technologies Corp.	619
281	Foodarama Supermarkets, Inc.	607
282	Alliance Capital Management L.P.	601
283	Charmer Industries, Inc.	600
284	Hunter Douglas, Inc.	600
285	Key Food Stores Cooperative, Inc.	600
286	Grey Advertising Inc.	593
287	Mayfair Supermarkets Inc.	591
288	Crompton & Knowles Corporation	590
289	Peerless Importers, Inc.	585
290	Skadden, Arps, Slate, Meagher & Flom	582
291	Brylane Inc.	579
292	King World Productions, Inc.	574
293	Tishman Realty & Construction Co.	572
294	Genovese Drug Stores, Inc.	570
295	General Host Corporation	568
296	Acclaim Entertainment, Inc.	567
297	Castle Oil Corporation	560
298	Finlay Enterprises, Inc.	552
299	Gemini Consulting, Inc.	551
300	Bloomberg L.P.	550

The New York 500: Largest Companies by Sales
in *Hoover's Guide to the Top New York Companies* (continued)

Rank	Company	Sales ($ mil.)	Rank	Company	Sales ($ mil.)
301	Horsehead Industries	550	351	Vitt Media International, Inc.	450
302	Benjamin Moore & Co.	547	352	Bed Bath & Beyond, Inc.	440
303	Petroleum Heat and Power Co.	547	353	MBIA Corporation	440
304	Fairchild Corporation	546	354	The Genlyte Group Incorporated	433
305	Griffon Corporation	546	355	Life Re Corporation	433
306	Continental Can Co.	537	356	Darby Group Companies, Inc.	430
307	Alliance Entertainment Corp.	535	357	Krasdale Foods Inc.	425
308	Leslie Fay Companies, Inc.	535	358	Titan Industrial Corporation	425
309	People's Bank	531	359	KCS Energy, Inc.	424
310	Goya Foods, Inc.	528	360	Donna Karan, Inc.	420
311	Catholic Medical Center of Brooklyn & Queens	526	361	Schein Pharmaceutical, Inc.	420
312	Drug Guild Distributors	520	362	Salant Corporation	419
313	Jetro Cash & Carry Enterprises	520	363	Century Communications Corp.	417
314	Sealed Air Corporation	519	364	Toresco Enterprises Inc.	412
315	Cygne Designs, Inc.	516	365	Associated Press	406
316	Cablevision Industries Corporation	515	366	Bozell, Jacobs, Kenyon & Eckhardt	405
317	Marvel Entertainment Group, Inc.	515	367	Forest Laboratories, Inc.	405
318	Duty Free International, Inc.	502	368	Western Publishing Group, Inc.	403
319	Galey & Lord, Inc.	502	369	Allied Building Products Corp.	400
320	Dress Barn, Inc.	501	370	Daniel F. Young Inc.	400
321	Barneys New York	500	371	Maidenform, Inc.	400
322	Frederick Atkins, Inc.	500	372	P.C. Richard & Son	400
323	Inserra Supermarkets	500	373	Lechters, Inc.	399
324	Morse Diesel International, Inc.	500	374	The Summit Bancorporation	394
325	W.W. Norton & Co.	500	375	Bowne & Co., Inc.	393
326	Ford Foundation	489	376	Butler International, Inc.	393
327	Henry Schein, Inc.	487	377	Loehmann's Holdings, Inc.	393
328	Audiovox Corporation	486	378	Harold Levinson Associates, Inc.	390
329	Global Directmail Corporation	484	379	United Jewish Appeal, Inc.	382
330	Chris-Craft Industries, Inc.	481	380	Pullman Company	381
331	NAC Re Corp.	478	381	Starter Corporation	380
332	Ethan Allen Interiors Inc.	476	382	Tingue Brown & Co.	380
333	BIC Corporation	475	383	Standard Microsystems Corp.	379
334	Clifford Paper, Inc.	475	384	CMP Publications, Inc.	378
335	Minerals Technologies Inc.	473	385	National RE Corporation	378
336	Playtex Products, Inc.	473	386	Chic by H.I.S, Inc.	376
337	Parsons Brinckerhoff, Inc.	470	387	NUI Corporation	376
338	A. L. Pharma Inc.	469	388	Bush Boake Allen Inc.	375
339	Symbol Technologies, Inc.	465	389	Bonjour Group, Inc.	370
340	Perry H. Koplik & Sons Inc.	462	390	IP Timberlands, Ltd.	369
341	Tops Appliance City, Inc.	462	391	Tower Air, Inc.	368
342	Harris Chemical Group	460	392	WR Acquisition, Inc.	368
343	Kinray, Inc.	460	393	Overseas Shipholding Group, Inc.	364
344	BHC Communications, Inc.	458	394	Career Horizons, Inc.	361
345	U.S. Trust Corporation	457	395	Fortunoff Fine Jewelry & Silverware	360
346	Gilman Paper Co.	455	396	Hudson County News Company	360
347	New Jersey Resources Corporation	455	397	United Retail Group, Inc.	358
348	New York Stock Exchange, Inc.	452	398	Shorewood Packaging Corporation	357
349	Dairy Enterprises, Inc.	450	399	Commons Brothers, Inc.	353
350	Pergament Home Centers, Inc.	450	400	D.B. Brown, Inc.	350

The New York 500: Largest Companies by Sales
in *Hoover's Guide to the Top New York Companies* (continued)

Rank	Company	Sales ($ mil.)	Rank	Company	Sales ($ mil.)
401	Rad Oil, Inc.	350	451	General Trading Co.	270
402	Herman's Sporting Goods, Inc.	349	452	Photocircuits Corporation	270
403	Fenway Partners Inc.	340	453	Tollman Hundley Hotels	270
404	Ampacet Corporation	335	454	Shearman & Sterling	268
405	GP Financial Corp.	332	455	Forbes, Inc.	267
406	John Wiley & Sons, Inc.	331	456	OMI Corp.	267
407	The Money Store Inc.	331	457	Cleary, Gottlieb, Steen & Hamilton	265
408	Chock full o'Nuts Corporation	330	458	The Topps Company, Inc.	265
409	Colorado Prime Corporation	330	459	Valley National Bancorp	265
410	Interep Radio Store	330	460	The Multicare Companies Inc.	262
411	Mendik Company	328	461	Horizon Paper Company	260
412	Syms Corp.	327	462	Southern Container Corporation	260
413	Blue Tee Corporation	325	463	Webcraft Technologies, Inc.	260
414	Duane Reade Holding Company	325	464	EnviroSource, Inc.	260
415	Sigma Plastics Group	325	465	J. Gerber & Co., Inc.	256
416	Staff Builders, Inc.	325	466	Davis Polk & Wardwell	254
417	Trans-Resources, Inc.	325	467	Park Electrochemical Corp.	253
418	Kings Super Markets, Inc.	320	468	Hooper Holmes, Inc.	252
419	Planned Parenthood of New York City, Inc.	320	469	AJ Contracting Company	251
420	Fedders Corporation	317	470	Atalanta Corporation	250
421	HFS Inc.	313	471	Calvin Klein, Inc.	250
422	Rockbottom Stores, Inc.	311	472	Celadon Group Inc.	250
423	Weil, Gotshal & Manges	311	473	Central Lewmar L.P.	250
424	Astoria Financial Corporation	308	474	Ellen Tracy, Inc.	250
425	Lone Star Industries, Inc.	307	475	Inteplast Corporation	250
426	Brooklyn Bancorp, Inc.	301	476	Refined Sugars, Inc.	250
427	FlightSafety International, Inc.	301	477	Thypin Steel Company	250
428	F. Schumacher & Company	300	478	Nautica Enterprises, Inc.	248
439	Ferolito, Vultaggio & Sons	300	479	Sid Tool Company	248
430	National Envelope Corporation	300	480	AEP Industries Inc.	243
431	Schott Corporation	300	481	Oxford Resources Corporation	243
422	W.P. Carey & Co.	300	482	Zurich Reinsurance Centre Holdings, Inc.	243
433	Sithe Energies Inc.	299	483	Cambrex Corporation	242
434	Sullivan & Cromwell	298	484	Information Builders, Inc.	240
435	Sbarro, Inc.	296	485	Milgray Electronics, Inc.	240
436	Long Island Bancorp	295	486	K & F Industries, Inc.	239
437	PennCorp Financial Group, Inc.	294	487	Allou Health & Beauty Care, Inc.	238
438	Physicians Health Services, Inc.	294	488	Modell's Sporting Goods, Inc.	238
439	Yankee Energy System, Inc.	294	489	Forstmann & Company, Inc.	237
440	PNY Electronics, Inc.	293	490	White & Case	233
441	United Water Resources Inc.	293	491	Connecticut Energy Corporation	232
442	EXECUTONE Information Systems	292	492	Prodigy Services Company	230
443	Western Beef, Inc.	292	493	Gartner Group, Inc.	229
444	Jordache Enterprises, Inc.	280	494	Seaman Furniture Company, Inc.	228
445	Russ Berrie & Company Inc.	278	495	Devon Group, Inc.	226
446	Dataflex Corporation	274	496	Max Kahan, Inc.	226
447	Infinity Broadcasting Corporation	274	497	AMBAC Inc.	225
448	Four M Corporation	272	498	Corinthian Communications, Inc.	225
449	Univision Holdings	272	499	Philipp Brothers Chemicals, Inc.	225
450	Bozell Worldwide, Inc.	271	500	The Riese Organization	225

The New York 500: Largest Companies by Employees
in *Hoover's Guide to the Top New York Companies*

Rank	Company	Employees
1	The Olsten Corporation	557,900
2	PepsiCo, Inc.	471,000
3	AT&T Corp.	304,500
4	General Electric Company	221,000
5	IBM	219,839
6	Career Horizons, Inc.	174,573
7	Philip Morris Companies Inc.	165,000
8	Woolworth Corporation	119,000
9	Melville Corporation	117,000
10	GTE Corporation	111,000
11	The Prudential Insurance Company of America	99,386
12	The Great Atlantic & Pacific Tea Company, Inc.	92,000
13	Xerox Corporation	87,600
14	AlliedSignal Inc.	87,500
15	Citicorp	82,600
16	Johnson & Johnson	81,500
17	AT&T Systems & Technology	76,125
18	American Home Products Corp.	74,009
19	American Express Company	72,412
20	KPMG Peat Marwick LLP	72,000
21	RJR Nabisco Holdings Corp.	70,600
22	International Paper Company	70,000
23	Viacom Inc.	70,000
24	Coopers & Lybrand L.L.P.	67,000
25	NYNEX Corporation	65,400
26	Ernst & Young LLP	65,000
27	Deloitte Touche Tohmatsu Intl.	59,000
28	ITT Industries, Inc.	58,400
29	Toys "R" Us, Inc.	58,000
30	Metropolitan Life Insurance Co.	53,000
31	Price Waterhouse LLP	53,000
32	Time Warner Inc.	53,000
33	The Travelers Inc.	52,000
34	Schlumberger N.V.	48,000
35	Bristol-Myers Squibb Company	47,700
36	Merck & Co., Inc.	47,500
37	The Dun & Bradstreet Corp.	47,000
38	Nabisco Holdings Corp.	45,000
39	Ogden Corporation	45,000
40	Merrill Lynch & Co., Inc.	44,000
41	MTA New York Transit	44,000
42	Chemical Banking Corporation	42,130
43	CPC International Inc.	41,900
44	New York City Health & Hospitals Corporation	41,711
45	Pfizer Inc.	40,800
46	American Standard Companies	38,500
47	Warner-Lambert Company	36,000
48	Ingersoll-Rand Company	35,932
49	Chase Manhattan Corp.	35,774
50	ITT Corporation	35,000

Rank	Company	Employees
51	American Brands, Inc.	34,820
52	Colgate-Palmolive Company	32,800
53	Pitney Bowes Inc.	32,792
54	American International Group	32,000
55	Avon Products, Inc.	30,400
56	Texaco Inc.	29,713
57	Pathmark Stores, Inc.	29,000
58	Loral Corporation	28,900
59	Dean Witter, Discover & Co.	28,475
60	Marsh & McLennan Companies	26,000
61	The City University of New York	25,800
62	Loews Corporation	25,400
63	Automatic Data Processing, Inc.	25,000
64	Champion International Corp.	24,615
65	The Caldor Corporation	24,000
66	Barnes & Noble, Inc.	23,500
67	Echlin Inc.	23,400
68	U.S. Industries, Inc.	23,230
69	Volt Information Sciences, Inc.	23,000
70	Dover Corporation	22,992
71	MacAndrews & Forbes Holdings	22,328
72	First Data Corporation	22,000
73	Hooper Holmes, Inc.	21,850
74	Schering-Plough Corporation	21,200
75	Capital Cities/ABC, Inc.	20,200
76	Metromedia Company	20,000
77	Petrie Retail, Inc.	19,500
78	Advance Publications, Inc.	19,000
79	Trump Organization	19,000
80	Union Camp Corporation	18,894
81	Becton, Dickinson and Co.	18,600
82	The Interpublic Group of Cos.	18,200
83	Praxair, Inc.	17,780
84	Lefrak Organization Inc.	17,400
85	Consolidated Edison Company of New York, Inc.	17,097
86	J.P. Morgan & Co. Incorporated	17,055
87	American Retail Group, Inc.	17,000
88	Paine Webber Group Inc.	16,300
89	Omnicom Group Inc.	16,100
90	Continental Grain Company	16,000
91	The Grand Union Company	16,000
92	New York Life Insurance Company	15,534
93	The Bank of New York Company, Inc.	15,477
94	The McGraw-Hill Companies	15,339
95	New York University	15,300
96	Pittston Services Group	15,100
97	The Warnaco Group, Inc.	14,800
98	Bankers Trust New York Corp.	14,529
99	Westvaco Corporation	14,170
100	EMCOR Group, Inc.	14,000

The New York 500: Largest Companies by Employees
in *Hoover's Guide to the Top New York Companies* (continued)

Rank	Company	Employees	Rank	Company	Employees
101	Franciscan Sisters of the		151	Empire Blue Cross/Blue Shield	7,900
	Poor Health System, Inc.	14,000	152	Alleghany Corporation	7,650
102	The Hearst Corporation	14,000	153	The Guardian Life Insurance	7,602
103	Phillips-Van Heusen Corp.	13,800	154	Computer Associates Intl.	7,500
104	The Equitable Companies Inc.	13,600	155	The Bear Stearns Companies	7,481
105	Alexander & Alexander Services	13,300	156	Hubbell Inc.	7,405
106	Helmsley Enterprises, Inc.	13,000	157	General Host Corporation	7,400
107	Avis, Inc.	12,800	158	The Goldman Sachs Group, L.P.	7,200
108	The New York Times Company	12,800	159	The Multicare Companies Inc.	7,000
109	Olin Corporation	12,800	160	Renco Group Inc.	7,000
110	Public Service Enterprise Group	12,390	161	Tollman Hundley Hotels	7,000
111	General Signal Corporation	12,200	162	Lehman Brothers Holdings Inc.	6,950
112	Union Carbide Corporation	12,004	163	Lechters, Inc.	6,911
113	First Fidelity Bancorporation	12,000	164	Federal Paper Board Company	6,890
114	Foster Wheeler Corporation	11,685	165	Bell Communications Research	6,624
115	McCrory Corporation	11,300	166	J. Crew Group Inc.	6,600
116	Triarc Companies, Inc.	11,250	167	Columbia University in the	
117	The Chubb Corporation	11,200		City of New York	6,570
118	Saks Holdings, Inc.	11,000	168	Arrow Electronics, Inc.	6,500
119	Crane Co.	10,700	169	Catholic Medical Center of	
120	General Public Utilities Corp.	10,534		Brooklyn & Queens	6,500
121	Dow Jones & Company, Inc.	10,300	170	Pall Corporation	6,500
122	The Dyson-Kissner-Moran Corp.	10,000	171	CBS Inc.	6,400
123	Maidenform, Inc.	10,000	172	Dress Barn, Inc.	6,400
124	Yale University	10,000	173	The Mutual Life Insurance Co.	6,400
125	Young & Rubicam Inc.	9,932	174	D'Arcy Masius Benton & Bowles	6,333
126	The Estée Lauder Companies	9,900	175	Finlay Enterprises, Inc.	6,250
127	Amerada Hess Corporation	9,858	176	Entex Information Services	6,200
128	Coltec Industries Inc.	9,800	177	The Reader's Digest Association	6,200
129	Southern New England		178	Midlantic Corporation	6,174
	Telecommunications	9,797	179	Allegheny Power System, Inc.	6,061
130	Morgan Stanley Group Inc.	9,685	180	Memorial Sloan-Kettering	
131	Reliance Group Holdings, Inc.	9,675		Cancer Center	6,050
132	The Port Authority of New York		181	Ethan Allen Interiors Inc.	6,048
	and New Jersey	9,200	182	Noel Group, Inc.	6,025
133	Sequa Corporation	9,200	183	CARQUEST Corp.	6,000
134	Sbarro, Inc.	9,100	184	McKinsey & Company	6,000
135	Salomon Inc	9,077	185	Pullman Company	6,000
136	Avnet, Inc.	9,000	186	Long Island Lighting Company	5,950
137	Johnson & Higgins	8,750	187	United States Surgical Corp.	5,922
138	C. R. Bard, Inc.	8,650	188	Perkin-Elmer Corporation	5,890
139	"21" International Holdings, Inc.	8,500	189	Engelhard Corporation	5,830
140	Colin Service Systems, Inc.	8,500	190	Brandon Systems Corporation	5,745
141	Montefiore Medical Center	8,223	191	WHX Corporation	5,684
142	Duracell International Inc.	8,100	192	Scholastic Corporation	5,636
143	UIS, Inc.	8,100	193	Republic New York Corporation	5,500
144	World Color	8,100	194	Amphenol Corporation	5,290
145	ASARCO Incorporated	8,000	195	J. M. Huber Corporation	5,163
146	Butler International, Inc.	8,000	196	Chic by H.I.S, Inc.	5,125
147	CUC International Inc.	8,000	197	Cygne Designs, Inc.	5,000
148	Liz Claiborne, Inc.	8,000	198	Cytec Industries Inc.	5,000
149	Rainbow Apparel Company	8,000	199	Lexmark International Group	5,000
150	Witco Corporation	7,955	200	Prime Hospitality Corp.	5,000

The New York 500: Largest Companies by Employees
in *Hoover's Guide to the Top New York Companies* (continued)

Rank	Company	Employees	Rank	Company	Employees
201	The Riese Organization	5,000	251	Fairchild Corporation	3,500
202	Securitas Lock Group, Inc.	5,000	252	New York Power Authority	3,500
203	Stone & Webster, Incorporated	5,000	253	Block Drug Company, Inc.	3,491
204	Towers Perrin	5,000	254	Tambrands Inc.	3,400
205	Big V Supermarkets Inc.	4,900	255	Tiffany & Co.	3,306
206	Handy & Harman	4,826	256	Doral Hotels & Resorts	
207	Parsons Brinckerhoff, Inc.	4,800		Management Company	3,300
208	Air Express International Corp.	4,783	257	Hudson General Corporation	3,300
209	Cablevision Systems Corporation	4,698	258	Standard Motor Products, Inc.	3,300
210	Donaldson, Lufkin & Jenrette	4,676	259	Ziff-Davis Publishing Company	3,300
211	International Flavors &		260	Ampal-American Israel Corp.	3,294
	Fragrances Inc.	4,570	261	Bozell, Jacobs, Kenyon &	
212	K-III Communications Corp.	4,550		Eckhardt	3,270
213	GAF Corporation	4,500	262	Skadden, Arps, Slate,	
214	King Kullen Grocery Company	4,500		Meagher & Flom	3,200
215	United Retail Group, Inc.	4,400	263	Associated Press	3,150
216	Leucadia National Corporation	4,374	264	Quantum Restaurant Group, Inc.	3,143
217	Hunter Douglas, Inc.	4,300	265	Federal Reserve Bank of New York	3,100
218	TLC Beatrice International		266	Forstmann & Company, Inc.	3,000
	Holdings, Inc.	4,300	267	Jordache Enterprises, Inc.	3,000
219	Citizens Utilities Company	4,294	268	Polo/Ralph Lauren Corporation	3,000
220	Nobody beats the Wiz	4,285	269	Sealed Air Corporation	3,000
221	First Brands Corporation	4,200	270	Smith Corona Corporation	3,000
222	Genovese Drug Stores, Inc.	4,200	271	Ultramar Corporation	3,000
223	Mayfair Supermarkets Inc.	4,200	272	Wakefern Food Corporation	3,000
224	PLY GEM Industries, Inc.	4,200	273	Griffon Corporation	2,900
225	Salant Corporation	4,200	274	Leslie Fay Companies, Inc.	2,900
226	Digital Solutions, Inc.	4,150	275	Terex Corporation	2,850
227	Bed Bath & Beyond, Inc.	4,100	276	A. L. Pharma Inc.	2,819
228	Big Flower Press Holdings, Inc.	4,100	277	Garan, Incorporated	2,800
229	UCAR International Inc.	4,074	278	National Envelope Corporation	2,800
230	Nine West Group Inc.	4,021	279	The Genlyte Group Incorporated	2,795
231	Coca-Cola Bottling Co. of		280	AT&T Capital Corporation	2,700
	New York	4,000	281	Bowne & Co., Inc.	2,700
232	Herman's Sporting Goods, Inc.	4,000	282	The Newark Group, Inc.	2,700
233	Silgan Holdings Inc.	4,000	283	People's Bank	2,700
234	Teachers Ins. and Annuity Assoc.	4,000	284	Rayonier Inc.	2,700
235	U.S. HomeCare Corporation	4,000	285	Rayonier Timberlands, L.P.	2,700
236	WR Acquisition, Inc.	4,000	286	Culbro Corporation	2,695
237	Hanover Direct, Inc.	3,900	287	Crompton & Knowles Corp.	2,652
238	UST Inc.	3,817	288	W. R. Berkley Corporation	2,607
239	Village Super Market, Inc.	3,800	289	Great American Recreation, Inc.	2,590
240	Western Publishing Group, Inc.	3,800	290	Petroleum Heat and Power Co.	2,574
241	AnnTaylor Stores Corporation	3,741	291	TIG Holdings, Inc.	2,550
242	Continental Can Co.	3,729	292	Fortunoff Fine Jewelry &	
243	The New York Public Library	3,680		Silverware, Inc.	2,500
244	Carter-Wallace, Inc.	3,670	293	Gilman Paper Co.	2,500
245	Tosco Corporation	3,613	294	Harris Chemical Group	2,500
246	Air & Water Technologies		295	Kings Super Markets, Inc.	2,500
	Corporation	3,600	296	The Metropolitan Museum of Art	2,500
247	Foodarama Supermarkets, Inc.	3,600	297	National Spinning Company	2,500
248	Wellman, Inc.	3,600	298	Pergament Home Centers, Inc.	2,500
249	Galey & Lord, Inc.	3,556	299	Schott Corporation	2,500
250	The Brooklyn Union Gas Co.	3,506	300	U.S. Trust Corporation	2,500

The New York 500: Largest Companies by Employees
in *Hoover's Guide to the Top New York Companies* (continued)

Rank	Company	Employees	Rank	Company	Employees
301	The Turner Corporation	2,499	351	Duty Free International, Inc.	2,000
302	ICC Industries Inc.	2,466	352	Esmark, Inc.	2,000
303	Bozell Worldwide, Inc.	2,450	353	Goya Foods, Inc.	2,000
304	Red Apple Group	2,425	354	Hofstra University	2,000
305	Innodata Corporation	2,420	355	Horsehead Industries	2,000
306	Loehmann's Holdings, Inc.	2,406	356	International Terminal Operating	
307	BIC Corporation	2,400		Company	2,000
308	Brylane Inc.	2,400	357	Overseas Shipholding Group	2,000
309	Eagle Electric Manufacturing	2,400	358	Pharmhouse Corporation	2,000
310	EXECUTONE Information		359	Photocircuits Corporation	2,000
	Systems, Inc.	2,400	360	Plaid Clothing Group, Inc.	2,000
311	Russ Berrie & Company Inc.	2,400	361	Potamkin Manhattan Corp.	2,000
312	United Merchants and		362	Bush Boake Allen Inc.	1,975
	Manufacturers, Inc.	2,400	363	MasterCard International	
313	Symbol Technologies, Inc.	2,387		Incorporated	1,975
314	The Alpine Group, Inc.	2,380	364	Sturm, Ruger & Company, Inc.	1,910
315	National Patent Development		365	Pace University	1,904
	Corporation	2,368	366	Devon Group, Inc.	1,900
316	Syms Corp.	2,364	367	I. Appel Corporation	1,900
317	General Re Corporation	2,360	368	United Industrial Corporation	1,900
318	Landstar Systems, Inc.	2,330	369	Macromedia Inc.	1,899
319	Benson Eyecare Corporation	2,300	370	PAXAR Corporation	1,891
320	Cablevision Industries Corp.	2,300	371	Family Bargain Corporation	1,870
321	Century Communications Corp.	2,300	372	The Care Group, Inc.	1,865
322	Inserra Supermarkets	2,300	373	EnviroSource, Inc.	1,850
323	Micro Warehouse, Inc.	2,300	374	Buck Consultants, Inc.	1,840
324	Modell's Sporting Goods, Inc.	2,300	375	Park Electrochemical Corp.	1,830
325	Movie Star, Inc.	2,300	376	Celadon Group Inc.	1,802
326	FlightSafety International, Inc.	2,246	377	A-P-A Transport Corporation	1,800
327	St. John's University	2,230	378	Fab Industries, Inc.	1,800
328	Baker & Taylor Inc.	2,200	379	Fedders Corporation	1,800
329	Barneys New York	2,200	380	Gemini Consulting, Inc.	1,800
330	Capital Mercury Shirt Corp.	2,200	381	Inteplast Corporation	1,800
331	Kinney System, Inc.	2,200	382	Marine Transport Lines, Inc.	1,800
332	Minerals Technologies Inc.	2,200	383	Parsons & Whittemore, Inc.	1,800
333	Shorewood Packaging		384	Schein Pharmaceutical, Inc.	1,800
	Corporation	2,200	385	Sigma Plastics Group	1,800
334	Staff Builders, Inc.	2,200	386	SLM International, Inc.	1,800
335	Tops Appliance City, Inc.	2,200	387	Ark Restaurants Corp.	1,797
336	American Banknote Corp.	2,155	388	Oxford Health Plans, Inc.	1,770
337	Computer Horizons Corp.	2,150	389	Information Builders, Inc.	1,750
338	IIC Industries Inc.	2,106	390	Donnkenny, Inc.	1,710
339	AmeriData Technologies, Inc.	2,100	391	AMREP Corporation	1,700
340	Hartz Group Inc.	2,100	392	Dime Bancorp, Inc.	1,700
341	HFS Inc.	2,100	393	Metallurg, Inc.	1,700
342	USLIFE Corporation	2,100	394	United Auto Group, Inc.	1,700
343	Louis Berger International, Inc.	2,036	395	John Wiley & Sons, Inc.	1,680
344	The Money Store Inc.	2,035	396	Western Beef, Inc.	1,660
345	American Nukem Corporation	2,000	397	Orange and Rockland	
346	Benjamin Moore & Co.	2,000		Utilities, Inc.	1,640
347	Bloomberg L.P.	2,000	398	The Summit Bancorporation	1,623
348	Brown Brothers Harriman & Co.	2,000	399	Duane Reade Holding	
349	Colorado Prime Corporation	2,000		Company	1,600
350	Darby Group Companies, Inc.	2,000	400	Henry Schein, Inc.	1,600

Rank	Company	Employees	Rank	Company	Employees
401	Katz Media Group, Inc.	1,600	451	MobileMedia Corporation	1,284
402	Magic Restaurants, Inc.	1,600	452	United Water Resources Inc.	1,282
403	Marvel Entertainment Group, Inc.	1,600	453	Rag Shops, Inc.	1,280
404	Nextel Communications, Inc.	1,600	454	Concurrent Computer Corp.	1,250
405	Playtex Products, Inc.	1,600	455	Lumex, Inc.	1,215
406	The Rockefeller University	1,600	456	Cleary, Gottlieb, Steen & Hamilton	1,200
407	Trans-Resources, Inc.	1,600	457	Conway Stores, Inc.	1,200
408	Warren Equities Inc.	1,600	458	Croscill, Inc.	1,200
409	Meridian Sports Incorporated	1,537	459	Fried, Frank, Harris, Shriver & Jacobson	1,200
410	GP Financial Corp.	1,528	460	Mendik Company	1,200
411	Danskin, Inc.	1,525	461	Peerless Importers, Inc.	1,200
412	Webcraft Technologies, Inc.	1,516	462	Wildlife Conservation Society	1,200
413	United Waste Systems, Inc.	1,507	463	Long Island Bancorp	1,188
414	Allied Digital Technologies Corp.	1,500	464	Del Laboratories, Inc.	1,175
415	Amerifoods Companies	1,500	465	K & F Industries, Inc.	1,173
416	Applied Graphics Technology	1,500	466	Lynch Corporation	1,173
417	The BISYS Group, Inc.	1,500	467	Forest Laboratories, Inc.	1,171
418	CMP Publications, Inc.	1,500	468	Valley National Bancorp	1,168
419	Curtiss-Wright Corporation	1,500	469	NUI Corporation	1,167
420	D'Agostino Supermarkets, Inc.	1,500	470	BHC Communications, Inc.	1,163
421	Dan's Supreme Supermarkets	1,500	471	Joule Inc.	1,160
422	F. Schumacher & Company	1,500	472	Napco Security Systems, Inc.	1,150
423	Fordham University	1,500	473	Square Industries, Inc.	1,139
424	Hayward Industries, Inc.	1,500	474	Dynamics Corporation of America	1,132
425	Health Insurance Plan of Greater New York	1,500	475	Infinity Broadcasting Corp.	1,114
426	Lone Star Industries, Inc.	1,500	476	LCS Industries, Inc.	1,112
427	March of Dimes Birth Defects Foundation	1,500	477	Audiovox Corporation	1,107
428	Orion Capital Corporation	1,500	478	Datascope Corporation	1,100
429	P.C. Richard & Son	1,500	479	Davis Polk & Wardwell	1,100
430	Remington Products, Inc.	1,500	480	Hudson County News Company	1,100
431	Global Directmail Corporation	1,489	481	ILC Industries, Inc.	1,100
432	The Jewish Board of Family & Children's Services Inc.	1,486	482	LeBoeuf, Lamb, Greene & MacRae	1,100
433	Alliance Capital Management	1,461	483	Rose Art Industries	1,100
434	New York Stock Exchange, Inc.	1,450	484	Starrett Corporation	1,100
435	Consolidated Technology Group	1,432	485	The Topps Company, Inc.	1,100
436	Alliance Entertainment Corp.	1,426	486	Synetic, Inc.	1,090
437	Plastic Specialties and Technologies, Inc.	1,420	487	Autotote Corporation	1,070
438	Grey Advertising Inc.	1,418	488	Hovnanian Enterprises, Inc.	1,070
439	Blyth Industries, Inc.	1,400	489	Baltek Corporation	1,065
440	Chock full o'Nuts Corporation	1,400	490	Baldwin Technology Company	1,055
441	Chris-Craft Industries, Inc.	1,385	491	Associated Merchandising Corp.	1,050
442	The United Illuminating Co.	1,377	492	Malcolm Pirnie, Inc.	1,050
443	Tower Air, Inc.	1,367	493	Queens Group, Inc.	1,050
444	Cambrex Corporation	1,336	494	AEP Industries Inc.	1,040
445	The Union Corporation	1,315	495	Dataflex Corporation	1,032
446	Donna Karan, Inc.	1,310	496	E-Z-EM, Inc.	1,020
447	Raytech Corporation	1,310	497	TransTechnology Corporation	1,014
448	Di Giorgio Corp.	1,305	498	Bernard Chaus, Inc.	1,009
449	Andover Togs, Inc.	1,300	499	TII Industries, Inc.	1,006
450	Cellular Communications, Inc.	1,300	500	Charmer Industries, Inc.	1,000

New York–Area Companies on the *FORTUNE* 500 List of Largest US Corporations

Rank	Company	Location	1994 Sales ($ mil.)	Employees
5	AT&T	New York, NY	75,094	304,500
6	General Electric	Fairfield, CT	64,687	221,000
7	Intl. Business Machines	Armonk, NY	64,052	243,039
10	Philip Morris	New York, NY	53,776	165,000
13	Prudential Ins. Co. of America	Newark, NJ	36,946	99,000
16	Texaco	White Plains, NY	33,768	30,042
17	Citicorp	New York, NY	31,650	82,600
20	PepsiCo	Purchase, NY	28,472	471,000
23	ITT	New York, NY	23,767	110,000
26	American International Group	New York, NY	22,386	32,000
27	Metropolitan Life Insurance	New York, NY	22,258	43,354
34	GTE	Stamford, CT	19,944	111,162
37	Travelers Inc.	New York, NY	18,465	52,000
40	Merrill Lynch	New York, NY	18,233	43,800
41	Xerox	Stamford, CT	17,837	87,600
52	Johnson & Johnson	New Brunswick, NJ	15,734	81,500
55	American Express	New York, NY	15,593	72,412
57	RJR Nabisco Holdings	New York, NY	15,366	70,600
59	Merck	Whitehouse Station, NJ	14,970	47,500
60	International Paper	Purchase, NY	14,966	70,000
64	Loews	New York, NY	13,515	28,100
67	NYNEX	New York, NY	13,307	65,400
72	AlliedSignal	Morris Township, NJ	12,817	87,500
74	Chemical Banking Corp.	New York, NY	12,685	42,130
84	New York Life Insurance	New York, NY	12,067	7,912
86	Bristol-Myers Squibb	New York, NY	11,984	47,700
87	J.P. Morgan & Co.	New York, NY	11,915	17,055
93	Melville	Rye, NY	11,286	117,414
95	Chase Manhattan Corp.	New York, NY	11,187	36,690
101	Teachers Ins. & Annuity Assn.	New York, NY	10,551	4,322
105	Great Atlantic & Pacific Tea	Montvale, NJ	10,384	94,000
118	Morgan Stanley Group	New York, NY	9,376	9,685
122	Lehman Brothers	New York, NY	9,190	8,512
130	American Home Products	Madison, NJ	8,966	74,009
131	Toys "R" Us	Paramus, NJ	8,746	58,000
137	American Brands	Old Greenwich, CT	8,442	34,820
143	Woolworth	New York, NY	8,293	119,000
144	Pfizer	New York, NY	8,281	40,800
153	Viacom	New York, NY	7,637	70,000
154	Colgate-Palmolive	New York, NY	7,588	32,800
155	Bankers Trust New York Corp.	New York, NY	7,503	14,529
157	CPC International	Englewood Cliffs, NJ	7,425	41,900
159	Time Warner	New York, NY	7,396	28,800
162	Supermarkets Genl. Hldgs.	Woodbridge, NJ	7,227	30,000
172	Amerada Hess	New York, NY	6,699	9,858
175	Dean Witter, Discover	New York, NY	6,603	28,475
178	Equitable	New York, NY	6,447	13,600
179	Warner-Lambert	Morris Plains, NJ	6,417	36,000
181	Capital Cities/ABC	New York, NY	6,379	20,200
182	Tosco	Stamford, CT	6,366	3,613

New York–Area Companies on the *FORTUNE* 500 List of Largest US Corporations (continued)

Rank	Company	Location	1994 Sales ($ mil.)	Employees
184	Salomon	New York, NY	6,278	9,077
188	Consolidated Edison of New York	New York, NY	6,240	17,097
190	Guardian Life Ins. Co. of America	New York, NY	6,134	5,395
202	Public Service Enterprise Group	Newark, NJ	5,916	11,919
207	Chubb	Warren, NJ	5,710	10,500
220	Champion International	Stamford, CT	5,318	24,600
222	Continental	New York, NY	5,164	9,400
234	Dun & Bradstreet	Wilton, CT	4,896	47,500
236	Union Carbide	Danbury, CT	4,865	12,004
248	Schering-Plough	Madison, NJ	4,657	21,200
249	Arrow Electronics	Melville, NY	4,649	6,426
259	Ingersoll-Rand	Woodcliff Lake, NJ	4,508	35,932
270	Avon Products	New York, NY	4,325	30,400
275	Bank of New York Co.	New York, NY	4,251	15,477
286	Loral	New York, NY	4,009	32,600
289	Paine Webber Group	New York, NY	3,964	16,600
298	General Re	Stamford, CT	3,826	3,282
300	Pitney Bowes	Stamford, CT	3,823	32,792
306	CBS	New York, NY	3,712	6,400
311	General Public Utilities	Parsippany, NJ	3,650	10,534
320	Avnet	Great Neck, NY	3,553	8,000
335	Bear Stearns	New York, NY	3,441	7,321
336	Marsh & McLennan	New York, NY	3,435	26,100
338	Union Camp	Wayne, NJ	3,396	18,894
361	Dover	New York, NY	3,085	22,992
362	Long Island Lighting	Hicksville, NY	3,067	5,947
366	Reliance Group Holdings	New York, NY	3,047	9,300
403	Reader's Digest Association	Pleasantville, NY	2,806	6,700
411	McGraw-Hill	New York, NY	2,761	15,339
414	Caldor	Norwalk, CT	2,749	24,000
419	Praxair	Danbury, CT	2,711	17,780
424	Pittston	Stamford, CT	2,667	17,829
426	Olin	Stamford, CT	2,658	12,800
428	Turner Corp.	New York, NY	2,639	2,400
431	Westvaco	New York, NY	2,613	14,170
441	Republic New York Corp.	New York, NY	2,560	5,500
442	Becton Dickinson	Franklin Lakes, NJ	2,560	18,600
445	First Fidelity Bancorp.	Newark, NJ	2,553	12,000
453	Grand Union Holdings	Wayne, NJ	2,477	17,000
454	Ultramar	Greenwich, CT	2,475	3,000
456	Automatic Data Proc.	Roseland, NJ	2,469	22,000
459	Allegheny Power System	New York, NY	2,452	6,061
468	Engelhard	Iselin, NJ	2,386	5,830
477	New York Times	New York, NY	2,358	12,800
488	Foster Wheeler	Clinton, NJ	2,271	11,685
489	Olsten	Melville, NY	2,260	7,900
493	Witco	Greenwich, CT	2,235	7,955
494	Echlin	Branford, CT	2,230	20,600

Source: *FORTUNE*; May 15, 1995

New York–Area Companies on the *Business Week* 1000 List of America's Most Valuable Companies

Rank	Company	Location	1995 Market Value ($ mil.)
1	General Electric	Fairfield, CT	93,402
2	AT&T	Morristown, NJ	81,000
6	Merck	Whitehouse Station, NJ	52,877
7	Philip Morris	New York, NY	52,317
9	International Business Machines	Armonk, NY	44,261
12	Johnson & Johnson	New Brunswick, NJ	36,490
16	American International Group	New York, NY	32,792
17	GTE	Stamford, CT	32,210
19	Bristol-Myers Squibb	New York, NY	31,388
21	PepsiCo	Purchase, NY	31,007
29	Pfizer	New York, NY	26,127
35	American Home Products	Madison, NJ	21,865
43	Citicorp	New York, NY	17,779
47	American Express	New York, NY	16,675
48	NYNEX	New York, NY	16,625
49	Texaco	White Plains, NY	16,431
50	Viacom	New York, NY	15,953
55	Time Warner	New York, NY	14,643
57	Schering-Plough	Madison, NJ	14,578
59	Schlumberger	New York, NY	13,777
61	Capital Cities/ABC	New York, NY	13,632
70	Travelers	New York, NY	12,304
71	J.P. Morgan	New York, NY	12,107
73	Xerox	Stamford, CT	11,729
77	AlliedSignal	Morris Township, NJ	10,724
79	General Re	Stamford, CT	10,664
82	ITT	New York, NY	10,303
83	Warner-Lambert	Morris Plains, NJ	10,297
85	Chemical Banking	New York, NY	9,806
90	International Paper	Purchase, NY	9,547
91	Colgate-Palmolive	New York, NY	9,314
94	Computer Associates International	Islandia, NY	9,160
101	Dun & Bradstreet	Wilton, CT	8,787
103	Automatic Data Processing	Roseland, NJ	8,692
115	CPC International	Englewood Cliffs, NJ	7,870
119	Toys "R" Us	Paramus, NJ	7,737
120	RJR Nabisco Holdings	New York, NY	7,659
125	American Brands	Old Greenwich, CT	7,495
126	Merrill Lynch	New York, NY	7,441
131	Public Service Enterprise Group	Newark, NJ	7,127
138	Dean Witter, Discover	New York, NY	6,861
139	Chubb	Warren, NJ	6,826
146	Chase Manhattan	New York, NY	6,504
148	Consolidated Edison Co. of N.Y.	New York, NY	6,489
152	Bank of New York	New York, NY	6,282
159	Marsh & McLennan	New York, NY	6,052
165	First Data	Hackensack, NJ	5,900
167	UST	Greenwich, CT	5,834
170	Loews	New York, NY	5,727
180	Pitney Bowes	Stamford, CT	5,370
181	International Flavors & Fragrances	New York, NY	5,364
186	Reader's Digest Association	Pleasantville, NY	5,213
190	Morgan Stanley Group	New York, NY	5,117
200	Bankers Trust New York	New York, NY	4,928
204	Duracell International	Bethel, CT	4,883

New York–Area Companies on the *Business Week* 1000 List of America's Most Valuable Companies (continued)

Rank	Company	Location	1995 Market Value ($ mil.)
218	Amerada Hess	New York, NY	4,556
229	Union Carbide	Danbury, CT	4,254
241	First Fidelity Bancorporation	Newark, NJ	4,090
246	CUC International	Stamford, CT	4,025
250	CBS	New York, NY	3,962
255	Avon Products	New York, NY	3,885
263	Champion International	Stamford, CT	3,837
265	Salomon	New York, NY	3,811
281	Union Camp	Wayne, NJ	3,605
285	Becton, Dickinson	Franklin Lakes, NJ	3,528
286	McGraw-Hill	New York, NY	3,502
288	General Public Utilities	Parsippany, NJ	3,485
290	Dow Jones	New York, NY	3,467
293	Loral	New York, NY	3,448
296	Melville	Rye, NY	3,431
299	Dover	New York, NY	3,374
300	Ingersoll-Rand	Woodcliff Lake, NJ	3,363
313	Equitable	New York, NY	3,186
318	Praxair	Danbury, CT	3,119
350	Allegheny Power System	New York, NY	2,803
365	Westvaco	New York, NY	2,653
367	Republic New York	New York, NY	2,624
369	Interpublic Group	New York, NY	2,609
375	MBIA	Armonk, NY	2,586
379	Citizens Utilities	Stamford, CT	2,545
388	Engelhard	Iselin, NJ	2,512
407	Pall	East Hills, NY	2,321
416	Forest Laboratories	New York, NY	2,264
448	Bear Stearns	New York, NY	2,106
460	Echlin	Branford, CT	2,055
466	Woolworth	New York, NY	2,020
484	Omnicom Group	New York, NY	1,937
488	Arrow Electronics	Melville, NY	1,916
489	Lehman Brothers Holdings	New York, NY	1,913
491	BHC Communications	New York, NY	1,910
494	Long Island Lighting	Hicksville, NY	1,895
528	Paine Webber Group	New York, NY	1,725
536	General Signal	Stamford, CT	1,688
557	Midlantic	Edison, NJ	1,614
559	Witco	Greenwich, CT	1,607
564	Tambrands	White Plains, NY	1,585
566	Avnet	Great Neck, NY	1,575
569	Marvel Entertainment Group	New York, NY	1,561
593	Oxford Health Plans	Norwalk, CT	1,449
599	AMBAC	New York, NY	1,430
604	Olsten	Melville, NY	1,427
607	C. R. Bard	Murray Hill, NJ	1,392
609	FlightSafety International	Flushing, NY	1,390
636	Transatlantic Holdings	New York, NY	1,318
637	Cablevision Systems	Woodbury, NY	1,317
641	King World Productions	New York, NY	1,310
642	Leucadia National	New York, NY	1,306
647	TIG Holdings	New York, NY	1,288
648	Hospitality Franchise Systems	Parsippany, NJ	1,285
663	Liz Claiborne	New York, NY	1,262

New York–Area Companies on the *Business Week* 1000 List of America's Most Valuable Companies (continued)

Rank	Company	Location	1995 Market Value ($ mil.)
666	Federal Paper Board	Montvale, NJ	1,259
670	Nextel Communications	Rutherford, NJ	1,250
684	Perkin-Elmer	Norwalk, CT	1,216
689	AT&T Capital	Morristown, NJ	1,213
698	Coltec Industries	New York, NY	1,197
699	U. S. Surgical	Norwalk, CT	1,194
708	Foster Wheeler	Clinton, NJ	1,173
710	Brooklyn Union Gas	Brooklyn, NY	1,166
716	ASARCO	New York, NY	1,146
723	Infinity Broadcasting	New York, NY	1,135
733	New Plan Realty Trust	New York, NY	1,105
742	Olin	Stamford, CT	1,094
744	Alleghany	New York, NY	1,089
763	Tosco	Stamford, CT	1,070
777	Pittston Services Group	Stamford, CT	1,040
789	Chris-Craft Industries	New York, NY	1,020
807	Ultramar	Greenwich, CT	991
813	Nine West Group	Stamford, CT	973
823	Alexander & Alexander Services	New York, NY	955
838	Ogden	New York, NY	932
855	Crane	Stamford, CT	907
857	Crompton & Knowles	Stamford, CT	900
861	Wellman	Shrewsbury, NJ	896
869	Rayonier	Stamford, CT	887
871	Barnes & Noble	New York, NY	886
872	Gartner Group	Stamford, CT	884
875	USLIFE	New York, NY	875
876	Sealed Air	Saddle Brook, NJ	874
905	Overseas Shipholding Group	New York, NY	837
916	Bed Bath & Beyond	Springfield, NJ	821
929	First Brands	Danbury, CT	806
941	Zurich Reinsurance Centre Holdings	New York, NY	790
945	Micro Warehouse	Norwalk, CT	788
946	Scholastic	New York, NY	784
955	Century Communications	New Canaan, CT	773
963	Kimco Realty	New Hyde Park, NY	762
964	AnnTaylor Stores	New York, NY	759
967	BIC	Milford, CT	757
968	Valley National Bancorp	Wayne, NJ	756
972	Roberts Pharmaceutical	Eatontown, NJ	748
977	Vornado Realty Trust	Saddle Brook, NJ	742
981	Great Atlantic & Pacific Tea	Montvale, NJ	736
992	International CableTel	New York, NY	724

Source: *Business Week*; March 27, 1995

New York–Area Companies on the *Forbes* List of the 500 Largest Private Companies in the US

Rank	Company	Location	Sales ($ mil.)	Employees
4	Continental Grain	New York, NY	13,500**	15,250
6	Goldman Sachs Group	New York, NY	10,910	8,750
12	Ernst & Young LLP	New York, NY	6,424**	65,000
13	KPMG Peat Marwick	New York, NY	6,405**	72,000
15	Coopers & Lybrand LLP	New York, NY	5,981**	67,000
17	Deloitte Touche Tohmatsu International	Wilton, CT	5,639**	56,600
23	Advance Publications	Staten Island, NY	4,855**	24,000
25	Price Waterhouse	New York, NY	4,460	53,000
29	Pathmark Stores	Woodbridge, NJ	4,182	9,000
30	MacAndrews & Forbes Holdings	New York, NY	4,143	32,510
36	AIOC*	New York, NY	3,500**	450
40	Estee Lauder Cos	New York, NY	2,899	9,900
48	Hearst	New York, NY	2,331**	13,500
50	Transammonia	New York, NY	2,321**	212
52	Red Apple Group	New York, NY	2,250	2,425
58	Polo Ralph Lauren	New York, NY	2,000**	3,000
68	TLC Beatrice International Holdings	New York, NY	1,822	4,500
71	Lexmark International	Greenwich, CT	1,800	5,000
75	Avis	Garden City, NY	1,700**	12,800
77	Metromedia	East Rutherford, NJ	1,700**	20,000
78	Helmsley Enterprises	New York, NY	1,698**	13,000
82	Renco Group	New York, NY	1,650	7,100
84	Lefrak Organization	Rego Park, NY	1,627**	16,000
99	Entex Information Services	Rye Brook, NY	1,500	3,500
100	McKinsey & Co	New York, NY	1,500	6,200
104	Trump Organization	New York, NY	1,439**	20,000
108	JM Huber	Edison, NJ	1,325	5,500
127	Parsons & Whittemore	Rye Brook, NY	1,181**	2,000
132	GAF	Wayne, NJ	1,156	4,500
147	Young & Rubicam	New York, NY	1,060	10,800
148	Connell	Westfield, NJ	1,050	200
149	Neuman Distributors	Ridgefield, NJ	1,050	625
158	Johnson & Higgins	New York, NY	1,009	8,400
166	Nobody Beats the Wiz	Carteret, NJ	1,000**	4,285
172	World Color Press	New York, NY	972	6,690
173	21 International Holdings	New York, NY	962**	4,500
182	DiGiorgio	Carteret, NJ	934	1,305
195	ICC Industries	New York, NY	886	2,466
198	Quality King Distributors	Ronkonkoma, NY	880	700
202	Silgan	Stamford, CT	861	4,000
207	McCrory	New York, NY	840	11,300
209	Gould Paper	New York, NY	830	405
211	UIS	Jersey City, NJ	830	8,097
216	Ziff-Davis Publishing	New York, NY	813**	3,000
224	Hartz Group	New York, NY	800	2,100
239	Towers Perrin	New York, NY	767	5,000
242	Big V Supermarkets	Florida, NY	754	4,900
247	J Crew	New York, NY	734	5,600
258	King Kullen Grocery	Westbury, NY	700	4,500
259	Newark Group	Cranford, NJ	700	2,900

New York-Area Companies on the *Forbes* List of the 500 Largest Private Companies in the US (continued)

Rank	Company	Location	Sales ($ mil.)	Employees
288	M Fabrikant & Sons	New York, NY	655	850
292	Bloomberg Financial Markets	New York, NY	650	2,100
299	Rickel Home Centers	South Plainfield, NJ	640	5,500
312	D'Arcy Masius Benton & Bowles	New York, NY	608	6,405
315	Charmer Industries	Long Island City, NY	605**	1,230
334	Peerless Importers	Brooklyn, NY	585**	1,200
335	Skadden, Arps, Slate, Meagher & Flom	New York, NY	582**	3,200
338	Brylane*	New York, NY	579	2,400
349	Schein Pharmaceutical	Florham Park, NJ	561**	2,500
354	Horsehead Industries	New York, NY	550	2,000
356	Tishman Realty & Construction	New York, NY	550**	575
358	Benjamin Moore & Co	Montvale, NJ	547	2,000
365	Goya Foods	Secaucus, NJ	528	2,000
380	Sansone Auto Network	Avenel, NJ	504	535
388	Inserra Supermarkets	Mahwah, NJ	500**	2,300
394	Drug Guild Distributors	Secaucus, NJ	494	328
406	Kinray*	New York, NY	480	200
408	Parsons Brinckerhoff*	New York, NY	477	4,700
415	Metallurg	New York, NY	472	1,242
419	Perry H Koplik & Sons	New York, NY	462	105
425	Harris Chemical Group*	New York, NY	460	2,500
428	Gilman Paper*	New York, NY	455**	2,500
431	Barneys New York	New York, NY	450	2,200
452	Darby Group Cos	Westbury, NY	430**	2,000
458	Krasdale Foods	White Plains, NY	425	600
461	Titan Industrial	New York, NY	425	175
465	Donna Karan	New York, NY	420	1,310
471	Toresco Enterprises	Springfield, NJ	416	798
474	Big M	Totowa, NJ	411**	3,367
482	Pullman	Lebanon, NJ	402**	3,000

Source: *Forbes*; December 4, 1995
* New in 1995
** Estimate

New York-Area Companies on the *Working Woman* 50

Rank	Company	Location	Owner/Executive	1994 Sales ($ mil.)
1	TLC Beatrice	New York, NY	Loida N. Lewis	1,820
7	Warnaco	New York, NY	Linda Wachner	789
8	Donna Karan	New York, NY	Donna Karan	465
24	J&R Music World	New York, NY	Rachelle Friedman	223
29	Bernard Chaus	New York, NY	Josephine Chaus	198
31	International Proteins	Fairfield, NJ	Celia Meilan	165
36	Andin International	New York, NY	Aya Azrielant	150
37	Adrienne Vittadini	New York, NY	Adrienne Vittadini	150
47	Joan & David	New York, NY	Joan Helpern	115
49	Turtle & Hughes	Linden , NJ	Suzanne Millard	114

Source: *Working Woman*, May 1995

New York–Area Companies on *Black Enterprise*'s List of Top 100 Black-Owned Industrial/Service Companies

Rank	Company	Location	1994 Sales ($ mil.)
1	TLC Beatrice International Holdings Inc.	New York, NY	1,800.0
9	Uniworld Group Inc.	New York, NY	104.1
17	Essence Communications Inc.	New York, NY	77.5
18	Granite Broadcasting Corp.	New York, NY	76.2
19	Marco International Inc.	Greenwich, CT	75.0
22	Rush Communications	New York, NY	65.0
31	The Mingo Group	New York, NY	49.2
58	Restoration Supermarket Corp.	Brooklyn, NY	29.3
59	Queen City Broadcasting Inc.	New York, NY	29.0
64	Inner City Broadcasting Corp.	New York, NY	27.9
72	Earl G. Graves Ltd.	New York, NY	24.8
82	Consolidated Beverage Corp.	New York, NY	21.1
87	American Urban Radio Networks	New York, NY	20.0

Source: *Black Enterprise*, June 1995

New York–Area Companies on the *Hispanic Business* 500

Rank	Company	Location	1994 Sales ($ mil.)
1	Goya Foods Inc.	Secaucus, NJ	527.0
21	Gaseteria Oil Corp.	Brooklyn, NY	101.0
27	Portfolio Acquisition Corp.	New York, NY	89.3
50	Popular Ford Sales Inc.	Brooklyn, NY	50.7
55	Spanish Broadcasting Syst. Inc.	New York, NY	49.1
75	Integral Construction Corp.	New York, NY	35.0
78	PAECO Inc.	New York, NY	34.0
143	Nelson Maintenance Services Inc.	Yonkers, NY	18.0
172	G & R Kings Holding Corp.	Brooklyn, NY	15.0
185	Somerset Investment Services Ltd.	Westport, CT	14.3
189	City Wide Security Services Inc.	Brooklyn, NY	14.0
211	Marsden Reproductions Inc.	New York, NY	13.0
214	La Rosa Del Monte Express Inc.	Bronx, NY	12.9
247	Metro Litho Inc.	Moonachie, NJ	10.7
252	Proftech Corp.	Elmsford, NY	10.5
256	Unalite Electric & Lighting Corp.	Long Island City, NY	10.2
269	Court Courier Systems Inc.	Edison, NJ	9.8
310	Fernandez Distributing Inc.	Elizabeth, NJ	8.2
344	CSR Construction Corp.	Nutley, NJ	7.2
388	Victory Wholesale Tobacco Dist. Inc.	Brooklyn, NY	6.2
415	Monti Moving & Storage Inc.	Brooklyn, NY	5.4
425	Lion Plastics Inc.	Clifton, NJ	5.3
433	Mast Distributors Inc.	Ronkonkoma, NY	5.1
447	Pamtours Great Neck Intl. Inc.	Great Neck, NY	5.0
462	Asensio Tours & Travel Corp.	New York, NY	4.5
463	Castro-Blanco, Piscioneri and Assoc.	New York, NY	4.5
474	Camin Cargo Control Inc.	Linden, NJ	4.4

Source: *Hispanic Business*, June 1995

New York–Area Companies on the *Inc.* 500 List of Fastest-Growing Private Companies

Rank	Company	Location	Sales Growth 1990–94 (% increase)	1994 Sales ($ mil.)
8	United Vision Group	Ossining, NY	13,238	28,009
42	PRT Corp. of America	New York, NY	2,910	13,876
79	CardMember Publishing	Stamford, CT	2,067	33,765
103	Transaction Information Systems	New York, NY	1,705	16,679
104	HRM Resources	New York, NY	1,694	3,767
105	Infinite Technology Group	Valley Stream, NY	1,691	4,066
275	Beechwood Data Systems	Clark, NJ	841	17,083
293	Executive Mortgage Bankers	Melville, NY	805	2,533
316	Energy Consortium	Iselin, NJ	732	4,008
348	Phonexpress	Fairfield, NJ	687	13,556
366	PNY Electronics	Moonachie, NJ	661	275,341
374	Programmed Solutions	Stamford, CT	651	3,304
396	Preferred Communications	Valley Stream, NY	620	1,628
403	MicroBiz	Mahwah, NJ	615	8,800
408	U.S. Computer Maintenance	Farmingdale, NY	602	14,443
440	Flash Creative Management	River Edge, NJ	561	2,077
496	Zeitech	New York, NY	518	25,460

Source: *Inc.*; October 17, 1995

New York–Area Companies on the *Forbes* 200 List of the Best Small Companies in America

Rank	Company	Location	5-Year Average Return (%)
5	Marisa Christina	New York, NY	66.5
12	Kenneth Cole Productions	New York, NY	40.7
26	Waterhouse Investor Services	New York, NY	34.0
28	American List	Mineola, NY	33.4
30	Blyth Industries	Greenwich, CT	32.4
34	Blimpie International	New York, NY	30.0
43	Ryan Beck & Co	West Orange, NJ	27.5
48	Hirsch International	Hauppauge, NY	26.6
58	Cheyenne Software	Roslyn Heights, NY	24.6
80	Hi-Tech Pharmacal	Amityville, NY	21.0
83	Wireless Telecom Group	Paramus, NJ	20.8
95	Jean Philippe Fragrances	New York, NY	19.5
134	Nu Horizons Electronics	Amityville, NY	16.8
138	First Central Financial	Lynbrook, NY	16.5
145	Brandon Systems	Lyndhurst, NJ	16.0
147	Nautica Enterprises	New York, NY	15.9
151	Vital Signs	Totowa, NJ	15.7
175	Paxar	White Plains, NY	14.3
188	Comverse Technology	Woodbury, NY	13.2

Source: *Forbes*; November 6, 1995

New York City Profile

CITY OF NEW YORK

OVERVIEW

New York, New York, was not named twice for emphasis, but ya wouldn't know it from the frenetic way life is lived there. The largest US city comprises a peninsula and numerous islands at the southernmost tip of New York State and includes the 5 boroughs of the Bronx, Brooklyn, Manhattan, Queens, and Staten Island. Its East Coast location belies the fact that New York City is the center of the universe: from Wall Street, the World Trade Center, and the United Nations, to Park Avenue, Broadway, and the Brooklyn Bridge, the Big Apple is the sun about which the worlds of finance, commerce, world politics, fashion, drama, and urban architecture revolve. (This might be disputed, but New Yorkers are firm in their conviction that it *is* a fact.) "Gotham" is the polyglot hub of a huge metropolitan area extending north to New Haven, Connecti-

cut, south to New Brunswick, New Jersey, and west to Wharton, New Jersey.

The "city that never sleeps" offers cultural attractions that range from classical music at Carnegie Hall to dancing in a sea of foam past 2 a.m. in a nightclub. Museums, art galleries, and architectural treasures are innumerable, and theatrical productions are widely varied.

The mayor is the one who sets the city's legislative agenda and forges its public image. Mayor Rudolph "Slasher of Budgets" Giuliani has spent 2 years in office campaigning for less government and more self-reliance (i.e., independence from federal and state subsidies). Controversial in this bastion of big-city liberalism, Giuliani has neverthless succeeded in reducing New York's payroll while maintaining "quality of life." Taxes have been reduced and the crime rate has fallen steeply.

WHEN

A large, sheltered bay at the mouth of the Hudson River enticed the Dutch West India Co. to establish Nieuw Amsterdam on the tip of Manhattan Island about 1625. Taverns outnumbered churches by 1640, and 18 different languages could be heard. In 1664 King Charles II of England granted his brother, the Duke of York, much of what is now New York State. The British sailed into New York Harbor and the Dutch yielded without a fight (though their influence is still felt in the helter-skelter layout of lower Manhattan's streets).

During the 18th century New York built cobblestone streets and established a paid police force. It briefly became the US capital after the Constitution was ratified in 1789. Three years later the "buttonwood agreement" established the New York Stock Exchange.

By 1820 the power of New York Harbor had driven its namesake past Philadelphia as the largest US city. New York had become the preeminent financial and trading center. In 1857 Frederick Olmstead began work on Central Park. During the Civil War, draft riots killed or injured 1,000 and caused serious damage.

Thomas Nast's famous political cartoons exposed the massive graft of Tammany Hall's Boss Tweed (who essentially ran city hall) in the 1870s. Robber barons such as J. P. Morgan (who acquired a vast railroad network) extended their power across the continent. In 1883 the Brooklyn Bridge was opened to traffic, and 3 years later the Statue of Liberty was unveiled. By 1890 New York's population had reached 1.4 million.

In 1897 the boroughs of Bronx, Brooklyn, Manhattan, Queens, and Staten Island were consolidated into one city. The lure of jobs during WWI induced southern blacks to move northward as the flow of overseas immigrants was cut off. In 1921 New York and New Jersey created the New York Port Authority to build and manage facilities in their shared port. Broadway theater grew to prominence, and jazz established itself uptown in Harlem. New York's importance as a banking center enticed companies to locate their headquarters there.

In 1929 the stock market crashed and the nation tumbled into the Depression. Fiorello La Guardia became mayor in 1933, and in a year he balanced the city's budget, dismantled its corruption, and secured federal projects.

After WWII a building boom and superhighways transformed the landscape. By the 1960s New York's financial community had eclipsed the importance of the port. In 1966 the city's mass transit system was completely shut down when transit workers walked out for 2 weeks.

In 1975 the city was saved from bankruptcy by a federal loan guarantee and budget cuts. Mayor Edward Koch was credited with turning the city around and attracting service businesses to replace lost industry. Nevertheless, during the 1980s the city lost big corporate headquarters to less expensive locations.

Mayor Rudolph Giuliani has taken a populist law-and-order approach to running the city's affairs. In 1995 productivity became a watchword as the mayor sought to maintain city services while slowing budget growth.

Form of government: Mayor/council
Fiscal year ends: June 30

WHO

Mayor: Rudolph W. Giuliani
Comptroller: Alan G. Hevesi
Public Advocate: Mark J. Green
Council Speaker and Majority Leader: Peter F. Vallone
Borough President, The Bronx: Fernando Ferrer
Borough President, Brooklyn: Howard Golden
Borough President, Manhattan: Ruth Messinger
Borough President, Queens: Claire Shulman
Borough President, Staten Island: Guy Molinari
Commissioner Personnel: Lillian Barrios-Paoli
Auditors: KPMG Peat Marwick LLP

WHERE

HQ: Office of the Mayor, New York, NY 10007
Phone: 212-788-9600
Fax: 212-406-3587 (Mayor's Office)
County: New York

New York City encompasses 309 square miles in Bronx, Kings, New York, Queens, and Richmond Counties at the southern tip of New York State.

Geographic area	1994 Employment NY–NJ Metropolitan Region % of total
New York City	47
New Jersey suburbs	31
New York suburbs	22
Total	**100**

WHAT

Selected Cultural Attractions and Institutions

Apollo Theatre	Metropolitan Opera
Broadway	Museum of Modern Art
Carnegie Hall	New York Public Library
Central Park	New York Stock Exchange
Chrysler Building	Radio City Music Hall
Coney Island	Rockefeller Center
Ed Sullivan Theatre	Statue of Liberty
Empire State Building	Times Square
Frick Collection	United Nations
Lincoln Center	Village Vanguard
Metropolitan Museum of Art	World Trade Center

Selected Schools	Major Professional Teams
City University of New York	New York Giants
Columbia University	New York Knickerbockers
Fordham University	New York Jets
Juilliard School	New York Mets
New York University	New York Rangers
Yeshiva University	New York Yankees

Industry	1994 Employment New York Metropolitan Region % of total
Services	33
Trade	20
Government	16
Manufacturing	11
Finance, insurance & real estate	9
Transportation, communications & public utilities	7
Construction	4
Total	**100**

	1994 City Government Revenues	
	$ mil.	% of total
Federal/state grants	10,810	34
Property tax	7,773	25
Income taxes	6,281	20
Sales & use taxes	2,855	9
Charges for services	1,277	4
Other taxes	1,206	4
Other revenues	1,151	4
Total	**31,353**	**100**

	1994 City Government Expenditures	
	$ mil.	% of total
Personal services	11,546	37
Other than personal services	8,170	26
Medicaid & welfare	5,066	16
Fringe benefits	2,718	9
Debt service	2,454	8
Pensions	1,394	4
Total	**31,348**	**100**

HOW MUCH

	Annual Growth	1985	1986	1987	1988	1989	1990	1991	1992	1993	1994
City revenue ($ mil.)	5.8%	18,808	20,020	21,390	22,426	24,489	25,937	27,481	29,022	30,116	31,353
Per capita debt ($)	8.9%	1,723	1,833	1,893	2,041	2,202	2,490	2,917	3,189	3,395	3,701
Population ($ thou.)	0.1%	7,233	7,277	7,292	7,290	7,314	7,323	7,310	7,312	7,326	7,331
Employment (thou.)	(0.1%)	2,965	2,983	3,058	3,082	3,105	3,136	3,027	2,939	2,936	2,926
Personal income ($)	6.4%	16,919	18,060	19,238	20,817	22,103	23,727	24,428	26,155	27,087	29,500
Market value of real estate ($ bil.)	14.7%	178	199	220	249	355	404	472	564	630	611
Employees	1.2%	212,000	220,276	225,238	231,982	238,383	243,090	243,208	234,108	238,439	235,752

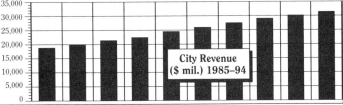

City Revenue ($ mil.) 1985–94

Top New York Companies

ADVANCE PUBLICATIONS, INC.

OVERVIEW

New York City–based Advance Publications is the holding company for one of the largest media groups in the US. Its holdings include books (Random House), magazines (Condé Nast), newspapers, and cable TV. Advance is owned by Si and Donald Newhouse, sons of the founder, who are known for their tight-lipped control of the company's operations.

Random House is the #1 consumer book publisher in the US, controlling the publishers Knopf, Ballantine, and Vintage, among others. Condé Nast is one of the leading US magazine publishers, with 15 titles, including *Vogue*, the *New Yorker,* and *Details.* Newhouse Newspapers publishes more than 20 newspapers,

including the Cleveland *Plain Dealer* and the New Orleans *Times-Picayune.*

In 1995 Advance formed a joint venture with Time Warner, combining Newhouse Broadcasting's cable systems, which serve 1.4 million subscribers, with Time Warner's systems in New York, North Carolina, and Florida. The deal comes as the cable industry is undergoing consolidation and preparing to compete with phone companies in the race to provide interactive television and other advanced communication services. Advance has also formed joint ventures to put many of its magazines and newspapers on-line.

WHEN

Solomon Neuhaus (who later became Samuel I. Newhouse) dropped out of school at age 13 because of family poverty. He went to work for a lawyer who received the *Bayonne* (New Jersey) *Times* as payment for a debt. At age 16 in 1911, Newhouse was put in charge of the failing newspaper; he turned the company around. In 1922 he bought the Staten Island *Advance,* the core of Advance Publications.

Newhouse used profits from the *Advance* to buy newspapers throughout the New York area, operating out of a briefcase rather than a headquarters suite. He purchased the *Long Island Press* (1932), the Newark *Star-Ledger* (1933), the *Long Island Star-Journal* (1938), and the *Syracuse Journal* (1939). He later acquired the *Syracuse Herald-Standard* (1941), the *Jersey Journal* (1945), and the Harrisburg *Patriot* (1948). In 1955 he expanded into the South by buying the *Birmingham News* and the *Huntsville Times.*

In 1959 Newhouse entered magazine publishing when he bought Condé Nast (*Vogue, Bride's, House & Garden*) as an anniversary gift for his wife, Mitzi (joking that she had asked for a fashion magazine, so he bought her *Vogue*). Continuing to build his newspaper empire, in 1962 he paid $42 million for the New Orleans *Times-Picayune* and *New Orleans States-Item,* a record price broken by his 1967 purchase of the Cleveland *Plain Dealer* for $54 million. By 1967 Newhouse had also established NewChannels, which owned several cable systems (10,000 subscribers). Newhouse set yet another newspaper purchase record in 1976 by buying the Booth chain of 8 Michigan newspapers for $304 million.

Newhouse died in 1979, leaving his sons Si and Donald as trustees of the company's 10

shares of voting stock. They claimed that the estate was worth $181.9 million, taxable at $48.7 million. The IRS contested that figure. When the case — the largest ever at the time — was decided in 1990, the IRS lost.

Meanwhile, the sons continued to expand Advance Publications. They entered book publishing by buying Random House, at that time the largest general-interest US book publisher, from RCA in 1980. Random House began in 1925 when Bennett Cerf bought the Modern Library from his boss. In 1927 Cerf and his partner, Donald Klopfer, began publishing luxury editions (chosen "at Random") in addition to the inexpensive Modern Library books. In 1966 RCA bought Random, but bureaucratic RCA and genteel Random did not mesh.

Advance resurrected *Vanity Fair* in 1983 and bought the *New Yorker* in 1985. In 1989 Advance bought Crown Publishing. In 1992 Si Newhouse moved *Vanity Fair* editor Tina Brown to the *New Yorker,* hoping to give an edge to the eccentric weekly. In 1993 Condé Nast bought Knapp Publications (*Architectural Digest, Bon Appetit*).

Also in 1993 the company joined with Brøderbund Software to create children's multimedia software and bought the electronic publishing division of Bantam Doubleday Dell. That year it also offered $500 million to QVC, backing its bid for Paramount (which QVC later lost to Viacom). The company acquired 25% of *Wired,* a leading multimedia magazine, in 1994. In 1995 Random House signed a deal with Planeta Internacional (the #1 book publisher in the Spanish-speaking world) to distribute Spanish-language books in the US and Canada, and Advance agreed to buy American City Business Journals for $269 million.

Private company
Fiscal year ends: December 31

Chairman and CEO: Samuel I. "Si" Newhouse Jr.,
  age 66
President: Donald E. Newhouse, age 64
Publisher: Richard Diamond
Chairman, President, and CEO, Random House:
  Alberto Vitale
President, Condé Nast Publications: Steven T. Florio
President, Newhouse Newspapers Metro-Suburbia:
  Edwin F. Russell
Editorial Director, Condé Nast Publications Inc.: James
  Truman

WHERE

HQ: 950 Fingerboard Rd., Staten Island, NY 10305
Phone: 718-981-1234
Fax: 718-981-1415

Advance Publications has newspapers and cable TV
groups in the US and book and magazine operations in
New York and Europe.

WHAT

The Condé Nast Publications Inc.

Allure	GQ
Architectural Digest	Mademoiselle
Bon Appetit	The New Yorker
Bride's	Parade
Condé Nast Traveler	Self
Details	Vanity Fair
Glamour	Vogue
Gourmet	

American City Business Journals (28 local weekly
  business newspapers and 3 auto-racing magazines)

Random House, Inc.

Alfred A. Knopf	Modern Library
Ballantine Books	Orion
Beginner Books	Pantheon Books
Crown Publishers	Random Century (UK)
Fawcett Books	Times Books
Fodor's Travel Publications	Villard Books
	Vintage Books

Newhouse Broadcasting
Cable television (1.4 million subscribers)

Newhouse Newspapers Metro-Suburbia (Selected)

Alabama
  Birmingham News
  Birmingham Post-Herald
  The Mobile Press
  The Mobile Press
  Register
  The Mobile Register
Louisiana
  The Times-Picayune (New
  Orleans)
Massachusetts
  Union-News & Sunday
  Republican (Springfield)
Michigan
  The Ann Arbor News
  The Flint Times
  The Grand Rapids
  Press
  Kalamazoo Gazette
  The Saginaw News
  Times (Bay City)
Mississippi
  Mississippi Press (Pascagoula)
Mississippi Press
  Register (Pascagoula)
New Jersey
  Jersey Journal (Jersey
  City)
  Star-Ledger (Newark)
  Times (Trenton)
New York
  Herald-American
  (Syracuse)
  The Post-Standard
  (Syracuse)
  Syracuse Herald-
  Journal
Ohio
  Plain Dealer (Cleveland)
Oregon
  The Oregonian
  (Portland)
Pennsylvania
  The Patriot-News
  (Harrisburg)

KEY COMPETITORS

ADVO	McGraw-Hill
American Express	New York Times
Bertelsmann	News Corp.
Cablevision	Pearson
Comcast	Pulitzer
Cox Communications	Reader's Digest
Cox Enterprises	Scholastic
Dow Jones	TCI
Electronic Arts	Time Warner
E. W. Scripps	Times Mirror
Gannett	Tribune
Harcourt General	Universal Press
Hearst	Syndicate
Houghton Mifflin	Viacom
John Wiley	Walt Disney
Knight-Ridder	Washington Post
Lagardère	W. W. Norton
McClatchey	

HOW MUCH

	Annual Growth	1985	1986	1987	1988	1989	1990	1991	1992	1993	1994
Estimated sales ($ mil.)	9.8%	2,030	2,200	2,482	2,655	2,882	3,040	3,095	4,287	4,416	4,690
Newspaper revenues ($ mil.)	4.0%	—	1,074	1,601	1,681	1,745	1,797	1,748	1,800	1,800	1,926
Newspapers	1.2%	26	27	26	36	26	30	32	28	26	29
Magazine revenues ($ mil.)	8.0%	—	544	678	745	842	845	941	975	970	1,008
Cable TV revenues ($ mil.)	13.9%	—	186	203	229	295	398	440	467	496	526
Cable subscribers (thou.)	4.8%	917	1,027	1,098	1,078	1,147	1,242	1,301	—	1,350	1,400
Employees	0.3%	18,500	18,500	19,000	19,000	19,000	19,500	19,000	19,000	19,000	19,000

Estimated Sales
($ mil.) 1985–94

R A N D O M
H O U S E

ALLIEDSIGNAL INC.

OVERVIEW

AlliedSignal finally has it together, thanks to CEO Lawrence Bossidy, who took over in 1991. Bossidy (*Financial World's* 1994 CEO of the year) trimmed unprofitable businesses while slashing employee and supplier rosters. For the first time in 7 years, in 1994 each of the Morristown, New Jersey–based company's 3 segments — Aerospace, Automotive, and Engineered Materials — had increased sales.

In 1994 and 1995 Allied continued to grow its core businesses through acquisitions and joint ventures. Acquisitions in 1994 included Ford Motor Company's UK spark plug operations and Textron's Lycoming Turbine Engine Division. The following year the company added Fiat Auto's braking business in Poland and the wheel and brake division of the Budd Co. Joint ventures include an airline maintenance center with TAECO (Hong Kong), manufacturing agreements for auto safety equipment with Jay Bharat Group (India), an auto safety radar system with Amerigon (US), and civilian aircraft parts with Aviation Corp. Rubin (Russia).

Attracted by Asia's high-growth potential, in 1994 Allied began building a $27 million truck engine turbocharger plant in Shanghai and pledged $100 million in investments in China. The following year Allied agreed to form a joint venture with China's 2nd largest car maker to produce hydraulic braking systems.

Nearly $9 million in stock options pushed Bossidy's pay to $12.4 million in 1994, making him the 6th-highest-paid CEO in the US.

WHEN

During WWI Germany controlled much of the world's chemical industry, causing shortages of such commodities as dyes and drugs. In response, in 1920 *Washington Post* publisher Eugene Meyer and scientist William Nichols organized the Allied Chemical & Dye Corporation from 5 existing companies.

In 1928 Allied opened a synthetic ammonia plant near Hopewell, Virginia, becoming the world's leading producer of ammonia. This represented the company's earliest venture into new markets. After WWII Allied began manufacturing other new products, including nylon 6 (for making everything from tires to clothes) and refrigerants. In 1958 it became Allied Chemical Corporation.

In 1962 Allied bought Union Texas Natural Gas, which owned oil and gas properties throughout the Americas. Allied regarded it mainly as a supplier of raw materials for its chemical products, but this changed in the early 1970s when CEO John Connor (secretary of commerce under Lyndon Johnson) sold many of Allied's unprofitable businesses and invested in oil and gas exploration. By 1979, when Edward Hennessy Jr. became CEO, Union Texas produced 80% of Allied's income.

Through purchases directed by Hennessy, Allied entered new fields, including electronics (Eltra, 1979; Bunker Ramo, 1981) and health and scientific products (Fisher Scientific, 1981). Under its new name, Allied Corporation (1981), the company went on to buy the Bendix Corporation, an aerospace and automotive company, in 1983. By 1984 Bendix generated 50% of Allied's income, while oil and gas generated 38%.

In 1985 Allied merged with the Signal Companies to form Allied-Signal (which changed its name to AlliedSignal in 1993). Founded by Sam Mosher in 1922 as the Signal Gasoline Company, Signal originally produced gasoline from natural gas. In 1928 the company changed its name to Signal Oil & Gas, entering into oil production the same year. Signal merged with the Garrett Corporation, a Los Angeles–based aerospace company, in 1964; acquired Mack Trucks in 1967 (spun off 1983); and in 1968 adopted the Signal Companies as its corporate name. Signal bought the Ampex Corporation in 1981.

The addition of Signal's Garrett division to Bendix made aerospace Allied's largest business sector. In 1985 the company sold 50% of Union Texas, and in 1986 it spun off 35 mostly unprofitable chemical and engineering businesses. Hennessy sold 7 more businesses in 1987, leaving Allied in aerospace, auto parts, and chemicals.

In 1992 Allied bought Westinghouse Electric's copper-laminates business and sold its 39% stake in Union Texas through a public offering. The following year the company signed a deal with the Russian government to help convert weapons-grade uranium from Russia's surplus missiles. Allied constructed a new laminates plant in Thailand in 1994.

In 1994 and 1995 the company scored several major contracts, including advanced systems and products for Boeing's 777s, radar warning systems for Singapore Airlines, avionics and maintenance contracts for Southwest Airlines, and turbofan engines for Raytheon's Hawker aircraft.

WHO

Chairman and CEO: Lawrence A. Bossidy, age 59,
$3,625,000 pay
EVP; President, AlliedSignal Engineered Materials:
Frederic M. Poses, age 52, $975,000 pay
EVP; President, AlliedSignal Aerospace:
Daniel P. Burnham, age 48, $806,670 pay
EVP; AlliedSignal Automotive: John W. Barter, age 48,
$802,500 pay (prior to promotion)
SVP and CFO: Richard Wallman, age 43
SVP, General Counsel, and Secretary: Peter M.
Kreindler, age 49, $725,000 pay
SVP and Chief Technology Officer: Isaac R. Barpal,
age 55
SVP International: Paul R. Schindler, age 53
SVP Quality and Productivity: James E. Sierk, age 56
SVP Public Affairs: David G. Powell, age 61
SVP Human Resources: Donald J. Redlinger,
age 50
VP Manufacturing: Richard P. Schroeder, age 43
VP Materials Management: Raymond C. Stark, age 52
Auditors: Price Waterhouse LLP

WHERE

HQ: 101 Columbia Rd., PO Box 4000, Morristown, NJ
07962-2497
Phone: 201-455-2000
Fax: 201-455-4807

AlliedSignal has 383 facilities in 40 countries.

	1994 Sales		1994 Net Income	
	$ mil.	% of total	$ mil.	% of total
US	9,739	76	654	86
Europe	2,283	18	65	9
Canada	202	1	23	3
Other regions	593	5	17	2
Total	**12,817**	**100**	**759**	**100**

WHAT

	1994 Sales		1994 Net Income	
	$ mil.	% of total	$ mil.	% of total
Aerospace	4,623	36	260	32
Automotive	4,922	38	223	27
Engineered Matls.	3,272	26	331	41
Adjustments	—	—	(55)	—
Total	**12,817**	**100**	**759**	**100**

Principal Business Areas

Aerospace
Aerospace Equipment Systems
AlliedSignal Engines
Commercial Avionics Systems
Government Electronic Systems

Automotive
Automotive aftermarket
Braking systems
Engine components
Safety restraint systems

Engineered Materials
Fibers
Fluorine Products
Laminate Systems
Performance Materials
Plastics

KEY COMPETITORS

American Standard	Hercules	Rolls-Royce
BASF	Hexcel	Siemens
Borg-Warner	Hoechst	Teledyne
Automotive	Honeywell	Tenneco
Coltec	ITT Industries	Textron
Dana	Litton Industries	Thomson SA
DuPont	Monsanto	TRW
Eaton	Morton	United
AB Electrolux	Robert Bosch	Technologies
General Electric	Rockwell	Westinghouse

HOW MUCH

	Annual Growth	1985	1986	1987	1988	1989	1990	1991	1992	1993	1994
Sales ($ mil.)	3.9%	9,115	11,794	11,116	11,909	11,942	12,343	11,831	12,042	11,827	12,817
Net income ($ mil.)	—	(279)	605	518	463	528	462	(273)	535	656	759
Income as % of sales	—	—	5.1%	4.7%	3.9%	4.4%	3.7%	—	4.4%	5.5%	5.9%
Earnings per share ($)	—	(1.64)	1.63	1.55	1.55	1.78	1.68	(1.00)	1.90	2.31	2.68
Stock price – high ($)	—	21.66	24.53	24.63	18.44	20.19	18.94	22.50	31.00	40.06	40.69
Stock price – low ($)	—	18.91	18.38	13.00	14.00	15.88	12.44	12.94	20.44	28.75	30.38
Stock price – close ($)	5.5%	21.03	20.06	14.13	16.25	17.44	13.50	21.94	30.25	39.50	34.00
P/E – high	—	—	15	16	12	11	11	—	16	17	15
P/E – low	—	—	11	8	9	9	7	—	11	12	11
Dividends per share ($)	(3.2%)	0.90	0.90	0.90	0.90	0.90	0.90	0.80	0.50	0.58	0.65
Book value per share ($)	(5.0%)	16.65	10.52	10.43	11.04	11.77	12.55	10.80	7.93	8.42	10.53
Employees	(5.4%)	143,800	137,200	115,300	109,550	107,100	105,800	98,300	89,300	86,400	87,500

1994 Year-end:
Debt ratio: 34.2%
Return on equity: 28.3%
Cash (mil.): $508
Current ratio: 1.35
Long-term debt (mil.): $1,424
No. of shares (mil.): 283
Dividends
  Yield: 1.9%
  Payout: 24.3%
Market value (mil.): $9,626

**Stock Price History
High/Low 1985–94**

AMERADA HESS CORPORATION

OVERVIEW

After 50 years of running oil and gas operations, 81-year-old Leon Hess turned over the reins of oil and gas giant Amerada Hess in 1995 to his son John. The younger Hess might count himself fortunate — Leon's father had stayed on the job until his death at age 92. The company president, 70-year-old Robert Wright, also stepped down as part of the company's 1995 reorganization.

The New York–based company has reserves of 670 million barrels of oil and 2.65 trillion cubic feet of natural gas. Its exploration activities are located primarily in the US, Canada, Gabon, and the North Sea. Amerada Hess refines an average of more than 250,000 barrels a day and sells gasoline in 541 HESS stations,

mainly in New York, New Jersey, and Florida. Of these stations, 155 operate HESS MART convenience stores.

Amerada Hess produces oil and gas at 9 major fields in the North Sea. Fifty-one percent of the company's crude oil is produced from these fields, along with 25% of its natural gas. Amerada Hess has updated its St. Croix, Virgin Islands, refinery, one of the largest in the world, spending $1 billion to satisfy the requirements of the Clean Air Act.

The $2.5 billion that management spent on reshaping the company in recent years left Amerada Hess with a heavy debt load. Leon Hess holds 12.9% of the company's stock; John Hess owns 1.7%.

WHEN

It was a logical match — Amerada Petroleum, which had been in the exploration and production business since the early part of the century, and Hess Oil and Chemical, involved in refining since the 1930s.

In 1919 oil entrepreneur Lord Cowdray formed Amerada Corporation to explore for oil in the US, Canada, and Central America. One of the first and most important people Cowdray hired was geophysicist Everette DeGolyer, a pioneer in oil geology research methods. DeGolyer's systematic methods — in a time when guesswork was still the norm — not only helped Amerada find oil deposits faster, but also helped the company pick up fields previously missed by competitors. DeGolyer became president of Amerada in 1929. He left the company in 1932 to work as an independent consultant. Amerada continued to make major discoveries in the US.

After WWII Amerada began exploring overseas, and during the 1950s the company entered into pipelining and refining. Amerada continued its overseas exploration through Oasis, a consortium formed with Marathon, Shell, and Continental to explore in Libya in 1964. At one time Oasis controlled half of Libya's oil production.

Leon Hess began to buy stock in Amerada in 1966. Hess started in the oil business during the Depression, selling "resid" — thick refining leftovers that the refineries thought were useless. Hess bought the resid cheap, kept it warm in heated trucks (so it would flow), and sold it as heating fuel to hotels and later to Public Service Electric & Gas. Hess also began speculating, buying oil cheap in the summer and selling it for a profit in the win-

ter. He also branched out into refining, gasoline retailing, transportation, and exploration.

All that expansion pushed debt up, so in 1962 Hess Oil and Chemical went public by merging with Cletrac Corporation. In 1966 Hess began building a refinery in St. Croix, Virgin Islands. After battling Phillips Petroleum and settling a suit brought by Amerada, Hess acquired Amerada in 1969.

During the 1970s Amerada Hess began drilling on Alaska's North Slope. In 1978 the company was one of 5 oil companies convicted of fixing retail gasoline prices.

The company took a roller coaster ride during the 1980s, posting sales of $10 billion in 1981, which then plunged, as oil prices plummeted, to only $4 billion in 1986, when Amerada Hess posted a loss of $219 million. Takeover rumors circulated as oilman T. Boone Pickens bought up a chunk of Amerada Hess's stock. However, the company rebounded, and Hess was able to fight off any takeover.

In 1989 Hurricane Hugo knocked out the company's refinery in St. Croix, which took a year to rebuild.

In 1993 Amerada Hess completed work on the Central Area Transmission System pipeline. The company owns 18% of the pipeline, which carries natural gas from the North Sea to the UK. In 1994 Amerada Hess's UK subsidiary began production in the South Scott oil field in the North Sea. Also that year the company began a consolidation of its US exploration and production operations in Houston, resulting in reduced staffing levels.

In 1995 Amerada Hess sold its 81% interest in Northstar, an undeveloped North Slope oil field in Alaska, to British Petroleum.

WHO

Chairman of the Executive Committee: Leon Hess,
age 81, $300,000 pay
Chairman and CEO: John B. Hess, age 40, $735,000 pay
(prior to promotion)
President and COO: W. Sam H. Laidlaw, age 39,
$575,000 pay (prior to promotion)
EVP and CFO: John Y. Schreyer, age 55, $550,000 pay
EVP Refining and Marketing: Michael W. Press, age 47
EVP and General Counsel: J. Barclay Collins II, age 50
SVP: Alan A. Bernstein, age 50
SVP: Marco B. Bianchi, age 55
SVP: James F. Cassidy, age 67
SVP: F. Lamar Clark, age 61
SVP: Charles H. Norz, age 57
SVP: Benedict J. O'Bryan, age 57
SVP: Rene L. Sagebien, age 54
SVP Human Resources: Neal Gelfand, age 50
Auditors: Ernst & Young LLP

WHERE

HQ: 1185 Avenue of the Americas, New York, NY 10036
Phone: 212-997-8500
Fax: 212-536-8390

Amerada Hess explores for oil and natural gas in the US,
Canada, Denmark, Egypt, Gabon, Namibia, Thailand,
and the North Sea. It has refineries in the US Virgin
Islands and in New Jersey and retail stations in the US.

	1994 Sales		1994 Operating Income	
	$ mil.	% of total	$ mil.	% of total
US	5,437	82	66	14
Europe	907	14	303	63
Other regions	258	4	112	23
Adjustments	97	—	—	—
Total	**6,699**	**100**	**481**	**100**

WHAT

	1994 Sales		1994 Operating Income	
	$ mil.	% of total	$ mil.	% of total
Refining & marketing	4,154	63	83	17
Exploration & production	2,263	34	368	77
Other	185	3	30	6
Adjustments	97	—	—	—
Total	**6,699**	**100**	**481**	**100**

Lines of Business
Marketing of refined products
Oil and gas exploration and production
Petroleum refining
Transportation of refined products

Selected Subsidiaries
Amerada Hess Canada Ltd.
Amerada Hess Ltd. (UK)
Amerada Hess Norge A/S (Norway)
Hess Oil Virgin Islands Corp.

KEY COMPETITORS

Amoco
Ashland, Inc.
Atlantic Richfield
British Petroleum
Broken Hill
Chevron
Circle K
Coastal
Elf Aquitaine
Exxon
Imperial Oil
Koch
Lyondell Petrochemical
Mobil
Occidental
Oryx

Panhandle Eastern
PDVSA
PEMEX
Pennzoil
Petrobrás
Petrofina
Phillips Petroleum
Repsol
Royal Dutch/Shell
Sinclair Oil
Southland
Sun Company
Texaco
TOTAL
Unocal
USX–Marathon

HOW MUCH

	Annual Growth	1985	1986	1987	1988	1989	1990	1991	1992	1993	1994
Sales ($ mil.)	(1.6%)	7,723	4,062	4,785	4,264	5,679	7,081	6,416	5,970	5,873	6,699
Net income ($ mil.)	—	(260)	(219)	230	124	476	483	84	8	(298)	74
Income as % of sales	—	—	—	4.8%	2.9%	8.4%	6.8%	1.3%	0.1%	—	1.1%
Earnings per share ($)	—	(3.08)	(2.60)	2.73	1.51	5.87	5.96	1.04	0.09	(3.22)	0.79
Stock price – high ($)	—	34.00	29.00	41.88	33.25	51.88	56.00	59.13	51.25	56.38	52.63
Stock price – low ($)	—	22.75	16.50	21.50	22.50	31.00	42.88	42.50	36.63	42.38	43.75
Stock price – close ($)	5.9%	27.25	23.75	24.88	31.50	48.75	46.38	47.50	46.00	45.13	45.63
P/E – high	—	—	—	15	22	9	9	57	—	—	67
P/E – low	—	—	—	8	15	5	7	41	—	—	55
Dividends per share ($)	(6.5%)	1.10	0.28	0.30	0.60	0.60	0.75	0.45	0.75	0.45	0.60
Book value per share ($)	2.3%	27.22	24.68	26.29	27.02	31.69	38.34	38.63	36.59	32.71	33.33
Employees	1.9%	8,290	7,776	7,890	8,151	16,638	9,645	10,317	10,263	10,173	9,858

1994 Year-end:
Debt ratio: 52.5%
Return on equity: 2.4%
Cash (mil.): $53
Current ratio: 1.43
Long-term debt (mil.): $3,235
No. of shares (mil.): 93
Dividends
  Yield: 1.3%
  Payout: 75.9
Market value (mil.): $4,243

Stock Price History
High/Low 1985–94

AMERICAN BRANDS, INC.

OVERVIEW

If American Brands isn't swallowed by an even bigger fish, and if it doesn't exit the tobacco business altogether (as some analysts predict), the Connecticut-based conglomerate should change its name: About 47% of the company's 1994 sales came from its UK-based subsidiary, Gallaher Tobacco, the #1 British tobacco company. American Brands sold its American Tobacco subsidiary, including the Pall Mall and Lucky Strike brands, to B.A.T Industries for $1 billion in late 1994.

American Brands is focusing on its nontobacco subsidiaries, all makers of leading consumer brands, including Jim Beam, the #2

US producer of distilled spirits; top pro golf equipment brands Titleist and Foot-Joy; ACCO office products; and faucet maker Moen.

The company continues to shed noncore operations. It gained $1.17 billion in early 1995 by selling Franklin Life Insurance to American General and announced it would sell its Forbuoys retail outlet chain and Prestige cookware, both based in the UK.

With proceeds from recent sales, the company has retired $1 billion in debt. It is also expected to buy back outstanding shares and make strategic acquisitions, possibly in the highly profitable distilled spirits division.

WHEN

American Brands began in 1864 as W. Duke and Sons, a small tobacco company started by Washington Duke, a North Carolina farmer. James Buchanan Duke joined his father's business at age 14 (1870) and by age 25 was its president. James Duke was the first to use the Bonsack cigarette rolling machine, which produced substantially cheaper cigarettes and allowed him to undercut competitors' prices. He advertised to expanding markets, bought rival tobacco firms, and by 1904 controlled the industry. That year he merged all the competitive groups as American Tobacco Company.

In a 1911 antitrust suit, the US Supreme Court dissolved American Tobacco into its original competitive firms, ordering them to operate independently.

Duke left American Tobacco in 1912 but remained president of British American Tobacco Company (now B.A.T, which he had founded in 1902). He also continued his work with Southern Power Company, which he had started in North Carolina in 1905. He later merged that company with Duke Power and Light. Duke established a $100 million trust fund, composed mainly of holdings in Duke Power and Light, for the local Trinity College, which became Duke University in 1924.

American Tobacco merely drifted under Duke's successor Percival Hill, but it found a dynamic new leader in George Washington Hill, who succeeded his father as president in 1925. For the next 19 years until his death, Hill proved himself a consummate ad man, pushing Lucky Strike, Pall Mall, and Tareyton cigarettes to top sales.

Research first linked cigarette smoking to lung cancer in 1953, and smokers switched to filter-tipped cigarettes in record numbers. American Tobacco, however, ignored the trend

and continued to rely on its popular filterless brands until the mid-1960s.

American Tobacco remained solely in the tobacco business until 1966, when it purchased Sunshine Biscuits (sold in 1988) and Jim Beam Distillery. Later came Swingline (office supplies, 1970) and Master Lock (1970). Reflecting its increasing diversity, the company became American Brands in 1970.

Threatened by a takeover by E-II Holdings (a conglomerate of brands split from Beatrice), American Brands bought E-II for $1.1 billion in 1988. The company kept 5 of E-II's companies — Day-Timers (time management products), Aristokraft (cabinets), Waterloo (tool storage), Twentieth Century (plumbing supplies), and Vogel Peterson (office partitions) — and sold the rest (Culligan and Samsonite) to Riklis Family Corporation.

Acquisitions in 1990 included Moen (faucets) and Whyte & Mackay (distillers). In 1991 the company bought 7 liquor brands from Seagram, including Kessler (whiskey), Ronrico (rum), and Leroux (cordials). Whyte & Mackay became the world's 3rd largest scotch whiskey producer in 1993 with the acquisition of the Invergordon Distillers Group.

In 1994 American Brands sold Dollond & Aitchison, its UK-based optical group. It also sold the rubber divison of Acushnet (leisure products) to members of that unit's top management. That same year it settled a false advertising charge filed by the FTC regarding American Tobacco's claim that its Carlton brand cigarettes deliver less tar and nicotine to smokers.

In 1995 Jim Beam, the world's top-selling bourbon, celebrated its 200th birthday. That year the company agreed to buy Cobra Golf for $700 million.

NYSE symbol: AMB
Fiscal year ends: December 31

WHO

Chairman and CEO: Thomas C. Hays, age 59,
$1,089,400 pay (prior to promotion)
President and COO: John T. Ludes, age 58,
$696,600 pay (prior to promotion)
SVP and CFO: Dudley L. Bauerlein Jr., age 48
SVP and Chief Accounting Officer: Robert L. Plancher,
age 63
SVP and General Counsel: Gilbert L. Klemann II, age 44
SVP and Chief Administrative Officer (HR): Steven C.
Mendenhall, age 46
Chairman and CEO, Gallaher Tobacco Limited: Peter
M. Wilson, age 53, $839,219 pay
Chairman and CEO, Jim Beam Brands Co.: Barry M.
Berish
President and CEO, Acco World Corp.: Norman H.
Wesley
President and CEO, Acushnet Co.: Walter R. Uihlein
President and CEO, Masterbrand Industries: Randall W.
Larrimore
Auditors: Coopers & Lybrand L.L.P.

WHERE

HQ: 1700 E. Putnam Ave., PO Box 811, Old Greenwich,
CT 06870-0811
Phone: 203-698-5000
Fax: 203-637-2580

American Brands is a holding company with subsidiaries
operating in Asia, Australia, Europe (principally the UK),
and North America.

	1994 Sales		1994 Operating Income	
	$ mil.	% of total	$ mil.	% of total
Europe	8,074	61	586	45
US	4,677	36	671	51
Other regions	396	3	55	4
Total	**13,147**	**100**	**1,312**	**100**

WHAT

	1994 Sales		1994 Operating Income	
	$ mil.	% of total	$ mil.	% of total
Tobacco products	7,764	59	765	58
Hardware & home imprvmt. prods.	1,271	10	176	13
Distilled spirits	1,268	10	221	17
Office products	1,050	8	75	6
Other businesses	1,794	13	75	6
Total	**13,147**	**100**	**1,312**	**100**

Selected Brands

Tobacco Products
Amber Leaf
Benson & Hedges (UK)
Berkeley
Old Holborn
Samson
Silk Cut

Kamchatka
Lord Calvert
Old Grand-Dad
Ronrico
Windsor Canadian
Wolfschmidt

Office Products
ACCO
Day-Timers
Kensington Microware
Perma Products
Swingline
Wilson Jones

Hardware and Home Improvement
Aristokraft (cabinets)
Master Lock (hardware)
Moen (faucets)
Waterloo (tool boxes)

Distilled Spirits
Gilbey's
Jim Beam

Other Products
Foot-Joy (golf shoes)
Titleist (golf equipment)

KEY COMPETITORS

Allied Domecq
American Standard
Bacardi
B.A.T
Black & Decker
Brown-Forman
Brunswick
Day Runner

Eastern Co.
Franklin Quest
Grand Metropolitan
Grohe
Guinness
Hillenbrand
Ingersoll-Rand
Kohler

Loews
Masco
Philip Morris
RJR Nabisco
Seagram
Stanley
U.S. Industries
Waxman

HOW MUCH

	Annual Growth	1985	1986	1987	1988	1989	1990	1991	1992	1993	1994
Sales ($ mil.)	6.7%	7,308	8,470	9,153	11,980	11,921	13,781	14,064	14,623	13,701	13,147
Net income ($ mil.)	6.4%	421	365	523	580	631	596	806	884	668	734
Income as % of sales	—	5.8%	4.3%	5.7%	4.8%	5.3%	4.3%	5.7%	6.0%	4.9%	5.6%
Earnings per share ($)	8.6%	1.80	1.56	2.24	2.76	3.04	2.84	3.74	4.13	3.23	3.77
Stock price – high ($)	—	17.50	26.25	30.00	35.88	40.94	41.63	47.63	49.88	40.63	38.38
Stock price – low ($)	—	13.31	15.66	18.25	21.13	30.63	30.88	35.63	39.00	28.50	29.38
Stock price – close ($)	9.6%	16.50	21.25	22.25	32.75	35.50	41.50	45.00	40.50	33.25	37.50
P/E – high	—	10	17	13	13	14	15	13	12	13	10
P/E – low	—	7	10	8	8	10	11	10	9	9	8
Dividends per share ($)	8.2%	0.98	1.02	1.06	1.16	1.26	1.41	1.59	1.81	1.97	1.99
Book value per share ($)	8.7%	10.86	11.57	13.32	13.34	15.03	18.13	20.42	21.14	21.09	22.93
Employees	(8.1%)	74,600	78,900	78,600	48,900	47,300	49,000	47,600	46,220	46,660	34,820

1994 Year-end:
Debt ratio: 32.4%
Return on equity: 16.5%
Cash (mil.): $110
Current ratio: 1.50
Long-term debt (mil.): $1,512
No. of shares (mil.): 202
Dividends
  Yield: 5.3%
  Payout: 52.8%
Market value (mil.): $7,560

**Stock Price History
High/Low 1985–94**

AMERICAN EXPRESS COMPANY

OVERVIEW

American Express, one of the US's largest financial services companies and the largest corporate travel agency, is continuing the drastic makeover it began in 1994 with the spinoff of Lehman Brothers.

Chairman Harvey Golub has trimmed the company to 3 units — Travel Related Services (TRS), American Express Financial Advisors (formerly IDS), and American Express Bank — and is now concentrating on wringing maximum performance from them by expanding services while cutting up to 6,000 jobs.

Though it is best known for American Express cards and Travelers Cheques, TRS operates a worldwide travel agency, with locations in 160 countries. It also publishes lifestyle and travel magazines and sells life insurance through AMEX Life Assurance. American Express Financial Services sells life and property/casualty insurance, annuities, investment funds, and financial advisory services. American Express Bank has offices in 37 countries.

In the 1980s American Express fell to a distant 3rd in the competition of the cards, behind Visa and MasterCard. It is now attempting to grow this business again, particularly in the areas of corporate travel and purchasing. After years of denigrating revolving credit cards, it has revamped its money-losing Optima card and plans to add up to 15 other credit card products to its lineup. But American Express has an uphill battle because of the proliferation of credit cards, its small merchant base, and its inexperience in credit underwriting.

The company has also reemphasized its travel agency services, which enjoy a tremendous synergy with its card products.

Warren Buffett owns 9.8% of American Express. In 1995 he applied for SEC permission to increase his interest to above 10%.

WHEN

In 1850 Henry Wells and his 2 main competitors combined delivery services to form American Express. When company directors refused to expand to California in 1852, Wells and VP William Fargo, while remaining at American Express, started Wells Fargo.

American Express merged with Merchants Union Express in 1868 and developed a money order to compete with the government's postal money order. Fargo's difficulty in cashing letters of credit in Europe led to the offering of Travelers Cheques in 1891. Services for US travelers overseas followed.

In WWI the US government nationalized and consolidated all express delivery services, compensating the owners. After the war American Express incorporated as an overseas freight (sold 1970) and financial services and exchange provider.

In 1958 the company introduced the American Express charge card (users had no credit limits and had to pay off balances each month). In 1968 the company bought Fireman's Fund American Insurance (sold gradually, 1985–89) and Equitable Securities.

James Robinson (CEO, 1977–93) expanded the company through acquisitions that included half of Warner Cable Communications (Warner Amex Cable, 1979; sold 1986), Shearson Loeb Rhoades (brokerage, 1981), the Boston Company (banking, 1981), Balcor (real estate, 1982; in liquidation), Lehman Brothers Holding Company and Investors Diversified Services (brokerage, 1984), and E.F. Hutton (brokerage, 1987). In 1987 the company introduced Optima, a revolving credit card, to compete with MasterCard and Visa. The financial units (except IDS) were combined as Shearson Lehman Brothers (SLB).

In 1989 American Express issued a public apology for having investigated and spread rumors about Edmond Safra, former chairman of American Express Bank. In connection with this settlement, the company paid $8 million to Safra's favorite charities. This action sparked a shareholder suit against management. Later that year the company acquired Lifeco Services Corporation, the 5th largest travel agency in the US. In 1993 American Express sold 3 magazines and turned over management of the rest of its magazines to Time Inc. The company also began an ad campaign for its Optima credit cards, lambasting Visa for its high interest rates, as Visa had lambasted American Express for its small merchant base. But the card was a failure because it was poorly underwritten.

American Express spun off Lehman Brothers in 1994 with a dowry of $1.1 billion to ensure its credit rating. The cultures had never fused, and Lehman had a way of snatching fiscal defeat from the jaws of victory. Also in 1994 the company bought the US offices and international accounts of Thomas Cook.

In 1995 president Jeffrey Stiefler resigned, reportedly dissatisfied by his reduced responsibilities. VC Kenneth Chenault is now considered the likely heir to chairman Harvey Golub.

NYSE symbol: AXP
Fiscal year ends: December 31

WHO

Chairman and CEO: Harvey Golub, age 56,
$2,840,000 pay
VC: Jonathan S. Linen, age 51, $1,400,000 pay
VC; President, U.S.A.-Travel Related Services: Kenneth
I. Chenault, age 43, $1,260,000 pay
President and CEO, American Express Financial: David
R. Hubers, age 52, $1,060,000 pay
President, International Travel Related Services:
R. Craig Hoenshell, age 50
Chairman and CEO, American Express Bank: Steven D.
Goldstein, age 43
EVP, CFO, and Treasurer: Michael P. Monaco, age 47
EVP and General Counsel: Louise M. Parent, age 44
EVP and Chief Information Officer: Allan Z. Loren,
age 56
EVP Quality and Human Resources: Joseph W. Keilty,
age 57
Auditors: Ernst & Young LLP

WHERE

HQ: American Express Tower, World Financial Center,
New York, NY 10285
Phone: 212-640-2000
Fax: 212-619-9802

American Express operates throughout the US and in
more than 160 countries.

	1994 Sales		1994 Pretax Income	
	$ mil.	% of total	$ mil.	% of total
US	10,801	73	1,150	61
Europe	1,858	12	364	19
Asia/Pacific	1,220	8	225	12
Other regions	1,028	7	152	8
Adjustments	(625)	—	—	—
Total	**14,282**	**100**	**1,891**	**100**

WHAT

	1994 Sales		1994 Pretax Income	
	$ mil.	% of total	$ mil.	% of total
Travel Related Svcs. American Express	10,256	71	1,396	65
Financial Advisors American Express	3,270	23	631	29
Bank	652	5	119	6
Other	188	1	(255)	—
Adjustments	(84)	—	—	—
Total	**14,282**	**100**	**1,891**	**100**

Selected Services
American Express Cards
American Express
   Travelers Cheques
Banking services
Corporate cards
Financial planning services
Property/casualty insurance
Revolving credit
   cards (Optima)
Travel planning

Magazines
Departures
Food & Wine
Travel & Leisure
Your Company

Selected Subsidiaries
American Express Bank
American Express
   Financial Advisors
AMEX Life Assurance Co.
Travel Related Services

KEY COMPETITORS

Advance Publications
Aetna
Allstate
AT&T Corp.
Barclays
Carlson
Charles Schwab
Chase Manhattan
Citicorp
Dean Witter, Discover
First Chicago
FMR
Hearst
Household International

John Hancock
Lagardère
Maritz Travel
MasterCard
Merrill Lynch
MetLife
New York Times
Prudential
Rosenbluth International
Thomas Cook
Thomson Corp.
Visa
World Travel

HOW MUCH

	Annual Growth	1985	1986	1987	1988	1989	1990	1991	1992	1993	1994
Sales ($ mil.)	2.1%	11,850	14,652	17,626	23,132	25,047	24,332	25,763	26,961	14,173	14,282
Net income ($ mil.)	6.4%	810	1,110	533	1,038	1,157	338	789	436	1,478	1,413
Income as % of sales	—	6.8%	7.6%	3.0%	4.5%	4.6%	1.4%	3.1%	1.6%	10.4%	9.9%
Earnings per share ($)	5.0%	1.78	2.46	1.20	2.43	2.70	0.69	1.59	0.83	2.92	2.75
Stock price – high ($)	—	27.50	35.06	40.63	30.38	39.38	35.25	30.38	25.38	36.63	33.13
Stock price – low ($)	—	17.94	25.25	20.75	22.88	26.38	17.50	18.00	20.00	22.38	25.25
Stock price – close ($)	1.2%	26.50	28.31	22.88	26.63	34.88	20.63	20.50	24.88	30.88	29.50
P/E – high	—	15	15	47	13	15	17	14	19	13	12
P/E – low	—	10	11	24	9	10	8	9	15	8	9
Dividends per share ($)	4.3%	0.65	0.68	0.75	0.76	0.84	0.92	0.94	1.00	1.00	0.95
Book value per share ($)	1.1%	11.41	12.60	10.11	11.39	12.90	13.21	14.43	14.58	17.42	12.57
Employees	0.3%	70,536	78,747	84,278	100,188	107,542	106,836	110,728	114,352	64,654	72,412

1994 Year-end:
Debt ratio: 77.4%
Return on equity: 19.1%
Cash (mil.): $3,433
Long-term debt (mil.): $7,162
No. of shares (mil.): 496
Dividends
   Yield: 3.2%
   Payout: 34.2%
Market value (mil.): $14,628
Assets (mil.): $97,006

**Stock Price History
High/Low 1985–94**

AMERICAN HOME PRODUCTS

OVERVIEW

Madison, New Jersey–based American Home Products (AHP) is a large diversified concern that is growing larger. Its major units produce pharmaceutical, consumer health care, animal health, agricultural, and food products, as well as medical supplies and diagnostics. In 1994 American Cyanamid, after initial resistance, merged with AHP in a deal valued at $9.6 billion to form the world's 4th largest pharmaceutical company with estimated sales of about $13 billion in 1995.

The combination broadens and diversifies the company's products and improves the company's standing in such areas as biotechnology, generics, and agricultural products. It also beefs up R&D, which will expand the long-term pipeline for new products.

The company boasts the leading US prescription drug company, by number of prescriptions dispensed, in its subsidiary Wyeth-Ayerst Laboratories. AHP's well-known divisional names include Whitehall Labs (Advil, Anacin) and A. H. Robins (Robitussin).

AHP maintains a leadership position in women's health care products. The company's lineup includes Premarin, an estrogen drug that is made from pregnant mares' urine and is the most prescribed drug in America. Use of Premarin for the treatment of symptoms of menopause and osteoporosis will continue to grow as the baby boomers age.

American Cyanamid brings to the merger its status as the largest US producer of childhood vaccines and its prominent Centrum multivitamins. Although the merger will be expensive, the company expects restructuring (including 4,000 job cuts) to result eventually in economies of scale.

WHEN

Incorporated in 1926, American Home Products consolidated several small companies that made proprietary medicinals such as Hill's Cascara Quinine and St. Jacob's Oil. AHP's history is one of continuous acquisitions.

During the Great Depression AHP bought over 30 food and drug companies. A sunburn oil acquired in 1935 became the hemorrhoid treatment Preparation H. Anacin was also acquired in the 1930s; Chef Boyardee was added in 1946. AHP purchased Canadian company Ayerst Laboratories in 1943 (cod liver oil, vitamins, and Premarin). Ayerst made penicillin for the Canadian armed forces in WWII.

In alliance with the British drug company Imperial Chemical Industries (ICI), Ayerst developed Inderal (1968), the first of the beta-blocker class of antihypertensives. AHP acquired Sherwood Medical Group (medical supplies) in 1982 and Bristol-Myers's animal health division in 1987. In 1988 it took over A. H. Robins, the company bankrupted by suits over the Dalkon Shield contraceptive device. In 1989, within 5 years of its introduction, Advil (AHP's OTC version of ibuprofen) outsold Bristol-Myers's Nuprin. In the 1980s AHP sold its non–health care businesses. In 1990 it completed integrating A. H. Robins, strengthening AHP's line of medical, veterinary, and consumer health products.

In 1993 the company expanded its generic drug making. In 1994 AHP began selling the antidepressant Effexor, claiming it has fewer side effects and works better than other antidepressants; it also bought American Cyanamid.

When Frank Washburn learned of a German process that extracted nitrogen, lime, and carbide to make cyanamid, a basic component of fertilizer, he bought the North American process rights, founded American Cyanamid in 1907, and began producing calcium cyanamide, the world's first synthetic fertilizer.

Washburn died in 1922, and his assistant, William Bell, became president. The company, which sold cyanide to the mining industry for extracting minerals from ore, diversified in the 1920s by buying chemical concerns.

During WWII American Cyanamid supplied US troops with typhus vaccine, dried blood plasma, and surgical sutures. In 1948 subsidiary Lederle discovered Aureomycin, an antibiotic. It diversified into consumer-related businesses in the 1950s and 1960s, buying Shulton (fragrances) in 1971. (It sold all its consumer businesses by 1990.)

In 1988 it introduced Novantrone (an anticancer drug). In 1992 it created an autonomous unit for its chemical operations, Cytec Industries (spun off in 1994). Also in 1992 it merged its oncology business with cancer drug maker Immunex. American Cyanamid paid $350 million and received 53.5% of Immunex. In 1994 it joined with Progenics Pharmaceuticals to develop drugs that destroy cells infected with HIV.

In 1995 AHP agreed to sell its Latin American oral health business (Kolynos) to Colgate-Palmolive for $1 billion and its Acufex Microsurgical unit to Smith & Nephew plc for $141 million.

NYSE symbol: AHP
Fiscal year ends: December 31

WHO

Chairman, President, and CEO: John R. Stafford,
age 57, $1,668,750 pay
EVP: Robert G. Blount, age 56, $814,875 pay
SVP: Fred Hassan, age 49, $738,000 pay
SVP: Stanley F. Barshay, age 55, $598,125 pay
SVP and General Counsel: Louis L. Hoynes Jr., age 59,
$564,038 pay
SVP: Joseph J. Carr, age 52
President, Wyeth-Ayerst Laboratories: Robert Essner
President, American Home Food Products: Charles E.
LaRosa
VP Finance (Principal Accounting Officer): John R.
Considine, age 44
VP Human Resources: René R. Lewin, age 48
VP Taxes: Thomas M. Nee, age 55
VP: E. Thomas Corcoran, age 47
VP: David Lilley, age 48
VP: William J. Murray, age 49
Auditors: Arthur Andersen & Co, SC

WHERE

HQ: American Home Products Corporation,
Five Giralda Farms, Madison, NJ 07940-0874
Phone: 201-660-5000
Fax: 201-660-6048

	1994 Sales		1994 Pretax Income	
	$ mil.	% of total	$ mil.	% of total
US	5,908	66	1,346	66
Europe & Africa	1,423	16	300	15
Canada &				
Latin America	1,022	11	271	13
Asia & Australia	613	7	113	6
Total	**8,966**	**100**	**2,030**	**100**

WHAT

	1994 Sales		1994 Pretax Income	
	$ mil.	% of total	$ mil.	% of total
Health care prod.	7,886	88	1,840	91
Food products	997	11	156	7
Agricultural prod.	83	1	17	1
Adjustments	—	—	17	1
Total	**8,966**	**100**	**2,030**	**100**

Selected Brands

Agricultural Products
Counter (insecticide)
Delan (fungicide)
Pursuit (herbicide)

Consumer Products
Advil
Anacin
Centrum (multivitamins)
Chef Boyardee
Denorex (shampoo)
Gulden's (mustard)
Jiffy Pop
Polaner (fruit spread)

Preparation H
Robitussin

Selected Pharmaceuticals
Cordarone (cardiovascular)
Effexor (antidepressant)
ISMO (angina treatment)
Minocin (antibiotic)
Norplant (contraceptive)
Orudis (anti-inflammatory)
Pipracil (antibiotic)
Premarin (estrogen
replacement)
Vaccines

KEY COMPETITORS

Abbott Labs	DuPont	PepsiCo
ALZA	Eli Lilly	Pfizer
Amgen	FMC	Procter & Gamble
BASF	Genentech	Quaker Oats
Baxter	Glaxo Wellcome	Rhône-Poulenc
Bayer	Heinz	Roche
Becton, Dickinson	Hoechst	St. Jude Medical
Block Drug	ICN	Sandoz
Bristol-Myers	Pharmaceuticals	Schering-Plough
Squibb	Imperial Chemical	SmithKline
Carter-Wallace	Johnson	Beecham
Chiron Corp.	& Johnson	Upjohn
Ciba-Geigy	Merck	U.S. Surgical
ConAgra	Nestlé	Warner-Lambert
C. R. Bard	Novo Nordisk	

HOW MUCH

	Annual Growth	1985	1986	1987	1988	1989	1990	1991	1992	1993	1994
Sales ($ mil.)	5.9%	5,358	5,684	5,850	6,401	6,747	6,775	7,079	7,874	8,305	8,966
Net income ($ mil.)	7.2%	818	866	928	996	1,102	1,231	1,375	1,151	1,469	1,528
Income as % of sales	—	15.2%	15.2%	15.9%	15.6%	16.3%	18.2%	19.4%	14.6%	17.7%	17.0%
Earnings per share ($)	7.7%	2.54	2.73	2.98	3.22	3.54	3.92	4.36	3.66	4.73	4.97
Stock price – high ($)	—	33.44	47.44	48.38	42.88	54.69	55.13	86.25	84.25	69.00	67.25
Stock price – low ($)	—	25.06	30.63	31.00	35.19	39.88	43.00	46.50	63.25	55.50	55.38
Stock price – close ($)	8.0%	31.44	38.44	36.38	41.63	53.75	52.63	84.63	67.50	64.75	62.75
P/E – high	—	14	18	17	13	15	14	20	23	15	14
P/E – low	—	11	12	11	11	11	11	11	17	12	11
Dividends per share ($)	8.2%	1.45	1.55	1.67	1.80	1.95	2.15	2.38	2.66	2.86	2.94
Book value per share ($)	7.0%	7.59	8.03	8.71	10.18	6.30	8.52	10.46	11.38	12.49	13.90
Employees	3.7%	53,337	49,896	50,623	51,464	50,816	48,700	47,938	50,653	51,399	74,009

1994 Year-end:
Debt ratio: 70.3%
Return on equity: 37.6%
Cash (mil.): $1,944
Current ratio: 1.69
Long-term debt (mil.): $9,973
No. of shares (mil.): 306
Dividends
  Yield: 4.7%
  Payout: 59.2%
Market value (mil.): $19,200

**Stock Price History
High/Low 1985–94**

AMERICAN INTERNATIONAL GROUP

OVERVIEW

American International Group (AIG) is the US's largest public property/casualty insurer and one of the largest insurance companies in the world. With a well-diversified product line (it specializes in property/casualty in the US but also has strong life insurance operations overseas, where it makes 52% of its money), AIG was able to withstand the natural disasters of the early 1990s better than many of its competitors. And its savvy investment strategy helped the company weather the US bond market collapse of 1994.

AIG has been branching into other lines in recent years, including personal auto (through its investment in 20th Century Industries, California's most efficient, though troubled, auto insurer), insurance brokerage (through the purchase of part of Alexander & Alexander), and health care (with new workers' compensation and health care management operations developed in-house).

The company is also continuing to expand overseas by adding commercial insurance operations in Russia and Uzbekistan, returning to Pakistan after a 20-year absence, and expanding its operations in China (where AIG was born and where it is the first US life insurer to be licensed since the 1950s).

WHEN

Former ice cream parlor owner Cornelius Starr founded casualty and property insurer C. V. Starr & Co. in Shanghai in 1919. For a few years Starr underwrote business for other insurers. Then in 1921 he began selling life insurance to the Chinese. In 1926 he opened a New York office to solicit insurance business on risks incurred outside the US by American companies. As WWII approached, Starr moved his base to the US; when the war in Europe cut off business there, he concentrated on Latin America. In the 1950s he developed an international benefits pool that provided disability, health, and life insurance and portable pension plans for employees who moved from country to country.

In 1967 Starr chose his successor, attorney Maurice Greenberg, and died the following year. By 1972 Greenberg had established American International Group as a holding company for Starr's worldwide collection of insurance companies. Greenberg is widely regarded as the true genius behind AIG.

AIG has always taken risks its competitors shun. During the mid-1970s AIG insured offshore oil rigs when other insurers would not, charging annual premiums as high as 10% of value. The company uses reinsurers around the world to help leverage otherwise risky ventures. AIG accepts larger single risks than most other insurers and therefore is the largest user of reinsurance in the US.

By 1975 it was the largest foreign life insurer in Hong Kong, Japan, Malaysia, the Philippines, Singapore, and Taiwan and the only insurer with sales and support facilities operating throughout the world.

From 1979 to 1984 the property/casualty business suffered heavy price competition that cost the industry almost $21 billion in underwriting losses, but during this period AIG outperformed all rivals in terms of its combined ratio (expenses plus losses divided by premiums). In 1986 the company again leveraged its international presence by offering services to foreign manufacturers interested in the American market.

The next year the company finally succeeded in cracking the Korean market, becoming only the 2nd US-owned company to do so (CIGNA was the first).

In the 1980s AIG began investment operations in Asia, increased its presence in health care, and formed a financial services group. In 1990 it bought International Lease Finance Corp., which leases and remarkets jets to airlines. AIG also became the first US insurer licensed to operate in Poland and Hungary (both joint ventures). In 1991 AIG began operating in Estonia.

The company resumed its Chinese operations in 1993 after triumphing over stiff opposition from local state monopolies. AIG is once again sending commissioned Chinese salespeople door-to-door to sell life insurance to their compatriots.

In 1994, a year in which many insurers suffered from the Northridge earthquake in California and other natural disasters, AIG enjoyed double-digit earnings growth. Its results will suffer little from the Kobe earthquake because earthquake insurance is not used in Japan.

AIG (along with most of the US insurance industry) welcomed the pro-business Republican landslide of 1994, which in 1995 resulted in the appointment of more sympathetic state insurance commissioners and in the introduction in Congress of legislation to relax antipollution laws and environmental liability regulations.

NYSE symbol: AIG
Fiscal year ends: December 31

Chairman and CEO: Maurice R. Greenberg, age 69,
$3,750,000 pay
VC Finance: Edward E. Matthews, age 63, $766,924 pay
VC Life Insurance: Ernest E. Stempel, age 78,
$475,000 pay
President: Thomas R. Tizzio, age 57, $716,239 pay
EVP Life Insurance: Edmund S. W. Tse, $470,834 pay
EVP: Evan Greenberg
SVP Domestic General-Brokerage: Kevin H. Kelley
SVP Life Insurance: R. Kendall Nottingham
SVP Administration: Lawrence W. English
SVP Worldwide Claims: John G. Hughes
SVP and Chief Investment Officer: Win J. Neuger
SVP Financial Services: Petros K. Sabatacakis
SVP and Comptroller: Howard I. Smith
**SVP Senior Casualty Actuary and Senior Claims
Officer:** Robert M. Sandler
SVP: Stephen Y. N. Tse
SVP Human Resources: Axel I. Freudmann
General Counsel: Florence A. Davis
Auditors: Coopers & Lybrand L.L.P

WHERE

HQ: American International Group, Inc., 70 Pine St.,
New York, NY 10270
Phone: 212-770-7000
Fax: 212-943-1125

AIG's property/casualty subsidiaries operate in all 50
states and approximately 130 countries.

	1994 Sales $ mil.	1994 Sales % of total	1994 Pretax Income $ mil.	1994 Pretax Income % of total
US & Canada	10,806	48	1,420	48
Asia	8,374	37	1,193	40
Other regions	3,262	15	339	12
Total	**22,442**	**100**	**2,952**	**100**

WHAT

1994 Assets	$ mil.	% of total
Cash & equivalents	76	0
State & municipal bonds	15,398	14
Corporate bonds	14,082	12
Foreign gov't securities	6,528	6
Stocks	5,658	5
Receivables & reinsurance	25,092	22
Mortgages & real estate	7,218	6
Flight equipment	10,723	9
Other	29,571	26
Total	**114,346**	**100**

	1994 Sales $ mil.	1994 Sales % of total	1994 Pretax Income $ mil.	1994 Pretax Income % of total
General insurance	11,774	50	1,635	42
Life insurance	8,559	37	952	24
Financial services	1,866	8	405	10
Agency & svc. fees	238	1	54	1
Corporate	900	4	900	23
Adjustments	(895)	—	(994)	—
Total	**22,442**	**100**	**2,952**	**100**

Selected Subsidiaries
AIG Europe S.A.
American Home
  Assurance Co.
American International
  Assurance Co., Ltd.
American Life Insurance Co.
Lexington Insurance Co.
Nan Shan Life Insurance
  Co., Ltd.
National Union Fire
  Insurance Co.
Philippine American
  Life Insurance Co.

KEY COMPETITORS

Aetna	General Re	Prudential
Allianz	John Hancock	Tokio Marine
Allstate	Kemper National	and Fire
Chubb	Lloyd's of London	Transamerica
CIGNA	Loews	Travelers
Equitable	New York Life	USF&G

HOW MUCH

	Annual Growth	1985	1986	1987	1988	1989	1990	1991	1992	1993	1994
Assets ($ mil.)	24.6%	15,845	21,473	29,555	37,317	46,037	58,202	69,389	92,722	101,015	114,346
Net income ($ mil.)	20.1%	420	791	1,033	1,209	1,367	1,442	1,553	1,625	1,918	2,176
Income as % of assets	—	2.7%	3.7%	3.5%	3.2%	3.0%	2.5%	2.2%	1.8%	1.9%	1.9%
Earnings per share ($)	18.7%	1.47	2.59	3.35	3.92	4.42	4.61	4.86	5.10	6.04	6.87
Stock price – high ($)	—	29.33	38.27	44.67	36.67	59.73	56.47	68.00	80.92	100.25	100.75
Stock price – low ($)	—	17.33	27.73	28.53	26.13	35.33	38.00	48.00	54.67	73.38	81.75
Stock price – close ($)	14.8%	28.27	32.60	32.00	36.13	55.20	51.25	65.59	77.33	87.75	98.00
P/E – high	—	22	18	15	10	14	12	14	16	17	15
P/E – low	—	13	13	9	7	8	8	10	11	12	12
Dividends per share ($)	15.2%	0.12	0.12	0.14	0.19	0.23	0.27	0.31	0.35	0.39	0.43
Book value per share ($)	17.7%	12.03	15.35	18.22	22.23	26.90	30.65	35.53	39.79	47.93	51.99
Employees	2.3%	26,100	28,000	31,000	31,000	33,000	33,000	33,600	32,000	33,000	32,000

1994 Year-end:
Equity as % of assets: 14.4%
Return on assets: 13.7%
Return on equity: 13.7%
Long-term debt (mil.): $13,730
No. of shares (mil.): 316
Dividends
  Yield: 0.4%
  Payout: 6.3%
Market value (mil.): $30,952
Sales (mil.): $22,442

**Stock Price History
High/Low 1985–94**

AMERICAN STANDARD COMPANIES INC.

OVERVIEW

While American Standard's profits have been in the toilet for years and its $2.1 billion debt has threatened to put the brakes on its breakneck expansion, investors have not cooled on the diversified manufacturer. The reasons? Piscataway, New Jersey–based American Standard — which makes plumbing products, braking systems for heavy trucks and buses, and air conditioning systems — is a globally diversified company with 94 plants in 32 countries, its sales are steadily rising, and its businesses are 1st or 2nd in each of its markets.

Its plumbing products unit offers a wide selection of products designed to fit the consumer tastes of individual countries. Its air-conditioning products unit makes products under the Trane brand name and emphasizes servicing, repair, and replacement over new construction. Its transportation products unit makes air brakes primarily for the commercial vehicle industries of Europe and Brazil.

The company's shift to demand flow technology (an improved version of just-in-time technology that greatly reduces product delivery time and improves product quality) has proved expensive to implement but should pay off in coming years.

The newly public company is controlled by Kelso ASI Partners (the firm that bought the company in 1988 and holds 59% of its stock). American Standard's employees own 14% through a stock ownership plan.

WHEN

In 1881 American Radiator was created in Buffalo to make steam and water heating equipment. J. P. Morgan acquired the company along with almost every other US heating equipment firm, consolidating them under the American Radiator name in 1899.

That same year Louisville-based Ahrens & Ott joined with Pittsburgh-based Standard Manufacturing to create Standard Sanitary, which produced enameled cast-iron plumbing parts and developed the one-piece lavatory, built-in bathtubs, and single taps for hot and cold running water.

Both American Radiator and Standard Sanitary grew through numerous acquisitions in the early decades of the 20th century. In 1929 the 2 companies merged to form American Radiator & Standard Sanitary, headquartered in New York City, which later that year bought CF Church (toilet seats). During the next 3 decades, the company expanded its operations across North and South America and into Europe. By the 1960s American Radiator & Standard Sanitary was the world's largest manufacturer of plumbing fixtures.

In 1967 the company changed its name to American Standard and then diversified out of the bathroom, acquiring a number of companies, the most important of which was Westinghouse Air Brake (WABCO, 1968). WABCO traces its history to Union Switch and Signal, begun in 1882. In 1917 Union Switch was bought by Westinghouse Air Brake. George Westinghouse had invented the airbrake before turning his attention to electrical products. Union Switch merged with its parent company and adopted the WABCO corporate name in 1951.

During the 1970s and 1980s American Standard consolidated its operations and sold off numerous businesses. It purchased Clayton Dewandre (truck brakes, 1977) and Queroy (faucets and fittings, 1982). In 1984 the company purchased Trane (air conditioners). In 1988 American Standard fought off a hostile takeover attempt by Black & Decker and then agreed to be purchased by ASI Holding (formed by the leveraged buyout firm Kelso & Co.) for $3 billion and taken private.

The transaction left American Standard deeply in debt. To raise cash in 1988, the company sold its Manhattan headquarters, its railway signal business ($105 million), and its Steelcraft division (steel doors, to Masco for $126 million). In 1989 the sale of American Standard's pneumatic controls business raised $102 million. The company sold its railway brake products operations to a group led by Investment AB Cardo (Sweden) in 1990. In 1991 it sold Tyler Refrigeration (refrigerated display cases) to a Kelso & Co. affiliate for $82 million, losing $22 million in the deal.

California's attorney general filed suit against American Standard in 1992 for allegedly violating EPA lead limits. In 1993 Dan Quayle joined American Standard's board.

In 1994 American Standard, in a joint venture agreement, acquired 70% of German manufacturer Deutsche Perrot-Bremsen's brake business. That same year it expanded its plumbing manufacturing business in China. The setting up of 6 joint ventures made the company the #1 full-line supplier of plumbing products in that country.

In February 1995 the company went public again through an IPO.

NYSE symbol: ASD
Fiscal year ends: December 31

WHO

Chairman, President, and CEO: Emmanuel A.
Kampouris, age 60, $1,200,000 pay
SVP Plumbing Products: George H. Kerckhove, age 57,
$491,000 pay
SVP Automotive Products: Horst Hinrichs, age 62,
$469,394 pay
VP and CFO: Fred A. Allardyce, age 53, $381,000 pay
VP; Group Executive, Plumbing Products, Europe:
Luigi Gandini, age 56, $368,369 pay
**VP; Group Executive, Air Conditioning Products,
Europe, Middle East, and Africa:** Daniel Hilger,
age 54
**VP; Group Executive, Plumbing Products, Worldwide
Fittings:** Wilfried Delker, age 54
VP; Group Executive, Plumbing Products, PRC: Gary A.
Brogoch, age 44
VP; Group Executive, Plumbing Products, Americas:
Alexander A. Apostolopoulos, age 52
**VP; Group Executive, Air Conditioning Products,
International:** William A. Klug, age 62
VP Air Conditioning Products, Compressor Business:
Bruce R. Schiller, age 50
VP, General Counsel, and Secretary: Richard A.
Kalaher, age 54
VP Systems and Technology: Cyril Gallimore, age 65
VP Human Resources: Adrian B. Deshotel, age 49
Auditors: Ernst & Young LLP

WHERE

HQ: One Centennial Ave., PO Box 6820, Piscataway,
NJ 08855-6820
Phone: 908-980-6000
Fax: 908-980-6120

The company operates 94 manufacturing facilities in 32
countries.

	1994 Sales		1994 Operating Income	
	$ mil.	% of total	$ mil.	% of total
US	2,465	54	168	47
Europe	1,572	34	144	41
Other regions	550	12	43	12
Adjustments	(130)	—	—	—
Total	**4,457**	**100**	**355**	**100**

WHAT

	1994 Sales		1994 Operating Income	
	$ mil.	% of total	$ mil.	% of total
Air-conditioning	2,480	56	182	51
Plumbing	1,218	27	111	31
Automotive	759	17	62	18
Total	**4,457**	**100**	**355**	**100**

Products

Plumbing
Bathroom and kitchen fittings and fixtures
Bathtubs

Automotive
Air brake and related systems

Air-Conditioning
Applied systems (custom-engineered and field-installed
components)
Mini-split systems (small unitary systems operating
without air ducts and generally used in residences)
Unitary systems (factory-assembled in one to 2 units for
residential and commercial use)

Major Brand Names

Plumbing
AMERICAN-STANDARD
IDEAL-STANDARD
STANDARD

Automotive
CLAYTON DEWANDRE
PERROT
WABCO
WABCO WESTINGHOUSE

Air-Conditioning
AMERICAN-STANDARD
TRANE

KEY COMPETITORS

AlliedSignal
American Brands
Black & Decker
Eaton
AB Electrolux
Eljer Industries
Fedders
Kohler
Lennox
Masco
Tecumseh Products
United Technologies
Watsco
Whitman
York International

HOW MUCH

	Annual Growth	1985	1986	1987	1988	1989	1990	1991	1992	1993	1994
Sales ($ mil.)	4.8%	2,912	2,998	3,400	3,716	3,334	3,637	3,595	3,792	3,830	4,457
Net income ($ mil.)	—	(3)	110	133	(26)	(34)	(54)	(111)	(57)	(209)	(86)
Income as % of sales	—	—	3.7%	3.9%	—	—	—	—	—	—	—
Employees	(0.6%)	40,000	38,900	39,300	34,100	33,300	32,900	32,000	33,500	36,000	38,000

1994 Year-end:
Debt ratio: 100.0%
Cash (mil.): $93
Current ratio: 0.99
Long-term debt (mil.): $2,152
Total assets (mil.): $3,156

American Standard Inc.

Net Income
($ mil.)
1985–94

ARROW ELECTRONICS, INC.

OVERVIEW

Through acquisitions, Melville, New York–based Arrow Electronics has hit the bull's-eye to become the world's largest distributor of electronic components and computer products. However, longtime rival Avnet remains on Arrow's tail feathers. Arrow sells such components and computer products as semiconductors, microcomputer boards, desktop computer systems, and peripherals to OEMs and industrial and commercial customers.

With its 1994 acquisition of Anthem Electronics, the US's 6th largest electronics distributor, Arrow can hit the target even more frequently. Its 160 sales facilities and 15 distribution centers in 28 countries provide on-schedule delivery of products in smaller quantities than what are usually available directly from the manufacturer.

Its inventory includes products from more than 350 electronics manufacturers and suppliers, including AMD, Intel (21% of purchases), and Texas Instruments (10% of purchases). About 65% of Arrow's inventory is semiconductors. It has 5 product-specific sales groups: Arrow/Schweber Electronics and Anthem Electronics both sell semiconductors and industrial subsystems; Capstone Electronics sells capacitors, relay switches, power supplies, and related components; Gates/Arrow Distributing sells computers and peripherals; and Zeus Electronics sells specialized semiconductors for the military.

Chairman and CEO Steve Kaufman wants revenues to reach $10 billion by the year 2000. He also wants to create a seamless worldwide inventory system that will allow any site to ship an order to any customer regardless of where the order originated. As part of this effort, he expects about half of Arrow products to have one worldwide price. Arrow expects to expand through acquisitions, especially in Asia.

WHEN

Arrow Radio began in 1935 in New York City as a used-radio-equipment outlet. In the mid-1960s the company was selling various home entertainment products and wholesaling electronic parts. However, in 1968, 3 Harvard Business School graduates got Arrow in their sights. Duke Glenn Jr., Roger Green, and John Waddell led a group of investors who acquired the company for $1 million in borrowed money. The 3 also bought a company that reclaimed lead from used car batteries.

With the money they made in the lead reclamation business, the trio expanded Arrow's inventory in its wholesale electronic distribution business. By 1971 Arrow was the 10th largest electronic parts distributor in the US. The company grew rapidly during the 1970s, primarily through internal growth. By 1977 Arrow had become the 4th largest distributor in the US. In 1979 Arrow bought the #2 US distributor, Cramer Electronics. While the purchase of the West Coast–based Cramer was financed with junk bonds and left the company deeply in debt, it also doubled its revenues. Also in 1979 Arrow had its initial public offering.

Tragedy struck in December 1980 when a hotel fire killed 13 members of Arrow's senior management, including Glenn and Green, who were having a budget meeting. Waddell had remained at company headquarters to answer questions about a stock split announced that day. He was named acting CEO.

Company stock fell 19% the first day it traded after the fire and another 14% before the end of the month. In the spring of 1981, a slump hit the electronics industry. Later in 1981 Arrow's board enticed Alfred Stein to leave Motorola to become the company's president and CEO. Waddell remained as chairman. However, Stein did not mesh with Arrow, and in early 1982 the board fired him and put Waddell in charge again. By 1983 the slump in the electronics industry was over, and Arrow was temporarily back in the black. However, another industry slump led to significant losses between 1985 and 1987.

In 1985, in a significant move, Arrow acquired a 40% interest in Germany's largest electronics distributor, Spoerle Electronic (it currently owns 70% of Spoerle). Steve Kaufman, who became CEO in 1986, continued the company's expansion, acquiring Kierulff Electronics, the 4th largest US distributor (1988) and Lex Electronics, the 3rd largest (1991).

In 1993 Kaufman expanded Arrow's operations into Asia with the acquisition of Hong Kong–based Components Agent Limited. Also that year the company acquired the semiconductor distribution business of Zeus Components for about $25 million. In 1994 it acquired 2 Scandinavian electronics distributors, Field Oy and Exatec A/S.

In early 1995 Spoerle acquired Germany's HED Heinrich Electronic Distribution.

NYSE symbol: ARW
Fiscal year ends: December 31

WHO

Chairman and CEO: Stephen P. Kaufman, age 53, $1,317,000 pay
VC: John C. Waddell, age 57
SVP, CFO, General Counsel, Secretary, and Treasurer: Robert E. Klatell, age 49, $566,400 pay
VP; Chairman and CEO, Anthem Electronics: Robert S. Throop, age 57, $826,889 pay
VP; President, Arrow/Schweber Electronics Group: Steven W. Menefee, age 50, $560,200 pay
VP; President, Anthem Electronics: John J. Powers III, age 40
VP; President, Capstone Electronics: Wesley S. Sagawa, age 47
VP; President, Zeus Electronics: Jan Salsgiver, age 38
VP: Don E. Burton
VP: Harriet Green
VP: Germano Fanelli
VP: Jurgen Saalwachter
VP: Betty Jane Scheihing
VP: John S. Smith
VP Human Resources: Tom Hallam
Auditors: Ernst & Young LLP

WHERE

HQ: 25 Hub Dr., Melville, NY 11747
Phone: 516-391-1300
Fax: 516-391-1644

Arrow has facilities in 28 countries.

	1994 Sales		1994 Operating Income	
	$ mil.	% of total	$ mil.	% of total
North America	3,339	72	224	71
Europe	1,147	25	90	28
Pacific Rim	163	3	4	1
Adjustments	—	—	(62)	—
Total	**4,649**	**100**	**256**	**100**

WHAT

	1994 Sales % of total
Semiconductors	66
Industrial & commercial computer prods.	25
Passive, electromechanical & connector prods.	9
Total	**100**

Selected Divisions and Subsidiaries
Ally (Taiwan)
Amitron-Arrow (Spain)
Anthem Electronics (semiconductors)
Arrow Electronics Ltd. (UK)
Arrow Electronique (France)
Arrow/Schweber Electronics Group (semiconductors)
ATD Electronica SA (Spain and Portugal)
Capstone Electronics (connecting devices and power supplies)
Components Agent Limited (Hong Kong)
Exatec A/S (Denmark)
Field Oy (Finland)
Gates/Arrow Distributing (industrial computer products distributor)
Lite-On Group (Taiwan)
Megachip (France)
Silverstar Ltd. SpA (Italy)
Spoerle Electronic Handelsgesellschaft mbH and Co. (70%, Germany)
Zeus Electronics (service to military and high-reliability components markets)

KEY COMPETITORS

Avnet
Bell Industries
Bell Microproducts
Future Electronics
Graybar Electric
Jaco Electronics
Marshall Industries
Nu Horizons
Pioneer-Standard Electronics
Premier Industrial
Richardson Electronics
Sterling Electronics
TTI
Western Micro Technology
Wyle Electronics

HOW MUCH

	Annual Growth	1985	1986	1987	1988	1989	1990	1991	1992	1993	1994
Sales ($ mil.)	27.2%	534	530	562	1,006	925	971	1,044	1,622	2,536	4,649
Net income ($ mil.)	—	(11)	(35)	(8)	18	(2)	5	4	41	81	112
Income as % of sales	—	—	—	—	1.8%	—	0.5%	0.4%	2.5%	3.2%	2.4%
Earnings per share ($)	—	(1.75)	(5.32)	(3.17)	1.55	(0.19)	0.44	0.28	1.54	2.43	2.31
Stock price – high ($)	—	18.25	17.13	12.13	10.75	6.75	7.00	16.50	30.50	43.13	45.13
Stock price – low ($)	—	11.25	3.00	4.88	5.38	3.13	3.63	3.63	14.38	26.50	33.63
Stock price – close ($)	9.6%	15.75	6.13	6.75	6.63	3.88	4.38	15.75	28.63	41.75	35.88
P/E – high	—	—	—	—	7	—	16	59	20	18	20
P/E – low	—	—	—	—	3	—	8	13	9	11	15
Dividends per share ($)	—	0.20	0.15	0.00	0.00	0.00	0.00	0.00	0.00	0.00	0.00
Book value per share ($)	5.9%	10.81	15.61	14.30	12.90	12.67	12.66	11.34	11.99	14.60	18.15
Employees	12.8%	2,200	2,200	2,900	2,775	2,475	2,280	4,200	4,100	4,600	6,500

1994 Year-end:
Debt ratio: 27.0%
Return on equity: 17.3%
Cash (mil.): $106
Current ratio: 2.26
Long-term debt (mil.): $224
No. of shares (mil.): 46
Dividends
  Yield: —
  Payout: —
Market value (mil.): $1,656

Stock Price History High/Low 1985–94

AT&T CORP.

OVERVIEW

New York City–based AT&T capped off the merger-filled summer of 1995 by doing what nobody expected it to do: announce that it was breaking up. By the end of 1996, the corporate giant plans to split into 3 companies: communications services (to be called AT&T Corp.), computer products and services (AT&T Global Information Solutions), and network products and R&D unit Bell Labs (AT&T Systems and Technology). In preparation for the split, the company took a $4 billion charge against 4th quarter 1995 earnings to eliminate 40,000 jobs over the next 3 years. About 70% of the layoffs, representing about 28,000 jobs, are expected to occur in 1996.

Even after the split, AT&T will remain one of the biggest companies in the US, with an estimated $50 billion in revenues. It has the largest long-distance network in the US and has stabilized its market share in this highly competitive market. The company continues to expand beyond traditional long-distance service as part of a strategy to eventually give consumers integrated telephony services that include cellular service, online access, paging, video, and electronic commerce services, all on one bill.

Alex Mandl, CEO of the communications services division, was tapped to become president and COO of the "new" AT&T.

WHEN

"Mr. Watson. Come here. I want you."

Alexander Graham Bell's legendary summons, the first words on a telephone, came as he was perfecting his invention in 1876. As demand for the new device spread, Bell's backers, fathers of deaf students he was tutoring, founded Bell Telephone (1877) and New England Telephone (1878), which were consolidated as National Bell Telephone in 1879.

After several years of litigation, National Bell barred rival Western Union from the telephone business in 1879. Western Union had tried to market Elisha Gray's competing patent, filed just hours after Bell's. In 1882 the Bell company wrested control of Western Electric, the US's #1 electrical equipment manufacturer, from Western Union.

Bell's patents expired in the 1890s, and independent phone companies raced into the market. Bell struggled to compete. After changing its name to American Telephone and Telegraph and moving its headquarters from Boston to New York in 1899, AT&T shifted its focus to swallowing smaller companies. It also blocked independents from access to Bell System phone lines.

J. P. Morgan and his allies gained control of AT&T and installed Theodore Vail as president in 1907. AT&T won control of Western Union in 1909; however, the Wilson administration threatened antitrust action. In the 1913 Kingsbury Commitment, AT&T agreed to sell Western Union, buy no more independent phone companies without regulatory approval, and grant independents access to its networks. Bell Labs, the heralded research and development division, was formed in 1925.

In 1949 the Justice Department sued to force AT&T to sell Western Electric. A 1956 settlement allowed AT&T to keep Western Electric but prohibited it from entering non-regulated businesses. FCC rulings stripped AT&T of its telephone equipment monopoly (1968) and allowed specialized carriers, such as MCI, to hook their microwave-based systems to the phone network (1969), injecting competition into the long-distance arena.

A government suit led to the settlement that, in 1984, spun off the 7 regional Bell companies. AT&T kept long-distance services and Western Electric. Since the breakup, CEO Robert Allen has cut jobs in order to remain competitive. In 1990 AT&T offered a consumer credit card (Universal Card) and acquired Western Union's business services group (electronic mail, telex). AT&T's 1991 acquisitions of computer manufacturers Teradata and NCR placed the company #7 among the world's computer makers.

In 1994 the company proposed opening local telecommunications markets in Illinois and gave up on its wireless communicator, shuttering the operation. Also in that year it formally adopted the name AT&T Corp. and relabeled its NCR unit AT&T Global Information Solutions. The company acquired McCaw Cellular, the nation's #1 cellular service, for $11.5 billion in that year, and it also bought Interchange Network Company, an online service, from Ziff-Davis Publishing.

In 1995 AT&T said it would pay $3.3 billion for the 48% of cellular communications company LIN Broadcasting that it did not already own. (It had acquired 52% of LIN when it bought McCaw Cellular.) Also in 1995, in preparation for its breakup, AT&T put its Paradyne data communications equipment unit on the auction block.

NYSE symbol: T
Fiscal year ends: December 31

Chairman and CEO: Robert E. Allen, age 59,
$3,362,600 pay
President and COO: Alex J. Mandl, age 51, $1,482,100
pay (prior to promotion)
SEVP General Counsel and Government Affairs:
John D. Zeglis, age 47
SEVP and CFO: Richard W. Miller, age 54
EVP; Chairman, Global Operations Team: Victor A.
Pelson, age 57, $1,657,600 pay
EVP Business Services Division: Gail McGovern, age 43
EVP Business Strategy: John Petrillo, age 46
EVP International Operations: Pier Carlo Falotti, age 53
EVP Consumer and Small Business Division: Joseph
Nacchio
EVP and Chief Information Officer: Ron J. Ponder,
age 53
SVP Human Resources: Harold W. Burlingame, age 54
Auditors: Coopers & Lybrand L.L.P.

WHERE

HQ: 32 Avenue of the Americas, New York, NY
10013-2412
Phone: 212-387-5400
Fax: 212-841-4715 (Public Relations)

	1994 Sales		1994 Operating Income	
	$ mil.	% of total	$ mil.	% of total
US	67,769	90	6,841	91
Other countries	7,325	10	677	9
Total	**75,094**	**100**	**7,518**	**100**

WHAT

	1994 Sales	
	$ mil.	% of total
Telecommunication services	43,425	58
Products & systems	21,161	28
Rentals & other services	7,391	10
Financial services & leasing	3,117	4
Total	**75,094**	**100**

Business Units

AT&T Solutions
Consulting
Systems integration

AT&T Universal Card Services Corp.

AT&T Wireless Services
Air-to-ground telephone services
Cellular services
Messaging services

Communication Services Group
Electronic mail
Long-distance services
Satellite transponder services
Toll-free and "800" services

KEY COMPETITORS

ACC	GTE
AirTouch	MCI
ALC Comm.	MFS Communications
ALLTEL	NYNEX
American Express	Pacific Telesis
Ameritech	SBC Communications
BCE	Sprint
Bell Atlantic	U.S. Long Distance
BellSouth	U S WEST
BT	Visa
Cable & Wireless	WorldCom

HOW MUCH

	Annual Growth	1985	1986	1987	1988	1989	1990	1991	1992	1993	1994
Sales ($ mil.)	8.9%	34,910	34,087	33,598	35,210	36,112	37,285	63,089	64,904	67,156	75,094
Net income ($ mil.)	13.1%	1,557	314	2,044	(1,669)	2,697	2,735	522	3,807	3,974	4,710
Income as % of sales	—	4.5%	0.9%	6.1%	—	7.5%	7.3%	0.8%	5.9%	5.9%	6.3%
Earnings per share ($)	9.1%	1.37	0.21	1.88	(1.55)	2.50	2.51	0.40	2.86	2.94	3.01
Stock price – high ($)	—	25.38	27.88	35.88	30.38	47.38	46.63	41.25	53.13	65.00	57.13
Stock price – low ($)	—	19.00	20.88	20.00	24.13	28.13	29.00	29.00	36.63	50.13	47.25
Stock price – close ($)	8.1%	25.00	25.00	27.00	28.75	45.50	30.13	39.13	51.00	52.50	50.25
P/E – high	—	19	133	19	—	19	19	103	19	22	19
P/E – low	—	14	99	11	—	11	12	73	13	17	16
Dividends per share ($)	1.1%	1.20	1.20	1.20	1.20	1.20	1.29	1.32	1.32	1.32	1.32
Book value per share ($)	(2.0%)	13.68	12.64	13.46	10.68	11.84	12.90	12.39	14.12	10.24	11.42
Employees	(3.0%)	399,600	378,900	365,000	364,700	339,500	328,900	317,100	312,700	308,700	304,500

1994 Year-end:
Debt ratio: 38.8%
Return on equity: 30.1%
Cash (mil.): $1,208
Current ratio: 1.22
Long-term debt (mil.):
$11,358
No. of shares (mil.): 1,569
Dividends
Yield: 2.6%
Payout: 43.9%
Market value (mil.): $78,843

Stock Price History
High/Low 1985–94

AT&T SYSTEMS AND TECHNOLOGY

OVERVIEW

When you are splitting up a $75 billion telecommunications conglomerate, sometimes it takes a while to work out the details — like a name. In late September 1995 AT&T announced plans to split into 3 companies. AT&T Systems and Technology is the interim name for a $20 billion chunk of that split. It consists of AT&T's Network Systems Group, its Multimedia Products Group, and Bell Labs.

Network Systems is the largest of the group, selling about $10 billion of network equipment, including switching systems, transmission systems, and cellular systems, and $2 billion of software to run it. The Multimedia Products Group makes and markets PBX systems, voice processing systems, video conferencing systems, telephones, security systems and other products. Bell Labs, which invented the transistor, the carbon dioxide laser, and microwave radio relay, provides R&D services.

AT&T split itself up in part to allow its equipment manufacturer to better compete in the telecommunications marketplace. In the past it had lost potential clients, such as long-distance providers, who were loath to buy products from a company that they were competing with. As part of the breakup, AT&T has announced plans to sell 15% of the systems and technology business to the public in 1996.

WHEN

AT&T's telecommunications equipment manufacturing roots reach back to 1856, before the telephone was invented, when Western Union bought several telegraph manufacturers. It paired the telegraph manufacturers with a Cleveland electrical equipment shop called Gray and Barton in 1872 and incorporated the group as Western Electric Manufacturing Company.

Western Union and Western Electric entered the telephone business in 1876, marketing a telephone invented by Elisha Gray, a founder of Gray and Barton. However, Gray's patent application arrived at the patent office just a few hours after Alexander Graham Bell's, so the Bell Telephone Company won the rights to the telephone. In 1879 Bell Telephone settled a suit barring Western Union and Western Electric from the telephone business. By that year Western Electric had become the largest electrical equipment manufacturer in the US. In 1881 Bell bought control of Western Electric, and in 1882 the 2 signed an agreement giving Western Electric the exclusive right to manufacture telephones for Bell. Bell changed its name to American Telephone and Telegraph in 1899.

Until 1908 Western Electric was not allowed to sell its equipment to non-AT&T companies, but that year AT&T, fearing antitrust action, changed the agreement to let Western Electric sell to independents. In 1925 AT&T and Western Electric set up Bell Laboratories to conduct research and development.

The Depression hurt AT&T, as lean times led many people to drop their phone service. With demand plummeting, Western Electric laid off 80% of its workforce. During WWII Western Electric and Bell Labs did work for the US military. Their work with radar would give AT&T an important advantage when the microwave relay became the primary method for transmitting long-distance calls. In 1947 Bell Labs introduced perhaps its most important invention, the transistor, for which its inventors, William Shockley, John Bardeen, and Walter Brattain, won the Nobel Prize for Physics in 1956.

In 1949 the Justice Department sued to force AT&T to sell Western Electric. A 1956 settlement allowed AT&T to keep Western Electric but prohibited it from entering nonregulated businesses. During the 1950s and 1960s AT&T and Bell Labs focused research activities and capital on an electronic switching system. The first unit, which greatly increased the speed and capacity of the phone system, was installed in 1965.

In 1974 the Justice Department filed an antitrust suit against AT&T. When the suit was finally settled in 1982, AT&T lost its regional operating companies (the 7 Baby Bells), but it was freed from its 1956 agreement prohibiting it from entering nonregulated businesses. When the split-up was completed in 1984, AT&T had 2 parts, long distance and Western Electric, which was renamed AT&T Technologies. Bell Labs continued to conduct research and development for the company.

Following the breakup, AT&T moved into the computer business. It also set up AT&T Network Systems to sell telephone switching equipment around the world.

In 1990 AT&T signed a deal to build a cellular telephone network for GTE. In 1995 Henry Schacht, an AT&T director and former head of Cummins Engine, was named CEO of the new systems and technology company.

Fiscal year ends: December 31

WHO

Chairman and CEO: Henry B. Schacht, age 61
President and COO: Richard A. McGinn, age 49
EVP and CFO: Donald K. Peterson, age 46
President, Bell Laboratories: Daniel C. Stanzione
EVP and CEO, Multimedia Products: William B.
Marx Jr., age 55

WHERE

HQ: 32 Avenue of the Americas, New York, NY
10013-2412
Phone: 212-387-5400
Fax: 212-841-4715 (Public Relations)

WHAT

Selected Products and Services

Bell Laboratories
Fundamental research
Product, systems, software, and services design and
development

Multimedia Products Group
Answering systems
Cellular telephones
Corded and cordless telephones
Fax machines
Installation, maintenance, and repair services
Modems
Multiplexers
PBX systems
Personal communications products
Security systems
Video conferencing systems
Voice messaging and voice processing systems

Network Systems Group
Asynchronous transfer mode switching systems
Digital switching systems
Microcells
Mobile switching centers
Radio base stations
Software support tools
Wireless data products
Wireless subscriber systems

KEY COMPETITORS

ADC Telecommunications
Alcatel Alsthom
Ascom
Bellcore
BT
DSC Communications
Ericsson
Fujitsu
GTE
Harris Corp.
Hitachi
Intel
Motorola
NEC
Norstan
Northern Telecom
Octel
Oki
Rockwell
Siemens
Telia
Tellabs
Toshiba
U.S. Robotics

HOW MUCH

	Annual Growth	1985	1986	1987	1988	1989	1990	1991	1992	1993	1994
Sales ($ mil.)	3.1%	15,782	15,476	15,132	15,439	15,275	15,548	15,941	16,579	17,925	21,161
Estimated employees	(3.0%)	99,900	94,725	91,250	91,175	84,875	82,225	79,275	78,175	77,175	76,125

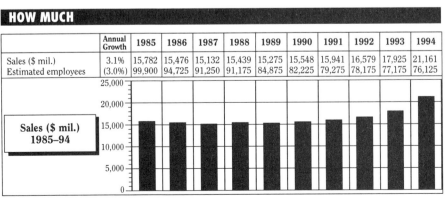

Sales ($ mil.) 1985–94

AVNET, INC.

OVERVIEW

Avnet, long the top global distributor of electronic components and computer products, dropped to #2 with rival Arrow Electronics's 1994 purchase of Anthem Electronics. The company's primary customers are OEMs that build a wide array of electronic equipment. Avnet has distribution agreements with DEC and Intel, among others, and it has 3 business segments: the Electronic Marketing Group, the Video Communications Group, and the Electrical and Industrial Group.

The first markets, assembles, and processes electronic components and computer products for industrial, commercial, and military use. It also offers value-added services including inventory replenishment systems, computer kits, connector and cable assembly, and semiconductor programming.

The Video Communications Group manufactures, assembles, and markets TV signal processing equipment including Direct Broadcast Satellite TV antennas, conventional TV roof antennas, and commercial satellite antenna systems.

The Electrical and Industrial Group distributes electric motors and motor parts, supplies for electronics production lines, and other related devices and supplies.

Avnet's customers use its cutting-edge POURS (Point of Use Replenishment System) bar code–based inventory system and its Electronic Data Interchange computerized ordering system to store parts and ensure automatic replacement.

Although Avnet has lost its place as the world's leading electronic component distributor, the company expects that its aggressive acquisitions, well-established industrial and military client base, high-tech inventory systems, and expansions into Europe and Asia will keep it on the heels of its longtime competitor Arrow Electronics.

WHEN

In 1921, before commercial battery-operated radios, Charles Avnet started a small ham radio replacement parts distributorship in lower Manhattan. The stock market crash in 1929 left the business strapped, and it went bankrupt in 1931. Later that decade Avnet had another company making car radio kits and antennas. But competition got the best of him, and again the company went bankrupt.

During WWII Charles Avnet and son Lester founded Avnet Electronic Supply to sell parts to government and defense contractors, since production of home radio sets was prohibited. After the war the company bought and sold surplus electrical and electronic parts. A contract from Bendix Aviation spurred company growth, and Avnet opened a West Coast warehouse. In 1955 the company incorporated as Avnet Electronics Supply Co., Inc. Sales reached $1 million that year although the company lost $17,000. In 1958 the company changed its name to Avnet Electronics Corp.

In 1960 Avnet made its first acquisition, British Industries Corp., and went public. The acquisitions continued with Hamilton Electro (1962), Fairmount Motor Production Co., Inc. (1963), and Valley Forge Products, Inc. (1964). Semiconductor maker Hamilton remained autonomous but buoyed Avnet's connector component business. To reflect its diversification into motors and other products, the company again changed its name, to Avnet, Inc., in 1964. Also in 1964 Charles Avnet died and

Lester became chairman and president. Avnet continued its acquisitions throughout the 1960s. In 1970 Lester Avnet died and director Simon Sheib became chairman and CEO.

The 1970s brought new opportunities to the company. In 1973 Intel, which had brought out the first microprocessor, signed Avnet as a distributor. By 1979 Avnet's sales had topped $1 billion. In 1980 Anthony Hamilton, founder of Hamilton Electro, became CEO, and Avnet took the top spot among US distributors of electronic components.

During 1991 and 1992 Avnet spent over $100 million for acquisitions in the European market, buying Access Group (UK), F.H. Tec Composants (France), and Nortec AB (Scandinavia). In 1992 DEC signed a 15-year distribution contract with Avnet. The next year the company outbid Wyle Laboratories for Hall-Mark Electronics, the US's 3rd largest distributor. It acquired Penstock, the top US distributor of microwave radio frequency products, in 1994.

Thanks to these acquisitions, Avnet was Europe's #2 electronics distributor in 1994 despite having had almost no European operations prior to 1990. As exemplified by the 1995 purchase of German electronics distributor Setron Schiffer-Electronik, which has a presence in eastern Europe, and the acquisition of 70% of Hong Kong distributor WKK Semiconductor, CEO Leon Machiz plans to continue the globalization of Avnet.

NYSE symbol: AVT
Fiscal year ends: Friday nearest June 30

WHO

Chairman and CEO: Leon Machiz, age 71,
$1,660,000 pay
VC, President, and COO: Roy Vallee, age 43,
$864,000 pay
VP: Steven C. Church, age 46, $499,481 pay
SVP and Secretary: Sylvester D. Herlihy, age 68,
$498,030 pay
SVP: Joseph W. Semmer, age 58, $487,876 pay
SVP: Burton Katz, age 53
SVP: Keith Williams, age 47
SVP and General Counsel: David R. Birk, age 48
SVP and Chief Information Officer: Anthony T. DeLuca,
age 45
SVP and CFO: Raymond Sadowski, age 41
Director Technical Operations: John Ashbaugh
VP: John A. Carfora, age 49
VP: John T. Clark, age 41
VP: Patrick Jewett, age 50
VP: Donald E. Sweet, age 58
VP: Morton M. Vogel, age 65
VP: Richard Ward, age 55
VP Human Resources: Robert Zierk
Auditors: Arthur Andersen & Co, SC

WHERE

HQ: 80 Cutter Mill Rd., Great Neck, NY 11021
Phone: 516-466-7000
Fax: 516-466-1203

Avnet operates throughout North America, Europe, and
the Asia/Pacific region.

WHAT

	1995 Sales	
	$ mil.	% of total
Electronic Marketing	3,873	90
Video Communications	246	6
Electrical and Industrial	181	4
Total	**4,300**	**100**

Electronic Marketing Group
Allied Electronics (electronic components and
maintenance and repair organization distribution)
Avnet Computer Marketing Group
Hamilton Hallmark (semiconductors)
Penstock (radio frequency/microwave components and
devices)
Time Electronics (interconnect products)

Video Communications Group
Channel Master
Channel Master (UK)

Electrical and Industrial Group
Avnet Industrial (maintenance and repair organization
products and services)
Brownell Electro (motor repair and industrial OEM
product services)

KEY COMPETITORS

Arrow Electronics
Bell Industries
Bell Microproducts
Future Electronics
Graybar Electric
Jaco Electronics
Marshall Industries
Nu Horizons

Pioneer-Standard Electronics
Premier Industrial
Richardson Electronics
Sterling Electronics
TTI
Western Micro Technology
Wyle Electronics

HOW MUCH

	Annual Growth	1986	1987	1988	1989	1990	1991	1992	1993	1994	1995
Sales ($ mil.)	13.1%	1,416	1,539	1,817	1,919	1,751	1,741	1,759	2,238	3,548	4,300
Net income ($ mil.)	21.7%	24	23	52	54	57	62	51	69	88	140
Income as % of sales	—	1.7%	1.5%	2.9%	2.8%	3.2%	3.5%	2.9%	3.1%	2.5%	3.3%
Earnings per share ($)	19.5%	0.67	0.64	1.46	1.51	1.57	1.72	1.42	1.91	2.16	3.32
Stock price – high ($)	—	40.38	39.25	28.13	32.75	33.50	30.00	36.00	42.25	45.00	55.63
Stock price – low ($)	—	25.00	18.50	19.00	20.63	21.50	23.25	23.50	29.00	30.75	35.75
Stock price – close ($)	6.3%	25.75	23.75	22.25	31.00	25.88	27.13	34.50	39.00	37.00	44.75
P/E – high	—	60	61	19	22	21	17	25	22	21	17
P/E – low	—	37	29	13	14	14	14	17	15	14	11
Dividends per share ($)	2.0%	0.50	0.50	0.50	0.50	0.58	0.60	0.60	0.60	0.60	0.60
Book value per share ($)	5.9%	18.20	18.44	19.54	20.60	21.46	22.60	23.56	24.35	27.26	30.38
Employees	(0.3%)	9,250	9,500	10,000	8,500	7,500	7,250	6,650	6,500	8,000	9,000

1995 Year-end:
Debt ratio: 25.3%
Return on equity: 12.0%
Cash (mil.): $49
Current ratio: 3.26
Long-term debt (mil.): $419
No. of shares (mil.): 41
Dividends
 Yield: 1.3%
 Payout: 18.1%
Market value (mil.): $1,835

Stock Price History
High/Low 1986–95

AVON PRODUCTS, INC.

OVERVIEW

Avon is calling on its traditional means of selling beauty products — direct sales — for its expansion into emerging markets. Based in New York City, Avon is the world's leading direct seller of beauty and related products, with 1.9 million independent representatives. Avon sold its Giorgio Beverly Hills retail subsidiary to Procter & Gamble for $150 million to focus on its global direct-selling business.

Since many emerging markets don't have developed infrastructures and distribution systems, Avon hires representatives to sell its products in such hard-to-reach locales as the Amazon basin. Avon now has 478,000 "beauty consultants" in Brazil and has more than doubled its Chinese sales force from 12,000 at the beginning of 1994 to 25,000 at year-end.

However, Avon has had difficulty competing with retail chains like Wal-Mart in the US and hypermarkets in Western Europe, which sell similar products at discount prices. In both markets, Avon has appointed new management to reinvigorate sales and marketing efforts. Avon is also improving its product line and cutting costs. The company began marketing a line of intimate and casual wear clothing through a brochure called Avon Style. It is mailing copies to its 415,000 representatives in the US and has recorded impressive sales of $120 million since the line's introduction. In its first-ever worldwide product launch, in 1994 Avon introduced Far Away, a women's fragrance, in all of its more than 100 markets.

WHEN

In the 1880s book salesman David McConnell gave small bottles of perfume to New York housewives who listened to his sales pitch. The perfume was more popular than the books, so in 1886 McConnell created the California Perfume Company (renamed Avon in 1950 after the Avon River in England) and hired women to sell door-to-door. Through the 1950s these women, mostly housewives seeking extra income, made Avon a major force in the cosmetics industry. The company still relies heavily on direct sales.

From the 1960s until the mid-1980s, Avon was the world's largest cosmetics company, known for its appeal to middle-class homemakers. Avon hit hard times in 1974, when recession made many of its products too pricey for blue-collar customers. Women were also leaving home for the work force, making door-to-door sales less viable. Avon discovered that its traditional products had little appeal for younger women. In response, president David Mitchell began to diversify and overhaul Avon's product line, introducing the Colorworks line for teenagers with the slogan "It's not your mother's makeup" and ads picturing active young women.

Avon acquired the Tiffany jewelry company to help improve the company's image in 1979, then sold it in 1984. The company also expanded into the health care field; acquisitions included Mallinckrodt (hospital supply and chemical company, 1982), Foster Medical (1984), and 60 other medical suppliers. The health care field soon proved unprofitable because of stricter reimbursement policies set by Medicare. Avon sold Mallinckrodt in 1986 and

continued to sell off its remaining health care companies through 1990.

To boost profits Avon entered the retail prestige fragrances business by launching a joint venture with Liz Claiborne (1985) and buying Giorgio (1987). When Avon bought Parfums Stern, a Claiborne competitor, in 1987 (sold in 1990), Claiborne dissolved the joint venture. That same year Avon sold 40% of Avon Japan (started in 1969) to the Japanese public for $218 million.

The company introduced Avon Color cosmetics in 1988 and sleepwear, preschool toys, and videos in 1989, the same year that Amway and Irwin Jacobs made an unsuccessful attempt to buy Avon. In 1990 the company expanded into Eastern Europe and China, and in 1991 it branched into direct mail in an attempt to boost domestic sales. Also in 1991 it reached a peaceful settlement with Chartwell Associates, ending the latter's 18-month attempt to gain control of Avon. Under the agreement Chartwell may not increase its Avon holdings beyond 4.9%.

Avon continued to expand its global reach in 1992 when it began direct sales in Poland. It also opened a showroom and service center in downtown Tokyo. That same year Avon introduced its highly successful new skin-care product called Anew Perfecting Complex, which uses alpha hydroxy acids to improve skin softness and smoothness. Avon expanded into Russia in 1993.

In 1995 Avon signed a joint licensing agreement with designer Diane Von Furstenberg to create a budget-to-moderate line of casual sportswear.

NYSE symbol: AVP
Fiscal year ends: December 31

WHO

Chairman and CEO: James E. Preston, age 61,
$1,050,412 pay
President and COO: Edward J. Robinson, age 54,
$1,038,300 pay
EVP Asia/Pacific: John I. Novosad, age 54, $398,832 pay
SVP; President, Avon US: Christina A. Gold, age 47,
$482,280 pay
SVP and CFO: Edwina D. Woodbury, age 43,
$406,520 pay
SVP, General Counsel, and Secretary: Ward M.
Miller Jr., age 62
SVP and Chief Information Officer: Ronald D.
Mastrogiovanni
SVP Global Human Resources and Corporate Affairs:
Marcia L. Worthing, age 52
President, Continental Europe: Alfredo Cuello, age 47
Group VP Taxes and Treasurer: Robert J. Corti, age 45
Auditors: Coopers & Lybrand L.L.P.

WHERE

HQ: 9 West 57th St., New York, NY 10019-2683
Phone: 212-546-6015
Fax: 212-546-6136

Avon makes beauty and related products in 18
manufacturing laboratories around the world. The
company operates subsidiaries in 40 countries and
distributes its products in 80 additional countries.

	1994 Sales		1994 Operating Income	
	$ mil.	% of total	$ mil.	% of total
US	1,535	36	201	35
Other Americas	1,416	33	274	47
Pacific	664	16	90	15
Europe	652	15	15	3
Adjustments	—	—	(146)	—
Total	**4,267**	**100**	**434**	**100**

WHAT

	1994 Sales	
	$ mil.	% of total
Cosmetics, fragrances & toiletries	2,604	61
Gift & decorative	769	18
Apparel	480	11
Fashion jewelry & accessories	413	10
Total	**4,267**	**100**

Selected Domestic and International Brands
Anew (skin care)
Avon Color (cosmetics)
Avon Fashions (lingerie and apparel)
Avon Life (vitamin and nutritional supplements)
Avon Style (lingerie and casual wear)
BioAdvance (skin care)
Boutique (jewelry and lingerie)
Daily Revival (skin care)
Far Away (fragrance)
Parfums Créatifs (fragrance)
Skin-So-Soft (lotion)
Triumph (cologne)

KEY COMPETITORS

Alberto-Culver	General Nutrition	Maybelline
Allou	Hasbro	MEM
American Home	Helene Curtis	Nature's
Products	Herbalife	Sunshine
Amway	International	Nordstrom
BeautiControl	J. C. Penney	Perrigo
Chattem	Jean Philippe	Pfizer
Colgate-	Fragrances	Premark
Palmolive	Johnson & Johnson	Procter &
Dep	Johnson Publishing	Gamble
Dillard	The Limited	Sandoz
Estée Lauder	L'Oréal	Shiseido
Forever Living	LVMH	Toys "R" Us
Frederick's of	Mary Kay	Unilever
Hollywood	Mattel	

HOW MUCH

	Annual Growth	1985	1986	1987	1988	1989	1990	1991	1992	1993	1994
Sales ($ mil.)	6.3%	2,470	2,883	2,763	3,063	3,300	3,454	3,593	3,810	4,008	4,267
Net income ($ mil.)	4.4%	163	159	183	96	55	195	136	175	240	241
Income as % of sales	—	6.6%	5.5%	6.6%	3.1%	1.7%	5.7%	3.8%	4.6%	6.0%	5.6%
Earnings per share ($)	5.8%	2.05	2.23	2.59	1.29	0.37	2.60	1.89	2.43	3.32	3.41
Stock price – high ($)	—	29.00	36.38	38.63	28.38	41.25	38.13	49.00	60.25	64.38	63.63
Stock price – low ($)	—	17.88	25.75	19.25	18.63	19.50	22.75	26.13	44.00	47.63	48.38
Stock price – close ($)	8.9%	27.63	27.00	25.75	19.50	36.88	29.38	46.00	55.38	48.63	59.75
P/E – high	—	14	16	15	22	—	15	26	25	19	19
P/E – low	—	9	12	7	14	—	9	14	18	14	14
Dividends per share ($)	(0.6%)	2.00	2.00	2.00	1.52	1.00	1.00	4.40	1.50	1.70	1.90
Book value per share ($)	(15.1%)	11.69	9.76	10.66	4.11	3.72	6.60	3.51	4.31	4.36	2.69
Employees	0.8%	28,200	28,500	28,600	28,800	30,100	30,300	30,500	29,700	29,800	30,400

1994 Year-end:
Debt ratio: 48.9%
Return on equity: 96.5%
Cash (mil.): $215
Current ratio: 1.01
Long-term debt (mil.): $117
No. of shares (mil.): 69
Dividends
  Yield: 3.2%
  Payout: 55.7%
Market value (mil.): $4,127

**Stock Price History
High/Low 1985–94**

THE BANK OF NEW YORK CO., INC.

OVERVIEW

The Bank of New York Company is continuing its strategy of business diversity and regional specialization by dominating the suburban New York and New Jersey retail banking market (with no immediate plans to expand its geographical territory), solidifying its role as an important US corporate and multinational banker, and increasing its role in several fee-generating specialty niches. Among these are factoring, securities transaction processing, trust services, and credit cards.

Other business lines include investment management, financial market services, investment banking, and international leasing. The Bank of New York Company is also one of the largest US sponsors of ADRs and a leader in government securities and international funds clearance.

All of these businesses have helped reduce the company's former dependence on loan income (which caused problems in the late 1980s and early 1990s).

In 1994, to ensure an orderly executive transition, chairman Carter Bacot announced that president and COO Thomas Renyi would succeed him upon his retirement in 1997.

WHEN

In 1784 Alexander Hamilton (at 27 already a Revolutionary War hero and early economic theorist) and a group of New York merchants and lawyers founded New York City's first bank, the Bank of New York. Hamilton saw a need to institute a credit system to finance the nation's growth and to establish credibility for the new nation's chaotic monetary system.

Hamilton became US secretary of the treasury in 1789 and soon negotiated the new US government's first loan, issued by Bank of New York for $200,000 (this would now be considered a highly suspect transaction). The bank also helped finance the War of 1812, by offering $16 million in subscription books, and the Civil War, by loaning the government $150 million (the strength of the returns for this latter transaction helped the bank raise its dividends to 5% in 1865). In 1878 the bank became a US Treasury depository for the sale of government bonds.

With its reputation for probity and conservative fiscal policies, the bank weathered numerous panics during the 19th century, but because Bank of New York emphasized commercial banking to select customers rather than competing for size with other banks, by 1904 it was no longer one of the largest in the US. In 1922 the bank merged with New York Life Insurance and Trust Co. (formed in 1830 by many of Bank of New York's directors) to form Bank of New York and Trust Co. and began to develop trust and investment services. The bank weathered the crash of 1929 and remained profitable, paying dividends throughout the Depression. In 1938 it changed its name back to Bank of New York.

In 1948 the bank acquired the Fifth Avenue Bank to get a mid-Manhattan location and to expand trust services. In 1966 it acquired Empire Trust Co., which specialized in lending to developing industries. The Bank of New York Co., Inc., a holding company created in 1968, expanded statewide. In 1980 the bank bought Empire National Bank (Newburgh), the #2 state branch network outside New York City.

In the 1980s, under the leadership of chairman and president J. Carter Bacot, Bank of New York relaxed its conservative lending policies to cash in on the economic boom. The bank bought New York competitor Irving Bank in a 1988 hostile takeover for $1.4 billion and in 1990 bought the credit card portfolios of First City Bancorp. of Texas and of Dreyfus Consumer Bank's Gold MasterCard. Bank of New York (Delaware), which manages these portfolios, is one of the US's largest credit card operations, specializing in low rate cards whose interest clock begins ticking at purchase rather than in the following month, and affinity cards, such as one for the AFL-CIO. Also in the late 1980s, Bank of New York began building up its fee-for-service side, beefing up its ADR business through direct solicitation of European companies, and going after government securities business as well.

As the economy cooled in the early 1990s, the bank suffered from its portfolio of highly leveraged transactions and nonperforming loans; in 1991 nonperforming assets peaked at $1.8 billion. Since then loan sales have reduced its nonperforming assets.

In 1994 and 1995 the company went on a very specialized buying spree, acquiring, among others, BankAmerica's securities processing business and the municipal bond administration business of Frost Bank (Texas). One business the bank is exiting, however, is mortgage servicing (although it will continue to originate mortgage loans in its home region); in 1995 it sold California-based mortgage servicing company ARCS Mortgage.

NYSE symbol: BK
Fiscal year ends: December 31

Chairman and CEO: J. Carter Bacot, age 62,
$2,700,000 pay
VC: Samuel F. Chevalier, age 61, $1,245,193 pay
VC: Alan R. Griffith, age 53, $783,846 pay
President; President and COO, The Bank of New York:
Thomas A. Renyi, age 49, $878,846 pay
SEVP; SEVP and CFO, The Bank of New York: Deno D.
Papageorge, age 56, $1,057,693 pay
**EVP Investment Co. Services and Operations, The
Bank of New York:** Thomas J. Perna
EVP: Richard D. Field, age 54
**SVP Public and Investor Relations, The Bank of New
York:** Paul J. Leyden
SVP Personnel, The Bank of New York: Frank L.
Peterson
Secretary and Chief Legal Officer: Phebe C. Miller,
age 45
Auditors: Deloitte & Touche LLP

WHERE

HQ: The Bank of New York Company, Inc., 48 Wall St.,
New York, NY 10286
Phone: 212-495-1784
Fax: 212-495-1398

The Bank of New York operates retail branch banks in
the Northeast with other businesses throughout the US
and in 24 countries.

	1994 Sales		1994 Pretax income	
	$ mil.	% of total	$ mil.	% of total
US	3,735	88	1,089	91
Asia	211	5	94	8
Europe	124	3	6	0
Other regions	181	4	9	1
Total	**4,251**	**100**	**1,198**	**100**

WHAT

	1994 Assets	
	$ mil.	% of total
Cash & equivalents	6,914	14
Treasurys	2,854	6
State & municipal bonds	776	2
Derivatives	522	1
Other securities	1,439	3
Net loans	32,291	66
Other	4,083	8
Total	**48,879**	**100**

	1994 Sales	
	$ mil.	% of total
Loan interest	2,405	57
Other interest	557	13
Trust & service charges	591	14
Processing fees	530	12
Other	168	4
Total	**4,251**	**100**

Selected Subsidiaries
The Bank of New York
(retail and corporate
banking, trusts and
investments, securities
processing)
The Bank of New York
(Delaware) (credit cards)

The Bank of New York
Mortgage Co.
BNY Associates, Inc.
(investment banking)
BNY Financial
Corp. (factoring)
BNY Leasing Corp.

KEY COMPETITORS

ADVANTA	Citicorp	J.P. Morgan
AT&T	CoreStates	KeyCorp
BankAmerica	Crédit Lyonnais	MBNA
Bankers Trust	Dime Bancorp	Mellon Bank
Barclays	First Chicago	NatWest
Bell Bancorp	First Interstate	Royal Bank of
BFS Bankorp	First Union	Canada
Canadian Imperial	Fleet	
Chase Manhattan	General Motors	

HOW MUCH

	Annual Growth	1985	1986	1987	1988	1989	1990	1991	1992	1993	1994
Assets ($ mil.)	11.4%	18,486	20,709	23,065	47,388	48,857	45,390	39,426	40,909	45,546	48,879
Net income ($ mil.)	21.2%	130	155	103	213	51	308	122	369	534	736
Income as % of assets	—	0.7%	0.7%	0.4%	0.4%	0.1%	0.7%	0.3%	0.9%	1.2%	1.5%
Earnings per share ($)	7.0%	2.01	2.27	1.41	2.61	0.14	1.99	0.64	2.12	2.72	3.70
Stock price – high ($)	—	17.47	23.39	22.94	18.63	27.50	20.88	18.06	27.31	31.25	33.25
Stock price – low ($)	—	11.63	16.42	12.25	12.94	18.38	6.63	8.25	15.00	25.31	24.94
Stock price – close ($)	6.3%	17.14	19.44	12.88	18.50	20.13	8.88	15.44	26.94	28.50	29.77
P/E – high	—	9	10	16	7	—	11	28	13	12	9
P/E – low	—	6	7	9	5	—	3	13	7	9	7
Dividends per share ($)	5.2%	0.70	0.78	0.86	0.92	0.99	1.06	0.84	0.76	0.86	1.10
Book value per share ($)	5.1%	14.20	15.88	16.83	18.67	17.44	17.96	17.93	19.26	20.18	22.26
Employees	8.2%	7,616	9,304	10,249	17,776	17,083	15,847	15,139	16,167	15,621	15,477

1994 Year-end:
Equity as % of assets: 8.5%
Return on assets: 3.0%
Return on equity: 18.5%
Long-term debt (mil.): $1,774
No. of shares (mil.): 188
Dividends
  Yield: 3.7%
  Payout: 29.7%
Market value (mil.): $5,586
Sales (mil.): $4,251

**Stock Price History
High/Low 1985–94**

BANKERS TRUST NEW YORK

OVERVIEW

Bankers Trust has had a few "difficulties." These included the crash of the US bond market in early 1994, which helped send income diving by 43%; the Mexican peso crash; lawsuits relating to derivatives sold to 2 longtime clients, Gibson Greetings and Procter & Gamble; a written supervisory agreement imposed by the Fed that restricts some of the firm's sales activities; and a $10 million fine imposed by the SEC and the Commodity Futures Trading Commission.

Bankers Trust remains committed to its specialty of risk management. But in the wake of all its tribulations it has determined to shift its emphasis from speculative derivatives plays aimed at making a killing, to using derivatives and other hedging strategies to shield itself and its clients from the worst vagaries of the market. As part of this change, Bankers Trust has shaken up management, not only of derivatives and asset management, but at the very top as well. Frank Newman, a former official of the Treasury Department, became president in 1995 and CEO in 1996.

Other business lines include fee-based businesses like trading, loan syndications, and international merchant banking. Bankers Trust has also begun cultivating customer relationships and improving interdepartmental communications to facilitate cross-selling.

WHEN

Bankers Trust Co. was founded in 1903 by a group of bankers led by Henry Davison to handle trust business for commercial banks. Within 5 years it began building a network of correspondent banks in other countries to handle international trust business. It soon began to expand domestically, acquiring Mercantile Trust (1911), Manhattan Trust (1912), and Astor Trust (1917). The 1913 Federal Reserve Act (which allowed all banks to offer trust services) eliminated the firm's competitive edge. So in 1917 Bankers Trust joined the Federal Reserve System and began offering a variety of banking services. In 1919 its securities department (started in 1916) began underwriting and distributing securities. In 1928 it became a subsidiary, but with the 1931 passage of the Glass-Steagall Act (which separated investment banking from commercial banking) the subsidiary was discontinued.

After WWII, Bankers Trust ventured into retail banking, offering savings and checking accounts and home improvement, auto, and unsecured business loans.

In 1950 it bought Lawyers Trust, Title Guaranty & Trust's banking division, and Flushing National Bank. By 1965 it had added 22 branches and bought several more banks.

By 1967 Bankers Trust had 89 offices in New York and 2 in London; within 8 years there were 200 offices. International operations expanded in the 1970s to more than 30 countries, and the firm's network of correspondent banks had grown to more than 1,200 banks in over 120 countries.

In the early 1980s the company sold its consumer banking business in order to focus on corporate services, particularly international commercial and merchant banking. It had not done much to cultivate traditional corporate clients, however, and gravitated to the high-risk, high-profit LBO arena, where it became a favorite of dealmakers like KKR. When the 1980s LBO craze faded, bad loan expenses rose as interest rates dropped. The bank lost money in 1989. A diminished customer base and a need for profits drove the bank deeper into proprietary trading and risk management.

Risk management involves hedging positions with derivatives, which can be as simple as "plain vanilla" options, but which can also be very complex (with names like "the ratio swap," "Spreadlock 1 and 2," and "Wedding Band 3 and 6") and contain multiple leveraging factors that vastly increase the potential for profit (and, as it turned out in 1994, for loss). These instruments were often stunningly profitable in 1993, when interest rates were falling, but many turned mean when rates rose in 1994.

Some of the firm's clients, suffering losses, turned against their bank, and 2 sued (although Gibson Greetings, facing a loss of $17.5 million, was unable to resist a last desperate gamble that added another $10 million to the tab). Later in 1994 the bank settled with Gibson (accepting only $6 million from the greeting card company instead of the $14 million Bankers Trust said it was owed) after a tape of 2 of the bank's employees discussing methods of concealing the extent of Gibson's losses was discovered. These problems have contributed to the firm's loss of share of a much-subdued derivatives market.

Several Bankers Trust executives left in 1995. Chairman Charles Sanford, the architect of the aggressive derivatives policy, announced that he would retire in 1996.

NYSE symbol: BT
Fiscal year ends: December 31

WHO

Chairman: Charles S. Sanford Jr., age 59
Chairman-designate, President, and CEO: Frank Newman
EVP and Chief Credit Officer: Joseph A. Manganello Jr., age 59, $832,100 pay
EVP and General Counsel: James J. Baechle, age 62, $757,100 pay
CFO: Richard Daniel
Chairman, Bankers Trust International: Yves de Balmann, age 48
Managing Director Corporate Human Resources: Mark Bieler
Auditors: Ernst & Young LLP

WHERE

HQ: Bankers Trust New York Corporation,
280 Park Ave., New York, NY 10017
Phone: 212-250-2500
Fax: 212-454-1704 (Public Relations)

Bankers Trust operates globally.

	1994 Sales		1994 Pretax Income	
	$ mil.	% of total	$ mil.	% of total
US	4,210	50	364	42
UK	1,546	18	144	17
Asia & the Pacific	1,167	14	218	25
Other Americas	896	11	103	12
Other regions	597	7	40	4
Adjustments	(913)	—	—	—
Total	**7,503**	**100**	**869**	**100**

WHAT

	1994 Assets	
	$ mil.	% of total
Cash & equivalents	24,059	25
Treas. & agency securities	13,314	14
Foreign govt. securities	9,828	10
Derivatives	14,071	15
Other securities	17,776	18
Net loans	11,249	11
Other	6,719	7
Total	**97,016**	**100**

	1994 Sales	
	$ mil.	% of total
Interest	5,030	67
Trading	465	6
Fiduciary & funds mgmt.	740	10
Fees & commissions	756	10
Other	512	7
Total	**7,503**	**100**

Financial Services
Commercial banking
Corporate finance
Fiduciary and securities services
Global operating and information services
International merchant banking
Investment management

Selected Subsidiaries
American Bank in Poland
Bankers Trust Australia Ltd.
BT Bank of Canada
Didier Philippe SA (France)
TISCO Securities Hong Kong Ltd.
Turk Merchant Bank AS
United Bank for Africa Ltd.
The WM Company PLC (UK)

KEY COMPETITORS

Bank of New York
BankAmerica
Bear Stearns
Chase Manhattan
Citicorp
Crédit Lyonnais
CS Holding
Dai-Ichi Kangyo
Deutsche Bank
First Chicago
Fleet
Goldman Sachs
HSBC
Industrial Bank of Japan
J.P. Morgan
Merrill Lynch
Morgan Stanley
NatWest
Paine Webber
Salomon
Union Bank of Switzerland

HOW MUCH

	Annual Growth	1985	1986	1987	1988	1989	1990	1991	1992	1993	1994
Assets ($ mil.)	7.5%	50,581	56,420	56,521	57,942	55,658	63,596	63,959	72,448	92,082	97,016
Net income ($ mil.)	6.2%	371	428	1	648	(987)	634	633	731	1,047	587
Income as % of assets	—	0.7%	0.8%	0.0%	1.1%	—	1.0%	1.0%	1.0%	1.1%	0.6%
Earnings per share ($)	3.2%	5.39	6.01	0.02	8.09	(12.10)	7.80	7.75	8.82	12.29	7.17
Stock price – high ($)	—	37.88	52.50	55.25	41.25	58.25	46.75	68.00	70.13	83.50	84.63
Stock price – low ($)	—	26.88	33.38	26.25	29.63	34.50	28.50	39.50	50.00	65.75	54.75
Stock price – close ($)	4.7%	36.75	45.25	31.75	35.00	41.38	43.38	63.75	68.50	79.13	55.38
P/E – high	—	7	9	—	5	—	6	9	10	7	12
P/E – low	—	5	6	—	4	—	4	5	7	5	8
Dividends per share ($)	11.9%	1.35	1.48	1.71	1.92	2.14	2.38	2.61	2.88	3.24	3.70
Book value per share ($)	5.4%	34.32	38.78	37.39	43.14	26.28	31.19	35.33	39.93	53.15	55.19
Employees	3.6%	10,543	11,069	12,292	12,558	13,485	13,315	12,088	12,917	13,571	14,529

1994 Year-end:
Equity as % of assets: 4.4%
Return on assets: 0.6%
Return on equity: 13.7%
Long-term debt (mil.): $6,455
No. of shares (mil.): 78
Dividends
  Yield: 6.7%
  Payout: 51.6%
Market value (mil.): $4,323
Sales (mil.): $7,503

Stock Price History
High/Low 1985–94

THE BEAR STEARNS COMPANIES INC.

OVERVIEW

Bear Stearns is one of the US's leading securities trading, investment banking, and brokerage firms. It serves an elite clientele of corporations, financial institutions, governments, and individuals.

It also has a major presence overseas, particularly in Latin America, where it holds a 66% share of equity offerings underwriting. It has operated in Europe for 40 years but arrived late in Asia. However, in the 1990s it has made great strides, especially in Japan. As the Chinese economy has opened, Bear Stearns has kept pace, expanding its Hong Kong office

to full branch status and opening representative offices in Beijing and Shanghai. Bear Stearns diversifies its income by performing trade clearing services. The company is known not only for its aggressive trading but also for its dedication to conforming to trading rules (it employs a staff of "ferrets" to look for infractions and swiftly punishes the guilty).

Bear Stearns was hurt by 1994's interest rate increases. Profits declined in fiscal 1995, and the company's bonus-heavy compensation fell accordingly; chairman Alan Greenberg's cash pay plummeted 47%, to $5.8 million.

WHEN

As the 1920s roared onto Wall Street, a fledgling brokerage firm opened in 1923 with $500,000 in capital. The partners were Joseph Ainslee Bear, Robert Stearns, and Harold Mayer. Their firm was Bear, Stearns & Co.

The firm grew rapidly and weathered the 1929 stock market crash with no layoffs. In the New Deal era, Bear Stearns aggressively promoted government bonds. Its arbitrage department, created in 1938, dealt in the securities of New York City transit systems.

In 1940 Bear Stearns opened its first branch office, in Chicago. The company's international department was created in 1948, and in 1955 Bear Stearns opened an office in Amsterdam. Other branches followed in Geneva (1963), San Francisco (1965), Paris (1967), and Los Angeles (1968).

Bear Stearns was guided in the 1950s and 1960s by colorful trader Salim "Cy" Lewis. Lewis began his career as a runner for Salomon Brothers. At Bear Stearns he climbed the ladder to chairman, becoming a Wall Street legend as the hard-charging, Scotch-drinking taskmaster of "The Bear," as the firm came to be known. During the 1950s Lewis originated block (large-scale) trading.

In 1973, after Bear Stearns moved to new headquarters, it found itself with additional space. It recruited independent brokers and gave them free rent if they would use the company for clearing — processing stock trades. Clearing grew to be a major contributor to the company's bottom line.

When Lewis died in 1978, Alan Greenberg became CEO and not only maintained his predecessor's reputation for aggressive trading but surpassed it. Greenberg, Kansas-born and Oklahoma-reared, had worked his way up from the risk arbitrage desk, to which he was assigned at the age of 25.

Under Greenberg the firm formed the government securities department (1979), the mortgage-backed securities department (1981), and Bear Stearns Asset Management and Custodial Trust, a New Jersey bank and trust company (1984).

In 1985 Bear Stearns formed a holding company called the Bear Stearns Companies Inc., which it took public. In the late 1980s Bear Stearns moved further into investment banking with hopes of becoming a leading US firm. In Latin America Bear Stearns became the leading equity underwriter in 1991. The firm also created Bear Stearns Securities Corporation to clear transactions for the company and for correspondent brokerages.

In 1992 Bear Stearns extended its industry coverage to include biotech, capital industry, and machinery stocks.

Along with the advantages of success and high visibility came difficulties. The company's volume of underwritings also prompted a deluge of lawsuits relating to junk bonds and hot IPOs that fizzled (matters still pending include suits relating to In-Store Advertising and Jenny Craig).

Bear Stearns has upgraded and expanded its information processing capabilities to provide all its locations with the most efficient systems possible.

In 1994 the company hired former Federal Reserve governor Wayne Angell as its chief economist. His experience with the Fed has been presumed to provide him with insight into the actions of that body (which was responsible for the 6 interest rate increases that produced the turmoil of 1994).

Also, Bear Stearns has become active in M&As, advising on deals like Raytheon's acquisition of E-Systems and the Martin Marietta/Lockheed merger in 1995.

NYSE symbol: BSC
Fiscal year ends: June 30

WHO

Chairman: Alan C. Greenberg, age 68, $5,827,980 pay
VC: E. John Rosenwald Jr.
President and CEO: James E. Cayne, age 61,
  $4,230,066 pay
COO and CFO: William J. Montgoris, age 48
EVP: Warren J. Spector, age 37, $3,925,976 pay
EVP: Alan D. Schwartz, age 45, $2,532,229 pay
EVP: Michael L. Tarnopol, age 59
EVP: Mark E. Lehman, age 44
Managing Director Personnel: Stephen A. Lacoff
Auditors: Deloitte & Touche LLP

WHERE

HQ: 245 Park Ave., New York, NY 10167
Phone: 212-272-2000
Fax: 212-272-8239 (Investor Relations)

Bear Stearns has offices in Atlanta, Boca Raton (Florida),
Boston, Chicago, Dallas, Los Angeles, New York,
Philadelphia, Princeton (New Jersey), San Francisco, and
Washington, DC. It also has offices in Beijing, Buenos
Aires, Geneva, Hong Kong, Karachi, London, Manila,
Paris, Sao Paulo, Shanghai, Singapore, and Tokyo.

WHAT

	1995 Sales	
	$ mil.	**% of total**
Commissions	547	15
Principal transactions	860	23
Investment banking	349	9
Interest & dividends	1,970	52
Other income	28	1
Total	**3,754**	**100**

Selected Services
Asset management
Brokerage
Clearing and custody services
Fiduciary services
Financing for securities transactions
Investment banking
Securities lending
Securities trading
Trust services

Selected Subsidiaries

Bear Stearns Argentina, Inc.	Bear, Stearns International Ltd. (UK)
Bear Stearns Asia, Ltd. (Hong Kong)	Bear Stearns Jahangir Siddiqui Ltd. (Pakistan)
Bear Stearns Bank GmbH (Germany)	Bear Stearns (Japan), Ltd. Bear Stearns Mortgage Capital Corp.
Bear Stearns do Brasil Ltda.	Bear Stearns S.A. (France)
Bear Stearns Fiduciary Services, Inc.	Bear, Stearns Securities Corp. Custodial Trust Co.

KEY COMPETITORS

AIG	Industrial Bank of Japan
Alex. Brown	KKR
American Express	Lehman Brothers
Bankers Trust	Merrill Lynch
Brown Brothers Harriman	Montgomery Securities Morgan Stanley
Canadian Imperial	Nomura Securities
Charles Schwab	Paine Webber
CS Holding	Prudential
Dai-Ichi Kangyo	Robertson-Stephens
Dean Witter, Discover	Royal Bank of Canada
Deutsche Bank	Safeguard Scientifics
Edward Jones	Salomon
Equitable	Travelers
Goldman Sachs	Union Bank of Switzerland

HOW MUCH

	Annual Growth	1986	1987	1988	1989	1990	1991	1992	1993	1994	1995
Sales ($ mil.)	6.3%	2,164	1,774	1,888	2,365	2,386	2,380	2,677	2,857	3,441	3,754
Net income ($ mil.)	6.9%	132	177	143	172	119	143	295	362	387	241
Income as % of sales	—	6.1%	9.9%	7.6%	7.3%	5.0%	6.0%	11.0%	12.7%	11.2%	6.4%
Earnings per share ($)	8.0%	0.85	1.14	0.87	1.09	0.74	1.02	2.22	2.59	2.75	1.70
Stock price – high ($)	—	8.29	14.08	12.08	10.69	9.78	13.78	16.74	23.56	22.43	23.38
Stock price – low ($)	—	6.45	7.48	4.45	6.87	5.32	6.64	11.60	13.59	14.04	14.53
Stock price – close ($)	11.9%	7.76	8.71	5.76	8.16	7.18	13.29	14.99	19.83	14.64	19.88
P/E – high	—	10	12	14	10	13	14	8	9	8	14
P/E – low	—	8	7	5	6	7	7	5	5	5	9
Dividends per share ($)	21.3%	0.10	0.24	0.27	0.36	0.34	0.41	0.50	0.50	0.53	0.57
Book value per share ($)	16.5%	4.12	5.11	5.77	6.42	6.72	7.31	9.10	11.36	14.51	16.32
Employees	4.7%	4,927	5,784	6,012	5,994	5,732	5,612	5,873	6,036	7,321	7,481

1995 Year-end:
Debt ratio: 94.7%
Return on equity: 13.2%
Cash (mil.): $701
Long-term debt (mil.): $4,060
No. of shares (mil.): 117
Dividends
  Yield: 2.9%
  Payout: 33.5%
Market value (mil.): $2,333

**Stock Price History
High/Low 1986–95**

BRISTOL-MYERS SQUIBB COMPANY

OVERVIEW

Bristol-Myers Squibb, based in New York City, is one of the largest pharmaceutical companies in the US; 58% of revenues come from its pharmaceutical division. The division concentrates on cardiovascular, anti-infective, and anticancer drugs. The company also has a consumer health products division (nutritional products), a medical devices division, and a toiletries and beauty aids division.

With the US and German patents for the company's prominent heart drug, Capoten (with about $1.5 billion in sales), expiring in 1995, Bristol-Myers hopes that sales of Pravachol, its cholesterol fighter, and TAXOL, an anticancer agent, will counteract this giant loss. The company's short-term drug pipeline is not flush with products, so it has begun licensing drugs in the final stages of development from other companies, including sorivudine, a SmithKline Beecham drug that combats shingles.

Since 1990 the company has cut employment by 8,500 workers. To improve company relations with managed care entities, the pharmaceutical division's 12 regional business units receive support from centralized managed care operations and marketing units.

Unlike many large drug companies (such as Merck, in its purchase of Medco), Bristol-Myers has refrained from buying a big drug benefit manager. Drug benefit management companies influence not only the drug choices of large insurers but also how much the insurers must pay for the drugs they choose.

WHEN

Bristol-Myers Squibb is a merger of 2 rivals. Squibb was founded by Dr. Edward Squibb in New York City in 1858. Squibb developed techniques for making pure ether and chloroform. He headed the business most of his life, turning it over to his sons in 1891. Theodore Weicker, one of Merck's founders, bought a major interest in Squibb in 1905.

Sales of $414,000 in 1904 grew to $13 million by 1928. Squibb supplied penicillin and morphine during WWII. In 1952 the company was bought by Mathieson Chemical, which in turn was bought by Olin Industries in 1953, forming Olin Mathieson Chemical. (Squibb maintained its separate identity.)

From 1968 to 1971 the company went through a series of reorganizations and changed its name to the Squibb Corporation. By 1975 sales had reached $1 billion. Capoten and Corgard, 2 major cardiovascular drugs, were introduced in the late 1970s. Capoten was the first drug engineered to attack a specific disease-causing mechanism rather than developed by the traditional method of trial and error. Squibb formed a joint venture with Denmark's Novo in 1982 to sell insulin.

William Bristol and John Myers founded Clinton Pharmaceutical in Clinton, New York, in 1887 (renamed Bristol-Myers in 1900) to sell bulk pharmaceuticals. Bristol-Myers made antibiotics after the 1943 purchase of Cheplin Biological Labs.

The company began overseas expansion in the 1950s with the purchase of English and German companies. Bristol-Myers bought Clairol (1959), Mead Johnson (drugs, infant and nutritional formula; 1967), and Zimmer (orthopedic implants, 1972). The company introduced new drugs for treating cancer (Platinol, 1978) and a new antianxiety drug (BuSpar, 1986). In 1986 the company acquired the biotech companies Oncogen and Genetic Systems. Bristol-Myers purchased Squibb in 1989 for $12.7 billion. In 1990 the company bought Concept (arthroscopy products, US), Orthoplant (implants, Germany), and an interest in Rueil-Malmaison (drugs, France). Bristol-Myers bought Astel Group, a producer of hip implants, in 1991.

In 1993 company scientists developed a compound that killed certain cancer cells in rats and mice. Also that year Bristol-Myers sold the Drackett Company, its household goods business, for $1.15 billion and joined Eastman Kodak and Elf Aquitaine in developing 2 new heart drugs. Demand for recently introduced drugs VIDEX (AIDS treatment) and TAXOL (anticancer) indicates that they will be substantial producers for the company. In August 1993 Bristol-Myers announced a 5-year sales agreement with American Healthcare Systems, alliance of over 1,000 nonprofit hospitals. Also in 1993 Axion Pharmaceuticals, a cancer treatment distributor, and Bristol-Myers formed a joint distribution venture.

President and CEO Charles Heimbold also took on the position of chairman of the board in 1995. Bristol Myers made Serzone, a new antidepressant with a low incidence of side effects, widely available in 1995. The company is being responsive to managed care providers and consumers by offering the new drug at a cost 10% to 20% below that of similar drugs used for the same purpose.

NYSE symbol: BMY
Fiscal year ends: December 31

WHO

Chairman, President, and CEO: Charles A. Heimbol Jr.,
age 61, $1,909,642 pay (prior to promotion)
EVP: Michael E. Autera, age 56, $1,092,851 pay
EVP; President, Pharmaceutical Group: Kenneth E.
Weg, age 56, $933,502 pay (prior to promotion)
President, Pharmaceutical Research Institute: L. E.
Rosenberg, age 62, $799,073 pay
President, Worldwide Consumer Medicines: Stephen E.
Bear, age 43
President, Bristol-Myers Squibb Pharmaceuticals US:
Samuel L. Barker, age 52
**President, Bristol-Myers Squibb Pharmaceuticals
Intercontinental:** Samuel A. Hamad, age 53
President, Mead Johnson Nutritional Group: Peter R.
Dolan, age 39
SVP and CFO: Michael F. Mee, age 52
SVP Human Resources: Charles G. Tharp, age 43
SVP and General Counsel: John L. McGoldrick, age 54
SVP Corporate Development: George P. Kooluris, age 50
SVP: E. Lynn Johnson, age 50
Auditors: Price Waterhouse LLP

WHERE

HQ: 345 Park Ave., New York, NY 10154-0037
Phone: 212-546-4000
Fax: 212-546-4020

	1994 Sales	
	$ mil.	% of total
US	7,846	59
Europe, Middle		
East & Africa	3,139	23
Pacific	1,320	10
Other Western Hemisphere	1,039	8
Adjustments	(1,360)	—
Total	**11,984**	**100**

WHAT

	1994 Sales	
	$ mil.	% of total
Prescription drugs	6,970	58
Consumer health	2,043	17
Medical devices	1,685	14
Toiletries/beauty aids	1,286	11
Total	**11,984**	**100**

Selected Pharmaceuticals
Azactam (antibiotic)
Capoten (cardiovascular)
Corgard (cardiovascular)
Glucophage (antidiabetic)
Monopril (cardiovascular)
Platinol (cancer drug)
Pravachol (cardiovascular)
Questran (cholesterol
  reducer)
Stadol (analgesic)
TAXOL (cancer drug)
VePesid (cancer drug)
VIDEX (AIDS treatment)

Selected Medical Devices
Minimally invasive surgery
  products
Orthopedic and surgical
  instruments

Consumer Health
Bufferin   Excedrin
Comtrex   Nuprin

Toiletries and Beauty Aids
Ban   Nice 'n Easy
Keri   Theragran
Miss Clairol Vavoom

KEY COMPETITORS

Abbott Labs	Gillette	Procter &
American	Glaxo Wellcome	Gamble
Home Products	Glycomed	Rhône-
Amgen	Hoechst	Poulenc
Ballard Medical	Immunex	Roche
Bayer	Johnson &	St. Jude
Biogen	Johnson	Medical
Biomet	L'Oréal	Sandoz
Chiron Corp.	Merck	Schering-
Ciba-Geigy	Mitek Surgical	Plough
Danek Group	Monsanto	SmithKline
Dial	Novo Nordisk	Beecham
Dow Chemical	Pfizer	U.S. Surgical
DuPont	Pharmacia &	Warner-
Eli Lilly	Upjohn	Lambert
Genentech		

HOW MUCH

	Annual Growth	1985	1986	1987	1988	1989	1990	1991	1992	1993	1994
Sales ($ mil.)	11.7%	4,444	4,836	5,401	5,973	9,189	10,300	11,159	11,156	11,413	11,984
Net income ($ mil.)	14.8%	531	590	710	829	747	1,748	2,056	1,603	1,959	1,842
Income as % of sales	—	12.0%	12.2%	13.1%	13.9%	8.1%	17.0%	18.4%	14.4%	17.2%	15.4%
Earnings per share ($)	7.2%	1.93	2.03	2.43	2.85	1.43	3.33	3.95	3.09	3.80	3.62
Stock price – high ($)	—	34.25	44.25	55.81	46.50	58.00	68.00	89.38	90.13	67.25	61.00
Stock price – low ($)	—	24.50	30.13	28.25	38.13	44.00	50.50	61.13	60.00	50.88	50.00
Stock price – close ($)	7.1%	31.13	41.31	41.63	45.25	56.00	67.00	88.25	67.38	58.25	57.88
P/E – high	—	18	18	23	16	41	20	23	29	18	17
P/E – low	—	13	15	12	13	31	15	16	19	13	14
Dividends per share ($)	13.4%	0.94	1.06	1.40	1.68	2.00	2.12	2.40	2.76	2.88	2.92
Book value per share ($)	2.7%	8.84	9.91	11.20	12.31	9.68	10.34	11.15	11.62	11.60	11.24
Employees	3.3%	35,700	34,900	34,100	35,200	54,100	52,900	53,500	52,600	49,500	47,700

1994 Year-end:
Debt ratio: 19.4%
Return on equity: 31.6%
Cash (mil.): $2,423
Current ratio: 1.57
Long-term debt (mil.): $644
No. of shares (mil.): 507
Dividends
  Yield: 5.0%
  Payout: 80.7%
Market value (mil.): $29,362

**Stock Price History
High/Low 1985–94**

THE CALDOR CORPORATION

OVERVIEW

Caldor Corporation, headquartered in Norwalk, Connecticut, has discount stores located throughout the Northeast and Mid-Atlantic corridors. The company is one of the largest discount retailers in the US. Caldor's stores offer a diverse line of private-label and branded merchandise, including housewares, electronics, furniture, toys, sporting goods, apparel, accessories, jewelry, and cosmetics.

Although the company's profits were up in fiscal 1995, weak sales, an overreliance on short-term financing, tightened credit by vendors and suppliers, and increased regional competition (especially from Wal-Mart, Kmart, and Target, a subsidiary of Dayton Hudson) led Caldor to voluntarily seek Chapter 11 protection in September 1995.

Some analysts blame Caldor's rapid expansion (while sales at existing stores declined)

for the company's problems. Same-store sales rose 2.2% in fiscal 1995 but began to decline in fiscal 1996. Plans for further expansion were put on hold. Analysts have also suggested that the increased penetration of national chains into Caldor's market means that the company's time as an independent retailer is likely to be short.

The Caldor strategy is to position itself between traditional discount stores and upscale department stores. The company emphasizes quality, branded products and emerging fashion and product trends. It projects an upscale appearance in the stores and at some locations offers restaurants such as Nathan's Famous Inc. franchises, as opposed to no-name snack bars. The company also locates its stores primarily in high-density urban and suburban markets.

WHEN

In 1951 Carl and Dorothy Bennett used their life savings to open the original Caldor discount house in a loft on the main square of Port Chester, New York. The store's name was created by combining the first 3 letters of each of their given names ("Cardor" was awkward, so they modified it to "Caldor"). The store sold brand-name housewares, luggage, and photographic equipment and supplies. It was a success in Port Chester, twice moving to larger accommodations.

In 1958 a 2nd Caldor opened in Norwalk, Connecticut. In the 1960s the chain opened more stores in Connecticut and New York and expanded into Massachusetts. Caldor opened its headquarters in Norwalk in 1965.

By the mid-1970s Caldor had 30 stores and was well known throughout the region. Hard goods, including housewares, electronics, and furniture, were the stores' mainstays. By 1980 annual sales had reached $666 million. The retail conglomerate Associated Dry Goods Corporation, owner of Lord & Taylor and other department store chains, acquired Caldor as Caldor continued to expand on the East Coast.

The company had 95 stores in 7 states and $1 billion in sales by 1983. Founder Carl Bennett retired as chairman in 1984, the year the company opened its 100th store.

Retail giant May Department Stores bought Associated Dry Goods for $2.5 billion in 1986. The large purchase was in part May's response to a changing retail market in which warehouse stores and off-price outlets were eroding

traditional department stores' market share. Through its acquisition May gained assets that included the upscale Lord & Taylor Stores along with the discount operations of Caldor and Loehmanns.

However, by 1988 May had further altered its strategy by discontinuing its discount operations — Loehmanns was sold that year, and Caldor was placed on the sales block. Many other retail operations were on the market at that point, and May failed to get its asking price for Caldor. So the Caldor Corporation, an investor group, including Odyssey Partners L.P., Caldor senior management, and investment bankers Donaldson, Lufkin, and Jenrette, bought Caldor in a $537 million LBO. This deal left the retailer more than $450 million in debt.

Caldor Corporation's initial public offering occurred in 1991, when the chain had 122 stores from Baltimore to Boston.

Seeing itself as a family-oriented chain, Caldor declined to sell New York radio personality Howard Stern's controversial memoir *Private Parts*, which hit the top of the *New York Times* best-sellers list in 1993. The company went so far as to alter the list in their stores, angering the newspaper and prompting an apology by the company. In 1994 Odyssey Partners L.P., a major player in the LBO, sold all its Caldor stock.

In 1995, falling sales, increased competition from national retailers, and skittish suppliers and bankers led to Caldor's bankruptcy filing, but business continued as usual.

NYSE symbol: CLD
Fiscal year ends: Saturday nearest January 31

WHO

Chairman and CEO: Don R. Clarke, age 49,
$808,661 pay
President: Marc I. Balmuth, age 47, $784,468 pay
SVP and CFO: Robert S. Schauman, age 51,
$415,426 pay
SVP Stores: Michael R. Lynch $372,994 pay
SVP Marketing: Gary S. Vasques, age 47, $361,846 pay
SVP General Merchandise Manager Softlines: Mark E.
Minsky, age 45
SVP General Merchandise Manager Softlines: Robert P.
Yorkus, age 46
SVP General Merchandise Manager Homelines: Thomas
G. Vellios, age 40
SVP Management Information Systems: William G.
Christie, age 46
**SVP Human Resources and Merchandise Distribution
and Replenishment:** Dennis M. Lee, age 45
VP and General Counsel: Bennett S. Gross, age 43
Auditors: Deloitte & Touche LLP

WHERE

HQ: 20 Glover Ave., Norwalk, CT 06856-5620
Phone: 203-846-1641
Fax: 203-849-2019

	1995 Stores
	No.
New York	53
Connecticut	31
New Jersey	25
Massachusetts	24
Maryland	12
Pennsylvania	9
Other states	9
Total	**163**

WHAT

	1995 Sales
	% of total
Hardlines	59
Softlines	41
Total	**100**

Merchandise Lines
Accessories
Apparel
Cosmetics
Electronics
Furniture
Home textiles
Housewares
Jewelry
Shoes
Toys

KEY COMPETITORS

Ames	The Limited
Bradlees	Melville
Dayton Hudson	Montgomery Ward
Edison Brothers	Price/Costco
Federated	Sears
Filene's Basement	Service Merchandise
Fred Meyer	Spiegel
The Gap	TJX
Hills Stores	Toys "R" Us
Home Depot	Venture
Jamesway	Waban
J. C. Penney	Wal-Mart
Kmart	Woolworth
Lechters	

HOW MUCH

	Annual Growth	1986	1987	1988	1989	1990	1991	1992	1993	1994	1995
Sales ($ mil.)	9.8%	—	—	—	1,568	1,671	1,772	1,873	2,128	2,414	2,749
Net income ($ mil.)	38.5%	—	—	—	6	2	4	2	37	30	44
Income as % of sales	—	—	—	—	0.4%	0.1%	0.2%	0.1%	1.8%	1.3%	1.6%
Earnings per share ($)	69.4%	—	—	—	—	0.19	0.38	0.17	2.54	1.84	2.65
Stock price – high ($)[1]	—	—	—	—	—	—	—	24.75	29.50	35.25	32.50
Stock price – low ($)[1]	—	—	—	—	—	—	—	12.63	13.38	21.13	21.38
Stock price – close ($)[1]	7.3%	—	—	—	—	—	—	18.00	29.50	25.50	22.25
P/E – high	—	—	—	—	—	—	—	146	12	19	12
P/E – low	—	—	—	—	—	—	—	74	5	11	8
Dividends per share ($)	—	—	—	—	—	—	—	0.00	0.00	0.00	0.00
Book value per share ($)	19.2%	—	—	—	—	—	—	11.92	14.08	17.65	20.19
Employees	15.7%	—	—	—	—	—	—	15,500	19,000	21,000	24,000

1995 Year-end:
Debt ratio: 50.8%
Return on equity: 14.1%
Cash (mil.): $7
Current ratio: 1.33
Long-term debt (mil.): $2.37
No. of shares (mil.): 17
Dividends
  Yield: —
  Payout: —
Market value (mil.): $372

Stock Price History[1]
High/Low 1992–95

[1] Stock prices are for the prior calendar year.

CHAMPION INTERNATIONAL

OVERVIEW

Champion International's timing has finally improved. The company, one of the US's largest manufacturers of paper and wood products, began modernizing its facilities and selling nonessential assets in the mid-1980s; however, expenses peaked in 1989, just as the US and European economies declined and paper prices fell. Finally, in mid-1994 rebounding paper prices and improving economies converged with Champion's newly streamlined operations, pulling the company out of a 5-year earnings slump. A year later Champion used its new-found profits to retire nearly $400 million in debt and to buy back nearly 10% of its outstanding shares.

With more than 5 million acres of timberland, Champion is one of the largest landholders in the US. The company produced over 6 million tons of packaging, paper, and pulp products in 1994, including newsprint, magazine papers, printing and writing papers, and beverage cartons. That same year the company produced over 2 million board feet of lumber and nearly 1.5 million square feet of plywood. Champion also has forests and pulp production operations in Brazil and Canada.

High demand had Champion's paper mills running close to full capacity in 1995. The modernization efforts begun in the mid-1980s have increased production capacity by 30%.

CEO Andrew Sigler, who orchestrated Champion's capital improvements program, is set to retire in 1996. Loews Corp. owns about 15% of the company.

WHEN

Champion International was formed by the 1967 merger of US Plywood and Champion Paper & Fibre. US Plywood, founded in New York by Lawrence Ottinger in 1919, started out selling glue and WWI surplus plywood. By 1932 the company had started manufacturing its own products, and it consolidated operations with Aircraft Plywood in 1937.

Champion Paper & Fibre, the other party in the merger, was created when Reuben Robertson, who founded Champion Fibre in Ohio in 1906, married the daughter of the founder of similarly named Champion Coated Paper, incorporated in Ohio in 1893.

The first years for US Plywood–Champion Paper, the name of the company resulting from the 1967 merger, were marked by internal quarrels between the paper and plywood divisions over such issues as allocation of the company's timber resources. During that same period the company diversified, buying Drexel Enterprises (furniture, 1968; sold in 1977), Trend Industries (carpet, 1969; sold in 1978), Path Fork Harlan Coal (to power the company's pulp and paper mills, 1970), and AW Securities (carpets, 1974; sold in 1980). It adopted its present name in 1972.

In 1974 director Karl Bendetson, who disapproved of plans to diversify Champion into chemicals, persuaded the board to fire CEO Thomas Willers. Andrew Sigler replaced Willers and quickly turned the company's focus back to forest products by selling more than a dozen nonforest businesses.

In 1977 Champion International bought Hoerner Waldorf, the 4th largest American producer of paper packaging products such as grocery bags and cardboard boxes. Hoerner Waldorf traces its roots back to the 1966 merger of Hoerner Boxes (formed in Keokuk, Iowa, in 1920) and Waldorf Paper (originated in St. Paul as part of Baker-Collins in 1886).

With the company's $1.8 billion acquisition of St. Regis in 1984, Champion narrowed its focus to pulp and paper production. The company sold its office products businesses (1984); 55 corrugated container plants, packaging plants, and paperboard mills (1986); and 2 Texas mills and its Columbus, Ohio, specialty paper plant (1987, 1988). In 1991 and 1992 Champion sold large tracts of its western timberlands that were not easily accessible to the company's pulp and paper mills.

Champion was a defendant in a $5 billion class-action lawsuit alleging the company's Canton, North Carolina, mill had discharged dioxins and other pollutants into the Pigeon River, but a mistrial was declared in 1992. In 1993 a judge approved a settlement calling for Champion to pay $6.5 million in restitution.

Also in 1993 Champion sold 870,000 acres of Montana woods to Plum Creek Timber and 2 wood products mills to Stimson Lumber.

In 1994 Champion lobbied the city of Houston to expand its recycling program to help the company feed its new Texas newsprint plant. Also in 1994 Champion announced a breakthrough in bleach filtrate recycling (BFR) technology that substantially reduces the waste of bleached pulp mills. Wheelabrator Technologies acquired exclusive licensing rights to the BFR process in 1995. That same year, continuing high demand allowed Champion to raise paper prices several times.

NYSE symbol: CHA
Fiscal year ends: December 31

	1994 Sales		1994 Operating Income	
	$ mil.	% of total	$ mil.	% of total
Paper	4,217	79	71	23
Wood products	1,101	21	242	77
Adjustments	—	—	(47)	—
Total	**5,318**	**100**	**266**	**100**

WHO

Chairman and CEO: Andrew C. Sigler, age 63, $1,525,000 pay
VC: Kenwood C. Nichols, age 55, $750,000 pay
President and COO: L. C. Heist, age 63, $950,000 pay
EVP: William H. Burchfield, age 59, $557,000 pay
EVP: Richard E. Olson, age 57, $541,000 pay
SVP and General Counsel: Marvin H. Ginsky, age 64
SVP Finance: Frank Kneisel
SVP Organizational Development and Human Resources: Mark V. Childers, age 42
President and CEO, Weldwood of Canada, Ltd.: Graham I. Bender
Auditors: Arthur Andersen & Co, SC

Selected Products

Paper and Board
Coated free sheet
Coated groundwood
Kraft paper
Linerboard
Liquid packaging board
Newsprint
Recycled fiber
Uncoated free sheet

Pulp
Bleached pulp
Groundwood/thermo-mechanical pulp
Unbleached pulp

Wood Chemicals
Tall oil
Turpentine

Wood Products
Chips
Lumber/studs
Plywood
Veneer
Waferboard

WHERE

HQ: Champion International Corporation, One Champion Plaza, Stamford, CT 06921
Phone: 203-358-7000
Fax: 203-358-2975

Champion's manufacturing facilities are located in Brazil, Canada, and the US.

Major Subsidiaries and Affiliates

Cariboo Pulp & Paper Co. (50/50 joint venture of Weldwood and Daishowa-Marubeni International Ltd.)
Champion Papel e Celulose Ltda. (99%, pulp and paper, Brazil)
Weldwood of Canada Ltd. (84%, bleached softwood kraft pulp)

Owned or Leased Timberlands	Acres (thou.)
Champion US	5,070
Champion Papel e Celulose	229
Total	**5,299**

	1994 Sales		1994 Operating Income	
	$ mil.	% of total	$ mil.	% of total
US	4,370	82	125	40
Canada	694	13	134	43
Brazil	254	5	54	17
Adjustments	—	—	(47)	—
Total	**5,318**	**100**	**266**	**100**

KEY COMPETITORS

Alco Standard	Georgia-Pacific	Rayonier
Boise Cascade	International	Reynolds Metals
Canadian Pacific	Paper	Scott
Consolidated	James River	Stone Container
Papers	Manville	Temple-Inland
Fletcher	Mead	Union Camp
Challenge	Potlatch	Weyerhaeuser
Fort Howard		

HOW MUCH

	Annual Growth	1985	1986	1987	1988	1989	1990	1991	1992	1993	1994
Sales ($ mil.)	(0.1%)	5,770	4,388	4,615	5,129	5,163	5,090	4,786	4,926	5,069	5,318
Net income ($ mil.)	(10.0%)	163	201	382	456	432	223	40	14	(149)	63
Income as % of sales	—	2.8%	4.6%	8.3%	8.9%	8.4%	4.4%	0.8%	0.3%	—	1.2%
Earnings per share ($)	(14.7%)	1.59	2.05	3.92	4.65	4.43	2.08	0.14	(0.15)	(1.90)	0.38
Stock price – high ($)	—	25.38	34.00	44.63	38.13	37.75	33.75	30.63	30.25	34.63	40.00
Stock price – low ($)	—	20.00	22.50	23.25	29.50	28.88	23.13	22.25	23.50	27.13	28.00
Stock price – close ($)	4.4%	24.88	30.75	34.50	32.13	32.00	25.63	24.00	28.75	33.38	36.50
P/E – high	—	16	17	11	8	9	16	—	—	—	105
P/E – low	—	13	11	6	6	7	11	—	—	—	74
Dividends per share ($)	(8.2%)	0.43	0.52	0.65	0.90	1.08	1.10	0.43	0.20	0.20	0.20
Book value per share ($)	2.1%	26.34	27.52	30.82	35.06	38.60	39.58	39.51	34.01	31.71	31.74
Employees	(6.0%)	43,000	32,200	30,700	30,400	29,500	28,500	27,500	27,300	25,250	24,615

1994 Year-end:
Debt ratio: 52.6%
Return on equity: 2.1%
Cash (mil.): $91
Current ratio: 1.14
Long-term debt (mil.): $2,889
No. of shares (mil.): 93.3
Dividends
  Yield: 0.5%
  Payout: 52.6%
Market value (mil.): $3,405

Stock Price History
High/Low 1985–94

CHASE MANHATTAN CORP.

OVERVIEW

In 1996, regulators willing, Chase Manhattan will take its old place as the US's largest banking company, but only by submerging itself into former arch-competitor, Chemical Banking Corp. The merger, announced after brief negotiations in 1995, creates a behemoth with combined assets of nearly $300 billion.

This is a merger in which some (those who work at Chemical) are more equal than others (those who work at Chase) because Chemical will clearly be the dominant partner. But the lower-level employees on both sides will be hard hit. The elimination of branch jobs and administrative redundancies are the primary motives for the merger. Up to 12,000 jobs will

be cut, which will deliver instant savings and increased profits.

In recent years, both banks have refined their businesses. Chemical has focused on mortgage banking, credit cards, and private banking as well as foreign currency, corporate financing, and debt and equity underwriting (it is one of the few US banks currently permitted to do this), while Chase competed in mortgages and credit cards, foreign exchange, foreign underwriting, and mutual funds.

But many analysts believe that the merger will not actually create growth because it does not address the primary problem of competition from non-bank financial institutions.

WHEN

Balthazar Melick, Mark Spenser, and Geradus Post founded the New York Chemical Manufacturing Co. in 1823, largely to be able to open a bank (the New York legislature was reluctant to grant charters to banks unaffiliated with other businesses). Chemical Bank opened in 1824. In 1844 the chemical firm was liquidated, but the bank continued. By 1900 Chemical was one of the US's largest banks.

In the years before WWI, Chemical Bank entered a period of drifting, losing clientele and market share. During WWI, however, new management and an upturn in business improved the bank's situation. In 1920 Chemical began to diversify into other services (like trusts). It opened its first branch in 1923 and its first foreign office in London in 1929. Chemical grew during the Depression; by 1941 assets were $1 billion.

In the 1960s Chemical concentrated primarily on domestic business, growing its consumer loan and mortgage lines. In 1968 Chemical formed a bank holding company.

Chemical used the 1980s' rash of bank and thrift failures to expand to Texas. In 1987 it bought Texas Commerce. In the late 1980s Chemical was hit by foreign loan losses, particularly in Argentina and Brazil. A few years later, Chemical was affected by the real estate crash that followed the foreign debt crisis.

In 1991 Chemical (then the 9th largest US bank company) moved a few rungs higher on the banking ladder by merging with Manufacturers Hanover, which created the US's 3rd largest banking company. Fully integrating the companies took 2 years, partly because of the difficulty in combining the firms' disparate data systems, and partly because of concerns about parity in this "merger of equals."

In 1877 John Thompson formed his bank, naming it Chase National for Salmon P. Chase, Abraham Lincoln's Secretary of the Treasury and the architect of the national bank system. But it did not rise to prominence until the 20th century.

In 1930 Chase merged with John D. Rockefeller's Equitable Trust, becoming the world's largest bank by assets and beginning a long relationship with the Rockefellers. Winthrop Aldrich, Rockefeller's brother-in-law, became head of the bank in 1932. Aldrich spearheaded Chase's expansion to Germany and Japan.

Chase continued its expansion after WWII. In 1955 it merged with the Bank of Manhattan (which had been founded in 1799 as part of a water utility). David Rockefeller became co-CEO 5 years later, and the bank took on an even greater internationalist focus. Chase continued to be the US's largest bank into the 1960s.

When soaring oil prices in the 1970s made energy-oriented loans attractive, Chase began having trouble. It invested in Penn Square, an obscure oil-patch bank and the first notable bank failure of the 1980s. Chase struggled in the 1980s with the aftereffects of its 1982 failure (litigation relating to the failure dragged on until 1993). Chase was also hit in 1987 with losses following the foreign loan crisis, and then by the real estate crash that left it with many nonperforming loans.

In 1991 Chase began a major round of cost cutting, including firings and asset sales. It sold noncore operations, particularly overseas. In 1995 Chase went looking for a partner while it still had the leverage to have some say in the matter. After talks with BankAmerica, it settled on Chemical.

NYSE symbol: CHL
Fiscal year ends: December 31

Chairman and CEO: Walter V. Shipley, age 59,
$2,496,154 pay
VC: William B. Harrison Jr., age 51, $1,746,154 pay
President: Edward D. Miller, age 54, $1,871,154 pay
**Chairman, President, and CEO, Texas Commerce Bank
National Association:** Marc J. Shapiro
SEVP: Michael Hegarty
SEVP: Donald H. Layton
SEVP: William H. Turner
EVP and CFO: Peter J. Tobin, $923,077 pay
EVP and Chief Credit Risk Policy Officer: William C.
Langley, $825,000 pay
EVP and General Counsel: William H. McDavid
EVP and Director Human Resources: Martin H.
Zuckerman
Auditors: Price Waterhouse LLP

WHERE

HQ: 270 Park Ave., New York, NY 10017
Phone: 212-270-6000
Fax: 212-270-2613

Chase Manhattan operates throughout the US and in 50
other nations.

	1994 Sales		1994 Pretax Income	
	$ mil.	% of total	$ mil.	% of total
US	9,530	75	1,470	66
Europe	1,638	13	348	16
Latin America & Caribbean	831	7	228	10
Asia & Pacific	567	4	167	8
Middle East & Africa	79	1	5	0
Other regions	40	0	(6)	—
Total	**12,685**	**100**	**2,212**	**100**

WHAT

	1994 Assets	
	$ mil.	% of total
Cash & equivalents	27,278	16
Treasury & agency securities	8,741	5
Foreign investments	7,720	5
Mortgage-backed securities & CMOs	16,325	9
Unrealized derivatives gains	17,709	10
Net loans	76,287	45
Other	17,363	10
Total	**171,423**	**100**

	1994 Sales	
	$ mil.	% of total
Loans	5,730	45
Securities interest	1,715	14
Other interest	1,643	13
Service & management fees	2,274	18
Trading account	645	5
Other	678	5
Total	**12,685**	**100**

Selected Subsidiaries
Chemical Bank
CIT (40%)
Geoserve, Inc.
Texas Commerce Bank
National Association

KEY COMPETITORS

American Express	Crédit Lyonnais	KeyCorp
Banc One	CS Holding	MBNA
Bank of New York	Deutsche Bank	Merrill Lynch
BankAmerica	Dime Anchor	Morgan Stanley
Bankers Trust	First Chicago	NationsBank
Barclays	First Fidelity	NatWest
Bear Stearns	First Interstate	Royal Bank of
Canadian Imperial	Fleet	Canada
Citicorp	General Electric	Salomon
Club Corp.	HSBC	Union Bank of
Countrywide Credit	J.P. Morgan	Switzerland

HOW MUCH

	Annual Growth	1985	1986	1987	1988	1989	1990	1991	1992	1993	1994
Assets ($ mil.)	13.0%	56,990	60,564	78,189	67,349	71,513	73,019	138,930	139,655	149,888	171,423
Net income ($ mil.)	14.2%	390	402	(854)	754	(482)	291	154	1,086	1,569	1,294
Income as % of assets	—	0.7%	0.7%	—	1.1%	—	0.4%	0.1%	0.8%	1.0%	0.8%
Earnings per share ($)	(4.7%)	7.15	7.42	(16.68)	12.02	(8.29)	2.38	0.11	3.90	5.63	4.64
Stock price – high ($)	—	46.25	56.25	49.50	33.88	41.13	31.38	30.13	39.50	46.38	42.13
Stock price – low ($)	—	33.13	40.75	20.25	20.00	28.50	9.63	10.50	21.88	35.00	33.63
Stock price – close ($)	(2.6%)	45.38	42.25	21.38	31.00	29.88	10.75	21.25	38.63	40.13	35.88
P/E – high	—	7	8	—	3	—	13	—	10	8	9
P/E – low	—	5	6	—	2	—	4	—	6	6	7
Dividends per share ($)	(4.8%)	2.45	2.57	2.69	2.72	2.72	2.72	1.00	1.20	1.29	1.58
Book value per share ($)	(3.3%)	51.17	56.14	25.96	31.31	24.32	24.25	26.28	32.43	37.61	37.88
Employees	8.8%	19,691	20,993	28,597	27,225	49,173	45,636	43,169	39,687	41,567	42,130

1994 Year-end:
Equity as % of assets: 6.2%
Return on assets: 0.8%
Return on equity: 13.8%
Long-term debt (mil.): $7,991
No. of shares (mil.): 245
Dividends
  Yield: 4.4%
  Payout: 34.1%
Market value (mil.): $8,773
Sales (mil.): $12,685

**Stock Price History
High/Low 1985–94**

Note: Financial data are for Chemical Banking Corp. only.

THE CHUBB CORPORATION

OVERVIEW

Chubb Corporation wants to grow through consolidation. It intends to become one of the 10 largest property/casualty insurers (by underwriting profit) in the US by the year 2000, and, because the US market is mature, it is targeting markets overseas for further growth. By 1994 it had almost attained its goal of deriving 25% of its sales from foreign business (it operates in most major markets in Europe, Asia, and Latin America).

As part of this effort, Chubb has been streamlining its operations by consolidating administrative offices in New York and Los Angeles and cutting the number of life insurance offices from 40 to 20. In the process the company is upgrading its technical systems and improving its customer services. Under the new system, customers will have one contact within the company, rather than having different contacts for every type of insurance.

Chubb's products, aimed at businesses and affluent individuals, include traditional property/casualty insurance as well as niche property products (like the winery coverage it offers in France) and life and health insurance (both group and individual). Its Chubb & Son subsidiary offers insurance company management services, and its Bellemead Development Corp. develops real estate.

In 1994 some of Chubb's segments showed lackluster results. Property/casualty was hit by losses due to the Northridge earthquake. Its employee benefits business (part of life and health) suffered from New York State's imposition of community ratings premiums, and Chubb's real estate units performed poorly.

WHEN

Thomas Caldecot Chubb and his son Percy formed Chubb & Son in New York in 1882 to underwrite cargo and ship insurance. The company soon became the US manager for Sea Insurance Co. of England and cofounded New York Marine Underwriters (NYMU). In 1901 NYMU became Chubb's chief property and casualty affiliate, Federal Insurance Co.

Chubb expanded in the 1920s, opening a Chicago office (1923) and, just before the 1929 crash, organizing Associated Aviation Underwriters. Growth slowed during the Depression, but Chubb recovered enough by 1939 to buy Vigilant Insurance Co.

Chubb bought Colonial Life in 1959 and Pacific Indemnity (which had written insurance for Fibreboard Corporation, later a major defendant in asbestos-related damage litigation) in 1967. In that year Chubb Corp. was formed as a holding company, with Chubb & Son as the manager of the property and casualty insurance businesses. In 1969 a takeover attempt by New York's First National City Corp. — predecessor of Citicorp — was foiled by federal regulators.

Chubb acquired Bellemead Development (1970) to expand its real estate portfolio. Following a strategy of insuring in specialty niches, in the 1970s Chubb launched insurance packages for the entertainment industry, including films and Broadway shows. After the Tylenol poisonings of 1982, Chubb developed insurance against product tampering and contamination (which it no longer offers).

In 1984 Chubb acquired Chattanooga-based Volunteer State Life. In this period Chubb focused on specialized property and casualty insurance lines and in 1985 retreated from medical malpractice insurance.

In 1988 Chubb authorized Good Weather International to write up to $30 million in drought insurance. Chubb discovered too late that Good Weather wrote more than 10 times that amount. Chubb promptly settled the matter, paying any claims that would have been due if the customers had received their policies.

In 1991 Chubb combined 3 subsidiaries into Chubb Life Insurance Co. of America. The next year Chubb subsidiary Pacific Indemnity settled a suit over Fibreboard Corp.'s asbestos liability (the settlement was revised in 1993 and extended in 1995). This resulted in a 1993 payment of $538 million into an escrow account set up to settle future asbestos-related damage claims. This contributed to a total charge for asbestos-related losses of $675 million and led to an earnings decrease in 1993.

Taking advantage of Lloyd's of London's financial problems and subsequent relaxation of rules relating to doing business with nonmembers, Chubb in 1993 opened an office at Lloyd's. It has also extended its insurance of the affluent to the UK by forming a joint venture with Sun Alliance. Chubb opened a new underwriting office at the Institute of London Underwriters in 1994.

In 1994 Chubb bought Personal Lines Insurance Brokerage and the personal lines business of Alexander & Alexander. In 1995 it opened offices in Munich and Hamburg and increased its holdings in Mexico.

NYSE symbol: CB
Fiscal year ends: December 31

WHO

Chairman: Dean R. O'Hare, age 52, $1,393,492 pay
VC and CFO: Percy Chubb III, age 60, $615,777 pay
VC and General Counsel: John J. Degnan, age 50
President: Robert P. Crawford Jr., age 53, $558,560 pay
EVP: George T. Van Gilder, age 51, $431,369 pay
EVP: Edward Dunlop, age 54
EVP: David S. Fowler, age 49
EVP: Frederick L. Hyer Jr.
EVP: Charles M. Luchs
SVP and Treasurer: Philip J. Sempier
SVP and Managing Director (HR): Baxter Graham
Auditors: Ernst & Young LLP

WHERE

HQ: 15 Mountain View Rd., PO Box 1615, Warren, NJ 07061-1615
Phone: 908-903-2000
Fax: 908-580-2027

Chubb operates in all 50 US states and the District of Columbia, Puerto Rico, and the Virgin Islands. It has 36 offices in 25 other countries.

WHAT

	1994 Assets	
	$ mil.	% of total
Cash & equivalents	6	0
Tax-exempt securities	5,680	28
Taxable bonds	3,376	16
Mortgage-backed securities	1,648	8
Real estate	1,740	8
Receivables & recoverables	2,768	13
Other	5,505	27
Total	**20,723**	**100**

	1994 Sales		1994 Operating Income	
	$ mil.	% of total	$ mil.	% of total
Life & health ins.	1,055	18	28	4
Real estate	205	4	(67)	—
Property/casualty insurance	4,402	77	607	94
Corporate	48	1	10	2
Total	**5,710**	**100**	**639**	**100**

Selected Subsidiaries and Affiliates

Associated Aviation Underwriters, Inc.
Bellemead Development Corp.
Chubb Asset Managers, Inc.
Chubb Capital Corp.
Chubb Customer Center, Inc.
Chubb de Colombia Compañía de Seguros, SA
Chubb de México, Compañía Afianzadora SA de SV

Chubb de México, Compañía de Seguros SA de SV
Chubb Programmer Resources, Inc.
Chubb Securities Corp.
Chubb Services Corp.
The Colonial Life Insurance Co. of America
Federal Insurance Co.
Great Northern Ins. Co.
Northwestern Pacific Indemnity Co.
Pacific Indemnity Co.
Seguros La Federación, CA
Texas Pacific Indemnity Co.
Vigilant Insurance Co.

KEY COMPETITORS

Aetna	General Re	Northwestern
AIG	ITT Hartford	Mutual
Allianz	John Hancock	Prudential
Allstate	Kolonia Conzern	State Farm
Axa	Liberty Mutual	Teachers
CIGNA	Lincoln National	Insurance
CNA Financial	Lloyd's of London	Tokio Marine
Commercial Union	MassMutual	and Fire
Equitable	MetLife	Travelers
GEICO	New York Life	USF&G

HOW MUCH

	Annual Growth	1985	1986	1987	1988	1989	1990	1991	1992	1993	1994
Assets ($ mil.)	13.2%	6,802	8,487	10,167	11,507	13,385	14,511	16,164	17,559	19,437	20,723
Net income ($ mil.)	25.0%	71	268	330	360	421	522	552	617	344	528
Income as % of assets	—	1.0%	3.2%	3.2%	3.1%	3.1%	3.6%	3.4%	3.5%	1.8%	2.6%
Earnings per share ($)	22.5%	0.96	3.53	3.97	4.27	4.91	6.07	6.32	6.96	3.91	5.95
Stock price – high ($)	—	28.81	39.06	36.75	31.69	49.75	54.75	78.00	91.00	95.75	83.18
Stock price – low ($)	—	16.58	27.00	25.44	25.63	28.81	34.63	50.00	62.38	76.63	68.63
Stock price – close ($)	12.2%	27.44	29.63	27.94	29.00	47.63	54.25	77.00	88.88	77.88	77.38
P/E – high	—	30	11	9	7	10	9	12	13	24	14
P/E – low	—	17	8	6	6	6	6	8	9	20	12
Dividends per share ($)	10.3%	0.76	0.80	0.89	1.08	1.16	1.32	1.48	1.60	1.72	1.84
Book value per share ($)	14.1%	14.88	20.06	23.85	27.54	30.84	35.19	40.74	45.18	47.84	48.92
Employees	2.5%	9,000	9,600	9,800	9,800	10,100	10,100	10,100	10,000	10,500	11,200

1994 Year-end:
Equity as % of assets: 20.5%
Return on assets: 2.6%
Return on equity: 12.5%
Long term debt (mil.): $1,268
No. of shares (mil.): 87
Dividends
  Yield: 2.4%
  Payout: 30.9%
Market value (mil.): $6,718
Sales (mil.): $5,710

Stock Price History High/Low 1985–94

CITICORP

OVERVIEW

Citicorp is the largest US banking company and the world's only global full-service consumer bank. It has more than 3,400 locations worldwide, including some 1,205 retail branches (complete with greeters) that are designed to look and perform uniformly. And Citicorp continues to expand. In 1994–95 it opened offices in South Africa, Kazakhstan, Tanzania, and Vietnam and brought its brand of consumer banking to Budapest.

Citicorp is still beating its way back from the problems it had in the early 1990s, when it fell victim to bad loans and management bloat. Poor results brought a loss in 1991 and a

subsequent decline in credit rating that the company is still working to improve.

As part of this effort, the bank is increasing its specialization, focusing on global retail banking (including, increasingly, the sale of financial services products such as mutual funds and annuities); credit card issuance and servicing (both for its own cards and many private-label cards); and the extremes of business banking (small business, which it defines as up to $20 million in sales, and giant international companies). Two areas it has decided to de-emphasize, however, are middle-market business and mortgage servicing.

WHEN

Colonel Samuel Osgood, first commissioner of the US Treasury, founded City Bank of New York in 1812 to serve cotton, sugar, metal, and coal merchants.

Opening offices in London and Shanghai in 1902 and in Buenos Aires in 1914, the bank (by then renamed National City Bank of New York) was a pioneer in expanding overseas. It moved into retail (consumer) banking in the 1920s and became the first commercial bank to make personal loans. In the 1920s and 1930s the bank's international operations grew. By 1939 it had 100 foreign offices.

James Rockefeller, who expanded the bank's retail banking in the late 1940s and early 1950s, became president in 1952. In 1955 the bank merged with First National (New York) to become First National City Bank. In 1961 the bank, under VP Walter Wriston, invented the certificate of deposit (CD), paying a higher interest rate on funds deposited for a specified period. CDs allowed the bank to compete against US government securities for funds. Wriston led the bank to international prominence (and into the morass of overseas debt markets) as president (1967–70) and as chairman (1970–84).

In 1968 First National City Corp. (renamed Citicorp in 1974) was created as a holding company; Citibank also passed Chase Manhattan as the largest New York City bank.

Citibank became a major issuer of VISA and MasterCard in the 1970s and acquired Carte Blanche in 1978 and Diners Club in 1981. In 1977 Citibank became the US's largest credit card issuer (it is still the market leader). It was the first bank to introduce automated teller machines (ATMs) on a large scale. John Reed, who developed the ATM and consumer banking markets, became chairman in 1984.

At the end of 1980, the bank passed BankAmerica to become the largest US bank. In the 1980s Citibank's acquisitions included institutions in San Francisco, Chicago, Miami, and Washington, DC. Under Reed, management jobs multiplied like cancer cells.

The bank's loans to other countries, particularly Brazil and Argentina, became a problem in the late 1980s, forcing Citicorp to make large loan loss provisions of $4 billion in 1987 and 1989. Then came the US's slide into recession and with it the collapse of the glutted commercial real estate market.

Hemorrhaging from real estate losses and the economic slowdown, Citicorp recapitalized in 1991 and 1992, raising $2.6 billion, nearly 1/4 of it from Saudi prince al-Waleed bin Talal (who in 1995 held rights to over 9% of Citicorp stock). The company also sold assets and eliminated dividends. In 1992 Citibank was placed under regulatory supervision, limiting its ability to make loans.

Citicorp resisted selling nonperforming real estate assets, hoping instead to manage them until the boom returned, but in 1993 it sold $600 million worth of them (about 62% of the portfolio's face value).

In 1994 friends of Reed and Citibank Argentina's president were found to have profited from the 1992 sale of shares in a stock fund created by a swap of Argentine government bonds for stocks in Argentine companies. Citicorp contended that this was not improper because the stocks might have proven worthless. No legal action was taken.

As part of its stress on customer services, Citicorp has upgraded its communications systems and is entering the electronic banking age, offering home computer banking systems in New York, Chicago, and Washington.

NYSE symbol: CCI
Fiscal year ends: December 31

WHO

Chairman: John S. Reed, age 56, $4,275,000 pay
VC: William R. Rhodes, age 59, $1,650,000 pay
VC: Christopher J. Steffen, age 53, $1,650,000 pay
VC: H. Onno Ruding, age 55, $1,415,000 pay
VC: Pei-yuan Chia, age 56, $1,415,000 pay
VC: Paul J. Collins, age 58, $1,225,000 pay
EVP and Principal Financial Officer: Thomas E. Jones, age 56
EVP Legal Affairs: John J. Roche, age 59
EVP Bankcards Europe and North America: Roberta J. Arena, age 46
EVP Asia/Pacific Global Finance: Shaukat Aziz, age 45
EVP North America Global Finance: Alan S. MacDonald, age 52
EVP European Global Finance: Ernst W. Brutsche, age 57
EVP Latin America Global Finance: Dionisio R. Martin, age 51
Senior Human Resources Officer: Lawrence R. Phillips, age 55
Auditors: KPMG Peat Marwick LLP

WHERE

HQ: 399 Park Ave., New York, NY 10043
Phone: 800-285-3000
Fax: 212-527-3277

Citicorp operates in the US and 93 other countries.

	1994 Sales % of total
US	51
Western Europe	16
Asia/Pacific	14
Latin America	13
Canada & Japan	3
Other regions	3
Total	**100**

WHAT

	1994 Assets	
	$ mil.	% of total
Cash & equivalents	20,327	8
US & foreign gov't. securities	19,077	8
Other securities	19,957	8
Unrealized derivatives gains	20,544	8
Net loans	147,265	59
Other	23,319	9
Total	**250,489**	**100**

	1994 Sales	
	$ mil.	% of total
Interest & fees on loans	16,241	52
Other interest	7,572	24
Fees & commissions	5,155	16
Other	2,682	8
Total	**31,650**	**100**

Selected Services
Asset management
Corporate finance
Credit cards
Foreign exchange
Retail and corporate banking
Securities trading

Selected Subsidiaries
Aspiration, Inc.
Citibank Mexico, S.A.
Grupo Financiero
Citibank
Citibank Overseas Investment Corporation
Citibank Privatkunden A.G.
Citicorp Holdings, Inc.
Citicorp Mortgage, Inc.
Citicorp North America, Inc.
Court Square Capital Ltd.

KEY COMPETITORS

American Express	Crédit Lyonnais	General Electric
BancOne	CS Holding	Great Western
Bank of New York	Dai-Ichi Kangyo	HSBC
BankAmerica	Dean Witter,	Industrial Bank
Bankers Trust	Discover	of Japan
Barclays	Deutsche Bank	J.P. Morgan
Canadian Imperial	First Chicago	NatWest
Charles Schwab	First Union	SunTrust
Chase Manhattan	Fleet	Wells Fargo

HOW MUCH

	Annual Growth	1985	1986	1987	1988	1989	1990	1991	1992	1993	1994
Assets ($ mil.)	4.2%	173,597	196,124	203,607	207,666	230,643	216,986	216,922	213,701	216,574	250,489
Net income ($ mil.)	14.7%	998	1,058	(1,138)	1,698	498	318	(914)	722	1,919	3,422
Income as % of assets	—	0.6%	0.5%	—	0.8%	0.2%	0.1%	—	0.3%	1.0%	1.4%
Earnings per share ($)	6.7%	3.56	3.57	(4.26)	4.87	1.16	0.57	(3.22)	1.35	3.53	6.40
Stock price – high ($)	—	25.88	31.88	34.19	27.00	35.50	29.63	17.50	22.50	39.75	47.75
Stock price – low ($)	—	18.44	23.44	15.88	18.00	24.63	10.75	8.50	10.38	20.50	36.00
Stock price – close ($)	5.9%	24.69	26.50	18.63	25.88	28.88	12.63	10.38	22.25	36.88	41.38
P/E – high	—	7	9	—	6	31	52	—	17	11	8
P/E – low	—	5	7	—	4	21	19	—	8	6	6
Dividends per share ($)	(9.5%)	1.11	1.21	1.32	1.45	1.59	1.74	0.75	0.00	0.00	0.45
Book value per share ($)	3.5%	25.31	27.96	22.83	25.93	25.36	24.34	21.22	21.74	26.04	34.38
Employees	0.2%	81,300	88,500	90,000	89,000	92,000	95,000	86,000	81,000	81,500	82,600

1994 Year-end:
Equity as % of assets: 7.1%
Return on assets: 1.5%
Return on equity: 15.3%
Long-term debt (mil.): $17,894
No. of shares (mil.): 395
Dividends
　Yield: 1.1%
　Payout: 7.0%
Market value (mil.): $16,348
Sales ($ mil.): $31,650

Stock Price History
High/Low 1985–94

THE CITY UNIVERSITY OF NEW YORK

OVERVIEW

City University of New York (CUNY) is a public university system with 20 campuses in the New York metropolitan area. With an open policy that guarantees admission to anyone who graduates from a New York City high school, CUNY has a total enrollment of more than 200,000 undergraduate and graduate students, about 92% of whom are from New York City. The university also teaches some 150,000 students in adult and continuing education programs.

Many of the university's students are immigrants, and about 47% of its first-year students speak a native language other than English. CUNY offers a wide variety of programs, including degrees in architecture and engineering, business, education, law, liberal arts, and nursing. The university's graduate school offers more than 30 doctoral programs.

CUNY is governed by a board of trustees (5 are appointed by the mayor of New York and 10 are appointed by the governor) and by the chairpersons of the university faculty senate and the university student senate. CUNY's support from public sources has dropped, cutting into revenues.

WHEN

The New York State Legislature first created a municipal-college system in New York City in 1926, when it formed the New York City Board of Higher Education to manage the operations of the City College of New York and Hunter College.

The City College has its roots in a mandate from the people of the City of New York to create an institution of higher learning. In 1847 New Yorkers passed a referendum that created the Free Academy, which was originally a tuition-free college. Hunter College was founded in 1870 as a women's college, and it was the first free normal school (teacher's college) in the US.

In 1926, with the authorization of the Board of Higher Education, City College created the Brooklyn Collegiate Center, a 2-year college for men; Hunter established a similar 2-year branch in Brooklyn for women. In 1930 the 2 schools were merged to create the Brooklyn College of the City of New York, the first public, coeducational liberal arts college in New York City.

Other schools were added to the municipal system, including Queens College (1937), New York City Community College (1947), Staten Island Community College (1955), Bronx Community College (1957), and Queensborough Community College (1958).

In 1961 the state legislature renamed New York City's municipal college system the City University of New York and ordered its board of trustees to expand the system's facilities and scope. One of the first actions was to create the graduate school.

CUNY expanded rapidly during the 1960s, chartering several new schools, including Borough of Manhattan Community College and Kingsborough Community College (both in 1963). In 1964 CUNY took over management of the New York State Institute of Applied Arts and Sciences (renamed New York City Technical College). That same year the university established the John Jay College of Criminal Justice. Other schools created during the 1960s included Richmond College (1965), York College (1966), Medgar Evers College (1968), Eugenio Maria de Hostos Community College (1968), and Fiorello H. LaGuardia Community College (1968).

In addition, in 1967 CUNY established an affiliation with Mount Sinai School of Medicine. In 1968 City College's School of Business and Public Administration was split off as Bernard M. Baruch College, and Herbert H. Lehman College was separated from Hunter College, where it had been a branch.

Despite all the expansion, CUNY had difficulty keeping up with demand, particularly after the university established its open admissions policy in 1970. Richmond College and Staten Island Community College became the College of Staten Island in 1976.

CUNY ran into serious budget problems in the mid-1970s as the City of New York ran into financial problems of its own. The budget crunch brought an end to CUNY's tradition of free tuition for all undergraduates who were New York City residents. To increase state financial support for CUNY, the legislature signed the City University Governance and Financing Act in 1979.

In 1983 the City University School of Law held its first classes. The following year the state board of regents authorized CUNY to offer a doctor of medicine degree. CUNY's law school received accreditation from the American Bar Association in 1992.

With enrollment increasing steadily, CUNY requested a 15% increase in state and city funding in 1995.

Private university
Fiscal year ends: June 30

Chairperson, Board of Trustees: James P. Murphy
VC, Board of Trustees: Edith B. Everett
Chancellor: W. Ann Reynolds
Deputy Chancellor: Laurence F. Mucciolo
Vice Chancellor for Academic Affairs: Richard M.
Freeland
Vice Chancellor for University Relations: Jay
Hershenson
Vice Chancellor for Student Affairs: Elsa Nunez-
Wormack
**Vice Chancellor for Budget, Finance, and Information
Services:** Richard F. Rothbard
**Vice Chancellor for Facilities Planning, Construction,
and Management:** Emma E. Macari
Vice Chancellor for Faculty and Staff Relations: Brenda
Richardson Malone
General Counsel and Vice Chancellor for Legal Affairs:
Robert E. Diaz
Finance Manager: Gerald Glick
Director Human Resources: J. Demby

WHERE

HQ: 535 E. 80th St., New York, NY 10021
Phone: 212-794-5555
Fax: 212-794-5397

The City University of New York has schools serving the
Bronx, Brooklyn, Manhattan, Queens, and Staten Island.

WHAT

	1995 Revenues	
	$ mil.	% of total
New York State appropriations	713	33
Tuition & fees	463	21
Federal grants & contracts	227	10
New York City appropriations	116	5
Private gifts, grants & contracts	60	3
New York City grants & contracts	38	2
New York State grants & contracts	37	2
Dormitory authority & other	515	24
Total	**2,169**	**100**

Campuses and Affiliated Institutions
Baruch College
Borough of Manhattan Community College
Bronx Community College
Brooklyn College
College of Staten Island
City College
CUNY Computing Information Services
CUNY Medical School
CUNY School of Law
Graduate School and University Center
Hostos Community College
Hunter College
John Jay College of Criminal Justice
Kingsborough Community College
LaGuardia Community College
Lehman College
Medgar Evers College
Mount Sinai School of Medicine
New York City Technical College
Queens College
Queensborough Community College
York College

HOW MUCH

	Annual Growth	1986	1987	1988	1989	1990	1991	1992	1993	1994	1995
Revenues ($ mil.)	7.3%	1,146	1,189	1,264	1,325	1,828	1,813	1,920	2,063	2,120	2,169
Endowment ($ mil.)	(0.9%)	39	44	20	26	28	32	34	38	36	36
Enrollment	1.4%	182,869	183,347	188,371	195,118	200,688	200,336	202,609	207,567	212,634	206,457
Faculty	(0.7%)	14,043	13,656	13,707	13,642	13,713	13,720	13,749	14,489	14,749	13,200
Employees	(0.9%)	27,975	27,443	27,750	26,338	26,643	26,140	26,010	27,799	28,609	25,800

Revenues ($ mil.)
1986–1995

COLGATE-PALMOLIVE COMPANY

OVERVIEW

Colgate-Palmolive is being squeezed in the US market but is swallowing more market share in Latin America and Asia. Based in New York, Colgate-Palmolive is a leading global consumer products company in the oral, personal, and household care and pet food markets.

While Colgate is #1 in toothbrushes and liquid soaps and #2 in toothpastes, many of Colgate's brands are trailing the competition in the US market. As retailers shrink store size and carry only the leading and private-label brands, Colgate has had to become more aggressive in the home market. Colgate is in-

creasing product development and advertising in higher-margin businesses like oral care.

With 2/3 of its revenues from outside the US, Colgate-Palmolive is an old pro in the international consumer market. In 1995 Colgate purchased Kolynos, a leading South American oral hygiene business, from American Home Products for $1 billion. With the purchase Colgate increases its share of the oral care market in Latin America from 54% to 79%. The company also bought Ciba-Geigy's oral hygiene business in India, increasing its share of that toothpaste market to 68%.

WHEN

In 1806 William Colgate founded the Colgate Company in Manhattan to produce soap, candles, and starch. The company moved to Jersey City in 1847. William Colgate died 10 years later, and the company passed to his son Samuel, who renamed it Colgate and Company. In 1877 the company introduced Colgate Dental Cream, which it began selling in a tube in 1890. By 1906 Colgate was making 160 kinds of soap, 625 perfumes, and 2,000 other products. The company went public in 1908.

In 1898 a Milwaukee soap maker, B. J. Johnson Soap Company (founded in 1864), introduced Palmolive, a soap made of palm and olive oils. It became so popular that the firm changed its name to the Palmolive company in 1917. In 1927 Palmolive merged with Peet Brothers, a Kansas City soap maker founded in 1872. Palmolive-Peet merged with Colgate in 1928, forming Colgate-Palmolive-Peet (shortened to Colgate-Palmolive in 1953). The stock market crash of 1929 prevented a planned merger of the company with Hershey and Kraft.

During the 1930s the company purchased French and German soap makers and opened branches in Europe. After WWII the Ajax, Colgate, and Palmolive brands were outselling rivals in Europe. The company expanded to the Far East in the 1950s, and by 1961 foreign sales were 52% of the total.

Colgate-Palmolive introduced several new products in the 1960s, including Cold Power detergent, Palmolive dishwashing liquid, Ultra Brite toothpaste, and Colgate with MFP. During the 1960s and 1970s, the company diversified by buying approximately 70 other companies, including Helena Rubenstein (1973), Ram Golf (1974), and Maui Divers

(1977). But the strategy failed, and most of these businesses were sold in the 1980s.

In the late 1980s the company launched a reorganization to focus on building Colgate-Palmolive's core businesses (personal care and household products), taking a $145 million charge against earnings in 1987 to cover reorganization costs.

Products introduced during the 1980s include Palmolive automatic dishwasher detergent (1986), Colgate Tartar Control toothpaste (1986), and Fab 1-Shot laundry detergent (1987). The company strengthened its hold on the global bleach market through its purchases of Cotelle (France, 1988), Klorin (Scandinavia, 1988), Unisol (Portugal, 1990), and Javex (Canada's #1 bleach producer, 1990). Other recent acquisitions include McKesson's veterinary distribution business (1989), Vipont Pharmaceutical (1990), the dental therapeutics unit of Scherer Laboratories (1990), and Murphy-Phoenix (maker of Murphy Oil Soap, 1991).

In 1992 Colgate expanded its presence in personal care products by paying $670 million for Mennen, maker of the leading US deodorant, Speed Stick. In 1993 Colgate-Europe purchased S.C. Johnson Wax's liquid soap products, becoming the global leader in liquid soap. In 1994 Colgate shifted from its traditional special-promotion pricing to everyday low pricing, resulting in a basic philosophy shift for its US retailers from promotion-induced purchases to actual-need purchases. As of the end of 1994, Colgate priced 50% of its business on an everyday low-price basis.

In 1995 Colgate continued its purchases of South American oral hygiene companies by buying 94% of the Argentinean dental care company Odol Saic.

NYSE symbol: CL
Fiscal year ends: December 31

WHO

Chairman and CEO: Reuben Mark, age 56,
$2,358,500 pay
President and COO: William S. Shanahan,
age 54, $1,296,667 pay
**Chief of Operations, Specialty Marketing and
International Business Development:** William G.
Cooling, age 50, $700,833 pay
SEVP and CFO: Robert M. Agate, age 59, $665,833 pay
President, Colgate-Europe: David A. Metzler, age 52,
$566,325 pay
President, Colgate-USA/Canada/Puerto Rico:
Lois Juliber, age 46
President, Colgate-Asia Pacific: Stephen A. Lister,
age 53
Chief Technological Officer: Craig B. Tate, age 49
SVP, General Counsel, and Secretary: Andrew D.
Hendry, age 47
SVP Human Resources: Douglas M. Reid, age 60
Auditors: Arthur Andersen & Co, SC

WHERE

HQ: 300 Park Ave., New York, NY 10022
Phone: 212-310-2000
Fax: 212-310-3284

Colgate-Palmolive operates 66 facilities in the
US and 235 in over 60 other countries.

	1994 Sales		1994 Operating Income	
	$ mil.	% of total	$ mil.	% of total
North America	2,400	31	306	31
Europe	2,043	27	202	21
Latin America	1,737	23	298	31
Asia & Africa	1,408	19	165	17
Total	**7,588**	**100**	**972**	**100**

WHAT

	1994 Sales % of total
Oral care	26
Personal care	24
Fabric care	18
Household surface care	17
Pet dietary care	11
Other	4
Total	**100**

Selected Brand Names

Personal Care	**Laundry Care**
Baby Magic	Ajax
Colgate	Axion
Irish Spring	Fab
Lady Speed Stick	Soupline/Suavitel
Mennen	Sta-Soft
Nouriché	
Optims	**Household Care**
Palmolive	Ajax
Protex	Fab
Skin Bracer	Fabuloso
Softsoap	Palmolive
Speed Stick	**Pet Care**
Total	Hill's Science Diet

KEY COMPETITORS

Abbott Labs	First Brands	Mars
American	Gillette	NCH
Home Products	Hartz	Nestlé
Amway	Heinz	Pet Ventures
Avon	Helene Curtis	Procter & Gamble
Brown-Forman	Henkel	Ralston Purina
Carter-Wallace	Iams	Group
Chattem	Johnson &	S.C. Johnson
Church & Dwight	Johnson	Shiseido
Clorox	Libbey	Unilever
Dial	L'Oréal	

HOW MUCH

	Annual Growth	1985	1986	1987	1988	1989	1990	1991	1992	1993	1994
Sales ($ mil.)	9.0%	3,489	3,769	4,366	4,734	5,039	5,691	6,060	7,007	7,141	7,588
Net income ($ mil.)	18.8%	123	115	1	153	280	321	125	477	548	580
Income as % of sales	—	3.5%	3.1%	0.0%	3.2%	5.6%	5.6%	2.1%	6.8%	7.7%	7.6%
Earnings per share ($)	18.5%	0.77	0.81	0.01	1.10	1.90	2.12	0.75	2.74	3.15	3.56
Stock price – high ($)	—	16.69	23.50	26.31	24.75	32.44	37.75	49.13	60.63	67.25	65.38
Stock price – low ($)	—	11.31	15.19	14.00	19.25	22.06	26.38	33.63	45.13	46.75	49.50
Stock price – close ($)	16.2%	16.38	20.44	19.63	23.50	31.75	36.88	48.88	55.75	62.38	63.38
P/E – high	—	16	19	—	22	17	18	66	22	21	18
P/E – low	—	11	12	—	17	12	12	45	16	15	14
Dividends per share ($)	10.1%	0.65	0.68	0.70	0.74	0.78	0.90	1.02	1.15	1.34	1.54
Book value per share ($)	5.0%	6.33	6.91	6.77	8.24	5.30	7.06	9.81	13.74	9.79	9.80
Employees	(2.3%)	40,600	37,900	37,400	24,700	24,100	24,800	24,900	28,800	28,000	32,800

1994 Year-end:
Debt ratio: 51.8%
Return on equity: 40.4%
Cash (mil.): $218
Current ratio: 1.42
Long-term debt (mil.): $1,752
No. of shares (mil.): 144
Dividends
  Yield: 2.4%
  Payout: 43.3%
Market value (mil.): $9,152

**Stock Price History
High/Low 1985–94**

COLUMBIA UNIVERSITY

OVERVIEW

The oldest institution of higher learning in the state of New York, Columbia University is one of the most prestigious schools in the US. The Ivy League member's list of graduates includes Alexander Hamilton and Theodore and Franklin Roosevelt, as well as Allen Ginsberg, Lou Gehrig, and James Cagney.

Columbia's main campus is located on 36 acres on Manhattan's Upper West Side. With a faculty of 6,400 (including 4 Nobel Prize winners), the university offers courses in 71 aca-

demic departments to nearly 20,000 students. The school has been recognized for its Core Curriculum program, which has been in place since 1919. The program, required of all students, provides a broad base of study in literature, philosophy, art, and music. Columbia's programs also include schools of business, engineering, law, medicine, and social work.

A private university, Columbia has one of the largest endowments in the US. It reached nearly $2 billion in fiscal 1994.

WHEN

Created by royal charter of King George II of England, Columbia was founded in 1754 as King's College. The school's first class of 8 students met in the vestry room in Trinity Church in Manhattan. The school soon moved to a site on a parcel of land at what is now Murray Street and West Broadway. Although chartered by the King of England, the school educated some of the American Revolution's leaders, including Alexander Hamilton and John Jay. In 1787 King's College was renamed Columbia College, in honor of a mythical patriotic figure.

In 1813 the school added the College of Physicians and Surgeons. Columbia moved to 49th Street and Madison Avenue in 1857. Following the move, several new courses of study were added, including the School of Law in 1858 and the School of Engineering in 1864. Columbia also added studies in political science (1880), philosophy (1890), and pure science (1892). Led by president Fredrick Barnard, Columbia established an affiliate school for women, Barnard College, in 1889.

With the expansion of the school's curriculum, Columbia's Board of Trustees authorized the school to change its name to Columbia University in 1896 (although the name did not officially change until 1912, when it was legalized by the state legislature). In 1897 the school moved to its present location on Manhattan's Upper West Side on a site formerly occupied by the Bloomingdale Insane Asylum. (However, Columbia retained the land of its old site, near what is now Rockefeller Center, until 1985.)

Led by president Nicholas Murray Butler, Columbia continued to expand during the early 20th century. In 1912 it added the School of Journalism, with funding from publishing magnate Joseph Pulitzer. The School of Business was opened in 1916, and Columbia

added the School of Dental and Oral Surgery in 1917 and the School of Public Health in 1921. Following WWII, the university added the School of International Affairs (1946) and the adult education School of General Studies (1947).

Butler was succeeded as president in 1948 by Dwight Eisenhower, who held the position until he became president of the US in 1953. Columbia continued to expand, adding the School of Social Work in 1959 and the School of the Arts in 1965. During the late 1960s Columbia gained a reputation for student political action, and in 1968 students closed down the university for several days in protest of the Vietnam War.

During the 1970s Columbia spent heavily on new construction. Among the projects completed were the Sherman Fairchild Center for Life Sciences and the Julius and Armand Hammer Health Sciences Center. In 1980 Michael Sovern, former dean of Columbia's law school, became president of the university. Sovern focused on increasing government funding for basic research and student aid and improving educational opportunities for minorities. In addition, in 1983 Columbia welcomed its first coeducational freshman class after 230 years as an all-male school.

In 1985 the university sold its land near Rockefeller Center for $400 million. However, by 1991 Columbia was facing economic pressures, including recession and cuts in government research spending. That year the school closed its linguistics and geography departments, saving $1.5 million.

In 1993 Sovern resigned to return to teaching law. He was succeeded by George Rupp, former president of Rice University.

In an effort to lower its electricity costs, Columbia began construction of a cogeneration plant on campus in 1995.

Private university
Fiscal year ends: June 30

Co-chairman Board of Trustees: Jerry I. Speyer
Co-chairman Board of Trustees: Lionel I. Pincus
President: George Rupp
Provost: Jonathan R. Cole
EVP Finance: John Masten
General Counsel: Elizabeth Head
Secretary: Corinne H. Rieder
VP Arts and Sciences: David Cohen
VP Health Sciences; Dean, Faculty of Medicine: Herbert Pardes
VP Facilities Management and Acting VP Administration: Lawrence R. Kilduff
VP Development and Alumni Relations: Richard K. Naum
VP Information Services and University Librarian: Elaine F. Sloan
VP Human Resources: Colleen Crooker
Auditors: Coopers & Lybrand L.L.P.

WHERE

HQ: Columbia University in the City of New York, Broadway and W. 116th St., 311 Dodge Hall, New York, NY 10027
Phone: 212-854-1754
Fax: 212-678-4817 (Office of Public Information)

Campuses
Arden House and Arden Homestead (Harriman, NY)
Columbia University (main campus, Morningside Heights, Manhattan)
Columbia-Presbyterian Medical Center (Washington Heights, Manhattan)
Lamont-Doherty Earth Observatory (Palisades, NY)
Nevis Laboratories (Irvington, NY)
Reid Hall (Paris, France)

WHAT

	1994 Revenues	
	$ mil.	% of total
Tuition & fees	278	25
Federal government grants & contracts	236	22
Private gifts, grants & contracts	199	18
Medical private practice plans	165	15
Investment income utilized	92	8
Local government grants & contracts	65	6
Sales & services of auxiliary enterprises	43	4
Other	25	2
Total	**1,103**	**100**

	1994 Expenditures	
	$ mil.	% of total
Instruction, research & educational administration	611	57
Medical private practice plans	165	16
University administration	60	6
Financial aid	57	5
Operation & maintenance of plant	57	5
Auxiliary enterprises	42	4
Library	29	3
Other	48	4
Total	**1,069**	**100**

KEY COMPETITORS

Brown University
Cornell University
Dartmouth College
Duke University
Georgetown University
Harvard University
MIT
New York University
Princeton University
Stanford University
University of Chicago
University of Pennsylvania
Yale University

HOW MUCH

	Annual Growth	1985	1986	1987	1988	1989	1990	1991	1992	1993	1994
Revenues ($ mil.)	8.1%	546	600	638	702	775	841	898	953	1,032	1,103
Endowment ($ mil.)	7.8%	989	1,283	1,403	1,358	1,443	1,516	1,548	1,708	1,883	1,952
Enrollment	0.9%	18,359	18,499	18,761	18,940	18,992	19,251	19,345	19,579	20,170	19,840
Faculty	(0.5%)	—	—	—	—	—	—	—	—	6,430	6,400
Employees	—	—	—	—	—	—	—	—	—	—	10,300

Revenues ($ mil.)
1985–94

1,200
1,000
800
600
400
200
0

CONSOLIDATED EDISON OF NEW YORK

OVERVIEW

Consolidated Edision (Con Ed) is one of the largest publicly owned gas and electric utilities in the US. Headquartered in New York City, the company provides electric power to more than 8 million people in a service area covering most of that city (except for parts of Queens) and most of Westchester County. Con Ed also supplies gas in Manhattan, the Bronx, and parts of Queens and Westchester and steam in part of Manhattan. It sells electricity to government customers through the New York Power Authority.

With deregulation of the electric and gas industries creating increased competition, Con Ed has concentrated on increasing efficiency. In the last decade it has cut employment by about 20%. It is also adding more value-added services and expanding its gas marketing and power purchasing programs.

Con Ed continues to shift the mix of its fuel sources away from oil toward natural gas and other sources. In 1994 oil produced 9% of the company's electricity, down from over 70% in the mid-1970s.

WHEN

A group of New York professionals, led by Timothy Dewey, founded the New York Gas Light Company in 1823 to provide utility service to a limited area of Manhattan. Various companies served other areas of New York City, and, in 1884, 5 of these joined with New York Gas Light to form the Consolidated Gas Company of New York.

This unification occurred on the heels of the introduction of Thomas Edison's incandescent lamp (1879). The Edison Electric Illuminating Company of New York was formed in 1880 to build the world's first commercial electric power station, financed by a group led by J. P. Morgan. Edison supervised this project, known as the Pearl Street Station, and in 1882 New York became the first major city to experience electric lighting.

Realizing that electric lighting would most certainly replace gas, Consolidated Gas began buying New York's electric companies, including Anthony Brady's New York Gas and Electric Light, Heat and Power Company (1900), which consolidated with Edison's Illuminating Company in 1901 to form the New York Edison Company. More than 170 other purchases followed, including that of the New York Steam Company in 1930 to provide a cheap source of steam for the company's electric turbines. In 1936 these utilities combined to form the Consolidated Edison Company of New York.

In 1962 Con Ed opened its first nuclear station at Indian Point. Environmentalists worried that Con Ed's proposed Cornwall pumped-storage plant at the foot of Storm King Mountain would damage the local ecosystem, and they managed to delay construction throughout the 1960s and early 1970s. A federal court ordered Con Ed to cease construction of the plant in 1974. In the meantime Con Ed had had trouble supplying

enough power to meet demand. Inflation and the OPEC oil embargo had driven up the price of oil (Con Ed's main energy source), and in 1974 the company skipped a dividend for the first time since 1885. The New York State Power Authority bought 2 of Con Ed's unfinished power plants, saving the company about $200 million.

Con Ed started buying power from various suppliers and in 1984 agreed to a 2-year rate freeze, a boon to New Yorkers, whose electric bills were nearly twice as high as those of most other big-city residents. In 1992 Con Ed formed a partnership with several other companies to build a 47-mile natural gas pipeline from New Jersey to Kennedy International Airport. Also in 1992 the New York State Public Service Commission approved a 3-year, 4.5% rate increase, the first since 1983.

In 1993 Indeck Energy Services, a co-generation facility operator, filed a breach-of-contract suit against Con Ed after Con Ed refused to buy electricity from a plant being built on a site it had not approved.

Con Ed canceled a long-term power purchase contract with Montreal-based Hydro-Quebec in 1994 after Hydro-Quebec came under fire from environmentalists (and Con Ed drew heat from its shareholders).

In 1995 the Public Service Commission (PSC) refused Con Ed's request for a $429 million electricity rate increase. In a deal struck with the PSC, however, the company will be allowed to defer differences between actual and projected amounts of certain expenses. Also in 1995 Con Ed was fined $2 million and given 3 years of probation after pleading guilty to concealing the fact that a 1989 manhole explosion had released more than 200 pounds of asbestos into a New York residential neighborhood.

NYSE symbol: ED
Fiscal year ends: December 31

Chairman, President, and CEO: Eugene R. McGrath, age 53, $839,066 pay
EVP and CFO: Raymond J. McCann, age 60, $480,776 pay
EVP Customer Service: Charles F. Soutar, age 58, $391,333 pay
EVP Central Operations: J. Michael Evans, age 49, $365,666 pay
SVP: Stephen B. Bram, age 52, $316,333 pay
SVP Gas Operations: Mary Jane McCartney, age 46
SVP Financial and Regulatory Matters: Carl W. Greene, age 59
SVP Public Affairs: Horace S. Webb, age 54
SVP and General Counsel: T. Bowring Woodbury II, age 57
SVP Central Services (Personnel): Thomas J. Galvin, age 56
Auditors: Price Waterhouse LLP

WHERE

HQ: Consolidated Edison Company of New York, Inc., 4 Irving Place, New York, NY 10003
Phone: 212-460-4600
Fax: 212-982-7816

Generating Facilities

Electric – Fossil Fueled	Electric – Gas Turbines
59th Street Station	Indian Point (Buchanan)
74th Street Station	Narrows (Brooklyn)
Arthur Kill (Staten Island)	
Astoria (Queens)	**Electric – Nuclear**
Bowline Point (Orange Co.)	Indian Point (Buchanan)
East River (Manhattan)	
Hudson Avenue (Brooklyn)	**Steam**
Ravenswood (Queens)	59th Street Station
Roseton (Newburgh)	74th Street Station
Waterside (Manhattan)	Hudson Avenue (Brooklyn)
	Ravenswood (Queens)

WHAT

	1994 Electricity Sales	
	$ mil.	% of total
Commercial & industrial	3,111	61
Residential	1,680	33
Public authorities	57	1
Sales to other utilities	49	1
Railroads	5	—
Delivery to NY Power Authority	238	4
Total	**5,140**	**100**

	1994 Sales		1994 Operating Income	
	$ mil.	% of total	$ mil.	% of total
Electric	5,140	81	881	85
Gas	890	14	117	11
Steam	343	5	38	4
Total	**6,373**	**100**	**1,036**	**100**

	1994 Fuel Sources
	% of total
Natural gas	34
Nuclear	19
Oil	9
Hydroelectric	5
Refuse	1
Purchased power	32
Total	**100**

KEY COMPETITORS

Brooklyn Union Gas
Central Hudson Gas and Electric
Cogen Technologies
Long Island Lighting
New York Power Authority
New York Public Utility Service
Niagara Mohawk
Selkirk Cogen Partners
Sithe Energies
Westchester County Public Service Agency

HOW MUCH

	Annual Growth	1985	1986	1987	1988	1989	1990	1991	1992	1993	1994
Sales ($ mil.)	1.7%	5,498	5,198	5,094	5,109	5,551	5,739	5,873	5,933	6,265	6,373
Net income ($ mil.)	3.2%	525	508	512	562	569	534	530	568	623	699
Income as % of sales	—	9.6%	9.8%	10.1%	11.0%	10.2%	9.3%	9.0%	9.6%	9.9%	11.0%
Earnings per share ($)	3.8%	2.13	2.13	2.21	2.47	2.49	2.34	2.32	2.46	2.66	2.98
Stock price – high ($)	—	19.81	26.44	26.00	23.75	29.88	29.25	28.75	32.88	37.75	32.38
Stock price – low ($)	—	14.69	18.81	18.75	20.44	22.19	19.75	22.50	25.00	30.25	23.00
Stock price – close ($)	3.0%	19.75	23.56	20.88	23.25	29.13	23.63	28.63	32.63	32.13	25.75
P/E – high	—	9	12	12	10	12	13	12	13	14	11
P/E – low	—	7	9	8	8	9	8	10	10	11	8
Dividends per share ($)	5.8%	1.20	1.34	1.48	1.60	1.72	1.82	1.86	1.90	1.94	2.00
Book value per share ($)	3.7%	16.35	17.03	17.59	18.44	19.21	19.73	20.18	20.89	21.63	22.62
Employees	(2.3%)	21,076	20,698	20,260	20,108	19,798	19,483	19,087	18,718	17,586	17,097

1994 Year-end:
Debt ratio: 43.5%
Return on equity: 13.5%
Cash (mil.): $245
Current ratio: 1.31
Long-term debt (mil.): $4,078
No. of shares (mil.): 235
Dividends
  Yield: 7.8%
  Payout: 67.1%
Market value (mil.): $6,049

Stock Price History
High/Low 1985–94

CONTINENTAL GRAIN COMPANY

OVERVIEW

One of the world's largest commodities traders and one of the US's biggest private companies, New York City–based Continental Grain racks up about $14 billion in annual sales of grain, cotton, chickens, pigs, and petroleum, among other things. Continental operates in more than 50 countries and is involved in feeding cattle and in milling, brokering, and shipping commodities as well as in financial services. The company's sales have held fairly steady for many years, leaving Continental to squeeze any profits from the same annual revenues derived from low-margin operations.

Continental continues to invest in ventures in China. In 1995 the company announced that it would control 52% of a $60 million venture with Shanghai Petrochemical (China's largest oil company) for the construction and operation of a facility in Shanghai to import and market liquid petroleum gas. When the plant begins operations in 1997, it will be the first of its kind in east China. Meanwhile, Continental controls 40% of a plastic packaging manufacturing plant in China in partnership with Huntsman Chemical.

Eighty-one-year-old chairman emeritus Michel Fribourg (the great-great-grandson of Continental's founder) and his family own the company as well as a stake in Overseas Ship Holding Group, the biggest independent owner and operator of tankers and commodity vessels in the US.

WHEN

In 1813 Simon Fribourg founded a commodity trading business in Belgium. The company operated primarily as a domestic concern until 1848, when a severe drought in Belgium caused the company to buy large stocks in Russian wheat.

As the Industrial Revolution swept across Europe and populations shifted toward the cities, people began consuming more traded grain. In the midst of such rapid changes, the company prospered.

After WWI, Russia, which had been Europe's primary grain supplier, ceased to be a major player in the trading game, and Western Hemisphere countries picked up the slack. Sensing the shift, Jules and René Fribourg reorganized the business as Continental Grain and opened the company's first US office in Chicago in 1921. Seven years later Continental leased a grain elevator in St. Louis (during the Depression the company bought US grain elevators wherever they could find them, often at low prices). In 1930 Continental leased a Galveston terminal from the Southern Pacific Railroad. Through its rapid purchases, the company built an elaborate North American grain network that included such important locations as Kansas City, Nashville, and Toledo.

Meanwhile, in Europe the Fribourgs were forced to weather constant political and economic upheaval, often profiting from it (the Fribourgs supplied food to the Republican forces during the Spanish Civil War). When the Nazis invaded Belgium in 1940, the Fribourgs were forced to flee but reorganized the business in New York City after the war.

During the postwar years, Continental conducted a lucrative grain trade with the Soviets and expanded its international presence. During the 1960s and 1970s, the company went on a buying spree, acquiring Allied Mills (feed milling, 1965) and absorbing several agricultural and transport businesses, including feedlots in Texas, an English soybean producer (sold in 1986), a bakery, and Quaker Oats's agricultural products unit.

During the 1980s the company slimmed down by selling its baking units (Oroweat and Arnold) as well as its commodities brokerage house. Michel Fribourg stepped down as CEO in 1988. Donald Staheli, the first nonfamily member to hold the position, succeeded him. Soon after, Continental realigned its international grain and oilseeds operations into the World Grain and Oilseeds Processing Group under the leadership of Michel's son Paul.

Continental in 1991 agreed with Scoular to enter a grain-handling and -merchandising joint venture. In 1992 Continental and Tosco formed a short-lived company to trade Russian oil. Because Continental uses futures contracts, it was well insulated from price swings caused by Mississippi River basin flooding in 1993. Continental ran into opposition to several proposed Missouri pork-producing plants in 1994. Local citizens, holding signs that read "Continental Grain, Go Home," were wary of land and air pollution and depressed land values.

In 1994 the company named CEO Staheli chairman and Paul Fribourg, widely seen as the next head of the company, as president and COO. The next year Staheli succeeded Michel Fribourg as chairman of the company's executive committee. Also in 1995 Continental merged its ContiMilling division into its ContiLatin trading unit.

Private company
Fiscal year ends: March 31

Chairman Emeritus: Michel Fribourg, age 81
Chairman and CEO: Donald L. Staheli, age 63
President and COO: Paul J. Fribourg. age 41
President, Commodity Marketing, The Americas: Vart Adjemian
President, Commodity Marketing, Europe and Far East: Poul Schroeder
President, Milling Group: Dale F. Larson
President, ContiFinancial: James E. Moore
EVP and CFO: James J. Bigham
SVP and Merchandising Manager: John Laesch
SVP: Bernard Steinweg
VP and General Counsel: Lawrence G. Weppler
VP and General Counsel, Commodity Marketing: David G. Friedman
VP Public Affairs: Daryl Natz
VP Human Resources: Dwight Coffin

WHERE

HQ: 277 Park Ave., New York, NY 10172-0002
Phone: 212-207-5100
Fax: 212-207-5181

Continental Grain has offices and facilities in more than 50 countries.

WHAT

Commodity Marketing Group
Astral International Shipping (shipping agents, New Orleans)
ContiCarriers & Terminals (transport, Chicago)
ContiChem (liquefied petroleum gases; Stamford, Connecticut)
ContiCotton (cotton merchandising, Memphis)
ContiLatin (Latin American trading unit, New York)
Continental Grain (Canada)
ContiQuincy Export (soybean merchandising partnership with Quincy Soybean, New York)
Finagrain (European trading unit, Geneva)
North American Grain Division (Chicago)
Rice Division (rice trading, New York)
Stellar Chartering and Brokerage (ocean vessels, Chicago)
World Grain and Oilseeds Merchandising (Chicago)

ContiFinancial
ContiFinancial Services (New York)
ContiMortgage Corp. (Horsham, Pennsylvania)
ContiTrade Services (New York)

Meat Group
Cattle Feeding Division (Chicago)
Dutch Quality House (poultry; Gainesville, GA)
Poultry Division (Atlanta)
Swine Marketing Services Division (Chicago)

Milling Group
Asian Agri Industries (Hong Kong)
Wayne Feed Division (Chicago)

KEY COMPETITORS

ADM
Ag Processing
Agway
BeefAmerica
Cargill
CENEX
Central Soya
ConAgra
Connell Co.
Countrymark Co-op
Farmland Industries
Gold Kist
Harvest States Co-ops
Hudson Foods
IBP
International Multifoods
Keystone Foods
Moorman Manufacturing
Perdue
Pilgrim's Pride
Pioneer Hi-Bred
Ralston Purina Group
Schreiber Foods
Scoular
Seaboard Corp.
Smithfield Foods
Tyson Foods

HOW MUCH

	Annual Growth	1986	1987	1988	1989	1990	1991	1992	1993	1994	1995
Estimated sales ($ mil.)	0.0%	14,000	13,500	13,000	13,500	14,850	15,000	15,000	15,000	15,000	14,000
Employees	3.2%	12,000	12,000	12,000	12,000	12,000	14,500	14,500	14,750	14,700	15,500	16,000

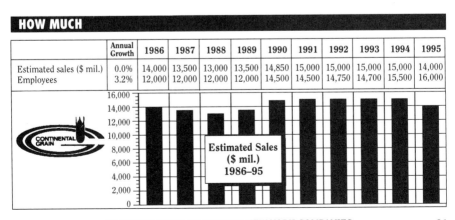

Estimated Sales
($ mil.)
1986–95

COOPERS & LYBRAND L.L.P.

OVERVIEW

Coopers & Lybrand is the 4th largest of the Big 6 accounting firms. It operates on a truly international scale, with offices in 130 countries. Although its primary business through its nearly 100 years of history has been auditing companies, in recent years the firm, like the other members of its fraternity, has been moving into the more lucrative area of business consulting. Not only has auditing become less profitable because of increased price competition (with Coopers & Lybrand a leading price-cutter), but in the hyperlitigious 1990s it is becoming downright dangerous. Coopers &

Lybrand is currently involved in a number of legal actions in which investors and government bodies have attempted to hold the firm accountable not only for the form of audited financial statements (which traditionally was all the auditor attested to) but for their veracity as well.

Consolidation of the accounting industry has been a factor in Coopers & Lybrand's international growth, as it has added overseas accounting firms. It also bought a number of consulting firms, including Coppi & Associates (construction management) in 1995.

WHEN

Coopers & Lybrand, the product of a 1957 transatlantic merger, literally wrote the book on auditing. Lybrand, Ross Bros. & Montgomery, as the US ancestor was known, had been formed in 1898 by 4 partners — William Lybrand, Edward Ross, Adam Ross, and Robert Montgomery. In 1912 Montgomery wrote *Montgomery's Auditing*, termed by many as the bible of the accounting profession.

In the early years the accounting firm grew slowly, and the Ross brothers' sister served as secretary, typist, and bookkeeper. In 1902 the company opened a New York office at 25 Broad Street. Other offices across the country followed — Pittsburgh (1908), Chicago (1909), and Boston (1915). WWI focused attention on Washington, DC, and the Lybrand firm opened an office there (1919) and then branched out to the new auto capital of Detroit (1920), to Seattle (1920), and to Baltimore (1924). A merger with the firm of Klink, Bean & Company gave the firm a window on California (1924). Another merger brought the firm into Dallas (1930), with an offshoot office in Houston a year later.

In Europe, Lybrand established offices in Berlin (1924, closed in 1938 as WWII loomed), Paris (1926), and London (1929). At the same time the UK firm of Cooper Brothers was also expanding in Europe.

Cooper Brothers had begun in 1854 when William Cooper, the oldest son of a Quaker banker, formed his accountancy at 13 George Street in London. He was quickly joined by his brothers, Arthur, Francis, and Ernest. The firm became Cooper Brothers & Company in 1861. After WWI Cooper Brothers branched out to Liverpool (1920), Brussels (1921), New York (1926), and Paris (1930). After WWII Cooper Brothers acquired 3 venerable firms — Alfred Tongue & Company; Aspell Dunn &

Company; and Rattray Brothers, Alexander & France.

In 1957 Coopers & Lybrand was formed by the amalgamation of the international accounting firms, and by 1973 the affiliated partnerships had largely adopted the Coopers & Lybrand name. In the 1960s the firm expanded into employee benefits consulting and introduced a new auditing method that included evaluating clients' systems of internal control. During the 1970s Coopers & Lybrand focused on integrating computer technology into the auditing process.

During the 1980s Coopers & Lybrand dropped from the top of the Big 8 to 5th in the Big 6 as several of its competitors paired off in a series of mergers. However, the firm unexpectedly benefited from merger mania, becoming a refuge for partners from the other firms. The mergers only increased the cutthroat nature of auditing competitions, and auditing became increasingly price driven.

In 1991 Coopers & Lybrand and IBM formed Meritus, a consulting service for the health care and consumer goods industries. In 1992 the firm agreed to pay $95 million to settle claims of defrauded investors in now-defunct disk drive maker MiniScribe. The next year it hired former SEC chairman Richard Breeden as VC of its domestic and foreign financial service groups.

Coopers & Lybrand introduced Telesim, a management simulation software package for the telecommunications industry, in 1994. Telesim was developed with Pacific Telesis, NYNEX, and software maker Thinking Tools.

In 1995 a former VC, Robert Caruso, was indicted on fraud charges. Caruso had allegedly converted to his own use funds obtained from Coopers & Lybrand for donation to Seton Hall University.

International partnership
Fiscal year ends: September 30

WHO

Chairman and CEO: Nicholas G. Moore
COO: William K. O'Brien
COO: John J. Roberts
VC Business Assurance: Patrick J. McDonnell
VC International: James T. Clarke
VC Coopers & Lybrand Consulting: John M. Jacobs
VC Tax: Alan L. LeBovidge
VC Financial Advisory Services: Raymond A. Ranelli
VC Human Resource Advisory: Reed A. Keller
National Director Marketing and Communications: Lee S. Pinkard Jr.
CFO: Frank V. Scalia
General Counsel: Harris J. Amhowitz

WHERE

HQ: 1251 Avenue of the Americas, New York, NY 10020
Phone: 212-536-2000
Fax: 212-536-3145

Coopers & Lybrand has offices in 130 countries.

	1995 Sales	
	$ mil.	**% of total**
US	1,905	39
Other countries	4,295	61
Total	**6,200**	**100**

WHAT

	1995 US Sales
	% of total
Accounting & auditing	45
Tax	20
Consulting & other	35
Total	**100**

Representative Clients
American Brands
AT&T
Ford
Johnson & Johnson
The Limited
3M
Philip Morris
Unilever

Selected Services

Business Assurance
ERISA
In-control services
Internal audit services
Regulatory and compliance services
Technology-related services

Coopers & Lybrand Consulting Units
Center for Operations Technology
Financial Management and Business Analysis
Integrated Management Services
Logistics/Systecon
Solutions Thru Technology
Technology Advisory Services

Financial Advisory Services
Business reorganization services
Corporate financial services
Litigation and claims services
Real estate services
Hospitality services

Human Resource Advisory
Communication services
Health care consulting
Human resource management
Human resource technology
Organizational effectiveness and development
Retirement plans
Total compensation services

Tax
Entertainment (Gelfand, Rennert & Feldman)
International tax services
Multistate tax services
Tax process management
Tax technology services
Wealth preservation services

KEY COMPETITORS

Alexander & Alexander
Arthur Andersen
Arthur D. Little
Bain & Co.
Booz, Allen
Boston Consulting
Deloitte & Touche
Delta Consulting
EDS
Ernst & Young
Gemini Consulting
Grant Thornton
H&R Block
Hewitt Associates
IBM
KPMG
Marsh & McLennan
McKinsey & Co.
Price Waterhouse
Towers Perrin
Wyatt Co.

HOW MUCH

	Annual Growth	1986	1987	1988	1989	1990	1991	1992	1993	1994	1995
Sales ($ mil.)	14.9%	1,780	2,076	2,520	2,977	4,136	4,959	5,350	5,220	5,542	6,200
Offices	4.0%	531	550	580	602	710	735	733	740	758	755
Partners	1.3%	—	—	—	—	—	—	—	5,091	5,243	5,228
Employees	6.9%	38,520	41,134	45,486	50,636	63,300	67,175	66,600	66,300	68,360	70,500

1995 Year-end:
Sales per partner:
$1,185,922

Sales ($ mil.)
1986–95

Coopers
&Lybrand

CPC INTERNATIONAL INC.

OVERVIEW

US sales may be sluggish for CPC, but the rest of the world has developed a taste for great American products like Skippy peanut butter. CPC is a consumer foods giant with over 1,700 trademark brands that include Skippy, Knorr soups, and Hellmann's and Best Foods mayonnaise. (Mayonnaise, in fact, accounted for over 11% of the company's sales in 1994.)

Globalization has been a major focus of CPC for over a quarter century; over 64% of its 1994 sales came from foreign markets. In recent years CPC has engaged in more than 20 foreign start-ups, acquisitions, and joint ventures, including new subsidiaries in China, eastern Europe, and Russia. In 1995 it bought Lesieur, one of France's top salad dressing makers.

CPC is a major corn refiner with operations in 17 countries. It produces Mazola corn oil, Karo corn syrup, and a variety of cornstarches, as well as ethanol for fuel. After severe flooding dampened the corn refining segment's business in 1993, new products and supplier relationships boosted 1994 sales. Analysts blame CPC's continuing domestic sales slump on a growing awareness of dietary fat. The company is countering with such new products as low-fat mayonnaise and reduced-fat peanut butter.

Acquisitions should also sweeten the company's domestic growth. In 1995 CPC agreed to acquire the bakery unit of Kraft (a subsidiary of Philip Morris), including the Entenmann's and Oroweat brands.

WHEN

In 1842 Thomas Kingsford developed a technique for separating starch from corn, and by 1890 the corn refining industry had emerged. Competition forced 20 cornstarch and syrup producers to band together as National Starch Manufacturing. The group established quotas and gained 70% of the cornstarch market, but their pool broke down and ruinous pricing competition resumed.

This pattern was typical of the unstable corn refining industry for the next decade. By 1906 price competition had forced Edward Bedford's New York Glucose to merge with Glucose Sugar Refining Company, of which National Starch was by then a part, forming Corn Products Refining Company. CPRC became the first stable corn refining company by improving refinery equipment and processes. In 1906 CPRC controlled 64% of the starch and 100% of the glucose output in the US.

For the first half of this century CPRC dominated corn refining, eliciting several antitrust actions. In 1916 Judge Learned Hand forced CPRC's eventual sale of portions of its business. In 1922 CPRC faced antitrust charges in connection with Karo syrup; the charges were dismissed. Between 1940 and 1942 the FTC filed antitrust charges against CPRC for "phantom freight" prices; to control prices, CPRC charged for shipping from places other than the actual point of origin. Removing phantom freight (1945) reduced industry concentration; by 1954 CPRC had only a 46% share of corn-grinding capacity.

Although the company produced some branded products (Mazola, Karo, Argo, and Kingsford's), CPRC remained largely a corn refinery until 1958. That year the company

merged with Best Foods, makers of Best Foods, Hellmann's, Rit, and Skippy brands, and bought C. H. Knorr (soups). During the 1960s CPRC bought 4 educational companies — MIND, the best known of these, made remedial training systems to improve workers' skills — but sold them all by 1980.

In 1969 the company was renamed CPC International to emphasize its international expansion. CPC bought S. B. Thomas (English muffins, 1969), C. F. Mueller (pasta, 1983), and Arnold Foods (crackers, 1986).

In 1986 CPC thwarted a takeover attempt by financier Ronald Perelman (MacAndrews & Forbes) and sold Bosco brand chocolate syrup.

Since 1988 CPC has spent nearly $1 billion to acquire over 50 companies, including Ambrosia (desserts, UK), Conimex (oriental foods, the Netherlands), Milwaukee Seasonings, and Fearn International (soups and sauces, US). In 1993 the company acquired Pfanni potato products, the largest such company in Europe, as well as new businesses in Costa Rica, Turkey, Denmark, and the Czech Republic.

In 1994 CPC began a 2-year restructuring program aimed at cutting costs. The plan includes consolidation of the company's North American and European operations and reduction of its work force. That same year CPC and General Mills formed a joint venture to market baking and dessert mixes in Latin America.

Also in 1994 CPC and Mexico-based Arancia formed a joint venture for corn refining. CPC CEO Charles Shoemate has targeted the company's Latin American business for expansion; development of a high-fructose corn syrup market in Mexico is one goal of the Arancia agreement.

NYSE symbol: CPC
Fiscal year ends: December 31

Chairman, President, and CEO: Charles R. Shoemate, age 55, $1,201,667 pay
EVP: Robert J. Gillespie, age 52, $668,750 pay
EVP; President, CPC Europe Division: Alain Labergère, age 60, $582,500 pay
SVP and General Counsel: Clifford B. Storms, age 62, $529,583 pay
SVP and CFO: Konrad Schlatter, age 59, $502,500 pay
President, Best Foods Grocery Products Group, Best Foods Division: Lawrence K. Hathaway
President, CPC Latin America Consumer Foods Division: Gordon F. Granger
President, Corn Refining Business: Bernard H. Kastory
VP; President, Best Foods Division: Axel Krauss, age 50
VP Human Resources: Richard P. Bergeman, age 56
Auditors: KPMG Peat Marwick LLP

WHERE

HQ: International Plaza, PO Box 8000, Englewood Cliffs, NJ 07632-9976
Phone: 201-894-4000
Fax: 201-894-2186

CPC has 27 operating plants in the US, 8 in Canada, 42 in Europe, 20 in Africa and the Middle East, 32 in Latin America, and 14 in Asia.

	1994 Sales		1994 Operating Income	
	$ mil.	% of total	$ mil.	% of total
Europe	2,933	40	181	25
North America	2,907	39	344	46
Latin America	1,273	17	166	22
Asia	312	4	49	7
Adjustments	—	—	(28)	—
Total	**7,425**	**100**	**712**	**100**

WHAT

	1994 Sales		1994 Operating Income	
	$ mil.	% of total	$ mil.	% of total
Consumer foods	6,203	84	552	75
Corn refining	1,222	16	188	25
Adjustments	—	—	(28)	—
Total	**7,425**	**100**	**712**	**100**

Major Brand Names

Baked Goods	Maizena	**Mayonnaise**
Arnold	Polly	Best Foods
Bran'nola	Vitamilho	Hellmann's
Brownberry		Telma
Sahara	**Desserts**	
Thomas'	Alsa	**Pasta**
	Ambrosia	Mueller's
Corn Oil	Yabon	Napolina
Mazola		Royal
	Dressings	
Corn Syrup	Henri's	**Peanut Butter**
Karo	Western	Lady's Choice
		Skippy
Cornstarch	**Jams**	
Argo	Fruco	**Soups, Sauces,**
Arrozina	Mateus	**and Bouillons**
Cremogema	Santa Rosa	Knorr
Kingsford's		Pfanni

KEY COMPETITORS

ADM	Danone	Nestlé
American	General Mills	PepsiCo
Brands	George Weston	Philip Morris
Associated Milk	Grand	Quaker Oats
Producers	Metropolitan	RJR Nabisco
Borden	Heinz	Sara Lee
Campbell Soup	Hershey	Tate & Lyle
Cargill	Hormel	TLC Beatrice
Chiquita Brands	Interstate Baking	Unilever
ConAgra	J.M. Smucker	
Continental	Mars	
Grain	Monsanto	

HOW MUCH

	Annual Growth	1985	1986	1987	1988	1989	1990	1991	1992	1993	1994
Sales ($ mil.)	6.5%	4,210	4,549	4,903	4,700	5,103	5,781	6,189	6,599	6,738	7,425
Net income ($ mil.)	10.4%	142	219	355	289	328	374	373	384	454	345
Income as % of sales	—	3.4%	4.8%	7.2%	6.2%	6.4%	6.5%	6.0%	5.8%	6.8%	4.6%
Earnings per share ($)	13.3%	0.73	1.15	2.17	1.84	2.11	2.42	2.40	2.47	2.95	2.25
Stock price – high ($)	—	13.31	22.13	29.25	29.19	36.88	42.38	46.75	51.63	51.13	55.63
Stock price – low ($)	—	9.56	11.63	13.00	19.75	24.69	31.00	36.00	39.75	39.88	44.25
Stock price – close ($)	17.2%	12.75	19.81	20.25	25.94	36.88	41.63	45.25	50.63	47.63	53.25
P/E – high	—	18	19	14	16	18	18	20	21	17	25
P/E – low	—	13	10	6	11	12	13	15	16	14	20
Dividends per share ($)	10.8%	0.55	0.55	0.62	0.74	0.85	0.98	1.08	1.18	1.28	1.38
Book value per share ($)	4.6%	7.05	5.79	6.81	7.62	6.73	8.30	9.46	9.72	10.45	10.60
Employees	1.1%	38,000	38,700	31,400	32,137	33,500	35,542	35,000	38,000	39,000	41,900

1994 Year-end:
Debt ratio: 49.8%
Return on equity: 44.4%
Cash (mil.): $125
Current ratio: 1.06
Long-term debt (mil.): $879
No. of shares (mil.): 146.7
Dividends
  Yield: 2.6%
  Payout: 61.3%
Market value (mil.): $7,813

Stock Price History
High/Low 1985–94

DEAN WITTER, DISCOVER & CO.

OVERVIEW

Dean Witter, Discover's watchwords are Profit and Growth. And the company, which was spun off from Allstate Insurance in 1993, pursues its goals with a combination of strict cost controls and market expansion.

The New York–based company's business is almost evenly balanced between its consumer credit operations — the Discover Card — and the financial services it offers through its Dean Witter Reynolds brokerage and investment banking operations.

The Discover Card was launched in 1986 by Sears in an attempt to build a financial services empire. The card's gimmick, cash back on purchases, helped it gain acceptance with 43 million users and an increasing number of merchants — including, as of 1995, the US Postal Service. This unit also includes credit transaction processing for private label cards, home mortgage and equity loans, and a co-branded (with NationsBank) MasterCard, the Prime Option card.

The other half of the business, Dean Witter Reynolds, engages in brokerage, mutual fund sales and management, investment advice, and investment banking. The company also has agreements with Allstate and ITT Hartford to sell their annuity products to its patrons.

WHEN

Dean Witter founded a brokerage in San Francisco in 1924. Witter, a broker of the old school, believed that serving his customers was a sacred trust and managed the firm accordingly for more than 40 years. The firm remained strongly regional, serving primarily wealthy retail customers.

In 1977 the company, under the leadership of Andrew Melton, merged with another regional, primarily retail, brokerage, Reynolds Securities International. Reynolds had been started by Richard Reynolds Jr., son of the founder of Reynolds Metals and grandnephew of the founder of Reynolds Tobacco company.

Melton hoped that the addition of Reynolds, whose retail offices did not compete with Dean Witter's, would provide a springboard for growing the company's investment banking activities. The newly combined company, Dean Witter Reynolds, became the US's 2nd largest brokerage (although it remained based in San Francisco) after Merrill Lynch, with more than 3,550 brokers.

The company then proceeded to transform itself into a full-service financial institution, building up its investment banking and block trading businesses. To do so, it lured brokers and traders away from other firms by offering top-dollar salaries.

In the late 1970s and early 1980s, the US economy was in trouble, interest rates were high, and banks and financial services companies needed new sources of capital. For Dean Witter, that source was Sears, which acquired Dean Witter (then one of the top 10 US investment firms) in 1981. Sears wanted to diversify into financial services and to make Dean Witter into a financial Allstate: an in-store, one-stop shopping center for Middle America's financial and investment needs. It was an ambition that contrasted with Dean Witter's recent successful effort to become a major underwriter. Sears replaced Melton with Robert Gardiner, who was oriented toward retail operations. It also cut staff and costs at Dean Witter in an effort to tailor the firm to fit into its stores. The apparent lack of interest of Sears's management in the investment side led to further staff reductions through resignations and hurt Dean Witter's investment operations, dragging down results.

In 1986 Sears and Dean Witter introduced the Discover Card, which was an almost instant success. Within a year Dean Witter was restructured and on an even keel again; even its investment business picked up.

But by the end of the 1980s, it was obvious that Sears was not going to be a financial giant — it was not even certain that it was going to continue to be a retail giant. Strapped for cash, it sold Allstate, Coldwell Banker, and the newly renamed Dean Witter, Discover.

Dean Witter and NationsBank entered into a brokerage joint venture, NationsSecurities, in 1992, but differences over sales policies led to the breakup of the venture in 1994. Dean Witter, Discover continues to provide services to NationsBank.

The company has fought a long battle to be allowed to issue Visa cards and MasterCards. It received permission (but only in partnership with NationsBank) to issue a MasterCard, Prime Option, in 1993. Access to Visa was denied in 1995, when the US Supreme Court let stand a lower court ruling that Visa's denial of the right to issue cards did not constitute a violation of the Sherman Antitrust Act. Dean Witter had hoped to gain access to the larger merchant base and overseas recognition enjoyed by the 2 major card consortia.

NYSE symbol: DWD
Fiscal year ends: December 31

WHO

Chairman and CEO: Philip J. Purcell, age 51, $2,700,000 pay
EVP; President and COO, Dean Witter Capital: Richard M. DeMartini, age 42, $1,760,000 pay
EVP; President and COO, Dean Witter Financial: James F. Higgins, age 46, $1,756,000 pay
EVP; President and COO, Discover Card Services: Thomas R. Butler, age 52, $770,000 pay
EVP and CFO: Thomas C. Schneider, age 57, $1,043,000 pay
EVP and Chief Administrative Officer: Mitchell M. Merin, age 41
EVP, General Counsel, and Secretary: Christine A. Edwards, age 42
SVP Human Resources: Michael Cunningham
Auditors: Deloitte & Touche LLP

WHERE

HQ: 2 World Trade Center, New York, NY 10048
Phone: 212-392-2222
Fax: 212-392-3118

Dean Witter, Discover has 353 offices nationwide, staffed by 8,044 brokers.

WHAT

	1994 Sales		1994 Pretax income	
	$ mil.	% of total	$ mil.	% of total
Credit services	3,460	52	672	45
Securities services	3,143	48	543	55
Total	**6,603**	**100**	**1,215**	**100**

	1994 Sales	
	$ mil.	% of total
Interest	2,507	38
Asset management fees	973	15
Merchant & cardmember fees	940	14
Commissions	874	13
Servicing fees	587	9
Principal transactions	422	6
Investment banking	198	3
Other	102	2
Total	**6,603**	**100**

Services
Asset management
Brokerage services
Consumer credit services
Home equity loans
Information processing
Insurance services
Investment banking
Mutual funds
Trust services

Selected Subsidiaries
Dean Witter InterCapital, Inc.
Dean Witter Realty, Inc.
Dean Witter Reynolds, Inc.
Demeter Management Corp.
Discover Card
Greenwood Trust Company
NOVUS Financial Corp.
Prime Option Services
SPS Transaction Services, Inc. (74%)

KEY COMPETITORS

A. G. Edwards
Alex. Brown
Allstate Financial
American Express
Bear Stearns
Beneficial
Brown Brothers Harriman
Charles Schwab
Chase Manhattan
Citicorp
Countrywide Credit
Donaldson Lufkin & Jenrette
Edward Jones
FMR

Goldman Sachs
Hambrecht & Quist
Household International
Lehman Brothers
MasterCard
Merrill Lynch
Morgan Stanley
Nomura Securities
Paine Webber
Quick & Reilly
Salomon
T. Rowe Price
Transamerica
Travelers
USAA
Visa

HOW MUCH

	Annual Growth	1985	1986	1987	1988	1989	1990	1991	1992	1993	1994
Sales ($ mil.)	10.0%	—	—	—	3,733	3,942	4,506	4,882	5,184	5,822	6,603
Net income ($ mil.)	43.2%	—	—	—	86	166	233	345	439	604	741
Income as % of sales		—	—	—	2.3%	4.2%	5.2%	7.1%	8.5%	10.4%	11.2%
Earnings per share ($)	30.1%	—	—	—	—	—	—	—	2.57	3.54	4.35
Stock price – high ($)	—	—	—	—	—	—	—	—	—	46.50	43.13
Stock price – low ($)	—	—	—	—	—	—	—	—	—	30.63	31.50
Stock price – close ($)	(2.2%)	—	—	—	—	—	—	—	—	34.63	33.88
P/E – high		—	—	—	—	—	—	—	—	13	10
P/E – low		—	—	—	—	—	—	—	—	8	7
Dividends per share ($)	66.7%	—	—	—	—	—	—	—	—	0.30	0.50
Book value per share ($)	19.3%	—	—	—	—	—	—	—	—	20.38	24.32
Employees	7.2%	—	—	—	—	—	—	—	—	26,564	28,475

1994 Year-end:
Debt ratio: 75.6%
Return on equity: 19.5%
Cash (mil.): $2,829
Long-term debt (mil.): $5,293
No. of shares (mil.): 169
Dividends
  Yield: 1.5%
  Payout: 11.5%
Market value (mil.): $5,721
Assets (mil.): $31,859

Stock Price History
High/Low 1993–94

DELOITTE TOUCHE TOHMATSU

OVERVIEW

In the daredevil new world of Big 6 accounting, Deloitte Touche Tohmatsu has won some and lost some — court cases, that is. The cases have arisen from the growing tendency to hold auditors responsible for the performances of the entities they audit. In the win column is the case in which Torrance, California, tried to hold the firm responsible for its investment losses. In the loss column, at least for now, is the $81.3 million judgment relating to the 1990 bankruptcy of Jacksonville, Florida–based Koger Properties, an audit client. Also in the losses column was the $312 million that the firm paid the US government in 1994 to settle malpractice cases arising from the S&L crisis of the 1980s.

Deloitte Touche Tohmatsu is the product of the 1989 merger of Deloitte Haskins & Sells and Touche Ross (whose Japanese affiliate's name, Ross Tohmatsu, rounds out the firm's name). In an industry that is becoming globally consolidated, the latter union gave the firm a truly international outlook. It still operates as Deloitte & Touche in the US.

Since the firm's original business, auditing, has become more driven by price rather than relationship, Deloitte Touche has branched into consulting and has grown by acquisitions.

In 1995 the firm began to revamp its operations, adopting a regional structure that is intended to make the firm more responsive to clients with far-flung operations.

WHEN

In 1845 William Welch Deloitte opened an accounting office in London. Deloitte's grandfather, Count de Loitte, had fled France during the Reign of Terror (1793–94) and supported himself by teaching French.

At first Deloitte, a former staff member of the Official Assignee in Bankruptcy of the City of London, solicited business from bankrupts. The development of joint stock companies in the mid-19th century fueled the rise of accounting in the UK (and in the US) because of the need for standardized financial reporting. Deloitte moved into the new field.

As the firm grew, it added partners, among them John Griffiths (1869). Griffiths visited the US in 1888, and in 1890 the firm opened a branch on Wall Street. Other branches followed in Cincinnati (1905), Chicago (1912), Montreal (1912), Boston (1930), and Los Angeles (1945). In 1952 the Deloitte firm formed an alliance with the accounting firm of Haskins & Sells, which operated 34 US offices.

Deloitte developed a reputation as a thorough, and therefore expensive, firm. Its aim was to be "the Cadillac, not the Ford" of accounting, but the firm, which became Deloitte Haskins & Sells in 1978, began to lose its conservatism as competition for auditing contracts and for management consulting clients became more intense. When the profession relaxed its restrictions on advertising, Deloitte Haskins & Sells was the first Big 8 firm with aggressive ads extolling its virtues.

In 1984, in a move that foreshadowed the merger mania to come, Deloitte Haskins & Sells tried to merge with Price Waterhouse. However, British partners in Price Waterhouse objected to the deal, and it was dropped.

In the US the Big 8 accounting firms became the Big 6 in 1989. Ernst & Whinney merged with Arthur Young to become Ernst & Young and the staid Deloitte Haskins & Sells teamed up with flamboyant Touche Ross to form Deloitte & Touche. Touche Ross was founded in New York in 1947 and had a reputation as the hard-charging, bare-knuckled bad boy of the Big 8. The merger was engineered by Deloitte's Michael Cook and Touche's Edward Kangas in part to unite the former firm's US and European strengths with the latter firm's Asian presence (Cook continues to oversee US operations and Kangas presides over international operations). But many affiliates, particularly in the UK, objected to the merger and defected to competing firms. In 1992 California regulators sued Deloitte & Touche, claiming that it had been the "auditor of choice" of a "daisy chain" linking Drexel Burnham junk-bond king Michael Milken to failed Executive Life. More legal grief came to Deloitte & Touche as the RTC began a series of actions designed to recover some of the losses brought about by the 1980s' S&L debacle.

The firm has been something of a pioneer in audit technology. In 1988 it introduced the A+ Audit Software System, which was largely instrumental in automating the firm's audits. It cut audit time by about 10% (which also reduced hourly billings).

Deloitte & Touche has made a concerted effort to accommodate women, devising a "mommy track" that actually leads to partnership.

In 1995 the SEC chose Michael Sutton, the firm's national director of auditing and accounting practice, as its chief accountant.

International partnership
Fiscal year ends: August 31

WHO

Chairman and CEO, Deloitte Touche Tohmatsu International: Edward A. Kangas
COO, Deloitte Touche Tohmatsu International: J. Thomas Presby
Chairman and CEO, Deloitte & Touche LLP: J. Michael Cook
VC, Deloitte & Touche LLP: John T. Cardis
Managing Partner, Deloitte & Touche LLP: James E. Copeland Jr.
National Managing Director of Finance, Deloitte & Touche LLP: Robert W. Pivik
National Director Marketing and Communications, Deloitte & Touche LLP: Gary Gerard
General Counsel, Deloitte & Touche LLP: Howard J. Krongard
National Director Human Resources, Deloitte & Touche LLP: James H. Wall

WHERE

HQ: Deloitte Touche Tohmatsu International, 1633 Broadway, New York, NY 10019
Phone: 212-492-4000
Fax: 214-492-4001
US HQ: Deloitte & Touche LLP, 10 Westport Rd., Wilton, CT 06897-0820
Phone: 203-761-3000
Fax: 203-834-2200

Deloitte Touche Tohmatsu operates offices in more than 655 cities in 124 countries worldwide.

WHAT

Selected Services
Accounting and auditing
Information technology consulting
Management consulting
Mergers and acquisitions consulting
Tax advice and planning

Representative Clients

Bank of New York	Mayo Foundation
BASF	Merrill Lynch
Boeing	MetLife
Bridgestone	Mitsubishi
Chrysler	Mitsui
Dow Chemical	Monsanto
Flagstar	PPG
General Motors	Procter & Gamble
Great A&P	RJR Nabisco
Litton Industries	Rockwell
Lowes	Sears

Selected Affiliates
Akintola Williams & Co. (Cameroon)
Braxton Associates (US)
C. C. Chokshi & Co. (India)
D&T Corporate Finance Europe Ltd.
Deloitte & Touche Eastern Europe
Goh, Tan & Co. (Brunei)
Hans Tuanakotta & Mustofa (Indonesia)
Nautilus Indemnity Holdings Ltd. (Bermuda)
PROFIT Project (US)
Shawki & Co. (Egypt)
Tohmatsu & Co. (Japan)
Vishnu Prasad & Co. (Fiji)

KEY COMPETITORS

Apogee Research	H&R Block
Arthur Andersen	Hewitt Associates
Arthur Little	IBM
Bain & Co.	KPMG
Booz, Allen	Marsh & McLennan
Boston Consulting Group	McKinsey & Co.
Carlson	Measured Marketing
Coopers & Lybrand	Services
Delta Consulting	Price Waterhouse
EDS	Right Management
Ernst & Young	Consultants
Gemini Consulting	Towers Perrin
Grant Thornton	Wyatt Co.

HOW MUCH

	Annual Growth	1986	1987	1988	1989	1990	1991	1992	1993	1994	1995
Sales ($ mil.)	11.0%	2,339	2,950	3,760	3,900	4,200	4,500	4,800	5,000	5,200	5,950
Deloitte Haskins & Sells	—	1,188	1,500	1,920	—	—	—	—	—	—	—
Touche Ross	—	1,151	1,450	1,840	—	—	—	—	—	—	—
Offices[1]	14.3%	205	195	196	126	630	647	647	653	655	680
Partners[1]	13.0%	1,600	1,590	1,600	1,652	4,900	4,700	4,600	4,600	4,600	4,650
Employees[1]	14.4%	17,521	18,252	19,276	19,668	59,700	56,000	56,000	56,000	56,600	59,000

Deloitte & Touche

Sales ($ mil.) 1986–95

[1] US only 1985–89

DIME BANCORP, INC.

OVERVIEW

A shiny new dime was minted in New York in 1995 — Dime Bancorp. The new Dime, the US's 4th largest thrift (and the largest based outside California), is the product of the merger of Dime Bancorp and Anchor Bancorp. Although both banks catered to a working- and middle-class clientele, the merger, which doubled Dime's size, allowed it to compete with banks like Chase Manhattan and Citicorp in such areas as commercial and business loans. It also positions it to become the area's preeminent bank for small businesses and middle-class and blue-collar consumers. This market is largely ignored by the mega-banks, which are more concerned with national and international operations and with competing for the patronage of wealthy individuals.

That the 2 survived to merge at all was noteworthy, as both were hit hard in the late 1980s and early 1990s, and both operated under regulatory supervision for years.

Dime and Anchor merged in order to realize the savings associated with consolidation (estimated at about $50 million and the reduction of about 500 jobs) of their overlapping operations. One of the merger's architects, Richard Parsons, was named president of Time Warner. He was replaced as chairman and CEO by Anchor's CEO, James Large. Dime was the surviving entity in the merger, and other Dime personnel have gained key positions in the new company.

The new Dime is expanding the variety of products it offers (in hopes of increasing fee-based income) in order to gain market share in the New York area by acquisitions and to diversify geographically by expanding its mortgage banking activities. In 1995 Dime agreed to acquire National Mortgage Investments, of Griffin, Georgia, and the mortgage origination business of First Commonwealth Savings Bank, of Alexandria, Virginia.

WHEN

Dime was founded in 1859 by William Edwards as a bank "for the common people," an institution where people could save money dime by dime (the bank's minimum deposit). In the Civil War, Dime pioneered banking by mail, allowing Union soldiers to deposit their pay. It remained a community bank serving the middle and working classes through wars and depressions. Dime vastly increased its size in 1949 by acquiring 42,000 loans from the New York State Home Owners Association. In 1951, as the suburbs developed, it opened a branch in Nassau County.

The number of branches increased to 11 by 1978 after several mergers and acquisitions, but Dime's real growth came in the 1980s, when thrifts were deregulated in response to soaring interest rates. Deregulation let thrifts make both larger and commercial loans. Dime went crazy, making low documentation loans. Among the information that was newly optional was the proof that the borrower could actually afford the monthly payments. As the economy turned down, loan defaults rose, reaching 10.8% of total assets shortly after the arrival in 1988 of Richard Parsons as president. He had no banking experience but had worked with Dime's chairman, Harry Albright, on Nelson Rockefeller's staff. Parsons rose to the challenge, turning Dime around by beefing up underwriting standards, managing or selling bad loans, cutting branches and staff, and outsourcing operations. In 1992 the bank

returned to the black for the first time since 1989. The low interest rates of 1993 returned Dime to profitability, and sales increased rapidly despite the interest rate hikes of 1994, when it began merger talks with Anchor.

Anchor Bancorp was founded in Brooklyn in 1869 as the Bay Ridge Savings Bank. It became the institution of choice for sailors serving New York's growing shipping industry. (This clientele was reflected in the anchor motif of the windows of its main office.) In 1926 Bay Ridge became the first New York to open a branch. Because of the Depression and WWII, it would be 40 years before the bank opened another. In 1968, seeking a less localized image, Bay Ridge changed its name to Anchor and in 1969 made its first acquisition. More followed in the 1970s and 1980s. Many were outside New York City and some were out of state. Anchor acquired several banks in Georgia and Florida, buying 13 S&Ls between 1981 and 1986 and moving into mortgages. Then came the real estate crash and new capital regulations, which raised defaults and forced the company to adopt tough new capital reserve standards.

Suddenly under-reserved and in the red, Anchor sold assets, first its out-of-state branches and then mortgage operations. Back in the black by 1992, Anchor aimed to gain market share. The Dime merger helped achieve this goal by making the new company one of the largest in the New York area.

WHO

Chairman and CEO: James M. Large Jr., age 62
President and COO: Lawrence J. Toal, age 57,
$535,000 pay
General Manager, Mortgage Banking: Jenne K. Britell,
age 52, $337,500 pay
General Manager, Consumer Banking Services: Cody T.
Sickle, age 45
General Counsel: Gene C. Brooks
Principal Financial Executive: John V. Brull, age 55
Treasurer and Asset/Liability Executive: D. James
Daras, age 41
External Affairs and Investor Relations Executive:
Franklin L. Wright
**Chief Human Resources Officer, Dime Savings Bank of
New York, FSB:** Arthur C. Bennett
Auditors: KPMG Peat Marwick LLP

WHERE

HQ: 598 Fifth Ave., New York, NY 10017
Phone: 212-326-6170
Fax: 212-326-6169

Dime Bancorp operates 85 retail branches in the
metropolitan New York area.

WHAT

	1994 Sales	
	$ mil.	% of total
Loans	427	65
Other interest	187	29
Service fees & charges	34	5
Other	4	1
Total	**652**	**100**

	1994 Assets	
	$ mil.	% of total
Cash & equivalents	80	1
Mortgage-backed securities	1,214	12
Collateralized mortgage obligations	1,723	17
State & municipal bonds	111	1
Other investments	283	3
Net loans	6,072	61
Other	513	5
Total	**9,996**	**100**

Selected Services
Business lending
Commercial real estate lending
Consumer banking
Insurance and securities brokerage services
Mortgage banking
Mortgage servicing
Portfolio investment

KEY COMPETITORS

Astoria Financial
Bank of New York
BFS Bankorp
Brooklyn Bancorp
Chase Manhattan
Citicorp
Commerical Bank of New York
First of Long Island
Gateway Bancorp
Greater New York Savings
Long Island Bancorp
Merchants Bank of New York
New York Bancorp.
North Fork Bancorporation
Queens County Bancorp
Reliance Bancorp
Republic New York
Sterling Bancorp
Suffolk Bancorp

HOW MUCH

	Annual Growth	1985	1986	1987	1988	1989	1990	1991	1992	1993	1994
Assets ($ mil.)	2.3%	8,151	8,367	10,944	12,007	11,652	10,842	9,898	8,773	9,276	9,996
Net income ($ mil.)	36.2%	5	85	70	46	(90)	(136)	(237)	10	45	84
Income as % of assets	—	0.1%	1.0%	0.65%	0.4%	—	—	—	0.1%	0.5%	0.8%
Earnings per share ($)	20.8%	0.27	3.77	3.08	2.00	(3.94)	(5.94)	(10.27)	0.44	0.93	1.48
Stock price – high ($)	—	—	18.25	26.38	21.25	17.75	10.75	6.75	7.38	10.50	10.75
Stock price – low ($)	—	—	14.13	12.88	12.00	8.75	2.13	1.19	3.13	5.75	7.38
Stock price – close ($)	(10.1%)	—	18.13	16.25	14.00	10.25	2.38	3.38	5.88	8.13	7.75
P/E – high	—	—	5	9	11	—	—	—	17	11	7
P/E – low	—	—	4	4	6	—	—	—	7	6	5
Dividends per share ($)	—	—	0.00	0.00	0.15	0.60	0.45	0.00	0.00	0.00	0.00
Book value per share ($)	(10.9%)	—	25.18	29.47	31.97	27.66	21.12	11.11	11.41	10.37	9.98
Employees	(8.6%)	—	3,500	4,100	3,300	2,640	2,338	2,345	2,214	2,345	1,700

1994 Year-end:
Equity as % of assets: 5.7%
Return on equity: 14.5%
Return on assets: 0.9%
Long-term debt (mil.): $231
No. of shares (mil.): 57
Dividends
  Yield: —
  Payout: —
Market value (mil.): $441
Sales (mil.): $652

**Stock Price History
High/Low 1986–94**

DOVER CORPORATION

OVERVIEW

Sales are going up at Dover Corp. The conglomerate is best known as a manufacturer of elevators, but there are more than 60 companies under the Dover umbrella, making everything from garbage trucks to manhole covers to pizza ovens. About 17% of the corporation's sales come from outside the US.

Dover has 5 business segments: Dover Elevator International is the US's 2nd largest elevator manufacturer (after Otis); Dover Industries makes products for the automotive service, bulk transport, commercial food service, machine tool, and waste-handling industries; Dover Resources produces equipment for the automotive, fuel handling, and petroleum industries; Dover Technologies International makes automated electronics assembly equipment; and Dover Diversified makes industrial assembly and production machinery, compressors, and heat transfer equipment.

Dover's unique corporate culture is often given credit for its success. The corporation's headquarters has a staff of only 22 and limits its role to providing corporate strategy, financial resources, and legal support. Each division has its own president and board of directors.

Dover is acquisition-driven; in 1994 it spent $188 million to buy 10 niche-market manufacturers. The corporation looks for small, low-tech companies that lead their industry. When Dover buys a company (usually for cash), it often leaves existing management in place, encouraging independent, aggressive growth.

Magalen Bryant, whose father founded Dover, owns more than 6% of the company's stock and is a company director.

WHEN

George Ohrstrom, a New York stockbroker, formed Dover Corp. in 1955 and took the corporation public that year. Dover, originally headquartered in Washington, DC, consisted of 4 companies: C. Lee Cook (compressor seals and piston rings), Peerless (space-venting heaters), Rotary Lift (automotive lifts), and W.C. Norris (components for oil wells). In 1958 Dover made the first of many acquisitions and entered the elevator industry when it bought Shepard Warner Elevator.

Through the 1960s Dover continued to diversify via acquisitions. In 1961 it bought OPW, a maker of gas pump nozzles. The following year it acquired De-Sta-Co, a producer of industrial clamps and valves. In 1964 OPW head Thomas Sutton became Dover's president. That same year the company moved its headquarters to New York City. Dover acquired Groen Manufacturing (food industry products) in 1967 and Ronningen-Petter (filter-strainer units) in 1968.

During the 1970s Dover expanded beyond its core industries (building materials, industrial components and equipment, and petroleum industry equipment). In 1975 it acquired Dieterich Standard, a maker of liquid measurement instruments. Dieterich Standard's president, Gary Roubos, became Dover's president and COO in 1977 and CEO in 1981. The company sold Peerless in 1977 and acquired Universal Instruments, a maker of electronics assembly equipment, in 1979.

During the 1980s electronics became an increasingly important part of Dover's business. In 1983 it acquired K&L Microwave, a maker of microwave filters used in satellite communications and cable TV equipment.

Between 1985 and 1990 Dover bought some 25 companies. Among those were Weldcraft Products (1985, welding equipment), Dielectric Laboratories (1985, microwave filter parts), NURAD (1986, microwave antennae), Wolfe Frostop (1987, salad bars), Weaver Corp. (1987, automotive lifts), General Elevator (1988), Texas Hydraulics (1988), Security Elevator (1990), and Marathon Equipment (1990, waste handling equipment). In 1989 Roubos became the company's chairman.

In 1992 Dover acquired 2 foreign elevator companies, Christian Hein GmbH of Germany and Deya Elevator Service of Puerto Rico.

The corporation spun off its DOVatron circuit board assembly subsidiary (formerly Dover Electronics Co.) to shareholders in 1993 after finding that DOVatron was competing with important Dover customers. Also in 1993 the company acquired Heil, a manufacturer of refuse trucks and trailerized tanks. That same year Dover Resources head Thomas Reece became Dover's president and COO.

Dover acquired 10 companies in 1994, including Hill Refrigeration (commercial refrigeration cases), Koolrad Design & Manufacturing (Canada, radiators for transformers), and Transmission Networks International (specialty transformers), plus certain assets of Mid-State Elevator. Reece became CEO that year.

In 1995 Dover negotiated 4 joint ventures for elevator installations in China. That same year the corporation acquired AT&T's Frequency Control Products division.

NYSE symbol: DOV
Fiscal year ends: December 31

WHO

Chairman: Gary L. Roubos, age 58, $750,000 pay
President and CEO: Thomas L. Reece, age 52,
$850,000 pay
VP; President, Dover Industries: Lewis E. Burns, age 56,
$640,000 pay
VP; President, Dover Diversified: Jerry W. Yochum,
age 56, $585,000 pay
VP Finance and Treasurer: John F. McNiff, age 52,
$560,000 pay
VP; President, Dover Resources: Rudolf J. Herrmann,
age 44, $550,000 pay
VP; President, Dover Technologies International: John
E. Pomeroy, age 53, $550,000 pay
VP; President, Dover Elevator International: John B.
Apple, age 60, $540,000 pay
Auditors: KMPG Peat Marwick LLP

WHERE

HQ: 280 Park Ave., New York, NY 10017
Phone: 212-922-1640
Fax: 212-922-1656

WHAT

	1994 Sales		1994 Operating Income	
	$ mil.	% of total	$ mil.	% of total
Dover Elevator	793	26	46	13
Dover Industries	691	22	81	23
Dover Technologies	603	20	76	21
Dover Resources	526	17	84	24
Dover Diversified	473	15	67	19
Adjustments	(1)	—	(47)	—
Total	**3,085**	**100**	**307**	**100**

Selected Subsidiaries

Dover Diversified, Inc.
A-C Compressor (compressors)
Belvac (canning equipment)
Thermal Equipment (autoclaves, industrial cleaning
equipment, medical waste treatment)

Dover Elevator International, Inc.
Dover Elevator Co. (elevator sales and installation)
Dover Elevator Systems (elevator manufacturer)
Hammond & Champness, Ltd (UK, elevator
manufacture, sales, and installation)

Dover Industries, Inc.
Bernard/Weldcraft (welding equipment)
Heil Co. (refuse collection vehicles)
Marathon Equipment (waste compaction, transporting,
and recycling equipment)
Randell (commercial refrigeration and pizza ovens)

Dover Resources, Inc.
Duncan Parking Systems (parking control products)
Norris (oil well components and servicing equipment)
OPW Fueling Components (gasoline nozzles and valves)
Petro Vend (key/card control systems and tank monitors)
Wittemann (carbon dioxide generation and recovery)

Dover Technologies International, Inc.
Novacap, Inc. (multilayer ceramic capacitators)
Quadrant Technologies (crystal oscillators)
Universal Instruments Corp. (automated assembly
products for printed circuit boards)

KEY COMPETITORS

American	Hitachi	Specialty
Standard	Honeywell	Equipment
Applied	Ingersoll-Rand	Teleflex
Materials	Keystone	Textron
Cawsl	International	TRW
Crawford	LG Group	United
Fitting	Mitsubishi	Technologies
FMC Corp.	Moog	Watkins-
General	Praxair	Johnson
Electric	Premark	Westinghouse
Handy & Harman	Siemens	Whitman

HOW MUCH

	Annual Growth	1985	1986	1987	1988	1989	1990	1991	1992	1993	1994
Sales ($ mil.)	8.8%	1,440	1,440	1,586	1,954	2,120	2,210	2,196	2,272	2,484	3,085
Net income ($ mil.)	8.1%	100	84	112	146	144	156	128	129	158	202
Income as % of sales	—	6.9%	5.8%	7.0%	7.5%	6.8%	7.0%	5.8%	5.7%	6.4%	6.6%
Earnings per share ($)	10.7%	1.42	1.21	1.66	2.22	2.28	2.55	2.15	2.23	2.77	3.54
Stock price – high ($)	—	22.00	24.25	38.94	36.63	39.50	41.25	43.75	47.63	61.88	66.88
Stock price – low ($)	—	16.06	18.50	21.88	26.63	27.25	27.50	34.50	38.25	45.00	49.75
Stock price – close ($)	11.0%	20.19	22.25	31.31	28.88	36.00	39.75	41.75	45.88	60.75	51.63
P/E – high	—	16	20	24	17	17	16	20	21	22	19
P/E – low	—	11	15	13	12	12	11	16	17	16	14
Dividends per share ($)	9.6%	0.43	0.45	0.51	0.62	0.70	0.76	0.82	0.86	0.90	0.98
Book value per share ($)	7.9%	8.88	9.26	10.14	11.37	12.00	13.13	14.05	14.10	15.22	17.56
Employees	4.1%	16,071	16,539	17,592	20,412	20,049	20,461	18,898	18,827	20,445	22,992

1994 Year-end:
Debt ratio: 34.2%
Return on equity: 21.7%
Cash (mil.): $90
Current ratio: 1.47
Long-term debt (mil.): $254
No. of shares (mil.): 57
Dividends
 Yield: 1.9%
 Payout: 27.7%
Market value (mil.): $2,929

**Stock Price History
High/Low 1985–94**

DOW JONES & COMPANY, INC.

OVERVIEW

Dow Jones, a multinational media company, specializes in business news and information and dispenses it in print, on-line, and by satellite, radio, TV, pager, and fax.

Dow Jones's many operations are grouped into 3 divisions. Information Services includes Dow Jones Telerate (on-line, real-time business and financial news, quotes, and analytical tools) and Dow Jones News/Retrieval (on-line business and legal news and information). Business Publications includes the company's flagship publication, the venerable daily *Wall Street Journal*; 2 companion editions, the *Asian Wall Street Journal* and the *Wall Street Journal Europe*; and the company's broadcasting operations. Dow also publishes *Barron's* (a weekly newspaper geared toward investors), the *Far Eastern Economic Review* (Asia's leading English-language weekly), and *SmartMoney* (a monthly magazine focusing on personal finance). Community Newspapers consists of the company's Ottaway Newspapers, 21 general-interest daily newspapers published in 11 states. Dow Jones also invests in information-based ventures, such as international and regional publications (*Texas Monthly* and Germany's *Handelsblatt*), newsprint mills, and satellite broadcasting (U.S. Satellite Broadcasting).

In 1994 Dow Jones began supplying foreign-language business inserts to leading newspapers in Latin America, Poland, and South Korea. It also added coverage of regional issues (*Southeast Journal* and *Florida Journal*), and moved on-line into consumer markets (eWorld and CompuServe). The company is building a worldwide business TV network, and in 1994 it began broadcasting its European Business News network from London.

Heirs of early owner Clarence Barron still own 69% of the voting interest and 47% of all the company's stock.

WHEN

Charles Dow, Edward Jones, and Charles Bergstresser, financial reporters, left the Kiernan News Agency and began Dow Jones & Company in 1882. Working out of an office next door to the NYSE, the company delivered handwritten bulletins of stock and bond trading news to subscribers in New York's financial districts. In 1883 Dow Jones started summarizing the trading day in the *Customers' Afternoon Letter*, which evolved into the *Wall Street Journal* (1889). Dow Jones offered more timely reports through its stock ticker service, acquired in 1897 from Kiernan.

Jones sold out to his partners in 1899; in 1902 Dow and Bergstresser sold the company to Clarence Barron, the company's Boston correspondent. Dow died later in 1902. *Journal* circulation grew from 7,000 in 1902 to over 50,000 in 1928, the year Barron died. In 1921 the company introduced *Barron's National Business and Financial Weekly*.

In 1941 managing editor Bernard Kilgore broadened the *Journal*'s coverage to include news summaries and in-depth business articles; he became president in 1945. By Kilgore's 1966 retirement, the *Journal* had a circulation of one million. In 1962 Dow Jones started the *National Observer*, a general-interest weekly, but the company closed it in 1977 after losing $16.2 million.

In 1975 Dow Jones began to offer same-day service to all US readers by transmitting copy via satellite to regional printing plants.

The *Journal*'s circulation began to drop after peaking in 1983, and the company turned its attention to computerized news delivery to keep pace with a changing marketplace. By the end of 1989, Dow Jones included several publications and an array of electronic news retrieval services, including Telerate, which the company had acquired through a series of stock purchases (1985–90) totaling $1.6 billion. In 1991 Telerate acquired equity interest in Minex, a Japanese consortium developing automated foreign exchange trading information. In 1992 Dow Jones and BellSouth tested a service providing telephone access to Dow Jones reports (discontinued in 1995), and the company and NYNEX entered into a venture to send video over telephone lines.

In 1993 the *Journal* began providing regional news coverage in its *Texas Journal* and introduced *SmartMoney* with Hearst Corp.

In 1994 Dow Jones joined with American City Business Journals to launch *BIZ*, a monthly magazine for small businesses (discontinued 1995). Also in 1994 the company bought a stake in direct broadcast TV (U.S. Satellite Broadcasting) and introduced the PC-based Telerate Workstation.

In 1995 the company added Japan's leading business publisher, Nikkei, to its on-line database and bought Charter Financial Publishing. With ITT Corp., it bought public TV station WNYC for $207 million; the station will become business and sports channel WBIS.

NYSE symbol: DJ
Fiscal year ends: December 31

WHO

Chairman and CEO; Publisher, *The Wall Street Journal*: Peter R. Kann, age 52, $1,050,000 pay
President and COO: Kenneth L. Burenga, age 50, $765,000 pay
SVP: Carl M. Valenti, age 56, $607,000 pay
SVP, General Counsel, and Secretary: Peter G. Skinner, age 50, $536,000 pay
SVP: James H. Ottaway Jr., age 57, $509,000 pay
VP Finance and CFO: Kevin J. Roche, age 60
VP Employee Relations: James A. Scaduto, age 40
Auditors: Coopers & Lybrand L.L.P.

WHERE

HQ: 200 Liberty St., New York, NY 10281
Phone: 212-416-2000
Fax: 212-732-8356

	1994 Sales		1994 Operating Income	
	$ mil.	% of total	$ mil.	% of total
US	1,489	71	234	62
Europe, Middle East, Africa	330	16	61	16
Asia/Pacific	225	11	78	21
Other regions	47	2	3	1
Adjustments	—	—	(18)	—
Total	**2,091**	**100**	**358**	**100**

WHAT

	1994 Sales		1994 Operating Income	
	$ mil.	% of total	$ mil.	% of total
Information services	977	47	199	53
Business publications	862	41	141	37
Community papers	252	12	36	10
Other	—	—	(18)	—
Total	**2,091**	**100**	**358**	**100**

Selected Information Services
AP-Dow Jones News Service (economic, business, and financial news wire, with the Associated Press)
Dow Jones Asian Equities Report (coverage of 12 Asian/Pacific stock markets)
Dow Jones News Service (business and financial news)
Dow Jones News/Retrieval (on-line business and financial news and information)
Dow Jones Telerate (market information)
DowVision (customized on-line news service)
Federal Filings (government and court news wire)
Personal Journal (electronic publication; personalized business news, world news, weather, and sports)
Professional Investor Report (financial news wire)
SportsTicker (20%, on-line sports information)
The Wall Street Journal Interactive Edition (extension of the *Wall Street Journal*)
The Wall Street Journal Report (radio and TV programs)

Selected Business Publications
American Demographics
The Asian Wall Street Journal (Hong Kong)
Asian Wall Street Journal Weekly (US)
Barron's
Central European Economic Review (Belgium)
Far Eastern Economic Review (Hong Kong)
National Business Employment Weekly
SmartMoney, The Wall Street Journal Magazine of Personal Business (monthly, with Hearst Corp.)
The Wall Street Journal (1,808,743 daily circulation)
The Wall Street Journal Europe (Belgium)

Community Newspapers
Ottaway Newspapers, Inc. (21 newspapers in 11 states)

KEY COMPETITORS

ADP	Investors	Reed Elsevier
America Online	Business Daily	Reuters
Bloomberg	Knight-Ridder	Times Mirror
Dun & Bradstreet	McGraw-Hill	Tribune
Forbes	Media General	Turner
Gannett	New York Times	Broadcasting
General	News Corp.	Washington Post
Electric	Pearson	Westinghouse

HOW MUCH

	Annual Growth	1985	1986	1987	1988	1989	1990	1991	1992	1993	1994
Sales ($ mil.)	8.1%	1,040	1,135	1,314	1,603	1,688	1,720	1,725	1,818	1,932	2,091
Net income ($ mil.)	3.0%	139	183	203	228	317	107	72	118	148	181
Income as % of sales	—	13.3%	16.2%	15.4%	14.2%	18.8%	6.2%	4.2%	6.5%	7.6%	8.7%
Earnings per share ($)	2.8%	1.43	1.89	2.10	2.35	3.15	1.06	0.71	1.17	1.48	1.83
Stock price – high ($)	—	33.34	42.13	56.25	36.50	42.50	33.75	30.63	35.38	39.00	41.88
Stock price – low ($)	—	24.50	28.00	28.00	26.75	29.25	18.13	21.63	24.50	26.75	28.13
Stock price – close ($)	(0.2%)	31.50	39.00	29.88	29.50	33.25	24.00	25.88	27.00	35.75	31.00
P/E – high	—	23	22	27	16	14	32	43	30	26	23
P/E – low	—	17	15	13	11	9	17	30	21	18	15
Dividends per share ($)	5.5%	0.52	0.55	0.64	0.68	0.72	0.76	0.76	0.76	0.80	0.84
Book value per share ($)	10.6%	6.21	7.52	8.77	11.95	13.94	14.23	14.21	14.41	14.91	15.33
Employees	4.5%	6,924	7,069	9,014	9,080	9,818	9,677	9,459	9,860	10,006	10,300

1994 Year-end:
Debt ratio: 16.9%
Return on equity: 12.2%
Cash (mil.): $11
Current ratio: 0.58
Long-term debt (mil.): $296
No. of shares (mil.): 96.6
Dividends
  Yield: 2.7%
  Payout: 45.9%
Market value (mil.): $2,995

**Stock Price History
High/Low 1985–94**

THE DUN & BRADSTREET CORPORATION

OVERVIEW

After decades of acquisitions that have made Dun & Bradstreet (D&B) a $4.9 billion conglomerate, the 155-year-old financial data and business services giant is splitting apart, having suffered years of lackluster earnings and weak stock prices. Its new manifestation will be 3 separate publicly traded companies.

Dun & Bradstreet Corp., headed by EVP Volney Taylor, will include the world's largest credit reporting agency, Dun & Bradstreet Information Services, which sells credit information on more than 38 million businesses in more than 30 countries; Moody's Investors Service, a leading publisher of financial information; and R. H. Donnelley, a publisher of telephone directories (*Yellow Pages*).

The financially troubled A.C. Nielsen, the world's #1 market research company, will now have to stand on its own in the face of stiffer competition. It has recently moved into Asia with the acquisition of the Survey Research Group, Asia's #1 market research information company.

D&B chairman Robert Weissman will head a new information services entity, Cognizant, which will be created with health care marketing research firm IMS International, broadcasting analyzer Nielsen Media Research, and high-tech services advisor Gartner Group.

The breakup will result in the sale of some problem operations: Dun & Bradstreet Software and American Credit Indemnity.

WHEN

Dun & Bradstreet originated in Lewis Tappan's Mercantile Agency, established in 1841 in New York City. The Mercantile Agency was one of the first commercial credit reporting agencies, and it supplied wholesalers and importers with information on their customers. Tappan's credit reporters, who prepared written reports on companies, included 4 men who became US presidents (Lincoln, Grant, Cleveland, and McKinley). In the 1840s Tappan opened offices in Boston, Philadelphia, and Baltimore and in 1857 established offices in Montreal and London. In 1859 Robert Dun took over the agency and changed its name to R.G. Dun & Co. The first edition of the *Dun's Book* (1859) contained information on 20,268 businesses; by 1886 the number had risen to over one million. John M. Bradstreet, a rival company founded in Cincinnati in 1849, merged with Dun in 1933; the company adopted the Dun & Bradstreet name in 1939.

In 1961 D&B bought Reuben H. Donnelley Corp., a direct-mail advertiser and publisher of the *Yellow Pages* (first published in 1886) and 10 trade magazines. In 1962 Moody's Investors Service (founded 1900) and Official Airline Guides (guides first published in 1929; sold in 1988) became part of D&B.

D&B's records were first computerized in the 1960s and eventually became the largest private database in the world. By 1975 the firm had a national network with a centralized database. Sales boomed when D&B created new products by repackaging information from its vast database (such as *Dun's Financial Profiles*, first published in 1979).

Since the late 1970s the company has purchased Technical Publishing (trade and professional publications, 1978), National CSS (computer services, 1979), and McCormack & Dodge (software, 1983). The addition of A.C. Nielsen (1984) and IMS International (pharmaceutical sales data, 1988) made D&B the largest marketing research company in the world. A 1987 attempt to buy Nielsen competitor Information Resources Inc. was nixed by regulators on antitrust grounds. In 1989 it bought Management Science America. That year reports surfaced that D&B was overcharging customers for credit reports; a resulting class-action suit was settled in 1994.

In 1990 D&B sold Zytron, Petroleum Information, and Neodata. In 1991 Donnelley Marketing, a direct marketer with an 85-million-household consumer information database, was sold, as were the IMS communications unit and Carol Wright Sales. D&B continued divestments in 1992, selling Datastream International and Information Associates.

Dun & Bradstreet acquired a majority interest in Gartner Group, an international market research firm, in 1993 and also formed D&B HealthCare Information to conduct health research. That same year the company introduced a restructuring program that was designed to improve efficiency in its spread-out information services businesses. It consolidated its 27 data centers worldwide to 4 automated centers and cut its headquarters staffing.

In 1994 D&B bought Pilot Software (online software) for around $35 million. In 1995 the company sold its Interactive Data Corporation unit (international financial information) to media group Pearson for $201 million.

NYSE symbol: DNB
Fiscal year ends: December 31

Chairman, President, and CEO: Robert E. Weissman,
age 54, $1,409,507 pay
**EVP; Chairman, Dun & Bradstreet Information
Services:** Volney Taylor, age 55, $973,922 pay
EVP Finance and CFO: Edwin A. Bescherer Jr., age 61,
$809,075 pay
EVP; Chairman, A.C. Nielsen Co.: Robert J. Lievense,
age 49
EVP; Chairman, IMS International: William G. Jacobi,
age 51
EVP: Dennis G. Sisco, age 48
SVP Communications and Government Affairs: Michael
F. Brewer, age 51
SVP and Controller: Thomas W. Young, age 56
SVP and General Counsel: Earl H. Doppelt, age 41
SVP Human Resources: Michael P. Connors, age 39
SVP: David Fehr, age 59
SVP: Frank R. Noonan, age 52
Auditors: Coopers & Lybrand L.L.P.

WHERE

HQ: 187 Danbury Rd., Wilton, CT 06897
Phone: 203-834-4200
Fax: 203-834-4201

	1994 Sales		1994 Operating Income	
	$ mil.	% of total	$ mil.	% of total
US	2,889	59	667	72
Europe	1,354	28	186	20
Other regions	653	13	73	8
Total	**4,896**	**100**	**926**	**100**

WHAT

	1994 Sales		1994 Operating Income	
	$ mil.	% of total	$ mil.	% of total
Marketing info. svcs.	2,043	42	285	26
Risk mgmt. & business mktg.	1,606	33	447	41
Directory info. svcs.	440	9	248	23
Software services	406	8	(4)	—
Business services	401	8	110	10
Adjustments	—	—	(160)	—
Total	**4,896**	**100**	**926**	**100**

Marketing Info. Services
IMS International (health
care market research)
A.C. Nielsen (marketing
and media research)

**Risk Mgmt. and Business
Marketing Info. Services**
Dun & Bradstreet
Information Services
(credit information and
insurance, receivables
management)
Moody's Investors Service,
Inc. (financial informa-
tion, bond rating)

Directory Info. Services
Reuben H. Donnelley

Software Services
Dun & Bradstreet Software
Services
Erisco (employee-benefits
software and services)
Pilot Software (software
solutions for online
analytical processing)
Sales Technologies (field
sales systems)

Business Services
Dataquest (high-tech
market research)
Dun & Bradstreet Pension
Services (health
insurance administration)
Gartner Group (50.6%
information technology)
NCH Promotional Services
(coupon processing)

KEY COMPETITORS

ADP	Information	PeopleSoft
American Business	Resources	Reed Elsevier
Information	M/A/R/C	Reuters
Dow Jones	McGraw-Hill	Thomson Corp.
Equifax	Morningstar	TRW
IBM	Pearson	Value Line

HOW MUCH

	Annual Growth	1985	1986	1987	1988	1989	1990	1991	1992	1993	1994
Sales ($ mil.)	6.5%	2,772	3,114	3,359	4,267	4,322	4,818	4,643	4,751	4,710	4,896
Net income ($ mil.)	8.8%	295	340	393	499	586	508	509	554	429	630
Income as % of sales	—	10.6%	10.9%	11.7%	11.7%	13.6%	10.5%	11.0%	11.7%	9.1%	12.9%
Earnings per share ($)	7.4%	1.94	2.24	2.58	2.67	3.14	2.80	2.85	3.10	2.42	3.70
Stock price – high ($)	—	43.94	60.19	71.75	57.50	60.25	48.63	58.00	59.13	68.50	64.00
Stock price – low ($)	—	31.38	40.38	44.50	45.88	41.25	36.13	39.13	50.63	55.75	51.88
Stock price – close ($)	3.1%	41.88	52.63	54.75	53.63	46.00	42.13	57.50	57.75	61.63	55.00
P/E – high	—	23	27	28	22	19	17	20	19	28	17
P/E – low	—	16	18	17	17	13	13	14	16	23	14
Dividends per share ($)	10.3%	1.06	1.24	1.45	1.68	1.94	2.09	2.15	2.25	2.40	2.56
Book value per share ($)	(1.5%)	8.92	9.79	10.95	11.18	11.80	11.65	12.11	12.10	6.53	7.77
Employees	(2.4%)	58,400	58,352	62,000	69,500	71,500	62,900	58,500	52,400	50,400	47,000

1994 Year-end:
Debt ratio: 27.5%
Return on equity: 51.8%
Cash (mil.): $362
Current ratio: 0.91
Long-term debt (mil.): $0
No. of shares (mil.): 170
Dividends
 Yield: 4.7%
 Payout: 69.2%
Market value (mil.): $9,337

**Stock Price History
High/Low 1985–94**

ECHLIN INC.

Echlin is making a large sum out of the (auto) parts it sells. Branford, Connecticut–based Echlin serves the global automotive aftermarket, that is, the owners of over 600 million used cars, trucks, and buses worldwide. Unlike businesses serving the new car market, Echlin actually benefits from economic downturns, as consumers tend to put off buying new cars and seek to maintain and repair their existing vehicles. It also gains from technological innovations in the auto industry such as antilock brakes, which cause brakes to wear out sooner than do earlier braking systems.

Echlin's products fall into 4 major areas. The bulk of its revenues are generated by brake system parts, including brake cables, brake shoes, and hydraulic brake master cylinders. Engine system parts (such as condensers, distributors, electronic voltage regulators, and solenoids) generate the next largest slice of revenue. The company also sells other vehicle parts such as engine mounts, mirrors, and water pumps and offers a line of nonvehicular products such as security access control products and small-engine parts.

The company has displayed a voracious appetite for expansion, having gobbled up more than 90 companies since 1965. With 2/3 of the world's autos outside the US, Echlin is seeking to expand its international sales from 1/3 of total revenues in 1995 to half by the year 2000. The company has operations in 10 European countries, and in 1994 it expanded its joint venture in India and opened an office in Hong Kong. Echlin is also anticipating strong growth in the US, where increased antilock brake and emissions regulations should benefit the company's sales.

Former shipboard wireless operator Jack Echlin joined his brother Earl's automotive repair business and established Echlin and Echlin in San Francisco in 1924. The brothers soon moved into making replacement parts. By 1926 the company's product line consisted of flywheel ring gears, igniter gears, and water pump shafts and impellers. Jack was the company's salesman, while Earl was in charge of the auto shop. Jack set up sales and technical clinics to teach salesmen the importance of replacement parts. These clinics helped build a national reputation for the company.

In 1928 the brothers secured a contract to supply the National Automotive Parts Association (NAPA) with oil pumps and gears. NAPA then distributed these parts to garages around the country. In 1929 Echlin and Echlin became the first to publish a complete catalog of ignition parts, in *Car Guide* magazine.

The company struggled economically during the Depression years, and Earl died in 1935. After struggling with high operating costs on the West Coast, Jack moved the headquarters to New Haven, Connecticut, in 1939. WWII found the company making parts for aircraft automatic pilots. Its name was changed to Echlin Manufacturing in 1959.

Jack stayed at the helm of the company until his retirement in 1969. During his tenure he posted an average annual growth rate of 15%. The company made a number of acquisitions during this time but never strayed outside its core business of automotive replacement parts.

Fred Mancheski (VP of manufacturing and engineering) took over as chairman and CEO following the departure of Jack Echlin and accelerated the company's acquisition strategy. Echlin acquired Ace Electric Co., a maker of alternators, generators, and starters, in 1970 and Berg Manufacturing & Sales Co., a maker of air brakes for trucks, in 1971. Both purchases paid off well for Echlin. In 1975 carmakers standardized electronic ignition systems, driving up demand for Echlin's components, and Berg's antiskid systems (produced in a joint venture with Fiat) became standard equipment on truck trailers during the 1970s. Echlin had similar success with its introduction of a selection of performance clutches and turbochargers.

The company expanded internationally under Mancheski, setting up subsidiaries in Australia, Brazil, Canada, South Africa, the UK, and Venezuela. In 1986 it set up a joint venture with leading British auto parts maker Lucas Girling to make and distribute brake parts across Europe.

In 1993 Echlin increased its investment in Europe with acquisitions, including that of the German clutch and brake division of FAG Kugelfischer. In 1994 it began a joint venture with China and bought US automotive hose maker Preferred Technical Group International for about $190 million. That year it also purchased Theodore Bargman Co.

Echlin acquired American Electronics Components in 1995 and the auto segment of Handy and Harman in 1996.

NYSE symbol: ECH
Fiscal year ends: August 31

WHO

Chairman and CEO: Frederick J. Mancheski, age 69,
$1,225,000 pay
President and COO: C. Scott Greer, age 45,
$495,000 pay
VP and Controller: Richard A. Wisot, age 49,
$237,000 pay
VP, General Counsel, and Corporate Secretary: Jon P.
Leckerling, age 47, $229,000 pay
VP Human Resources: Milton J. Makoski, age 49,
$222,000 pay
VP Materials: James A. G. Krupp
VP Marketing: Richard J. Spelleri
VP Engineering: David G. Lee
VP and Treasurer: Joseph A. Onorato, age 46
VP Corporate Development: Robert F. Tobey, age 50
Auditors: Price Waterhouse LLP

WHERE

HQ: 100 Double Beach Rd., Branford, CT 06405
Phone: 203-481-5751
Fax: 203-481-6485

The company operates 28 major manufacturing facilities
in Australia, Brazil, Canada, Germany, Mexico, South
Africa, Spain, the UK, and the US.

	1995 Sales		1995 Operating Income	
	$ mil.	% of total	$ mil.	% of total
North America	2,001	74	161	70
Europe	589	22	61	26
Other regions	128	4	9	4
Total	**2,718**	**100**	**231**	**100**

WHAT

	1995 Sales
	% of total
Brake system parts	44
Power transmission, steering & suspension systems components	28
Engine system parts	25
Nonvehicular products	3
Total	**100**

Selected Products

Brake System Parts
Antilock brake systems
Brake cables
Brake shoes
Disc pads
Hoses
Hydraulic brake master
cylinders
Push rods
Repair kits
Rotors

Engine System Parts
Condensers
Contacts
Control modules
Distributors

Electronic voltage
regulators
Ignition coils
Sensors
Solenoids

Other Vehicle Parts
Bell housings
Engine mounts
Mirrors
Water pumps

Nonvehicular Products
Security access control
products
Small-engine parts

KEY COMPETITORS

APS Holding
Arrow Automotive
Borg-Warner
Automotive
Champion Parts
Eaton
F & B Manufacturing
Federal-Mogul Corp.
General Motors

Genuine Parts
Hastings Manufacturing
Hughes Electronics
ITT Industries
Republic Automotive Parts
Robert Bosch
Rockwell
Standard Motor Products
TRW

HOW MUCH

	Annual Growth	1986	1987	1988	1989	1990	1991	1992	1993	1994	1995
Sales ($ mil.)	13.0%	902	1,100	1,294	1,455	1,601	1,686	1,783	1,945	2,230	2,718
Net income ($ mil.)	13.7%	49	48	62	44	47	42	64	94	121	154
Income as % of sales	—	5.4%	4.1%	4.8%	3.1%	2.9%	2.5%	3.6%	4.8%	5.4%	5.7%
Earnings per share ($)	9.9%	1.11	0.88	1.12	0.80	0.85	0.75	1.15	1.60	2.06	2.60
Stock price – high ($)	—	20.63	25.38	18.75	18.38	16.38	14.88	23.63	34.63	35.25	39.63
Stock price – low ($)	—	14.25	10.75	14.00	13.25	9.38	9.88	13.50	22.50	24.50	29.88
Stock price – close ($)	7.2%	19.50	14.00	16.50	15.63	11.25	14.38	23.38	33.25	30.00	36.50
P/E – high	—	19	29	17	23	19	20	21	22	17	15
P/E – low	—	13	12	13	17	11	13	12	14	12	12
Dividends per share ($)	5.9%	0.47	0.53	0.59	0.66	0.70	0.70	0.70	0.70	0.73	0.79
Book value per share ($)	6.3%	8.79	10.88	11.39	11.48	11.87	11.63	12.34	12.13	13.52	15.25
Employees	8.9%	10,900	13,500	14,700	16,200	17,300	17,800	17,900	18,600	20,600	23,400

1995 Year-end:
Debt ratio: 35.8%
Return on equity: 18.1%
Cash (mil.): $28
Current ratio: 2.22
Long-term debt (mil.): $482
No. of shares (mil.): 60
Dividends
  Yield: 2.2%
  Payout: 30.4%
Market value (mil.): $2,176

Stock Price History
High/Low 1986–95

THE EQUITABLE COMPANIES

OVERVIEW

At Equitable, *on parle français*. Because in 1995 French insurance giant Axa exercised its prerogative to convert its preferred stock to common, thus raising its equity stake in the New York–based insurer to 60%.

Axa's $1 billion 1991 investment was responsible for Equitable's Lazarus-like rise from moribund mutual company to profitable public company, and Equitable's new status makes it a partner in Axa's global empire.

Spearheading the company's rise to profitability since its demutualization has been Equitable Life Assurance Co. Focusing on the retirement and investment needs of baby boomers, the subsidiary has offered investment and annuity products that have reinvigo-

rated Equitable's insurance operations. These products fit well with the company's other operations, which include Alliance Capital Management (mutual funds and cash management, in addition to institutional services).

Most of the company's 7,800 insurance agents are also licensed stockbrokers, making them qualified to sell the full range of Equitable's products. The company is also a major manager and developer of commercial real estate .

Donaldson, Lufkin & Jenrette, Equitable's brokerage and investment banking unit, lagged behind Equitable's other businesses in 1994, which contributed to the company's decision to sell 20% of it in a 1995 IPO.

WHEN

As a student in Catskill, New York, Henry Hyde was advised by his teacher, General John Johnston (founder of Northwestern Mutual Life Insurance Co. in 1857), to go into life insurance. Hyde joined Mutual Life of New York and left in 1859 at age 25 to found the Equitable Life Assurance Society in New York, a joint stock company named after the Equitable Life Assurance Society of London.

Business boomed during the Civil War, and Equitable expanded to Asia, Europe, South America, and the Middle East. It grew faster than the insurance industry overall and by 1899 was the world's first company to have $1 billion of life insurance in force.

Revelations in 1905 about the company's financial condition led to the resignation of management and, in 1917, its conversion to a mutual company. It was the first company to write group insurance (Montgomery Ward, 1911) and to develop a method for apportioning dividends within a particular group, which was adopted by others in the industry.

After the boom of the 1920s, Equitable weathered the Depression and WWII. It continued to grow in the postwar boom.

The 1970s saw diversification into computers, mining, and real estate. Equitable also pioneered guaranteed investment contracts (GICs) — retirement plans that guaranteed principal and returns of up to 18% and allowed contributions for the life of the contract. This forced the company to pay inflationary rates even after interest rates fell in the 1980s. To cover the difference, the company invested in risky, high-yield junk bonds and real estate. Diversification continued with the acquisition of Donaldson, Lufkin &

Jenrette and the formation of an HMO (Equicor, with Hospital Corp. of America, 1986; sold 1990). When the mid-1980s boom faded in the late 1980s, the company was left with $15 billion in GIC obligations.

In a total management change in May 1990, Richard Jenrette became CEO and began cutting costs, seeking new capital, and investing in new areas. Equitable formed COMPASS (property leasing and management), acquired an interest in Europolis (European property markets), and expanded Capital Management (now owned by subsidiary Alliance Capital Management) to London and Tokyo. By 1991 GIC obligations were down to $10 billion (they were further reduced to under $3 billion in 1993, and by 1994 were less than $2 billion). Yet rumors of Equitable's demise brought a run of policy redemptions, further increasing the need for cash. As a mutual it had no way to raise capital, so Jenrette took it public in 1992.

Since then, cost cutting and an economic upturn have helped turn the tide. But a little asset shuffling hasn't hurt either. In 1993 the parent company capitalized the Life Assurance unit by buying 61% of Donaldson, Lufkin & Jenrette from it, and in 1994 the corporation improved its asset quality by selling (through Alliance) $700 million of collateralized below–investment grade bonds, some of which the company then repurchased.

The Axa transaction improved Equitable's balance sheet, and the company continued to seek ways to improve its financial condition, including increased cost cutting and the sale of assets like shopping malls. The Donaldson, Lufkin & Jenrette IPO brought Equitable $196 million.

NYSE symbol: EQ
Fiscal year ends: December 31

WHO

Chairman and CEO: Richard H. Jenrette, age 65,
$7,730,000 pay
President and COO: Joseph J. Melone, age 62,
$2,600,000 pay
SEVP: James M. Benson, age 48, $2,000,000 pay
EVP and CFO: Jerry M. de St. Paer, age 53,
$1,350,000 pay
EVP and Chief Administrative Officer: William T.
McCaffrey, age 58, $1,025,000 pay
EVP and Chief Investment Officer: Brian S. O'Neil,
age 42
EVP and General Counsel: Robert E. Garber, age 45
EVP and Chief Agency Officer: José S. Suquet
SVP and Chief Information Officer: Leon B. Billis
SVP and Chief Marketing Officer: Michael E. Fisher
SVP and Chief Compliance Officer: Richard V. Silver
President, Income Management Group: Jerome Golden
President and CEO, Donaldson, Lufkin & Jenrette:
John S. Chalsty
**Chairman and CEO, Equitable Real Estate Investment
Management:** George R. Puskar
Chairman and CEO, Alliance Capital Management:
Dave H. Williams
VP Human Resources: Janet Friedman
Auditors: Price Waterhouse LLP

WHERE

HQ: The Equitable Companies Incorporated,
787 Seventh Ave., New York, NY 10019
Phone: 212-554-1234
Fax: 212-315-2825

The Equitable operates throughout the US.

WHAT

	1994 Assets	
	$ mil.	% of total
Cash & equivalents	1,268	1
Corporate bonds	10,349	11
Trading accounts	8,970	9
Other securities	13,321	14
Mortgage loans & real estate	10,078	11
Broker-dealer receivables	13,982	15
Separate accounts	20,470	22
Other	16,202	17
Total	**94,640**	**100**

	1994 Sales		1994 Pretax income	
	$ mil.	% of total	$ mil.	% of total
Individual ins. & annuities	3,111	48	246	43
Investment svcs.	2,908	45	307	54
Group pension	359	5	16	3
Other	111	2	(85)	—
Adjustments	(42)	—	(2)	—
Total	**6,447**	**100**	**482**	**100**

Selected Subsidiaries
Alliance Capital Management L.P. (60%)
Donaldson, Lufkin & Jenrette, Inc. (80%)
The Equitable Life Assurance Society of the United States
Equitable Real Estate Investment Management, Inc.
The Equitable Variable Life Insurance Co. (EVLICO)

KEY COMPETITORS

Aetna	JMB Realty	Prudential
Allstate	John Hancock	State Farm
Charles Schwab	MetLife	T. Rowe Price
Chubb	New York Life	Transamerica
CIGNA	Northwestern	Travelers
FMR	Mutual	USF&G

HOW MUCH

	Annual Growth	1985	1986	1987	1988	1989	1990	1991	1992	1993	1994
Assets ($ mil.)	7.1%	51,168	54,577	56,794	60,934	68,574	69,789	74,918	78,869	98,991	94,640
Net income ($ mil.)	9.2%	—	—	—	144	133	(454)	(898)	(148)	169	244
Income as % of sales	—	—	—	—	0.2%	0.2%	—	—	—	0.2%	0.3%
Earnings per share ($)	—	—	—	—	—	—	—	—	(0.08)	1.09	1.38
Stock price – high ($)	—	—	—	—	—	—	—	—	14.38	31.50	30.00
Stock price – low ($)	—	—	—	—	—	—	—	—	7.13	13.38	16.75
Stock price – close ($)	13.8%	—	—	—	—	—	—	—	14.00	27.00	18.13
P/E – high	—	—	—	—	—	—	—	—	—	29	20
P/E – low	—	—	—	—	—	—	—	—	—	12	11
Dividends per share ($)	41.4%	—	—	—	—	—	—	—	0.10	0.20	0.20
Book value per share ($)	(1.1%)	—	—	—	—	—	—	—	14.51	15.78	14.20
Employees	5.2%	—	—	—	—	—	—	—	12,300	13,100	13,600

1994 Year-end:
Equity as % of assets: 2.8%
Return on assets: 0.3%
Return on equity: 10.0%
Long-term debt (mil.): $2,926
No. of shares (mil.): 184
Dividends
  Yield: 1.1%
  Payout: 13.1%
Market value (mil.): $3,330
Sales (mil.): $6,447

**Stock Price History
High/Low 1992–94**

ERNST & YOUNG LLP

OVERVIEW

Ernst & Young, one of the Big 6 accounting firms, has an image problem. It doesn't really have an image. One contributing factor has been the long period of consolidation after its 1989 merger. In 1995 Ernst & Young was still closing offices and reassigning people to streamline its operations. The firm has used this process to upgrade its internal communications; it has been integrating its systems to achieve worldwide access to its data.

Like its competitors, Ernst & Young offers accounting and auditing services as well as management, regulatory, human resources services consulting, and other services. Accounting firms have been jolted by the ten-

dency to blame auditors for the performance of their clients (in 1992 Ernst & Young paid $400 million to settle claims arising from the S&L debacle). So they have diversified into consulting. But there are perils there, too. In 1995 Ernst & Young was hit with a $42 million judgment relating to its actions as a litigation loss consultant in a California case.

In 1995 the firm took a step to help differentiate it from its competitors, merging with Kenneth Leventhal & Co., a real estate consulting firm. The resulting unit, Ernst & Young Kenneth Leventhal Real Estate Group, will make Ernst & Young one of the preeminent real estate consultancies in the US.

WHEN

While the 1494 publication in Venice of Luca Pacioli's *Summa di Arithmetica* — the first published work dealing with double-entry bookkeeping — boosted the accounting profession, it wasn't until well after the Industrial Revolution in England that accountants developed their craft.

Frederick Whinney joined the UK firm of Harding & Pullein in 1849. R. P. Harding reputedly had been a hat maker whose business ended up in court. The ledgers he produced were so well kept that an official advised him to take up accounting, which was a growth field as stock companies proliferated.

Whinney's name was added to the firm in 1859, and later his sons also became partners. The firm's name changed to Whinney, Smith & Whinney in 1894. The name became the longest-lived of the firm's many incarnations, not yielding until 1965.

After WWII, Whinney, Smith & Whinney formed an alliance with the American firm of Ernst & Ernst. Ernst & Ernst had been founded in Cleveland in 1903 by brothers Alwin and Theodore Ernst. The alliance, which recognized that the accountants' business clients were getting larger and more international in orientation, provided that each firm would operate in the other's behalf within their respective markets.

In 1965 the Whinney firm merged with Brown, Fleming & Murray to become Whinney Murray. The merger also included the fledgling computer department — the harbinger of electronic accounting systems — set up by Brown, Fleming & Murray to serve British Petroleum. Whinney Murray also formed joint ventures with other accounting firms to provide consulting services.

In 1979 Whinney Murray and Turquands Barton Mayhew — itself the product of a merger that began with a cricket match — united with Ernst & Ernst to form Ernst & Whinney, a firm with an international scope.

Ernst & Whinney, a merger melting pot, wasn't finished with its combinations. Having grown to the world's 4th largest accounting firm by 1989, it merged with the 5th largest, Arthur Young. Arthur Young had taken its name from the Scottish immigrant who had founded a partnership with C. U. Stuart in Chicago in 1894. When Stuart withdrew, Young took brother Stanley as a partner. Arthur Young — the firm — was long known as the "old reliable" of the accounting giants. In 1984 the spotlight shone on it as vice-presidential candidate Geraldine Ferraro chose the firm to sort out her tax troubles.

The new firm of Ernst & Young faced a rocky start. At the end of 1990, it was forced to defend itself from rumors of collapse. In 1991 it pared back the payroll, thinning the ranks of partners and others. That same year it agreed to pay the RTC $41 million to settle claims stemming from its involvement with Charles Keating's Lincoln Savings and Loan.

The next year Ernst & Young agreed to pay $400 million for allegedly mishandling the audits of 4 failed S&Ls. In early 1994 a federal judge in Rhode Island ordered Ernst & Young and the state to settle a suit arising from the collapse of the state's credit union system.

In 1994 Ernst & Young slashed its legal staff by half and replaced its head, Carl Riggio, with Kathryn Oberly. Riggio had built up the department and preferred to fight cases to the end rather than settle. Ernst & Young had sales of nearly $6.9 billion in 1995.

International partnership
Fiscal year ends: September 30

Chairman: Philip A. Laskawy
Co-chairman: William L. Kimsey
CEO, International: Michael A. Henning
VC Finance and Administration: Hilton Dean
VC Human Resources: Robert Center
General Counsel: Kathryn A. Oberly

HQ: 787 Seventh Ave., New York, NY 10019
Phone: 212-773-3000
Fax: 212-773-6350

Ernst & Young has more than 670 offices in over 130 countries.

	1995 Sales	
	$ mil.	% of total
US	2,974	43
Other countries	3,893	57
Total	**6,867**	**100**

	1995 US Revenues
	% of total
Accounting & auditing	43
Tax	22
Management consulting	35
Total	**100**

Representative Clients

American Express	Lockheed-Martin
Apple Computer	McDonald's
BankAmerica	Mobil
Coca-Cola	The Reference Press
Eli Lilly	Time Warner
Hanson	USF&G
Knight-Ridder	Wal-Mart

US Services

Accounting and auditing services	Insurance actuarial services
Capital markets services	Insurance regulatory services
Cash management services	
Continuous improvement	International tax compliance and consulting services
Corporate finance services	
Corporate real estate advisory services	Investment services
Corporate tax	Litigation services
Environmental consulting	Management consulting
Federal and state regulatory risk management	Organization alignment
	Organizational change management
Financial and accounting systems	Outsourcing services
Financial products services	Performance improvement
Process improvement	Personal financial counseling
Government relations and contract services	Relocation services
	Restructuring and reorganization services
Health care consulting	
Health care legislative services	Tax policy and legislative services
Human resources services	Tax services
Expatriate tax services	Valuation services
Industry services	
Information technology services	

Arthur Andersen
Andersen Consulting
Bain & Co.
Booz, Allen
Coopers & Lybrand
CSC
Deloitte & Touche
Hewitt
KPMG
McKinsey & Co.
Price Waterhouse

	Annual Growth	1986	1987	1988	1989	1990	1991	1992	1993	1994	1995
Sales ($ mil.)	10.0%	2,919	3,480	4,244	4,200	5,006	5,406	5,701	5,839	6,020	6,867
Arthur Young	—	1,427	1,702	2,053	—	—	—	—	—	—	—
Ernst & Whinney	—	1,492	1,778	2,191	—	—	—	—	—	—	—
Offices	0.9%	—	—	—	—	642	673	660	663	680	670
Partners	(0.8%)	—	—	—	—	5,609	5,665	5,300	5,318	5,228	5,392
Employees	2.1%	—	—	—	—	61,591	61,173	58,900	58,377	61,287	68,452

1995 Year-end:
Sales per partner:
$1,273,500

≡ ERNST & YOUNG

Sales ($ mil.)
1986–95

7,000
6,000
5,000
4,000
3,000
2,000
1,000
0

THE ESTÉE LAUDER COMPANIES INC.

OVERVIEW

Estée Lauder is rejuvenating, remodeling, and recapitalizing its brands — Aramis, Clinique, Estée Lauder, Origins, and Prescriptives. Under these brands the company markets about 700 skin care, makeup, and fragrance products and captures almost 40% of all US department and specialty store cosmetics sales.

During the past year all of the Estée Lauder companies have either launched new products or entered new markets. Aramis introduced a new fragrance called tommy through a licensing agreement with Tommy Hilfiger. With this fragrance Aramis hopes to attract a younger consumer, similar to Hilfiger's core clientele —

men aged 14 to 40. Estée Lauder spokesmodel Elizabeth Hurley received international attention and sympathy in 1995 when her boyfriend, actor Hugh Grant, was arrested with a Los Angeles prostitute.

Prescriptives had been trimming its product line since 1993 and now plans to focus on its reputation for color cosmetics to double its sales in the next 3–5 years. Origins continues to launch new products (which generate 15–20% of its sales) to build its business.

Estée Lauder ended 49 years of private ownership in 1995 with an IPO that raised $365 million. The Lauder family kept an 86.6% stake.

WHEN

Estée Lauder (then Josephine Esther Mentzer) started her beauty career by selling skin care products formulated by her Hungarian uncle, John Schotz, during the 1930s. Eventually she packaged and peddled her variations of Schotz's formulas, which included an all-purpose face cream and a cleansing oil.

With the help of her husband, Joseph Lauder, she set up her first office in Queens, New York, in 1944 and added lipstick, eye shadow, and face powder to the line. Joseph oversaw production and Estée sold her wares to beauty salons and department stores, using samples and gifts to persuade customers to buy her products. At one Manhattan beauty salon, Estée Lauder asked the owner where she had bought her blouse. The owner replied that Lauder didn't need to know because she would never be able to afford it. Lauder has been driven ever since. Throughout the 1950s Lauder traveled cross-country, at first to sell her line to high-profile department stores like Neiman-Marcus, I. Magnin, and Saks and later to train saleswomen in the same stores.

Estée Lauder created her first fragrance, a bath oil called Youth Dew, in 1953. In the late 1950s many of the large cosmetics houses in the US introduced "European" skin care lines that had scientific-sounding names and supposedly advanced skin repair properties. Estée Lauder's contribution was Re-Nutriv cream. It sold for $115 a pound in 1960, the same year the company hit the million-dollar profit mark. The advertising campaign for the cream established the "Lauder look": aristocratic, sophisticated, and tastefully wealthy, an image that Estée Lauder herself cultivated.

In 1964 the company introduced Aramis, a fragrance for men, and in 1968, with the help of a *Vogue* editor, launched Clinique, one of

the first hypoallergenic skin care lines. In 1972 Estée Lauder's son Leonard became president, although Estée remained CEO.

By 1978 Aramis cologne and aftershave accounted for 50–80% of men's fragrance sales in some department stores. Also in 1978 the company introduced 2 fragrances for women, White Linen and Cinnabar. In 1979 Estée Lauder created Prescriptives, skin care and makeup for young professional women.

Between 1978 and 1983 the company focused R&D on skin care products, resulting in Night Repair, one of the company's largest-selling formulas. Leonard Lauder was named CEO in 1983. By 1988 the company captured 1/3 of the US market in prestige cosmetics.

Leonard's brother, Ronald, who had left the company in 1983 to become deputy assistant secretary for defense, returned after losing an expensive bid to become mayor of New York in 1989 (reportedly spending $350 per vote).

During the early 1990s Estée Lauder unveiled its new Origins line of environmentally safe cosmetics. In 1990 the company recruited former Calvin Klein executive Robin Burns to head its domestic branch — Estée Lauder (U.S.A). Burns made her mark by breathing life back into the company's traditionally conservative advertising. The company launched the All Skins cosmetics line in 1991. In late 1993 the company introduced Resilience, a skin care product designed to combat signs of premature aging. The following year Clinique opened 2 counters in South Korea and one in Russia.

Leonard Lauder became chairman in 1995. Also that year Estée Lauder introduced its newest fragrance, Pleasures, and Thigh-Zone Body Streamlining Complex, a cream made especially for women's thighs.

NYSE symbol: EL
Fiscal year ends: June 30

WHO

Founding Chairman: Estée Lauder, $3,757,572 pay
Chairman and CEO: Leonard A. Lauder, age 62, $2,309,977 pay
President and COO: Fred H. Langhammer, age 51, $4,450,000 pay
Chairman, Clinique Laboratories, Inc. and Estée Lauder International, Inc.: Ronald S. Lauder, age 51, $2,472,830 pay
SVP, General Counsel, and Secretary: Saul H. Magram, age 64, $1,559,550 pay
SVP and CFO: Robert J. Bigler
SVP Corporate Human Resources: Andrew J. Cavanaugh, age 48
President, Clinique (U.S.A.): Daniel J. Brestle, age 50
President, Estée Lauder (U.S.A.): Robin R. Burns
President, Origins Natural Resources, Inc.: William P. Lauder, age 35
President, Aramis (U.S.A.) and Prescriptives (U.S.A.): Robert A. Nielsen, age 65
Auditors: Arthur Andersen & Co, SC

WHERE

HQ: 767 Fifth Ave., New York, NY 10153
Phone: 212-572-4200
Fax: 212-572-3941

	1995 Sales		1995 Operating Income	
	$ mil.	% of total	$ mil.	% of total
US	1,543	51	94	41
Europe, the Middle East & Africa	861	28	72	31
Asia/Pacific	534	18	63	27
Other Americas	85	3	2	1
Adjustments	(124)	—	—	—
Total	**2,899**	**100**	**231**	**100**

WHAT

	1995 Sales	
	$ mil.	% of total
Skin care	1,216	42
Makeup	1,003	35
Fragrance	680	23
Total	**2,899**	**100**

Selected Brands and Products

Aramis
Aramis 900 (fragrance)
Aramis Classic (fragrance)
Lab Series (skin care)
New West (fragrance)
Tuscany (fragrance)

Clinique
Aromatics (fragrance)
Balanced Makeup Base
Chemistry (fragrance)
Daily Eye Benefits
Re-Moisturizing Lipstick
Turnaround Cream

Estée Lauder
Advanced Night Repair
Enlighten (makeup)
Knowing (fragrance)
Re-Nutriv Lipstick
White Linen (fragrance)

Origins
Bite Your Lips (makeup)
Peace of Mind (skin care)
Sensory Therapy (fragrance)
Skin Care Pairs (skin care)
Spring Fever (fragrance)
Underwear for Lashes (makeup)

Prescriptives
All You Need (skin care)
Calyx (fragrance)
Classic Lipstick
Color Senses (8 separate fragrances)
Custom Blended Powders and Foundations
Exact Color Foundation
Flight Cream

KEY COMPETITORS

Alberto-Culver	Helen of Troy	Nature's
Allou	Helene Curtis	Sunshine
Amway	Jean Philippe	Perrigo
Avon	Fragrances	Playtex
BeautiControl	Johnson & Johnson	Procter &
Body Shop	L'Oréal	Gamble
Chattem	LVMH	Shiseido
Colgate-Palmolive	MacAndrews & Forbes	Tristar
Gillette	Mary Kay	Unilever

HOW MUCH

	Annual Growth	1986	1987	1988	1989	1990	1991	1992	1993	1994	1995[1]
Sales ($ mil.)	8.9%	1,350	1,600	1,730	1,865	2,010	2,100	2,250	2,448	2,576	2,899
Net income ($ mil.)	25.5%	—	—	—	—	—	39	51	58	70	96
Income as % of sales	—	—	—	—	—	—	1.8%	2.3%	2.4%	2.7%	3.3%
Earnings per share ($)	—	—	—	—	—	—	—	—	—	—	0.83
Stock prices – high ($)	—	—	—	—	—	—	—	—	—	—	36.75
Stock prices – low ($)	—	—	—	—	—	—	—	—	—	—	31.75
Stock prices – close ($)	—	—	—	—	—	—	—	—	—	—	34.88
P/E – high	—	—	—	—	—	—	—	—	—	—	44
P/E – low	—	—	—	—	—	—	—	—	—	—	38
Dividends per share ($)	—	—	—	—	—	—	—	—	—	—	0.00
Book value per share ($)	—	—	—	—	—	—	—	—	—	—	2.91
Employees[2]	(0.1%)	10,000	10,000	10,000	10,000	10,000	12,000	12,000	12,000	10,000	9,900

1995 Year-end:
Debt ratio: 36.7%
Return on equity: 21.0%
Cash (mil.): $281
Current ratio: 1.58
Long-term debt (mil.): $66

**Stock Price History
High/Low 1995**

40
35
30
25
20
15
10
5
0

[1] Initial public offering subsequent to fiscal year-end.   [2] 1986–94 estimates

GENERAL ELECTRIC COMPANY

OVERVIEW

Industrial behemoth General Electric (GE) makes everything from lightbulbs to locomotives, power generators, and jet engines. The manufacturer ranks among the world's 10 largest industrial companies and is #1 among US electronics firms.

Diversity has protected GE's bottom line from recent fluctuations in its primary markets: automobile electronics, aircraft engines, and power generation are down; materials (especially plastics), financial services (GE Capital Corp.), and ad rates at NBC are up. Other GE businesses include appliances, lighting, medical systems, and information services.

Like other international companies, GE is reacting to global competition by reducing its work force and streamlining its operations while expanding its global reach. In 1994 GE Capital acquired Minebea Credit (Japan), and

GE Power Generation acquired 80% of turbine maker Nuovo Pignone (Italy). The company's aircraft engines unit won important orders from Air Canada and Singapore Airlines. In Europe and the Middle East, over 60 million homes tuned in to the NBC Super Channel.

GE's operations hit some turbulence in 1995 when CEO Jack Welch underwent triple bypass surgery, raising questions about the company's line of succession. Later that year delivery of the GE90 engine, used to power British Airways's new Boeing 777s, was delayed when the engine failed to meet FAA testing.

On an up note, in 1994 GE sold scandal-plagued Kidder, Peabody to Paine Webber for a package valued at $670 million. In 1995 the company announced that it had developed a new electric power generator that converts a record 60% of fuel to energy.

WHEN

General Electric was established in 1892 in New York, the result of a merger between the Thomson-Houston Company and the Edison General Electric Company. Charles Coffin was GE's first president and Thomas Edison, who left the company in 1894, one of its directors.

GE's financial strength (backed by the Morgan banking house) and focus on research (it started one of the first corporate research laboratories in 1900) led to the company's success. Products included elevators (1885), trolleys, motors, the lightbulb, and toasters (1905) and other appliances under the GE and Hotpoint labels. In the 1920s GE joined AT&T and Westinghouse in a radio broadcasting joint venture, Radio Corporation of America (RCA). GE sold off its RCA holdings (1930) because of an antitrust ruling (one of 65 antitrust actions against GE between 1911 and 1967).

From 1940 to 1952 annual sales increased sixfold to $2.6 billion. GE entered the computer industry in 1956 but sold the business in 1970 to Honeywell because of operating losses. By 1980 GE's revenues had reached $25 billion from sales of plastics, consumer electronics, nuclear reactors, and jet engines.

In the 1980s GE's strategy was to pursue only high-performance ventures. Between 1980 and 1989 GE sold operations that accounted for 25% of its 1980 sales and focused on medical equipment, financial services, and high-performance plastics and ceramics. GE shed its air-conditioning (1982), housewares (1984), mining (1984), and semiconductor (1988) businesses. It acquired Employers

Reinsurance in 1984 ($1.1 billion); RCA, including NBC, in 1986 ($6.4 billion); investment bankers Kidder, Peabody (completed in 1990); and CGR medical equipment from Thomson of France in 1987 as part of an exchange for GE's consumer electronics division.

GE entered Eastern Europe in 1990, taking a majority interest in the Hungarian lighting company Tungsram. In 1991 GE acquired a stake in THORN Light Source in the UK. The 2 purchases increased GE's European share of the lamp market to 20%. In 1992 GE entered a lighting equipment joint venture with Hitachi, giving GE access to the Japanese company's distribution network. In 1993 GE moved into the mutual fund business, buying mutual fund wholesaler GNA for $525 million and gaining SEC permission to allow GE Investment Management, which runs GE's pension assets, to sell mutual funds to the public.

In 1994 GE fired its top government bond trader for allegedly making phony trades at Kidder, Peabody that led to a $350 million charge. The debacle, which also resulted in the resignation of Kidder CEO Michael Carpenter, reignited rumors that GE would sell off the unit. GE talked with Disney and Turner Broadcasting in 1994 about buying NBC, but neither deal panned out.

The doctor with the first patent for magnetic resonance imaging (MRI) won an $111 million patent infringement award from GE in 1995. GE claimed that it had independently developed MRI technology and said it expected the judgment to be thrown out on appeal.

NYSE symbol: GE
Fiscal year ends: December 31

WHO

Chairman and CEO: John F. (Jack) Welch Jr., age 59, $4,350,000 pay
VC and Executive Officer: Paolo Fresco, age 61, $2,125,000 pay
VC: John D. Opie, age 57
SVP Finance: Dennis D. Dammerman, age 49, $1,475,000 pay
SVP, General Counsel, and Secretary: Benjamin W. Heineman Jr., age 51, $1,427,500 pay
SVP GE Power Systems: David C. Genever-Watling, age 49
SVP GE Lighting: W. James McNerney Jr., age 45
SVP GE Aircraft Engines: Eugene F. Murphy, age 59
SVP GE Plastics: Gary L. Rogers, age 50
SVP GE Appliances: J. Richard Stonesifer, age 58
SVP GE Medical Systems: John M. Trani, age 50
SVP Research and Development: Lewis S. Edelheit, age 52
SVP Human Resources: William J. Conaty, age 49
Auditors: KPMG Peat Marwick LLP

WHERE

HQ: 3135 Easton Tnpk., Fairfield, CT 06431-0001
Phone: 203-373-2211
Fax: 203-373-3131

GE has 145 manufacturing plants in 31 states and Puerto Rico and 113 plants in 25 other countries.

	1994 Sales		1994 Operating Income	
	$ mil.	% of total	$ mil.	% of total
US	49,920	79	8,445	87
Other countries	13,290	21	1,268	13
Adjustments	(3,101)	—	5	—
Total	**60,109**	**100**	**9,718**	**100**

WHAT

	1994 Sales		1994 Operating Income	
	$ mil.	% of total	$ mil.	% of total
GE Capital				
Financing	14,932	24	2,662	25
Other	4,943	8	287	3
Industrial products	9,038	15	1,328	12
Power generation	5,962	10	1,238	11
Aircraft engines	5,889	9	935	9
Major appliances	5,671	9	683	6
Materials	5,638	9	967	9
Technical	4,267	7	787	7
Broadcasting	3,361	5	500	5
Other	2,348	4	1,346	13
Adjustments	(1,940)	—	(2,072)	—
Total	**60,109**	**100**	**8,661**	**100**

Products and Services
Aircraft engines (engines and replacement parts)
Appliances (kitchen and laundry equipment)
Broadcasting (National Broadcasting Co. [NBC])
Industrial products and systems (lighting, electrical distribution, and control equipment)
Materials (plastics, silicones, laminates, and abrasives)
Power generation (products for generating electricity)
Technical products and services (medical and network-based information services)

KEY COMPETITORS

ABB	Hitachi	Siemens
AB Electrolux	Ingersoll-Rand	Time Warner
Alcatel Alsthom	Matsushita	Toshiba
CBS	Maytag	Turner
CS Holding	Mitsubishi	Broadcasting
AB Electrolux	Mitsui	United Technologies
Fried. Krupp	News Corp.	Viacom
GEC	Philips	Walt Disney
General Motors	Raytheon	Westinghouse
General Re	Rockwell	Whirlpool
GTE	Rolls-Royce	

HOW MUCH

	Annual Growth	1985	1986	1987	1988	1989	1990	1991	1992	1993	1994
Sales ($ mil.)	8.7%	28,285	35,210	39,315	38,793	54,574	58,414	60,236	57,073	60,562	60,109
Net income ($ mil.)	8.1%	2,336	2,492	2,119	3,386	3,939	4,303	4,435	4,725	5,177	4,726
Income as % of sales	—	8.3%	7.1%	5.4%	8.7%	7.2%	7.4%	7.4%	8.3%	8.5%	7.9%
Earnings per share ($)	8.9%	1.29	1.37	1.17	1.88	2.18	2.43	2.55	2.76	3.03	2.77
Stock price – high ($)	—	18.47	22.19	33.19	23.94	32.38	37.75	39.06	43.75	53.50	54.88
Stock price – low ($)	—	13.91	16.63	19.38	19.19	21.75	25.00	26.50	36.38	40.44	45.00
Stock price – close ($)	12.1%	18.19	21.50	22.06	22.38	32.25	28.69	38.25	42.75	52.44	51.00
P/E – high	—	14	16	28	13	15	16	15	16	18	20
P/E – low	—	11	12	17	10	10	10	10	13	13	16
Dividends per share ($)	11.7%	0.55	0.58	0.65	0.70	0.82	0.94	1.02	1.12	1.26	1.49
Book value per share ($)	8.2%	7.62	8.29	9.13	10.23	11.54	12.42	12.55	13.71	15.09	15.47
Employees	(3.5%)	304,000	359,000	302,000	298,000	292,000	298,000	284,000	231,000	222,000	221,000

1994 Year-end:
Debt ratio: 78.0%
Return on equity: 18.1%
Cash (mil.): $2,591
Current ratio: 1.74
Long-term debt (mil.): $36,979
No. of shares (mil.): 1,706
Dividends
  Yield: 2.9%
  Payout: 53.8%
Market value (mil.): $87,004

Stock Price History
High/Low 1985–94

GENERAL RE CORPORATION

OVERVIEW

Stamford, Connecticut–based General Re is the parent company of General Reinsurance, the largest property/casualty reinsurer in the US and one of the 3 largest in the world.

Primary insurers use reinsurance to cover their own risks. General Re writes most of its business on an excess-of-loss basis, meaning that the company pays only after the primary insurer's losses exceed a specific sum. Most policies are written by the company through direct contact with the purchasing insurers.

In the past 4 years, the insurance business has been shaken by an unprecedented series of natural and man-made disasters. This has made it difficult for General Re to make an underwriting profit (a profit from premium sales alone).

In 1994 the major culprit in its underwriting loss was the Northridge earthquake in California. Fortunately the company's investment income has boosted results.

Other segments of General Re's business include insurance consulting, aviation insurance, securities, and derivatives trading in the US and overseas.

Although the US reinsurance market is mature, there is room for growth in overseas markets, where new business is on the rise. To take advantage of this growing market, in 1995 General Re formed an alliance with Germany's Colonia Konzern (a subsidiary of Union des Assurances de Paris), by forming a joint venture to buy Colonia's subsidiary, Cologne Re.

WHEN

In 1921, when Duncan Reid became president of the newly organized General Casualty and Surety Reinsurance Corp. of New York, the reinsurance field was virtually nonexistent in the US. By 1923 the company's name had changed to General Reinsurance Corp.; Carl Hansen, an underwriting expert, became VP and general manager. By 1925 Hansen and 2 partners controlled the company, which began providing property and casualty reinsurance — its domain to this day.

Reinsurance was a small market, and business grew slowly. It began to take off when, in 1945, the Mellon family united its privately owned Mellon Indemnity with General Re and took over operations. Edward Lowry Jr. was brought in as head in 1946. Reinsurers then paid claims on losses but provided no other services. Lowry, recognizing that reinsurers were the first to know when a branch of the industry was at risk, began offering management consulting services, which remain important to General Re in customer retention.

After the merger General Re held a near monopoly on reinsurance. From 1945 to 1980 General Re was able to charge the highest premiums in the business and was consistently the most profitable US reinsurer.

Lowry retired in 1960. Successor James Cathcart began international expansion in 1962, starting Zurich-based International Reinsurance and buying Stockholm's Swedish Atlas Reinsurance and an interest in Reinsurance Company of Australasia. In the 1960s and 1970s General Re expanded its facultative group (companies that insure against specific risks), started in 1954. Beginning

from a small revenue base, the group contributed half of General Re's premium income by 1978. In the mid-1970s the company also began reinsuring against medical malpractice and equipment leasing losses.

By 1978 General Re was suffering price competition from startups; concurrently, about a dozen senior managers left, some to form competitor Trenwick Re.

In 1980 General Re formed a holding company for its operations and began investing in other insurers such as British-based Trident Insurance Group (sold in 1985) and Monarch Insurance Co. of Ohio (1985).

General Re did not join the 1980s stampede into risky investments. It kept noninvestment grade bonds to under 1% of its portfolio.

General Re's US Aviation subsidiary was the leader of a 15-member syndicate that carried 30% of the insurance on the plane involved in the 1988 Pan Am 103 bombing, about which there was considerable litigation.

In 1993 General Re and the W.R. Berkley Corporation agreed to form a holding company for their respective wholly owned subsidiaries, North Star and Signet Reinsurance. General Re owns 40% of the new company, Signet Star Holdings, Inc.

In accordance with the company's plans to expand overseas, the 1994 acquisition of part of Colonia Konzern's Cologne Re will give General Re easier access to the European reinsurance market.

Cologne Re is the world's oldest reinsurance company. It was founded in 1846 and was the 5th largest reinsurer in the world in 1994.

NYSE symbol: GRN
Fiscal year ends: December 31

Chairman, President, and CEO: Ronald E. Ferguson, age 53, $1,457,917 pay
VC: John C. Etling, age 59, $1,016,250 pay
President and COO, General Reinsurance Corp.: Tom N. Kellogg, age 58
Chairman and CEO, General Reinsurance Corp.: James E. Gustafson, age 48
VP and Chief Investment Officer: Ernest C. Frohboese, age 54, $564,167 pay
VP and CFO: Joseph P. Brandon, age 36, $410,000 pay
VP, General Counsel, and Secretary: Charles F. Barr, age 45, $317,258 pay
Controller: Elizabeth A. Monrad, age 40
SVP Information Systems, General Re Services Corp.: Stephen P. Raye, age 52
SVP Human Resources, General Re Services Corp.: Theron S. Hoffman Jr., age 47
Auditors: Coopers & Lybrand L.L.P.

WHERE

HQ: 695 E. Main St., PO Box 10351, Stamford, CT 06904-2351
Phone: 203-328-5000
Fax: 203-328-5329

General Re conducts business in the US and in 13 other countries worldwide.

	1994 Sales		1994 Pretax Income	
	$ mil.	% of total	$ mil.	% of total
US	3,381	88	741	93
Other countries	456	12	53	7
Total	**3,837**	**100**	**794**	**100**

WHAT

	1994 Assets	
	$ mil.	% of total
Cash & equivalents	1,274	4
US Treasurys	1,702	6
Foreign govt. securities	5,215	17
State & municipal bonds	5,224	18
Corporate bonds	1,160	4
Stocks	2,977	10
Other securities	4,329	15
Receivables & recoverables	3,488	12
Other assets	4,228	14
Total	**29,597**	**100**

Selected Domestic Subsidiaries
General Re Asset Management, Inc.
General Star Indemnity Co.
General Star National Insurance Co.
Genesis Indemnity Insurance Co.
Genesis Insurance Co.
United States Aviation Underwriters, Inc.

International Operations
General Re-CKAG Reinsurance & Investments SARL (Luxembourg)
General Re Compañia de Reaseguros, SA (Argentina)
General Re Correduría de Reaseguros, SA (Spain)
General Re Europe Ltd.
General Re Financial Products (Japan) Inc.
General Re Financial Products, Ltd. (UK)
General Re Financial Securities, Ltd. (UK)
General Re Underwriting Services, Ltd. (Bermuda)
General Reinsurance Australasia Ltd. (Australia, New Zealand, Singapore)

KEY COMPETITORS

Aetna	Marsh & McLennan
AIG	Prudential
Allianz	Swiis Re
American Re	Tokio Marine and Fire
CIGNA	USF&G
Lloyd's of London	

HOW MUCH

	Annual Growth	1985	1986	1987	1988	1989	1990	1991	1992	1993	1994
Assets ($ mil.)	19.4%	6,005	8,078	8,902	9,394	10,390	11,033	12,416	14,700	18,469	29,597
Net income ($ mil.)	19.3%	136	329	511	480	599	614	657	596	697	665
Income as % of assets	—	2.3%	4.0%	5.7%	5.1%	5.8%	5.6%	5.3%	4.1%	3.8%	2.2%
Earnings per share ($)	20.8%	1.45	3.22	5.04	5.04	6.52	6.89	7.46	6.84	8.11	7.97
Stock price – high ($)	—	52.50	68.88	68.38	59.25	95.75	93.00	101.88	123.13	133.38	129.13
Stock price – low ($)	—	30.57	49.44	48.75	45.88	55.00	69.00	84.88	78.63	104.75	101.75
Stock price – close ($)	10.6%	50.06	55.50	55.88	55.25	87.13	93.00	101.88	115.75	107.00	123.50
P/E – high	—	36	21	14	12	15	14	14	18	16	16
P/E – low	—	21	15	10	9	8	10	11	11	13	13
Dividends per share ($)	10.5%	0.78	0.88	1.00	1.20	1.36	1.52	1.68	1.80	1.88	1.92
Book value per share ($)	13.8%	18.48	23.47	26.20	29.04	34.28	37.50	45.14	49.89	56.93	59.32
Employees	0.9%	2,185	2,332	2,426	2,363	2,379	2,496	2,513	2,413	2,397	2,360

1994 Year-end:
Equity as % of assets: 16.4%
Return on assets: 2.8%
Return on equity: 13.8%
Long-term debt (mil.): $157
No. of shares (mil.): 82
Dividends
  Yield: 1.6%
  Payout: 24.1%
Market value (mil.): $10,111
Sales (mil.): $3,837

Stock Price History High/Low 1985–94

THE GOLDMAN SACHS GROUP, L.P.

OVERVIEW

Goldman Sacks! For the first time since the late 1980s, Wall Street's last major private partnership laid off staff in 1995. The 1994 bond crash and a decline in new debt issues were to blame. The layoffs and other cost cutting actions (plus the 1995 bond rebound and 1995's continuing bull market) helped the firm double its earnings for fiscal 1995. But some of New York–based Goldman Sachs's problems won't be solved by economizing and waiting for an up-cycle.

As it has grown, the firm has stretched its partnership (an intimate form of organization) to globe-straddling size, and some of its business has shifted from client-centered investment banking to firm-centered proprietary trading. Many feel the firm has lost some of its family feeling and become more anonymous.

The 1994 retirement of senior partner Stephen Friedman (whom some considered responsible for the firm's turmoil) sparked a rash of partner retirements. Because partners can begin to cash out only when they leave, this raised concerns about the company's future capital strength. Recent good fortune has stemmed this worry for now, but the firm's capital structure is still vulnerable, and rumors persist that the company might go public.

Goldman Sachs's core areas are research, investment (trading and market making, derivatives), municipal and corporate financing (underwriting debt and equity issues), mergers and acquisitions, foreign exchange and commodities, and real estate.

The Kamehameha Schools/Bishop Estate of Hawaii owns over 20% of Goldman Sachs.

WHEN

Philadelphia retailer Marcus Goldman moved to New York in 1869 and began buying customers' promissory notes from jewelers and reselling them to commercial banks. Samuel Sachs, Goldman's son-in-law, joined the business in 1882, and the firm became Goldman, Sachs & Company in 1885.

In 1887 Goldman Sachs, through British merchant bankers Kleinwort Sons, offered its clients US–UK foreign exchange and currency services. To serve clients like Sears, Roebuck, the firm expanded to Chicago and St. Louis. In 1896 it joined the NYSE.

In the late 1890s and early 1900s, the firm increased its contacts in Europe. Goldman's son Henry made the firm a major source of financing for US industry. In 1906 the firm comanaged its first public offering, $4.5 million for United Cigar Manufacturers (later General Cigar). By 1920 the firm had arranged the IPOs of Sears, May Department Stores, Jewel Tea, B.F. Goodrich, and Merck.

Sidney Weinberg became a partner in 1927 and remained a leader until his death in 1969. In the 1930s the firm started a securities dealer (rather than agent) operation and sales departments. Since WWII it has been a leader in investment banking. It comanaged Ford's IPO in 1956. In the 1970s Goldman Sachs was the first firm to buy blocks of stock for resale.

Under Sidney's son, John Weinberg (co–senior partner with John Whitehead beginning in 1976, retired in 1991), Goldman Sachs expanded its international operations, became a leader in mergers and acquisitions (M&A), and acquired First Dallas, Ltd. (1982, landed mer-

chant banking). By 1982 it was the largest M&A lead manager with $24.7 billion in mergers, including U.S. Steel–Marathon Oil, Occidental Petroleum–Cities Service, and Connecticut General–INA. Another acquisition, J. Aron Co. (1981), the world's largest coffee trader, gave Goldman a significant presence in precious metals. Contacts made through Aron have been instrumental in Goldman's growth in South America.

In the late 1980s and the 1990s, Goldman sought capital, raising over $500 million from Sumitomo for a nonparticipatory 12.5% interest. The Kamehameha Schools/Bishop Estate (a Hawaiian educational trust) has invested approximately $500 million in the firm (most recently in 1994, when Goldman Sachs sought more capital after a bruising year).

In the 1990s the firm expanded rapidly overseas but ran into problems with some of these ventures. An investment project in China fell through after the firm asked for a greater share than the Chinese were willing to grant; the Hong Kong office ballooned to more than 500 employees; and in Russia the company hitched its star to a government official who was booted out of office.

As a partnership, Goldman Sachs is reluctant to divulge its financial results, but offering documents that fell into the hands of the press showed record profits in 1993. Partners' bonuses (a large part of the appeal of working for the company) were more than $3 million.

In 1995 the firm continued to raise capital, borrowing over $250 million in the private debt markets — but at high interest rates.

Private partnership
Fiscal year ends: Last Friday in November

WHO

Senior Partner and Chairman of the Management Committee: Jon S. Corzine, age 48
VC of the Management Committee and COO: Henry M. Paulson Jr., age 48
Chairman, Goldman Sachs International: Peter Sutherland, age 49
Partner and Co–General Counsel: Robert J. Katz
Partner and Co–General Counsel: Gregory K. Palm
Partner, International Comptroller: David W. Blood
Partner, Personnel: Jonathan L. Cohen
Auditors: Coopers & Lybrand L.L.P.

WHERE

HQ: 85 Broad St., New York, NY 10004
Phone: 212-902-1000
Fax: 212-902-1512

Goldman Sachs operates as an equities and fixed income broker and underwriter, investment banker, asset manager, and commodities trader in Belgium, France, Germany, Japan, Singapore, the UK, and the US.

	Offices
	No.
US	11
Asia/Pacific	9
Europe	7
Other	4
Total	**31**

WHAT

Services

Asset Management

Investment Banking
Advisory services
Mergers and acquisitions
Underwriting
  Bonds
  State and municipal issues
  Stocks

Real estate
Mortgage-backed securities
Real estate investment trusts

Research

Trading
Bonds
Commodities
Currency
Derivatives and custom products
Stocks
US Treasury instruments (primary trader)

Selected Subsidiaries

Goldman, Sachs & Co. Finanz GmbH (Frankfurt)
Goldman, Sachs & Co. (Zurich)
Goldman Sachs (Asia) Ltd.
Goldman Sachs (Australia) Ltd
Goldman Sachs International Ltd. (UK)
Goldman Sachs (Japan) Corp.
Goldman Sachs (Singapore) Pte. Ltd

KEY COMPETITORS

AIG
Alex. Brown
Bankers Trust
Bear Stearns
Brown Brothers Harriman
CS Holding
Dean Witter, Discover
Deutsche Bank
Donaldson, Lufkin & Venrette
Hambrecht & Quist
ING Group
J.P. Morgan
KKR
Lehman Brothers
Merrill Lynch
Morgan Stanley
Nomura Securities
Paine Webber
Prudential
Salomon
Travelers
Yamaichi Securities

HOW MUCH

	Annual Growth	1986	1987	1988	1989	1990	1991	1992	1993	1994	1995
Estimated sales ($ mil.)	16.7%	3,600	4,200	4,000	3,400	4,600	5,290	8,500	13,200	11,440	14,470
Net income	10.6%	—	—	—	750	886	1,150	1,500	2,700	508	1,370
Net income as % of sales	—	—	—	—	22.1%	19.3%	21.7%	17.6%	20.5%	4.4%	9.5%
Partners' capital ($ mil.)	17.7%	1,104	1,656	1,876	2,145	2,477	3,010	3,714	5,008	4,800	4,800
Employees	5.3%	4,516	6,087	6,500	6,400	5,800	6,600	6,733	7,000	9,000	7,200

Goldman Sachs

Net Income
($ mil.) 1989–95

GOYA FOODS, INC.

OVERVIEW

Goya has created a masterpiece out of the production and distribution of traditional Hispanic foodstuffs. Based in Secaucus, New Jersey, the family-owned and -operated company makes and distributes more than 1,000 grocery products, including a wide variety of canned and dried beans, olives and olive oil, rice specialty mixes, seasonings, condiments, and tropical fruit nectars and juices. Goya also has a line of frozen foods that features favorite Caribbean entrees like Jamaican beef pie and guava pound cake.

The largest Hispanic-owned company in the US, Goya controls more than 50% of the Hispanic grocery market in the Northeast and Florida. (Some analysts put the figure closer to 80%). The company's products are favored by a community made up predominantly of Puerto Rican, Cuban, Dominican, and other Latin Caribbean immigrants, although the sizable Mexican and Central American population of the Southwest has provided growth in recent years.

Increasing health consciousness and a growing interest in ethnic foods throughout the US has further strengthened Goya's position, with crossover products such as extra virgin olive oil, beans, salsas, and rice specialty mixes, in particular, enjoying popularity.

Goya's future looks bright, if increasingly competitive. With census figures showing that the Hispanic population is the nation's fastest growing, food giants like Campbell Soup have stepped up their efforts to tap the market, releasing lines of Spanish specialties. Goya has responded by widening its own selection, and the company continues to court consumers by its involvement in community affairs.

WHEN

Goya Foods was founded in New York City in 1936 by the husband/wife team of Prudencio Unanue and Carolina Casal. Immigrants from Spain by way of Puerto Rico, the couple missed the foods of their homeland and began importing sardines, olives, and olive oil from Spain for local distribution. When the Spanish Civil War (1936–39) resulted in the interruption of the company's supplies, the couple began importing from Morocco.

In 1949 Goya established its first cannery, in Bayamón, Puerto Rico. The company initially distributed its Puerto Rican imports through warehouses in Manhattan to a local market of immigrants from the West Indies. Each of the couple's 4 sons eventually joined the family business, and in 1958, Goya relocated to Brooklyn. Operations were moved to the present New Jersey headquarters in 1974.

In 1976 Joseph Unanue was named company president and CEO. Along with his brother Frank, president of Goya–Puerto Rico, Joseph began a cautious expansion campaign, beginning by adding traditional products to the company's existing line of Latin Caribbean and Spanish favorites.

Buoyed by the growing popularity of Mexican food, Goya decided to venture beyond its traditional customer base in 1982. The company began distributing its products in Houston, targeting the Southwest's sizable Mexican and Central American markets and hoping for crossover customers from the region's Anglo community. The move at first proved a disaster, however. The company's products, while certainly possessing a Latin flair, were not suited to the Mexican palate, which preferred spicier foods and flavors. Likewise, a similar move to capture a portion of Florida's huge Cuban market share initially met with only moderate success, but Goya persevered, eventually turning the tables in its favor.

From 1982 to 1988 the company also attempted to woo the non-Hispanic market. While Goya's cream of coconut — an essential ingredient in piña colada cocktails — successfully crossed over into a broader market, its ad campaign featuring obscure actress Zohra Lampert did little to attract a large following of non-Hispanic customers.

Success in that market came in the 1990s. America's interest in the reportedly healthier "Mediterranean diet" boosted sales of Goya's extra virgin olive oil, and health experts' recommendations to cut fat and boost dietary fiber led to the company's launch of the "For Better Meals, Turn to Goya" campaign. In 1994 it spent an estimated $1–$1.5 million on English-language TV ads in the New York City area, and print ads featured recipes calling for Goya products.

In late 1995 the company released its new Goya Tropical Blast line of juice-based beverages, anticipating that the products would be successful crossovers. That same year a study revealed that Goya's traditional Hispanic customers are enjoying a significant increase in purchasing power — up from $94.1 billion in 1984 to a projected $228.1 billion in 1996.

Private company
Fiscal year ends: May 31

WHO

President and CEO: Joseph A. Unanue, age 70
President, GOYA de Puerto Rico: Francisco J. Unanue
CFO and Controller: Luis Perez
VP Marketing: Conrad O. Colon
VP Purchasing: Joseph Perez
VP Computer Information Services: David Kinkela
General Counsel: Carlos Ortiz
Director-Sales: Tony Santamaria
Director-Public Relations: Ralph Toro
Manager-Personnel: Gilberto Otero
Assistant, Public Relations: Carmen Hernandez
Auditors: Polakoff & Leen

WHERE

HQ: 100 Seaview Dr., Secaucus, NJ 07096
Phone: 201-348-4900
Fax: 201-348-6600

WHAT

Business Units
Angola Distribution Center (Angola, New York)
CPA Products, Inc. (City of Industry, California)
CPR, International (Miami, Florida)
GOYA Foods (Bensenville, Illinois)
GOYA Foods (Houston, Texas)
GOYA Foods (Miami, Florida)
GOYA Foods (Bayamón, Puerto Rico)
GOYA Foods (Seville, Spain)
GOYA Foods (Tampa, Florida)
GOYA Foods (Webster, Massachusetts)
GOYA Foods (West Deptford, New Jersey)
Productora Quisquenyana (Santo Domingo, Dominican
  Republic)

Selected Beverages
Fruit juices
Jamaican-style ginger beer
Malta goya
Piña colada mix
Tropical Blast fruit drinks
  Caribbean Punch
  Guava Gusto
  Mango Mambo
  Papaya Plunge
  Passion Splash
  Tropical fruit nectars
  Tropi-Cola champagne
    soda

**Selected Foods and Other
  Products**
Bread pudding
Canned beans
Cheese
Chorizos
Corn masa mix
Corn oil
Cornmeal
Devotional candles
Dried beans
Flan
Flavorings and spices
  Adobo
  Chili powder
  Cinnamon sticks
  Ground cumin
  Jamaican curry powder
  Sazón
Frozen Caribbean entrees
Guacamole
Guava paste
Imported sardines
Imported Spanish olive
  oil
Rice specialty mixes
Salsas
Snack foods
  Sesame crackers
  Tortilla chips
  Whole wheat crackers
Stuffed olives
Vegetable oil

KEY COMPETITORS

Bell-Carter Foods
Borden
Campbell Soup
Chiquita Brands
ConAgra
CPC International
Del Monte
Dole
Grand Metropolitan
Heinz
Maizoro
Nestlé
Ocean Spray
PepsiCo
Philip Morris
Pro-Fac
RJR Nabisco
Seneca Foods
TriValley Growers
Unilever

HOW MUCH

	Annual Growth	1986	1987	1988	1989	1990	1991	1992	1993	1994	1995
Sales ($ mil.)	8.5%	—	275	—	300	300	330	410	453	480	528
Employees	4.9%	—	—	—	1,500	1,500	1,600	1,600	1,800	2,000	2,000

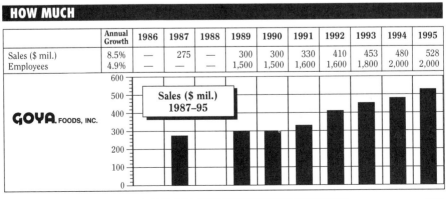

GOYA. FOODS, INC.

Sales ($ mil.)
1987–95

GREAT ATLANTIC & PACIFIC TEA CO.

OVERVIEW

A&P's 1,108 stores — 1,107 of which are not located in New York's Trump Palace — make the Montvale, New Jersey–based chain one of the top food retailers in North America. The company is Ontario's #1 grocer, but don't remind CEO James Wood. Troubles there in 1993 and 1994 included tough, lower-cost competition and a 14-week strike that shut down 63 stores. A&P converted 25 Ontario stores to low-price Super Fresh formats but still finished fiscal 1995 in the red because of its Canadian operations. The company no doubt hopes Trump Palace's swanky Food Emporium is more indicative of its direction.

The company has supermarkets in 22 states, the District of Columbia, and Ontario under 15 names, the best known being A&P. The company is the top grocery chain in New York City and Detroit. Strong markets for A&P in 1994 included Michigan (where the company has spent $123 million in capital improve-

ments in the past 5 years) and Atlanta (where the weaker stores obtained in a 1992 acquisition have been unloaded). In 1994 A&P opened 16 stores and renovated 55 while shuttering 87; the company plans to open about 30 stores annually for several years.

The company has been consolidating its variety of private-label brand names under the America's Choice moniker. In addition to the Eight O'Clock, Bokar, and Royale brands of coffee (sold not only by A&P but by other retailers outside its markets), A&P manufactures baked goods, deli products, and ice cream. Private-label products account for over 22% of A&P's sales, not far from the company's goal of 25%.

Tengelmann, a German firm that owns almost 54% of A&P, has been applying the company's name to grocery stores it owns in the Netherlands, where the name has previously been a known product brand.

WHEN

George Gilman and George H. Hartford of Augusta, Maine, set up shop in 1859 on New York City's docks to sell tea at a 50% discount by eliminating middlemen. The Great American Tea Company advertised by drawing a red wagon through the city's streets. By 1869 the company, renamed The Great Atlantic & Pacific Tea Company, had 11 stores offering discounted items.

Gilman retired in 1878, and Hartford brought in his sons George and John. In 1912, when the company had 400 stores, John opened a store on a low-price, cash-and-carry format, without customer credit or premiums, which proved popular. When the company passed to the sons in 1916, A&P had over 1,000 cash-and-carry stores and a strategy of having "a store on every corner."

During the 1920s and 1930s, the company grew to more than 15,000 stores; however, there was a movement by small retailers to restrict chain stores in general and A&P in particular. To improve the company's image, John Hartford initiated innovative marketing and customer service policies. A&P grew in the 1940s by converting its stores to supermarkets, but an antitrust suit in 1949 and the company's reluctance to carry more nonfood items pushed A&P into decline. Management shut stores in California and Washington to shore up the northeastern stores.

In 1975, after a long period of poor sales and failed discount format attempts, the board

chose a new CEO: former Albertson's president Jonathan Scott (who eventually left A&P to become president and CEO of American Stores). Scott cut costs by closing stores and reducing the work force, but his efforts proved ineffective. The company's 1978 sales increases failed to keep ahead of inflation, and A&P posted a $52 million loss.

In 1979 the Hartford Foundation sold its A&P holdings to the German Tengelmann Group, which appointed English-born James Wood as CEO (1980). A&P has since acquired Super Fresh (1982), Kohl's (1983), Pantry Pride (1984), Borman's (1989), Ontario's Miracle Food Mart (1990), and Atlanta's Big Star (1992).

The company entered the 1990s trying to fend off the effects of the recession and increasing competition from warehouse-type stores. Rivals' larger, newer, and cleaner supermarkets have stripped away market share in New York City, Detroit, and Long Island. In response, A&P has closed hundreds of old stores, planned openings of larger stores, and tried its hand at emphasizing ethnic and gourmet foods and unusual produce.

A&P in 1994 transplanted its Farmer Jack store name from Michigan to Virginia, where it is being used for a new produce-intensive store concept. In 1995 customers of A&P's 6 New York City Food Emporium stores were given the option of ordering their groceries from home via America Online.

NYSE symbol: GAP
Fiscal year ends: Last Saturday in February

WHO

Chairman and CEO: James Wood, age 65,
$1,160,500 pay
VC, CFO, and Treasurer: Fred Corrado, age 55,
$488,500 pay
President and COO: Christian W. E. Haub, age 30
EVP Development and Strategic Planning: Peter J.
O'Gorman, age 56, $374,712 pay
EVP Marketing and Merchandising: Gerald L. Good,
age 52
**Chairman and CEO, The Great Atlantic & Pacific
Company of Canada, Ltd.:** John D. Moffatt, age 47
SVP and Chief Merchandising Officer: George Graham,
age 45, $384,712 pay
SVP and General Counsel: Robert G. Ulrich, age 60
SVP and COO, US Operations: J. Wayne Harris, age 56
SVP and Chief Services Officer: Ivan K. Szathmary,
age 58
SVP Human Resources: H. Nelson "Bud" Lewis
Auditors: Deloitte & Touche LLP

WHERE

HQ: The Great Atlantic & Pacific Tea Company, Inc.,
2 Paragon Dr., Montvale, NJ 07645
Phone: 201-573-9700
Fax: 201-930-8106

A&P operates 1,108 supermarkets in 22 states in the
eastern, southern, and midwestern US, the District of
Columbia, and Ontario.

	1995 Sales		1995 Operating Income	
	$ mil.	% of total	$ mil.	% of total
US	8,541	83	138	—
Canada	1,791	17	(196)	—
Total	**10,332**	**100**	**(58)**	**—**

	No. of Stores
Ontario	235
New York	196
New Jersey	115
Michigan	100
Connecticut	62
Wisconsin	56
Virginia	53
Maryland	51
Pennsylvania	48
Georgia	46
Louisiana	32
North Carolina	29
Massachusetts	28
South Carolina	13
Delaware	9
West Virginia	8
Alabama	7
Mississippi	6
Other states	14
Total	**1,108**

WHAT

Store Names

A&P	Food Bazaar	Miracle Food Mart
Compass Foods	Food Emporium	Sav-A-Center
Dominion	Food Mart	Super Fresh
Family Mart	Futurestore	Ultra Mart
Farmer Jack	Kohl's	Waldbaum's

KEY COMPETITORS

Albertson's	Grand Union	Rite Aid
American Stores	J Sainsbury	Roundy's
Bruno's	Kroger	Ruddick
D'Agostino	Loblaw	Safeway
DeMoulas Super	Meijer	Star Market
Markets	Pathmark	Stop & Shop
Food Lion	Penn Traffic	Walgreen
Giant Eagle	Publix	Wegmans
Giant Food	Red Apple Group	Winn-Dixie

HOW MUCH

	Annual Growth	1986	1987	1988	1989	1990	1991	1992	1993	1994	1995
Sales ($ mil.)	5.1%	6,615	7,835	9,532	10,068	11,148	11,391	11,591	10,500	10,384	10,332
Net income ($ mil.)	—	56	69	103	128	147	151	71	(99)	4	(167)
Income as % of sales	—	0.8%	0.9%	1.1%	1.3%	1.3%	1.3%	0.6%	—	—	—
Earnings per share ($)	—	1.48	1.82	2.71	3.34	3.84	3.95	1.85	(2.58)	0.10	(4.36)
Stock price – high ($)[1]	—	22.00	27.75	46.88	48.13	65.38	61.75	57.75	35.25	35.00	27.38
Stock price – low ($)[1]	—	14.38	19.25	23.63	31.88	44.25	37.75	25.50	21.38	22.50	17.38
Stock price – close ($)[1]	(2.1%)	21.88	23.50	37.50	44.63	58.88	44.13	28.38	23.88	27.00	18.13
P/E – high	—	15	15	17	14	17	16	31	—	—	—
P/E – low	—	10	11	9	10	12	10	14	—	—	—
Dividends per share ($)	23.1%	0.10	0.40	0.48	0.58	0.68	0.78	0.80	0.80	0.80	0.65
Book value per share ($)	1.6%	17.63	19.85	22.32	25.42	28.59	31.96	32.79	27.06	26.02	20.27
Employees	4.9%	60,000	81,500	83,000	92,000	91,000	99,300	94,600	90,000	94,000	92,000

1995 Year-end:
Debt ratio: 53.3%
Return on equity: —
Cash (mil.): $129
Current ratio: 1.09
Long-term debt (mil.): $759
No. of shares (mil.): 38
Dividends
  Yield: 3.6%
  Payout: —
Market value (mil.): $693

Stock Price History[1]
High/Low 1986–95

[1]Stock prices are for the prior calendar year.

GTE CORPORATION

OVERVIEW

Based in Stamford, Connecticut, GTE is the 4th largest publicly owned telecommunications company in the world. It is the leading local telephone company in the US and provides traditional wireline telephone services in 28 states. Through its Mobilnet and Contel Cellular units, GTE is also the #2 cellular provider in the US. It recently purchased the 10% of Contel Cellular that it did not already own.

GTE is now combining wireline and wireless communications by offering Tele-Go, the first personal communications service (PCS) for the US residential market. Tele-Go is a cordless phone that can receive calls over wireline and cellular networks. Through its alliance with SBC Communications, GTE is able to offer both wireline and wireless telecommunications services in its Texas market.

In addition, it is extending its wireless services through its purchase of the broadband spectrum licenses necessary for PCS in Atlanta, Seattle, Cincinnati, and Denver.

The company has received construction approval from the FCC for its video-dialtone networks in 3 initial markets — Ventura County, California; Pasco and Pinellas Counties, Florida; and Honolulu. GTE plans to deliver video programming to 900,000 homes by the end of 1997.

GTE has numerous investments overseas, currently holding stakes in telephone companies in Argentina, Canada, the Dominican Republic, and Venezuela. It has signed an agreement with China United Telecommunications (UNICOM) to develop a 2nd telecommunications network in that country.

WHEN

Two former staff members of the Wisconsin Railroad Commission — Sigurd Odegard and John O'Connell — formed Richland Center Telephone in Wisconsin dairy country in 1918.

With backing from a utilities executive and a Paine Webber partner, Odegard and O'Connell created Associated Telephone Utilities in 1926. That year they bought a Long Beach telephone company, which Odegard, while on a California vacation, had noticed was up for sale. Associated Telephone grew rapidly, but the company was caught with too much debt in the Depression. Lenders took control in 1932 and moved headquarters from Chicago to New York. Still beset by problems, Associated was forced into bankruptcy and emerged as General Telephone (GT) in 1935.

Attorney David Power, named CEO in 1951, guided post-WWII growth as GT acquired Theodore Gary and Company (1955) and Sylvania (1959). When GT purchased Sylvania, which had been founded in 1901 by Frank Poor as a company that refilled burned-out light bulbs, it became a manufacturer and developer of lighting and electronics and was renamed General Telephone and Electronics.

The company, long the largest phone company independent of the Bell group, expanded with the purchase of phone companies in Florida (1957), the Southwest (1964), and Hawaii (1967). GTE sold its US consumer electronics business to North American Philips in 1981, and GTE Mobilnet was formed in 1982 to provide cellular telephone service. Under chairman James (Rocky) Johnson, it sold most of its US Sprint long-distance service, purchased in 1983 from Southern Pacific, to partner United Telecommunications in 1989. Concentrating again on its lucrative local phone businesses, GTE jettisoned PBX (private branch telephone exchange) maker Automatic Electric as AG Communication Systems, creating a joint venture to be owned by AT&T.

In 1991 the company merged with Contel ($3 billion in annual sales), which consisted of 30 telephone companies serving more than 2 million people in 30 states and the Caribbean. The historic merger made GTE the largest US local telephone utility (adding 2.6 million to GTE's 15.1 million lines) and the 2nd largest cellular telephone provider (nearly doubling GTE's cellular properties).

After acquiring about 20% of the Venezuelan phone company in 1991, GTE sold its remaining interest in Sprint in 1992 to United Telecommunications (now Sprint). It sold its electrical products business in 1993 and agreed to sell its GTE Spacenet satellite unit to GE in 1994. In the same year a GTE-led consortium won its bid for Argentinian cellular licenses.

In 1995 GTE chose 15 states, including Florida, Hawaii, and California, for video operations center (VOC) installations to support video-conferencing service for business. It also began selling telephone equipment for the home and office in its newly introduced GTE Phone Mart on CompuServe's on-line Electronic Mall. In addition, GTE Government Systems Corp., Sun Microsystems, and 2 other companies won a $200 million US government contract to provide the army's next generation of computer systems for the battlefield.

NYSE symbol: GTE
Fiscal year ends: December 31

Chairman and CEO: Charles R. Lee, age 55,
$2,004,115 pay
VC; President, GTE Telephone Operations: Kent B.
Foster, age 51, $1,525,508 pay
VC: Michael T. Masin, age 50, $1,271,077 pay
SVP Finance: J. Michael Kelly, age 38
SVP Corporate Planning and Development: Robert C.
Calafell, age 53
SVP and General Counsel: William P. Barr, age 44
VP Taxes: John P. Z. Kent, age 54
VP and Treasurer: Dan J. Cohrs
VP Public Affairs and Communications: G. Bruce
Redditt, age 44
VP Government Affairs: Samuel F. Shawhan Jr., age 62
VP and Controller: Lawrence R. Whitman, age 43
VP Human Resources and Administration: J. Randall
MacDonald, age 46
Auditors: Arthur Andersen & Co, SC

WHERE

HQ: One Stamford Forum, Stamford, CT 06904
Phone: 203-965-2000
Fax: 203-965-2277

GTE has telecommunications operations in 28 states,
Argentina, Canada, the Dominican Republic, and
Venezuela.

	1994 Sales	
	$ mil.	% of total
US	17,363	87
Other countries	2,581	13
Total	**19,944**	**100**

WHAT

	1994 Sales		1994 Operating Income	
	$ mil.	% of total	$ mil.	% of total
Telephone ops.	15,905	80	4,238	87
Telecomm prods. & svcs.	4,039	20	608	13
Total	**19,944**	**100**	**4,846**	**100**

Major Operations

**Selected Products
and Services**
GTE Airfone
GTE Government Systems
GTE Information Services
Personal Communications
Services

Telephone Operations
Local network services
Long-distance services
Network access services

Selected Subsidiaries and Affiliates
AG Communication Systems (20%)
BC TEL (51%)
BELGACOM Directory Services (20%, Belgium)
Compañía de Teléfonos del Interior (26%, Argentina)
Compañía Anónima Nacional Teléfonos
de Venezuela (20%)
Compañía Dominicana de Teléfonos, C. por A.
Contel Cellular Inc.
GTE Mobilnet
Québec Telephone (51%)

KEY COMPETITORS

AirTouch
Ameritech
AT&T Corp.
BCE
Bell Atlantic
BellSouth
Cable & Wireless
Century Telephone
Dun & Bradstreet
Ericsson

Frontier Corp.
Goeken Group
MCI
MFS
Communications
Motorola
Nextel
NYNEX
Pacific Telesis

SBC
Communications
Sprint
Telephone and
Data Systems
U.S. Long
Distance
U S WEST
WorldCom

HOW MUCH

	Annual Growth	1985	1986	1987	1988	1989	1990	1991	1992	1993	1994
Sales ($ mil.)	2.7%	15,732	15,112	15,421	16,460	17,424	18,374	19,621	19,984	19,748	19,944
Net income ($ mil.)	—	(161)	1,184	1,119	1,225	1,417	1,541	1,580	1,739	990	2,451
Income as % of sales	—	—	7.8%	7.3%	7.4%	8.1%	8.4%	8.1%	8.7%	5.0%	12.3%
Earnings per share ($)	—	(0.32)	1.72	1.61	1.77	2.08	2.26	1.75	1.90	1.03	2.55
Stock price – high ($)	—	15.47	21.30	22.38	22.94	35.56	36.00	35.00	35.75	39.88	35.25
Stock price – low ($)	—	12.72	15.09	8.81	16.88	21.44	23.50	27.50	28.88	34.13	29.50
Stock price – close ($)	7.9%	15.34	19.47	17.69	22.25	35.00	29.25	34.63	34.63	35.00	30.38
P/E – high	—	—	12	14	13	17	16	20	19	39	14
P/E – low	—	—	9	6	10	10	10	16	15	33	12
Dividends per share ($)	6.9%	1.03	1.06	1.23	1.28	1.37	1.49	1.61	1.73	1.84	1.88
Book value per share ($)	0.1 %	10.75	11.61	11.90	12.45	12.01	12.90	12.21	10.61	10.14	10.86
Employees	(5.4%)	183,033	160,463	161,224	159,000	158,000	177,477	162,000	131,000	117,446	111,000

1994 Year-end:
Debt ratio: 57.3%
Return on equity: 24.4%
Cash (mil.): $323
Current ratio: 0.69
Long-term debt (mil.): $12,163
No. of shares (mil.): 965
Dividends
  Yield: 6.2%
  Payout: 73.7%
Market value (mil.): $29,319

**Stock Price History
High/Low 1985–94**

(chart: 40–0)

GUARDIAN LIFE INSURANCE

OVERVIEW

New York City–based Guardian Life Insurance is what its name implies — a zealous steward of the interests of its policyholders. Its conservative investment policy left it undamaged by the 1994 bond market crash and allowed the company, despite decreased sales of group insurance policies, to complete its 127th consecutive year of dividend payments.

Guardian, which operates in all 50 states and the District of Columbia, offers group and individual life and health insurance, disability and medical and dental coverage (through indemnity policies, HMOs, and PPOs), and variable annuities. Its Guardian Asset Management and Guardian Investor Services units offer a variety of financial services, including the flagship Guardian Park Avenue Fund, the Baillie Gifford International Fund (international investment fund), and a variety of other equity, money market, and bond funds. The company also provides life, credit, and annuity reinsurance to other insurers.

In 1994 the company added to its financial services segment by creating a new division to sell and service group pensions, particularly 401(k)s. This is a market that Guardian feels is underdeveloped but will grow as the baby boomers age.

WHEN

Hugo Wesendonck made his way to Philadelphia in 1850, having escaped from Germany, where he had been sentenced to death for his part in the abortive revolution of 1848. After working in the silk business in Philadelphia, he moved to New York, which had the 3rd largest concentration of ethnic Germans in the world (after Berlin and Vienna).

In 1860 Wesendonck and several fellow expatriates formed an insurance company to serve the needs of the German-American community. Germania Life Insurance was chartered as a mixed company (a stock mutual), which paid dividends both to shareholders and policy owners. Wesendonck became the first president and led it through its formative years. The outbreak of the US Civil War blocked the company's growth among Germans in the South, but the company expanded within the rest of the US and its territories and, by 1867, had even penetrated South America.

After the Civil War many insurance companies foundered, victims of high costs. Wesendonck battled this problem by instituting strict cost controls and limiting commissions. This allowed the company to continue issuing dividends, which, in turn, kept shareholders happy and gave what amounted to a rebate on its policyholders' premiums.

In the 1870s Germania opened offices in Europe, and for the next decades much of the company's growth was concentrated in Europe. By 1910, 46% of sales originated in Europe. Germania's original clientele decreased between the 1890s and WWI, as German immigration slowed, as Germans were assimilated into the population, and as the greatest influx of immigrants in US history brought in millions of people from eastern and southern Europe. Germania's market share dropped from 9th place in 1880 to 21st in 1910.

When WWI began in Europe, the company lost contact with much of its business. American anti-German sentiment even before US entry into the war prodded Germania's officers to consider changing the company's name. Germania became the Guardian Life Insurance Company of America in 1917.

After WWI the company began winding down its German business, but it did not completely disentangle itself until 1952, when it bought out its last policyholders there.

In 1924 Guardian began mutualizing but could not complete the process until 1944. The delay was caused by the probate of one shareholder's estate.

After WWII Guardian began offering noncancelable medical insurance (1955) and group insurance (1957). In 1969 Guardian formed Guardian Investor Services to offer mutual funds. Two years later it established Guardian Insurance & Annuity to sell variable contracts. In 1989 it organized Guardian Asset Management to handle pension funds.

In 1993 the company joined Private Health Care Systems, Inc., a consortium of commercial insurance carriers offering managed health care products and services. This allowed Guardian to offer the services of 97,000 doctors at 1,035 hospitals throughout the US.

Guardian's health care segment continued to grow in 1994, when it signed a managed indemnity agreement with Juniper Healthcare Containment Systems. In 1995 it made a joint marketing agreement with Physicians Health Services (an HMO), which will give Guardian's clients access to these HMO services and Physicians Health Services's clients access to Guardian's products.

Mutual company
Fiscal year ends: December 31

Chairman and CEO: Arthur V. Ferrara
President: Joseph D. Sargent
EVP and CFO: Peter L. Hutchings
EVP and Chief Investment Officer: Frank J. Jones
SVP and General Counsel: Edward K. Kane
SVP Reinsurance and Taxes: Thomas G. Kabele
VP Group Medical and Managed Care Products: John D. DeRosa
VP Group Pension: Gary B. Lenderink
VP Group Insurance Procedure: John J. Pallotta Jr.
VP Group National Claims Policy Procedure and Customer Service: Michael J. Chiaffitella
VP Disability Insurance: John M. Sawyer
VP Group Pricing and Standards: Sanford B. Herman
VP Office Services: Hugh A. Howell
VP Life Insurance Marketing: Michael A. Schiffman
VP Human Resources and Administrative Support: Douglas C. Kramer
Auditors: Price Waterhouse LLP

HQ: The Guardian Life Insurance Company of America, 201 Park Avenue South, New York, NY 10003
Phone: 212-598-8000
Fax: 212-598-8813

Guardian Life Insurance is licensed in all 50 states and the District of Columbia.

	1994 Sales	
	$ mil.	% of total
Premiums	5,281	87
Net investment income	599	10
Service fees	73	1
Other	138	2
Total	**6,091**	**100**

	1994 Assets	
	$ mil.	% of total
Cash & equivalents	22	0
State & municipal bonds	2,114	16
Other bonds	4,244	31
Stocks	1,217	9
Mortgage loans	778	6
Real estate	124	1
Policy loans	767	6
Other investments	176	1
Separate account assets	3,402	25
Receivables	189	1
Other	534	4
Total	**13,567**	**100**

Services
Asset management
Group and individual disability insurance
Group and individual life insurance
Group and individual medical and dental coverage
Variable annuities

Subsidiaries
Guardian Asset Management Corp.
Guardian Baillie Gifford, Ltd. (UK)
Guardian Insurance & Annuity Co.
Guardian Investor Services Corp.

Aetna	Northwestern Mutual
Blue Cross	Oxford Health Plans
Charles Schwab	Pacific Mutual Life
Chubb	PacifiCare
CIGNA	Paine Webber
Equitable Cos.	Provident Life
FMR	Prudential
Health Systems	Salomon
Household International	T. Rowe Price
Humana	Transamerica
John Hancock	Travelers
Kemper Corp.	United HealthCare
MassMutual	U.S. Healthcare
Merrill Lynch	USF&G
MetLife	WellPoint
New York Life	

	Annual Growth	1985	1986	1987	1988	1989	1990	1991	1992	1993	1994
Assets ($ mil.)	15.9%	—	—	—	5,611	6,715	7,523	8,861	10,271	12,336	13,567
Net income ($ mil.)	16.7%	—	—	—	57	134	236	186	132	249	144
Income as % of assets	—	—	—	—	1.0%	2.0%	3.1%	2.1%	1.3%	2.0%	1.1%
Employees	7.7%	4,472	4,930	3,149	4,704	3,420	6,845	7,175	7,502	7,126	7,602

1994 Year-end:
Equity as % of assets: 7.4%
Return on equity: 14.4%
Sales (mil.): $6,091

The Guardian

Assets ($ mil.) 1988–94

THE HEARST CORPORATION

OVERVIEW

The Hearst Corporation's presence in newspapers, magazines, books, and broadcasting makes it one of the world's largest diversified media companies. Still controlled by descendants of William Randolph Hearst, the closely held, New York–based company owns 12 daily and 5 weekly newspapers (such as the *San Antonio Express-News* and *San Francisco Examiner*); 15 US consumer magazines (including *Popular Mechanics*, *Good Housekeeping*, and *Redbook*); stakes in 4 cable TV networks; 6 TV and 6 radio stations; and major book and business publishers.

Hearst intends to be a big wheel on the information autobahn. It opened a New Media Center to inspire staff and showcase advanced media. In 1995 it joined 8 other large newspaper companies to create New Century Network, a national on-line array of newspaper services still under development. Hearst is already selling magazine subscriptions, videos, and other products in cyberspace on the Multimedia Newsstand and plans to create on-line editions of 6 magazines and the *Houston Chronicle*. It bought stakes in Netscape Communications (Internet software developer) and KidSoft (educational software company).

Hearst's magazines, which supply almost half of the company's revenues, successfully launched *Marie Claire* in 1994. The company created a new unit to hunt for magazine ideas both inside and outside the company.

WHEN

William Randolph Hearst, son of a California mining magnate, started his empire as a reporter, having been expelled from Harvard in 1884 for playing jokes on professors. He became editor of the *San Francisco Examiner*, which his father had obtained as payment for a gambling debt, in 1887. Hearst's sensationalist style brought financial success to the paper. In 1895 he bought the *New York Morning Journal* and competed against the *New York World*, owned by Joseph Pulitzer, Hearst's first employer. The "yellow journalism" resulting from that rivalry characterized American journalism at the turn of the century. Hearst used his newspapers as a forum for his personal and political views for more than 30 years.

The company branched out into magazines (1903), film (1913), and radio (1928). The Hearst organization owned 13 newspapers and 7 magazines by 1920 and pioneered film journalism throughout the 1920s with the Hearst-Selig News Pictorial. In 1935 the company was at its peak, with newspapers in 19 cities (nearly 14% of total US daily and 24% of Sunday circulation), the largest syndicate (King Features), international news and photo services, 13 magazines, 8 radio stations, and 2 motion picture companies. Two years later Hearst had to relinquish control of the company to avoid bankruptcy. Movie companies, radio stations, magazines, and, later, most of his San Simeon estate were sold to reduce debt. Hearst inspired Orson Welles's 1941 film *Citizen Kane*.

When Hearst died in 1951, Richard Berlin, in charge of the company since 1940, became CEO. During his tenure Berlin sold off failing newspapers but also moved into television and acquired more magazines. The Hearst family retained control through a family trust.

Frank Bennack Jr., president and CEO since 1979, expanded the company, acquiring daily and weekly newspapers (in Los Angeles, Houston, and Seattle, among other cities), publishing companies (notably William Morrow, 1981), 3 TV stations (in 1981, 1982, and 1986), magazines (*Redbook*, 1982; *Esquire*, 1986), and 20% of cable sports network ESPN (1991). Hearst branched into video via a joint venture with Capital Cities/ABC (1981) and helped launch the Lifetime and Arts & Entertainment cable channels (1984). It closed the Los Angeles *Herald Examiner* in 1989.

Hearst teamed up with *Izvestia* (1990) to start a newspaper in Russia and with Dow Jones (1992) to publish *SmartMoney*, a personal finance magazine. Also in 1992 Hearst closed the *Light* in San Antonio after buying its competitor, the *Express-News*, and launched a New England news network with Continental Cablevision. Hearst hired former FCC chairman Alfred Sikes, who quickly moved the company onto the information superhighway.

In 1993 Hearst joined with Canadian cable company Le Groupe Vidéotron to experiment in interactive TV; bought a stake in a California electronic publisher to put Hearst magazines on-line; and created an interactive home service (HomeArts). Hearst also bought other companies for their medical databases. That same year founder Hearst's son and namesake, who was chairman of the executive committee, died at age 85.

Hearst planned to launch a weekly magazine with ESPN in 1995 called *Total Sports*.

Private company
Fiscal year ends: December 31

WHO

Chairman: Randolph A. Hearst, age 80
President and CEO: Frank A. Bennack Jr., age 62
EVP and COO: Gilbert C. Maurer, age 66
SVP, CFO, and Chief Legal Officer: Victor F. Ganzi, age 47
VP; General Manager, Hearst Broadcasting: John G. Conomikes
VP; General Manager, Hearst Newspapers: Robert J. Danzig
VP; Group Head, Hearst New Media and Technology: Alfred C. Sikes, age 55
VP and General Counsel: Jon E. Thackeray
VP and Director Human Resources: Kenneth A. Feldman

WHERE

HQ: 959 Eighth Ave., New York, NY 10019
Phone: 212-649-2000
Fax: 212-765-3528 (corporate communications)

Hearst products are available throughout the US and in more than 80 countries.

WHAT

Selected Businesses

US Magazines

Colonial Homes	House Beautiful	Redbook
Cosmopolitan	Marie Claire	SmartMoney
Country Living	Motor Boating	Sports Afield
Esquire	& Sailing	Town &
Good Housekeeping	Popular	Country
Harper's Bazaar	Mechanics	Victoria

Broadcasting

KMBC-TV, Kansas City, MO	WISN-TV, Milwaukee
WBAL (AM) Baltimore	WIYY (FM), Baltimore
WBAL-TV, Baltimore	WLTQ (FM), Milwaukee
WCVA-TV, Boston	WTAE (AM), Pittsburgh
WDTN-TV, Dayton, OH	WTAE-TV, Pittsburgh
WISN (AM), Milwaukee	WVTY (FM), Pittsburgh

Book Publishing
Avon Books
William Morrow & Co.

Business Publishing
American Druggist
Black Book series (auto guides)
HDG International (UK partnership with R.R. Donnelley Co.)
Motor magazine
Official Guides to Walt Disney World/Disneyland
Retirement Advisors Inc.
United Technical Publications

Electronic Publishing
Camdat Corp. (medical information software)
First DataBank (drug database)
N-Squared Computing
Professional Drug Systems

Entertainment and Syndication
Arts & Entertainment Network (37.5%)
ESPN (20%)
Hearst/ABC Video Services (joint venture)
Hearst Entertainment Distribution
Hearst Entertainment Productions

King Features Syndicate
Lifetime Television (50%)
New England Cable News (joint venture)
North America Syndicate

New Media/Technology
Books That Work (minority stake)
Hearst Interactive Canada
Hearst Multimedia Publishing
Hearst New Media Center
HomeArts (on-line home and garden information)
KidSoft, Inc. (29%)
Netscape Communications (minority stake)
New Century Network
UBI (interactive TV, with Le Groupe Vidéotron and 4 others, Canada)

Newspapers (Major)
Albany (NY) Times Union
Houston Chronicle
San Antonio Express-News
San Francisco Examiner
Seattle Post-Intelligencer

Other
Associated Publishing Co. (telephone directories)
Hearst Broadcasting Productions
Hearst Magazines Enterprises

KEY COMPETITORS

Advance Publications	Cox Enterprises	Reader's Digest
American Media	E.W. Scripps	Reed Elsevier
Bertelsmann	Gannett	Time Warner
Bloomberg	Heritage Media	Times Mirror
Capital Cities/ABC	Lagardère	Tribune
CBS	McGraw-Hill	Viacom
Chronicle Publishing	MediaNews	Walt Disney
	New York Times	Washington Post
	News Corp.	

HOW MUCH

	Annual Growth	1985	1986	1987	1988	1989	1990	1991	1992	1993	1994
Sales ($ mil.)	4.6%	1,540	1,529	1,886	1,986	2,094	2,138	1,888	1,973	2,174	2,299
Newspaper revenues ($ mil.)	8.9%	—	390	650	689	700	715	680	701	720	770
Magazine revenues ($ mil.)	5.9%	—	780	873	919	992	1,022	1,002	1,062	1,200	1,236
Broadcast revenues ($ mil.)	0.5%	—	280	262	263	270	290	206	210	254	292
Cable TV revenues ($ mil.)	—	—	9	11	15	21	—	—	—	—	—
Other revenues ($ mil.)	—	—	70	90	100	111	111	—	—	—	—
Employees	1.7%	12,000	12,000	15,000	15,000	14,000	13,950	14,000	13,000	13,500	14,000

The Hearst Corporation

Sales ($ mil.)
1985–94

HELMSLEY ENTERPRISES, INC.

OVERVIEW

In a classic New York–style 1995 remake of *King Kong*, Donald Trump battled Leona Helmsley over the Empire State Building. Which one played King Kong and which Fay Wray was unclear. Leona and Harry Helmsley control more than 100,000 apartments, 13,000 hotel rooms, and 100 million square feet of commercial space across the US, including the Empire State Building. Trump, who bought a stake in the New York landmark in 1994, sued the Helmsleys in 1995 for $100 million, alleging that they had let the building become "second rate" and "rodent infested." In a countersuit the Helmsleys sued Trump for $100 million, alleging that Trump was trying to extort money from them. Lawsuits and notoriety are no strangers to Helmsley Enterprises. Its well-publicized brushes with the law

include Leona Helmsley's conviction and jailing on income tax evasion charges and a 1994 kickback scandal involving its Brown, Harris, Stevens real estate brokerage and co-op management company.

Subsidiaries Helmsley-Spear and Helmsley-Noyes manage several hundred office and apartment buildings in New York and across the US, in most of which Harry Helmsley has a stake. Deco Purchasing is the purchasing arm for Helmsley Hotels, and Owners & Maintenance holds cleaning contracts with many Helmsley properties.

Although Harry Helmsley was declared mentally unfit to stand trial for 47 counts of fraud and tax evasion in 1989, the 85-year-old billionaire is still nominally in charge of the Helmsley empire.

WHEN

Harry Helmsley began his career as a Manhattan rent collector in 1925. Rent collecting, then handled in person, gave Helmsley contact with building owners and an ability to evaluate a building. When the real estate market crashed in 1929, Helmsley obtained property at bargain prices. He paid $1,000 down for a building with a $100,000 mortgage and later quipped that he did so to provide a job for his father, whom he hired as superintendent. In 1946 he sold the building for $165,000.

In 1949 Helmsley teamed up with lawyer Lawrence Wien. Helmsley located property; Wien found financing. During the 1950s Helmsley bought into many office buildings, including the Flatiron (1951), Berkeley (1953), and Equitable (1957). He bought the property management firm of Leon Spear in 1955. In 1961 Helmsley bought the Empire State Building for $65 million and sold it to Prudential for $29 million, obtaining a 114-year leaseback. A public offering for the newly created Empire State Building Co. made up the balance.

In the mid-1960s he began developing properties, beginning with a 52-story office tower on Broadway. By 1967 Helmsley was investing in shopping centers. In 1969 he bought the trust of Furman and Wolfson, which held about 30 buildings nationwide, for $165 million. To finance the trust, Helmsley borrowed $78 million in cash on his reputation — the largest signature loan ever.

Helmsley's association with Spear precipitated a meeting with successful real estate broker Leona Roberts, from whom Spear had purchased an apartment. Spear arranged for

them to meet in 1969; Helmsley hired Leona, promoted her to SVP, and divorced his wife to marry her in 1971.

Helmsley became interested in hotels in the 1970s, although the Manhattan market for luxury hotels was considered saturated. In 1974 he leased a historical building (later called the Helmsley Palace) from the Catholic church and began renovation; the Palace opened in 1980. Beginning in 1979 Harry invested in Florida, first building Miami Palace and, in a later project that went bankrupt, Helmsley Center.

During the 1980s Harry's empire began to crumble as Leona gained control. Lawsuits, lackadaisical bookkeeping, shoddy maintenance (a ceiling collapsed at the Helmsley Windsor, killing a guest), and extravagant spending culminated in indictments for tax evasion. In 1989 Leona was convicted, fined $7.1 million, and sentenced to 30 months in jail.

In 1990 the Helmsleys sold their Helmsley-Greenfield subsidiary. In 1991 the limited partners of the Helmsley Palace sued to remove the Helmsleys from control of the hotel. In 1993 the Helmsleys gave up control of the hotel, renamed the New York Palace.

In 1994 Leona Helmsley was released from federal prison after serving a 21-month stint. No longer a Helmsley executive (New York law prohibits convicted felons from trafficking in alcohol, i.e., managing hotels that serve liquor), she is seen as an active behind-the-scenes manager of the hotel business.

In 1995 Helmsley sold its troubled Brown, Harris, Stevens real estate brokerage.

Private company
Fiscal year ends: December 31

WHO

Chairman, President, and CEO: Harry B. Helmsley, age 85
SVP: Joseph Licari, age 58
VP and Assistant Secretary: Alvin Schwartz, age 74
VP and Assistant Secretary: Irving Schneider, age 76
Treasurer, Secretary, and CFO: Martin S. Stone
Controller: Josephine Keenan
Manager Human Resources: Jennie Voscina
Auditors: Eisner & Lubin

WHERE

HQ: 60 E. 42nd St., New York, NY 10165-0001
Phone: 212-687-6400
Fax: 212-687-6437

Helmsley operates primarily in Manhattan but has holdings elsewhere across the US.

WHAT

Major Subsidiaries
77 Park Inc. (real estate)
Basic Estates, Inc. (real estate)
Boardwalk & Missouri Corp. (hotel management)
California Jewelry Mart Realty Corp. (office building management)
Carlton House Inc. (hotel management)
Charles F. Noyes Co. Inc. (real estate management and brokerage)
Deco Purchasing Co. (purchasing)
H 33 Manor Corp. (real estate)
H 321 Cloister Corp. (real estate)
Helmsley Hotels Inc. (hotel management)
Helmsley-Noyes Co., Inc. (real estate)
Helmsley-Spear Conversion Sales Corp. (real estate)
Helmsley-Spear Inc. (restaurants, hotels, and other real estate)
Hospitality Motor Inns (motel management)
John J. Reynolds, Inc. (real estate)
Moritz Inc. (hotel management)
National Realty Corp.
Owners & Maintenance Corp. (real estate services)
Park Lane Hotel Inc. (hotel management)
Parkmerced Corp. (real estate)
Supervisory Management Corp. (management and consulting services)
Willoughby Properties Inc. (real estate)

Selected Hotels
Carlton House Hotel (New York, NY)
Harley of Enfield (Hartford, CT)
Harley of Grand Rapids (MI)
Harley of Lexington (KY)
The Helmsley (New York, NY)
The Helmsley Middletown (New York, NY)
The Helmsley Park Lane (New York, NY)
Helmsley Windsor (New York, NY)
Holiday Inn (Atlantic City, NJ)
Hospitality Motor Inns (Cleveland, OH)
Hotel St. Moritz (New York, NY)
Park Lane Hotel (New York, NY)

KEY COMPETITORS

Alexander's
Bass
Carlson
Four Seasons
HFS
Hilton
Hyatt
ITT Corp.
JMB Realty
Lefrak
Loews
Marriott International
Melvin Simon
Promus Hotels
Ritz-Carlton
Rockefeller Group
Rouse
Taubman
Tishman Speyer Properties
Trammell Crow
Trump Organization

HOW MUCH

	Annual Growth	1985	1986	1987	1988	1989	1990	1991	1992	1993	1994
Estimated sales ($ mil.)	6.1%	1,000	1,700	1,430	1,400	1,480	1,435	1,327	1,200	1,200	1,700
Employees	3.0%	10,000	13,000	13,000	13,000	13,000	13,000	13,000	13,000	13,000	13,000

Estimated Sales
($ mil.)
1985–94

INGERSOLL-RAND COMPANY

OVERVIEW

With 42% of its sales destined for overseas markets in 1994, the Woodcliff Lake, New Jersey–based Ingersoll-Rand Company is poised to take advantage of the growing economies in Asia and Europe. The company is a leading manufacturer of nonelectrical industrial machinery and air compression systems, antifriction bearings, construction equipment, air tools, pumps, and other industrial tools.

Ingersoll-Rand operates 3 major business segments: standard machinery (32% of 1994 sales), which makes air compressors and construction and mining machinery; engineered equipment (21%), which sells pump and processing systems; and bearings, locks, and tools (47%). The firm also owns 49% of Dresser-Rand, which primarily sells compressors.

Ingersoll-Rand places a strong emphasis on technological innovation and invested a record $154.6 million in R&D in 1994. The company has registered 440 US patents in the past 5 years, including 98 in 1994.

Acquisitions have also been a key part of the company's growth strategy. In 1995 the company agreed to shell out $1.5 billion to acquire the $950-million-in-sales Clark Equipment Co. The acquisition makes Ingersoll-Rand a major player in the market for small and medium-sized construction machines, such as those used in road repair.

WHEN

Simon Ingersoll invented the steam-driven rock drill in New York City in 1871. In 1874 he sold the patent to José Francisco de Navarro, who financed the organization of the Ingersoll Rock Drill Company. Three years later the company merged with Sergeant Drill, a company created by Navarro's former foreman, Henry Clark Sergeant.

In 1871, at the same time Ingersoll was inventing his drill, Albert, Jasper, and Addison Rand were forming the Rand Drill Company. Both companies continued to make drills and other equipment through the turn of the century. In 1905 they merged to become Ingersoll-Rand.

During the next several years, Ingersoll-Rand started producing air compressors in addition to its basic line of rock drills. In 1912 the company added centrifugal compressors and turbo blowers to its product line. Further diversification occurred with the purchase of A. S. Cameron Steam Pump Works and Imperial Pneumatic Tool Company (portable air tools). For several decades the company continued to grow as a major manufacturer of compressed-air tools, sold mostly to the mining industry.

After WWII Ingersoll-Rand expanded its operations to Canada, Europe, South America, and Africa. During the 1960s it diversified into new specialized machinery. Acquisitions included Aldrich Pump (high-pressure plunger pumps, 1961), Pendleton Tool (mechanics' service tools, 1964), and Torrington (antifriction bearings and textile machine needles, 1969). Diversification continued during the 1970s and 1980s with the acquisitions of DAMCO (truck-mounted drilling rigs, 1973); Schlage Lock (lock and door hardware,

1974); California Pellet (1974); Western Land Roller (vertical water pumps, 1977); and Fafnir Bearings, the purchase of which made Ingersoll-Rand the largest US bearing manufacturer (1986).

During this time the company developed several new products, including small air compressors and water jet systems capable of cutting steel and concrete. In 1986 Ingersoll-Rand formed a partnership with Dresser Industries (Dresser-Rand, 49%) to produce gas turbines, compressors, and similar equipment. In 1992 the companies combined their pump businesses (Ingersoll-Dresser Pump, 51%). Ingersoll-Rand bought Aro (air-powered tools, 1990) from Todd Shipyards and German ABG (paving-equipment maker, 1990) and sold Schlage Electronics (1991) to Westinghouse.

After 5 years at the company's helm, Theodore Black retired in 1993 and was replaced by 16-year veteran James Perrella. In 1993 Ingersoll-Rand bought the German needle and cylindrical bearing business of FAG Kugelfischer Georg Schäfer for $43 million and agreed to buy a 12% interest in Nuovo Pignone (turbines, compressors, pumps, valves) from Italy's ENI. That same year the company sold its underground coal-mining machinery business to Long-Airdox and its domestic jet engine bearing operation to MPB. In 1994 Ingersoll-Rand agreed to buy ECOAIR, a unit of MAN GHH, and formed a joint venture (50%) with MAN GHH to produce rotary-screw airends.

In 1994 the firm purchased Montabert SA, a French maker of rock-breaking and drilling equipment, for $18.4 million, and French industrial toolmaker SA Charles Maire.

NYSE symbol: IR
Fiscal year ends: December 31

WHO

Chairman, President, and CEO: James E. Perrella,
age 59, $1,245,417 pay
EVP; President, Production Equipment Group: J. Frank
Travis, age 59, $613,625 pay
EVP: William G. Mulligan, age 64, $516,667 pay
SVP and CFO: Thomas F. McBride, age 59, $466,667
VP; President, Air Compressor Group: Paul L. Bergren,
age 45, $436,417 pay
VP; President, Bearing and Components Group: Allen
M. Nixon, age 54
VP; President, IDP: Frederick W. Hadfield, age 58
VP; President, Construction and Mining Group:
R. Barry Uber, age 49
VP; President, Process Systems Group: Larry H. Pitsch,
age 54
VP and Treasurer: William J. Armstrong, age 53
VP and General Counsel: Patricia Nachtigal, age 48
VP Human Resources: Donald H. Rice, age 50
Auditors: Price Waterhouse LLP

WHERE

HQ: 200 Chestnut Ridge Rd., Woodcliff Lake, NJ 07675
Phone: 201-573-0123
Fax: 201-573-3448

The company operates 47 plants in the US, 6 in Canada,
27 in Europe, 5 in the Far East, 5 in Latin America, 2 in
Asia, and one in Africa.

	1994 Sales		1994 Operating Income	
	$ mil.	% of total	$ mil.	% of total
US	2,810	62	336	81
Europe	1,254	28	43	11
Other regions	444	10	35	8
Adjustments	—	—	(37)	—
Total	**4,508**	**100**	**377**	**100**

WHAT

	1994 Sales		1994 Operating Income	
	$ mil.	% of total	$ mil.	% of total
Bearings, locks & tools	2,135	47	257	62
Standard machinery	1,446	32	122	30
Engineered equip.	927	21	35	8
Adjustments	—	—	(37)	—
Total	**4,508**	**100**	**377**	**100**

Selected Products

Air compressors	Mining machinery
Air motors	Paving equipment
Air tools	Pellet mills
Asphalt compactors	Pneumatic valves
Automotive components	Portable generators
Ball and roller bearings	Pulp-processing machinery
Construction equipment	Road-building machinery
Door hardware	Roller mills
Engine-starting systems	Rotary drills
Fluid-handling equipment	Rough-terrain forklifts
Food-processing equipment	Separation equipment
Industrial pumps	Soil compactors
Lubrication equipment	Spray-coating systems
Material-handling equip.	Waterjet cutting systems
	Winches

KEY COMPETITORS

American Brands	Flow International	Masco
AMSTED	FMC	Newell Co.
Anglo American	Friedrich Krupp	Raytheon
Baker Hughes	General Signal	Robert Bosch
Black & Decker	Goulds Pumps	Rolls-Royce
Caterpillar	Harnischfeger	Stanley Works
Cooper Industries	Industries	Teledyne
Deere	Hillenbrand	Texas
Dover	Honda	Instruments
Eaton	Honeywell	Thermo Electron
Emerson	Illinois Tool Works	TRINOVA
Fiat	ITT Industries	Willcox & Gibbs

HOW MUCH

	Annual Growth	1985	1986	1987	1988	1989	1990	1991	1992	1993	1994
Sales ($ mil.)	6.1%	2,637	2,800	2,648	3,021	3,447	3,738	3,586	3,784	4,021	4,508
Net income ($ mil.)	11.4%	80	101	108	162	202	185	151	116	164	211
Income as % of sales	—	3.0%	3.6%	4.1%	5.3%	5.9%	5.0%	4.2%	3.1%	4.1%	4.7%
Earnings per share ($)	11.4%	0.76	0.95	0.99	1.50	1.89	1.78	1.46	1.11	1.56	2.00
Stock price – high ($)	—	11.34	13.78	22.88	22.31	25.13	30.25	27.50	34.25	39.88	41.63
Stock price – low ($)	—	8.84	10.17	11.25	15.50	16.81	14.25	17.50	25.00	28.75	29.50
Stock price – close ($)	12.7%	10.70	11.16	17.75	17.13	25.13	18.63	27.50	29.13	38.25	31.50
P/E – high	—	15	15	23	15	13	17	19	31	26	21
P/E – low	—	12	11	11	10	9	8	12	23	18	15
Dividends per share ($)	3.7%	0.52	0.52	0.52	0.52	0.58	0.63	0.66	0.69	0.70	0.72
Book value per share ($)	3.2%	10.61	11.05	10.98	12.04	13.37	14.53	15.21	12.36	12.82	14.03
Employees	0.4%	34,740	29,857	29,556	30,284	31,623	33,722	31,117	35,308	35,143	35,932

1994 Year-end:
Debt ratio: 17.1%
Return on equity: 14.7%
Cash (mil.): $207
Current ratio: 1.93
Long-term debt (mil.): $316
No. of shares (mil.): 109
Dividends
  Yield: 2.3%
  Payout: 36.0%
Market value (mil.): $3,437

Stock Price History
High/Low 1985–94

INTERNATIONAL BUSINESS MACHINES

OVERVIEW

Big Blue is back in the pink. IBM, the world's #1 computer company (hardware and software), showed a profit in 1994 after 3 years of losses totaling more than $15 billion.

IBM acquired software pioneer Lotus, developer of the *1-2-3* spreadsheet, for $3.52 billion in 1995. IBM, which has failed to sell PC users on its own OS/2 operating system, hopes to challenge the dominance of Microsoft Windows with Lotus's *Notes*, which links PCs regardless of operating system. Lotus also gives IBM a commanding presence in desktop software.

The Lotus acquisition is the most flamboyant chapter in IBM's recent effort to recapture slipping market share after a drop in mainframe and minicomputer sales during the early 1990s. Ironically, it was a mid-1990s resurgence in high-end products (mainframes,

minicomputers, and data-storage products) that pulled the company back into the black. To boost sales, IBM is also broadening its focus to include PCs, software, networking, and client/server products.

Under Louis Gerstner, who became CEO in 1993, IBM has begun trimming overhead by shutting plants, selling real estate, and laying off workers. In 1995 the company said it will also cut costs by buying more parts from outside sources and by expanding its contract manufacturing. IBM intends to reduce annual expenses by $8 billion by mid-1996.

Gerstner is changing IBM's tone with new products, a growing service unit, and a casual dress code that replaces the long-standard dark suits. The company is cash rich, so more acquisitions could be in store.

WHEN

In 1914 National Cash Register's star salesman, 40-year-old Thomas Watson, left to rescue the flagging Computing-Tabulating-Recording Company. Watson aggressively marketed C-T-R's Hollerith machine (a punch card tabulator) and supplied tabulators to the US government during WWI, tripling C-T-R's revenues to almost $15 million by 1920.

Watson expanded operations to Europe, Latin America, and the Far East. The company became International Business Machines in 1924 and soon dominated the market for tabulators, time clocks, and electric typewriters. It was the US's largest office machinery firm by 1940, with sales approaching $50 million.

IBM perfected electromechanical calculation (the Harvard Mark I, 1944) but initially dismissed the potential of computers. When Remington Rand's commercial computer (UNIVAC, 1951) began replacing IBM machines, IBM quickly responded, using its superior R&D and marketing to build a market share near 80% in the 1960s and 1970s; competitors scattered to niches on the periphery.

Triumphs achieved under Thomas Watson Jr. (president in 1952) included IBM's first computer (the 701, 1952), the STRETCH systems (which eliminated vacuum tubes, 1960), and the first compatible family of computers (System/360, 1964; System/370, 1970). Accompanying innovations included the FORTRAN programming language (1957) and floppy disk storage (1971). IBM later moved into midrange systems (System/38, 1978; AS/400, 1988). The IBM PC (1981) spawned entirely new PC-related industries.

The shift to open, smaller systems, along with greater competition in all of IBM's segments, caused wrenching change. After posting profits of $6.6 billion in 1984, IBM began a slow slide. The company began reducing its work force and by 1992 had cut worldwide employment by 100,000 through attrition and early retirement. IBM also sold many noncomputer businesses, such as its copier division (to Kodak, 1988); Rolm telecommunications (to Siemens, 1988); and its typewriter, keyboard, personal printer, and supplies business (Lexmark, to Clayton & Dubilier, 1991).

IBM restructured in 1991, and in 1992 it set up a European unit to sell low-cost clones of its own computers. Also in 1992 the company formed a joint venture with Sears called Advantis to provide voice-and-data network services. In 1993 IBM and Groupe Bull entered a joint venture to develop software.

In 1994 IBM sold its Federal Systems unit, which provides computer systems and services to the government, to Loral for $1.5 billion. That same year, in a challenge to Intel's dominance of the microprocessor business, IBM agreed to manufacture computer chips designed by Cyrix.

Several of IBM's highest-ranking executives, including chief strategist James Cannavino and Lotus head Jim Manzi, left the company in 1995 as Gerstner continued to clean house. That same year Apple released its first Power Mac computers that use the PowerPC chip developed by Apple, IBM, and Motorola. Also in 1995 IBM agreed to purchase DMR, a Canadian provider of information technology services.

NYSE symbol: IBM
Fiscal year ends: December 31

WHO

Chairman and CEO: Louis V. Gerstner Jr., age 53, $4,600,000 pay
CEO, Lotus Development: Michael D. Zisman, age 46
COO, Lotus Development: Jeffrey Papows, age 41
SVP and CFO: G. Richard Thoman, age 50
SVP and Group Executive, Worldwide Sales and Services: Ned C. Lautenbach, age 51, $1,065,000 pay
SVP and Group Executive, Software Group: John M. Thompson, age 53, $1,008,000 pay
SVP and Group Executive, Technology Group: Patrick A. Toole, age 57
SVP and Group Executive, Server Group: Nicholas M. Donofrio, age 50
SVP Research: James C. McGroddy, age 57
SVP Strategy: J. Bruce Harreld, age 44
SVP and General Counsel: Lawrence Ricciardi, age 54
SVP Human Resources: J. Thomas Bouchard
Auditors: Price Waterhouse LLP

WHERE

HQ: International Business Machines Corporation, One Old Orchard Rd., Armonk, NY 10504
Phone: 914-765-1900
Fax: 914-288-1147 (HR)

IBM sells its products worldwide.

	1994 Sales		1994 Net Income	
	$ mil.	% of total	$ mil.	% of total
US	24,118	38	969	31
Europe/Middle East/Africa	23,034	36	1,086	35
Asia/Pacific	11,365	18	567	18
Americas	5,535	8	498	16
Adjustments	—	—	(183)	—
Total	**64,052**	**100**	**2,937**	**100**

WHAT

	1994 Sales	
	$ mil.	% of total
Workstations	13,038	21
Software	11,346	18
Processors	9,784	15
Services	9,715	15
Maintenance	7,222	11
Storage & other peripherals	5,557	9
OEM hardware	3,248	5
Financing & other	4,142	6
Total	**64,052**	**100**

Business Units

Application Solutions	Personal Computer Company
AS/400	Personal Software Products
Large Scale Computing	Power Personal Systems
Microelectronics	Printing Systems Company
Networking Hardware	RISC System/6000
Networking Software	Storage Systems

KEY COMPETITORS

AMD	Hewlett-Packard
Amdahl	Hitachi
Apple	Intel
Arthur Andersen	Intergraph
AST	Machines Bull
AT&T Global Information	Matsushita
Canon	Microsoft
Ceridian	NEC
Compaq	Oracle
Computer Associates	Packard Bell
Cray Research	Seagate Technology
Cyrix	Siemens
Data General	Silicon Graphics
DEC	Storage Technology
Dell	Sun Microsystems
EDS	Tandem
EMC	Texas Instruments
Fujitsu	Toshiba
Gateway 2000	Unisys

HOW MUCH

	Annual Growth	1985	1986	1987	1988	1989	1990	1991	1992	1993	1994
Sales ($ mil.)	2.6%	50,718	52,160	55,256	59,598	62,654	68,931	64,766	64,523	62,716	64,052
Net Income ($ mil.)	(8.5%)	6,555	4,789	5,258	5,451	3,722	5,967	(598)	(6,865)	(7,940)	2,937
Income as % of sales	—	13.1%	9.3%	9.7%	9.1%	5.9%	8.7%	—	—	—	4.6%
Earnings per share ($)	(8.0%)	10.67	7.81	8.72	9.20	6.41	10.42	(1.05)	(12.03)	(14.02)	5.02
Stock price – high ($)	—	158.50	161.88	175.88	129.50	130.88	123.13	139.75	100.38	59.88	76.38
Stock price – low ($)	—	117.38	119.25	102.00	104.50	93.38	94.50	83.50	48.75	40.63	51.38
Stock price – close ($)	(8.0%)	155.50	120.00	115.50	121.88	94.13	113.00	89.00	50.38	56.50	73.50
P/E – high	—	15	21	20	14	20	12	—	—	—	15
P/E – low	—	11	15	12	11	14	9	—	—	—	10
Dividends per share ($)	(15.2%)	4.40	4.40	4.40	4.40	4.73	4.84	4.84	4.84	1.58	1.00
Book value per share ($)	(3.4%)	51.98	56.73	64.09	66.99	67.01	76.43	64.20	48.31	33.95	38.00
Employees	(6.6%)	405,535	407,080	389,348	387,112	383,220	373,816	344,396	301,542	256,207	219,839

1994 Year-end:
Debt ratio: 49.8%
Return on equity: 14.3%
Cash (mil.): $10,554
Current ratio: 1.41
Long-term debt (mil.): $12,548
No. of shares (mil.): 599
Dividends
  Yield: 1.4%
  Payout: 19.9%
Market value (mil.): $43,197

Stock Price History High/Low 1985–94

INTERNATIONAL PAPER COMPANY

OVERVIEW

International Paper is both living up to its name and trying to change its image at the same time. The world's leading producer of forest products and one of the US's largest industrial corporations went on an international shopping spree in 1995, buying a controlling interest in New Zealand's leading forest products company, Carter Holt Harvey, for $1.15 billion and offering to buy Swiss paper distribution firm Holvis for approximately $350 million. At the same time the firm has diversified its business away from overdependence on paper and packaging products (76% of 1986 revenues, 52% of 1994 sales) to a broader product line that includes distribution services, forest products, printing paper, industrial and consumer packaging, and spe-

cialty items ranging from photographic film to oil and natural gas. International Paper is a leading distributor of paper and office supply products.

The company has invested $9.4 billion in capital projects in the past 10 years and has transformed its once inefficient US mills into more competitive ones, with increased energy self-sufficiency and with many plants producing pulp on-site. International Paper has also invested in other overseas acquisitions, buying forest product companies and paper mills in Europe, Canada, and Israel.

The absorption of Carter and Holvis will increase foreign sales to 45% of total revenue and give the firm greater access to markets in South America, Europe, and the Pacific Rim.

WHEN

In 1898, 18 northeastern pulp and paper companies consolidated to lower operating costs. The resulting International Paper Company started with 20 mills in Maine, New Hampshire, Vermont, Massachusetts, and New York.

These mills depended on the forests of the northeastern US and those in neighboring Canada for wood pulp. However, Canadian provinces were enacting legislation to prevent the export of pulpwood, wanting instead to export finished products. Thus in 1919 International Paper formed Canadian International Paper, which bought Riordon (a Canadian paper company) in 1925.

In the 1920s International Paper built a hydroelectric plant on the Hudson River, and between 1928 and 1941 the company called itself International Paper & Power. The company entered the kraft (German for strength) paper market (e.g., paper sacks) in 1925 with the purchase of the Bastrop Pulp & Paper kraft paper mill (Louisiana). Mass production of paper was made possible by the Fourdrinier paper machine, which could make paper in a continuous sheet (patented by Henry and Sealy Fourdrinier in England about 1807). International Paper first mass-produced kraft containerboard in 1931.

During the 1940s and 1950s, International Paper bought Agar Manufacturing (shipping containers, 1940), Single Service Containers (Pure-Pak milk containers, 1946), and Lord Baltimore Press (folding cartons, 1958). The company diversified in the 1960s and 1970s, buying Davol (hospital products, 1968; sold to C. R. Bard in 1980), American Central (land development, 1968; assets sold to developers

in 1974), and General Crude Oil (gas and oil, 1975; sold to Mobil Oil in 1979).

In the 1980s International Paper modernized its plants to change its business mix to less cyclical products and became the industry's low-cost producer. After selling Canadian International Paper in 1981, the company went on a buying spree, starting with Hammermill Paper (office paper, 1986), Arvey (paper manufacturer and distributor, 1987), and Masonite (composite wood products, 1988). In 1989 International Paper entered the European paper market by buying Aussedat Rey (France), Ilford Group (UK), and Zanders (West Germany). The company's 1990 acquisitions included Dixon Paper (paper and graphic arts supply distributor), Nevamar (laminates), and the UK's Cookson Group (printing plates).

In 1991 International Paper enhanced its US distribution network by buying Dillard Paper and Leslie Paper; in Europe it bought Scaldia-Papier (the Netherlands). Acquisitions in 1992 included Western Paper; a $258 million investment in Carter Holt Harvey, a New Zealand forest products company; and 11% (up to 12% in 1993) of Israel's Scitex, the world's #1 maker of electronic prepress systems. In 1993 the company began building a paper machine for recycled paper production at its Selma, Alabama, mill.

In 1994 International Paper formed a joint venture to build and operate a liquid packaging plant in China; it also acquired 2 Mexican paper distributing companies.

In late 1995 the company agreed to acquire Federal Paper Board in a deal valued at $2.7 billion in stock and cash.

NYSE symbol: IP
Fiscal year ends: December 31

WHO

Chairman and CEO: John A. Georges, age 64, $2,068,750 pay
President and COO: John T. Dillon, age 56, $800,000 pay (prior to promotion)
EVP Legal and External Affairs and General Counsel: James P. Melican, age 54, $765,000 pay
EVP Distribution, Forest and Specialty Products: Mark A. Suwyn, age 52, $708,500 pay
EVP Printing Papers: C. Wesley Smith, age 55, $668,750 pay
President, International Paper Europe: W. Michael Amick
SVP Industrial Packaging: Victor A. Casebolt
SVP Specialty Products: Milan J. Turk
SVP and CFO: Marianne M. Parrs
Controller: Andrew R. Lessin, age 52
SVP Human Resources: Robert M. Byrnes, age 57
VP Manufacturing Programs: J. Alan Day
Auditors: Arthur Andersen & Co, SC

WHERE

HQ: 2 Manhattanville Rd., Purchase, NY 10577
Phone: 914-397-1500
Fax: 914-397-1596

International Paper has production facilities in 27 countries. The company sells its products in 130 countries.

	1994 Sales		1994 Operating Income	
	$ mil.	% of total	$ mil.	% of total
US	11,965	79	915	89
Europe	2,958	19	97	9
Other regions	354	2	21	2
Adjustments	(311)	—	—	—
Total	**14,966**	**100**	**1,033**	**100**

WHAT

	1994 Sales		1994 Operating Income	
	$ mil.	% of total	$ mil.	% of total
Printing papers	4,400	28	20	2
Distribution	3,470	22	74	7
Packaging	3,375	22	293	28
Specialty products	2,590	17	268	26
Forest products	1,715	11	378	37
Adjustments	(584)	—	—	—
Total	**14,966**	**100**	**1,033**	**100**

Pulp and Paper
Coated publication papers (Hudson Web, Zanders)
Copy paper (Aussedat Rey, Springhill, Hammermill)
File folders, posters
Magazine papers (Aerial, Aussedat Rey)
Market pulp
Printing, writing, and artistic papers (Beckett, Strathmore, Ward)

Distribution Businesses
Office products
Packaging and industrial supplies
Paper

Paperboard and Packaging
Cartons
Containerboard
Food packaging (Akrosil, Nicolet, Thilmany)
Kraft packaging papers
Linerboards (Pineliner, ColorBrite)

Specialty Products
Chemicals (Arizona Chemical)
Nonwoven fabrics (Veratec)
Oil and gas production
Photographic films and plates (Anitec, Horsell, Ilford)
Specialty panels (Masonite, CraftMaster, OmniWood)

Forest Products
Fiberboard
Logs and lumber
Particleboard and siding
Treated poles

KEY COMPETITORS

Alco Standard
Arjo Wiggins
Appleton
Boise Cascade
Canadian Pacific
Champion International
Fletcher Challenge
Fort Howard
Georgia-Pacific
James River
Jefferson Smurfit
Kimberly-Clark
Mead
3M
Rayonier
Stone Container
Stora
Union Camp
Westvaco
Weyerhaeuser

HOW MUCH

	Annual Growth	1985	1986	1987	1988	1989	1990	1991	1992	1993	1994
Sales ($ mil.)	14.3%	4,502	5,500	7,763	9,533	11,378	12,960	12,703	13,598	13,685	14,966
Net income ($ mil.)	14.2%	131	305	407	754	864	569	399	136	289	432
Income as % of sales	—	3.0%	5.5%	5.2%	7.9%	6.0%	4.4%	3.1%	1.0%	2.1%	2.9%
Earnings per share ($)	13.9%	1.07	2.90	3.68	6.57	7.72	5.21	3.61	1.12	2.34	3.46
Stock price – high ($)	—	28.88	40.06	57.81	49.38	58.75	59.75	78.25	78.50	69.88	80.50
Stock price – low ($)	—	22.13	24.19	27.00	36.50	45.13	42.75	50.50	58.50	56.63	60.63
Stock price – close ($)	12.9%	25.38	37.56	42.25	46.38	56.50	53.50	70.75	66.63	67.75	75.38
P/E – high	—	27	14	16	8	8	12	22	70	30	23
P/E – low	—	21	8	7	6	6	8	14	52	24	18
Dividends per share ($)	3.8%	1.20	1.20	1.23	1.28	1.53	1.68	1.68	1.68	1.68	1.68
Book value per share ($)	5.0%	33.34	35.05	36.35	41.17	47.35	51.34	51.01	50.44	50.24	51.74
Employees	9.1%	32,000	44,000	45,500	55,500	63,500	69,000	70,500	73,000	72,500	70,000

1994 Year-end:
Debt ratio: 50.1%
Return on equity: 6.8%
Cash (mil.): $270
Current ratio: 1.20
Long-term debt (mil.): $4,464
No. of shares (mil.): 126
Dividends
  Yield: 2.2%
  Payout: 48.6%
Market value (mil.): $9,490

**Stock Price History
High/Low 1985–94**

THE INTERPUBLIC GROUP

OVERVIEW

If you need an advertising firm, the Interpublic Group is the real thing. The New York–based enterprise is a holding company for a group of advertising agencies and other media firms, including McCann-Erickson (creator of several 1970s Coke ads), Lintas Worldwide, the Lowe Group, and Western International Media. Interpublic is the world's 2nd largest advertising business behind UK-based WPP Group.

The company's agencies plan and create ad programs for their clients and place the ads in media including television, radio, and print. Interpublic also provides direct marketing, market research, and other marketing services. By operating as a cluster of competing agencies within a holding company, the subsidiaries are able to serve rival clients while using the resources and worldwide connections of the parent. The group concept also has been an effective way for Interpublic to allow creative independence while keeping financial control.

By holding down costs and choosing its acquisitions carefully, Interpublic has experienced steady and strong growth even in the face of lower ad spending and the loss of several major accounts, including one that Coke awarded to Creative Artists Agency in 1993.

Although its main subsidiaries, McCann-Erickson and Lintas, have been criticized as uncreative, veteran chairman Philip Geier maintains that his focus is on achieving better sales results for clients instead of winning awards with bold and aggressive ads.

Interpublic's recent strategic alliances and minority investments have included an exploration of interactive technologies with Silicon Valley–based communications company CKS.

WHEN

The Interpublic Group's history began in 1911 with Harrison McCann, an advertising executive for Standard Oil who opened his own agency when the petroleum trust was split up. Standard Oil of New Jersey (now Exxon) was his first client, and as the automobile and petroleum products became integral parts of American life, McCann's ad business boomed.

In 1930 McCann's firm merged with Alfred Erickson's agency, forming the McCann-Erickson Company. At the end of the decade, the ad firm hired Marion Harper, a top Yale graduate, as a mail room clerk. He quickly rose through the ranks, and by 1948 he succeeded McCann as president of the agency.

Harper, an advocate of the research-oriented approach to advertising, used social science techniques to determine what motivated people to buy. He also began acquiring other ad agencies, and by 1961 Harper controlled more than 20 companies. That year he unveiled his concept of a holding company for various advertising subsidiaries that would use the parent company's financial and informational resources but operate separately, allowing them to work on accounts for competing products. He named the company the Interpublic Group, after a German research company that was owned by the former H. K. McCann Co.

The advertising conglomerate continued its rapid expansion, buying Afamal (the largest ad firm in Africa) in 1962 and Erwin, Wasey, Ruthrauff & Ryan in 1963, making it the biggest agency in the world. However, Harper's management capabilities weren't up to the task. With the company facing bankruptcy, the board of directors chose Robert Healy to replace Harper in 1967. (Harper died in 1990, having lived his last 20 years as a recluse.) By borrowing from employees, securing advance payments from clients, and cutting costs, Healy was able to save the company and return it to profitability. In 1971 Interpublic went public.

The 1970s were fruitful years for the company, whose ad teams created memorable campaigns for Coke ("Its the Real Thing" and "Have a Coke and a Smile") and Miller Beer ("Miller Time" and Miller Lite ads).

Philip Geier became chairman in 1980 and presided over continued expansion, adding agencies such as Lintas International and Dailey & Associates. With 60% of its billings coming from overseas, Interpublic was sufficiently diversified to withstand declines in regional businesses or even the loss of major clients and was able to achieve double-digit growth during the last half of the 1980s.

Interpublic bought UK-based Lowe Group and sailed through the global recession of the early 1990s with few problems until 1993, when Coca-Cola (a client since 1942) hired Creative Artists Agency to develop a new image.

In 1994 the firm purchased Western International Media, the largest independent media buyer in the US, and Ammirati & Puris, a New York firm respected for its creativity. In 1995 Interpublic purchased Mark Goodson Productions, the game show producer, through a joint venture with All American Communications.

NYSE symbol: IPG
Fiscal year ends: December 31

WHO

Chairman, President, and CEO: Philip H. Geier Jr.,
age 60, $1,515,000 pay
Chairman, Lowe Group: Frank B. Lowe, age 53,
$1,035,000 pay
Chairman, McCann-Erickson Worldwide: Robert L.
James, age 58, $850,000 pay
Chairman and CEO, Lintas Worldwide: Kenneth L.
Robbins, age 59, $525,000 pay
EVP Finance and Operations and CFO: Eugene P.
Beard, age 59, $975,000 pay
SVP, General Counsel, and Secretary: Christopher
Rudge, age 57
SVP Financial Operations: Thomas J. Volpe, age 59
SVP Human Resources: C. Kent Kroeber, age 56
Auditors: Price Waterhouse LLP

WHERE

HQ: The Interpublic Group of Companies, Inc.,
1271 Avenue of the Americas, New York, NY 10020
Phone: 212-399-8000
Fax: 212-399-8130

The Interpublic Group of Companies provides
international advertising services through offices in
more than 60 countries worldwide.

	1994 Sales	
	$ mil.	% of total
US	714	36
Europe	720	36
Far East	268	14
Latin America	153	8
Other regions	129	6
Total	**1,984**	**100**

WHAT

Selected Subsidiaries
Ammirati & Puris, Inc. (New York)
Dailey & Associates (Los Angeles)
Lintas Campbell-Ewald Co. (Detroit)
Lintas, Inc. (New York)
Mark Goodson Productions
McCann-Erickson USA, Inc. (New York)
Western International Media (Los Angeles)

Services
Advertising
Direct marketing
Market research
Media buying
Media placement
Product development
Sales promotion
Telemarketing

Selected Clients
AT&T	Mercedes
Bertoli	Nestlé
Coca-Cola	Renault
Fidelity Investments	SEGA
General Motors	Unilever
Marriott International	

KEY COMPETITORS

Bozell, Jacobs, Kenyon & Eckhardt
Cordiant
Creative Artists
D'Arcy Masius
Dentsu Inc.
Grey Advertising
King World
Leo Burnett
Omnicom Group
True North
WPP Group
Young & Rubicam

HOW MUCH

	Annual Growth	1985	1986	1987	1988	1989	1990	1991	1992	1993	1994
Sales ($ mil.)	12.9%	667	814	943	1,192	1,257	1,368	1,678	1,804	1,794	1,984
Net income ($ mil)	13.6%	37	41	49	60	71	80	95	112	125	115
Income as % of sales	—	5.5%	5.0%	5.2%	5.0%	5.6%	5.9%	5.6%	6.2%	7.0%	5.8%
Earnings per share ($)	11.8%	0.56	0.63	0.75	0.91	1.05	1.19	1.30	1.50	1.67	1.53
Stock price – high ($)	—	7.31	10.17	14.50	12.34	18.94	19.00	28.63	35.75	35.63	35.88
Stock price – low ($)	—	5.53	7.00	7.59	3.30	12.17	14.63	16.88	25.75	23.88	27.50
Stock price – close ($)	18.2%	7.16	9.13	10.59	12.25	16.31	17.50	28.63	34.88	32.00	32.13
P/E – high	—	13	16	19	14	18	16	22	24	21	24
P/E – low	—	10	11	10	4	12	12	13	17	14	18
Dividends per share ($)	13.2%	0.18	0.20	0.22	0.26	0.32	0.37	0.41	0.45	0.49	0.55
Book value per share ($)	11.3%	3.18	3.65	4.23	4.77	5.32	6.94	7.78	6.81	7.53	8.36
Employees	4.5%	12,200	12,600	13,300	14,700	14,700	16,800	16,800	16,800	17,600	18,200

1994 Year-end:
Debt ratio: 28.6%
Return on equity: 19.0%
Cash (mil.): $442
Current ratio: 1.03
Long-term debt (mil.): $131
No. of shares (mil.): 78
Dividends
  Yield: 1.7%
  Payout: 35.9%
Market value (mil.): $2,497

Stock Price History
High/Low 1985–94

ITT CORPORATION

OVERVIEW

ITT Corp. has a new destination: profits based on hospitality, gambling, and sports entertainment. When ITT restructures in late 1995 (spinning off its insurance unit and its electronics and defense segment), the parent company will keep its ITT Destinations subsidiary. The 425-hotel Sheraton chain will serve as the centerpiece of the new ITT Corp.

In 1994 ITT Corp. bought the exclusive Phoenician Hotel in Scottsdale, Arizona, and 70% of CIGA SpA, an Italian luxury hotel chain. The company confirmed its commitment to the hospitality industry in 1995 when it paid $1.7 billion for the 3 Caesars World hotel/casinos, including the chain's flagship, the 1,500-room Caesars Palace in Las Vegas.

In 1995 ITT Corp. became a big-league player in the sports entertainment industry when it bought a 50% stake in Madison Square Garden (MSG) from Viacom; Cablevision Systems is co-owner. The $1 billion joint purchase includes the sports and entertainment arena, the 5,600-seat Paramount Theater, the MSG Network (cable sports), and the New York Knicks (basketball) and New York Rangers (hockey) professional sports teams.

ITT Corp.'s Communications and Information (COINS) segment includes ITT World Directories, which creates telephone directories in 9 countries, and ITT Educational Services, which has 20,000 students in 58 trade schools. It sold off about 17% of ITT Educational to the public in 1994.

After orchestrating ITT's breakup, Rand Araskog, who has led the company for 16 years, chose to stay with the hospitality segment.

WHEN

Colonel Sosthenes Behn founded the International Telephone and Telegraph Corp. in 1920, intending to build a global telephone company. Over the next 4 decades ITT grew into an international powerhouse with business and political interests on several continents. During the 1940s the company sold its telephone services to focus on telecommunications equipment manufacturing. Harold Geneen became CEO in 1959 and diversified ITT by buying such companies as Aetna Finance, the Sheraton hotels, and Continental Baking. By the time Rand Araskog took over in 1979, ITT had become a floundering giant, embroiled in political scandals in South America and at home. Araskog sold all or part of 250 companies, including the last of ITT's telecommunications operations.

The Sheraton chain was founded by Harvard classmates Ernest Henderson and Robert Moore, who pooled their WWI war bonuses to invest in real estate. When they bought the Sheraton Hotel in Boston, they decided it would be too costly to replace the electric sign, so they took the name for their company.

Sheraton bought and refurbished hotels along the East Coast, including Boston's famed Copley Plaza (1941). The company introduced several innovations, including a telex reservation network (1948), a centralized electronic reservation system (1958), and a toll-free reservation number (1970). As the US became more mobile after WWII, Sheraton expanded its luxury hotels and its motor inns. It also went international, buying properties in Canada (1949); Israel, Jamaica, and Puerto Rico (1961); and Venezuela (1963). By the 1960s it was the

#1 hotel owner in the US. Henderson died in 1967, and ITT acquired the company in 1968. In the 1980s ITT Sheraton opened the first US-based hotels in China and Eastern Europe.

The $1 million grand opening of Jay Sarno's Caesars Palace in 1966 featured champagne and movie stars. Sarno had made his fortune with the Cabana motel chain. In 1969 Caesars was sold to Clifford and Stuart Perlman (originators of Lum's fast-food restaurants) who named the company Caesars World. With the end of Atlantic City's gambling ban, Caesars added the Boardwalk Regency (now Caesars Atlantic City) in 1979; Caesars Tahoe also opened that year. In 1981 Caesars World shareholders bought the Perlmans' 18% stake for twice its value to rid the company of the brothers' questionable contacts.

Madison Square Garden began as P. T. Barnum's Hippodrome in 1874. It took the MSG name in 1879. The current Garden, the 4th, was opened in 1968 and acquired by Gulf + Western in 1987 (that company became Paramount in 1989). During its various incarnations MSG has hosted rodeos, boxing matches, and concert performances by Frank Sinatra, Judy Garland, and Mick Jagger. Paramount abandoned plans to rebuild MSG and instead gave it a $200 million facelift in 1991.

During the early 1990s Sheraton opened its 10th Hawaiian hotel and its 1,500-room Walt Disney World location. The company also entered the gaming industry in 1993 when it bought the Desert Inn in Las Vegas. In 1995 Sheraton said it would convert several hotels to a new, mid-priced brand, Four Points Hotels.

Fiscal year ends: December 31

Chairman and CEO: Rand V. Araskog, age 63,
$4,030,000 pay
President and COO: Robert A. Bowman, age 40,
$928,000 pay
Chairman and CEO, ITT Sheraton: John Kapioltas,
age 67, $910,417 pay
EVP, General Counsel, and Corporate Secretary:
Richard S. Ward, age 54, $695,624 pay
CFO: Ann N. Reese, age 42
Chairman and CEO, ITT Educational Services: Rene
Champagne, age 53
Chairman and CEO, World Directories: Gerald C.
Crotty, age 43
President and COO, Caesars World: Peter Boynton,
age 52
SVP and Director Human Resources: Ralph W. Pausig
Auditors: Arthur Andersen & Co, SC

WHERE

HQ: 1330 Avenue of the Americas, New York, NY
10019-5490
Phone: 212-258-1000
Fax: 212-489-5196

WHAT

	1994 Sales		1994 Cash Flow	
	$ mil.	% of total	$ mil.	% of total
ITT Sheraton	3,927	13	258	8
Caesars	1,005	3	193	6
COINS	833	3	181	5
MSG	353	1	12	0
Adjustment	(1,358)	—	(220)	—
Subtotal	**4,760**	**20**	**424**	**21**
Spun-off business	18,860	80	1,595	79
Total	**23,620**	**100**	**2,019**	**100**

Operating Segments

Caesars World (hotel/casinos)
Caesars Atlantic City
Caesars Palace (Las Vegas)
Caesars Tahoe

ITT Communications and Information Services
(COINS)
ITT Educational Services (83%; 58 technical schools in
25 states)
ITT World Directories (telephone directories in the
Caribbean, Europe, Japan, and South Africa)

ITT Sheraton (casinos, hotels, and resorts; 425
properties in 63 countries)

Madison Square Garden (50%, entertainment)
Madison Square Garden (20,000-seat arena)
MSG Network (sports cable network)
New York Knicks (professional basketball team)
New York Rangers (professional hockey team)
Paramount Theater (5,600-seat theater in NYC)

KEY COMPETITORS

Accor	Four Seasons	MGM Grand
Apollo Group	Griffin Gaming	Mirage Resorts
Aztar	Harrah's	National
Bally	Entertainment	Education
Entertainment	Helmsley	Nestlé
Bass	HFS	Rank
Boomtown	Hilton	Ritz-Carlton
Boyd Gaming	Hollywood	Sahara Gaming
Canadian Pacific	Casinos	Sands Regent
Carlson	Hyatt	Showboat
Carnival Corp.	Loews	Tata Enterprises
Circus Circus	Marriott	Trump
Computer Learning	International	Westin Hotel
Centers	Mashantucket	WMS Industries
DeVRY	Pequot Gaming	Wyndham Hotel

HOW MUCH

	Annual Growth	1985	1986	1987	1988	1989	1990	1991	1992	1993	1994
Sales ($ mil.)	7.9%	11,871	7,596	8,551	19,355	20,005	20,604	20,421	21,651	22,762	23,620
Net income ($ mil.)	15.0%	294	494	1,085	817	922	958	817	(260)	913	1,033
Income as % of sales	—	2.5%	6.5%	12.7%	4.2%	4.6%	4.6%	4.0%	—	4.0%	4.4%%
Earnings per share ($)	17.6%	1.89	3.23	7.20	5.70	6.30	6.85	6.05	(2.19)	6.90	8.11
Stock price – high ($)	—	38.88	59.50	66.38	54.88	64.50	60.88	63.00	72.13	94.88	104.25
Stock price – low ($)	—	28.38	35.38	41.75	43.25	49.75	40.25	44.88	54.75	69.00	77.00
Stock price – close ($)	9.9%	38.00	53.38	44.50	50.38	58.88	48.00	57.75	72.00	91.25	88.63
P/E – high	—	21	217	9	10	10	9	10	—	14	13
P/E – low	—	15	10	6	8	8	6	7	—	10	9
Dividends per share ($)	7.9%	1.00	1.00	1.00	1.00	1.25	1.48	1.60	1.72	1.81	1.98
Book value per share ($)	0.4%	43.75	48.28	55.52	58.05	57.67	66.33	71.72	55.10	58.00	45.46
Employees	8.0%	232,000	123,000	120,000	227,000	119,000	114,000	110,000	106,000	98,000	110,000

1994 Year-end:
Debt ratio: 74.4%
Return on equity: 17.5%
Cash (mil.): $1,136
Current ratio: —
Long-term debt (mil.): $13,940
No. of shares (mil.): 106
Dividends
  Yield: 2.2%
  Payout: 24.4%
Market value (mil.): $9,365

Stock Price History
High/Low 1985–94

ITT INDUSTRIES, INC.

OVERVIEW

ITT Industries is one of a trio of companies formed by the breakup of ITT Corporation in late 1995. ITT Corporation's 3 manufacturing companies — ITT Automotive, ITT Defense & Electronics, and ITT Fluid Technology — now make up ITT Industries.

ITT Automotive, the largest of the 3 companies, is one of the world's leading suppliers of automobile components and systems. The company makes assemblies for antilock brakes, doors, windows, windshield wipers, and car seats. In 1994 ITT Automotive bought General Motors's actuators and motors business, renaming it ITT Automotive Electrical Systems.

ITT Defense & Electronics develops and manufactures high-tech electronics for commercial and defense applications. It is a leading supplier of audio/video signal processors, combat radios, radar, night-vision devices, and air

traffic control systems. The US government accounted for nearly 60% of ITT Defense & Electronics's 1994 sales.

ITT Fluid Technology produces pumps, controls, valves, and other fluid-handling devices for use principally in the construction, manufacturing, and water and wastewater treatment industries.

Each of ITT's manufacturing companies is pursuing growth in emerging markets. In 1994 ITT Automotive established a manufacturing facility in Hungary and became 40% owner of a joint venture with Shanghai Automotive Brake Systems. Also in 1994 ITT Fluid Technology formed joint ventures to manufacture pumps in Brazil and China.

Travis Engen, who studied aeronautics and astronautics at MIT and who had served as CEO of ITT Defense, heads ITT Industries.

WHEN

Colonel Sosthenes Behn founded the International Telephone and Telegraph Corporation (ITT) in 1920 to manage Cuban and Puerto Rican telephone companies. By 1925 Behn had added 3 other small telephone companies. ITT bought International Western Electric (renamed International Standard Electric, or ISE) from AT&T in 1925, making ITT a major international phone equipment manufacturer. In the late 1920s ITT bought Mackay, a US holding company involved in telegraph, cable, radio, and equipment manufacturing. During WWII, ISE scientists who had fled Europe gravitated to the company's New York laboratory. Their work laid the foundation for ITT's high-tech electronics business.

As WWII began to cause losses at ITT's considerable foreign interests (more than 2/3 of company revenues had come from overseas), Behn determined that ITT should rely less on foreign income sources. To increase US opportunities, Behn arranged for a Mackay subsidiary, Federal Telegraph (later Federal Electric), to become part of ITT. Behn took charge of Federal, creating the Federal Telephone & Radio Laboratories. By 1944 Federal had $90 million in sales. Its primary products were radio and telephone systems and military equipment.

By the 1950s ITT was a diverse and unwieldy collection of companies. In the mid-1950s ISE was the company's biggest segment, developing advanced telephone switching equipment. ITT Laboratories pioneered transistor technology, although management failed to capitalize on the lab's products.

In 1956 the aging Behn resigned as chairman of ITT. He died a year later. Former Raytheon executive Harold Geneen took the reins of ITT in 1959.

During the 1960s and 1970s, ITT added several companies that would evolve into ITT Industries. Auto parts makers included Teves (car brakes, West Germany), Ulma (auto trim, Italy), and Altissimo (auto lights and accessories, Italy). Electronics acquisitions included Cannon Electric (a leading manufacturer of electrical connectors) and National Computer Products (electronics for satellite communications). Fluid technology companies included Bell & Gossett (the US's largest maker of commercial and industrial pumps) and Flygt (pumps and mixers, Sweden). When ITT acquired Sheraton in 1968, it also got Thompson Industries, a supplier of auto parts. By 1977 ITT's Engineered Products division consisted of nearly 80 companies making automotive and electrical products.

In the 1980s ITT established itself as a leading supplier of antilock brakes (viewed as the most significant auto safety development of the decade), a top manufacturer of semiconductors and defense electronics, and (with the 1988 purchase of Allis-Chalmers's pump business) an international force in fluid technology. In 1990 ITT Fluid Technology passed the $1 billion sales mark.

During the early 1990s ITT's Defense & Electronics segment earned major military contracts to manufacture equipment for use in the Persian Gulf War.

NYSE symbol: IIN
Fiscal year ends: December 31

WHO

Chairman, President, and CEO: D. Travis Engen,
age 51, $1,246,583 pay
SVP; President, ITT Automotive: Timothy D. Leuliette,
age 45, $785,417 pay
SVP; President, ITT Defense & Electronics: Louis J.
Giuliano, age 48, $613,814 pay
SVP; President, ITT Fluid Technology: Bertil T.
Nilsson, age 63, $517,100 pay
SVP and Director Human Resources: James P.
Smith Jr., age 52, $325,000 pay
SVP and CFO: Heidi Kunz, age 40
SVP and Controller: Richard J. M. Hamilton, age 45
SVP, Secretary, and General Counsel: Vincent A.
Maffeo, age 44
SVP and Director Corporate Development: Martin
Kamber, age 47
Auditors: Arthur Andersen & Co, SC

WHERE

HQ: 4 West Red Oak Ln., White Plains, NY 10604
Phone: 914-641-2000
Fax: 914-696-2950

	1994 Sales % of total
US	50
Western Europe	38
Canada	6
Asia/Pacific	3
Other regions	3
Total	**100**

WHAT

	1994 Sales		1994 Operating Income	
	$ mil.	% of total	$ mil.	% of total
Automotive	4,784	62	328	63
Defense & Electronics	1,498	19	96	18
Fluid Technology	1,125	14	99	19
Other	351	5	—	—
Total	**7,758**	**100**	**523**	**100**

Companies and Selected Products

ITT Automotive
Brake and Chassis Systems
  Antilock brakes
  Chassis systems
  Fluid-handling components
  Foundation brake components
  "Koni" brand shock absorbers
  Traction-control systems
Body and Electrical Systems
  Air management systems
  Door and window assemblies
  Fractional horsepower DC motors
  Seat systems
  Switches
  Wiper module assemblies

ITT Defense & Electronics
Electronic warfare systems
Interconnect products
Night-vision devices
Operations and management services
Radar
Space payloads
Tactical communications equipment

ITT Fluid Technology
Controls and instruments
Heat exchangers
Mixers
Pumps
Valves

KEY COMPETITORS

Alliant Techsystems	Lear Seating
AlliedSignal	Litton
Arvin	Loral
Autocam	Mannesmann
British Aerospace	Olin
BW/IP	Raytheon
Core Industries	Rockwell
Crawford Fitting	SCI Systems
Dana	Texas Instruments
Daniel Industries	Thomson SA
Echlin	Tracor
FMC	TRW
GenCorp	Unisys
Hughes Electronics	U.S. Industries
Johnson Controls	Watts Industries

HOW MUCH

	Annual Growth	1985	1986	1987	1988	1989	1990	1991	1992	1993	1994
Sales ($ mil.)	(3.1%)	10,314	5,870	6,626	7,464	7,741	8,057	7,342	6,845	6,621	7,758
Net income ($ mil.)	—	—	—	—	—	—	—	—	(260)	913	1,033
Income as % of sales	—	—	—	—	—	—	—	—	—	13.8%	13.3%
Employees	—	—	—	—	—	—	—	—	—	—	58,400

1994 Year-end:
Debt ratio: 32.6%
Return on equity: 17.5%
Cash (mil.): $322
Current ratio: 0.99
Long-term debt (mil.): $1,712

Net Income ($ mil.)
1992–94

1,200
1,000
800
600
400
200
0
-200
-400

JOHNSON & JOHNSON

OVERVIEW

Johnson & Johnson (J&J), based in New Brunswick, New Jersey, is a company in continual transition. Between 1989 and 1994 J&J acquired 24 businesses, sold 13 others, consolidated 47 units, and closed more than 25 plants. One of the world's largest and most diversified health care products makers, it owns industry-leading products, ranging from a leading pain reliever (Tylenol) to the world's leading contact lens brand (Acuvue).

The company operates in 3 sectors: consumer products (with brands like Band-Aid and Reach toothbrushes), professional products (ranging from surgical instruments to joint replacements), and pharmaceuticals. J&J's ability to discover, develop, or acquire new products and get them to penetrate markets quickly has served it well during world-

wide changes in the health care industry. The company is known for the autonomy it allows its business units. International expansion is an important strategy. In 1994, for the 2nd year in a row, J&J's Xian-Janssen was named the most successful joint venture in China.

Increased private-label competition in consumer products and pressure by managed care organizations and governments to limit price increases continue to limit profit margins and encourage the company to improve productivity. To improve business relations, at the end of 1994 J&J created Johnson and Johnson Health Care Systems to assist its managed care customers in better serving their clients. Also that year the company purchased Eastman Kodak's Clinical Diagnostics segment to advance its diagnostics business position.

WHEN

Brothers James and Edward Mead Johnson founded the medical products company that bears the family name in 1885 in New Brunswick, New Jersey. In 1886 Robert Johnson joined his brothers to make and sell the antiseptic surgical dressings he developed.

In 1897 Edward left to found the drug company Mead Johnson (now a part of Bristol-Myers Squibb). In 1916 J&J bought gauze maker Chicopee Manufacturing. A byproduct of Johnson's dressing, the Band-Aid, was introduced in 1921 along with Johnson's Baby Cream.

In 1932 Robert Johnson Jr. became chairman and served until 1963. An Army general in WWII, he believed in decentralization; managers were given substantial freedom, a principle still used today. Early product lines, now business units, included Ortho (birth-control products) and Ethicon (sutures) in the 1940s. In 1959 J&J bought McNeil Labs, which launched Tylenol (acetaminophen) as an over-the-counter drug in 1960. Foreign acquisitions included Switzerland's Cilag-Chemie (1959) and Belgium's Janssen (1961).

J&J bought Iolab Corporation, a developer of intraocular lenses used in cataract surgery (1980), and Lifescan, a maker of blood glucose monitoring systems for diabetics (1986). J&J's sales had grown to nearly $5 billion by 1980. But there have since been problems: the drug Zomax (for arthritis pain) was linked to 5 deaths and was pulled in 1983. When someone laced Tylenol capsules with cyanide in 1982, killing 8 people, it cost the company $240 mil-

lion in recalls, advertising, and repackaging and cut Tylenol's profits by nearly 50%. J&J's immediate recall of 31 million bottles and its openness in dealing with the problem saved the Tylenol brand. Now sold as tablets and caplets to prevent tampering, Tylenol is still a leader in the over-the-counter analgesic market.

New products in the 1980s included Acuvue (a disposable contact lens), Retin-A (skin treatment), and Eprex (a bioengineered treatment for anemia). In 1989 J&J began a venture with Merck to sell Mylanta and other drugs bought from ICI Americas. In 1990 it entered the Eastern European market.

In late 1991 the company formed a joint venture with Fujisawa to market a new antibiotic. In 1992 J&J took a mandated down charge of over $600 million relating to future pensions. Key products that year included Prepulsid (digestion aid), Eprex (anti-anemia agent), and One Touch II (blood glucose monitor). J&J paid 3M $116 million in 1992 in a patent infringement suit concerning fiberglass tape used in orthopedic casts.

In 1993 the company introduced the first daily-wear, disposable contact lenses and opened its 2nd Chinese production facility in Shanghai. In 1994 J&J purchased soap and skin cream maker Neutrogena to enhance its consumer product line. To diversify its product line and better compete for hospital business, the company acquired Mitek Surgical Products in 1995 in a deal worth $128 million. Also in 1995 J&J agreed to acquire Cordis, a medical equipment maker, for $1.8 billion.

NYSE symbol: JNJ
Fiscal year ends: Sunday nearest December 31

WHO

Chairman and CEO: Ralph S. Larsen, age 56,
$1,506,714 pay
VC: Robert N. Wilson, age 54, $1,178,967 pay
Corporate VP: Frank H. Barker
Chairman, Pharmaceutical and Diagnostics Group:
Ronald G. Gelbman, age 47
VP Finance and CFO: Clark H. Johnson, age 59,
$642,087 pay
VP Science and Technology: Robert Z. Gussin
VP and General Counsel: George S. Frazza, age 61
VP Administration (Personnel): Roger S. Fine, age 52
Auditors: Coopers & Lybrand L.L.P.

WHERE

HQ: One Johnson & Johnson Plaza, New Brunswick, NJ
08933
Phone: 908-524-0400
Fax: 908-214-0332

The company has operations in 50 countries and sells
items in more than 175 countries.

	1994 Sales		1994 Operating Income	
	$ mil.	% of total	$ mil.	% of total
US	7,812	50	1,534	52
Europe	4,504	28	1,050	35
Africa & Asia/Pacific	1,907	12	198	7
Canada & Latin America	1,511	10	173	6
Adjustments	—	—	(274)	—
Total	**15,734**	**100**	**2,681**	**100**

WHAT

	1994 Sales		1994 Operating Income	
	$ mil.	% of total	$ mil.	% of total
Professional prods.	5,325	34	843	29
Consumer prods.	5,251	33	443	15
Pharmaceuticals	5,158	33	1,669	56
Other	—	—	(274)	—
Total	**15,734**	**100**	**2,681**	**100**

Consumer Products
Acuvue (contact lens)
Baby Oil
Baby Shampoo
Band-Aid
Clean & Clear (skin care)
Imodium A-D (anti-diarrheal)
Monistat 7 (yeast infection treatment)
Mylanta (antacid)
Neutrogena (skin & hair products)
Reach (toothbrush)
Tylenol (pain reliever)

Pharmaceuticals
Duragesic (analgesic)
Eprex (anti-anemia agent)
Ergamisol (cancer treatment)
Floxin (antibacterial)
Hismanal (antihistamine)
Ortho-Novum (birth control)
Propulsid (digestive aid)
Retin-A (acne cream)
Risperdal (anti-psychotic)

Professional Products
Hepatitis testing systems
Joint replacements
Surgical instruments

KEY COMPETITORS

Abbott Labs
ALZA
American Home Products
Amgen
Bausch & Lomb
Baxter
Bayer
Becton, Dickinson
Bristol-Myers Squibb
Carter-Wallace

Ciba-Geigy
Clorox
Colgate-Palmolive
Dial
Eli Lilly
Genentech
Gillette
Glaxo Wellcome
Hoechst
James River
Kimberly-Clark
Medtronic
Merck

3M
Nestlé
Novo Nordisk
Pfizer
Pharmacia & Upjohn
Procter & Gamble
Rhône-Poulenc
St. Jude Medical
Sandoz
Unilever
U.S. Surgical

HOW MUCH

	Annual Growth	1985	1986	1987	1988	1989	1990	1991	1992	1993	1994
Sales ($ mil.)	10.5%	6,421	7,003	8,012	9,000	9,757	11,232	12,447	13,753	14,138	15,734
Net income ($ mil.)	14.1%	614	330	833	974	1,082	1,143	1,461	1,625	1,787	2,006
Income as % of sales	—	9.6%	4.7%	10.4%	10.8%	11.1%	10.2%	11.7%	11.8%	12.6%	12.7%
Earnings per share ($)	15.7%	0.84	0.47	1.21	1.43	1.63	1.72	2.20	2.46	2.74	3.12
Stock price – high ($)	—	13.81	18.56	26.34	22.03	29.75	37.06	58.13	58.69	50.38	56.50
Stock price – low ($)	—	8.78	11.44	13.75	17.31	20.75	25.56	32.69	43.00	35.63	36.00
Stock price – close ($)	17.2%	13.16	16.41	18.72	21.28	29.69	35.88	57.25	50.50	44.88	54.75
P/E – high	—	16	40	22	15	18	22	26	24	18	18
P/E – low	—	11	24	11	12	13	15	15	18	13	12
Dividends per share ($)	15.0%	0.32	0.35	0.41	0.48	0.56	0.66	0.77	0.89	1.01	1.13
Book value per share ($)	10.3%	4.58	4.08	5.06	5.26	6.23	7.36	8.44	7.89	8.66	11.08
Employees	0.9%	74,900	77,100	78,200	81,300	83,100	82,200	82,700	84,900	81,600	81,500

1994 Year-end:
Debt ratio: 54.5%
Return on equity: 31.6%
Cash (mil.): $636
Current ratio: 1.57
Long-term debt (mil.): $2,199
No. of shares (mil.): 643
Dividends
 Yield: 2.1%
 Payout: 36.2%
Market value (mil.): $35,205

Stock Price History
High/Low 1985–94

J.P. MORGAN & CO. INCORPORATED

OVERVIEW

One short year after touting its increased investment in people, J.P. Morgan, one of the US's premier international banking companies, embarked in 1995 on a restructuring that would cut costs by cutting jobs. With the possibility of 5–10% staff reductions, this will be J.P. Morgan's first-ever layoff (previous staff reductions have largely been accomplished through attrition). There are 2 factors in the timing of this action, the first being the generally poor year for the financial industry due in part to the decline of the bond market in early 1994. The 2nd is the changing of the guard following the retirement of Dennis

Weatherstone and his replacement as chairman and CEO by Douglas Warner.

J.P. Morgan's primary subsidiary is Morgan Guaranty Trust. The company is a primary dealer in government securities and also deals in derivatives and currencies for a worldwide clientele. The bank, traditionally client-centered, has in recent years derived an increasing amount of income from trading for its own account. Over the years, rapid growth has resulted in inefficiencies and duplications. The restructuring is intended to eliminate some of these problems and refocus the bank on relationship banking.

WHEN

J.P. Morgan & Co. was born into international capitalism and has lived there ever since. Junius Spencer Morgan became a partner in Londoner George Peabody's banking house in 1854. Morgan assumed control and renamed the firm J. S. Morgan and Co. when Peabody retired in the early 1860s.

Morgan's son began his own firm, J. Pierpont Morgan and Co., in New York in 1862. Connections on both sides of the Atlantic led to profits and power as the firm funneled European capital into the US. Early in its career the firm came to the rescue of the US government. When Congress bickered over the Hayes-Tilden election in 1877 and didn't get around to paying the army, a Morgan affiliate came up with the funds until Congress reconvened.

After Junius's death in 1890, his son reorganized his businesses in London and New York as J.P. Morgan & Co. The firm had already financed and restructured much of the American railroad network, and J. P. Morgan, who became the personification of Wall Street, helped devise the deals that created U.S. Steel, General Electric, and International Harvester.

In 1907 J.P. Morgan acted as the country's de facto central bank, leading a group of bankers to stop a financial panic. Its influence was pervasive. In 1912 a congressional investigation panel found that Morgan partners held 72 directorships in 47 corporations, with total resources of $10 billion.

Morgan's son J. P. Morgan Jr. became senior partner of the firm upon his father's death in 1913. He yielded day-to-day control to partner Thomas Lamont, who tried in 1929, just as J. P. Morgan Sr. had in 1907, to stem national financial collapse; however, the stock crash overwhelmed the effort.

In 1933 the Glass-Steagall Act forced the company to split its activities. J.P. Morgan remained a commercial bank, and a spinoff entity — Morgan Stanley — became the securities underwriter.

In 1959 J.P. Morgan merged with Guaranty Trust Co. of New York and in 1969 became a holding company. In the 1960s Morgan was the most active trader in government securities and intensified its international efforts. After a 1987 restructuring, the company pushed into mergers and acquisitions.

In 1991 an arm of the Morgan organization, J.P. Morgan Securities, served as underwriter for a $56 million equity issue for Amsco, a health products manufacturer. The event was historic — the first time since the Glass-Steagall Act that an affiliate of a commercial bank was permitted both to trade and to underwrite corporate equities.

J.P. Morgan pushed into the uncharted territory of Eastern Europe in 1993 when it was chosen to advise the Czech Republic on the privatization of its telephone company.

The bank entered 1994 in high spirits, on the heels of its record-breaking performance in 1993. Then in February came the decline of the US bond market as interest rates rose and financing activity declined. In response, J.P. Morgan began tightening its belt, deciding after 1994's earnings decline to lay off workers (which entailed a significant shift of culture for the company). Reporting relationships to the new chairman and CEO were also changed through the creation of regional executives with added responsibilities and autonomy. The bank has opened new offices in Beijing, Shanghai, Prague, Warsaw, and Mexico City and received authorization to begin branch banking operations in Australia.

NYSE symbol: JPM
Fiscal year ends: December 31

Chairman, President, and CEO: Douglas A. Warner III,
age 48, $1,949,600 pay
VC: Roberto G. Mendoza, age 49, $1,778,400 pay
VC: Kurt F. Viermetz, age 55, $1,778,400 pay
VC: Rodney B. Wagner, age 63, $1,504,000 pay
CFO: John Meyer, age 55
Chief Administrative Officer: Michael E. Patterson
Corporate Risk Management: Peter B. Smith
Corporate Risk Management: Stephen G. Thieke
Controller: David H. Sidwell
Technology and Operations: Michael Enthoven
Corporate Services: Ronald H. Menaker
General Counsel: Edward J. Kelly III
Auditor: Edward F. Murphy
Managing Director Human Resources: Herbert J. Hefke
Auditors: Price Waterhouse LLP

WHERE

HQ: 60 Wall St., New York, NY 10260-0060
Phone: 212-483-2323
Fax: 212-648-5193

J.P. Morgan conducts banking and investment
operations at offices in 7 US cities and in 35 other cities
around the world.

	1994 Sales		1994 Pretax Income	
	$ mil.	% of total	$ mil.	% of total
US	6,485	55	955	51
Europe, the Middle East & Africa	4,432	37	890	48
Asia/Pacific	617	5	(47)	—
Other Western Hemisphere	381	3	27	1
Total	11,915	100	1,825	100

WHAT

	1994 Assets	
	$ mil.	% of total
Cash & equivalents	37,049	24
Treasury & agency securities	25,276	16
Foreign investments	21,576	14
Swaps, options & other derivatives	19,495	13
Other securities	13,375	9
Net loans	20,949	14
Other assets	17,197	11
Total	**154,917**	**100**

	1994 Sales	
	$ mil.	% of total
Interest	8,379	70
Trading	1,019	8
Corporate finance	434	4
Fees	1,267	11
Other	816	7
Total	**11,915**	**100**

Services	Selected Subsidiaries
Asset and liability management	J.P. Morgan Benelux S.A.
	J.P. Morgan España S.A.
Asset management and servicing	J.P. Morgan Securities Asia, Ltd. (Singapore)
Equity investments	J.P. Morgan Sterling
Finance and advisory	Securities Ltd. (UK)
Sales and trading	Société de Bourse J.P. Morgan S.A. (France)

KEY COMPETITORS

American Express
BankAmerica
Bankers Trust
Barclays
Bear Stearns
Canadian Imperial
Chase Manhattan
Citicorp
Crédit Lyonnais
CS Holding
Dai-Ichi Kangyo
Deutsche Bank
Goldman Sachs
HSBC
Merrill Lynch
Morgan Stanley
NatWest
Paine Webber
Royal Bank of Canada
Salomon
Union Bank of Switzerland

HOW MUCH

	Annual Growth	1985	1986	1987	1988	1989	1990	1991	1992	1993	1994
Assets ($ mil.)	9.3%	69,375	76,039	75,414	83,923	88,964	93,103	103,468	102,941	133,888	154,917
Net income ($ mil.)	6.2%	705	873	83	1,002	(1,275)	775	1,114	1,382	1,723	1,215
Income as % of assets	—	1.0%	1.1%	0.1%	1.2%	—	0.8%	1.1%	1.3%	1.3%	0.8%
Earnings per share ($)	4.9%	3.91	4.74	0.39	5.38	(7.04)	3.99	5.63	6.92	8.48	6.02
Stock price – high ($)	—	33.00	48.00	53.63	40.25	48.13	47.25	70.50	70.50	79.38	72.00
Stock price – low ($)	—	19.13	29.50	27.00	30.75	34.00	29.63	40.50	51.50	59.38	55.13
Stock price – close ($)	6.4%	32.06	41.25	36.25	34.88	44.00	44.38	68.63	65.75	69.38	56.13
P/E – high	—	8	10	—	8	—	12	13	10	9	12
P/E – low	—	5	6	—	6	—	7	7	7	7	9
Dividends per share ($)	10.6%	1.10	1.23	1.36	1.50	1.66	1.82	1.98	2.18	2.40	2.72
Book value per share ($)	8.2%	23.70	27.64	26.32	30.52	21.78	25.29	29.41	34.30	48.50	48.34
Employees	2.6%	13,506	14,518	15,731	15,363	14,207	12,968	13,323	14,368	15,193	17,055

1994 Year-end:
Equity as % of assets: 6.2%
Return on assets: 0.8%
Return on equity: 13.2%
Long-term debt (mil.): $6,802
No. of shares (mil.): 188
Dividends
  Yield: 4.8%
  Payout: 45.2%
Market value (mil.): $10,536
Sales (mil.): $11,915

Stock Price History
High/Low 1985–94

KOHLBERG KRAVIS ROBERTS & CO.

OVERVIEW

After choking on RJR Nabisco, Kohlberg Kravis Roberts & Co. (KKR) is hoping that Borden will go down easier. The New York City–based corporate takeover specialist swapped shares of the tobacco and food company for Borden in 1994. Since then KKR has unloaded the rest of its RJR shares, exiting the tobacco business completely.

One of the bigger Wall Street sharks during the LBO feeding frenzy of the 1980s, KKR is now having to make do with more bite-sized acquisitions. With the firm facing more competition from new buyout firms (there are now more than 200), the ability to charge exorbitant fees is under pressure. In addition, the improved health of companies overall

means fewer opportunities for huge profits through turnarounds. With the latest boom in the stock market, even finding healthy companies that are undervalued is more difficult.

To make up for the lack of takeover targets in the US, KKR is looking in Canada and Europe. The firm is also using a strategy called the leveraged buildup, where it builds a company in a promising industry by assembling a group of related enterprises. One example is K-III Communications, a media and publishing business made up of over 40 companies, including Channel One (the in-school broadcaster), several magazines, and Funk & Wagnalls. KKR registered in 1995 to take the media conglomerate public.

WHEN

In 1976 Jerome Kohlberg left investment bank Bear Stearns, where he had orchestrated leveraged buyouts, to form his own firm. With him he brought Henry Kravis and Kravis's cousin George Roberts. They formed Kohlberg Kravis Roberts & Co. (KKR).

Kohlberg believed LBOs, by giving management ownership stakes in their companies, would result in greater efficiency and productivity. KKR put together friendly buyouts funded by investor groups and large amounts of debt. In 1979 KKR made its first buyout of an NYSE company, Houdaille Industries, a machine tool manufacturer, for $335 million.

In the purchase of the American Forest Products division of Bendix in 1981, KKR lost $93 million. By 1984 KKR had raised its 4th LBO fund and made the first $1 billion buyout, of Wometco Enterprises.

In 1985 KKR turned mean with a hostile takeover of Beatrice ($6.2 billion). The deal depended upon junk bond financing provided by Drexel Burnham Lambert's Michael Milken and on the sale of pieces of the company. KKR funded the acquisitions of Safeway Stores ($5.2 billion) and Owens-Illinois ($4.4 billion) in 1986 from the same investment pool. The firm bought out Jim Walter Homes (now Walter Industries, $2.4 billion) in 1987 and Stop & Shop ($1.2 billion) in 1988.

In 1987 Kohlberg, unhappy with the firm's hostile image, left to form Kohlberg & Co. His suit against KKR over alleged undervaluing of companies in relation to his departure settlement was settled for an undisclosed amount.

The Beatrice LBO had triggered a rash of LBOs as the financial industry sought fat fees. The frenzy culminated in 1988 with the

RJR Nabisco buyout, which provided KKR with $75 million in fees.

After 1989, as the US slid into recession, LBO activities died out and KKR turned to managing its LBOs. RJR Nabisco, caught in tobacco price wars and in a downturn of consumer brand loyalty, required more cash. Infusing an extra $3 billion in RJR doubled KKR investors' equity stakes and halved return on equity. Before it got rid of its shares in RJR in 1994–95, KKR had invested over 50% of the 1987 investment pool and 39% of all KKR investment funds in the company. Other troubled companies include Seamans furniture and Hillsborough Holdings, which went into Chapter 11 bankruptcy in 1989 after profitable operations were sold to service debt and the company was hit with asbestos claims.

In 1991, with partner Fleet/Norstar (now Fleet Financial Group), KKR bought the Bank of New England from the FDIC for $625 million. In 1992 KKR bought 47% of TW Holdings restaurant group (now Flagstar; Denny's and Hardee's) for $300 million and the refinancing of $950 million in old debt.

KKR acquired troubled food giant Borden in 1994 for half of its RJR stock. In early 1995 KKR installed Robert Kidder, former CEO of Duracell (which is also controlled by KKR), as the new head of Borden. By March of that year the firm had traded in the rest of its RJR shares. Other KKR purchases in 1995 included Medco Behavioral Care Corp. for $340 million, Bruno's Inc. (whose supermarkets include Food World and Piggly Wiggly) for nearly $1 billion, and Reed Elsevier's UK regional newspaper publishing group for $320 million. The Reed purchase was its first European venture.

Private partnership

WHO

Founding Partner: Henry R. Kravis, age 51
Founding Partner: George R. Roberts, age 51
General Partner: R. Theodore Ammon, age 41
General Partner: Saul Fox, age 37
General Partner: Edward Gilhuly, age 35
General Partner: Perry Golkin, age 41
General Partner: James H. Greene Jr., age 42
General Partner: Robert I. MacDonnell
General Partner: Michael W. Michelson
General Partner: Paul E. Raether
General Partner: Clifton S. Robbins, age 36
General Partner: Scott Stuart, age 35
General Partner: Michael T. Tokarz, age 43

WHERE

HQ: 9 W. 57th St., Ste. 4200, New York, NY 10019
Phone: 212-750-8300
Fax: 212-593-2430 (public relations firm)

WHAT

Largest LBO Deals	Final Value ($ mil.)
RJR Nabisco	30,600
Beatrice	6,100
Safeway	5,340
Borden	4,640
Owens-Illinois	3,640

Selected Investment Holdings
American Re-Insurance Co.
AutoZone (43.1%, automotive parts retailer)
Bank of New England (14.1%, in partnership with Fleet
   Financial Group)
Bruno's (grocery retail)
Canadian General Insurance Group
Duracell (33.97%, batteries)
First Interstate Bancorp (8.26%)
Flagstar (60.94%, restaurants)
Fred Meyer (38%)
IDEX Corp. (29.9%, industrial products)
K-III (87%, publishing)
Marley Co. (water towers, heating systems)
Medco Behavioral Care Corp.
Neway Anchorlok International (brakes and suspension
   systems)

Owens-Illinois (30.2%, glass containers)
Reliance Comm/Tec (telecommunications equipment)
PacTrust (Pacific Realty trust)
Safeway (61.6%, grocery stores)
Seaman Furniture
The Stop & Shop Cos. (62.2%)
Union Texas Petroleum (25%)
Walter Industries (11.7%, construction products)
World Color Press

Investors in KKR Partnerships
Insurance companies
Nonprofit organizations
State pension funds
   Montana Investment Board
   Oregon Public Employees Retirement Fund
   Washington State Investment Board

KEY COMPETITORS

AEA Investors	HSBC
American Financial	Interlaken Capital
Apollo Advisors	Jordan Co.
Barclays	Lehman Brothers
Bear Stearns	Loews
Berkshire Hathaway	MacAndrews & Forbes
Blackstone Group	Merrill Lynch
Canadian Imperial	Morgan Stanley
Clayton Dubilier & Rice	National Westminster
Crédit Lyonnais	Nomura Securities
CS Holdings	Odyssey Partners
Dai-Ichi Kangyo	Paine Webber
Deutsche Bank	Prudential
Forstmann Little	Royal Bank of Canada
General Electric	Salomon
Goldman Sachs	Thomas H. Lee
Hanson	Union Bank of
Heico Acquisitions	Switzerland
Hicks, Muse, Tate & Furst	

HOW MUCH

	Annual Growth	1985	1986	1987	1988	1989	1990	1991	1992	1993	1994
Value of major new investments ($ mil.)	—	10,800	9,290	2,400	32,930	405	2,300	966	1,700	110	4,840[1]
No. of major investments	—	3	2	1	4	2	1	3	2	2	2

KKR

Value of Major
New Investments
($ mil.) 1985–94

35,000
30,000
25,000
20,000
15,000
10,000
5,000
0

[1] Includes total value of Borden transaction

KPMG

OVERVIEW

Klynveld Peat Marwick Goerdeler (KPMG) is the most international of the Big 6 accounting firms, doing more than 2/3 of its business outside the US. It is also the one that is still most tied to its auditing business. The combination of overseas recessions, exchange imbalances, and increased price competition in auditing in the 1990s has brought repeated rounds of layoffs and cost cutting, including the firing of 65 junior auditors just in time for the glad new fiscal year of 1995.

But in 1995 the firm began a counteroffensive designed to remind potential clients of its preeminence overseas and to change the nature of its relationship with its clients. The firm launched *Worldbusiness,* a new magazine version of its quarterly newsletter. KPMG Peat Marwick, the US affiliate, admitted 127 new partners, each of whom will specialize in a specific area. The firm believes clients will appreciate the advantage of using auditors who actually know something about the industries they are dealing with.

KPMG has also made a number of strategic alliances with producers of computer hardware and software, which the company believes will contribute to both its accounting and consulting work.

WHEN

KPMG was formed in 1987 when Peat, Marwick, Mitchell, & Copartners joined KMG, an international federation of accounting firms. The combined firms immediately jumped to #1 in worldwide revenues.

Peat Marwick was founded in 1911, when William Peat, a respected London accountant, met James Marwick on a westbound crossing of the Atlantic. Marwick and fellow University of Glasgow alumnus S. Roger Mitchell had formed Marwick, Mitchell & Company in New York in 1897. Peat and Marwick agreed to join their firms under an agreement that was to terminate in 1919. In 1925 they merged permanently as Peat, Marwick, Mitchell, & Copartners.

In 1947 William Black became senior partner, a position he held until 1965. He guided the firm's 1950 merger with Barrow, Wade, Guthrie, the oldest and most prestigious US firm, and built up the firm's management consulting practice. Peat Marwick restructured its international practice as PMM&Co. (International) in 1972 and reformed it as Peat Marwick International in 1978.

In 1979 a group of European accounting firms led by Klynveld Kraayenhoff (the Netherlands) and Deutsche Treuhand (Germany) discussed the formation of an international accounting federation to serve multinationals. At that time 2 American firms that had been founded around the turn of the century, Main Lafrentz and Hurdman Cranstoun, agreed to merge in order to combat the growing reach of the Big 8. The Europeans needed an American member for their federation and encouraged the formation of the new firm, Main Hurdman & Cranstoun. By 1980 Main Hurdman had joined the Europeans to form Klynveld Main Goerdeler (KMG), named after 2 of the member firms and the chairman of Deutsche Treuhand, Dr. Reinhard Goerdeler. Other federation members were C. Jespersen (Denmark), Thorne Riddel (Canada), Thomson McLintok (UK), and Fides Revision (Switzerland). KMG immediately became one of the world's largest accounting firms, breaking the dominance of the Anglo-US firms.

In 1987 Peat Marwick merged with KMG to form Klynveld Peat Marwick Goerdeler (KPMG). As a result of the merger, KPMG lost 10% of its business owing to the departure of competing companies that had formerly been clients of Peat Marwick or KMG; but the firm nevertheless became #1 worldwide in 1987.

KPMG in 1992 established the first joint accounting venture in China and opened an office in Estonia. In that same year the RTC sued KPMG Peat Marwick for alleged negligence and breach of contract in auditing Pennsylvania-based Hill Financial S&L. There were several other such suits. In 1994 the firm settled its S&L/banking suits with the US government for $187 million.

In 1993 the firm was named by the Agency for International Development to head a consortium providing technical assistance to 12 countries of the former Soviet Union, as those countries attempt to privatize their economies.

KPMG's Australian affiliate agreed to pay $97 million in 1994 to settle a suit brought by the Australian state of Victoria. The state claimed that faulty audits were to blame in the collapse of Tricontinental Group, a subsidiary of the State Bank of Victoria.

As part of its drive to improve the quality of its auditing and consulting, in 1995 KPMG allied with both Integral and Hyperion for the promotion of client/server software. Fiscal 1995 sales rose to $7.5 billion worldwide.

International partnership
Fiscal year ends: June 30

WHO

Chairman, KPMG; Chairman, KPMG Peat Marwick LLP: Jon C. Madonna
Administration and Finance Partner, KPMG Peat Marwick LLP: Joseph E. Heintz
General Counsel, KPMG Peat Marwick LLP: Claudia L. Taft
Human Resources, KPMG Peat Marwick LLP: Howard R. Marcus

WHERE

HQ: Klynveld Peat Marwick Goerdeler, PO Box 74555, 1070 BC Amsterdam, The Netherlands
Phone: +31-20-656-7890
Fax: +31-20-656-7000
US HQ: KPMG Peat Marwick LLP, 767 Fifth Ave., New York, NY 10153
US Phone: 212-909-5000
US Fax: 212-909-5299

KPMG has offices in 142 countries. KPMG Peat Marwick LLP has 124 offices in the US.

	1995 Sales % of total
US	31
Other countries	69
Total	**100**

WHAT

Selected Services
Financial services
Health care and life sciences
Information, communications, and entertainment
Manufacturing, retailing, and distribution
Public services

Representative Clients
Aetna
American Cyanamid
BMW
British Aerospace
Citicorp
Daimler-Benz
First Union
General Mills
Gillette
Hasbro
Heineken
J. C. Penney
Kemper Corp.
Koch Industries
Motorola
Nestlé
Norfolk Southern
PepsiCo
Pfizer
Polaroid
Ryder
Siemens
TCI
Union Carbide
USAir
Wells Fargo
Xerox

Affiliated Firms
Century Audit Corp. (Japan)
KPMG Deutsche Treuhand-Gesellschaft (Germany)
KPMG Klynveld (The Netherlands)
KPMG Peat Marwick (Belgium)
KPMG Peat Marwick (UK)
KPMG Peat Marwick (US)
KPMG Peat Marwick Huazhen (China)
KPMG Peat Marwick Thorne (Canada)
KPMG Reviconsult (Russia)

KEY COMPETITORS

Andersen Worldwide
Arthur D. Little
Bain & Co.
Booz, Allen
Boston Consulting
Coopers & Lybrand
Deloitte & Touche
Delta Consulting
EDS
Ernst & Young
Gemini Consulting
H&R Block
IBM
Marsh & McLennan
McKinsey & Co.
Perot Systems
Price Waterhouse
Wyatt Co.

HOW MUCH

	Annual Growth	1986	1987	1988	1989	1990	1991	1992	1993	1994	1995
Sales ($ mil.)	18.1%	1,672	3,250	3,900	4,300	5,368	6,011	6,150	6,000	6,600	7,500
Offices	13.9%	342	620	637	700	800	820	819	1,100	1,100	1,100
Partners	9.4%	2,726	5,150	5,050	5,300	6,300	6,100	6,004	6,100	6,100	6,100
Employees	9.8%	32,183	60,000	63,700	68,000	77,300	75,000	73,488	76,200	76,200	74,400

1995 Year-end:
Sales per partner: $1,229,500

Note: Figures prior to 1987 are for Peat Marwick only; sales prior to 1994 are net of reimbursable expenses.

LEFRAK ORGANIZATION INC.

OVERVIEW

The Lefrak Organization has followed its founder Samuel LeFrak's golden rule: "He who has the gold makes the rules." Unlike Donald Trump and other high rollers of the 1980s New York real estate market who borrowed other people's gold to make high-priced deals, Lefrak stuck to its policy of buying low and selling high. Many others ran into trouble when the market slumped in the 1990s.

The Lefrak Organization is one of the US's largest private landlords; it owns more than 90,000 apartments in the New York boroughs and controls millions of square feet of commercial space.

The company also has a significant presence in entertainment. Lefrak Entertainment operates LMR, the record label that launched

Barbra Streisand. It also owns stage and movie theaters and produces television shows, movies, and Broadway shows (such as the 1982 Tony-award-winning musical *Nine*). Lefrak Oil & Gas Organization (LOGO) engages in petroleum exploration. In 1994 the company bought 200 oilfields to build up its reserves of gas and home-heating oil.

Samuel LeFrak used the money he earned building low-cost housing in the postwar era to invest in a variety of other fields, including mining and forestry. The billionaire is also an active philanthropist, sponsoring oceanographic studies by Jacques Cousteau, endowing a library at St. Cross College, Oxford, and giving $10 million to the Guggenheim Museum in New York.

WHEN

Harry Lefrak and his father, both builders, came to the US around the turn of the century and began building tenements to house the flood of immigrants then pouring into New York City. In 1905 they started what is now known as the Lefrak Organization. It diversified into glass and for some time provided glass for the lamps of Louis Comfort Tiffany. After WWI the glass factory was sold, and the company expanded into Brooklyn, where it developed housing and commercial space in Bedford-Stuyvesant, among other areas.

Samuel, Harry's son, began working in the business early, assisting tradesmen at building sites. He then attended the University of Maryland and returned to the business.

After WWII, business took off as the company began providing low-cost housing for returning veterans and their burgeoning families. Samuel took over the company in 1948. To keep down expenses over the years, Samuel bought up clay and gypsum quarries, as well as forests, and operated his own lumber mills and cement plants, eventually achieving 70% vertical integration of his operations.

The 1950s building boom was in part spurred by new laws in New York authorizing the issue of state bonds dedicated to financing low-interest construction loans. Lefrak built more than 2,000 apartments in previously undeveloped coastal sections of Brooklyn. At its peak Lefrak could turn out an apartment every 16 minutes for projected rents as low as $21 per room.

In 1960 Lefrak began its greatest project to that date, Lefrak City, a 6,000-apartment development built on 40 acres in Queens. The

privately financed development featured air-conditioned units at rents of $40 per room.

The next decade brought a real estate slump that endangered the organization's then-current project, Battery Park. In order to save it, Lefrak had to issue public bonds. In a time when all about him were losing their heads, Samuel LeFrak remained cool and solvent and picked up a few more properties. During this period Samuel Lefrak capitalized the "F" in his family name but not the company name. (He later said that he did this to distinguish himself from other Lefraks at his club who had been posted for nonpayment of dues.)

In the Roaring '80s LeFrak's son Richard became increasingly involved in the business. The organization's big new project, Newport City, began construction on 400 acres near Jersey City, New Jersey. The project included commercial and retail space, a marina, and nearly 10,000 apartments. Newport City ran into problems with local authorities. LeFrak refused to pay taxes on the property because the city did not supply police and fire services for the facilities he had finished, which included more than 2,000 occupied apartments and commercial and retail space. This sent him into technical default, which he disputed by escrowing the tax money until Jersey City began providing the Newport community the municipal services to which it was entitled.

In 1995 LeFrak (and Leon Charney, of Charney Communications) acquired TV and motion picture rights for *The Secret War Against the Jews*, a book which claims Western government complicity in anti-Israeli activities.

Private company
Fiscal year ends: Last Sunday in November

WHO

Chairman and CEO: Samuel J. LeFrak, age 77
President and COO: Richard S. LeFrak
EVP: Arthur Klein
SVP Marketing, Advertising, and Public Relations:
Edward Cortese
VP Acquisitions/Investments: Richard Papert
VP Management: Charles Hehlman
VP Commercial Leasing: Irwin Granville
VP Commercial Leasing: Marsilia Boyle
VP: Harrison LeFrak
VP: James LeFrak
Director Human Resources: John Farelly

WHERE

HQ: 97-77 Queens Blvd., Rego Park, NY 11374
Phone: 718-459-9021
Fax: 718-897-0688

The company engages primarily in real estate
development and management in the New York
metropolitan area.

WHAT

Energy
LOGO (Lefrak Oil & Gas Organization; 700 properties)

Entertainment
Lefrak Entertainment Co.

Real Estate Developments
Battery Park City (2,200 units, 1973)
Commercial (5 million square feet)
Lefrak City (6,000 units, 1960)
Newport City (2,000 units, in progress)
Residential (200,000 units built to date)
Retail (5 million square feet)

KEY COMPETITORS

Apache
Ashland Inc.
Barrett Resources
Corporate Property Investors
Edward J. DeBartolo
Exxon
Helmsley
Investment Properties Associates
JMB Realty
King World
Lincoln Property
Melvin Simon & Associates
Nederlander Organization
News Corp.
Pembrook Management
Rockefeller Group
Rouse
Rudin Management
Shubert Organization
Sony
Sun Co.
Taubman Centers
Tenneco
Texaco
Time Warner
Tishman Speyer Properties
Trammell Crow
Trump Organization
USX-Delhi
Viacom
Walt Disney
Westinghouse
Zeckendorf

HOW MUCH

	Annual Growth	1985	1986	1987	1988	1989	1990	1991	1992	1993	1994
Estimated sales ($ mil.)	13.4%	1,000	2,000	2,600	3,000	2,875	2,900	3,100	3,200	3,200	3,100
Employees	(0.3%)	18,000	18,000	18,000	18,000	18,000	18,000	18,000	18,000	18,000	17,500

Estimated Sales
($ mil.)
1985–94

LEHMAN BROTHERS HOLDINGS INC.

OVERVIEW

"Free at last, free at last, thank God Almighty, free at last." That was how most people at New York–based Lehman Brothers felt in May of 1994, when American Express spun off the venerable investment bank to stockholders and the public. After more than 10 years with American Express, the company is making its way as a public company for the first time in its 145-year history.

Lehman Brothers is a leading investment bank, with offices in the US, Latin America, Europe, the Middle East, and Asia. It raises money for corporate, institutional, and government clients through underwriting and placing securities, and it provides a variety of advisory and investment management services to its clientele of corporations, governments and individuals. Lehman also trades stocks, currency, derivatives, and commodities.

Lehman gained its independence in one of the worst years in recent memory for the financial industry, as the Federal Reserve raised interest rates 6 times in 1994 alone. This played havoc with the firm's bond business (it is one of the US's leading corporate debt underwriters).

But a severe round of cost cutting, including massive layoffs, lifted Lehman into the black for the year. Simultaneously with its cost cutting, the firm is expanding into such emerging markets as China and India. It is also targeting markets in Europe: Lehman was authorized as a primary trader in Italian government bonds in 1994.

Lehman's share price got off to a rocky start (but insiders have bought stock on the open market). Nippon Life, which lent the firm money in 1987, owns 11.5% of the stock.

WHEN

Henry Lehman came to the US in 1844. After a year in New York, he moved to Montgomery, Alabama, and opened a dry goods store. His 2 younger brothers, Emanuel and Mayer, had joined him by 1850. Their Lehman Brothers store prospered on the strength of the pre–Civil War cotton boom. The brothers often accepted raw cotton instead of cash in return for merchandise, and they developed a thriving cotton business on the side. Soon cotton trading dominated the firm, and in 1858 (2 years after Henry's death) the company opened a New York office.

Despite the effects of the Civil War, in 1862 the remaining Lehman brothers joined with another cotton merchant, John Durr, to form Lehman, Durr & Co. This company helped finance Alabama's postwar reconstruction. In 1870 Lehman Brothers led in the formation of the New York Cotton Exchange.

Lehman Brothers continued to grow and diversify, underwriting its first IPO in 1899 for the International Steam Pump Company. Seven years later Lehman joined with Goldman Sachs to take Sears public. In the 1920s and even during the Depression, Lehman continued its investment operations, pioneering private placements during the long eclipse of the stock market in the 1930s.

The firm remained under family management until the death of Robert Lehman (Emanuel's grandson) in 1969. There followed a period of drifting.

In 1977 Lehman Brothers merged with Kuhn Loeb & Co., a firm of similar vintage,

which had helped finance the development of the railroad industry. Kuhn Loeb had significant business overseas dating from the turn of the century, when it had helped the Japanese government to finance the Russo-Japanese War (which the Japanese won).

But the late 1970s were a precarious time in the financial world; in addition the 2 firms did not meld well. By 1984 Lehman Brothers Kuhn Loeb was rent by infighting among its partners and managers and ripe for a sellout to the right suitor. Along came Sanford Weill, who had sold out his Shearson brokerage to American Express and become that company's president. He was attempting to assemble a financial supermarket and needed an investment banking firm.

Lehman Brothers Kuhn Loeb had trouble adjusting to Shearson, and there were mass defections. Shearson instilled a more go-getting ethos than Lehman had previously known, and results improved. But they remained spotty, and Lehman was notoriously free-spending on employee perks.

In 1992 American Express began to refocus on its core businesses and divest financial services, splitting the unit by business lines. Lehman Brothers kept investment banking but lost brokerage, with its network of sales offices, and mutual funds. American Express gave it $1 billion to shore up its balance sheet.

In 1995 Lehman made plans to enter the mutual funds field, with its potentially lucrative (and steady) fee income, and began beefing up its equities trading operations.

NYSE symbol: LEH
Fiscal year ends: November 30

Chairman and CEO: Richard S. Fuld Jr., age 48,
$1,425,000 pay
President and COO: T. Christopher Pettit, age 49,
$1,237,500 pay
Chief Administrative Officer: John L. Cecil, age 40,
$1,600,000 pay
Chief Legal Officer: Thomas A. Russo, age 51,
$1,275, 000 pay
CFO: Robert Matza, age 38, $900,000 pay
**Managing Director Fixed Income Division, Lehman
Brothers:** Joseph M. Gregory
**Managing Director Investment Banking Division,
Lehman Brothers:** Mel A. Shaftel
Managing Director Lehman Brothers: Bruce R.
Lakefield
Managing Director Human Resources: Maryanne
Rasmussen
Auditors: Ernst & Young LLP

WHERE

HQ: 3 World Financial Center, New York, NY 10285
Phone: 212-526-7000
Fax: 212-526-3738

Lehman Brothers has 46 offices in Argentina, Bahrain,
Canada, Chile, China, Dubai, France, Germany, Hong
Kong, Israel, Italy, Japan, Korea, Mexico, Singapore,
Switzerland, Taiwan, the UK, the US, and Venezuela.

	1994 Sales		1994 Pretax Income	
	$ mil.	% of total	$ mil.	% of total
US	8,020	87	225	95
Europe	846	9	(43)	—
Asia/Pacific	324	4	11	5
Total	**9,190**	**100**	**193**	**100**

WHAT

	1994 Sales	
	$ mil.	% of total
Interest & dividends	6,761	74
Principal transactions	1,345	15
Investment banking	572	6
Commissions	445	5
Other	67	0
Total	**9,190**	**100**

Services
Asset management
Commodities and futures trading
Derivatives origination and trading
Foreign exchange services
Merchant banking
Research
Securities trading and underwriting

KEY COMPETITORS

Bankers Trust
Bear Stearns
Brown Brothers Harriman
Chase Manhattan
CS Holding
Dai-Ichi Kangyo
Dean Witter, Discover
Deutsche Bank
Equitable
Fannie Mae
Goldman Sachs
Industrial Bank of Japan
J.P. Morgan
Merrill Lynch
Morgan Stanley
Nomura Securities
Paine Webber
Royal Bank of Canada
Salomon
Travelers

HOW MUCH

	Annual Growth	1985	1986	1987	1988	1989	1990	1991	1992	1993	1994[1]
Sales ($ mil.)	(3.1%)	—	—	—	—	10,776	8,750	9,830	10,611	10,586	9,190
Net income ($ mil.)	(4.4%)	—	—	—	—	110	(809)	207	(116)	(102)	88
Income as % of sales	—	—	—	—	—	1.0%	—	2.1%	—	—	1.0%
Earnings per share ($)	—	—	—	—	—	—	—	—	—	—	0.81
Stock price – high ($)	—	—	—	—	—	—	—	—	—	—	20.88
Stock price – low ($)	—	—	—	—	—	—	—	—	—	—	13.75
Stock price – close ($)	—	—	—	—	—	—	—	—	—	—	14.75
P/E – high	—	—	—	—	—	—	—	—	—	—	26
P/E – low	—	—	—	—	—	—	—	—	—	—	17
Dividends per share ($)	—	—	—	—	—	—	—	—	—	—	0.18
Book value per share ($)	—	—	—	—	—	—	—	—	—	—	25.70
Employees	(25.3%)	—	—	—	—	—	—	—	—	9,300	6,950

1994 Year-end:
Debt ratio: 84.4%
Return on equity: 4.4%
Cash (mil.): $2,384
Current ratio: 1.15
Long-term debt (mil.): $11,321
No. of shares (mil.): 105
Dividends
Yield: 1.2%
Payout: 21.6%
Market value (mil.): $1,542

**Stock Price History
High/Low 1994**

[1] 11-month fiscal year

LOEWS CORPORATION

OVERVIEW

Larry Tisch got upstaged by a rodent in 1995. Loews, the holding company run by Tisch and his brother Bob, owned 18% of CBS and was at the center of the decision to sell the network to Westinghouse for $5.4 billion. Network chairman Larry's announcement of the sale, however, came one day after Walt Disney agreed to buy Capital Cities/ABC for $19 billion — making the CBS deal look rather Mickey Mouse by comparison.

Most of Loews's revenue comes from insurance. The company's 84%-owned CNA Financial holding company provides health, life, and professional insurance; 36% of premiums are from workers' compensation. Catastrophic losses related to the Northridge earthquake in California and severe winter weather hurt CNA's profits in 1994. CNA acquired the Conti-

nental Corp. in 1994 and Alexsis in 1995, making it the US's 7th largest insurance provider.

A discount pricing strategy is firing up sales at wholly owned Lorillard, which makes the Kent, Newport, and True cigarette brands. Lorillard, the US's 4th largest cigarette maker, had 7.5% of the US cigarette market in 1994.

Smaller Loews holdings include Loews Hotels, which has 12 US hotels plus one each in Canada and Monaco; Bulova, the watch and clock maker; and 49-rig Diamond Offshore Drilling. (Loews announced in 1995 that it would offer 26% of Diamond Offshore to the public.) Loews owns 49% of Hellespont, which operates 6 crude oil tankers.

The Tisch brothers each own 16% of the company and have involved their sons — a total of 5 Tisches sit on the company's board.

WHEN

In 1946 Larry Tisch, who had received an NYU business degree at age 18, dropped out of Harvard Law and with his younger brother Bob bought a Lakewood, New Jersey, resort hotel, with help from their parents. Tisch Hotels, the new entity, bought Atlantic City's Traymore and Ambassador Hotels in the early 1950s and 10 others by 1955. In the early 1960s the brothers erected 6 hotels simultaneously in New York City.

Moving beyond hotels, the brothers bought money-losing companies saddled with poor management. Discarding the management along with underperforming divisions, they quickly tightened operational control and eliminated frills such as fancy offices, company planes, and even memos.

In 1960 Tisch Hotels gained control of MGM's ailing Loew's Theaters division and sold the real estate underneath many of the elegant one-screen theaters to developers. The company name became Loews in 1971; it sold its remaining theater operations in 1985.

In 1968 the company bought Lorillard, shed pet food and candy operations, and regained its slipping tobacco market share by introducing low-tar brands (Kent III, True). CNA Financial (bought in 1974) was next: the Tisch method turned losses of $208 million in 1974 to $110 million in profits the next year.

Bulova Watch (acquired in 1979), guided by Larry's son Andrew, combated a nagging image problem with sleek new watch styles; profitability returned in 1984.

In 1985 Loews helped CBS fend off a takeover attempt by Ted Turner and ended up with

almost 25% of the company (7% was later sold); Larry became president of CBS.

Loews's deep pockets allowed the purchase of 6 used tankers for $5.5 million apiece (average construction cost: $60 million) during a period of depressed supertanker prices in the early 1980s. In 1990 Loews sold 3 of the tankers for $133 million to Hellespont and exchanged the other 3 for 49% interest in that company. Loews bought offshore drilling rig operator Diamond M in 1989.

Loews's caution during the hotel overexpansion of the 1980s later enabled the company to purchase some bargains (e.g., Loews Giorgio, Denver; 1989). In 1989 Loews also entered a joint venture with Covia, a United Airlines affiliate, to create a new computer reservation service for hotels. Diamond M bought Odeco Drilling for $372 million in 1992. CNA Financial increased its reserves for asbestos claims to $1.5 billion in 1993, in part to cover claims associated with asbestos producer Fireboard, which CNA insured from 1957 to 1959. Also in 1993 CNA's drilling activities were grouped as Diamond Offshore Drilling. In 1994, 5 US tobacco companies, including Lorillard, were hit with a $5 billion lawsuit following allegations that cigarette manufacturers manipulated nicotine levels.

In 1995 Bulova sold its industrial and defense products segment (36% of 1994 revenues) for about $21 million. That same year a West Virginia judge dismissed 8 of 10 counts in a suit against Lorillard and other cigarette makers seeking recovery of that state's Medicaid payments for smokers' health problems.

NYSE symbol: LTR
Fiscal year ends: December 31

WHO

Co-chairman and Co-CEO: Laurence A. Tisch, age 72, $601,660 pay
Co-chairman and Co-CEO: Preston Robert Tisch, age 68, $1,555,448 pay
President and COO: James S. Tisch, age 42, $697,443 pay
Chairman and CEO, Lorillard Tobacco: Alexander Spears III
VP; President and CEO, Loews Hotels: Jonathan M. Tisch, age 41, $696,432 pay
Chairman, CNA Insurance: Dennis H. Chookaszian
President, Diamond Offshore Drilling: Robert E. Rose
SVP and CFO: Roy E. Posner, age 61
SVP; President, Bulova: Herbert C. Hofmann, age 52
VP Personnel: Kenneth Abrams, age 61
Auditors: Deloitte & Touche LLP

WHERE

HQ: 667 Madison Ave., New York, NY 10021-8087
Phone: 212-545-2000
Fax: 212-545-2498

WHAT

	1994 Sales		1994 Operating Income	
	$ mil.	% of total	$ mil.	% of total
Insurance	10,992	81	(14)	—
Cigarettes	1,916	14	584	86
Drilling	304	2	(14)	—
Hotels	217	2	49	7
Watches & clocks	151	1	4	0
CBS	—	—	46	7
Investments	(90)	—	(94)	—
Adjustments & other	25	—	(16)	—
Total	**13,515**	**100**	**545**	**100**

Major Holdings

CNA Financial (84%)
Alexsis
Continental Assurance
Continental Casualty
Continental Corporation

Lorillard, Inc. (Cigarette Brands)
Kent
Newport
Old Gold
Style
True

Diamond Offshore Drilling, Inc.
Drilling rigs

Loews Hotels
Days Hotel (NYC)
Howard Johnson Hotel (NYC)
Loews Anatole (Dallas)

Loews Annapolis
Loews Coronado Bay Resort (San Diego)
Loews Giorgio (Denver)
Loews Le Concorde (Quebec City)
Loews L'Enfant Plaza (DC)
Loews Monte Carlo
Loews New York
Loews Santa Monica Beach
Loews Vanderbilt Plaza (Nashville)
Loews Ventana Canyon Resort (Tucson)
Regency (NYC)

Bulova Corporation (97%)
Clocks
Jewelry
Watches

Hellespont (49%)
Crude oil tankers

KEY COMPETITORS

Accor	Hanson	Nestlé
Aetna	Helmsley	North American
Allstate	Hilton	Watch
Baker Hughes	Home	Philip Morris
Bass	Holdings	Promus Hotels
B.A.T	Hyatt	Prudential
Canadian	Imasco	Rank
Pacific	Ingram	Ritz-Carlton
Carlson	ITT Corp.	RJR Nabisco
Casio	ITT Hartford	SAFECO
Chubb	Kemper National	Seiko
CIGNA	Insurance	SMH Group
Citizen Watch	Liggett	Tidewater
Fossil	Marriott	Travelers
GEICO	International	USF&G
Halliburton	MetLife	Westin Hotel

HOW MUCH

	Annual Growth	1985	1986	1987	1988	1989	1990	1991	1992	1993	1994
Sales ($ mil.)	8.5%	6,475	8,405	9,254	10,514	11,437	12,637	13,620	13,691	13,687	13,515
Net income ($ mil.)	(8.4%)	589	546	696	909	907	805	904	(22)	594	268
Income as % of sales	—	3.7%	2.9%	3.1%	3.5%	2.8%	2.3%	2.3%	—	4.3%	2.0%
Earnings per share ($)	(5.2%)	7.23	6.69	8.92	11.94	12.07	11.01	13.14	(0.33)	9.27	4.45
Stock price – high ($)	—	56.25	72.38	96.25	83.13	135.00	126.88	112.88	126.50	120.25	102.75
Stock price – low ($)	—	32.97	53.75	58.00	62.00	77.00	75.00	88.50	103.50	86.75	84.50
Stock price – close ($)	5.3%	54.50	58.25	66.63	78.88	124.25	98.13	109.50	120.13	93.00	86.88
P/E – high	—	8	11	11	7	11	12	9	—	13	23
P/E – low	—	5	8	7	5	6	7	7	—	9	19
Dividends per share ($)	(11.5%)	3.00	1.00	1.00	1.00	1.00	1.00	1.00	1.00	1.00	1.00
Book value per share ($)	13.2%	29.96	36.07	42.56	53.20	64.09	72.10	84.18	84.90	99.59	91.67
Employees	1.7%	21,900	22,950	23,900	24,500	26,800	26,600	26,800	28,100	27,100	25,400

1994 Year-end:
Debt ratio: 28.4%
Return on equity: 4.6%
Cash (mil.): $8,598
Current ratio: —
Long-term debt (mil.): $2,144
No. of shares (mil.): 59
Dividends
　Yield: 1.2%
　Payout: 22.5%
Market value (mil.): $5,123

Stock Price History
High/Low 1985–94

LONG ISLAND LIGHTING COMPANY

OVERVIEW

Ensconced on an island it views as a fortress against the threat of competition, Long Island Lighting (Lilco) is nevertheless fighting an insurrection and battling with state officials over fair surrender terms. The Hicksville, New York–based utility generates, transmits, and sells electricity to more than one million customers on Long Island. The company also buys, distributes, and sells natural gas to about 450,000 customers in the same area.

In 1995 Lilco charged about 16.8 cents per kilowatt-hour (kWh) — twice the national average. (Lilco has been granted several rate hikes to recoup the $4.6 billion it invested in the unused Shoreham nuclear plant.) Customer uproar has propelled local politicians into action: Nassau County has petitioned state regulators to allow retail competition for all electric customers in the county. In

addition, several Long Island towns are considering the formation of municipal power authorities to replace Lilco.

The response of William Catacosinos, the chairman, president, and CEO, has been simple: he has cut costs and vehemently opposed power municipalization efforts. Lilco insists that its service territory's small industrial base, together with limited transmission connections to the mainland, makes it unlikely the company will lose much to local cogenerators or cheaper public utilities.

Nevertheless, Lilco finds itself being appraised. The goal of the Long Island Power Authority (LIPA, a state agency) is to acquire and restructure the utility to bring about lower rates. Meanwhile, Catacosinos is holding out for the best possible terms: a good price for shareholders and a future for Lilco.

WHEN

Engineer Ellis Phillips, investor George Olmstead, and former generating equipment supplier Clarence Dean formed the Long Island Lighting Co. (Lilco) in 1910 by merging 4 small Suffolk County utilities. Phillips became general manager (retiring as chairman in 1945). In the 1910s and 1920s the firm acquired several electric and gas companies and expanded its territory to include all of Suffolk County and parts of adjacent Nassau County. Additional acquisitions effectively made it a monopoly by the onset of the Depression.

During the 1930s and 1940s Lilco battled state and federal regulators by initiating a local public relations campaign, giving plant tours and emphasizing employees' community involvement. After WWII the company struggled with the SEC over the implications of the Public Utility Holding Company Act of 1935 (which ushered in the current era of regulated local utility monopolies). Finally, in the midst of the postwar boom, Lilco was allowed to consolidate its subsidiaries.

The utility built several plants in the 1950s and 1960s and connected its transmission facilities to the northeastern US grid. In 1965 Lilco proposed a 540 megawatt (MW), $75 million nuclear plant at Shoreham, Long Island. Within a few years the rapid growth in demand led the firm to expand the project to 820 MW.

Lilco began construction of Shoreham in 1973 — the same year the OPEC oil embargo sent oil prices skyrocketing. (The company had converted its plants from coal to oil in the

previous decade.) Shoreham's construction costs also rose dramatically, to $1.2 billion in 1977, then $4.6 billion in 1986. Lilco raised its rates 13 times in 12 years to keep pace.

Meanwhile, the March 1979 accident at the Three Mile Island nuclear plant in Pennsylvania revitalized Shoreham's opponents over the issue of emergency evacuation. One by one, political leaders began to oppose completion of the project. The company's bond ratings fell and Lilco faced bankruptcy. In the midst of this maelstrom in 1984, William Catacosinos became head of Lilco. He immediately instituted a draconian cost control program, cutting employment by 17%.

In 1985 the company won Nuclear Regulatory Agency approval to test Shoreham. But the Chernobyl disaster in 1986 gave impetus to state legislation that created LIPA (charged with taking over Lilco and closing Shoreham). In 1989 Lilco agreed to turn over the completed (but unused) plant to LIPA in return for a decade of 4.6% annual rate increases to cover its $4.6 billion investment.

Passage of the federal Energy Policy Act in 1992 required the company to open its transmission lines to independent power producers. In 1994 Lilco lost about $90 million to cogenerators, although a new round of cost cutting and lower fuel costs enabled it to request a rate freeze for 1995–96. In June 1995 the utility rejected LIPA's bid of $17.50 a share. In October of that year, LIPA requested proposals from utilities, investment banks, and others regarding a renewed bid to take over Lilco.

WHO

Chairman, President, and CEO: William J. Catacosinos, age 65, $579,654 pay
COO and EVP: James T. Flynn, age 61, $235,178 pay
SVP Electric Business: Edward J. Youngling, age 50, $169,512 pay
SVP and CFO: Anthony Nozzolillo, age 46, $157,678 pay
VP Human Resources: Robert X. Kelleher
Auditors: Ernst & Young LLP

WHERE

HQ: 175 E. Old Country Rd., Hicksville, NY 11801
Phone: 516-755-6650
Fax: 516-931-3165

Long Island Lighting owns 5 steam electric plants and 42 internal combustion units on Long Island. The company also has an 18% interest in the Nine Mile Point nuclear plant (Unit 2) near Oswego, New York.

WHAT

	1994 Sales	
	$ mil.	% of total
Electric operations		
Residential	1,202	39
Commercial & industrial	1,196	39
Other	68	2
Wholesale	15	1
Subtotal	**2,481**	**81**
Gas operations		
Residential	369	12
Commercial & industrial	161	5
Other	29	1
Interruptible revenues	27	1
Subtotal	**586**	**19**
Total	**3,067**	**100**

1994 Electricity Marketed		
	kWh (mil.)	% of total
Commercial & industrial	8,394	51
Residential	7,159	44
Wholesale	372	2
Other	457	3
Total	**16,382**	**100**

1994 Generating Capacity		
	MW	% of total
Gas/oil steam generator	2,012	41
Internal combustion units	1,352	27
Purchased	616	13
Oil steam generator	471	10
Gas steam generator	228	5
Nuclear	189	4
Total	**4,868**	**100**

1994 Gas Marketed		
	Dekatherm (thou.)	% of total
Residential	38,844	53
Commercial & industrial	20,045	27
Off-system sales	7,232	10
Interruptible sales	6,914	10
Total	**73,035**	**100**

KEY COMPETITORS

Brooklyn Union Gas
Central Hudson Gas & Electric
Con Ed
Destec Energy
New York State Electric & Gas
Niagara Mohawk Power
Rochester Gas & Electric
Sithe Energies

HOW MUCH

	Annual Growth	1985	1986	1987	1988	1989	1990	1991	1992	1993	1994
Sales ($ mil.)	4.7%	2,034	1,977	2,072	2,138	2,348	2,447	2,549	2,622	2,881	3,067
Net income ($ mil.)	(5.9%)	524	317	270	299	(96)	320	306	302	297	302
Income as % of sales	—	25.8%	16.0%	13.0%	14.0%	—	13.1%	12.0%	11.5%	10.3%	9.8%
Earnings per share ($)	(6.6%)	3.97	2.13	1.73	2.02	(1.57)	2.26	2.15	2.14	2.15	24.25
Stock price – high ($)	—	9.38	14.63	12.38	17.13	20.25	21.75	25.00	25.88	29.63	24.25
Stock price – low ($)	—	5.75	8.00	6.13	7.13	12.63	17.50	19.00	22.13	23.25	15.00
Stock price – close ($)	7.5%	8.00	10.13	7.13	12.75	20.25	21.38	24.63	25.75	24.38	15.38
P/E – high	—	2	7	7	9	—	10	12	12	14	11
P/E – low	—	1	4	4	4	—	8	9	10	11	7
Dividends per share ($)	—	0.00	0.00	0.00	0.00	0.25	1.13	1.55	1.71	1.75	1.78
Book value per share ($)	(2.9%)	26.84	29,68	32.10	19.61	17.45	18.57	19.13	19.58	19.88	20.66
Employees	0.6%	5,414	6,200	6,400	6,200	6,250	6,600	6,600	6,500	6,300	5,950

1994 Year-end:
Debt ratio: 62.6%
Return on equity: 13.1%
Cash (mil.): $186
Current ratio: 1.41
Long-term debt (mil.): $5,163
No. of shares (mil.): 116
Dividends
  Yield: 11.6%
  Payout: 82.8%
Market value (mil.): $1,782

Stock Price History
High/Low 1985–94

LORAL CORPORATION

OVERVIEW

Loral is a leading manufacturer of defense electronics and telecommunications and space systems, and with its 1995 acquisition of the defense systems business of Unisys, the New York–based company continues to beef up its systems integration business as well. The $800 million purchase of the Unisys unit (which includes air traffic control; command, control, and communications; and naval computers) follows the company's 1994 purchase of IBM's Federal Systems unit. The moves are part of CEO Bernard Schwartz's strategy of diversifying within defense- and government contract–related businesses. While more than 80% of the company's sales go to the US government, no program represents more than 6% of sales,

and Loral plans to continue to diversify its operations.

Loral's defense electronics business includes a variety of high-tech military equipment, from radar-jamming devices to weapons guidance systems. The company also provides electronic reconnaissance and satellite tracking systems for the DOD, and mission and operations support for NASA. Loral affiliate Space Systems/Loral builds telecommunications satellites.

Loral also holds a 32% interest in Globalstar, a wireless telephone system joint venture with Qualcomm, Alcatel-Alsthom, and other investors. Globalstar plans to have worldwide voice and data service by 1998.

WHEN

Loral was founded in 1948 by William Lorenz and Leon Alpert (the "Lor" and "Al" in Loral). Lorenz and Alpert set about creating a conglomerate, acquiring a variety of companies, including a toymaker, a copper wire business, and an industrial meter manufacturer. However, many of the acquisitions proved less than successful, and by the early 1970s the company was floundering. In 1972 the company was in the process of posting a $3 million loss, was in default on its loans, and was being threatened with delisting by the New York Stock Exchange. That's when Bernard Schwartz stepped in.

Schwartz, who had been president of computer leasing company Leasco, came on board as Loral's chairman and president. He worked out new agreements with Loral's creditors and sold off its weaker subsidiaries. Within a year Schwartz had the company back in the black and focused on defense electronics systems. To attract the talented engineers he needed to move Loral up among the leaders in electronic warfare, Schwartz offered stock options in the company.

Schwartz's timing proved impeccable. When Egypt shot down nearly 100 Israeli planes with Soviet-made radar-guided weapons during the 1973 Yom Kippur War, the US and its allies took notice, and the electronic defense industry took off.

Loral's breakthrough came with the ALR56 radar-warning receiver for the F-15 fighter plane. Previously, when a radar receiver was updated to cope with new enemy radar signals, the system had to be rewired, which took over 3 weeks. Loral's system, which used programmable software, took only 20 minutes. The

company also took its business overseas, signing a deal to develop an integrated system that provided radar warning and jamming for the Belgian Air Force in 1975. It was the first such system designed and manufactured by a single company.

While Loral has had its share of technological breakthroughs, its growth has been spurred through acquisitions. Led by Schwartz it acquired 13 companies between 1980 and 1992, including Xerox's electro-optical defense and aerospace business (1983), Rolm's military computer unit (1985), and Goodyear Aerospace (1987). Schwartz's biggest deal came in 1990 when he bought Ford Aerospace (annual sales of $1.8 billion) for $715 million, more than doubling Loral's size.

Like many defense contractors, Loral was swept up in the General Accounting Office's Operation Ill Wind investigation of defense procurements, and in 1989 it pleaded guilty to 3 charges and had to give up part of a contract to provide radar warning systems for the F-16 fighter plane.

In 1991 Loral sold 49% of Space Systems/Loral to a consortium of European space system manufacturers. Loral bought LTV's missile business in 1992 for $254 million.

In 1994 Loral moved into systems integration with its $1.5 billion acquisition of IBM's Federal Systems unit. Federal Systems, which had sales of about $2.2 billion in 1993, builds large computer systems for government agencies, including the FAA and the IRS.

In 1995 Loral Air Traffic Control won a $955 million contract with the US Department of Transportation to upgrade the FAA's air traffic control system.

NYSE symbol: LOR
Fiscal year ends: March 31

Chairman and CEO: Bernard L. Schwartz, age 69,
$6,244,191 pay
President and COO: Frank C. Lanza, age 63,
$3,247,179 pay
SVP Finance: Michael P. DeBlasio, age 58, $954,633 pay
SVP and Controller: Robert V. LaPenta, age 49,
$883,979 pay
SVP and Secretary: Michael B. Targoff, age 50,
$874,427 pay
Group VP Telemetry: Hugh Bennett, age 63
Group VP Missiles: Felix W. Fenter, age 68
Group VP; President, Federal Systems: Arthur E.
Johnson, age 48
**Group VP Microwave; President, Loral Microwave-
Narda:** Bernard Leibowitz, age 65
VP Washington Operations: Jimmie V. Adams, age 59
VP Technology: Lawrence H. Schwartz, age 57
VP Special Projects: William F. Gates, age 73
VP Communications: Joanne Hvala, age 44
VP and Treasurer: Nicholas C. Moren, age 48
VP and General Counsel: Eric J. Zahler, age 44
VP Administration (HR): Stephen L. Jackson, age 53
Auditors: Coopers & Lybrand L.L.P.

WHERE

HQ: 600 Third Ave., New York, NY 10016
Phone: 212-697-1105
Fax: 212-661-8988

	1995 Sales	
	$ mil.	% of total
US	4,463	81
Europe	616	11
Asia	234	4
Middle East	151	3
Other regions	20	1
Total	**5,484**	**100**

WHAT

	1995 Sales	
	$ mil.	% of total
US government agencies	3,548	64
Foreign and export	1,021	19
Other	915	17
Total	**5,484**	**100**

**Command, Control,
Communications, and
Intelligence/
Reconnaissance**
Data and voice recorders
("black boxes")
Information processing
and display hardware
Satellite communication
terminals

Electronic Combat
Electronic jamming and
radar warning systems
Forward-Looking Infrared
(FLIR) targeting and
weapon delivery pod

Systems Integration
Display System
Replacement (air traffic
control)
Document Processing
System (for the IRS)
NEXRAD weather-
detection system

Tactical Weapons
Digital Scene Matching Area
Correlation guidance
system
Extended Range Interceptor
missile
Multiple Launch Rocket
System (MLRS)

**Telecommunications and
Space Systems**
Mission control and
operations support
Telecommunications
satellites

Training and Simulation
Close Combat Tactical
Trainer (computer-based
trainer)
Flight and weapons
simulators for F-15 and
F-15E
Multiple Integrated Laser
Engagement System
(MILES)

KEY COMPETITORS

AlliedSignal	Hughes Electronics	Orbital Sciences
Boeing	Lockheed Martin	Raytheon
EDS	McDonnell Douglas	Rockwell
EG&G	Motorola	Teledyne
GEC	Northrop	Thomson SA
General Electric	Grumman	TRW

HOW MUCH

	Annual Growth	1986	1987	1988	1989	1990	1991	1992	1993	1994	1995
Sales ($ mil.)	26.4%	664	690	1,441	1,187	1,274	2,127	2,882	3,335	4,009	5,484
Net income ($ mil.)	20.7%	53	58	74	88	78	90	122	159	228	288
Income as % of sales	—	8.0%	8.3%	5.2%	7.4%	6.1%	4.3%	4.2%	4.8%	5.7%	5.3%
Earnings per share ($)	13.5%	1.08	1.14	1.46	1.69	1.51	1.71	1.93	2.02	2.72	3.38
Stock price – high ($)[1]	—	19.50	24.38	24.63	20.25	18.94	17.44	22.75	23.69	38.75	42.75
Stock price – low ($)[1]	—	12.13	16.94	12.50	15.25	13.75	12.06	16.06	15.38	22.25	33.50
Stock price – close ($)[1]	8.5%	18.25	19.19	15.75	16.13	14.81	16.75	19.69	23.00	37.75	37.88
P/E – high	—	18	21	17	12	13	10	12	12	14	13
P/E – low	—	11	15	9	9	9	7	8	8	8	10
Dividends per share ($)	9.5%	0.26	0.29	0.24	0.35	0.39	0.43	0.47	0.50	0.55	0.59
Book value per share ($)	13.2%	6.53	7.56	8.66	10.15	11.41	12.95	15.64	14.39	16.57	19.86
Employees	15.2%	8,100	14,500	13,700	13,700	12,700	23,750	22,000	24,500	32,600	28,900

1995 Year-end:
Debt ratio: 43.8%
Return on equity: 18.8%
Cash (mil.): $126
Current ratio: 1.53
Long-term debt (mil.): $1,316
No. of shares (mil.): 85
Dividends
  Yield: 1.6%
  Payout: 17.5%
Market value (mil.): $3,219

**Stock Price History[1]
High/Low 1986–95**

[1]Stock prices are for the prior calendar year.

MACANDREWS & FORBES HOLDINGS

OVERVIEW

Murdoch has it; Ted Turner, too. So why shouldn't fellow billionaire Ronald Perelman have the media bug? Perelman, whose MacAndrews & Forbes holding company is one of the US's largest private firms, spent the last few years creating his own media empire. In 1993 MacAndrews & Forbes acquired 37.5% of TV infomercial producer Guthy-Renker and SCI Television's 7 stations, merging them to create New World Television. That company was combined with TV syndicator Genesis Entertainment and TV production house New World Entertainment to create New World Communications Group, which Perelman took public in 1994.

MacAndrews & Forbes (i.e., Perelman) oversees an eclectic portfolio of public and private companies, including Coleman (camping gear), Marvel (the US's top comic book publisher), and Revlon (cosmetics). In 1995 the company announced an IPO for Revlon. Revlon has lost money since 1991, and Perelman has sold several of the cosmetics maker's product lines and drastically cut its workforce.

Since 1994 New World Communications has purchased 4 TV stations from Great American Communications and, as part of a deal that brought a $500 million investment from Rupert Murdoch in exchange for switching its stations to Fox, bought 4 stations from Argyle Television. In 1995 former NBC executive Brandon Tartikoff became chairman of New World Entertainment. The company also bought Cannell Television, a producer of television programming.

WHEN

Ron Perelman grew up working in his father's Philadelphia-based conglomerate, Belmont Industries, but left it at the age of 35 to seek his fortune in New York. In 1978 he bought 40% of jewelry store operator Cohen-Hatfield Industries. In 1979 Cohen-Hatfield bought a minority interest in MacAndrews & Forbes (licorice flavoring). It acquired the rest of the company the next year, then took MacAndrews & Forbes Group as its name.

In 1982 MacAndrews & Forbes bought 82% of Technicolor, a motion picture processor (sold in 1988). After going private in 1983, the company bought control of video production company Compact Video. In 1984 Perelman reshuffled his assets, creating MacAndrews & Forbes Holdings and making it the owner of MacAndrews & Forbes Group. Perelman's holding company acquired control of Pantry Pride, a Florida-based supermarket chain, in 1985. Later that year Pantry Pride announced a $1.8 billion hostile takeover bid for Revlon.

Revlon had been #1 in US cosmetics until founder Charles Revson died in 1975. His successor, Michel Bergerac, cut R&D spending and used beauty division earnings to buy health care and pharmaceutical companies. After Perelman acquired Revlon in 1985, he sold all its health care businesses except for National Health Laboratories. In the late 1980s he added several other cosmetics vendors (including Max Factor and Yves Saint Laurent's fragrance and cosmetic lines). MacAndrews & Forbes took Revlon private in 1987.

In 1988 MacAndrews & Forbes Holdings agreed to invest $315 million in 5 failing Texas S&Ls, which Perelman combined and named First Gibraltar (sold to BankAmerica in 1993, when Perelman sold 2.6 million shares of BankAmerica). The next year MacAndrews & Forbes bought the Coleman Company.

The company bought a controlling interest in Marvel Entertainment Group from New World Entertainment in 1988, buying the rest of New World in 1989. Between 1988 and 1992 MacAndrews & Forbes sold 80% of National Health Laboratories. In 1991 Perelman took Marvel public and sold Revlon's Max Factor and Betrix units to Procter & Gamble for over $1 billion. In 1992 he sold the Halston and Princess Marcella Borghese brands.

MacAndrews & Forbes increased its stake in Marvel from 60% to 80% in 1993. That same year New World Communications was formed. In 1994 its First Madison Bank bought Ford's First Nationwide, the US's 5th largest S&L.

In 1995 MacAndrews & Forbes subsidiaries Mafco Worldwide Corp. and Consolidated Cigar Corp. merged with Abex (aircraft parts) to create Mafco Consolidated Group; New World Communications and Hachette Filipacchi joined forces to buy the entertainment magazine *Premiere*; and National Health Laboratories merged with Roche's clinical laboratory to create Laboratory Corp. of America, the US's largest operator of medical testing labs.

Also in 1995 former CFO Fred Tepperman accused Perelman of firing him for taking time off to care for his wife, who suffers from Alzheimer's disease. After early trial testimony painted less than flattering portraits of the parties, the case was settled.

Private company
Fiscal year ends: December 31

Chairman and CEO: Ronald O. Perelman, age 52
VC: Howard Gittis
VC: Donald G. Drapkin
President: Bruce Slovin
EVP: Meyer Laskin
EVP and General Counsel: Barry F. Schwartz
CFO: Erwin Engelman
Auditors: KPMG Peat Marwick LLP

WHERE

HQ: MacAndrews & Forbes Holdings, Inc.,
35 E. 62nd St., New York, NY 10021
Phone: 212-688-9000
Fax: 212-572-8400

MacAndrews & Forbes's entertainment and consumer
products operations are principally in the US.

WHAT

Groups

Entertainment and Publishing
New World Communications Group, Inc. (37%)
  Genesis Entertainment (TV syndication)
  Guthy-Renker Corp. (37%, infomercial production)
  Marvel Entertainment Group (81%, comic book
    publishing)
      Fleer Trading Cards
      Toy Biz (46%, toys)
  New World Entertainment, Ltd. (TV production and
    distribution)
  New World Sales and Marketing, Inc. (advertising
    representation)
  New World Television, Inc. (TV broadcasting)
  Four Star International (film library)

Industrial and Consumer Products
MacAndrews & Forbes Group, Inc.
  Mafco Consolidated Group (80%, cigars and licorice
    flavoring used in cigarettes)
  NWL Aerospace (10%, aerospace products)
Revlon Group, Inc.
  Revlon, Inc. (cosmetics and fragrances)
    Almay, Inc. (cosmetics)
    Charles of the Ritz Group Ltd. (cosmetics and
      fragrances)
    Germaine Monteil Cosmetiques (cosmetics)
  Laboratory Corporation of America (12%, medical
    testing services)

Financial Services
First Nationwide Bank (based in San Francisco; over 150
  branches in 8 states)
Recreation Products Companies
Coleman Co., Inc. (83%; camping equipment, portable
  generators, power washers, and recreational
  accessories)
Meridian Sports, Inc. (65%)
  Boston Whaler (boats)
  Mastercraft Boats
  O'Brien International (water skis and accessories)
  Skeeter Products (boats)
  Wet Jet International

KEY COMPETITORS

Actava	Helene Curtis
Alberto-Culver	Honda
Amway	Igloo
Avon	Jean Philippe Fragrances
Banc One	Johnson Publishing
BancFlorida Financial	Kellwood
BankAmerica	KeyCorp
Bayer	Liz Claiborne
BeautiControl	L'Oréal
Black & Decker	LVMH
Body Shop	Mary Kay
Bristol-Myers Squibb	McGraw-Hill
Brunswick	NationsBank
Capital Bancorp	Nature's Sunshine
Chase Manhattan	Outboard Marine
Chattem	Procter & Gamble
Citicorp	RJR Nabisco
Cosmair	Rubbermaid
Colgate-Palmolive	Shiseido
Cox Communications	Suzuki
Dayton Hudson	Time Warner
Estée Lauder	Tribune
First Chicago	Turner Broadcasting
First Interstate	Unilever
Fleetwood	Union Bank
Fountain Powerboat	Yamaha
Gannett	Warner-Lambert
General Electric	Washington Post
Hearst	Wells Fargo

HOW MUCH

	Annual Growth	1985	1986	1987	1988	1989	1990	1991	1992	1993	1994
Estimated sales ($ mil.)	16.8%	750	552	2,440	2,500	5,325	5,381	4,521	3,496	2,748	3,030
Employees	25.0%	3,000	3,000	28,000	24,582	44,000	44,000	38,100	25,700	23,500	22,328

REVLON

**Estimated Sales
($ mil.)
1985–94**

MARSH & MCLENNAN COMPANIES, INC.

OVERVIEW

It's a good news/bad news situation for Marsh & McLennan Companies. Its Marsh & McLennan unit is the world's top insurance brokerage service. Other units include Guy Carpenter & Company (reinsurance), the Mercer Consulting Group (management consulting), and Putnam Investments (money management, with over $95 billion in assets in 1994). Its Frizzell Financial Services is the UK's leading provider of group insurance programs; Seabury & Smith is the same in the US.

The good news for Marsh & McLennan is that as companies move to improve competitiveness and operating efficiency, Mercer Consulting Group is seeing consulting revenues increase. The bad news is that insurance premiums are declining and competition is intense, keeping insurance revenues depressed. Meanwhile, the volatile financial markets are dampening investors' appetite for risk.

Marsh & McLennan is looking overseas for relief. In 1994 Mercer Consulting expanded in the Netherlands and Latin America, while Marsh & McLennan improved operations in Germany and the UK. In 1995 Mercer acquired MID SA, a French consulting firm.

The Trident Partnership, an investment partnership formed by Marsh & McLennan Risk Capital, had won over $600 million in capital commitments by the end of 1994.

WHEN

Marsh & McLennan evolved from 3 turn-of-the-century midwestern firms: Marsh Ullmann & Co. (led by Henry Marsh, who pioneered insurance brokering and in 1901 set up U.S. Steel's self-insurance program), Manley-McLennan of Duluth (specialists in railroad insurance), and D.W. Burrows (a small Chicago-based railroad insurance firm).

In 1904, after discovering that they had both been promised the Burlington Northern Railroad account, Donald McLennan and Marsh joined forces with Daniel Burrows to form the world's largest insurance brokerage, with $3 million in premiums. In 1906 the firm became Marsh & McLennan, with Marsh as the chief, McLennan overseeing the railroad business, and a new partner, Charles Seabury, handling technical and support services.

In the early 20th century, Marsh won AT&T's business by arranging to meet the company's president on an Atlantic crossing; McLennan landed the Armour Meat Packing account by chatting with P. D. Armour while on a commuter train to Chicago.

In 1923 Marsh & McLennan became a closely held corporation. As the business became more technical, Marsh lost interest; he sold out to McLennan in 1935. The company weathered the Depression without major layoffs by cutting pay and branching into life insurance and employee-benefits consulting after passage of the Social Security Act (1935).

Until the late 1930s the company never billed for consulting services that were expected to lead to insurance placements. This changed when the president of American Can insisted on paying for the time of the company's employees. In 1946 the company won Ford Motor Company's business.

In the 1950s, as the company grew through acquisitions, interoffice rivalries developed. In 1962 it went public and in 1969 it organized a holding company that became Marsh & McLennan Companies. In the 1970s the company began to diversify, buying The Putnam Cos. (investment management).

Marsh & McLennan set up its employee-benefits consulting business in 1975 as a separate subsidiary, William M. Mercer, and in 1980 acquired a foothold in the UK with C.T. Bowring Reinsurance. In 1982 Marsh & McLennan formed Seabury & Smith to manage its insurance programs.

As the insurance business stagnated in the 1980s, the financial and consulting fields grew. In 1992 the company formed Mercer Consulting Group to encompass its various consulting companies.

Also in 1992 Marsh & McLennan continued its expansion program, acquiring The Frizzell Group of the UK. It also added Marsh & McLennan Risk Capital Corp., which oversees investments in insurance companies.

The company formed Mid Ocean Reinsurance and Underwriters Capital (Merrett) Ltd. with J.P. Morgan in 1993.

In 1994 the Trident Fund (also formed with J.P. Morgan) began accepting subscriptions for investments that capitalize on the restructuring occurring in the insurance industry.

In 1994 Putnam president Lawrence Lasser was awarded a $10.5 million bonus based on that company's successful growth. However, early in 1995 Putnam and Alliance Capital Management, who together own $50 million in Orange County notes, lost a court ruling to have the bankrupt California county set aside payments for notes coming due.

NYSE symbol: MMC
Fiscal year ends: December 31

Chairman and CEO: A. J. C. Smith, age 60, $1,825,000 pay
VC: Philip L. Wroughton, age 61
Chairman and CEO, Guy Carpenter & Company, Inc.: Richard H. Blum, age 56, $850,000 pay
Chairman, Marsh & McLennan, Inc.: David D. Holbrook, age 56, $840,000 pay
President and CEO, Putnam Investments, Inc.: Lawrence J. Lasser, age 52, $11,320,000 pay
President, Mercer Consulting Group, Inc.: Peter Coster, age 55, $875,000 pay
President and CEO, Marsh & McLennan, Inc.: John T. Sinnott, age 55, $840,000 pay
SVP and CFO: Frank J. Borelli, age 59
SVP Human Resources and Administration: Francis N. Bonsignore, age 48
General Counsel and Secretary: Gregory F. Van Gundy, age 49
Auditors: Deloitte & Touche LLP

WHERE

HQ: 1166 Avenue of the Americas, New York, NY 10036-2774
Phone: 212-345-5000
Fax: 212-345-4838 (Public Affairs)

Marsh & McLennan operates in more than 80 countries.

	1994 Sales		1994 Operating Income	
	$ mil.	% of total	$ mil.	% of total
US	2,227	65	478	67
Europe	910	26	181	25
Canada	165	5	35	5
Other regions	133	4	16	2
Adjustments	—	—	(40)	—
Total	**3,435**	**100**	**670**	**100**

WHAT

	1994 Sales		1994 Operating Income	
	$ mil.	% of total	$ mil.	% of total
Insurance services	1,887	55	406	57
Consulting	933	27	96	14
Investment mgmt.	615	18	208	29
Other	—	—	(40)	—
Total	**3,435**	**100**	**670**	**100**

Selected Subsidiaries

The Frizzell Group Limited (insurance, finance, and financial planning programs for affinity groups; UK)
Guy Carpenter & Co., Inc. (reinsurance)
Marsh & McLennan, Inc. (insurance brokerage)
Marsh & McLennan Risk Capital Corp. (insurance industry investments and advisory services)
Mercer Consulting Group, Inc. (management consulting, Europe and North America)
Putnam Investments, Inc. (investment management)
Seabury & Smith, Inc. (insurance program management services; Canada, the UK, and the US)

KEY COMPETITORS

AIG	General Electric
Alexander & Alexander	General Re
Allianz	Johnson & Higgins
American Express	Kemper Corp.
American Re	KPMG
Andersen Consulting	Lloyd's of London
Arthur Gallagher	McKinsey & Co.
Booz, Allen	MDC Holding
Charles Schwab	Merrill Lynch
Chubb	Nomura Securities
CIGNA	Paine Webber
Coopers & Lybrand	Price Waterhouse
Deloitte & Touche	Prudential
Ernst & Young	T. Rowe Price
First Fidelity	Tokio Marine and Fire
FMR	Transnational Re
Franklin Resources	USF&G

HOW MUCH

	Annual Growth	1985	1986	1987	1988	1989	1990	1991	1992	1993	1994
Sales ($ mil.)	10.8%	1,368	1,804	2,147	2,272	2,428	2,723	2,779	2,937	3,163	3,435
Net income ($ mil.)	9.9%	163	243	302	296	295	304	306	304	332	382
Income as % of sales	—	11.9%	13.5%	14.1%	13.0%	12.1%	11.2%	11.0%	10.3%	10.5%	11.1%
Earnings per share ($)	9.8%	2.23	3.30	4.06	4.09	4.10	4.15	4.18	4.21	4.52	5.19
Stock price – high ($)	—	41.75	76.75	72.00	59.75	89.75	81.00	87.25	94.50	97.63	88.75
Stock price – low ($)	—	28.25	40.63	43.75	45.25	55.13	59.75	69.13	71.25	77.00	71.25
Stock price – close ($)	7.7%	40.75	60.75	49.50	56.25	78.00	78.00	81.38	91.38	81.25	79.25
P/E – high	—	19	23	18	15	22	20	21	22	22	17
P/E – low	—	13	12	11	11	13	14	17	17	17	14
Dividends per share ($)	9.5%	1.24	1.57	2.15	2.43	2.50	2.55	2.60	2.65	2.70	2.80
Book value per share ($)	12.3%	7.02	8.64	10.71	10.56	12.06	14.77	14.41	15.05	18.47	19.95
Employees	4.4%	17,700	19,900	22,700	22,800	23,600	24,400	23,400	25,800	25,600	26,000

1994 Year-end:
Debt ratio: 21.9%
Return on equity: 27.0%
Cash (mil.): $295
Current ratio: 1.04%
Long-term debt (mil.): $409
No. of shares (mil.): 73
Dividends
  Yield: 3.5%
  Payout: 53.9%
Market value (mil.): $5,801

Stock Price History High/Low 1985–94

THE MCGRAW-HILL COMPANIES, INC.

OVERVIEW

If this is, indeed, the Information Age, then McGraw-Hill is in the right place at the right time. The New York City–based company's commodity is information, served up a variety of ways for the ever-expanding assortment of media humans keep inventing to communicate. McGraw-Hill serves customers ranging from elementary school students to corporate executives. It serves the business, professional, consumer, government, and education markets through print (books, magazines, newsletters), via digital formats (electronic networks, software, CD-ROMs), and over the air (the company owns 4 TV stations).

McGraw-Hill's sales have blossomed thanks to its 1993 acquisition of full control of joint venture MacMillan/McGraw-Hill School Pub-

lishing from MacMillan. The company, now part of McGraw-Hill's Educational and Professional Publishing division, has helped to make McGraw-Hill the US's #1 schoolbook publisher.

Subsidiary Standard & Poor's (S&P) is a leading provider of credit ratings and also publishes directories of corporate information. The company's Information and Media Services division publishes *Business Week*, *BYTE*, and other consumer and trade magazines.

McGraw-Hill is focusing on paying down the debt left over from its MacMillan/McGraw acquisition, and it is also looking to expand internationally. It hopes to have about 30% of its revenue come from outside the US by the end of the decade, up from 18% in 1994.

WHEN

In 1909 magazine publishers James McGraw (*Street Railway Journal*) and John Hill (*American Machinist*, *Locomotive Engineer*) formed the McGraw-Hill Book Company to publish scientific and technical books. Initially the 2 kept their magazines separate, but following Hill's death in 1916 the magazine segments were merged with McGraw-Hill.

In the 1920s McGraw-Hill pioneered the risky but successful "send-no-money" plan, giving customers a free 10-day examination of its books. In 1929, 2 months before the stock market crash, McGraw-Hill started *Business Week* magazine, in which it expressed concerns about the economy's health — a view contrary to general opinion.

During the 1930s and 1940s, McGraw-Hill continued to expand as a publisher of trade journals and college textbooks. It had entered trade publishing in 1930 under the Whittlesey House name (changed to McGraw-Hill in 1950), but it was not until the 1950s that the trade division earned some distinction. Its biggest commercial success was *Betty Crocker's Picture Cook Book* (1947), which sold 2.3 million copies in its first 2 years.

In the 1960s and 1970s, McGraw-Hill acquired Standard & Poor's (S&P), an investment information service (1966); 4 TV stations from Time Inc. (1972); Datapro Research Corporation, a product information service (1976); and Data Resources Inc. (DRI), an economic forecasting service (1979). In 1979 it successfully fended off American Express's attempt at an $830 million takeover.

In the 1980s McGraw-Hill expanded its electronic information services and acquired

small, industry-specific publishing and information service companies. In 1989 it sold its trade books division, and S&P downgraded its parent company's common stock rating to A⁻ because of a restructuring charge associated with McGraw-Hill's reorganization.

Also in 1989 McGraw-Hill (in partnership with Kodak and R. R. Donnelley) produced the first computerized college textbook, which allows instructors to select contents for custom publications from McGraw-Hill's Primis database.

In 1990 the company bought J.J. Kenny, a provider of municipal securities information. In 1991 its joint venture MacMillan/McGraw-Hill acquired Computer Systems Research and its integrated learning system for instruction in basic mathematics, reading, and writing.

In 1993 McGraw-Hill bought MacMillan's half of the 1989 MacMillan/McGraw-Hill School Publishing Co. textbook and educational software joint venture, sold for $337.5 million as part of MacMillan parent Maxwell Communication's bankruptcy. Also in 1993 McGraw-Hill bought 25% of Liberty Brokerage, Inc. (New York), which gave McGraw-Hill access to US Treasury securities pricing information.

Reflecting the growing interest in overseas markets, S&P Ratings Group opened a branch in Hong Kong in 1994 and announced plans to open one in Singapore in 1995.

In 1995 the company established a new information services group to focus on the development of the company's information products and publications and of new media opportunities.

NYSE symbol: MHP
Fiscal year ends: December 31

WHO

Chairman and CEO: Joseph L. Dionne, age 61,
$1,539,480 pay
President and COO: Harold W. "Terry" McGraw III,
age 46, $929,404 pay
EVP and CFO: Robert J. Bahash, age 49, $638,368 pay
EVP Administration: Thomas J. Sullivan, age 59,
$586,934 pay
EVP New Ventures: Michael K. Hehir, age 47,
$483,268 pay
SVP Taxes: Frank J. Kaufman, age 50
SVP and Executive Assistant to the Chairman: Barbara
A. Munder, age 49
SVP Treasury Operations: Frank D. Penglase, age 54
SVP and General Counsel: Kenneth M. Vittor
VP Human Resources: Patrick Pavelski
Auditors: Ernst & Young LLP

WHERE

HQ: 1221 Avenue of the Americas, New York, NY 10020
Phone: 212-512-2000
Fax: 212-512-4871

McGraw-Hill has operations worldwide.

WHAT

	1994 Sales		1994 Operating Income	
	$ mil.	% of total	$ mil.	% of total
Educational & professional pub.	1,162	42	126	28
Info. & media svcs.	853	31	108	24
Financial services	746	27	217	48
Total	**2,761**	**100**	**451**	**100**

Selected Operations and Publications

Educational and Professional Publishing
Macmillan/McGraw School Division
McGraw-Hill Continuing Education Center
McGraw-Hill Home Software
Osborne Books
Primis Custom Publishing (college publishing)
Schaum (college publishing)
Shepard's/McGraw-Hill (legal information)
TAB Books

Financial Services
DRI/McGraw-Hill (business and financial advising)
Equity Services
J.J. Kenny Drake (securities information)
Kenny S&P Information Services (securities and commodities data)
Liberty Brokerage Investment Corp. (25%)
Standard & Poor's Ratings Group (financial information & credit ratings)

Information and Media Services
Architectural Record
Aviation Week & Space Technology
Business & Commercial Aviation
Business Week
Business Week International
BYTE
Chemical Engineering
Datapro Information Services (database)
Electrical World
Engineering News-Record
F.W. Dodge (construction information)
KERO-TV (Bakersfield)
KGTV (San Diego)
KMGH-TV (Denver)
Newsletters/On-line
Postgraduate Medicine
Power
Tower Group International (custom broker, freight forwarder, trade-related services)
World Aviation Directory
WRTV (Indianapolis)

KEY COMPETITORS

Advance Publications
American Financial
Bertelsmann
Bloomberg
CCH
Dow Jones
Dun & Bradstreet
Forbes
Harcourt General
Houghton Mifflin
John Wiley
Knight-Ridder
Media General
Morningstar
News Corp.
Pearson
Primark
Reed Elsevier
Reuters
Thomson Corp.
Time Warner
Times Mirror
TRW
Value Line
Viacom
West Publishing

HOW MUCH

	Annual Growth	1985	1986	1987	1988	1989	1990	1991	1992	1993	1994
Sales ($ mil.)	7.1%	1,491	1,577	1,751	1,818	1,789	1,939	1,943	2,051	2,196	2,761
Net income ($ mil.)	3.6%	147	154	165	186	40	173	148	153	11	203
Income as % of sales	—	9.9%	9.8%	9.4%	10.2%	2.2%	8.9%	7.6%	7.5%	0.5%	7.4%
Earnings per share ($)	3.8%	2.92	3.04	3.27	3.83	0.82	3.53	3.03	3.13	0.23	4.10
Stock price – high ($)	—	52.00	64.00	84.50	76.00	86.13	61.13	64.75	66.50	75.25	77.25
Stock price – low ($)	—	39.75	46.50	43.00	46.75	53.50	39.88	49.75	53.00	55.25	62.50
Stock price – close ($)	3.8%	48.00	54.63	48.25	62.25	56.75	52.63	57.38	61.38	67.63	66.88
P/E – high	—	18	21	26	20	—	17	21	21	—	19
P/E – low	—	14	15	13	12	—	11	16	17	—	15
Dividends per share ($)	5.8%	1.40	1.52	1.68	1.84	2.05	2.16	2.20	2.24	2.28	2.32
Book value per share ($)	2.0%	15.40	17.04	16.33	17.94	18.08	19.50	20.37	18.58	16.66	18.38
Employees	0.7%	14,345	15,232	15,892	16,255	14,461	13,868	13,539	13,393	15,661	15,339

1994 Year-end:
Debt ratio: 45.5%
Return on equity: 23.4%
Cash (mil.): $8
Current ratio: 1.12
Long-term debt (mil.): $658
No. of shares (mil.): 50
Dividends
  Yield: 3.5%
  Payout: 56.6%
Market value (mil.): $3,322

**Stock Price History
High/Low 1985–94**

MELVILLE CORPORATION

OVERVIEW

One of the largest diversified specialty retailers in the US, Melville Corporation is planning some selling of a different kind. In late 1995 the Rye, New York–based company announced plans to spin off its footwear (Footaction, Medisco, Thom McAn) and toys (Kay-Bee) divisions. The company also announced plans to sell its Marshall's discount clothing stores to TJX, and it said it was looking for buyers for its Wilson leather goods store and its This End Up home furnishings stores.

Melville plans to retain its CVS drugstores, Linens 'n Things home textiles and furnishings stores, and Bob's casual clothing stores. The company focuses on being a low-cost pro-

vider for value-conscious customers, and almost all of its stores are located in "strip" shopping centers or malls.

CVS, which sells prescription drugs and health and beauty aids, is the company's biggest revenue generator. Melville has worked to improve CVS's operations by investing in new computer systems. The company planned to add about 75 new stores in 1995.

Linens 'n Things, which focuses primarily on home textiles, is shifting to a larger store format, opening bigger stores and closing smaller ones. It planned to add about one million square feet of selling space in 1995. Melville's planned to open 12 Bob's in 1995.

WHEN

In 1892 shoe supplier Frank Melville formed Melville Shoe by taking over 3 New York shoe stores when their owner left town owing him money. During WWI Ward Melville, Frank's son and vice-president of the firm, served in the Quartermaster Corps's shoe and leather division under shoe manufacturer J. Frank McElwain. The 2 men devised the merchandising scheme of mass-producing shoes for distribution through a chain of low-price stores. Melville opened the first of its Thom McAn (named after a Scottish professional golfer) stores, for which McElwain provided the shoes, in New York in 1922. There were 370 stores in the chain by 1927.

By 1931 Melville operated 476 shoe stores and had income of $1.2 million on sales of over $26 million. In 1939 Melville bought the McElwain factory, consolidating production and distribution into one corporation. By 1958 Melville was operating 1,034 stores, 796 of them Thom McAn stores, but profits were declining because of changes in customer tastes and shifting populations.

Melville met the challenge of change, moving stores from urban areas to the suburbs and adding more fashionable merchandise to existing lines. Its Meldisco division began leasing space for shoe sales in S. S. Kresge's Kmart discount department stores in 1961. In 1968 the company launched Chess King (young men's apparel) and bought Foxwood (young women's apparel, renamed Foxmoor) stores. Melville bought the Consumer Value Stores (CVS) drugstore chain in 1969.

In 1975 Kresge demanded a 49% equity interest in all Meldisco subsidiaries operating in Kmart stores. Melville accepted the terms of

the new agreement rather than lose one of its largest divisions. The company purchased Marshalls (discount department stores, 1976), Mack Drug (1977), Kay-Bee Toy and Hobby Shops (1981), Freddy's (deep-discount drugstores, 1984), Prints Plus (1985), This End Up Furniture (1985), and Accessory Lady (1987), and it sold Foxmoor (1985).

In 1990 Melville added 823 stores by buying Bob's Stores (apparel and footwear "superstores"), People's Drug Stores (merged with CVS), and Circus World toys (merged with Kay-Bee). The acquisitions made Melville the 5th largest drugstore operator in the US and one of the largest toy retailers.

In 1991 the company acquired the 128-store FootAction chain and the 136-store K&K toy store chain. The acquisitions strengthened Melville's presence in the Southeast and the Sunbelt.

In 1992 Melville initiated a massive restructuring aimed at sharpening its focusing on its most successful operations. Targeted for downsizing were the company's Thom McAn and Kay-Bee stores. The company also announced plans to convert many of its Linens 'n Things stores to a larger format.

Melville sold its Prints Plus framing stores to CPI Corporation and the men's clothier Chess King to Merry-Go-Round Enterprises in 1993. It sold its 114 Accessory Lady stores to Woolworth Corp. later that year.

In 1994 Melville created PharmaCare Management Services to provide pharmacy services and managed-care drug programs.

Warren Feldberg resigned as chairman and CEO of Marshalls in 1995, prior to the agreement with TJX.

NYSE symbol: MES
Fiscal year ends: December 31

WHO

Chairman and CEO: Stanley P. Goldstein, age 60,
$1,541,400 pay
President and COO: Harvey Rosenthal, age 52,
$1,042,500 pay
EVP: Jerald S. Politzer, age 49, $829,750 pay
SVP Human Resources: Jerald L. Maurer, age 52,
$343,640 pay
SVP and Acting CFO: Gary L. Crittenden, age 41
SVP; President, Melville Realty: Daniel B. Katz, age 49
VP and Treasurer: Philip C. Galbo, age 44
VP and Corporate Secretary: Arthur V. Richards, age 56
Auditors: KPMG Peat Marwick LLP

WHERE

HQ: One Theall Rd., Rye, NY 10580
Phone: 914-925-4000
Fax: 914-925-4026

WHAT

	1994 Sales		1994 Operating Income	
	$ mil.	% of total	$ mil.	% of total
Prescription drugs, health & beauty aids	4,330	38	228	35
Apparel	3,539	31	161	25
Footwear	1,840	16	159	25
Toys & household furnishings	1,577	14	99	15
Total	**11,286**	**100**	**647**	**100**

	No. of Stores	1994 Sales ($ mil.)
Meldisco (footwear)	2,778	1,281
CVS (drugstores)	1,328	4,330
Kay-Bee (toys)	996	1,012
Wilsons (leather apparel)	628	475
Marshalls (apparel)	484	2,775
FootAction	439	332
Thom McAn (footwear)	323	227
This End Up (furniture)	237	125
Linens 'n Things	145	440
Bob's (apparel & footwear)	20	289
Total	**7,378**	**11,286**

KEY COMPETITORS

50-Off Stores	L.L. Bean
American Stores	Luxottica
Arbor Drugs	May
The Athlete's Foot	Men's Wearhouse
Bed Bath & Beyond	Merck
Big B	Merry-Go-Round
Brown Group	NIKE
Dayton Hudson	Nine West
Eckerd	Reebok
Edison Brothers	Revco
The Gap	Rite Aid
Genovese Drug Stores	Spiegel
J. Crew	Sports Authority
J. C. Penney	Thriftway Food & Drug
Jos. A. Bank	Toys "R" Us
Just For Feet	VF
Kmart	Walgreen
L.A. Gear	Wal-Mart
Lands' End	Woolworth
The Limited	
Liz Claiborne	

HOW MUCH

	Annual Growth	1985	1986	1987	1988	1989	1990	1991	1992	1993	1994
Sales ($ mil.)	10.0%	4,775	5,262	5,930	6,780	7,554	8,687	9,886	10,433	10,435	11,286
Net income ($ mil.)	4.3%	210	238	285	355	398	385	347	156	332	307
Income as % of sales	—	4.4%	4.5%	4.8%	5.2%	5.3%	4.4%	3.5%	1.5%	3.2%	2.7%
Earnings per share ($)	3.9%	1.95	2.20	2.63	1.63	3.56	3.59	3.20	1.34	3.00	2.75
Stock price – high ($)	—	26.44	36.88	42.00	38.31	53.63	57.75	55.25	55.00	54.75	41.63
Stock price – low ($)	—	17.63	24.63	22.13	26.63	36.88	32.75	38.25	42.50	38.88	29.50
Stock price – close ($)	2.3%	25.25	27.00	26.50	37.19	44.63	42.00	44.50	53.13	40.63	30.88
P/E – high	—	14	17	16	24	15	16	17	41	18	15
P/E – low	—	9	11	8	16	10	9	12	32	13	11
Dividends per share ($)	8.7%	0.72	0.78	0.88	1.05	1.30	1.42	1.44	1.48	1.52	1.52
Book value per share ($)	9.1%	10.20	11.64	13.41	15.66	12.11	15.65	19.93	19.67	21.15	22.42
Employees	4.9%	76,011	80,394	90,500	96,554	100,541	119,590	110,148	115,644	111,082	117,000

1994 Year-end:
Debt ratio: 18.2%
Return on equity: 13.4%
Cash (mil.): $117
Current ratio: 1.61
Long-term debt (mil.): $331
No. of shares (mil.): 106
Dividends
 Yield: 4.9%
 Payout: 55.3%
Market value (mil.): $3,262

Stock Price History
High/Low 1985–94

MERCK & CO., INC.

OVERVIEW

With the merger of competitors Glaxo and Wellcome, Merck is now only the 2nd largest pharmaceutical company in the world. Vasotec, its biggest-selling drug (with sales of $2.2 billion), is the world's leading cardiovascular treatment. Two of the company's cholesterol-lowering drugs, Mevacor and Zocor, each has sales of over $1 billion.

The New Jersey–based company also makes pesticides and animal health products, but it sold its specialty chemical concerns to Bristol-Myers and Monsanto to concentrate on core businesses. In 1993 Merck bought Medco Containment Services, the largest pharmacy benefits management company in the US. Medco,

which processes and ships the prescriptions of more than 41 million Americans, is helping Merck capture a larger share of the growing managed-care market. Merck drugs account for about 12% of Medco's available pharmaceuticals, up from 10%.

Merck spends about 8.2% of sales on R&D. Among the drugs Merck has in the research pipeline are treatments for schizophrenia (with Swedish partner Astra), osteoporosis, and asthma. It expects growth to come from new drugs and expansion of Medco, not from acquisition. Chairman Raymond Gilmartin says that Merck's goal is to again be the world's largest pharmaceutical company.

WHEN

Merck was started in 1887 when chemist Theodore Weicker came to the US from Germany to set up an American branch of E. Merck AG of Germany. George Merck (grandson of the German company's founder) came in 1891 and entered into a partnership with Weicker. At first the firm imported and sold drugs and chemicals from Germany, but in 1903 it opened a plant in Rahway, New Jersey, to manufacture alkaloids. Weicker sold out to Merck in 1904 and bought a controlling interest in competitor Squibb. During WWI Merck gave the US government the 80% of company stock owned by family in Germany (George kept his shares). After the war the stock was sold to the public.

Merck merged with Powers-Weightman-Rosengarten of Philadelphia (a producer of the antimalarial quinine) in 1927. At its first research lab, established in 1933, Merck scientists did pioneering work on vitamin B-12 and developed the first steroid (cortisone, 1944). Five Merck scientists received Nobel prizes in the 1940s and 1950s. In 1953 Merck merged with Sharp & Dohme of Philadelphia, which brought with it a strong sales force.

Merck introduced Diuril (antihypertensive) in 1958 and other drugs in the early 1960s (Indocin, Aldomet), but for nearly 10 years there were few new drugs. John Horan, who took over in 1976, accelerated R&D in an effort to create new products. By the late 1970s the company had produced Clinoril (antiarthritic), Flexeril (muscle relaxant), and Timoptic (for glaucoma).

Biochemist Roy Vagelos, who joined Merck in 1976 as head of research and became CEO in 1985, continued the commitment to R&D. Merck introduced 10 major new drugs in the

1980s, including Mevacor for high cholesterol and Vasotec for high blood pressure.

In 1990 Merck bought the nonprescription drug segment of ICI Americas, whose drugs it markets through a joint venture with Johnson & Johnson. Merck and DuPont formed a joint venture in 1991 to market drugs in the US and Europe.

In 1993 Merck paid $6.6 billion in stock and cash for Medco Containment Services. Medco traces its roots to National Pharmacies, a mail order pharmacy founded in 1969. Investor Martin Wygod bought National Pharmacies from corporate raider Victor Posner in 1983 for about $30 million. A year later Wygod sold 20% of the company to the public and changed its name to Medco Containment.

In 1985 Medco bought retail drug claim processor Paid Prescriptions for $29 million. The acquisition gave Medco access to information from a network of more than 40,000 drugstores. To attract more customers, Medco introduced its Prescriber's Choice program in 1991. The program tracks its clients' prescriptions. When Medco finds a cheaper equivalent (such as a generic version) that could be prescribed, it contacts the doctor, notifying him or her of the cheaper alternative. About 40% of the doctors contacted prescribe the cheaper version.

In 1994 the company established new subsidiaries in Cyprus, Germany, Holland, Peru, and South Korea and began a joint venture in China to manufacture and sell Merck products. Also that year the FDA cleared Trusopt as the first topical treatment for elevated intraocular pressure in patients with ocular hypertension or glaucoma. In 1995 the FDA issued a license for Merck's chicken pox vaccine, Varivax.

NYSE symbol: MRK
Fiscal year ends: December 31

WHO

Chairman, President, and CEO: Raymond V. Gilmartin, age 54, $1,541,671 pay
EVP Science and Technology; President, Merck Research Laboratories: Edward M. Scolnick, age 54, $1,209,996 pay
EVP: Jerry T. Jackson, $1,135,004 pay
EVP: Francis H. Spiegel Jr., $1,009,749 pay
EVP Worldwide Basic Research, Merck Research Laboratories: Bennett M. Shapiro, age 55, $633,946 pay
President, Human Health US and Canada: David W. Anstice, age 46, $681,589 pay
President, Merck Vaccines: R. Gordon Douglas Jr., age 60
SVP and CFO: Judy C. Lewent, age 46, $684,996 pay
SVP and General Counsel: Mary M. McDonald, age 50
VP Planning and Development: Clifford S. Cramer, age 43
VP Human Resources: Steven M. Darien, age 52
Auditors: Arthur Andersen & Co, SC

WHERE

HQ: PO Box 100, Whitehouse Station, NJ 08889-0100
Phone: 908-423-1000
Fax: 908-594-4662

Merck has operations around the world.

	1994 Sales	
	$ mil.	% of total
North America	10,561	70
Europe	2,553	17
Asia/Pacific	1,587	11
Other regions	269	2
Total	**14,970**	**100**

WHAT

	1994 Sales	
	$ mil.	% of total
Cardiovasculars	5,352	36
Anti-ulcerants	1,566	10
Animal health/ crop protection	1,027	7
Antibiotics	827	6
Vaccines/biologicals	485	3
Ophthalmologicals	482	3
Specialty chemicals	422	3
Anti-inflammatories/ analgesics	271	2
Other Merck human health	433	3
Other human health	4,104	27
Total	**14,970**	**100**

Selected Products

Heartgard (canine heartworm prevention)	Prinivil (cardiovascular)
	Proscar (benign prostate
Indocin (anti-inflammatory)	enlargement)
Mevacor (cardiovascular)	Recombivax HB (hepatitis
M-M-R II (measles, mumps,	B vaccine recombinant)
and rubella virus vaccine)	Vasotec (cardiovascular)
Pepcid (anti-ulcerant)	Zocor (cardiovascular)
Primaxin (antibiotic)	

KEY COMPETITORS

Abbott Labs	Glaxo	Rhône-Poulenc
American Home	Wellcome	Rite Aid
Products	Hoechst	Roche
American Stores	J. C. Penney	Sandoz
Amgen	Johnson &	Schering-Plough
Baxter	Johnson	SmithKline
Bayer	Longs	Beecham
Bristol-Myers	McKesson	Upjohn
Squibb	Melville	Walgreen
Ciba-Geigy	Monsanto	Wal-Mart
Eli Lilly	Pfizer	Warner-
FoxMeyer Health	Procter	Lambert
Genentech	& Gamble	

HOW MUCH

	Annual Growth	1985	1986	1987	1988	1989	1990	1991	1992	1993	1994
Sales ($ mil.)	17.3%	3,548	4,129	5,061	5,940	6,551	7,672	8,603	9,663	10,498	14,970
Net income ($ mil.)	21.0%	540	676	906	1,207	1,495	1,781	2,122	2,447	2,166	2,997
Income as % of sales	—	15.2%	16.4%	17.9%	20.3%	22.8%	23.2%	24.7%	25.3%	20.6%	20.0%
Earnings per share ($)	21.3%	0.42	0.54	0.74	1.02	1.26	1.52	1.83	2.12	1.87	2.38
Stock price – high ($)	—	7.65	14.39	24.78	19.88	26.92	30.38	55.67	56.58	44.13	39.50
Stock price – low ($)	—	5.01	7.46	13.56	16.00	18.75	22.33	27.33	40.50	28.63	28.13
Stock price – close ($)	19.6%	7.61	13.76	17.61	19.25	25.83	29.96	55.50	43.38	34.38	38.13
P/E – high	—	18	27	34	19	21	20	30	27	24	17
P/E – low	—	12	14	18	16	15	15	15	19	15	12
Dividends per share ($)	22.8%	0.18	0.21	0.27	0.43	0.55	0.64	0.77	0.92	1.03	1.14
Book value per share ($)	17.9%	2.03	2.03	1.73	2.41	2.96	3.27	4.24	4.34	7.99	8.93
Employees	4.9%	30,900	30,700	31,100	32,000	34,400	36,900	37,700	38,400	47,100	47,500

1994 Year-end:
Debt ratio: 10.4%
Return on equity: 28.3%
Cash (mil.): $2,270
Current ratio: 1.27
Long-term debt (mil.): $1,146
No. of shares (mil.): 1,248
Dividends
  Yield: 3.0%
  Payout: 47.9%
Market value (mil.): $47,573

Stock Price History High/Low 1985–94

MERRILL LYNCH & CO., INC.

OVERVIEW

Merrill Lynch managed to keep its income above the $1 billion mark despite turbulent markets that brought earnings declines in its foreign operations and static-to-declining revenues in 3 of its 4 major business categories (brokerage, proprietary trading, and investment banking). The firm had rising results in asset and portfolio management. Merrill Lynch, the US's largest brokerage firm and the leader in US and foreign equities underwriting, is unique in combining a retail brokerage and cash management business with investment banking. Other lines include clearing services, retail banking, and insurance.

In 1994 and 1995 Merrill Lynch was hit with at least a dozen suits related to the bankruptcy of Orange County, California, because it had sold the county the derivatives whose loss in value had precipitated the bankruptcy. In addition to suits alleging misconduct in the sale of the instruments to the county, the firm is named as a defendant in suits by investors who bought Merrill Lynch's California and other municipal bond funds or the county bonds themselves, and in suits by Merrill Lynch stockholders because of the firm's potential liability in all these suits. In turn, Merrill Lynch sued several ex-employees.

WHEN

Wall Street bond salesman Charles Merrill opened an underwriting firm in 1914 and within 6 months took on his friend Edmund Lynch as partner. In the 1920s the new firm pursued nontraditional investors (i.e., the small investor) by stressing personal service. Merrill became known as the man who brought Wall Street to Main Street. During the 1920s the firm took a lead in financing the new supermarkets that were providing consumers with more service and variety.

In 1930 the company sold its retail business to Wall Street's largest brokerage firm, E. A. Pierce, and survived the Depression as an investment banking firm. Merrill Lynch reacquired the retail business in a 1940 merger with Pierce, and in 1941 the company merged with Fenner and Beane. Winthrop Smith, an employee transferred to Pierce in 1930, became a partner in 1958.

The company continued to grow by pursuing new investor groups, aiming information and advertising campaigns at small investors. Merrill Lynch was the first NYSE member to incorporate (1959) and go public (1971). In the 1960s it diversified into government securities, real estate financing (and sales in the 1970s), and asset management and consulting. In the 1970s, under Donald Regan (Ronald Reagan's secretary of the treasury and chief of staff), the company introduced the patented Cash Management Account and built up its investment banking, insurance, and foreign operations.

In the 1980s Merrill Lynch's underwriting business boomed. It became the global leader in offerings and advised on the largest of them all, Kohlberg Kravis Roberts's LBO of RJR Nabisco.

After the 1987 crash, Merrill Lynch retrenched and reorganized, jettisoning or trimming less profitable segments (merchant banking, real estate, and its mortgage insurance business) and closing some overseas offices. In addition to increasing the proportion of earnings from management and other fees and reducing dependence on commissions, Merrill Lynch moved to reduce its holdings of junk bonds and curtail its granting of bridge loans to ailing companies. In 1990, to reduce staff turnover (14–15% of its professional staff annually), the company introduced new training and pay procedures to reward long service and reduce dependency by inexperienced staff members on commission earnings. In 1991 Merrill Lynch received permission to buy a seat on the Seoul exchange.

In 1990 the stock market rebounded, followed in 1991 and 1992 by a recovery in merchant and investment banking, with a record number of new issues worldwide. Many of the issues were related to the privatization of formerly state-owned companies in Eastern and southern Europe and in South America, as well as to a burgeoning number of US IPOs.

Although Merrill Lynch cut back its Japanese operations because of the recession there, it has continued to expand in Asia, opening offices in Beijing and Thailand. In 1995 it entered into a joint venture with India's largest investment bank, DSP Financial Consultants. However, its operations in Latin America, where it is a major underwriter of new issues, were hurt in late 1994 and into 1995 by the effects of the collapse of the Mexican peso.

In 1995, in order to boost brokerage sales and compete with regional full-service brokerages, Merrill Lynch announced that it would open up to 250 new branches in small towns throughout the US to bring personal service to wealthy individuals in smaller markets.

NYSE symbol: MER
Fiscal year ends: Last Friday in December

WHO

Chairman and CEO: Daniel P. Tully, age 63,
$4,840,000 pay
President and COO: David H. Komansky, age 55,
$3,200,000 pay
VC and General Counsel: Stephen L. Hammerman,
age 56, $2,800,000 pay
EVP Private Client Group: John L. Steffens, age 53,
$3,200,000 pay
EVP Corporate and Institutional Business Group:
Herbert M. Allison Jr., age 51, $3,200,000 pay
EVP Asset Management Group: Arthur Zeikel, age 62,
$2,800,000 pay
EVP International: Winthrop H. Smith Jr., age 45
EVP; Chairman, Investment Banking: Barry S.
Friedberg
SVP and CFO: Joseph T. Willet, age 43
SVP Human Resources: Patrick J. Walsh
Auditors: Deloitte & Touche LLP

WHERE

HQ: World Financial Center, North Tower,
250 Vesey St., New York, NY 10281-1332
Phone: 212-449-1000
Fax: 212-236-4384

	1994 Sales		1994 Pretax Income	
	$ mil.	% of total	$ mil.	% of total
US	13,754	73	1,342	78
Europe & Middle East	3,464	19	176	10
Asia/Pacific	963	5	75	4
Canada & Latin America	617	3	137	8
Adjustments	(565)	—	—	—
Total	**18,233**	**100**	**1,730**	**100**

WHAT

	1994 Sales	
	$ mil.	% of total
Commissions	2,871	16
Interest & dividends	9,578	52
Trading	2,335	13
Investment banking	1,239	7
Asset management & portfolio service fees	1,739	9
Other	471	3
Total	**18,233**	**100**

Selected Subsidiaries	Financial Services
Merrill Lynch Asset Management, L.P.	Cash management accounts
ML Bank & Trust Co.	Commodity futures
ML Capital Services, Inc.	Government and municipal securities
ML Derivative Products, Inc.	Investment banking and underwriting
ML Futures Investment Partners Inc.	Life insurance and annuity products
ML Government Securities Inc.	Mutual funds
ML International Inc.	Securities and economic research
ML Money Markets Inc.	Securities brokerage
ML, Pierce, Fenner & Smith Inc.	

KEY COMPETITORS

A. G. Edwards
Alex. Brown
Bankers Trust
Bear Stearns
Brown Brothers Harriman
Charles Schwab
CS Holding
Dean Witter, Discover
Deutsche Bank

Edward Jones
Equitable
FMR
Goldman Sachs
Hambrecht & Quist
ING Bank
J.P. Morgan
Lehman Brothers
Mellon Bank
Morgan Stanley
Nomura Securities

Paine Webber
Piper Jaffray
Prudential
Quick & Reilly
Raymond James Financial
Salomon
T. Rowe Price
Travelers

HOW MUCH

	Annual Growth	1985	1986	1987	1988	1989	1990	1991	1992	1993	1994
Sales ($ mil.)	11.0%	7,117	9,475	11,036	10,547	11,273	11,147	12,353	13,413	16,588	18,233
Net income ($ mil.)	18.3%	224	469	391	463	(213)	192	696	952	1,394	1,017
Income as % of sales	—	3.2%	5.0%	3.5%	4.4%	—	1.7%	5.6%	7.1%	8.4%	5.6%
Earnings per share ($)	17.5%	1.11	2.14	1.76	2.11	(1.16)	0.80	2.95	4.17	6.11	4.74
Stock price – high ($)	—	18.38	21.88	23.38	14.19	18.38	13.63	30.44	33.38	51.13	45.63
Stock price – low ($)	—	12.75	16.19	9.75	11.06	11.75	8.06	9.56	22.19	28.00	32.25
Stock price – close ($)	8.5%	17.19	18.25	11.19	12.00	13.13	10.38	29.56	29.75	42.00	35.75
P/E – high	—	17	10	13	7	—	17	10	8	8	10
P/E – low	—	12	8	6	5	—	10	3	5	5	7
Dividends per share ($)	9.3%	0.40	0.40	0.48	0.50	0.50	0.50	0.50	0.58	0.70	0.89
Book value per share ($)	10.3%	11.49	13.28	15.83	17.65	15.34	14.95	17.43	20.92	24.85	27.67
Employees	(0.3%)	44,900	47,900	43,400	41,800	41,200	39,000	38,300	40,100	41,900	43,800

1994 Year-end:
Debt ratio: 95.7%
Return on equity: 18.0%
Cash (mil.): $9,590
Long-term debt (mil.): $14,863
No. of shares (mil.): 188
Dividends
  Yield: 2.5%
  Payout: 18.8%
Market value (mil.): $6,718
Assets (mil.): $163,749

**Stock Price History
High/Low 1985–94**

METROPOLITAN LIFE INSURANCE CO.

OVERVIEW

Get Met — It pays. New York–based Metropolitan Life Insurance uses this motto to assure customers that its insurance (and annuity products) will pay off as expected. In recent years, however, it has seemed like the slogan of insurance regulators investigating the sales practices of some of MetLife's agents and levying fines against the company for not policing itself. The over $100 million in fines and restitution payments to customers in 13 states (who had bought insurance after being told that it was a retirement investment) adversely affected 1994's results and shook customer confidence.

MetLife (the largest North American life insurer, with over $1.2 trillion of life insurance in force) is trying to end such abuses, possibly by making agents less dependent on commissions. It has also begun to refocus on life insurance and related financial services.

In 1995 MetLife announced that it would merge with Boston-based New England Mutual, whose upper-income clientele would complement MetLife's middle-class customer base. MetLife's financial strength, meanwhile, would help reduce the effects of New England's portfolio of troubled real estate and commercial mortgages.

WHEN

Simeon Draper, a New York merchant, tried to form National Union Life and Limb Insurance to cover Union soldiers in the Civil War, but investors were scared off by heavy casualties. After several reorganizations and name changes, the company emerged in 1868 as Metropolitan Life Insurance, a stock company.

Sustained at first by business from mutual assistance societies for German immigrants, Metropolitan went into industrial insurance with workers' burial policies. Metropolitan agents combed working-class neighborhoods, collecting small premiums. This nickel-and-dime business could be particularly profitable during the recessions of the late 19th century because if a worker missed one payment the company could cancel the policy and keep all premiums paid, a practice outlawed in 1900.

Aggressive sales were a Metropolitan hallmark. The company even imported polished British salesmen when no suitable Americans could be found.

Metropolitan became a mutual company, owned by policyholders, in 1915 and in 1917 offered group insurance. Metropolitan expanded to Canada in 1924.

After being led by the conservative Frederick Eckers and his son Frederick Jr. from 1929 to 1963, Metropolitan began to change, dropping industrial insurance in 1964. In 1974 Metropolitan began offering automobile and homeowner's insurance.

The company began to diversify in the 1980s (along with most insurers). It bought State Street Research & Management (1983), which founded the first US mutual fund; Century 21 Real Estate (1985); London-based Albany Life Assurance (1985); and Allstate's group life and health business (1988). In 1987 Metropolitan took over the annuities segment

of the failed Baldwin United Co. and expanded into Spain and Taiwan in 1988.

In 1989 MetLife bought J. C. Penney's casualty insurance portfolio, United Resources Insurance Services (retirement and financial programs), and Texas Life Insurance. Metropolitan also launched a "Family Reunion" program to contact holders of old industrial insurance policies still in force.

With the economy in recession in the early 1990s, Metropolitan began to cut costs, trimming jobs and transferring thousands of others from New York City. The company also reemphasized insurance products and added new ones, such as long-term care insurance.

In 1992 Metropolitan continued expanding despite the costs of natural disasters like Hurricane Andrew. In addition to joint ventures in Mexico and Portugal, MetLife added the 30,000 policyholders of United Mutual Life Insurance Company, which, until its merger into MetLife, was New York's only African-American life insurance company.

The next year MetLife was hit by charges of improper sales practices by agents in 13 states. Improprieties included misrepresentation of life insurance policies as retirement accounts and churning (persuading policyholders to buy more expensive policies to replace old ones). Legal fees, fines, and refunds in these cases exceeded $100 million, and bad publicity had a chilling effect on policy sales in 1994.

MetLife has added an array of services, including mutual funds and employee benefits administration, and has subtracted other operations. In 1993 it combined its health plans with Travelers's to form MetraHealth, but in 1995 this joint venture was bought by United Health. Also sold were Century 21 and MetLife's Canadian trust business.

Mutual company
Fiscal year ends: December 31

Chairman and CEO: Harry P. Kamen
President and COO: Ted Athanassiades
SEVP and CFO: Stewart G. Nagler
EVP and Chief Investment Officer: Gerald Clark
EVP and Chief Legal Officer: Gary A. Beller
EVP: Robert J. Crimmins
EVP: John D. Moynahan Jr.
EVP: William G. Poortvliet
EVP: Anthony C. Cannatella
EVP: C. Robert Henrikson
SVP and General Counsel: Richard M. Blackwell
SVP Human Resources: Anne E. Hayden
Auditors: Deloitte & Touche LLP

WHERE

HQ: Metropolitan Life Insurance Company,
One Madison Ave., New York, NY 10010-3690
Phone: 212-578-2211
Fax: 212-578-3320

MetLife and its affiliated companies operate in Canada,
Mexico, Portugal, South Korea, Spain, Taiwan, the UK,
and the US.

	1994 Life Insurance Premiums	
	$ mil.	% of total
New York	877	14
California	471	8
Illinois	372	6
Michigan	359	6
New Jersey	361	6
Pennsylvania	351	6
Texas	332	5
Florida	251	4
Ohio	243	4
Connecticut	127	3
Massachusetts	191	3
Missouri	109	2
Other US	1,766	29
Canada	259	4
Total	**6,069**	**100**

WHAT

	1994 Assets	
	$ mil.	% of total
Cash & equivalents	2,334	2
Treasury & agency securities	9,807	7
Foreign government securities	1,931	2
Mortgage-backed securities	17,485	13
Corporate bonds	31,262	24
State & municipal bonds	1,483	1
Stocks	3,672	3
Mortgage loans	14,524	11
Real estate	10,417	8
Policy loans	3,964	3
Separate account assets	25,424	19
Other	8,874	7
Total	**131,177**	**100**

	1994 Sales	
	$ mil.	% of total
Premiums & deposits	19,881	66
Investments	7,143	24
Supplementary contracts		
& dividends	2,879	10
Other	80	0
Total	**29,983**	**100**

Selected Affiliates
Albany Life Assurance Company Ltd. (UK)
Farmers National Co.
GFM International Investors Ltd. (UK)
MetLife HealthCare Management Corp.
MetLife (UK) Limited
MetLife Securities, Inc.
Metropolitan Property and Casualty Insurance Co.
Metropolitan Tower Life Insurance Co.
Metropolitan Trust Company of Canada
Seguros Génesis, S.A. (Mexico)

KEY COMPETITORS

Aetna	ITT Hartford	Pacific Mutual
Allstate	John Hancock	Life
Berkshire Hathaway	Kemper Corp.	Prudential
Blue Cross	MassMutual	State Farm
Equitable	Mutual of Omaha	Tokio Marine
GEICO	New York Life	and Fire
Guardian Life	Northwestern	Travelers
Insurance	Mutual	USAA

HOW MUCH

	Annual Growth	1985	1986	1987	1988	1989	1990	1991	1992	1993	1994
Assets ($ mil.)	6.6%	73,803	78,773	88,140	94,232	98,740	103,228	110,799	118,178	128,225	131,177
Net income ($ mil.)	(25.2%)	—	—	809	836	494	360	237	225	133	106
Income as % of assets	—	—	—	—	0.9%	0.9%	0.5%	0.3%	0.2%	0.1%	0.0%
Employees	4.7%	35,000	33,000	33,000	37,000	42,464	45,342	58,000	57,000	55,000	53,000

1994 Year-end:
Equity as % of
assets: 4.8%
Return on equity: 1.7%
Sales (mil.): $29,983

Net Income ($ mil.)
1987–94

MetLife

MORGAN STANLEY GROUP INC.

OVERVIEW

In 1995 New York City–based Morgan Stanley got a 2nd chance. By changing its fiscal year-end to November 30 from January 31, the investment banking and brokerage company was able to report results twice in one year. The first fiscal 1995 was bad news, the 2nd much brighter. The company made the change so that year-end accounting will not interfere with budget and compensation planning, especially as it affects bonuses.

Rebounding from the bond and investment traumas of 1994, Morgan Stanley has added to its head count, but primarily overseas. In addition to opening new offices in Beijing, Montreal, Sydney, Geneva, and Johannesburg (in the former pariah nation South Africa), the firm is expanding its established operations in other nations. It has recently upgraded its operations in Germany, Italy, and France and has won authorization for brokerage operations in Mexico.

In addition to brokerage services and investment banking, Morgan Stanley offers its clients mergers and acquisitions, merchant banking, custody and clearing, and asset management services.

WHEN

Morgan Stanley split from the J.P. Morgan banking company after the 1934 Glass-Steagall Act required banks to separate commercial banking (deposit-taking and lending) from investment banking activities (issuing and trading securities).

In 1935 Henry Morgan, Harold Stanley, and others established Morgan Stanley as an investment banking firm. Capitalizing on old ties to major corporations, the company handled $1 billion in issues in its first year.

By the time Morgan Stanley became a partnership in 1941 so it could join the New York Stock Exchange, it had managed 25% of all bond issues underwritten since the Glass-Steagall Act took effect.

In the 1950s Morgan Stanley was known as a well-managed firm that handled issues by itself and rarely participated with other firms. Despite having only $3 million in capital, the partnership was the investment bank for such major US corporations as General Motors, U.S. Steel, General Electric, and DuPont.

Morgan Stanley chose not to help finance the merger wave of the 1960s, since its blue-chip clients were not involved. But in the early 1970s it entered the mergers and acquisitions world, forming Wall Street's first M&A department. In 1974 Morgan Stanley handled its first hostile takeover, International Nickel's takeover of ESB, the world's largest battery manufacturer. Competing investment banking firms then became involved in hostile takeovers.

When Morgan Stanley went public in 1986, its managing directors and principals retained 81% of its stock. The firm amassed a $1.6 billion investment pool and bought Burlington Industries for $46.3 million in cash and $2.2 billion in debt (1987). Burlington's best assets were sold to service the debt, and the company reaped over $176 million in fees and dividends.

Although the 1987 crash sent the financial world into a tailspin and tipped the Northeast into recession, Morgan Stanley escaped virtually unscathed. It was, in fact, the only one of its New York peers to see its earnings rise in 1987, and it was not forced to lay off any employees.

In the 1990s Morgan Stanley became mired in numerous lawsuits arising from investor dissatisfaction with its M&A and LBO activities in the 1980s. In 1991 a jury awarded investors a $16 million settlement for the firm's role in the 1987 formation of First RepublicBank Corp, whose collapse was the costliest in US history. In a suit arising from the 1987 stock crash, Morgan Stanley was ordered in 1995 to reimburse West Virginia for over $32 million in pension fund losses. The firm was West Virginia's financial advisor, and the losses arose from prohibited speculative trades by the state. The firm has appealed the judgment.

In 1992 Morgan Stanley's Real Estate Fund bought interests in resorts in California and Colorado. In 1994 the firm unsuccessfully engaged in merger talks with London-based S. G. Warburg Group, an investment bank. During the 1990s Morgan Stanley has lost market share, slipping out of the top 5 in its class. The 1993 defection of star banker Robert Greenhill and several others (to the Travelers's Smith Barney) was a blow, and the firm began taking corrective action, bringing in Joseph Perella (formerly of Wasserstein Perella) and otherwise upgrading its operations. By 1995 Morgan Stanley was able to lure other high-profile staff, raiding 6 members of CS First Boston's Houston office to help beef up its energy banking capacities.

Morgan Stanley rode 1995's bull market, reporting earnings of $600 million for the 10-month fiscal year ending November 30.

NYSE symbol: MS
Fiscal year ends: November 30

WHO

Chairman and Managing Director: Richard B. Fisher,
age 58, $2,637,500 pay
President and Managing Director: John J. Mack, age 50,
$2,575,000 pay
Managing Director: Peter F. Karches, age 43,
$2,325,000 pay
Managing Director: Barton M. Biggs, age 62,
$2,150,000 pay
Managing Director and CFO: Philip N. Duff, age 38
Managing Director, General Counsel, and Secretary:
Jonathan M. Clark, age 57
Treasurer: Charles B. Hintz
Director Human Resources: William Higgins
Auditors: Ernst & Young LLP

WHERE

HQ: 1585 Broadway, New York, NY 10036
Phone: 212-703-4000
Fax: 212-703-6503

Morgan Stanley operates in Chicago, Los Angeles, New
York, and San Francisco and has offices in Beijing,
Bombay, Frankfurt, Geneva, Hong Kong, Johannesburg,
London, Luxembourg, Madrid, Melbourne, Milan,
Montreal, Moscow, Paris, Seoul, Shanghai, Singapore,
Sydney, Taipei, Tokyo, Toronto, and Zurich.

	1995[1] Sales		1995[1] Pretax Income	
	$ mil.	% of total	$ mil.	% of total
North America	8,332	65	527	89
Europe	3,942	30	11	2
Asia	603	5	56	9
Adjustments	(3,501)	—	—	—
Total	**9,376**	**100**	**594**	**100**

WHAT

	1995[1] Sales	
	$ mil.	% of total
Interest & dividends	6,406	68
Trading & investing	1,243	13
Investment banking	919	10
Commissions	449	5
Asset management	350	4
Other	9	0
Total	**9,376**	**100**

Financial Services
Asset management
Corporate finance
Futures, option, foreign exchange, and commodities
trading
Investment banking
Securities distribution and trading
Securities underwriting
Stock brokerage and research

KEY COMPETITORS

Alex. Brown	FMR
Alliance Capital	General Electric
Bankers Trust	Goldman Sachs
Barclays	HSBC
Bear Stearns	John Nuveen
Brown Brothers	ING Group
Harriman	Lehman Brothers
Canadian Imperial	Mellon Bank
Charles Schwab	Merrill Lynch
Chase Manhattan	Nomura Securities
Citicorp	Paine Webber
CS Holding	Prudential
Dean Witter, Discover	Salomon
Deutsche Bank	T. Rowe Price
Equitable	Travelers

HOW MUCH

	Annual Growth	1986[1]	1987[1]	1988[1]	1989[1]	1990[1]	1991[1]	1992[1]	1993[1]	1994[1]	1995[1]
Sales ($ mil.)	20.2%	1,795	2,463	3,148	4,109	5,831	5,869	6,785	7,382	9,176	9,376
Net income ($ mil.)	15.8%	106	201	231	395	443	270	475	511	786	395
Income as % of sales	—	5.9%	8.2%	7.3%	9.6%	7.6%	4.6%	7.0%	6.9%	8.6%	4.2%
Earnings per share ($)	9.5%	1 78	2.81	3.00	5.13	5.61	3.38	5.61	5.71	9.16	4.03
Stock price – high ($)[2]	—	—	27.34	28.64	28.31	39.75	37.75	65.00	67.88	89.63	80.38
Stock price – low ($)[2]	—	—	20.47	12.75	15.59	27.44	23.56	26.00	45.88	54.00	55.00
Stock price – close ($)[2]	13.4%	—	21.64	17.09	27.69	32.31	27.19	63.75	55.75	70.75	59.00
P/E – high	—	—	10	10	6	7	11	12	12	10	20
P/E – low	—	—	7	4	3	5	7	5	8	6	14
Dividends per share ($)	33.4%	—	0.12	0.27	0.48	0.50	0.75	0.80	0.96	1.08	1.20
Book value per share ($)	28.7%	5.11	10.53	13.44	19.09	23.92	24.48	30.13	37.71	49.03	49.62
Employees	10.0%	4,100	7,000	6,517	6,414	6,640	7,122	7,053	7,421	8,273	9,685

1995[1] Year-end:
Debt ratio: 94.1%
Return on equity: 10.7%
Cash (mil.): $4,626
Long-term debt (mil.): $8,814
No. of shares (mil.): 75
Dividends
  Yield: 2.0%
  Payout: 29.8%
Market value (mil.): $4,443
Assets (mil.): $116,694

Stock Price History[2]
High/Low 1987–95

[1] For fiscal year ending January 31   [2] Stock prices are for the prior calendar year.

MTA

OVERVIEW

The Metropolitan Transportation Authority's rate hike has given it just enough rope to tie itself to the tracks — in front of a union-run train. The MTA, based in Manhattan, is the largest public-transit provider in the Americas. A subsidiary agency, MTA New York City Transit, provides bus service to all 5 New York City boroughs and subway service to the Bronx, Brooklyn, Manhattan, and Queens. It also operates the Staten Island Railway. MTA Long Island Bus and MTA Long Island Rail Road provide bus and railway service to Long Island. MTA Metro-North Railroad serves outlying counties in New York and Connecticut. MTA also maintains 7 bridges and 2 tunnels.

MTA chairman Virgil Conway's aim is to move the agency toward self-reliance (and perhaps partial privatization) since federal, state, and city budgets are coming under increased pressure and subsidies are being reduced. The authority has hiked bus and subway fares by 25¢ to $1.50. However, Conway was criticized in late 1995 for sinking his own austerity plan by conceding a 10.4% wage hike over 4 years to Metro-North's unions (thus setting a shaky stage for talks with MTA New York City Transit's unions, where Conway plans to seek the largest cuts). MTA's multibillion-dollar capital improvement program, however, appears to remain on track.

WHEN

Mass transit began in New York City in the 1820s and 1830s with the introduction of horse-drawn omnibuses (local stagecoaches) run by small private firms. By 1832 a horse-drawn railcar began operating on Fourth Avenue and offered a smoother and faster ride than its street-bound rivals.

By 1864 residents were complaining that horsecars and buses were overcrowded and that drivers were intolerably rude. (Horsecars were transporting 45 million passengers annually.) In 1870 a short pneumatic subway under Broadway was opened to the public, but it was never more than an amusement. Elevated steam railways were built, but people resisted them because of the smoke, noise, and danger of explosions. Cable cars provided a limited transit solution in the 1880s, and by the 1890s electric streetcars became important.

Construction of the first commercial subway line was completed in 1904. It was operated by Interborough Rapid Transit Co. (IRT), which had leased the primary elevated rail line in 1903 and thus had effective control of rail transit in Manhattan and the Bronx. In 1905 the IRT merged with the Metropolitan Street Railway, which operated almost all surface railways in Manhattan, giving the new firm almost complete control of the city's rapid transit. Public protests caused the city to grant licenses to Brooklyn Rapid Transit (later BMT), creating the Dual System. The 2 rail firms quickly covered most of the city.

By the 1920s the transit system was again in crisis, largely because the 2 lines were not allowed to raise their 5¢ fare. In 1932 both the IRT and the BMT were in receivership; the city decided to own and operate part of the rail system and organized the Independent (IND)

rail line. Pressure for public ownership and operation of the transit system resulted in the city's purchase of all the IRT's and BMT's assets in 1940 for $326 million. The 3 lines were managed by the Transit Commission of the New York State Department of Public Service.

In 1953 the state legislature created the New York City Transit Authority, to which the city leased all transit facilities, creating the first unified system. During the 1950s ridership declined as people moved to the suburbs.

Transit workers walked out for almost 2 weeks in 1966, and people found it almost impossible to negotiate the ensuing gridlock. The union won higher wages but lost the public relations battle to the mayor. Two years later the Metropolitan Transit Authority was created to coordinate the city's transit activities with other commuter services.

The 1970s and 1980s saw the city's transit infrastructure and service deteriorate while crime, accidents, graffiti, and fares rose. But by the early 1990s a multibillion-dollar modernization program had begun to make noticeable improvements: subway stations were repaired, graffiti was erased, and service was extended. In 1994 MTA introduced an automated fare card. The authority also reported subway crime was down 50% from 1990.

The ever-politicized agency lost a fight with the mayor in early 1995 when its transit police department was merged into the city police department. Virgil Conway was appointed chairman by Governor George Pataki in April 1995. Budget cuts followed, which led to service reductions and staff cuts. Later that year token-booth firebombings (reflecting a scene in the movie *Money Train*) left one clerk dead and provoked a national debate.

Public-benefit corporation
Fiscal year ends: December 31

Chairman: E. Virgil Conway
Executive Director: Marc Shaw
President, MTA New York City Transit: Lawrence Reuter
President, MTA Long Island Rail Road: Thomas F. Prendergast
President, MTA Long Island Bus: Helena E. Williams
President, MTA Metro-North Railroad: Donald N. Nelson
President, MTA Bridges and Tunnels: Michael C. Ascher
President, MTA Card Company: Judith Squire
CFO: Stephen Reitano
Director Human Resources: David Knapp
Auditors: Ernst & Young LLP

WHERE

HQ: Metropolitan Transportation Authority, 347 Madison Ave., New York, NY 10017
Phone: 212-878-7000
Fax: 212-878-7031

MTA Metro-North Railroad has rail lines to outlying counties in New York and Connecticut. MTA Long Island Bus operates buses in Nassau, Queens, and Suffolk Counties. MTA Long Island Rail Road has rail lines to Nassau and Suffolk Counties. MTA New York Transit operates buses and subways in the Bronx, Brooklyn, Manhattan, and Queens. It also operates buses on Staten Island. The MTA Staten Island Railway runs from the Staten Island Ferry landing 14 miles south to Tottenville.

WHAT

	1994 Revenues	
	$ mil.	% of total
Operating revenues	2,494	48
State/regional taxes	987	19
Tolls	725	14
Local subsidies	310	6
Federal & state subsidies	295	6
Other	378	7
Total	**5,189**	**100**

1994 Ridership		
	Riders (mil. approx.)	% of total
New York City subway	1,081	64
New York City bus	451	27
Long Island Rail Road	73	4
Metro-North Railroad	62	4
Long Island Bus	19	1
Staten Island Railway	5	0
Total	**1,691**	**100**

1994 Agency Statistics

Rolling Stock
Long Island Bus: 318 buses
Long Island Rail Road: 1,120 railcars
Metro-North Railroad: 815 railcars
New York City bus system: 3,707 buses
New York City subway system: 5,806 railcars
Staten Island Railway: 64 railcars

Number of Lines or Routes
Long Island Bus: 51
Long Island Rail Road: 11
Metro-North Railroad: 8
New York City bus system: 231
New York City subway system: 25
Staten Island Railway: 1

Bridges

Bronx Whitestone	Triborough
Cross Bay	Verrazano-Narrows
Henry Hudson	
Marine Parkway	**Tunnels**
Throgs Neck	Brooklyn Battery
	Queens Midtown

Subsidiary Agencies

MTA Bridges and Tunnels
MTA Card Co. (automated fare-collection system)
MTA Long Island Bus
MTA Long Island Rail Road
MTA Metro-North Railroad
MTA New York City Transit
MTA Staten Island Railway

KEY COMPETITORS

Gray Line Air Shuttle	Laidlaw Transit
Jamaica Buses	Queens Surface Corp.

HOW MUCH

	Annual Growth	1985	1986	1987	1988	1989	1990	1991	1992	1993	1994
Revenues ($ mil.)	3.5%	—	—	—	—	—	—	—	4,845	5,036	5,189
Passenger revenue ($ mil.)	2.5%	—	—	—	—	—	—	—	2,374	2,435	2,494
Net income ($ mil.)	—	—	—	—	—	—	—	—	(173)	(136)	(156)
Income as % of revenues	—	—	—	—	—	—	—	—	—	—	—
Employees	1.0%	—	—	—	—	—	—	—	—	64,838	65,465

Revenues
($ mil.) 1992–94

MUTUAL LIFE OF NEW YORK

OVERVIEW

Mutual Life of New York (MONY) is the oldest mutual insurance company in the US. Always choosy about its clientele, the company targets upper-income individuals and small-business groups for the sale of a variety of life, disability income, annuity, and mutual fund products. MONY was one of the first companies to use an agency force for sales, and it has developed a long tradition of careful training and supervision of its agents (though in the 1990s some unethical ones have surfaced). The company operates throughout the US and has agents overseas, primarily to serve US military personnel stationed abroad.

In addition to its insurance operations, MONY has several subsidiaries that offer financial management, investment, and advisory services (Enterprise Capital Management, MONY Brokerage, MONY Securities, and 1740 Advisers Inc.). Other subsidiaries manage the company's own investments. MONY has turned some of these operations into profit centers by offering their services to other institutions. In 1995 the company merged its real estate management operations into its ARES property management subsidiary to offer 3rd-party clients a full range of real estate management services.

Managing real estate is something MONY has had a lot of experience with in the 1990s, as it was caught by the real estate crash and the following recession with a lot of defaulted mortgages. Rather than selling the properties, MONY managed them and began disposing of them as the commercial real estate markets rebounded. To prevent a recurrence of this problem, MONY has avoided new mortgages in recent years. But high returns remain alluring to the company, which makes investments in such exotica as securities backed by subprime auto paper, manufactured-home mortgages, and franchise leases.

WHEN

The Mutual Life Insurance Co. of New York was founded in 1842 by a group that included Elihu Townsend, a prominent member of the New York Stock Exchange; Morris Robinson, a banker; and Alfred Pell, an insurance underwriter who became acquainted with the idea of the mutual insurance company while visiting England. It sold its first policy in 1843 and the next year paid its first death benefit, on Jane Coit, a Connecticut tuberculosis victim (most insurers did not sell coverage for women).

MONY grew quickly, using career agents (including women) and applying stringent underwriting standards. Recognizing the statistical correlation between pulmonary disease and smoking or working with lead, the company either refused coverage or raised premiums in such cases. It also refused to pay off on clients who made hazardous journeys without permission. In 1868 the company adopted the first mortality table in the US insurance industry. Emphasis on prevention continued in the 1870s, when MONY distributed health guides to its policyholders.

The company began international expansion, opening an office in Mexico City in 1886. By 1906 it had offices in 25 foreign cities (all of them were closed during WWI — the last one, in London, in 1917; some of this business was still on the books in the 1980s).

In 1898 MONY's most prominent employee joined the organization. Composer Charles Ives and his partner, Julian Myrick, founded an agency that later became the company's most successful.

By 1900 MONY was the world's largest insurer. Five years later it was under investigation by the State of New York for sales abuses and imprudent investment policies. One of the resultant reforms was the transition of general agents from straight commission to salaried branch managers.

The company grew through the 1920s and even expanded modestly during the Depression and WWII. After the war the company began offering group insurance for small businesses, including pension plans (1954) and variable annuities (1965).

In 1969 MONY entered the financial services field. The following 2 decades saw a proliferation of financial services subsidiaries and the acquisition of other insurance companies (by 1987 there were 33 subsidiaries).

Then came the 1987 stock market crash and the real estate bust, which depressed results. The company began reorganizing and cutting internal costs. It also began boosting capital by selling assets, among them its group pensions business (to Aegon in 1993).

In 1994, combining a technical upgrade program with its search for new income sources, MONY joined with Computer Sciences Corp., of California, to launch the Insurance Technology Center, which will develop and market new technological tools for use by the insurance industry.

Mutual company
Fiscal year ends: December 31

Chairman and CEO: Michael I. Roth
President and COO: Samuel J. Foti
EVP and Chief Investment Officer: Kenneth M. Levine
EVP and CFO: Richard D'addario
General Counsel: Richard Mulroy
Assistant VP Human Resources: Linda Kramer
Auditors: Coopers & Lybrand L.L.P.

WHERE

HQ: The Mutual Life Insurance Company of New York,
1740 Broadway, New York, NY 10019
Phone: 212-708-2000
Fax: 212-708-2056

Mutual Life of New York is licensed in all 50 states, the
District of Columbia, Puerto Rico, and the Virgin
Islands.

WHAT

	1994 Sales	
	$ mil.	% of total
Premiums, annuity considerations & fund deposits	1,880	66
Net investment income	682	24
Revenue from ceded reinsurance	155	6
Other	122	4
Total	**2,839**	**100**

	1994 Assets	
	$ mil.	% of total
Cash & equivalents	258	2
Bonds	4,577	32
Stocks	212	1
Mortgage loans	2,112	15
Real estate	2,038	14
Policy loans	1,221	9
Other investments	349	3
Separate accounts	2,834	20
Other	565	4
Total	**14,166**	**100**

Subsidiaries
1740 Advisers Inc. (investment advice)
ARES, Inc. (real estate management)
Bell Investment Acquisition Corp. (origination and
servicing of land and agricultural loans)
Enterprise Capital Management Inc. (investment advice)
MONY Bank & Trust Co. of the Americas, Ltd.
MONY Brokerage Inc. (life insurance brokerage)
MONY Life Insurance Co. of America
MONY Life Insurance Co. of the Americas, Ltd.
(international life insurance)
MONY Securities Corp. (securities brokerage)

KEY COMPETITORS

American Bankers Insurance
American General
American National Insurance
Connecticut Mutual Life
Conseco
Equitable Cos.
First Colony
General American Life Insurance
Guardian Life
Household International
Jefferson-Pilot
John Hancock
Lincoln National
MassMutual
Met Life
Minnesota Mutual
Mutual of Omaha
New York Life
Northwestern Mutual
Pacific Mutual Life
Principal Financial
Provident Life
Providian
Prudential
ReliaStar Financial
Torchmark

HOW MUCH

	Annual Growth	1985	1986	1987	1988	1989	1990	1991	1992	1993	1994
Assets ($ mil.)	3.8%	10,138	11,249	13,976	15,757	17,181	17,996	19,115	18,727	16,866	14,166
Net income ($ mil.)	(9.0%)	—	—	—	151	154	141	207	117	112	86
Income as % of assets	—	—	—	—	1.0%	0.9%	0.8%	1.1%	0.6%	0.7%	0.6%
Employees	(1.6%)	7,400	—	7,000	—	5,200	5,163	4,479	7,681	6,357	6,400

1994 Year-end:
Equity as % of assets:
4.8%
Return on equity: 13.5%
Return on assets: 0.6%

Assets ($ mil.)
1985–94

NEW YORK LIFE INSURANCE COMPANY

OVERVIEW

New York Life has taken the high road in addressing the problem of deceptive sales practices. It had to, after a Texas jury awarded $21 million to an aggrieved customer and Florida also began investigating the company. But unlike some of the other insurers involved in such cases, New York Life, one of the largest US life insurers, moved decisively to forestall further problems by ordering a comprehensive review of all sales materials in use throughout the country. As a result, it issued standardized materials and prohibited any other from being used to make sales.

New York Life offers a wide variety of life, health, and disability insurance policies; annuities; mutual funds and other investments; and health care management services. In 1995 it was authorized to open a trust bank, which will aid its benefits and mutual funds operations.

Although New York Life closed its operations in Canada in 1994, it is expanding elsewhere in the world, opening a representative office in Shanghai. It expects its business in Mexico to grow, fueled by demand in a country where only 2% of the people are insured.

WHEN

In 1841 actuary Pliny Freeman and 56 New York businessmen founded Nautilus Insurance Co., the 3rd US mutual (policyholder-owned) company. It began operating in 1845 and became New York Life in 1849.

In 1846 the company had the first life insurance agent west of the Mississippi River. Although cut off from its southern business by the Civil War, New York Life honored all its obligations and renewed lapsed policies when the war ended. By 1887 the company had developed its branch office system.

By 1900 the company had established the NYLIC Plan for compensating agents, which featured a lifetime income after 20 years of service. New York Life had moved into Europe in the late 1800s but withdrew after WWI.

Much of the company's growth and product development has occurred since WWII. In the early 1950s the company simplified insurance policy forms, slashed premiums, and replaced mortality tables of the 1860s with more up-to-date data. These actions resulted in new company sales records and were widely copied by competitors. In 1956 the company became the first life insurance firm to use data processing equipment on a large scale.

In the 1960s New York Life was instrumental in developing variable life insurance, a new product with variable benefits and level premiums. In 1968 the company added variable annuities. Steady growth continued until the late 1970s, when high interest rates led to heavy policyholder borrowing. Jarred by the outflow of money, the company sought to make its products more competitive as investments.

In 1981 the company offered single- and flexible-premium deferred annuities, and in 1982 it added a universal life product. New York Life also formed New York Life and Health Insurance Co. in 1982.

The company acquired MacKay-Shields Financial, which now oversees its MainStay mutual funds, in 1984. This, along with a modernization program, caused income to plummet. Also in 1984 NYLIFE Realty offered the company's first pure investment product, a real estate limited partnership.

Expansion continued in 1987 with the purchase of a controlling interest in Hillhouse Associates Insurance (3rd-party administrator of insurance plans) and Madison Benefits Administrators (group insurance programs). The company also acquired Sanus Corp. Health Systems, the largest privately held manager of health care programs in the US. It returned to Europe in 1988, opening an office in Ireland.

New York Life entered a joint venture to provide insurance in Indonesia in 1992, when it also began operations in Korea and Taiwan. The next year it bought Aetna UK's life insurance operations.

In a climate of increased scrutiny of insurance industry sales practices in 1993 and 1994, New York Life was investigated by the state of Florida and faced several suits in Texas. The company also launched its own investigations, which won praise from the state regulators involved. In late 1994 it increased its health care holdings, adding ETHIX Corp. (utilization review) and Avanti Health Systems (physician practice management).

In early 1995 president George Bundschuh announced his retirement in October. He was succeeded by EVP Seymour Sternberg. As part of the expansion of its overseas business, New York Life entered into a joint venture with St. James's Place Capital, PLC, to form Life Assurance Holding Corp. That same year New York Life and Oracle Systems began developing client/server database software specifically for the insurance industry.

Mutual company
Fiscal year ends: December 31

WHO

Chairman and CEO: Harry G. Hohn
VC and President: Seymour Sternberg, age 51
VC and EVP: Lee M. Gammill Jr., age 61
EVP Human Resources: George J. Trapp, age 47
EVP: Frederick J. Sievert, age 47
SVP and General Counsel: Michael J. McLaughlin, age 51
SVP and Chief Information Officer: Lee Lapioli, age 53
SVP and Chief Actuary: Stephen N. Steinig
SVP Corporate Office of Business Conduct: Richard A. Hansen
SVP, Deputy General Counsel, and Secretary: Melbourne Nunes
VP and Controller: Marc J. Chalfin
VP and General Auditor: Thomas J. Warga
Auditors: Price Waterhouse LLP

WHERE

HQ: 51 Madison Ave., New York, NY 10010
Phone: 212-576-7000
Fax: 212-576-8145

New York Life operates in Argentina, Bermuda, China, Hong Kong, Indonesia, Korea, Mexico, Taiwan, the UK, and the US.

WHAT

	1994 Assets	
	$ mil.	% of total
Cash & equivalents	2,506	4
Treasury & agency securities	6,682	10
Municipal bonds	11,992	18
Foreign governments' securities	1,699	2
Corporate bonds	22,740	33
Other bonds	2,187	3
Stocks	1,789	2
Mortgage loans	5,990	9
Real estate	1,290	2
Policy loans	5,380	8
Separate account assets	3,580	5
Other	3,091	4
Total	**68,926**	**100**

	1994 Sales	
	$ mil.	% of total
Premiums	10,255	65
Net investment income	4,679	30
Other income	873	5
Total	**15,807**	**100**

Business Units
Asset Management
Group Operations
Individual Operations
Investments

Selected Products
Annuities
Disability insurance
Group pensions
Life insurance
MainStay (mutual funds)

Selected Subsidiaries
Las Buenos Aires New York Life
New York Life and Health Insurance Co.
New York Life Insurance and Annuity Corp.
New York Life Worldwide (Bermuda) Ltd.
New York Life Worldwide Holding, Inc.
NYL Benefit Services, Inc. (employee benefit consulting)
NYLIFE Distributors, Inc. (brokerage)
NYLIFE Insurance Company of Arizona
Sanus Corp. Health Systems (HMO)

KEY COMPETITORS

Aetna	Kaiser Foundation
Allstate	Health Plan
American National	Kemper Corp.
Insurance	MassMutual
Berkshire Hathaway	Mellon Bank
Blue Cross	Merrill Lynch
Charles Schwab	MetLife
Chubb	Mutual of Omaha
CIGNA	Northwestern Mutual
CNA Financial	Oxford Health Plans
Dean Witter, Discover	Paine Webber
Equitable	Prudential
Guardian Life Insurance	State Farm
ITT Hartford	T. Rowe Price
John Alden Financial	Transamerica
John Hancock	USF&G

HOW MUCH

	Annual Growth	1985	1986	1987	1988	1989	1990	1991	1992	1993	1994
Assets ($ mil.)	9.0%	31,740	35,087	38,877	43,417	46,648	50,126	54,066	59,169	66,791	68,926
Net income ($ mil.)	32.5%	32	194	92	204	57	290	280	271	.368	404
Income as % of assets	—	0.1%	0.6%	0.2%	0.5%	0.1%	0.6%	0.5%	0.5%	0.6%	0.6%
Employees	(4.4%)	—	—	—	—	19,438	18,200	18,848	17,406	17,169	15,534

1994 Year-end:
Equity as % of assets: 5.4%
Return on equity: 11.3%
Sales (mil.): $15,807

Net Income ($ mil.)
1985–94

THE NEW YORK TIMES COMPANY

OVERVIEW

The New York Times Company is a sprawling, $2.4 billion media and communications conglomerate with interests in newspapers, magazines, broadcasting, and information services. It publishes one of the world's most respected newspapers, the *New York Times*, which is also the US's #1 metropolitan daily. The company owns the *Boston Globe*, 21 smaller daily newspapers (plus 5 weeklies) in 10 states, half of the *International Herald Tribune*, 2 newspaper distributors, and a stake in 2 US and Canadian paper mills. Newspapers represented 83% of 1994 revenues. The company also operates 6 TV stations and 2 New York radio stations; publishes 10 sports and leisure magazines; sells wire and photo services (it is the world's largest supplemental news service); repackages information and news for fax,

CD-ROM, microform, and online services; and licenses trademarks and copyrighted material from the *Times*.

A traditional print publisher (90% of its profits are from print properties), the Times Co. is now moving quickly into multimedia. Previously hamstrung by an exclusive contract with online information provider LEXIS/NEXIS, the company regained control of the electronic rights to the *Times* in late 1994. In 1995 the company teamed up with 8 other major newspaper companies to distribute the *Times* online through a new service, New Century Network, which is expected to be operational by late 1995. The company intends to further explore other news outlets, especially TV, and look for opportunities in local TV stations and national cable TV programming.

WHEN

In 1851 George Jones and Henry Raymond, 2 former *New York Tribune* staffers, started the *New York Times*. The paper began a long tradition of political coverage during the Civil War and of investigative reporting with the Tammany Hall scandals, but by the late 1800s it had lost popularity to the yellow journalism of the Hearst and Pulitzer papers.

In 1896 Adolph Ochs, a newspaperman from Chattanooga, bought the *Times*. Continuing hard news and business coverage and eschewing diversification, Ochs added the newspaper's now-famous slogan: "All the News That's Fit to Print." Ochs's son-in-law Arthur Hays Sulzberger, who ran the paper from 1935 to 1961, diversified the company with the purchase of 2 New York City radio stations (1944). Sulzberger's son-in-law Orvil Dryfoos was publisher until his death in 1963, leaving Adolph's grandson Arthur Ochs "Punch" Sulzberger in charge.

In the 1960s declining ad revenues from Manhattan stores and a newspaper strike sent the company into the red. To regain strength Punch built the largest news-gathering staff of any newspaper. The *Times*'s coverage of the Vietnam War helped change public sentiment, and the newspaper won a Pulitzer Prize in 1972 for publishing the Pentagon Papers.

In the meantime Punch had taken the company public (1967), though the family retained solid control through ownership of most of the Class B stock. In the 1970s the Times Co. bought magazines, publishing houses, television stations, smaller newspapers, and cable TV systems and began co-

publishing, with the Washington Post Co., the *International Herald Tribune*. To contain costs the company bought interests in 3 pulp and paper companies.

In the 1980s the *Times* added feature sections to compete with suburban papers. The company bought *Golf World* in 1988, and in 1989 it bought *McCall's* (sold in 1994) and sold its cable systems. In 1990 the company started *TimesFax*, a summary of the *Times* sent to subscribers' fax machines worldwide.

Family members are still active on the board and in publishing activities. In 1992 Arthur Ochs Sulzberger Jr. succeeded his father as *Times* publisher; Punch remained Times Co. chairman and CEO.

In 1993 the Times Co. bought Affiliated Publications, owner of the *Boston Globe*, for a record $1.1 billion. Started in 1872, the *Globe* found its footing in 1878 under the financing of Eben Jordan (one of 6 *Globe* cofounders and founder of Jordan Marsh department stores) and the management of Charles Taylor. By selling to the Times Co., Affiliated avoided a possible hostile takeover in 1996, the year the Jordan and Taylor family trusts were to expire. In 1994 the Times Co. sold the 1/3 interest in BPI Communications (specialty magazines) that had come with the Affiliated purchase.

In 1994 the company began construction on a new, state-of-the-art printing plant. The company also sold its women's and 3 UK golf magazines. In 1995 the Times Co. agreed to buy a majority stake in Video News International, a video news-gathering company, and launched 2 cable news channels in Arkansas.

AMEX symbol: NYTA
Fiscal year ends: December 31

WHO

Chairman and CEO: Arthur Ochs "Punch" Sulzberger, age 69, $962,200 pay
President and COO: Lance R. Primis, age 48, $1,100,800 pay
Publisher, *The New York Times*: Arthur Ochs Sulzberger Jr., age 43, $918,200 pay
SVP and CFO: Diane P. Baker
SVP and Deputy COO: David L. Gorham, age 62, $683,400 pay
Publisher, *The Boston Globe*: William O. Taylor, age 62, $550,451 pay
SVP Broadcasting, Corporate Development, and Human Resources: Katharine P. Darrow, age 51
VP Operations and Planning: Gordon Medenica, age 43
VP and General Counsel: Solomon B. Watson IV, age 50
Auditors: Deloitte & Touche LLP

WHERE

HQ: 229 W. 43rd St., New York, NY 10036
Phone: 212-556-1234
Fax: 212-556-3722

WHAT

	1994 Sales	
	$ mil.	% of total
Newspapers	1,969	83
Magazines	280	12
Broadcasting & information svcs.	109	5
Total	**2,358**	**100**

Major Newspapers
Boston Globe (498,400 average daily circulation)
International Herald Tribune (50%, with the Washington Post Co.)
New York Times (1,129,600 average daily circulation)

Magazines
Cruising World   *Sailing World*
Golf Digest   *Snow Country*
Golf Shop Operations   *Snow Country Business*
Golf World   *Tennis*
Sailing Business   *Tennis Buyer's Guide*

Broadcasting
KFSM-TV, Fort Smith, AR   WQEW (AM), New York
NYT Video Productions   WQXR (FM), New York
Video News International   WREG-TV, Memphis
WHNT-TV, Huntsville, AL   WTKR-TV, Norfolk, VA
WNEP-TV, Wilkes-Barre/
  Scranton, PA
WQAD-TV, Moline, IL

Information Services
The New York Times Syndication Sales Corp.
  The New York Times News Service (650 newspaper
    and magazine customers)
  Special Features (supplemental news and information)
  TimesFax (fax-, satellite-, and PC-delivered *Times*
    summary)
NYT Business Information Services
  The New York Times Index
  New York Times on Dow Jones News/Retrieval and
    LEXIS/NEXIS
NYT New Media/New Products
  @*times* on America Online
  NYT Custom Publishing (custom magazines)

Forest Products
Donohue Malbaie Inc. (49%, Canada)
Madison Paper Industries

KEY COMPETITORS

Advance   Gannett   Pearson
  Publications   Hearst   Reuters
Associated Press   Herald Media   Thomson Corp.
Bloomberg   Knight-Ridder   Time Warner
Cox Enterprises   Lagardère   Times Mirror
Daily News   Media General   Tribune
Dow Jones   Meredith Corp.   Viacom
E.W. Scripps   News Corp.   Washington Post

HOW MUCH

	Annual Growth	1985	1986	1987	1988	1989	1990	1991	1992	1993	1994
Sales ($ mil.)	6.0%	1,394	1,565	1,690	1,700	1,769	1,777	1,703	1,774	2,020	2,358
Net income ($ mil.)	7.0%	116	132	160	168	267	65	47	(11)	6	213
Income as % of sales	—	8.3%	8.4%	9.5%	9.9%	15.1%	3.6%	2.8%	—	0.3%	9.0%
Earnings per share ($)	3.9%	1.45	1.63	1.96	2.08	3.39	0.85	0.61	(0.14)	0.07	2.05
Stock price – high ($)	—	25.44	42.00	49.63	32.75	34.75	27.50	25.25	32.13	31.25	29.50
Stock price – low ($)	—	17.50	23.31	24.75	24.38	24.50	16.88	18.25	22.63	22.38	21.25
Stock price – close ($)	(1.1%)	24.50	35.50	31.00	26.88	26.50	20.63	23.63	26.38	26.25	22.13
P/E – high	—	18	26	25	16	10	32	41	—	—	14
P/E – low	—	12	14	13	12	7	20	30	—	—	10
Dividends per share ($)	8.0%	0.28	0.32	0.38	0.45	0.49	0.67	0.42	0.70	0.56	0.56
Book value per share ($)	9.0%	7.24	8.64	10.04	10.44	13.63	13.68	13.70	12.53	14.96	15.71
Employees	2.4%	10,350	10,000	10,500	10,700	10,600	10,400	10,100	10,100	13,000	12,800

1994 Year-end:
Debt ratio: 25.4%
Return on equity: 13.6%
Cash (mil.): $41
Current ratio: 0.91
Long-term debt (mil.): $523
No. of shares (mil.): 98
Dividends
  Yield: 2.5%
  Payout: 27.3%
Market value (mil.): $2,174

**Stock Price History
High/Low 1985–94**

NYNEX CORPORATION

OVERVIEW

Based in New York City, NYNEX provides local telecommunications services in New York and New England. With one of the oldest telephone networks in the US, NYNEX has been busy defending its lucrative New York City market from competitors. In preparation for the competitive future of telecommunications, NYNEX has begun improving both its cost structure, by cutting 16,800 positions through 1996, and its system, by spending $2.5 billion in 1994 on capital improvements.

NYNEX also is combining its cellular telephone operations with those of Bell Atlantic. Due to its smaller customer base, NYNEX will own approximately 38% of the combined business. The NYNEX-Bell Atlantic partnership also has joined forces with U S WEST and AirTouch Communications (formerly the cellular operations of Pacific Telesis), to develop

a national brand and marketing strategy for their cellular operations. The foursome has successfully acquired licenses to offer personal communications services in 11 markets.

NYNEX also has been developing ways of obtaining the content as well as the means of delivering entertainment and information services to its customers. Along with Bell Alantic and Pacific Telesis, NYNEX has formed a new media company with the assistance of Creative Artists Agency to purchase and develop the content for its network. In addition, NYNEX and Bell Atlantic are investing $100 million in CAI Wireless Systems, a wireless cable provider in Albany, Buffalo, New York City, Rochester, Syracuse, NY; Boston, MA; Hartford, CT; Norfolk, VA; and Providence, RI. NYNEX has chosen Ivan Seidenberg as its new chairman, president, and CEO.

WHEN

NYNEX's 2 telephone divisions, New York Telephone and New England Telephone and Telegraph, began as arms of AT&T. New York Telephone was incorporated in 1896 and grew out of 2 small, independent telephone companies, Metropolitan Telephone & Telegraph and Westchester Telephone. Gardiner Hubbard, Alexander Bell's father-in-law, formed New England Telephone Company in 1878 with a plan to offer switching hardware. Half interest was later sold to a group that included Colonel William Forbes, who merged New England Telephone into the Bell system.

In 1984 the Bell companies were split from AT&T as part of the AT&T antitrust suit settlement, and NYNEX became a separate operating entity. At the time, NYNEX received 1/7 of Bell Communications Research (Bellcore) and cellular rights for its telephone territory.

In 1986 NYNEX purchased IBM's computer retailing operations. It then invested in financial services software, buying Business Intelligence Services (1987) and AGS Computers (1988). NYNEX tried to enter the international long distance market between 1986 and 1988 but failed to receive the necessary approvals.

NYNEX has suffered a number of setbacks since its formation. Over 60,000 laborers went on strike in 1989, and NYNEX Materiel Enterprises came in for regulatory scrutiny in 1990. While a Massachusetts audit found no improprieties, an FCC inquiry led to $35.5 million being paid in customer rebates and $1.4 million being paid to the government. NYNEX Materiel and NYNEX Service merged in late

1990, forming Telesector Resources. NYNEX sold its 77 computer stores in 1991.

In 1992 NYNEX bought an interest in TelecomAsia, which is expanding Bangkok's telephone network by 2 million lines. NYNEX joined with Dow Jones that year to form a model to provide programming and information services over NYNEX's telephone system.

In 1993 NYNEX and the leading European electronics company (Philips) formed a joint venture to develop information services for residential use on visual display telephones. In 1993 and 1994 NYNEX sold its UK software unit, BIS Group, and AGS Computers, Inc. Also in those years, NYNEX invested heavily in NYNEX CableComms, which is building a telecommunications and cable network in the United Kingdom.

In 1993 NYNEX bought $1.2 billion of Viacom preferred stock in support of Viacom's successful battle to buy Paramount Communications. In 1994 NYNEX and Times Mirror formed a joint venture to offer electronic shopping services in New York City by combining the company's directory listings and the newspaper group's advertising and news services. In the same year NYNEX changed the names of its New England Telephone and New York Telephone companies to NYNEX.

In 1995 NYNEX established a joint venture with Reliance Industries to acquire licenses for basic and cellular telephone services in India. The company also made its Yellow Pages accessible over the Internet to 7500 universities and public libraries in the US.

NYSE symbol: NYN
Fiscal year ends: December 31

Chairman, President, and CEO: Ivan G. Seidenberg, age 48, $729,000 pay (prior to promotion)
VC Finance and Business Development: Frederic V. Salerno, age 51, $769,000 pay
EVP, General Counsel and Secretary: Raymond F. Burke, age 61, $609,000 pay
EVP and CFO: Alan Z. Senter, age 53
EVP and General Counsel: Morrison DeS. Webb, age 47
President and Group Executive - NYNEX Telecommunications: Richard A. Jalkut, age 50
President and Group Executive - NYNEX Worldwide Services Group: Richard W. Blackburn, age 52
President and Group Executive - NYNEX External Affairs and Corporate Communications: Donald B. Reed, age 50
EVP and Group Executive - Network Services: Arnold J. Eckelman, age 51
VP Human Resources: Donald J. Sacco, age 53, $445,300 pay
Auditors: Coopers & Lybrand L.L.P.

WHERE

HQ: 1095 Avenue of the Americas, New York, NY 10036
Phone: 212-395-2121
Fax: 212-921-2684 (Investor Relations)

NYNEX offers telecommunications services in Connecticut, Maine, Massachusetts, New Hampshire, New York, Rhode Island, and Vermont. Cellular service is provided throughout the northeastern US. Major international operations and investments are located in the Czech Republic, Gibraltar, Greece, Indonesia, Japan, Poland, Slovakia, Thailand, and the UK.

WHAT

	1994 Sales		1994 Operating Income	
	$ mil.	% of total	$ mil.	% of total
Telecommunications	11,511	86	1,875	91
Publishing	894	7	66	3
Cellular	720	5	51	3
Financial services	89	1	69	3
Other	93	1	(135)	—
Adjustments	—	—	(170)	—
Total	**13,307**	**100**	**1,756**	**100**

Major Subsidiaries

Telecommunications
Bell Communications Research, Inc. (1/7)
NYNEX New England Telephone
NYNEX New York Telephone
NYNEX Science & Technology, Inc.
Telesector Resources Group, Inc.

Publishing
NYNEX Information Resources Co.

Cellular
NYNEX Mobile Communications Co.

Financial Services
NYNEX Capital Funding Co.
NYNEX Credit Co.
NYNEX Trade Finance Co.

Other Diversified Operations
NYNEX CableComms Ltd.
NYNEX Network Systems Co.

KEY COMPETITORS

American Business Information
Ameritech
AT&T Corp.
BellSouth
BT
Cable & Wireless
Cellular Communications, Inc.
Century Communications
Frontier Corp.
GTE
MCI
MFS Communications
Nextel
Pacific Telesis
SBC Communications
Sprint
Teleport
U.S. Long Distance
U S WEST
WorldCom

HOW MUCH

	Annual Growth	1985	1986	1987	1988	1989	1990	1991	1992	1993	1994
Sales ($ mil.)	2.9%	10,314	11,342	12,084	12,661	13,211	13,582	13,229	13,155	13,408	13,307
Net income ($ mil.)	(3.5%)	1,095	1,215	1,277	1,315	808	949	601	1,311	(272)	793
Income as % of sales	—	10.6%	10.7%	10.6%	10.4%	6.1%	7.0%	4.5%	10.0%	—	6.0%
Earnings per share ($)	(4.0%)	2.72	3.01	3.13	3.32	2.05	2.39	1.49	3.20	(0.66)	1.89
Stock price – high ($)	—	24.63	36.63	39.19	35.44	46.00	45.50	40.38	44.25	48.88	41.38
Stock price – low ($)	—	18.22	23.22	29.00	30.44	32.63	33.56	33.50	34.56	40.13	33.25
Stock price – close ($)	4.6%	24.44	32.06	32.13	33.00	45.69	35.56	40.38	41.94	40.13	36.75
P/E – high	—	9	12	13	11	22	19	27	14	—	22
P/E – low	—	7	8	9	9	16	14	23	11	—	18
Dividends per share ($)	4.6%	1.58	1.71	1.86	1.99	2.14	2.26	2.28	2.31	2.35	2.36
Book value per share ($)	1.2%	18.18	21.88	22.82	23.91	23.78	22.86	22.48	24.61	20.39	20.26
Employees	(3.4%)	89,600	90,200	95,300	97,400	95,400	93,800	83,900	82,500	76,200	65,400

1994 Year-end:
Debt ratio: 59.5%
Return on equity: 9.3%
Cash (mil.): $138
Current ratio: 0.65
Long-term debt (mil.): $7,785
No. of shares (mil.): 424
Dividends
  Yield: 6.4%
  Payout: 124.9%
Market value (mil.): $15,567

Stock Price History High/Low 1985–94

PAINE WEBBER GROUP INC.

OVERVIEW

It was a quiet wedding for Wall Street. In 1994 Paine Webber and Kidder, Peabody joined forces. The bride, Kidder, Peabody, was given away by GE and will take the groom's name. In this way Paine Webber's less-than-stellar investment banking operations will receive a boost and GE rids itself of a drag on earnings.

New York–based Paine Webber serves a varied clientele, offering retail brokerage services, investment banking, municipal securities underwriting, real estate services, institutional stock and bond trading, asset management (through its Mitchell Hutchins subsidiaries), and transaction services.

The cost of the Kidder, Peabody transaction, though a relatively modest $670 million (plus GE's acquisition of 21.6% of Paine Webber's stock), contributed to an 87% decline in earnings for 1994 (to $32 million). But the primary factor in this stunning reduction was the bond market crash and the subsequently reduced volume of bond and equity issues. The effect of the crash was so severe for one of Paine Webber's bond mutual funds (primarily because of derivatives-related losses) that the company felt forced to support the fund's value, at a cost of a $34 million charge against earnings.

WHEN

William Paine and Wallace Webber, 2 former clerks at Boston's Blackstone National Bank, opened a brokerage house in 1880. The firm joined the New York Stock Exchange in 1890 and bought seats on the Chicago Board of Trade in 1909 and the Chicago Stock Exchange in 1916.

The company opened its first branch in 1899, in Houghton, Michigan, the headquarters of copper companies that Paine Webber had helped underwrite. After WWI the company expanded rapidly during the bull market of the 1920s. The Depression forced the firm to eliminate offices.

In 1942 Paine Webber merged with another Boston brokerage house, Jackson and Curtis, formed by Charles Cabot Jackson and Laurence Curtis in 1879. Paine, Webber, Jackson & Curtis moved its offices from Boston to New York in 1963 and broadened its national scope by buying Kansas City brokerage Barret Fitch North (1967) and Richmond, Virginia–based Abbott, Proctor & Paine (no relation; 1970). The firm also launched overseas offices in London and Tokyo (1973).

Paine Webber converted from a partnership to a corporation in 1970 and went public in 1972, creating a holding company for its operations — Paine Webber Group Inc. The company added Mitchell Hutchins (equity research, 1977) and Blyth Eastman Dillon (investment banking, 1979). Blyth executives defected, taking customers with them, and Paine Webber was late bringing its new bank into play during the M&A craze of the 1980s.

Donald Marron, named CEO in 1980, continued to expand the company, buying Houston-based Rotan Mosle and First Mid America, a Nebraska company. After the 1987 stock market crash, Marron, who had begun his career running his own investment bank at age 25, aggressively restructured the company and sold operations, including the commercial paper business (1987) and its venture capital unit (1988). In late 1987 Japanese insurance company Yasuda injected capital for an equity stake that grew to 20% by 1990. A bridge loan to financially beleaguered Federated Department Stores (1988) dogged Paine Webber into 1990, when the company curtailed merchant banking and increased reserves against bad loans.

In the early 1990s the stock market bounced back with a vengeance, and Paine Webber Inc. expanded its sales force, hiring 350 new brokers in 1991.

Since the 1987 crash the company has diversified to reduce its dependence on commissions and increase the amount of money it derives from fee-producing services.

The company was hit in 1993 by the departure of key personnel from Mitchell Hutchins Institutional Investors. It suffered still more personnel problems that year when it was directed by NASD arbitrators to pay an award to 5 brokers who said they had been forced from their jobs for refusing to direct investors into inappropriate proprietary mutual funds.

The 1994 bond crash and its aftermath had a profound effect on the company's bottom line and led to layoffs of a projected 5% of its staff just months after the company had spent heavily on compensation for personnel from Kidder, Peabody, the investment banking firm it acquired in 1994.

Paine Webber has spent heavily on technology recently, introducing an in-house system in 1995 to monitor trading activities as they occur on its state-of-the-art workstation system.

WHO

Chairman and CEO: Donald B. Marron, age 60,
$2,525,000 pay
Chairman, PaineWebber International: John A. Bult,
age 58
President, PaineWebber International: Joseph J.
Grano Jr., age 47, $1,320,000 pay
EVP Administration (HR): Ronald M. Schwartz
VP, General Counsel, and Secretary: Theodore
A. Levine, age 50, $850,000 pay
VP and CFO: Regina A. Dolan, age 40, $655,000 pay
Treasurer: Pierce R. Smith, age 51
Auditors: Ernst & Young LLP

WHERE

HQ: 1285 Avenue of the Americas, New York, NY 10019
Phone: 212-713-2000
Fax: 212-713-4924

Paine Webber Group operates 295 offices in the US and
Puerto Rico, France, Hong Kong, Japan, Switzerland,
and the UK.

	1994 Offices
	No.
Southern US	75
Western US	63
Central US	59
Mid-Atlantic US	59
Northeast US	31
Outside US	8
Total	**295**

WHAT

	1994 Sales	
	$ mil.	% of total
Interest	1,695	43
Commissions	970	24
Principal transactions	519	13
Investment banking	285	7
Asset management	356	9
Other	139	4
Total	**3,964**	**100**

Selected Services
Asset management
Commodities
Corporate and government
bonds
Insurance
Investment banking
Listed securities
Mortgage securities
Municipal securities
Mutual funds
Options and futures
Research services
Retail brokerage

Selected Subsidiaries
Mitchell Hutchins Asset
Management Inc.
Mitchell Hutchins
Institutional Investors
Inc.
PaineWebber Capital Inc.
PaineWebber Incorporated
PaineWebber International
Bank Ltd.
PaineWebber International
(UK) Ltd.
PaineWebber Life Insurance
PW Trust Company

KEY COMPETITORS

A.G. Edwards
Alex. Brown
Alliance Capital
Bankers Trust
Bear Stearns
Brown Brothers
Harriman
Canadian Imperial
Charles Schwab
Chase Manhattan
Citicorp
CS Holding
Dai-Ichi Kangyo

Dean Witter,
Discover
Equitable
Fannie Mae
FMR
General Electric
Goldman Sachs
Hambrect &
Quist
J. P. Morgan
Kemper Corp.
Lehman
Brothers

Merrill Lynch
Morgan Stanley
Nomura
Securities
Prudential
Royal Bank of
Canada
Salomon
Stephens
T. Rowe Price
Transamerica
Travelers
USAA

HOW MUCH

	Annual Growth	1985	1986	1987	1988	1989	1990	1991	1992	1993	1994
Sales ($ mil.)	8.6%	1,885	2,385	2,437	2,512	2,926	2,979	3,166	3,364	4,005	3,964
Net income ($ mil.)	(0.7%)	34	72	75	42	52	(57)	151	213	246	32
Income as % of sales	—	1.8%	3.0%	3.1%	1.7%	1.8%	—	4.8%	6.3%	6.1%	0.8%
Earnings per share ($)	(4.3%)	0.61	1.09	1.00	0.26	0.47	(1.43)	1.67	2.37	2.95	0.41
Stock price – high ($)	—	15.35	17.41	17.41	8.40	10.51	9.18	16.51	17.84	23.09	19.76
Stock price – low ($)	—	8.98	11.30	5.84	6.40	6.95	5.12	4.89	10.51	14.08	12.75
Stock price – close ($)	2.1%	12.46	14.01	6.40	7.17	7.51	6.12	15.59	16.26	18.01	15.00
P/E – high	—	25	16	17	32	22	—	10	8	8	48
P/E – low	—	15	10	6	25	15	—	3	4	5	31
Dividends per share ($)	9.1%	0.21	0.21	0.29	0.23	0.23	0.23	0.23	0.29	0.36	0.46
Book value per share ($)	8.3%	7.49	9.17	10.58	11.06	11.61	10.06	16.58	13.51	15.51	15.41
Employees	4.5%	—	—	12,000	13,000	12,900	12,700	12,900	13,600	14,400	16,300

1994 Year-end:
Debt ratio: 93.5%
Return on equity: 2.3%
Cash (mil.): $629
Long-term debt (mil.): $2,315
No. of shares (mil.): 99
Dividends
Yield: 3.1%
Payout: 112.2%
Market value (mil.): $1,490
Assets (mil.): $35,856

**Stock Price History
High/Low 1985–94**

PATHMARK STORES, INC.

OVERVIEW

Grocery shoppers in the New York, New Jersey, and Philadelphia metro areas know well the path to Pathmark. The Woodbridge, New Jersey–based chain, operated by Pathmark Stores, has 143 supermarkets in the Northeast and is one of the region's most dominant grocery retailers.

Pathmark also operates pharmacies. However, the company is now limiting that business mainly to its food stores, most of which already have pharmacies. In 1995 Pathmark agreed to sell its 30 New York City–area freestanding drugstores to Rite Aid. Pathmark has 6 discount drugstores in Connecticut.

Pathmark is benefiting from the growing willingness of urbanites to shop at large grocery superstores, such as the chain's 62,000-square-foot Super Centers. The latest twist to Pathmark's Super Centers is the upscale Pathmark 2000 store format, which emphasizes produce selection and offers wider aisles, better access to information, and more in-store help. The chain expects to have 50 Pathmark 2000 stores by the end of 1995.

This upscale emphasis extends to Pathmark's 3,300-item private-label grocery program, which the company believes is one of the biggest in the nation. Pathmark has introduced its first premium private-label brand, Pathmark Preferred, to go with its established Pathmark and No Frills brands.

In 1994 Pathmark began offering free home delivery of health, beauty, and pharmacy products as well as general merchandise.

WHEN

After WWII, supermarket operators in New York and New Jersey banded together to form a cooperative to combat chain grocers, and the Wakefern Cooperative was born. Members enjoyed enhanced buying power and, with some stores sharing the name Shop-Rite, extended advertising reach.

Three participants in the cooperative — Alex Aidekman, Herbert Brody, and Milton Perlmutter — combined in a smaller group to form Supermarkets Operating Company in 1956. Supermarkets Operating's stores continued to use the Shop-Rite name and the Wakefern Cooperative's services.

In 1966 Supermarkets Operating merged with General Super Markets to become Supermarkets General Corporation.

Supermarkets General left Wakefern in 1968 and renamed its stores Pathmark. The company branched into small-town department stores with the purchase of Genung's, which operated chains under the names Steinbach (New Jersey) and Howland (New York and New England). In 1969 the company added to its department store holdings with the purchase of Baltimore retailer Hochschild, Kohn & Co. and entered the home improvement market by purchasing the 6-store Rickel chain. The company grew steadily in the 1970s, pioneering large supermarket and grocery/drug combinations in densely populated areas of New York, New Jersey, and Connecticut. The company's aggressive discounting and experimentation gained it a reputation as one of the US's best-run supermarket chains.

Value House, a catalog showroom that grew to 20 locations, was sold in 1978. In 1983 Leonard Lieberman became CEO. Supermarkets General acquired Boston's Purity Supreme, operator of Purity Supreme and Heartland grocery stores and Li'l Peach convenience stores, for $80 million (1984; sold 1991). In 1985 the company opened superstores, under both the Pathmark and Purity Supreme names, which offered a great variety of merchandise. The company boosted its New England market share when it bought Angelo's Supermarkets in 1986. Also that year it sold its department store operations, and Aidekman stepped down as chairman.

Supermarkets General's expansion slowed when the Haft family's Dart Group made a $1.62 billion raid on the company in 1987. Merrill Lynch Capital Partners stepped in with an LBO, retaining control of Supermarkets General after the company was taken private. In 1989 CEO Kenneth Peskin, who had replaced Lieberman, resigned, and Jack Futterman took his place.

In 1991 the company sold its Purity Operations to Freeman Spogli & Co. for about $265 million, retaining a 10% interest in Purity.

Pathmark Stores, Inc., became the successor company to Supermarkets General in 1993, but a plan to go public was shelved when executives did not believe shares would garner a worthy price. Instead, the company was recapitalized, with ownership of Pathmark transferred to a newly formed holding company, Newco, and the Rickel Home Center chain spun off to a new entity, Plainbridge, Inc.

In 1995 president and CFO Anthony Cuti said he expected the supermarket chain to go public soon.

Private company
Fiscal year ends: Saturday nearest January 31

WHO

Chairman and CEO: Jack Futterman, age 61,
$583,473 pay
President and CFO: Anthony J. Cuti, age 49,
$364,266 pay
EVP Marketing: Neill Crowley, age 52
EVP and CFO: Ron Marshall, age 41
SVP Merchandising: Ronald Rallo, age 57, $221,526 pay
SVP Operations: Robert Joyce, age 49, $199,183 pay
SVP Retail Development: Harvey M. Gutman, age 49,
$189,801 pay
VP and Controller: Joseph W. Adelhardt, age 48
VP, General Counsel, and Secretary: Marc A. Strassler,
age 46
VP and General Counsel, Real Estate: Myron D.
Waxberg, age 61
VP Human Resources: Maureen McGurl, age 47
Auditors: Deloitte & Touche LLP

WHERE

HQ: 301 Blair Rd., PO Box 5301, Woodbridge, NJ
07095-0915
Phone: 908-499-3000
Fax: 908-499-3072

The company operates 143 Pathmark supermarkets in
Connecticut, Delaware, New Jersey, New York, and
Pennsylvania and 6 deep-discount drugstores in
Connecticut. The company also has distribution or
processing facilities in the New Jersey cities of Avenel,
Dayton, Edison, Somerset, and Woodbridge.

WHAT

	1995 Sales	
	$ mil.	% of total
Supermarkets	4,006	96
Other	176	4
Total	**4,182**	**100**

Supermarkets and Drugstores
Deep-discount drugstores (6)
Supermarkets (143)
    Super Centers (108)
    Pathmark 2000 (29)
    Conventional supermarkets (6)

Distribution Facilities
Dry grocery (Woodbridge, NJ)
Frozen food (Dayton, NJ)
General merchandise (health and beauty care products,
    pharmaceuticals, tobacco; Edison, NJ)
Meat, dairy, deli, produce (Woodbridge, NJ)

Processing Facilities
Banana ripening (Avenel, NJ)
Delicatessen products (Somerset, NJ)

Private-Label Brands
No Frills
Pathmark
Pathmark Preferred

KEY COMPETITORS

American Stores
Big V Supermarkets
Circle K
Eckerd
Fay's
Genovese Drug Stores
Giant Eagle
Golub
Grand Union
Great A&P
Inserra Supermarkets
J Sainsbury
Key Food
King Kullen Grocery
Kmart
Mayfair Supermarkets
Melville
Penn Traffic
Red Apple Group
Rite Aid
Southland
Stop & Shop
Victory Markets
Village Supermarkets
Walgreen
Wal-Mart
Wegmans Food Markets
Weis Markets

HOW MUCH

	Annual Growth	1986	1987	1988	1989	1990	1991	1992	1993	1994	1995
Sales ($ mil.)	(2.2%)	5,123	5,508	5,767	5,962	5,475	4,481	4,378	4,340	4,207	4,182
Net income ($ mil.)	(7.7%)	64	63	(66)	(59)	(74)	(18)	(197)	(623)	(132)	31
Income as % of sales	—	1.2%	1.1%	—	—	—	—	—	—	—	0.7%
Employees	(6.3%)	52,000	53,000	53,000	52,000	51,000	46,000	31,000	27,000	28,000	29,000

1995 Year-end:
Debt ratio: 100%
Return on equity: —
Cash (mil.): $7
Current ratio: 0.57
Long-term debt (mil.): $1,399

Net Income ($ mil.)
1986–95

PEPSICO, INC.

OVERVIEW

Although PepsiCo is the world's #1 fast-food chain (KFC, Taco Bell, and Pizza Hut) and the #1 chip maker (Frito-Lay), it is still #2 in the cola wars. But it is challenging Coca-Cola's lead outside the US. Over the last 3 years, the company has invested more than $2 billion in its worldwide bottling operations. Even though Coke brands have 42% of the market (to Pepsi's 32%) international markets are less saturated and offer a huge potential for growth.

In 1994 Pepsi-Cola International (PCI) formed a joint venture with Brazil's BAESA to market products in South America. The following year PCI launched Atlantis bottled water in Asia and Mexico. Other recent investments include plants in China and India. Pepsi Max, which contains an artificial sweetener not available in the US, is marketed in over 50 countries.

Pepsi is also diversifying its product line. In a joint venture with Lipton, it has won over 30% of the ready-to-drink tea market, a part of the so-called "new age" beverage segment. The company also has a pact with Ocean Spray to market fruit juices. In 1995 Pepsi began testing Mazagran, a coffee-based drink codeveloped with Starbucks.

The fast-food industry is also ripe for PepsiCo's innovations. In 1995 Pizza Hut, the top pizza chain with $4.6 billion in 1994 sales, introduced "stuffed crust" pizza and quickly began setting sales records. Pizza Hut is now set to enter India. In mid-1995 Taco Bell gave away $12 million worth of food to push its "border light" menu. KFC also began adding Taco Bell units to 50 of its restaurants.

Sales from PepsiCo's other segment, salty snack foods, jumped 7% in 1994 on the strong performance of Frito-Lay, which has 43% of its market. The chip maker is investing $225 million to develop reduced-fat snacks, including baked chips and fat-free pretzels.

WHEN

In New Bern, North Carolina, pharmacist Caleb Bradham invented Pepsi in 1898. He named his new drink Pepsi-Cola (claiming it cured dyspepsia) and registered the trademark in 1903.

Following Coca-Cola's example, Bradham developed a system of bottling franchises. By WWI 300 bottlers had signed up. After the war Bradham stockpiled sugar to safeguard against rising costs. In 1920 sugar prices plunged, forcing Bradham to sell the company in 1923.

Pepsi existed on the brink of ruin under various owners for the next decade, until the Loft Candy Company bought it in 1931. The company's fortunes took a turn for the better in 1934 when, in the midst of the Depression, it doubled the size of its bottles to 12 ounces without raising the 5¢ price. In 1939 Pepsi introduced the world's first radio jingle. In 1941 Loft Candy merged with its Pepsi subsidiary and became the Pepsi-Cola Company.

Pepsi started to produce drinks in cans in 1948. Former Coca-Cola executive Alfred Steele became president 2 years later. Steele introduced the slogan "Be Sociable, Have a Pepsi" and in 1954 put his wife, actress Joan Crawford, to work as a Pepsi spokesperson.

Donald Kendall, who became president of Pepsi in 1963, persuaded Soviet premier Nikita Khrushchev to down a Pepsi for the cameras at the Moscow Trade Fair and turned Pepsi's attention to young people ("The Pepsi Generation").

In 1965 Pepsi acquired Frito-Lay and became PepsiCo. Dallas-based Frito-Lay had been created when Elmer Doolin (who had discovered Fritos at a cafe near the Mexican border in 1932) and Herman Lay (HW Lay & Company) joined efforts in 1960.

During the early 1970s Kendall broke into the Soviet market by agreeing to distribute Stolichnaya vodka in the US in exchange for Pepsi distribution in the USSR. With the purchases of Pizza Hut (1977), Taco Bell (1978), and Kentucky Fried Chicken (1986), PepsiCo became a major force in the fast-food industry.

When Coca-Cola changed its formula in 1985, Pepsi stepped up the competition with its longtime archrival, claiming victory in the cola wars. Coke and Pepsi expanded their rivalry to tea in 1991 when Pepsi formed a venture with #1 Lipton in response to Coke's announced venture with Nestlé (Nestea).

In 1993 the company successfully refuted claims that syringes had been found in Pepsi cans. After slow sales Pepsi began scaling back plans for its double drive-through Hot 'n Now burger stands in 1994. Also that year Mountain Dew, the #6 carbonated beverage, grew more than any of its competitors, topping 500 million cases sold.

Courting the interest of Generation X, in 1995 Pepsi began US testing of Pepsi XL, which has 50% sugar and 50% aspartame, a combination that supposedly masks aspartame's bitter taste while still cutting calories.

NYSE symbol: PEP
Fiscal year ends: Last Saturday in December

WHO

Chairman and CEO: D. Wayne Calloway, age 59, $2,943,269 pay
VC; Chairman, PepsiCo Worldwide Restaurants: Roger A. Enrico, age 50, $1,347,134 pay
EVP and CFO: Robert G. Dettmer, age 63, $830,163 pay
SVP, General Counsel, and Secretary: Edward V. Lahey Jr., age 56, $600,642 pay
SVP and Controller: Robert L. Carleton, age 54, $485,460 pay
SVP Personnel: William Bensyl
Chairman and CEO, Taco Bell Corp.: John E. Martin
President and CEO, PepsiCo Restaurants International: James H. O'Neal
President and CEO, Frito-Lay, Inc.: Steven S. Reinemund, age 46
President and CEO, Pepsi-Cola North America: Craig E. Weatherup, age 49
President and CEO, PepsiCo Foods and Beverages International: Christopher A. Sinclair, age 44
President and CEO, Pizza Hut Inc.: Allan S. Huston
President and CEO, Kentucky Fried Chicken Corp.: David C. Novak, age 42
Auditors: KPMG Peat Marwick LLP

WHERE

HQ: Purchase, NY 10577-1444
Phone: 914-253-2000
Fax: 914-253-2070

	1994 Sales		1994 Operating Income	
	$ mil.	% of total	$ mil.	% of total
US	20,246	71	2,706	81
Canada & Mexico	3,267	11	343	10
Europe	2,177	8	17	1
Other regions	2,782	10	258	8
Total	**28,472**	**100**	**3,324**	**100**

WHAT

	1994 Sales		1994 Operating Income	
	$ mil.	% of total	$ mil.	% of total
Restaurants	10,521	37	730	22
Beverages	9,687	34	1,217	37
Snack foods	8,264	29	1,377	41
Total	**28,472**	**100**	**3,324**	**100**

Selected Subsidiaries
Frito-Lay North America (snack foods, including Chee•tos, Doritos, Fritos, Lay's, Ruffles, and Tostitos brands)
KFC Corp. (2,250 restaurants, 100 licensed outlets, and 3,600 franchises in the US and Canada)
PepsiCo Foods International (snack food manufacturing and marketing outside the US and Canada, including Chee•tos, Doritos, Fritos, Gamesa, Ruffles, Sabritas, Sonric's, Sunchips, and Walkers Crisps brands)
Pepsi-Cola International (beverage bottling and marketing outside the US and Canada, including Pepsi-Cola, Mirinda, Pepsi Max, and 7Up brands)
Pepsi-Cola North America (beverage bottling and marketing, including Pepsi-Cola, Mountain Dew, Slice, Mug, and, in Canada, 7Up, brands)
Pizza Hut, Inc. (5,990 restaurants and other outlets and 2,650 franchises in the US and Canada)
Taco Bell Corp. (3,270 restaurants, 960 specialty outlets, and 1,500 franchises in the US and Canada)

KEY COMPETITORS

Borden	Ferolito, Vultaggio	Nestlé
Boston Chicken	Flagstar	Procter &
Cadbury Schweppes	Foodmaker	Gamble
Celestial	General Mills	Quaker Oats
Seasonings	Grand	Rally's
Checker's Drive-In	Metropolitan	Seagram
Clearly Canadian	Lance	Sonic Corp.
Coca-Cola	Little Caesars	Triarc
Dairy Queen	McDonald's	Wendy's
Domino's Pizza	Nabisco Holdings	

HOW MUCH

	Annual Growth	1985	1986	1987	1988	1989	1990	1991	1992	1993	1994
Sales ($ mil.)	15.1%	8,057	9,291	11,485	13,007	15,242	17,803	19,608	21,970	25,021	28,472
Net income ($ mil.)	14.1%	544	458	595	762	901	1,077	1,080	1,302	1,588	1,784
Income as % of sales	—	6.7%	4.9%	5.2%	5.9%	5.9%	6.0%	5.5%	5.9%	6.3%	6.3%
Earnings per share ($)	14.6%	0.65	0.58	0.76	0.97	1.13	1.35	1.35	1.61	1.96	2.22
Stock price – high ($)	—	8.36	11.86	14.07	14.53	21.94	27.88	35.63	43.38	43.63	41.13
Stock price – low ($)	—	4.51	7.32	6.83	9.99	12.57	17.98	23.50	30.50	34.50	29.25
Stock price – close ($)	18.2%	8.06	8.66	11.11	13.15	21.31	26.00	33.88	41.50	40.88	36.25
P/E – high	—	13	20	19	15	19	21	26	27	22	19
P/E – low	—	7	13	9	10	11	13	17	19	18	13
Dividends per share ($)	18.3%	0.15	0.21	0.22	0.25	0.31	0.37	0.44	0.50	0.58	0.68
Book value per share ($)	15.8%	2.32	2.63	3.21	4.02	4.91	6.22	7.03	6.70	7.94	8.68
Employees	13.6%	150,000	214,000	225,000	235,000	266,000	308,000	338,000	372,000	423,000	471,000

1994 Year-end:
Debt ratio: 58.1%
Return on equity: 27.0%
Cash (mil.): $1,488
Current ratio: 0.96
Long-term debt (mil.): $8,841
No. of shares (mil.): 790
Dividends
  Yield: 1.9%
  Payout: 30.6%
Market value (mil.): $28,634

Stock Price History High/Low 1985–94

PFIZER INC.

OVERVIEW

Pfizer's relies on its pharmaceuticals for 70% of its net sales. It concentrates on cardiovascular agents, anti-infectives, central nervous system drugs, anti-inflammatories, and diabetes treatments. Procardia XL remains a leading US heart drug, with sales of $1.2 billion in 1994. Pfizer also manufactures medical products (pumps and catheters), consumer health products (Visine), food science products (such as the bulking agent polydextrose for dietetic foods), and veterinary drugs.

In 1994 Pfizer agreed to buy Smith-Kline Beecham's animal health business for $1.45 billion in cash. The acquisition will create the largest animal drug maker, controlling about 10% of the market, and will overtake Merck.

The company continues its commitment to pharmaceutical health care products; it has a number of drugs in the late trial phases and expects to enlarge its product pipeline through a 20% increase in the 1995 research budget, to about $1.4 billion. Also in 1995 Pfizer announced investments of about $115 million in 2 small US-based biotechnology firms (Myco Pharmaceuticals and Immusol) and in 2 UK-based ones (AEA Technology and Oxford Asymmetry).

Pfizer's US pharmaceutical marketing division is organized along disease category lines to improve relations with the powerful US managed-care sector.

WHEN

Charles Pfizer and his cousin, confectioner Charles Erhart, started to manufacture chemicals in Brooklyn in 1849. Pfizer's products included camphor, citric acid (business sold in 1990), and santonin (an early antiparasitic). The company was incorporated in 1900 as Chas. Pfizer & Co. Pfizer was propelled into the modern drug business when the company was asked to mass-produce penicillin for the war effort in 1941.

After WWII Pfizer continued to make penicillin as well as streptomycin, most of which it sold to other companies. Pfizer researchers discovered Terramycin, which the company introduced in 1950. Pfizer bought the drug firm Roerig in 1953, its first major acquisition. In the early 1950s the company opened branches in Canada, Mexico, Cuba, the UK, and Belgium and began manufacturing in Europe, Japan, and South America. By the mid-1960s Pfizer had worldwide sales of over $200 million in 100 countries.

Beginning in the late 1950s, Pfizer made Salk and Sabin polio vaccines and added new pharmaceuticals, including Diabinese (antidiabetic, 1958) and Vibramycin (antibiotic, 1967). Pfizer acquired 14 other companies in the early 1960s, including makers of specialty metals, consumer products (Ben-Gay, Desitin), and cosmetics (Coty, sold in 1992). The company bought its first hospital products company, Howmedica, in 1972 and heart-valve maker Shiley in 1979.

Growth slowed during the 1970s, although sales had reached $2 billion by 1977. A new chairman, Edmund Pratt, increased R&D expenditures, which resulted in several new

drugs, including Minipress (antihypertensive, 1975), Feldene (arthritis pain reliever, 1982), and Glucotrol (antidiabetic, 1984). Licensing agreements with foreign companies allowed Pfizer to sell Procardia (for angina and hypertension, developed by Bayer in Germany) and Cefobid (antibiotic, from Japan). In the 1980s Pfizer expanded its hospital products division, buying 18 product lines or companies. It bought Plax (mouthwash) in 1988, of which it sold the international part in 1991. In 1990 Pfizer acquired the license to market the anticancer drug D-99 being developed by the Liposome Company.

In 1991 Pfizer established a joint venture with Hungarian drug company Biogal to market drugs in Europe. Suits filed over the failure of about 500 Shiley heart valves and the alleged falsification of quality-control records led Pfizer to divest Shiley in 1992. Drugs released in 1992 included the antidepressant Zoloft, the antibiotic Zithromax, and the cardiovascular agent Norvasc.

In 1993 Pfizer collaborated with 14 other leading drug makers to work on finding an AIDS cure. That year the company expanded distribution capabilities by purchasing Charwell Pharmaceuticals, an over-the-counter drug distributor in the UK, and by buying an interest in Koshin Medical Corporation, a Japanese hospital products distributor.

In 1994 Pfizer began a jointly owned managed care unit with Connecticut-based Value Health, Inc. In 1995 a team of Pfizer scientists discovered a genetic technique that may help in developing better methods to prevent Type II (adult-onset) diabetes.

NYSE symbol: PFE
Fiscal year ends: December 31

Chairman and CEO: William C. Steere Jr., age 58, $2,941,667 pay
VC: Edward C. Bessey, age 60, $1,206,000 pay
EVP; President, Hospital Products Group: Henry A. McKinnell Jr., age 52, $1,049,333 pay
EVP Research and Development: John F. Niblack, age 56, $947,000 pay
EVP; President, International Pharmaceuticals Group: Robert Neimeth, age 59, $946,500 pay
President, US Pharmaceuticals Group: Karen L. Katen, age 46
SVP Corporate Affairs, Secretary, and Corporate Counsel: C. L. Clemente
SVP and General Counsel: Paul S. Miller, age 56
CFO: David Shedlarz, age 47
VP Personnel: Bruce R. Ellig, age 58
Auditors: KPMG Peat Marwick LLP

WHERE

HQ: 235 E. 42nd St., New York, NY 10017-5755
Phone: 212-573-2323
Fax: 212-573-7851

The company's products are manufactured in 30 countries and are available in more than 140 countries.

	1994 Sales		1994 Operating Income	
	$ mil.	% of total	$ mil.	% of total
US	4,411	53	1,427	67
Europe	1,817	22	535	25
Asia	1,249	15	115	5
Canada/Latin Amer.	619	8	45	2
Africa/Mid. East	185	2	12	1
Adjustments	—	—	(45)	—
Total	**8,281**	**100**	**2,089**	**100**

WHAT

	1994 Sales		1994 Operating Income	
	$ mil.	% of total	$ mil.	% of total
Health care	6,963	84	1,977	95
Animal health	605	7	47	2
Consumer products	409	5	34	2
Food science	304	4	31	1
Total	**8,281**	**100**	**2,089**	**100**

Selected Drugs
Cardura (cardiovascular)
Cefobid (antibiotic)
Diflucan (antifungal)
Feldene (antiarthritic)
Glucotrol (antidiabetic)
Minipress (antihypertensive)
Norvasc (cardiovascular)
Procardia XL (cardiovascular)
Unasyn (antibiotic)
Zithromax (antibiotic)
Zoloft (antidepressive)

Hospital Products Group Division
American Medical Systems (penile implants)
Schneider (angioplasty devices)

Consumer Products
Barbasol (shaving creams)
Ben-Gay (analgesic cream)
Desitin (diaper rash cream)
Plax (dental rinse)
Rid (antilice products)
Visine (eye drops)

KEY COMPETITORS

Abbott Labs	Colgate-	Merck
American	Palmolive	Monsanto
Home Products	C. R. Bard	Novo Nordisk
Amgen	DuPont	Pharmacia Upjohn
Ballard Medical	Eli Lilly	Rhône-Poulenc
Bausch & Lomb	Genentech	Roche
Baxter	Gillette	St. Jude Medical
Bayer	Glaxo Wellcome	Sandoz
Becton, Dickinson	Hoechst	Schering-Plough
Biogen	Immunex	SmithKline
Bristol-Myers	Johnson &	Beecham
Squibb	Johnson	Unilever
Carter-Wallace	LVMH	U.S. Surgical
Ciba-Geigy	Medtronic	Warner-Lambert

HOW MUCH

	Annual Growth	1985	1986	1987	1988	1989	1990	1991	1992	1993	1994
Sales ($ mil.)	8.3%	4,025	4,476	4,920	5,385	5,672	6,406	6,950	7,230	7,478	8,281
Net income ($ mil.)	9.4%	580	660	690	791	681	801	722	1,094	658	1,298
Income as % of sales	—	14.4%	14.7%	14.0%	14.7%	12.0%	12.5%	10.4%	15.1%	8.8%	15.7%
Earnings per share ($)	10.4%	1.72	1.95	2.04	2.35	2.02	2.38	2.13	3.25	2.05	4.19
Stock price – high ($)	—	28.13	36.44	38.50	30.13	37.88	40.88	86.13	87.00	75.63	79.38
Stock price – low ($)	—	18.81	23.13	20.63	23.69	27.00	27.25	36.75	65.13	52.50	53.13
Stock price – close ($)	13.2%	25.31	30.50	23.31	29.00	34.75	40.38	84.00	72.50	69.00	77.25
P/E – high	—	16	19	19	13	19	17	40	27	37	19
P/E – low	—	11	12	10	10	13	11	17	20	26	13
Dividends per share ($)	10.9%	0.74	0.82	0.90	1.00	1.00	1.10	1.20	1.32	1.48	1.88
Book value per share ($)	4.9%	8.93	10.35	11.80	13.00	13.72	15.42	15.25	14.51	12.04	13.76
Employees	0.4%	39,200	40,000	40,700	40,900	42,100	42,500	44,100	40,700	40,500	40,800

1994 Year-end:
Debt ratio: 39.5%
Return on equity: 31.7%
Cash (mil.): $2,019
Current ratio: 1.20
Long-term debt (mil.): $604
No. of shares (mil.): 314
Dividends
  Yield: 2.4%
  Payout: 44.9%
Market value (mil.): $24,274

Stock Price History High/Low 1985–94

PHILIP MORRIS COMPANIES INC.

OVERVIEW

There's a new Marlboro Man in town: Geoff Bible, a smoker and drinker recently named CEO of Philip Morris. Bible has already made heroic strides to revive the sagging tobacco-and-food giant. Now he's standing tall against forces attacking the tobacco industry.

In addition to top tobacco brands, Philip Morris owns Kraft Foods, the US's #2 food business (after ConAgra), and Miller Brewing, the world's #3 beer producer (after Anheuser-Busch and Heineken). Its Philip Morris Capital Corp. subsidiary is involved in financial services and real estate investment.

After several years of slowing growth, in early 1995 Philip Morris started streamlining its North American food business. It merged Kraft and General Foods to form Kraft Foods. It has also been cutting noncore subsidiaries, selling Kraft's bakery business (which included the Entenmann's and Oroweat brands) to food giant CPC and Kraft Foodservice to buyout firm Clayton, Dubilier & Rice.

Bible is fighting to redeem the company's tobacco products. Suits filed by Philip Morris challenge the EPA's findings regarding secondhand smoke and challenge Florida's and San Francisco's antismoking regulations. Meanwhile, a 1995 recall of more than 7 billion cigarettes contaminated with an irritant cost the company $100 million.

WHEN

Philip Morris opened a London tobacco store in 1847; by 1854 he was making his own cigarettes. When Morris died in 1873, the company passed to his brother and widow, who sold it to William Thomson just before the turn of the century. In 1902 Thomson introduced his company's cigarettes to the US. American investors purchased the rights to the Philip Morris Cambridge, Oxford Blues, English Ovals, Marlboro, and Players brands in 1919 and 10 years later began manufacturing cigarettes in Richmond, Virginia.

When the original members of the old Tobacco Trust (broken up by the federal government in 1911) raised their prices in 1930, Philip Morris countered by introducing inexpensive cigarettes popular with Depression-weary consumers. A popular ad campaign in 1933 featured bellhop Johnny Roventini chanting the slogan "Call for Philip Morris."

Philip Morris acquired Benson & Hedges and its president, Joseph Cullman III, in 1954. Cullman, assigned to market the filtered Marlboro brand, enlisted the help of advertiser Leo Burnett, who created a simple red-and-white box and the hugely successful Marlboro Man. In 1968 the company introduced Virginia Slims, a cigarette targeted at women. Under Cullman, Philip Morris experienced tremendous overseas expansion.

In 1970 Philip Morris purchased Miller Brewing Company (formed in 1855 by Frederic Miller) and with aggressive marketing vaulted it from the #7 world position in beer to the #2 position by 1980.

Philip Morris paid $5.6 billion in 1985 for food and coffee giant General Foods. General Foods traces its roots back to acquisitions made by C.W. Post's cereal company, including Jell-O (1925) and Maxwell House Coffee (1928). The Post company then acquired the General Foods Company from frozen foods pioneer Clarence Birdseye, and changed its own name to General Foods, in 1929.

In 1988 Philip Morris spent $12.9 billion to purchase Kraft, which had been created in 1930 when Thomas McInnerney's National Dairy Products bought Kraft-Phenix (formed in 1903 by cheese wholesaler James Kraft). In 1991 chairman Hamish Maxwell retired, and Kraft executive Michael Miles became the first nontobacco man to fill the post.

In 1993 the company acquired RJR Nabisco's North American cold cereal operation for $448 million, chocolatier Terry's Group from the UK's United Biscuits Holdings for $295 million, Scandinavian candy maker Freia Marabou for $1.3 billion, and a 20% interest in Molson (Canada's largest brewer) and 100% of Molson Breweries USA for $320 million. That same year it sold Bird's Eye frozen foods to Dean Foods for $140 million.

Also in 1993 Philip Morris cut the price on Marlboro cigarettes to fend off low-priced competitors. The 40¢-per-pack price cut resulted in a 46% drop in domestic tobacco profits but boosted market share for Marlboro and other Philip Morris brands in the US. The profit decline in domestic tobacco was partially offset by stronger 1993 earnings on food, beer, and international cigarette sales.

Amid price pressures and political attacks, CEO Michael Miles suddenly stepped down in mid-1994, shortly after the board rejected a proposal to split Philip Morris into separate tobacco and food companies.

NYSE symbol: MO
Fiscal year ends: December 31

WHO

Chairman and CEO: Geoffrey C. Bible, age 57, $1,875,000 pay
EVP Worldwide Foods: James M. Kilts, age 47, $1,178,077 pay
EVP and CFO: Hans G. Storr, age 63, $1,200,000 pay
SVP Human Resources and Administration: Lawrence A. Gates, age 57
Auditors: Coopers & Lybrand L.L.P.

WHERE

HQ: 120 Park Ave., New York, NY 10017
Phone: 212-880-5000
Fax: 212-878-2167

	1994 Sales $ mil.	1994 Sales % of total	1994 Operating Income $ mil.	1994 Operating Income % of total
US	35,936	55	7,306	74
Europe	19,888	31	1,914	19
Other regions	9,301	14	671	7
Adjustments	—	—	(442)	—
Total	**65,125**	**100**	**9,449**	**100**

WHAT

	1994 Sales $ mil.	1994 Sales % of total	1994 Operating Income $ mil.	1994 Operating Income % of total
Food	31,669	48	3,108	32
Tobacco	28,671	44	6,162	62
Beer	4,297	7	413	4
Finance/real estate	488	1	208	2
Adjustments	—	—	(442)	—
Total	**65,125**	**100**	**9,449**	**100**

Selected Brands

Kraft Foods
Breakstone's
Bull's-Eye
Cheez Whiz
Chiffon
Claussen
Cool Whip
Country Time
Cracker Barrel
DiGiorno
Freihofer's
Jell-O
Knudsen
Lender's
Log Cabin
Louis Rich
Lunchables
Maxim
Maxwell House
Minute
Miracle Whip
Oscar Mayer
Parkay
Philadelphia Brand

Post
Sanka
Seven Seas
Shake 'N Bake
Tombstone
Velveeta
Yuban

Kraft Foods International
Callard & Bowser
Côte d'Or
Daim
Dairylea
El Caserío
Estrella
Freia
Frisco
Hollywood
Kibon
Marabou
Milka
Mirácoli
Q-Refres-Ko
Suchard

Terry's of York
Tobler
Toblerone
Vegemite

Miller Brewing
Löwenbräu
Meister Bräu
Miller
Milwaukee's Best
Molson
Red Dog
Sharp's

Philip Morris
Alpine
Basic
Benson & Hedges
Bristol
Cambridge
Chesterfield
Marlboro
Merit
Parliament
Players
Virginia Slims

KEY COMPETITORS

Adolph Coors
Allied Domecq
American Brands
Anchor Brewing
Anheuser-Busch
Bass
B.A.T
Ben & Jerry's
Boston Beer
Cadbury Schweppes
Carlsberg
Clorox
Coca-Cola

CPC
Danone
Foster's Brewing
George Weston
Grand Metropolitan
Guinness
Heileman
Heineken
Heinz
Hershey
Hormel
Imasco
Interbrew
John Labatt

Kellogg
Kirin
Loews
Mars
Nestlé
Procter & Gamble
Quaker Oats
RJR Nabisco
S&P
Sara Lee
Stroh
Unilever

HOW MUCH

	Annual Growth	1985	1986	1987	1988	1989	1990	1991	1992	1993	1994
Sales ($ mil.)	16.9%	15,964	25,409	27,695	31,742	44,759	51,169	56,458	59,131	60,901	65,125
Net income ($ mil.)	15.9%	1,255	1,478	1,842	2,337	2,946	3,540	3,972	4,939	3,568	4,725
Inc ... e as % of sales	—	7.9%	5.8%	6.7%	7.4%	6.6%	6.9%	7.0%	8.4%	5.9%	7.3%
Earnings per share ($)	17.2%	1.31	1.55	1.94	2.51	3.18	3.83	4.24	5.45	4.06	5.45
Stock price – high ($)	—	11.91	19.50	31.13	25.50	45.50	52.00	81.75	86.63	77.63	64.50
Stock price – low ($)	—	9.00	11.00	17.25	20.13	25.00	36.00	41.75	69.50	45.00	47.25
Stock price – close ($)	20.1%	11.06	17.97	21.34	25.47	41.63	51.75	80.25	77.13	55.63	57.50
P/E – high	—	9	13	16	10	14	14	19	16	19	12
P/E – low	—	7	7	9	8	8	9	10	13	11	9
Dividends per share ($)	22.1%	0.48	0.56	0.75	0.96	1.19	1.46	1.82	2.23	2.60	2.86
Book value per share ($)	13.1%	4.96	5.94	7.21	8.31	10.31	12.90	13.60	14.07	13.26	14.99
Employees	4.2%	114,000	111,000	113,000	155,000	157,000	168,000	166,000	161,000	173,000	165,000

1994 Year-end:
Debt ratio: 56.3%
Return on equity: 38.7%
Cash (mil.): $184
Current ratio: 1.07
Long-term debt (mil.): $14,975
No. of shares (mil.): 853
Dividends
　Yield: 5.0%
　Payout: 52.5%
Market value (mil.): $49,039

Stock Price History High/Low 1985–94

PITNEY BOWES INC.

OVERVIEW

Based in Stamford, Connecticut, Pitney Bowes is the world's #1 producer of mailing equipment and postage meters. The company is restructuring its operations to focus on its core business of mailing systems and office products. As part of this program, in 1995 Pitney Bowes sold its Dictaphone Corp. (voice processing systems) to Stonington Partners, a New York investment group, for $450 million. The company is also selling its Monarch Marking Systems subsidiary (bar code equipment) and reorganizing its German operations.

Pitney Bowes is trimming costs by eliminating about 2,000 nontechnical positions and adding around 850 skilled employees to serve its new software-driven equipment and systems. These new products were developed through Pitney Bowes's own research and joint ventures with partners such as IBM. Although businesses are increasingly using electronic mail, business-to-consumer correspondence is still delivered via the traditional mail channels. As a result, Pitney Bowes is pursuing opportunities as a contractor of outsourced mailroom services.

Pitney Bowes is planning for the eventual retirement of George Harvey, the company's chairman, president, and CEO. The company named Michael Critelli and Marc Breslawsky as vice-chairmen in 1994. They will eventually assume the roles of chairman and CEO, and president and COO, respectively.

WHEN

In 1912 English-born Walter Bowes, an addressing machine salesman, obtained control of the Universal Stamping Machine Company (Stamford, Connecticut), which became a major producer of post office stamp canceling machines. In 1920 Bowes formed a partnership with Arthur Pitney, who had been developing a postage metering machine for 14 years. In 1921 Pitney received his final patent, congressional legislation authorizing the use of his invention was passed, and the Pitney-Bowes Postage Meter Company began leasing its new machines to customers.

In 1929 Pitney-Bowes expanded to overseas markets, and by 1932 revenues totaled almost $1.5 million. In 1945 the company adopted its current name. It continued to grow in the postage meter and letter handling business throughout the 1940s and 1950s.

In the 1960s, with a focus on accelerated growth and diversification, Pitney Bowes began marketing a new line of internally produced copiers (1967) and bought Monarch Marking Systems (price marking and inventory control products, 1968) and Malco Plastics (credit and ID cards, 1968). The company wrote off its 4-year joint venture with Alpex (point-of-sale terminals) in 1973, resulting in its first loss in 54 years. In 1979 Pitney Bowes bought Dictaphone Corporation, including subsidiaries Data Documents (computer supplies) and Grayarc (office supplies), for $124 million. In 1981 it consolidated Grayarc with the Drawing Board (office supply catalog, 1980) to form the Wheeler Group, a direct-mail marketer of office supplies.

To support the financing needs of its US customers, Pitney Bowes set up a leasing organization, Pitney Bowes Financial Services (PBFS), in 1977. As Pitney Bowes grew, so did PBFS, extending its coverage to Canada, the UK, Australia, France, and Germany. PBFS broke even in its 2nd year of business and has increased its profits every year since.

In 1982 Pitney Bowes began designing, marketing, and selling high-end, sophisticated facsimile machines to corporate customers. By 1991 its sales force and extensive support network had brought the company approximately 45% of the large corporate market for fax machines. The machines are serviced by Pitney Bowes's Facsimile Systems' National Diagnostic Centers, which handle most customer problems via telephone.

Pitney Bowes stopped remanufacturing old copiers in 1990 and started selling new, higher-margin copiers (such as its 9000 series, introduced in 1991) to larger businesses. The same year it decided to sell the Wheeler Group, completing the sale in 1992.

New products for 1991 included automated freight management software programs, address and mail list management software, and a medical records transcription network. In 1993 Pitney Bowes's contribution to US postal history was featured in the new National Postal Museum in Washington, DC.

In 1994 the company's successful Paragon mailing system was introduced in Germany, the world's 2nd largest postage meter market. In addition, Pitney Bowes signed an agreement with the Chinese Ministry of Telecommunications and Posts and the Mexican Post Office to assist in the modernization of their postal systems. In 1995 Pitney Bowes opened sales and service offices in France and Spain.

NYSE symbol: PBI
Fiscal year ends: December 31

WHO

Chairman, President, and CEO: George B. Harvey,
  age 63, $1,390,417 pay
VC: Marc C. Breslawsky, age 52, $888,825 pay
VC: Michael J. Critelli, age 46, $632,610 pay
President and CEO, Pitney Bowes Business Services:
  Carole F. St. Mark, age 52, $667,317 pay
VP Finance and Administration and Treasurer:
  Carmine F. Adimando, age 50, $593,850 pay
VP Controller: Steven J. Green, age 43
**VP Communications and Planning, Secretary, and
  General Counsel:** Douglas A. Riggs, age 50
VP Personnel: Johnna G. Torsone, age 44
Auditors: Price Waterhouse LLP

WHERE

HQ: One Elmcroft Rd., Stamford, CT 06926-0700
Phone: 203-356-5000
Fax: 203-351-6303 (Public Relations)

Pitney Bowes products are sold worldwide. The company
has manufacturing facilities in Connecticut and the UK.

	1994 Sales		1994 Operating Income	
	$ mil.	% of total	$ mil.	% of total
US	2,851	84	655	97
Europe	293	9	(13)	—
Other countries	231	7	19	3
Adjustments	(104)	—	(9)	—
Total	**3,271**	**100**	**652**	**100**

WHAT

	1994 Sales		1994 Operating Income	
	$ mil.	% of total	$ mil.	% of total
Business equip. & services	2,586	79	425	65
Financial services	685	21	227	35
Total	**3,271**	**100**	**652**	**100**

Business Equipment and Services
Copier systems (SmartTouch, Value Added Maintenance
  System [VAMS] 2)
Facsimile systems (PrintScan software for Model 9720)
Mailing systems (Addressright, Business Basics, E530
  and E540, PARAGON, Postage by Phone)
Management services (image-based litigation support,
  records management, document services)
Production mail systems (SPECTRUM and 7 and 8 Series
  inserting systems)
Shipping and weighing systems (ARRIVAL, SEND-IT,
  STAR 460/470)

Financial Services
Pitney Bowes financial services (lease financing
  programs for Pitney Bowes and other products)

KEY COMPETITORS

Alcatel Alsthom	Matsushita
AM International	Merrill Corp.
Bell & Howell	3M
Brother	Minolta
Canon	Moore Products
Copifax	NEC
Eastman Kodak	Oki
Fuji Photo	Olivetti
GEC	Sharp
Harris Corp.	Smith Corona
Hewlett-Packard	Varitronic
Hitachi	Xerox
IBM	

HOW MUCH

	Annual Growth	1985	1986	1987	1988	1989	1990	1991	1992	1993	1994
Sales ($ mil.)	6.7%	1,832	1,987	2,251	2,650	2,876	3,196	3,333	3,434	3,543	3,271
Net income ($ mil.)	11.3%	150	168	199	243	187	213	295	315	353	394
Income as % of sales	—	8.2%	8.5%	8.9%	9.2%	6.5%	6.7%	8.9%	9.2%	10.0%	12.0%
Earnings per share ($)	11.2%	0.96	1.06	1.27	1.54	1.19	1.34	1.85	1.98	2.22	2.50
Stock price – high ($)	—	12.47	19.13	25.13	23.75	27.38	26.75	32.75	41.00	44.50	46.38
Stock price – low ($)	—	8.41	11.38	14.81	16.88	20.44	13.50	19.00	28.00	36.25	29.25
Stock price – close ($)	11.3%	12.13	18.31	19.13	21.38	23.75	19.88	31.56	39.88	41.38	31.75
P/E – high	—	13	18	20	15	23	20	18	21	20	19
P/E – low	—	9	11	12	11	17	10	10	14	16	12
Dividends per share ($)	14.8%	0.30	0.33	0.38	0.46	0.52	0.60	0.68	0.78	0.90	1.04
Book value per share ($)	9.3%	5.17	4.83	6.48	8.09	9.07	9.93	11.31	10.50	11.81	11.52
Employees	1.4%	28,995	29,166	29,460	29,316	31,404	29,942	29,421	28,958	32,539	32,792

1994 Year-end:
Debt ratio: 66.1%
Return on equity: 21.8%
Cash (mil.): $76
Current ratio: 0.52
Long-term debt (mil.): $779
No. of shares (mil.): 151
Dividends
  Yield: 3.3%
  Payout: 41.6%
Market value (mil.): $4,803

**Stock Price History
High/Low 1985–94**

PORT AUTHORITY OF NY AND NJ

OVERVIEW

The Port Authority of New York and New Jersey is trying to bridge some turbulent waters. The New York City–based, bistate agency operates and maintains tunnels, bridges, airports, a commuter rail system, shipping terminals, and other facilities within the Port District, an area centered around the Statue of Liberty and comprised of 17 counties in New York and New Jersey. The governors of the 2 states each appoint 6 of the 12 members of the Board of Commissioners. The board's decisions are reviewed by both governors.

The Port Authority has been under attack from its bosses (the governors) for inefficiency — anathema in an era of governmental belt tightening. So executive director George Marlin has cut operating costs to preserve an ambitious, multibillion-dollar capital program intended to transport the authority into the 21st century. Marlin is also shaking its foundations by restructuring the organization while returning it to its original mission: facilitating the movement of people and goods.

The agency's facilities include such international symbols of transportation and commerce as the George Washington Bridge, the Holland Tunnel, John F. Kennedy International Airport, the New York-New Jersey port, and the World Trade Center.

The Port Authority's revenue is derived from user fees. Marlin succeeded in closing a $100 million deficit for 1996 through budget cuts and the largest layoffs in the agency's history. A privatization proponent, Marlin sold the World Trade Center's Vista Hotel to Host Marriott for $141.5 million and is studying the prospect of selling other Port Authority properties to maximize their profitability.

WHEN

New York and New Jersey spent much of the 19th century fighting over their common waterways. While the Treaty of 1834 settled a boundary dispute along the Hudson River and in New York Harbor, the states' efforts to tax each other's interstate goods and their competing port facilities created constant conflict.

At the close of WWI the 2 states formed a commission to study better ways of administering the port. In 1921 the treaty creating a single, bistate agency (the Port of New York Authority) was ratified by the New York and New Jersey state legislatures (over the protests of the New Jersey governor).

The agency struggled at first, although its early projects, such as the Goethals Bridge (1928, linking Staten Island to New Jersey), were far from timid. It merged with the Holland Tunnel Commission in 1930, bringing a steady source of revenue. In 1931 the George Washington Bridge (spanning the Hudson River from Manhattan to New Jersey) was completed. The Lincoln Tunnel (also linking Manhattan to New Jersey) opened in 1937.

After WWII, the Port Authority broadened its focus to include commercial aviation. In 1947 the agency took over La Guardia Airport. The following year it dedicated the New York International Airport at Idlewild, Queens.

As trucking supplanted railroads in the late 1950s, the Port Authority began experimenting with a more efficient means of transferring cargo. In 1962 it built the first containerport in the world, at its Elizabeth, New Jersey, terminal. That same year the agency acquired a commuter rail line, which became the Port Authority Trans-Hudson Corporation (PATH), connecting Newark, New Jersey, and nearby suburbs to Manhattan. In December 1963 New York International was renamed the John F. Kennedy International Airport.

In the early1970s the Port Authority completed the World Trade Center (including the world's 2 tallest buildings at the time). In 1972 the agency changed its name to the Port Authority of New York and New Jersey, reflecting its role in mass transit between the 2 states.

By the mid-1980s the Port Authority was raking it in. As part of its regional development program, it bought a fleet of buses for mass transit use in suburban New Jersey and New York. However, it also invested in several industrial parks that lost millions. Critics frequently accused the Port Authority of being little more than a giant pork barrel from which the state governors doled out wasteful construction projects. By the 1990s recession, its heavy spending caught up with it.

Executive director Stanley Brezenoff began to cut costs by 1993. That same year terrorists detonated a truck bomb in the World Trade Center, killing 6 and injuring over 1,000. By 1994 the Port Authority had largely recovered: it spent more than $300 million (much of it from insurance) for renovations, and its occupancy rate was higher than in 1993.

In early 1995 George Marlin became executive director. That same year the authority began testing a monorail connecting Newark International Airport's 3 passenger terminals.

Interstate agency
Fiscal year ends: December 31

Chairperson: Lewis M. Eisenberg
VC: Charles A. Gargans
Executive Director: George J. Marlin
Deputy Executive Director: John J. Haley Jr.
Chief Technical Officer: Karen Antion
Chief Administrative Officer: Paul Blanco
Chief Operations Officer: John J. Collura
Acting CFO: Charles M. McClafferty
Acting Director Corporate Policy and Planning: Cruz C. Russell
Acting Director Interstate Transportation: Ernesto Butcher
Acting Director PATH: Michael A. Scott
Director Port Commerce: Lillian C. Borrone
Director World Trade: Charles Maikish
Director Aviation: Gerald P. Fitzgerald
Director Human Resources: Louis J. LaCapra
Auditors: Deloitte & Touche LLP

HQ: The Port Authority of New York and New Jersey, One World Trade Center, New York, NY 10048
Phone: 212-435-7000
Fax: 212-435-4660

The Port Authority's jurisdiction extends in a 25-mile radius from the Statue of Liberty and comprises 17 counties in New Jersey and New York.

	1994 Bridges and Tunnels	
	Eastbound vehicles (thou.)	% of total
George Washington Bridge	46,120	42
Staten Island bridges	27,538	25
Lincoln Tunnel	19,657	18
Holland Tunnel	15,681	15
Total	**108,996**	**100**

Selected Facilities

Aviation
John F. Kennedy International Airport (New York)
La Guardia Airport (New York)
Newark International Airport (New Jersey)
Port Authority Heliports (New York)
Teterboro Airport (New Jersey)

Interstate Transportation
Bayonne Bridge (Staten Island to Bayonne)
Ferry transportation (Manhattan to Hoboken)
George Washington Bridge (Manhattan to Ft. Lee)
Goethals Bridge (Staten Island to Elizabeth)
Holland Tunnel (Manhattan to Jersey City)
Lincoln Tunnel (Manhattan to Union City)
Outerbridge Crossing (Staten Island to Perth Amboy)
Port Authority Bus Terminal (Manhattan)
Port Authority Trans-Hudson System (PATH)

Port
New York City Passenger Ship Terminal (Manhattan)
Oak Point Rail Freight Link (Bronx)
Port Authority Marine Terminals
  Auto (Bayonne, New Jersey)
  Brooklyn/Red Hook
  Elizabeth (New Jersey)
  Greenville Yard (Jersey City)
  Port Newark (New Jersey)

Regional Development
Bathgate Industrial Park (Bronx)
Essex County Resource Recovery Facility (New Jersey, municipal waste-to-energy electric generation plant)
Industrial Park at Elizabeth (New Jersey)
New Jersey Waterfront Development
Newark Legal Center (New Jersey, office development)
The Teleport (Staten Island, business park and satellite communications center)

World Trade
World Trade Center (Manhattan)

	1994 Revenues	
	$ mil.	% of total
Air terminals		
JFK International	446	23
Newark International	297	15
La Guardia	186	9
Other	2	0
Subtotal	**931**	**47**
Interstate transportation		
G.W. Bridge & Bus Station	218	11
Lincoln Tunnel	82	4
Holland Tunnel	68	3
PATH	64	3
Other	140	7
Subtotal	**572**	**28**
World Trade Center & Vista Hotel	288	15
Marine & other	97	5
Regional development	92	5
Total	**1,980**	**100**

	Annual Growth	1985	1986	1987	1988	1989	1990	1991	1992	1993	1994
Revenues ($ mil.)	6.7%	1,101	1,170	1,331	1,437	1,527	1,691	1,857	1,934	1,921	1,980
Net income ($ mil.)	10.3%	63	39	84	74	108	31	60	144	108	153
Income as % of revenue	—	5.8%	3.3%	6.3%	5.1%	7.1%	1.8%	3.2%	7.5%	5.6%	7.7%
Employees	(1.4%)	—	—	—	10,000	9,950	9,700	9,500	9,500	9,350	9,200

1994 Year-end:
Debt ratio: 66.3%
Return on equity: 5.1%
Cash (mil.): $35
Long-term
  debt (mil.): $6,069

Revenues
($ mil.) 1985–94

PRAXAIR, INC.

OVERVIEW

Praxair is in its element when it comes to oxygen, argon, helium, nitrogen, or any of a number of industrial gases that it produces and distributes. The Danbury, Connecticut–based company is the largest supplier of industrial gases in North and South America and is the 3rd largest gas producer in the world behind the French gas giant L'Air Liquide and the British company BOC.

Formerly a unit of Union Carbide before its 1992 spin-off, Praxair produces industrial gases used in a wide range of industries, including chemicals, food processing, electronics, metal fabrication, oil and gas, petroleum refining, and printing and pulp. Praxair's surface technologies business supplies wear-resistant metallic and ceramic powders and coatings to many industries, including aircraft, paper, and petrochemicals. Praxair also sells a wide range of specialty gases and the equipment used to produce industrial gases.

In recent years the company has developed and commercialized noncryogenic technologies that make use of air separation mechanisms and membranes. These techniques produce gases at prices as much as 30% lower than the industry-standard cryogenic (extremely low temperature) processes used to separate gases. Praxair claims to lead the market in noncryogenic technologies.

The company uses 3 distribution methods. For customers with large and regular gas demand, Praxair builds gas plants on or adjacent to their factories. For medium-demand customers the company supplies gas in liquid form via tankers. Small-volume buyers are supplied with gas in cylinders.

With 54% of its 1994 sales originating outside the US, Praxair has made international sales a priority. It is building the world's largest oxygen plant for Jindal Vijayanagar Steel, a customer in the Indian state of Karnataka.

WHEN

The origins of Praxair date back to the work of Karl von Linde, a professor of mechanical engineering at the College of Technology in Munich, Germany, in the late 1800s. In 1895 he pioneered the cryogenic air liquefier. He built his first oxygen production plant in 1902 and a nitrogen plant in 1904. The scientist-cum-entrepreneur established a number of air separation plants throughout Europe in the first decade of the 20th century.

In 1907 von Linde founded Linde Air Products in Cleveland, the first US company to extract oxygen from the air using a cryogenic process. In 1911 Linde joined with rival Union Carbide (formed in 1898) to experiment in the production of acetylene. The gas had been extensively used in gas lighting until Thomas Edison's light bulb made the technology passé. Fortunately, a French researcher discovered that oxygen mixed with acetylene produced an effective metal-cutting flame. This find launched a whole new industry for the gas.

In 1917 Linde became a unit of Union Carbide. America's war effort and the subsequent economic expansion in the 1920s spurred the rapid development of new applications of industrial gases, such as for the creation of corrosion-resistant ferroalloys. Union Carbide's Linde unit also made a contribution to the development of the atomic bomb in the 1940s. Its scientists perfected a refining process for treating uranium concentrates through gaseous diffusion.

The Linde division rode the back of Union Carbide's global expansion in the 1950s and 1960s and retained its position as America's #1 producer of industrial gases. In the 1960s the growth of oxygen-fired furnaces for steel production and the increased use of nitrogen in refrigerators expanded Linde's markets.

By the early 1980s Linde accounted for 11% of Union Carbide's $9 billion in annual sales. In the 1980s competitor Air Products and Chemicals overtook Linde as the top producer of nitrogen and hydrogen. Linde made another technological breakthrough with the introduction of noncryogenic, vacuum-pressure swing adsorption (VPSA), an economical air separation technology that is expected to capture a major share of the market.

A disastrous chemical accident at Union Carbide's plant in Bhopal, India, in 1984 resulted in a $470 million settlement. This, coupled with heavy debt and falling sales, forced Union Carbide to reorganize.

In 1992 Linde was spun off to Union Carbide shareholders as the independent company Praxair. William Lichtenberger, former president of Union Carbide, headed the new company. Lichtenberger has been pushing global expansion, particularly in China, India, Indonesia, South Korea, and other growth markets. In 1994 Praxair set up China's first helium transfill plants for the magnetic resonance imaging market. In 1995 Praxair succeeded in its bid to buy rival CBI Industries.

NYSE symbol: PX
Fiscal year ends: December 31

Chairman and CEO: H. William Lichtenberger, age 59,
$1,278,360 pay
President: Edgar G. Hotard, age 51, $770,035 pay
VP and CFO: John A. Clerico, age 53, $578,796 pay
VP, General Counsel, and Secretary: David H. Chaifetz,
age 52, $372,070 pay
VP and Controller: J. Robert Vipond, age 49,
$197,098 pay
President, Praxair Asia: R. Natarajan
**VP North American Packaged Gases; President, Praxair
Canada:** Jose R. Rivero
VP North American Merchant Gases: Thomas H. Cable
VP Procurement and Materials Management: S. Kay
Phillips
VP and Treasurer: James S. Sawyer
VP Human Resources: Barbara R. Harris, age 48
Auditors: Price Waterhouse LLP

HQ: 39 Old Ridgebury Rd., Danbury, CT 06810-5113
Phone: 203-837-2000
Fax: 203-837-2454

Praxair has 131 cryogenic air separation plants in the US
and 210 such plants worldwide. The company operates
21 surface technologies plants in Denmark, France,
Germany, Italy, Japan, Singapore, Switzerland, the UK,
and the US.

	1994 Sales		1994 Operating Profit	
	$ mil.	% of total	$ mil.	% of total
US	1,242	46	206	44
South America	595	22	139	30
Europe	432	16	69	15
Other regions	442	16	49	11
Adjustments	—	—	(16)	—
Total	**2,711**	**100**	**447**	**100**

	1994 Sales by Distribution Methods
	% of total
Merchant (deliverable liquids)	39
Packaged gases (cylinders)	28
On-site (including noncryogenic)	24
Surface technologies	7
Other	2
Total	**100**

Selected Products

Equipment for the Production of Industrial Gases	Nitrogen Oxygen Specialty gases

Industrial Gases	
Acetylene	**Surface Technologies**
Argon	Ceramic coatings and powders
Helium	Metallic coatings and powders
Hydrogen	

Selected Subsidiaries

Altair Gases and Equipment, Inc. (packaged gases)
Amko Service Co. (cryogenic equipment repair)
Innovative Membrane Systems, Inc. (membrane R&D
and manufacture)
Linde de México SA de CV
Praxair Argentina SA
Praxair Canada, Inc.
Wellnite Services (partnership with Halliburton Oil Well
Services)

AGA
Air Products
and Chemicals
Airgas
BOC

Interlake
L'Air Liquide
Scott Specialty Gases
Teleflex

	Annual Growth	1985	1986	1987	1988	1989	1990	1991	1992	1993	1994
Sales ($ mil.)	6.8%	—	—	—	1,826	2,073	2,420	2,469	2,604	2,438	2,711
Net income ($ mil.)	24.7%	—	—	—	54	43	120	107	84	143	203
Income as % of sales	—	—	—	—	3.0%	2.1%	5.0%	4.3%	3.2%	5.9%	7.5%
Earnings per share ($)	20.0%	—	—	—	—	—	—	0.84	0.64	1.06	1.45
Stock price – high ($)	—	—	—	—	—	—	—	—	17.50	18.63	24.63
Stock price – low ($)	—	—	—	—	—	—	—	—	13.63	14.13	16.25
Stock price – close ($)	10.6%	—	—	—	—	—	—	—	16.75	16.63	20.50
P/E – high	—	—	—	—	—	—	—	—	27	18	17
P/E – low	—	—	—	—	—	—	—	—	21	13	11
Dividends per share ($)	—	—	—	—	—	—	—	—	0.00	0.00	0.00
Book value per share ($)	21.1%	—	—	—	—	—	—	—	4.15	4.72	6.09
Employees	0.1%	—	—	—	17,638	19,547	20,034	19,992	18,592	16,776	17,780

1994 Year-end:
Debt ratio: 60.1%
Return on equity: 27.5%
Cash (mil.): $63
Current ratio: 0.94
Long-term debt (mil.): $893
No. of shares (mil.): 138
Dividends
Yield: —
Payout: —
Market value (mil.): $2,826

Stock Price History
High/Low 1992–94

PRICE WATERHOUSE LLP

OVERVIEW

Price Waterhouse (PW) is the smallest of the Big 6 accounting firms, the best known (thanks to decades of tallying the votes for the Academy Awards), and traditionally the most prestigious. But in the 1990s the firm's luster has been tarnished by the involvement of its UK branch with the Bank of Credit & Commerce Intl. (BCCI), which failed spectacularly in 1992 amid charges of fraud and double-dealing throughout the world. The UK branch faces suits for billions of dollars in damages brought by BCCI's liquidator, Touche Ross (the UK branch of Big 6 rival Deloitte Touche Tohmatsu). Other world partners would not be liable for monetary payment in a judgment

against the UK firm, but full recovery of damages could put an important link in PW's operations out of business.

In addition to auditing, PW offers a full range of management consulting services.

In 1995 the firm embarked on a sweeping restructuring, separating the offices of US and world chairpersons, rooting out a layer of middle management, and reorganizing its practice along business lines, to ensure that auditors and consultants are specialists in the fields they work in. New areas of specialization include entertainment, media, and communications; high tech; energy; and individual product groups like food and health.

WHEN

In 1850 Samuel Lowell Price founded an accounting firm in London, and in 1865 he took on Edwin Waterhouse as a partner. The firm quickly attracted several important accounts and a group of prestigious partners that included 4 Knights of the British Empire. Aided by the explosive industrial growth in Britain and the rest of the world, Price Waterhouse expanded rapidly (as did the accounting industry as a whole) and by the late 1800s had established itself as the most renowned accounting firm in the world, providing its services in accounting, auditing, and business consulting.

By the 1890s the firm's dealings in America (where it kept tabs on the US investments of Britons) had grown sufficiently to warrant permanent representation, so Lewis Jones and William Caesar were sent to open offices in New York City and Chicago. United States Steel chose Price Waterhouse as its auditors in 1902.

Through the next several decades, PW's London office initiated tremendous expansion into other countries. By the 1930s, 57 PW offices boasting 2,500 employees operated globally. The growth of PW in New York was largely due to the Herculean efforts of partner Joseph Sterrett, and PW, along with other accounting firms, benefited from SEC audit requirements. The firm's reputation was enhanced further in 1935 when it was chosen to handle the Academy Awards balloting. Its prestige attracted several important clients, notably large oil and steel interests.

During WWII, PW recruited and trained women with college experience to fill its depleted ranks for the duration; some remained with the firm after the end of the hostilities. In

1946 the firm started a management consulting service.

While PW tried to coordinate and expand its international offices after the war, the firm lost its dominance in the 1960s. The company came to be viewed as the most traditional and formal of the major firms. PW tried to show more aggressiveness in the 1980s.

In 1989 the firm made plans to merge with Arthur Andersen, but the 2 managements were unable to come to terms. When the deal fell through, the firm expanded internationally, merging with Swiss firm Revisuisse and opening an office in Budapest that same year.

In 1992 PW lost a $338 million judgment in a suit brought by Standard Chartered PLC (UK). Standard Chartered had sued the firm for negligence in its audits of Arizona-based United Bank, which Standard Chartered had bought in 1987. The judgment was thrown out in late 1992, and a new trial was ordered.

In 1993 PW achieved some notoriety when it was revealed that it had charged US thrift regulators 67¢ a page for copying more than 10 million documents in reviewing the assets of a failed S&L. But it remained the only Big 6 firm not sued by the FDIC or RTC.

It was not so lucky overseas. In addition to the BCCI litigation, in 1994 the firm was sued by stockholders in Banco Español de Crédito, charging that PW did not reveal the bank's financial problems. Similar complaints were made after the near bankruptcy of Italy's Montedison, a food and chemical conglomerate. Yet another suit, arising from the bankruptcy of a Hong Kong property company, was settled out of court. Also in 1994 the firm was granted a license to start up operations in Vietnam.

Limited liability partnership
Fiscal year ends: June 30

WHO

US Chairman: James J. Schiro, age 49
Chairman, PW World Firm Limited: Dominic A.
Tarantino, age 63
VC, International Accounting and Emerging Markets:
James E. Daley
VC, National Business Units: Willard W. Brittain Jr.
VC, Partnership Affairs and Human Resources
Strategies and Programs: Lennart S. Lindegren
VC, National Risk Management and Practice Protection
Policies and Programs: Peter B. Frank
General Counsel: Lawrence Keeshan

WHERE

HQ: Southwark Towers, 32 London Bridge St.,
London SE1 9SY, UK
Phone: +44-(01)71-939-3000
Fax: +44-(01)71-378-0467
US HQ: 1251 Avenue of the Americas, New York, NY
10020
US Phone: 212-596-7000
US Fax: 212-790-6620

Price Waterhouse maintains 434 offices in 119 countries
and territories.

	1995 Revenues	
	$ mil.	% of total
US	1,770	40
Other countries	2,690	60
Total	**4,460**	**100**

WHAT

	1995 US Revenues	
	$ mil.	% of total
Auditing & accounting	708	40
Management consulting	551	31
Tax	417	24
Other	94	5
Total	**1,770**	**100**

Selected Services
Audit and business advisory services
Dispute analysis and corporate recovery services
Employee benefits services
Government services
Industry services
International business development services
International trade services
Inventory services
Investment management and securities operations
consulting
Litigation and reorganization consulting
Management consulting services
Merger and acquisition services
Partnership services
Personal financial services
Tax services
Valuation services

Representative Clients
AlliedSignal
Amoco
Anheuser-Busch
Baxter
Bristol-Myers Squibb
Campbell Soup
Caterpillar
Chase Manhattan
Chemical Banking
Chevron
CIGNA
Compaq
Dresser
DuPont
Eastman Kodak
Exxon
Goodyear
Hewlett-Packard
IBM
J. P. Morgan
Kellogg
Kmart
NIKE
Ralston Purina
United Technologies
Walt Disney
Warner-Lambert
Washington Post
W. R. Grace

KEY COMPETITORS

Arthur Andersen
A. T. Kearny
Bain & Co.
Booz, Allen
Boston Consulting Group
Coopers & Lybrand
Deloitte & Touche
EDS
Ernst & Young
Gemini Consulting
Grant Thornton
H&R Block
Hewitt
IBM
KPMG
Marsh & McLennan
MCI
McKinsey & Co.
Perot Systems

HOW MUCH

	Annual Growth	1986	1987	1988	1989	1990	1991	1992	1993	1994	1995
Sales ($ mil.)	13.0%	1,488	1,804	2,097	2,468	2,900	3,603	3,781	3,890	3,980	4,460
Offices	1.5%	381	400	412	420	448	458	453	448	447	434
Partners	3.9%	2,300	2,297	2,526	2,680	3,007	3,227	3,221	3,242	3,045	3,246
Employees	41.6%	32,794	33,236	37,120	40,869	46,406	49,461	48,600	48,781	50,122	52,699

1995 Year-end:
Sales per partner:
$1,373,998

Price Waterhouse

Sales ($ mil.)
1986–95

THE PRUDENTIAL INSURANCE CO.

OVERVIEW

A few million in fines here, a few million in customer restitution there, and pretty soon it adds up to real money, enough to send Prudential into the red, especially when combined with a year for disasters (like 1994, with the Northridge earthquake in California).

Since 1991 the company has paid more than $1 billion in fines, restitution, and legal fees resulting from the sale of risky real estate partnerships wrongly represented by employees of Prudential Securities as low-risk investments. The company has also been stung by allegations of systematic misrepresentation of insurance policies as retirement accounts and of account churning. Many of these investigations are still open and may result in even more fines and charges.

The effects on Prudential's business have been widespread: the company is re-examining its quest for leadership in the worldwide financial services field; Prudential Securities is operating at reduced strength because of staff departures; and Prudential has also decided to shed some other financial businesses, including Residential Services Corp., its residential mortgage operation, and Prudential Reinsurance, which it hopes to take public.

On the plus side, Prudential's health care segment (which underwrites the AARP's health insurance products) is doing well.

Guiding the company through these changes is a new CEO, Arthur Ryan, formerly of Chase Manhattan, who replaced Robert Winters upon his retirement.

WHEN

In 1873 John Dryden founded the Widows and Orphans Friendly Society in New Jersey to sell workers industrial insurance (life insurance with small face values and premiums paid weekly). In 1875 he changed the name to the Prudential Friendly Society, naming it after the successful Prudential Assurance Co. of England. In 1876 he visited the English company and copied some of its methods, such as recruiting agents from neighborhoods where insurance was to be sold. In 1877 the company adopted its current name.

Prudential began issuing ordinary whole life insurance in addition to industrial insurance in 1886 and by the end of 1890 was selling more than 2,000 ordinary life policies a year. By this time the company had 3,000 field agents in 8 states. In 1896 Dryden commissioned the J. Walter Thompson advertising agency to design a company trademark. The product was the famed Rock of Gibraltar logo.

Prudential issued its first group life policy in 1916 (the company became a major group life insurer in the 1940s). In the 1920s it was a pioneer in shifting the burden of group life record keeping to the client company.

In 1928 Prudential introduced 3 new insurance policies. An Intermediate Monthly Premium Plan combined some features of the industrial and ordinary life policies. The Modified 3 policy was a whole life policy with a rate change after 3 years. The addition of an Accidental Death Benefit to weekly premium policies cost the company an extra $3 million in benefits in the next year alone.

In 1943 Prudential became a mutual insurance company (owned by the policyholders).

In the 1940s President Carroll Shanks began to decentralize the company's operations. When the system proved successful, other companies copied Prudential. Later the company introduced a Property Investment Separate Account (PRISA), which gave pension plans a real estate investment option. By 1974, 20 of the country's largest 100 corporations were PRISA contract holders, and Prudential was the US's group pension leader.

Prudential acquired the Bache Group (renamed Prudential Securities), a securities brokerage, for $385 million in 1981. Bache's forte was retail investments, an area expected to blend well with Prudential's insurance business. Under George Ball the company tried to become a major investment banker — but failed. In 1991, after losing almost $260 million and facing lawsuits relating to the sale of real estate limited partnerships, Ball resigned.

In 1993 losses caused by Hurricane Andrew led Prudential to seek permission from the state of Florida to allow 25,000 homeowners' policies to lapse.

Despite the 1992 settlement of the real estate partnership suit, Prudential found itself under increasing scrutiny in 1993 and 1994. There were several state investigations into its insurance sales practices, including allegations of churning (persuading policyholders to buy costlier policies, thus generating a large new commission). In 1995 Prudential was hit by new suits in Connecticut and Florida.

In 1995 Prudential Securities opened a representative office in Shanghai, and Prudential joined with Wausau Insurance to provide a workers' compensation managed care plan.

Mutual company
Fiscal year ends: December 31

Chairman, President, and CEO: Arthur F. Ryan
VC: Garnett L. Keith Jr.
CFO: Mark Grier, age 43
Chairman and CEO Group Operations: William P. Link
President and CEO, Prudential Securities Inc.:
  Hardwick Simmons
President and CEO, Prudential Asset Management Group: Eric A. Simonson
Operations and Systems Executive Officer: John V. Scicutella
Chief Communications Officer: Elizabeth R. Krupnick
SVP and Chief Ethics Officer: Stephen R. Braswell
SVP and General Counsel: James R. Gillen
SVP Human Resources: Donald C. Mann
Auditors: Deloitte & Touche LLP

WHERE

HQ: The Prudential Insurance Company of America,
  751 Broad St., Newark, NJ 07102-3777
Phone: 201-802-6000
Fax: 201-802-6092

Prudential operates in Canada, China, Italy, Japan,
South Korea, Spain, Taiwan, the UK, and the US.

WHAT

	1994 Assets	
	$ mil.	% of total
Cash & equivalents	11,739	6
Trading account	6,218	3
Treasury & agency securities	13,624	7
Foreign govt. securities	3,101	1
Mortgage-backed securities	4,889	2
State & municipal bonds	2,776	1
Corporate bonds	54,144	26
Stocks	2,327	1
Broker-dealer receivables	7,311	3
Mortgage loans & real estate	27,799	13
Policy loans	6,631	3
Other investments	10,947	5
Separate account assets	48,633	23
Other	11,763	6
Total	**211,902**	**100**

	1994 Sales	
	$ mil.	% of total
Premiums & annuities	29,698	68
Net investment income	9,595	22
Broker-dealer revenues	3,677	8
Realized investment losses	(450)	—
Other	1,037	2
Total	**43,557**	**100**

Product Lines
Annuities
Asset management
Credit card services
Deposit accounts
Estate and financial planning
Life, health, and property insurance
Reinsurance
Residential real estate services

Selected Subsidiaries
Capital Management Group
Prudential Asset Management Group
Prudential Health Care System
Prudential International Insurance
Prudential Preferred Financial Services
The Prudential Realty Group
Prudential Securities, Inc.
Prudential Select

KEY COMPETITORS

Aetna	FMR	Northwestern
AIG	Foundation Health	Mutual
Alliance Capital	General Electric	Oxford Health
Management	General Re	Plans
Allianz	Goldman Sachs	Paine Webber
Allstate	Guardian Life	RE/MAX
American	Insurance	Salomon
Financial	Health Systems	Sierra Health
Bankers Trust	ITT Hartford	Services
Bear Stearns	John Hancock	State Farm
Blue Cross	John Nuveen	T. Rowe Price
Coldwell Banker	Kaiser	Trammell
Canadian Imperial	Foundation	Crow
Charles Schwab	Health Care	Residential
Chase Manhattan	Liberty Mutual	Transamerica
Chubb	MassMutual	Travelers
CIGNA	Merrill Lynch	United
Citicorp	MetLife	HealthCare
Equitable	Morgan Stanley	USF&G
First Chicago	New York Life	

HOW MUCH

	Annual Growth	1985	1986	1987	1988	1989	1990	1991	1992	1993	1994
Assets ($ mil.)	9.8%	91,706	133,733	140,931	153,023	163,967	169,046	189,148	199,625	218,440	211,902
Net income ($ mil.)	—	—	—	967	829	743	113	2,280	347	879	(1,175)
Income as % of assets	—	—	—	0.7%	0.5%	0.5%	0.1%	1.2%	0.2%	0.4%	—
Employees	2.2%	81,634	85,503	93,290	98,009	105,063	104,847	103,284	101,000	105,534	99,386

1994 Year-end:
Equity as % of assets: 3.5%
Return on equity: —
Sales (mil.): $43,557

Net Income
($ mil.) 1987-94

PUBLIC SERVICE ENTERPRISE GROUP

OVERVIEW

Public Service Enterprise Group (Enterprise) is the parent company of Public Service Electric and Gas Company (PSE&G), New Jersey's largest electric and natural gas utility.

PSE&G provides services to about 300 cities and towns, including Newark, Trenton, and Camden. Through its subsidiary, Enterprise Diversified Holdings (EDHI), the company is also involved in nonutility businesses, including oil and gas exploration, independent power projects, and commercial real estate development in several states.

With deregulation of the utility industry increasing competition, Enterprise has reorganized PSE&G, creating separate business units for generation, transmission, and customer service. It also formed a new subsidiary, Enterprise Ventures and Services, to develop products and services that it can sell outside its traditional boundaries. The changes are part of a strategy focused on improving efficiency and increasing flexibility.

Since the passage of the Energy Policy Act, which opens the utility market up to independent power producers, Enterprise (along with other utilities) has had to compete for large corporate accounts. In 1995 the company requested a rate decrease of about $7.3 million annually for its 2nd largest customer, Co-Steel Raritan.

WHEN

Newark, New Jersey, was the scene of a tragedy in 1903 when a trolley car full of high school students collided with a Delaware, Lackawanna and Western train. While investigating the accident, state attorney general Thomas McCarter discovered the underlying financial weakness of the trolley company and many of New Jersey's other transportation, gas, and electric companies. Planning to buy and consolidate these companies, McCarter resigned as attorney general. He and several colleagues then established the Public Service Corporation (1903).

The company originally formed separate divisions for gas utilities, trolley and other transportation companies, and electric utilities. Management spent most of its energies on the trolley company, reasoning that these operations would be the most profitable. Indeed, during its first full year of operation, the trolley company generated almost half of Public Service's total sales.

In 1924 the gas and electric companies consolidated as Public Service Electric and Gas (PSE&G). A new company formed to operate buses that year and merged with the trolley company in 1928 to form Public Service Coordinated Transport (later Transport of New Jersey). PSE&G signed interconnection agreements with 2 Pennsylvania electric companies in 1928 to form the world's first integrated power pool — later known as the Pennsylvania–New Jersey–Maryland (PJM) Interconnection when Baltimore Gas & Electric joined in 1956. Four more companies joined in 1965.

PSE&G began exploring new gas fields in Texas and Louisiana in response to the 1972 Arab oil embargo and formed a research subsidiary in 1977 to develop solar and other non–fossil fuel energy sources.

The state of New Jersey, which had been subsidizing Transport of New Jersey, bought it from PSE&G in 1980. Public Service Enterprise Group, a holding company, was formed in 1985 to allow PSE&G to diversify into nonutility enterprises. A new subsidiary, Enterprise Diversified Holdings, was formed in 1989 to handle these activities, which included commercial real estate development (Enterprise Group Development) and 94 oil- and gas-producing properties in West Texas and the Gulf of Mexico (Energy Development Corporation). In 1989 Energy Development bought Pelto Oil Company (oil and gas exploration) from Houston-based Southdown.

Community Energy Alternatives, Enterprise's independent power production subsidiary, and 3 partners acquired a 650-megawatt power station near Buenos Aires, Argentina, in 1993. In 1994 Energy Development announced an agreement with the Chinese government to evaluate and analyze an oil block in the East China Sea.

In 1995 PSE&G and AT&T said they planned to develop an interactive customer communications system that will provide services such as automatic and remote meter reading and energy-use monitoring. After a test in New Jersey, the 2 companies plan to market the system worldwide. Also in 1995 PSE&G's Salem Generating Station nuclear plant agreed to pay the state of Delaware $10.5 million to offset the costs of damage to aquatic life caused by the plant's use of water from the Delaware River.

WHO

Chairman, President, and CEO: E. James Ferland, age 52, $652,492 pay
President and COO, PSE&G: Lawrence R. Codey, age 50, $398,468 pay
President and COO, EDHI: Paul H. Way, age 57, $308,813 pay
SVP Electric, PSE&G: Robert J. Dougherty Jr., age 43, $273,946 pay
SVP Customer Operations, PSE&G: Thomas M. Crimmins Jr., age 51
SVP External Affairs, PSE&G: Howard W. Borden Jr., age 50
Chief Nuclear Officer and President Nuclear Business Unit, PSE&G: Leon R. Eliason, age 55
VP and CFO: Robert C. Murray, age 49, $353,832 pay
VP and General Counsel: R. Edwin Selover, age 49
VP Human Resources, PSE&G: Martin P. Mellet
Auditors: Deloitte & Touche LLP

WHERE

HQ: Public Service Enterprise Group Incorporated, 80 Park Plaza, PO Box 1171, Newark, NJ 07101-1171
Phone: 201-430-7000
Fax: 201-430-5983

Selected Generating Facilities

Oil and Gas	Mercer (NJ)
Bayonne (NJ)	National Park (NJ)
Bergen (NJ)	Salem (NJ)
Burlington (NJ)	Sewaren (NJ)
Conemaugh (22.5%, PA)	
Edison (NJ)	**Nuclear**
Essex (NJ)	Hope Creek (95.0%, NJ)
Hudson (NJ)	Peach Bottom (42.5%, PA)
Kearny (NJ)	Salem (42.6%, NJ)
Keystone (22.8%, PA)	**Pumped Storage**
Linden (NJ)	Yards Creek (50.0%, NJ)

WHAT

	1994 Sales	
	$ mil.	% of total
Electric	3,733	63
Gas	1,779	30
Nonutility activities	404	7
Total	**5,916**	**100**

	1994 Electricity Fuel Sources
	% of total
Nuclear	45
Interchange & 2-party purchases	27
Coal	19
Natural gas	7
Residual oil	2
Total	**100**

Selected Subsidiaries

Enterprise Diversified Holdings Incorporated
Community Energy Alternatives Inc. (investment in and development of cogeneration and small power plants)
Energy Development Corporation (oil and gas exploration, development, and production)
Enterprise Group Development Corporation (commercial real estate development)

Enterprise Ventures and Services Corporation
Public Service Conservation Resources Corporation (energy management products and services)
U.S. Energy Partners (gas marketing partnership with Cincinnati Gas and Electric Company)

Public Service Electric and Gas Company

KEY COMPETITORS

AES	Columbia Gas	Koch
Associated Natural Gas	Consolidated Edison	Occidental
California Energy	Destec Energy	Panhandle Eastern
Coastal	Enron	Tenneco

HOW MUCH

	Annual Growth	1985	1986	1987	1988	1989	1990	1991	1992	1993	1994
Sales ($ mil.)	3.3%	4,428	4,498	4,211	4,395	4,805	5,357	5,092	5,357	5,706	5,916
Net income ($ mil.)	6.1%	400	378	520	529	523	404	543	504	596	679
Income as % of sales	—	9.0%	8.4%	12.3%	12.0%	11.0%	8.4%	10.7%	9.4%	10.4%	11.5%
Earnings per share ($)	2.7%	2.18	1.90	2.55	2.57	2.53	1.90	2.43	2.17	2.48	2.78
Stock price – high ($)	—	22.08	32.20	30.50	26.88	29.38	29.75	29.38	31.38	36.13	32.00
Stock price – low ($)	—	16.92	20.50	20.00	22.00	23.00	22.50	25.25	25.38	30.00	23.88
Stock price – close ($)	2.6%	21.08	26.83	23.88	24.50	29.25	26.38	29.38	30.88	32.00	26.50
P/E – high	—	10	17	12	10	12	16	12	14	15	12
P/E – low	—	8	11	8	9	9	12	10	12	12	9
Dividends per share ($)	1.6%	1.87	1.95	1.99	2.01	2.05	2.09	2.13	2.16	2.16	2.16
Book value per share ($)	2.2%	17.87	17.92	18.54	19.11	19.48	19.44	20.04	20.32	21.07	21.70
Employees	(0.9%)	13,500	13,800	13,800	12,832	13,113	13,383	13,116	13,115	13,115	12,390

1994 Year-end:
Debt ratio: 54.0%
Return on equity: 13.0%
Cash (mil.): $68
Current ratio: 0.73
Long-term debt (mil.): $5,234
No. of shares (mil.): 245
Dividends
  Yield: 8.2%
  Payout: 77.7%
Market value (mil.): $6,484

Stock Price History
High/Low 1985–94

THE READER'S DIGEST ASSOCIATION

OVERVIEW

The Reader's Digest Association is the company that parlayed condensed reprints of journal articles into a global publishing and entertainment empire with nearly $3 billion in sales. Its flagship publication, *Reader's Digest*, is the world's most widely read magazine; 47 editions are published in 18 languages and read by 100 million people. The New York–based company also produces a wide range of books, music, videos, and special-interest magazines whose traditional values inspire, inform, and entertain legions of worldwide customers. Reader's Digest is one of the leading European book and magazine publishers. In 1995, 61% of the company's revenues were from international sales. Reader's Digest markets its products through sophisticated direct

mailings and an extensive consumer database that is considered one of the best in the world.

The company, which sold 52 million copies of cookbooks and reference, do-it-yourself, series, and condensed books in 1995, has moved into multimedia. A new director was hired in 1994 to expand the company's video operations; its history, travel, and comedy videos have won 3 Emmys and 26 awards for excellence since the business line was launched in 1986. Reader's Digest has teamed up with software giant Microsoft to produce a line of CD-ROM products. It is making its magazines, such as *Family Handyman* and *Travel Holiday*, available online, and the company intends to expand its presence in the electronic publishing marketplace.

WHEN

The first edition of DeWitt ("Wally") and Lila Wallace's monthly *Reader's Digest* appeared in 1922 and was an immediate success. Within 3 years circulation had almost quintupled, and the Wallaces moved from New York City to Pleasantville, New York. The idea of condensing material from other magazines into a compact, readable form proved to be popular, and the *Digest* grew enormously. It expanded from mail subscriptions only to newsstand sales in 1929 and reached a circulation of one million by 1935. In 1939 the company moved to Chappaqua, New York, but kept Pleasantville as a mailing address.

In the 1940s the *Digest* expanded internationally (the first overseas edition started in England in 1938), opening company offices on 5 continents and providing foreign-language translations. During that decade Wally began to write his own articles (partly because some magazines had stopped allowing him reprint rights), giving the *Digest* its conservative, optimistic style.

In 1950 the first Reader's Digest Condensed Book was published. In 1955 the *Digest* accepted its first advertising but did not carry liquor ads until 1978 and has never carried cigarette ads. The *Digest* published articles in the mid-1950s examining the link between smoking and cancer.

The company added the Recorded Music Division in 1959 and General Books in 1963. Reader's Digest was the first publisher to use direct-mail advertising with "personalized" letters to promote its products. Its huge mailing list was later used for promotions such as the Reader's Digest Sweepstakes.

The Wallaces continued to manage the company until 1973. Wally died in 1981; Lila died 3 years later. Their voting stock in the company passed to trust funds, and about 6 million nonvoting shares were given to 10 organizations, including Lincoln Center, the Metropolitan Museum of Art, and the New York Zoological Society.

George Grune took over as chairman and CEO in 1984. He cut staff by 20% and disposed of unprofitable subsidiaries, ushering in an era of increased profitability for the company. Reader's Digest added a line of specialty magazines by purchasing *Travel Holiday* in 1986, *Family Handyman* in 1988, *50 Plus* (first renamed *New Choices for Retirement Living* and then *New Choices: Living Even Better After 50*) in 1988, and *American Health* in 1990. The company bought 50% of British publisher Dorling Kindersley in 1987.

Following a 1990 public offering, Reader's Digest made a transition from nearly a public trust to a profit-oriented company. Most of the voting shares are owned by the DeWitt Wallace–Reader's Digest Fund and the Lila Wallace–Reader's Digest Fund (36% each).

In 1993 "Reader's Digest: On Television" aired on network TV. The one-hour special was the company's first venture into TV (excepting home video production) since 1955.

James Schadt succeeded Grune as CEO in 1994 and as chairman in 1995. In 1995 the company launched a Polish edition of *Reader's Digest*, upping to 18 the number of local-language editions. Former RJR Nabisco CFO Stephen Wilson joined Reader's Digest after SVP and CFO Anthony Ruggiero resigned.

NYSE symbol: RDA
Fiscal year ends: June 30

WHO

Chairman and CEO: James P. Schadt, age 56,
$975,866 pay (prior to promotion)
President and COO; President, Reader's Digest USA:
Kenneth A. H. Gordon, age 57, $766,154 pay (prior to promotion)
EVP and CFO: Stephen R. Wilson, age 48
SVP Global Direct Marketing: Peter J. C. Davenport, age 54
SVP Human Resources: Joseph M. Grecky, age 55, $432,808 pay
SVP; Editor-in-Chief, *Reader's Digest* Magazine:
Kenneth Y. Tomlinson, $431,154 pay
VP; President, US Magazine Publishing: Thomas M. Kenney, age 47, $571,038 pay
VP; President, Reader's Digest Pacific: Martin J. Pearson, age 47, $457,346 pay
VP; President, Reader's Digest Europe: Heikki K. Helenius, age 52
VP; President, Special Markets Group: William H. Willis, age 43
VP Operations: Bruce G. Koe, age 51
Auditors: KPMG Peat Marwick LLP

WHERE

HQ: The Reader's Digest Association, Inc., Reader's Digest Rd., Pleasantville, NY 10570-7000
Phone: 914-238-1000
Fax: 914-238-4559

	1995 Sales		1995 Operating Income	
	$ mil.	% of total	$ mil.	% of total
Europe	1,456	47	225	50
US	1,197	39	152	34
Other regions	425	14	71	16
Adjustments	(9)	—	(56)	—
Total	**3,069**	**100**	**392**	**100**

WHAT

	1995 Sales		1995 Operating Income	
	$ mil.	% of total	$ mil.	% of total
Books, CDs, cassettes & videos	2,100	68	339	76
Reader's Digest	733	24	78	17
Special-interest magazines	96	3	—	—
Other	144	5	31	7
Adjustments	(4)	—	(56)	—
Total	**3,069**	**100**	**392**	**100**

Books and Home Entertainment Products
General-interest books and CDs (how-to and reference books, cookbooks, and songbooks; 12 languages)
Reader's Digest Condensed Books (popular fiction; 15 editions in 12 languages)
Recorded music (original and licensed recordings)
Series books (multiple volumes; 9 languages)
Videocassettes and original video productions

Magazines
American Health
The Family Handyman
Moneywise (UK)
New Choices: Living Even Better After 50
Reader's Digest (47 editions in 18 languages)
Travel Holiday

Other Operations
Fund-raising products and services for school and youth groups (QSP, Inc.)
Sweepstakes direct-mail promotion
Other direct marketing (language courses, globes)

KEY COMPETITORS

AARP	Hearst	Sony
Advance	K-III	Time Warner
Publications	Lagardère	Viacom
Bertelsmann	New York Times	Virgin Group
Cox Enterprises	News Corp.	

HOW MUCH

	Annual Growth	1986	1987	1988	1989	1990	1991	1992	1993	1994	1995
Sales ($ mil.)	10.4%	1,255	1,420	1,712	1,832	2,010	2,345	2,614	2,869	2,806	3,069
Net income ($ mil.)	15.4%	73	95	141	152	176	209	234	258	272	264
Income as % of sales	—	5.8%	7.6%	8.2%	8.3%	8.8%	8.9%	9.0%	9.0%	9.7%	8.6%
Earnings per share ($)	16.6%	0.59	0.78	1.18	1.28	1.48	1.74	1.95	2.16	2.34	2.35
Stock price – high ($)	—	—	—	—	—	29.50	49.00	56.38	55.88	49.38	52.00
Stock price – low ($)	—	—	—	—	—	21.00	26.13	43.00	36.13	39.88	38.25
Stock price – close ($)	11.7%	—	—	—	—	29.50	48.38	54.00	45.00	49.13	51.25
P/E – high	—	—	—	—	—	20	28	29	26	21	22
P/E – low	—	—	—	—	—	14	15	22	17	17	16
Dividends per share ($)	32.5%	—	—	—	—	0.38	0.57	0.80	1.15	1.35	1.55
Book value per share ($)	2.2%	—	—	—	—	5.07	6.12	7.57	6.65	6.70	5.66
Employees	(2.9%)	—	—	—	7,400	7,400	7,400	7,400	7,400	7,300	6,700	6,200

1995 Year-end:
Debt ratio: 0.0%
Return on equity: 38.4%
Cash (mil.): $532
Current ratio: 1.13
Long-term debt (mil.): $0
No. of shares (mil.): 108
Dividends
  Yield: 3.5%
  Payout: 66.0%
Market value (mil.): $5,545

**Stock Price History
High/Low 1990–95**

RELIANCE GROUP HOLDINGS, INC.

OVERVIEW

Reliance is still trying to deliver on its promise (following a $148 million loss in 1991) to remake itself as a profit powerhouse. In the past few years, the New York City–based property/casualty and title insurer has restructured its business, its strategies, and its culture. And although it has returned to profitability, the company remains extremely sensitive to the cycles of its main businesses.

Through its insurance subsidiaries — Reliance National, Reliance Insurance, Reliance Reinsurance, and Reliance Surety — the company provides a wide range of property/casualty coverages for *FORTUNE* 500 businesses, including specialty lines and nonstandard risks. It offers reinsurance services primarily to small to midmarket specialty insurers. Reliance also provides surety bonds for contractors and financial institutions.

This commercial emphasis is relatively new, resulting from the company's withdrawal from personal lines. However, its specialty focus, particularly on environmental coverage, potentially exposes Reliance to almost unlimited liability for past site contamination. The company reduces this risk through careful underwriting and meticulously written contracts.

The company's Commonwealth Land Title is one of the 3 largest title insurers in the US. This segment contributed to Reliance's return to profitability in 1993, when interest rates were low and the real estate market was booming. However, it helped drag down earnings in 1994, when rates increased.

Reliance is the flagship operation of Saul Steinberg's financial empire. Two of his brothers are involved in management, and the family owns about 50% of the company.

WHEN

Ben Franklin organized the first fire brigade in Philadelphia, the Union Fire Company, in 1736. In the decades that followed, brigades multiplied. Firefighting became a competitive and chaotic affair in which triumphing over the flames was often less important than winning the brawls that flared between rival companies responding to alarms. By 1817 there were 49 fire companies in the city. In that year Caleb Carmalt attempted to bring order to the situation by uniting a number of them as the Fire Association of Philadelphia. They also decided to offer fire insurance. After a 3-year fight (which involved unseating some members of the state legislature), the company won a state charter. The association's owners were its component fire companies.

The Fire Association survived and grew despite frequent fires and 2 major conflagrations in Philadelphia, one of which, in 1850, almost put it out of business.

But the Fire Association's true challenge was Philadelphia's decision to form a professional fire department. The association could focus on its home market when it was a private fire department-cum-insurance company, but it had to expand geographically in order to survive purely as a stock insurer. Fortunately, Mrs. O'Leary's cow got frisky in October of 1871 and burned Chicago to a crisp. The resulting mass bankruptcy of fire insurers left a niche for the Fire Association (which had no business in Chicago) as it went national.

The Fire Association's standard product until the Depression was the single-premium

Perpetual Policy, which transferred from owner to owner. The company added new coverage, including marine and auto, and opened an office in Montreal in 1917.

In 1921 the association bought rival Reliance Insurance Co. of Philadelphia (founded in 1841). The company prospered in the 1920s and even expanded in the 1930s. In 1958 the Fire Association officially merged with its subsidiary, Reliance, and took the Reliance name.

In that year, Saul Steinberg, with a year to go until graduation from the Wharton School, was already in the computer leasing business. In 1961 the 22-year-old Steinberg incorporated under the name Leasco Data Processing Equipment Corp. Four years later the company went public. In 1968 Steinberg bought 91% of Reliance. He changed Leasco's name to Reliance Group, Inc., in 1973 and began shifting the company's focus from leasing to financial services (forming Commonwealth Land Title in 1976 as part of this effort). In 1981 Steinberg acquired the remainder of Reliance Insurance, taking it private. He relaunched the company, now Reliance Group Holdings, as a 20% public company in 1986.

Since then Reliance has been buffeted by the effects of the stock crash of 1987, the real estate crash that followed, and an unusual string of natural disasters that continued into 1994. The company lost money in 1991 and 1992 as it strove to remake itself and return to profitability.

Steinberg suffered a mild stroke in 1995 but apparently suffered no impairment.

NYSE symbol: REL
Fiscal year ends: December 31

WHO

Chairman and CEO: Saul P. Steinberg, age 55,
$3,725,000 pay
President and COO: Robert M. Steinberg, age 52,
$2,465,000 pay
EVP and Controller: George E. Bello, age 59,
$1,362,500 pay
SVP Investments: James E. Yacobucci, age 43,
$2,500,000 pay
SVP and CFO: Lowell C. Freiberg, age 55,
$1,260,000 pay
SVP, General Counsel, and Secretary: Howard E.
Steinberg, age 50
VP Human Resources: Joel H. Rothwax
Auditors: Deloitte & Touche LLP

WHERE

HQ: 55 E. 52nd St., New York, NY 10055
Phone: 212-909-1100
Fax: 212-909-1864

Reliance's property/casualty companies write insurance
in all 50 states, the District of Columbia, Guam, Puerto
Rico, and the Virgin Islands as well as in Argentina,
Canada, Mexico, the Netherlands, Spain, and the UK.

	1994 Sales
	% of total
California	18
New York	9
Texas	7
Pennsylvania	6
Florida	5
Other	55
Total	**100**

WHAT

	1994 Assets	
	$ mil.	% of total
Cash & equivalents	279	3
Treasury & agency securites	495	5
Public untility bonds	625	7
Corporate bonds	1,393	15
Stocks	1,056	11
Real estate	292	3
Receivables	1,263	13
Reinsurance recoverables	2,929	31
Other	1,329	12
Total	**9,370**	**100**

	1994 Sales	
	$ mil.	% of total
Property/casualty insurance	2,018	66
Title & mortgage insurance	884	29
Other	145	5
Total	**3,047**	**100**

Selected Subsidiaries
Commonwealth Land Title Co., Inc.
Reliance Insurance Co.
Reliance National Insurance Co.
Reliance Reinsurance Corp.
Reliance Surety Co.

KEY COMPETITORS

Aetna	Lincoln National
AIG	Nationwide Enterprises
Alleghany Corp.	St. Paul Cos.
American Family	Sentry Insurance
Insurance	State Farm
American Re	TIG Holdings
CIGNA	Torchmark
CNA Financial	Transamerica
General Re	Travelers
Investors Title	Unitrin
ITT Hartford	UNUM
Liberty Mutual	USF&G

HOW MUCH

	Annual Growth	1985	1986	1987	1988	1989	1990	1991	1992	1993	1994
Assets ($ mil.)	7.1%	5,057	6,079	7,180	9,045	10,383	11,011	11,253	5,760	8,856	9,370
Net income ($ mil.)	0.1%	43	104	126	24	22	118	(148)	(39)	86	44
Income as % of assets	—	0.9%	1.7%	1.8%	0.3%	0.2%	1.1%	—	—	1.0%	0.5%
Earnings per share ($)	6.8%	0.21	1.14	1.68	0.32	0.29	1.58	(2.00)	(0.52)	0.92	0.38
Stock price – high ($)	—	—	10.63	11.50	7.50	8.63	6.63	7.50	7.13	10.38	8.13
Stock price – low ($)	—	—	7.50	4.50	4.50	4.25	4.25	3.75	3.50	5.63	4.88
Stock price – close ($)	(5.1%)	—	7.88	5.75	4.63	5.13	4.63	4.13	6.13	8.00	5.19
P/E – high	—	—	9	7	23	30	4	—	—	11	21
P/E – low	—	—	7	3	14	15	3	—	—	6	13
Dividends per share ($)	29.7%	—	0.04	0.18	0.26	0.32	0.24	0.32	0.32	0.32	0.32
Book value per share ($)	(3.0%)	—	4.35	4.13	4.91	4.66	5.96	2.94	2.99	4.65	3.42
Employees	1.6%	—	8,500	9,450	9,200	8,900	9,200	12,500	9,350	9,765	9,675

1994 Year-end:
Equity as % of assets:4.1%
Return on equity: 9.7%
Return on assets: —
Long-term debt (mil.): $872
No. of shares (mil.): 113
Dividends
  Yield: 6.2%
  Payout: 84.2%
Market value (mil.): $587
Sales (mil.): $3,047

**Stock Price History
High/Low 1986–94**

RJR NABISCO HOLDINGS CORP.

OVERVIEW

With the split of its food and tobacco companies and the departure of the LBO firm Kohlberg Kravis Roberts (KKR), RJR Nabisco Holdings has recently undergone major structural and ownership changes. Based in New York, RJR Nabisco separated its 2 companies by selling 19.5% of Nabisco to the public in early 1995. The resulting $1 billion will likely be used to pay down debt and begin an annual common stock dividend. The split of its food and tobacco companies will also help to shield Nabisco from litigation resulting from RJR's tobacco business. KKR concluded the final episode of its historic LBO of RJR Nabisco, which took place in 1989, by selling its $4 billion stake in the company for what, in the end, was only a modest profit of about 11 cents a share for KKR shareholders.

With sales growth of 10% in 1994, Nabisco generated sales of $7.7 billion with such strong food brands as Oreo, A.1. Steak Sauce, Life Savers, and SnackWell's (its successful reduced-fat and fat-free snack line). In contrast, RJR is experiencing both operational and legal troubles. Its leading brand of cigarettes (Winston) is losing market share in the US, declining by about a point to 5.8%. Along with other cigarette makers, RJR is also facing an increasingly hostile regulatory and legal environment. As a result, RJR plans to rely on its 81% ownership in Nabisco and a rapidly growing international tobacco market. In addition, the company announced a 1-for-5 reverse stock split in February 1995 and hopes the higher price per share will enhance interest among institutional investors.

WHEN

R. J. Reynolds formed the R.J. Reynolds Tobacco Company in 1875 in Winston, North Carolina, to produce chewing tobacco. In the late 1890s James Duke of the American Tobacco trust forced Reynolds to sell out to him for $3 million. Reynolds regained control in 1911 after Duke's trust was dismantled by the government. In 1913 the company introduced Camel, its best-selling cigarette. After Reynolds died in 1918, leadership passed to Bowman Gray, whose family ran the company for the next 50 years.

With the success of Camel, R.J. Reynolds became the largest domestic cigarette company. During the 1930s and 1940s, Camel and Lucky Strike (American Tobacco Company) vied for the #1 cigarette position. In response to growing health concerns in the 1950s, the company introduced its filtered Winston (1954) and Salem (1956) brands.

Growing antismoking sentiment led to diversification in the 1960s and 1970s. Acquisitions included Chun King (1966; sold 1989), Patio Foods (1967), American Independent Oil (1970; sold 1984), and Del Monte (1979; sold 1990). In 1970 the company became R.J. Reynolds Industries; it acquired Heublein in 1982. Heublein's Kentucky Fried Chicken chain was sold to PepsiCo in 1986 and its liquor business to Grand Metropolitan in 1987.

In 1985 the company bought Nabisco Brands for $4.9 billion and renamed itself RJR Nabisco. The National Biscuit Company had been formed by the 1898 consolidation of several baking companies by Adolphus Green, Nabisco's first president. Products included

Fig Newtons, Oreo, and Premium Saltines. Nabisco acquired Shredded Wheat (1929), Milk-Bone (1931), Dromedary (1954), Cream of Wheat (1961), James Welch (candy, 1963), and Standard Brands (Planters nuts, Blue Bonnet margarine, beer, wine; 1981). Standard Brands's CEO, Ross Johnson, became CEO of Nabisco and then of RJR Nabisco.

In 1987 Johnson attempted an LBO; KKR outbid him, acquiring the company for $29.6 billion in 1989, and Louis Gerstner became CEO. To reduce the LBO debt, the company sold Nabisco's European food business (1989).

After an American Medical Association report determined that RJR Nabisco's controversial 1991 cigarette-ad campaign featuring Joe Camel, a cartoon character, appealed to children (implying the ad encouraged children to smoke), the FTC considered banning the spokescamel altogether in 1993.

In 1992 the company acquired Stella D'oro (pastries) and New York Style Bagel Chips. In 1993 RJR sold its cold cereal business to Kraft and brought new tobacco processing plants on line in Poland and Turkey. Also in 1993 Charles Harper, former ConAgra head, became CEO.

In a series of transactions in late 1994 and early 1995, KKR unloaded its 35% stake in RJR Nabisco. KKR exchanged approximately 3/4 of its stake in RJR Nabisco to acquire 100% of Borden then sold off its remaining 8%.

In late 1995 investors Carl Icahn and Bennett LeBow joined forces to buy a 4.8% stake in RJR. Icahn and LeBow pledged to launch a proxy fight, if necessary, to force RJR to sell its Nabisco food business.

WHO

Chairman and CEO: Charles M. Harper, age 67,
$3,010,000 pay
VC: James W. Johnston, age 49, $2,425,000 pay (prior to
promotion)
President and General Counsel: Steven F. Goldstone,
age 49
President and CEO; President and CEO, Nabisco, Inc.:
H. John Greeniaus, age 50, $1,683,430 pay
SVP and Treasurer: John J. Delucca, age 51
**President and CEO, R.J. Reynolds Tobacco
International:** Anthony J. Butterworth, age 57
President and CEO, Nabisco International: James J.
Postl, age 49
CFO: Robert S. Roath, age 52
SVP and Controller: Richard G. Russell, age 49
**SVP and Deputy Head, Human Resources and
Administration:** Gerald Angowitz, age 45
Auditors: Deloitte & Touche LLP

WHERE

HQ: 1301 Avenue of the Americas, New York, NY 10019
Phone: 212-258-5600
Fax: 212-969-9173

The company sells its products in more than 160
countries around the world.

	1994 Sales		1994 Operating Income	
	$ mil.	% of total	$ mil.	% of total
US	11,144	69	2,159	78
Europe	1,934	12	272	10
Other regions	3,039	19	326	12
Adjustments	(751)	—	(207)	—
Total	**15,366**	**100**	**2,550**	**100**

WHAT

	1994 Sales		1994 Operating Income	
	$ mil.	% of total	$ mil.	% of total
Tobacco	7,667	50	1,826	66
Food	7,699	50	931	34
Adjustments	—	—	(207)	—
Total	**15,366**	**100**	**2,550**	**100**

Selected Product Names

Cigarettes	Cookies, Crackers, and Cereals	Teddy Grahams
Camel	Barnum's Animal	Triscuit
Century	Crackers	Wheat Thins
Doral	Better Cheddar	
Gold Coast	Cheese Nips	**Other**
Magna	Chicken in a Biskit	A.1. Steak Sauce
More	Chips Ahoy!	Blue Bonnet
NOW	Cream of Wheat	College Inn
Salem	Granola Bars	Fleischmann's
Sterling	Harvest Crisps	Grey Poupon
Vantage	Mr. Phipps	Knox
Winston	Nabisco Honey Maid	Milk-Bone
	Grahams	Move Over
Candy, Gum, and Nuts	Newtons	Butter
Beech-Nut	Nilla Wafers	My*T*Fine
Breath Savers	Nutter Butter	New York
Bubble Yum	Oreo	Style Bagel
Care*Free	Premium	Ortega
Life Savers	Ritz	Pita Chips
Now and Later	SnackWell's	Regina
Planters	Stella D'oro	Royal
		Vermont Maid

KEY COMPETITORS

American Brands	Heinz	Philip Morris
B.A.T	Hershey	Procter & Gamble
Borden	Imasco	Quaker Oats
Campbell Soup	Inflo Holdings	Tootsie Roll
ConAgra	Kellogg	Unilever
Danone	Loews	UST
General Mills	Mars	Wrigley

HOW MUCH

	Annual Growth	1985	1986	1987	1988	1989	1990	1991	1992	1993	1994
Sales ($ mil.)	1.4%	13,533	15,978	15,766	16,956	12,764	13,879	14,989	15,734	15,104	15,366
Net income ($ mil.)	(9.0%)	910	962	1,179	1,378	(976)	(429)	195	268	(213)	388
Income as % of sales	—	6.7%	6.0%	7.5%	8.1%	—	—	1.3%	1.7%	—	2.5%
Earnings per share ($)	—	—	—	—	—	(3.21)	(1.19)	0.22	0.20	(0.15)	0.25
Stock price – high ($)	—	—	—	—	—	—	—	12.88	11.75	9.25	8.13
Stock price – low ($)	—	—	—	—	—	—	—	5.50	7.88	4.38	5.38
Stock price – close ($)	(20.0%)	—	—	—	—	—	—	10.75	8.63	6.38	5.50
P/E – high	—	—	—	—	—	—	—	59	59	—	33
P/E – low	—	—	—	—	—	—	—	25	39	—	22
Dividends per share ($)	—	—	—	—	—	—	—	0.00	0.00	0.00	0.00
Book value per share ($)	(2.7%)	—	—	—	—	—	—	7.51	7.38	6.65	6.91
Employees	(7.9%)	147,513	124,617	120,334	116,881	48,000	55,000	56,000	63,000	66,500	70,600

1994 Year-end:
Debt ratio: 54.2%
Return on equity: 4.6%
Cash (mil.): $423
Current ratio: 0.78
Long-term debt (mil.): $8,883
No. of shares (mil.): 1,362
Dividends
  Yield: —
  Payout: —
Market value (mil.): $7,489

**Stock Price History
High/Low 1991–94**

SALOMON INC

OVERVIEW

Can Warren Buffett's wisdom be described as Salomonic? Since the New York–based investment firm's 1991 Treasury bond scandal, Salomon has experienced low morale and high-level defections — not so much as a result of the scandal as because of the efforts of dominant shareholder Warren Buffett and his handpicked management team to transform the firm's "me first" culture into one more communal and client-oriented. A recent attempt to link compensation with firm performance for client-driven operations led to more departures (including that of founding-family member Robert Salomon) and a reorganization of the operating committee.

This turmoil combined with the 1994 bond market crash (and the resulting slowdown in securities activity) to plunge the company into the red. Results later improved, but the rift between Buffett and some in the company seemed to widen amid rumors of growing executive contempt for Buffett. But Salomon remains dependent upon Buffett's good graces. Word that he might divest part of his interest led to lower stock prices that cut the value of executives' holdings. Buffett decreased his share (from 20% to 17% in 1995).

Salomon's primary income source is trading; its Phibro operations are petroleum- and commodities-oriented.

WHEN

Arthur, Herbert, and Percy Salomon founded Salomon Brothers as a money brokerage firm in 1910. In 1917 the company became a US government securities dealer. Until the 1960s it specialized in bond trading.

In the 1950s and 1960s, Salomon expanded its trading department, entered stock underwriting, and added a corporate finance department. The firm opened branches in London and Tokyo in 1970.

In 1978 John Gutfreund, head of corporate finance, became managing partner. He sought capital in 1981 by selling the firm to Phibro Corporation, an international oil and commodities trader. The companies remained autonomous, and Gutfreund and Phibro's John Tendler became co-CEOs. Gutfreund became sole CEO in 1984. As the economy boomed in the 1980s, Salomon's staff grew exponentially.

When Salomon suffered losses in mortgage-backed securities and in the stock market crash, Gutfreund sought capital from Warren Buffett. Salomon withdrew from municipal bonds and commercial paper and went into LBOs. Two LBOs, Southland and Revco, ended in Chapter 11. Salomon sold its interest in the 3rd, Grand Union, in 1992.

In 1991 rumors circulated that Salomon was violating regulations that prohibited any one company from buying more than 35% of Treasury instrument issues; Salomon had bought up most of the February auction by using clients' names without authorization. In April, Gutfreund and others became aware of the violation. Complaints prompted an SEC investigation, which found that Salomon had bought 94% of the May auction.

When this became public, Gutfreund resigned. Investor Warren Buffett became chairman and installed Robert Denham (Buffett's lawyer) and Deryck Maughan (a Salomon administrator) as the top executives. Buffett made a full revelation of Salomon's actions and took disciplinary action. Following the scandal, Salomon sold assets to continue operating as credit became more difficult to obtain. Morale plunged and employees left.

Afterward the company's brokerage business rebounded, but Salomon's energy business became a major problem. In 1992 the company broke up Phibro Energy. It turned the commodities business into a division of Salomon, grouped the refineries operations together as Phibro USA, and separated a joint venture with Russia (the largest US venture in Russia) into Phibro Energy Production, Inc. (PEPI). After the joint venture was begun, Russia imposed new taxes. Although PEPI received an exemption from these taxes in 1994, the question of whether Salomon can recoup its investment, despite significantly increased oil production, remains open. Phibro USA, which operates oil refineries, is subject to the fluctuations of the oil market. Salomon as a whole also retains an undetermined amount of potential environmental liability attributable to Phibro's former smelting (and current refinery) operations.

In 1995, after announcing a new, stricter compensation plan for client-side personnel (while leaving the firm's proprietary traders untouched), Maughan was forced to modify it after the departure of nearly 10% of the firm's 200 managing directors.

Meanwhile, litigation arising from the scandal wound its way through the courts. In 1995 Salomon shareholders were offered a $40 million settlement of their class action suit.

WHO

Chairman and CEO: Robert E. Denham, age 49,
$1,000,000 pay
EVP; Chairman and CEO, Salomon Brothers Inc:
Deryck C. Maughan, age 47, $838,000 pay
EVP and General Counsel: Robert H. Mundheim,
age 62, $1,048,000 pay
CFO: Jerome H. Bailey, age 42, $1,000,000 pay
President, Phibro Division: Andrew J. Hall,
$1,000,000 pay
Treasurer: John G. Macfarlane, age 40, $1,000,000 pay
Managing Director Planning and Resources (HR):
Matthew Levitan
Auditors: Arthur Andersen & Co, SC

WHERE

HQ: 7 World Trade Center, New York, NY 10048
Phone: 212-783-7000
Fax: 212-783-2110

	1994 Sales		1994 Pretax Income	
	$ mil.	% of total	$ mil.	% of total
North America	4,449	71	(119)	—
Europe	1,332	21	(841)	—
Asia & other regions	497	8	129	—
Total	**6,278**	**100**	**(831)**	**—**

WHAT

	1994 Sales		1994 Pretax Income	
	$ mil.	% of total	$ mil.	% of total
Salomon Brothers	5,751	92	(963)	—
Phibro Division	208	3	81	—
Phibro USA	87	1	18	—
Corporate & other	232	4	33	—
Total	**6,278**	**100**	**(831)**	**—**

	1994 Sales	
	$ mil.	% of total
Interest & dividends	5,902	86
Investment banking	486	7
Commissions	336	5
Principal transactions	(560)	—
Other	114	2
Total	**6,278**	**100**

Salomon Brothers
Asset and money
management
Financial research and
advice
Investment banking
Mutual funds
Securities and
currency trading
Securities underwriting

The Mortgage Corp. (UK)

Phibro Division
Commodities trading

**Phibro Energy Production,
Inc. (PEPI)**
Russian oil joint venture

Phibro USA
Oil refining

Salomon Swapco Inc
Derivatives subsidiary

KEY COMPETITORS

ADM
Alex. Brown
Amerada Hess
American Express
Amoco
Ashland, Inc.
Atlantic Richfield
Bear Stearns
Brown Brothers
Harriman
Cargill
Chevron
Coastal
ConAgra
Continental Grain
CS Holding
Dean Witter,
Discover

Equitable
Exxon
Goldman Sachs
Hambrecht &
Quist
ING Group
KKR
Koch
Lehman Brothers
Merrill Lynch
Mobil
Morgan Stanley
Nomura Securities
Occidental
Oryx
Paine Webber
Pennzoil

Phillips
Petroleum
Prudential
Raymond
James
Financial
Rothschilds
Stephens
Sun Company
Swiss Bank
Texaco
Transamerica
Travelers
Unocal
USX–Marathon
Yamaichi
Securities

HOW MUCH

	Annual Growth	1985	1986	1987	1988	1989	1990	1991	1992	1993	1994
Sales ($ mil.)	1.1%	5,701	6,789	6,003	6,146	8,999	8,946	9,175	8,183	8,799	6,278
Net income ($ mil.)	—	557	516	142	280	470	303	507	550	864	(399)
Income as % of sales	—	9.8%	6.7%	2.4%	4.6%	5.2%	3.4%	5.5%	6.7%	9.8%	—
Earnings per share ($)	—	3.60	3.32	0.86	1.63	3.20	2.05	3.79	4.05	6.57	(4.31)
Stock price – high ($)	—	46.75	59.38	44.50	28.38	29.38	27.00	37.00	39.00	51.88	52.75
Stock price – low ($)	—	30.00	37.38	16.63	19.38	20.50	20.00	20.75	26.63	34.38	35.00
Stock price – close ($)	(1.6%)	43.50	38.38	19.63	24.13	23.38	24.38	30.63	38.13	47.63	37.50
P/E – high	—	13	18	52	17	9	13	10	10	8	—
P/E – low	—	8	11	19	12	6	10	6	7	5	—
Dividends per share ($)	1.9%	0.54	0.62	0.64	0.64	0.64	0.64	0.64	0.64	0.64	0.64
Book value per share ($)	5.7%	20.02	22.72	21.15	21.82	24.08	25.68	28.31	32.34	39.06	32.88
Employees	4.1%	6,300	7,800	8,000	8,400	8,924	8,883	8,917	8,631	8,640	9,077

1994 Year-end:
Debt ratio: 96.5%
Return on equity: —
Cash (mil.): $3,539
Long-term debt (mil.): $18,228
No. of shares (mil.): 106
Dividends
  Yield: 1.7%
  Payout: —
Market value (mil.): $3,969
Assets (mil.): $172,732

**Stock Price History
High/Low 1985–94**

SCHERING-PLOUGH CORPORATION

OVERVIEW

Schering-Plough produces pharmaceuticals, consumer health products, and animal health products. The company's top-selling product is Claritin, with worldwide sales that increased 71% in 1994. Claritin is #1 in the US for new prescriptions for plain antihistamines. The Madison, New Jersey–based company also makes such top-selling drugs as Proventil (an antiasthmatic that is experiencing generic competition) and Eulexin (treatment for advanced prostate cancer). Over-the-counter products include Coricidin, Afrin, Dr. Scholl's, Coppertone, and Solarcaine.

Schering-Plough spends about 1/4 of its R&D expenditures on biotechnology research. The company believes the key to cost-effective quality medical care is continued biomedical innovation. It has developed a joint venture with Canji Inc. to research new cancer treatments based on Canji's new p53 gene therapy technology. The company has an agreement with Corvas to develop oral antithrombotic drugs to treat cardiovascular disorders. Schering-Plough has more products in the early development stages and fewer ones close to the production stage.

Chairman Robert Luciano's continual restructuring, downsizing efforts, and increased attention to managed care organizations have resulted in a lean and well-managed company. Shering-Plough is expanding worldwide (almost half of its sales are foreign). It has built new plants in Ireland and is working on plants in China, Mexico, and Singapore.

WHEN

Schering takes its name from Ernst Schering, a Berlin chemist who formed the company in 1864 to sell chemicals to apothecary shops. By 1880 the German company was exporting pharmaceuticals to the US. An American subsidiary was established in 1928, and during the 1930s it developed processes for the mass production of sex hormones. At the outbreak of WWII the US government seized the subsidiary and appointed government attorney Francis Brown director. Brown put together a research team whose efforts led to development of new postwar drugs, including Chlor-Trimeton, one of the first antihistamines, and the cold medicine Coricidin.

In 1952 the government sold Schering to Merrill Lynch, which took it public. Its most profitable products in the 1950s were new steroids. In 1957 Schering bought White Labs. In the 1960s the company introduced Tinactin (antifungal, 1965), Garamycin (antibiotic, 1964), and Afrin (decongestant, 1967).

The 1971 merger with Plough, Inc., expanded the product line to include cosmetics and consumer items such as Coppertone and Di-Gel. Plough had originated in Memphis, Tennessee, in 1908. Abe Plough, its founder, borrowed $125 from his father to create an "antiseptic healing oil" consisting of cottonseed oil, carbolic acid, and camphor. Plough sold his concoction door-to-door and went on to acquire 28 companies. He served as chairman of newly merged Schering-Plough until 1976. Known for his philanthropy in Memphis, Plough died in 1984 at the age of 92.

Schering-Plough introduced many products after the merger, including Lotrimin AF (anti-fungal, 1975), Drixoral (cold remedy, made nonprescription in 1982), and the antiasthmatics Vanceril (1976) and Proventil (1981). When Garamycin's patent expired in 1980, the company introduced a similar antibiotic, Netromycin.

Schering-Plough was one of the first of the drug giants to make significant investments in biotechnology: it owns a portion of Biogen of Cambridge, Massachusetts, and acquired DNAX Research Institute of Palo Alto, California, in 1982. In 1993 Intron A, a biotechnology drug to treat chronic hepatitis C, was the company's top-selling product.

Acquisitions in the late 1970s and 1980s included Scholl (foot care, 1979), Key Pharmaceuticals (cardiovascular drugs, 1986), and Cooper Companies (eye care, 1988). The company sold Maybelline (cosmetics) to Playtex in 1990 and received FDA approval to sell Gyne-Lotrimin (a treatment for yeast infections) as an over-the-counter product.

In April 1993 Schering-Plough began marketing its nonsedating antihistamine, Claritin, in the US. By year's end domestic sales had reached an impressive $130 million. In 1994 the company gained FDA approval to market the first colored disposable contact lenses. In late 1994 the company received FDA permission for Claritin-D, which adds a decongestant to the top-selling product.

Schering-Plough's Robert Luciano resigned as CEO in 1995 but will retain his chairmanship until his contract expires in 1998. Company president and COO Richard Kogan was chosen to succeed Luciano as CEO.

NYSE symbol: SGP
Fiscal year ends: December 31

Chairman: Robert P. Luciano, age 61, $2,274,100 pay
President and CEO: Richard J. Kogan, age 53,
$1,366,500 pay (prior to promotion)
EVP Administration: Hugh A. D'Andrade, age 56,
$879,125 pay
EVP; President, Schering-Plough HealthCare Products:
Donald R. Conklin, age 58, $880,000 pay
EVP Finance: Jack L. Wyszomierski, age 40
EVP; President, Schering-Plough Pharmaceuticals:
Raul E. Cesan, age 47
**SVP Investor Relations and Corporate
Communications:** Geraldine U. Foster, age 52
SVP Taxes: Daniel A. Nichols, age 54
SVP Human Resources: Gordon C. O'Brien, age 54
SVP and General Counsel: Joseph C. Connors, age 46
VP Administration and Business Development:
J. Martin Comey, age 60
VP Corporate Information Services: Robert S. Lyons
Auditors: Deloitte & Touche LLP

WHERE

HQ: One Giralda Farms, Madison, NJ 07940-1000
Phone: 201-822-7000
Fax: 201-822-7447

	1994 Sales		1994 Operating Income	
	$ mil.	% of total	$ mil.	% of total
US	2,553	55	878	65
Europe, Middle East & Africa	1,064	23	232	17
Canada & Asia/ Pacific	646	14	138	10
Latin America	394	8	102	8
Total	**4,657**	**100**	**1,350**	**100**

WHAT

	1994 Sales		1994 Operating Income	
	$ mil.	% of total	$ mil.	% of total
Pharmaceuticals	4,001	86	1,191	88
Health care prods.	656	14	159	12
Total	**4,657**	**100**	**1,350**	**100**

Selected Pharmaceuticals
Celestone (anti-inflammatory)
Claritin (antihistamine)
Elocon (dermatological)
Eulexin (for prostate cancer)
Garamycin (antibiotic)
Intron A (cancer treatment)
Nitro-Dur (antianginal)
Normodyne
 (antihypertensive)
Proventil (antiasthmatic)
Theo-Dur (antiasthmatic)
Vancenase AQ (antiallergy)
Vanceril (antiasthmatic)

**Selected Consumer
Health Care**
Afrin (decongestant)
Coppertone (suncare)
Coricidin (decongestant)
Dr. Scholl's (foot care)
Drixoral (decongestant)
Durasoft (contact lenses)
Gyne-Lotrimin
 (antifungal)
Lotrimin AF (antifungal)
Solarcaine (sunburn pain)
Tinactin (antifungal)

Holiday Products
Paas (egg coloring)

KEY COMPETITORS

Abbott Labs
ALZA
American Home Products
Amgen
Bausch & Lomb
Bayer
Biogen
Bristol-Myers Squibb
Carter-Wallace
Chiron Corp.
Ciba-Geigy
Eli Lilly
Genentech
Glaxo Wellcome

Hoechst
Johnson & Johnson
Merck
Nestlé
Novo Nordisk
Pfizer
Pharmacia & Upjohn
Procter & Gamble
Rhône-Poulenc
Roche
Sandoz
SmithKline Beecham
Warner-Lambert

HOW MUCH

	Annual Growth	1985	1986	1987	1988	1989	1990	1991	1992	1993	1994
Sales ($ mil.)	9.4%	2,079	2,399	2,699	2,969	3,158	3,323	3,616	4,056	4,341	4,657
Net income ($ mil.)	19.1%	192	266	316	390	471	565	646	720	825	922
Income as % of sales	—	9.2%	11.1%	11.7%	13.1%	14.9%	17.0%	17.9%	17.8%	19.0%	19.8%
Earnings per share ($)	22.1%	0.80	1.09	1.37	1.74	2.09	2.50	3.01	3.60	4.23	4.82
Stock price – high ($)	—	16.63	22.00	27.63	29.69	43.00	50.75	67.13	70.13	71.00	75.88
Stock price – low ($)	—	8.81	14.00	15.63	22.63	27.69	36.94	40.75	49.88	51.75	54.50
Stock price – close ($)	19.8%	14.53	19.75	23.50	28.38	42.75	44.38	65.75	63.63	68.50	74.00
P/E – high	—	21	20	20	17	21	20	22	20	17	16
P/E – low	—	11	13	11	13	13	15	14	14	12	11
Dividends per share ($)	18.8%	0.42	0.45	0.51	0.70	0.89	1.07	1.27	1.50	1.74	1.98
Book value per share ($)	1.9%	7.15	6.24	6.17	7.46	8.64	9.37	6.67	8.00	8.17	8.46
Employees	(1.0%)	23,200	23,500	21,700	22,400	21,300	19,700	20,200	21,100	21,600	21,200

1994 Year-end:
Debt ratio: 38.1%
Return on equity: 58.4%
Cash (mil.): $161
Current ratio: 0.86
Long-term debt (mil.): $186
No. of shares (mil.): 186
Dividends
 Yield: 2.7%
 Payout: 41.1%
Market value (mil.): $13,765

**Stock Price History
High/Low 1985–94**

SCHLUMBERGER N.V.

OVERVIEW

New York–based Schlumberger packs a one-two punch, combining oil field services and exploration with a sophisticated electronics and technology business. With extensive operations worldwide and 75% of sales and income derived from business outside the US, Schlumberger discovered that the world was a dangerous place in 1994. In Algeria 2 of its engineers were killed by terrorists. Political unrest caused the company to curtail its activities in Algeria and Nigeria, while political confusion in the former Soviet Union forced the company to pull back on investment plans in that region, leading to a 22-year low in the number of active drilling rigs outside North America.

Schlumberger's Oilfield Services unit includes wireline logging, well testing, seismic surveying, geoscience software and computing services, drilling and pumping services, and cementing and stimulation services for enhanced well productivity.

Schlumberger's Measurement & Systems unit makes such diverse products as utility meters, automatic testing equipment for the semiconductor industry, fuel dispensing systems for gas stations, point-of-sale payment systems, and parking management systems. Schlumberger Technology's ATE Division is the world leader in engineering-based electron beam probing systems (used in the testing of integrated circuits).

WHEN

Conrad and Marcel Schlumberger were Alsatian scientists who believed that electrical resistance could be used to measure the earth's subsurface. Paul Schlumberger, their father and fellow scientist, thought a business would follow and offered capital for the venture (1919); the brothers' Paris home became the site of Schlumberger.

Their theories were proven by the mid-1920s, but no application developed until 1927, when Pechelbronn Oil became interested in using their technique to search for oil. Conrad asked his son-in-law, Henri Doll, to design a tool for the purpose, and the process of wireline logging, akin to an X-ray for charting where oil and gas lie in a well, was born. Doll turned out to be a tremendous asset — upon his 1967 retirement it was estimated that 40% of Schlumberger revenues stemmed from his inventions.

Conrad died in 1936, leaving Marcel in charge until 1953; Marcel's death resulted in factionalism. Different family members controlled the 4 divisions (North American, South American/Middle Eastern, European, and Doll's US technical development), creating disorganization. Marcel's son Pierre took the company public, merged foreign operations with North American headquarters in Houston, and restructured the company in 1956 as Schlumberger Ltd, incorporated in the Netherlands Antilles. In 1965 Pierre ended nepotism, giving leadership of Schlumberger to another Frenchman, Jean Riboud. That year Riboud moved the headquarters to New York, where it remains today.

Riboud began a series of acquisitions, including the Compagnie des Compteurs, a

French electric-meter manufacturer (1970). Envisioning a company that would provide information as well as oil field services, he purchased Fairchild Camera & Instrument in 1979, believing that semiconductors would play an important future role. Today 35% of revenues are derived from non–oil field products and services. In 1982 Riboud bought Applicon, a producer of computer-aided design and manufacturing software (sold in 1993).

Through a series of acquisitions, Schlumberger invested in artificial intelligence technology, which it introduced in 1982. Known for providing state-of-the-art equipment to the oil industry, Schlumberger in 1986 bought GECO, a Norwegian geophysical company noted for marine seismic analysis. In 1991 Schlumberger acquired 51% of Prakla Seismos (and the remaining 49% in 1993), which had strong onshore seismic operations, from the German government and folded it into its GECO unit.

In 1992 Schlumberger acquired oil field service businesses Seismograph Service Limited and GeoQuest Systems from Raytheon. The next year the company acquired semiconductor manufacturing supplier TLA Technology. Also in 1993 Schlumberger acquired Dow Chemical's half of well cementing and stimulation joint venture Dowell Schlumberger, giving it full ownership.

In 1994 GeoQuest acquired CPS, which makes mapping software for oil and gas exploration and production.

In 1995 the company announced that it had teamed up with Cable and Wireless to form Omnes, a global communications and information system for the oil and gas industry.

NYSE symbol: SLB
Fiscal year ends: December 31

Chairman, President, and CEO: D. Euan Baird, age 57, $1,600,000 pay
EVP Oilfield Services: Victor E. Grijalva, age 56, $830,000 pay
EVP Measurement and Systems: Clermont A. Matton, age 53, $660,000 pay
EVP Finance and CFO: Arthur Lindenauer, age 57, $650,000 pay
EVP Health, Safety, and Environment: Alain Roger, age 64, $520,646 pay
EVP Technology and Communication: Ian Strecker, age 55
VP Business Development and Treasurer: Michel Soublin, age 49
VP Personnel: Pierre E. Bismuth, age 50
VP: Patrick J. B. Corser, age 51
VP: Jean-Marc Perraud, age 47
Secretary and General Counsel: David S. Browning, age 55
Auditors: Price Waterhouse LLP

WHERE

HQ: 277 Park Ave., New York, NY 10172-0266
Phone: 212-350-9400
Fax: 212-350-9564

Schlumberger operates 930 facilities in 100 countries.

	1994 Sales		1994 Operating Income	
	$ mil.	% of total	$ mil.	% of total
US	1,650	25	177	27
France	690	10	58	10
Other Europe	1,609	24	(9)	—
Other countries	2,748	41	410	63
Adjustments	—	—	(43)	—
Total	**6,697**	**100**	**593**	**100**

WHAT

	1994 Sales		1994 Operating Income	
	$ mil.	% of total	$ mil.	% of total
Oilfield Services	4,362	65	495	80
Measurement & Systems	2,335	35	121	20
Adjustments	—	—	(23)	—
Total	**6,697**	**100**	**593**	**100**

Oilfield Services
Anadrill (directional drilling, logging while drilling, measurements while drilling)
Dowell (coiled tubing services, drilling fluid services, pumping services, well cementing and stimulation)
GECO-Prakla (exploration services, marine and land seismic acquisition, seismic data processing)
GeoQuest (data services and software products)
Sedco Forex (contract drilling and operation)
Wireline & Testing (borehole measurements, corrosion evaluation services, production monitoring services, well testing)

Measurement and Systems
Automatic test equipment (semiconductors and circuit boards test systems)
Electricity management (electricity meters, management services)
Electronic transactions (fuel dispensing systems, parking management systems, public pay phones)
Gas management (gas meters, management services)
Water management (water meters, management services)

KEY COMPETITORS

Baker Hughes	Ingram	Nabors Industries
BJ Services	Intergraph	Tektronix
Dresser	Kaneb Services	Teledyne
Emerson	Litton	Teradyne
Fluor	Industries	Vishay
Halliburton	LTV	Intertechnology
Hewlett-Packard	McDermott	Western Atlas

HOW MUCH

	Annual Growth	1985	1986	1987	1988	1989	1990	1991	1992	1993	1994
Sales ($ mil.)	1.0%	6,119	4,568	4,402	4,925	4,686	5,306	6,145	6,332	6,706	6,697
Net income ($ mil.)	4.8%	351	(2,018)	283	454	420	570	816	662	583	536
Income as % of sales	—	5.7%	—	6.4%	9.2%	9.0%	10.7%	13.3%	10.4%	8.7%	8.0%
Earnings per share ($)	7.3%	1.17	(7.02)	1.02	1.72	1.77	2.40	3.42	2.75	2.40	2.21
Stock price – high ($)	—	43.88	37.75	51.00	38.75	50.50	69.88	74.00	70.63	68.88	63.00
Stock price – low ($)	—	32.38	27.25	26.00	28.50	32.00	43.50	50.50	52.63	55.38	50.00
Stock price – close ($)	3.6%	36.50	31.75	28.75	32.63	49.13	57.88	62.38	57.25	59.13	50.38
P/E – high	—	38	—	50	23	29	29	22	26	26	29
P/E – low	—	28	—	26	17	18	18	15	19	19	23
Dividends per share ($)	0.0%	1.20	1.20	1.20	1.20	1.20	1.20	1.20	1.20	1.20	1.20
Book value per share ($)	(2.3%)	23.24	14.67	14.09	11.59	12.19	13.67	16.06	17.50	18.09	18.92
Employees	(2.6%)	61,000	50,000	50,000	48,000	46,000	50,000	53,000	51,000	48,000	48,000

1994 Year-end:
Debt ratio: 19.4%
Return on equity: 11.9%
Cash (mil.): $1,232
Current ratio: 1.37
Long-term debt (mil.): $394
No. of shares (mil.): 242
Dividends
  Yield: 2.4%
  Payout: 54.3%
Market value (mil.): $12,204

Stock Price History
High/Low 1985–94

TEACHERS INSURANCE

OVERVIEW

The giant is stirring. Teachers Insurance and Annuity Association–College Retirement Equities Fund (TIAA-CREF) is beginning to use its investment might to influence the management of the companies in which it invests. As one of the US's largest insurance companies and the world's largest private pension system, TIAA-CREF has the muscle to succeed in this endeavor: it is estimated that the association owns about 1% of US stocks. In 1994 the association used its influence to help oust the chairman of W.R. Grace. It also started a corporate assessment program, headed by Kenneth West, formerly of Harris Bancorp in Chicago, to further good corporate governance procedures.

TIAA-CREF provides portable insurance and retirement benefits to the often-transient employees of educational and research organizations. It gains new clients primarily through the adoption of its services by new institutions, as part of an increasing menu of benefit plans available to a formerly underserved group. In recent years the organization has increased its scope to include public school teachers.

One of TIAA-CREF's strengths is its unusually low overhead: about 0.25% for TIAA and 0.4% for CREF.

WHEN

The Carnegie Foundation for the Advancement of Teaching established TIAA in New York City in 1905 with an endowment of $15 million to provide retirement benefits and other forms of financial security to employees of educational and research organizations. The original endowment was found to be insufficient, and in 1918 the fund was reorganized into a defined contribution plan with another $1 million from Carnegie. TIAA, now the major pension system of higher education in the US, was the first portable pension plan, allowing participants to move between institutions without losing retirement benefits and offering a fixed annuity. But the fund kept requiring cash from the foundation until 1947.

In 1952 CEO William Greenough pioneered the first variable annuity, based on common stock investments, and established the College Retirement Equities Fund (CREF) to offer it. Designed to supplement TIAA's fixed-dollar annuity, CREF invested participants' premiums in stocks. CREF, like TIAA, was subject to New York insurance regulations but not SEC regulation.

In the 1950s TIAA led the fight for Social Security benefits for university employees and began offering group total disability coverage (1957) and group life insurance (1958).

In 1971 TIAA-CREF established the Common Fund to help colleges boost investment returns from their endowments; TIAA went on to help manage endowments. TIAA facilitated the establishment in 1972 of the Investor Responsibility Research Center, which provides objective information on making socially responsible investments.

For 70 years TIAA-CREF members had no way to exit the system other than retirement. Members had only 2 investment choices:

stocks through CREF or a one-way transfer into TIAA's annuity accounts based on long-term bond, real estate, and mortgage investments. In the 1980s CREF indexed its funds to the S&P average. By the 1987 stock crash, the organization had one million members, many of whom wanted protection from stock market fluctuations and more investment options. In 1988 CREF added a money market fund, but this required SEC oversight, and the SEC required complete transferability, even outside of TIAA-CREF.

Since transferability made TIAA-CREF vulnerable to competition, it began to add investment options (the TIAA Interest Payment Retirement Option; CREF Bond Market and Social Choice accounts; and Global Equities, Growth, and Equity Index accounts) and to offer long-term care plans.

With about 40% of its investments in mortgages and real estate, TIAA was somewhat affected by the cycles of the commercial real estate sector, but less so than other insurers because of its policy of direct investment in such projects as the Mall of America.

In 1993 chairman and CEO Clifton Wharton resigned after being named US deputy secretary of state and was replaced by John Biggs.

In addition to investment activism, in 1994 TIAA-CREF began a major educational campaign to acquaint its members with basic principles of retirement planning and investment. One the most important elements in the campaign is its emphasis on long-term results. This may help persuade members not to switch their funds to flashy short-term investments outside the TIAA-CREF system and not to panic during cyclical events like the 1994 bond crash, which depressed income.

Nonprofit organization
Fiscal year ends: December 31

WHO

Chairman and CEO: John H. Biggs
President and COO: Thomas W. Jones
EVP Finance and Planning: Richard L. Gibbs
EVP Law and General Counsel: Charles H. Stamm
EVP TIAA Investments: J. Daniel Lee Jr.
EVP CREF Investments: James S. Martin
EVP Pension and Annuity Services: John J. McCormack
EVP Insurance Services: Thomas G. Walsh
EVP Operations Support: John A. Putney Jr.
EVP External Affairs: Don W. Harrell
EVP Human Resources: Matina S. Horner
Auditors: Deloitte & Touche LLP

WHERE

HQ: Teachers Insurance and Annuity Association–
College Retirement Equities Fund, 730 Third Ave.,
New York, NY 10017-3206
Phone: 212-490-9000
Fax: 212-916-6231

TIAA-CREF is licensed in 33 states, is exempt from
licensing in 17 states, and is licensed in Canada.

WHAT

	1994 TIAA Assets	
	$ mil.	% of total
Cash & equivalents	432	1
US, Canadian & other government bonds	2,424	3
Utility bonds	8,016	11
Corporate bonds	19,022	26
Mortgage- & asset-backed securities	13,911	19
Stocks	163	0
Mortgage loans	20,217	27
Real estate	7,075	10
Other	2,088	3
Total	**73,348**	**100**

	1994 CREF Assets	
	$ mil.	% of total
Stock account	54,761	88
Money Market account	2,919	5
Bond Market account	619	1
Social Choice account	782	1
Global Equities	2,745	4
Growth fund	309	1
Equity Index	72	0
Total	**62,207**	**100**

CREF Investment Accounts
Bond Market account
Global Equities account
Money Market account
Social Choice account
Stock account

Selected TIAA Investments

African Development Bank	J. C. Penney
Alco Standard	Kmart
AT&T	May Stores
BankAmerica	MCI
Circus Circus	Panhandle Eastern
Coca Cola	Pipeline Co.
Cox Enterprises	Sears
Enron	Sprint
Federal Express	Sun Microsystems
First Union Corp.	Time Warner
General Mills	Viacom

TIAA Insurance Products
Group life insurance
Group total disability insurance
Individual life insurance
Long-term care insurance
Retirement and group retirement annuities

KEY COMPETITORS

Aetna	MassMutual
American Express	Merrill Lynch
Berkshire Hathaway	MetLife
Chubb	New York Life
CIGNA	Northwestern Mutual
Citicorp	Prudential
Equitable	T. Rowe Price
Fleet	Transamerica
FMR	Travelers
John Hancock	USAA

HOW MUCH

	Annual Growth	1985	1986	1987	1988	1989	1990	1991	1992	1993	1994
TIAA assets ($ mil.)	13.7%	23,159	27,887	33,210	38,631	44,374	49,894	55,576	61,777	67,483	73,348
TIAA sales ($ mil.)	6.8%	5,774	6,839	7,735	8,414	9,046	9,370	10,067	10,300	10,400	10,413
TIAA increase in reserves ($ mil.)	2.7%	—	—	—	—	—	240	232	178	(63)	268
CREF assets ($ mil.)	12.4%	21,651	26,191	25,510	31,700	39,515	38,055	48,450	52,064	60,737	62,207
Employees	4.9 %	2,600	2,800	3,200	3,500	3,500	3,700	3,800	3,800	4,000	4,000

1994 Year-end:
TIAA equity
as % of assets: 4.7%

TIAA CREF

TIAA Assets
($ mil.) 1985–94

80,000
70,000
60,000
50,000
40,000
30,000
20,000
10,000
0

TEXACO INC.

OVERVIEW

Among integrated petroleum firms, White Plains, New York–based Texaco trails only Exxon and Mobil in the *FORTUNE* 500. Over the past 2 years, the oil giant has reorganized its operations in order to focus on its core oil and gas businesses. Texaco sold its chemical operations to a joint venture controlled by John Huntsman (of Huntsman Chemical) and Kerry Packer (owner of Australia's Consolidated Press Holdings) in 1993. Texaco also cut overhead costs by almost $200 million in 1994 and disposed of 300 scattered, nonstrategic US oil and gas producing properties in early 1995.

Despite a sluggish market for oil and gas and a drop in sales in 1994, the company is actively investing in developing new fields and upgrading old ones. In 1994 the company in-creased worldwide oil production by 66,000 barrels a day and plans to pour $19 billion into its oil and gas businesses over the next 5 years.

Internationally, the company is exploring high-potential areas in Russia, China, and Colombia. It is also investing in high technology to increase its output in oil fields in the North Sea, and it is continuing to develop fields in the Gulf of Martaban, the Gulf of Mexico, and the Permian Basin of Texas.

Caltex Petroleum, Texaco's 50-50 refining and marketing joint venture with Chevron, operates in 61 countries. It is currently upgrading refineries and expanding its retail outlets; in 1994 Caltex renovated 177 existing service stations and built an additional 119.

WHEN

"Buckskin Joe" Cullinan came to Texas in 1897 and, relying on sales to old friends from his days as a Standard Oil worker in Pennsylvania, began his own oil company.

When the Spindletop gusher hit in 1901, some 200 "oil companies" swarmed onto the scene. Cullinan decided the way to make money was to sell oil other people had found. He enlisted the support of Arnold Schlaet, who managed investments for 2 New York leather merchants. Cullinan and the Schlaet interests formed Texas Fuel in 1902. In a few months they changed the name to the Texas Company, selling under the Texaco brand.

The colorful Cullinan was deposed in a 1916 fight with New York executives. From its New York base, the Texas Company quickly expanded across the globe. When Standard of California's discoveries in Saudi Arabia proved more than it could handle, it summoned the Texas Company, and the 2 companies spawned Caltex for overseas marketing in 1936.

In the 1930s the Texas Company, partly through a company controlled by political boss Huey Long's family, leased a million acres of state-owned, oil-rich marshland in Louisiana. With such resources it became the only oil company with service stations in all states. In the 1940s it began sponsoring radio opera and Milton Berle's TV show. Its ads urged, "You can trust your car to the man who wears the star," a reference to the company logo. But Texaco (renamed in 1959) fell from atop the oil industry in the 1960s and 1970s as US wells dried up. Also it passed up drilling in Alaska's Prudhoe Bay and lost overseas supplies to nationalizations by developing countries.

Texaco thought it had found a source of oil in the $8.6 billion purchase of Getty Oil in 1983, but Getty had already agreed to be acquired by Pennzoil. A Texas court ordered Texaco to pay Pennzoil $10.53 billion in damages, and Texaco sought bankruptcy protection in 1987. After a $3 billion settlement with Pennzoil later that year, Texaco emerged from bankruptcy — just in time to fend off raider Carl Icahn. After those battles, Texaco raised about $7 billion, partly by selling its West German subsidiary and Texaco Canada (1988). It shucked 2,500 unprofitable gas stations, pulling out of 11 states.

In 1989 it launched a joint venture, Star Enterprise, with Saudi Arabia. Texaco put in 60% of its US refining and marketing operations, and the Saudis chipped in $812 million in cash and a steady flow of crude. The Persian Gulf War highlighted the weakness in that arrangement: 60% of Texaco's refinery output relied on Saudi crude.

In 1993 James Kinnear, who had led Texaco back from bankruptcy and streamlined the company's operations, retired. He was succeeded by Alfred DeCrane.

In 1994, hoping to take advantage of the deregulation of the natural gas industry, Texaco created the Gulf Coast Star Center, a natural gas system with transportation, storage, processing, and marketing operations providing a "one-stop shop" for customers.

In 1995 Texaco and Huntsman announced plans to form a joint venture to run Texaco's worldwide lubricant additives line. Texaco also launched a major advertising campaign to promote its gas, oil, and antifreeze products.

NYSE symbol: TX
Fiscal year ends: December 31

Chairman and CEO: Alfred C. DeCrane Jr., age 63, $1,522,635 pay
VC: Allen J. Krowe, age 62, $1,023,705 pay
SVP: James L. Dunlap, age 57, $581,723 pay
SVP: Peter I. Bijur, age 52, $523,379 pay
SVP: C. Robert Black, age 59, $514,212 pay
SVP and CFO: William C. Bousquette, age 58
SVP: William K. Tell Jr., age 61
SVP and General Counsel: Stephen M. Turner, age 56
VP Human Resources: John D. Ambler, age 60
VP and Secretary: Carl B. Davidson, age 61
VP Investor Relations and Shareholder Services: Elizabeth P. Smith, age 45
General Tax Counsel: Michael N. Ambler, age 58
Treasurer: James F. Link, age 50
Comptroller: Robert C. Oelkers, age 50
Auditors: Arthur Andersen & Co, SC

WHERE

HQ: 2000 Westchester Ave., White Plains, NY 10650
Phone: 914-253-4000
Fax: 914-253-7753

Texaco conducts exploration and production activities in the US, Europe, Latin America, western Africa, the Middle East, and the Far East.

	1994 Sales		1994 Operating Income	
	$ mil.	% of total	$ mil.	% of total
US	15,936	49	522	69
Europe	8,479	26	65	9
Other countries	8,125	25	171	22
Total	**32,540**	**100**	**758**	**100**

WHAT

	1994 Sales % of total
Refined products	54
Crude oil	30
Natural gas	8
Other	8
Total	**100**

Selected Subsidiaries and Affiliates
Caltex Petroleum Corp. (50%, refining and marketing venture with Chevron, Asia-Pacific region and Africa)
Star Enterprise (50%, refining and marketing venture with Saudi Arabian Oil, 26 eastern and Gulf Coast states)
Texaco Oil Trading and Supply Company
Texaco Refining and Marketing Inc. (gas stations, 23 midwestern and western states)
Texaco Trading and Transportation Inc. (pipeline and trucking operations)
Timan Pechora Co. LLC (Russian oil exploration partnership with Amoco, Exxon, and Norsk Hydro)

KEY COMPETITORS

Amerada Hess	E-Z Serve	Phillips
Amoco	Imperial Oil	Petroleum
Ashland, Inc.	Kerr-McGee	Racetrac
Atlantic Richfield	Koch	Petroleum
British Gas	Kroger	Repsol
British Petroleum	Mobil	Royal Dutch/Shell
Broken Hill	Norsk Hydro	Sinclair Oil
Chevron	Occidental	Southland
Circle K	Panhandle	Sun Company
Coastal	Eastern	TOTAL
Columbia Gas	PDVSA	Unocal
Diamond	PEMEX	USA Petroleum
Shamrock	Pennzoil	USX–Delhi
Elf Aquitaine	Petrobrás	USX–Marathon
Enron	Petrofina	World Oil
Exxon		

HOW MUCH

	Annual Growth	1985	1986	1987	1988	1989	1990	1991	1992	1993	1994
Sales ($ mil.)	(3.8%)	46,297	31,613	34,372	33,544	32,416	40,899	37,271	36,812	33,245	32,540
Net income ($ mil.)	(3.3%)	1,233	725	(4,407)	1,304	2,413	1,450	1,294	1,012	1,068	910
Income as % of sales	—	2.7%	2.3%	—	3.8%	7.3%	3.5%	3.4%	2.7%	3.2%	2.8%
Earnings per share ($)	(4.6%)	4.85	3.01	(18.15)	5.19	8.74	5.08	4.55	3.53	3.74	3.17
Stock price – high ($)	—	40.88	37.13	47.50	52.75	59.00	68.50	70.00	66.88	69.50	68.13
Stock price – low ($)	—	27.00	26.00	23.50	35.63	48.50	55.00	55.50	56.13	57.63	58.13
Stock price – close ($)	8.0%	30.00	35.88	37.25	51.13	58.88	60.50	61.25	59.75	64.75	59.88
P/E – high	—	8	12	—	10	7	14	15	19	19	21
P/E – low	—	6	9	—	7	6	11	12	16	15	18
Dividends per share ($)	0.7%	3.00	3.00	0.75	2.25	10.10	3.05	3.20	3.20	3.20	3.20
Book value per share ($)	(5.5%)	57.04	56.71	37.76	33.27	34.65	33.84	35.51	36.04	37.18	34.42
Employees	(6.5%)	54,481	51,978	50,164	41,820	37,067	39,199	40,181	37,582	32,514	29,713

1994 Year-end:
Debt ratio: 42.0%
Return on equity: 10.3%
Cash (mil.): $464
Current ratio: 1.20
Long-term debt (mil.): $5,564
No. of shares (mil.): 260
Dividends
  Yield: 5.3%
  Payout: 100.9%
Market value (mil.): $15,541

Stock Price History High/Low 1985–94

TIME WARNER INC.

OVERVIEW

With its proposed merger with Turner Broadcasting, New York–based Time Warner is vying with Walt Disney for the top spot among media conglomerates. Known for its formidable assets and famous brand names, Time Warner has a portfolio of such industry giants as Time Inc. (the US's #1 magazine publisher); Warner Bros. (the world's #1 producer and distributor of movies, TV programs, and videos); Warner Music Group (the world's #1 music publisher, Warner/Chappell, plus 49 record labels); Home Box Office (the #1 pay cable TV service); Little, Brown and Co. and Warner Books (leading book publishers); and Time Warner Cable (the #2 US cable system).

Time Warner also owns stakes in cable TV programming through Turner Broadcasting (19.6%) and other networks such as Cinemax, Court TV (55%), Comedy Central (50%), and the SEGA Channel (33%, video games). The company considered buying NBC but instead launched WB Network in 1995 as an outlet for its library of films, TV programs, and cartoons. It also is investing heavily in cable in the US (enough to vie with #1 Tele-Communications) and in Japan's fledgling industry. Concentrated in major metropolitan and suburban areas, its cable operation expects to provide a wide range of services (pay-per-view, interactive TV, and telephone) and online outlets for its huge treasury of magazines, movies, TV programs, and books.

The company has pledged to reduce its debt from the 1989 merger of Time and Warner. In 1995 it sold a 51% stake in its Six Flags amusement parks as part of its plan to sell $2–$3 billion in noncore businesses. The proposed Turner merger would make Time Warner larger than the proposed Walt Disney–Capital Cities/ABC marriage but has been muddied by a legal challenge from partner US WEST and complaints from Turner stockholders.

WHEN

Time Warner was created in 1989 when Time Inc. merged with Warner Communications Inc. Henry Luce had founded Time Inc. with Briton Hadden in 1922. Their first magazine, *Time*, summarized a week's worth of news. In the 1930s they added *FORTUNE*, *Life*, and other magazines. Luce, a controversial business manager, stepped down as editor-in-chief in 1964; he died in 1967.

During the 1970s and 1980s Time Inc. explored new ventures. It entered the cable TV market with Home Box Office (1972) and bought Book-of-the-Month Club (1977). In magazines, *Money* (1972) was a moderate success and *People* (1974) was a hit, but *TV-Cable Week* lasted only 5 months.

Warner Brothers, founded by Harry, Albert (Abe), Jack, and Sam Warner, was one of Hollywood's largest movie studios. Warner Brothers made such classics as *Little Caesar* (1930), *Casablanca* (1942), and *Rebel Without a Cause* (1955). Sam died in 1927; Harry and Abe retired in 1951; and Jack remained until 1967, when Seven Arts Ltd. bought the studio. Steven Ross's Kinney National Services, owner of Famous Agency (talent) and National Periodical Publications (*Superman* and *Batman* comics and *Mad* magazine), bought the studio in 1969.

Kinney sold the pre-1948 movies to United Artists and shared the studios with Columbia. The company changed its name to Warner Communications Inc. in 1972. During the 1970s and early 1980s, Warner made most of its money with its game subsidiary, Atari (1976), but losses in this field led Warner to sell most of Atari in 1984.

Under the pressure of a possible takeover, Time agreed to merge with Warner, effective in 1990, at a cost of $14 billion, most of it in debt. During the 1990s the new conglomerate launched *Entertainment Weekly*, *Martha Stewart Living*, *In Style*, and *Vibe*. In 1992 the company created Time Warner Entertainment, a limited partnership for its film, TV programming, and cable businesses. Time Warner retained a 63% stake but sold interests to U S WEST, a regional Bell telephone company, and 2 Japanese companies, ITOCHU and Toshiba.

In 1993 Gerald Levin, former Time Inc. VC and one of the architects of the merger, became chairman, shortly after Ross's death from cancer. Time Warner announced plans to start a US network of broadcast stations in some markets and cable systems in others.

When Canadian spirits maker Seagram increased its holdings in Time Warner in 1994 to 14.9%, the company adopted a "poison pill" plan to discourage more purchases. Also that year the Warner Books unit of Time Warner bought a minority stake in The Reference Press, publisher of this profile.

In 1995 Seagram, the company's largest shareholder, bought rival studio MCA. That September Time Warner sold its stake in controversial rap music house Interscope Records.

NYSE symbol: TWX
Fiscal year ends: December 31

WHO

Chairman and CEO: Gerald M. Levin, age 55, $5,050,000 pay
President: Richard D. Parsons, age 46
EVP, General Counsel, and Secretary: Peter R. Haje, age 60, $1,650,000 pay
SVP and CFO: Richard J. Bressler, age 37
Editor in Chief: Norman Pearlstine, age 52
President and CEO, Time Inc.: Don Logan, age 51
Chairman, President, and CEO, Home Box Office: Jeffrey Bewkes
Chairman and Co-CEO, Warner Bros. and Warner Music: Robert A. Daly
Chairman and Co-CEO, Warner Bros. and Warner Music: Terry S. Semel
Chairman and CEO, Time Warner Cable: Joseph J. Collins, age 50
VP Administration (HR): Carolyn McCandless
Auditors: Ernst & Young LLP

WHERE

HQ: 75 Rockefeller Plaza, New York, NY 10019
Phone: 212-484-8000
Fax: 212-484-8734 (Corporate Communications)

	1994 Sales		1994 Operating Income	
	$ mil.	% of total	$ mil.	% of total
Time Warner Inc.				
US	4,944	31	494	32
Europe	1,445	9	108	7
Pacific Rim	724	5	74	5
Other regions	283	2	37	2
Subtotal	**7,396**	**47**	**713**	**46**
Entertainment Group	—	—	852	54
US	6,816	43	—	—
Other countries	1,693	10	—	—
Total	**15,905**	**100**	**1,565**	**100**

WHAT

	1994 Sales		1994 Operating Income	
	$ mil.	% of total	$ mil.	% of total
Time Warner Inc.				
Music	3,986	25	366	23
Publishing	3,433	21	347	22
Adjustments	(23)	—	—	—
Subtotal	**7,396**	**46**	**713**	**45**
Entertainment Group				
Films/TV	5,041	31	275	18
Cable	2,242	14	340	22
Programming/HBO	1,513	9	237	15
Adjustments	(287)	—	—	—
Total	**15,905**	**100**	**1,565**	**100**

Selected Operations

Cable	Little, Brown and Co.
Time Warner Cable	*People*
Film	*Sports Illustrated*
Warner Bros.	*Time*
Warner Home Video	Warner Books, Inc.
Music	**Other Interests**
The Atlantic Group	Columbia House (50%, music/video club)
Elektra Entertainment	Pathfinder (on-line services)
Publishing	Six Flags Entertainment (49%)
FORTUNE	Turner Broadcasting (19.6%)

KEY COMPETITORS

Advance Publications	Forbes	Sony
Bertelsmann	General Electric	TCI
Cablevision Systems	Lagardère	Thorn EMI
Capital Cities/ABC	MCA	Times Mirror
Comcast	McGraw-Hill	Viacom
Continental Cablevision	Metro Goldwyn Mayer	Walt Disney
Cox Communications	News Corp.	Washington Post
	Philips	Westinghouse

HOW MUCH

	Annual Growth	1985	1986	1987	1988	1989	1990	1991	1992	1993	1994
Sales ($ mil.)	9.0%	3,404	3,762	4,193	4,507	7,642	11,517	12,021	13,560	6,581[1]	7,396[1]
Net income ($ mil.)	—	200	376	250	289	(256)	(786)	(692)	(542)	(339)	(104)
Income as % of sales	—	5.9%	10.0%	6.0%	6.4%	—	—	—	—	—	—
Earnings per share ($)	—	0.79	1.49	1.05	1.25	(1.08)	(3.42)	(2.40)	(1.46)	(0.90)	(0.27)
Stock price – high ($)	—	16.31	22.84	29.22	30.63	45.69	31.16	16.53	19.44	28.75	44.25
Stock price – low ($)	—	10.63	14.38	16.44	19.69	25.91	16.53	19.44	21.63	28.75	31.50
Stock price – close ($)	9.5%	15.53	17.50	20.56	26.75	30.16	21.44	21.88	29.25	44.25	35.13
P/E – high	—	21	15	28	24	—	—	—	—	—	—
P/E – low	—	14	10	16	16	—	—	—	—	—	—
Dividends per share ($)	4.1%	0.25	0.25	0.25	0.25	0.25	0.25	0.26	0.27	0.31	0.36
Book value per share ($)	(5.1%)	4.82	5.40	5.98	5.99	—	—	—	—	3.62	3.02
Employees	12.1%	19,000	21,500	20,000	21,000	34,700	41,000	41,700	44,000	50,000	53,300

1994 Year-end:
Debt ratio: 88.9%
Return on equity: —
Cash (mil.): $282
Current ratio: 0.95
Long-term debt (mil.): $8,839
No. of shares (mil.): 379
Dividends
 Yield: 1.0%
 Payout: —
Market value (mil.): $13,323

Stock Price History High/Low 1985–94

[1] The company stopped consolidating Time Warner Entertainment Group sales.

TOSCO CORPORATION

OVERVIEW

Stamford, Connecticut–based Tosco is refining its business strategy in order to stay profitable in the highly competitive US oil industry. With 3 refineries in California, New Jersey, and Washington, Tosco — the country's 2nd largest independent refiner of unbranded petroleum products after Sun Co. — moved into retail marketing in 1994 with the purchase of British Petroleum's gas stations in the Pacific Northwest and northern California and Exxon's Arizona retail business. As a result, Tosco sells 3 million gallons of gasoline per day at BP- and Exxon-branded retail outlets in Arizona, California, Oregon, and Washington.

On the more traditional side of its business, refining, the company is restructuring and consolidating to cut costs. In 1994 low refining margins in the US and high maintenance costs at its Avon (San Francisco Bay) and Bayway (New York harbor) refineries hurt the company's financial performance. In 1995 Tosco combined its Avon and Ferndale (Puget Sound) refineries and its retail unit into a single business unit to improve efficiency.

The company also has interests in more than 43,000 acres of undeveloped oil shale properties in Colorado and Utah.

Tosco has set its sights on expanding its retail business through further acquisitions. It hopes to boost sales in the West to 4 million gallons per day in 1995 and to gain a foothold in the retail market on the East Coast.

WHEN

Tosco began as a company built around the idea of extracting oil from oil shale (a process whereby oil is distilled from the fine-grained shale rock). Led by Hein Koolsbergen, a group of investors set up Oil Shale Corporation in 1955 in Los Angeles as an entrepreneurial venture. One of its early projects — developing shale oil in Brazil to help the country reduce its oil imports — fell through for lack of financial support.

In 1965 the company joined with Atlantic Richfield to form the Colony Shale Oil Project, an oil extraction scheme involving 7,000 acres of Colorado's rich oil shale reserves. However, the development of the project was slowed by strict environmental regulations and the high cost of the extraction process.

Oil Shale moved into the mainstream oil refining business with the purchase of the Signal Oil & Gas refinery in Bakersfield, California, in 1970 for $22.5 million and Monsanto's petroleum business in 1972 for $25 million.

The company took several bold moves in 1976. Morton Winston, a law school graduate and Oil Shale executive since 1964, ousted Koolsbergen as CEO. The company was renamed Tosco (an acronym of The Oil Shale Co.) and paid out $222 million for Phillips Petroleum's West Coast assets, including its Avon refinery. This purchase made Tosco one of the top 3 independent refiners in the US and the largest supplier of petroleum products to independent marketers on the West Coast.

The oil price hikes of the 1970s prompted Tosco to reinvest in developing its domestic oil shale properties as an alternative to expensive imported crude oil. However, the daunting cost of developing the Colony Project was too rich for Atlantic Richfield's taste, and it sold its 60% share to Exxon for $300 million in 1980. Unable to get government funding to support the massive costs required to develop shale oil, Exxon threw in the towel on the project in 1982, effectively bringing it to an end. In the wake of this collapse Tosco faced serious financial problems. Winston stepped down in 1983 and was replaced as CEO by Matthew Talbot; Talbot resigned in 1986 and was succeeded by Tosco chairman Clarence Frame. The company went through a shaky period in the mid-1980s as it struggled with heavy debt and slumping oil and gas prices.

In 1988 Argus Energy, an investment concern led by Thomas O'Malley, bought a 40% stake in the company. O'Malley was promoted to CEO of Tosco in 1989. He then served notice that Tosco was open to takeover bids, attracting British Petroleum among other suitors. In 1991 Tosco declared that it would remain independent.

In that year Tosco made a strategic move to expand its operations to the East Coast by moving its headquarters to Connecticut, home of Argus Energy. In 1993 it acquired Exxon's Bayway, New Jersey, refinery for $175 million.

As part of the company's restructuring, Tosco sold its fertilizer subsidiary to Cargill in 1993 for $150 million. In 1995 it expanded its retail operations in the Pacific Northwest by landing a contract with Car Wash Enterprises to operate and rebrand (as BP) 27 car washes and 16 gas stations.

NYSE symbol: TOS
Fiscal year ends: December 31

Chairman, President, and CEO: Thomas D. O'Malley,
age 53, $1,475,000 pay
EVP, Treasurer, and CFO: Jefferson F. Allen, age 49,
$738,750 pay
SVP; President, Tosco Northwest: Robert J. Lavinia,
age 48, $1,186,750 pay
SVP; President, Tosco Refining: James M. Cleary,
age 49, $446,250 pay
SVP; President, Bayway Refining: Dwight L. Wiggins,
age 54, $446,250 pay
VP and General Counsel; SVP, Tosco Refining: Wilkes
McClave III, age 47
VP: George E. Ogden, age 52
VP: Richard W. Reinken
VP; SVP Tosco Refining: Peter A. Sutton, age 49
Chief Accounting Officer: Robert I. Santo
VP Human Resources, Tosco Refining: Timothy J.
McGarvey
Auditors: Coopers & Lybrand L.L.P.

WHERE

HQ: 72 Cummings Point Rd., Stamford, CT 06902
Phone: 203-977-1000
Fax: 203-964-3187

The company has operations in Arizona, California, New
Jersey, and Washington in the US as well as in Singapore
and the UK.

	1994 Crude Oil Refined	
	Barrels per day	% of total
Bayway, NJ	196,660	45
Avon, CA	147,450	34
Ferndale, WA	88,840	21
Total	**432,950**	**100**

WHAT

	1994 Sales
	% of total
Wholesale gasoline	44
Distillates	29
Other	27
Total	**100**

Products and Services
Convenience stores
Oil shale property management
Petroleum refining (diesel, gasoline, heating oil, and jet
fuel)
Petroleum retail marketing

KEY COMPETITORS

Amerada Hess
Amoco
Ashland, Inc.
Atlantic Richfield
British Petroleum
Chevron
Coastal
Crown Central Petroleum
Diamond Shamrock
Exxon
FINA
Global Petroleum
Mobil
Occidental
Phillips Petroleum
Shell Oil
Sinclair Oil
Star Enterprise
Sun Co.
Texaco
TOTAL
Ultramar
Unocal
USX-Marathon
Valero Energy

HOW MUCH

	Annual Growth	1985	1986	1987	1988	1989	1990	1991	1992	1993	1994
Sales ($ mil.)	17.3%	1,513	780	1,187	1,143	1,441	2,158	1,980	1,861	3,559	6,366
Net income ($ mil.)	28.3%	9	(56)	28	55	41	123	75	(91)	81	84
Income as % of sales	—	0.6%	—	2.3%	4.8%	2.8%	5.7%	3.8%	—	2.3%	1.3%
Earnings per share ($)	5.0%	1.45	(10.65)	0.80	1.65	1.24	3.94	2.35	(2.85)	2.33	2.24
Stock price – high ($)	—	25.00	23.13	16.25	18.13	25.88	24.63	25.88	30.75	32.75	35.00
Stock price – low ($)	—	5.00	8.13	5.63	8.13	3.13	14.50	14.63	16.38	18.88	26.75
Stock price – close ($)	4.6%	19.38	10.00	8.75	15.63	22.75	15.00	25.63	20.50	29.13	29.13
P/E – high	—	17	—	20	11	21	6	11	—	14	16
P/E – low	—	3	—	7	5	3	4	6	—	8	12
Dividends per share ($)	—	0.00	0.00	0.00	0.00	0.30	0.60	0.60	0.60	0.60	0.62
Book value per share ($)	—	(46.95)	(10.58)	(2.97)	4.10	7.25	11.15	12.90	9.22	11.79	14.53
Employees	15.5%	990	898	860	850	870	905	879	994	2,729	3,613

1994 Year-end:
Debt ratio: 54.4%
Return on equity: 17.0%
Cash (mil.): $24
Current ratio: 1.79
Long-term debt (mil.): $687
No. of shares (mil.): 40
Dividends
  Yield: 2.1%
  Payout: 27.7%
Market value (mil.): $1,154

Stock Price History
High/Low 1985–94

TOYS "R" US, INC.

OVERVIEW

Although Toys "R" Us is the world's #1 toy retailer, it is not all fun and games at the Paramus, New Jersey–based chain. The company, which operates 618 toy superstores and 204 Kids "R" Us children's clothing stores in the US and 293 toy stores overseas, is feeling the heat from major competitors, such as Wal-Mart, that have expanded their toy businesses to attract more young families.

Toys "R" Us holds a 22% share of the US toy market, but the company saw domestic same-store sales rise a meager 2% in fiscal 1995. The retailer has struggled with both competition and a flagging video game market, which fell into a slump as video game enthusiasts waited for the new 64-bit game systems to be released.

The company's sales and net income have continued to grow as it adds more stores, but with the US market saturated, the company is looking for growth overseas. In addition to opening corporate-owned stores, Toys "R" Us has begun making franchise arrangements in other countries. Its success overseas is due to both the popularity of things American and the fact that toys know no language.

To compete more effectively against the big US discounters, Toys "R" Us is cutting prices, increasing advertising and promotions, and adding computer software to its product mix. It is also establishing several in-store specialty shops, including Books "R" Us bookstores, the Lego Store, and the Learning Center, which carries learning aids and PC software.

WHEN

Charles Lazarus entered retailing in 1948, adding his $2,000 savings to a $2,000 bank loan to convert his father's Washington, DC, bicycle-repair shop into a children's furniture store. Customers persuaded him to add toys. He renamed the store Children's Supermart. Lazarus added a 2nd store, which he later converted to cash-and-carry self-service, but it was with his 3rd store that he established the pattern for his success. Opened in 1958, this 25,000-square-foot discount toy store offered a wider variety of toys than other retailers at 20–50% lower prices.

By 1966 sales had reached $12 million, but Lazarus had added only one store and needed cash to expand, so he sold his company to discount-store operator Interstate Stores for $7.5 million with the condition that he would retain control of the toy operation. Initially the arrangement worked, but after a 1969 high of $11 million profit on $589 million in sales, Interstate began to feel the competition from stronger chains like Kmart. By 1974, although Lazarus had expanded to 47 stores and $130 million yearly sales, the parent had lost $92 million and filed for bankruptcy.

Lazarus kept increasing sales in the toy division. His approach of selling toys year-round (not just during the Christmas season) was encouraged by toy manufacturers in the form of generous credit terms. By 1978 he had generated enough profit to pull Interstate out of bankruptcy. Now under his control, the company adopted a new name: Toys "R" Us, with the R backwards to grab attention. With 72 toy stores (and 10 department stores remaining from Interstate) and a 5% share of the toy market, Toys "R" Us posted a $36 million pretax profit on $349 million in sales that year.

From 1978 to 1983 net earnings grew at an annual rate of 40%, market share climbed to 12.5%, and the number of toy stores grew to 169. The company diversified by opening 2 Kids "R" Us children's clothing stores in 1983, copying the toy stores' success formula of huge discount stores.

In 1991 the company won a major victory when it successfully penetrated the notoriously bureaucratic and xenophobic Japanese retail market.

Stiff competition from Toys "R" Us was partially responsible for causing rivals Child World and Lionel to seek Chapter 11 bankruptcy in 1992. In 1993 Kids Central, Service Merchandise's experiment in the children's apparel and accessory market, also folded. That same year Toys "R" Us continued its international expansion, opening more stores outside the US than in it, including its first stores in Australia, Belgium, the Netherlands, Portugal, and Switzerland.

In 1994 Lazarus retired from daily involvement with Toys "R" Us, giving up his CEO hat but remaining chairman. He will continue to work with the company on a consulting basis. Also in 1994, to boost its sales outside the Christmas rush, Toys "R" Us circulated a mid-year coupon catalog.

In 1995 the company opened its first franchise store, in Dubai, United Arab Emirates.

NYSE symbol: TOY
Fiscal year ends: Saturday nearest January 31

WHO

Chairman: Charles Lazarus, age 71, $7,862,530 pay
VC and CEO: Michael Goldstein, age 53, $1,202,700 pay
President and COO: Robert C. Nakasone, age 47,
$1,202,700 pay
EVP; General Merchandise Manager, Toys "R" Us US:
Roger V. Goddu, age 44, $516,574 pay
SVP Finance and CFO: Louis Lipschitz, age 50
SVP Human Resources: Jeffrey S. Wells
VP; President, Toys "R" Us International: Larry D.
Bouts, age 46, $569,667 pay
VP; President, Kids "R" Us Division: Richard L.
Markee, age 42, $516,420 pay
Auditors: Ernst & Young LLP

WHERE

HQ: 461 From Rd., Paramus, NJ 07652
Phone: 201-262-7800
Fax: 201-262-7606

	No. of US Stores	
	Toys "R" Us	Kids "R" Us
California	77	25
Texas	50	7
New York	41	20
Florida	39	8
Illinois	34	20
Pennsylvania	29	14
Ohio	28	19
Michigan	23	13
New Jersey	21	17
Virginia	18	7
Maryland	17	8
North Carolina	16	—
Georgia	14	4
Other states	211	42
Total	**618**	**204**

	No. of Stores
	Toys "R" Us
US	618
Canada	56
Germany	53
UK	49
France	29
Japan	24
Spain	20
Other countries	62
Total	**911**

	1995 Sales		1995 Pretax Income	
	$ mil.	% of total	$ mil.	% of total
US	6,645	76	779	85
Other countries	2,101	24	141	15
Adjustments	—	—	(76)	—
Total	**8,746**	**100**	**844**	**100**

WHAT

Books "R" Us (bookstores located within company
toy stores)
Kids "R" Us (children's apparel)
Toys "R" Us (toys, games, sporting goods)

KEY COMPETITORS

Ames	Melville
Baby Superstore	Montgomery Ward
Barnes & Noble	Noodle Kidoodle
Caldor	Sears
CompUSA	Service Merchandise
Crown Books	Sports Authority
Dayton Hudson	Tandy
The Gap	Time Warner
Gymboree	Wal-Mart
Hills Stores	Walt Disney
Kmart	Woolworth
May	Zany Brainy

HOW MUCH

	Annual Growth	1986	1987	1988	1989	1990	1991	1992	1993	1994	1995
Sales ($ mil.)	18.0%	1,976	2,445	3,137	4,000	4,788	5,510	6,124	7,169	7,946	8,746
Net income ($ mil.)	18.0%	120	152	204	268	321	326	340	438	483	532
Income as % of sales	—	6.1%	6.2%	6.5%	6.7%	6.7%	5.9%	5.5%	6.1%	6.1%	6.1%
Earnings per share ($)	18.2%	0.41	0.52	0.69	0.91	1.09	1.11	1.15	1.47	1.63	1.85
Stock price – high ($)[1]	—	12.24	15.32	19.01	18.01	26.85	35.00	36.00	41.00	42.88	40.88
Stock price – low ($)[1]	—	7.50	9.75	9.80	13.34	16.01	19.88	22.00	30.38	32.38	29.63
Stock price – close ($)[1]	12.7%	10.42	12.80	14.01	16.51	23.93	22.50	32.75	40.13	40.88	30.63
P/E – high	—	30	30	28	20	25	32	31	28	26	22
P/E – low	—	18	19	14	15	15	18	19	21	20	16
Dividends per share ($)	—	0.00	0.00	0.00	0.00	0.00	0.00	0.00	0.00	0.00	0.00
Book value per share ($)	18.9%	2.58	3.22	3.95	4.95	5.95	7.11	8.39	9.87	10.66	12.21
Employees	2.8%	45,200	54,000	52,000	63,200	73,400	73,000	78,000	87,000	55,000	58,000

1995 Year-end:
Debt ratio: 20.9%
Return on equity: 16.2%
Cash (mil.): $370
Current ratio: 1.18
Long-term debt (mil.): $785
No. of shares (mil.): 281
Dividends
  Yield: —
  Payout: —
Market value (mil.): $8,604

**Stock Price History[1]
High/Low 1986–95**

[1] Stock prices are for the prior calendar year.

THE TRAVELERS INC.

OVERVIEW

Travelers has undergone a period of consolidation and adjustment since its 1993 acquisition by Sanford Weill's Primerica (which took the Travelers name and its distinctive red umbrella logo) and the addition of Smith Barney, the US's 2nd largest brokerage and investment bank (after Merrill Lynch), which Primerica also bought in 1993. These additions diversified the company into life and property/casualty insurance and brokerage and investment banking (Weill wanted to build an investment powerhouse like Merrill Lynch).

The company has streamlined itself along business lines. These include investment services (Smith Barney), consumer finance (Commercial Credit), credit cards (Travelers Bank, formerly Primerica Bank), and mutual funds (Primerica Financial Services). Insurance operations include Travelers Insurance (insurance and retirement products) and Travelers Indemnity (personal and commercial property/casualty insurance).

In the process, Travelers jettisoned several businesses, including mutual fund manager American Capital Management, specialty auto insurer Shippers Insurance Company, and its health care joint venture (with MetLife), MetraHealth, sold to United Health.

WHEN

In 1864 James Batterson and 9 other Hartford businessmen founded Travelers as the first accident insurance company in the US. The company began using its red umbrella logo as early as 1870.

The company diversified into life insurance (1865), annuities (1884), and liability insurance (1889). In 1897 it issued the first auto policy, and in 1919 it sold President Woodrow Wilson the first air travel policy.

The company added group life insurance coverage in 1913, with the Victor Co. (later part of RCA) as one of its first clients.

A decision on the eve of the 1929 crash to sell gold stocks and buy federal bonds helped the company survive the Depression. In 1940 the company began insuring government projects carried out by civilian contractors.

Travelers prospered during the post-WWII boom and issued the first space travel accident insurance, covering the Apollo 11 astronauts in their historic lunar landing.

In the late 1970s and early 1980s, the company bought Keystone (mutual funds, 1979; sold 1989) and Dillon, Read (investment banking, 1986; sold 1991). As the real estate market, in which the company had invested heavily, turned sour in the late 1980s and early 1990s, Travelers sold Travelers Mortgage Services (home mortgage and relocation business) in 1990 to focus on its investment and insurance business.

In the 1990s Travelers began cutting jobs and withdrawing from unprofitable business areas. These and other cost-control measures made Travelers attractive to the profit-driven management of Primerica.

One of Primerica's antecedents, American Can, had started life in 1901 as a canning company in New Jersey. By the 1930s it was an industry leader, but by the 1960s it had to diversify into other areas (paper and forest products). In the 1970s it went still farther afield and bought Musicland (record stores, sold 1988) and Fingerhut (catalog sales). In 1981 American Can bought life insurance company Associated Madison. Five years later it jettisoned its container operations and became a financial services company. In 1987 it became Primerica.

The next year Primerica was bought by Sanford Weill's much smaller company, Commercial Credit. Weill had started out by building Shearson Loeb Rhoades and selling it to American Express, of which he later became president. Later still, he engineered a buyout of Control Data. Commercial Credit had been founded in 1912 to deal in commercial acceptances and receivables.

When Weill bought Primerica, he got rid of the noncore businesses; finding no buyer for Fingerhut, Primerica gradually reduced its share of the company, selling its last 2% interest in 1993. Weill soon began the same process at Travelers.

The $4 billion merger of Primerica and Travelers was no union of equals. Primerica dominated. New management members included Weill's son Marc (as chief investment officer) and Robert Greenhill (whom Weill hired from J.P. Morgan to lead Smith Barney).

The consolidation of Smith Barney was rocky. Although 1994's down results improved in 1995, rumors of dissension between Greenhill and his new recruits and Smith Barney's veterans continued to fly. In 1995, after some of his duties were taken away, Greenhill left Smith Barney to form his own firm and was replaced by Travelers's president and COO, James Dimon.

NYSE symbol: TRV
Fiscal year ends: December 31

WHO

Chairman and CEO: Sanford I. Weill, age 61,
$3,678,750 pay
VC; Group Chief Executive, Travelers Insurance:
Robert I. Lipp, age 56, $2,189,375 pay
**VC; Group Chief Executive, Primerica Financial
Services:** Joseph J. Plumeri II, age 51, $1,960,375 pay
**President and COO; Chairman and CEO, Smith Barney
Inc.:** James Dimon, age 38, $2,774,375 pay
EVP Marketing: Edwin M. Cooperman, age 51
EVP Strategic Planning: Michael A. Carpenter, age 47
SVP and CFO: Heidi G. Miller
SVP, General Counsel, and Secretary: Charles O.
Prince III, age 45
**SVP Corporate Communications and Investor
Relations:** Mary McDermott
SVP and Chief Information Officer: Richard F.
Morrison
SVP Human Resources: Barry L. Mannes
Auditors: KPMG Peat Marwick LLP

WHERE

HQ: 388 Greenwich St., New York, NY 10013
Phone: 212-816-8000
Fax: 212-816-8913

WHAT

	1994 Sales	
	$ mil.	% of total
Premiums	7,590	41
Investment income	3,637	19
Commissions & fees	2,691	15
Other charges & fees	2,725	15
Other	1,822	10
Total	**18,465**	**100**

	1994 Assets	
	$ mil.	% of total
Cash & equivalents	1,227	1
Treasury & agency securities	7,900	7
Mortgage-backed securities	4,913	4
Corporate bonds	15,567	14
Other securities	10,270	9
Securities under resale agreements	25,655	22
Receivables & recoverables	20,010	17
Mortgage & policy loans	6,997	6
Other assets	22,758	20
Total	**115,297**	**100**

Selected Services
Brokerage services
Consumer finance
Credit cards
Investment banking
Life insurance
Mutual funds
Property/casualty
insurance

Selected Subsidiaries
Commercial Credit
The MetraHealth
Companies
Primerica Financial
Services, Inc.
RCM Capital Management
Travelers Bank
Travelers Insurance
Company

KEY COMPETITORS

ADVANTA
Aetna
AFLAC
Alex. Brown
Allstate
American
Express
American
Financial
Bear Stearns
Berkshire
Hathaway
Brown Brothers
Harriman
Chubb
CIGNA
Citicorp

CNA Financial
CS Holding
Dean Witter,
Discover
Equitable
FMR
GEICO
Goldman Sachs
ING Group
ITT Hartford
John Hancock
Kemper Corp.
Lehman Brothers
MassMutual
Merrill Lynch
MetLife
Morgan Stanley

New York Life
Nomura
Securities
Northwestern
Mutual
Paine Webber
Prudential
Raymond James
Financial
Rothschilds
Salomon
State Farm
Swiss Bank
T. Rowe Price
Transamerica
USAA
USF&G

HOW MUCH

	Annual Growth	1985	1986	1987	1988	1989	1990	1991	1992	1993	1994
Assets ($ mil.)	38.3%	6,235	4,864	4,306	14,435	17,955	19,689	21,561	23,397	101,360	115,297
Net income ($ mil.)	—	(5)	46	34	162	289	373	479	756	951	1,326
Income as % of assets	—	—	0.9%	0.6%	1.1%	1.6%	1.9%	2.2%	3.2%	0.9%	1.2%
Earnings per share ($)	—	(0.07)	0.59	0.24	1.81	1.43	1.64	2.14	3.34	3.88	3.86
Stock price – high ($)	—	—	11.38	17.32	14.51	15.01	18.88	20.07	24.95	49.50	43.13
Stock price – low ($)	—	—	9.88	8.50	10.26	10.13	8.44	10.94	17.88	24.07	30.38
Stock price – close ($)	13.6%	—	10.26	11.19	10.88	14.26	11.44	19.70	24.20	38.88	32.38
P/E – high	—	—	19	72	8	11	12	9	8	13	11
P/E – low	—	—	17	35	6	7	5	5	5	6	8
Dividends per share ($)	43.8%	—	0.03	0.12	0.14	0.14	0.18	0.23	0.36	0.49	0.55
Book value per share ($)	11.5%	—	9.20	7.67	10.14	11.77	13.21	15.10	17.70	25.68	24.46
Employees	6.4%	29,822	33,353	33,000	36,000	35,000	34,000	32,000	30,000	65,000	52,000

1994 Year-end:
Equity as % of assets: 6.8%
Return on assets: 1.2%
Return on equity: 16.4%
Long-term debt (mil.): $7,075
No. of shares (mil.): 317
Dividends
  Yield: 1.7%
  Payout: 14.2%
Market value (mil.): $10,249
Sales (mil.): $18,465

**Stock Price History
High/Low 1986–94**

TRUMP ORGANIZATION

OVERVIEW

With a new casino venture and his first IPO, Donald Trump has proven that his name still has cachet with gamblers and investors. But how long can "The Donald" continue to charm the bankers who control the huge debt on Trump properties (over $400 million on Trump Plaza alone)? Trump's hotel, gambling, and real estate empire epitomized the high-flying '80s, but "The Donald" crashed in the early 1990s, losing several of his glitziest assets — including his Trump Shuttle airline and much of his stake in New York's Plaza Hotel.

In mid-1995 Trump took 2 big steps on the comeback trail. First he took Trump Hotels & Casino Resorts public (under the stock ticker "DJT") in a stock-and-debt offering that raised $280 million; Trump retained the majority

stake. Then his creditor banks gave Trump a 3-year extension on $115 million in personal debt that was coming due.

The cash infusion and debt relief may help Trump salvage some of his tattered empire, which now centers around the Trump Plaza hotel and casino in Atlantic City and the Trump Indiana riverboat casino south of Chicago. About $100 million from the offering is being used to upgrade and expand the Plaza, with $60 million tagged for the Indiana casino.

Another Trump investment being salvaged involves a 75-acre tract on Manhattan's Upper West Side. A deal with the Hong Kong investors who acquired a defaulted bank loan on the property lets Trump retain a minority stake and play a role in the property's development.

WHEN

Donald Trump, the 4th of 5 children, was an aggressive boy who at age 13 was sent to New York Military Academy. His father, Fred, was a successful builder in Queens and Brooklyn.

Trump graduated from the Wharton School of Finance in 1968. His first job was the turnaround of a 1,200-unit foreclosed apartment building in Cincinnati that Fred had purchased for $6 million with no money down.

Managing the Cincinnati job gave Trump a distaste for the nonaffluent. He wanted to get out of the boroughs and into Manhattan to meet all the right people. Operating as the Trump Organization (which then had no legal existence), in 1973 he contacted Victor Palmieri, who was selling Penn Central's real estate assets. In 1974 Trump took options on 2 Hudson River sites for no money down and began lobbying the city to finance his construction of a convention center. The center was built, but not by Trump, who did get about $800,000 and priceless publicity. Trump next took control of a site near Grand Central Station and began his first Manhattan job, the Grand Hyatt Hotel, in which he had a 49% interest, again with no money down. In 1977 Trump married fashion model Ivana Zelnicek.

By the late 1980s Trump owned the Plaza Hotel in Manhattan, 3 Atlantic City casinos, the Eastern air shuttle, the world's largest private yacht, and part of the Grand Hyatt Hotel in Manhattan. He built the posh Trump Tower on Fifth Avenue under a tax abatement program for moderate-income housing. Trump also joined with Holiday Inn, for no money down, to build the Trump Plaza casino using public issue bonds. Trump then bought out

Holiday Inn's interest. He personally guaranteed a loan to acquire the Trump Castle from Hilton and began a battle with Merv Griffin for Resorts International. Griffin won Resorts International, and Trump was left with the unfinished Taj Mahal in Atlantic City, the world's largest casino. In 1987 Trump published *The Art of the Deal,* and in 1988 he bought the famed Plaza Hotel.

Back in Atlantic City, the Taj was a sensation, but it stole business from Trump's other casinos and still could not make interest payments to its bondholders. Trump took the Taj into Chapter 11 bankruptcy, from which he emerged in nominal control. The other casinos also flirted with default.

As the 1990s dawned, people finally looked at Trump's balance sheet, finding it loaded with debt that could not be serviced from cash flow. At the same time, his marriage to the flamboyant Ivana broke up in a splash of publicity. Trump's 70 creditor banks consolidated and restructured his debt and put him on a monthly allowance. In 1991 they reduced his personal recourse debt to $155 million. Since then he has worked to reduce that debt and regain his credibility. In 1993 Trump married Marla Maples, mother of his daughter Tiffany.

In 1994 Trump announced his intention to develop a 75-acre tract along the Hudson River at 59th Street. The following year Trump surrendered his majority stake in the Plaza Hotel in exchange for continuing his role in the hotel. Trump is expected to receive a fixed equity position of 20% in the hotel from the new owners — a Saudi prince and a hotel company based in Singapore.

Private company
Fiscal year ends: December 31

WHO

Chairman: Donald J. Trump, age 48
President and CEO, Trump Hotels & Casino Resorts:
Nicholas L. Ribis, age 50, $822,917 pay
President and COO, Plaza Associates: Barry J. Cregan,
age 41, $153,945 pay
**EVP Corporate and Legal Affairs, Trump Hotels &
Casino Resorts:** Robert M. Pickus, age 40,
$196,259 pay
EVP Casino Operations, Plaza Associates: James A.
Rigot, age 43, $113,461 pay
EVP Hotel Operations, Plaza Associates: Shinji Tanaka,
age 47
SVP Finance and Administration, Plaza Associates:
Francis X. McCarthy Jr., age 42, $244,394 pay
SVP Marketing, Plaza Associates: Fred A. Buro, age 38
VP and General Counsel, Plaza Associates: Kevin S.
Smith, age 38
Auditors: Arthur Andersen & Co, SC

WHERE

HQ: 725 Fifth Ave., New York, NY 10022-2519
Phone: 212-832-2000
Fax: 212-935-0141

WHAT

	Primary Deals	
	Year	$ mil.
Grand Hyatt Hotel (49%)*	1979	100
Trump Tower	1982	190
Trump Plaza Hotel & Casino	1984	218
59th St. Railyard	1984	100
Trump Castle casino	1985	320
Mar-A-Lago	1985	8
Plaza Hotel	1988	408
Trump Princess*	1988	29
Trump Shuttle*	1989	365
Trump Taj Mahal	1989	230
Trump Indiana	1995	60

* Sold

Trump Hotels & Casino Resorts, Inc.
Plaza Associates (entity that owns Trump Plaza)
   Trump Plaza (555-room hotel casino, Atlantic City)
   Trump Plaza East (349-room hotel casino)
   Trump Plaza West (500-room hotel casino)
Trump Indiana (mooring for the Trump Princess,
   280-foot yacht casino; Buffington Harbor, IN)

Other Holdings
Mar-A-Lago (estate, Palm Beach)
Park South Assoc.
The Trump Corp.
Trump Enterprises Inc.
Trump Taj Mahal (50%, hotel casino, Atlantic City)
Trump Tower (apartment tower and retail space,
   New York)
Trump's Castle (hotel casino, Atlantic City)

KEY COMPETITORS

Aztar
Bally
Circus Circus
Four Seasons
Griffin Gaming
Harrah's
Helmsley
Hilton
Hollywood Casino
Hyatt
ITT Corp.
Lefrak
Loews
Marriott International
Mashantucket Pequot Gaming
Mirage Resorts
Players
Pratt
Rank
Ritz-Carlton
Sahara
Showboat

HOW MUCH

	Annual Growth	1985	1986	1987	1988	1989	1990	1991	1992	1993	1994
Estimated sales ($ mil.)	4.1%	1,000	850	700	1,359	1,494	1,340	1,400	2,040	1,720	1,450
Employees	4.0%	14,000	14,000	20,000	25,000	25,000	20,000	17,000	15,000	15,000	20,000

Estimated Sales
($ mil.)
1985–94

TRUMP

UNION CARBIDE CORPORATION

OVERVIEW

Like the gas cloud that once lingered over Bhopal, India, Union Carbide's financial woes have dissipated. The world's #1 producer of ethylene oxide and ethylene glycol (used to make antifreeze and polyester fibers), Union Carbide is also one of the largest manufacturers of polyethylene, the most widely used plastic in the world, and is a maker of solvents, coatings, latex, resins, emulsions, and plasticizers. The company is emerging profitably from a troubled decade in which it was buffeted by the Bhopal disaster and an abortive takeover by Samuel Heyman's GAF Corp.

In the 1980s, as the company was reeling under heavy debt, CEO Robert Kennedy took the ax to the organization, slashing nearly 90% of the work force and selling a number of businesses, including its Eveready, Praxair industrial gases, and consumer products units.

The company is positioning itself to make major inroads into the Asian plastics market with the building of a $1.5 billion petrochemical complex in Kuwait with the Kuwaiti government. In close proximity to the Asian markets, the plant, the firm claims, which will have access to the low-cost oil needed to compete against Saudi Arabian petrochemical firms, will produce the world's cheapest plastic when it comes onstream in 1997.

Kennedy stepped down as chairman and CEO in 1995, and president William Joyce took over.

WHEN

Union Carbide Corporation traces its origins back to 2 chemical companies: National Carbon Company (1886), which manufactured carbons for street lights and began the Eveready trademark, and Union Carbide (1898), which manufactured calcium carbide. In 1917 the 2 companies — along with Linde Air Products (oxygen), Prest-O-Lite (calcium carbide), and Electro Metallurgical (metals) — joined to form Union Carbide & Carbon Corporation (UCC).

In 1919 the company began forming subsidiaries in Canada and in 1925 expanded overseas with the purchase of a Norwegian hydroelectric power plant. UCC expanded into chemical manufacturing and in 1920 established its own chemicals division, which developed ethylene glycol (antifreeze), eventually marketed as Prestone. The company bought vanadium interests in Colorado from U.S. Vanadium in 1926. UCC continued to grow with further purchases, including Acheson Graphite (1928) and Bakelite (an early developer of plastics, 1939). In the 1940s the company entered the atomic field and ran the US government's nuclear laboratories in Oak Ridge, Tennessee, and in Paducah, Kentucky, until 1984.

UCC bought Visking (food casings) in 1956. In 1957 the company changed its name to Union Carbide Corporation and in the early 1960s introduced Glad plastic household products (sold in 1985).

In 1975 the company built a pesticide plant in Bhopal, India, and kept 51% ownership (giving 49% to Indian companies). In 1984 a tank at the plant leaked 5 tons of poisonous methyl isocyanate gas, killing more than 3,000 people and permanently injuring 50,000 — the world's worst recorded industrial accident. Resulting legal action against Union Carbide led to a $470 million settlement in India's Supreme Court in 1989.

In 1985 GAF (chemicals and roofing materials) tried to take over Union Carbide; in response the company went into debt by $3 billion, which it used to buy back 55% of its stock to defeat the attempt. In 1986 Union Carbide sold its battery division (including Eveready) to Ralston Purina, its agricultural products business to Rhône-Poulenc, and its home and auto products business to First Brands in order to concentrate on its 3 core businesses: chemicals and plastics, industrial gases, and carbon products.

In 1992 the company spun off its industrial gases unit, Praxair, to shareholders. That same year, in legal proceedings related to the Bhopal case, a court in India seized the assets of Union Carbide's Indian operations. In 1993 an Indian court ordered 8 employees of the firm's Indian subsidiary, plus its Hong Kong subsidiary, the parent company, and former chairman Warren Anderson, to stand trial for "culpable homicide." With the case still pending, the firm sold its Indian subsidiary in 1994 for $92 million.

In 1994 Union Carbide announced plans to build a rubber manufacturing plant in Seadrift, Texas. The plant (estimated to cost $94 million) will have an annual capacity of 200 million pounds of ethylene-propylene rubber. In 1995 Union Carbide set up a joint venture with Elf Aquitaine (in Europe) to produce specialty polyethylene resins and products for the cable and wire, pipe, and other industries.

NYSE symbol: UK
Fiscal year ends: December 31

Chairman, President and CEO: William H. Joyce,
age 59, $910,833 pay (prior to promotion)
VP, General Counsel, and Secretary: Joseph E.
Geoghan, age 57, $615,000 pay
VP Corporate Ventures & Purchasing: Joseph C.
Soviero, age 56, $503,333 pay
VP; General Manager - UNIPOL: Roger B. Staub, age 60,
$470,000 pay
VP, Controller, and Principal Accounting Officer: John
K. Wulff, age 46, $444,167 pay
VP; General Manager, Solvents and Intermediates:
James F. Flynn, age 52
VP; General Manager, Ethylene Oxide/Glycol: Lee P.
McMaster, age 52
VP and Principal Financial Officer: Gilbert E. Playford,
age 47
VP Human Resources: Malcolm A. Kessinger, age 51
Auditors: KPMG Peat Marwick LLP

WHERE

HQ: 39 Old Ridgebury Rd., Danbury, CT 06817
Phone: 203-794-2000
Fax: 203-794-4336

Union Carbide operates in 14 countries.

	1994 Sales		1994 Operating Income	
	$ mil.	% of total	$ mil.	% of total
US	3,535	73	433	88
Europe	474	10	12	2
Latin America	218	4	16	3
Canada	136	3	14	3
Far East & other	502	10	17	13
Adjustments	—	—	59	—
Total	**4,865**	**100**	**551**	**100**

WHAT

	1994 Sales	
	$ mil.	% of total
Polyolefins	1,562	32
Solvents, intermediates & emulsion systems	1,344	27
Olefins, ethylene oxide, glycol & derivatives	1,253	26
Specialty polymers & prods.	706	15
Total	**4,865**	**100**

Selected Products

Polyolefins	**Olefins, Ethylene Oxide,**
Polyethylenes	**Glycol, and Derivatives**
Recycled plastics	Aircraft and runway de-icing
(Curbside Blend)	fluids (UCAR)
Resins	Fluids and lubricants (UCON)
Wire insulation,	Specialty surfactants
semiconducting, and	(TERGITOL, TRITON)
jacketing compounds	

Solvents, Intermediates,
and Emulsion Systems
Acids
Acrylics
Alcohols
Esters
Glycol ethers
Latex products (UCAR)

Specialty Polymers and
Products
Hydroxyethyl cellulose
(CELLOSIZE)
Plasticizers (FLEXOL)
Polyester modifiers
(NEULON)
Water-soluble resins
(POLYOX)

KEY COMPETITORS

Akzo Nobel	Eastman Chemical	Mitsubishi
Atlantic	Exxon	Mobil
Richfield	Formosa Plastics	Monsanto
BASF	Hanson	Occidental
Bayer	Hercules	Phillips
British	Hoechst	Petroleum
Petroleum	Huntsman Chemical	Rhône-Poulenc
Chevron	Imperial Chemical	Royal Dutch/
Dow Chemical	Lyondell	Shell
DuPont	Petrochemical	Texaco

HOW MUCH

	Annual Growth	1985	1986	1987	1988	1989	1990	1991	1992	1993	1994
Sales ($ mil.)	(6.6%)	9,003	6,244	6,914	8,324	8,744	5,238	4,877	4,872	4,640	4,865
Net income ($ mil.)	—	(599)	135	232	662	573	308	(9)	186	165	389
Income as % of sales	—	—	2.2%	3.4%	8.0%	6.6%	5.9%	—	3.8%	3.6%	8.0%
Earnings per share ($)	—	(2.86)	1.30	1.76	4.66	3.92	2.13	(0.22)	1.27	1.00	2.27
Stock price – high ($)	—	10.28	13.78	13.52	11.80	13.83	10.35	10.09	17.13	23.13	35.88
Stock price – low ($)	—	4.99	7.80	6.45	7.07	9.46	5.88	6.40	8.37	16.00	21.50
Stock price – close ($)	12.9%	9.82	9.36	9.05	10.66	9.67	6.81	8.42	16.63	22.38	29.38
P/E – high	—	—	11	8	3	4	5	—	14	23	16
P/E – low	—	—	6	4	2	2	3	—	7	16	10
Dividends per share ($)	(4.5%)	1.13	1.50	1.50	1.15	1.00	1.00	1.00	0.88	0.75	0.75
Book value per share ($)	(6.9%)	19.82	7.87	9.35	13.34	16.83	16.06	17.55	9.32	9.49	10.45
Employees	(20.2%)	91,459	50,292	43,119	43,992	45,987	37,756	16,705	15,075	13,051	12,004

1994 Year-end:
Debt ratio: 38.5%
Return on equity: 26.5%
Cash (mil.): $109
Current ratio: 1.26
Long-term debt (mil.): $899
No. of shares (mil.): 144
Dividends
  Yield: 2.6%
  Payout: 33.0%
Market value (mil.): $4,243

Stock Price History
High/Low 1985–94

U.S. INDUSTRIES, INC.

OVERVIEW

Like Athena, U.S. Industries (USI) sprang full-grown from its parent's brow. Now the company, which was spun off from British conglomerate Hanson PLC in 1995, is creating offspring of its own as it works to focus its corporate identity and pare the huge debt ($1.4 billion) Hanson sent along.

Iselin, New Jersey–based USI started with 34 subsidiaries — all small companies bought by Hanson between 1975 and 1993. The company has 3 business segments: building products, consumer products, and industrial products.

By late 1995 USI had already sold furniture makers Anderson Hickey and United Chair (both to Haworth) as well as several of its niche market manufacturers in building products and sporting goods. Its "keeper" subsid-

iaries include whirlpool maker Jacuzzi and toolmaker Ames, while "for sale" tags went up on Universal Gym Equipment and cookware manufacturer Farberware. Still other subsidiaries were being combined; for example, Progress Lighting and Spaulding Lighting were to become parts of a new subsidiary, Lighting Corp. of America. The company has also sold its minority stake in Beazer Homes.

USI is headed by champion yachtsman David Clarke, who was VC of Hanson and CEO of that company's US operations (Hanson Industries). Taking a page from the book of his mentor, Lord Hanson, Clarke has indicated that he intends to keep paying off debt by cutting USI down to its strongest components. He then plans to make strategic acquisitions to bolster those segments.

WHEN

USI was created in 1995 to help raise funds for its parent, the UK-based industrial conglomerate Hanson PLC. Hanson was started in the early 1960s by James Hanson (now Lord Hanson) and Gordon White and grew through numerous acquisitions into one of Britain's leading enterprises — encompassing chemicals, consumer products, mining, and tobacco. Hanson's US arm, Hanson Industries, included Cavenham Forest Industries (the lumber producer formerly known as Crown Zellerbach), Peabody Holding (the US's top coal producer), and Quantum Chemical (the US's #1 maker of polyethylene, a plastic used in packaging). But with profits falling off and debt rising in the mid-1990s, Hanson began looking for ways to raise money for more acquisitions.

Hanson acquired many of its USI subsidiary companies in 1987 when it bought Kidde (formerly Walter Kidde & Co.), a New York City–based conglomerate, for $1.7 billion. Kidde, which dates to the turn of the century, started as a manufacturer of fire safety equipment and had grown to over 100 businesses when it was bought by Hanson. Two of the best-known subsidiaries the Kidde acquisition gave Hanson were top-selling cookware maker Farberware and whirlpool bath pioneer Jacuzzi.

Farberware was started in New York City in 1900 by Simon Farber, an immigrant who had managed a copper cookware factory in Russia. In New York, Farber set up his own factory in a basement and began making brass cooking vessels by hand. Farberware, a line of nickel- and silver-plated cookware, was introduced in 1910. The company added a line of chrome-

plated utensils in the mid-1920s and stainless steel products in the 1950s. Kidde acquired the Farberware line in 1966.

The Jacuzzi family's California business was started in the early 1900s by 7 brothers who immigrated from Italy. The company made airplane propellers and industrial pumps. When a family member needed hydrotherapy in the mid-1950s, engineers at Jacuzzi created a whirlpool effect using a company pump. The firm then began marketing a small portable pump, the J-300, for use in homes and hospitals. Roy Jacuzzi joined the family firm in the late 1960s. With technology from the J-300, he patented the "hydromassage" system and marketed a whirlpool bathtub. Jacuzzi was acquired by Kidde in 1979.

Other Kidde companies that became part of USI included Bear (archery equipment), Piedmont Moulding, Ertl (toys), Progress Lighting, Rexair (vacuum cleaners), Spartus (clocks), Universal Gym Equipment, and Valley Recreation Products (pinball machines and pool tables).

USI's spin-off from Hanson included nearly 30% of the stock of builder Beazer Homes; Hanson had purchased Beazer in 1993.

Upon its spin-off USI immediately announced its intention to sell some of its holdings in order to pare debt. In mid-1995 the company gained $44.7 million from the sale of its interest in Beazer Homes. That same year a group of companies that included Bear, MW Manufacturers (building products), Teters Floral Products, and Valley Recreation was sold to Fenway Partners for $200 million.

NYSE symbol: USN
Fiscal year ends: September 30

WHO

Chairman and CEO: David H. Clarke, age 54, $437,498 pay
President and COO: John G. Raos, age 46, $291,665 pay
Group VP: John S. Oldford, age 52, $138,833 pay
Group VP: John A. Mistretta, age 49, $123,958 pay
SVP Corporate Development: Christian R. Guntner, age 41, $127,083 pay
SVP and CFO: Frank R. Reilly, age 38
SVP, General Counsel, and Secretary: George H. MacLean, age 60
VP Administration (HR): Dorothy E. Sander, age 42
Auditors: Ernst & Young LLP

WHERE

HQ: 101 Wood Ave. South, Iselin, NJ 08830
Phone: 908-767-0700
Fax: 908-767-2222

U.S. Industries operates mainly in the US. Revenues from foreign operations are derived primarily from the operations of Jacuzzi affiliates in Italy and Brazil.

	1995 Sales	
---	---:	
	% of total	
US operations	88	
Export sales	12	
Total	**100**	

WHAT

	1995 Sales	
	$ mil.	% of total
Consumer Group	1,062	47
Building Products Group	775	34
Industrial Products Group	447	19
Total	**2,284**	**100**

Selected Companies and Products

Consumer Group
Ertl Co., Inc. (toys, die-cast miniatures, and model kits)
Farberware, Inc. (cookware and kitchen appliances)
Georgia Boot, Inc. (work, hiking, and Western boots)
Lehigh Safety Shoe Co. (protective footwear)
O. Ames Co. (lawn, garden, and industrial hand tools)
Rexair (Rainbow vacuum cleaners and accessories)
Spartus Corp. (alarm, decorator, and radio clocks)
Tommy Armour Golf Co. (golf clubs and accessories)
Universal Gym Equipment, Inc. (exercise equipment)

Building Products Group
Jacuzzi, Inc. (whirlpool baths and spas)
Progress Lighting, Inc. (residential lighting)
Spaulding Lighting, Inc. (commercial/industrial and outdoor lighting)

Industrial Group
Garden State Tanning (leather for auto interiors)
Huron Inc. (metal automotive components)
Leon Plastics, Inc. (plastic automotive components)
SCM Metal Products, Inc. (copper specialty products)

KEY COMPETITORS

Action Performance	L.L. Bean
Amer Group	Masco
American Brands	Maxim Group
Andersen Corp.	Metromedia International
Berkshire Hathaway	Pella
Black & Decker	Phillips-Van Heusen
Brunswick	Premark
Callaway Golf	Revell Monogram
CML	Salomon S.A.
Cooper Industries	Spalding
Corning	Sunbeam
Electrolux	Tandy
Foamex	Thomas Industries
Genesco	Timberland
Health o meter	Toastmaster
Huffy	Toro
Justin	Tyco Toys
Karsten	Wolverine World Wide
Lear Seating	

HOW MUCH

	Annual Growth	1986	1987	1988	1989	1990	1991	1992	1993	1994	1995
Sales ($ mil.)	(1.0%)	—	—	—	—	2,407	2,352	2,628	2,908	2,994	2,284
Net income ($ mil.)		—	—	—	—	34	2b	54	61	81	(89)
Income as % of sales		—	—	—	—	1.4%	1.1%	2.1%	2.1%	2.7%	—
Earnings per share ($)		—	—	—	—	—	—	—	—	—	(1.84)
Stock prices – high ($)		—	—	—	—	—	—	—	—	—	18.38
Stock prices – low ($)		—	—	—	—	—	—	—	—	—	12.63
Stock prices – close ($)		—	—	—	—	—	—	—	—	—	18.38
P/E – high		—	—	—	—	—	—	—	—	—	—
P/E – low		—	—	—	—	—	—	—	—	—	—
Dividends per share ($)		—	—	—	—	—	—	—	—	—	0.00
Book value per share ($)		—	—	—	—	—	—	—	—	—	7.68
Employees	(19.8%)	—	—	—	—	—	—	—	—	23,230	18,640

1995 Year-end:
Debt ratio: 70.7%
Return on equity: —
Cash (mil.): $51
Current ratio: 1.83
Long-term debt (mil.): $834
No. of shares (mil.): 54
Dividends
   Yield: —
   Payout: —
Market value (mil.): $986

Stock Price History
High/Low 1995

VIACOM INC.

OVERVIEW

Viacom, one of the world's largest media companies, is the medium *and* the message. A major force in TV, it owns such cable channels as MTV, VH1, Nickelodeon/Nick at Nite, pay movie channels (Showtime, the Movie Channel, and Flix), and 50% of USA Network, Comedy Central, the Sci-Fi Channel, and the All News Channel. It is a major producer of leading TV shows (*Entertainment Tonight* and *Frasier*, among others); a syndicator of popular TV programs (the *Star Trek* series, *Cheers*, and *Taxi*); a major movie producer (*Forrest Gump*); a leading book publisher (Simon & Schuster); and the world's top video and music retailer (Blockbuster Video and Blockbuster Music). The diversified entertainment giant also owns a score of radio and TV stations, presides over a library of TV programs and feature films, operates regional theme parks, and owns movie theaters in the US, Canada, and Europe.

New York–based Viacom emerged as a world-class company in 1994 when its chairman, Sumner Redstone, won a bidding war for Paramount and subsequently bought Blockbuster Video (Redstone owns about 1/2 of Viacom's common stock through his company, National Amusements).

To offset the debt incurred for the Paramount purchase, Redstone sold off Madison Square Garden, along with the Knicks (basketball), the Rangers (hockey), the Paramount Theater, and a cable sports station, and agreed in principle to sell Viacom's cable system. The company plans to sell its 78% stake in Spelling Entertainment (*Melrose Place* and *Beverly Hills 90210*) and may put other non-core assets on the block to cut debt. Viacom intends to exploit its many copyrights in movies, TV, toys, games, and books, and may enter the fast-growing music business.

WHEN

CBS formed Viacom in 1970 after the FCC ruled that TV networks could not own cable systems and TV stations in the same market. Viacom took over CBS's program syndication division. In the early 1970s Viacom bought cable systems in 5 states. In 1978 it formed Showtime, a subscription TV service, with Teleprompter, becoming full owner in 1982.

Paramount was started in 1912 by Adolph Zukor, becoming Paramount Pictures after merging with Famous Players-Lasky, a studio formed by Jesse Lasky, Samuel Goldwyn (né Goldfish), and Cecil B. DeMille. In the 1940s the government forced Paramount to divest its theater holdings. Movie attendance slipped as TV grew, and in 1966 Gulf + Western bought the struggling Paramount Pictures.

Gulf + Western began in 1956 when Charles G. Bluhdorn bought Michigan Plating and Stamping (Studebaker rear bumpers). Two years later he merged his company with Beard & Stone Electric and in 1959 adopted the name Gulf + Western Industries. The company acquired many diverse firms. When Bluhdorn died in 1983, his successor, Martin Davis, sold off all the other businesses except Associates Investment (auto loans, later sold in 1989), Simon & Schuster (1975), and Madison Square Garden (1977, sold 1995). In 1989 Gulf + Western became Paramount Communications, the same year it made an unsuccessful $200-per-share bid for Time.

In the late 1970s and early 1980s, Viacom purchased TV and radio stations in 5 states.

Viacom and Warner/Amex combined Showtime with The Movie Channel to form Showtime Networks in 1983. American Express left the Warner/Amex venture in 1986, and Viacom bought Warner's share of Showtime Networks and MTV Networks, including cable's first all-music video channel. Viacom also began producing series for network TV and bought a St. Louis TV station.

Sumner Redstone's National Amusements, a movie theater chain, bought 83% of Viacom for $3.4 billion in 1987 after a bidding war against Carl Icahn and a Viacom management group. In 1988 Viacom tried unsuccessfully to buy Orion Pictures.

In the early 1990s Paramount bought TV station operator TVX, King's Entertainment (theme parks), and a Detroit TV station. In 1993 Viacom bought ICOM Simulations (CD-ROM and video game software).

The 1994 acquisition of Paramount ultimately could bring Viacom $200 million in profits from Academy Award–winner *Forrest Gump*'s stunning box office success. In early 1995 Viacom launched a new TV network (United Paramount Network) with New York–based Chris-Craft. Congress's repeal of an FCC tax credit program for minorities killed Viacom's planned sale of its cable system (Viacom Cable Television) to Mitgo, a partnership with a black entrepreneur and major institutional investors. Viacom now will sell the system to an affiliate of Tele-Communications.

AMEX symbol: VIA
Fiscal year ends: December 31

WHO

Chairman: Sumner M. Redstone, age 71
VC; Chairman, Blockbuster Entertainment Group:
H. Wayne Huizenga, age 57
President and CEO: Frank J. Biondi Jr., age 50,
$3,991,895 pay
**EVP, General Counsel, Chief Administrative Officer,
and Secretary:** Philippe P. Dauman, age 41,
$2,159,465 pay
**EVP Finance, Corporate Development, and
Communications:** Thomas E. Dooley, age 38,
$2,155,912 pay
SVP and CFO: George S. Smith Jr., age 46
SVP; Chairman and CEO, Viacom Interactive Media:
Edward D. Horowitz, age 47, $938,400 pay
SVP Human Resources and Administration: William A.
Roskin, age 52
Auditors: Price Waterhouse LLP

WHERE

HQ: 1515 Broadway, New York, NY 10036
Phone: 212-258-6000
Fax: 212-258-6597

WHAT

	1994 Sales		1994 Operating Income	
	$ mil.	% of total	$ mil.	% of total
Entertainment	2,285	31	(88)	—
Networks	1,855	25	357	43
Publishing	1,787	24	194	23
Video/music/parks	1,070	15	199	24
Cable TV	406	5	79	10
Adjustments	(40)	—	(133)	—
Total	**7,363**	**100**	**608**	**100**

Selected Holdings

Entertainment
Movie theaters in the US,
Canada, and Europe
Paramount Pictures
Paramount Television
Spelling Entertainment
Group (78%)
Republic Pictures
Spelling Television
Virgin Interactive
Entertainment (90%)
Worldvision Enterprises
Viacom Interactive Media

**Networks and
Broadcasting**
All News Channel (50%)
Comedy Central (50%)
MTV Networks
MTV: Music Television
Nickelodeon/Nick at Nite
VH1 Music First
Showtime Networks
Flix
The Movie Channel
Showtime

USA Networks (50%)
Sci-Fi Channel
USA Network

Publishing
Simon & Schuster
Allyn and Bacon
Educational Management
Group, Inc.
MacMillan Publishing
USA
Pocket Books
Prentice Hall
Scribner
Simon & Schuster

Video/Music/Theme Parks
Block Party (entertainment
centers)
Blockbuster Music
Blockbuster Video
Discovery Zone, Inc.
(49.6%)
Paramount Parks (5 theme
parks in US and Canada)

KEY COMPETITORS

Advance
Publications
Bertelsmann
Capital Cities/ABC
CBS
Cineplex Odeon
Discovery
Communications
DreamWorks SKG
Gaylord
Entertainment
Harcourt General
Hearst
Heritage Media

Hollywood
Entertainment
K-III
King World
MCA
McGraw-Hill
Metro Goldwyn
Mayer
Metromedia
International
News Corp.
Pearson
Reed Elsevier
Six Flags

Sony
Thomson Corp.
Thorn EMI
Ticketmaster
Time Warner
Tribune
Turner
Broadcasting
United Artists
Theatre
Walt Disney
Washington
Post

HOW MUCH

	Annual Growth	1985	1986	1987	1988	1989	1990	1991	1992	1993	1994
Sales ($ mil.)	36.6%	444	919	1,011	1,259	1,436	1,600	1,712	1,865	2,005	7,363
Net income ($ mil.)	(9.5%)	37	(10)	(124)	(123)	131	(90)	(50)	49	158	15
Income as % of sales	—	8.3%	—	—	—	9.1%	—	—	2.6%	7.9%	0.2%
Earnings per share ($)	—	—	(0.13)	(1.64)	(1.77)	1.07	(0.84)	(0.44)	0.41	1.23	0.07
Stock price – high ($)	—	—	—	14.25	15.69	32.62	29.56	35.38	44.00	67.50	49.75
Stock price – low ($)	—	—	—	5.00	8.87	15.25	15.63	23.50	28.13	37.13	24.50
Stock price – close ($)	24.3%	—	—	9.06	15.56	28.75	26.25	34.25	44.00	48.88	41.63
P/E – high	—	—	—	—	—	31	—	—	104	55	—
P/E – low	—	—	—	—	—	14	—	—	69	30	—
Dividends per share ($)	—	—	—	0.00	0.00	0.00	0.00	0.00	0.00	0.00	0.00
Book value per share ($)	28.9%	—	—	4.98	3.21	4.27	3.43	5.82	6.28	7.60	29.45
Employees	37.8%	3,900	4,700	4,800	4,400	4,900	5,000	4,900	5,000	17,500	70,000

1994 Year-end:
Debt ratio: 46.9%
Return on equity: 1.9%
Cash (mil.): $598
Current ratio: 1.27
Long-term debt (mil.): $10,402
No. of shares (mil.): 360
Dividends
Yield: —
Payout: —
Market value (mil.): $14,972

**Stock Price History
High/Low 1987–94**

WARNER-LAMBERT COMPANY

OVERVIEW

Diversified Warner-Lambert is committed to becoming the world's leading provider of consumer health care products (54% of sales in 1994 were international) and keeping its pharmaceutical pipeline full. Through an initial $30 million, 3-year investment, Warner-Lambert will establish a confectionery and consumer health care products operation in China. With a Chinese partner the company will build and run a manufacturing plant in Guangzhou (formerly Canton).

The Morris Plains, New Jersey–based company has numerous drugs in various development phases. Most brands are marketed under the Parke-Davis and Goedecke names. The firm's 72 generic drugs (including the generic

equivalent of its former blockbuster cholesterol reducer Lopid) are made by its Warner Chillcott Laboratories Division. Warner-Lambert spent 7% of 1994 sales on R&D.

Domestically, the company estimates that more than 50% of its pharmaceutical sales are to managed-care organizations, including governmental units and hospitals. Warner-Lambert has plans to develop a marketing group to deal exclusively with managed-care organizations' specific needs.

Neurontin (a drug for treating epilepsy) received FDA approval in 1993 and contributed to overall sales growth in 1994. Worldwide sales of cardiovascular drug Accupril increased by 36% in 1994.

WHEN

In 1856 pharmacist William Warner opened a drugstore in Philadelphia and soon made his mark by sugar-coating pills and tablets. In 1886 he began drug production by opening William R. Warner & Co. In 1908 St. Louis–based Pfeiffer Chemical bought the company, adopted the Warner name, and moved it to New York in 1916. By 1945 the company had several overseas operations and over 50 businesses, including Sloan's (liniment), Corn Husker's (lotion), and Hudnut (cosmetics).

In 1950 the company, under the leadership of Elmer Bobst, changed its name to Warner-Hudnut and went public. Two years later Warner bought Chilcott Labs (founded in 1874 as the Maltine Company). Warner Chilcott is now the part of Warner-Lambert responsible for producing generic drugs. In 1955 the company assumed its current name following the purchase of Lambert Pharmacal (founded in 1884 by Jordan Lambert after he acquired the formula for Listerine antiseptic).

Acquisitions continued throughout the next 2 decades and included Emerson Drugs (Bromo-Seltzer, 1956), Nepera Chemical (antihistamines, 1956), American Chicle (chewing gum, 1962), and Schick (razors, 1970). The purchase of Parke-Davis in 1970 resulted in an antitrust investigation and the selling of certain product lines in 1976 (thyroid preparations, blood products, vaccines, and others). Founded in Detroit in 1866, Parke-Davis was the first company to make "biologicals" (vaccines). It later introduced Dilantin (anticonvulsant, 1938), Benadryl (antihistamine, 1946), and Chloromycetin (antibiotic, 1949), all still sold today.

Because of slipping profits in the 1970s, unprofitable divisions were sold and others consolidated in the early 1980s. In 1985 the divestitures and restructuring caused the company to take a $553 million write-down. The restructuring, however, along with new, efficient robotic manufacturing methods, resulted in annual savings of over $300 million and led to generally profitable bottom lines throughout the rest of the 1980s. In 1992 Warner-Lambert introduced Cool Mint Listerine and formed a partnership with British company Xenova to test and develop pharmaceuticals from natural compounds. Also that year Accupril's market numbers grew.

In 1993, to sharpen its consumer health care products line, Warner-Lambert purchased Wilkinson Sword, the razor and toiletries maker, to augment its Schick razor line (#2, after Gillette). In that year it began research partnerships with biotechnology firms Ribozyme and Neurex. Also in 1993 the company agreed to buy consumer health care products concern Fisons PLC, with operations in Australia and New Zealand, for $23 million.

In 1994 Warner-Lambert began joint ventures with Wellcome and Glaxo (now Glaxo-Wellcome) to market OTC versions of their products (including Sudafed, Actifed, and Zantac) in the US, Australia, and Europe. Also that year the Parke-Davis Division restructured to improve relationships with managed care organizations and address patent expirations. Warner-Lambert continues its worldwide expansion, especially in China, India, and eastern Europe. In 1995 the company agreed to buy Glaxo-Wellcome's share of the joint venture producing Sudafed and Actifed.

NYSE symbol: WLA
Fiscal year ends: December 31

Chairman and CEO: Melvin R. Goodes, age 59,
$1,686,250 pay
President and COO: Lodewijk J. R. de Vink, age 50,
$1,116,500 pay
EVP; President, Consumer Healthcare Sector: John F.
Walsh, age 52, $718,333 pay
VP External Relations: Joseph E. Smith, age 55,
$573,000 pay
VP and CFO: Ernest J. Larini, age 52, $543,967 pay
VP; President, Confectionery Sector: J. Frank Lazo,
age 47
VP; Chairman, Parke-Davis Research: Ronald M.
Cresswell, age 60
VP; President, Parke-Davis Research: Pedro M.
Cuatrecasas, age 58
VP and General Counsel: Gregory L. Johnson, age 48
VP Human Resources: Raymond M. Fino, age 52
Auditors: Price Waterhouse LLP

WHERE

HQ: 201 Tabor Rd., Morris Plains, NJ 07950-2693
Phone: 201-540-2000
Fax: 201-540-3761

The company has 72 production facilities in 34
countries.

	1994 Sales		1994 Operating Income	
	$ mil.	% of total	$ mil.	% of total
US	2,954	46	844	50
Americas & Far East	1,845	29	422	25
Europe, Middle East & Africa	1,618	25	428	25
Adjustments	—	—	(456)	—
Total	**6,417**	**100**	**1,238**	**100**

WHAT

	1994 Sales		1994 Operating Income	
	$ mil.	% of total	$ mil.	% of total
Consumer health care	2,970	46	649	53
Pharmaceuticals	2,079	33	241	19
Confectionery	1,368	21	348	28
Total	**6,417**	**100**	**1,238**	**100**

Consumer Health Care
Benadryl (antihistamine)
Benylin (cough syrup)
Halls (cough tablets)
Listerine (mouthwash)
Lubriderm (skin lotion)
Rolaids (antacid)

Pharmaceuticals
Accupril (cardiovascular product)
Chloromycetin (antibiotic)
Cognex (treatment for Alzheimer's)
Dilantin (anticonvulsant)
ERYC (erythromycin, antibiotic)
Gemfibrozil (generic of Lopid, lipid regulator)

Loestrin (contraceptive)
Neurontin (anticonvulsant)

Confectionery
Bubblicious
Certs
Chiclets
Cinn*A*Burst
Clorets
Dentyne
Trident

Other
Capsugel (empty gelatin capsules)
Schick (razors)
Tetra (aquarium supplies)
Wilkinson Sword (razors)

KEY COMPETITORS

ALZA
American Home Products
Amway
Bausch & Lomb
Bristol-Myers Squibb
Carter-Wallace
Colgate-Palmolive
Dow Chemical

Eastman Chemical
Gillette
Hoechst
Hershey
Johnson & Johnson
Merck
Nestlé
Novo Nordisk

Pharmacia & Upjohn
Procter & Gamble
Rhône-Poulenc
Nabisco Holdings
Schering-Plough
SmithKline Beecham
Unilever
Wrigley

HOW MUCH

	Annual Growth	1985	1986	1987	1988	1989	1990	1991	1992	1993	1994
Sales ($ mil.)	8.0%	3,200	3,103	3,485	3,908	4,196	4,687	5,059	5,598	5,794	6,417
Net income ($ mil.)	12.7%	237	262	298	340	413	485	141	644	285	694
Income as % of sales	—	7.4%	8.4%	8.5%	8.7%	9.8%	10.3%	2.8%	11.5%	4.9%	10.8%
Earnings per share ($)	14.5%	1.53	1.77	2.08	2.50	3.05	3.61	1.05	4.78	2.11	5.17
Stock price – high ($)	—	24.63	31.63	43.75	39.75	59.38	70.38	82.25	79.25	76.38	86.75
Stock price – low ($)	—	16.63	22.50	24.13	29.94	37.25	49.63	61.75	58.38	59.75	60.00
Stock price – close ($)	14.0%	23.75	29.31	33.75	39.19	57.75	67.50	77.63	69.13	67.50	77.00
P/E – high	—	16	18	21	16	19	19	78	17	36	17
P/E – low	—	11	13	12	12	12	14	59	12	28	12
Dividends per share ($)	14.0%	0.75	0.80	0.89	1.08	1.28	1.52	1.76	2.04	2.28	2.44
Book value per share ($)	6.4%	5.89	6.32	6.37	7.36	8.38	10.44	8.70	11.29	10.36	10.32
Employees	(0.9%)	39,000	33,200	33,500	33,000	33,000	34,000	34,000	34,000	35,000	36,000

1994 Year-end:
Debt ratio: 51.2%
Return on equity: 49.9%
Cash (mil.): $465
Current ratio: 1.07
Long-term debt (mil.): $535
No. of shares (mil.): 134
Dividends
    Yield: 3.2%
    Payout: 47.2%
Market value (mil.): $10,364

**Stock Price History
High/Low 1985–94**

WOOLWORTH CORPORATION

OVERVIEW

The question remains: what is Woolworth? Founded as a general merchandiser, the company is abandoning its roots to concentrate on building its eclectic collection of specialty stores. One of the few major retailers still based in New York City, Woolworth has struggled to reinvent itself. Its revenues dropped over 13% in fiscal 1995, reflecting the closure of many of its US five-and-dimes and the sale of 122 Canadian Woolco stores.

Leading the charge into specialty retailing is new CEO Roger Farah, a former executive with R. H. Macy. Farah is the first non-Woolworth executive to be named CEO of the company.

Farah plans to continue the company's shift to specialty retailing, which includes athletic and dress shoes, costume jewelry and accessories, casual apparel, and home furnishings and accessories. He also plans to sell some underperforming specialty chains and is looking for other ways to cut costs. In 1995 the company announced plans to reduce employment by 2,000, and it eliminated the dividend on its common stock for the first time in 92 years.

WHEN

With the idea of selling merchandise priced at no more than 5 cents, Frank Woolworth opened The Great Five Cent Store in Utica, New York, in 1879. It failed. That same year he moved to Lancaster, Pennsylvania, and created the first five-and-dime.

Woolworth moved his headquarters to New York City (1886) and spent the rest of the century acquiring other dime-store chains. He later expanded to Canada (1897), England (1909), France (1922), and Germany (1927).

With $10 million in sales, the 120-store chain incorporated as F.W. Woolworth & Company in 1905, with Frank Woolworth as president. In 1912 Woolworth merged with 5 rival chains and went public with 596 stores, making $52 million in sales the first year.

Frank Woolworth built lavish homes and corporate headquarters. In 1913, paying $13.5 million in cash, he finished construction of the Woolworth Building, then the world's tallest building (792 feet). When Woolworth died in 1919, the chain had 1,081 stores, with sales of $119 million.

Woolworth became more competitive after WWII by advertising, establishing revolving credit and self-service, moving stores to the suburbs, and expanding merchandise selections. In 1962 Woolworth opened Woolco, a US and Canadian discount chain. The US stores were closed in 1982.

Since the 1960s the company has become a specialty retailer, growing by acquiring and expanding US, Canadian, Australian, and European chains. Acquisitions included G.R. Kinney (shoes, 1963), Richman Brothers (men's clothing, 1969), Holtzman's Little Folk Shop (children's clothing, 1983), Champs (sporting goods, 1987), Moderna Shuh Center (shoes, Germany, 1988), Mathers (shoes, Australia, 1988), and Profoot (the Netherlands and Belgium, 1990).

In 1974 the company introduced Foot Locker, the athletic-shoe chain, later developing Lady Foot Locker (1982) and Kids Foot Locker (1987). Woolworth Express (1987) was a smaller version of the original dime store that has since been discontinued.

Since 1980 Woolworth's specialty stores have increased dramatically, while general merchandise stores have decreased sharply. In 1990 the company "reopened" a German store, in Halle, that it had operated before WWII. It was the first opened by any US retailer in eastern Germany.

In 1993 CFO William Lavin replaced retiring CEO Harold Sells. Lavin launched an ambitious restructuring plan, abandoning general merchandise in favor of becoming a diverse collection of specialty stores (primarily apparel and shoes). Although the company had been heading in this direction for years, in 1993 it took important steps to cut its general merchandise segment in half, closing 400 stores in the US and selling 122 Canadian Woolco stores to Wal-Mart. It also closed about 300 underperforming shoe stores.

The realignment was interrupted by an accounting scandal in 1994, when it was discovered that quarterly results had been overstated. An investigation found no intentional wrongdoing and no effect on annual results but noted that accountants were under pressure by management to show good results. CFO Charles Young was fired. The scandal prompted a deluge of shareholders lawsuits and an SEC investigation. The lawsuits and the investigation are pending. Later in 1994 Lavin was forced to resign by the board of directors, which was dissatisfied with the turnaround of the company.

In June 1995 Woolworth sold its Kids Mart/ Little Folks children's wear chain to investor group LFS Acquisition.

NYSE symbol: Z
Fiscal year ends: Last Saturday in January

WHO

Chairman and CEO: Roger N. Farah, age 42, $2,000,000 pay
President and COO: Dale W. Hilpert, age 52
VC, Kinney Shoe Corporation: Harold C. Rowen, $330,000 pay
EVP Worldwide Specialty Operations: Ronald J. Berens, age 55, $375,630 pay
SVP and Chief Administrative Officer: W. Barry Thomson, age 42, $280,000 pay
SVP and CFO: Andrew P. Hines, age 55
SVP Corporate Planning and Development: C. Jackson Gray, age 47
VP and Treasurer: John H. Cannon, age 53
VP Real Property: Gary H. Brown, age 55
VP Public Affairs: Frances E. Trachter, age 49
VP, General Counsel, and Secretary: Gary M. Bahler, age 43
VP Human Resources: Patricia A. Peck, age 44
Auditors: Price Waterhouse LLP

WHERE

HQ: 233 Broadway, New York, NY 10279-0003
Phone: 212-553-2000
Fax: 212-553-2042

Woolworth operates over 8,000 specialty and general merchandise stores in 23 countries worldwide.

	1995 Sales		1995 Operating Income	
	$ mil.	% of total	$ mil.	% of total
US	5,444	66	266	91
Europe	1,745	21	20	7
Canada	772	9	(16)	—
Pacific Rim	222	3	5	2
Mexico	110	1	(1)	—
Total	**8,293**	**100**	**274**	**100**

WHAT

	1995 Sales		1995 Operating Income	
	$ mil.	% of total	$ mil.	% of total
Specialty stores	5,017	60	258	94
General merch.	3,276	40	16	6
Total	**8,293**	**100**	**274**	**100**

1995 Specialty Stores	No.
Foot Locker (athletic footwear)	1,828
AfterThoughts/Carimar/Rubin/ Reflexions (boutiques)	1,082
Kinney (shoes)	826
Lady Foot Locker (athletic footwear)	595
Champs Sports (sporting goods)	539
Northern Reflections (women's casual wear)	466
Other formats	1,889
Total	**7,225**

1995 General Merchandise Stores	No.
Woolworth	812
The Bargain! Shop (low-priced apparel & household items)	194
Other formats	65
Total	**1,071**

KEY COMPETITORS

50-Off Stores	Just For Feet	Sears
Ames	Kmart	Sports Authority
Brown Group	The Limited	The Athlete's Foot
Dayton Hudson	Luxottica	TJX
Dillard	May	Venture
Edison Brothers	Melville	Wal-Mart
Federated	Merry-Go-Round	
The Gap	Montgomery Ward	
Gymboree	Nine West	
J. C. Penney	Price/Costco	

HOW MUCH

	Annual Growth	1986	1987	1988	1989	1990	1991	1992	1993	1994	1995
Sales ($ mil.)	3.7%	5,958	6,501	7,134	8,088	8,820	9,789	9,914	9,962	9,626	8,293
Net income ($ mil.)	(13.7%)	177	214	251	288	329	317	(53)	280	(495)	47
Income as % of sales	—	3.0%	3.3%	3.5%	3.6%	3.7%	3.2%	—	2.8%	—	0.6%
Earnings per share ($)	(13.9%)	1.38	1.63	1.91	2.24	2.56	2.45	(0.41)	2.14	(3.76)	0.36
Stock price – high ($)[1]	—	15.63	24.50	29.81	30.38	36.13	36.63	36.38	35.00	32.75	26.25
Stock price – low ($)[1]	—	9.16	14.53	14.75	17.06	24.19	22.88	23.50	26.00	20.50	12.88
Stock price – close ($)[1]	0.0%	15.00	19.31	17.25	25.88	31.94	30.25	26.50	31.63	25.38	15.00
P/E – high	—	11	15	16	14	14	15	—	16	—	73
P/E – low	—	7	9	8	8	9	9	—	12	—	36
Dividends per share ($)	6.7%	0.49	0.55	0.66	0.78	0.91	1.02	1.07	1.11	1.15	0.88
Book value per share ($)	0.8%	9.55	11.32	13.01	14.41	16.08	18.04	15.57	15.67	10.22	10.25
Employees	0.0%	119,000	121,000	125,000	132,000	138,000	141,000	142,000	145,000	111,000	119,000

1995 Year-end:
Debt ratio: 46.7%
Return on equity: 3.5%
Cash (mil.): $72
Current ratio: 1.21
Long-term debt (mil.): $309
No. of shares (mil.): 133
Dividends
    Yield: 5.9%
    Payout: —
Market value (mil.): $1,988

**Stock Price History[1]
High/Low 1986–95**

[1] Stock prices are for the prior calendar year.

XEROX CORPORATION

OVERVIEW

The Document Company — Xerox — focuses on the intersection of the paper and digital worlds by producing, marketing, servicing, and financing a wide range of copiers, scanners, printers, and document processing software. Based in Stamford, Connecticut, Xerox sold its Xerox Financial Services Life Insurance Company to General American Life Insurance Company in 1995 and is in the process of selling its remaining nondocument processing companies, primarily in the insurance sector.

Xerox is also adjusting its ownership in one of its international joint ventures and the division of its global markets. Xerox has raised its stake in Rank Xerox, its European subsidiary, from 51% to 71% by purchasing additional shares from the Rank Organisation for $960 million. Also, Xerox is now forming a production venture in China with Fuji Xerox that would allow Fuji Xerox to compete directly with its Japanese rivals already in China. Xerox has historically controlled the production and sales operations in China along with North and South America.

Xerox's $900 million R&D program is concentrating on 3 developing markets: digital printing, color systems, and network systems.

WHEN

The Haloid Company was incorporated in 1906 to make and sell photographic paper. In 1935 it bought the Rectigraph Company (photocopiers). This purchase led Haloid to acquire a license for a new process called electrophotography (later renamed xerography from the ancient Greek words for *dry* and *writing*) from the Battelle Memorial Institute in 1947. Battelle had backed inventor Chester Carlson, who had labored since 1937 to perfect a process of transferring electrostatic images from a photoconductive surface to paper.

Haloid commercialized the process, introducing the Model A copier in 1949 and the Xerox Copyflo in 1955. By 1956 xerographic products represented 40% of the company's sales. The company became Haloid Xerox in 1958 and in 1959 introduced the Xerox 914, the first simplified office copier. The 914 took the world by storm, beating out such competing technologies as mimeograph (A.B. Dick), thermal paper (3M), and damp copy (Kodak). Xerox's revenues soared from $37 million in 1960 to $268 million in 1965. The firm dropped Haloid from its name in 1961.

Xerox branched out in the 1960s, buying 3 publishing firms and one computer company, all of which were later sold or disbanded.

In the 1970s Xerox bought companies that made printers (Diablo, 1972), plotters (Versatec, 1975), and disk drives (Shugart, 1977; sold in 1984); it also bought record carrier Western Union International (1979; sold in 1982). In 1974 the FTC, believing Xerox was too dominant in its market, forced the company to license its xerographic technology to other manufacturers.

In the 1980s Xerox bought companies in optical character recognition (Kurzweil, 1980), scanning and fax (Datacopy, 1988), and desktop publishing (Ventura, 1990; sold to Corel Corp. in 1993). It also diversified into financial services, buying insurance companies (Crum and Forster, 1983) and investment banking companies (Van Kampen Merritt, 1984), among others.

After becoming CEO in 1990, Paul Allaire embarked on a major restructuring program to focus Xerox's operations on its core document processing business. In 1992 Xerox reorganized into 9 independent business divisions and 3 geographical customer operations units. Also in 1992 the company eliminated 2,500 jobs, with savings of $150 million. With an eye to future alliances, Xerox signed agreements to supply print engines to computer companies Compaq (1992) and Apple (1993). The Apple contract was a particular coup, as Canon, a chief US competitor, had been Apple's sole print engine supplier since 1985.

In 1993 Xerox sold 2 financial companies, Van Kampen Merritt for $360 million and Furman Selz for $99 million. In late 1993 Xerox announced plans to cut an additional 10,000 jobs by 1996 (more than 10% of its total work force). A surge of new products accompanied the cost cutting, indicating better use of its R&D centers. Xerox's R&D had a reputation for great inventions (the laser printer, PC networking, the graphical computer screen) but slow implementation. Xerox also formed partnerships with Lotus, Microsoft, and Novell to market its technology faster.

In 1995 Xerox introduced a new family of networked color laser printers and a host of software products. These products include DocuWeb and InterDoc, which allow documents to be printed via the Internet and the World Wide Web. Xerox also announced a multiple-site printing service with AT&T.

NYSE symbol: XRX
Fiscal year ends: December 31

Chairman and CEO: Paul A. Allaire, age 56,
$3,294,284 pay
EVP and CFO: Barry D. Romeril, age 51, $1,920,904 pay
EVP Operations: A. Berry Rand, age 50, $1,539,055 pay
EVP Operations: Peter van Cuylenburg, age 47,
$1,402,498 pay
EVP; Chairman and CEO, Xerox Financial Services:
Stuart B. Ross, age 57
SVP Corporate Strategic Services: Allan E. Dugan,
age 54, $1,273,371 pay
SVP Corporate Research and Technology: Mark B.
Myers, age 56
SVP and Chief Staff Officer: William F. Buehler, age 55
SVP and General Counsel: Richard S. Paul, age 53
VP Treasurer and Secretary: Eunice M. Filter, age 54
VP Controller: Philip D. Fishbach, age 53
VP Human Resources: Anne M. Mulcahy
Auditors: KPMG Peat Marwick LLP

WHERE

HQ: 800 Long Ridge Rd., PO Box 1600,
Stamford, CT 06904
Phone: 203-968-3000
Fax: 203-968-4312 (Public Relations)

Xerox, in conjunction with jointly owned subsidiaries
Rank Xerox and Fuji Xerox, operates offices,
manufacturing plants, and other facilities worldwide.

	1994 Sales		1994 Net Income	
	$ mil.	% of total	$ mil.	% of total
US	10,571	59	386	49
Europe	4,633	26	215	27
Other regions	2,633	15	193	24
Total	**17,837**	**100**	**794**	**100**

WHAT

	1994 Sales	
	$ mil.	% of total
Sales	7,853	44
Service & rentals	6,229	35
Insurance	2,749	15
Equipment financing	1,006	6
Total	**17,837**	**100**

Business Divisions
Desktop Document Systems (digital desktop devices)
Office Document Products (copiers)
Office Document Systems (laser and ink-jet printers)
Personal Document Products (personal/convenience
copiers)
Xerox Business Services (document management
services)
Xerox Engineering Systems (document systems for
engineering and scientific applications)
Xerox Production Systems (publishing and printing
systems)
XSoft (software for document management and other
applications)

Other
Insurance services

KEY COMPETITORS

AM International	Matsushita
Brother	3M
Canon	Minolta
Casio	Mitsubishi
Copifax	Moore Corp.
Eastman Kodak	NEC
GEC	Océ
General Binding	Olivetti
Harris Corp.	Pitney Bowes
Hewlett-Packard	Polaroid
Hitachi	Sharp
Lexmark	Siemens
Machines Bull	

HOW MUCH

	Annual Growth	1985	1986	1987	1988	1989	1990	1991	1992	1993	1994
Sales ($ mil.)	8.1%	8,838	9,355	10,320	31,234	33,148	17,973	17,830	18,261	17,410	17,837
Net income ($ mil.)	5.9%	475	423	578	388	704	243	454	(1,074)	(126)	794
Income as % of sales	—	5.4%	4.5%	5.6%	1.2%	2.1%	1.4%	2.5%	—	—	4.5%
Earnings per share ($)	4.2%	4.44	3.85	5.35	3.50	6.41	1.66	3.86	(3.32)	(1.84)	6.44
Stock price – high ($)	—	60.50	72.25	85.00	63.00	69.00	58.88	69.75	82.25	90.00	112.75
Stock price – low ($)	—	37.25	48.63	50.00	50.25	54.38	29.00	35.25	66.50	69.88	87.75
Stock price – close ($)	5.8%	59.75	60.00	56.63	58.38	57.25	35.50	68.50	79.25	89.38	99.00
P/E – high	—	14	19	16	18	11	36	18	—	—	18
P/E – low	—	8	13	9	14	9	18	9	—	—	14
Dividends per share ($)	0.0%	3.00	3.00	3.00	3.00	3.00	3.00	3.00	3.00	3.00	3.00
Book value per share ($)	(1.6%)	45.47	48.00	51.00	52.22	54.66	54.76	55.36	40.76	38.15	39.41
Employees	(1.7%)	102,396	100,400	99,200	100,000	99,000	99,000	100,900	99,300	97,000	87,600

1994 Year-end:
Debt ratio: 72.0%
Return on equity: 19.5%
Cash (mil.): $35
Current ratio: 1.35
Long-term debt (mil.): $7,596
No. of shares (mil.): 106
Dividends
  Yield: 3.0%
  Payout: 46.6%
Market value (mil.): $10,493

Stock Price History
High/Low 1985–94

Selected New York Companies

ACCLAIM ENTERTAINMENT, INC.

OVERVIEW

Playing is serious business for Acclaim Entertainment, one of the US's largest independent makers of entertainment software for SEGA and Nintendo game systems. Acclaim's games, mainly targeted for 11- to 17-year-old boys, include WWF Raw, NFL Quarterback Club, and The Simpsons. The company's Acclaim Comics is a major publisher of comic books. Founders Gregory Fischbach and James Scoroposki own 14% and 13% of Acclaim's stock, respectively.

Acclaim was founded in 1986 to design and sell video games, mostly for Nintendo's NES system. The company went public in 1988 and 2 years later acquired LJN Toys from MCA. In 1989 Acclaim began making software for Nintendo's Game Boy.

In 1992 the company entered the SEGA game market by buying Mirrorsoft, a European designer of software for SEGA's Genesis and Game Gear systems. While Acclaim sank $3 million that year into a failed television venture, it benefited from a price war between Nintendo and SEGA that caused both companies to lower their prices.

The company diversified into comic books with the purchase of Voyager Communications (renamed Acclaim Comics) in 1994. That year it contracted with Warner Bros. Studios to create special effects for the movie *Batman Forever* using video game technology. This convergence of technologies allows more cross-marketing between movies and games.

The company is vulnerable to technological advances in its market. The rise of interactive PC games for home use and the introduction of 32- and 64-bit systems has made some of its products obsolete, which contributed to a slight decline in earnings in 1995.

In late 1995 the company acquired Lazer-Tron (which makes coin-operated redemption games) and video-game makers Probe Entertainment and Sculptured Software.

WHO

Co-chairman and CEO: Gregory E. Fischbach, age 53, $3,550,000 pay
Co-chairman, EVP, Secretary, and Treasurer: James Scoroposki, age 47, $2,850,000 pay
President, COO, and General Manager: Robert Holmes, age 42, $2,900,000 pay
EVP Finance and CFO: Anthony R. Williams, age 37, $270,000 pay
VP Planning and Operations (HR): John Ma
Attorney: Bernard Fischbach, age 49
Auditors: Grant Thornton, LLP

WHERE

HQ: One Acclaim Plaza, Glen Cove, NY 11542
Phone: 516-656-5000   **Fax:** 516-656-2040

	1995 Sales	
	$ mil.	% of total
North America	443.9	78
Europe	95.5	17
Asia	27.3	5
Total	**566.7**	**100**

WHAT

	1995 Sales
	% of total
16-bit game software	74
CD software	10
Portable game software	10
Other	6
Total	**100**

Selected Software Titles

Batman Forever	NFL Quarterback	StarGate
Mortal Kombat II	Club	True Lies
NBA Jam	The Simpsons	Warlock

KEY COMPETITORS

7th Level	id Software	SEGA
Accolade	Interplay	Sierra On-Line
Activision	Productions	Sony
Atari	LucasArts	Spectrum
Brøderbund	Marvel	HoloByte
Electronic Arts	Microsoft	Time Warner
Cyan	Nintendo	WMS Industries

HOW MUCH

Nasdaq symbol: AKLM FY ends: August 31	Annual Growth	1990	1991	1992	1993	1994	1995	1995 Year-end: Debt ratio: 8.5%
Sales ($ mil.)	32.0%	141.5	122.1	214.6	327.1	480.8	566.7	Return on equity: 17.9%
Net income ($ mil.)	25.8%	14.2	(5.8)	13.8	28.2	45.1	44.8	Cash (mil.): $44.7
Income as % of sales	—	10.0%	—	6.4%	8.6%	9.4%	7.9%	Current ratio: 2.59
Earnings per share ($)	11.0%	0.51	(0.21)	0.37	0.63	1.00	0.86	Long-term debt (mil.): $0.4
Stock price – high ($)	—	10.67	4.25	12.26	31.75	27.25	28.63	No. of shares (mil.): 46.3
Stock price – low ($)	—	2.08	1.92	3.00	10.67	12.88	10.75	Dividends
Stock price – close ($)	30.7%	3.25	3.08	12.09	21.25	14.38	12.38	Yield: —
P/E – high	—	21	—	33	50	27	33	Payout: —
P/E – low	—	4	—	8	17	13	13	Market value (mil.): $573.0
Dividends per share ($)	—	0.00	0.00	0.00	0.00	0.00	0.00	
Book value per share ($)	37.9%	1.41	1.17	1.85	2.60	4.45	7.03	
Employees	60.5%	75	89	133	193	295	800	

THE ALPINE GROUP, INC.

OVERVIEW

The Alpine Group is finding new mountains to climb. Formerly focused on electronic flat panel display technology, it has shifted to other areas in the hopes that it will find Mount Profits. Alpine, which has posted losses since Ronald Reagan was president, is now a diversified industrial company, manufacturing copper wire and cable for the telecommunications industry, electronic products for military and commercial applications, and special refractory products for a variety of applications, including iron and steel, aluminum, and glass manufacturing. CEO Steven Elbaum owns 8.8% of the company's common stock.

Alpine was founded in 1957 by researchers from Columbia University, several of whom lived in Alpine, New Jersey. The company, which went public in 1964, focused on marine geodetic surveys and marine transportation until the early 1980s. Elbaum, who became CEO in 1983, led Alpine through a series of acquisitions and divestitures, including Precision Products (machine shop, acquired in 1984 and sold in 1991) and Rochester Button (acquired in 1984 and sold in 1989).

In 1987 Alpine bought the technology for flat panel display manufacturing and shifted its focus. It acquired firms in related fields, including DNE Technologies (1992), a maker of aerospace controllers and secured communications devices, and Superior TeleTec (1993), a maker of telecommunications cable, as part of a strategy to market its flat panel display technology to niche markets such as aircraft makers, who need cockpit instrument panels.

However, Alpine changed its strategy and began to focus more on industrial products in mature markets. In 1994 it bought a maker of specialty refractory products, Adience. In 1995 Alpine spun off its flat panel display technology and several other companies as PolyVision to shareholders.

WHO

Chairman and CEO: Steven S. Elbaum, age 46, $381,785 pay
EVP and COO: Stephen Johnson, age 46
EVP and Secretary: Bragi F. Schut, age 54, $220,532 pay
SVP: Alan J. Nickerson, age 45, $184,752 pay
Treasurer and CFO: David S. Aldridge, age 40, $99,927 pay
Office Manager (HR): Elaine McKee
Auditors: Arthur Andersen & Co, SC

WHERE

HQ: 1790 Broadway, New York, NY 10019-1412
Phone: 212-757-3333   **Fax:** 212-757-3423

WHAT

Selected Products
Communications products
Copper telephone cable
Electronic printers
Military avionics
Multiplexers
Outside service wire
Premises wire
Refractory products

KEY COMPETITORS

ADC Telecommunications
Anixter International
A.P. Green Industries
AT&T Systems & Technology
Cable Design Technologies
Encore Wire
Essex Holdings
Honeywell
Hughes Electronics
Loral
Matsushita
McDonnell Douglas
National Refractories
North American Refractories
Northrop Grumman
Premier Refractories & Chemicals
Wassall

HOW MUCH

AMEX symbol: AGI FY ends: April 30	Annual Growth	1990	1991	1992	1993	1994	1995
Sales ($ mil.)	90.5%	7.9	6.3	10.3	32.1	73.6	198.1
Net income ($ mil.)	—	(16.1)	(2.0)	(8.0)	(12.5)	(30.1)	(6.8)
Income as % of sales	—	—	—	—	—	—	—
Earnings per share ($)	—	(3.20)	(0.35)	(1.08)	(1.40)	(2.16)	(0.38)
Stock price – high ($)[1]	—	6.50	2.88	7.13	14.88	12.25	8.75
Stock price – low ($)[1]	—	1.38	1.00	1.75	5.38	6.63	4.13
Stock price – close ($)[1]	20.1%	2.00	2.13	6.38	7.50	8.63	5.00
P/E – high	—	—	—	—	—	—	—
P/E – low	—	—	—	—	—	—	—
Dividends per share ($)	—	0.00	0.00	0.00	0.00	0.00	0.00
Book value per share ($)	—	(0.14)	(0.11)	0.08	0.57	2.31	1.59
Employees	95.2%	84	90	270	290	434	2,380

[1] Stock prices are for the prior calendar year.

1995 Year-end:
Debt ratio: 72.7%
Return on equity: —
Cash (mil.): $17.0
Current ratio: 1.08
Long-term debt (mil.): $84.0
No. of shares (mil.): 17.2
Dividends
 Yield: —
 Payout: —
Market value (mil.): $86.0

AMERIDATA TECHNOLOGIES, INC.

OVERVIEW

AmeriData Technologies offers PC users everything but the kitchen sink. The diversified computer services company (formerly Sage Technologies) provides end-users not only with new computers, but also with a wide range of computer hardware and software, network integration, technological support, and consulting and training services. AmeriData also owns Sage Alerting Systems, Inc. (specialists in emergency response technologies), and radio stations in Vermont and Texas.

Founded as Sage Broadcasting (radio stations) in 1985 by Leonard Fassler and Gerald Poch (now co-chairmen of AmeriData), the company formed Sage Alerting Systems in 1990 and took its stock public in 1991. In 1992 Sage Alerting Systems formed a subsidiary (Sage DataCom, Inc.) to acquire computer firms. Among its acquisitions was AmeriData, which became the company's chief operating unit. Early in 1994 Sage DataCom became AmeriData Technologies. Since 1992, AmeriData has completed at least 25 acquisitions, beefing up its computer systems and services group. In late 1994, AmeriData Consulting and AmeriData Computer Rental were established.

The future looks bright for AmeriData despite increasing industry competition. Acquisition of Bohdan Associates (renamed AmeriData Federal Systems) promises the company a piece of Uncle Sam's information technology market. Recent designation by IBM as one of 5 authorized vendors of EduQuest, a classroom network, assures AmeriData a share of the estimated $2 billion market. And expansion abroad is imminent. In early 1995 AmeriData formed an international subsidiary, InterData Inc., which — pending the $34 million acquisition of selected Control Data Systems businesses — expects to have operations in Canada, Mexico, Europe, and Asia.

WHO

Co-chairman, President, and CEO: Gerald A. Poch, age 48, $770,000 pay
Co-chairman: Leonard J. Fassler, age 63, $770,000 pay
Co-chairman; President and CEO, AmeriData: James K. McCleary, age 53, $770,000 pay
VP Finance, CFO, Treasurer, and Director Human Resources: Richard H. McDevitt, age 57, $190,000 pay
President, Sage Alerting Systems, Inc.: Gerald M. LeBow, age 49, $150,000 pay
General Counsel: Gwen M. Higgins
Director Human Resources: Sharon Berglund
Auditors: Ernst & Young LLP

WHERE

HQ: 700 Canal St., Stamford, CT 06902
Phone: 203-357-1464   **Fax:** 203-357-1531

WHAT

Alerting Business	**Computer Systems Rental Services**
Computer Systems and Service	
Document imaging	**Consulting Services**
Enhancements	Application solutions
Installation of electrical & telecomm. wire	Business performance improvement
Local- and wide-area networking	Business systems consulting
Outsourcing	Education and training solutions
Personal computers, hardware, and software	Information technology architecture solutions
Systems integration	Information technology management
Technical support and maintenance	Strategic research services
Training	**Radio Stations**

KEY COMPETITORS

American Management
Andersen Consulting
Booz, Allen
CompuCom
Computer Data Systems
Computer Sciences
Control Data Systems

Entex
Gemini Consulting
Intelligent Electronics
MicroAge
Technology Solutions
Vanstar

HOW MUCH

NYSE symbol: ADA FY ends: December 31	Annual Growth	1989	1990	1991	1992	1993	1994	1994 Year-end:
Sales ($ mil.)	873.3%	—	—	1.1	6.4	219.7	1,018.5	Debt ratio: 54.6% Return on equity: 14.9%
Net income ($ mil.)	—	—	—	(0.6)	0.0	4.3	13.9	Cash (mil.): $17.9
Income as % of sales	—	—	—	0.6%	1.9%	1.4%		Current ratio: 1.13
Earnings per share ($)	—	—	—	(0.20)	0.01	0.35	0.78	Long-term debt (mil.): $36.2
Stock price – high ($)	—	—	—	2.17	4.67	30.50	23.25	No. of shares (mil.): 19.0
Stock price – low ($)	—	—	—	1.58	2.17	4.31	9.50	Dividends
Stock price – close ($)	71.0%	—	—	2.00	4.58	19.25	10.00	Yield: —
P/E – high	—	—	—	—	—	87	30	Payout: —
P/E – low	—	—	—	—	—	12	12	Market value (mil.): $190.5
Dividends per share ($)	—	—	—	0.00	0.00	0.00	0.00	
Book value per share ($)	79.2%	—	—	1.11	1.02	4.51	6.38	
Employees	309.9%	—	—	—	—	1,600	2,100	

BED BATH & BEYOND INC.

OVERVIEW

A look at Bed Bath & Beyond's expansion history and plans makes it clear that the domestics superstore chain is not napping on the job. Rather, the bed linens, bath accessories, and home furnishings retailer is energetically approaching its next growth surge — 16 new stores planned for 1995 and 22 for 1996. The company expanded its retail space by almost 56% in 1994 and planned to debut in 4 states (Indiana, Kansas, Oklahoma, and Washington) in 1995.

The Springfield, New Jersey, retailer has awakened with a start in the 1990s after its sleepy beginnings in 1971. That was when co-founders Warren Eisenberg and Leonard Feinstein (who each own about 17% of the company) opened 2 small linens stores named bed n bath. Expansion moved at a drowsy pace with just 13 new locations added by 1985. With consumers focusing more on their homes, the partners decided on a superstore retail concept. The company went public as Bed Bath & Beyond Inc. in 1992.

Bed Bath & Beyond stores operate in a warehouse-like setting, offering up to 30,000 department store quality items at discounts of up to 40%. The warehouse concept, which features floor-to-ceiling displays of merchandise, is part of the retailer's cost-cutting strategy. The company foregoes central distribution centers and separate warehouses. Individual stores control stocking by keeping tabs on local sales trends.

The company also saves by locating in strip shopping centers, freestanding buildings, and off-price malls rather than in pricier regional malls. The frugality extends to advertising, with word-of-mouth and inexpensive direct delivery circulars the favored tools. Despite the company's rapid growth, its market share remains at less than 1%, with sales dominated by department stores and chains.

WHO

Chairman and Co-CEO: Warren Eisenberg, age 64, $750,000 pay
President and Co-CEO: Leonard Feinstein, age 58, $750,000 pay
CFO and Treasurer: Ronald Curwin, age 65
Director Real Estate and General Counsel: Steven H. Temares
Director Human Resources: Wayne Sarrow
Auditors: KPMG Peat Marwick LLP

WHERE

HQ: 715 Morris Ave., Springfield, NJ 07081
Phone: 201-379-1520   **Fax:** 201-379-1731

	1995 Stores	
	No.	% of total
California	10	16
New York	7	11
Florida	6	10
New Jersey	6	10
Illinois	5	8
Texas	5	8
Other states	23	37
Total	**62**	**100**

WHAT

	1995 Sales
	% of total
Bed linens	21
Other	79
Total	**100**

KEY COMPETITORS

Dayton Hudson	Kmart	Price/Costco
Dillard	Lands' End	Sears
Euromarket	Lechters	Strouds
Designs	Melville	Tuesday Morning
Federated	Montgomery	Venture Stores
Home Express	Ward	Wal-Mart
HomePlace	Nordstrom	Williams-Sonoma
Ikea	Pacific Linen	
J. C. Penney	Pier 1	

HOW MUCH

Nasdaq symbol: BBBY FY ends: Sun. nearest Feb. 28	Annual Growth	1990	1991	1992	1993	1994	1995	1995 Year-end: Debt ratio: 16.6%
Sales ($ mil.)	33.8%	102.7	134.2	167.6	216.7	305.8	440.3	Return on equity: 32.2%
Net income ($ mil.)	28.6%	8.5	10.4	12.0	16.0	21.9	30.0	Cash (mil.): $6.5
Income as % of sales	—	8.3%	7.7%	7.2%	7.4%	7.2%	6.8%	Current ratio: 2.56
Earnings per share ($)	33.0%	—	—	0.37	0.48	0.64	0.87	Long-term debt (mil.): $21.6
Stock price – high ($)[1]	—	—	—	—	19.00	35.50	34.50	No. of shares (mil.): 33.9
Stock price – low ($)[1]	—	—	—	—	7.00	13.00	22.75	Dividends
Stock price – close ($)[1]	27.3%	—	—	—	18.50	34.50	30.00	Yield: —
P/E – high	—	—	—	—	40	56	40	Payout: —
P/E – low	—	—	—	—	15	20	26	Market value (mil.): $1,016.5
Dividends per share ($)	—	—	—	—	0.00	0.00	0.00	
Book value per share ($)	40.9%	—	—	—	1.62	2.29	3.22	
Employees	36.8%	—	—	1,600	2,400	3,200	4,100	

[1] Stock prices are for the prior calendar year.

BENSON EYECARE CORPORATION

Benson CEO Martin Franklin is a man with vision, and what he sees is a growing market for his company's products. An aging baby boomer population bodes well for Benson, whose Foster Grant Group is the US's largest distributor of ready-to-wear reading glasses. More than 90% of Americans over 45 wear corrective lenses, and that age group is expected to grow by 23% by the year 2000. Foster Grant is also the #1 distributor of value-priced sunglasses. Benson's Omega Group is the largest operator of independent wholesale optical laboratories, providing prescription eyewear, contact lenses, and related products. It sells nonprescription eyewear through leading mass merchandisers (including Wal-Mart, which accounted for 15% of sales in 1994) and drugstores.

The company's namesake, Benson Optical, was a troubled prescription eyewear firm that changed hands a number of times. In 1992 it was bought by Franklin (who learned the investment business from his father, Roland Franklin, partner of European financier Sir James Goldsmith) and Warren Kanders. The young duo (Franklin was 27, Kanders was 34) bought the company through a shell firm with no assets and changed its name to Benson Eyecare Corporation. Between 1992 and 1994 Benson acquired 11 companies specializing in prescription eyewear, ready-to-wear eyewear, and ophthalmic services. Franklin and Kanders own about 23% of Benson's stock.

Benson gained entry to the continental European market in 1994 when Eyecare Products plc (of which Benson owns 26% through another investment) bought L'Amy SA, France's #1 ophthalmic frame maker. Benson and Eyecare Products are cooperating in marketing efforts in the US and Europe. In 1995 Benson announced it would purchase sunglasses maker Bolle America.

WHO

Chairman, President, and CEO: Martin E. Franklin, age 30, $381,610 pay
VC: Warren B. Kanders, age 37
CFO and Director: Ian G. H. Ashken, age 34, $213,120 pay
Chief Operating Officer and Executive VP Operations: William T. Sullivan, age 51
Secretary and General Counsel: Peter H. Trembath
Director Human Resources: Fran Scibora
Auditors: Price Waterhouse LLP

WHERE

HQ: 555 Theodore Fremd Ave., Ste. B302, Rye, NY 10580
Phone: 914-967-9400   **Fax:** 914-967-9405

WHAT

	1994 Sales
	% of total
Nonprescription eyewear	60
Prescription eyewear	17
Other	23
Total	**100**

Nonprescription Reading Glass Brands
FosterGrant   PennOptics

Sunglasses Brands
ABC Sports
Bain de Soleil
Coppertone
FosterGrant
Gitano
International Eyewear
Opti-Ray
Revlon
Spalding

KEY COMPETITORS

Allergan   National Vision
American Greetings   NuVision
Bausch & Lomb   Oakley
BMC Industries   Sears
Corning   STAAR Surgical
Gentex   Sunglass Hut
Grand Metropolitan

HOW MUCH

NYSE symbol: EYE FY ends: December 31	Annual Growth	1989	1990	1991	1992	1993	1994
Sales ($ mil.)	83.2%	8.2	7.4	7.6	16.7	82.1	169.1
Net income ($ mil.)	—	(0.3)	0.5	(0.0)	(1.8)	(2.5)	8.2
Income as % of sales	—	—	6.4%	—	—	—	4.9%
Earnings per share ($)	—	(1.80)	2.55	(0.07)	(0.47)	(0.16)	0.41
Stock price – high ($)	—	—	—	—	6.13	10.38	8.50
Stock price – low ($)	—	—	—	—	0.25	5.38	6.13
Stock price – close ($)	11.8%	—	—	—	6.00	6.88	7.50
P/E – high	—	—	—	—	—	—	21
P/E – low	—	—	—	—	—	—	15
Dividends per share ($)	—	—	—	—	0.00	0.00	0.00
Book value per share ($)	177.2%	—	—	—	0.49	2.16	3.78
Employees	102.1%	—	—	—	563	1,145	2,300

1994 Year-end:
Debt ratio: 53.3%
Return on equity: 12.0%
Cash (mil.): $11.6
Current ratio: 1.05
Long-term debt (mil.): $59.8
No. of shares (mil.): 25.8
Dividends
    Yield: —
    Payout: —
Market value (mil.): $193.5

THE BISYS GROUP, INC.

OVERVIEW

Little Falls, New Jersey–based BISYS Group is one of a growing number of outsourcing companies serving the financial industry. It offers transaction processing, document imaging, and mutual fund and retirement plan administration services to more than 5,000 banks, thrifts, insurance companies, and corporations in all 50 states. The company also provides financial database services for marketers.

The firm was established in 1966 as United Data Processing, the forerunner of the banking and thrift data processing businesses of Automatic Data Processing (ADP). In 1989 a group of investors led by ADP veteran Lynn Mangum formed BISYS and acquired ADP's financial data processing operations in an LBO. Mangum was appointed chairman and CEO. In 1989 BISYS bought Data Systems Corporation, a data processing company in the Southeast. BISYS went public in 1992. The company expanded its range of services with the acquisition of Litton Mortgage Servicing Center (a Texas loan servicing company, 1991) and the Barclay Group (an investment services firm, 1993).

In 1995 the company acquired document processing software maker Document Solutions. It also merged with Concord Holding, a leading administrator of mutual funds, making BISYS the largest bank mutual fund service firm. The company is expanding its management of 401(k) plans, specializing in those sponsored by businesses with fewer than 1,000 employees, the fastest-growing segment of the 401(k) market.

The expenses associated with its mergers and the sale of the company's mortgage servicing operations (which the company concluded were not part of its core business) helped drive BISYS into the red for fiscal 1995 despite increased sales generated by an aggressive marketing campaign.

WHO

Chairman and CEO: Lynn J. Mangum, age 53, $582,557 pay
President and COO: Paul H. Bourke, age 49, $381,731 pay
EVP and CFO: Robert J. McMullan, age 41, $400,385 pay
SVP Human Resources: Mark J. Rybarczyk, age 40, $212,023 pay
VP, General Counsel, and Secretary: Catherine T. Dwyer, age 43, $193,426 pay
Auditors: Coopers & Lybrand L.L.P.

WHERE

HQ: 150 Clove Rd., Little Falls, NJ 07424
Phone: 201-812-8600   **Fax:** 201-812-1217

WHAT

Information Services
Commercial banking services
Credit/loan administration
Document processing
Financial management support
Marketing support

Investment Services
401(k) marketing support and administration
Mutual fund marketing and administration

Major Client Categories
Commercial banks
Corporations
Insurance companies
Mutual savings banks
Thrift institutions

KEY COMPETITORS

Affiliated Computer
ALLTEL
AT&T GIS
EDS
Federated Investors
First Data
Fiserv

Marshall & Ilsley
Newtrend
Perot Systems
SEI
Systems & Computer Technolgy

HOW MUCH

Nasdaq symbol: BSYS FY ends: June 30	Annual Growth	1990	1991	1992	1993	1994	1995
Sales ($ mil.)	29.7%	54.7	62.9	74.5	88.3	136.7	200.5
Net income ($ mil.)	—	(21.3)	(18.8)	(23.7)	3.4	13.8	(6.5)
Income as % of sales	—	—	—	—	3.8%	10.1%	—
Earnings per share ($)	—	(4.32)	(3.01)	(2.71)	0.23	0.86	(0.27)
Stock price – high ($)	—	—	—	20.00	24.50	31.13	
Stock price – low ($)	—	—	—	9.88	16.00	17.00	17.00
Stock price – close ($)	15.9%	—	—	19.75	17.25	22.13	30.75
P/E – high	—	—	—	—	107	26	—
P/E – low	—	—	—	—	70	20	—
Dividends per share ($)	—	—	—	0.00	0.00	0.00	0.00
Book value per share ($)	65.5%	—	—	1.09	4.64	5.56	4.96
Employees	28.1%	—	—	714	1,000	1,250	1,500

1995 Year-end:
Debt ratio: 6.8%
Return on equity: —
Cash (mil.): $13.9
Current ratio: 1.11
Long-term debt (mil.): $0.0
No. of shares (mil.): 23.1
Dividends
  Yield: —
  Payout: —
Market value (mil.): $710.5
R&D as % of sales: 4.7%

BLOOMBERG L.P.

OVERVIEW

Bloomberg is an international, multimedia business news and information service that rivals Reuters and Dow Jones. The New York City–based company began as an online financial data service for investment professionals but has quickly mushroomed to include magazines and national TV, radio, and newspaper wire services. With 350 reporters and more than 600 researchers in 55 bureaus worldwide, Bloomberg has supplanted Dow Jones as the source of business information in such venerable newspapers as the *New York Times*. But at the heart of the operations are the high-tech Bloomberg terminals, easy-to-use computers that transmit up-to-the-minute financial data, analyses, news, sports, and advertising to 42,000 institutional investors who lease them for $1,200 a month. Linked to the company's giant mainframes, the terminals feature conventional text, sound, and pictures as well as Internet access and something close to video-on-demand; they were the first to offer sophisticated analytical software that produced forecasts of prices and values. Founder and CEO Michael Bloomberg owns 70% of the company and Merrill Lynch, 30%.

Educated in engineering as well as business, Bloomberg was a partner at Salomon Brothers, where he was chief of equity trading and sales and later chief of systems. Fired in 1981 for criticizing management, Bloomberg designed the prototype of his computer terminal and pitched it to former colleagues and clients; in exchange for a 30% stake, Merrill Lynch helped bankroll its development and bought the first 20 terminals.

The company built a news operation from scratch, later hiring reporters from the *Wall Street Journal*, *Forbes*, *Business Week*, and the like. In 1992 the company bought a New York radio station and converted it to an all-news format. In 1993 Bloomberg built an in-house TV studio and created a business news show for PBS. In 1994 it debuted a satellite TV station and launched a slick Sunday newspaper supplement that focused on personal finance. In 1995 Bloomberg teamed up with Salomon, its founder's former employer, to launch an online bond trading service in Europe.

WHO

President and CEO: Michael R. Bloomberg, age 53
COO: Susan Friedlaender
CFO: Wolf Boehm
Editor-in-Chief, Bloomberg Business News: Matthew Winkler
VP Marketing: Elisabeth DeMarse
VP Development: Tom Secunda
Bloomberg Information Radio: Bob Leverone
New York Sales: Lou Eccleston
London Sales: Stuart Bell
Tokyo Sales: Ian Fallman
Hong Kong Sales: Mark Daly
Sydney Sales: Trevor Jarrett
Auditors: Grant Thornton LLP

WHERE

HQ: 499 Park Ave., New York, NY 10022
Phone: 212-318-2000   **Fax:** 212-980-2480

WHAT

Bloomberg Media

Bloomberg (monthly business magazine, also published in Japanese; 100,000 circulation)

Bloomberg Business News (radio and TV program broadcast to 35 radio and 188 TV stations)

Bloomberg Business News Service (news service featuring financial and market information and analysis, general news, sports, and advertising; carried on Bloomberg Financial Markets terminals and in major newspapers)

Bloomberg Financial Markets (financial information and analysis relayed to 42,000 dedicated terminals)

Bloomberg Forum (interviews with leading business executives; on USA Network and Bloomberg terminals)

Bloomberg Information Radio (WBBR-AM, New York City, also syndicated and carried by satellite to Bloomberg Information Television subscribers)

Bloomberg Information Television (24-hour video cable channel)

Bloomberg Personal (monthly magazine on personal finance, carried as a Sunday supplement in regional newspapers; 5.5 million circulation)

KEY COMPETITORS

ADP	Knight-Ridder
Associated Press	News Corp.
Baseline	Reuters
Bridge Information	Times Mirror
CBS	Tribune
Dow Jones	Turner Broadcasting
General Electric	UPI

HOW MUCH

Private company FY ends: December 31	Annual Growth	1989	1990	1991	1992	1993	1994
Estimated sales ($ mil.)	42.4%	94.0	140.0	192.0	290.0	370.0	550.0
Terminals	41.1%	7,500	10,500	13,500	21,000	34,000	42,000
Sales per terminal ($)	0.9%	12,533	13,333	16,000	13,810	10,882	13,095
Employees	33.0%	—	—	850	1,100	1,800	2,000

Bloomberg
FINANCIAL MARKETS
COMMODITIES
NEWS

THE BROOKLYN UNION GAS COMPANY

OVERVIEW

Brooklyn Union is looking to heat up its profits by forming a new holding company to manage its diverse businesses. The utility distributes natural gas to about 1.1 million customers in Brooklyn, Queens, and Staten Island, New York. The firm also explores for and markets natural gas, and it develops cogeneration projects through its subsidiaries. CEO Robert Catell wants to pursue nonutility businesses (which offer greater profitability), so he is trying to warm up state regulators to the idea of allowing Brooklyn Union to reorganize. He also wants to restructure its gas rates.

Brooklyn Union's roots extend to a charter first granted in 1825 to the Brooklyn Gas Light Co. However, the borough refused to sign a streetlight contract, and the "company" was defunct until 1847. Two years later it began supplying manufactured gas. For half a century it fought a running battle with as many as 15 rivals. In 1895 Brooklyn Gas Light, Fulton Municipal Gas Co., and 5 other gas utilities formed Brooklyn Union Gas. The firm conceded lighting to electricity providers and focused on heating new buildings.

An emphasis on home heating and cooking helped the company survive the Great Depression. By 1952 cheap natural gas had arrived, allowing Brooklyn Union's aggressive conversion of residential heating systems from oil to gas, which became its main sales catalyst. The firm diversified in the late 1970s and 1980s, forming several nonutility businesses.

In 1992 federal regulators fundamentally changed the gas industry by allowing retail competition. The company responded in 1994 by opening the New York Market Hub, a gas market for large-volume customers.

In 1995 Brooklyn Union filed a reorganization plan with state regulators and examined its options for enhancing or selling off its cogeneration interests.

WHO

President and CEO: Robert B. Catell, age 58, $586,999 pay
EVP: Helmut W. Peter, age 63, $374,798 pay
EVP: Craig G. Matthews, age 52, $370,608 pay
SVP: Anthony J. DiBrita, age 54, $234,335 pay
SVP and CFO: Vincent D. Enright, age 51, $230,010 pay
SVP Human Resources: Wallace P. Parker Jr.
Auditors: Arthur Andersen & Co, SC

WHERE

HQ: One MetroTech Center, New York, NY 11201-3850
Phone: 718-403-2000   **Fax:** 718-852-4643

WHAT

	1995 Sales	
	$ mil.	% of total
Utility	1,152.3	95
Gas production & other	64.0	5
Total	1,216.3	100

Selected Subsidiaries
BRING Gas Services Corp. (gas marketing and transportation services)
Fuel Resources, Inc. (gas exploration and production subsidiaries)
Fuel Resources Production and Development Co., Inc. (interests in Texas and West Virginia gas wells)
Gas Energy, Inc., and Gas Energy Cogeneration, Inc. (designing, building, owning, and operation of gas-fired cogeneration facilities)
Houston Exploration Co. (gas exploration in the Gulf of Mexico)
North East Transmission Co. (owns 11.4% interest in Iroquois Gas Transmission System, a 375-mile gas pipeline supplying the Northeast)

KEY COMPETITORS

Burnside Coal and Oil	Gassmon Coal and Oil
Consolidated Edison	Long Island Lighting
Destec Energy	National Fuel Gas
Enron	Sithe Energies

HOW MUCH

NYSE symbol: BU FY ends: September 30	Annual Growth	1990	1991	1992	1993	1994	1995
Sales ($ mil.)	4.1%	993.9	990.5	1,074.9	1,205.5	1,338.6	1,216.3
Net income ($ mil.)	10.2%	56.4	61.8	59.9	76.6	87.4	91.5
Income as % of sales	—	5.7%	6.2%	5.6%	6.4%	6.5%	7.5%
Earnings per share ($)	5.8%	1.43	1.45	1.35	1.73	1.85	1.90
Stock price – high ($)	—	21.51	20.84	23.51	27.93	28.63	29.63
Stock price – low ($)	—	16.68	18.01	18.68	21.59	21.50	22.00
Stock price – close ($)	8.2%	19.68	20.26	22.34	27.38	22.25	29.25
P/E – high	—	15	14	17	16	16	16
P/E – low	—	12	12	14	13	12	12
Dividends per share ($)	2.6%	1.22	1.26	1.29	1.31	1.34	1.39
Book value per share ($)	4.4%	13.69	14.38	14.56	15.55	16.27	16.94
Employees	(1.5%)	3,651	3,651	3,626	3,711	3,506	3,378

1995 Year-end:
Debt ratio: 47.9%
Return on equity: 11.4%
Cash (mil.): $40.5
Current ratio: —
Long-term debt (mil.): $720.6
No. of shares (mil.): 48.8
Dividends
  Yield: 4.8%
  Payout: 73.2%
Market value (mil.): $1,427.1

CANNONDALE CORPORATION

OVERVIEW

For Cannondale, aluminum is gold. The Georgetown, Connecticut–based company makes high-performance, aluminum-frame bicycles as well as bicycling accessories. Recent national and global racing titles have earned Cannondale a presence at the 1996 Olympics.

Joe Montgomery, who grew up on a farm and dropped out of college 3 times, had been sailing charter boats for a living when he sank one night in shark-infested waters. This sobering experience prompted Montgomery's 1964 decision to become a Wall Street analyst. In 1970 he left high finance and, with funding from his partnership in a trendy New York bar, started the company that in 1977 became Cannondale. His first office was in an old pickle factory near the Cannondale, Connecticut, train stop.

Cannondale started out making bike trailers, but sales were modest. When the company added bike clothing and bags, the products were picked up by the L.L. Bean catalog, providing Montgomery with enough capital to begin making aluminum-frame bikes. The company introduced one of the first affordable aluminum-frame bicycles in 1983 and added mountain bikes to its line in 1984. In 1991 Scott Montgomery, Joe's son, established a sales division in Tokyo. The company is now the largest US supplier of bikes to Japan and also has a branch in Europe.

Cannondale went public in late 1994. Joe Montgomery owns 23.4% of the company's stock. Scott, who is VP of marketing (his business cards say "Vice President of Listening"), owns 6.5%.

To pump up its bikes' high-performance image, Cannondale cosponsors teams with Volvo, New Balance, and Timex. In 1995 teams cosponsored by Cannondale won US National Championship and World Championship titles.

WHO

Chairman, President, and CEO: Joseph S. Montgomery, age 55, $267,688 pay
VP Finance, Treasurer, and CFO: William A. Luca, age 51, $178,808 pay
VP Technology Development: Richard J. Resch, age 52, $144,000 pay
VP Marketing and VP Japanese Operations: James Scott Montgomery, age 34, $135,000 pay
VP Sales US and VP European Operations: Daniel C. Alloway, age 36, $127,231 pay
Director Human Resources: Jean Benson
Auditors: Ernst & Young LLP

WHERE

HQ: 9 Brookside Place, Georgetown, CT 06829
Phone: 203-544-9800   **Fax:** 203-852-9081

Cannondale sells its products in more than 60 countries.

WHAT

	1996 Bicycle Models
	No.
Mountain bikes	23
Road bikes	11
Specialty	9
Hybrid	7
Touring	3
Total	**53**

Selected Bicycling Accessories

Apparel	Pumps
Bicycle bags	Racks
Gloves	Tools
Helmets	Trailers

KEY COMPETITORS

Anthony Industries	Giro	Schwinn
Bell Sports	GT Bicycles	Shimano
Bridgestone	Huffy	Softride
Easton	Litespeed	Specialized
First Team Sports	Titanium	Tompkins
	Manitou	Trek
	Roadmaster	Yakima

HOW MUCH

Nasdaq symbol: BIKE FY ends: Sat. nearest June 30	Annual Growth	1990[1]	1991	1992	1993[2]	1994	1995
Sales ($ mil.)	33.4%	28.9	54.5	76.9	80.8	102.1	122.1
Net income ($ mil.)	58.2%	0.8	1.2	(4.6)	(3.6)	(1.6)	7.5
Income as % of sales	—	2.6%	2.1%	—	—	—	6.2%
Earnings per share ($)	38.8%	0.21	0.28	(1.08)	(0.83)	(0.37)	1.08
Stock price – high ($)	—	—	—	—	—	14.50	19.50
Stock price – low ($)	—	—	—	—	—	9.75	10.25
Stock price – close ($)	54.9%	—	—	—	—	10.25	15.88
P/E – high	—	—	—	—	—	—	18
P/E – low	—	—	—	—	—	—	9
Dividends per share ($)	—	—	—	—	—	0.00	0.00
Book value per share ($)	—	—	—	—	—	0.76	5.08
Employees	11.0%	—	—	—	—	746	828

[1] 8-month fiscal year   [2] 10-month fiscal year

1995 Year-end:
Debt ratio: 45.6%
Return on equity: 22.9%
Cash (mil.) $2.3
Current ratio: 1.53
Long-term debt (mil.): $5.6
No. of shares (mil.): 3.8
Dividends
  Yield: —
  Payout: —
Market value (mil.): $61.0
R&D as % of sales: 1.4%

CENTENNIAL CELLULAR CORP.

OVERVIEW

Centennial Cellular, based in New Canaan, Connecticut, serves more than 170,000 cellular subscribers in 11 states and Puerto Rico under the Cellular One service mark. The company also offers a variety of alternative communications services, including paging, specialized mobile radio, and conventional mobile telephone.

Originally called Century Cellular, Centennial got its start in 1988 as a subsidiary of Century Communications, the cable television operator founded by Leonard Tow in 1973. In 1989 Century Communications purchased Citizens Cellular, a subsidiary of Citizens Utilities, a diversified utilities provider. (At the same time, Tow acquired a large stake in Citizens Utilities, and in 1990 he became its chairman and CEO.) Citizens Cellular and Century Cellular were merged in 1991. When the company went public late that year, it operated 13 cellular franchises. The company changed its name to Centennial Cellular in 1992. Through their holdings in Century Communications and Citizens Utilities, Tow and his wife, Claire, own 90.9% of Centennial Cellular voting stock.

Since its founding, Centennial has added markets through franchises and acquisitions; in recent years it has begun consolidating its holdings into market clusters. Losses are the result of continuing costs associated with the construction and development of the company's cellular system.

Centennial added nearly 48,000 subscribers in fiscal 1995. That year the company added markets in Indiana, Iowa, Louisiana, Michigan, and Mississippi. It also paid $54.5 million for the license to build a personal communications services (PCS) system in Puerto Rico and the US Virgin Islands. PCS systems combine a variety of digital, wireless telecommunications technologies.

WHO

Chairman and CEO: Bernard P. Gallagher, age 48
President and COO: Rudy J. Graf, age 46, $250,000 pay
SVP Operations: Phillip Mayberry, age 42, $190,000 pay
SVP, CFO, and Treasurer: Scott N. Schneider, age 37
SVP Engineering: Michael G. Harris, age 49
VP Engineering: Thomas Cogar, age 38, $170,000 pay
VP Human Resources: Geoff Broom
Auditors: Deloitte & Touche LLP

WHERE

HQ: 50 Locust Ave., New Canaan, CT 06840
Phone: 203-972-2000   **Fax:** 203-966-9228

Centennial Cellular operates in 11 states, Puerto Rico, and the US Virgin Islands.

Largest Majority-owned Markets (% ownership)

Beaumont/Port Arthur, TX (100%)	Fort Wayne, IN (100%)
Beauregard, LA (100%)	Kalamazoo, MI (100%)
Cass, MI (85.74%)	Newaygo, MI (100%)
	South Bend, IN (100%)

Selected Minority-owned Markets

Lake Charles, LA	San Francisco, CA
Lawrence, PA	San Jose, CA
Reno, NV	Santa Cruz, CA
Sacramento, CA	Stockton, CA

WHAT

	1995 Sales	
	$ mil.	% of total
Service	78.5	92
Equipment	4.1	5
Other	2.8	3
Total	**85.4**	**100**

KEY COMPETITORS

AirTouch	GTE
ALLTEL	Palmer Wireless
AT&T Corp.	SBC
Bay Area Cellular	Sprint
Cellular Communications	U.S. Cellular
of Puerto Rico	U S WEST

HOW MUCH

Nasdaq symbol: CYCL FY ends: May 31	Annual Growth	1990	1991	1992	1993	1994	1995
Sales ($ mil.)	48.3%	11.9	19.8	31.3	43.2	56.4	85.4
Net income ($ mil.)	—	(35.6)	(36.6)	(37.2)	(36.8)	(39.5)	(45.4)
Income as % of sales	—	—	—	—	—	—	—
Earnings per share ($)	—	(5.42)	(5.57)	(4.10)	(3.28)	(3.28)	(1.93)
Stock price – high ($)	—	—	17.75	22.00	24.25	24.00	20.13
Stock price – low ($)	—	—	15.75	9.25	11.50	14.00	13.00
Stock price – close ($)	1.3%	—	16.25	13.50	24.25	17.00	17.13
P/E – high	—	—	—	—	—	—	—
P/E – low	—	—	—	—	—	—	—
Dividends per share ($)	—	—	0.00	0.00	0.00	0.00	0.00
Book value per share ($)	—	—	(14.62)	(8.05)	(10.63)	(10.96)	0.48
Employees	25.2%	—	—	275	255	338	540

1995 Year-end:
Debt ratio: 65.0%
Return on equity: —
Cash (mil.): $121.6
Current ratio: 2.13
Long-term debt (mil.): $350.0
No. of shares (mil.): 26.2
Dividends
  Yield: —
  Payout: —
Market value (mil.): $448.7

CHEYENNE SOFTWARE, INC.

OVERVIEW

Cheyenne Software's sales are anything but soft. The company is the #1 producer of data storage management solutions for LAN-based systems. Cheyenne also makes software for network imaging, communications, management, and security. OEMs that pre-install Cheyenne software include Hewlett-Packard, IBM, and Intel.

The company's founders were still looking for a name as they flew to Delaware to file for incorporation in 1983. Overhearing their conversation, the flight attendant suggested Cheyenne, from the model of airplane on which they were flying. The company went public in 1985. It acquired Freeman-Owings and FA Components, both computer distributors, in 1987. Cheyenne introduced its flagship product, ARCserve, a data storage manager for Novell networks, in 1989; it entered into an OEM agreement with Hewlett-Packard and into a partnership with Novell in 1990. These moves and the burgeoning use of networks have been key factors in the firm's growth.

In 1992 Cheyenne introduced 2 new products, InocuLAN and FAXserve, and purchased 5% of CompuLink, a communications software developer. The next year it formed a subsidiary, Cheyenne Communications, to focus on network communications.

In 1994 Cheyenne introduced ARCserve for Mac and acquired NETstor, an HSM (hierarchical storage management) software developer. The company also announced OEM agreements with Fujitsu and Mitsubishi. NEC said it would bundle Cheyenne software with its Express products distributed in Japan.

In 1995 Cheyenne introduced BitWare for Windows, a fax, voice mail, and data communications software package. That same year the company formed a technology and marketing alliance with Computer Associates and acquired 2 small storage management software developers, Chile Pepper and Media Blitz.

WHO

Chairman, President, and CEO: ReiJane Huai, age 36, $205,000 pay
EVP, Senior Financial Officer, and Treasurer: Elliot Levine, age 59, $180,000 pay
EVP Sales and Secretary: Alan W. Kaufman, age 57, $180,000 pay
EVP Business Development: James P. McNiel, age 32, $180,000 pay
EVP: Yuda Doron, $159,653 pay
VP Engineering: Robert Daly
Director Human Resources: Andy Boyland
Auditors: KPMG Peat Marwick LLP

WHERE

HQ: 3 Expressway Plaza, Roslyn Heights, NY 11577
Phone: 516-484-5110   **Fax:** 516-484-7106

	1995 Sales	
	$ mil.	% of total
US	68.3	53
Europe	48.8	38
Canada	2.2	2
Other regions	8.6	7
Total	**127.9**	**100**

WHAT

	1995 Sales	
	$ mil.	% of total
Distribution	94.1	74
OEM	15.3	12
Other	18.5	14
Total	**127.9**	**100**

Selected Products
ARCserve (network data storage management)
Bit Software (network communications)
FAXserve (network communications)
InocuLAN (network security)
Monitrix (network management)

KEY COMPETITORS

Brooktrout Technology	Intel	Novell
Conner	Legato	Seagate
Peripherals	Systems	Symantec
EMC Corp.	Microsoft	Tecmar

HOW MUCH

AMEX symbol: CYE FY ends: June 30	Annual Growth	1990	1991	1992	1993	1994	1995
Sales ($ mil.)	137.3%	1.7	7.2	17.9	56.7	97.7	127.9
Net income ($ mil.)	—	(2.1)	2.1	9.1	20.6	32.5	38.5
Income as % of sales	—	—	29.1%	50.8%	40.7%	33.3%	30.1%
Earnings per share ($)	—	(0.06)	0.06	0.24	0.53	0.82	0.97
Stock price – high ($)	—	2.44	5.30	15.89	26.83	30.25	27.88
Stock price – low ($)	—	0.96	2.19	4.17	10.90	6.00	12.38
Stock price – close ($)	60.7%	2.44	5.15	13.39	18.50	13.75	26.13
P/E – high	—	—	88	66	51	37	29
P/E – low	—	—	36	17	21	7	13
Dividends per share ($)	—	0.00	0.00	0.00	0.00	0.00	0.00
Book value per share ($)	55.1%	0.33	0.37	0.75	1.62	2.71	2.96
Employees	60.1%	59	170	107	229	430	621

1995 Year-end:
Debt ratio: 0.0%
Return on equity: 34.8%
Cash (mil.): $30.7
Current ratio: 5.93
Long-term debt (mil.): $0.0
No. of shares (mil.): 39.3
Dividends
  Yield: —
  Payout: —
Market value (mil.): $1,027.1
R&D as % of sales: 12.8%

CHOCK FULL O'NUTS CORPORATION

OVERVIEW

Chock full o'Nuts is chock full o'beans — coffee beans, that is — and ready to challenge the leaders of the coffee bar business. Although it had previously run coffee shops, the company shifted in the 1980s to processing and selling coffees and teas to restaurants and groceries under the Chock full o'Nuts, LaTouraine, and Cain's labels. CEO Marvin Haas owns 4.5% of the company.

In the roaring '20s William Black began selling shelled nuts from a pushcart and then from a basement in New York's theater district; his nutty empire grew to 18 stores. Chock full o'Nuts was incorporated in 1932. During the Depression he added coffee and date-nut breads. Black was a pioneer in franchising, and by the 1940s there were full-service Chock full o'Nuts restaurants in New York, New Jersey, and Pennsylvania. In 1953 the company began selling coffee in supermarkets. It went public in 1958.

By the late 1960s there were 115 restaurants, but growing competition from fast-food chains devastated the restaurants and the last company-owned store closed in 1983, the year after Black died.

Black's successor (and personal physician), Leon Pordy, expanded into gourmet coffees, teas, and cocoas and promoted the company's nonchemical decaffeination process. He also emphasized the wholesale side of the business, selling to institutions and restaurants and buying private-label coffee companies. Pordy stepped down as chairman in 1992.

In 1994 Chock full o'Nuts took advantage of a renewed interest in coffee shops to acquire Quikava, a Boston-based drive-through company that specializes in coffee and bakery goods that it has begun to franchise. Later that year Chock full o'Nuts opened an upscale specialty coffeehouse, its first quick-service cafe in 12 years; 4 others followed in 1995.

WHO

Chairman: Norman E. Alexander, age 81
President and CEO: Marvin I. Haas, age 53, $388,000 pay
SVP and CFO: Howard M. Leitner, age 54, $327,000 pay
SVP Retail Sales and Marketing: Anthony Fazzari, $267,000 pay
VP, Secretary, and Treasurer: Martin J. Cullen, age 61, $276,000 pay
VP; President and CEO, Cain's Coffee Company: Thomas Donnell, $247,000 pay
VP Labor Relations: Peter Baer
Auditors: Ernst & Young LLP

WHERE

HQ: 370 Lexington Ave., New York, NY 10017
Phone: 212-532-0300   **Fax:** 212-532-0864

WHAT

	1995 Sales		1995 Operating income	
	$ mil.	% of total	$ mil.	% of total
Food products	328.4	99	15.5	97
Real estate rentals	2.0	1	0.5	3
Adjustments	—	—	(0.4)	—
Total	**330.4**	**100**	**15.6**	**100**

Selected Brands	Restaurants
Cain's	Chock full o'Nuts
Chock full o'Nuts	Quikava
LaTouraine	
Safari	

KEY COMPETITORS

Au Bon Pain	Philip Morris
Barnes & Noble	Procter & Gamble
Brothers Gourmet Coffees	Quaker Oats
Circle K	Regency Coffee
Coca-Cola	Sara Lee
Farmers Bros.	Southland
Green Mountain Coffee	Starbucks
McDonald's	Stop & Shop
Nestlé	Whole Foods Market

HOW MUCH

NYSE symbol: CHF FY ends: Fri. nearest July 31	Annual Growth	1990	1991	1992	1993	1994	1995
Sales ($ mil.)	6.1%	245.7	270.2	259.9	253.5	265.7	330.4
Net income ($ mil.)	2.0%	4.4	8.8	(4.1)	(1.0)	7.9	4.9
Income as % of sales	—	1.8%	3.3%	—	—	3.0%	1.5%
Earnings per share ($)	(0.5%)	0.44	0.62	(0.41)	(0.10)	0.56	0.42
Stock price – high ($)	—	7.66	8.23	8.48	9.95	8.61	7.25
Stock price – low ($)	—	3.33	4.33	5.27	6.80	5.00	4.97
Stock price – close ($)	0.7%	5.22	7.67	8.13	7.77	5.75	5.25
P/E – high	—	17	13	—	—	15	17
P/E – low	—	8	7	—	—	9	12
Dividends per share ($)	—	0.00	0.00	0.00	0.00	0.00	0.00
Book value per share ($)	5.5%	5.69	6.67	5.77	5.14	5.59	6.05
Employees	0.0%	1,150	1,100	1,035	1,400	1,150	1,150

1995 Year-end:
Debt ratio: 62.1%
Return on equity: 7.9%
Cash (mil.): $15.4
Current ratio: 4.33
Long-term debt (mil.): $106.6
No. of shares (mil.): 10.7
Dividends
  Yield: —
  Payout: —
Market value (mil.): $56.4
Advertising as % of sales: 1.2%

CYGNE DESIGNS, INC.

OVERVIEW

Cygne Designs, a leading designer and maker of private-label clothing, has matured from an ugly duckling to a swan. Despite a weak retail market for women's apparel, the company's sales continue to soar as it broadens its product line, adds new customers, and acquires new companies.

Cygne (French for "swan" and pronounced "see-nya") basically serves as a middleman by designing and manufacturing private-label clothing for such leading retailers as Ann Taylor, Intimate Brands (including Victoria's Secret), the Limited (including Lane Bryant, Lerner, and Express), and U.S. Shoe (including Casual Corner). While Cygne specializes in making women's career sportswear, casual sportswear, intimate apparel, and shoes, it also manufactures men's casual sportswear. In 1995 Ann Taylor and the Limited together accounted for 75% of sales.

Irving Benson founded Cygne in 1975 and then sold it to a subsidiary of the Limited in 1984. In 1988 he teamed up with Amvent, a European investment group led by Bernard Manuel, to spin off Cygne as a private company.

Cygne suffered major cash flow problems in 1988 and 1989, primarily because of its inability to meet deadlines for the delivery of quality products, which resulted in charge-backs and rejections of shipments. The company steadily reorganized its production operations, bringing on board more reliable, cost-efficient suppliers and extending its product line. The company went public in 1993. Manuel and his wife own 14.4% of the stock and Benson and his wife own 11.46%.

In 1994 Cygne acquired GJM International Limited, a Hong Kong–based manufacturer of intimate apparel, and Fenn, Wright & Manson (FW&M), a British designer. In 1995 Cygne sold FW&M to a group led by Colin Fenn, who had been VC of Cygne and president of FW&M.

WHO

Chairman and CEO: Bernard M. Manuel, age 47, $452,115 pay
VC and President: Irving Benson, age 56, $452,115 pay
VC and CEO, GJM International Ltd.: W. Glynn Manson, age 50
SVP Manufacturing: Gary C. Smith, age 44, $253,846 pay
SVP, CFO, and Treasurer: Roy E. Green, age 62, $220,000 pay
VP, General Counsel, and Secretary: Paul Baiocchi, age 47
Director Human Resources: Remy Nicholas
Auditors: Ernst & Young LLP

WHERE

HQ: 1372 Broadway, New York, NY 10018
Phone: 212-354-6474   **Fax:** 212-921-8318

WHAT

	1995 Sales % of total
Ann Taylor	38
The Limited	37
Other	25
Total	**100**

Women's Apparel	Men's Apparel
Career sportswear	Casual sportswear
Casual sportswear	
Dresses	
Intimate apparel	
Shoes	

KEY COMPETITORS

Benetton	Hartmarx Corp.	NIKE
Bernard Chaus	Jones Apparel	Oxford Industries
Calvin Klein	Kellwood	Phillips-Van
Carole Little	Koret	Heusen
Donna Karan	L.A. Gear	Polo/Ralph Lauren
Ellen Tracy	Lands' End	Reebok
Esprit de Corp.	Leslie Fay	Salant
Fruit of the Loom	Levi Strauss	VF Corp.
Haggar Corp.	Liz Claiborne	Warnaco Group

HOW MUCH

Nasdaq symbol: CYDS FY ends: Sat. nearest Jan. 31	Annual Growth	1990	1991	1992	1993	1994	1995	1995 Year-end:
Sales ($ mil.)	76.4%	30.2	41.9	70.4	124.7	220.2	516.1	Debt ratio: 22.9%
Net income ($ mil.)	—	(5.6)	0.4	0.1	3.1	6.1	10.8	Return on equity: 12.3%
Income as % of sales	—	—	0.9%	0.1%	2.5%	2.8%	2.1%	Cash (mil.): $14.2
Earnings per share ($)	—	(1.06)	0.07	0.02	0.59	0.92	0.93	Current ratio: 1.45
Stock price – high ($)[1]	—	—	—	—	—	20.75	27.00	Long-term debt (mil.): $1.5
Stock price – low ($)[1]	—	—	—	—	—	10.00	10.00	No. of shares (mil.): 13.0
Stock price – close ($)[1]	(27.6%)	—	—	—	—	19.00	13.75	Dividends
P/E – high	—	—	—	—	—	23	29	Yield: —
P/E – low	—	—	—	—	—	11	11	Payout: —
Dividends per share ($)	—	—	—	—	—	0.00	0.00	Market value (mil.): $178.5
Book value per share ($)	153.5%	—	—	—	—	4.31	10.92	
Employees	203.0%	—	—	—	—	1,650	5,000	

[1] Stock prices are for the prior calendar year.

DIAL-A-MATTRESS

This company's CEO did time for tax fraud in 1995, and radio bad boy Howard Stern is the leading pitchman for its products. A recipe for disaster? Not in New York, and not for Dial-A-Mattress. Unlike store-based competitors in the traditional retail mattress business (such as Sears and Montgomery Ward), Dial sells over the telephone and via the online services of Bloomberg and CompuServe. Urban customers can order brand-name beds at low prices, sight unseen, 24 hours a day, by dialing 1-800-MATTRES or by accessing online sites. Insomniacs are good buyers too: the New York office receives 80 calls daily in the postmidnight hours. The New York area accounts for 80% of sales. All phone orders are processed by telemarketers at Dial's headquarters. Dial sells in other cities such as Boston, Chicago, and Los Angeles, where orders are fulfilled by local franchise owners and distributors who pay Dial royalties for sales generated by Dial.

Furniture salesman Napoleon Barragan, an Ecuadorean immigrant, came up with the idea for Dial-A-Mattress in 1976. While traveling on a New York train he noticed an ad for home-delivered steaks purchased by phone and realized the same approach could be used to sell mattresses. Dial was founded in 1977, when Barragan began running classified ads offering customers home delivery of mattresses for $29.99. Orders began to flood in. In 1991 Dial went nationwide.

Dial was a pioneer of phone shopping, offering harried consumers the option of buying through toll-free calls from their homes. Key to this strategy has been direct response advertising; 75% of Dial's advertising budget is spent on TV ads. Dial's strategy also eliminates store display costs, allowing it to undercut competitors' prices.

In 1994 Dial launched 1-800-FURNITURE, a national shopping network for furniture, and created the first home furnishing sites on the Internet. Also that year Barragan ran afoul of the law and was sentenced to a year in jail and fined $1 million for sales tax fraud.

In 1995, in an attempt to increase its number of laid-back customers, Dial pushed an advertising campaign aimed at ethnic and niche markets, such as gays, Koreans, Japanese, Hispanics, Jews, brides, and new movers.

CEO: Napoleon Barragan
CFO: Manny Martinez
EVP and General Manager: Joseph Vicens
Director Data Processing: John Leon
Director Human Resources: Zorida Cook

HQ: Dial-A-Mattress Operating Corporation, 31-10 48th Ave., Long Island City, NY 11101
Phone: 718-472-1200   **Fax:** 718-472-1310

Selected Cities Served
Boston
Chicago
Los Angeles
Miami
New York

Major Services
1-800-4-FURNITURE (a national shopping network for furniture purchase and delivery service)
1-800-MATTRES (national shopping telephone network for mattress purchase and delivery service)
beds.com (Internet site for bed purchase and delivery service)
mattress.com (Internet site for mattress purchase and delivery service)

Major Mattress Brands
Sealy
Serta
Simmons

Subsidiary
Factory Network Direct

Art Van
Federated
Haverty Furniture
Heilig-Meyers
J. C. Penney
Levitz
Mattress Discounters
Montgomery Ward
Nationwide Discount Sleep Centers
Rhodes
Rockaway
Sears
Sleepy's
Slumberland
Smith's Home Furnishings
West Co.

Private company FY ends: December 31	Annual Growth	1989	1990	1991	1992	1993	1994
Sales ($ mil.)	61.0%	6.0	7.5	14.0	27.5	40.6	64.9
Employees	24.0%	—	—	—	195	267	300

DIALOGIC CORPORATION

Dialogic is the world's leading manufacturer of PC-based telephony products — components that let computers speak or recognize speech. The company's products are key components in voice mail and voice response telephone systems and will become part of personal computers in the near future. Dialogic has more than 2,500 customers in 43 countries.

Nicholas Zwick, James Shinn, and Kenneth Burkhardt founded Dialogic in 1983. Zwick had been a technical manager and applications engineer with Advanced Micro Devices, Shinn a general manager of AMD's Japanese subsidiary, and Burkhardt a systems architect for Unisys. Within 10 years of start-up, Dialogic had shipped over a million signal processing ports to customers worldwide. In 1993 Dialogic began promoting a software standard known as Signal Computing System Architecture (SCSA) to encourage compatibility among components of information processing systems; more than 260 manufacturers now support SCSA. The company went public in April 1994. Chairman Zwick owns 23.9%, EVP Burkhardt owns 14.3%, and Shinn, a company director, owns 12.9%.

Strategic alliances have fueled Dialogic's success. The company has worked with AT&T, Swedish telecommunications equipment manufacturer Ericsson, and IBM, among others, and with call processing leaders such as Active Voice and Brite Voice. In 1994 Dialogic and Radish Communication Systems agreed to codevelop a visual interface for call processing systems that guides PC users with voice and on-screen prompts. Microsoft's Windows 95 incorporates the visual interface.

In 1994 Dialogic acquired GammaLink, a provider of facsimile boards and software products. The following year Dialogic purchased Digital Equipment Corp.'s telephony technology and said it would create a new division based on the acquisition.

WHO

Chairman: Nicholas Zwick, age 42
President and CEO: Howard G. Bubb, age 40, $202,670 pay
EVP New Business Development: Kenneth J. Burkhardt Jr., age 49
VP Sales and Service, the Americas: John G. Alfieri, age 35, $154,037 pay
VP, CFO, Treasurer, and Secretary: Edward B. Jordan, age 34, $145,357 pay
VP Marketing: John Landau, age 41, $143,790 pay
VP Product Development: Robert N. Heymann, age 33, $123,193 pay
VP Human Resources: Steven P. Wentzell
Auditors: Deloitte & Touche LLP

WHERE

HQ: 1515 Rt. 10, Parsippany, NJ 07054
Phone: 201-993-3000   **Fax:** 201-993-3093

	1994 Sales	
	$ mil.	% of sales
North America	103.3	81
Europe	16.3	13
Asia/Pacific	7.6	6
Total	**127.2**	**100**

WHAT

Selected Products
Facsimile and data products
Network interfaces
Open buses
Open signal processing platform (Antares)
Speech recognition and speech synthesis products
System software
Voice processing products

KEY COMPETITORS

Active Voice	Microlog
Brooktrout Technology	Motorola
Communications Systems	Natural MicroSystems
DEC	Octel
EXECUTONE	Sierra Semiconductor
Inter-Tel	Symantec

HOW MUCH

Nasdaq symbol: DLGC FY ends: December 31	Annual Growth	1989	1990	1991	1992	1993	1994	1994 Year-end: Debt ratio: 4.1%
Sales ($ mil.)	37.2%	26.2	46.6	50.1	65.4	95.6	127.2	Return on equity: 23.4%
Net income ($ mil.)	34.8%	3.1	4.7	4.2	4.5	8.5	13.6	Cash (mil.): $30.0
Income as % of sales	—	11.7%	10.1%	8.3%	6.8%	8.8%	10.7%	Current ratio: 5.45
Earnings per share ($)	36.2%	—	—	—	—	0.69	0.94	Long-term debt (mil.): $2.5
Stock price – high ($)	—	—	—	—	—	—	23.50	No. of shares (mil.): 14.7
Stock price – low ($)	—	—	—	—	—	—	10.75	Dividends
Stock price – close ($)	—	—	—	—	—	—	23.50	Yield: —
P/E – high	—	—	—	—	—	—	25	Payout: —
P/E – low	—	—	—	—	—	—	11	Market value (mil.): $345.7
Dividends per share ($)	—	—	—	—	—	—	0.00	R&D as % of sales: 10.3%
Book value per share ($)	—	—	—	—	—	—	4.54	
Employees	42.7%	—	—	—	—	370	528	

EIS INTERNATIONAL, INC.

OVERVIEW

EIS enables salespeople to get their foot in the door, electronically speaking. The next time you find a stranger on the telephone pitching you a product, think of EIS. It is more than likely that EIS, the leading supplier of outbound calling systems, is facilitating the phone call. EIS provides automatic phone-calling equipment to credit card companies, market researchers, fund-raisers, and other organizational representatives who want to inundate their chosen target audience with questions and spiels. EIS's computer/telephone systems perform multiple tasks, from dialing calls to providing callers with on-screen data to routing phone call traffic. By 1995 EIS had installed 39,000 agent workstations at 700 call centers worldwide.

EIS is an offshoot of Dun & Bradstreet's 1986 attempt to enter the telemarketing arena. D&B hired consultant Robert Jesurum to develop its computerized telemarketing system. When the project died, Jesurum continued to work with call processing technology. He founded Electronic Information Systems and introduced his first automated call processors in 1988. Jesurum retired in 1991. CEO Joseph Porfeli was VP of Telenet Communications and EVP of Centex Telemanagement before he joined Electronic Information in 1989. The company became EIS International when it merged with publicly held International Telesystems in 1993. Executives and directors own 27.8% of company stock.

In 1994 EIS introduced new client/server software, Centenium, which Porfeli sees as key to EIS's future growth. Centenium lets phone operators switch between incoming and outgoing calls. This allows EIS customers to shift from surveying and telemarketing to receiving customer service queries.

The company set up a technical support center in the Netherlands in 1995 and introduced Centenium internationally that year.

WHO

Chairman and CEO: Joseph J. Porfeli, age 47, $340,264 pay
President and COO: E. Kevin Dahill, age 47, $262,788 pay
EVP Worldwide Sales and Marketing: Edward J. Sarkisian, age 56, $235,715 pay
SVP Strategic Business Development: Robert F. Kelly, age 47, $174,716 pay
SVP Strategic Technology Development and Chief Technical Officer: Jacob W. Jorgensen, age 42, $168,616 pay
SVP Finance, CFO, and Treasurer: Frederick C. Foley, age 49
SVP Marketing: Jodi M. Wallace, age 37
Director Human Resources: Jo Lovell
Auditors: KPMG Peat Marwick LLP

WHERE

HQ: 1351 Washington Blvd., Stamford, CT 06902
Phone: 203-351-4800   **Fax:** 203-961-8632

WHAT

	1994 Sales	
	$ mil.	% of total
Products	52.5	81
Services	12.4	19
Total	**64.9**	**100**

Products
Call Processing System (supports up to 96 agents)
Centenium (client/server software that allows EIS systems to interface with systems from other vendors)
OCM (call and data management)
System 7000 (supports up to 80 agents)

Services
Maintenance contracts   Remote diagnostics
On-site service   Telephone consultation

KEY COMPETITORS

Davox   Melita
Digital Systems   Northern Telecom
InterVoice   Rockwell

HOW MUCH

Nasdaq symbol: EISI FY ends: December 31	Annual Growth	1989	1990	1991	1992	1993	1994
Sales ($ mil.)	50.9%	8.3	17.7	20.5	26.0	50.7	64.9
Net income ($ mil.)	27.5%	2.3	2.1	1.3	3.2	4.7	7.6
Income as % of sales	—		27.2%	11.8%	6.4%	12.3%	9.3%	11.7%
Earnings per share ($)	11.5%	0.51	0.45	0.28	0.59	0.58	0.88
Stock price – high ($)	—	—	—	—	9.25	14.38	15.75
Stock price – low ($)	—	—	—	—	4.75	7.75	9.13
Stock price – close ($)	29.3%	—	—	—	9.13	13.25	15.25
P/E – high	—	—	—	—	16	25	18
P/E – low	—	—	—	—	8	13	10
Dividends per share ($)	—	—	—	—	0.00	0.00	0.00
Book value per share ($)	38.6%	—	—	2.60	2.85	3.42	5.48
Employees	15.1%	—	—	—	—	258	297

1994 Year-end:
Debt ratio: 0.0%
Return on equity: 20.5%
Cash (mil.): $21.2
Current ratio: 3.56
Long-term debt (mil.): $0.0
No. of shares (mil.): 8.9
Dividends
   Yield: —
   Payout: —
Market value (mil.): $136.3
R&D as % of sales: 10.1%

FEROLITO, VULTAGGIO & SONS

OVERVIEW

Lake Success, New York–based Ferolito, Vultaggio & Sons has a lakeful of successful beverages, including fruit juices, cocktails, iced teas, and malt liquors. Since it introduced AriZona Iced Teas in 1992, the brand has become the hottest item in the fast-growing ready-to-drink iced tea segment of the beverage industry. AriZona — distinguished from its rivals by its 24-ounce can with funky graphics — has vaulted to #3 in the category (after Snapple and PepsiCo's Lipton tea and ahead of Coca-Cola's Nestea). Even more startling, the brand gained its 12.6% share of the $1 billion market with 80% of its sales coming from 4 markets (New York, New Jersey, Florida, and Detroit).

John Ferolito and Don Vultaggio started out in 1972 as beer wholesalers in Brooklyn, working days and nights looking for success. In 1986 the pair launched Midnight Dragon, a malt liquor they marketed with a poster featuring a scantily clad woman whose provocative utterance ("I could suck on this all night") drew howls from the National Organization of Women. Crazy Horse, a malt liquor introduced in 1991, received a similarly hostile reception from Native Americans. But it was the success of New York–based Snapple that prompted the 2 "beer guys" to develop a competing product. AriZona Iced Teas, named after the state because of its hot climate, made its debut in distinctive cans in mid-1992. AriZona Iced Teas saw its caseload sales soar fifteenfold within a year.

The company has kept its overhead down by limiting advertising to billboards and buses. It has also contracted out the making of its beverages. Profits have been reinvested to fuel growth, but the company expected to fund future growth through an IPO. Its strategy calls for capitalizing on its brand-name recognition through licensing agreements and new products. To that end, in 1994 it made a deal with Leader Candies in Brooklyn to market AriZona lollipops and freezer pops. The company also went national with its AriZona Iced Teas that year. After a brief courtship by G. Heileman (the brewing unit of Hicks, Muse, Tate & Furst) in 1995, the company rejected a $400 million takeover overture.

WHO

Chairman: Don Vultaggio
President: John Ferolito
COO: Michael B. Schott, age 47
CFO: Rick Adonaillo
Auditors: Maier, Markey, Manashi

WHERE

HQ: 5 Dakota Dr., Ste. 205, Lake Success, NY 11042
Phone: 516-327-0002   **Fax:** 516-326-4988

WHAT

Selected Products

Cowboy Cocktails	Ginseng
(punch drinks)	Natural Peach Flavor
Grape Kiwi	Natural Raspberry
Kiwi Strawberry	Tropical
Mucho Mango	With Lemon
Strawberry Punch	With Real Lemon Juice
Freez-A-Pops	Lollipops
Lemon	Lemon Tea
Raspberry	Peach Tea
Fruit Juices	Raspberry Tea
Lemonade	Tropical Tea
Pink Lemonade	Malt Liquors
Iced Teas	Crazy Horse
Decaf Light	Midnight Dragon
Diet with Lemon	

KEY COMPETITORS

Allied Domecq
Cable Car Beverage
Cadbury Schweppes
Celestial Seasonings
Coca-Cola
Danone
Dole
Heileman
National Beverage
Nestlé
Ocean Spray
PepsiCo
Quaker Oats
RJR Nabisco
Seagram
Stroh
Triarc
Unilever
Veryfine
Whitman

HOW MUCH

Private company FY ends: December 31	Annual Growth	1989	1990	1991	1992	1993	1994
Estimated revenues ($ mil.)	447.7%	—	—	—	10.0	100.0	300.0
Cases – AriZona (thou.)	421.0%	—	—	—	700	10,000	19,000
Employees	—	—	—	—	—	200	200

Ferolito, Vultaggio & Sons

THE FORSCHNER GROUP, INC.

OVERVIEW

The Forschner Group is slicing and dicing as it diversifies its product line. Although it has built its business around being the exclusive North American marketer of the world-famous Swiss Army Knife (made by Victorinox of Switzerland for more than 100 years), the knife is no longer Forschner's primary product. The company's sales of high-quality Swiss-made products (watches, compasses, and sunglasses) carrying the Swiss Army Brand label accounted for over half of 1994 revenues. Forschner also sells quality cutlery for consumer and professional use.

Founded in 1855 as a manufacturer of butcher scales, the company became a major customer for Victorinox's Swiss Army Knife in 1937. In 1974 the company was bought by investor Louis Marx (who still owns 31.2%). In 1975 Forschner stopped selling butcher scales, and it switched from selling pocket knives to wholesalers to selling directly to retail stores. Without a cent spent on advertising, the Swiss Army Knife became a cult item, and sales rose from $800,000 in 1974 to $11 million in 1981. Marx took the company public in 1983.

Forschner's exclusive distribution of the Excalibur of pocket knives (a deal it formalized in 1983) has been the core strength of the enterprise, although it successfully branched into Swiss Army Brand watches and sunglasses in 1989.

In 1993 the company signed an exclusive distribution agreement with Victorinox for the Caribbean area and opened a sales and distribution center in Switzerland to handle foreign sales of its Swiss Army Brand watch. In 1994 the company invested $7 million in Forschner Enterprises, a privately held investment group. In that year 25% of Forschner's sales went to Cyrk, Inc., a Massachusetts-based marketer of sports and promotional items.

In 1995 Forschner sued 3 New York retailers for counterfeiting its branded watches.

WHO

Co-chairman and CEO: James W. Kennedy, age 44, $375,000 pay
Co-chairman and CEO: M. Leo Hart, age 46, $345,000 pay
EVP: Stanley G. Mortimer III, age 52, $320,000 pay
EVP and CFO: Thomas D. Cunningham, age 45, $274,308 pay
SVP, Controller, Secretary, and Treasurer: Thomas M. Lupinski, age 42
VP: Michael J. Belleveau, age 38, $195,746 pay
Director Personnel: Lesley Olsen
Auditors: Arthur Andersen & Co, SC

WHERE

HQ: One Research Dr., Shelton, CT 06484
Phone: 203-929-6391　　　**Fax:** 203-929-3786

WHAT

	1994 Sales
	% of total
Swiss Army Brand products	52
Original Swiss Army Knife	35
Cutlery	13
Total	**100**

Products
Original Swiss Army Knife
Professional and consumer cutlery
　Cuisine de France Sabatier
　R.H. Forschner
Swiss Army Brand products
　Compasses
　Sunglasses
　Watches

KEY COMPETITORS

Alpha Store	Loews
Arrow Trading	North American Watch
Bausch & Lomb	Oakley
Benson Eyecare	Precise International
Casio	Seiko
Cooper Development	Servotronics
Fossil	SMH
L.L. Bean	T-Shirt Plaza

HOW MUCH

Nasdaq symbol: FSNR FY ends: December 31	Annual Growth	1989	1990	1991	1992	1993	1994
Sales ($ mil.)	26.9%	43.8	50.2	60.1	74.1	102.5	144.4
Net income ($ mil.)	24.8%	3.1	2.1	2.0	4.9	7.5	9.4
Income as % of sales	—	7.1%	4.2%	3.3%	6.6%	7.1%	6.5%
Earnings per share ($)	9.1%	0.75	0.51	0.45	0.80	1.04	1.16
Stock price – high ($)	—	13.25	12.50	12.75	16.00	18.25	16.25
Stock price – low ($)	—	5.38	4.50	5.75	9.50	12.00	10.25
Stock price – close ($)	2.1%	11.25	6.00	11.25	12.50	15.25	12.50
P/E – high	—	18	25	28	20	18	14
P/E – low	—	7	9	13	12	12	9
Dividends per share ($)	—	0.00	0.00	0.00	0.00	0.00	0.00
Book value per share ($)	39.0%	1.94	2.72	3.22	6.70	8.66	10.07
Employees	15.2%	94	100	99	126	160	191

1994 Year-end:
Debt ratio: 0.0%
Return on equity: 13.2%
Cash (mil.): $18.0
Current ratio: 3.29
Long-term debt (mil.): $0.0
No. of shares (mil.): 8.2
Dividends
　Yield: —
　Payout: —
Market value (mil.): $102.3

HEALTH MANAGEMENT, INC.

OVERVIEW

Health Management (HMI), formerly called Homecare Management, provides home drug therapy, case management, and support services, primarily for organ transplant patients — who require daily drugs for the rest of their lives. The company also serves other patients with chronic conditions, including schizophrenia, cancer, and AIDS. Its collection of services is known as Lifecare. HMI is a leader in the fragmented transplant patient care market. As the population ages and managed-care firms attempt to control costs by getting people out of the hospital and keeping them out, HMI's markets for transplant recipients (and especially patients with chronic conditions) will grow rapidly.

Chairman Clifford Hotte, a licensed pharmacist, began Homecare Management in 1985 as a home health company, taking it public in 1988. In 1990 the company began its Lifecare program services for transplant patients at their homes. In 1992 Homecare received accreditation from the Joint Commission on Accreditation of Healthcare Organizations, increasing its standing with transplant centers. Hotte and his family own 12% of the company's stock. In 1995 Homecare changed its name to Health Management.

To expand services to individuals with chronic diseases, during 1994 the company acquired the Murray Group (cancer, HIV/AIDS, and infertility services) and Pharmaceutical Marketing Alliance (services to multiple sclerosis patients). HMI cares for approximately 7,000 transplant patients through its preferred providers agreements with transplant centers around the country.

In 1995 HMI acquired Caremark's Clozaril Patient Management Business, for approximately $23 million. The purchase established HMI as the #1 US provider of health management services to schizophrenics.

WHO

Chairman, President, and CEO: Clifford E. Hotte, age 48, $220,000 pay
EVP and COO: Michael R. Norman, age 47, $95,077 pay
CFO, Corporate Development Officer, Treasurer, and Secretary: Drew W. Bergman, age 39, $100,000 pay
VP: Robert C. Clifton, age 41, $149,600 pay
VP Sales and Marketing: Lloyd N. Myers, age 35
Director Personnel and Human Services: Virginia Belloise, age 48
Auditors: BDO Seidman LLP

WHERE

HQ: 4250 Veterans Memorial Hwy., Holbrook, NY 11741
Phone: 516-981-0034 **Fax:** 516-981-0522

WHAT

	1995 Sales % of total
Private insurance & other payors	60
Medicaid & other state programs	26
Medicare & other federal programs	14
Total	**100**

	1995 Sales % of total
Transplant services	65
Other	35
Total	**100**

Selected Subsidiaries
Health Reimbursement Corp.
HMI Illinois, Inc.
HMI Maryland, Inc.
HMI Pennsylvania, Inc.
HMI PMA Inc.
HMI Retail Corp. Inc.
Home Care Management, Inc.

KEY COMPETITORS

Chronimed	Medco Containment
Coram Healthcare	Merck
Diagnostek	Stadtlanders Drug
J. C. Penney	Systemed

HOW MUCH

Nasdaq symbol: HMIS FY ends: April 30	Annual Growth	1990	1991	1992	1993	1994	1995
Sales ($ mil.)	73.4%	5.7	7.8	14.6	26.4	44.2	89.3
Net income ($ mil.)	102.4%	0.2	0.6	1.1	2.2	4.0	6.8
Income as % of sales	—	3.5%	7.7%	7.5%	8.3%	9.0%	7.6%
Earnings per share ($)	—	0.06	0.12	0.22	0.35	0.53	0.73
Stock price – high ($)[1]	64.8%	—	2.06	6.94	14.13	16.13	20.00
Stock price – low ($)[1]	—	—	0.75	1.13	4.50	7.63	12.25
Stock price – close ($)[1]	88.7%	—	1.41	6.38	13.75	13.63	17.88
P/E – high	—	—	17	32	40	30	27
P/E – low	—	—	6	5	13	14	17
Dividends per share ($)	—	—	0.00	0.00	0.00	0.00	0.00
Book value per share ($)	112.4%	—	0.28	0.52	1.61	4.84	5.70
Employees	120.4%	—	30	50	85	194	413

1995 Year-end:
Debt ratio: 33.1%
Return on equity: 14.0%
Cash (mil.): $4.6
Current ratio: 3.31
Long-term debt (mil.): $23.2
No. of shares (mil.): 9.3
Dividends
  Yield: —
  Payout: —
Market value (mil.): $166.6

[1] Stock prices are for the prior calendar year.

HFS INC.

HFS Inc. (formerly Hospitality Franchise Systems), the world's #1 hotel franchisor, has expanded into the real estate business. In 1995 it purchased Century 21, the world's largest residential real estate organization, and also welcomed Electronic Realty Associates.

HFS's hotel brands include Days Inn, Howard Johnson, Park Inns, Ramada, Super 8, Villager Lodge, and a new chain, Wingate Inns. HFS owns no units outright; rather, it collects franchise and other fees from more than 4,000 hotels. In exchange, it provides national marketing systems and centralized reservation systems. HFS also oversees marketing for 10 casinos and owns Casino & Credit Services, a provider of gambler credit information.

Henry Silverman learned about the hotel business during the 1980s, when he helped transform Days Inn from a small chain of roadside hotels into the world's 3rd largest hotel franchisor. In 1990 he joined the Blackstone Group and led the LBO specialist into buying the Howard Johnson and Ramada chains. Two years later Blackstone bought Days Inn, taking it and the other 2 chains public as Hospitality Franchise Systems. (The name was changed to HFS Inc. in 1995.) Over the next year the company bought Super 8 Motels and Park Inn International.

In 1994 it formed National Gaming Corp. to acquire and develop casinos, then spun it off to shareholders later that year. In 1995 HFS and National Gaming purchased Forte PLC's North American Travelodge hotel unit, National Gaming bought 16 hotel/motel properties and obtained joint-venture interests in 96 other motels, and HFS acquired the Travelodge trademark and franchise systems of some 450 hotels. That same year National Gaming failed to obtain casino licenses and switched to the hotel business. It was renamed National Lodging Corp.

WHO

Chairman and CEO: Henry R. Silverman, age 54, $1,370,837 pay
President and COO: John D. Snodgrass, age 38, $1,073,093 pay
EVP, CFO, and Treasurer: Stephen P. Holmes, age 38, $473,911 pay
EVP, General Counsel, and Assistant Secretary: James E. Buckman, age 50, $471,116 pay
Director Compensation and Benefits: Jim LaBella
Auditors: Deloitte & Touche LLP

WHERE

HQ: 339 Jefferson Rd., Parsippany, NJ 07054
Phone: 201-428-9700   **Fax:** 201-428-6057

WHAT

	1994 Sales	
	$ mil.	% of total
Franchise	283.2	91
Gaming	8.5	2
Other	20.8	7
Total	**312.5**	**100**

Franchise Brands

Days Inn (3rd largest lodging brand in the US, with 1,586 properties)
Howard Johnson (9th largest lodging brand in the US, with 582 properties)
Park Inns International (midmarket chain, with 45 properties)
Ramada (4th largest lodging brand in the US, with 775 properties)
Super 8 Motel (a leading national franchisor in economy segment, with 1,220 properties)
Villager Lodge (extended-stay, budget-price motels)
Wingate Inns (limited-service hotels)

KEY COMPETITORS

Accor	La Quinta Inns	Prime Hospitality
Bass	Manor Care	Prudential
Best Western	Marriott	Red Lion
Coldwell Banker	International	Red Roof Inns
Hilton	Microtel	RE/MAX
ITT Corp.	Pratt Hotel	ShoLodge

HOW MUCH

NYSE symbol: HFS FY ends: December 31	Annual Growth	1989	1990[1]	1991	1992	1993	1994
Sales ($ mil.)	45.1%	—	51.5	102.2	203.0	257.1	312.5
Net income ($ mil.)	—	—	(1.9)	(5.4)	18.2	21.5	53.5
Income as % of sales	—	—	—	—	9.0%	8.4%	17.1%
Earnings per share ($)	—	—	(0.09)	(0.25)	0.42	0.43	1.06
Stock price – high ($)	—	—	—	—	10.13	26.88	33.50
Stock price – low ($)	—	—	—	—	9.00	9.38	20.75
Stock price – close ($)	65.9%	—	—	—	9.63	26.50	26.50
P/E – high	—	—	—	—	24	63	32
P/E – low	—	—	—	—	21	22	20
Dividends per share ($)	—	—	—	—	0.00	0.00	0.00
Book value per share ($)	6.9%	—	—	—	5.30	6.06	6.06
Employees	19.9%	—	—	—	1,460	1,270	2,100

[1] 6-month fiscal year

1994 Year-end:
Debt ratio: 55.4%
Return on equity: 19.5%
Cash (mil.): $6.0
Current ratio: 1.09
Long-term debt (mil.): $347.4
No. of shares (mil.): 46.3
Dividends
 Yield: —
 Payout: —
Market value (mil.): $1,227.0

HIRSCH INTERNATIONAL CORP.

OVERVIEW

Hirsch International is reaping what it sews as it keeps its customers in stitches. Hirsch distributes embroidery machinery to makers of apparel and soft goods. In addition to selling and leasing machinery, it develops software for automating the embroidery design process and provides a range of embroidery supplies.

Hirsch competes with leader MacPherson (its main rival, with which it shares about 85% of the US embroidery market). Its machines are used by such apparel makers as Carter, Gerber, Oshkosh B'Gosh, and Russell. Hirsch distributes machines made by Japanese manufacturers Brother and Tajima.

The company was founded in 1968 by Harry Hirsch, a knitter from Europe, as a servicer of knitting machines. The company stuck to its knitting lines through 1975, when a slump in the knitting machine industry prompted Hirsch to look into other business lines, including embroidery machines. A distribution contract with Tajima resulted in 1976. Henry Arnberg, who became a stockholder in the firm's holding company in 1977, was named CEO when Hirsch died in 1980. Arnberg became sole owner shortly thereafter. He sold a 45% stake to colleague (and current COO) Paul Levine in 1981. The pair then focused the firm on embroidery and sold its knitting units.

In 1993 Hirsch launched HAPL Leasing, its equipment leasing subsidiary (by 1995 this unit had closed $26.7 million in annual lease agreements). In 1994 the company purchased Pulse Microsystems, a Canadian designer of computer programs for embroidery, which had supplied it with software packages since 1991. Hirsch went public in 1994. Rapid acceptance of the company's software and its position as the only one-stop shop in the field have helped expand its customer base and sales.

In 1995 Hirsch developed software that uses bar codes to recognize embroidery designs.

WHO

Chairman, President, and CEO: Henry Arnberg, age 52, $850,752 pay
EVP, COO, and Secretary: Paul Levine, age 42, $850,106 pay
VP; President, Pulse Microsystems Ltd.: Tas Tsonis, age 43, $416,917 pay
VP; EVP, Pulse Microsystems Ltd.: Brian Goldberg, age 35, $416,917 pay
VP Finance and CFO: Kenneth Shifrin, age 37, $292,476 pay
VP Midwest Sales: Kristof Janowski, age 42
VP HAPL Leasing Co.: Theodore Pawelec, age 44
Corporate Controller: Michael P. Petaja, age 29
Manager Human Resources: Susan Lange, age 45
Auditors: Deloitte & Touche LLP

WHERE

HQ: 200 Wireless Blvd., Hauppauge, NY 11788
Phone: 516-436-7100   **Fax:** 516-436-7054

WHAT

	1995 Sales	
	$ mil.	% of total
Embroidery machines (includes Pulse software)	60.8	84
Embroidery supplies	1.4	2
Other	10.1	14
Total	**72.3**	**100**

Operating Groups
Embroidery Supply Warehouse (embroidery supplies)
HAPL Leasing (equipment leasing)
Pulse Microsystems (embroidery design software)

Major Suppliers
Brother (Japan)
Tajima (Japan)

KEY COMPETITORS

Gunold & Stickma
Happy Sewing Machine
MacPherson
Saurer
Singer Industrial Machine Equipment
Wilcom
ZSK

HOW MUCH

Nasdaq symbol: HRSH FY ends: January 31	Annual Growth	1990	1991	1992	1993	1994	1995	1995 Year-end:
Sales ($ mil.)	28.9%	—	26.2	29.9	43.6	50.5	72.3	Debt ratio: 12.8%
Net income ($ mil.)	—	—	(0.1)	1.0	1.9	4.2	4.8	Return on equity: 26.3% Cash (mil.): $2.7
Income as % of sales	—	—	—	2.6%	4.2%	8.3%	6.7%	Current ratio: 1.73
Earnings per share ($)	—	—	(0.03)	0.22	0.54	0.76	1.03	Long-term debt (mil.): $2.7
Stock price – high ($)[1]	—	—	—	—	—	—	7.59	No. of shares (mil.): 4.8
Stock price – low ($)[1]	—	—	—	—	—	—	5.53	Dividends
Stock price – close ($)[1]	—	—	—	—	—	—	7.20	Yield: —
P/E – high	—	—	—	—	—	—	7	Payout: —
P/E – low	—	—	—	—	—	—	5	Market value (mil.): $34.3
Dividends per share ($)	—	—	—	—	—	—	0.00	
Book value per share ($)	—	—	—	—	—	—	4.33	
Employees	—	—	—	—	—	—	141	

[1] Stock prices are for the prior calendar year.

HYPERION SOFTWARE CORPORATION

Hyperion Software helps businesses balance their checkbooks. The Stamford, Connecticut–based firm is the #3 developer of financial software for client/server networks (after Oracle and SAP). Its products — including accounting, budgeting, and forecasting software — are used by more than 2,300 corporations in 25 countries. CEO James Perakis owns 5.8% of Hyperion's stock.

The company was founded as IMRS in 1981 by Robert Thomson and shipped its first product, Micro Control, in 1983. Perakis came aboard as CEO in 1985. Thomson eased out of the business, stepping down as president in 1987, but remains a consultant and director. Demand for the company's Hyperion products has been driven by the spread of PC networks. In 1988 IMRS began standardizing the development of its software around Windows. The next year IMRS bought FASTAR, a competing product, from Hoechst Celanese. The company went public in 1991 and that year released its Hyperion line of Windows software (it now has more than 80% of the Windows market for financial software).

IMRS realized early on that business information could be handled on LANs. It has grown internationally by designing multilingual programs so that multinational companies can use the same programs everywhere. One of its most effective means of promotion is forming alliances with the consulting arms of the Big 6 accounting firms, which recommend its products to clients.

In 1995 IMRS changed its name to capitalize on the success of its Hyperion product line. Later that year it released Hyperion Financials, a corporate accounting software package. Also in 1995 the company acquired its exclusive Scandinavian distributor, now called Hyperion Software Nordic AB, and Pillar Corp., a developer of budgeting and planning software.

WHO

Chairman, President, and CEO: James A. Perakis, age 51, $360,000 pay
EVP: Terence W. Rogers, age 53, $312,000 pay
SVP: David M. Sample, age 47, $341,000 pay
SVP and CFO: Lucy Rae Ricciardi, age 53
VP Hyperion Enterprise Business Group: Gordon O. Rapkin, age 40, $208,000 pay
VP Products and Services and Secretary: Craig M. Schiff, age 40, $192,000 pay
Director Human Resources: Paul Avalone
Auditors: Ernst & Young LLP

WHERE

HQ: 900 Long Ridge Rd., Stamford, CT 06902-1247
Phone: 203-703-3000   **Fax:** 203-322-3904

	1995 Sales	
	$ mil.	% of total
US	98.6	72
UK	13.3	10
Other countries	25.2	18
Total	**137.1**	**100**

WHAT

	1995 Sales	
	$ mil.	% of total
Software licenses	78.0	57
License renewals & services	59.1	43
Total	**137.1**	**100**

Selected Products
Hyperion Enterprise and Micro Control (financial data consolidation and reporting)
Hyperion Financials (business transaction collecting and reporting)
Hyperion OnTrack (graphical data presentation)
Hyperion Pillar (budgeting and forecasting)

KEY COMPETITORS

American Software	Fourth Shift	SAP AG
Computer Associates	IBM	System Software Associates
Consilium	Marcam	Systeme
Dun & Bradstreet	Oracle	Andwendungen
	PeopleSoft	Produkt
	Ross Systems	

HOW MUCH

Nasdaq symbol: HYSW FY ends: June 30	Annual Growth	1990	1991	1992	1993	1994	1995
Sales ($ mil.)	41.6%	24.1	34.3	46.0	61.0	84.4	137.1
Net income ($ mil.)	48.8%	1.7	2.7	4.2	4.3	8.5	12.1
Income as % of sales	—	6.9%	7.7%	9.1%	7.0%	10.0%	8.9%
Earnings per share ($)	35.9%	0.15	0.23	0.31	0.29	0.55	0.70
Stock price – high ($)	—	—	11.00	12.50	13.88	20.13	28.38
Stock price – low ($)	—	—	6.00	6.88	5.63	9.00	15.63
Stock price – close ($)	21.5%	—	9.75	12.38	12.75	19.75	21.25
P/E – high	—	—	48	41	49	37	41
P/E – low	—	—	26	23	20	17	22
Dividends per share ($)	—	—	0.00	0.00	0.00	0.00	0.00
Book value per share ($)	50.1%	—	0.88	2.56	2.93	2.81	4.47
Employees	34.8%	190	262	335	419	580	846

1995 Year-end:
Debt ratio: 11.9%
Return on equity: 19.4%
Cash (mil.): $45.5
Current ratio: 1.60
Long-term debt (mil.): $8.9
No. of shares (mil.): 16.1
Dividends
  Yield: —
  Payout: —
Market value (mil.): $341.2
R&D as % of sales: 15.3%

INFINITY BROADCASTING

OVERVIEW

Being bad has been good business for Infinity Broadcasting. The New York City–based company employs Watergate burglar G. Gordon Liddy and "shock jock" Howard Stern, whose controversial on-air remarks have garnered a large national following, premium advertisers, and $1.9 million in fines from the FCC. Only CBS can compete with Infinity's ability to deliver to advertisers a radio-listening audience in each of the top 10 markets. With its stable of 27 stations, Infinity is the nation's largest operator of radio stations, serving 13 of the US's largest markets and accounting for $2.7 billion in radio advertising revenues — 27% of the national total.

Founded in 1972 by Michael Wiener and Gerald Carrus, the company bought its first radio station in 1973. Mel Karmazin, who had spent 10 years with Metromedia's radio division, joined the company in 1981 and championed the push to capture major markets. Infinity grew by buying underperforming radio stations in key markets and turning them around. The company acquired stations in New York, Chicago, Boston, and Houston before going public in 1986. Wiener, Carrus, and Karmazin took the company private in 1988 when it merged with WCK Acquisition. The trio took Infinity public again in 1992 with an IPO that raised just over $100 million; that year Infinity bought WFAN-AM, the flagship station for the New York Mets, Knicks, and Rangers, for a whopping $70 million. In 1993 the company had a 2nd public offering. Wiener, Carrus, and Karmazin own 82% of Infinity's voting stock.

In 1994 Infinity merged with Westwood One, becoming the US's largest syndicator of radio programming. Also that year it committed $51 million to buy KLUV-FM in Dallas, the 7th-largest US radio market; Infinity's purchase was approved by the FCC in 1995.

WHO

Chairman and Treasurer: Gerald Carrus, age 69, $250,000 pay
Co-chairman and Secretary: Michael A. Wiener, age 57, $250,000 pay
President and CEO: Mel Karmazin, age 51, $2,425,000 pay
VP Finance and CFO: Farid Suleman, age 43, $700,000 pay
Business Manager (HR): Tom Gesimondo
Auditors: KPMG Peat Marwick LLP

WHERE

HQ: Infinity Broadcasting Corporation, 600 Madison Ave., New York, NY 10022
Phone: 212-750-6400   **Fax:** 212-888-2959

WHAT

Markets and Stations
Atlanta (WZGC-FM)
Baltimore (WJFK-AM, WLIF-FM)
Boston (WBCN-FM, WZLX-FM)
Chicago (WJMK-FM/WJJD-AM, WUSN-FM)
Dallas/Fort Worth (KDMM-AM/KVIL-FM, KLUV-FM)
Detroit (WXYT-AM/WOMC-FM)
Houston (KXYZ-AM)
Los Angeles (KROQ-FM, KRTH-FM)
New York (WFAN-AM, WZRC-AM, WXRK-FM)
Philadelphia (WIP-AM, WYSP-FM)
San Francisco/San Jose (KOME-FM)
Tampa/St. Petersburg (WQYK-AM/FM)
Washington, DC (WJFK-FM, WPGC-AM/FM)

KEY COMPETITORS

A. H. Belo	E.W. Scripps
Associated Group	EZ Communications
Barden Communications	Gannett
BHC Communications	Hearst
Broadcast Partners	Heritage Media
CBS	SFX Broadcasting
Chris-Craft	Tribune
Clear Channel	Viacom
Communications	Walt Disney
Cox Enterprises	Washington Post

HOW MUCH

Nasdaq symbol: INFTA FY ends: December 31	Annual Growth	1989	1990	1991	1992	1993	1994
Sales ($ mil.)	20.7%	107.2	112.2	118.0	150.2	204.6	274.1
Net income ($ mil.)	—	(43.6)	(39.7)	(6.0)	(9.4)	14.3	33.2
Income as % of sales	—	—	—	—	—	7.0%	12.1%
Earnings per share ($)	—	(5.03)	(3.93)	(0.41)	(0.69)	0.35	0.74
Stock price – high ($)	—	—	—	—	13.25	35.63	33.75
Stock price – low ($)	—	—	—	—	7.88	10.13	20.25
Stock price – close ($)	69.2%	—	—	—	11.00	30.25	31.50
P/E – high	—	—	—	—	—	102	46
P/E – low	—	—	—	—	—	29	27
Dividends per share ($)	—	—	—	—	0.00	0.00	0.00
Book value per share ($)	—	—	—	—	(5.84)	(0.74)	(0.80)
Employees	38.4%	—	—	420	420	675	1,114

1994 Year-end:
Debt ratio: —
Return on equity: —
Cash (mil.): $7.7
Current ratio: 1.52
Long-term debt (mil.): $531.8
No. of shares (mil.): 31.8
Dividends
  Yield: —
  Payout: —
Market value (mil.): $1,001.9

JEAN PHILIPPE FRAGRANCES, INC.

OVERVIEW

Would a perfume by another name smell as sweet? Jean Philippe Fragrances would say yes. The company specializes in low-cost imitations of high-dollar designer perfumes, known as "alternative designer fragrances." Jean Philippe also holds exclusive distribution rights to other name-brand perfumes, including Burberrys, Chaz, and Jordache, and it manufactures and markets cosmetics, including Cutex nail enamel and lip color products.

Founded in 1985, Jean Philippe was named after its 2 cofounders: Jean Madar, a Frenchman who came to New York with $8,000 after working in marketing for Inter Parfums (Paris), and Philippe Benacin, current president of Inter Parfums. (Madar and Benacin own 31.4% and 27.8% of Jean Philippe, respectively.) In 1990 Jean Philippe bought the fragrance and cosmetics division of Jordache Enterprises and obtained an exclusive license to manufacture and market Jordache fragrances. In 1991 it bought a controlling interest in Inter Parfums and an affiliated French fragrance company, Selective Industrie.

The company has aggressively expanded its markets and product line. In 1994 it acquired trademarks for a variety of fragrances from Parfums Molyneux and Parfums Weil, bought the worldwide trademark for Intimate and Chaz from Revlon, and acquired rights to Cutex nail enamel and lipsticks from Chesebrough-Pond's. The acquisition of Cutex's product lines has brought Jean Philippe greater access to mass merchandise channels, including Wal-Mart and Kmart.

In 1995 the company introduced several new mass-market alternative fragrances, including Romantic Illusions, a collection of 8 perfumes (among them knockoffs of Calvin Klein's Obsession and Elizabeth Taylor's White Diamonds) packed in cartons designed to look like romance novels.

WHO

Chairman; Director General, Inter Parfums: Jean Madar, age 34, $133,250 pay
VC, President, and CEO; President, Inter Parfums: Philippe Benacin, age 36, $81,360 pay
EVP: Bruce Elbilia, age 35, $162,000 pay
EVP: Wayne C. Hamerling, age 38, $159,449 pay
EVP and CFO: Russell Greenberg, age 38, $158,250 pay
Controller (HR): Henry Dominentz
Auditors: Richard A. Eisner & Company LLP

WHERE

HQ: 551 Fifth Ave., New York, NY 10176
Phone: 212-983-2640   **Fax:** 212-983-4197

	1994 Sales		1994 Net Income	
	$ mil.	% of total	$ mil.	% of total
US	48.4	61	6.3	83
Europe	30.7	39	1.3	17
Adjustments	(4.0)	—	(0.3)	—
Total	**75.1**	**100**	**7.3**	**100**

WHAT

Selected Alternative Designer Fragrances	Brand-Name and Licensed Fragrances and Cosmetics
Dakota	Burberrys
Elite 2	Chaz
Fire	Cutex
Fleur de Paris	Intimate
Gold	Jordache
Memphis	Ombre Rose
Possession	Parfums Jean Desprez
Radiance	Parfums Molyneux
Snow Silk	Parfums Weil

KEY COMPETITORS

Avon	Gillette	Parfum de Coeur
Benckiser	Liz Claiborne	Perfumania
Colgate-Palmolive	L'Oréal	Pfizer
Del Labs	MacAndrews &	Procter &
Estée Lauder	Forbes	Gamble
Fragrance	Mary Kay	Roche Group
Impressions	Maybelline	Unilever

HOW MUCH

Nasdaq symbol: JEAN FY ends: December 31	Annual Growth	1989	1990	1991	1992	1993	1994
Sales ($ mil.)	71.2%	5.1	8.6	25.5	43.7	59.5	75.1
Net income ($ mil.)	71.0%	0.5	0.9	1.9	4.3	7.1	7.3
Income as % of sales	—	9.8%	10.5%	7.5%	9.8%	11.9%	9.7%
Earnings per share ($)	42.2%	0.12	0.20	0.27	0.50	0.70	0.70
Stock price – high ($)	—	2.19	2.42	7.25	14.13	18.00	12.88
Stock price – low ($)	—	1.46	0.75	2.33	6.34	10.50	6.75
Stock price – close ($)	36.9%	1.56	2.42	6.92	12.50	12.38	7.50
P/E – high	—	18	12	27	28	26	18
P/E – low	—	12	4	9	13	15	10
Dividends per share ($)	—	0.00	0.00	0.00	0.00	0.00	0.00
Book value per share ($)	41.0%	0.78	1.00	1.09	2.12	3.41	4.34
Employees	63.8%	10	19	55	70	107	118

1994 Year-end:
Debt ratio: 14.7%
Return on equity: 18.6%
Cash (mil.): $5.3
Current ratio: 2.34
Long-term debt (mil.): $0.9
No. of shares (mil.): 10.2
Dividends
  Yield: —
  Payout: —
Market value (mil.): $76.8

KCS ENERGY, INC.

OVERVIEW

KCS is an energy company that has 3 main businesses: oil and gas exploration and production, natural gas transportation, and energy marketing and services. Natural gas makes up about 85% of the Edison, New Jersey–based company's oil and gas reserves. Most of the company's exploration is done onshore on the US Gulf Coast and in the Rocky Mountain region. KCS has working interests in 862 wells and operates 406 of them. KCS's main transportation asset is a 150-mile, high-pressure transmission system owned by company subsidiary KCS Pipeline Systems. The company has 325 industrial and commercial customers in 34 states and Canada. A 20-year contract signed in 1979 with a Tenneco subsidiary calls for Tenneco to purchase 85% of the supply of natural gas produced in KCS's Bob West Field at a set price (a great deal more than the going rate on the spot market). This contract accounts for about 1/3 of KCS's total production.

NUI Corp., a New Jersey–based gas distribution company, diversified in the late 1960s and early 1970s into exploration, production, transportation, and marketing. It also had holdings in propane distribution and utilities data processing. KCS was formed in 1988 and then spun off from NUI. This spin-off included the nonutility operations; KCS quickly sold its unprofitable data processing company and propane distributor. Chairman Stewart Kean owns almost 15% of company stock.

KCS's long-term goal is to rank among the top 50 domestic oil and gas companies. It has targeted a minimum annual growth rate of 20%. To meet this goal, the company is expanding geographically. In 1995 KCS acquired the oil and gas assets of the Natural Gas Processing Co. (more than 30 fields in the Rocky Mountain region). That year it also purchased oil and gas reserves in Michigan for $31 million.

WHO

Chairman: Stewart B. Kean, age 61
President and CEO: James W. Christmas, age 47, $344,750 pay
VP Oil and Gas Operations; President, KCS Resources, Inc.: C. R. Devine, age 49, $201,000 pay
VP, CFO, and Secretary: Henry A. Jurand, age 46, $198,175 pay (prior to promotion)
President, KCS Energy Marketing, Inc.; President, KCS Michigan Resources, Inc; President, KCS Pipeline Systems, Inc.: Harry Lee Stout, age 47, $165,025 pay
Director Human Resources and Treasurer: Kathryn M. Kinnamon, age 31
Auditors: Arthur Andersen & Co, SC

WHERE

HQ: 379 Thornall St., Edison, NJ 08837
Phone: 908 632-1770   **Fax:** 908-603-8960

WHAT

	1995 Sales	
	$ mil.	% of total
Energy marketing & services	328.2	75
Oil & gas exploration & production	84.6	19
Natural gas transportation	24.5	6
Adjustments	(13.7)	—
Total	**423.6**	**100**

Selected Producing Fields
Birdie Field (Karnes County, TX)
Bob West Field (Zapata and Starr Counties, TX)
Cypress Deep and Langham Creek Fields (Harris County, TX)

KEY COMPETITORS

Amoco	Lyondell	Sterling
Apache	Petrochemical	Chemicals
Chevron	Mitchell Energy &	Tejas Gas
DuPont	Development	Tenneco
Enron	Mobil	Texaco
Exxon	Royal Dutch/Shell	Unocal
Gulf Oil	Phillips Petroleum	Wainoco Oil
Howell	Santa Fe Energy	

HOW MUCH

NYSE symbol: KCS FY ends: September 30	Annual Growth	1990	1991	1992	1993	1994	1995
Sales ($ mil.)	42.4%	72.2	98.9	143.7	271.7	335.6	423.6
Net income ($ mil.)	56.8%	2.4	2.5	3.3	13.7	23.3	22.8
Income as % of sales	—	3.3%	2.5%	2.3%	5.0%	6.9%	5.4%
Earnings per share ($)	53.2%	0.23	0.23	0.30	1.19	1.97	1.94
Stock price – high ($)	—	2.30	2.20	11.68	32.75	29.00	22.25
Stock price – low ($)	—	1.75	1.50	2.08	9.00	12.25	9.88
Stock price – close ($)	50.9%	1.92	2.17	10.68	26.75	16.25	15.00
P/E – high	—	10	10	39	28	15	11
P/E – low	—	8	7	7	8	6	5
Dividends per share ($)	—	0.00	0.00	0.03	0.04	0.08	0.12
Book value per share	30.8%	2.18	2.42	2.68	4.51	6.45	8.33
Employees	4.8%	68	69	72	71	86	86

1995 Year-end:
Debt ratio: 48.7%
Return on equity: 26.9%
Cash (mil.): $4.2
Current ratio: 0.95
Long-term debt (mil.): $90.8
No. of shares (mil.): 11.5
Dividends
  Yield: 0.8%
  Payout: 6.2%
Market value (mil.): $172.3

MARVEL ENTERTAINMENT GROUP, INC.

OVERVIEW

Marvel may be the poor man's Disney. The world's #1 comic-book publisher, Marvel is now a diversified entertainment company, with stakes in sports trading cards, children's magazines, licensing, and toys. Marvel is best known for its roster of 3,500 proprietary characters such as Spider-Man, X-Men, Captain America, and the Incredible Hulk. The fabled comic-book operations have lost circulation and are now eclipsed by Marvel's sports trading cards, which cover professional athletes and sports teams (baseball, basketball, football, and hockey), its own superheroes, and Disney and *Star Trek* figures. The company also has vigorously licensed its characters for TV, film, toys, and multimedia. Financier and chairman Ron Perelman owns 80% of the company stock.

Marvel was founded in 1932 as Western Publishing. Its first Marvel comics were issued in 1939. Two years later Captain America was introduced to fight Nazis, and Stanley Martin Lieber (Stan Lee, the creator of Spider-Man, Hulk, Fantastic Four, and X-Men) came on board. The company was incorporated as Marvel Entertainment Group in 1986. Perelman bought a stake in Marvel in 1988 and the rest in 1989 through a subsidiary of MacAndrews & Forbes. Marvel went public in 1991.

The company doubled in size in 1992 by acquiring trading card and confectionery maker Fleer. In 1993 Marvel bought a stake in toy designer and manufacturer Toy Biz. One year later it bought rival Malibu Comics Entertainment, Welsh Publishing Group (now Marvel Family Publishing), Panini stickers and adhesives, and the distribution operations of Superhero Enterprises' (Heroes World). Also in 1994 the company signed deals with Planet Hollywood (to create a chain of restaurants) and MCA (to develop theme park rides). In 1995 Marvel bought trading card competitor SkyBox International for $150 million and announced plans to expand its toy operations.

WHO

Chairman: Ronald O. Perelman, age 52
VC: Terry C. Stewart, age 49, $629,808 pay
President and CEO: William C. Bevins, age 48, $250,000 pay
Chairman, Marvel Comics and Marvel Films: Stan Lee
EVP and President, Fleer Corp.: Jeffrey L. Kaplan, age 33, $404,385 pay
EVP, General Counsel, and Chief Administrative Officer: Paul E. Shapiro, age 53, $400,000 pay
EVP and President, Marvel Comics Group: Gerard S. Calabrese, age 46, $367,365 pay (prior to promotion)
EVP and CFO: Bobby G. Jenkins, age 33
Director Human Resources: Jacquelyn Green
Auditors: Ernst & Young LLP

WHERE

HQ: 387 Park Ave. South, New York, NY 10016
Phone: 212-696-0808   **Fax:** 212-576-8598

	1994 Sales		1994 Operating Income	
	$ mil.	% of total	$ mil.	% of total
US & Canada	427.5	81	95.7	83
Foreign	97.5	19	19.4	17
Adjustments	(10.2)	—	—	—
Total	**514.8**	**100**	**115.1**	**100**

WHAT

Selected Operations
Fleer Corp. (sports and entertainment trading cards; confectioneries)
Malibu Comics Entertainment, Inc.
Marvel Comics (10 million per month circulation)
Marvel Family Publishing (children's magazines)
Panini SpA (children's activity sticker collections)
SkyBox International Inc. (trading cards)
Superhero Enterprises' Inc. (distributor and marketer of comic books and cartoon character–related cards, games, and toys)
Toy Biz, Inc. (36.6%, toy designer and distributor)

KEY COMPETITORS

Acclaim Entertainment	Hasbro Image	RJR Nabisco Score Board	Viacom Warner-Lambert
Harvey Entertainment	Comics Mattel	Time Warner Topps	Wrigley

HOW MUCH

NYSE symbol: MRV FY ends: December 31	Annual Growth	1989	1990	1991	1992	1993	1994
Sales ($ mil.)	49.6%	68.6	81.1	115.1	223.8	415.2	514.8
Net income ($ mil.)	91.5%	2.4	5.4	16.1	32.6	56.0	61.8
Income as % of sales	—	3.5%	6.7%	14.0%	14.6%	13.5%	12.0%
Earnings per share ($)	82.1%	0.03	0.06	0.16	0.33	0.55	0.60
Stock price – high ($)	—	—	—	6.09	13.00	35.75	30.38
Stock price – low ($)	—	—	—	2.27	5.44	8.56	13.50
Stock price – close ($)	35.6%	—	—	5.72	12.56	27.38	14.25
P/E – high	—	—	—	35	39	65	51
P/E – low	—	—	—	14	16	16	23
Dividends per share ($)	—	—	—	0.00	0.00	0.00	0.00
Book value per share ($)	67.9%	—	—	0.51	0.88	1.51	2.41
Employees	47.4%	230	230	278	775	725	1,600

1994 Year-end:
Debt ratio: 61.3%
Return on equity: 31.7%
Cash (mil.): $18.1
Current ratio: 1.48
Long-term debt (mil.): $364.1
No. of shares (mil.): 100.7
Dividends
  Yield: —
  Payout: —
Market value (mil.): $1,434.3

MICRO WAREHOUSE, INC.

OVERVIEW

There's nothing small about Connecticut-based Micro Warehouse. More than 1.3 million customers bought one of the 20,000 computer products offered in the 54 million catalogs it mailed in 1994. The company sells Apple Macintosh and PC clone computers, software, and accessories primarily through its highly descriptive, full-color monthly catalogs *MacWAREHOUSE* and *MicroWAREHOUSE*. Micro Warehouse also places its stock in specialty catalogs (*Data CommWAREHOUSE*; data communication and networking), outbound telemarketing to businesses, and the acquisition of foreign computer catalogers to build its global presence. The company buys 70% of its products in large volumes directly from manufacturers (such as Apple, Toshiba, Hewlett-Packard, and Microsoft), allowing it to set prices at 30–60% below retail. Chairman and CEO Peter Godfrey owns 12.04% of the firm's stock; cofounder Felix Dennis has 6.9%.

Godfrey got together with Robert Bartner in 1974 to run Fiona Press, a publisher of adult magazines (sold to Paragon Publishing in 1992). In 1985 they founded *MacUser* magazine (along with Felix Dennis), which they sold to Ziff-Davis the following year. In 1987 they founded Micro Warehouse and launched *MacWAREHOUSE* to sell products to Macintosh computer users. In 1990 the firm added *MicroWAREHOUSE* to sell to PC users. The company expanded into the UK in 1991, and in 1992 it went public.

In 1994 and 1995 Micro Warehouse focused on balancing its Macintosh- (55% of 1994 revenues) and PC-related sales and expanding internationally. It acquired Technomatic (UK) in May 1995 and Mac Direct (Australia) and Castle Computing (Australia) 2 months later. Micro Warehouse incorporated *CDRomWAREHOUSE* into *MacWAREHOUSE* and *MicroWAREHOUSE* and launched *Mac SystemsWAREHOUSE* in August 1995.

WHO

Chairman, President, and CEO: Peter Godfrey, age 49, $415,000 pay
EVP and COO: Melvin Seiler, age 52, $510,000 pay
VP Finance, CFO, and Treasurer: Steven Purcell, age 44, $359,000 pay
VP Worldwide Advertising: Stephen F. England, age 41, $245,620 pay
VP Marketing: Adam Shaffer, age 29, $220,000 pay
VP Human Resources: Michael Kurtz
Auditors: KPMG Peat Marwick LLP

WHERE

HQ: 535 Connecticut Ave., Norwalk, CT 06854
Phone: 203-899-4000   **Fax:** 203-899-4203

	1994 Sales		1994 Operating Income	
	$ mil.	% of total	$ mil.	% of total
North America	652.1	84	46.4	—
Europe	124.3	16	(1.1)	—
Total	**776.4**	**100**	**45.3**	**—**

WHAT

	1994 Sales
	% of total
Hardware	46
Software	40
Supplies & accessories	14
Total	**100**

Selected Catalogs and Services

Data CommWAREHOUSE
Mac SystemsWAREHOUSE
MacWAREHOUSE
Micro SuppliesWAREHOUSE
MicroWAREHOUSE

Paper designWAREHOUSE (laser printers and supplies)
WAREHOUSE-On-Line

KEY COMPETITORS

Best Buy	ELEK-TEK	Office Depot
CDW Computer	Gateway 2000	OfficeMax
Centers	InaCom	Packard Bell
CompuCom	Intelligent	PC and Mac
CompUSA	Electronics	Connection
Damark	J&R Music	Tandy
Dell	MicroAge	Tiger Direct
Egghead	NeoStar	

HOW MUCH

Nasdaq symbol: MWHS FY ends: December 31	Annual Growth	1989	1990	1991	1992	1993	1994
Sales ($ mil.)	71.3%	52.6	123.7	163.6	269.6	450.4	776.4
Net income ($ mil.)	—	(0.2)	(0.1)	1.4	0.2	15.0	28.0
Income as % of sales	—	—	—	0.9%	0.1%	3.3%	3.6%
Earnings per share ($)	66.2%	—	—	0.22	0.39	0.64	1.01
Stock price – high ($)	—	—	—	—	13.25	21.38	36.25
Stock price – low ($)	—	—	—	—	10.81	9.63	17.75
Stock price – close ($)	69.0%	—	—	—	12.25	20.81	35.00
P/E – high	—	—	—	—	34	33	36
P/E – low	—	—	—	—	28	15	18
Dividends per share ($)	—	—	—	—	0.00	0.00	0.00
Book value per share ($)	74.9%	—	—	—	2.65	3.91	8.11
Employees	78.6%	—	—	—	721	1,496	2,300

1994 Year-end:
Debt ratio: 0.3%
Return on equity: 16.6%
Cash (mil.): $74.5
Current ratio: 4.63
Long-term debt (mil.): $0.6
No. of shares (mil.): 29.5
Dividends
  Yield: —
  Payout: —
Market value (mil.): $1,033.7

THE MONEY STORE INC.

OVERVIEW

If you need a few odds and ends, you go to a convenience store; it's a little more expensive, but it's just easier. The Money Store, based in Union, New Jersey, is a convenience store for money (for those with a house and willing to pay higher interest). The company is a leading originator, buyer, servicer, and seller of home equity loans (2nd mortgages). It is the #1 lender of Small Business Administration–guaranteed loans and also offers guaranteed student loans and sub-prime used-auto loans.

Alan Turtletaub founded Modern Acceptance Corp. in 1967 to make 2nd-mortgage loans to people with subpar credit histories. With careful underwriting and aggressive servicing, Turtletaub profited in a niche most banks avoided and provided money for people who needed to consolidate debt or make home improvements. Turtletaub (whose son, Marc, is now CEO) moved into other unpopular niches, like SBA loans and student loans (starting with loans to foreign students and dental students, which other lenders neglected). In 1971 the company became the Money Store, and in 1991 it went public.

Since 1989 the company has securitized its loans on a pass-through basis (which lets it sell the risk as well). Formerly, it sold the loans themselves but had to retain the risk of default. Many of these loans are still on its books, increasing its vulnerability to economic downturns. But a large percentage of its loans (FHA, SBA, and student loans) have an element of guarantee, leaving the company liable only for unguaranteed portions of loans.

The Money Store has expanded in recent years, aiming to become fully national. It advertises heavily, using former baseball great Jim Palmer as spokesman. In 1995, after Clinton-administration laws began phasing out the guaranteed student loan program, the Money Store started making used-car loans.

WHO

Chairman: Alan Turtletaub, age 81, $300,000 pay
President and CEO: Marc Turtletaub, age 49, $450,000 pay
EVP, CFO, and Secretary: Morton Dear, age 57, $419,900 pay
EVP: Anthony R. Medici, age 64, $272,700 pay
SVP: William S. Templeton, age 46, $294,600 pay
VP Human Resources: Charlotte L. Moffett
Auditors: KPMG Peat Marwick LLP

WHERE

HQ: 2840 Morris Ave., Union, NJ 07083
Phone: 908-686-2000   **Fax:** 908-686-6907

The Money Store has more than 155 offices in 40 states, the District of Columbia, and Puerto Rico.

WHAT

	1994 Sales	
	$ mil.	% of total
Sales of receivables	259.9	79
Finance income & fees	68.1	21
Insurance commissions	2.5	0
Total	**330.5**	**100**

	1994 Loans
	% of total
Mortgages (home equity)	72
Small Business Administration loans	15
Student loans	13
Total	**100**

Primary Operations
Educaid (student loans)
The Money Store (home equity loans)
The Money Store Auto Finance (sub-prime car loans)
The Money Store Investment Corp. (Small Business Administration-guaranteed loans)

KEY COMPETITORS

AT&T Capital	Fleet	KeyCorp
Beneficial	Freddie Mac	Mercury Finance
Credit Acceptance	Household	Norwest Corp.
Fannie Mae	International	Student Loan Corp.

HOW MUCH

Nasdaq symbol: MONE FY ends: December 31	Annual Growth	1989	1990	1991	1992	1993	1994
Sales ($ mil.)	24.7%	109.7	121.8	140.3	157.3	219.8	330.5
Net income ($ mil.)	15.7%	15.1	8.1	11.4	15.2	21.8	31.3
Income as % of sales	—	13.7%	6.6%	8.1%	9.7%	9.9%	9.5%
Earnings per share ($)	25.5%	—	0.62	0.82	0.84	1.20	1.54
Stock price – high ($)	—	—	—	9.22	10.06	12.22	14.83
Stock price – low ($)	—	—	—	5.56	4.56	6.89	10.33
Stock price – close ($)	24.2%	—	—	6.44	7.22	10.72	12.33
P/E – high	—	—	—	11	12	10	10
P/E – low	—	—	—	7	5	6	7
Dividends per share ($)	—	—	—	0.00	0.02	0.09	0.12
Book value per share ($)	15.8%	—	—	6.16	6.98	8.13	9.56
Employees	31.3%	—	—	900	1,050	1,375	2,035

1994 Year-end:
Debt ratio: 78.3%
Return on equity: 17.4%
Cash (mil.): $161.3
Current ratio: —
Long-term debt (mil.): $700.4
No. of shares (mil.): 20.3
Dividends
  Yield: 1.0%
  Payout: 7.8%
Market value (mil.): $250.5
Advertising as % of sales: 12.2%

THE MULTICARE COMPANIES, INC.

OVERVIEW

Multicare has many ways to care for its patients. The Hackensack, New Jersey–based company operates almost 60 nursing home facilities with about 6,800 beds in 8 states. Serving those who require long-term institutional medical care, including the fastest-growing segment of the US population (those over 85 years old), it provides supervision for patients needing subacute care, such as for stroke or cardiac recovery. Other medical services include skilled nursing, Alzheimer's care, ventilator care, intravenous therapy, and various forms of coma, pain, and wound management. Multicare does not employ doctors (patients are directly billed by their visiting physicians), allowing the company to provide less-expensive long-term care than to hospitals.

Brothers Moshael and Daniel Straus inherited 4 nursing homes from their father, who died in 1978. They took over the management of these family assets in 1984 and formed their own company, Multicare. The company grew through acquisitions, and in 1992 it acquired 13 long-term facilities from Adventist Living Centers for $30 million. Multicare went public in 1993. By the end of that year it was operating 35 nursing facilities in 5 states.

In 1994 Multicare acquired Providence Health Care, an Ohio-based provider of long-term nursing care with 16 care facilities (with 1,400 beds) for $29 million. That year the company also completed construction on 2 nursing care facilities in New Jersey.

Multicare in 1995 acquired an institutional pharmacy serving 6,000 outside beds (non-company facilities), and expanded its in-house pharmacy to provide infusion therapy and prescription drugs. That same year it signed a deal to acquire 5 facilities from Great American Nursing Center for $37 million.

In 1996 Multicare agreed to acquire Concord Health Group for about $70.7 million.

WHO

Chairman and Co-CEO: Moshael J. Straus, age 42, $902,500 pay
President and Co-CEO: Daniel E. Straus, age 38, $902,500 pay
EVP and CFO: Stephen R. Baker, age 39, $280,422 pay
EVP and General Counsel: Paul J. Klausner, age 37, $280,422 pay
VP Operations: James P. Ignarski, age 34, $127,731 pay
VP Finance: Robert S. Anderson, age 33, $121,054 pay
VP Human Resources: Ronald G. Clarendon, age 51
Auditors: KPMG Peat Marwick LLP

WHERE

HQ: 411 Hackensack Ave., Hackensack, NJ 07601
Phone: 201-488-8818   **Fax:** 201-525-5954

	1994 Medical Facilities	
	No.	% of total
New Jersey	19	32
Ohio	14	24
Illinois	9	15
Other states	17	29
Total	**59**	**100**

WHAT

	1994 Sales
	% of total
Medicaid	39
Private insurance & other payors	37
Medicare	24
Total	**100**

Selected Services

Basic patient services	Rehabilitation services
Pharmacy services	Subacute care

KEY COMPETITORS

Advocat	Horizon/CMS	Sisters of Charity
Arbor Health Care	Healthcare	Health Care
Beverly	Life Care	Star MultiCare
Enterprises	Centers	Services
Columbia/HCA	Living Centers	Sun Healthcare
Franciscan Sisters	of America	TheraTx
Health Care	Manor Care	Universal Health
Geriatric & Medical	Mercy Health	Services
Cos.	System	Vencor

HOW MUCH

NYSE symbol: MUL FY ends: December 31	Annual Growth	1989	1990	1991	1992	1993	1994
Sales ($ mil.)	35.8%	56.8	74.8	88.0	126.0	162.4	262.4
Net income ($ mil.)	—	(0.0)	(1.1)	(0.5)	1.8	3.3	15.4
Income as % of sales	—	—	—	—	1.4%	2.0%	5.9%
Earnings per share ($)	132.1%	—	—	—	0.18	0.29	0.97
Stock price – high ($)	—	—	—	—	—	18.25	21.75
Stock price – low ($)	—	—	—	—	—	10.00	15.00
Stock price – close ($)	8.2%	—	—	—	—	18.25	19.75
P/E – high	—	—	—	—	—	63	22
P/E – low	—	—	—	—	—	34	15
Dividends per share ($)	—	—	—	—	—	0.00	0.00
Book value per share ($)	151.8%	—	—	—	—	2.25	5.67
Employees	45.8%	—	—	—	—	4,800	7,000

1994 Year-end:
Debt ratio: 61.0%
Return on equity: 23.3%
Cash (mil.): $8.0
Current ratio: 1.82
Long-term debt (mil.): $153.5
No. of shares (mil.): 17.7
Dividends
   Yield: —
   Payout: —
Market value (mil.): $348.8

NATHAN'S FAMOUS, INC.

OVERVIEW

Nathan's Famous, one of the world's best-known hot dog chains, has lost a little of its sizzle in the competitive fast-food market. Declining sales in some of the company-owned restaurants (which are older and larger than many of the franchised locations) took a bite out of profits during fiscal 1995.

Nathan's has over 150 franchised units (including 15 carts, kiosks, and snack bars) in 17 states — mostly in the Eastern US — and Puerto Rico. Most of the 24 company-owned restaurants are in the New York metropolitan area. Nathan's plans to increase net income by opening franchised and company-owned restaurants in nontraditional locations, including universities, airports, racetracks, and convenience stores. In 1995 the company opened 3 units in Home Depot stores in the Northeast.

The company, which claims to be the country's oldest fast-food operator, sells hot dogs that contain the original secret blend of spices created by Ida Handwerker, who with her husband, Nathan, opened the first restaurant on Coney Island in 1916. In 1957 the Handwerker family opened the 2nd restaurant and continued to operate Nathan's until Equicor Group bought the chain in 1987. For the next 3 years the company experienced difficult times and a record loss in fiscal 1990. A turnaround led by Wayne Norbitz, who took over as president in 1989, helped restore stability. Norbitz's management team includes SVP William Handwerker, a grandson of the founders. Equity Assets Management, Inc., owns 21.8% of the common shares.

Nathan's is best known for its 100% beef hot dogs and fresh crinkle-cut French fries. Recognizing that consumers want alternatives, including low fat foods, Nathan's has tried out such new items as salads, fruits, and chicken sandwiches.

WHO

Chairman and CEO: Howard M. Lorber, age 46
President and COO: Wayne Norbitz, age 47, $250,000 pay
EVP: Janice Ellis, age 39, $204,902 pay
SVP Corporate Services: William Handwerker, age 41, $120,002 pay
SVP Franchise and Real Estate Development: Carl Paley, age 58, $120,000 pay
VP Finance, CFO, and Secretary: Ronald G. DeVos, age 40
VP Architecture and Construction: Donald P. Schedler, age 42
VP Operations: Bharat Varma, age 50
Director Personnel and Training: Karen C. Brown
Auditors: KPMG Peat Marwick LLP

WHERE

HQ: 1400 Old Country Rd., Ste. 400, Westbury, NY 11590
Phone: 516-338-8500   **Fax:** 516-338-7220

WHAT

	Restaurants	
	No.	% of total
Operated by franchisees	159	87
Operated by the company	24	13
Total	**183**	**100**

KEY COMPETITORS

A&W Restaurants	McDonald's
Blimpie	PepsiCo
Boston Chicken	Rally's Hamburgers
Checkers Drive-In	Sbarro
Dairy Queen	Schlotzsky's
Domino's	Sonic Corp.
Foodmaker	Subway
Grand Metropolitan	Wendy's
Imasco	Whataburger
Little Caesar's	White Castle

HOW MUCH

Nasdaq symbol: NATH FY ends: Last Sun. in March	Annual Growth	1990	1991	1992	1993	1994	1995
Sales ($ mil.)	3.7%	21.9	21.8	20.9	21.7	25.1	26.2
Net income ($ mil.)	—	(6.1)	0.9	1.3	1.8	1.5	(0.5)
Income as % of sales	—	—	3.9%	6.2%	8.2%	5.8%	—
Earnings per share ($)	—	(2.04)	0.28	0.43	0.56	0.31	(0.11)
Stock price – high ($)[1]	—	—	—	—	—	12.00	8.88
Stock price – low ($)[1]	—	—	—	—	—	6.25	4.63
Stock price – close ($)[1]	(45.1%)	—	—	—	—	8.88	4.88
P/E – high	—	—	—	—	—	39	—
P/E – low	—	—	—	—	—	20	—
Dividends per share ($)	—	—	—	—	—	0.00	0.00
Book value per share ($)	(1.5%)	—	—	—	—	5.91	5.82
Employees	5.2%	445	384	470	495	537	573

1995 Year-end:
Debt ratio: 0.3%
Return on equity: —
Cash (mil.): $8.2
Current ratio: 2.64
Long-term debt (mil.): $0.1
No. of shares (mil.): 4.7
Dividends
  Yield: —
  Payout: —
Market value (mil.): $23.0

[1] Stock prices are for the prior calendar year.

NAUTICA ENTERPRISES, INC.

OVERVIEW

Nautica Enterprises is sailing on smooth seas. The upscale men's sportswear clothier has seen its sales boosted by international expansion and the trend of dressing down in the corporate world. The company runs 2 wholly owned subsidiaries, Nautica International (men's sportswear, outerwear, and activewear) and State-O-Maine (men's dress shirts, robes, loungewear, swimwear, and sportswear). Nautica sells its pricey products at over 700 in-store shops in major US department stores. In addition, it operates 29 factory outlet stores in the US, an international licensing operation, and freestanding retail outlets in Asia, Australia, Central and South America, Europe, and the Pacific Rim.

Nautica was founded in 1971 as State-O-Maine, Inc. Harvey Sanders, once a company sales trainee, took over as CEO in 1977. In 1984 State-O-Maine launched the successful, yachting-inspired line of Nautica casualwear designed by David Chu. The company changed its corporate name from State-O-Maine to Nautica Enterprises in 1993 to be more closely associated with its most-recognized brand.

Image is important to Nautica. The company seduces its active crew of customers through ads in fashion and lifestyle magazines, including *Conde Nast Traveler*, *GQ*, *Esquire*, and *Vanity Fair*. Nautica augments this strategy with sponsorships of sporting events, including the outfitting of the Pact '95/ Young America and US sailing teams and the sponsoring of a number of Senior PGA tours.

Plans to keep Nautica on course in the future include the release of activewear lines featuring new fabric technologies. The company's patented, waterproof Nautex fabric is being tested by the Pact/Young America Team, and the new Nautech fleece was introduced in the fall 1995 collection.

WHO

Chairman, CEO, and President: Harvey Sanders, age 45, $1,288,680 pay
EVP; President, Nautica Apparel and Nautica International: David Chu, age 40, $1,118,400 pay
President, Nautica Retail USA: John Wetzler, age 49, $319,000 pay
President, State-O-Maine: Charles Zona, age 45, $308,000 pay
VP and Chief Administrative Officer: Donald W. Pennington
VP Distribution: Larry Ingram
VP Finance: Neal Nackman
VP Management Information Systems: Larry Brenner
Auditors: Grant Thornton LLP

WHERE

HQ: 40 W. 57th St., New York, NY 10019
Phone: 212-541-5757   **Fax:** 212-977-4348

Nautica operates some 726 in-store units in the US and licenses Nautica apparel for wholesale distribution in Australia, Belgium, Brazil, Canada, the Caribbean, Chile, Colombia, Greece, Hong Kong, Italy, Japan, Korea, Mexico, New Zealand, Panama, Peru, Taiwan, Thailand, the UK, and Venezuela. There are over 53 international Nautica retail stores and 28 outlet stores in the US.

WHAT

Nautica International	State-O-Maine, Inc.
Men's activewear	Loungewear
Men's outerwear	Men's dress furnishings
Men's sportswear	Robes
	Sportswear and
	swimwear

KEY COMPETITORS

Authentic Fitness	Lands' End	Salant
G-III Apparel	The Limited	Spiegel
Gander Mountain	L.L. Bean	Stage II
The Gap	Oxford Industries	Supreme
Haggar	Phillips/	International
Hartmarx	Van Heusen	Tommy Hilfiger
J. Crew	Polo/Ralph Lauren	VF

HOW MUCH

Nasdaq symbol: NAUT FY ends: Last day in Feb.	Annual Growth	1990	1991	1992	1993	1994	1995
Sales ($ mil.)	23.5%	86.2	95.4	121.2	151.0	192.9	247.6
Net income ($ mil.)	32.8%	5.8	2.2	7.5	10.5	16.8	24.0
Income as % of sales	—	6.7%	2.3%	6.2%	6.9%	8.7%	9.7%
Earnings per share ($)	27.6%	0.34	0.13	0.43	0.60	0.90	1.15
Stock price – high ($)[1]	—	5.03	4.22	5.85	8.22	18.17	21.67
Stock price – low ($)[1]	—	3.20	1.15	1.63	4.67	6.33	13.00
Stock price – close ($)[1]	37.7%	4.08	1.85	4.95	6.83	17.67	20.17
P/E – high	—	15	32	14	14	20	19
P/E – low	—	9	9	4	8	7	11
Dividends per share ($)	—	0.00	0.00	0.00	0.00	0.00	0.00
Book value per share ($)	14.6%	3.59	3.87	4.57	5.55	5.88	7.10
Employees	24.9%	250	200	—	380	550	760

1995 Year-end:
Debt ratio: 0.2%
Return on equity: 18.9%
Cash (mil.): $49.2
Current ratio: 4.97
Long-term debt (mil.): $0.3
No. of shares (mil.): 19.6
Dividends
  Yield: —
  Payout: —
Market value (mil.): $395.9

[1]Stock prices are for the prior calendar year.

NEXTEL COMMUNICATIONS, INC.

OVERVIEW

"I feel exactly like someone who wrote a play and is now going to see it performed," says Nextel chairman Morgan O'Brien. He has assembled a massive network of radio dispatch systems into the #1 specialized mobile radio (SMR) service in 9 of the 10 largest metropolitan areas in the US. However, O'Brien's script does not end with his company providing 2-way radio service to cabs and truck fleets. He plans to parlay all the FCC radio licenses Nextel has picked up to create a major cellular network that covers 85% of the US population by replacing the analog systems with digital ones. Both Motorola and Comcast hold major investments in Nextel.

A former FCC staffer who oversaw SMR licensing during the 1970s, O'Brien founded Fleet Call (changed to Nextel in 1993) in 1987. He saw a "value gap" between prices being paid for cellular phone systems and those paid for radio dispatch systems that use the same radio spectrum, so he and his partners began quietly buying up US radio dispatch companies. In 1991 the company received FCC approval to begin building Digital Mobile networks. The company went public in 1992, and in 1993 it got a major boost when it signed a deal to acquire licenses owned by Motorola in 21 states.

Nextel first began service in Los Angeles in 1994, but there have been complaints of inferior quality. Also, MCI, which had agreed to invest $1.3 billion and provide marketing assistance, pulled out of the deal, citing fears over the quality of Nextel's service. However, the company is undeterred; it plans to spend $2 billion by 1997 to construct 4,000 digital cells across the US. Wireless communication pioneer Craig McCaw and his family agreed in 1995 to buy a stake of up to 23.5% in Nextel, paying up to $1.1 billion in a series of payments over the next 6 years.

WHO

Chairman: Morgan E. O'Brien, age 50, $686,000 pay
President: Brian D. McAuley, age 54, $686,000 pay
Acting CEO: Dennis Weibling
EVP and COO; President, SMR Operations: Joel A. Schleicher, age 42, $275,000 pay
SVP Government Affairs: Robert S. Foosaner, age 51, $370,000 pay
SVP; President, Digital Mobile Operations: James M. Dixon, age 46, $297,000 pay
CFO: Louis Salamone Jr., age 47
Treasurer and Secretary (Principal Financial Officer): Elizabeth G. Long, age 34
Director Human Resources: Lane Foster
Auditors: Deloitte & Touche LLP

WHERE

HQ: 201 Rte. 17 North, Rutherford, NJ 07070
Phone: 201-438-1400   **Fax:** 201-438-5540

Selected Markets

Baltimore	Minneapolis-St. Paul
Boston	New York City
Chicago	Philadelphia
Dallas-Fort Worth	Phoenix
Houston	Sacramento
Los Angeles	San Francisco
Milwaukee	

WHAT

	1994 Sales	
	$ mil.	% of total
Radio service	50.2	60
Equipment sales & maintenance	33.5	40
Total	**83.7**	**100**

KEY COMPETITORS

Air Touch	GTE
Ameritech	MCI
AT&T Corp.	Pacific Telesis
Bell Atlantic	SBC Communications
BellSouth	Sprint
Contel Cellular	U S West

HOW MUCH

Nasdaq symbol: CALL FY ends: December 31	Annual Growth	1989	1990	1991	1992	1993	1994[1]
Sales ($ mil.)	18.2%	36.3	53.9	52.5	53.0	67.9	83.7
Net income ($ mil.)	—	(10.1)	(7.7)	(28.4)	(9.6)	(56.9)	(125.8)
Income as % of sales	—	—	—	—	—	—	—
Earnings per share ($)	—	(0.44)	(0.33)	(1.05)	(0.16)	(0.73)	(1.25)
Stock price – high ($)	—	—	—	—	18.75	54.88	46.75
Stock price – low ($)	—	—	—	—	9.00	17.88	13.25
Stock price – close ($)	(11.9%)	—	—	—	18.50	37.25	14.38
P/E – high	—	—	—	—	—	—	—
P/E – low	—	—	—	—	—	—	—
Dividends per share ($)	—	—	—	—	0.00	0.00	0.00
Book value per share ($)	72.5%	—	—	—	4.04	9.98	12.02
Employees	69.3%	—	—	330	550	773	1,600

[1] 9-month fiscal year

1994 Year-end:
Debt ratio: 47.9%
Return on equity: —
Cash (mil.): $474.0
Current ratio: 2.33
Long-term debt (mil.): $1,163.2
No. of shares (mil.): 105.6
Dividends
  Yield: —
  Payout: —
Market value (mil.): $1,517.6

NOBODY BEATS THE WIZ

OVERVIEW

Billing itself as the Northeast's largest consumer electronics total entertainment retailer, Nobody beats the Wiz takes its name seriously. The company, which is commonly known as the Wiz, blankets its market area — New York, New Jersey, Connecticut, and Pennsylvania — with radio, television, and print ads. Using pitchmen such as Joe Namath and Patrick Ewing, the company spends more on advertising (on a per-store basis) than almost all of its rivals, trying to make sure everyone's heard of the Wiz. Headquartered in Carteret, New Jersey, the company sells TVs, VCRs, stereos, PCs, cellular phones, and a variety of other electronic products as well as software, CDs, and videocassettes through about 60 retail stores. It also sells computer products via direct marketing (primarily to businesses).

While it may be that nobody in the Northeast beats the company in consumer electronic sales or advertising, it may also be true that nobody beats the Wiz in mystery. For example, extensive advertising for the company's Founder's Day sale made a point of omitting the founder's name. The company is controlled by the reclusive Jemal family. CEO Lawrence Jemal's father started in Brooklyn in 1976 with a 5,000-square-foot store on Fulton Street. The Wiz continued to expand throughout the New York metropolitan area. By 1986 it had 11 stores, and by 1988 it had more than 20 outlets.

The Wiz found its yellow brick road littered with rivals during the early 1990s as the highly competitive New York market took its toll on competitors, including Crazy Eddie and Newmark & Lewis. The company continued to expand, adding new, bigger stores and enlarging its older ones. The Wiz moved into Connecticut in 1993, opening 5 large-format stores. By early 1994 the company had a total of 40 stores.

With the burgeoning market for PCs and other computer products, the Wiz has begun to boost its offerings in that product category, in part to compete with a new round of rivals entering the New York market, such as CompUSA and Tandy's Computer City and Incredible Universe. The company also continues to expand geographically. In 1995 it announced plans to move into Massachusetts.

WHO

President and CEO: Lawrence Jemal
EVP: Marvin Jemal
EVP: Stephen Jemal
SVP: Mark Bernstein
CFO: Stan Berg
VP and Chief Merchandising Officer: Tasso Koken
VP Real Estate: Lon Rubatkin
VP Advertising: Richard Block
VP Human Resources: Bob Brummer

WHERE

HQ: 1300 Federal Blvd., Carteret, NJ 07008
Phone: 908-602-1900   **Fax:** 908-634-6856

WHAT

Selected Merchandise
Answering machines
Audio components
Camcorders
Cameras
Cellular phones and pagers
Compact discs
Computer software
Computers and peripherals
Fax machines
Televisions
VCRs
Videocassettes

KEY COMPETITORS

47th Street Photo
Ames
CompUSA
Dayton Hudson
Egghead
Fretter
J&R Music
Kmart
MTS
Musicland
NeoStar
Office Depot
OfficeMax
PC and Mac Connection
P. C. Richard & Sons
Price/Costco
Sears
Sharper Image
Staples
Tandy
Tops Appliance City
Wal-Mart

HOW MUCH

Private company **FY ends:** Last day of Feb.	Annual Growth	1990	1991	1992	1993	1994	1995
Estimated sales ($ mil.)	41.0%	—	—	—	504.0	750.0	1,000.0
Employees	2.0%	—	—	—	—	4,200	4,285

NU HORIZONS ELECTRONICS CORP.

OVERVIEW

Nu Horizons strives to be an electrical engineer's genie: granting wishes for smaller, faster, and more efficient gadgets. The Amityville, New York–based company is a leading distributor of such electronic components as memory chips, microprocessors, and resistors. Nu Horizons has agreements with more than 55 manufacturers (including Cirrus Logic and Toshiba) to sell components to OEMs that make anything with a circuit board (such as computers and telecommunications equipment). The company's strategy is to take advantage of its wide inventory, thorough product knowledge, and a growing nationwide presence. Its NIC Components subsidiary is the exclusive North American sales outlet for Nippon Industries. The com-pany's Nu Visions Manufacturing subsidiary assembles circuit boards.

Irving Lubman, Arthur Nadata, and Richard Schuster had a cumulative 56 years in the electronic components distribution business when they left Diplomat Electronics to found Nu Horizons and NIC in 1982. The firm went public in 1983, and 3 years later Nu Horizons International was formed. Initially, the company derived most of its sales from military OEMs, and marketing efforts were focused on the East Coast. However, by 1993 military OEMs represented just 7% of total sales, and the company began moving west.

In 1994 Nu Horizons bought Merit Electronics (now subsidiary Nu Horizons/Merit Electronics), based in San Jose, California. This capped the company's aggressive expansion to the Midwest and the West. In 1995 Nu Horizons signed a franchise agreement with Cirrus Logic and won industry recognition for its quality assurance system. The company also planned to open several sales offices that year in the Midwest and on the West Coast.

WHO

Chairman and CEO: Irving Lubman, age 56, $489,731 pay
President and Treasurer: Arthur Nadata, age 49, $489,731 pay
VP and Secretary; President, NIC Components: Richard S. Schuster, age 46, $489,731 pay
VP Finance: Paul Durando, age 51, $125,000 pay
Executive Corporate Assistant Human Resources: Pattie Englert
Auditors: Lazar, Levine & Company LLP

WHERE

HQ: 6000 New Horizons Blvd., Amityville, NY 11701
Phone: 516-226-6000   **Fax:** 516-226-5505

The company has sales offices in Alabama, California, Florida, Georgia, Maryland, Massachusetts, Minnesota, New Jersey, New York, Ohio, and Texas.

WHAT

Subsidiaries

NIC Components	Nu Horizons/Merit
Nu Horizons International	Electronics
	Nu Visions Manufacturing

Products Distributed

Active Components	**Passive Components**
Digital and linear circuits	Capacitors
Diodes	Resistors
Fiber-optic components	
Memory chips	
Microprocessors	
Microwave components	
Transistors	

Products Assembled

Circuit boards
Related electromechanical devices

KEY COMPETITORS

Arrow Electronics	Marshall Industries
Avnet	Pioneer-Standard Electronics
Bell Industries	Premier Industries
Insight Electronics	Wyle Electronics

HOW MUCH

Nasdaq symbol: NUHC FY ends: Last day in February	Annual Growth	1990	1991	1992	1993	1994	1995
Sales ($ mil.)	27.2%	39.2	39.0	42.2	60.5	92.4	130.3
Net income ($ mil.)	37.4%	0.9	0.2	0.3	1.5	5.0	4.4
Income as % of sales	—	2.3%	0.5%	0.7%	2.5%	5.4%	3.4%
Earnings per share ($)	39.1%	0.10	0.02	0.04	0.20	0.65	0.52
Stock price – high ($)[1]	—	1.81	1.81	1.28	4.13	16.50	12.25
Stock price – low ($)[1]	—	1.13	0.68	0.68	0.98	3.33	5.75
Stock price – close ($)[1]	46.8%	1.21	0.68	0.98	3.49	11.00	8.25
P/E – high	—	18	91	32	21	25	24
P/E – low	—	11	34	17	5	5	11
Dividends per share ($)	—	0.00	0.00	0.00	0.00	0.00	0.00
Book value per share ($)	15.3%	1.43	1.44	1.47	1.76	2.35	2.91
Employees	24.7%	102	124	156	175	252	307

[1] Stock prices are for the prior calendar year.

1995 Year-end:
Debt ratio: 47.4%
Return on equity: 21.7%
Cash (mil.): $0.5
Current ratio: 5.08
Long-term debt (mil.): $20.0
No. of shares (mil.): 7.7
Dividends
  Yield: —
  Payout: —
Market value (mil.): $63.8

NYCOR, INC.

Some like it hot. But NYCOR's businesses have been built on the fact that most like it cold. The company's Rotorex subsidiary manufactures rotary compressors for use in air conditioners; leading US room–air conditioner manufacturer Fedders has been the major customer of ROTOREX compressors for 20 years and is committed to buy 80% of its compressors from the company.

NYCOR's 2nd business, Melcor, is the world's #1 producer of solid-state thermoelectric cooling and heating modules, which are typically used where space is limited or where there are lightweight cooling requirements or special environmental conditions. These modules are used in a range of products including bottled water coolers, fiber-optic equipment, computers, scientific and laboratory instruments, and beverage dispensers. Melcor's products are sold under the FRIGICHIP brand.

NYCOR was spun off from Fedders in 1987 as an acquisition vehicle by Salvatore Giordano, an octogenarian who is chairman of both companies. NYCOR is about 22%-owned by the Giordanos. Considered "a balance sheet in search of a business," NYCOR bought an 8% stake in Zenith in 1990 and tried to take control of the firm. Such overtures met with resistance from Zenith management, and NYCOR sold its stake for a gain of $4 million in 1992. That year NYCOR bought Fedders's long-term supplier Rotorex for $72.8 million and Melcor for $14.9 million.

Fedders's supply agreement has provided a solid sales base for NYCOR, but the company is looking to wean itself from its dependency on Fedders through international expansion. By 1994 NYCOR had 3 Chinese licensees for its compressor technology and one each in South Korea and Taiwan.

In 1995 NYCOR opened a representative office in Beijing to boost its China strategy.

Chairman: Salvatore Giordano, age 84, $295,244 pay
VC: Sal Giordano Jr., age 56, $237,660 pay
President: Joseph Giordano, age 62, $211,604 pay
VP Finance, Secretary, and General Counsel (HR): Kent E. Hansen, age 47, $211,604 pay
VP Business Planning and Development: Salvatore Giordano III
VP International: Stewart Pei
Corporate Controller: Edwin Diaz
Treasurer: Gerald Solomon
Auditors: Ernst & Young LLP

HQ: 287 Childs Rd., Basking Ridge, NJ 07920
Phone: 908-953-8200   **Fax:** 908-953-0100

Operating Companies and Products

Materials Electronic Products Corporation (Melcor)
Thermoelectric cooling and heating modules for use in fiber-optic, photonic, and laser equipment; computers; PC board electronics; laboratory and scientific instruments; medical and pharmaceutical equipment; chilled food and beverage dispensers; bottled water coolers; portable refrigerators; and beverage coolers for auto, home, marine, and recreational vehicles

Rotorex Company, Inc.
Rotary compressors
   39 Frame series
   48 Frame series

Brand Names
FRIGICHIP
MELCOR
ROTOREX

Armstrong World
Continental Materials
De Mar
Goodman Manufacturing
Lennox
Marley
Mestek
Scotsman Industries
TCC Industries
United Technologies
York International

NYSE symbol: NYCO FY ends: December 31	Annual Growth	1989	1990	1991	1992	1993	1994
Sales ($ mil.)	69.3%	5.4	6.0	6.4	14.2	59.2	75.2
Net income ($ mil.)	(30.5%)	3.7	5.4	4.1	5.2	3.6	0.6
Income as % of sales	—	67.9%	90.0%	64.1%	36.6%	6.1%	0.8%
Earnings per share ($)	—	0.24	0.98	0.30	0.48	0.21	(0.17)
Stock price – high ($)	—	7.25	7.38	6.00	4.50	6.75	5.50
Stock price – low ($)	—	5.63	5.00	3.38	2.00	2.13	2.13
Stock price – close ($)	(14.4%)	6.00	5.50	3.69	2.13	4.13	2.75
P/E – high	—	30	8	20	9	32	—
P/E – low	—	23	15	11	4	10	—
Dividends per share ($)	(100.0%)	0.08	0.16	0.16	0.12	0.00	0.00
Book value per share ($)	0.3%	10.13	20.65	10.46	10.81	10.65	10.26
Employees	(0.8%)	—	—	—	825	800	812

1994 Year-end:
Debt ratio: 0.0%
Return on equity: 0.8%
Cash (mil.): $2.0
Current ratio: 2.18
Long-term debt (mil.): $0.0
No. of shares (mil.): 7.6
Dividends
   Yield: —
   Payout: —
Market value (mil.): $20.8
R&D as % of sales: 1.9%

OXFORD HEALTH PLANS, INC.

OVERVIEW

Mr. Wiggins has got it — more members, that is, for his Oxford Health Plans. Membership in the company's health plans more than doubled from 217,300 in 1993 to 482,500 in 1994. Oxford Health Plans is a managed health care company providing benefit plans through its HMOs in New York, New Jersey, and Connecticut and through its Oxford Health Insurance company. Oxford anticipates continued growth from increased use of managed care products by small employers and Medicaid and Medicare recipients.

The most popular product of Oxford Health Plans is the point-of-service Freedom Plan, which allows members to choose physicians outside the network. The company also offers traditional HMOs, a more economical point-of-service plan called the Liberty Plan, Medicare and Medicaid plans, third-party administration of self-funded health plans, and dental plans. Oxford is expanding into new markets in the northeast, including Philadelphia; Hartford, Connecticut; and New Hampshire.

Oxford Health Plans was founded in New Jersey in 1984 by chairman and CEO Stephen Wiggins, who had previously founded a Minneapolis nonprofit organization to operate long-term care facilities for disabled people and had developed 4 retirement communities. Oxford entered the New York market after state regulations allowed the operation of for-profit HMOs in 1986. The company became profitable in 1990 and went public in 1991. It entered the Medicaid and Medicare markets in 1992 and introduced its Liberty Plan in 1993.

Oxford is also growing through acquisitions. In 1993 it bought SmokEnders, a company that helps people quit smoking. In 1995 the company agreed to acquire OakTree Health Plan, a Philadelphia HMO, in a stock swap valued at $66 million, accelerating Oxford's entry into the Philadelphia market.

WHO

Chairman and CEO: Stephen F. Wiggins, age 38, $810,000 pay
EVP Operations: Robert M. Smoler, age 38, $384,178 pay
EVP Marketing, Medical Delivery Systems, and Government Programs: David B. Snow Jr., age 40, $383,767 pay
EVP Sales: William M. Sullivan, age 31, $364,891 pay
EVP and General Counsel: Donald V. Barrett, age 45
CFO: Andrew B. Cassidy, age 49, $282,562 pay
VP Information Systems: Edward A. Kremer, age 37
VP Medical Affairs: Frank N. Medici, age 59
VP Marketing and Communications: Jay L. Silverstein, age 35
VP Medical Delivery Systems: Thomas A. Travers, age 46
VP Human Resources: Jeanne D. Wisniewski, age 36
Auditors: KPMG Peat Marwick LLP

WHERE

HQ: 800 Connecticut Ave., Norwalk, CT 06854
Phone: 203-852-1442   **Fax:** 203-851-2464

WHAT

	1994 Sales	
	$ mil.	% of total
Freedom Plan	491.7	68
HMOs	112.4	16
Medicare	50.3	7
Medicaid	48.3	7
Third-party administration	10.9	1
Other	7.1	1
Total	**720.7**	**100**

KEY COMPETITORS

Aetna	MetLife
Blue Cross	New York Life
CIGNA	Physicians Health Services
Health Insurance of NY	Prudential
Healthsource	Travelers
John Hancock	U.S. Healthcare
M.D. Enterprises	Value Health

HOW MUCH

Nasdaq symbol: OXHP FY ends: December 31	Annual Growth	1989	1990	1991	1992	1993	1994
Sales ($ mil.)	74.1%	45.0	61.4	94.9	155.7	311.9	720.7
Net income ($ mil.)	—	(2.6)	1.6	4.7	8.0	14.9	27.9
Income as % of sales	—	—	2.6%	5.0%	5.1%	4.8%	3.9%
Earnings per share ($)	—	(0.17)	0.06	0.21	0.26	0.45	0.82
Stock price – high ($)	—	—	—	6.13	14.19	28.00	41.75
Stock price – low ($)	—	—	—	3.44	4.31	7.81	19.75
Stock price – close ($)	94.6%	—	—	5.38	14.13	26.50	39.63
P/E – high	—	—	—	30	55	62	51
P/E – low	—	—	—	17	17	17	24
Dividends per share ($)	—	—	—	0.00	0.00	0.00	0.00
Book value per share ($)	36.4%	—	—	1.57	2.17	2.92	3.99
Employees	94.9%	—	—	239	348	720	1,770

1994 Year-end:
Debt ratio: 0.0%
Return on equity: 25.6%
Cash (mil.): $191.1
Current ratio: 1.36
Long-term debt (mil.): $0.0
No. of shares (mil.): 31.8
Dividends
  Yield: —
  Payout: —
Market value (mil.): $1,261.1

ROBERTS PHARMACEUTICAL

OVERVIEW

Roberts Pharmaceutical markets postdiscovery drugs in a few selected medical areas. The company both licenses and acquires drugs, concentrating on therapeutic drugs in the cardiovascular, respiratory, gynecology, endocrinology, urology, oncology, and gastroenterology fields. Roberts has 2 other business segments: Homecare/Medical Products and Contract Clinical Research. The company markets drugs in Belgium, Canada, Ireland, Luxembourg, the Netherlands, the UK, and the US. Robert Vukovich (chairman, president, and CEO) owns 12.0% of the company's stock and Yamanouchi U.S.A. owns 27.2%.

The drug company was founded in 1983 and acquired its first license, to sell Amatine, in 1984. In 1988 it established Monmouth Pharmaceuticals in the UK. During 1990 Roberts went public and purchased US and Canadian rights to several nonprescription product lines from Upjohn. In 1991 the company acquired subsidiary IV Therapy Associates.

Roberts's strategy focuses on acquiring and developing pharmaceuticals in late-stage testing and acquiring already marketed prescription and nonprescription products that it feels have not been marketed to their potential. Recently acquired drugs include Tigan (antinausea), Eminase (blood clotter), and Noroxinn (for urinary tract infections).

In 1993 the company acquired rights from Bristol-Myers Squibb to a line of US and Canadian prescription and nonprescription products, including Colace/Peri-Colace and Squibb Mineral Oil and Cod Liver Oil. In 1994 Roberts agreed to acquire the US rights to sell Nitrodisc, a nitroglycerin skin patch made by G. D. Searle, and announced its expansion into France through its subsidiary Laboratoires Pharmaceutique Roberts. The company expects FDA approval in 1996 for Agrelin (high blood platelet treatment) and Pro-Amatine (low blood pressure drug.)

WHO

Chairman, President, and CEO: Robert A. Vukovich, age 51, $1,069,038 pay
VP, CFO, and Treasurer: Anthony P. Maris, age 61, $330,284 pay
VP and COO: Robert W. Loy, age 56, $252,458 pay
VP, General Counsel, and Secretary: Anthony A. Rascio, age 52, $136,100 pay
VP Marketing and Sales: Richard J. Caulfield
VP International Operations: Stuart Goss
VP Manufacturing: Moises Saporta
VP Developmental Therapeutics: Jerome Wilson
VP Administrative Services (HR): Laura J. DiMichele
Auditors: Coopers & Lybrand L.L.P.

WHERE

HQ: Roberts Pharmaceutical Corporation, Meridian Center II, 4 Industrial Way West, Eatontown, NJ 07724
Phone: 908-389-1182   **Fax:** 908-389-1014

WHAT

	1994 Sales	
	$ mil.	% of total
Sales	95.1	85
Contract research & other	17.1	15
Total	**112.2**	**100**

Selected Subsidiaries
Geriatric Pharmaceuticals
Infusion Specialists, Inc.
IV Therapy Associates
Laboratoires Pharmaceutique Roberts (France)
Mallard Pharmaceuticals
Monmouth Pharmaceuticals, Ltd.(UK)
Pronetics Healthcare, Inc.
Roberts Pharmaceutical Canada, Inc.
VRG International/NCRC

KEY COMPETITORS

Barr Labs	Copley	Pharmaceutical
Biocraft Labs	Pharmaceutical	Resources
BioCryst	Halsey Drug	Purepac
Pharmaceuticals	Hi-Tech	Watson
Caremark	Pharmacal	Pharmaceuticals
	Mylan Labs	Zenith Labs

HOW MUCH

Nasdaq symbol: RPCX FY ends: December 31	Annual Growth	1989	1990	1991	1992	1993	1994	1994 Year-end: Debt ratio: 17.9%
Sales ($ mil.)	103.7%	3.2	2.1	13.5	33.0	89.7	112.2	Return on equity: 7.8%
Net income ($ mil.)	—	—	(6.4)	(5.1)	(8.8)	7.2	19.4	Cash (mil.): $36.5
Income as % of sales	—	—	—	—	—	8.1%	17.3%	Current ratio: 1.78
Earnings per share ($)	—	—	(0.92)	(0.58)	(0.64)	0.46	1.04	Long-term debt (mil.): $22.4
Stock price – high ($)	—	—	8.00	33.00	36.75	42.50	40.00	No. of shares (mil.): 18.0
Stock price – low ($)	—	—	2.50	4.00	13.50	15.25	19.75	Dividends
Stock price – close ($)	62.4%	—	4.56	32.13	22.63	39.75	31.75	Yield: —
P/E – high	—	—	—	—	—	92	38	Payout: —
P/E – low	—	—	—	—	—	33	19	Market value (mil.): $569.6
Dividends per share ($)	—	—	0.00	0.00	0.00	0.00	0.00	R&D as % of sales: 8.5%
Book value per share ($)	93.3%	—	1.03	2.55	8.33	13.32	14.37	
Employees	62.6%	50	62	119	326	452	568	

ROBOTIC VISION SYSTEMS, INC.

OVERVIEW

Robotic Vision Systems, Inc. (RVSI), has an eye for detail. Actually, it has hundreds of them. The company is a leading manufacturer of 3D machine-based vision systems, which are used for quality control and precise measurements. Its core product is the LS Lead Scanning System, which can detect whether the tiny leads that run from a semiconductor are out of place. RVSI's products are used by IBM, Intel, and other major semiconductor makers. The company's vision systems products are also used by the US Navy to inspect propellers, and RVSI is developing an automated aircraft ice-detection system. General Motors owns 10.5% of the company.

RVSI was founded (as Solid Photography) in 1977 by Paul DiMatteo as a spinoff of Dynell Electronics. The company provided 3D images that were used to make portrait sculptures. In 1980 the company changed its name to Robotic Vision Systems and won a navy contract to provide propeller inspections for submarines. In 1984 RVSI signed a deal with General Motors to provide the car maker with automatic welding systems for its plants. That year DiMatteo left the company; he was succeeded by Pat Costa. By 1989 RVSI began posting a series of losses. In order to right itself, the company decided to concentrate on products for the semiconductor industry, selling its robotic welding systems business to Cybo Systems.

The company returned to profitability in 1992. RVSI also began to look for new uses for its vision system. In 1993 the company completed the initial development of its ID-1 aircraft ice-detection system, and in 1994 the FAA awarded RVSI a contract to continue developing and testing the system.

In 1995 RVSI acquired the machine-based vision firm Acuity Imaging, which more than doubled RVSI's sales.

WHO

Chairman, President, and CEO: Pat V. Costa, age 51, $212,702 pay
EVP: Steven J. Bilodeau, age 36, $170,260 pay
EVP, Secretary, and Treasurer: Robert H. Walker, age 59, $137,715 pay
SVP and Technical Director: Howard Stern, age 57, $143,787 pay
VP Electronics Group: Earl H. Rideout, age 48, $125,627 pay
VP New Product Development: William E. Yonescu, age 52
Director Human Resources: Pat Jennison
Auditors: Deloitte & Touche LLP

WHERE

HQ: 425 Rabro Dr. East, Hauppauge, NY 11788
Phone: 516-273-9700 **Fax:** 516-273-1167

	1995 Sales	
	$ mil.	% of total
Asia/Pacific Rim	34.0	54
North America	22.6	35
Europe	7.0	11
Total	**63.6**	**100**

WHAT

Products and Services
Ice-detection systems
Semiconductor lead inspection systems
Ship propeller inspection and machining

KEY COMPETITORS

Applied Intelligent Systems
Cognex
CyberOptics
Epix
KLA Instruments
Perceptron
Siemens
Synthetic Vision Systems
View Engineering

HOW MUCH

Nasdaq symbol: ROBV FY ends: September 30	Annual Growth	1990	1991	1992	1993	1994	1995
Sales ($ mil.)	41.3%	11.3	8.5	13.3	19.9	24.6	63.6
Net income ($ mil.)	—	(5.5)	(2.4)	0.2	1.6	3.1	10.0
Income as % of sales	—	—	—	1.7%	8.0%	12.6%	15.6%
Earnings per share ($)	—	(0.87)	(0.38)	0.03	0.14	0.24	0.61
Stock price – high ($)	—	4.25	1.88	1.75	5.75	8.13	27.75
Stock price – low ($)	—	1.13	0.44	0.50	1.25	4.38	5.50
Stock price – close ($)	74.3%	1.50	0.69	1.25	5.25	6.25	24.13
P/E – high	—	—	—	58	41	34	45
P/E – low	—	—	—	17	9	18	9
Dividends per share ($)	—	0.00	0.00	0.00	0.00	0.00	0.00
Book value per share ($)	101.8%	0.06	(4.53)	(2.97)	0.15	0.78	2.01
Employees	35.0%	66	79	87	109	128	302

1995 Year-end:
Debt ratio: —
Return on equity: 46.0%
Cash (mil.): —
Current ratio: —
Long-term debt (mil.): —
No. of shares (mil.): 15.9
Dividends
  Yield: —
  Payout: —
Market value (mil.): $383.4
R&D as % of sales: 15.2%

STANDARD MICROSYSTEMS

OVERVIEW

Standard Microsystems Corp. (SMC) wants to make PC networking easier and less expensive. The Hauppauge, New York–based company makes network interface cards that support such open technologies as "plug-and-play" and a variety of platforms, including ARCNET, Ethernet, FDDI, and Token Ring. VLSI (very large scale integrated) circuits manufactured by SMC are used for PC input/output control and LAN and industrial networking.

SMC was founded in 1971. (Paul Richman, one of the founding staff, is the chairman.) The company started supplying communications components in 1971 and built its business around computer peripheral–related chips, such as those used to design and make IBM's original PCs. After the semiconductor depression of 1985 and 1986 dragged down SMC's sales, Micron Technology bought a 14% stake in the company and tried to merge with it. Richman and other executives resisted the challenge, and Micron eventually sold its stake. In 1988 SMC laid off 10% of its work force and appointed a new CEO, Victor Trizzino (previously SMC's CFO). Under Trizzino the company expanded, buying Western Digital's LAN business, a move that doubled SMC's size, in 1991 and Sigma Network Systems, a high-end enterprise-switching hub maker, in 1992.

In 1994 SMC introduced upgraded software for its ES/1 EliteSwitch hubs. The following year it introduced the industry's first dual-channel PCI adapter card (for connecting peripherals) and products for Fast Ethernet networking.

In late 1995 Cabletron Systems agreed to pay $77.5 million for SMC's Enterprise Networks Business Unit, which makes LAN switches and wiring hubs. Difficulty selling and delivering the unit's products had hurt the company's bottom line, despite the success of its other units.

WHO

Chairman: Paul Richman, age 52, $773,000 pay
President and CEO: Victor F. Trizzino, age 54, $697,281 pay
EVP: Arthur Sidorsky, age 61, $481,000 pay
EVP: Gerald E. Gollub, age 52, $287,500 pay
VP Finance and CFO: Anthony M. D'Agostino, age 37, $263,606 pay
VP Human Resources: Ernest W. Sern
Auditors: Arthur Andersen & Co, SC

WHERE

HQ: Standard Microsystems Corporation, 80 Arkay Dr., Hauppauge, NY 11788
Phone: 516-435-6000   **Fax:** 516-273-5550

	1995 Sales
	% of total
US	53
Other countries	47
Total	**100**

WHAT

	1995 Sales	
	$ mil.	% of total
System products		
Network interface cards	206.1	54
Hubs and LAN switches	55.2	15
Component products	117.4	31
Total	**378.7**	**100**

Selected Products
Internetworking products	Support software
Network interface cards	VLSI circuits

KEY COMPETITORS

3Com	Chipcom	Novell
Apple	Cisco Systems	Olicom
Artisoft	Hewlett-Packard	Optical Data
Asanté	IBM	Systems
AT&T GIS	Madge	Oracle
Bay Networks	Microdyne	Proteon
Cabletron	Microsoft	Tandem
Cheyenne	Newbridge	Tech Data
Software	Networks	U.S. Robotics

HOW MUCH

Nasdaq symbol: SMSC FY ends: Last day in February	Annual Growth	1990	1991	1992	1993	1994	1995	1995 Year-end: Debt ratio: 0.0%
Sales ($ mil.)	37.4%	77.2	87.0	132.7	250.5	322.6	378.7	Return on equity: 15.2%
Net income ($ mil.)	38.8%	4.7	1.2	0.6	15.8	19.9	24.2	Cash (mil.): $29.5
Income as % of sales		6.1%	1.4%	0.5%	6.3%	6.2%	6.4%	Current ratio: 3.75
Earnings per share ($)	34.7%	0.41	0.10	0.05	1.27	1.52	1.82	Long-term debt (mil.): $0.0
Stock price – high ($)[1]	—	7.50	9.88	7.25	26.25	27.00	30.38	No. of shares (mil.): 13.2
Stock price – low ($)[1]	—	4.63	4.13	3.63	6.38	12.50	13.38	Dividends
Stock price – close ($)[1]	36.9%	6.25	5.00	6.63	26.00	21.50	30.00	Yield: —
P/E – high		18	99	145	21	18	17	Payout: —
P/E – low		11	41	73	5	8	7	Market value (mil.): $396.7
Dividends per share ($)	—	0.00	0.00	0.00	0.00	0.00	0.00	R&D as % of sales: 7.5%
Book value per share ($)	12.1%	7.43	7.65	7.71	9.50	11.18	13.16	
Employees	12.0%	488	454	605	649	728	861	

[1] Stock prices are for the prior calendar year.

TIFFANY & CO.

OVERVIEW

They say big presents come in small packages, and that's still true at Tiffany. But lately CEO William Chaney has been trying to get the word out that customers can get gifts costing $50 as well as $500,000 in the company's famous robin's-egg-blue boxes. While he has not forsaken Tiffany's image of glamour and exclusive clientele, Chaney has been looking to boost profits lately by broadening the company's appeal. Tiffany sells fine jewelry, timepieces, sterling silverware, china, crystal, and other fine gifts and accessories. It operates in over 80 stores and boutiques around the world, but nearly 20% of the company's sales come from its flagship store on Fifth Avenue. Japanese department store company Mitsukoshi owns 13.6% of Tiffany.

Charles Lewis Tiffany and John P. Young founded Tiffany in 1837 in New York as a stationery and fancy goods store. In 1845 the company introduced its first catalog. The firm built a reputation for quality and craftsmanship, particularly in silver and jewelry design. However, by the 1950s it had begun to lose money. In 1955 Walter Hoving was hired to rejuvenate the company. He held Tiffany's first clearance sale and introduced new designs. During the 1960s the company began adding stores across the US, and in the 1970s it moved into Japan. In 1979 Avon Products acquired the company, hurting Tiffany's reputation with the firm's exclusive clientele. In 1984 Chaney, an Avon executive, led an LBO of the company, and in 1987 Tiffany went public.

Chaney restored the luster to the company's image, but the recession in the early 1990s brought a drop in profits. He began a drive to attract more downscale customers, promoting the company's less-expensive items through heavy newspaper advertising. By 1995 profits had rebounded. Chaney plans to continue adding stores both in the US and abroad.

WHO

Chairman, President, and CEO: William R. Chaney, age 62, $839,692 pay
EVP: Michael J. Kowalski, age 43, $354,124 pay
EVP: James E. Quinn, age 43, $324,260 pay
SVP and Design Director: John R. Loring, age 55, $315,315 pay
SVP Merchandising: Jeanne B. Daniel, age 39, $229,544 pay
SVP Finance and CFO: James N. Fernandez, age 39
SVP, General Counsel, and Secretary: Patrick B. Dorsey, age 44
VP Human Resources: Michael H. Mitchell
Auditors: Coopers & Lybrand L.L.P.

WHERE

HQ: 727 Fifth Ave., New York, NY 10022
Phone: 212-755-8000 **Fax:** 212-605-4465

Tiffany operates in over 80 locations in Australia, Canada, Germany, Guam, Hong Kong, Italy, Japan, the Philippines, Singapore, South Korea, Switzerland, Taiwan, the UK, the United Arab Emirates, and the US.

WHAT

	1995 Sales
	% of total
Jewelry	67
Tableware	11
Timepieces	8
Other	14
Total	**100**

Merchandise

China	Stationery
Crystal	Sterling silverware
Fine jewelry	Ties
Fragrances	Timepieces
Leather goods	Writing instruments
Scarves	

KEY COMPETITORS

Dayton Hudson	Nordstrom
Harry Winston	Saks
LVHM	Van Cleef & Arpels
Neiman Marcus	

HOW MUCH

NYSE symbol: TIF FY ends: January 31	Annual Growth	1990	1991	1992	1993	1994	1995
Sales ($ mil.)	12.2%	384.0	455.7	491.9	486.4	566.5	682.8
Net income ($ mil.)	(2.5%)	33.3	36.7	31.8	15.7	(10.2)	29.3
Income as % of sales	—	8.7%	8.1%	6.5%	3.2%	—	4.3%
Earnings per share ($)	(2.8%)	2.13	2.34	2.01	1.00	(0.65)	1.85
Stock price – high ($)[1]	—	61.25	53.75	57.50	52.88	38.00	43.63
Stock price – low ($)[1]	—	26.00	27.50	32.63	22.63	24.13	28.50
Stock price – close ($)[1]	(3.6%)	46.75	35.38	45.25	34.63	31.88	39.00
P/E – high	—	29	23	29	53	—	24
P/E – low	—	12	12	16	23	—	15
Dividends per share ($)	10.5%	0.17	0.26	0.28	0.28	0.28	0.28
Book value per share ($)	9.7%	8.89	11.46	12.85	13.11	12.08	14.12
Employees	9.7%	2,085	2,379	2,735	2,865	3,133	3,306

1995 Year-end:
Debt ratio: 46.1%
Return on equity: 14.3%
Cash (mil.): $105.9
Current ratio: 2.40
Long-term debt (mil.): $129.1
No. of shares (mil.): 15.7
Dividends
  Yield: 0.7%
  Payout: 15.1%
Market value (mil.): $612.4

[1] Stock prices are for the prior calendar year.

TOWER AIR, INC.

OVERVIEW

With a remarkable ecumenical pragmatism, Tower Air transports business executives to Tel Aviv, pilgrims to Mecca, and US troops to war zones. The Jamaica, New York–based company's main business is long-haul scheduled passenger service from New York to 11 domestic and international locations, including Bombay, Los Angeles, São Paulo, and Tel Aviv. The Israel market is Tower's largest passenger revenue source (24% of the total). The company also provides commercial charter service to tour operators (18% of 1994 revenues) and charter service to the military (Tower helped fly US troops to and from Somalia in 1993).

Key to the company's growth strategy is its ability to tailor its services to appeal to the dominant group of passengers on each flight. The New York–Tel Aviv flight offers kosher meals and Israel-based flight attendants; Indian flights have India-based attendants; and the company's US flights offer low fares and no-frills service to stay competitive.

Originally a travel agency that developed into a tour packager and wholesaler and then a chartered aircraft tour operator, Tower Air was incorporated as an airline in 1982 by Morris Nachtomi and 3 other investors. The company began offering scheduled passenger services to Israel in 1983 on its one leased 747-100. Nachtomi, a 30-year veteran of Israel's state airline (El Al), became president in 1986 and chairman and CEO in 1989. He bought out his partners during the first 10 years of operation and took the company public in 1993. The Nachtomi Family Limited Partnership owns 77% of company stock.

By 1994 the company was operating 15 passenger 747s and 2 cargo 747s and had become the 3rd-busiest US carrier at JFK International Airport. In 1995 Tower added Rio de Janeiro as a new South American destination.

WHO

Chairman, President, and CEO: Morris K. Nachtomi, age 58, $1,000,000 pay
VP and CFO: Clinton V. Meserole III, age 51, $163,654 pay
VP Maintenance and Engineering: William J. Cain, age 38, $131,571 pay
VP Marketing: Christian A. Frankel, age 41, $126,531 pay
VP Operations: L. Nicholas Lacey, age 48, $113,000 pay
VP Aircraft Scheduling and Military Contracts: Mark T. Hayes, age 60
VP Marketing, Services, and Planning: Robert W. Mann Jr., age 41
Director Human Resources: Pamela Marett
Auditors: Ernst & Young LLP

WHERE

HQ: John F. Kennedy International Airport, Hangar #17, Jamaica, NY 11430-2478
Phone: 718-553-4300   **Fax:** 718-553-4312

WHAT

	1994 Sales	
	$ mil.	% of total
Scheduled services		
Passenger	206.6	56
Cargo	22.1	6
Nonscheduled services		
Commercial charters	67.2	18
Military charters	66.8	18
Other	5.3	2
Total	**368.0**	**100**

Flight Equipment	Owned	Leased
Boeing 747-100	7	2
Boeing 747-200	—	8
Total	**7**	**10**

KEY COMPETITORS

Aer Lingus	Delta
Air France	El Al
Air-India	KLM
AMR	Northwest Airlines
Atlantic Southeast Airlines	TWA
Atlas Air	UAL
British Airways	USAir
Continental Airlines	Varig

HOW MUCH

Nasdaq symbol: TOWR FY ends: December 31	Annual Growth	1989	1990	1991	1992	1993	1994
Sales ($ mil.)	21.1%	141.4	172.3	245.8	247.2	341.8	368.0
Net income ($ mil.)	(28.8%)	3.1	5.4	7.0	1.2	9.9	0.6
Income as % of sales	—	2.2%	3.1%	2.9%	0.5%	2.9%	0.2%
Earnings per share ($)	(45.1%)	—	0.44	0.57	0.10	0.78	0.04
Stock price – high ($)	—	—	—	—	—	16.00	17.75
Stock price – low ($)	—	—	—	—	—	13.00	6.75
Stock price – close ($)	(44.8%)	—	—	—	—	14.50	8.00
P/E – high	—	—	—	—	—	21	444
P/E – low	—	—	—	—	—	17	169
Dividends per share ($)	—	—	—	—	—	0.00	0.00
Book value per share ($)	(3.5%)	—	—	—	—	4.59	4.43
Employees	23.5%	475	432	551	850	1,176	1,367

1994 Year-end:
Debt ratio: 32.2%
Return on equity: 0.8%
Cash (mil.): $15.7
Current ratio: 0.59
Long-term debt (mil.): $21.1
No. of shares (mil.): 15.3
Dividends
  Yield: —
  Payout: —
Market value (mil.): $122.3

UNITED WASTE SYSTEMS, INC.

OVERVIEW

United Waste makes frequent pickups. Since its founding in 1989, the company has picked up 59 acquisitions, 10 in the first half of 1995 alone. One of the fastest-growing solid waste collection companies in the US, United Waste collects trash, hauls it to transfer stations, and disposes of it, often in its own landfills. It also has recycling and composting operations.

The company was founded by Bradley Jacobs, who had previously been an international trader and oil broker. From the beginning its strategy was to grow primarily through acquisitions. The company's growth was sped along by the passage of the Resource Conservation and Recovery Act in 1991, which imposed strict regulations on the design, construction, and operation of landfills and forced many mom-and-pop garbage companies out of business. These smaller companies sold out to companies like United Waste, which had deeper pockets, increasing the pace of industry consolidation. United Waste went public in 1992 to raise cash for further acquisitions. Jacobs owns 7.6% of the company.

United Waste's strategy is to concentrate on midsized cities and more sparsely populated areas (like Michigan's Upper Peninsula), where there is less competition from the mammoths of the industry. Emphasizing these markets allows the company to pick up operations for less money and charge higher fees because of the lack of pricing pressure. United Waste has also followed a strategy of vertical integration, acquiring a landfill in an area and then adding local collection services to maximize volume. The company has major market shares in northern Michigan and central Massachusetts. In 1995 it acquired Waste Systems Corp. and its affiliate, Wasteco, bringing United Waste significant market share in northern Iowa and southern Minnesota, including the Minneapolis-St. Paul area.

WHO

Chairman and CEO: Bradley S. Jacobs, age 38, $263,750 pay
VC, SVP, Chief Acquisition Officer, Treasurer, and Secretary: John N. Milne, age 36, $208,250 pay
President and COO: Edward T. Sheehan, age 52, $257,500 pay
EVP: Richard A. Volonino, age 52, $172,500 pay
CFO: Michael J. Nolan, age 34, $142,500 pay
Director Human Resources: Anna Petersen
Auditors: Ernst & Young LLP

WHERE

HQ: 4 Greenwich Office Park, Greenwich, CT 06830
Phone: 203-622-3131   **Fax:** 203-622-6080

	1994 Sales % of total
Traverse City, MI	26
Central Massachusetts	24
Upper Peninsula of Michigan	18
Grand Rapids, MI	14
Western Pennsylvania	11
South	7
Total	**100**

WHAT

	1994 Sales % of total
Collection operations	52
Landfill disposal fees	38
Waste reuse & reduction programs	4
Fees paid by municipalities	1
Other services	5
Total	**100**

KEY COMPETITORS

Browning-Ferris
Mid-American Waste
Sanifill
USA Waste Services

HOW MUCH

Nasdaq symbol: UWST FY ends: December 31	Annual Growth	1989	1990	1991	1992	1993	1994
Sales ($ mil.)	60.5%	10.0	9.2	13.5	26.5	77.5	106.6
Net income ($ mil.)	174.4%	0.1	(1.6)	(3.3)	0.2	10.0	15.6
Income as % of sales	—	0.5%	—	—	0.8%	12.9%	14.6%
Earnings per share ($)	—	—	—	(1.00)	(0.64)	0.98	1.24
Stock price – high ($)	—	—	—	—	13.00	17.00	25.50
Stock price – low ($)	—	—	—	—	11.75	9.25	14.75
Stock price – close ($)	42.9%	—	—	—	12.25	15.50	25.00
P/E – high	—	—	—	—	—	17	21
P/E – low	—	—	—	—	—	9	12
Dividends per share ($)	—	—	—	—	0.00	0.00	0.00
Book value per share ($)	16.0%	—	—	—	7.35	8.30	9.89
Employees	82.2%	—	—	—	367	825	1,218

1994 Year-end:
Debt ratio: 33.8%
Return on equity: 15.3%
Cash (mil.): $0.5
Current ratio: 0.77
Long-term debt (mil.): $57.7
No. of shares (mil.): 12.1
Dividends
   Yield: —
   Payout: —
Market value (mil.): $303.4

WATERHOUSE INVESTOR SERVICES, INC.

OVERVIEW

Waterhouse Investor Services is the US's 5th largest discount brokerage, offering its customers round-the-clock, low-priced execution of their orders. In 1995 the company opened Waterhouse National Bank, which, in addition to retail banking services, allows Waterhouse Investor to offer its customers a range of money management services, including cash management-type accounts, lines of credit, and credit cards.

The company was founded by Lawrence Waterhouse (who owns 22.6% of the company), a Chemical Bank employee turned financial advisor. After brokerage commissions were deregulated in 1975, he placed a small ad for discount brokerage in a newspaper. The response was gratifying, and he incorporated in 1979. The company grew in the hot market of the 1980s, opening offices outside New York, where competition was less intense. In 1987 its stock began trading, and it listed on the NYSE in 1992.

Part of the impetus for the company's development in the early 1990s as a hot stock in its own right was its practice of offering even deeper discounts for the purchase of its own stock. This helped drive up the company's stock price (as well as generate extra profits).

Waterhouse Investors has added a variety of new products to remain competitive, particularly against powerhouse Charles Schwab. One such line is a group of no-load mutual funds. It has also upgraded its services, opening a nationwide phone trading and quotation service. And despite a drop-off in trading activity in 1994, the company continued to expand, opening 12 offices in fiscal 1995.

The company benefited from the bull market of 1995, posting record profits for fiscal 1995. Waterhouse also announced the formation of new subsidiaries for transaction clearing and mutual fund management.

WHO

Chairman and CEO: Lawrence M. Waterhouse Jr., age 58, $1,154,000 pay
President and COO: Frank J. Petrilli, age 45, $403,000 pay
EVP, General Counsel, and Secretary: Richard H. Neiman, age 45, $310,000 pay
EVP and CFO: M. Bernard Siegel
SVP; President, Waterhouse Securities: John H. Chapel, age 43, $330,000 pay
SVP; EVP, Waterhouse Securities: Peter A. Wigger, age 48, $330,000 pay
SVP Human Resources, Waterhouse Securities: Karen L. Buck
Auditors: Price Waterhouse LLP

WHERE

HQ: 100 Wall St., New York, NY 10005
Phone: 212-806-3500   **Fax:** 212-809-0274

	1995 Offices
	No.
California	9
New York	7
Florida	5
New Jersey	4
Texas	4
Other states	43
Total	**72**

WHAT

	1995 Sales	
	$ mil.	% of total
Commissions & clearing fees	103.4	70
Interest	28.2	15
Mutual fund management	9.8	6
Other	1.6	9
Total	**143.0**	**100**

KEY COMPETITORS

Accutrade	Edward Jones	Piper Jaffray
Ceres Securities	Hoenig	Quick & Reilly
Charles Schwab	Merrill Lynch	Raymond James
Dean Witter,	M. H. Meyerson	Financial
Discover	Paine Webber	RKS Financial

HOW MUCH

NYSE symbol: WHO FY ends: August 31	Annual Growth	1990	1991	1992	1993	1994	1995	1995 Year-end:
Sales ($ mil.)	43.5%	23.5	31.4	55.6	84.2	107.6	143.0	Debt ratio: 56.9%
Net income ($ mil.)	72.2%	1.3	3.2	8.5	14.4	15.7	19.4	Return on equity: 33.3%
Income as % of sales	—	5.4%	10.1%	15.3%	17.0%	14.6%	13.5%	Cash (mil.): $117.2
Earnings per share ($)	66.6%	0.12	0.30	0.75	1.26	1.30	1.54	Current ratio: —
Stock price – high ($)	—	1.19	8.11	12.42	29.27	19.59	26.70	Long-term debt (mil.): $48.5
Stock price – low ($)	—	0.69	0.77	4.91	7.63	9.20	9.91	No. of shares (mil.): 11.4
Stock price – close ($)	93.8%	0.91	7.83	8.75	17.00	9.80	24.75	Dividends
P/E – high	—	10	27	17	23	15	17	Yield: 0.8%
P/E – low	—	6	3	7	6	7	6	Payout: 13.0%
Dividends per share ($)	38.0%	0.04	0.05	0.09	0.14	0.16	0.20	Market value (mil.): $283.3
Book value per share ($)	42.8%	0.98	1.12	1.86	3.12	4.34	5.83	Advertising as % of sales: 4.9%
Employees	29.8%	205	300	420	657	756	756	

XPEDITE SYSTEMS, INC.

OVERVIEW

An idle fax machine is Xpedite's workshop. The company is the #1 independent fax broadcasting service. Using Xpedite's high-tech fax broadcast system, a financial institution can send a notice of a change in interest rates, a PR firm can send a press release, or a trade organization can send a newsletter to hundreds of recipients simultaneously. The company also offers gateway messaging, which sends a document to a single recipient at each of a variety of destinations, including electronic mail systems, fax machines, and telex systems. For example, a hotel chain can send specific confirmation of reservations to a variety of customers. Insiders own 42% of the company's stock.

Xpedite was founded in 1988 by a group that was working to create a word processing communications program. CEO Roy Andersen, who had worked for Electronic Courier Systems and Western Union, joined the company that same year and redirected its focus toward fax broadcast. Xpedite unveiled its fax broadcast service in 1989, and the company grew rapidly as the fax machine became a more essential business tool. Between 1990 and 1994 the faxes it delivered rose from 5 million pages to 108 million pages.

In the beginning Xpedite focused on fax broadcasting, but in 1993 it expanded its gateway messaging business when it acquired hardware, software, and customer accounts from Pacific Telecom subsidiary TRT/FTC Communications. Xpedite went public in 1994.

Xpedite's rapid growth was fueled by the increasing popularity of the fax machine and by the company's aggressive sales force.

In 1995 the company introduced fax-on-demand. The service allows clients to store documents in Xpedite's computers. The documents can be accessed by the client's customers when they want information.

WHO

President and CEO: Roy B. Andersen Jr., age 46, $332,357 pay
VP Sales and Marketing: Max A. Slifer, age 47, $224,582 pay
VP Operations and Engineering: Dennis Schmaltz, age 47, $201,024 pay
VP Finance, CFO, and Secretary: Stuart S. Levy, age 53, $187,589 pay
Administration Manager (Personnel): Jane Droge
Auditors: Ernst & Young LLP

WHERE

HQ: 446 Hwy. 35, Eatontown, NJ 07724
Phone: 908-389-3900 **Fax:** 908-935-9667

WHAT

	1994 Sales	
	$ mil.	% of total
Fax broadcast	31.0	75
Gateway messaging	8.5	21
System sales & other	1.9	4
Total	**41.4**	**100**

Fax Broadcast
Single transmission to multiple recipients, for customers such as banks, finance companies, public relations firms, and investor relations groups

Gateway Messaging
Single document to single recipient at a variety of destinations, for customers such as hotel chains, airlines, cruise lines, and shipping companies

Fax-on-Demand
Single document to single recipient at recipient's request, for a variety of customers

KEY COMPETITORS

Ameritech	Newport
AT&T	Sprint
Cable & Wireless	Technology Solutions
Epigraphx	U S WEST
FaxLand	World Data Delivery
MCI	Systems

HOW MUCH

Nasdaq symbol: XPED FY ends: December 31	Annual Growth	1989	1990	1991	1992	1993	1994	1994 Year-end:
Sales ($ mil.)	94.9%	1.5	3.9	6.1	10.0	29.1	41.4	Debt ratio: 2.2%
Net income ($ mil.)	—	(3.2)	(3.3)	(1.6)	(0.5)	1.7	4.7	Return on equity: 43.2%
Income as % of sales	—	—	—	—	—	5.8%	11.4%	Cash (mil.): $10.3
Earnings per share ($)	108.8%	—	—	—	—	0.34	0.71	Current ratio: 3.28
Stock price – high ($)	—	—	—	—	—	—	22.75	Long-term debt (mil.): $0.0
Stock price – low ($)	—	—	—	—	—	—	12.00	No. of shares (mil.): 6.4
Stock price – close ($)	—	—	—	—	—	—	20.25	Dividends
P/E – high	—	—	—	—	—	—	32	Yield: —
P/E – low	—	—	—	—	—	—	17	Payout: —
Dividends per share ($)	—	—	—	—	—	—	0.00	Market value (mil.): $129.7
Book value per share ($)	—	—	—	—	—	—	4.23	R&D as % of sales: 6.8%
Employees	42.8%	—	57	—	—	173	245	

Key New York Companies

IIC INDUSTRIES INC.

420 Lexington Ave., Ste. 300
New York, NY 10170
Phone: 212-297-6132
Fax: 212-681-7431

CEO: Bernard Schreier
CFO: —
HR: —
Employees: 2,106

1994 Sales: $245.2 million
1-Yr. Sales Change: -2.2%
Exchange: Nasdaq (SC)
Symbol: IICR

Wholesale distribution - tractors & other heavy equipment, agricultural products, electrical equipment & consumer products

4 KIDS ENTERTAINMENT, INC.

1414 Avenue of the Americas
New York, NY 10019
Phone: 212-758-7666
Fax: 212-980-0933

CEO: Alfred R. Kahn
CFO: Joseph P. Garrity
HR: Tom O'Connor
Employees: 56

1994 Sales: $9.2 million
1-Yr. Sales Change: -15.6%
Exchange: Nasdaq
Symbol: KIDE

Product licensing services, including toys, games, food, toiletries, apparel & footwear

"21" INTERNATIONAL HOLDINGS, INC.

153 E. 53rd St., Ste. 5900
New York, NY 10022
Phone: 212-230-0400
Fax: 212-593-1363

CEO: Marshall S. Cogan
CFO: Robert H. Nelson
HR: Barry Zimmerman
Employees: 8,500

1994 Sales: $2,400 million
1-Yr. Sales Change: 41.2%
Ownership: Privately Held

Diversified operations - foam rubber (Foamex); auto interior parts & auto dealerships

A & J PRODUCE CORPORATION

138-144 NYC Terminal Market
New York, NY 10474
Phone: 718-589-7877
Fax: 718-378-1095

CEO: John Tramutola
CFO: —
HR: —
Employees: 167

1994 Sales: $190 million
1-Yr. Sales Change: 15.2%
Ownership: Privately Held

Fresh fruits & vegetables

A&E TELEVISION NETWORKS

235 E. 45th St.
New York, NY 10017
Phone: 212-661-4500
Fax: 212-210-1308

CEO: Nickolas Davatzes
CFO: Seymour Seylesser
HR: Marisa Famulare
Employees: 315

1994 Sales: $214.1 million
1-Yr. Sales Change: 22.9%
Ownership: Privately Held

Broadcasting - cable TV station

ABSOLUTE ENTERTAINMENT, INC.

10 Mountainview Rd., Ste. 300 South	CEO: Garry E. Kitchen	1994 Sales: $19 million
Upper Saddle River, NJ 07458	CFO: Sigurd C. Kirk	1-Yr. Sales Change: 52.0%
Phone: 201-818-4800	HR: Christine Galvin	Exchange: OTC
Fax: 201-818-3324	Employees: 44	Symbol: ABSO

Computers - interactive video game software (filed for Chapter 7 bankruptcy)

ACCLAIM ENTERTAINMENT, INC.

One Acclaim Plaza	CEO: Gregory Fischbach	1995 Sales: $566.7 million
Glen Cove, NY 11542	CFO: Anthony Williams	1-Yr. Sales Change: 17.9%
Phone: 516-656-5000	HR: John Ma	Exchange: Nasdaq
Fax: 516-656-2040	Employees: 800	Symbol: AKLM

Video game cartridges (WWF Raw, NFL Quarterback Club, The Simpsons), PC CD-ROM games (StarGate, Batman Forever) & comic books (Ninjak, Bloodshot)

 See page 252 for a full profile of this company.

ACETO CORPORATION

One Hollow Ln.	CEO: Arnold J. Frankel	1995 Sales: $164.8 million
Lake Success, NY 11042	CFO: Donald Horowitz	1-Yr. Sales Change: 10.0%
Phone: 516-627-6000	HR: Terry Steinberg	Exchange: Nasdaq
Fax: 516-627-6093	Employees: 100	Symbol: ACET

Chemicals - specialty for agricultural, health care, plastics & research industries

ACME UNITED CORPORATION

75 Kings Hwy. Cutoff	CEO: Walter Johnsen	1994 Sales: $53 million
Fairfield, CT 06430	CFO: Walter Bajda	1-Yr. Sales Change: 1.1%
Phone: 203-332-7330	HR: Ralph Mastrony	Exchange: AMEX
Fax: 203-576-0022	Employees: 561	Symbol: ACU

Housewares - scissors, shears, rulers, knives & first-aid kits for school, office & home; disposable medical scissors & instruments, dressings, germicides, wound-care products, IV products

ACTRADE INTERNATIONAL, LTD.

7 Penn Plaza, Ste. 422	CEO: Amos Aharoni	1995 Sales: $16.4 million
New York, NY 10001	CFO: Henry Seror	1-Yr. Sales Change: 35.5%
Phone: 212-563-1036	HR: Betty Melnik	Exchange: Nasdaq (SC)
Fax: 212-563-3271	Employees: —	Symbol: ACRT

Financial - international trade & finance, exporter of American products utilizing a package or grouping concept; financing purchases of international buyers

ACTV, INC.

1270 Avenue of the Americas, Ste. 2401	CEO: William C. Samuels	1994 Sales: $0.9 million
New York, NY 10020	CFO: Christopher C. Cline	1-Yr. Sales Change: 350.0%
Phone: 212-262-2570	HR: Denice Bloomer	Exchange: Nasdaq (SC)
Fax: 212-459-9548	Employees: 17	Symbol: IATV

Leisure & recreational products - interactive TV entertainment system

ADM TRONICS UNLIMITED, INC.

224 S. Pegasus Ave.	CEO: Alfonso DiMino	1995 Sales: $1.6 million
Northvale, NJ 07647	CFO: Andre DiMino	1-Yr. Sales Change: 14.3%
Phone: 201-767-6040	HR: Andre DiMino	Exchange: Nasdaq (SC)
Fax: 201-784-0620	Employees: 9	Symbol: ADMT

Chemicals - specialty, water-based primers & adhesives, coatings & resins

ADVANCE PUBLICATIONS, INC.

950 Fingerboard Rd.	CEO: Samuel I. "Si" Newhouse Jr.	1994 Sales: $4,690 million
Staten Island, NY 10305	CFO: Arthur Silverstein	1-Yr. Sales Change: 6.2%
Phone: 718-981-1234	HR: —	Ownership: Privately Held
Fax: 718-981-1415	Employees: 19,000	

Publishing - newspapers, books (Random House), magazines (Conde Nast); cable TV

 See pages 38–39 for a full profile of this company.

ADVANCED ORTHOPEDIC TECHNOLOGIES, INC.

151 Hempstead Turnpike	CEO: Andrews H. Meyers	1994 Sales: $13.2 million
West Hempstead, NY 11552	CFO: Jesse Z. Fink	1-Yr. Sales Change: 37.5%
Phone: 516-481-9670	HR: —	Exchange: Nasdaq (SC)
Fax: 516-481-3725	Employees: 125	Symbol: AOTI

Medical services - orthotic & prosthetic rehabilitation services

ADVANCED TECHNOLOGY MATERIALS, INC.

7 Commerce Dr.	CEO: Eugene G. Banucci	1994 Sales: $19.8 million
Danbury, CT 06810-4169	CFO: Daniel P. Sharkey	1-Yr. Sales Change: 92.2%
Phone: 203-794-1100	HR: Phyllis Banucci	Exchange: Nasdaq
Fax: 203-792-8040	Employees: 109	Symbol: ATMI

Industrial processing - diamond & silicon carbide semiconductors, chemical vapor deposition technology

ADVANCED VOICE TECHNOLOGY

639 Lexington Ave.
New York, NY 10017
Phone: 212-599-2062
Fax: 212-697-9236

CEO: Gwyeth Smith
CFO: Philip Brettschneider
HR: —
Employees: 15

1994 Sales: $0.7 million
1-Yr. Sales Change: —
Exchange: Nasdaq (SC)
Symbol: HMWK

Computers - hardware & software applications that allow teachers & school administrators to communicate with parents & students on a daily basis

AEA INVESTORS INC.

65 E. 55th St.
New York, NY 10022
Phone: 212-644-5900
Fax: 212-888-1459

CEO: Vincent A. Mai
CFO: Tom Salice
HR: Izzy Leizerowitz
Employees: 42

1995 Sales: —
1-Yr. Sales Change: —
Ownership: Privately Held

Financial - investment group (Caressa, Dal-Tile, Sola Group Ltd.)

THE AEGIS CONSUMER FUNDING GROUP, INC.

525 Washington Blvd.
Jersey City, NJ 07310
Phone: 201-418-7300
Fax: 201-418-7393

CEO: Angelo R. Appierto
CFO: Dina L. Penepent
HR: Kate Fitzpatrick
Employees: 130

1995 Sales: $17.8 million
1-Yr. Sales Change: 58.9%
Exchange: Nasdaq
Symbol: ACAR

Financial - consumer loans

AEP INDUSTRIES INC.

125 Phillips Ave.
South Hackensack, NJ 07606-1546
Phone: 201-641-6600
Fax: 201-807-2490

CEO: J. Brendan Barba
CFO: Paul M. Feeney
HR: Judy Lipman
Employees: 1,040

1995 Sales: $242.9 million
1-Yr. Sales Change: 31.5%
Exchange: Nasdaq
Symbol: AEPI

Chemicals - stretch films used to wrap & secure products on wooden pallets for shipping & industrial films for trash bags & other products

AFP IMAGING CORPORATION

250 Clearbrook Rd.
Elmsford, NY 10523
Phone: 914-592-6100
Fax: 914-592-6148

CEO: Donald Rabinovich
CFO: David Vozick
HR: Aida McKinney
Employees: 169

1995 Sales: $26.6 million
1-Yr. Sales Change: -12.8%
Exchange: Nasdaq (SC)
Symbol: AFPC

Electro/optical imaging equipment & supplies for medical/dental, industrial & graphic arts industries

AGP AND COMPANY INC.

530 Fifth Ave., 10th Fl.	CEO: Steven W. Bingaman	1994 Sales: $12.2 million
New York, NY 10036	CFO: Steven W. Bingaman	1-Yr. Sales Change: 1,009%
Phone: 212-302-0999	HR: —	Exchange: Nasdaq (SC)
Fax: 212-302-6161	Employees: 7	Symbol: AGPC

Financial - investment banking; manufacture & distribution of wedding & bridal accessories

AID AUTO STORES, INC.

275 Grand Blvd.	CEO: Philip L. Stephen	1994 Sales: $24.2 million
Westbury, NY 11590	CFO: James Mazzarella	1-Yr. Sales Change: -2.8%
Phone: 516-338-7889	HR: James Mazzarella	Exchange: Nasdaq (SC)
Fax: 516-338-7943	Employees: 113	Symbol: AIDA

Auto parts - retail, wholesale & franchisor

AIOC CORPORATION

230 Park Ave.	CEO: Alan Clingman	1994 Est. Sales: $3,500 mil.
New York, NY 10169	CFO: Don Nickbarg	1-Yr. Sales Change: 16.7%
Phone: 212-949-0600	HR: Phyllis Lee	Ownership: Privately Held
Fax: 212-599-0159	Employees: 450	

Metal products - trading

AIR & WATER TECHNOLOGIES CORPORATION

PO Box 1500	CEO: Claudio Elia	1995 Sales: $618.9 million
Somerville, NJ 08876	CFO: Alain Brunais	1-Yr. Sales Change: 18.4%
Phone: 908-685-4600	HR: Alan Simpson	Exchange: AMEX
Fax: 908-685-4050	Employees: 3,600	Symbol: AWT

Air & water pollution control systems

AIR EXPRESS INTERNATIONAL CORPORATION

120 Tokeneke Rd.	CEO: Guenter Rohrmann	1994 Sales: $997.4 million
Darien, CT 06820	CFO: Dennis M. Dolan	1-Yr. Sales Change: 37.4%
Phone: 203-655-7900	HR: Billie Raisides	Exchange: Nasdaq
Fax: 203-655-5779	Employees: 4,783	Symbol: AEIC

Transportation - air & sea freight forwarder

AJ CONTRACTING COMPANY

470 Park Ave. South	CEO: Charles Uribe	1994 Sales: $251 million
New York, NY 10016	CFO: James Capalino	1-Yr. Sales Change: 43.4%
Phone: 212-889-9100	HR: Ann Sue Mushmick	Ownership: Privately Held
Fax: 212-889-8889	Employees: 130	

Building - general contracting & construction management

A. L. PHARMA INC.

One Executive Dr., PO Box 1399	CEO: Einar W. Sissener	1994 Sales: $469.3 million
Fort Lee, NJ 07024	CFO: Jeffrey E. Smith	1-Yr. Sales Change: 16.5%
Phone: 201-947-7774	HR: Loraine Catarcio	Exchange: NYSE
Fax: 201-947-5541	Employees: 2,819	Symbol: ALO

Drugs - pharmaceuticals & animal-health products

ALCIDE CORPORATION

One Willard Rd.	CEO: Joseph A. Sasenick	1995 Sales: $9.2 million
Norwalk, CT 06851-4414	CFO: John P. Richards	1-Yr. Sales Change: 21.1%
Phone: 203-847-2555	HR: —	Exchange: Nasdaq
Fax: 203-846-3331	Employees: 11	Symbol: ALCD

Chemicals - specialty

ALEXANDER & ALEXANDER SERVICES INC.

1185 Avenue of the Americas	CEO: Frank G. Zarb	1994 Sales: $1,323.9 mil.
New York, NY 10036	CFO: Edward F. Kosnik	1-Yr. Sales Change: -1.3%
Phone: 212-840-8500	HR: Mark Schneiderman	Exchange: NYSE
Fax: 212-444-4559	Employees: 13,300	Symbol: AAL

Insurance - brokerage & management consulting

ALEXANDER'S, INC.

Park 80 West	CEO: Steven Roth	1994 Sales: $11.6 million
Saddle Brook, NJ 07663	CFO: Steven Santora	1-Yr. Sales Change: 107.1%
Phone: 201-587-8541	HR: —	Exchange: NYSE
Fax: 201-587-0061	Employees: 13	Symbol: ALX

Real estate development - property development on former sites of Alexander's retail stores

ALFIN, INC.

720 Fifth Ave.	CEO: Jean Farat	1995 Sales: $32.2 million
New York, NY 10019	CFO: Michael D. Ficke	1-Yr. Sales Change: 9.5%
Phone: 212-333-7700	HR: —	Exchange: AMEX
Fax: 212-246-7423	Employees: 129	Symbol: AFN

Fragances (Fracas, Bandit, Baghari, Cravache, Musk Blanc); cosmetics & other beauty products

ALLCITY INSURANCE COMPANY

122 Fifth Ave.	CEO: Andrew W. Attivissimo	1994 Sales: $107.3 million
New York, NY 10011	CFO: Robert Iacona	1-Yr. Sales Change: 13.4%
Phone: 212-387-3000	HR: James Boylan	Exchange: Nasdaq
Fax: 212-691-6374	Employees: 650	Symbol: ALCI

Insurance - property & casualty

ALLEGHANY CORPORATION

Park Avenue Plaza	CEO: John J. Burns Jr.	1994 Sales: $1,827.1 mil.
New York, NY 10055	CFO: Peter R. Sismondo	1-Yr. Sales Change: -4.3%
Phone: 212-752-1356	HR: —	Exchange: NYSE
Fax: 212-759-8149	Employees: 7,650	Symbol: Y

Financial - title insurance (#1 worldwide: Chicago Title and Trust) & financial services (Sacramento Savings Bank, Underwriters Reinsurance Co.); industrial minerals (World Minerals); heads & steel fastener distribution (Heads and Threads)

ALLEGHENY POWER SYSTEM, INC.

12 E. 49th St.	CEO: Klaus Bergman	1994 Sales: $2,451.7 mil.
New York, NY 10017-1028	CFO: Stanley I. Garnett II	1-Yr. Sales Change: 5.2%
Phone: 212-752-2121	HR: Richard J. Gagliardi	Exchange: NYSE
Fax: 212-836-4340	Employees: 6,061	Symbol: AYP

Utility - electric power

ALLEGRO NEW MEDIA, INC.

16 Passaic Ave., Unit 6	CEO: Barry A. Cinnamon	1994 Sales: $1 million
Fairfield, NJ 07004	CFO: Mark E. Leininger	1-Yr. Sales Change: 100.0%
Phone: 201-808-1992	HR: —	Exchange: Nasdaq
Fax: 201-808-2645	Employees: 30	Symbol: ANMI

Publishing - interactive how-to, business & instructional CD-ROMs (Learn To Do, Berlitz Executive Travel, Entrepreneur Magazine, Business Reference, InPrint Art Library)

ALLIANCE CAPITAL MANAGEMENT L.P.

1345 Avenue of the Americas	CEO: Dave H. Williams	1994 Sales: $601 million
New York, NY 10105	CFO: Robert H. Joseph Jr.	1-Yr. Sales Change: 20.3%
Phone: 212-969-1000	HR: Rosanne Peress	Exchange: NYSE
Fax: 212-969-2229	Employees: 1,461	Symbol: AC

Financial - investment management

ALLIANCE ENTERTAINMENT CORP.

110 E. 59th St.	CEO: Joseph J. Bianco	1994 Sales: $535.2 million
New York, NY 10022	CFO: Anil K. Narang	1-Yr. Sales Change: 166.9%
Phone: 212-750-2303	HR: Ken Butler	Exchange: NYSE
Fax: 212-935-6620	Employees: 1,426	Symbol: CDS

Leisure & recreational services - prerecorded music & entertainment-related products such as blank tapes, laser discs & licensed apparel

ALLIED BUILDING PRODUCTS CORPORATION

15 E. Union Ave.	CEO: Bob Feury	1994 Sales: $400 million
East Rutherford, NJ 07073	CFO: Jack Bickel	1-Yr. Sales Change: 6.7%
Phone: 201-507-8400	HR: —	Ownership: Privately Held
Fax: 201-507-3850	Employees: 1,000	

Building products - wholesale

ALLIED DEVICES CORPORATION

2365 Milburn Ave.	CEO: Mark Hopkinson	1994 Sales: $12.2 million
Baldwin, NY 11510-3321	CFO: P. K. Bartow	1-Yr. Sales Change: 14.0%
Phone: 516-223-9100	HR: Phyllis Paley	Exchange: Nasdaq (SC)
Fax: 800-338-4232	Employees: 160	Symbol: ALDV

Machinery - servo & drive-train assemblies, instrument-related fasteners, gears & gear products

ALLIED DIGITAL TECHNOLOGIES CORPORATION

15 Gilpin Ave.	CEO: George N. Fishman	1995 Sales: $115.4 million
Hauppauge, NY 11788	CFO: Charles P. Kavanagh	1-Yr. Sales Change: 85.2%
Phone: 516-234-0200	HR: Larry Henry	Exchange: AMEX
Fax: 516-234-0346	Employees: 1,500	Symbol: ADK

Business services - compact disc, analog & videocassette replication

ALLIEDSIGNAL INC.

101 Columbia Rd., PO Box 4000
Morristown, NJ 07962-2497
Phone: 201-455-2000
Fax: 201-455-4807

CEO: Lawrence A. Bossidy
CFO: Richard Wallman
HR: Donald J. Redlinger
Employees: 87,500

1994 Sales: $12,817 million
1-Yr. Sales Change: 8.4%
Exchange: NYSE
Symbol: ALD

Diversified operations - aerospace, automotive & engineered products

 See pages 40–41 for a full profile of this company.

ALLOU HEALTH & BEAUTY CARE, INC.

50 Emjay Blvd.
Brentwood, NY 11717
Phone: 516-273-4000
Fax: 516-273-5318

CEO: Victor Jacobs
CFO: David Shamilzadeh
HR: Kathy Calzente
Employees: 180

1995 Sales: $237.5 million
1-Yr. Sales Change: 15.6%
Exchange: AMEX
Symbol: ALU

Cosmetics & toiletries

ALL-PRO PRODUCTS, INC.

555 White Plain Rd.
Tarrytown, NY 10591
Phone: 914-631-9400
Fax: 914-631-9487

CEO: Lawrence Taylor
CFO: Michael Stone
HR: Sandra Vitelli
Employees: 20

1994 Sales: $1.8 million
1-Yr. Sales Change: —
Exchange: Nasdaq (SC)
Symbol: ALPROU

Computers - virtual reality games software; corrugated packaging systems

ALPHA HOSPITALITY CORPORATION

12 E. 49th St.
New York, NY 10017
Phone: 212-750-3500
Fax: 212-750-3508

CEO: Stanley S. Tollman
CFO: James A. Cutler
HR: Tom Damewood
Employees: 662

1994 Sales: $46.1 million
1-Yr. Sales Change: 5,022%
Exchange: Nasdaq (SC)
Symbol: ALHY

Casinos (Bayou Caddy's Jubilee Casino)

THE ALPINE GROUP, INC.

1790 Broadway
New York, NY 10019-1412
Phone: 212-757-3333
Fax: 212-757-3423

CEO: Steven S. Elbaum
CFO: David S. Aldridge
HR: Elaine McKee
Employees: 2,380

1995 Sales: $198.1 million
1-Yr. Sales Change: 189.2%
Exchange: AMEX
Symbol: AGI

Wire & cable products - copper wire & cable for the telecommunications industry; refractory products
for the iron, steel, aluminum & glass industries; data & electronic products

 See page 253 for a full profile of this company.

ALPINE LACE BRANDS, INC.

111 Dunnell Rd.	CEO: Carl T. Wolf	1994 Sales: $132.4 million
Maplewood, NJ 07040	CFO: Arthur Karmel	1-Yr. Sales Change: -26.7%
Phone: 201-378-8600	HR: Arthur Karmel	Exchange: Nasdaq
Fax: 201-378-8887	Employees: 136	Symbol: LACE

Food - cheeses (Alpine Lace) that are generally lower in sodium, fat & cholesterol than those made from whole milk

ALTEON, INC.

170 Williams Dr.	CEO: James J. Mauzey	1994 Sales: $1.8 million
Ramsey, NJ 07446-2907	CFO: Kenneth I. Moch	1-Yr. Sales Change: -14.3%
Phone: 201-934-5000	HR: Christina Blicharz	Exchange: Nasdaq
Fax: 201-934-8880	Employees: 74	Symbol: ALTN

Drugs - pharmaceutical R&D of theraputic & diagnostic products to treat complications of diabetes & aging

AMBAC INC.

One State St. Plaza	CEO: Phillip B. Lassiter	1994 Sales: $225 million
New York, NY 10004	CFO: Frank J. Bivona	1-Yr. Sales Change: -31.3%
Phone: 212-668-0340	HR: Janice A. Reals	Exchange: NYSE
Fax: 212-363-9049	Employees: 578	Symbol: ABK

Insurance - municipal bond insuror (AMBAC Indemnity, AMBAC Capital Management, AMBAC Financial Services, HCIA Inc.)

AMERADA HESS CORPORATION

1185 Avenue of the Americas	CEO: John B. Hess	1994 Sales: $6,698.8 mil.
New York, NY 10036	CFO: John Y. Schreyer	1-Yr. Sales Change: 14.1%
Phone: 212-997-8500	HR: Neal Gelfand	Exchange: NYSE
Fax: 212-536-8390	Employees: 9,858	Symbol: AHC

Oil & gas - US integrated

 See pages 42–43 for a full profile of this company.

AMEREX (USA) INCORPORATED

350 Fifth Ave.	CEO: Frederick R. Shvetz	1994 Sales: $110 million
New York, NY 10118	CFO: Stuart M. Cohen	1-Yr. Sales Change: 0.0%
Phone: 212-967-3330	HR: Karen Tombacher	Ownership: Privately Held
Fax: 212-499-9300	Employees: 200	

Apparel - men's, women's & children's outerwear & sportswear

AMERICAN BANKNOTE CORPORATION

51 W. 52nd St.	CEO: Morris Weissman	1994 Sales: $208.1 million
New York, NY 10019	CFO: John T. Gorman	1-Yr. Sales Change: 4.0%
Phone: 212-582-9200	HR: JoAnne O. Martinez	Exchange: NYSE
Fax: 212-582-9201	Employees: 2,155	Symbol: ABN

Printing - counterfeit-resistant documents, coupons, securities, holographic debit cards & lithographic undertints

AMERICAN BRANDS, INC.

1700 E. Putnam Ave., PO Box 811	CEO: Thomas C. Hays	1994 Sales: $13,146.5 mil.
Old Greenwich, CT 06870-0811	CFO: Dudley L. Bauerlein Jr.	1-Yr. Sales Change: -4.0%
Phone: 203-698-5000	HR: Steven C. Mendenhall	Exchange: NYSE
Fax: 203-637-2580	Employees: 34,820	Symbol: AMB

Diversified operations - liquor (Gilbey's, Jim Beam, Windsor Canadian); office products (ACCO, Swingline); golfing equipment (Titleist); locks (Master Lock)

 See pages 44–45 for a full profile of this company.

AMERICAN CLAIMS EVALUATION, INC.

One Jericho Plaza	CEO: Gary Gelman	1995 Sales: $5.4 million
Jericho, NY 11753-1635	CFO: Gary J. Knauer	1-Yr. Sales Change: -6.9%
Phone: 516-938-8000	HR: —	Exchange: Nasdaq
Fax: 516-938-0405	Employees: 67	Symbol: AMCE

Business services - insurance claim verification; vocational rehabilitation & disability management services (RPM Rehabilitation & Associates, Inc., American Rehabilitation Services, Inc.)

AMERICAN EXPRESS COMPANY

World Financial Center	CEO: Harvey Golub	1994 Sales: $14,282 million
New York, NY 10285	CFO: Michael P. Monaco	1-Yr. Sales Change: 0.8%
Phone: 212-640-2000	HR: Joseph W. Keilty	Exchange: NYSE
Fax: 212-619-9802	Employees: 72,412	Symbol: AXP

Financial - business services

 See pages 46–47 for a full profile of this company.

AMERICAN FUEL CORP.

8 W. 38th St., 10th Fl.	CEO: Robert Barra	1994 Sales: $0
New York, NY 10018	CFO: Elizabeth Buccigrossi	1-Yr. Sales Change: —
Phone: 212-302-7389	HR: —	Exchange: Nasdaq (SC)
Fax: 212-302-7837	Employees: 5	Symbol: COAL

Financial - funding for & development of coal properties

AMERICAN HOLDINGS, INC.

PO Box 74
Bedminster, NJ 07921
Phone: 908-234-9220
Fax: 908-234-9355

CEO: Paul O. Koether
CFO: John W. Galuchie Jr.
HR: —
Employees: 104

1994 Sales: $1.8 million
1-Yr. Sales Change: -87.7%
Exchange: Nasdaq
Symbol: HOLD

Real estate - manager of RTC properties

AMERICAN HOME PRODUCTS CORPORATION

5 Giralda Farms
Madison, NJ 07940-0874
Phone: 201-660-5000
Fax: 201-660-6048

CEO: John R. Stafford
CFO: John E. Considine
HR: Rene R. Lewin
Employees: 74,009

1994 Sales: $8,966.2 mil.
1-Yr. Sales Change: 8.0%
Exchange: NYSE
Symbol: AHP

Drugs & consumer health care products - pharmaceuticals (Anacin, Dristan, Chapstick, Centrum); canned food (Chef Boyardee); herbicides (acquired American Cyanamid Corp.)

 See pages 48–49 for a full profile of this company.

AMERICAN INTERNATIONAL GROUP, INC.

70 Pine St.
New York, NY 10270
Phone: 212-770-7000
Fax: 212-943-1125

CEO: Maurice R. Greenberg
CFO: Edward E. Matthews
HR: Axel I. Freudmann
Employees: 32,000

1994 Sales: $22,441.7 mil.
1-Yr. Sales Change: 11.5%
Exchange: NYSE
Symbol: AIG

Insurance - property & casualty

 See pages 50–51 for a full profile of this company.

AMERICAN INTERNATIONAL PETROLEUM CORPORATION

444 Madison Ave
New York, NY 10022-6102
Phone: 212-688-3333
Fax: 212-956-4917

CEO: George N. Faris
CFO: Denis J. Fitzpatrick
HR: Denis J. Fitzpatrick
Employees: 41

1994 Sales: $3.5 million
1-Yr. Sales Change: -12.5%
Exchange: Nasdaq
Symbol: AIPN

Oil & gas - US exploration & production

AMERICAN LIST CORPORATION

330 Old Country Rd.
Mineola, NY 11501
Phone: 516-248-6100
Fax: 516-248-6364

CEO: Martin Lerner
CFO: Martin Lerner
HR: —
Employees: 25

1995 Sales: $15.5 million
1-Yr. Sales Change: 23.0%
Exchange: AMEX
Symbol: AMZ

Business services - mailing lists of children & students throughout the country

AMERICAN LUNG ASSOCIATION

1740 Broadway	CEO: Jacqueline F. McLeod	1994 Sales: $35.6 million
New York, NY 10019-4374	CFO: Charles Toder	1-Yr. Sales Change: 1.4%
Phone: 212-315-8700	HR: Austin Brown	Ownership: Privately Held
Fax: 212-315-8641	Employees: 200	

Foundation - support for the prevention of tuberculosis, asthma, smoking-related illness & air pollution

AMERICAN MEDICAL ALERT CORP.

3265 Lawson Blvd.	CEO: Howard M. Siegel	1994 Sales: $5.4 million
Oceanside, NY 11572	CFO: Howard M. Siegel	1-Yr. Sales Change: 38.5%
Phone: 516-536-5850	HR: Howard M. Siegel	Exchange: Nasdaq (SC)
Fax: 516-536-5276	Employees: 75	Symbol: AMAC

Computers - emergency response services systems

AMERICAN MUSEUM OF NATURAL HISTORY

Central Park West at W. 79th St.	CEO: Ellen V. Futter	1994 Sales: $61.2 million
New York, NY 10024-5192	CFO: Charles H. Mott	1-Yr. Sales Change: 11.7%
Phone: 212-769-5100	HR: Richard MacKewice	Ownership: Privately Held
Fax: 212-769-5006	Employees: 750	

Natural history museum

AMERICAN NUKEM CORPORATION

1200 MacArthur Blvd.	CEO: Steve Beck	1994 Sales: $180 million
Mahwah, NJ 07430	CFO: Tony Horncastle	1-Yr. Sales Change: 0.0%
Phone: 201-818-0900	HR: —	Ownership: Privately Held
Fax: 201-818-0900	Employees: 2,000	

Refuse systems

AMERICAN REAL ESTATE PARTNERS, L.P.

100 S. Bedford Rd.	CEO: Carl C. Icahn	1994 Sales: $61.6 million
Mt. Kisco, NY 10549	CFO: John P. Saldarelli	1-Yr. Sales Change: 2.3%
Phone: 914-242-7700	HR: —	Exchange: NYSE
Fax: 914-242-9282	Employees: 17	Symbol: ACP

Real estate operations

AMERICAN RETAIL GROUP, INC.

1114 Avenue of the Americas
New York, NY 10036
Phone: 212-391-4141
Fax: 212-302-4381

CEO: Roland Brenninkmeyer
CFO: Jim Painter
HR: Tom Elliott
Employees: 17,000

1994 Sales: $2,120 million
1-Yr. Sales Change: 0.0%
Ownership: Privately Held

Retail - apparel (Byrons, EMS, Maurices, Miller's Outpost, Modern Woman, Steinbach, Uptons, Women's World)

AMERICAN STANDARD COMPANIES INC.

One Centennial Ave.
Piscataway, NJ 08855-6820
Phone: 908-980-6000
Fax: 908-980-6120

CEO: Emmanuel A. Kampouris
CFO: Fred A. Allardyce
HR: Adrian B. Deshotel
Employees: 38,500

1994 Sales: $4,457 million
1-Yr. Sales Change: 16.4%
Exchange: NYSE
Symbol: ASD

Building products - bathroom & kitchen fixtures & fittings; air conditioning systems; auto braking systems

 See pages 52–53 for a full profile of this company.

AMERICAN STOCK EXCHANGE, INC.

86 Trinity Place
New York, NY 10006-1881
Phone: 212-306-1000
Fax: 212-306-1644

CEO: Richard F. Syron
CFO: William D. Strauss
HR: Lee J. Murray
Employees: 708

1994 Sales: $143.6 million
1-Yr. Sales Change: 9.6%
Ownership: Privately Held

Stock exchange

AMERICAN TECHNICAL CERAMICS CORP.

17 Stepar Place
Huntington Station, NY 11746-2102
Phone: 516-547-5700
Fax: 516-547-5748

CEO: Victor Insetta
CFO: James Condon
HR: Susan Vignali
Employees: 429

1995 Sales: $28.6 million
1-Yr. Sales Change: 22.2%
Exchange: AMEX
Symbol: AMK

Electrical components - ceramic & porcelain capacitors

AMERICAN TOYS, INC.

448 W. 16th St.
New York, NY 10011
Phone: 212-391-2272
Fax: 212-391-4129

CEO: Ilan Arbel
CFO: Allean Goode
HR: Allean Goode
Employees: 317

1995 Sales: $25.5 million
1-Yr. Sales Change: 25.0%
Exchange: Nasdaq (SC)
Symbol: ATOY

Toys - children's & adult toys, games, bicycles & other sporting goods, electronic & video games, records & books

AMERIDATA TECHNOLOGIES, INC.

700 Canal St.	CEO: Gerald A. Poch	1994 Sales: $1,019 million
Stamford, CT 06902	CFO: John Harvatine	1-Yr. Sales Change: 363.8%
Phone: 203-357-1464	HR: Sharon Burglund	Exchange: NYSE
Fax: 203-357-1531	Employees: 2,100	Symbol: ADA

Computers - 18 computer hardware, software & service companies

 See page 254 for a full profile of this company.

AMERIFOODS COMPANIES

E. 80 Rte. 4	CEO: John Wilcha	1994 Sales: $210 million
Paramus, NJ 07652	CFO: —	1-Yr. Sales Change: 7.7%
Phone: 201-567-4700	HR: David Russell	Ownership: Privately Held
Fax: 201-712-0597	Employees: 1,500	

Food - bread, baking products & snacks

AMNEX, INC.

101 Park Ave., Ste. 2507	CEO: Peter M. Izzo Jr.	1994 Sales: $108.7 million
New York, NY 10178	CFO: Sharon Vanzant	1-Yr. Sales Change: 95.9%
Phone: 212-867-0166	HR: Missy Kessinger	Exchange: Nasdaq (SC)
Fax: 212-867-0092	Employees: 468	Symbol: AMXI

Telecommunications services - operator-assisted & direct-dial long distance telephone services

AMPACET CORPORATION

660 White Plains Rd.	CEO: David S. Weil	1994 Sales: $335 million
Tarrytown, NY 10591	CFO: Donald Fleischman	1-Yr. Sales Change: 6.3%
Phone: 914-631-6600	HR: Janet Segatti	Ownership: Privately Held
Fax: 914-631-7197	Employees: 665	

Chemicals - color concentrates for plastics

AMPAL-AMERICAN ISRAEL CORPORATION

1177 Avenue of the Americas	CEO: Lawrence Lefkowitz	1994 Sales: $80.9 million
New York, NY 10036	CFO: Alan L. Schaffer	1-Yr. Sales Change: 10.5%
Phone: 212-782-2100	HR: Alvia Miller	Exchange: AMEX
Fax: 212-782-2114	Employees: 3,294	Symbol: AISA

Financial - SBIC & commercial

AMPHENOL CORPORATION

358 Hall Ave.
Wallingford, CT 06492-7530
Phone: 203-265-8900
Fax: 203-265-8793

CEO: Lawrence J. DeGeorge
CFO: Edward G. Jepsen
HR: William Hough Jr.
Employees: 5,290

1994 Sales: $692.7 million
1-Yr. Sales Change: 14.7%
Exchange: NYSE
Symbol: APH

Electronic connectors & cabling systems

AMREP CORPORATION

641 Lexington Ave.
New York, NY 10022
Phone: 212-541-7300
Fax: 212-705-4740

CEO: Anthony B. Gliedman
CFO: Mohan Vachani
HR: Pat Bradley
Employees: 1,700

1995 Sales: $152.5 million
1-Yr. Sales Change: 20.9%
Exchange: NYSE
Symbol: AXR

Real estate development - single-family homes in Rio Rancho, NM & Denver, CO; publication
subscription fulfillment services; environmental & economic consulting & project management

ANADIGICS, INC.

35 Technology Dr.
Warren, NJ 07059
Phone: 908-668-5000
Fax: 908-668-5068

CEO: Ronald Rosenzweig
CFO: John F. Lyons
HR: Andrea Soster
Employees: 270

1994 Sales: $34.8 million
1-Yr. Sales Change: 20.0%
Exchange: Nasdaq
Symbol: ANAD

Electrical components - gallium arsenide semiconductors

ANDERSON, KILL, OLICK & OSHINSKY L.L.P.

1251 Avenue Of The Americas
New York, NY 10020
Phone: 212-278-1000
Fax: 212-278-1733

CEO: Thomas M. Murphy
CFO: —
HR: Patricia M. O'Brien
Employees: 616

1995 Sales: $83 million
1-Yr. Sales Change: -1.8%
Ownership: Privately Held

Law firm

ANDOVER TOGS, INC.

One Penn Plaza
New York, NY 10119
Phone: 212-244-0700
Fax: 212-239-0709

CEO: William L. Cohen
CFO: Alan Kanis
HR: Susan Rosenman
Employees: 1,300

1994 Sales: $73.8 million
1-Yr. Sales Change: -17.4%
Exchange: Nasdaq
Symbol: ATOG

Apparel - children's sportswear, including tops, dresses, warm-up suits & jeans

ANDREA ELECTRONICS CORPORATION

11-40 45th Rd.
Long Island City, NY 11101
Phone: 718-729-8500
Fax: 718-729-8500

Telecommunications equipment

CEO: Frank A. D. Andrea Jr.
CFO: Patrick Pilch
HR: Frank A. D. Andrea Jr.
Employees: 75

1994 Sales: $3.3 million
1-Yr. Sales Change: -49.2%
Exchange: AMEX
Symbol: AND

ANDREW SPORTS CLUB, INC.

1407 Broadway
New York, NY 10018
Phone: 212-764-6225
Fax: 212-840-3078

Apparel - clothing for women & children

CEO: Andrew Kirpalani
CFO: Andrew Kirpalani
HR: —
Employees: 85

1994 Sales: $110 million
1-Yr. Sales Change: 0.0%
Ownership: Privately Held

ANNTAYLOR STORES CORPORATION

142 W. 57th St.
New York, NY 10019
Phone: 212-541-3300
Fax: 212-541-3298

Retail - women's apparel, shoes & accessories

CEO: Sally Frame Kasaks
CFO: Paul E. Francis
HR: Gerri Feemster
Employees: 3,741

1995 Sales: $658.8 million
1-Yr. Sales Change: 31.3%
Exchange: NYSE
Symbol: ANN

A-P-A TRANSPORT CORPORATION

2100 88th St.
North Bergen, NJ 07047
Phone: 201-869-6600
Fax: 201-869-1017

Transportation - long-distance & local trucking

CEO: Armand Pohan
CFO: Fred Astle
HR: Joe Whelan
Employees: 1,800

1994 Sales: $160 million
1-Yr. Sales Change: 0.0%
Ownership: Privately Held

APOLLO ADVISORS

2 Manhattanville Rd.
Purchase, NY 10577
Phone: 914-694-8000
Fax: 914-694-8067

Financial - investment management

CEO: Leon Black
CFO: Tony Tortorelli
HR: —
Employees: 50

1995 Sales: —
1-Yr. Sales Change: —
Ownership: Privately Held

APPLIED GRAPHICS TECHNOLOGY, INC.

28 W. 23rd. St.
New York, NY 10010
Phone: 212-929-4111
Fax: 212-929-2787

Printing - prepress

CEO: Fred Drasner
CFO: Al Stoddart
HR: Bonni Rhodes
Employees: 1,500

1994 Sales: $220 million
1-Yr. Sales Change: 10.0%
Ownership: Privately Held

APPLIED MICROBIOLOGY INC.

771 Saw Mill River Rd.
Tarrytown, NY 10591
Phone: 914-347-5767
Fax: 914-347-6370

Biomedical & genetic products

CEO: Fredric D. Price
CFO: —
HR: —
Employees: 100

1995 Sales: $11.3 million
1-Yr. Sales Change: 76.6%
Exchange: Nasdaq
Symbol: AMBI

AQUARION COMPANY

835 Main St.
Bridgeport, CT 06601-2353
Phone: 203-335-2333
Fax: 203-337-5938

Utility - water supply

CEO: Richard K. Schmidt
CFO: Janet M. Hansen
HR: Charles V. Firlotte
Employees: 679

1994 Sales: $122 million
1-Yr. Sales Change: 13.6%
Exchange: NYSE
Symbol: WTR

ARIEL CORPORATION

433 River Rd.
Highland Park, NJ 08904
Phone: 908-249-2900
Fax: 908-249-2123

Computers - digital signal processing hardware & software

CEO: Anthony M. Agnello
CFO: Gerard E. "Rod" Dorsey
HR: —
Employees: 49

1994 Sales: $6.9 million
1-Yr. Sales Change: 19.0%
Exchange: Nasdaq (SC)
Symbol: ADSP

ARISTA INVESTORS CORP.

116 John St.
New York, NY 10038
Phone: 212-964-2150
Fax: 212-608-6473

Insurance - accident & health

CEO: Bernard Kooper
CFO: Susan J. Hall
HR: Peter Norton
Employees: 54

1994 Sales: $13.6 million
1-Yr. Sales Change: -37.3%
Exchange: Nasdaq (SC)
Symbol: ARINA

ARISTO INTERNATIONAL CORPORATION

152 W. 57th St., 29th Fl.
New York, NY 10019
Phone: 212-586-2400
Fax: 212-586-1652

CEO: Mouli Cohen
CFO: Ed Hughes
HR: Grace Russo
Employees: 10

1995 Sales: —
1-Yr. Sales Change: —
Exchange: Nasdaq (SC)
Symbol: ATSP

Computers - software tools, games & online multiplayer systems for the entertainment industry

ARISTOTLE CORPORATION

129 Church St., Ste. 810
New Haven, CT 06510
Phone: 203-867-4090
Fax: —

CEO: John J. Crawford
CFO: George H. Brooks-Gonyer
HR: —
Employees: 40

1994 Sales: $21.7 million
1-Yr. Sales Change: 294.5%
Exchange: Nasdaq
Symbol: ARTL

Financial - savings & loans

ARK RESTAURANTS CORP.

85 Fifth Ave.
New York, NY 10003-3019
Phone: 212-206-8800
Fax: 212-206-8845

CEO: Michael Weinstein
CFO: Andrew Kuruc
HR: Vincent Pascal
Employees: 1,797

1995 Sales: $73 million
1-Yr. Sales Change: 20.9%
Exchange: Nasdaq
Symbol: ARKR

Retail - restaurants in New York (An American Place, B. Smith's, Ernie's, Rodeo Bar), Boston, Florida & Washington, DC (Sequoia)

AROMAT CORPORATION

629 Central Ave.
New Providence, NJ 07974
Phone: 908-464-3550
Fax: 908-771-5658

CEO: Phil Yamamoto
CFO: Martin Sato
HR: Michael Gleason
Employees: 500

1995 Sales: $125 million
1-Yr. Sales Change: 19.0%
Ownership: Privately Held

Electronics - manufacturing relays & electronic equipment

ARROW ELECTRONICS, INC.

25 Hub Dr.
Melville, NY 11747
Phone: 516-391-1300
Fax: 516-391-1644

CEO: Stephen P. Kaufman
CFO: Robert E. Klatell
HR: Thomas Hallam
Employees: 6,500

1994 Sales: $4,649.2 mil.
1-Yr. Sales Change: 83.4%
Exchange: NYSE
Symbol: ARW

Electronics - parts distribution

 See pages 54–55 for a full profile of this company.

ARX, INC.

35 S. Service Rd.
Plainview, NY 11803
Phone: 516-694-6700
Fax: 516-752-5664

CEO: Harvey R. Blau
CFO: Michael Gorin
HR: Corrine Colombi
Employees: 670

1995 Sales: $71.1 million
1-Yr. Sales Change: 8.4%
Exchange: NYSE
Symbol: ARX

Electronics - mechanical & electronic components for military weapons, communications &
surveillance systems

ASARCO INCORPORATED

180 Maiden Ln.
New York, NY 10038
Phone: 212-510-2000
Fax: 212-510-1855

CEO: Richard de J. Osborne
CFO: Kevin R. Morano
HR: David B. Woodbury
Employees: 8,000

1994 Sales: $2,031.8 mil.
1-Yr. Sales Change: 17.0%
Exchange: NYSE
Symbol: AR

Metal ores - copper, lead, zinc, silver & gold mining

ASOMA CORPORATION

105 Corporate Park Dr.
White Plains, NY 10624
Phone: 914-251-5400
Fax: 914-251-1073

CEO: Colin H. Benjamin
CFO: Salvador Purpura
HR: Nancy Kovar
Employees: 55

1994 Sales: $200 million
1-Yr. Sales Change: 0.0%
Ownership: Privately Held

Metal products - steel trading

ASSOCIATED MERCHANDISING CORPORATION

1440 Broadway
New York, NY 10018
Phone: 212-596-4000
Fax: 212-575-2993

CEO: Zachary Solomon
CFO: Richard Kuznich
HR: —
Employees: 1,050

1994 Sales: $800 million
1-Yr. Sales Change: 8.1%
Ownership: Privately Held

Business Services - product development & sourcing for private-label merchandise

ASSOCIATED PRESS

50 Rockefeller Plaza
New York, NY 10020
Phone: 212-621-1500
Fax: 212-621-5447

CEO: Louis D. Boccardi
CFO: Patrick O'Brien
HR: James Donna
Employees: 3,150

1994 Sales: $406 million
1-Yr. Sales Change: 6.3%
Ownership: Privately Held

Business services - news, photos, graphics, photo technology, information & satellite services

ASTORIA FINANCIAL CORPORATION

One Astoria Federal Plaza
Lake Success, NY 11042-1085
Phone: 516-327-3000
Fax: 516-327-7610

Financial - savings & loans

CEO: George L. Engelke Jr.
CFO: Monte N. Redman
HR: Rhoda Baisi
Employees: 836

1994 Sales: $307.6 million
1-Yr. Sales Change: 12.5%
Exchange: Nasdaq
Symbol: ASFC

ASTROSYSTEMS, INC.

6 Nevada Dr.
Lake Success, NY 11042
Phone: 516-328-1600
Fax: 516-328-1658

CEO: Seymour Barth
CFO: Gilbert H. Steinberg
HR: Ann Mulvey
Employees: 151

1995 Sales: $12.3 million
1-Yr. Sales Change: -8.2%
Exchange: Nasdaq
Symbol: ASTR

Instruments power conversion devices & electronic products for measurement & display

ATALANTA CORPORATION

Atalanta Plaza
Elizabeth, NJ 07206
Phone: 908-351-8000
Fax: 908-351-0761

Food - importer

CEO: George Gellert
CFO: Tim Davies
HR: Conrad Uy
Employees: 200

1994 Sales: $250 million
1-Yr. Sales Change: 0.0%
Ownership: Privately Held

ATALANTA/SOSNOFF CAPITAL CORPORATION

101 Park Ave.
New York, NY 10178-0695
Phone: 212-867-5000
Fax: 212-922-1820

CEO: Martin T. Sosnoff
CFO: Anthony G. Miller
HR: Toni Sosnoff
Employees: 47

1994 Sales: $17.4 million
1-Yr. Sales Change: 8.1%
Exchange: NYSE
Symbol: ATL

Financial - investment management, brokerage & related services

AT&T CAPITAL CORPORATION

44 Whippany Rd.
Morristown, NJ 07962-1983
Phone: 201-397-3000
Fax: 201-397-3240

CEO: Thomas C. Wajnert
CFO: Edward M. Dwyer
HR: Sara R. McAuley
Employees: 2,700

1994 Sales: $1,384 million
1-Yr. Sales Change: 1.8%
Exchange: NYSE
Symbol: TCC

Financial - equipment leasing & finance

AT&T CORP.

32 Avenue of the Americas
New York, NY 10013-2412
Phone: 212-387-5400
Fax: 212-841-4715

CEO: Robert E. Allen
CFO: Richard W. Miller
HR: Harold W. Burlingame
Employees: 304,500

1994 Sales: $75,094 million
1-Yr. Sales Change: 11.8%
Exchange: NYSE
Symbol: T

Telecommunications services - long-distance carrier (#1 in US); telecommunications equipment; credit cards (Universal); cellular (McCaw); online service (Interchange Network)

 See pages 56–57 for a full profile of this company.

AT&T SYSTEMS AND TECHNOLOGY

32 Avenue of the Americas
New York, NY 10013-2412
Phone: 212-387-5400
Fax: 212-841-4715

CEO: Henry B. Schacht
CFO: Donald K. Peterson
HR: —
Employees: 76,125

1994 Sales: $21,161 million
1-Yr. Sales Change: 18.1%
Ownership: Division

Telecommunications equipment - private branch exchanges (PBXs); voice processing systems & voice messaging systems; video conferencing systems (division of AT&T Corp.)

 See pages 58–59 for a full profile of this company.

ATC ENVIRONMENTAL INC.

104 E. 25th St., 10th Fl.
New York, NY 10010-2917
Phone: 212-353-8280
Fax: 212-353-8306

CEO: Morry F. Rubin
CFO: Richard Pruitt
HR: —
Employees: 632

1995 Sales: $36.3 million
1-Yr. Sales Change: 36.0%
Exchange: Nasdaq (SC)
Symbol: ATCE

Pollution control - assessment, monitoring, training, analytical & management services for environmental projects

ATLANTIC MARKETING FORCES, INC.

270 G. Duffy Ave.
Hicksville, NY 11801
Phone: 516-931-6200
Fax: 516-931-6349

CEO: Robert D. Petersen
CFO: —
HR: —
Employees: 30

1994 Sales: $115 million
1-Yr. Sales Change: 0.0%
Ownership: Privately Held

Food broker

AUDIOVOX CORPORATION

150 Marcus Blvd.
Hauppauge, NY 11788
Phone: 516-231-7750
Fax: 516-231-2968

CEO: John J. Shalam
CFO: Charles M. Stoehr
HR: Liz O'Connell
Employees: 1,107

1994 Sales: $486.4 million
1-Yr. Sales Change: 25.0%
Exchange: AMEX
Symbol: VOX

Auto parts - retailer of sound, cellular & electronic equipment

AUDITS AND SURVEYS WORLDWIDE, INC.

650 Avenue of the Americas	CEO: Solomon Dutka	1994 Sales: $43.9 million
New York, NY 10011	CFO: Allan Ritter	1-Yr. Sales Change: 9.2%
Phone: 212-627-9700	HR: Kathy Murphy	Exchange: AMEX
Fax: 212-627-2034	Employees: —	Symbol: ASW

Business services - services & information to commercial, industrial, institutional & academic clients used in the development of marketing, advertising & investment strategies

AUTOINFO, INC.

1600 Rte. 208	CEO: Scott Zecher	1995 Sales: $4.8 million
Fair Lawn, NJ 07410	CFO: William I. Wunderlich	1-Yr. Sales Change: -76.7%
Phone: 201-703-0500	HR: —	Exchange: Nasdaq
Fax: 201-703-1777	Employees: 7	Symbol: AUTO

Telecommunications services - long-distance telephone communications services to approximately 2,000 customers throughout the US at discounted rates

AUTOMATIC DATA PROCESSING, INC.

One ADP Blvd.	CEO: Josh S. Weston	1995 Sales: $2,893.7 mil.
Roseland, NJ 07068-1728	CFO: Fred D. Anderson Jr.	1-Yr. Sales Change: 17.2%
Phone: 201-994-5000	HR: Michael R. Holmes	Exchange: NYSE
Fax: 201-994-5387	Employees: 25,000	Symbol: AUD

Business services - computing services, payroll & online information, employer, brokerage, dealer & claims services

AUTOTOTE CORPORATION

888 Seventh Ave.	CEO: A. Lorne Weil	1995 Sales: $153.2 million
New York, NY 10106-1894	CFO: Thomas C. DeFazio	1-Yr. Sales Change: 2.7%
Phone: 212-541-6440	HR: Cathy Angle	Exchange: Nasdaq
Fax: 212-754-2372	Employees: 1,070	Symbol: TOTE

Gambling equipment - computerized pari-mutuel wagering systems for racetracks

AVALON PROPERTIES, INC.

11 Burtis Ave.	CEO: Richard L. Michaux	1994 Sales: $74.3 million
New Canaan, CT 06840-5504	CFO: Thomas J. Sargeant	1-Yr. Sales Change: 25.3%
Phone: 203-972-4000	HR: —	Exchange: NYSE
Fax: 203-966-8438	Employees: 600	Symbol: AVN

Real estate investment trust

AVIS, INC.

900 Old Country Rd.
Garden City, NY 11530
Phone: 516-222-3000
Fax: 516-222-4381

Leasing - autos

CEO: Joseph V. Vittoria
CFO: Lawrence Ferezy
HR: Donald L. Korn
Employees: 12,800

1995 Sales: $1,700 million
1-Yr. Sales Change: 21.4%
Ownership: Privately Held

AVITAR, INC.

556 Washington Ave., Ste. 202
North Haven, CT 06473
Phone: 203-234-7737
Fax: 203-234-0199

Health maintenance organization

CEO: Douglas W. Scott
CFO: Jay C. Leatherman
HR: —
Employees: 23

1994 Sales: $1.5 million
1-Yr. Sales Change: 275.0%
Exchange: Nasdaq (SC)
Symbol: AVIT

AVNET, INC.

80 Cutter Mill Rd.
Great Neck, NY 11021-3107
Phone: 516-466-7000
Fax: 516-466-1203

CEO: Leon Machiz
CFO: Raymond Sadowski
HR: Robert Zierk
Employees: 9,000

1995 Sales: $4,300 million
1-Yr. Sales Change: 21.2%
Exchange: NYSE
Symbol: AVT

Electronic part & computer product distribution for industrial & military customers; TV & audio
equipment manufacturing

 See pages 60–61 for a full profile of this company.

AVON PRODUCTS, INC.

9 W. 57th St.
New York, NY 10019-2683
Phone: 212-546-6015
Fax: 212-546-6136

CEO: James E. Preston
CFO: Edwina D. Woodbury
HR: Marcia L. Worthing
Employees: 30,400

1994 Sales: $4,266.5 mil.
1-Yr. Sales Change: 6.5%
Exchange: NYSE
Symbol: AVP

Cosmetics & toiletries

 See pages 62–63 for a full profile of this company.

BAKER & TAYLOR INC.

300 First Stamford Place
Stamford, CT 06902
Phone: 203-462-7000
Fax: 203-961-8343

Wholesale - books, videos & software

CEO: Craig M. Richards
CFO: Edward H. Gross
HR: Jeanne P. Rudell
Employees: 2,200

1995 Est. Sales: $785 mil.
1-Yr. Sales Change: -1.9%
Ownership: Privately Held

BALCHEM CORPORATION

PO Box 175, Rts. 6 & 284
Slate Hill, NY 10973
Phone: 914-355-2861
Fax: 914-355-6314

Chemicals - specialty

CEO: Herb Weiss
CFO: Herb Weiss
HR: Larry Brest
Employees: 97

1994 Sales: $18.9 million
1-Yr. Sales Change: 28.6%
Exchange: AMEX
Symbol: BCP

BALDWIN TECHNOLOGY COMPANY, INC.

65 Rowayton Ave.
Rowayton, CT 06853
Phone: 203-838-7470
Fax: 203-359-8631

CEO: Wendell M. Smith
CFO: William J. Lauricella
HR: Helen Mitchell
Employees: 1,055

1995 Sales: $222.3 million
1-Yr. Sales Change: 12.2%
Exchange: AMEX
Symbol: BLD

Machinery - material handling, accessory, control & prepress equipment for the printing industry

BALTEK CORPORATION

10 Fairway Ct., PO Box 195
Northvale, NJ 07647-0195
Phone: 201-767-1400
Fax: 201-387-6631

Building products - wood

CEO: Jacques Kohn
CFO: Benson J. Zeikowitz
HR: —
Employees: 1,065

1994 Sales: $40.1 million
1-Yr. Sales Change: 23.8%
Exchange: Nasdaq
Symbol: BTEK

BANCORP CONNECTICUT, INC.

121 Main St.
Southington, CT 06489
Phone: 203-628-0351
Fax: 203-276-9429

CEO: Robert D. Morton
CFO: Anthony Priore Jr.
HR: Donna M. Schaefer
Employees: 130

1994 Sales: $24.2 million
1-Yr. Sales Change: -2.0%
Exchange: Nasdaq
Symbol: BKCT

Financial - savings & loans (Southington Savings Bank)

BANFI PRODUCTS CORPORATION

1111 Cedar Swamp Rd.
New York, NY 11545
Phone: 516-626-9200
Fax: 516-626-6282

Beverages - wine & sherry

CEO: John Mariani
CFO: Vincent Aprigliano
HR: Judi Rifkin
Employees: 200

1994 Sales: $175 million
1-Yr. Sales Change: 0.0%
Ownership: Privately Held

THE BANK OF NEW YORK COMPANY, INC.

48 Wall St.
New York, NY 10286
Phone: 212-495-1784
Fax: 212-495-1398

Banks - Northeast

CEO: J. Carter Bacot
CFO: Deno D. Papageorge
HR: Frank L. Peterson
Employees: 15,477

1994 Sales: $4,251 million
1-Yr. Sales Change: 11.2%
Exchange: NYSE
Symbol: BK

 See pages 64–65 for a full profile of this company.

THE BANK OF SOUTHINGTON

130 N. Main St.
Southington, CT 06489-0670
Phone: 203-620-5000
Fax: 203-620-5288

Banks - Northeast

CEO: Bryan P. Bowerman
CFO: Peter Pfau
HR: Peter Pfau
Employees: 50

1994 Sales: $7.8 million
1-Yr. Sales Change: 20.0%
Exchange: AMEX
Symbol: BSO

BANKERS CORP.

210 Smith St.
Perth Amboy, NJ 08861
Phone: 908-442-4100
Fax: 908-442-9570

Banks - Northeast

CEO: Joseph P. Gemmell
CFO: Howard S. Garfield II
HR: Francine R. Thomas
Employees: 351

1994 Sales: $108.3 million
1-Yr. Sales Change: 3.2%
Exchange: Nasdaq
Symbol: BKCO

BANKERS TRUST NEW YORK CORPORATION

280 Park Ave.
New York, NY 10017
Phone: 212-250-2500
Fax: 212-454-1704

Banks - money center

CEO: Frank Newman
CFO: Timothy T. Yates
HR: Mark Bieler
Employees: 14,529

1994 Sales: $7,503 million
1-Yr. Sales Change: -3.8%
Exchange: NYSE
Symbol: BT

 See pages 66–67 for a full profile of this company.

BARNES & NOBLE, INC.

122 Fifth Ave.
New York, NY 10011-5605
Phone: 212-633-3300
Fax: 212-675-0413

CEO: Leonard Riggio
CFO: Richard Daniel
HR: Don Lapp
Employees: 23,500

1995 Sales: $1,622.7 mil.
1-Yr. Sales Change: 21.3%
Exchange: NYSE
Symbol: BKS

Retail - book retailer (#1 in US) operating superstores (Barnes & Noble, Bookstop, Bookstar) & mall stores (B. Dalton, Doubleday, Scribner's)

BARNEYS NEW YORK

106 Seventh Ave.
New York, NY 10011
Phone: 212-593-7800
Fax: 212-886-1767

Retail - apparel

CEO: Gene Pressman
CFO: Irvin Rosenthal
HR: Janice Cartwright
Employees: 2,200

1994 Est. Sales: $500 mil.
1-Yr. Sales Change: 17.6%
Ownership: Privately Held

BARR LABORATORIES, INC.

2 Quaker Rd., PO Box 2900
Pomona, NY 10970-0519
Phone: 914-362-1100
Fax: 914-353-3476

Drugs - generic pharmaceuticals

CEO: Bruce L. Downey
CFO: Paul M. Bisaro
HR: Catherine F. Higgins
Employees: 357

1995 Sales: $199.7 million
1-Yr. Sales Change: 83.0%
Exchange: AMEX
Symbol: BRL

BARRINGER TECHNOLOGIES INC.

219 South St.
New Providence, NJ 07974
Phone: 908-665-8200
Fax: 908-665-8298

Pollution control - environmental monitoring & radon gas detection systems, geochemical analysis & image processing

CEO: Stanley S. Binder
CFO: Richard S. Rosenfield
HR: —
Employees: 56

1994 Sales: $11.9 million
1-Yr. Sales Change: -10.5%
Exchange: Nasdaq (SC)
Symbol: BARR

BAY RIDGE BANCORP, INC.

7500 Fifth Ave.
New York, NY 11209
Phone: 718-745-6100
Fax: 718-680-7034

Banks - Northeast

CEO: Donald A. Cordano
CFO: Tormey J. Santolli
HR: Frank Dellacamera
Employees: 117

1994 Sales: $40.5 million
1-Yr. Sales Change: 1.8%
Exchange: Nasdaq
Symbol: BRBC

BAYSIDE FUEL OIL DEPOT CORPORATION

1776 Shore Pkwy.
New York, NY 11214
Phone: 718-372-9800
Fax: 718-266-3744

Oil & gas - wholesale petroleum bulk station & terminal

CEO: Alfred Allegretti
CFO: Alfred Allegretti
HR: —
Employees: 285

1994 Sales: $135 million
1-Yr. Sales Change: 0.0%
Ownership: Privately Held

BCAM INTERNATIONAL

1800 Walt Whitman Rd.
Melville, NY 11747
Phone: 516-752-3550
Fax: 516-752-3550

CEO: Michael Stauss
CFO: Daniel Benjamin
HR: Mike Cataro
Employees: 14

1994 Sales: $1.3 million
1-Yr. Sales Change: -7.1%
Exchange: Nasdaq (SC)
Symbol: BCAM

Engineering - biomechanical & ergonomic design services

THE BEAR STEARNS COMPANIES INC.

245 Park Ave.
New York, NY 10167
Phone: 212-272-2000
Fax: 212-272-8239

CEO: James E. Cayne
CFO: William J. Montgoris
HR: Stephen A. Lacoff
Employees: 7,481

1995 Sales: $3,753.6 mil.
1-Yr. Sales Change: 9.1%
Exchange: NYSE
Symbol: BSC

Financial - investment bankers

 See pages 68–69 for a full profile of this company.

BECTON, DICKINSON AND COMPANY

One Becton Dr.
Franklin Lakes, NJ 07417-1880
Phone: 201-847-6800
Fax: 201-847-6475

CEO: Clateo Castellini
CFO: Edward J. Ludwig
HR: Rosemary Mede
Employees: 18,600

1995 Sales: $2,712.5 mil.
1-Yr. Sales Change: 6.0%
Exchange: NYSE
Symbol: BDX

Medical supplies - needles, syringes, IVs & diagnostic equipment

BED BATH & BEYOND INC.

715 Morris Ave.
Springfield, NJ 07081
Phone: 201-379-1520
Fax: 201-379-1731

CEO: Leonard Feinstein
CFO: Ronald Curwin
HR: Wayne Sarrow
Employees: 4,100

1995 Sales: $440.3 million
1-Yr. Sales Change: 44.0%
Exchange: Nasdaq
Symbol. BBBY

Retail - bed, bath, kitchen & other household furnishings

 See page 255 for a full profile of this company.

BEECHWOOD DATA SYSTEMS

100 Walnut Ave.
Clark, NJ 07066
Phone: 908-382-5400
Fax: 908-382-5575

CEO: Donald Rankin
CFO: Bob Mayes
HR: Sandy Swanson
Employees: 184

1994 Sales: $17 million
1-Yr. Sales Change: 142.9%
Ownership: Privately Held

Computers - analysis, software & training services for the telecommunications industry

BEL FUSE INC.

198 Van Vorst St.
Jersey City, NJ 07302
Phone: 201-432-0463
Fax: 201-432-9542

Electrical components

CEO: Elliot Bernstein
CFO: Colin Dunn
HR: Miriam Martinez
Employees: 707

1994 Sales: $45.7 million
1-Yr. Sales Change: -3.8%
Exchange: Nasdaq
Symbol: BELF

BELL COMMUNICATIONS RESEARCH INC.

445 South St.
Morristown, NJ 07960-6438
Phone: 201-740-3000
Fax: 201-740-6877

CEO: George H. Heilmeier
CFO: Edward G. Grogan
HR: Gwen P. Taylor
Employees: 6,624

1994 Sales: $1,052.9 mil.
1-Yr. Sales Change: -3.0%
Ownership: Privately Held

Engineering - R&D services (Bellcore); owned by the 7 regional Bell operating companies

BENJAMIN MOORE & CO.

51 Chestnut Ridge Rd.
Montvale, NJ 07645
Phone: 201-573-9600
Fax: 201-573-0046

Paints & allied products

CEO: Richard Roob
CFO: William Fritz
HR: Charles Vail
Employees: 2,000

1994 Sales: $547 million
1-Yr. Sales Change: 6.8%
Ownership: Privately Held

BENSON EYECARE CORPORATION

555 Theodore Fremd Ave., Ste. B302
Rye, NY 10580-1437
Phone: 914-967-9400
Fax: 914-967-9405

CEO: Martin E. Franklin
CFO: Ian G. H. Ashken
HR: Desiree DeStefano
Employees: 2,300

1994 Sales: $169.1 million
1-Yr. Sales Change: 106.0%
Exchange: NYSE
Symbol: EYE

Retail - nonprescription & prescription eyecare products

 See page 256 for a full profile of this company.

BERES INDUSTRIES, INC.

1785 Swarthmore Ave.
Lakewood, NJ 08701
Phone: 908-367-5700
Fax: 908-277-0344

CEO: Charles Beres Jr.
CFO: Charles Beres Jr.
HR: —
Employees: 66

1995 Sales: $4.7 million
1-Yr. Sales Change: -14.5%
Exchange: OTC
Symbol: BERS

Chemicals - precision-engineered molds for plastic products & parts

BERNARD CHAUS, INC.

1410 Broadway
New York, NY 10018
Phone: 212-354-1280
Fax: 212-302-8713

Apparel - women's clothing

CEO: Andrew Grossman
CFO: Wayne S. Miller
HR: Robin Santelia
Employees: 1,009

1995 Sales: $181.7 million
1-Yr. Sales Change: -11.9%
Exchange: NYSE
Symbol: CHS

BERNARD HALDANE ASSOCIATES INC.

444 Park Ave. South, Ste. 503
New York, NY 10016
Phone: 212-679-3360
Fax: 212-532-0059

Schools - vocational & career advancement offices

CEO: Jerold P. Weinger
CFO: Jerold P. Weinger
HR: —
Employees: 5

1995 Sales: $2 million
1-Yr. Sales Change: 33.3%
Exchange: Nasdaq (SC)
Symbol: BHAL

BEST MANUFACTURING, INC.

1633 Broadway
New York, NY 10019
Phone: 212-974-1100
Fax: 212-245-0385

Apparel - washable service clothing & textiles

CEO: Irving Miles
CFO: Irving Miles
HR: Gary Wool
Employees: 1,000

1994 Sales: $136 million
1-Yr. Sales Change: 3.0%
Ownership: Privately Held

BFS BANKORP, INC.

110 William St.
New York, NY 10038
Phone: 212-227-4040
Fax: 212-227-9639

banks - Northeast

CEO: James A. Randall
CFO: Gerard A. Perri
HR: Mary Kay Callahan
Employees: 151

1994 Sales: $40.6 million
1-Yr. Sales Change: 1.0%
Exchange: Nasdaq
Symbol: BFSI

BHC COMMUNICATIONS, INC.

600 Madison Ave.
New York, NY 10022
Phone: 212-421-0200
Fax: 212-935-8462

Broadcasting - radio & TV

CEO: Herbert J. Siegel
CFO: Joelin Merkel
HR: —
Employees: 1,163

1994 Sales: $457.5 million
1-Yr. Sales Change: 11.0%
Exchange: AMEX
Symbol: BHC

BIC CORPORATION

500 BIC Dr.
Milford, CT 06460
Phone: 203-783-2000
Fax: 203-783-2660

CEO: Bruno Bich
CFO: Robert L. Macdonald
HR: Paul Russo
Employees: 2,400

1994 Sales: $475.1 million
1-Yr. Sales Change: 8.1%
Exchange: NYSE
Symbol: BIC

Diversified - pens; shavers; lighters

BIG FLOWER PRESS HOLDINGS, INC.

3 E. 54th St.
New York, NY 10022
Phone: 212-521-1600
Fax: 212-223-4074

CEO: Theodore Ammon
CFO: Andrew P. Kaplan
HR: Marlene Gurrola
Employees: 4,100

1995 Sales: $896.6 million
1-Yr. Sales Change: 43.5%
Exchange: NYSE
Symbol: BGF

Publishing - advertising circulars, newspaper TV listing guides, Sunday comics & magazines &/or special supplements for approximately 2/3 of the most widely circulated US newspapers

BIG V SUPERMARKETS INC.

176 N. Main St.
Florida, NY 10921
Phone: 914-651-4411
Fax: 914-651-7048

CEO: Joseph Fisher
CFO: Gary Koppele
HR: —
Employees: 4,900

1994 Sales: $754 million
1-Yr. Sales Change: 11.7%
Ownership: Privately Held

Retail - supermarkets

BIOCRAFT LABORATORIES, INC.

18-01 River Rd.
Fair Lawn, NJ 07410
Phone: 201-703-0400
Fax: 201-703-3756

CEO: Harold Snyder
CFO: Steven J. Sklar
HR: Bob Rooney
Employees: 800

1995 Sales: $140.8 million
1-Yr. Sales Change: -0.4%
Exchange: NYSE
Symbol: BCL

Drugs - generic

BIOMATRIX, INC.

65 Railroad Ave.
Ridgefield, NJ 07657
Phone: 201-945-9550
Fax: 201-945-0363

CEO: Endre A. Balazs
CFO: Brian J. Hayden
HR: Joann Caha
Employees: 101

1994 Sales: $9 million
1-Yr. Sales Change: 157.1%
Exchange: Nasdaq
Symbol: BIOX

Biomedical & genetic products

BIOPHARMACEUTICS, INC.

990 Station Rd.
Bellport, NY 11713
Phone: 516-286-5900
Fax: 516-286-5803
Drugs

CEO: Edward Fine
CFO: Marc Feldman
HR: —
Employees: 35

1994 Sales: $2.7 million
1-Yr. Sales Change: 22.7%
Exchange: OTC
Symbol: BIOP

BIO-REFERENCE LABORATORIES, INC.

481 Edward H. Ross Dr.
Elmwood Park, NJ 07407
Phone: 201-791-2600
Fax: 201-791-1941

CEO: Marc D. Grodman
CFO: Sam Singer
HR: Carol Rusert
Employees: —

1994 Sales: $22.9 million
1-Yr. Sales Change: 21.8%
Exchange: Nasdaq (SC)
Symbol: BRLI

Biomedical - medical testing laboratory designed for gene probe technology, flow cytometry & tumor marking used in diagnosis & evaluations

BIOSPECIFICS TECHNOLOGIES CORP.

35 Wilbur St.
Lynbrook, NY 11563
Phone: 516-593-7000
Fax: 516-593-7039

CEO: Edwin H. Wegman
CFO: Albert Horcher
HR: —
Employees: 45

1995 Sales: $4.9 million
1-Yr. Sales Change: -12.5%
Exchange: Nasdaq
Symbol: BSTC

Drugs - production of collagenase for the healing process associated with infected wounds, dermal ulcers, burns & various other skin problems

BIO-TECHNOLOGY GENERAL CORP.

70 Wood Ave. South
Iselin, NJ 08830
Phone: 908-632-8800
Fax: 908-632-8844

CEO: Sim Fass
CFO: Yehuda Sternlicht
HR: Gwen Harning
Employees: 162

1994 Sales: $17.4 million
1-Yr. Sales Change: 25.2%
Exchange: Nasdaq
Symbol: BTGC

Biomedical & genetic products

BIRMINGHAM UTILITIES, INC.

230 Beaver St., PO Box 426
Ansonia, CT 06401
Phone: 203-735-1888
Fax: 203-732-2616

CEO: Aldore J. Rivers
CFO: Paul V. Erwin
HR: —
Employees: 19

1994 Sales: $4.1 million
1-Yr. Sales Change: 2.5%
Exchange: Nasdaq (SC)
Symbol: BIRM

Utility - water supply for domestic, commercial & industrial uses in Ansonia, Derby & Seymour, CT

BISCAYNE APPAREL, INC.

1373 Broad St.	CEO: John E. Pollack	1994 Sales: $72.4 million
Clifton, NJ 07013	CFO: Peter Vandenberg Jr.	1-Yr. Sales Change: 10.9%
Phone: 201-473-3240	HR: —	Exchange: AMEX
Fax: 201-473-5401	Employees: 496	Symbol: BHA

Apparel - women & children's clothing (OshKosh B'Gosh, BonJour, Andy John's, KAOS)

THE BISYS GROUP, INC.

150 Clove Rd.	CEO: Lynn J. Mangum	1995 Sales: $200.5 million
Little Falls, NJ 07424	CFO: Robert J. McMullan	1-Yr. Sales Change: 46.7%
Phone: 201-812-8600	HR: Mark J. Rybarczyk	Exchange: Nasdaq
Fax: 201-812-1217	Employees: 1,500	Symbol: BSYS

Business services - image & data processing outsourcing for banks

See page 257 for a full profile of this company.

BLACK CLAWSON COMPANY

405 Lexington Ave.	CEO: Carl C. Landegger	1994 Sales: $130 million
New York, NY 10174	CFO: Dale Parker	1-Yr. Sales Change: 0.0%
Phone: 212-916-8000	HR: William Coyler	Ownership: Privately Held
Fax: 212-916-8057	Employees: 1,000	

Machinery - pulp & paper machinery

THE BLACKSTONE GROUP LP

345 Park Ave.	CEO: Stephen A. Schwarzman	1995 Sales: —
New York, NY 10154	CFO: Michael Puglisi	1-Yr. Sales Change: —
Phone: 212-935-2626	HR: Veronica Buckley	Ownership: Privately Held
Fax: 212-754-8713	Employees: 170	

Financial - investment bankers

BLIMPIE INTERNATIONAL, INC.

740 Broadway	CEO: Anthony P. Conza	1995 Sales: $27 million
New York, NY 10003	CFO: Robert S. Sitkoff	1-Yr. Sales Change: 63.6%
Phone: 212-673-5900	HR: Pam Gower	Exchange: Nasdaq
Fax: 212-995-2566	Employees: 51	Symbol: BMPE

Business services - restaurant franchising & marketing (Blimpie Subs & Salads)

BLOCK DRUG COMPANY, INC.

257 Cornelison Ave.
Jersey City, NJ 07302-9988
Phone: 201-434-3000
Fax: 201-434-5739

CEO: Thomas R. Block
CFO: Melvin Kopp
HR: Thomas J. McNamara
Employees: 3,491

1995 Sales: $692.9 million
1-Yr. Sales Change: 8.8%
Exchange: Nasdaq
Symbol: BLOCA

Drugs - consumer & professsional dental products (Polident, Sensodyne, Poli-grip), over-the-counter products (Nytol, Phazyme), household products (2000 Flushes, X-14) & pharmaceuticals

BLOOMBERG L.P.

499 Park Ave.
New York, NY 10022
Phone: 212-318-2000
Fax: 212-980-4585

CEO: Michael R. Bloomberg
CFO: Wolf Boehm
HR: Geri Ingram
Employees: 2,000

1994 Est. Sales: $550 mil.
1-Yr. Sales Change: 48.6%
Ownership: Privately Held

Business services - online financial information; print, radio & TV news network

 See page 258 for a full profile of this company.

BLUE CHIP COMPUTERWARE, INC.

27-B Dubon Ct.
Farmingdale, NY 11735
Phone: 516-777-7130
Fax: 516-777-7133

CEO: Victor M. Caron
CFO: Chris Mellious
HR: —
Employees: 68

1994 Sales: $19.7 million
1-Yr. Sales Change: -3.0%
Exchange: Nasdaq (SC)
Symbol: BCHP

Computers - microcomputer systems for businesses & individuals; automotive neon products & accessories

BLUE TEE CORPORATION

250 Park Ave. South
New York, NY 10003
Phone: 212-598-0880
Fax: 212-598-0896

CEO: Richard Secrist
CFO: Glen Smith
HR: —
Employees: 900

1994 Sales: $325 million
1-Yr. Sales Change: 30.0%
Ownership: Privately Held

Wholesale distribution - steel & scrap metal

BLYTH INDUSTRIES, INC.

2 Greenwich Plaza
Greenwich, CT 06830
Phone: 203-661-1926
Fax: 203-661-1969

CEO: Robert B. Goergen
CFO: Howard E. Rose
HR: Erik Sprotte
Employees: 1,400

1995 Sales: $214.8 million
1-Yr. Sales Change: 36.4%
Exchange: NYSE
Symbol: BTH

Housewares - scented candles, outdoor citronella candles & fragrance products

BNH BANCSHARES, INC.

209 Church St.
New Haven, CT 06510
Phone: 203-498-3500
Fax: 203-799-8229
Banks - Northeast

CEO: F. Patrick McFadden Jr.
CFO: John F. Trentacosta
HR: —
Employees: 138

1994 Sales: $23.3 million
1-Yr. Sales Change: 4.0%
Exchange: Nasdaq
Symbol: BNHB

BONJOUR GROUP, INC.

1411 Broadway
New York, NY 10018
Phone: 212-398-1000
Fax: 212-921-3813
Financial - licenses trademark to other companies

CEO: Charles Dayan
CFO: Chris Miller
HR: Michael Jacobs
Employees: 30

1994 Sales: $370 million
1-Yr. Sales Change: 5.7%
Ownership: Privately Held

BONTEX, INC.

15 Nuttman St.
Newark, NJ 07103
Phone: 201-642-3547
Fax: 201-642-1961
Rubber & plastic products - uncoated & coated elastomeric wet web–impregnated fiberboard products

CEO: James C. Kostelni
CFO: Jeffrey C. Kostelni
HR: Brenda Clark
Employees: 206

1995 Sales: $51 million
1-Yr. Sales Change: 6.9%
Exchange: Nasdaq
Symbol: BOTX

BOURAS INDUSTRIES, INC.

PO Box 662
Summit, NJ 07901
Phone: 908-277-1617
Fax: 908-277-1619
Building products - metal roof & floor decking

CEO: Nicholas J. Bouras
CFO: Gary Ruckleshaus
HR: —
Employees: 500

1994 Sales: $175 million
1-Yr. Sales Change: 34.6%
Ownership: Privately Held

BOWNE & CO., INC.

345 Hudson St.
New York, NY 10014
Phone: 212-924-5500
Fax: 212-229-3400
Printing - world's largest financial printer, specializing in documentation for securities offerings, corporate restructurings & other financial transactions including electronic filings

CEO: Richard H. Koontz
CFO: James P. O'Neil
HR: Allen D. Marold
Employees: 2,700

1995 Sales: $392.7 million
1-Yr. Sales Change: 3.2%
Exchange: AMEX
Symbol: BNE

BOXHILL SYSTEMS CORPORATION

161 Avenue of the Americas	CEO: Philip Black	1995 Sales: $41 million
New York, NY 10013	CFO: Richard Tom	1-Yr. Sales Change: —
Phone: 212-989-4455	HR: —	Ownership: Privately Held
Fax: 212-989-6817	Employees: 100	

Computers - redundant arrays of independent disks (RAID) storage subsystems for Sun Microsystems servers

BOZELL, JACOBS, KENYON & ECKHARDT

40 W. 23rd St.	CEO: Charles D. Peebler Jr.	1994 Sales: $405 million
New York, NY 10010	CFO: Ramesh Rajan	1-Yr. Sales Change: 18.1%
Phone: 212-727-5000	HR: Michael Bruce	Ownership: Privately Held
Fax: 212-463-8419	Employees: 3,270	

Advertising agency

BOZELL WORLDWIDE, INC.

40 W. 23rd St.	CEO: David Bell	1994 Sales: $271 million
New York, NY 10010	CFO: Ramesh Rajan	1-Yr. Sales Change: 0.4%
Phone: 212-727-5000	HR: Joanne Conforti	Ownership: Privately Held
Fax: 212-645-9173	Employees: 2,450	

Advertising

BP PRUDHOE BAY ROYALTY TRUST

101 Barcay St., 21st Fl. West	CEO: Walter Gitlin	1994 Sales: $32.4 million
New York, NY 10286	CFO: —	1-Yr. Sales Change: -37.3%
Phone: 212-815-5092	HR: —	Exchange: NYSE
Fax: 212-815-5915	Employees: —	Symbol: BPT

Oil & gas - royalty trust

BRADLEY PHARMACEUTICALS INC.

383 Rte. 46 West	CEO: Daniel Glassman	1994 Sales: $20.1 million
Fairfield, NJ 07004-2402	CFO: Alan V. Gallantar	1-Yr. Sales Change: 356.8%
Phone: 201-882-1505	HR: Karen Krampf	Exchange: Nasdaq
Fax: 201-575-5366	Employees: 208	Symbol: BPRXA

Drugs & sundries - wholesale over-the-counter & prescription drugs & health related products

BRANDON SYSTEMS CORPORATION

One Harmon Plaza	CEO: Ira B. Brown	1995 Sales: $80.6 million
Secaucus, NJ 07094	CFO: Peter Lordi	1-Yr. Sales Change: 20.3%
Phone: 201-392-0800	HR: Robert J. Hanas	Exchange: AMEX
Fax: 201-392-0405	Employees: 5,745	Symbol: BRA

Computers - programming & technical support services

BRANFORD SAVINGS BANK

45 S. Main St.	CEO: Robert J. Mariano	1994 Sales: $13 million
Branford, CT 06405	CFO: Albert Otto	1-Yr. Sales Change: -5.8%
Phone: 203-481-3471	HR: Elaine Reed	Exchange: Nasdaq
Fax: 203-488-6730	Employees: 77	Symbol: BSBC

Banks - Northeast

BRIDGEPORT MACHINES, INC.

500 Lindley St.	CEO: Dan L. Griffith	1995 Sales: $148.8 million
Bridgeport, CT 06606	CFO: Walter C. Lazarcheck	1-Yr. Sales Change: 39.1%
Phone: 203-367-3651	HR: Denise Masulli	Exchange: Nasdaq
Fax: 203-335-0151	Employees: 917	Symbol: BPTM

Metal cutting machine tools & accessories

BRISTOL-MYERS SQUIBB COMPANY

345 Park Ave.	CEO: Charles A. Heimbold Jr.	1994 Sales: $11,983.6 mil.
New York, NY 10154-0037	CFO: Michael F. Mee	1-Yr. Sales Change: 5.0%
Phone: 212-546-4000	HR: Charles G. Tharp	Exchange: NYSE
Fax: 212-546-4020	Employees: 47,700	Symbol: BMY

Drugs & medical devices

 See pages 70–71 for a full profile of this company.

BROAD NATIONAL BANCORPORATION

905 Broad St.	CEO: Donald M. Karp	1994 Sales: $33.4 million
Newark, NJ 07102	CFO: James Boyle	1-Yr. Sales Change: 3.4%
Phone: 201-624-2300	HR: Ellen K. Rogoff	Exchange: Nasdaq
Fax: 201-624-5395	Employees: 265	Symbol: BNBC

Banks - Northeast (Broad National Bank)

BROOKLYN ACADEMY OF MUSIC

30 Lafayette Ave.
New York, NY 11217
Phone: 718-636-4111
Fax: 718-857-2021

School - music theater

CEO: Harvey Lichtenstein
CFO: Arthur J. Shaw
HR: Liz Sharp
Employees: 115

1994 Sales: $14.7 million
1-Yr. Sales Change: 8.9%
Ownership: Privately Held

BROOKLYN BANCORP, INC.

211 Montague St.
New York, NY 11201
Phone: 718-780-0400
Fax: 718-780-6254

Banks - Northeast

CEO: Richard A. Kraemer
CFO: Jonathon G. Matuscak
HR: Bruce Franzese
Employees: 890

1994 Sales: $301 million
1-Yr. Sales Change: -19.6%
Exchange: Nasdaq
Symbol: BRKB

THE BROOKLYN UNION GAS COMPANY

One MetroTech Center
New York, NY 11201-3850
Phone: 718-403-2000
Fax: 718-852-4643

Utility - gas distribution

CEO: Robert B. Catell
CFO: Vincent D. Enright
HR: Wallace P. Parker Jr.
Employees: 3,506

1995 Sales: $1,216.3 mil.
1-Yr. Sales Change: -9.1%
Exchange: NYSE
Symbol: BU

 See page 259 for a full profile of this company.

BROWN & WOOD

One World Trade Center
New York, NY 10048-0001
Phone: 212-839-5300
Fax: 212-839-5598

Law firm

CEO: Daniel Setomer
CFO: Frank Campagna
HR: —
Employees. 761

1994 Sales: $102 million
1-Yr. Sales Change: 5.2%
Ownership: Privately Held

BROWN BROTHERS HARRIMAN & CO.

59 Wall St.
New York, NY 10005
Phone: 212-483-1818
Fax: 212-493-8526

Financial - investment bankers

CEO: Anthony T. Enders
CFO: George Gage
HR: Alan B. Wechsler
Employees: 2,000

1995 Sales: —
1-Yr. Sales Change: —
Ownership: Privately Held

BRT REALTY TRUST

60 Cutter Mill Rd.
Great Neck, NY 11021
Phone: 516-466-3100
Fax: 516-466-3132

CEO: Israel Rosenzweig
CFO: David W. Kalish
HR: Myron Ginsberg
Employees: 9

1994 Sales: $22 million
1-Yr. Sales Change: 21.5%
Exchange: NYSE
Symbol: BRT

Real estate investment trust

BRYLANE INC.

463 Seventh Ave.
New York, NY 10018
Phone: 212-613-9500
Fax: 212-613-9513

CEO: Sheila Garelik
CFO: Sheila Garelik
HR: —
Employees: 2,400

1994 Sales: $579 million
1-Yr. Sales Change: —
Ownership: Privately Held

Retail - catalog retailer of special-size women's apparel

BUCK CONSULTANTS, INC.

2 Penn Plaza
New York, NY 10121-0047
Phone: 212-330-1000
Fax: 212-695-4184

CEO: Joseph A. LoCicero
CFO: Gary S. Stephen
HR: William M. Brackley
Employees: 1,840

1995 Sales: $196 million
1-Yr. Sales Change: 12.0%
Ownership: Privately Held

Consulting - employee benefits, actuarial & compensation consulting services

BULL & BEAR GROUP, INC.

11 Hanover Sq., Ste. 1100
New York, NY 10005
Phone: 212-785-0900
Fax: 212-785-0400

CEO: Bassett S. Winmill
CFO: Mark C. Winmill
HR: Thomas A. Winmill
Employees: 35

1994 Sales: $5.6 million
1-Yr. Sales Change: -9.7%
Exchange: Nasdaq (SC)
Symbol: BNBGA

Financial - mutual fund investment management

BUREAU OF ELECTRONIC PUBLISHING, INC.

141 New Rd.
Parsippany, NJ 07054
Phone: 201-808-2700
Fax: 201-808-2676

CEO: Larry Shiller
CFO: William P. Fox
HR: Brent Subkowsky
Employees: 23

1994 Sales: $2.8 million
1-Yr. Sales Change: 0.0%
Exchange: Nasdaq (SC)
Symbol: BEPI

Publishing - interactive multimedia CD-ROMs for the consumer & library/education markets (Inside the White House, Much Ado About Shakespeare, Multimedia World Factbook)

BUSH BOAKE ALLEN INC.

7 Mercedes Dr.	CEO: Julian W. Boyden	1994 Sales: $375 million
Montvale, NJ 07645-1855	CFO: Fred W. Brown	1-Yr. Sales Change: 11.5%
Phone: 201-391-9870	HR: John J. Lawless	Exchange: NYSE
Fax: 201-391-0860	Employees: 1,975	Symbol: BOA

Chemicals - flavors, fragrances & aromas for food & turpentine

BUTLER INTERNATIONAL, INC.

110 Summit Ave.	CEO: Edward M. Kopko	1994 Sales: $393.3 million
Montvale, NJ 07645	CFO: Michael C. Hellriegel	1-Yr. Sales Change: 27.8%
Phone: 201-573-8000	HR: Barbara A. Spindel	Exchange: Nasdaq
Fax: 201-573-9723	Employees: 8,000	Symbol: BUTL

Personnel - skilled technical staffing services

BUTTERICK COMPANY, INC.

161 Avenue of the Americas	CEO: John E. Lehmann	1994 Sales: $105 million
New York, NY 10013	CFO: Jay Stein	1-Yr. Sales Change: 0.0%
Phone: 212-620-2500	HR: Sheila Wahlers	Ownership: Privately Held
Fax: 212-620-2736	Employees: 900	

Printing - pattern making

BYRON PREISS MULTIMEDIA COMPANY, INC.

24 W. 25th St.	CEO: Byron Preiss	1994 Sales: $3.1 million
New York, NY 10010	CFO: James R. Dellomo	1-Yr. Sales Change: 287.5%
Phone: 212-989-6252	HR: Lois Brown	Exchange: Nasdaq (SC)
Fax: 212-989-6550	Employees: 49	Symbol: CDRM

Computers - interactive multimedia software on CD-ROM & other multimedia formats for online delivery & other non–CD-ROM forms

CABLEVISION INDUSTRIES CORPORATION

One Cablevision Center	CEO: Alan Gerry	1995 Est. Sales: $515 mil.
Liberty, NY 12754	CFO: Keith G. Svehnholz	1-Yr. Sales Change: 3.6%
Phone: 914-292-7550	HR: Nick Speranza	Ownership: Privately Held
Fax: 914-295-2721	Employees: 2,300	

Cable TV - multiple-system operation

CABLEVISION SYSTEMS CORPORATION

One Media Crossways
Woodbury, NY 11797
Phone: 516-364-8450
Fax: 516-496-1780

Cable TV

CEO: James L. Dolan
CFO: Barry J. O'Leary
HR: Joyce E. Mancini
Employees: 4,698

1994 Sales: $837.2 million
1-Yr. Sales Change: 25.6%
Exchange: AMEX
Symbol: CVC

CACHE, INC.

1460 Broadway
New York, NY 10036
Phone: 212-840-4242
Fax: 212-840-4225

Retail - apparel & shoes

CEO: Andrew M. Saul
CFO: Thomas E. Reinckens
HR: Carol Garrymore
Employees: 1,000

1994 Sales: $104.7 million
1-Yr. Sales Change: 20.9%
Exchange: Nasdaq
Symbol: CACH

CADAPULT GRAPHIC SYSTEMS INC.

110 Commerce St.
Allendale, NJ 07401
Phone: 201-236-1100
Fax: 201-236-9320

Computers - prepress, imaging & digital media systems integration

CEO: Michael Levin
CFO: Michael Levin
HR: Frances Bianco
Employees: 17

1994 Sales: $6.5 million
1-Yr. Sales Change: 18.2%
Ownership: Privately Held

CADWALADER, WICKERSHAM & TAFT

100 Maiden Ln.
New York, NY 10038-4818
Phone: 212-504-6000
Fax: 212-504-6666

Law firm

CEO: Calvin Trowbridge
CFO: Mitchell Wallsh
HR: Maryanne Braverman
Employees: 500

1995 Sales: $121 million
1-Yr. Sales Change: 2.5%
Ownership: Privately Held

CAHILL GORDON & REINDEL

80 Pine St.
New York, NY 10005
Phone: 212-701-3000
Fax: 212-269-5420

Law firm

CEO: Mary Forcellon
CFO: Thomas Walsh
HR: Mary Forcellon
Employees: 300

1994 Sales: $117 million
1-Yr. Sales Change: -1.3%
Ownership: Privately Held

THE CALDOR CORPORATION

20 Glover Ave.
Norwalk, CT 06856-5620
Phone: 203-846-1641
Fax: 203-849-2019

CEO: Don R. Clarke
CFO: Robert S. Schauman
HR: Dennis M. Lee
Employees: 24,000

1995 Sales: $2,748.6 mil.
1-Yr. Sales Change: 13.9%
Exchange: NYSE
Symbol: CLD

Retail - discount & variety

 See pages 72–73 for a full profile of this company.

CALI REALTY CORPORATION

11 Commerce Dr.
Cranford, NJ 07016
Phone: 908-272-8000
Fax: 908-272-6755

CEO: John J. Cali
CFO: Thomas A. Rizk
HR: Nicholas Mitarotondo
Employees: 50

1994 Sales: $50.5 million
1-Yr. Sales Change: 5.4%
Exchange: NYSE
Symbol: CLI

Real estate investment trust - office buildings

CALTON, INC.

500 Craig Rd.
Manalapan, NJ 07726-8790
Phone: 908-780-1800
Fax: 908-780-7257

CEO: Douglas T. Noakes
CFO: Bradley A. Little
HR: Bradley A. Little
Employees: 175

1994 Sales: $168.7 million
1-Yr. Sales Change: 5.5%
Exchange: AMEX
Symbol: CN

Real estate development - single-family homes

CALVIN KLEIN INDUSTRIES, INC.

205 W. 39th St., 5th Fl.
New York, NY 10018
Phone: 212-719-2600
Fax: 212-730-4818

CEO: Barry K. Schwartz
CFO: Richard Martin
HR: Kathy Kavanagh
Employees: —

1994 Sales: $250 million
1-Yr. Sales Change: -10.7%
Ownership: Privately Held

Apparel - fashion marketing & manufacturing, including men's underwear

CAM DESIGNS, INC.

460 Park Ave.
New York, NY 10022
Phone: 212-836-4935
Fax: 212-688-2870

CEO: John R. Davidson
CFO: Robert A. Righton
HR: —
Employees: 180

1995 Sales: $0
1-Yr. Sales Change: —
Exchange: Nasdaq
Symbol: CMDA

Engineering - automotive & aerospace engineering & design

CAMBREX CORPORATION

One Meadowlands Plaza	CEO: James A. Mack	1994 Sales: $241.6 million
East Rutherford, NJ 07073	CFO: Peter Tracey	1-Yr. Sales Change: 22.5%
Phone: 201-804-3000	HR: Steven Klosk	Exchange: AMEX
Fax: 201-804-9852	Employees: 1,336	Symbol: CBM

Chemicals - specialty & fine chemicals for industrial & medical use; intermediate commodities used in farm chemicals; vitamins & bulk active intermediates for generic drugs

CANDIE'S, INC.

2975 Westchester Ave.	CEO: Neil Cole	1995 Sales: $20 million
Purchase, NY 10577	CFO: Gary Klein	1-Yr. Sales Change: 51.5%
Phone: 914-694-8600	HR: Laura Leva	Exchange: Nasdaq
Fax: 914-694-8608	Employees: 31	Symbol: CAND

Shoes & related apparel - women's & girls' casual, outdoor & fashion footwear (Candie's)

CANNONDALE CORPORATION

9 Brookside Place	CEO: Joseph S. Montgomery	1995 Sales: $122.1 million
Georgetown, CT 06829-0122	CFO: William A. Luca	1-Yr. Sales Change: 19.6%
Phone: 203-544-9800	HR: Jean Benson	Exchange: Nasdaq
Fax: 203-852-9081	Employees: 828	Symbol: BIKE

Leisure & recreation products - bicycles with hand-welded lightweight aluminum frames

 See page 260 for a full profile of this company.

CANTEL INDUSTRIES, INC.

1135 Broad St.	CEO: James P. Reilly	1995 Sales: $31.1 million
Clifton, NJ 07013	CFO: James P. Reilly	1-Yr. Sales Change: 6.1%
Phone: 201-470-8700	HR: —	Exchange: Nasdaq
Fax: 201-471-0054	Employees: 111	Symbol: CNTL

Medical instruments - flexible & rigid endoscopes, endoscope washers & disinfectors, air cleaning & surgical equipment & related accessories, precision instruments & industrial technology equipment

CAPITAL CITIES/ABC, INC.

77 W. 66th St.	CEO: Thomas S. Murphy	1994 Sales: $6,379.2 mil.
New York, NY 10023-6298	CFO: Ronald J. Doerfler	1-Yr. Sales Change: 12.4%
Phone: 212-456-7777	HR: William J. Wilkinson	Exchange: NYSE
Fax: 212-456-6850	Employees: 20,200	Symbol: CCB

Broadcasting - radio & TV; publishing

CAPITAL MERCURY SHIRT CORPORATION

1372 Broadway
New York, NY 10018
Phone: 212-704-4800
Fax: 212-764-4342

CEO: Jay Schwartz
CFO: Vincent Pecoraro
HR: Vincent Pecoraro
Employees: 2,200

1994 Sales: $220 million
1-Yr. Sales Change: 10.0%
Ownership: Privately Held

Apparel - men's & women's shirts & blouses

CAPITAL RE CORPORATION

1325 Avenue of the Americas
New York, NY 10019
Phone: 212-974-0100
Fax: 212-581-3268

CEO: Michael E. Satz
CFO: David A. Buzen
HR: Ivana Grillo
Employees: 49

1994 Sales: $101.5 million
1-Yr. Sales Change: 27.7%
Exchange: NYSE
Symbol: KRE

Insurance - property & casualty

THE CARE GROUP, INC.

One Hollow Ln.
Lake Success, NY 11042
Phone: 516-869-8383
Fax: 516-869-8401

CEO: Ann T. Mittasch
CFO: Pat H. Celli
HR: Dolores Wenger
Employees: 1,865

1994 Sales: $36.4 million
1-Yr. Sales Change: 23.4%
Exchange: Nasdaq
Symbol: CARE

Health care - outpatient & home

CAREER HORIZONS, INC.

177 Crossways Park Dr.
Woodbury, NY 11797
Phone: 516-496-2300
Fax: 516-496-1008

CEO: Walter W. Macauley
CFO: Michael T. Druckman
HR: —
Employees: 174,573

1995 Sales: $361 million
1-Yr. Sales Change: 14.4%
Exchange: Nasdaq
Symbol: CARH

Temporary personnel services

CARNEGIE CORPORATION OF NEW YORK

437 Madison Ave.
New York, NY 10022
Phone: 212-371-3200
Fax: 212-753-0395

CEO: David A. Hamburg
CFO: Jeanmarie C. Grisi
HR: Idalia Holder
Employees: —

1994 Sales: $126.7 million
1-Yr. Sales Change: -14.5%
Ownership: Privately Held

Foundation whose goals are education & healthy development of children, strengthening human resources in developing countries & cooperative security among nations

CARNEGIE HALL CORPORATION

881 Seventh Ave.
New York, NY 10019
Phone: 212-903-9600
Fax: 212-581-6539

CEO: Judith Arron
CFO: Richard Matlaga
HR: Joan Goldstone
Employees: 300

1995 Sales: $32 million
1-Yr. Sales Change: 6.7%
Ownership: Privately Held

Real estate operations - Carnegie Hall & other properties

CARQUEST CORP.

580 White Plains Rd.
Tarrytown, NY 10591
Phone: 914-332-1515
Fax: 914-332-8504

CEO: Daniel Bock
CFO: Daniel Bock
HR: Nikki Bellizze
Employees: 6,000

1994 Sales: $860 million
1-Yr. Sales Change: 0.0%
Ownership: Privately Held

Auto parts - wholesale parts & accessories

CARTER-WALLACE, INC.

1345 Avenue of the Americas
New York, NY 10105-0021
Phone: 212-339-5000
Fax: 212-339-5100

CEO: Henry H. Hoyt Jr.
CFO: Paul A. Veteri
HR: Thomas B. Moorhead
Employees: 3,670

1995 Sales: $670 million
1-Yr. Sales Change: 0.0%
Exchange: NYSE
Symbol: CAR

Drugs & personal care products

CARVER FEDERAL SAVINGS BANK

121 W. 125th St.
New York, NY 10027
Phone: 212-876-4747
Fax: 212-666-8340

CEO: Thomas L. Clark Jr.
CFO: Biswarup Mukherjee
HR: Margaret Lewis
Employees: 102

1995 Sales: $20.4 million
1-Yr. Sales Change: 6.3%
Exchange: Nasdaq
Symbol: CARV

Financial - savings & loan

THE CASABLANCA GROUP

45 Enterprise Ave. SA
Secaucus, NJ 07094
Phone: 201-392-1100
Fax: 201-392-1728

CEO: Sam Silber
CFO: Michael Rubin
HR: Rae Brown
Employees: 250

1994 Sales: $155 million
1-Yr. Sales Change: 8.4%
Ownership: Privately Held

Apparel - women's & misses' outerware

CASTLE OIL CORPORATION

500 Mamaroneck Ave.
Harrison, NY 10528
Phone: 914-381-6500
Fax: 914-381-2877

CEO: Mauro C. Romita
CFO: Tom Vitti
HR: Monica Roney
Employees: 300

1994 Sales: $560 million
1-Yr. Sales Change: 0.0%
Ownership: Privately Held

Oil refining & marketing - petroleum products

CATHOLIC HEALTHCARE NETWORK

1011 First Ave.
New York, NY 10022
Phone: 212-371-1000
Fax: 212-371-1269

CEO: Mary Healey-Sedutto
CFO: —
HR: —
Employees: —

1994 Sales: $860.5 million
1-Yr. Sales Change: 5.7%
Ownership: Privately Held

Hospitals - not-for-profit system run by the Archdiocese of New York

CATHOLIC MEDICAL CENTER OF BROOKLYN & QUEENS

88-25 153rd St.
Jamaica, NY 11432
Phone: 718-558-6900
Fax: 718-326-2918

CEO: Mark Lane
CFO: Daniel Rinaldi
HR: Patrick McEneaey
Employees: 6,500

1994 Sales: $526.2 million
1-Yr. Sales Change: 7.0%
Ownership: Privately Held

Hospitals - not-for-profit system serving Brooklyn & Queens

CBC BANCORP INC.

128 Amity Rd.
Woodbridge, CT 06525
Phone: 203-389-2800
Fax: 203-389-9123

CEO: Charles Pignatelli
CFO: David Munzer
HR: —
Employees: 50

1994 Sales: $9.1 million
1-Yr. Sales Change: -41.3%
Exchange: Nasdaq (SC)
Symbol: CBCB

Banks - Northeast

CBS INC.

51 W. 52nd St.
New York, NY 10019-6188
Phone: 212-975-4321
Fax: 212-975-7133

CEO: Peter A. Lund
CFO: Peter W. Keegan
HR: Joan Showalter
Employees: 6,400

1994 Sales: $3,711.9 mil.
1-Yr. Sales Change: 5.7%
Ownership: Subsidiary

Broadcasting - radio & TV (subsidiary of Westinghouse)

CCA INDUSTRIES, INC.

200 Murray Hill Pkwy.
East Rutherford, NJ 07073
Phone: 201-330-1400
Fax: 201-935-0675

Cosmetics & toiletries

CEO: David Edell
CFO: John Bingman
HR: John Merritt
Employees: 127

1994 Sales: $47.7 million
1-Yr. Sales Change: 7.7%
Exchange: Nasdaq
Symbol: CCAM

CEL COMMUNICATIONS, INC.

655 Third Ave.
New York, NY 10016
Phone: 212-557-3400
Fax: 212-481-6356

CEO: Peter Collins
CFO: Martin Katz
HR: —
Employees: 17

1994 Sales: $1.8 million
1-Yr. Sales Change: -5.3%
Exchange: Nasdaq (SC)
Symbol: CELC

Broadcasting - original programming for commercial, public & cable TV & educational & home video markets

CELADON GROUP INC.

888 7th Ave.
New York, NY 10106-1591
Phone: 212-977-4447
Fax: 212-315-5281

CEO: Stephen Russell
CFO: Brian L. Reach
HR: Peter Bennet
Employees: 2,040

1995 Sales: $250.3 million
1-Yr. Sales Change: 38.4%
Exchange: Nasdaq
Symbol: CLDN

Transportation - trucking, logistics & freight forwarding, especially long-haul, full-truckload service between the US & Mexico

CELGENE CORPORATION

7 Powder Horn Dr.
Warren, NJ 07059
Phone: 908-271-1001
Fax: 908-271-4184

CEO: Richard G. Wright
CFO: Robert B. Eastty
HR: Lisa Desnoyers
Employees: 47

1994 Sales: $2.8 million
1-Yr. Sales Change: 0.0%
Exchange: Nasdaq
Symbol: CELG

Immunotherapeutic drugs designed to control serious disease states; chiral intermediates used in advanced therapeutic compounds

CELLULAR COMMUNICATIONS, INC.

110 E. 59th St., 26th Fl.
New York, NY 10022
Phone: 212-906-8440
Fax: 212-752-1157

CEO: William B. Ginsberg
CFO: J. Barclay Knapp
HR: Beth Wilson
Employees: 1,300

1994 Sales: $58.9 million
1-Yr. Sales Change: 23.7%
Exchange: Nasdaq
Symbol: COMMA

Telecommunications services - cellular systems in Indiana, Kentucky, Michigan & Ohio

CELLULAR COMMUNICATIONS INTERNATIONAL, INC.

110 E. 59th St., 26th Fl.	CEO: William B. Ginsberg	1994 Sales: $0.2 million
New York, NY 10022	CFO: Stanton Williams	1-Yr. Sales Change: -50.0%
Phone: 212-906-8480	HR: Beth Wilson	Exchange: Nasdaq (SC)
Fax: 212-752-1157	Employees: 19	Symbol: CCIL

Telecommunications services - cellular systems

CELLULAR COMMUNICATIONS OF PUERTO RICO, INC.

110 E. 59th St., 26th Fl.	CEO: George S. Blumenthal	1994 Sales: $67.1 million
New York, NY 10022	CFO: J. Barclay Knapp	1-Yr. Sales Change: 130.6%
Phone: 212-906-8440	HR: Beth Wilson	Exchange: Nasdaq
Fax: 212-752-1157	Employees: 250	Symbol: CCPR

Telecommunications services - cellular & paging systems in the Commonwealth of Puerto Rico & the US Virgin Islands

CENTENNIAL CELLULAR CORP.

50 Locust Ave.	CEO: Bernard P. Gallagher	1995 Sales: $85.4 million
New Canaan, CT 06840	CFO: Scott N. Schneider	1-Yr. Sales Change: 51.4%
Phone: 203-972-2000	HR: Geoff Broom	Exchange: Nasdaq
Fax: 203-972-2085	Employees: 540	Symbol: CYCL

Telecommunications services - paging & specialized mobile radio business & conventional mobile telephone business

 See page 261 for a full profile of this company.

CENTRAL JERSEY FINANCIAL CORPORATION

591 Cranbury Rd., PO Box 789	CEO: L. Doris Fritsch	1995 Sales: $29.7 million
East Brunswick, NJ 08816	CFO: John J. Doherty	1-Yr. Sales Change: 0.0%
Phone: 908-254-6600	HR: Ted Munley	Exchange: Nasdaq
Fax: 908-254-5364	Employees: 125	Symbol: CJFC

Financial   savings & loans

CENTRAL LEWMAR L.P.

60 McClellan St.	CEO: David Berkowitz	1994 Sales: $250 million
Newark, NJ 07114	CFO: Mark Auerbach	1-Yr. Sales Change: 22.0%
Phone: 201-622-6377	HR: —	Ownership: Privately Held
Fax: 201-623-4323	Employees: 325	

Wholesale distribution - fine paper

CENTRAL NATIONAL-GOTTESMAN, INC.

3 Manhattanville Rd.
Purchase, NY 10577
Phone: 914-696-9000
Fax: 914-696-1066

CEO: James G. Wallach
CFO: James G. Wallach
HR: Louise Caputo
Employees: 900

1994 Sales: $2,000 million
1-Yr. Sales Change: 33.3%
Ownership: Privately Held

Wholesale distribution - industrial & personal service paper

CENTRAL PARK CONSERVANCY, INC.

The Arsenal, Central Park
New York, NY 10021
Phone: 212-315-0385
Fax: 212-315-0869

CEO: Karen Putnam
CFO: J. V. Cossaboom
HR: Carol Steinberg
Employees: 184

1994 Sales: $13.7 million
1-Yr. Sales Change: 5.4%
Ownership: Privately Held

Foundation supporting the preservation & maintenance of Central Park

CENTURY BUSINESS CREDIT CORPORATION

119 W. 40th St., 10th Fl.
New York, NY 10018
Phone: 212-703-3500
Fax: 212-703-3250

CEO: Stanley Tananbaum
CFO: Andrew H. Tananbaum
HR: Robert Swanzey
Employees: 135

1994 Sales: $2,000 million
1-Yr. Sales Change: 25.0%
Ownership: Privately Held

Financial - factoring & accounts receivable financing

CENTURY COMMUNICATIONS CORP.

50 Locust Ave.
New Canaan, CT 06840
Phone: 203-972-2000
Fax: 203-966-9228

CEO: Leonard Tow
CFO: Leonard Tow
HR: Claire L. Tow
Employees: 2,300

1995 Sales: $416.7 million
1-Yr. Sales Change: 11.2%
Exchange: Nasdaq
Symbol: CTYA

Ownership & operation of cable television systems, wireless telephone systems & radio stations

CHADBOURNE & PARKE

30 Rockefeller Plaza, 23rd Fl.
New York, NY 10112
Phone: 212-408-5100
Fax: 212-541-5406

CEO: Neil Bianco
CFO: John Vlachos
HR: Carol Hampton
Employees: 600

1994 Sales: $122 million
1-Yr. Sales Change: 1.7%
Ownership: Privately Held

Law firm

CHAMPION INTERNATIONAL CORPORATION

One Champion Plaza	CEO: Andrew C. Sigler	1994 Sales: $5,318.1 mil.
Stamford, CT 06921	CFO: Frank Kneisel	1-Yr. Sales Change: 4.9%
Phone: 203-358-7000	HR: Mark V. Childers	Exchange: NYSE
Fax: 203-358-2975	Employees: 24,615	Symbol: CHA

Paper & paper products

 See pages 74–75 for a full profile of this company.

CHARMER INDUSTRIES, INC.

19-50 48th St.	CEO: Charles Merinoff	1995 Sales: $600 million
Long Island City, NY 11105	CFO: Steve Meresmen	1-Yr. Sales Change: -0.8%
Phone: 718-726-2500	HR: Annette Perry	Ownership: Privately Held
Fax: 718-726-3101	Employees: 1,000	

Beverages - wine & liquor wholesaler

CHASE MANHATTAN CORP.

270 Park Ave.	CEO: Thomas G. Labrecque	1994 Sales: $11,187 million
New York, NY 10017	CFO: Arjun K. Mathrani	1-Yr. Sales Change: -2%
Phone: 212-270-6000	HR: John J. Farrell	Exchange: NYSE
Fax: 212-270-2613	Employees: 35,774	Symbol: CHL

Banks - money center

 See pages 76–77 for a full profile of this company.

CHEF'S INTERNATIONAL, INC.

62 Broadway	CEO: Anthony C. Papalia	1995 Sales: $31.9 million
Point Pleasant Beach, NJ 08742	CFO: Anthony C. Papalia	1-Yr. Sales Change: 182.3%
Phone: 908-295-0350	HR: Anne Liss	Exchange: Nasdaq (SC)
Fax: 908-295-4514	Employees: —	Symbol: CHEF

Retail - restaurants

CHELSEA GCA REALTY, INC.

103 Eisenhower Pkwy.	CEO: David C. Bloom	1994 Sales: $53.1 million
Roseland, NJ 07068	CFO: Leslie T. Chao	1-Yr. Sales Change: 36.9%
Phone: 201-228-6111	HR: Alexandra M. Smorodin	Exchange: NYSE
Fax: 201-228-3891	Employees: 140	Symbol: CCG

Real estate investment trust

CHEMEX PHARMACEUTICALS, INC.

660 White Plains Rd., Ste. 400
Tarrytown, NY 10591
Phone: 201-944-1449
Fax: 201-944-9474

Drugs - skin disease treatment & research

CEO: Herbert H. McDade Jr.
CFO: Leonard F. Stigliano
HR: —
Employees: 10

1994 Sales: $3.2 million
1-Yr. Sales Change: 88.2%
Exchange: OTC
Symbol: CHMX

CHEMICAL BANKING CORPORATION

270 Park Ave.
New York, NY 10017-2036
Phone: 212-270-6000
Fax: 212-270-2613

Banks - money center

CEO: Walter V. Shipley
CFO: Peter J. Tobin
HR: Martin H. Zuckerman
Employees: 42,130

1994 Sales: $12,685 million
1-Yr. Sales Change: 2.1%
Exchange: NYSE
Symbol: CHL

 See pages 76–77 for a full profile of this company.

CHEYENNE SOFTWARE, INC.

3 Expressway Plaza
Roslyn Heights, NY 11577
Phone: 516-484-5110
Fax: 516-484-7106

Computers - LAN & WAN software products

CEO: ReiJane Huai
CFO: Elliot Levine
HR: Andy Boyland
Employees: 621

1995 Sales: $127.9 million
1-Yr. Sales Change: 30.9%
Exchange: AMEX
Symbol: CYE

 See page 262 for a full profile of this company.

CHIC BY H.I.S., INC.

1372 Broadway
New York, NY 10018
Phone: 212-302-6400
Fax: 212-819-9172

Apparel - men's & women's jeans (Chic, H.I.S.)

CEO: Burton M. Rosenberg
CFO: John Chin
HR: —
Employees: 5,125

1995 Sales: $376.1 million
1-Yr. Sales Change: 6.2%
Exchange: NYSE
Symbol: JNS

CHIEF CONSOLIDATED MINING COMPANY

866 2nd Ave.
New York, NY 10017
Phone: 212-688-8130
Fax: 212-758-1764

Metal ores - mining

CEO: Leonard Weitz
CFO: Edward R. Schwartz
HR: Leonard Weitz
Employees: —

1994 Sales: $0
1-Yr. Sales Change: —
Exchange: Nasdaq (SC)
Symbol: CFCM

CHILDROBICS, INC.

200 Smith St.
Farmingdale, NY 11735
Phone: 516-694-0999
Fax: 516-694-1062

CEO: Salvatore Casaccio
CFO: A. Joseph Melnick
HR: —
Employees: 300

1995 Sales: $4.2 million
1-Yr. Sales Change: 600.0%
Exchange: Nasdaq (SC)
Symbol: CHLD

Leisure & recreational services - family-oriented indoor/outdoor recreation & entertainment centers

CHOCK FULL O'NUTS CORPORATION

370 Lexington Ave.
New York, NY 10017
Phone: 212-532-0300
Fax: 212-532-0864

CEO: Marvin I. Haas
CFO: Howard M. Leitner
HR: Peter Baer
Employees: 1,400

1995 Sales: $330.4 million
1-Yr. Sales Change: 24.4%
Exchange: NYSE
Symbol: CHF

Food - coffee & tea (Chock full o'Nuts, La Touraine, Cain's); cafés

See page 263 for a full profile of this company.

CHRIS-CRAFT INDUSTRIES, INC.

600 Madison Ave.
New York, NY 10022
Phone: 212-421-0200
Fax: 212-935-8462

CEO: Herbert J. Siegel
CFO: Laurence M. Kashdin
HR: —
Employees: 1,385

1994 Sales: $481.4 million
1-Yr. Sales Change: 9.5%
Exchange: NYSE
Symbol: CCN

Broadcasting - radio & TV

CHROMATICS COLOR SCIENCES INTERNATIONAL, INC.

5 E. 80th St., First Fl.
New York, NY 10021
Phone: 212-717-6544
Fax: 212-717-6675

CEO: Darby S. Macfarlane
CFO: Leslie Foglesong
HR: —
Employees: 8

1994 Sales: $1.9 million
1-Yr. Sales Change: 850.0%
Exchange: Nasdaq (SC)
Symbol: CCSI

Medical services - color science clinic research in the detection & monitoring of infant jaundice

THE CHUBB CORPORATION

15 Mountain View Rd., PO Box 1615
Warren, NJ 07061-1615
Phone: 908-903-2000
Fax: 908-580-2027

CEO: Dean R. O'Hare
CFO: Percy Chubb III
HR: Baxter Graham
Employees: 11,200

1994 Sales: $5,709.5 mil.
1-Yr. Sales Change: 3.8%
Exchange: NYSE
Symbol: CB

Insurance - property & casualty

 See pages 78–79 for a full profile of this company.

CHYRON CORPORATION

5 Hub Dr.
Melville, NY 11747
Phone: 516-845-2000
Fax: 516-845-2090

CEO: Michael Wellesley-Wesley
CFO: Patricia A. Lampe
HR: Caroline Zix
Employees: 183

1994 Sales: $42.8 million
1-Yr. Sales Change: 14.4%
Exchange: NYSE
Symbol: CHY

Video equipment - digital electronic-graphics equipment

CITICORP

399 Park Ave.
New York, NY 10043
Phone: 800-285-3000
Fax: 212-527-3277

CEO: John S. Reed
CFO: Thomas E. Jones
HR: Lawrence R. Phillips
Employees: 82,600

1994 Sales: $31,650 million
1-Yr. Sales Change: -1.7%
Exchange: NYSE
Symbol: CCI

Banks - money center

 See pages 80–81 for a full profile of this company.

CITIZENS UTILITIES COMPANY

High Ridge Park, PO Box 3801
Stamford, CT 06905
Phone: 203-329-8800
Fax: 203-322-7186

CEO: Leonard Tow
CFO: Alessandro V. Ross
HR: Alex Roff
Employees: 4,294

1994 Sales: $916 million
1-Yr. Sales Change: 47.9%
Exchange: NYSE
Symbol: CZNB

Utility - telephone

THE CITY UNIVERSITY OF NEW YORK

535 E. 80th St.
New York, NY 10021
Phone: 212-794-5555
Fax: 212-397-5685

CEO: W. Ann Reynolds
CFO: Gerald Glick
HR: J. Demby
Employees: 28,100

1995 Sales: $1,721.9 mil.
1-Yr. Sales Change: —
Ownership: Privately Held

Public university offering undergraduate & graduate degree programs in the arts & sciences

 See pages 82–83 for a full profile of this company.

CLARE ROSE, INC./CLARE ROSE OF NASSAU

72 West Ave.
New York, NY 11772
Phone: 516-475-1840
Fax: 516-475-1836

CEO: Fredric Rosen
CFO: Paul Clough
HR: Sue Sullivan
Employees: 172

1994 Sales: $136 million
1-Yr. Sales Change: 0.0%
Ownership: Privately Held

Beverages - beer & ale distribution

CLAYTON, DUBILIER & RICE, INC.

375 Park Ave.
New York, NY 10152
Phone: 212-407-5200
Fax: 212-407-5252

Financial - investors

CEO: Joseph L. Rice III
CFO: —
HR: —
Employees: 20

1995 Sales: —
1-Yr. Sales Change: —
Ownership: Privately Held

CLEARY, GOTTLIEB, STEEN & HAMILTON

One Liberty Plaza
New York, NY 10006
Phone: 212-225-2000
Fax: 212-225-3999

Law firm

CEO: Ned B. Stiles
CFO: John H. Slattery
HR: Nancy Roberts
Employees: 1,200

1994 Sales: $265 million
1-Yr. Sales Change: 0.8%
Ownership: Privately Held

CLIFFORD PAPER, INC.

600 W. Crescent Ave.
Upper Saddle River, NJ 07458
Phone: 201-934-5115
Fax: 201-934-5188

Wholesale distribution - printing & writing paper

CEO: John Clifford
CFO: John Clifford
HR: —
Employees: 38

1995 Sales: $475 million
1-Yr. Sales Change: 9.2%
Ownership: Privately Held

CMP PUBLICATIONS, INC.

600 Community Dr.
Manhasset, NY 11030-3847
Phone: 516-562-5000
Fax: 516-562-5718

Publishing - technology- & computer-related publications (HomePC, NetGuide, WINDOWS magazine,
Electronic Engineering Times, Interactive Age), trade shows, convention management & online services

CEO: Michael S. Leeds
CFO: Joseph E. Sichler
HR: —
Employees: 1,500

1995 Sales: $378 million
1-Yr. Sales Change: 19.2%
Ownership: Privately Held

COCA-COLA BOTTLING CO. OF NEW YORK

PO Box 1820
Greenwich, CT 06836
Phone: 203-625-4000
Fax: 203-622-0142

Beverages - bottling of soft drinks, iced teas & sports drinks

CEO: Ted Highberger
CFO: W. Lamar Chesney
HR: Donna Horton
Employees: 4,000

1994 Sales: $850 million
1-Yr. Sales Change: 1.2%
Ownership: Privately Held

CODENOLL TECHNOLOGY CORPORATION

1086 N. Broadway	CEO: Michael H. Coden	1994 Sales: $2.5 million
Yonkers, NY 10701	CFO: —	1-Yr. Sales Change: -62.1%
Phone: 914-965-6300	HR: Sandi Rosenthal	Exchange: Nasdaq (SC)
Fax: 914-965-9811	Employees: 18	Symbol: CODN

Computers - high performance networking & connectivity equipment based primarily on fiber-optic & related software, electronic, semiconductor & optoelectronic technology

COGNITRONICS CORPORATION

3 Corporate Dr.	CEO: Brian J. Kelley	1994 Sales: $14.6 million
Danbury, CT 06810-4130	CFO: Garrett Sullivan	1-Yr. Sales Change: -11.0%
Phone: 203-830-3400	HR: Janet Freund	Exchange: AMEX
Fax: 203-830-3405	Employees: 75	Symbol: CGN

Computers - voice processing & optical scanning peripherals

COIN BILL VALIDATOR, INC.

425-B Oser Ave.	CEO: William H. Wood	1995 Sales: $14.1 million
Hauppauge, NY 11788	CFO: Henry Kayser	1-Yr. Sales Change: 45.4%
Phone: 516-231-1177	HR: Maureen Harold	Exchange: Nasdaq
Fax: 516-434-1771	Employees: 80	Symbol: CBVI

Electrical components - paper currency validators & related paper currency stackers for use in gaming & vending machines

COLGATE-PALMOLIVE COMPANY

300 Park Ave.	CEO: Reuben Mark	1994 Sales: $7,587.9 mil.
New York, NY 10022-7499	CFO: Robert M. Agate	1-Yr. Sales Change: 6.3%
Phone: 212-310-2000	HR: Douglas M. Reid	Exchange: NYSE
Fax: 212-310-3284	Employees: 32,800	Symbol: CL

Soap & cleaning preparations (Ajax, Fab, Palmolive, Softsoap), toothpaste (Colgate), personal-care products (Mennen) & pet food (Hill's)

 See pages 84–85 for a full profile of this company.

COLIN SERVICE SYSTEMS, INC.

One Brockway Place	CEO: Larry H. Colin	1995 Sales: $144 million
White Plains, NY 10601	CFO: Bernie Blum	1-Yr. Sales Change: 8.3%
Phone: 914-328-0800	HR: Bob Kinsley	Ownership: Privately Held
Fax: 914-328-7849	Employees: 8,500	

Building - housekeeping services

COLONIAL COMMERCIAL CORP.

3601 Hempstead Turnpike
Levittown, NY 11756-1315
Phone: 516-796-8400
Fax: 516-796-8696

CEO: Bernard Korn
CFO: James W. Stewart
HR: —
Employees: 4

1994 Sales: $0.3 million
1-Yr. Sales Change: -57.1%
Exchange: Nasdaq (SC)
Symbol: CCOM

Consulting - consumer accounts receivable consulting services

COLORADO PRIME CORPORATION

One Michael Ave.
New York , NY 11735
Phone: 516-694-1111
Fax: 800-694-4064

CEO: John Masciandaro Jr.
CFO: Bill Dordelman
HR: Christine Smith
Employees: 2,000

1994 Sales: $330 million
1-Yr. Sales Change: 0.0%
Ownership: Privately Held

Retail - kitchen appliances, including refrigerators & grills

COLTEC INDUSTRIES INC.

430 Park Ave.
New York, NY 10022-3597
Phone: 212-940-0400
Fax: 212-940-0598

CEO: John W. Guffey Jr.
CFO: Paul G. Schoen
HR: Laurence H. Polsky
Employees: 9,800

1994 Sales: $1,326.8 mil.
1-Yr. Sales Change: -0.6%
Exchange: NYSE
Symbol: COT

Various systems & components for commercial & military aircraft; engines for naval ships & power plants; automotive fuel, transmission, suspension parts; industrial seals, gaskets & bearings

COLUMBIA UNIVERSITY IN THE CITY OF NEW YORK

Broadway & W. 116th St.
New York, NY 10027
Phone: 212-854-1754
Fax: 212-749-0397

CEO: George Rupp
CFO: John Masten
HR: Robert S. Early
Employees: 6,570

1994 Sales: $1,031.6 mil.
1-Yr. Sales Change: -6.5%
Ownership: Privately Held

Public university offering 80 undergraduate & 110 graduate degree programs

 See pages 86–87 for a full profile of this company.

COMMAND CREDIT CORPORATION

100 Garden City Plaza, Ste. 200
Garden City, NY 11530
Phone: 516-739-8800
Fax: 516-739-8821

CEO: William G. Lucas
CFO: Philip A. Leone
HR: —
Employees: —

1995 Sales: $0.9 million
1-Yr. Sales Change: 350.0%
Exchange: Nasdaq (SC)
Symbol: CDMD

Financial - credit card issuance

COMMERCIAL BANK OF NEW YORK

301 Park Ave.
New York, NY 10022
Phone: 212-735-0010
Fax: 212-688-3068

Banks - Northeast

CEO: Jacob Berman
CFO: Donald J. Linton
HR: —
Employees: 122

1994 Sales: $54 million
1-Yr. Sales Change: -2.5%
Exchange: Nasdaq
Symbol: CBNY

COMMONS BROTHERS, INC.

55 Hunter Lane
Elmsford, NY 10523
Phone: 914-279-2031
Fax: 914-347-2182

Drugs & sundries - wholesale

CEO: Robert Castello
CFO: —
HR: —
Employees: 240

1994 Sales: $353 million
1-Yr. Sales Change: 0.0%
Ownership: Privately Held

COMMUNITY MEDICAL TRANSPORT, INC.

45 Morris St.
Yonkers, NY 10705
Phone: 914-963-6666
Fax: 914-963-7896

CEO: Dean L. Sloane
CFO: Dean L. Sloane
HR: Craig V. Sloane
Employees: 90

1994 Sales: $4.1 million
1-Yr. Sales Change: 28.1%
Exchange: Nasdaq
Symbol: CMTI

Medical services - ambulance & specialized medical transportation services

COMPETITIVE TECHNOLOGIES, INC.

1465 Post Rd. East, PO Box 901
Westport, CT 06881-0901
Phone: 203-255-6044
Fax: 203-254-1102

CEO: George M. Stadler
CFO: Frank R. McPike Jr.
HR: —
Employees: 9

1995 Sales: $1.7 million
1-Yr. Sales Change: -63.8%
Exchange: AMEX
Symbol: CTT

Diversified operations - education services; patent & license royalties

COMPLINK, LTD.

175 Community Dr.
Great Neck, NY 11021
Phone: 516-829-1883
Fax: 516-829-5001

CEO: Neil Luden
CFO: Neil Luden
HR: —
Employees: 28

1994 Sales: $0.5 million
1-Yr. Sales Change: 0.0%
Exchange: Nasdaq (SC)
Symbol: CLNK

Computers - software applications for the office automation market, including electronic messaging & networking gateway products

COMPREHENSIVE ENVIRONMENTAL SYSTEMS, INC.

72 A Cabot St.	CEO: Donald Kessler	1995 Sales: $8.3 million
West Babylon, NY 11704	CFO: David Behanna	1-Yr. Sales Change: 137.1%
Phone: 516-694-7060	HR: —	Exchange: Nasdaq (SC)
Fax: 516-694-7067	Employees: 30	Symbol: COEV

Pollution control - asbestos & lead remediation services, hazardous waste transportation & sludge removal

COMPUTER ASSOCIATES INTERNATIONAL, INC.

One Computer Associates Plaza	CEO: Charles B. Wang	1995 Sales: $2,623 million
Islandia, NY 11788-7000	CFO: Peter A. Schwartz	1-Yr. Sales Change: 22.1%
Phone: 516-342-5224	HR: Lisa Mars	Exchange: NYSE
Fax: 516-342-5329	Employees: 7,500	Symbol: CA

Computers - mainframe data processing management & personal finance software

COMPUTER CONCEPTS CORP.

80 Orville Dr.	CEO: Daniel DelGiorno Sr.	1994 Sales: $13.7 million
Bohemia, NY 11716	CFO: Gary Kolesar	1-Yr. Sales Change: 45.7%
Phone: 516-244-1500	HR: —	Exchange: Nasdaq (SC)
Fax: 516-563-8085	Employees: 131	Symbol: CCEE

Computers - systems management & information delivery software products, including end-user data access tools for personal & client/server environments

COMPUTER HORIZONS CORPORATION

49 Old Bloomfield Ave.	CEO: John J. Cassese	1994 Sales: $152.2 million
Mountain Lakes, NJ 07046-1495	CFO: Bernhard Hubert	1-Yr. Sales Change: 25.2%
Phone: 201-402-7400	HR: Michelle Friedberg	Exchange: Nasdaq
Fax: 201-402-7988	Employees: 2,150	Symbol: CHRZ

Computers - contract programming services

COMPUTER OUTSOURCING SERVICES, INC.

360 W. 31st St.	CEO: Zach Lonstein	1994 Sales: $15.8 million
New York, NY 10001	CFO: Roger Kaufman	1-Yr. Sales Change: 38.6%
Phone: 212-564-3730	HR: Ronald Green	Exchange: Nasdaq
Fax: 212-564-0591	Employees: 265	Symbol: COSI

Computers - payroll & data processing services

COMPUTRON SOFTWARE, INC.

301 Rte. 17 North
Rutherford, NJ 07070
Phone: 201-935-3400
Fax: 201-935-4531

CEO: Andreas Typaldos
CFO: David A. Gerth
HR: Theresa Santualli
Employees: 379

1994 Sales: $35 million
1-Yr. Sales Change: 44.0%
Exchange: Nasdaq
Symbol: CTRN

Computers - financial, workflow & archival data management software for mission-critical applications in large organizations for a broad range of industries worldwide

COMTECH TELECOMMUNICATIONS CORP.

105 Baylis Rd.
Melville, NY 11747
Phone: 516-777-8900
Fax: 516-777-8877

CEO: Fred V. Kornberg
CFO: J. Preston Windus Jr.
HR: —
Employees: 155

1995 Sales: $16.4 million
1-Yr. Sales Change: 10.1%
Exchange: Nasdaq
Symbol: CMTL

Telecommunications equipment - antenna products, frequency converters, solid-state power amplifiers & microwave subsystems

COMVERSE TECHNOLOGY, INC.

170 Crossways Park Dr.
Woodbury, NY 11797
Phone: 516-677-7200
Fax: 516-677-7355

CEO: Kobi Alexander
CFO: Igal Nissim
HR: Teri Caperna
Employees: 722

1994 Sales: $98.8 million
1-Yr. Sales Change: 40.3%
Exchange: Nasdaq
Symbol: CMVT

Computers - integrated voice & fax mail systems (TRILOGUE) & data surveillance CD products

CONCORD CAMERA CORPORATION

35 Mileed Way
Avenel, NJ 07001-2403
Phone: 908-499-8280
Fax: 908-499-0697

CEO: Ira B. Lampert
CFO: Gary M. Simon
HR: —
Employees: 152

1995 Sales: $62.1 million
1-Yr. Sales Change: 13.3%
Exchange: Nasdaq
Symbol: LENS

Photographic equipment & supplies

CONCORD FABRICS INC.

1359 Broadway
New York, NY 10018
Phone: 212-760-0300
Fax: 212-967-7025

CEO: Earl Kramer
CFO: Martin Wolfson
HR: —
Employees: 565

1995 Sales: $180.2 million
1-Yr. Sales Change: -8.9%
Exchange: AMEX
Symbol: CIS

Textiles - mill products

CONCURRENT COMPUTER CORPORATION

2 Crescent Place
Oceanport, NJ 07757
Phone: 908-870-4500
Fax: 908-870-4249

CEO: John T. Stihl
CFO: Roger J. Mason
HR: David L. Vienneau
Employees: 1,250

1995 Sales: $140.1 million
1-Yr. Sales Change: -21.7%
Exchange: Nasdaq
Symbol: CCUR

Computers - real-time systems & solutions

CONDAL DISTRIBUTORS INC.

531 Dupont St.
New York, NY 10474
Phone: 718-589-1100
Fax: 718-589-9200

CEO: Nestor Fernandez
CFO: Idefi Graves
HR: —
Employees: 100

1994 Sales: $84 million
1-Yr. Sales Change: -11.6%
Ownership: Privately Held

Food - wholesale grocery products

CONESCO INDUSTRIES, LTD.

214 Gates Rd.
Little Ferry, NJ 07643
Phone: 201-641-6500
Fax: 201-641-6254

CEO: Charles J. Trainor
CFO: Alan A. Pearson
HR: —
Employees: 51

1994 Sales: $10 million
1-Yr. Sales Change: 17.6%
Exchange: Nasdaq (SC)
Symbol: CNSC

Construction - cement & concrete; forming equipment, accessories

CONESTOGA BANCORP, INC.

1075 Northern Blvd.
Roslyn, NY 11576
Phone: 516-365-8000
Fax: 516-940-0598

CEO: John W. Boyle
CFO: James J. Korona
HR: Gerald Friedfertig
Employees: 118

1995 Sales: $28.5 million
1-Yr. Sales Change: 8.4%
Exchange: Nasdaq
Symbol: CONE

Financial - savings & loans (Pioneer Savings Bank)

CONNECTICUT ENERGY CORPORATION

855 Broad St.
Bridgeport, CT 06604
Phone: 203-579-2732
Fax: 203-382-8120

CEO: J. R. Crespo
CFO: Carol A. Forest
HR: Frank L. Esposito
Employees: 572

1995 Sales: $232.1 million
1-Yr. Sales Change: -3.7%
Exchange: NYSE
Symbol: CNE

Utility - gas distribution

CONNECTICUT WATER SERVICE, INC.

93 W. Main St.
Clinton, CT 06413
Phone: 203-669-8636
Fax: 203-669-9326

Utility - water supply

CEO: Marshall T. Chiaraluce
CFO: Bertram L. Lenz
HR: Linda Mahon
Employees: 164

1994 Sales: $38.1 million
1-Yr. Sales Change: 0.0%
Exchange: Nasdaq
Symbol: CTWS

THE CONNELL COMPANY

45 Cardinal Dr.
Westfield, NJ 07090
Phone: 908-233-0700
Fax: 908-233-1070

Leasing - heavy equipment; rice exporting

CEO: Grover Connell
CFO: Terry Connell
HR: Rosalie Fleming
Employees: 200

1994 Sales: $1,100 million
1-Yr. Sales Change: 4.8%
Ownership: Privately Held

CONOLOG CORPORATION

5 Columbia Rd.
Somerville, NJ 08876-3588
Phone: 908-722-8081
Fax: 908-722-5461

CEO: Robert S. Benou
CFO: Arpad J. Havasy
HR: —
Employees: 41

1995 Sales: $2.1 million
1-Yr. Sales Change: 5%
Exchange: Nasdaq
Symbol: CNLG

Electronic & electromagnetic components & subassemblies for use in telephone, radio & microwave transmission

CONSOLIDATED EDISON COMPANY OF NEW YORK, INC.

4 Irving Place
New York, NY 10003
Phone: 212-460-4600
Fax: 212-982-7816

Utility - electric power

CEO: Eugene R. McGrath
CFO: Raymond J. McCann
HR: Thomas J. Galvin
Employees: 17,097

1994 Sales: $6,373.1 mil.
1-Yr. Sales Change: 1.7%
Exchange: NYSE
Symbol: ED

 See pages 88–89 for a full profile of this company.

CONSOLIDATED TECHNOLOGY GROUP LTD.

160 Broadway, 9th Fl.
New York, NY 10038
Phone: 212-233-4500
Fax: 212-233-5023

CEO: Lewis S. Schiller
CFO: George W. Mahoney
HR: —
Employees: 1,432

1994 Sales: $15.7 million
1-Yr. Sales Change: 313.2%
Exchange: Nasdaq (SC)
Symbol: COTG

Medical services - magnetic resonance imaging centers; electromechanical & electro-optical products; telecommunication services

CONSTRUCTION SPECIALTIES, INC.

55 Winans Ave.
Cranford , NJ 07016
Phone: 908-272-5200
Fax: 908-272-6038

Construction - architectural metalwork

CEO: Ronald Dadd
CFO: Ronald Dadd
HR: Lee Dirubbo
Employees: —

1994 Sales: $110 million
1-Yr. Sales Change: 10.0%
Ownership: Privately Held

CONTINENTAL CAN CO.

One Aerial Way
Syosset, NY 11791
Phone: 516-822-4940
Fax: 516-931-6344

Containers - paper & plastic

CEO: Donald J. Bainton
CFO: Marshal L'Hommedieu
HR: Abdo Yazgi
Employees: 3,729

1994 Sales: $537.1 million
1-Yr. Sales Change: 11.5%
Exchange: NYSE
Symbol: CAN

CONTINENTAL CHOICE CARE, INC.

25-B Vreeland Rd.
Florham Park, NJ 07932
Phone: 201-593-0500
Fax: 201-593-0024

Medical services - in-home dialysis-related services

CEO: Alvin S. Trenk
CFO: Ronald A. Lefkon
HR: Larry Trenk
Employees: 61

1994 Sales: $9.3 million
1-Yr. Sales Change: 0.0%
Exchange: Nasdaq
Symbol: CCCI

CONTINENTAL GRAIN COMPANY

277 Park Ave.
New York, NY 10172-0002
Phone: 212-207-5100
Fax: 212-207-5181

Food - commodity merchandising & processing

CEO: Donald L. Staheli
CFO: James J. Bigham
HR: Dwight Coffin
Employees: 16,000

1995 Sales: $14,000 million
1-Yr. Sales Change: -6.7%
Ownership: Privately Held

 See pages 90–91 for a full profile of this company.

THE CONTINUUM GROUP, INC.

380 Ludlow Ave.
Cranford, NJ 07016-3228
Phone: 908-709-0011
Fax: 908-709-0641

Leisure & recreational products - music recordings (Roger Daltrey, Ronnie Wood, Charlie Watts)

CEO: Harrison Weaver
CFO: Theodore Weis
HR: —
Employees: 21

1994 Sales: $3.3 million
1-Yr. Sales Change: 37.5%
Exchange: Nasdaq
Symbol: CNUUQ

CONVERGENT SOLUTIONS, INC.

100 Metro Park South
Laurence Harbor, NJ 08878
Phone: 908-290-0090
Fax: 908-290-1494

Computers - software

CEO: Tom Bosanko
CFO: Mitch Lindenfeldar
HR: Deborah Marraro
Employees: 182

1994 Sales: $9.7 million
1-Yr. Sales Change: 19.8%
Exchange: Nasdaq (SC)
Symbol: KTIE

CONWAY STORES, INC.

One Penn Plaza
New York, NY 10119
Phone: 212-967-5300
Fax: 212-967-6740

Retail - discount stores (18 units)

CEO: Ricky Cohen
CFO: Ricky Rudy
HR: Dan Uebbing
Employees: 1,200

1994 Sales: $175 million
1-Yr. Sales Change: 0.0%
Ownership: Privately Held

COOPER LIFE SCIENCES, INC.

160 Broadway
New York, NY 10038
Phone: 212-791-5362
Fax: 212-791-5367

Wholesale - products for professional athletes

CEO: Steven Rosenberg
CFO: Steven Rosenberg
HR: —
Employees: 21

1994 Sales: $9.6 million
1-Yr. Sales Change: 77.8%
Exchange: Nasdaq (SC)
Symbol: ZAPS

COOPERS & LYBRAND L.L.P.

1251 Avenue of the Americas
New York, NY 10020
Phone: 212-536-2000
Fax: 212-536-3145

Business services - accounting, auditing & consulting services

CEO: Nicholas G. Moore
CFO: Frank V. Scalia
HR: Reed A. Keller
Employees: 70,500

1995 Sales: $6,200 mil.
1-Yr. Sales Change: 11.9%
Ownership: Privately Held

 See pages 92–93 for a full profile of this company.

COPYTELE, INC.

900 Walt Whitman Rd.
Huntington Station, NY 11746
Phone: 516-549-5900
Fax: 516-549-5974

Electrical products - video displays

CEO: Denis A. Krusos
CFO: Gerald J. Bentivegna
HR: —
Employees: 25

1994 Sales: $0
1-Yr. Sales Change: —
Exchange: Nasdaq
Symbol: COPY

CORINTHIAN COMMUNICATIONS, INC.

845 Third Ave.
New York, NY 10022
Phone: 212-371-5225
Fax: 212-752-6594

Advertising

CEO: Larry Miller
CFO: Claire Pride
HR: —
Employees: 65

1994 Sales: $225 million
1-Yr. Sales Change: -25.0%
Ownership: Privately Held

CORNICHE GROUP, INC.

145 Rte. 46 West
Wayne, NJ 07470
Phone: 201-377-0400
Fax: 201-785-0649

Medical instruments - image-processing devices & electrocardiographs

CEO: Michael O'Shea
CFO: Barbara Knapp
HR: —
Employees: 18

1995 Sales: $21 million
1-Yr. Sales Change: 500.0%
Exchange: OTC
Symbol: CGII

CORPORATE RENAISSANCE GROUP, INC.

1185 Avenue of the Americas, 18th Fl.
New York, NY 10036
Phone: 212-730-2000
Fax: 212-843-5949

Financial - closed-end management investment company for business development

CEO: Martin D. Sass
CFO: Hugh R. Lamle
HR: —
Employees: —

1995 Sales: $0.2 million
1-Yr. Sales Change: —
Exchange: Nasdaq (SC)
Symbol: CREN

COUDERT BROTHERS

200 Park Ave.
New York, NY 10166
Phone: 212-626-4400
Fax: 212-626-4120

Law firm

CEO: Robert N. Hornick
CFO: Louis S. Bernstein
HR: Geraldine DeFranco
Employees: 500

1994 Sales: $121 million
1-Yr. Sales Change: 26.7%
Ownership: Privately Held

COVINGTON FABRICS CORPORATION

15 E. 26th St.
New York, NY 10010
Phone: 212-689-2200
Fax: 212-689-5131

Textiles - piece goods & notions

CEO: Abby Gilmore
CFO: George Curtis
HR: Meredith Pinkett
Employees: 150

1994 Est. Sales: $100 mil.
1-Yr. Sales Change: 0.0%
Ownership: Privately Held

CPC INTERNATIONAL INC.

International Plaza	CEO: Charles R. Shoemate	1994 Sales: $7,425.4 mil.
Englewood Cliffs, NJ 07632-9976	CFO: Konrad Schlatter	1-Yr. Sales Change: 10.2%
Phone: 201-894-4000	HR: Richard P. Bergeman	Exchange: NYSE
Fax: 201-894-2186	Employees: 41,900	Symbol: CPC

Food - soups & sauces (Knorr), pastas, baked goods (Thomas' English muffins, Arnold breads), peanut butter (Skippy), mayonnaise (Hellman's) & corn oil (Mazola)

 See pages 94–95 for a full profile of this company.

CPI AEROSTRUCTURES, INC.

1900 Ocean Ave.	CEO: Arthur August	1994 Sales: $5 million
Ronkonkoma, NY 11779	CFO: Theodore J. Martines	1-Yr. Sales Change: -18.0%
Phone: 516-737-4700	HR: Josephine Domanico	Exchange: Nasdaq
Fax: 516-737-4041	Employees: 26	Symbol: CPIA

Aerospace - aircraft equipment

CPT HOLDINGS, INC.

1430 Broadway St., 13th Fl.	CEO: William L. Remley	1995 Sales: $31.2 million
New York, NY 10018	CFO: William L. Remley	1-Yr. Sales Change: 437.9%
Phone: 212-382-1313	HR: —	Exchange: Nasdaq (SC)
Fax: 212-391-1393	Employees: 313	Symbol: CPTH

Metal products - fabrication, lightweight structural steel shapes for the manufactured housing, truck trailer & highway safety systems industries, primarily in the Northeast, Southeast & Mid-Atlantic regions

C. R. BARD, INC.

730 Central Ave.	CEO: William H. Longfield	1994 Sales: $1,018.2 mil.
Murray Hill, NJ 07974	CFO: William C. Bopp	1-Yr. Sales Change: 4.9%
Phone: 908-277-8000	HR: Hope Greenfield	Exchange: NYSE
Fax: 908-277-8240	Employees: 8,650	Symbol: BCR

Medical & dental supplies

CRANE CO.

100 First Stamford Place	CEO: Robert S. Evans	1994 Sales: $1,653.5 mil.
Stamford, CT 06902	CFO: David S. Smith	1-Yr. Sales Change: 26.2%
Phone: 203-363-7300	HR: Richard B. Phillips	Exchange: NYSE
Fax: 203-363-7295	Employees: 10,700	Symbol: CR

Diversified operations - aerospace & defense products & millwork

CRAVATH, SWAINE & MOORE

825 Eighth Ave.
New York, NY 10019
Phone: 212-474-1000
Fax: 212-474-3700

Law firm

CEO: S. Charleston Butler
CFO: —
HR: Margarette Luberda
Employees: 308

1994 Sales: $186 million
1-Yr. Sales Change: -7.7%
Ownership: Privately Held

CREATIVE LEARNING PRODUCTS, INC.

150 Morris Ave.
Springfield, NJ 07081
Phone: 201-467-0266
Fax: 201-467-5650

CEO: Peter J. Jegou
CFO: Walter J. Krzanowski
HR: —
Employees: 17

1995 Sales: $1.5 million
1-Yr. Sales Change: 275.0%
Exchange: Nasdaq (SC)
Symbol: CLPI

Publishing - educational audio & videocassettes, cards, placemats & workbooks

CREATIVE TECHNOLOGIES CORP.

170 53rd St., 3rd Fl.
New York, NY 11232
Phone: 718-492-8400
Fax: 718-492-3878

CEO: David Guttmann
CFO: Richard Helfman
HR: —
Employees: 130

1994 Sales: $30.1 million
1-Yr. Sales Change: 88.1%
Exchange: Nasdaq (SC)
Symbol: CRTV

Housewares - pasta machines, indoor grill (Grill Express) & steamers

CROMPTON & KNOWLES CORPORATION

One Station Place
Stamford, CT 06902
Phone: 203-353-5400
Fax: 203-353-5424

Chemicals - specialty

CEO: Vincent A. Calarco
CFO: Charles J. Marsden
HR: Ester Mattson
Employees: 2,652

1994 Sales: $589.7 million
1-Yr. Sales Change: 5.6%
Exchange: NYSE
Symbol: CNK

CROSCILL, INC.

261 Fifth Ave.
New York, NY 10016
Phone: 212-689-7222
Fax: 212-481-8656

Textiles - curtains & other home furnishings

CEO: Mike Kahn
CFO: Anthony Cassella
HR: —
Employees: 1,200

1994 Sales: $150 million
1-Yr. Sales Change: 0.0%
Ownership: Privately Held

CRYSTAL CLEAR INDUSTRIES

2 Bergen Turnpike	CEO: Abraham Lefkowitz	1994 Est. Sales: $95 mil.
Ridgefield Park, NJ 07660	CFO: Morty Roth	1-Yr. Sales Change: 14.5%
Phone: 201-440-4200	HR: —	Ownership: Privately Held
Fax: 201-440-1758	Employees: 260	

Housewares - crystal giftware & dinnerware (American Atelier)

CUC INTERNATIONAL INC.

707 Summer St.	CEO: Walter A. Forbes	1995 Sales: $1,044.7 mil.
Stamford, CT 06901	CFO: Cosmo Corigliano	1-Yr. Sales Change: 18.8%
Phone: 203-324-9261	HR: Fran Johnson	Exchange: NYSE
Fax: 203-348-4528	Employees: 8,000	Symbol: CU

Retail - membership-based consumer services, shopping, travel, dining & other services & products offered by mail order, phone & online network (Comp-U-Card)

CULBRO CORPORATION

387 Park Ave. South	CEO: Edgar M. Cullman Sr.	1994 Sales: $185.4 million
New York, NY 10016-8899	CFO: Jay M. Green	1-Yr. Sales Change: -86.4%
Phone: 212-561-8700	HR: Mary Raffaniello	Exchange: NYSE
Fax: 212-561-8791	Employees: 2,695	Symbol: CUC

Cigars; disposable lighter distribution; packaging & labeling systems; nursery products; real estate development

CURATIVE HEALTH SERVICES, INC.

14 Research Way, PO Box 9052	CEO: Russell B. Whitman	1994 Sales: $40.6 million
East Setauket, NY 11733-9052	CFO: John C. Prior	1-Yr. Sales Change: 29.7%
Phone: 516-689-7000	HR: Denise Smith	Exchange: Nasdaq
Fax: 516-689-7067	Employees: 366	Symbol: CURE

Health care - outpatient treatment centers specializing in chronic wounds

CURTISS-WRIGHT CORPORATION

1200 Wall St. West	CEO: David Lasky	1994 Sales: $166.2 million
Lyndhurst, NJ 07071-0635	CFO: Robert Bosi	1-Yr. Sales Change: -2.4%
Phone: 201-896-8400	HR: —	Exchange: NYSE
Fax: 201-438-5680	Employees: 1,500	Symbol: CW

Aerospace - precision components to operate electro- & hydromechanical devices; industrial heat treating & shot peening of metals

CUSTOMEDIX CORPORATION

53 N. Plains Industrial Rd.
Wallingford, CT 06492
Phone: 203-284-9079
Fax: 203-265-7662

CEO: Gordon S. Cohen
CFO: Barry L. Kosowsky
HR: —
Employees: 166

1995 Sales: $51.1 million
1-Yr. Sales Change: 8.0%
Exchange: AMEX
Symbol: CUS

Dental & medical health care products & supplies

CUTCO INDUSTRIES, INC.

125 S. Service Rd., PO Box 265
Jericho, NY 11753
Phone: 516-334-8400
Fax: 516-334-8575

CEO: Don von Liebermann
CFO: Michael Kramer
HR: —
Employees: 500

1995 Sales: $13.2 million
1-Yr. Sales Change: 8.2%
Exchange: Nasdaq (SC)
Symbol: CUTC

Retail - hair salons (Haircrafters, Great Expectations, Precision Haircutters)

CYGNE DESIGNS, INC.

1372 Broadway
New York, NY 10018
Phone: 212-354-6474
Fax: 212-921-8318

CEO: Bernard M. Manuel
CFO: Roy E. Green
HR: Remy Nicholas
Employees: 5,000

1995 Sales: $516.1 million
1-Yr. Sales Change: 134.4%
Exchange: Nasdaq
Symbol: CYDS

Apparel - women's & men's apparel

 See page 264 for a full profile of this company.

CYTEC INDUSTRIES INC.

5 Garret Mountain Plaza
West Paterson, NJ 07424-1599
Phone: 201-357-3100
Fax: 201-357-3058

CEO: Darryl D. Fry
CFO: J. P. Cronin
HR: James W. Hirsch
Employees: 5,000

1994 Sales: $1,101.3 mil.
1-Yr. Sales Change: 9.2%
Exchange: NYSE
Symbol: CYT

Specialty chemicals for water treatment & the appliance, automotive & paper industries

CZARNIKOW-RIONDA

One William St.
New York, NY 10004
Phone: 212-806-0700
Fax: 212-968-0825

CEO: Daniel Gutman
CFO: Jean-Max Mozes
HR: Joseph Torres
Employees: 48

1994 Sales: $650 million
1-Yr. Sales Change: 24.8%
Ownership: Privately Held

Food - international sugar trader

D'AGOSTINO SUPERMARKETS, INC.

1385 Boston Post Rd.	CEO: Nicholas D'Agostino Jr.	1994 Sales: $203 million
Larchmont, NY 10538	CFO: Nicholas D'Agostino Jr.	1-Yr. Sales Change: 0.0%
Phone: 914-833-4000	HR: Frank Argento	Ownership: Privately Held
Fax: 914-833-4060	Employees: 1,500	
Retail - supermarkets		

DAIRY ENTERPRISES, INC.

750 Union Ave.	CEO: James Schreiber	1994 Sales: $450 million
Union, NJ 07083	CFO: Tom Zanautreve	1-Yr. Sales Change: 20.0%
Phone: 908-851-5180	HR: Don Griffin	Ownership: Privately Held
Fax: 908-687-5130	Employees: 1,000	
Food - milk production		

DALE CARNEGIE TRAINING, INC.

1475 Franklin Ave.	CEO: Stuart Levine	1995 Est. Sales: $100 mil.
New York, NY 11530	CFO: Marc Johnston	1-Yr. Sales Change: —
Phone: 516-248-5100	HR: Kathleen Gambino	Ownership: Privately Held
Fax: 516-877-0627	Employees: 195	
School - leadership training; book publishing (The Leader In You)		

DALIL FASHIONS

1400 Broadway	CEO: Stephen Montifiore	1994 Sales: $100 million
New York, NY 10018	CFO: Jeff White	1-Yr. Sales Change: 0.0%
Phone: 212-382-1414	HR: —	Ownership: Privately Held
Fax: 212-764-6165	Employees: 200	
Apparel - women's & juniors' dresses		

DANIEL F. YOUNG INC.

17 Battery Place	CEO: Joseph G. Kearns	1994 Sales: $400 million
New York, NY 10004	CFO: Rita Bentley	1-Yr. Sales Change: 0.0%
Phone: 212-248-1700	HR: —	Ownership: Privately Held
Fax: 212-509-3934	Employees: 400	
Transportation - freight forwarding		

DANIELSON HOLDING CORPORATION

767 Third Ave., 5th Fl.
New York, NY 10017-2023
Phone: 212-888-0347
Fax: 212-888-6704

CEO: C. Kirk Rhein Jr.
CFO: Michael T. Carney
HR: —
Employees: 264

1994 Sales: $110.3 million
1-Yr. Sales Change: 7.7%
Exchange: AMEX
Symbol: DHC

Insurance underwriting - property, casualty & workers compensation

DAN'S SUPREME SUPERMARKETS, INC.

474 Fulton Ave.
New York, NY 11550
Phone: 516-483-7046
Fax: 516-483-1586

CEO: Frank Grobman
CFO: Donald Gross
HR: Harold Kroebel
Employees: 1,500

1994 Sales: $165 million
1-Yr. Sales Change: -17.5%
Ownership: Privately Held

Retail - supermarkets

DANSKIN, INC.

111 W. 40th St.
New York, NY 10018
Phone: 212-764-4630
Fax: 212-764-7265

CEO: Howard D. Cooley
CFO: Beverly Eichel
HR: Lynn Golubchik
Employees: 1,525

1995 Sales: $128.1 million
1-Yr. Sales Change: -2.6%
Exchange: Nasdaq
Symbol: DANS

Apparel - women's exercise clothes & hosiery (Danskin, Round-the-Clock, Anne Klein, Christian Dior)

DARBY GROUP COMPANIES, INC.

865 Merrick Ave.
New York, NY 11590
Phone: 516-683-0000
Fax: 516-832-7101

CEO: Michael Ashkin
CFO: —
HR: Janice Gilman
Employees: 2,000

1994 Est. Sales: $430 mil.
1-Yr. Sales Change: —
Ownership: Privately Held

Medical & dental supplies - distribution

D'ARCY MASIUS BENTON & BOWLES, INC.

1675 Broadway
New York, NY 10019
Phone: 212-468-3622
Fax: 212-468-4385

CEO: Roy J. Bostock
CFO: Craig D. Brown
HR: William L. Clayton
Employees: 6,333

1995 Sales: $626 million
1-Yr. Sales Change: 2.9%
Ownership: Privately Held

Advertising

DATA SYSTEMS & SOFTWARE INC.

200 Rte. 17	CEO: George Morgenstern	1994 Sales: $79.7 million
Mahwah, NJ 07430	CFO: George Morgenstern	1-Yr. Sales Change: 37.7%
Phone: 201-529-2026	HR: Elihu Levino	Exchange: Nasdaq
Fax: 201-529-3163	Employees: 915	Symbol: DSSI

Computers - real-time systems integrator & consultants; semiconductor fabrication

DATAEASE SAPPHIRE INTERNATIONAL INC.

7 Cambridge Dr.	CEO: James Falanga	1994 Sales: $16 million
Trumbull, CT 06611	CFO: Douglas Meny	1-Yr. Sales Change: -44.8%
Phone: 203-374-8000	HR: Julee Agresta	Ownership: Privately Held
Fax: 203-365-2397	Employees: 170	

Computers - PC relational database systems for corporate users

DATAFLEX CORPORATION

3920 Park Ave.	CEO: Richard C. Rose	1995 Sales: $274 million
Edison, NJ 08820	CFO: Raymond DioGuardi	1-Yr. Sales Change: 124.0%
Phone: 908-321-1100	HR: Nancy Ebery	Exchange: Nasdaq
Fax: 908-321-6590	Employees: 1,032	Symbol: DFLX

Computers - direct marketing of desktop computer equipment & related products supplied primarily by major manufacturers

DATALOGIX INTERNATIONAL INC.

100 Summit Lake Dr.	CEO: Richard C. Giordanella	1995 Sales: $43.2 million
Valhalla, NY 10595	CFO: Rick L. Smith	1-Yr. Sales Change: 74.9%
Phone: 914-747-2900	HR: Patricia L. Anderson	Exchange: Nasdaq
Fax: 914-747-2987	Employees: 250	Symbol: DLGX

Computers - client/server–based applications software for the information management needs of the process manufacturing industry (CIMPRO, DATALOGIX & GEMMS)

DATASCOPE CORPORATION

14 Philips Pkwy.	CEO: Lawrence Saper	1995 Sales: $195.7 million
Montvale, NJ 07645	CFO: Richard L. Smernoff	1-Yr. Sales Change: 7.1%
Phone: 201-391-8100	HR: Richard Monastersky	Exchange: Nasdaq
Fax: 201-265-8562	Employees: 1,100	Symbol: DSCP

Medical instruments

DAVIS POLK & WARDWELL

One Chase Manhattan Plaza, 39th Fl.
New York, NY 10005
Phone: 212-450-4000
Fax: 212-450-5541

Law firm

CEO: Henry L. King
CFO: David Krenkel
HR: Jeannie Gratta
Employees: 1,100

1994 Sales: $254 million
1-Yr. Sales Change: -5.9%
Ownership: Privately Held

DAXOR CORPORATION

350 Fifth Ave., Ste. 7120
New York, NY 10022
Phone: 212-244-0555
Fax: 212-244-0806

CEO: Joseph Feldschuh
CFO: Octavia Atanasiu
HR: Chris Kable
Employees: 48

1994 Sales: $4.6 million
1-Yr. Sales Change: -4.2%
Exchange: AMEX
Symbol: DXR

Medical services - long-term frozen autologous blood banking services

D.B. BROWN, INC.

400 Port Carteret Dr.
Carteret, NJ 07008
Phone: 908-541-0200
Fax: 908-969-6042

CEO: W. Paul Brogowski
CFO: Stu Lipkin
HR: —
Employees: 210

1994 Sales: $350 million
1-Yr. Sales Change: 40.0%
Ownership: Privately Held

Food - wholesale meat, meat products & seafood

DEAN WITTER, DISCOVER & CO.

2 World Trade Center
New York, NY 10048
Phone: 212-392-2222
Fax: 212-392-3118

CEO: Philip J. Purcell
CFO: Thomas C. Schneider
HR: Michael Cunningham
Employees: 28,475

1994 Sales: $6,602.6 mil.
1-Yr. Sales Change: 13.4%
Exchange: NYSE
Symbol: DWD

Financial - securities brokerage (Dean Witter, Reynolds), investment banker & credit card issuer
(Discover)

 See pages 96–97 for a full profile of this company.

DEBEVOISE & PLIMPTON

875 Third Ave.
New York, NY 10022
Phone: 212-909-6000
Fax: 212-909-6836

Law firm

CEO: Barry Bryan
CFO: Richard Depalma
HR: Rachael Kagen
Employees: 419

1994 Sales: $181.5 million
1-Yr. Sales Change: 6.8%
Ownership: Privately Held

DEL ELECTRONICS CORPORATION

One Commerce Park
Valhalla, NY 10595
Phone: 914-686-3600
Fax: 914-686-5425

CEO: Leonard A. Trugman
CFO: Michael Taber
HR: Doris Doherty
Employees: 335

1995 Sales: $32.6 million
1-Yr. Sales Change: 34.2%
Exchange: AMEX
Symbol: DEL

Electrical products - high-voltage power conversion systems

DEL LABORATORIES, INC.

565 Broad Hollow Rd.
Farmingdale, NY 11735
Phone: 516-844-2020
Fax: 516-293-1515

CEO: Dan K. Wassong
CFO: Melvyn C. Goldstein
HR: Charlie Schnek
Employees: 1,175

1994 Sales: $190.1 million
1-Yr. Sales Change: 14.2%
Exchange: AMEX
Symbol: DLI

Cosmetics & toiletries

DELOITTE TOUCHE TOHMATSU INTERNATIONAL

10 Westport Rd.
Wilton, CT 06897-0820
Phone: 203-761-3000
Fax: 203-834-2200

CEO: J. Michael Cook
CFO: Robert W. Pivik
HR: James H. Wall
Employees: 59,000

1995 Est. Sales: $5,950 mil.
1-Yr. Sales Change: 14.4%
Ownership: Privately Held

Business services - accounting & consulting

 See pages 98–99 for a full profile of this company.

DENDRITE INTERNATIONAL, INC.

1200 Mount Kemble Ave.
Morristown, NJ 07960-6797
Phone: 201-425-1200
Fax: 201-425-1919

CEO: John E. Bailye
CFO: Chuck Warczakowski
HR: Steve Van Houten
Employees: 480

1994 Sales: $39.4 million
1-Yr. Sales Change: 43.8%
Exchange: Nasdaq
Symbol: DRTE

Computers - sales management software for the pharmaceutical industry

DESIGNATRONICS INC.

2101 Jericho Tpke., Box 5416
New Hyde Park, NY 11042-5416
Phone: 516-328-3300
Fax: 516-326-8827

CEO: Martin Hoffman
CFO: Frank Buchsbaum
HR: Barbara Schmidt
Employees: 265

1994 Sales: $25 million
1-Yr. Sales Change: 5.5%
Exchange: OTC
Symbol: DSGT

Machinery - mechanical, electromechanical & linear motion components & subassemblies

DETOMASO INDUSTRIES, INC.

107 Monmouth St., PO Box 856
Red Bank, NJ 07701
Phone: 908-842-7200
Fax: 908-842-1219

CEO: Howard E. Chase
CFO: Catherine D. Germano
HR: Diane Kuhrt
Employees: 303

1994 Sales: $52 million
1-Yr. Sales Change: 24.1%
Exchange: Nasdaq (SC)
Symbol: DTOM

Automotive manufacturing - Italian cars & motorcycles (GBM, Lita)

DEVLIEG-BULLARD, INC.

One Gorham Island
Westport, CT 06880
Phone: 203-221-8201
Fax: 203-221-0780

CEO: William O. Thomas
CFO: Lawrence M. Murray
HR: —
Employees: 625

1995 Sales: $78.2 million
1-Yr. Sales Change: 23.0%
Exchange: Nasdaq
Symbol: DVLG

Machinery - general industrial machine tools & related products

DEVON GROUP, INC.

281 Tresser Blvd., Ste. 501
Stamford, CT 06901-3227
Phone: 203-964-1444
Fax: 203-964-1036

CEO: Marne Obernauer Jr.
CFO: Bruce K. Koch
HR: Bruce K. Koch
Employees: 1,900

1995 Sales: $225.7 million
1-Yr. Sales Change: 18.3%
Exchange: Nasdaq
Symbol: DEVN

Printing - advertising & editorial production, computerized typesetting, composition, color separation, printing, binding & related services

DEWEY BALLANTINE

1301 Avenue of the Americas
New York, NY 10019
Phone: 212-259-8000
Fax: 212-259-6333

CEO: Harvey Kurzweil
CFO: Marc Kessler
HR: Jean Shatiloss
Employees: —

1994 Sales: $164 million
1-Yr. Sales Change: -0.6%
Ownership: Privately Held

Law firm

DI GIORGIO CORP.

380 Middlesex Ave.
Carteret, NJ 08873
Phone: 908-541-5555
Fax: 908-451-3590

CEO: Arthur M. Goldberg
CFO: Richard B. Neff
HR: Jackie Simmons
Employees: 1,305

1994 Sales: $934 million
1-Yr. Sales Change: 19.4%
Ownership: Privately Held

Food - wholesale

DIAGNOSTIC/RETRIEVAL SYSTEMS, INC.

5 Sylvan Way	CEO: Mark S. Newman	1995 Sales: $69.9 million
Parsippany, NJ 07054	CFO: Nancy R. Pitek	1-Yr. Sales Change: 20.9%
Phone: 201-898-1500	HR: Andrea Hayward	Exchange: AMEX
Fax: 201-898-4730	Employees: 565	Symbol: DRSA

Electronics - military signal processors & display systems, trainer & simulator systems, data storage & playback systems, optics, manufacturing & technical services

DIAL-A-MATTRESS OPERATING CORPORATION

31-10 48th Ave.	CEO: Napoleon Barragan	1994 Sales: $64.9 million
Long Island City, NY 11101	CFO: Louis Kurpis	1-Yr. Sales Change: 59.9%
Phone: 718-472-1200	HR: Zorida Cook	Ownership: Privately Held
Fax: 718-472-1310	Employees: 300	

Retail - nationwide discount mattress delivery

 See page 265 for a full profile of this company.

DIALOGIC CORPORATION

1515 Rte. 10	CEO: Howard G. Bubb	1994 Sales: $127.2 million
Parsippany, NJ 07054	CFO: Edward B. Jordan	1-Yr. Sales Change: 33.1%
Phone: 201-993-3000	HR: Steven P. Wentzell	Exchange: Nasdaq
Fax: 201-993-3093	Employees: 370	Symbol: DLGC

Telecommunications equipment - hardware & software signal computing components for call processing systems

 See page 266 for a full profile of this company.

DIAMOND FLOWER (NORTHEAST), INC.

7 Elkins Rd.	CEO: Rocky Liu	1995 Sales: $35 million
East Brunswick, NJ 08816-2006	CFO: Connie Jian	1-Yr. Sales Change: 52.2%
Phone: 908-390-2815	HR: —	Ownership: Privately Held
Fax: 908-390-2817	Employees: 87	

Computers - mainframe systems & parts

DIANON SYSTEMS, INC.

200 Watson Blvd.	CEO: Richard A. Sandberg	1994 Sales: $41 million
Stratford, CT 06497	CFO: Carl R. Iberger	1-Yr. Sales Change: 7.0%
Phone: 203-381-4000	HR: David Bryant	Exchange: Nasdaq
Fax: 203-380-4158	Employees: 361	Symbol: DIAN

Medical services - oncology testing & diagnostic information services

DIGITAL NETWORK ASSOCIATES INC.

110 Wall St., 25th Fl.
New York, NY 10005
Phone: 212-425-8000
Fax: 212-425-0809

CEO: Eric B. Schwartz
CFO: Joseph B. Goeller
HR: Robert M. Johnson
Employees: 40

1995 Est. Sales: $16 mil.
1-Yr. Sales Change: 19.4%
Ownership: Privately Held

Computers - network integration services linking dissimiliar host & client environments

DIGITAL SOLUTIONS, INC.

4041-F Hadley Rd.
South Plainfield, NJ 07080
Phone: 908-561-1200
Fax: 908-561-5348

CEO: Raymond J. Skiptunis
CFO: Kenneth P. Brice
HR: Louis J. Monari
Employees: 4,150

1994 Sales: $38 million
1-Yr. Sales Change: 158.5%
Exchange: Nasdaq (SC)
Symbol: DGSI

Personnel - payroll processing, personnel placement, employee leasing & insurance services

DILLON, READ & COMPANY

535 Madison Ave.
New York, NY 10022
Phone: 212-906-7000
Fax: 212-486-8077

CEO: Franklin W. Hobbs IV
CFO: David Niemiec
HR: Lori Hinchman
Employees: 600

1995 Sales: —
1-Yr. Sales Change: —
Ownership: Privately Held

Financial - investment bankers

DIME BANCORP, INC.

589 Fifth Ave.
New York, NY 10017
Phone: 212-326-6170
Fax: 212-326-6169

CEO: James M. Large Jr.
CFO: John V. Brull
HR: —
Employees: 1,700

1994 Sales: $654.2 million
1-Yr. Sales Change: 9.4%
Exchange: NYSE
Symbol: DME

Financial - savings & loans

See pages 100–101 for a full profile of this company.

DIME FINANCIAL CORPORATION

95 Barnes Rd., PO Box 700
Wallingford, CT 06492
Phone: 203-269-8881
Fax: 203-284-1091

CEO: Richard H. Dionne
CFO: Albert E. Fiacre Jr.
HR: Karen Pinchook
Employees: 253

1994 Sales: $48.2 million
1-Yr. Sales Change: -8.5%
Exchange: Nasdaq
Symbol: DIBK

Banks - Northeast

DIPLOMAT CORPORATION

25 Kay Fries Dr.	CEO: Sheldon R. Rose	1994 Sales: $10.3 million
Stony Point, NY 10980	CFO: Irwin Oringer	1-Yr. Sales Change: 25.6%
Phone: 914-786-5552	HR: Michael Lichtenstein	Exchange: Nasdaq (SC)
Fax: 914-786-8727	Employees: 55	Symbol: DIPL

Textiles - cloth diapers, diaper covers, bedding, furniture covers, infant & toddler car seat covers & other accessories (Ecology Kids, Lamaze from AMI/Ecology Kids)

DIRECT CONNECT INTERNATIONAL INC.

700 Godwin Ave., Ste. 110	CEO: Joseph M. Salvani	1995 Sales: $3.9 million
Midland Park , NJ 07432-1460	CFO: Barry A. Rosner	1-Yr. Sales Change: -59.4%
Phone: 201-445-2101	HR: —	Exchange: OTC
Fax: 201-445-3839	Employees: 7	Symbol: KIDZ

Toys - infant & preschool toy products, including soft toys & sound-activated toys

DIRECT MARKETING ENTERPRISES, INC.

1200 Shames Dr.	CEO: Jerry Williams	1994 Sales: $150 million
Westbury, NY 11590	CFO: —	1-Yr. Sales Change: 7.1%
Phone: 516-997-8881	HR: —	Ownership: Privately Held
Fax: 516-997-8315	Employees: 450	

Retail - catalog & mail-order low-priced jewelry, perfume, collectors items & cookware

DIVERSIFAX, INC.

39 Stringham	CEO: Irwin A. Horowitz	1994 Sales: $6 million
Valley Stream, NY 11580	CFO: Kevin J. Coffey	1-Yr. Sales Change: 25.0%
Phone: 516-872-0650	HR: Susan Reckhart	Exchange: Nasdaq (SC)
Fax: 516-872-0904	Employees: 106	Symbol: DFAX

Office automation - coin & debit card pay-per-copy photocopy machines, microfilm reader-printers & accessory equipment

DNX CORPORATION

575 Rte. 28	CEO: Paul J. Schmitt	1994 Sales: $26.5 million
Raritan, NJ 08869	CFO: John G. Cooper	1-Yr. Sales Change: 11.8%
Phone: 908-722-7900	HR: —	Exchange: Nasdaq
Fax: 908-722-6677	Employees: 301	Symbol: DNXX

Biomedical & genetic products - genetically altered animal organs for human transplant

DONALDSON, LUFKIN & JENRETTE, INC.

140 Broadway
New York, NY 10005
Phone: 212-504-3000
Fax: 212-504-4009

Financial - investment banking

CEO: John S. Chalsty
CFO: Anthony Daddino
HR: Gerald Rigg
Employees: 4,676

1994 Sales: $2,290 million
1-Yr. Sales Change: 37.1%
Exchange: NYSE
Symbol: DLJ

DONNA KARAN, INC.

550 Seventh Ave.
New York, NY 10018
Phone: 212-789-1500
Fax: 212-789-9410

Apparel - women's designer clothing (DKNY)

CEO: Donna Karan
CFO: Patrick Spainhour
HR: —
Employees: 1,310

1994 Sales: $420 million
1-Yr. Sales Change: 2.9%
Ownership: Privately Held

DONNKENNY, INC.

1411 Broadway
New York, NY 10018
Phone: 212-730-7770
Fax: 212-398-1787

Apparel - women's coordinated separates, sportswear & sleepwear

CEO: Richard Rubin
CFO: Edward T. Creevy
HR: Edward T. Creevy
Employees: 1,710

1994 Sales: $158.8 million
1-Yr. Sales Change: 10.2%
Exchange: Nasdaq
Symbol: DNKY

DORAL HOTELS & RESORTS MANAGEMENT COMPANY

122 E. 42nd St.
New York, NY 10168
Phone: 212-557-3300
Fax: 212-557-3410

Hotels & resorts

CEO: Bruce Blum
CFO: —
HR: Wendy Lundsten
Employees: 3,300

1994 Sales: $220 million
1-Yr. Sales Change: 4.8%
Ownership: Privately Held

DOVER CORPORATION

280 Park Ave.
New York, NY 10017-1292
Phone: 212-922-1640
Fax: 212-922-1656

Diversified - a group of 70 diverse industrial manufacturing companies

CEO: Thomas L. Reece
CFO: John F. McNiff
HR: —
Employees: 22,992

1994 Sales: $3,085.3 mil.
1-Yr. Sales Change: 24.2%
Exchange: NYSE
Symbol: DOV

 See pages 102–103 for a full profile of this company.

DOW JONES & COMPANY, INC.

200 Liberty St.	CEO: Peter R. Kann	1994 Sales: $2,091 million
New York, NY 10281	CFO: Kevin J. Roche	1-Yr. Sales Change: 8.2%
Phone: 212-416-2000	HR: James A. Scaduto	Exchange: NYSE
Fax: 212-732-8356	Employees: 10,300	Symbol: DJ

Publishing - newspapers & online business information

 See pages 104–105 for a full profile of this company.

DRESS BARN, INC.

30 Dunnigan Dr.	CEO: Elliot S. Jaffe	1995 Sales: $500.8 million
Suffern, NY 10901	CFO: Armand Correia	1-Yr. Sales Change: 9.5%
Phone: 914-369-4500	HR: David Montieth	Exchange: Nasdaq
Fax: 914-369-4829	Employees: 6,400	Symbol: DBRN

Retail - apparel & shoes

DREW INDUSTRIES INCORPORATED

200 Mamaroneck Ave.	CEO: Leigh J. Abrams	1994 Sales: $83 million
White Plains, NY 10601	CFO: Fredric M. Zinn	1-Yr. Sales Change: -36.5%
Phone: 914-428-9098	HR: —	Exchange: AMEX
Fax: 914-428-4581	Employees: 988	Symbol: DW

Building products - aluminum windows & skylights

DRIVER-HARRIS COMPANY

308 Middlesex St.	CEO: Frank L. Driver III	1994 Sales: $60.6 million
Harrison, NJ 07029	CFO: Thomas Carey	1-Yr. Sales Change: -27.9%
Phone: 201-483-4802	HR: —	Exchange: AMEX
Fax: 201-483-4806	Employees: 427	Symbol: DRH

Metals - nonferrous

DRUG GUILD DISTRIBUTORS

350 Meadowland Pkwy.	CEO: Roman Englander	1994 Sales: $520 million
Secaucus, NJ 07094	CFO: Jay Reba	1-Yr. Sales Change: 15.6%
Phone: 201-348-3700	HR: Irene Sclafane	Ownership: Privately Held
Fax: 201-608-3893	Employees: 310	

Drugs & sundries

DS BANCOR, INC.

33 Elizabeth St.
Derby, CT 06418
Phone: 203-736-1000
Fax: 203-732-5785

Financial - savings & loans

CEO: Harry DiAdamo Jr.
CFO: Harry DiAdamoJr.
HR: Bonnie Smith
Employees: 312

1994 Sales: $80.4 million
1-Yr. Sales Change: -1.5%
Exchange: Nasdaq
Symbol: DSBC

DUALSTAR TECHNOLOGIES CORPORATION

150 E. 42nd St.
New York, NY 10017
Phone: 212-986-9186
Fax: 212-949-9325

CEO: Gregory Cuneo
CFO: Stephen J. Yager
HR: —
Employees: 170

1995 Sales: $65.1 million
1-Yr. Sales Change: 122.9%
Exchange: Nasdaq
Symbol: DSTR

Instruments - mechanical systems & services; electronic & control systems & services

DUANE READE HOLDING COMPANY

49-29 30th Place
Long Island City, NY 11101
Phone: 718-391-4800
Fax: 718-391-4875

Retail - drugstores

CEO: Barry Weston
CFO: Bill Lang
HR: —
Employees: 1,600

1995 Sales: $325 million
1-Yr. Sales Change: 16.1%
Ownership: Privately Held

THE DUN & BRADSTREET CORPORATION

187 Danbury Rd.
Wilton, CT 06897
Phone: 203-834-4200
Fax: 203-834-4201

CEO: Robert E. Weissman
CFO: Edwin A. Bescherer Jr.
HR: Michael P. Connors
Employees: 47,000

1994 Sales: $4,895.7 mil.
1-Yr. Sales Change: 3.9%
Exchange: NYSE
Symbol. DNB

Business services - marketing & credit information, software & financial services

 See pages 106–107 for a full profile of this company.

DURACELL INTERNATIONAL INC.

Berkshire Corporate Park
Bethel, CT 06801
Phone: 203-796-4000
Fax: 203-796-4187

CEO: Charles R. Perrin
CFO: G. Wade Lewis
HR: Nancy A. Reardon
Employees: 8,100

1995 Sales: $2,079 million
1-Yr. Sales Change: 11.1%
Exchange: NYSE
Symbol: DUR

Electrical products - alkaline batteries (#1 worldwide: Duracell)

DUTY FREE INTERNATIONAL, INC.

63 Copps Hill Rd.	CEO: Alfred Carfora	1995 Sales: $501.8 million
Ridgefield, CT 06877	CFO: Gerald F. Egan	1-Yr. Sales Change: 33.3%
Phone: 203-431-6057	HR: Becky Bahlman	Exchange: NYSE
Fax: 203-438-1356	Employees: 2,000	Symbol: DFI

Retail - leading operator of duty-free stores along the US, Canadian & Mexican borders & in international airports throughout the US

DVL INC.

24 River Rd., PO Box 408	CEO: Alan E. Casnoff	1994 Sales: $3.8 million
Bogota, NJ 07603	CFO: Joel Zbar	1-Yr. Sales Change: 22.6%
Phone: 201-487-1300	HR: Meena Bhatia	Exchange: OTC
Fax: 201-487-2089	Employees: 23	Symbol: DVLN

Real estate investment trust - commercial, office & industrial properties

DYNAMICS CORPORATION OF AMERICA

475 Steamboat Rd.	CEO: Andrew Lozyniak	1994 Sales: $96.5 million
Greenwich, CT 06830-7197	CFO: Patrick J. Dorme	1-Yr. Sales Change: -4.7%
Phone: 203-869-3211	HR: Josephine Vitale	Exchange: NYSE
Fax: 203-869-8708	Employees: 1,132	Symbol: DYA

Diversified operations - appliances, metal & environmental systems

THE DYSON-KISSNER-MORAN CORPORATION

230 Park Ave., Ste. 659	CEO: Robert R. Dyson	1995 Sales: $1,370 million
New York, NY 10169	CFO: M.J. Zilinskas	1-Yr. Sales Change: 0.0%
Phone: 212-661-4600	HR: Louise Donahue	Ownership: Privately Held
Fax: 212-599-5105	Employees: 10,000	

Diversified operations - real estate development; crafts; plumbing & heating; electronics

E & B MARINE INC.

201 Meadow Rd.	CEO: Kenneth G. Peskin	1994 Sales: $101.8 million
Edison, NJ 08818	CFO: Walfrido A. Martinez	1-Yr. Sales Change: 9.8%
Phone: 908-819-7400	HR: —	Exchange: Nasdaq (SC)
Fax: 908-819-4771	Employees: 750	Symbol: EBMA

Retail - mail-order marine supplies & apparel

E. GLUCK CORPORATION

2010 Thompson Ave.
Long Island City, NY 11101
Phone: 718-784-0700
Fax: 718-706-6326

CEO: Eugene Gluck
CFO: Renee Jacobs
HR: Robert Nublin
Employees: —

1994 Sales: $175 million
1-Yr. Sales Change: —
Ownership: Privately Held

Precious metals & jewelry - watches (Anne Klein, Annitron)

EAGLE ELECTRIC MANUFACTURING COMPANY

45-31 Court Sq.
Long Island City, NY 11101
Phone: 718-937-8000
Fax: 718-482-0160

CEO: Neal Kluger
CFO: Nick Vertuzzi
HR: Sophia Stratis
Employees: 2,400

1994 Sales: $180 million
1-Yr. Sales Change: 0.0%
Ownership: Privately Held

Wire & cable products - current-carrying wiring devices

EASTCO INDUSTRIAL SAFETY CORP.

130 W. 10th St.
Huntington Station, NY 11746-1616
Phone: 516-427-1802
Fax: 516-427-1840

CEO: Alan E. Densen
CFO: Anthony P. Towell
HR: Arthur Wasserspring
Employees: 200

1995 Sales: $24 million
1-Yr. Sales Change: 15.9%
Exchange: Nasdaq (SC)
Symbol: ESTO

Protection - disposable safety wear, such as protective clothing & lab coats

ECCS, INC.

One Sheila Dr.
Tinton Falls, NJ 07724
Phone: 908-747-6995
Fax: 908-747-6542

CEO: Michael E. Faherty
CFO: Louis Altieri
HR: Sharon Wallace
Employees: 119

1994 Sales: $42.7 million
1-Yr. Sales Change: -17.2%
Exchange: Nasdaq
Symbol: ECCS

Computers - hardware & mass-storage peripherals

ECHLIN INC.

100 Double Beach Rd.
Branford, CT 06405
Phone: 203-481-5751
Fax: 203-481-6485

CEO: Frederick J. Mancheski
CFO: Richard A. Wisot
HR: Milton J. Makoski
Employees: 23,400

1995 Sales: $2,717.9 mil.
1-Yr. Sales Change: 21.9%
Exchange: NYSE
Symbol: ECH

Automotive & trucking - brake, engine, power transmission & steering & suspension parts

 See pages 108–109 for a full profile of this company.

ECONOMIC CHEMICAL DISTRIBUTION, INC.

PO Box 15038
Jersey City, NJ 07305
Phone: 201-333-1138
Fax: —

Chemicals - industrial; inorganic

CEO: Clarence Nixon
CFO: —
HR: —
Employees: 800

1994 Est. Sales: $150 mil.
1-Yr. Sales Change: -3.2%
Ownership: Privately Held

EDISON CONTROL CORPORATION

140 Ethel Rd. West
Piscataway, NJ 08854
Phone: 908-819-8800
Fax: 908-985-9598

Electrical products - fault indicators

CEO: Mary McCormack
CFO: Jack Miller
HR: —
Employees: 19

1994 Sales: $1.4 million
1-Yr. Sales Change: 16.7%
Exchange: Nasdaq
Symbol: EDCO

EDO CORPORATION

14-04 111th St.
College Point, NY 11356-1434
Phone: 718-321-4000
Fax: 718-321-4194

Electronics - military

CEO: Frank A. Fariello
CFO: Kenneth A. Paladino
HR: Bruce A. Henkle
Employees: 843

1994 Sales: $91 million
1-Yr. Sales Change: -13.1%
Exchange: NYSE
Symbol: EDO

EIS INTERNATIONAL, INC.

1351 Washington Blvd.
Stamford, CT 06902
Phone: 203-351-4800
Fax: 203-961-8632

Telecommunications equipment - inbound & outbound telemarketing/call processing systems

CEO: Joseph J. Porfeli
CFO: Frederick C. Foley
HR: Jo Lovell
Employees: 297

1994 Sales: $64.9 million
1-Yr. Sales Change: 28.0%
Exchange: Nasdaq
Symbol: EISI

 See page 267 for a full profile of this company.

ELECTRIC FUEL CORPORATION

885 Third Ave., Ste. 2900
New York, NY 10022
Phone: 212-230-2172
Fax: 212-230-3299

Automotive & trucking - advanced zinc-air battery based systems for powering electric vehicles

CEO: Yehuda Harats
CFO: Robert S. Ehrlich
HR: —
Employees: 93

1994 Sales: $4.9 million
1-Yr. Sales Change: 32.4%
Exchange: Nasdaq
Symbol: EFCX

ELECTRO-CATHETER CORPORATION

2100 Felver Ct.
Rahway, NJ 07065
Phone: 908-382-5600
Fax: 908-382-7107

CEO: Ervin Schoenblum
CFO: Joseph P. Macaluso
HR: Emily Gordon
Employees: 127

1995 Sales: $7.3 million
1-Yr. Sales Change: -3.9%
Exchange: Nasdaq (SC)
Symbol: ECTH

Medical instruments - catheters & related devices

ELECTRONIC ASSOCIATES, INC.

185 Monmouth Pkwy.
West Long Branch, NJ 07764-9989
Phone: 908-229-1100
Fax: 908-229-1329

CEO: Joseph R. Spalliero
CFO: Stanley O. Jester
HR: Barbara Evenson
Employees: 334

1994 Sales: $30.5 million
1-Yr. Sales Change: 17.3%
Exchange: NYSE
Symbol: EA

Computers - contract manufacturing of electronic products & systems

ELECTRONIC RETAILING SYSTEMS INTERNATIONAL, INC.

372 Danbury Rd.
Wilton, CT 06897
Phone: 203-761-7900
Fax: 203-761-9928

CEO: Bruce F. Failing Jr.
CFO: William Fischer
HR: Virginia Menz
Employees: 57

1994 Sales: $2.4 million
1-Yr. Sales Change: 118.2%
Exchange: Nasdaq
Symbol: ERSI

Computers - electronic shelf-labeling systems for supermarkets

ELLEN TRACY, INC.

575 Seventh Ave.
New York, NY 10018
Phone: 212-944-6999
Fax: 212-398-1678

CEO: Herbert Gallen
CFO: Youram Arieven
HR: Roberta Rooney
Employees: —

1994 Est. Sales: $250 mil.
1-Yr. Sales Change: 25.0%
Ownership: Privately Held

Apparel - bridgewear (industry segment between designers such as Donna Karan & moderately priced lines such as Liz Claiborne)

EMBRYO DEVELOPMENT CORPORATION

750 Lexington Ave., Ste. 2750
New York, NY 10022
Phone: 212-355-8484
Fax: 212-486-0831

CEO: Donn M. Gordon
CFO: Donn M. Gordon
HR: —
Employees: 1

1995 Sales: $0
1-Yr. Sales Change: —
Exchange: Nasdaq (SC)
Symbol: EMBR

Medical products - biomedical devices

EMCOR GROUP, INC.

101 Merritt Seven Corporate Park
Norwalk, CT 06851-1060
Phone: 203-849-7800
Fax: 203-849-7900

CEO: Frank T. MacInnis
CFO: Leicle E. Chesser
HR: Jim Murphy
Employees: 14,000

1994 Sales: $1,764 million
1-Yr. Sales Change: -19.6%
Exchange: OTC
Symbol: EMCG

Diversified operations - electrical & HVAC contracting; water supply

EMERSON RADIO CORP.

9 Entin Rd., PO Box 430
Parsippany, NJ 07054-0430
Phone: 201-884-5800
Fax: 201-428-2022

CEO: Geoffrey P. Jurick
CFO: Eugene I. Davis
HR: Linda Schwartz
Employees: 550

1995 Sales: $654.7 million
1-Yr. Sales Change: 34.3%
Exchange: AMEX
Symbol: MSN

Electronics - parts distribution, video & consumer electronics & microwave oven products

EMISPHERE TECHNOLOGIES, INC.

15 Skyline Dr.
Hawthorne, NY 10532
Phone: 914-347-2220
Fax: 914-347-2498

CEO: Michael M. Goldberg
CFO: Michael M. Goldberg
HR: Joseph Poveromo
Employees: 56

1995 Sales: $0
1-Yr. Sales Change: —
Exchange: Nasdaq
Symbol: EMIS

Drugs - oral drug delivery products

EMPIRE BLUE CROSS AND BLUE SHIELD

622 Third Ave.
New York, NY 10017-6758
Phone: 212-476-1000
Fax: 212-370-0575

CEO: Michael A. Stocker
CFO: Ramesh Punwani
HR: Michael L. Kent
Employees: 7,900

1994 Sales: $4,798.4 mil.
1-Yr. Sales Change: -10.9%
Ownership: Privately Held

Insurance - health, hospital & medical service plans

EMPIRE OFFICE EQUIPMENT, INC.

21 Murray St.
New York, NY 10007
Phone: 212-349-5530
Fax: 212-766-2328

CEO: Lawrence L. Gaslow
CFO: Joel Rosenberg
HR: Perlita Konikoff
Employees: 200

1994 Sales: $150 million
1-Yr. Sales Change: -6.8%
Ownership: Privately Held

Wholesale distribution - contract office equipment

EMPRESS INTERNATIONAL LTD.

10 Harbor Park Dr.
Port Washington, NY 11050
Phone: 516-621-5900
Fax: 516-621-8318

Food - importer of frozen seafood

CEO: Joel Kolen
CFO: Ronald Carvalho
HR: —
Employees: 33

1995 Sales: $108 million
1-Yr. Sales Change: 20.0%
Ownership: Privately Held

ENERGY RESEARCH CORPORATION

3 Great Pasture Rd.
Danbury, CT 06813
Phone: 203-792-1460
Fax: 203-798-2945

CEO: Bernard S. Baker
CFO: Louis P. Barth
HR: Rena Cherry
Employees: 156

1995 Sales: $34 million
1-Yr. Sales Change: 13.0%
Exchange: Nasdaq (SC)
Symbol: ERCC

Electrical products - electrochemical technologies, fuel cells & batteries

ENGELHARD CORPORATION

101 Wood Ave.
Iselin, NJ 08830
Phone: 908-205-5000
Fax: 908-321-1161

CEO: Orin R. Smith
CFO: William E. Nettles
HR: William M. Dugle
Employees: 5,830

1994 Sales: $2,385.8 mil.
1-Yr. Sales Change: 10.9%
Exchange: NYSE
Symbol: EC

Chemicals - specialty; engineered materials & precious metals management services to the automotive, petroleum & paper industries

ENHANCE FINANCIAL SERVICES GROUP, INC.

335 Madison Ave.
New York, NY 10017
Phone: 212-983-3100
Fax: 212-682-5377

CEO: Daniel J. Gross
CFO: Robert M. Rosenberg
HR: —
Employees: 79

1994 Sales: $96.4 million
1-Yr. Sales Change: -12.5%
Exchange: NYSE
Symbol: EFS

Insurance - property & casualty

ENTERACTIVE, INC.

110 W. 40th St., Ste. 2100
New York, NY 10018
Phone: 212-221-6559
Fax: 212-730-6045

CEO: Andrew Gyenes
CFO: Kenneth Gruber
HR: —
Employees: 48

1995 Sales: $0.4 million
1-Yr. Sales Change: -83.3%
Exchange: Nasdaq (SC)
Symbol: ENTR

Computers - interactive multimedia products for the home & school markets

ENTERTAINMENT/MEDIA ACQUISITION CORPORATION

745 Fifth Ave.	CEO: Jeffrey A. Rochlis	1994 Sales: $0
New York, NY 10151	CFO: Kevin M. Kelley	1-Yr. Sales Change: —
Phone: 212-888-4700	HR: Jana R. Josel	Exchange: OTC
Fax: 212-888-9178	Employees: 3	Symbol: EMAC

Financial - media business acquisitions

ENTEX INFORMATION SERVICES

6 International Dr.	CEO: John A. McKenna Jr.	1995 Est. Sales: $1,500 mil.
Rye Brook, NY 10573	CFO: Wayne D. Stinnett Jr.	1-Yr. Sales Change: 7.1%
Phone: 914-935-3600	HR: Philip R. Johnson	Ownership: Privately Held
Fax: 914-935-3750	Employees: 6,200	

Computers - reseller of PCs to large corporations & PC systems integration (#1 privately owned in the US)

ENVIRONMENTAL SERVICES OF AMERICA, INC.

937 E. Hazelwood Ave., Bldg. 2	CEO: Jon Colin	1994 Sales: $32.8 million
Rahway, NJ 07065	CFO: Kathleen P. LeFevre	1-Yr. Sales Change: 37.8%
Phone: 908-381-9229	HR: Susan Yuseff	Exchange: Nasdaq
Fax: 908-381-7887	Employees: 345	Symbol: ENSA

Pollution control equipment & services - waste disposal services, environmental consulting; remediation of hazardous waste sites; air quality testing

ENVIRONMENTAL TECHNOLOGIES CORP.

550 James St.	CEO: George Cannan Sr.	1995 Sales: $28.7 million
Lakewood, NJ 08701-4021	CFO: Richard Schmeling	1-Yr. Sales Change: 44.9%
Phone: 908-370-3400	HR: —	Exchange: Nasdaq
Fax: 908-370-3088	Employees: 45	Symbol: EVTC

Chemicals - refrigerants & refrigerant reclaiming services

ENVIROSOURCE, INC.

5 High Ridge Park, PO Box 10309	CEO: Louis A. Guzzetti Jr.	1994 Sales: $259.5 million
Stamford, CT 06904-2309	CFO: James C. Hull	1-Yr. Sales Change: -4.2%
Phone: 203-322-8333	HR: Donna Robbins	Exchange: Nasdaq
Fax: 203-968-1039	Employees: 1,850	Symbol: ENSO

Pollution control equipment & services - waste disposal services

ENZO BIOCHEM, INC.

60 Executive Blvd.
Farmingdale, NY 11735
Phone: 516-755-5500
Fax: 516-755-5561

CEO: Elazar Rabbani
CFO: Shahram K. Rabbani
HR: June Tedesco
Employees: 232

1995 Sales: $31.7 million
1-Yr. Sales Change: 38.4%
Exchange: AMEX
Symbol: ENZ

Biomedical & genetic products - diagnostics to detect sexually transmitted diseases & other infectious diseases

ENZON, INC.

40 Kingsbridge Rd.
Piscataway, NJ 08854-3998
Phone: 908-980-4500
Fax: 908-980-5911

CEO: Pete Tombros
CFO: Ken Geureubersil
HR: —
Employees: 244

1995 Sales: $15.8 million
1-Yr. Sales Change: 6.8%
Exchange: Nasdaq
Symbol: ENZN

Biomedical & genetic products

THE EQUITABLE COMPANIES INCORPORATED

787 Seventh Ave.
New York, NY 10019
Phone: 212-554-1234
Fax: 212-315-2825

CEO: Richard H. Jenrette
CFO: Jerry M. de St. Paer
HR: Janet Friedman
Employees: 13,600

1994 Sales: $6,447.3 mil.
1-Yr. Sales Change: -0.5%
Exchange: NYSE
Symbol: EQ

Insurance - life, financial services (Donaldson, Lufkin & Jenrette, Alliance Capital Management)

 See pages 110–111 for a full profile of this company.

ERD WASTE CORPORATION

70 Water St.
Long Beach, NY 11561
Phone: 516-543-0606
Fax: 516-543-0678

CEO: Robert Rubin
CFO: Kathryn Kohsiek
HR: Kathryn Kohsiek
Employees: 50

1995 Sales: $6.7 million
1-Yr. Sales Change: 857.1%
Exchange: Nasdaq
Symbol: ERDI

Pollution control - industrial & commercial waste disposal & management

ERNST & YOUNG LLP

787 Park Ave.
New York, NY 10019
Phone: 212-773-3000
Fax: 212-773-1996

CEO: Phil Laskaway
CFO: Hilton Dean
HR: Bruce J. Mantia
Employees: 65,000

1995 Sales: $6,870 million
1-Yr. Sales Change: 14.1%
Ownership: Privately Held

Business services - accounting & consulting

 See pages 112–113 for a full profile of this company.

ESMARK, INC.

111 W. 40th St.	CEO: Howard Cooley	1994 Sales: $140 million
New York, NY 10018	CFO: Beverly Eichel	1-Yr. Sales Change: 0.0%
Phone: 212-764-4630	HR: Amy Baron	Ownership: Privately Held
Fax: 212-764-7265	Employees: 2,000	

Leisure & recreational equipment - sporting & athletic goods

ESQUIRE COMMUNICATIONS LTD.

342 Madison Ave.	CEO: Malcolm L. Elvey	1994 Sales: $12.8 million
New York, NY 10173	CFO: Malcolm L. Elvey	1-Yr. Sales Change: 128.6%
Phone: 212-687-8010	HR: Vasan Thatham	Exchange: Nasdaq (SC)
Fax: 212-572-5972	Employees: 310	Symbol: ESQS

Business services - court reporting, providing printed & computerized transcripts, video recordings of testimony from depositions & speech recognition systems

ESSENCE COMMUNICATIONS INC.

1500 Broadway	CEO: Edward Lewis	1994 Sales: $77.5 million
New York, NY 10036	CFO: Harry Dedyo	1-Yr. Sales Change: 9.0%
Phone: 212-642-0600	HR: Elaine P. Williams	Ownership: Privately Held
Fax: 212-921-5173	Employees: 102	

Publishing - magazines; TV production; direct-mail catalogs

THE ESTÉE LAUDER COMPANIES INC.

767 Fifth Ave.	CEO: Leonard A. Lauder	1995 Sales: $2,899 million
New York, NY 10153	CFO: Robert J. Bigler	1-Yr. Sales Change: 12.5%
Phone: 212-572-4200	HR: Andrew J. Cavanaugh	Exchange: NYSE
Fax: 212-572-3941	Employees: 9,900	Symbol: EL

Cosmetics (Estée Lauder, Clinique, Aramis, Prescriptives, Origins)

See pages 114–115 for a full profile of this company.

ETHAN ALLEN INTERIORS INC.

Ethan Allen Dr.	CEO: M. Farooq Kathwari	1995 Sales: $476.1 million
Danbury, CT 06811	CFO: Edward P. Schade	1-Yr. Sales Change: 8.9%
Phone: 203-743-8000	HR: Charles J. Farfaglia	Exchange: NYSE
Fax: 203-743-8298	Employees: 6,048	Symbol: ETH

Retail - furniture; wood furnishings, upholstered products & home furnishing accessories

ETIENNE AIGNER, INC.

712 Fifth Ave.
New York, NY 10019
Phone: 212-246-8660
Fax: 212-956-6146

CEO: Robert B. Chavez
CFO: Michael Cangemi
HR: Eileen Stewart
Employees: 450

1994 Sales: $135 million
1-Yr. Sales Change: 0.0%
Ownership: Privately Held

Leather & related products - handbags & women's shoes

E'TOWN CORPORATION

600 South Ave.
Westfield, NJ 07090
Phone: 908-654-1234
Fax: 908-232-2719

CEO: Robert W. Kean, Jr.
CFO: Andrew M. Chapman
HR: Henry S. Patterson III
Employees: 386

1994 Sales: $102 million
1-Yr. Sales Change: 2.0%
Exchange: NYSE
Symbol: ETW

Utility - water supply

EV ENVIRONMENTAL, INC.

1465 Post Road East
Westport, CT 06880
Phone: 203-256-9596
Fax: 203-259-2507

CEO: Michael R. Cox
CFO: Dan L. Scroggins
HR: Ralph Armstrong
Employees: 105

1994 Sales: $9.8 million
1-Yr. Sales Change: 5.4%
Exchange: Nasdaq (SC)
Symbol: EVEN

Filtration - products used to treat water & waste water

EXCEL TECHNOLOGY, INC.

45 Adams Ave.
Hauppauge, NY 11788
Phone: 516-273-6900
Fax: 516-273-6958

CEO: Rama Rao
CFO: J. Donald Hill
HR: Karen Kujawski
Employees: 196

1994 Sales: $33.6 million
1-Yr. Sales Change: 15.9%
Exchange: Nasdaq
Symbol: XLTC

Lasers - systems & components

EXECUTIVE TELECARD, LTD.

8 Avenue C
Nanuet, NY 10954
Phone: 914-627-2060
Fax: 914-627-3631

CEO: Anthony Balinger
CFO: Allen Mandel
HR: Robert Schuck
Employees: 83

1995 Sales: $30.6 million
1-Yr. Sales Change: 70.0%
Exchange: Nasdaq
Symbol: EXTL

Telecommunications services - telephone charge card

EXECUTONE INFORMATION SYSTEMS, INC.

478 Wheelers Farms Rd.	CEO: Alan Kessman	1994 Sales: $292 million
Milford, CT 06460	CFO: Anthony R. Guarascio	1-Yr. Sales Change: -3.7%
Phone: 203-876-7600	HR: Elizabeth Hinds	Exchange: Nasdaq
Fax: 203-882-0398	Employees: 2,400	Symbol: XTON

Telecommunications equipment - hospital, voice & data communications equipment

EXOGEN, INC.

10 Constitution Ave., PO Box 6860	CEO: John P. Ryaby	1995 Sales: $1.9 million
Piscataway, NJ 08855	CFO: Richard H. Reisner	1-Yr. Sales Change: —
Phone: 908-981-0990	HR: Mark McNulty	Exchange: Nasdaq
Fax: 908-981-0003	Employees: 36	Symbol: EXGN

Medical instruments - devices for noninvasive treatment musculoskeletal injury & disease

E-Z-EM, INC.

717 Main St.	CEO: Daniel R. Martin	1995 Sales: $97.6 million
Westbury, NY 11590-5021	CFO: Dennis J. Curtin	1-Yr. Sales Change: 3.4%
Phone: 516-333-8230	HR: Sandra D. Baron	Exchange: AMEX
Fax: 516-333-8278	Employees: 1,020	Symbol: EZMA

Medical instruments - diagnostic imaging products for assisting radiologists in the detection of physical abnormalities & gastrointestinal diseases

F. SCHUMACHER & COMPANY

79 Madison Ave.	CEO: Philip P. Puschel	1994 Sales: $300 million
New York, NY 10016	CFO: Joe Meth	1-Yr. Sales Change: 9.1%
Phone: 212-213-7900	HR: James Hinthorn	Ownership: Privately Held
Fax: 212-213-7711	Employees: 1,500	

Textiles - fabrics & wall coverings

FAB INDUSTRIES, INC.

200 Madison Ave.	CEO: Samson Bitensky	1994 Sales: $189.8 million
New York, NY 10016	CFO: Howard Soren	1-Yr. Sales Change: 0.1%
Phone: 212-592-2700	HR: Marilyn Ende	Exchange: AMEX
Fax: 212-689-6929	Employees: 1,800	Symbol: FIT

Textiles - knitting mills

FAIRCHILD CORPORATION

110 E. 59th St.
New York, NY 10022
Phone: 212-308-6700
Fax: 212-888-5674

Aerospace - aircraft equipment

CEO: Jeffrey J. Steiner
CFO: Michael T. Alcox
HR: Maureen Rickbeil
Employees: 3,500

1995 Sales: $546.3 million
1-Yr. Sales Change: 23.0%
Exchange: NYSE
Symbol: FA

FAMILY BARGAIN CORPORATION

315 E. 62nd St.
New York, NY 10021
Phone: 212-980-9670
Fax: 212-593-4586

Retail - off-price apparel

CEO: John A. Selzer
CFO: William W. Mowbray
HR: —
Employees: 1,870

1995 Sales: $146.5 million
1-Yr. Sales Change: 51.8%
Exchange: Nasdaq (SC)
Symbol: FBAR

FAMILY GOLF CENTERS, INC.

225 Broadhollow Rd.
Melville, NY 11747
Phone: 516-694-1666
Fax: 516-694-0918

Leisure & recreational services - golf-related recreational facilities

CEO: Dominic Chang
CFO: Krishnan P. Thampi
HR: Krishnan P. Thampi
Employees: 133

1994 Sales: $6.3 million
1-Yr. Sales Change: 142.3%
Exchange: Nasdaq (SC)
Symbol: FGCI

FARMERS & MECHANICS BANK

237 Main St.
Middletown, CT 06457
Phone: 203-346-9677
Fax: 203-638-4468

Financial - savings & loans

CEO: John F. Beckert
CFO: Joel E. Hyman
HR: Sheila M. Privott
Employees: 220

1994 Sales: $35.4 million
1-Yr. Sales Change: -1.1%
Exchange: Nasdaq
Symbol: FMCT

FARMLAND DAIRIES, INC.

520 Main Ave.
Wallington, NJ 07057
Phone: 201-777-2500
Fax: 201-361-3127

Agricultural operations - dairy & milk depot

CEO: Jacob Goldman
CFO: William Black
HR: Lisa Annunziata
Employees: 328

1994 Sales: $150 million
1-Yr. Sales Change: -3.2%
Ownership: Privately Held

FARREL CORPORATION

25 Main St.
Ansonia, CT 06401
Phone: 203-736-5500
Fax: 203-735-6267

CEO: Rolf K. Liebergesell
CFO: Rolf K. Liebergesell
HR: —
Employees: 550

1994 Sales: $75.5 million
1-Yr. Sales Change: -0.4%
Exchange: Nasdaq
Symbol: FARL

Machinery - mixers, extruders, pelletizers & pumps for rubber & plastics

FEDDERS CORPORATION

505 Martinsville Rd., PO Box 813
Liberty Corner, NJ 07938
Phone: 908-604-8686
Fax: 908-604-0715

CEO: Salvatore Giordano Jr.
CFO: Robert L. Laurent Jr.
HR: —
Employees: 1,800

1995 Sales: $316.5 million
1-Yr. Sales Change: 36.7%
Exchange: NYSE
Symbol: FJC

Building products - window, through-the-wall & split ductless room air conditioners

FEDERAL PAPER BOARD COMPANY, INC.

75 Chestnut Ridge Rd.
Montvale, NJ 07645
Phone: 201-391-1776
Fax: 201-307-6125

CEO: John R. Kennedy
CFO: Quentin J. Kennedy
HR: Barry Smedstad
Employees: 6,890

1994 Sales: $1,569.6 mil.
1-Yr. Sales Change: 13.2%
Exchange: NYSE
Symbol: FBO

Paper & paper products

FEDERAL RESERVE BANK OF NEW YORK

33 Liberty St.
New York, NY 10045
Phone: 212-720-5000
Fax: 212-720-6947

CEO: William J. McDonough
CFO: Ernest T. Patrikias
HR: Donald Vangel
Employees: 3,100

1994 Sales: $7,133.1 mil.
1-Yr. Sales Change: 11.8%
Ownership: Privately Held

Regional federal banking institution for the creation of US monetary policy

FENWAY PARTNERS INC.

152 W. 57th St.
New York, NY 10019
Phone: 212-698-9400
Fax: 212-757-0609

CEO: Peter Lamm
CFO: Stuart Diamond
HR: Stuart Diamond
Employees: —

1994 Est. Sales: $340 mil.
1-Yr. Sales Change: —
Ownership: Privately Held

Financial - investment banking (Valley Recreational Products, Teters Floral Products, Bear Archery, M.W. Manufacturers, Brown Moulding, Halkey-Roberts)

FEROLITO, VULTAGGIO & SONS

5 Dakota Dr., Ste. 205
Success, NY 11042
Phone: 516-327-0002
Fax: 516-326-4988

CEO: John Ferolito
CFO: Rick Adonaillo
HR: —
Employees: 200

1994 Sales: $300 million
1-Yr. Sales Change: 130.8%
Ownership: Privately Held

Beverages - iced tea & fruit drinks (AriZona)

 See page 268 for a full profile of this company.

FINANCIAL BANCORP, INC.

42-25 Queens Blvd.
Long Island City, NY 11104
Phone: 718-729-5002
Fax: 718-937-6326

CEO: Stuart G. Hoffer
CFO: P. James O'Gorman
HR: Robert Adamec
Employees: 60

1994 Sales: $13.4 million
1-Yr. Sales Change: 11.7%
Exchange: Nasdaq
Symbol: FIBC

Financial - savings & loan

FINANCIAL FEDERAL CORPORATION

400 Park Ave., 8th Fl.
New York, NY 10022-4406
Phone: 212-888-3344
Fax: 212-888-0695

CEO: Clarence Y. Palitz Jr.
CFO: Michael C. Palitz
HR: —
Employees: 110

1995 Sales: $35 million
1-Yr. Sales Change: 35.1%
Exchange: AMEX
Symbol: FIF

Financial - financing & leasing of equipment & machinery, especially construction, over-the-road-transportation, waste management & disposal equipment & machine tools

FINANCIAL SECURITY ASSURANCE HOLDINGS LTD.

350 Park Ave., 13th Fl.
New York, NY 10022
Phone: 212-826-0100
Fax: 212-339-0820

CEO: Robert P. Cochran
CFO: John A. Harrison
HR: Margaret M. McGovern
Employees: 160

1994 Sales: $109.4 million
1-Yr. Sales Change: -14.3%
Exchange: NYSE
Symbol: FSA

Financial - insurer of asset-backed securities & municipal bonds

FINANCIAL SERVICES ACQUISITION CORPORATION

667 Madison Ave.
New York, NY 10021
Phone: 212-246-1000
Fax: 212-246-1514

CEO: Gilbert Scharf
CFO: Michael J. Scharf
HR: —
Employees: 2

1994 Sales: $0
1-Yr. Sales Change: —
Exchange: OTC
Symbol: FSAC

Financial - business acquisitions

FIND/SVP, INC.

625 Avenue of the Americas, 2nd Fl.
New York, NY 10011
Phone: 212-645-4500
Fax: 212-645-7681

Consulting & information services

CEO: Andrew P. Garvin
CFO: Peter J. Fiorillo
HR: —
Employees: 220

1994 Sales: $24.4 million
1-Yr. Sales Change: 20.2%
Exchange: Nasdaq (SC)
Symbol: FSVP

FINLAY ENTERPRISES, INC.

521 5th Ave.
New York, NY 10175
Phone: 212-382-7400
Fax: 212-557-3848

Retail - jewelry outlets in department stores

CEO: David B. Cornstein
CFO: Barry D. Schecker
HR: Joyce Manning
Employees: 6,250

1995 Sales: $552.1 million
1-Yr. Sales Change: 9.2%
Exchange: Nasdaq
Symbol: FNLY

FIRETECTOR INC.

262 Duffy Ave.
Hicksville, NY 11801-0000
Phone: 516-433-4700
Fax: 516-433-1131

Protection - life safety, security, energy management & audio/video communication systems for office buildings, hotels, apartment buildings & other structures

CEO: Richard Axelsen
CFO: Marc Palker
HR: —
Employees: 133

1994 Sales: $12.1 million
1-Yr. Sales Change: 28.7%
Exchange: Nasdaq (SC)
Symbol: FTEC

FIRST BRANDS CORPORATION

83 Wooster Heights Rd., PO Box 1911
Danbury, CT 06813-1911
Phone: 203-731-2300
Fax: 203-731-2518

Retail - distribution of consumer products for the household & automotive markets, soap & cleaning preparations, plastic wrap (Glad), engine additive products (STP) & car polish (Simoniz)

CEO: William V. Stephenson
CFO: Donald A. DeSantis
HR: Ronald F. Dainton
Employees: 4,200

1995 Sales: $1,036.5 mil.
1-Yr. Sales Change: -4.6%
Exchange: NYSE
Symbol: FBR

FIRST CENTRAL FINANCIAL CORPORATION

266 Merrick Rd., PO Box 7014
Lynbrook, NY 11563-7014
Phone: 516-593-7070
Fax: 516-593-8880

Insurance - property & casualty

CEO: Martin J. Simon
CFO: Joan M. Locascio
HR: Ray Barancaccio
Employees: 136

1994 Sales: $56.3 million
1-Yr. Sales Change: 14.0%
Exchange: AMEX
Symbol: FCC

FIRST DATA CORPORATION

401 Hackensack Ave.	CEO: Henry C. "Ric" Duques	1994 Sales: $1,652.2 mil.
Hackensack, NJ 07601	CFO: Lee Andrean	1-Yr. Sales Change: 10.9%
Phone: 201-525-4702	HR: Donald F. Crowley	Exchange: NYSE
Fax: 201-342-0402	Employees: 22,000	Symbol: FDC

Financial - credit card processing & worldwide money-transfer services (Western Union)

FIRST FIDELITY BANCORPORATION

550 Broad St.	CEO: Anthony P. Terracciano	1994 Sales: $2,553.1 mil.
Newark, NJ 07102	CFO: Wolfgang Schoellkopf	1-Yr. Sales Change: 5.1%
Phone: 201-565-3200	HR: William A. Karmen	Exchange: NYSE
Fax: 201-565-3359	Employees: 12,000	Symbol: FFB

Banks; insurance & stock brokerage; automobile & equipment leasing

THE FIRST OF LONG ISLAND CORPORATION

10 Glen Head Rd.	CEO: J. William Johnson	1994 Sales: $28.3 million
Glen Head, NY 11545	CFO: William J. White	1-Yr. Sales Change: 6.0%
Phone: 516-671-4900	HR: Barbara Whitebook	Exchange: Nasdaq (SC)
Fax: 516-671-4842	Employees: 187	Symbol: FLIC

Banks - Northeast (The First National Bank of Long Island)

FIRST STATE FINANCIAL SERVICES, INC.

1120 Bloomfield Ave., Ste. CN 2449	CEO: Michael J. Quigley III	1994 Sales: $35.2 million
West Caldwell, NJ 07007-2449	CFO: Emil J. Butchko	1-Yr. Sales Change: 1.7%
Phone: 201-575-5800	HR: Elizabeth Hubble	Exchange: Nasdaq
Fax: 201-244-4012	Employees: 173	Symbol: FSFI

Financial - savings & loans

FLASH CREATIVE MANAGEMENT

1060 Main St.	CEO: David Blumenthal	1994 Sales: $2 million
River Edge, NJ 07661-2013	CFO: David Blumenthal	1-Yr. Sales Change: 0.0%
Phone: 201-489-2500	HR: David Blumenthal	Ownership: Privately Held
Fax: 201-489-6750	Employees: 25	

Computers - consulting services, including business process improvement, strategic information systems development & developer-level training services

THE FLEMINGTON NATIONAL BANK AND TRUST COMPANY

56 Main St., PO Box 231
Flemington, NJ 08822
Phone: 908-782-3151
Fax: 908-284-4916

Banks - Northeast

CEO: Nathan C. Collins
CFO: Thomas Pickel
HR: Judy D'Aluto
Employees: —

1994 Sales: $19.6 million
1-Yr. Sales Change: -3.4%
Exchange: Nasdaq (SC)
Symbol: FLNB

FLIGHTSAFETY INTERNATIONAL, INC.

La Guardia Airport
Flushing, NY 11371-1061
Phone: 718-565-4100
Fax: 718-565-4134

Schools - aircraft operator training

CEO: Albert L. Ueltschi
CFO: Kenneth W. Motschwiller
HR: Thomas W. Riffe
Employees: 2,246

1994 Sales: $301.3 million
1-Yr. Sales Change: 1.4%
Exchange: NYSE
Symbol: FSI

FOILMARK, INC.

40 Melville Park Rd.
Melville, NY 11747
Phone: 516-694-7773
Fax: 516-694-6836

Machinery - foil & stamping equipment, tooling & dies

CEO: Frank J. Olsen Jr.
CFO: Philip Leibel
HR: Philip Leibel
Employees: 224

1994 Sales: $30.6 million
1-Yr. Sales Change: 10.9%
Exchange: Nasdaq
Symbol: FLMK

FONAR CORPORATION

110 Marcus Dr.
Melville, NY 11747-4292
Phone: 516-694-2929
Fax: 516-694-5434

Medical instruments - magnetic resonance imaging (MRI) scanners

CEO: Raymond V. Damadian
CFO: David B. Terry
HR: Fred Peipman
Employees: 154

1995 Sales: $14.1 million
1-Yr. Sales Change: -23.8%
Exchange: Nasdaq (SC)
Symbol: FONR

FOOD COURT ENTERTAINMENT NETWORK, INC.

34-12 36th St.
Astoria, NY 11106
Phone: 718-937-5757
Fax: 718-706-5388

Broadcast - direct advertising via satellite into mall food courts (Cafe USA)

CEO: Stephen G. Bowen
CFO: Stephen G. Bowen
HR: —
Employees: 6

1994 Sales: $0
1-Yr. Sales Change: —
Exchange: Nasdaq
Symbol: FCENA

FOODARAMA SUPERMARKETS, INC.

303 W. Main St.
Freehold, NJ 07728
Phone: 908-462-4700
Fax: 908-294-2313

CEO: Joseph J. Saker
CFO: Michael Shapiro
HR: Robert Spiers
Employees: 3,600

1994 Sales: $606.5 million
1-Yr. Sales Change: -9.5%
Exchange: AMEX
Symbol: FSM

Retail - supermarkets (Shop-Rite) in New Jersey & Pennsylvania

FORBES, INC.

60 Fifth Ave.
New York, NY 10011
Phone: 212-620-2200
Fax: 212-206-5534

CEO: Timothy C. Forbes
CFO: Joel Redler
HR: Rose Ateniese
Employees: 900

1994 Sales: $266.5 million
1-Yr. Sales Change: 8.7%
Ownership: Privately Held

Publishing - magazines (Forbes, Forbes FYI, Forbes ASAP, Audacity, American Heritage); books; weekly
newspapers in suburban New Jersey (Forbes Newspapers)

FORD FOUNDATION

320 E. 43rd St.
New York, NY 10017
Phone: 212-573-5000
Fax: 212-599-4584

CEO: Susan V. Berresford
CFO: Nicholas M. Gabriel
HR: Bruce D. Stuckey
Employees: 597

1994 Sales: $489 million
1-Yr. Sales Change: -38.6%
Ownership: Privately Held

Charitable foundation

FORDHAM UNIVERSITY

441 E. Fordham Rd.
New York, NY 10458
Phone: 718-817-4950
Fax: 718-817-4965

CEO: Joseph O'Hare
CFO: Donald Cipullo
HR: Tony Ruggiero
Employees: 1,500

1995 Sales: $186.7 million
1-Yr. Sales Change: 6.9%
Ownership: Privately Held

Jesuit-run Catholic university offering 38 undergraduate & 76 graduate degree programs

FOREST LABORATORIES, INC.

909 3rd Ave.
New York, NY 10022
Phone: 212-421-7850
Fax: 212-750-9152

CEO: Howard Solomon
CFO: Kenneth E. Goodman
HR: Bernard McGovern
Employees: 1,171

1995 Sales: $404.8 million
1-Yr. Sales Change: 12.0%
Exchange: AMEX
Symbol: FRX

Drugs

THE FORSCHNER GROUP, INC.

One Research Dr.	CEO: Peter Gilson	1994 Sales: $144.4 million
Shelton, CT 06484-6226	CFO: Thomas D. Cunningham	1-Yr. Sales Change: 40.9%
Phone: 203-929-6391	HR: Lesley Olsen	Exchange: Nasdaq
Fax: 203-929-3786	Employees: 193	Symbol: FSNR

Housewares - Swiss Army Knife importing & cutlery manufacturing

See page 269 for a full profile of this company.

FORSTMANN & COMPANY, INC.

1185 Avenue of the Americas	CEO: Robert N. Dangremond	1994 Sales: $237.1 million
New York, NY 10036	CFO: —	1-Yr. Sales Change: 1.6%
Phone: 212-642-6900	HR: Robert Christian	Exchange: OTC
Fax: 212-642-6870	Employees: 3,000	Symbol: FSTMQ

Textiles - wool & wool-blend fabrics

FORSTMANN LITTLE & CO.

767 Fifth Ave.	CEO: Theodore Forstmann	1995 Sales: —
New York, NY 10153	CFO: Theodore Forstmann	1-Yr. Sales Change: —
Phone: 212-355-5656	HR: —	Ownership: Privately Held
Fax: 212-759-9059	Employees: —	

Financial - investments (Gulfstream Aerospace, Pullman, Thompson Minwax, General Instrument & other companies)

FORTUNOFF FINE JEWELRY & SILVERWARE, INC.

70 Charles Lindbergh Blvd.	CEO: Alan Fortunoff	1994 Sales: $360 million
New York, NY 11553	CFO: Leonard Tabs	1-Yr. Sales Change: 2.9%
Phone: 516-832-9000	HR: Richard Farber	Ownership: Privately Held
Fax: 516-237-1703	Employees: 2,500	

Retail - jewelry & silverware

FOSTER WHEELER CORPORATION

Perryville Corporate Park	CEO: Richard J. Swift	1994 Sales: $2,271.1 mil.
Clinton, NJ 08809-4000	CFO: David J. Roberts	1-Yr. Sales Change: -14.4%
Phone: 908-730-4000	HR: James E. Schessler	Exchange: NYSE
Fax: 908-730-4315	Employees: 11,685	Symbol: FWC

Diversified - engineering & construction, energy equipment & power systems

FOUR M CORPORATION

115 Stevens Ave.
Valhalla, NY 10595
Phone: 914-747-2600
Fax: 914-747-2774

CEO: Dennis Mehiel
CFO: Timothy McMillan
HR: Isabel Solomon
Employees: 997

1995 Sales: $272 million
1-Yr. Sales Change: 18.8%
Ownership: Privately Held

Paper & paper products - corrugated cartons, solid-fiber partitions & paper plates & cups

FRANCISCAN SISTERS OF THE POOR HEALTH SYSTEM, INC.

708 3rd Ave., Ste. 200
New York, NY 10017
Phone: 212-818-1987
Fax: 212-808-0096

CEO: Joanne Schuster
CFO: Paul N. MacGiffert
HR: June Casterton
Employees: 14,000

1994 Sales: $963.2 million
1-Yr. Sales Change: 6.3%
Ownership: Privately Held

Hospitals - not-for-profit system

FRANCOSTEEL CORPORATION

345 Hudson St.
New York, NY 10014
Phone: 212-633-1010
Fax: 212-633-1398

CEO: Michel Lonchampt
CFO: Bob Tamburrino
HR: —
Employees: 240

1994 Sales: $650 million
1-Yr. Sales Change: -18.8%
Ownership: Privately Held

Wholesale distribution - importer & exporter of carbon steel products

THE FRANKLIN HOLDING CORPORATION

450 Park Ave.
New York, NY 10022
Phone: 212-486-2323
Fax: 212-755-5451

CEO: Stephen L. Brown
CFO: Stephen L. Brown
HR: —
Employees: —

1994 Sales: $0.7 million
1-Yr. Sales Change: -22.2%
Exchange: AMEX
Symbol. FKL

Financial - SBIC & commercial

FREDERICK ATKINS, INC.

1515 Broadway
New York, NY 10036
Phone: 212-840-7000
Fax: 212-536-7355

CEO: Bernard Olsoff
CFO: Wayne Greer
HR: Patricia McNamara
Employees: 400

1995 Sales: $500 million
1-Yr. Sales Change: 6.8%
Ownership: Privately Held

Wholesale distribution - products to department stores

FREQUENCY ELECTRONICS, INC.

55 Charles Lindbergh Blvd.	CEO: Joseph P. Franklin	1995 Sales: $24.1 million
Mitchel Field, NY 11553	CFO: Dawn R. Johnston	1-Yr. Sales Change: -12.4%
Phone: 516-794-4500	HR: Bob Klomp	Exchange: AMEX
Fax: 516-794-4340	Employees: 266	Symbol: FEI

Electronics - precision time & frequency control products for military use

THE FRESH JUICE COMPANY, INC.

350 Northern Blvd.	CEO: Steven Smith	1994 Sales: $8.2 million
Great Neck, NY 11021	CFO: Kathy Siegel	1-Yr. Sales Change: -1.2%
Phone: 516-482-5190	HR: —	Exchange: Nasdaq (SC)
Fax: 516-482-5453	Employees: 20	Symbol: FRSH

Food - frozen Florida orange juice, grapefruit juice, apple juice & other noncarbonated beverages (Just Pik't) distribution to supermarkets

THE FRICK COLLECTION

One E. 70th St.	CEO: Charles Ryskamp	1994 Sales: $8.1 million
New York, NY 10021	CFO: Robert Goldsmith	1-Yr. Sales Change: 1.3%
Phone: 212-288-0700	HR: —	Ownership: Privately Held
Fax: 212-861-7347	Employees: 140	

Museum

FRIED, FRANK, HARRIS, SHRIVER & JACOBSON

One New York Plaza, 28th Fl.	CEO: Peter Z. Cobb	1994 Sales: $162 million
New York, NY 10004	CFO: —	1-Yr. Sales Change: 15.7%
Phone: 212-859-8177	HR: —	Ownership: Privately Held
Fax: 212-859-8588	Employees: 1,200	

Law firm

FULTON COMPUTER PRODUCTS & PROGRAMMING LTD.

212 Merrick Rd.	CEO: Barry Weinstein	1994 Sales: $40 million
Rockville Centre, NY 11570	CFO: Kurt Spears	1-Yr. Sales Change: 25.0%
Phone: 516-764-2822	HR: Kurt Spears	Ownership: Privately Held
Fax: 516-764-3873	Employees: 48	

Computers - hardware, software & peripheral equipment

FUTTER LUMBER CORPORATION

100 Merrick Rd., Ste. 200W	CEO: Bernard Futter	1994 Sales: $125 million
New York, NY 11570	CFO: Kenneth Futter	1-Yr. Sales Change: 6.8%
Phone: 516-764-4445	HR: —	Ownership: Privately Held
Fax: 516-764-0579	Employees: 18	

Building products - wholesale lumber

GABELLI EQUITY TRUST INC.

One Corporate Center	CEO: Mario J. Gabelli	1994 Sales: $22.3 million
Rye, NY 10580	CFO: Bruce N. Alpert	1-Yr. Sales Change: 9.9%
Phone: 914-921-5100	HR: —	Exchange: NYSE
Fax: 914-921-5118	Employees: 2	Symbol: GAB

Real estate investment trust

GAF CORPORATION

1361 Alps Rd.	CEO: Samuel J. Heyman	1994 Sales: $1,156.2 mil.
Wayne, NJ 07470	CFO: James P. Rogers	1-Yr. Sales Change: 8.2%
Phone: 201-628-3000	HR: Jim Strupp	Ownership: Privately Held
Fax: 201-628-3311	Employees: 4,500	

Diversified operations - specialty derivative chemicals, mineral products, filter products & advanced materials; asphalt roofing products & accessories; commercial radio broadcasting

GALEY & LORD, INC.

980 Avenue of the Americas	CEO: Arthur C. Wiener	1995 Sales: $502.2 million
New York, NY 10018	CFO: Michael R. Harmon	1-Yr. Sales Change: 11.3%
Phone: 212-465-3000	HR: Terrence Bowman	Exchange: NYSE
Fax: 212-465-3025	Employees: 3,556	Symbol: GNL

Textiles - woven cotton & cotton-blend apparel fabrics, primarily for manufacturers of sportswear & commercial uniforms

GANIN TIRE, INC.

1421 38th St.	CEO: Saul Ganin	1994 Sales: $100 million
New York, NY 11218	CFO: —	1-Yr. Sales Change: 0.0%
Phone: 718-633-0600	HR: —	Ownership: Privately Held
Fax: 718-438-6301	Employees: 120	

Auto parts - retail car & truck tires

GARAN, INCORPORATED

350 Fifth Ave.
New York, NY 10118
Phone: 212-563-2000
Fax: 212-564-7994

CEO: Seymour Lichtenstein
CFO: William J. Wilson
HR: Dana Therese
Employees: 2,800

1995 Sales: $141.3 million
1-Yr. Sales Change: -18.3%
Exchange: AMEX
Symbol: GAN

Apparel & other finished products

GARTNER GROUP, INC.

56 Top Gallant Rd., PO Box 10212
Stamford, CT 06904-2212
Phone: 203-964-0096
Fax: 203-316-1100

CEO: Manuel A. Fernandez
CFO: John F. Halligan
HR: Lindon Smith
Employees: 1,175

1995 Sales: $229.2 million
1-Yr. Sales Change: 35.5%
Exchange: Nasdaq
Symbol: GART

Business services - subscription research services to users of advanced technology

GASETERIA OIL CORPORATION

364 Maspeth Ave.
New York, NY 11211
Phone: 718-782-4200
Fax: 718-782-5175

CEO: Oscar Porcelli
CFO: Louis Fresolone
HR: Raul Delmonte
Employees: 450

1994 Sales: $101 million
1-Yr. Sales Change: -6.5%
Ownership: Privately Held

Retail - gas stations in the New York metro area

GEMINI CONSULTING, INC.

25 Airport Rd.
Morristown, NJ 07960
Phone: 201-285-9000
Fax: 201-285-9586

CEO: Pierre Hessler
CFO: Nick Zaccaria
HR: Joseph DeGennero
Employees: 1,800

1994 Sales: $551 million
1-Yr. Sales Change: 6.8%
Ownership: Privately Held

Consulting - management & information

GENERAL ELECTRIC COMPANY

3135 Easton Tnpk.
Fairfield, CT 06431-0001
Phone: 203-373-2211
Fax: 203-373-3497

CEO: John "Jack" F. Welch Jr.
CFO: Dennis D. Dammerman
HR: William J. Conaty
Employees: 221,000

1994 Sales: $60,109 million
1-Yr. Sales Change: -0.7%
Exchange: NYSE
Symbol: GE

Diversified operations - financing (GE Capital); aircraft engines; locomotives; appliances; broadcasting
(NBC); plastics; power generation; lighting; medical systems; insurance; online service (Genie)

 See pages 116–117 for a full profile of this company.

GENERAL HOST CORPORATION

One Station Place	CEO: Harris J. Ashton	1995 Sales: $568.1 million
Stamford, CT 06902	CFO: Robert M. Lovejoy	1-Yr. Sales Change: -0.1%
Phone: 203-357-9900	HR: Carol Cox	Exchange: NYSE
Fax: 203-357-0148	Employees: 7,400	Symbol: GH

Retail - gardening, crafts, Christmas merchandise (265 Frank's Nursery & Crafts stores in 16 states)

GENERAL MAGNAPLATE CORPORATION

1331 US Rte. 1	CEO: Charles P. Covino	1995 Sales: $10 million
Linden, NJ 07036	CFO: Charles P. Covino	1-Yr. Sales Change: 1.0%
Phone: 908-862-6200	HR: —	Exchange: Nasdaq
Fax: 908-862-6110	Employees: 125	Symbol: GMCC

Metal processing & fabrication

GENERAL MEDIA INTERNATIONAL, INC.

277 Park Ave.	CEO: Bob Guccione	1994 Est. Sales: $170 mil.
New York, NY 10172	CFO: Patrick Gavin	1-Yr. Sales Change: -4.5%
Phone: 212-702-6000	HR: Iris Frank	Ownership: Privately Held
Fax: 212-702-6262	Employees: 350	

Publishing - periodicals (Penthouse, Omni, Stock Car Racing, Women's Forum); pay-per-view TV channel

GENERAL MICROWAVE CORPORATION

5500 New Horizons Blvd.	CEO: Mitchell Tuckman	1995 Sales: $22.3 million
Amityville, NY 11701	CFO: Arnold H. Levine	1-Yr. Sales Change: -1.8%
Phone: 516-226-8900	HR: Sylvia Weisbard	Exchange: AMEX
Fax: 516-226-8966	Employees: 295	Symbol: GMW

Electrical components - microwave, electronic & fiber-optic equipment & components

GENERAL PUBLIC UTILITIES CORPORATION

100 Interpace Pkwy.	CEO: James R. Leva	1994 Sales: $3,649.5 mil.
Parsippany, NJ 07054-1149	CFO: John G. Graham	1-Yr. Sales Change: 1.5%
Phone: 201-263-6500	HR: J.J. Westervelt	Exchange: NYSE
Fax: 201-263-6822	Employees: 10,534	Symbol: GPU

Utility - electric power

GENERAL RE CORPORATION

695 E. Main St.
Stamford, CT 06904-2351
Phone: 203-328-5000
Fax: 203-328-5329

CEO: Ronald E. Ferguson
CFO: Joseph P. Brandon
HR: Theron S. Hoffman Jr.
Employees: 2,360

1994 Sales: $3,837 million
1-Yr. Sales Change: 7.8%
Exchange: NYSE
Symbol: GRN

Insurance - property & casualty; reinsurance

 See pages 118–119 for a full profile of this company.

GENERAL SIGNAL CORPORATION

High Ridge Park, PO Box 10010
Stamford, CT 06904
Phone: 203-329-4100
Fax: 203-329-4159

CEO: Edmund M. Carpenter
CFO: Terence D. Martin
HR: George Falconer
Employees: 12,200

1994 Sales: $1,527.7 mil.
1-Yr. Sales Change: -0.2%
Exchange: NYSE
Symbol: GSX

Instruments - control

GENERAL TRADING CO.

455 16th St.
Carlstadt, NJ 07072
Phone: 201-935-7717
Fax: 201-438-6353

CEO: George Abad
CFO: Joey Goetting
HR: Carol Tirella
Employees: 400

1994 Est. Sales: $270 mil.
1-Yr. Sales Change: 0.0%
Ownership: Privately Held

Food - wholesale to grocers

THE GENLYTE GROUP INCORPORATED

100 Lighting Way
Secaucus, NJ 07096-1508
Phone: 201-864-3000
Fax: 201-392-3784

CEO: Larry Powers
CFO: Neil M. Bardach
HR: Donna Ratliff
Employees: 2,795

1994 Sales: $432.7 million
1-Yr. Sales Change: 0.8%
Exchange: Nasdaq
Symbol: GLYT

Building products - lighting fixtures, commercial, industrial & residential (Lightolier)

GENOVESE DRUG STORES, INC.

80 Marcus Dr.
Melville, NY 11747
Phone: 516-420-1900
Fax: 516-845-8378

CEO: Leonard Genovese
CFO: Jerome Stengel
HR: Sue Crickmore
Employees: 4,200

1995 Sales: $570 million
1-Yr. Sales Change: 16.5%
Exchange: AMEX
Symbol: GDXA

Retail - drugstores

GEOTEK COMMUNICATIONS, INC.

20 Craig Rd.
Montvale, NJ 07645
Phone: 201-930-9305
Fax: 201-930-9614

CEO: Yaron I. Eitan
CFO: Michael McCoy
HR: Lou Zanoni
Employees: 200

1994 Sales: $73 million
1-Yr. Sales Change: 49.0%
Exchange: Nasdaq
Symbol: GOTK

Telecommunications services - wireless mobile communications services

GETTY PETROLEUM CORP.

125 Jericho Tpke.
Jericho, NY 11753
Phone: 516-338-6000
Fax: 516-338-6062

CEO: Leo Liebowitz
CFO: John J. Fitteron
HR: Maureen S. Hunstein
Employees: 778

1995 Sales: $785.2 million
1-Yr. Sales Change: -2.7%
Exchange: NYSE
Symbol: GTY

Oil refining, marketing & distribution of petroleum products to retail & wholesale markets

G-III APPAREL GROUP, LTD.

345 W. 37th St.
New York, NY 10018
Phone: 212-629-8830
Fax: 212-967-1487

CEO: Morris Goldfarb
CFO: Alan Feller
HR: —
Employees: 334

1995 Sales: $171.4 million
1-Yr. Sales Change: -18.0%
Exchange: Nasdaq
Symbol: GIII

Apparel - leather apparel, men's & women's outerwear & sportswear

GILMAN & CIOCIA, INC.

475 Northern Blvd.
Great Neck, NY 11021
Phone: 516-482-4860
Fax: 516-482-5014

CEO: James Ciocia
CFO: Ralph V. Esposito
HR: —
Employees: 79

1995 Sales: $9.9 million
1-Yr. Sales Change: 32.0%
Exchange: Nasdaq (SC)
Symbol: GTAX

Financial - preparation of federal, state & local income tax returns; insurance agent, mortgage broker & securities broker

GILMAN PAPER CO.

111 W. 50th St.
New York, NY 10020
Phone: 212-246-3300
Fax: 212-582-7610

CEO: Howard Gilman
CFO: Howard Gilman
HR: —
Employees: 2,500

1994 Sales: $455 million
1-Yr. Sales Change: 13.8%
Ownership: Privately Held

Paper & paper products - envelopes & specialty paper

GIRL SCOUTS OF THE UNITED STATES OF AMERICA

420 5th Ave.	CEO: Mary Rose Main	1994 Sales: $43 million
New York, NY 10018	CFO: Florence Corsello	1-Yr. Sales Change: 0.0%
Phone: 212-852-8000	HR: Priscilla Vazquez	Ownership: Privately Held
Fax: 212-852-6514	Employees: 500	

Membership organization for girls

GLASGAL COMMUNICATIONS, INC.

151 Veterans Dr.	CEO: Isaac J. Gaon	1995 Sales: $35.2 million
Northvale, NJ 07647	CFO: James M. Caci	1-Yr. Sales Change: 214.3%
Phone: 201-768-8082	HR: Mary Simon	Exchange: Nasdaq (SC)
Fax: 201-768-2947	Employees: 144	Symbol: GLAS

Computers - systems integrator of local & wide area networks utilizing computer hardware, networking systems & software products; distributes data communications equipment

GLOBAL DIRECTMAIL CORPORATION

22 Harbor Park Dr.	CEO: Richard Leeds	1994 Sales: $484.2 million
Port Washington, NY 11050	CFO: Richard Leeds	1-Yr. Sales Change: 23.0%
Phone: 516-625-1555	HR: Lillian Berman	Exchange: NYSE
Fax: 516-625-0038	Employees: 1,489	Symbol: GML

Computers - direct marketer of brand-name & private-label computer-related products, office products & industrial products (Global, Misco)

GLOBAL MARKET INFORMATION INC.

56 Pine St.	CEO: Barry Hertz	1994 Sales: $8.9 million
New York, NY 10005	CFO: Martin Kaye	1-Yr. Sales Change: 64.8%
Phone: 212-422-4300	HR: —	Exchange: Nasdaq
Fax: 212-612-2241	Employees: 84	Symbol: GMKT

Business services - electronically transmitted information for individuals & institutions involved in financial markets

GLOBAL TELECOMMUNICATION SOLUTIONS, INC.

40 Elmont Rd.	CEO: Shelly Finkel	1994 Sales: $1.4 million
New York, NY 11003	CFO: Maria Bruzzese	1-Yr. Sales Change: 1,300%
Phone: 516-326-1940	HR: Fred Cortmann	Exchange: Nasdaq (SC)
Fax: 516-326-6106	Employees: 21	Symbol: GTST

Telecommunications equipment - prepaid phone cards (some licensed by Marvel Entertainment Group, Major League Baseball, National Hockey League, Led Zeppelin, Upper Deck Co.)

THE GOLDMAN SACHS GROUP, L.P.

85 Broad St.
New York, NY 10004
Phone: 212-902-1000
Fax: 212-902-1512

CEO: Jon S. Corzine
CFO: David W. Blood
HR: Jonathan L. Cohen
Employees: 7,200

1995 Est. Sales: $14,470 mil.
1-Yr. Sales Change: 26.5%
Ownership: Privately Held

Financial - investment banking & securities brokerage

 See pages 120–121 for a full profile of this company.

THE GOLODETZ GROUP

142 W. 57th St., 8th Fl.
New York, NY 10019
Phone: 212-887-1600
Fax: 212-887-1650

CEO: Marc Ginzberg
CFO: Sharon Roth
HR: William Maguire
Employees: 350

1994 Sales: $1,250 million
1-Yr. Sales Change: -7.4%
Ownership: Privately Held

Diversified operations - trading, agriculture, real estate, venture capital

GOODTIMES ENTERTAINMENT WORLDWIDE

16 E. 40th St.
New York, NY 10016
Phone: 212-951-3000
Fax: 212-213-9319

CEO: Joe Cayre
CFO: Maria Haggerty
HR: Lily Rettis
Employees: 1,000

1994 Sales: $1,000 million
1-Yr. Sales Change: 42.9%
Ownership: Privately Held

Leisure & recreational products - diversified multimedia entertainmment, including videos (Cindy Crawford Workouts, Animated Classics), children's & family TV programming, children's books (Berenstain Bears), infomercials (Richard Simmons) & feature film production

GOULD PAPER CORPORATION

315 Park Ave. South, 19th Fl.
New York, NY 10010
Phone: 212-505-1000
Fax: 212-505-0345

CEO: Harry E. Gould Jr.
CFO: D. J. Lala
HR: —
Employees: 425

1994 Sales: $830 million
1-Yr. Sales Change: 62.7%
Ownership: Privately Held

Wholesale distribution - printing & fine writing paper

GOYA FOODS, INC.

100 Seaview Dr.
Secaucus, NJ 07096
Phone: 201-348-4900
Fax: 201-348-6600

CEO: Joseph A. Unanue
CFO: Luis Perez
HR: Gilberto Otero
Employees: 2,000

1995 Sales: $528 million
1-Yr. Sales Change: 10.0%
Ownership: Privately Held

Food - canned vegetables & meats

 See pages 122–123 for a full profile of this company.

GP FINANCIAL CORP.

41-60 Main St.	CEO: Thomas S. Johnson	1994 Sales: $332.3 million
Flushing, NY 11355	CFO: Charles P. Richardson	1-Yr. Sales Change: 21.9%
Phone: 718-670-7500	HR: Eugene Phillippi	Exchange: Nasdaq
Fax: 718-463-2381	Employees: 1,528	Symbol: GNPT

Banks - Northeast (The Green Point Savings Bank)

GRAFF PAY-PER-VIEW INC.

536 Broadway	CEO: J. Roger Faherty	1994 Sales: $40.4 million
New York, NY 10012	CFO: Philip Callaghan	1-Yr. Sales Change: 97.1%
Phone: 212-941-1434	HR: Joan Simari	Exchange: Nasdaq
Fax: 212-941-4746	Employees: 100	Symbol: GPPV

Cable TV - adult entertainment channels (Spice, Spice 2); pay-per-view movie channels (Cable Video Store, Theatre VisioN)

GRAHAM-FIELD HEALTH PRODUCTS, INC.

400 Rabro Dr. East	CEO: Irwin Selinger	1994 Sales: $94.5 million
Hauppauge, NY 11788	CFO: Gary M. Jacobs	1-Yr. Sales Change: 2.1%
Phone: 516-582-5900	HR: Kathleen Natalie	Exchange: NYSE
Fax: 516-582-5608	Employees: 534	Symbol: GFI

Medical instruments - diagnostic & surgical instruments & home health care products

THE GRAND UNION COMPANY

201 Willowbrook Blvd.	CEO: Joseph J. McCaig	1995 Sales: $2,391.7 mil.
Wayne, NJ 07470	CFO: Kenneth R. Baum	1-Yr. Sales Change: -3.5%
Phone: 201-890-6000	HR: Charles Barrett	Exchange: Nasdaq
Fax: 201-890-6671	Employees: 16,000	Symbol: GUCO

Retail - supermarkets (231 units: Grand Union) in 6 northeastern states

GRANITE BROADCASTING CORPORATION

767 Third Ave.	CEO: W. Don Cornwell	1994 Sales: $62.9 million
New York, NY 10017	CFO: Lawrence I. Wills	1-Yr. Sales Change: 67.7%
Phone: 212-826-2530	HR: —	Exchange: Nasdaq
Fax: 212-826-2858	Employees: 590	Symbol: GBTVK

Broadcasting - radio & TV

THE GREAT AMERICAN BACKRUB STORE, INC.

958 Third Ave.
New York, NY 10022
Phone: 212-832-1766
Fax: 212-758-7671

Retail - back rubs

CEO: Terrance C. Murray
CFO: Steven J. Thompson
HR: Bob Napodano
Employees: 31

1994 Sales: $0.7 million
1-Yr. Sales Change: 600.0%
Exchange: Nasdaq (SC)
Symbol: RUBB

GREAT AMERICAN RECREATION, INC.

PO Box 848
McAfee, NJ 07428
Phone: 201-827-2000
Fax: 201-209-3342

Leisure & recreational services - ski hill & school & summer action park

CEO: Richard Pye
CFO: Joseph R. Bellantoni
HR: —
Employees: 2,590

1995 Sales: $20.2 million
1-Yr. Sales Change: -26.3%
Exchange: OTC
Symbol: GRAR

THE GREAT ATLANTIC & PACIFIC TEA COMPANY, INC.

2 Paragon Dr., PO Box 418
Montvale, NJ 07645
Phone: 201-573-9700
Fax: 201-930-8106

Retail - supermarkets

CEO: James Wood
CFO: Fred Corrado
HR: H. Nelson "Bud" Lewis
Employees: 92,000

1995 Sales: $10,332 million
1-Yr. Sales Change: -0.5%
Exchange: NYSE
Symbol: GAP

 See pages 124–125 for a full profile of this company.

GREATER NEW YORK SAVINGS BANK

One Penn Plaza
New York, NY 10119
Phone: 212-613-4000
Fax: 212-613-4194

Financial - savings & loans

CEO: Gerard C. Keegan
CFO: Gerard C. Keegan
HR: Caroline Fredericks
Employees: 650

1994 Sales: $176.4 million
1-Yr. Sales Change: -4.3%
Exchange: Nasdaq
Symbol: GRTR

GREENSTONE ROBERTS ADVERTISING, INC.

One Huntington Quadrangle, Ste. 1C14
Melville, NY 11747
Phone: 516-249-2121
Fax: 516-249-6641

Advertising - marketing, consulting, market & product research & direct mail advertising

CEO: Ronald M. Greenstone
CFO: Gregory A. Rice
HR: Jean Mostaccio
Employees: 116

1994 Sales: $10.5 million
1-Yr. Sales Change: -6.3%
Exchange: Nasdaq (SC)
Symbol: GRRI

GREG MANNING AUCTIONS, INC.

775 Passaic Ave.
West Caldwell, NJ 07006
Phone: 201-882-0004
Fax: 201-882-3499

CEO: Greg Manning
CFO: Dan Kaplan
HR: Bob Jesso
Employees: 31

1995 Sales: $11.6 million
1-Yr. Sales Change: 16.0%
Exchange: Nasdaq (SC)
Symbol: GMAI

Retail - public auctions of rare stamps, stamp collections & stocks

GREY ADVERTISING INC.

777 3rd Ave.
New York, NY 10017
Phone: 212-546-2000
Fax: 212-546-1495

CEO: Edward H. Meyer
CFO: Steven G. Felsher
HR: Kevin Bergin
Employees: 1,418

1994 Sales: $593.3 million
1-Yr. Sales Change: 4.6%
Exchange: Nasdaq
Symbol: GREY

Advertising

GRIFFON CORPORATION

100 Jericho Quadrangle
Jericho, NY 11753
Phone: 516-938-5544
Fax: 516-938-5644

CEO: Harvey R. Blau
CFO: Robert Balemien
HR: Susan Roland
Employees: 2,900

1995 Sales: $546.4 million
1-Yr. Sales Change: 11.7%
Exchange: NYSE
Symbol: GFF

Diversified operations - customized plastic films; garage doors

GROWTH FINANCIAL CORP

1500 Rte. 202, PO Box 401
Basking Ridge, NJ 07920-0401
Phone: 201-425-2500
Fax: 201-425-8989

CEO: Dale G. Potter
CFO: George J. McGuinness
HR: —
Employees: 59

1994 Sales: $8 million
1-Yr. Sales Change: 29.0%
Exchange: Nasdaq (SC)
Symbol: GRFC

Banks - Northeast

GRYPHON HOLDINGS INC.

30 Wall St.
New York, NY 10005-2201
Phone: 212-825-1200
Fax: 212-825-0200

CEO: Stephen A. Crane
CFO: Robert P. Cuthbert
HR: Robert Coffee
Employees: 99

1994 Sales: $72.7 million
1-Yr. Sales Change: -3.5%
Exchange: Nasdaq
Symbol: GRYP

Insurance - property & casualty

GTE CORPORATION

One Stamford Forum
Stamford, CT 06904
Phone: 203-965-2000
Fax: 203-965-2277

CEO: Charles R. Lee
CFO: J. Michael Kelly
HR: J. Randall MacDonald
Employees: 111,000

1994 Sales: $19,944 million
1-Yr. Sales Change: 1.0%
Exchange: NYSE
Symbol: GTE

Utility - telephone service, cellular communications, information services, in-flight telephone service (Airfone)

 See pages 126–127 for a full profile of this company.

THE GUARDIAN LIFE INSURANCE COMPANY OF AMERICA

201 Park Ave. South
New York, NY 10003
Phone: 212-598-8000
Fax: 212-598-8813

CEO: Arthur V. Ferrara
CFO: Peter L. Hutchings
HR: Douglas C. Kramer
Employees: 7,602

1994 Sales: $6,091.3 mil.
1-Yr. Sales Change: -13.8%
Ownership: Privately Held

Insurance - multiline & miscellaneous

 See pages 128–129 for a full profile of this company.

GUEST SUPPLY, INC.

720 US Hwy. One
North Brunswick, NJ 08902
Phone: 908-246-3011
Fax: 908-828-2342

CEO: Clifford W. Stanley
CFO: Paul T. Xenis
HR: Joan Constanzo
Employees: 706

1995 Sales: $159.5 million
1-Yr. Sales Change: 37.1%
Exchange: Nasdaq
Symbol: GEST

Cosmetics & toiletries - miniature soaps, shampoos & personal care items for hotel rooms

GYRODYNE COMPANY OF AMERICA, INC.

17 Flowerfield, Ste. 15
St. James , NY 11780-1551
Phone: 516-584-5400
Fax: 516-584-7075

CEO: Dimitri P. Papadakos
CFO: Joseph L. Dom
HR: John Rohrs
Employees: 21

1995 Sales: $1.7 million
1-Yr. Sales Change: 0.0%
Exchange: Nasdaq (SC)
Symbol: GYRO

Diversified operations - real estate operations; oil & gas production; citrus grove; helicopter rotor blades

THE HAIN FOOD GROUP

50 Charles Lindberg Blvd.
Uniondale, NY 11553
Phone: 516-237-6200
Fax: 516-237-6240

CEO: Irwin D. Simon
CFO: Jack Kaufman
HR: —
Employees: 35

1995 Sales: $58.1 million
1-Yr. Sales Change: 287.3%
Exchange: Nasdaq
Symbol: NOSH

Food - wholesale natural food lines marketed to supermarkets, natural food stores, food distributors, mass merchandisers, drugstores & other independent retailers by food brokers & distributors

HALSEY DRUG CO., INC.

1827 Pacific St.	CEO: Rosendo Ferran	1994 Sales: $24.1 million
New York, NY 11233	CFO: Rosendo Ferran	1-Yr. Sales Change: -33.1%
Phone: 718-467-7500	HR: —	Exchange: AMEX
Fax: 718-467-4261	Employees: 423	Symbol: HDG
Drugs - generic		

HALSTON BORGHESE, INC.

767 5th Ave.	CEO: David Horner	1994 Sales: $170 million
New York, NY 10153	CFO: Paul Lawer	1-Yr. Sales Change: 0.0%
Phone: 212-572-3100	HR: Jerry Aiello	Ownership: Privately Held
Fax: 212-572-3180	Employees: 1,000	

Cosmetics & toiletries - fragrances (Nautica, Catalyst) & skin treatment products (Cura Vitale)

HANDEX ENVIRONMENTAL RECOVERY, INC.

500 Campus Dr.	CEO: Curtis L. Smith Jr.	1994 Sales: $52.5 million
Morganville, NJ 07751	CFO: John T. St. James	1-Yr. Sales Change: 35.7%
Phone: 908-536-8500	HR: Camille Sorensen	Exchange: Nasdaq
Fax: 908-536-7751	Employees: 600	Symbol: HAND

Pollution control equipment & services - groundwater clean up

HANDY & HARMAN

250 Park Ave.	CEO: Richard N. Daniel	1994 Sales: $781.4 million
New York, NY 10177	CFO: John M. McLoone	1-Yr. Sales Change: 18.7%
Phone: 212-661-2400	HR: Bernard Lishinsky	Exchange: NYSE
Fax: 212-309-0691	Employees: 4,826	Symbol: HNH

Precious metals - fabrication, precision plating & refining; fuel handling systems; fluid & air management systems; mechanical controls; specialty wire & tubing

HANOVER DIRECT, INC.

1500 Harbor Blvd.	CEO: Jack E. Rosenfeld	1994 Sales: $768.9 million
Weehawken, NJ 07087	CFO: Wayne P. Garten	1-Yr. Sales Change: 19.7%
Phone: 201-863-7300	HR: Ralph Boyd	Exchange: AMEX
Fax: 201-392-5035	Employees: 3,900	Symbol: HNV

Retail - mail-order catalogs (#6 US) for home furnishings (Company Store, Domestications, Gump's, Hanover House), woodworking (Leichtung Workshops), kitchen products (Kitchen & Home, Colonial Garden Kitchens) golf (Austad's), home safety products (Safety Zone) & apparel (Tweed's)

HAPPINESS EXPRESS INC.

One Harbor Park Dr.
Port Washington, NY 11050
Phone: 516-484-3700
Fax: 516-484-3750

CEO: Joseph A. Sutton
CFO: Michael A. Goldberg
HR: Michael A. Goldberg
Employees: 50

1995 Sales: $60 million
1-Yr. Sales Change: 49.6%
Exchange: Nasdaq
Symbol: HAPY

Housewares - children's lamps, nightlights, banks & dolls of licensed characters (Lion King, Barney, Power Rangers)

HARBOR FOOTWEAR GROUP

55 Harbor Park Dr.
Port Washington, NY 11050
Phone: 516-621-8400
Fax: 516-621-4957

CEO: Dennis Lazar
CFO: Israel Weintraub
HR: —
Employees: 103

1994 Est. Sales: $100 mil.
1-Yr. Sales Change: 0.0%
Ownership: Privately Held

Men's & boys' footwear (Pierre Cardin)

HAROLD LEVINSON ASSOCIATES, INC.

One Enterprise Place
Hicksville, NY 11801
Phone: 516-822-0068
Fax: 516-822-2182

CEO: Ed Berro
CFO: Andrew DeFranciso
HR: Liz Flaherty
Employees: 130

1994 Sales: $390 million
1-Yr. Sales Change: 121.6%
Ownership: Privately Held

Tobacco & tobacco products

HARRIS CHEMICAL GROUP

399 Park Ave.
New York, NY 10022
Phone: 212-207-6400
Fax: 212-207-6450

CEO: D. George Harris
CFO: Emanuel Viteresi
HR: —
Employees: 2,500

1994 Sales: $460 million
1-Yr. Sales Change: —
Ownership: Privately Held

Chemicals - salt, soda products, boron chemicals & specialty fertilizer

HARTZ GROUP INC.

667 Madison Ave.
New York, NY 10021
Phone: 212-308-3336
Fax: 212-644-5987

CEO: Leonard N. Stern
CFO: Curtis B. Schwartz
HR: Charlotte Camino
Employees: 2,100

1994 Sales: $800 million
1-Yr. Sales Change: 17.6%
Ownership: Privately Held

Diversified operations - pet supplies (Hartz Mountain); real estate; publishing (The Village Voice)

HARVEY GROUP INC.

600 Secaucus Rd.
Secaucus, NJ 07094
Phone: 201-865-3418
Fax: 201-865-0342

Retail - consumer electronics

CEO: Arthur Shulman
CFO: Joseph J. Calabrese Jr.
HR: Mary Benio
Employees: 110

1995 Sales: $23 million
1-Yr. Sales Change: 5.5%
Exchange: OTC
Symbol: HRVA

HAUPPAUGE DIGITAL, INC.

91 Cabot Ct.
Hauppauge, NY 11788
Phone: 516-434-1600
Fax: 516-434-3198

Computers - digital video boards for the PC-based digital video market (Win/TV)

CEO: Kenneth Plotkin
CFO: Gerald Tucciarone
HR: Cheryl Willins
Employees: 33

1995 Sales: $11.6 million
1-Yr. Sales Change: 176.2%
Exchange: Nasdaq (SC)
Symbol: HAUP

HAVEN BANCORP, INC.

93-22 Jamaica Ave.
Woodhaven, NY 11421
Phone: 718-847-7041
Fax: 718-441-0512

Financial - savings & loans

CEO: Philip S. Messina
CFO: Catherine Califano
HR: Nancy Pacione
Employees: 321

1994 Sales: $88 million
1-Yr. Sales Change: 2.7%
Exchange: Nasdaq
Symbol: HAVN

HAYWARD INDUSTRIES, INC.

900 Fairmount Ave.
Elizabeth, NJ 07207
Phone: 908-351-5400
Fax: 908-351-0604

Filtration products - swimming pool filtration equipment & industrial fluid handling products

CEO: Anthony T. Castor III
CFO: Ruben Har-Even
HR: Wayne Wilson
Employees: 1,500

1994 Sales: $210 million
1-Yr. Sales Change: 7.7%
Ownership: Privately Held

HEALTH INSURANCE PLAN OF GREATER NEW YORK

7 W. 34th St.
New York, NY 10001
Phone: 212-630-5000
Fax: 212-630-8747

Not-for-profit health maintenance organization

CEO: Anthony L. Watson
CFO: Bernard J. Neeck
HR: Fred Blickman
Employees: 1,500

1994 Sales: $1,713.8 mil.
1-Yr. Sales Change: 8.3%
Ownership: Privately Held

HEALTH MANAGEMENT, INC.

4250 Veterans Memorial Hwy.
Holbrook, NY 11741
Phone: 516-981-0034
Fax: 516-981-0522

CEO: Clifford E. Hotte
CFO: Paul S. Jurewicz
HR: Virginia Belloise
Employees: 413

1995 Sales: $89.3 million
1-Yr. Sales Change: 101.6%
Exchange: Nasdaq
Symbol: HMIS

Health care - integrated health management services for patients with chronic medical conditions & for health care professionals, drug manufacturers & 3rd-party payers

 See page 270 for a full profile of this company.

HEALTH MANAGEMENT SYSTEMS, INC.

401 Park Ave. South
New York, NY 10016
Phone: 212-685-4545
Fax: 212-889-8776

CEO: Paul J. Kerz
CFO: Scott A. Remley
HR: Lewis D. Levetown
Employees: 421

1995 Sales: $86.7 million
1-Yr. Sales Change: 45.2%
Exchange: Nasdaq
Symbol: HMSY

Business services - information management & data processing services for hospitals, health care providers & government health services agencies

HEALTHCARE IMAGING SERVICES, INC.

200 Schulz Dr.
Middletown, NJ 07701
Phone: 908-224-9292
Fax: 908-224-9329

CEO: Elliott H. Vernon
CFO: —
HR: Volores Lessone
Employees: 61

1994 Sales: $11.4 million
1-Yr. Sales Change: -13.6%
Exchange: Nasdaq
Symbol: HISS

Medical services - MRI (magnetic resonance imaging) centers

HEALTH-CHEM CORPORATION

1212 Avenue of the Americas
New York, NY 10036
Phone: 212-398-0700
Fax: 212-398-0884

CEO: Marvin M. Speiser
CFO: Paul R. Moeller
HR: Joyce Montalvo
Employees: 220

1994 Sales: $46.9 million
1-Yr. Sales Change: 4.5%
Exchange: AMEX
Symbol: HCH

Textiles - synthetic fabrics including laminating & coating materials for products for the pharmaceutical, health care, industrial, agricultural & environmental markets

HEALTHPLEX, INC.

60 Charles Lindbergh Blvd.
Uniondale, NY 11553-3634
Phone: 516-794-3000
Fax: 516-794-3186

CEO: Martin Kane
CFO: George Kane
HR: —
Employees: 54

1994 Sales: $10.7 million
1-Yr. Sales Change: 11.5%
Exchange: Nasdaq (SC)
Symbol: HPLX

Business services - marketing, management, claims processing, printing, consulting & related services for dental health companies

HEALTHRITE, INC.

200 Madison Ave., 2nd Fl.
New York, NY 10016
Phone: 212-953-0100
Fax: 212-953-0626

CEO: John Teeger
CFO: John Teeger
HR: —
Employees: 179

1994 Sales: $9.4 million
1-Yr. Sales Change: 27.0%
Exchange: Nasdaq (SC)
Symbol: HLRT

Vitamins & nutritional products - natural dietary supplements, herbal-based products, weight loss products & vitamins; distribution of snacks, beverages & related products

THE HEARST CORPORATION

959 Eighth Ave.
New York, NY 10019
Phone: 212-649-2000
Fax: 212-765-3528

CEO: Frank A. Bennack Jr.
CFO: Victor F. Ganzi
HR: Kenneth A. Feldman
Employees: 14,000

1994 Sales: $2,299 million
1-Yr. Sales Change: 5.7%
Ownership: Privately Held

Publishing - magazines, newspapers & books; broadcasting & cable

 See pages 130–131 for a full profile of this company.

HELM RESOURCES, INC.

93 Mason St.
Greenwich, CT 06830
Phone: 203-629-1400
Fax: 203-629-1961

CEO: Herbert M. Pearlman
CFO: Daniel T. Murphy
HR: —
Employees: 160

1994 Sales: $14.2 million
1-Yr. Sales Change: -5.3%
Exchange: AMEX
Symbol: HHH

Diversified operations - thermoplastic resins; seismic survey licensing

HELMSLEY ENTERPRISES, INC.

60 E. 42nd St.
New York, NY 10165-0001
Phone: 212-687-6400
Fax: 212-687-6437

CEO: Harry B. Helmsley
CFO: Martin S. Stone
HR: Jennie Voscina
Employees: 13,000

1994 Sales: $1,698 million
1-Yr. Sales Change: 41.5%
Ownership: Privately Held

Real estate operations - brokerage & management; hotels

 See pages 132–133 for a full profile of this company.

HELMSTAR GROUP, INC.

2 World Trade Center, Ste. 2112
New York, NY 10048-0203
Phone: 212-775-0400
Fax: 212-775-0901

CEO: George W. Benoit
CFO: Roger J. Burns
HR: —
Employees: 49

1994 Sales: $2.9 million
1-Yr. Sales Change: 3.6%
Exchange: AMEX
Symbol: HLM

Financial - investment bankers

HENRY SCHEIN, INC.

135 Duryea Rd.
Melville, NY 11747
Phone: 516-843-5500
Fax: 516-843-5658

CEO: Stanley M. Bergman
CFO: Steven Paladino
HR: Leonard A. David
Employees: 1,600

1994 Sales: $486.6 million
1-Yr. Sales Change: 17.1%
Exchange: Nasdaq
Symbol: HSIC

Medical & dental supplies - products & services for office-based health care practitioners, primarily dental practices & laboratories, physician practices, veterinary clinics & institutions

HERMAN'S SPORTING GOODS, INC.

2 Germak Dr.
Carteret, NJ 07008
Phone: 908-541-1550
Fax: 908-969-4669

CEO: Alfred F. Fasola Jr.
CFO: Alan Weiss
HR: Scott Knowles
Employees: 4,000

1994 Sales: $349 million
1-Yr. Sales Change: 12.6%
Ownership: Privately Held

Retail - sporting goods

HE-RO GROUP, LTD.

550 Seventh Ave.
New York, NY 10018
Phone: 212-840-6047
Fax: 212-764-6108

CEO: Della Rounick
CFO: Sam D. Kaplan
HR: Mary Ann Pulver
Employees: 325

1995 Sales: $57.2 million
1-Yr. Sales Change: -34.3%
Exchange: NYSE
Symbol: HRG

Apparel - women's & juniors'

HFS INC.

339 Jefferson Rd.
Parsippany, NJ 07054
Phone: 201-428-9700
Fax: 201-428-6057

CEO: Henry R. Silverman
CFO: Stephen P. Holmes
HR: Jim LaBella
Employees: 2,100

1994 Sales: $312.5 million
1-Yr. Sales Change: 21.5%
Exchange: NYSE
Symbol: HFS

Hotel & motel franchisor (#1 worldwide: Days Inn, Howard Johnson, Park Inns, Ramada, Super 8)

 See page 271 for a full profile of this company.

HILLSIDE BEDDING, INC.

1952 E. Jericho Tnpk.
Northport, NY 11731
Phone: 516-462-6700
Fax: 516-462-6223

CEO: Surinder Rametra
CFO: Ashok Rametra
HR: —
Employees: 33

1995 Sales: $29.7 million
1-Yr. Sales Change: 16.5%
Exchange: Nasdaq (SC)
Symbol: ATEC

Retail - bedding stores

HIMMEL EQUITIES & HIMMEL INC.

450 Park Ave., Ste. 501	CEO: Jeffrey Himmel	1994 Est. Sales: $50 mil.
New York, NY 10022	CFO: Jeffrey Himmel	1-Yr. Sales Change: —
Phone: 212-688-1301	HR: —	Ownership: Privately Held
Fax: 212-308-2578	Employees: 25	

Business services - marketing (Bromo Seltzer, Doan's Pills, Ovaltine, Topol Smoker's Toothpolish)

HIRSCH INTERNATIONAL CORP.

200 Wireless Blvd.	CEO: Henry Arnberg	1995 Sales: $72.3 million
Hauppauge, NY 11788	CFO: Kenneth Shifrin	1-Yr. Sales Change: 43.2%
Phone: 516-436-7100	HR: Susan Lange	Exchange: Nasdaq
Fax: 516-436-7054	Employees: 141	Symbol: HRSH

Machinery - computerized embroidery equipment

 See page 272 for a full profile of this company.

HI-SHEAR INDUSTRIES INC.

3333 New Hyde Park Rd.	CEO: David A. Wingate	1995 Sales: $58.6 million
North Hills, NY 11042	CFO: Victor J. Galgano	1-Yr. Sales Change: 3.7%
Phone: 516-627-8600	HR: —	Exchange: NYSE
Fax: 516-365-8629	Employees: 625	Symbol: HSI

Aerospace - structural fasteners & installation tools used for commercial & military aircraft

HI-TECH PHARMACAL CO., INC.

369 Bayview Ave.	CEO: Bernard Seltzer	1995 Sales: $16.4 million
Amityville, NY 11701	CFO: Arthur S. Goldberg	1-Yr. Sales Change: 23.3%
Phone: 516-789-8228	HR: Carole Wood	Exchange: Nasdaq
Fax: 516-789-8429	Employees: 118	Symbol: HITK

Drugs - products in liquid & semisolid form, over-the-counter pharmaceuticals, prescription drug products & nutritional preparations for the private-label market

HMG WORLDWIDE CORPORATION

475 10th Ave.	CEO: Michael Wahl	1994 Sales: $55.6 million
New York, NY 10018	CFO: Robert V. Cuddihy Jr.	1-Yr. Sales Change: 172.5%
Phone: 212-736-2300	HR: Debra Eccles	Exchange: Nasdaq (SC)
Fax: 212-629-8587	Employees: 251	Symbol: HMGC

Advertising - in-store marketing (point-of-sale)

HOENIG & CO. INC.

4 International Dr.
Rye Brook, NY 10573
Phone: 914-935-9000
Fax: 914-935-9146

CEO: Joseph A. D'Andrea
CFO: Alan B. Herzog
HR: —
Employees: 95

1994 Sales: $58.9 million
1-Yr. Sales Change: -5.9%
Exchange: Nasdaq
Symbol: HOEN

Financial - securities brokerage

HOFFMANN-LA ROCHE, INC.

340 Kingsland St.
Nutley, NY 07110
Phone: 201-235-5000
Fax: 201-562-2208

CEO: Patrick J. Zenner
CFO: Martin F. Spadler
HR: Martin F. Spadler
Employees: —

1994 Sales: $3,039 million
1-Yr. Sales Change: 8%
Ownership: Subsidiary

Drugs, vitamins & fine chemicals (subsidiary of Roche Group)

HOFSTRA UNIVERSITY

Hempstead Tnpk. South
Hempstead, NY 11550
Phone: 516-463-6600
Fax: 516-463-5421

CEO: James Shuart
CFO: James McCue
HR: Janet Lenaghan
Employees: 2,000

1995 Est. Sales: $135 mil.
1-Yr. Sales Change: —
Ownership: Privately Held

Private university offering 91 undergraduate & 88 graduate degree programs

HOLOPAK TECHNOLOGIES, INC.

9 Cotters Ln.
East Brunswick, NJ 08816
Phone: 908-238-2883
Fax: 908-613-9653

CEO: Harry Parker
CFO: David W. Jaffin
HR: —
Employees: 282

1995 Sales: $45.9 million
1-Yr. Sales Change: 1.1%
Exchange: Nasdaq
Symbol: HOLO

Paper & paper products - hot stamping foils, holographic foils & metallized paper for decoration or protection against counterfeiting

HOME STATE HOLDINGS, INC.

3 S. Revmont Dr.
Shrewsbury, NJ 07702
Phone: 908-935-2600
Fax: 908-935-0156

CEO: Robert Abidor
CFO: Kenneth E. Edwards
HR: Geraldine Dohanyos
Employees: 138

1994 Sales: $38.1 million
1-Yr. Sales Change: 38.5%
Exchange: Nasdaq
Symbol: HOMS

Insurance - property & casualty, personal & commercial auto insurance in several eastern states

HOMETOWN BANCORPORATION, INC.

20 West Ave.
Darien, CT 06820
Phone: 203-656-2265
Fax: 203-662-2531

Banks - Northeast

CEO: Kevin E. Gage
CFO: Albert T. Jaronczyk
HR: Agnes Kung
Employees: 79

1994 Sales: $13.5 million
1-Yr. Sales Change: 17.4%
Exchange: Nasdaq
Symbol: HTWN

HONEY FASHIONS, LTD.

417 5th Ave.
New York, NY 10016
Phone: 212-686-4424
Fax: 212-696-9568

Apparel   women's clothing & accessories

CEO: Norman Elowitz
CFO: Norman Elowitz
HR: —
Employees: 220

1994 Sales: $125 million
1-Yr. Sales Change: 25.0%
Ownership: Privately Held

HOOPER HOLMES, INC.

170 Mt. Airy Rd.
Basking Ridge, NJ 07920
Phone: 908-766-5000
Fax: 908-766-5073

Health care - home

CEO: James M. McNamee
CFO: Fred Lash
HR: Frank Stiner
Employees: 21,850

1994 Sales: $251.8 million
1-Yr. Sales Change: 34.4%
Exchange: AMEX
Symbol: HH

HORIZON PAPER COMPANY

230 Park Ave.
New York, NY 10169
Phone: 212-682-5820
Fax: 212-986-0689

Paper & paper products

CEO: Gerry L. Martin
CFO: Jeff Hansen
HR: —
Employees: 26

1994 Sales: $260 million
1-Yr. Sales Change: 23.8%
Ownership: Privately Held

HORNELL BREWING COMPANY

4501 Glenwood Rd.
New York, NY 11203
Phone: 718-284-1200
Fax: 718-484-0174

Beverages - malt liquor (Crazy Horse)

CEO: John Ferolito
CFO: Rick Adonailo
HR: —
Employees: 100

1994 Sales: $200 million
1-Yr. Sales Change: 0.0%
Ownership: Privately Held
Symbol: 114

HORSEHEAD INDUSTRIES

110 E. 59th St.
New York, NY 10022
Phone: 212-527-3000
Fax: 212-527-3008

CEO: William E. Flaherty
CFO: —
HR: John Brown
Employees: 2,000

1994 Sales: $550 million
1-Yr. Sales Change: 0.0%
Ownership: Privately Held

Metals - zinc, carbon & graphite; environmental services

HOSPOSABLE PRODUCTS, INC.

100 Readington Rd.
Somerville, NJ 08876
Phone: 908-707-1800
Fax: 908-707-1606

CEO: Joseph Weinkam
CFO: John Zisko
HR: —
Employees: 207

1994 Sales: $34.5 million
1-Yr. Sales Change: 15.4%
Exchange: Nasdaq
Symbol: HOSP

Medical & dental supplies

HOST APPAREL, INC.

1430 Broadway
New York, NY 10018
Phone: 212-302-0800
Fax: 212-302-8570

CEO: Howard Cohen
CFO: Al Bonzer
HR: Jim Rolek
Employees: 600

1994 Sales: $105 million
1-Yr. Sales Change: -4.5%
Ownership: Privately Held

Apparel - men's & women's sleepwear (Christian Dior), robes & boxer shorts

HOVNANIAN ENTERPRISES, INC.

10 Hwy. 35, PO Box 500
Red Bank, NJ 07701
Phone: 908-747-7800
Fax: 908-747-7159

CEO: Kevork S. Hovnanian
CFO: J. Larry Sorsby
HR: Timothy Mason
Employees: 1,070

1994 Sales: $704.4 million
1-Yr. Sales Change: 64.1%
Exchange: AMEX
Symbol: HOV

Building - residential

HRE PROPERTIES

321 Railroad Ave.
Greenwich, CT 06830
Phone: 203-863-8200
Fax: 203-861-6755

CEO: Charles J. Urstadt
CFO: James R. Moore
HR: —
Employees: 16

1994 Sales: $19 million
1-Yr. Sales Change: 17.3%
Exchange: NYSE
Symbol: HRE

Real estate investment trust - shopping centers, single-tenant retail stores, office buildings & service & distribution facilities in 15 states throughout the US

HUBBELL INC.

584 Derby Milford Rd.
Orange, CT 06477-4024
Phone: 203-799-4100
Fax: 203-799-4254

CEO: G. J. Ratcliffe
CFO: Harry B. Rowell Jr.
HR: George Zurman
Employees: 7,405

1994 Sales: $1,013.7 mil.
1-Yr. Sales Change: 21.8%
Exchange: NYSE
Symbol: HUBB

Electrical products - electrical wiring devices, industrial controls

HUBCO, INC.

1000 MacArthur Blvd.
Mahwah, NJ 07430
Phone: 201-236-2600
Fax: 201-866-7986

CEO: Kenneth T. Neilson
CFO: Eugene Malinowski
HR: Karen A. Foley
Employees: 679

1994 Sales: $93.9 million
1-Yr. Sales Change: 22.9%
Exchange: Nasdaq
Symbol: HUBC

Banks - Northeast (Hudson United Bank)

HUDSON COUNTY NEWS COMPANY

1305 Paterson Plank Rd.
N. Bergen, NJ 07047
Phone: 201-867-3600
Fax: 201-867-0067

CEO: Robert B. Cohen
CFO: Howard Joroff
HR: Lynn Stanton
Employees: 1,100

1994 Sales: $360 million
1-Yr. Sales Change: 2.3%
Ownership: Privately Held

Wholesale distribution - newspapers & magazines (#1 on the East Coast)

HUDSON GENERAL CORPORATION

111 Great Neck Rd.
Great Neck, NY 11021
Phone: 516-487-8610
Fax: 516-487-4855

CEO: Jay B. Langner
CFO: Michael Rubin
HR: Robert T. Cavaliere
Employees: 3,300

1995 Sales: $135.5 million
1-Yr. Sales Change: -4.6%
Exchange: AMEX
Symbol: HGC

Transportation - aviation services, including aircraft marshaling, baggage loading & off-loading, freight & commissary items, passenger ticketing & porter & wheelchair services

HUDSON TECHNOLOGIES, INC.

25 Torne Valley Rd., PO Box 1187
Hillburn, NY 10931-9900
Phone: 914-368-4990
Fax: 914-368-2540

CEO: Kevin J. Zugibe
CFO: Stephen J. Cole-Hatchard
HR: Deborah L. Bulson
Employees: 55

1994 Sales: $1.3 million
1-Yr. Sales Change: 550.0%
Exchange: Nasdaq (SC)
Symbol: HDSN

Pollution control - refrigerant reclamation services (Zugibeast)

HUGHES HUBBARD & REED

One Battery Park Plaza, 12th Fl.
New York, NY 10004
Phone: 212-837-6000
Fax: 212-422-4726

Law firm

CEO: Chalres H. Scherer
CFO: Joan Clark
HR: Nancy Albanese
Employees: 537

1994 Sales: $78 million
1-Yr. Sales Change: 5.4%
Ownership: Privately Held

HUNGARIAN BROADCASTING CORP.

90 West St.
New York, NY 10006
Phone: 212-571-7400
Fax: 212-571-2051

CEO: Peter E. Klenner
CFO: Peter E. Klenner
HR: —
Employees: 13

1995 Sales: $0.1 million
1-Yr. Sales Change: —
Ownership: Privately Held

Broadcasting - acquisition of interests in companies that have commercial broadcasting licenses to operate TV stations in Hungary (Magyar TV 1, MTV 2, DUNA TV)

HUNGARIAN TELEPHONE AND CABLE CORP.

90 West St.
New York, NY 10006
Phone: 212-571-7400
Fax: 212-571-2051

CEO: Robert Genova
CFO: Frank R. Cohen
HR: —
Employees: 233

1994 Sales: $0.6 million
1-Yr. Sales Change: 500.0%
Exchange: Nasdaq (SC)
Symbol: HTCC

Telecommunications services in Hungary

HUNTER DOUGLAS, INC.

2 Upper Pkwy. & Rte. 17 South
Upper Saddle River , NJ 07458
Phone: 201-327-8200
Fax: 201-327-1965

CEO: Marvin Hopkins
CFO: James Conkling
HR: Betty Lou Smith
Employees: 4,300

1994 Est. Sales: $600 mil.
1-Yr. Sales Change: 0.0%
Ownership: Privately Held

Building products   custom window blinds & coverings

HYPERION SOFTWARE CORPORATION

777 Long Ridge Rd.
Stamford, CT 06902-1247
Phone: 203-321-3500
Fax: 203-322-3904

CEO: James A. Perakis
CFO: Lucy Rae Ricciardi
HR: Paul Avalone
Employees: 580

1995 Sales: $137.1 million
1-Yr. Sales Change: 62.4%
Exchange: Nasdaq
Symbol: HYSW

Computers - executive information systems software

 See page 273 for a full profile of this company.

I. APPEL CORPORATION

136 Madison Ave.
New York, NY 10016
Phone: 212-592-8600
Fax: 212-592-8799

Apparel - robes & dressing gowns

CEO: N. Katz
CFO: Howard Kaufer
HR: —
Employees: 1,900

1994 Sales: $135 million
1-Yr. Sales Change: 0.0%
Ownership: Privately Held

ICC INDUSTRIES INC.

720 Fifth Ave.
New York, NY 10019
Phone: 212-903-1700
Fax: 212-903-1794

Chemicals - diversified

CEO: John J. Farber
CFO: John Oram
HR: —
Employees: 2,466

1994 Sales: $1,050 million
1-Yr. Sales Change: 18.4%
Ownership: Privately Held

IDM ENVIRONMENTAL CORP.

396 Whitehead Ave., PO Box 388
South River, NJ 08882
Phone: 908-390-9550
Fax: 908-390-9545

Pollution control - environmental remediation, plant decommissioning services & relocation &
re-erection of process plants

CEO: Joel A. Freedman
CFO: Michael B. Killeen
HR: —
Employees: 193

1994 Sales: $28.5 million
1-Yr. Sales Change: 49.2%
Exchange: Nasdaq
Symbol: IDMC

ILC INDUSTRIES, INC.

105 Wilbur Place
New York, NY 11716
Phone: 516-567-5600
Fax: 516-567-6357

Electrical components - semiconductors & electronic coils

CEO: Clifford P. Lane
CFO: Ken Sheed
HR: Martha Solowey
Employees: 1,100

1994 Sales: $120 million
1-Yr. Sales Change: -4.0%
Ownership: Privately Held

IMCLONE SYSTEMS, INC.

180 Varick St.
New York, NY 10014
Phone: 212-645-1405
Fax: 212-645-2054

Biomedical & genetic products

CEO: Samuel D. Waksal
CFO: Peter M. Rogalin
HR: —
Employees: 96

1994 Sales: $0.9 million
1-Yr. Sales Change: -83.3%
Exchange: Nasdaq
Symbol: IMCL

IMMUNOMEDICS, INC.

150 Mt. Bethel Rd.
Warren, NJ 07059
Phone: 201-605-8200
Fax: 201-605-8282

CEO: David W. Ortlieb
CFO: David W. Ortlieb
HR: Donna Bobb
Employees: 85

1995 Sales: $3.2 million
1-Yr. Sales Change: -23.8%
Exchange: Nasdaq
Symbol: IMMU

Biomedical & genetic products - antibody selection, modification & chemistry products for the detection & treatment of cancers & infectious diseases

INDEPENDENCE BANCORP, INC.

1100 Lake St.
Ramsey, NJ 07446
Phone: 201-825-1000
Fax: 201-818-9818

CEO: A. Roger Bomsa
CFO: Kevin J. Killian
HR: Cindy M. Schroeder
Employees: 161

1994 Sales: $19.1 million
1-Yr. Sales Change: -3.5%
Exchange: Nasdaq (SC)
Symbol: IBNJ

Banks - Northeast (Independence Bank of NJ)

INDEPENDENCE HOLDING COMPANY

96 Cummings Point Rd.
Stamford, CT 06904
Phone: 203-358-8000
Fax: 203-348-3103

CEO: Edward Netter
CFO: Roy T. K. Thung
HR: Nancy Howe
Employees: 440

1994 Sales: $98.4 million
1-Yr. Sales Change: -0.4%
Exchange: Nasdaq
Symbol: INHO

Financial - business services, primarily insurance services; commercial signs

INDIVIDUAL INVESTOR GROUP, INC.

333 Seventh Ave., 5th Fl.
New York, NY 10001
Phone: 212-843-2777
Fax: 212-843-2789

CEO: Jonathan L. Steinberg
CFO: Scot A. Rosenblum
HR: Deirdre Cavanaugh
Employees: 28

1994 Sales: $6.6 million
1-Yr. Sales Change: 43.5%
Exchange: Nasdaq (SC)
Symbol: INDI

Publishing - market & financial information for individual investors (Individual Investor)

INDUSTRIAL ACOUSTICS CO., INC.

1160 Commerce Ave.
New York, NY 10462
Phone: 718-931-8000
Fax: 718-863-1138

CEO: Martin Hirschorn
CFO: Robert N. Bertrand
HR: Raymond E. Svana
Employees: 780

1995 Sales: $71.7 million
1-Yr. Sales Change: -3.4%
Exchange: Nasdaq
Symbol: IACI

Building products - noise-suppression materials

INDUSTRIAL TECHNOLOGIES, INC.

One Trefoil Dr.
Trumbull, CT 06611
Phone: 203-268-8000
Fax: 203-268-2538

CEO: Gerald W. Stewart
CFO: Joseph Schlig
HR: Nancy Wilkins
Employees: 45

1994 Sales: $6.6 million
1-Yr. Sales Change: -7.0%
Exchange: Nasdaq (SC)
Symbol: INTI

Computers - sensing, monitoring, processing & inspection technologies designed to improve
industrial operations; standard inspection & industrial-strength computers for harsh conditions

INFINITY BROADCASTING CORPORATION

600 Madison Ave.
New York, NY 10022
Phone: 212-750-6400
Fax: 212-888-2959

CEO: Mel Karmazin
CFO: Farid Suleman
HR: Tom Gesimondo
Employees: 1,114

1994 Sales: $274.1 million
1-Yr. Sales Change: 34.0%
Exchange: Nasdaq
Symbol: INFTA

Broadcasting - radio broadcasting (#1 in US)

 See page 274 for a full profile of this company.

INFORMATION BUILDERS, INC.

1250 Broadway, 38th Fl.
New York, NY 10001-3782
Phone: 212-736-4433
Fax: 212-967-6406

CEO: Gerald D. Cohen
CFO: Harry Lerner
HR: Lila Goldberg
Employees: 1,750

1994 Sales: $240 million
1-Yr. Sales Change: 5.7%
Ownership: Privately Held

Computers - database software (Focus)

INFORMATION MANAGMENT TECHNOLOGIES CORP.

130 Cedar St., 4th Fl.
New York, NY 10006-1016
Phone: 212-306-6100
Fax: 212-962-4551

CEO: Ted E. Prince
CFO: Joseph A. Gitto Jr.
HR: Michelle Romero
Employees: 190

1995 Sales: $21.2 million
1-Yr. Sales Change: -22.9%
Exchange: Nasdaq (SC)
Symbol: IMTAC

Business services - information & facilities management services

INFOSAFE SYSTEMS, INC.

342 Madison Ave., Ste. 622
New York, NY 10173
Phone: 212-867-7200
Fax: 212-867-7227

CEO: Thomas H. Lipscomb
CFO: Alan N. Alpern
HR: Alistair Wier
Employees: 17

1995 Sales: $0.1 million
1-Yr. Sales Change: -75.0%
Exchange: Nasdaq (SC)
Symbol: ISFEA

Computers - secure electronic distribution systems (Infosafe System) for publishers & other information
providers to prevent theft of digital information, video, graphics & software

INFU-TECH, INC.

900 Sylvan Ave.
Englewood Cliffs, NJ 07632
Phone: 201-567-4600
Fax: 201-567-1072

Medical services

CEO: Jack Rosen
CFO: Gary Finkel
HR: Geraldine Kelly
Employees: 120

1994 Sales: $16.3 million
1-Yr. Sales Change: -4.1%
Exchange: Nasdaq
Symbol: INFU

INGERSOLL-RAND COMPANY

200 Chestnut Ridge Rd.
Woodcliff Lake, NJ 07675
Phone: 201-573-0123
Fax: 201-573-3448

Machinery - engineered equipment & bearings, locks & tools

CEO: James E. Perrella
CFO: Thomas F. McBride
HR: Donald H. Rice
Employees: 35,932

1994 Sales: $4,507.5 mil.
1-Yr. Sales Change: 12.1%
Exchange: NYSE
Symbol: IR

 See pages 134–135 for a full profile of this company.

INNODATA CORPORATION

95 Rockwell Place
New York, NY 11217
Phone: 718-625-7750
Fax: 718-522-9235

CEO: Barry Hertz
CFO: Martin Kaye
HR: Jack Cohen
Employees: 2,420

1994 Sales: $14.3 million
1-Yr. Sales Change: 49.0%
Exchange: Nasdaq
Symbol: INOD

Data collection & systems - data entry & conversion, scanning, indexing & abstracting services for customers in the US & Europe

INNOVIR LABORATORIES, INC.

510 E. 73rd St.
New York, NY 10021
Phone: 212-249-4703
Fax: 212-249-4513

CEO: Allan R. Goldberg
CFO: Gary Pokrassa
HR: Kathleen E. Pickering
Employees: 23

1994 Sales: $0.1 million
1-Yr. Sales Change: —
Exchange: Nasdaq (SC)
Symbol: INVR

Biomedical & genetic products - development of biopharmaceutical therapeutic agents, primarily ribozyme-based (catalytic RNA) drugs, for the treatment of a wide array of human diseases

INSERRA SUPERMARKETS

20 Ridge Rd.
Mahwah, NJ 07430
Phone: 201-529-5900
Fax: 201-529-1189

CEO: Lawrence R. Inserra
CFO: Frank Festa
HR: Marie Larson
Employees: 2,300

1994 Sales: $500 million
1-Yr. Sales Change: 9.6%
Ownership: Privately Held

Retail - supermarkets (23 units: ShopRite)

INSTITUTE OF INTERNATIONAL EDUCATION

809 United Nations Plaza	CEO: Richard M. Krasno	1994 Sales: $85.4 million
New York, NY 10017-3580	CFO: Madeline H. McWhinney	1-Yr. Sales Change: -7.9%
Phone: 212-883-8200	HR: Joan Wall	Ownership: Privately Held
Fax: 212-984-5452	Employees: 365	

Foundation - international exchange programs; publications, census, counseling, library & reference services

INTEGRATED BRANDS INC.

4175 Veterans Highway	CEO: Richard E. Smith	1994 Sales: $33.8 million
Ronkonkoma, NY 11779	CFO: Gary P. Stevens	1-Yr. Sales Change: -6.6%
Phone: 516-737-9700	HR: Sue Yurman	Exchange: Nasdaq
Fax: 516-737-9797	Employees: 196	Symbol: IBIN

Food - ice cream (Steve's, Swensen's, American Glace, Chilly Things), yogurt distribution (Yoplait); owns & operates restaurants & ice cream stores (Swensen's)

INTEPLAST CORPORATION

9 Peach Tree Hill Rd.	CEO: John Young	1994 Sales: $250 million
Livingston, NJ 07039	CFO: Benjamin Tsao	1-Yr. Sales Change: 150.0%
Phone: 201-992-2090	HR: George Karlis	Ownership: Privately Held
Fax: 201-994-8090	Employees: 1,800	

Chemicals - unsupported plastics, film & sheet

INTERCHANGE FINANCIAL SERVICES CORPORATION

Park 80 West/Plaza Two	CEO: Anthony S. Abbate	1994 Sales: $36.4 million
Saddle Brook, NJ 07663	CFO: Robert N. Harris	1-Yr. Sales Change: 6.7%
Phone: 201-703-2265	HR: Amanda C. Pascale	Exchange: AMEX
Fax: 201-845-4640	Employees: 181	Symbol: ISB

Banks - Northeast (Interchange State Bank)

INTERCHEM TRADING CORPORATION

120 Rte. 17 North	CEO: Joseph Pizza	1994 Sales: $125 million
Paramus, NJ 07652	CFO: Vincent Durante	1-Yr. Sales Change: 25.0%
Phone: 201-261-7333	HR: Vincent Durante	Ownership: Privately Held
Fax: 201-261-7339	Employees: 55	

Drugs & sundries

INTEREP RADIO STORE

100 Park Ave.
New York, NY 10017
Phone: 212-916-0700
Fax: 212-916-0772

CEO: Ralph Gild
CFO: Michael Tsavaris
HR: —
Employees: 500

1994 Sales: $330 million
1-Yr. Sales Change: 0.0%
Ownership: Privately Held

Advertising - radio advertising representative

INTERFERON SCIENCES, INC.

783 Jersey Ave.
New Brunswick, NJ 08901
Phone: 908-249-3250
Fax: 908-249-6895

CEO: Samuel H. Ronel
CFO: Donald W. Anderson
HR: Sarah Walker
Employees: 55

1994 Sales: $1.1 million
1-Yr. Sales Change: 1,000%
Exchange: Nasdaq (SC)
Symbol: IFSC

Medical services - alpha-interferon pharmaceutical production

INTERIORS, INC.

320 Washington St.
Mt. Vernon, NY 10553
Phone: 914-665-5400
Fax: 914-665-5469

CEO: Theodore Stevens
CFO: Robert M. Schildkraut
HR: Sharon Watson
Employees: 134

1995 Sales: $7.1 million
1-Yr. Sales Change: 9.2%
Exchange: Nasdaq (SC)
Symbol: INTXA

Antique & contemporary picture frames for museums, art galleries, designers, collectors & frame
retailers; traditional & contemporary mirrors through retail furniture & department stores

INTERLAKEN INVESTMENT PARTNERS L.P.

165 Mason St.
Greenwich, CT 06830
Phone: 203-629-8750
Fax: 203-629-8554

CEO: William R. Berkley
CFO: Charlie Martin
HR: Margaret Crawford
Employees: 15

1995 Sales: —
1-Yr. Sales Change: —
Ownership: Privately Held

Financial - investment bankers

INTERNATIONAL BUSINESS MACHINES CORPORATION

One Old Orchard Rd.
Armonk, NY 10504
Phone: 914-765-1900
Fax: 914-288-1147

CEO: Louis V. Gerstner Jr.
CFO: G. Richard Thoman
HR: J. Thomas Bouchard
Employees: 219,839

1994 Sales: $64,052 million
1-Yr. Sales Change: 2.1%
Exchange: NYSE
Symbol: IBM

Computers - mainframes, minis, micros, processors, software & peripherals

See pages 136–137 for a full profile of this company.

INTERNATIONAL CABLETEL, INC.

150 E. 58th St.
New York, NY 10155
Phone: 212-371-3714
Fax: 212-752-1157

Telecommunications services

CEO: George S. Blumenthal
CFO: Gregg Gorelick
HR: Beth Wilson
Employees: 190

1994 Sales: $13.7 million
1-Yr. Sales Change: 35.6%
Exchange: Nasdaq
Symbol: ICTL

INTERNATIONAL FLAVORS & FRAGRANCES INC.

521 W. 57th St.
New York, NY 10019-2960
Phone: 212-765-5500
Fax: 212-708-7132

Chemicals - specialty

CEO: Eugene P. Grisanti
CFO: Thomas H. Hoppel
HR: William A. Myers Jr.
Employees: 4,570

1994 Sales: $1,315.2 mil.
1-Yr. Sales Change: 10.6%
Exchange: NYSE
Symbol: IFF

INTERNATIONAL PAPER COMPANY

2 Manhattanville Rd.
Purchase, NY 10577
Phone: 914-397-1500
Fax: 914-397-1596

Paper & paper products; specialty products; wood & timber

CEO: John A. Georges
CFO: Marianne M. Parrs
HR: Robert M. Byrnes
Employees: 70,000

1994 Sales: $14,966 million
1-Yr. Sales Change: 9.4%
Exchange: NYSE
Symbol: IP

 See pages 138–139 for a full profile of this company.

INTERNATIONAL POST LIMITED

545 5th Ave.
New York, NY 10017
Phone: 212-986-6300
Fax: 212-986-1364

CEO: Martin Irwin
CFO: Jeffrey J. Kaplan
HR: Carla Moxham
Employees: 227

1995 Sales: $38.3 million
1-Yr. Sales Change: 37.8%
Exchange: Nasdaq
Symbol: POST

Motion pictures & services - film-to-tape transfer, electronic video editing & computer-generated graphics primarily for the TV advertising & international program distribution industries

INTERNATIONAL PROTEINS CORPORATION

PO Box 1169
Fairfield, NJ 07007
Phone: 201-227-2710
Fax: 201-227-6533

Financial - commodities trading

CEO: Eric Jackson
CFO: Bob Pastore
HR: —
Employees: 50

1994 Sales: $150 million
1-Yr. Sales Change: -9.1%
Ownership: Privately Held

INTERNATIONAL RESCUE COMMITTEE

122 E. 42nd St.	CEO: Robert P. DeVecchi	1994 Sales: $93.3 million
New York, NY 10168-1289	CFO: Joan Koenig	1-Yr. Sales Change: —
Phone: 212-551-3000	HR: Louise Shea	Ownership: Privately Held
Fax: 212-551-3180	Employees: 490	

Voluntary not-for-profit organization providing relief, protection & resettlement services for refugees & victims of oppression or violent conflict

INTERNATIONAL TERMINAL OPERATING COMPANY

One Evertrust Plaza	CEO: James Field	1994 Sales: $212 million
Jersey City, NJ 07302	CFO: Gus Hatcichristos	1-Yr. Sales Change: 0.0%
Phone: 201-915-3100	HR: Pat Tomasull	Ownership: Privately Held
Fax: 201-915-3109	Employees: 2,000	

Transportation - marine cargo handling

INTERNATIONAL VITAMIN CORPORATION

500 Halls Mill Rd.	CEO: A. Edell	1995 Sales: $49.3 million
Freehold, NJ 07728	CFO: Joseph Edell	1-Yr. Sales Change: 13.3%
Phone: 908-308-3000	HR: —	Exchange: Nasdaq (SC)
Fax: 908-308-9793	Employees: 315	Symbol: IVCO

Drugs

THE INTERPUBLIC GROUP OF COMPANIES, INC.

1271 Avenue of the Americas	CEO: Philip H. Geier Jr.	1994 Sales: $1,984.3 mil.
New York, NY 10020	CFO: Eugene P. Beard	1-Yr. Sales Change: 10.6%
Phone: 212-399-8000	HR: C. Kent Kroeber	Exchange: NYSE
Fax: 212-399-8130	Employees: 18,200	Symbol: IPG

Advertising

See pages 140–141 for a full profile of this company.

INVESTMENT TECHNOLOGY GROUP, INC.

900 Third Ave.	CEO: Raymond L. Killian Jr.	1994 Sales: $58.9 million
New York, NY 10022	CFO: John R. MacDonald	1-Yr. Sales Change: 16.2%
Phone: 212-755-6800	HR: Susan Nelson	Exchange: Nasdaq
Fax: 212-444-6290	Employees: 94	Symbol: ITGI

Financial - automated securities trade execution & analysis services

IP TIMBERLANDS, LTD.

2 Manhattanville Rd.
Purchase, NY 10577
Phone: 914-397-1500
Fax: 914-397-1928

Building products - wood

CEO: John A. Georges
CFO: Marianne M. Parrs
HR: Robert M. Byrnes
Employees: —

1994 Sales: $369.3 million
1-Yr. Sales Change: -13.3%
Exchange: NYSE
Symbol: IPT

IPC INFORMATION SYSTEMS, INC.

Wall Street Plaza, 88 Pine St.
New York, NY 10005
Phone: 212-825-9060
Fax: 212-509-7888

CEO: S. T. "Terry" Clontz
CFO: Gregory Riedel
HR: Jody Tracey
Employees: 510

1995 Sales: $206.3 million
1-Yr. Sales Change: 26.0%
Exchange: Nasdaq
Symbol: IPCI

Telecommunications equipment - specialized systems for the financial services industry; design &
implementation of local (LAN) & wide area network (WAN) for voice, data & video networking

ISAAC MIZRAHI & CO., L.P.

104 Wooster St.
New York, NY 10012
Phone: 212-334-0055
Fax: 212-334-9569

Apparel - women's clothing

CEO: Isaac Mizrahi
CFO: Krisann Tallman
HR: —
Employees: 70

1995 Est. Sales: $10 mil.
1-Yr. Sales Change: —
Ownership: Privately Held

ISOMEDIX INC.

11 Apollo Dr.
Whippany, NJ 07981
Phone: 201-887-4700
Fax: 201-887-1476

Medical & dental supplies

CEO: Peter Mayer
CFO: Thomas J. DeAngelo
HR: Thomas J. De Angelo
Employees: 335

1994 Sales: $47.2 million
1-Yr. Sales Change: 9.3%
Exchange: NYSE
Symbol: ISO

ISRAMCO, INC.

800 5th Ave., Ste. 21-D
New York, NY 10021
Phone: 212-683-4890
Fax: 212-679-1184

Oil & gas - exploration & production in Israel

CEO: Joseph Elmaleh
CFO: Joseph Elmaleh
HR: —
Employees: 10

1994 Sales: $2.2 million
1-Yr. Sales Change: -53.2%
Exchange: Nasdaq (SC)
Symbol: ISRL

ITT CORPORATION

1330 Avenue of the Americas	CEO: Rand V. Araskog	1994 Sales: $4,760 million
New York, NY 10019-5490	CFO: Ann N. Reese	1-Yr. Sales Change: 14.2%
Phone: 212-258-1000	HR: Ralph W. Pausig	Exchange: NYSE
Fax: 212-258-1297	Employees: 35,000	Symbol: ITT

Hotels (Sheraton, Four Points); gambling resorts & casinos (Caesars Palace); professional sports teams (New York Knicks & Rangers) & sports arena (Madison Square Garden); telephone directories

 See pages 142–143 for a full profile of this company.

ITT INDUSTRIES, INC.

4 West Red Oak Ln.	CEO: D. Travis Engen	1994 Sales: $7,758 million
White Plains, NY 10604	CFO: Heidi Kunz	1-Yr. Sales Change: 17.2%
Phone: 914-641-2000	HR: James P. Smith Jr.	Exchange: NYSE
Fax: 914-696-2950	Employees: 58,400	Symbol: IIN

Automotive & trucking - brakes, chassis, door & window assemblies, seats & electrical systems for auto & truck makers & related products for the aftermarket; defense & electronics; fluid technology

 See pages 144–145 for a full profile of this company.

IVF AMERICA, INC.

One Manhattanville Rd.	CEO: Jerry Canet	1994 Sales: $17.6 million
Purchase, NY 10577	CFO: Dwight P. Ryan	1-Yr. Sales Change: 10.0%
Phone: 914-253-8000	HR: —	Exchange: Nasdaq
Fax: 914-253-8008	Employees: 113	Symbol: IVFA

Medical services - assisted reproductive technology (ART) services

J & R MUSIC WORLD

23 Park Row	CEO: Joe Friedman	1994 Sales: $165 million
New York, NY 10038	CFO: Vvi Hirsch	1-Yr. Sales Change: 10.0%
Phone: 212-732-8600	HR: —	Ownership: Privately Held
Fax: 212-238-9191	Employees: 350	

Retail - consumer electronics, computers & office supplies & equipment

J. CREW GROUP INC.

625 Sixth Ave.	CEO: Arthur Cinader	1995 Sales: $725 million
New York, NY 10011	CFO: Michael P. McHugh	1-Yr. Sales Change: 14.0%
Phone: 212-886-2500	HR: Marianne Ruggiero	Ownership: Privately Held
Fax: 212-886-2666	Employees: 6,600	

Retail - mail-order & retail apparel & home furnishings

J. GERBER & CO., INC.

11 Penn Plaza	CEO: Geoffrey Clain	1995 Sales: $256 million
New York, NY 10001	CFO: Martin B. Egnal	1-Yr. Sales Change: 37.6%
Phone: 212-631-1200	HR: —	Ownership: Privately Held
Fax: 212-631-1316	Employees: 70	

Food - exporter of meat & poultry products; residential, commercial & auto air conditioning; specialty wire products

J. MICHAELS, INC.

182 Smith St.	CEO: James Michaels	1995 Sales: $7.2 million
New York, NY 11201	CFO: Martin Kasman	1-Yr. Sales Change: -15.3%
Phone: 718-852-6100	HR: Arthur Fettner	Exchange: Nasdaq (SC)
Fax: 718-858-0396	Employees: —	Symbol: MICH

Retail - home furnishings, furniture retail & leasing

JACK SCHWARTZ SHOES, INC.

155 Sixth St.	CEO: Bernard Schwartz	1994 Sales: $140 million
New York, NY 10013	CFO: Bernard Schwartz	1-Yr. Sales Change: 0.0%
Phone: 212-691-4700	HR: —	Ownership: Privately Held
Fax: 212-691-5350	Employees: 90	

Wholesale distribution - athletic footwear

JACLYN, INC.

635 59th St.	CEO: Robert Chestnov	1995 Sales: $73.9 million
West New York, NJ 07093	CFO: Anthony Christon	1-Yr. Sales Change: -10.7%
Phone: 201-868-9400	HR: Virginia Piacentini	Exchange: AMEX
Fax: 201-868-3047	Employees: 284	Symbol: JLN

Apparel - vinyl, leather & fabric handbags; apparel lines, vests, loungewear, sleepwear, dresses, sportswear, slippers, footwear & lingerie

JACO ELECTRONICS, INC.

145 Oser Ave.	CEO: Joel H. Girsky	1995 Sales: $138.7 million
Hauppauge, NY 11788	CFO: Jeffrey D. Gash	1-Yr. Sales Change: 31.8%
Phone: 516-273-5500	HR: Karen Blankmeyer	Exchange: Nasdaq
Fax: 516-273-5528	Employees: 280	Symbol: JACO

Electronics - parts distribution

JACOBSON MANUFACTURING COMPANY

One Mark Rd.
Kenilworth, NJ 07033
Phone: 908-686-0200
Fax: 908-686-0248

Containers - custom packaging

CEO: Harvey Jacobson
CFO: Charles Sundstrom
HR: Christine Sapienza
Employees: 600

1994 Sales: $112 million
1-Yr. Sales Change: 24.4%
Ownership: Privately Held

JAMES D. WOLFENSOHN, INC.

599 Lexington Ave.
New York, NY 10022
Phone: 212-909-8100
Fax: 212-909-0831

Financial - investment bankers

CEO: Paul Volcker
CFO: Robert Bertolid
HR: Joseph Heenan
Employees: 110

1995 Sales: —
1-Yr. Sales Change: —
Ownership: Privately Held

J&R COMPUTER WORLD

15 Park Row
New York, NY 10038
Phone: 212-238-9000
Fax: 212-238-9191

Computer superstore in New York City; mail-order sales

CEO: Rachelle Friedman
CFO: Zvi Hirsch
HR: Dean Shilenok
Employees: 600

1994 Est. Sales: $135 mil.
1-Yr. Sales Change: —
Ownership: Privately Held

JAYDOR CORPORATION

16 Bleeker St.
Millburn, NJ 07041
Phone: 201-379-1234
Fax: 201-379-1913

Beverages - distribution of wines, spirits, specialty foods & gourmet beer

CEO: Michael D. Silverman
CFO: Louis Healey
HR: Carolyn White
Employees: 300

1994 Sales: $140 million
1-Yr. Sales Change: 7.7%
Ownership: Privately Held

JEAN PHILIPPE FRAGRANCES, INC.

551 Fifth Ave.
New York, NY 10176
Phone: 212-983-2640
Fax: 212-983-4197

Cosmetics & toiletries

CEO: Philippe Benacin
CFO: Russell Greenberg
HR: Henry Dominentz
Employees: 118

1994 Sales: $75.1 million
1-Yr. Sales Change: 26.2%
Exchange: Nasdaq
Symbol: JEAN

 See page 275 for a full profile of this company.

JETRO CASH & CARRY ENTERPRISES

575 Eighth Ave.
New York, NY 10018
Phone: 212-594-5360
Fax: 212-971-6661

Retail - grocery stores

CEO: Stanley Fleishman
CFO: Richard Kirchner
HR: Stuart Kipilman
Employees: 1,000

1994 Sales: $520 million
1-Yr. Sales Change: 0.0%
Ownership: Privately Held

THE JEWISH BOARD OF FAMILY & CHILDREN'S SERVICES INC.

120 W. 57th St.
New York, NY 10019
Phone: 212-582-9100
Fax: 212-246-2680

CEO: Seymour R. Askin Jr.
CFO: Theodore Wengrofsky
HR: Diana Torres
Employees: 1,486

1995 Sales: $87.4 million
1-Yr. Sales Change: 10.5%
Ownership: Privately Held

Charitable organization - mental health & social services (#1 in US) through community-based
programs, residential facilities & day treatment centers

JIM HJELM'S PRIVATE COLLECTION, LTD.

225 W. 37th St., 5th Fl.
New York, NY 10018
Phone: 212-921-7058
Fax: 212-921-7608

Apparel - bridal wear & accessories

CEO: Joseph L. Murphy
CFO: Jody Chesnov
HR: Cindy Cole
Employees: 35

1994 Sales: $5.8 million
1-Yr. Sales Change: 1.8%
Exchange: Nasdaq (SC)
Symbol: JHPC

JIMLAR CORPORATION

160 Great Neck Rd.
New York, NY 11021
Phone: 516-829-1717
Fax: 516-829-2970

Wholesale distribution - shoes

CEO: James Tarica
CFO: Frank Vigonola
HR: Frank Vigonola
Employees: 160

1994 Sales: $130 million
1-Yr. Sales Change: 0.0%
Ownership: Privately Held

J. M. HUBER CORPORATION

333 Thornall St.
Edison, NJ 08818
Phone: 908-549-8600
Fax: 908-549-2239

CEO: Peter T. Francis
CFO: Susan Tohbe
HR: Joseph P. Matturro
Employees: 5,163

1994 Sales: $1,325 million
1-Yr. Sales Change: 10.4%
Ownership: Privately Held

Diversified operations - engineered minerals; chemicals; electronics

JOHN WILEY & SONS, INC.

605 Third Ave.
New York, NY 10158-0012
Phone: 212-850-6000
Fax: 212-850-6088

CEO: Charles R. Ellis
CFO: Robert D. Wilder
HR: William J. Arlington
Employees: 1,680

1995 Sales: $331.1 million
1-Yr. Sales Change: 12.5%
Exchange: NYSE
Symbol: JWA

Publishing - scientific & technical books & journals; electronic publishing

JOHNSON & HIGGINS

125 Broad St.
New York, NY 10004
Phone: 212-574-7000
Fax: 212-574-7190

CEO: David A. Olsen
CFO: Joseph D. Roxe
HR: James R. Reardon
Employees: 8,750

1994 Sales: $1,050 million
1-Yr. Sales Change: 9.1%
Ownership: Privately Held

Insurance - risk management consulting & insurance brokerage

JOHNSON & JOHNSON

One Johnson & Johnson Plaza
New Brunswick, NJ 08933
Phone: 908-524-0400
Fax: 908-214-0332

CEO: Ralph S. Larsen
CFO: Clark H. Johnson
HR: Roger S. Fine
Employees: 81,500

1994 Sales: $15,734 million
1-Yr. Sales Change: 11.3%
Exchange: NYSE
Symbol: JNJ

Cosmetics & toiletries - baby shampoo (Johnson's), pain killers (Tylenol), bandages (Band-Aid), toothbrushes (Reach), powder (Shower to Shower) & soap (Neutrogena); clinical diagnostics

 See pages 146–147 for a full profile of this company.

JORDACHE ENTERPRISES, INC.

226 W. 39th St.
New York, NY 10018
Phone: 212-643-8400
Fax: 212-714-6801

CEO: Joseph Nakash
CFO: Steve Tuccillo
HR: Kalinly Wilson
Employees: 3,000

1994 Sales: $280 million
1-Yr. Sales Change: 0.0%
Ownership: Privately Held

Apparel - men's, women's & children's jeans

THE JORDAN CO.

9 W. 57th St., 40th Fl.
New York, NY 10019
Phone: 212-572-0800
Fax: 212-755-5263

CEO: John W. Jordan II
CFO: Paul Rodzevik
HR: —
Employees: 16

1995 Sales: —
1-Yr. Sales Change: —
Ownership: Privately Held

Financial - investment bankers (affiliated with Jordan Industries; 100% interest in Duromed, Jackson Products, Flex-O-Lite Inc., Tee Jay's Manufacturing Co.)

JORDAN, MCGRATH, CASE & TAYLOR

445 Park Ave.
New York, NY 10022
Phone: 212-326-9100
Fax: 212-326-9357

Advertising

CEO: Patrick McGrath
CFO: Thomas Finneran
HR: Chris Martin
Employees: 350

1994 Sales: $47 million
1-Yr. Sales Change: 1.1%
Ownership: Privately Held

JOULE INC.

1245 US Rte. One South
Edison, NJ 08837
Phone: 908-548-5444
Fax: 908-494-9261

Personnel - temporary technical, clerical & maintenance staff

CEO: Emanuel N. Logothetis
CFO: Bernard G. Clarkin
HR: Ralph Cimato
Employees: 1,160

1995 Sales: $43.6 million
1-Yr. Sales Change: 20.4%
Exchange: AMEX
Symbol: JOL

JOYCE INTERNATIONAL, INC.

114 5th Ave.
New York, NY 10011
Phone: 212-463-9044
Fax: —

Furniture, fixtures & office products

CEO: G. L. Shostack
CFO: —
HR: —
Employees: 1,050

1994 Sales: $150 million
1-Yr. Sales Change: -27.9%
Ownership: Privately Held

J.P. MORGAN & CO. INCORPORATED

60 Wall St.
New York, NY 10260-0060
Phone: 212-483-2323
Fax: 212-648-5193

Banks - money center

CEO: Douglas A. Warner III
CFO: John Meyer
HR: Herbert J. Hefke
Employees: 17,055

1994 Sales: $11,915 million
1-Yr. Sales Change: -0.2%
Exchange: NYSE
Symbol: JPM

See pages 148–149 for a full profile of this company.

JSB FINANCIAL, INC.

303 Merrick Rd.
Lynbrook, NY 11563-2574
Phone: 516-887-7000
Fax: 516-599-8061

Financial - savings & loans

CEO: Park T. Adikes
CFO: Thomas R. Lehmann
HR: John J. Conroy
Employees: 425

1994 Sales: $109.8 million
1-Yr. Sales Change: -0.5%
Exchange: Nasdaq
Symbol: JSBF

THE JUILLIARD SCHOOL

60 Lincoln Center Plaza
New York, NY 10023
Phone: 212-799-5000
Fax: 212-873-4085

CEO: Joseph Polisi
CFO: Charles C. Lucas Jr.
HR: Caryn Doktor
Employees: 530

1994 Sales: $30.2 million
1-Yr. Sales Change: 6.7%
Ownership: Privately Held

College offering professional training in the performing arts

JUNIPER FEATURES LTD.

111 Great Neck Rd., Ste. 604
Great Neck, NY 11021-5402
Phone: 516-829-4670
Fax: 516-829-4691

CEO: Paul V. Hreijanovic
CFO: Paul V. Hreijanovic
HR: —
Employees: 14

1994 Sales: $2.6 million
1-Yr. Sales Change: 23.8%
Exchange: Nasdaq (SC)
Symbol: JUNI

Motion pictures & services - feature film distribution; music & jingles for advertising

JUST TOYS, INC.

50 W. 23rd St.
New York, NY 10010
Phone: 212-645-6335
Fax: 212-741-8793

CEO: Morton J. Levy
CFO: Michael Vastola
HR: Julia Nichols
Employees: 45

1994 Sales: $23.9 million
1-Yr. Sales Change: -43.9%
Exchange: Nasdaq
Symbol: JUST

Toys - games & hobby products (Air Zone, Bend-Ems)

J. W. MAYS, INC.

9 Bond St.
New York, NY 11201
Phone: 718-624-7400
Fax: 718-935-0378

CEO: Max L. Shulman
CFO: Alex Slobodin
HR: —
Employees: 30

1995 Sales: $8.3 million
1-Yr. Sales Change: -12.6%
Exchange: Nasdaq
Symbol: MAYS

Retail - regional department stores

JYACC INC.

116 John St.
New York, NY 10038
Phone: 212-267-7722
Fax: 212-608-6753

CEO: Robert Ismach
CFO: Peter Stoll
HR: —
Employees: 229

1994 Est. Sales: $20 mil.
1-Yr. Sales Change: —
Ownership: Privately Held

Client/server development software

K & F INDUSTRIES, INC.

600 Third St.
New York, NY 10016
Phone: 212-297-0900
Fax: 212-867-1182

CEO: Bernard L. Schwartz
CFO: Kenneth Schwartz
HR: —
Employees: 1,173

1994 Sales: $239 million
1-Yr. Sales Change: 5.8%
Ownership: Privately Held

Aerospace - wheels, brakes & brake management systems for commercial, general aviation & military aircraft

K-III COMMUNICATIONS CORPORATION

745 5th Ave.
New York, NY 10151
Phone: 212-745-0100
Fax: 212-745-0169

CEO: William F. Reilly
CFO: Charles G. McCurdy
HR: Michaelanne C. Discepolo
Employees: 4,550

1994 Sales: $964.6 million
1-Yr. Sales Change: 14.2%
Exchange: NYSE
Symbol: KCC

Publishing - periodicals (New York, Chicago, Seventeen, Soap Opera Digest, New Woman) & books (World Almanac); educational TV programming (Channel One)

KANE/MILLER CORPORATION

555 White Plains Rd.
Tarrytown, NY 10591
Phone: 914-630-6900
Fax: 914-631-6901

CEO: Stanley B. Kane
CFO: Michael Raffia
HR: —
Employees: 750

1994 Sales: $185 million
1-Yr. Sales Change: 0.5%
Ownership: Privately Held

Food - meat processing; children's book publishing

KATZ MEDIA GROUP, INC.

125 W. 55th St.
New York, NY 10019
Phone: 212-424-6000
Fax: 212-424-6110

CEO: Thomas E. Olson
CFO: Richard E. Vendig
HR: Anne Strafaci
Employees: 1,600

1994 Sales: $184.8 million
1-Yr. Sales Change: 17.8%
Exchange: AMEX
Symbol: KTZ

Business services - national, local & network advertising time sales to radio, TV & cable stations

KAYE, SCHOLER, FIERMAN, HAYS & HANDLER

425 Park Ave.
New York, NY 10022
Phone: 212-836-8000
Fax: 212-836-8760

CEO: Andrew McDonald
CFO: Clifford Hook
HR: Edwina McGonghlin
Employees: 500

1994 Sales: $153 million
1-Yr. Sales Change: 1.3%
Ownership: Privately Held

Law firm

KCS ENERGY, INC.

379 Thornall St.
Edison, NJ 08837
Phone: 908-632-1770
Fax: 908-603-8960

CEO: James W. Christmas
CFO: Henry A. Jurand
HR: Kathy Kinnamon
Employees: 86

1995 Sales: $423.6 million
1-Yr. Sales Change: 26.2%
Exchange: NYSE
Symbol: KCS

Oil & gas - oil exploration & production, natural-gas transportation & gas marketing

 See page 276 for a full profile of this company.

KELLEY DRYE & WARREN

101 Park Ave.
New York, NY 10178-0001
Phone: 212-808-7800
Fax: 212-808-7898

CEO: Merrill B. Stone
CFO: Tom Carty
HR: Molly McEney
Employees: 841

1994 Sales: $108 million
1-Yr. Sales Change: -7.7%
Ownership: Privately Held

Law firm

KENNETH COLE PRODUCTIONS, INC.

152 W. 57th St.
New York, NY 10019
Phone: 212-265-1500
Fax: 212-265-1662

CEO: Kenneth D. Cole
CFO: Stanley A. Mayer
HR: Paul Blum
Employees: 285

1994 Sales: $84.9 million
1-Yr. Sales Change: 39.6%
Exchange: NYSE
Symbol: KCP

Shoes & related apparel (Kenneth Cole, Unlisted); retail stores

KENT FINANCIAL SERVICES, INC.

367 Main St., PO Box 74
Bedminster, NJ 07921
Phone: 908-234-0078
Fax: 908-234-9355

CEO: Paul O. Koether
CFO: John W. Galuchie Jr.
HR: —
Employees: 50

1994 Sales: $8.9 million
1-Yr. Sales Change: -21.2%
Exchange: Nasdaq (SC)
Symbol: KENT

Financial - securities broker-dealer buying & selling securities for customer accounts, over-the-counter market, financial services, underwritings, private placements, mergers & acquisitions

KEY ENERGY GROUP INC.

257 Livingston Ave.
New Brunswick, NJ 08901
Phone: 908-247-4822
Fax: 908-247-5148

CEO: Francis D. John
CFO: Francis D. John
HR: —
Employees: 434

1995 Sales: $44.7 million
1-Yr. Sales Change: 29.2%
Exchange: AMEX
Symbol: KEG

Oil & gas - production

KEY FOOD STORES COOPERATIVE, INC.

8925 Ave. D
New York, NY 11236
Phone: 718-451-1000
Fax: 718-451-1202

CEO: Allen Newman
CFO: Sam Kristal
HR: —
Employees: 500

1994 Sales: $600 million
1-Yr. Sales Change: 0.0%
Ownership: Privately Held

Retail - cooperative of supermarkets in New York (140 units)

KIMCO REALTY CORPORATION

3333 New Hyde Park Rd.
New Hyde Park, NY 10042-0020
Phone: 516-869-9000
Fax: 516-869-9001

CEO: Milton Cooper
CFO: Louis J. Petra
HR: Toni Calandrino
Employees: 62

1994 Sales: $125.3 million
1-Yr. Sales Change: 26.7%
Exchange: NYSE
Symbol: KIM

Real estate operations - neighborhood & community shopping centers

KING KULLEN GROCERY COMPANY INC.

1194 Prospect Ave.
Westbury, NY 11590
Phone: 516-333-7100
Fax: 516-333-7929

CEO: John B. Cullen
CFO: J. D. Kennedy
HR: Thomas Nagle
Employees: 4,500

1995 Sales: $706 million
1-Yr. Sales Change: -1.7%
Ownership: Privately Held

Retail - supermarkets

KING WORLD PRODUCTIONS, INC.

1700 Broadway, 35th Fl.
New York, NY 10019
Phone: 212-315-4000
Fax: 212-247-7674

CEO: Michael King
CFO: Steven A. LoCascio
HR: Patsy Bundy
Employees: 430

1995 Sales: $574.2 million
1-Yr. Sales Change: 19.5%
Exchange: NYSE
Symbol: KWP

Broadcasting - first-run syndicated programs, TV station & advertising

KINGS SUPER MARKETS, INC.

2 Dedrick Place
Caldwell, NJ 07006
Phone: 201-575-3320
Fax: 201-575-3297

CEO: James Meister
CFO: Peter Davis
HR: Edward Lowenfish
Employees: 2,500

1994 Est. Sales: $320 mil.
1-Yr. Sales Change: 15.1%
Ownership: Privately Held

Retail - upscale supermarkets

KINNEY SYSTEM, INC.

60 Madison Ave.
New York, NY 10010
Phone: 212-889-4444
Fax: 212-889-2053

Public parking lot management

CEO: Lewis Katz
CFO: Michael Michalofsky
HR: Jeffrey Goldmacher
Employees: 2,200

1995 Sales: $170 million
1-Yr. Sales Change: 17.2%
Ownership: Privately Held

KINRAY, INC.

152-35 10th Ave.
New York, NY 11537
Phone: 718-767-1234
Fax: 718-767-4388

Drugs & sundries - wholesale

CEO: Stewart Rahr
CFO: Bill Ball
HR: Diane Newell
Employees: 170

1994 Sales: $460 million
1-Yr. Sales Change: 29.6%
Ownership: Privately Held

KIWI INTERNATIONAL AIRLINES

Hemisphere Center
Newark, NJ 07114-0006
Phone: 201-645-1133
Fax: 201-645-1161

Transportation - airline serving the East Coast & Chicago

CEO: Jerry Murphy
CFO: James Player
HR: Esther Bar
Employees: —

1994 Est. Sales: $116 mil.
1-Yr. Sales Change: —
Ownership: Privately Held

KNOGO NORTH AMERICA INC.

350 Wireless Blvd.
Hauppauge, NY 11788
Phone: 516-232-2100
Fax: 516-232-2812

Protection - safety equipment & services, systems used to detect the unauthorized movements of articles & persons

CEO: Thomas A. Nicolette
CFO: Robert T. Abbott
HR: Diana Houck
Employees: 251

1994 Sales: $29.6 million
1-Yr. Sales Change: -68.6%
Exchange: AMEX
Symbol: KNA

KOCH INTERNATIONAL L.P.

2 Tri-Harbor Ct.
Port Washington, NY 11050
Phone: 516-484-1000
Fax: 516-484-4746

Prerecorded music

CEO: Michael Koch
CFO: Liz Jones
HR: Nancy Young
Employees: 143

1995 Sales: $60 million
1-Yr. Sales Change: 15.4%
Ownership: Privately Held

KOHLBERG KRAVIS ROBERTS & CO.

9 W. 57th St., Ste. 4200
New York, NY 10019
Phone: 212-750-8300
Fax: 212-593-2430

CEO: Henry R. Kravis
CFO: George R. Roberts
HR: —
Employees: —

1995 Sales: —
1-Yr. Sales Change: —
Ownership: Privately Held

Financial - investment in operating companies

 See pages 150–151 for a full profile of this company.

KOO KOO ROO, INC.

75 Rte. 27
Iselin, NJ 08830
Phone: 908-494-2555
Fax: 908-321-6522

CEO: Kenneth Berg
CFO: Morton J. Wall
HR: Anastacia Gibbs
Employees: 280

1995 Sales: $13.2 million
1-Yr. Sales Change: 106.3%
Exchange: Nasdaq (SC)
Symbol: KKRO

Retail - casual dining restaurants featuring roasted chicken & turkey

KPMG PEAT MARWICK LLP

767 Fifth Ave.
New York, NY 10153
Phone: 212-909-5000
Fax: 212-909-5299

CEO: Jon C. Madonna
CFO: Joseph E. Heintz
HR: Mary L. Dupont
Employees: 72,000

1995 Est. Sales: $6,405 mil.
1-Yr. Sales Change: 5.0%
Ownership: Privately Held

Business services - accounting & consulting

 See pages 152–153 for a full profile of this company.

KRANTOR CORPORATION

120 E. Industry Ct.
Deer Park, NY 11729
Phone: 516-586-7500
Fax: 516-586-0690

CEO: Henry J. Platek Jr.
CFO: Mair Fabish
HR: Mair Fabish
Employees: 17

1994 Sales: $32 million
1-Yr. Sales Change: -26.1%
Exchange: Nasdaq (SC)
Symbol: KRAN

Food, general merchandise & health & beauty aids distribution to grocers

KRASDALE FOODS INC.

65 W. Red Oak Ln.
White Plains, NY 10022
Phone: 914-694-6400
Fax: 914-697-5225

CEO: Charles A. Krasne
CFO: Brian Cassidy
HR: Ralph Zampini
Employees: 550

1994 Sales: $425 million
1-Yr. Sales Change: 0.0%
Ownership: Privately Held

Food distribution

KRYSTALTECH INTERNATIONAL INC.

555 W. 57th St., Ste. 1750
New York, NY 10017-2925
Phone: 212-261-0400
Fax: 212-262-0414

Computers - parts & peripherals reseller

CEO: Dan Tochner
CFO: Kevin Khoo
HR: —
Employees: 43

1994 Sales: $55.1 million
1-Yr. Sales Change: 57.4%
Ownership: Privately Held

LAFAYETTE AMERICAN BANK AND TRUST COMPANY

1087 Broad St.
Bridgeport, CT 06604
Phone: 203-336-6200
Fax: 203-287-1064

Banks - Northeast

CEO: Robert B. Goldstein
CFO: Phillip J. Mucha
HR: Patricia Antonelli
Employees: 310

1994 Sales: $48.9 million
1-Yr. Sales Change: -1.6%
Exchange: Nasdaq
Symbol: LABK

LAFAYETTE INDUSTRIES, INC.

140 Hinsdale St.
New York, NY 11207
Phone: 718-346-3099
Fax: 718-346-6824

CEO: Robert L. Jessen
CFO: Joseph A. Rubino
HR: —
Employees: 214

1994 Sales: $12.5 million
1-Yr. Sales Change: 52.4%
Exchange: Nasdaq (SC)
Symbol: LAFI

Furniture - store fixtures & merchandising systems for retail stores, including display racks, showcases, cabinets & wall display units

LAKELAND INDUSTRIES, INC.

711-2 Koehler Ave.
Ronkonkoma, NY 11779-7410
Phone: 516-981-9700
Fax: 516-981-9751

CEO: Raymond J. Smith
CFO: James M. McCormick
HR: —
Employees: 124

1995 Sales: $35.2 million
1-Yr. Sales Change: 16.9%
Exchange: Nasdaq
Symbol: LAKE

Apparel - disposable & limited-use garments, including suits for toxic waste cleanup teams, fire- & heat-protective apparel, safety & industrial work gloves & industrial & medical woven-cloth garments

LAKEVIEW FINANCIAL CORP.

1117 Main St.
Paterson, NJ 07503
Phone: 201-742-3060
Fax: 201-890-3182

CEO: Kevin J. Coogan
CFO: Anthony G. Gallo
HR: Sandy Coulthart
Employees: 103

1995 Sales: $35.6 million
1-Yr. Sales Change: 64.8%
Exchange: Nasdaq
Symbol: LVSB

Financial - savings & loans (Lakeview Savings Bank)

LANCIT MEDIA PRODUCTIONS, LTD.

601 W. 50th St.
New York, NY 10019
Phone: 212-977-9100
Fax: 212-477-9164

CEO: Cecily Truett
CFO: Gary Appelbaum
HR: JoAnn Pezzella
Employees: 43

1995 Sales: $17.9 million
1-Yr. Sales Change: 96.7%
Exchange: Nasdaq
Symbol: LNCT

Broadcasting - children's TV programming (The Puzzle Place, Backyard Safari); film production

LAND N SEA, INC.

375 Broadway
New York, NY 10018
Phone: 212-444-6000
Fax: 212-444-6019

CEO: Seymour Sobel
CFO: Thomas Mangum
HR: —
Employees: 900

1994 Est. Sales: $100 mil.
1-Yr. Sales Change: 0.0%
Ownership: Privately Held

Apparel - women's & children's clothing

LANDSTAR SYSTEMS, INC.

1000 Bridgeport Ave.
Shelton, CT 06484-0898
Phone: 203-925-2900
Fax: 203-925-2916

CEO: Jeffrey C. Crowe
CFO: Henry H. Gerken
HR: Linda Carroll
Employees: 2,500

1994 Sales: $984.4 million
1-Yr. Sales Change: 26.1%
Exchange: Nasdaq
Symbol: LSTR

Transportation - truck

THE LANGER BIOMECHANICS GROUP, INC.

450 Commack Rd.
Deer Park, NY 11729
Phone: 516-667-1200
Fax: 516-667-1203

CEO: Gary L. Grahn
CFO: Donald M. Carbone
HR: Kathy Park
Employees: 157

1995 Sales: $10.5 million
1-Yr. Sales Change: -11.0%
Exchange: Nasdaq (SC)
Symbol: GAIT

Medical products - foot- & gait-related biomechanical products, primarily orthotic devices

THE LANTIS CORPORATION

461 5th Ave.
New York, NY 10017
Phone: 212-686-1500
Fax: 212-685-4453

CEO: Lon Moellentine
CFO: Dave Gordon
HR: —
Employees: 500

1994 Sales: $125 million
1-Yr. Sales Change: 25.0%
Ownership: Privately Held

Sunglasses (Solargenics, DKNY)

LASER VIDEO NETWORK, INC.

645 5th Ave., East Wing
New York, NY 10022
Phone: 212-888-0617
Fax: 212-755-5992

CEO: Peter Kauff
CFO: Alan Pearl
HR: —
Employees: 16

1994 Sales: $0.7 million
1-Yr. Sales Change: 133.3%
Exchange: Nasdaq (SC)
Symbol: LVNI

Leisure & recreational products - video jukeboxes

LAWRENCE INSURANCE GROUP, INC.

500 Fifth Ave., 56th Fl.
New York, NY 10110-0002
Phone: 212-944-8242
Fax: 212-944-8328

CEO: F. Herbert Brantlinger
CFO: Albert F. Kilts
HR: Carm Roberson
Employees: 273

1994 Sales: $7.9 million
1-Yr. Sales Change: -93.6%
Exchange: AMEX
Symbol: LWR

Insurance - property & casualty

LAZARE KAPLAN INTERNATIONAL INC.

529 5th Ave.
New York, NY 10017
Phone: 212-972-9700
Fax: 212-972-8561

CEO: Leon Tempelsman
CFO: Sheldon L. Ginsberg
HR: Ruth Kassanga
Employees: 658

1995 Sales: $178.1 million
1-Yr. Sales Change: -12.7%
Exchange: AMEX
Symbol: LKI

Precious metals & jewelry - diamond cutting & polishing

LAZARUS AUTO GROUP, INC.

124 Green Ave.
Amityville, NY 11701
Phone: 516-264--2244
Fax: 516-798-0686

CEO: Michael Lazarus
CFO: Mike Minella
HR: Mike Minella
Employees: 288

1994 Sales: $195 million
1-Yr. Sales Change: 21.1%
Ownership: Privately Held

Retail - new & used cars

LCS INDUSTRIES, INC.

120 Brighton Rd.
Clifton, NJ 07012
Phone: 201-778-5588
Fax: 201-778-6001

CEO: Arnold J. Scheine
CFO: Pat R. Frustaci
HR: Monica A. Mahon
Employees: 1,112

1995 Sales: $78.9 million
1-Yr. Sales Change: 25.4%
Exchange: Nasdaq
Symbol: LCSI

Computers - direct-response, fulfillment & list marketing services for computer companies

LEARONAL, INC.

272 Buffalo Ave.
Freeport, NY 11520
Phone: 516-868-8800
Fax: 516-868-8824

CEO: Ronald F. Ostrow
CFO: David Rosenthal
HR: Joan Rappa
Employees: 600

1995 Sales: $177 million
1-Yr. Sales Change: 17.1%
Exchange: NYSE
Symbol: LRI

Chemicals - products, including specialty additives for the connector, printed circuit board, semiconductor & industrial metal-finishing industries; precious metal electroplating processes

LEBOEUF, LAMB, GREENE & MACRAE

125 W. 55th St., 12th Fl.
New York, NY 10019
Phone: 212-424-8000
Fax: 212-424-8500

CEO: Donald J. Greene
CFO: David Marshall
HR: Carl Garaffo
Employees: 1,100

1994 Sales: $161 million
1-Yr. Sales Change: 4.5%
Ownership: Privately Held

Law firm

LECHTERS, INC.

One Cape May St.
Harrison, NJ 07029-9998
Phone: 201-481-1100
Fax: 201-481-5493

CEO: Steen Kanter
CFO: John W. Smolak
HR: Robert J. Harloe
Employees: 6,911

1995 Sales: $399.3 million
1-Yr. Sales Change: 14.0%
Exchange: Nasdaq
Symbol: LECH

Retail - discount & variety

LECROY CORPORATION

700 Chestnut Ridge Rd.
Chestnut Ridge, NY 10977
Phone: 914-425-2000
Fax: 914-578-6061

CEO: Lutz P. Henckels
CFO: Joseph J. Migliozzi
HR: Lori Peters
Employees: 420

1995 Sales: $82.3 million
1-Yr. Sales Change: 29.0%
Exchange: Nasdaq
Symbol: LCRY

Electronics - measuring instruments, signal analyzers & digital oscilloscopes

LEFRAK ORGANIZATION INC.

97-77 Queens Blvd.
Rego Park, NY 11374
Phone: 718-459-9021
Fax: 718-897-0688

CEO: Samuel J. LeFrak
CFO: Arthur Klein
HR: John Farelly
Employees: 17,400

1995 Sales: $3,300 million
1-Yr. Sales Change: 6.5%
Ownership: Privately Held

Real estate development & management; entertainment; oil & gas exploration

See pages 154–155 for a full profile of this company.

LEHIGH GROUP INC.

810 Seventh Ave.
New York, NY 10019
Phone: 212-333-2620
Fax: 212-333-7240

CEO: Salvatore J. Zizza
CFO: Salvatore J. Zizza
HR: —
Employees: 48

1994 Sales: $12.2 million
1-Yr. Sales Change: -5.4%
Exchange: NYSE
Symbol: LEI

Building - retail electrical conduit, switches, outlets, cables, fittings, panels & wire

LEHMAN BROTHERS HOLDINGS INC.

3 World Financial Center
New York, NY 10285
Phone: 212-526-7000
Fax: 212-526-3738

CEO: Richard S. Fuld Jr.
CFO: Robert Matza
HR: Maryanne Rasmussen
Employees: 6,950

1995 Sales: $13,476 million
1-Yr. Sales Change: 46.6%
Exchange: NYSE
Symbol: LEH

Financial - investment bankers

 See pages 156–157 for a full profile of this company.

LESLIE BUILDING PRODUCTS, INC.

200 Mamaroneck Ave.
White Plains, NY 10601
Phone: 914-421-2545
Fax: 914-428-4581

CEO: Leigh J. Abrams
CFO: Fredric M. Zinn
HR: —
Employees: 417

1994 Sales: $71.1 million
1-Yr. Sales Change: 11.6%
Exchange: OTC
Symbol: LBPI

Building products - specialty for the do-it-yourself home remodeling & home construction industry (spinoff of Drew Industries Inc.)

LESLIE FAY COMPANIES, INC.

1400 Broadway
New York, NY 10018
Phone: 212-221-4000
Fax: 212-221-4146

CEO: John J. Pomerantz
CFO: John S. Dubel
HR: Susan Tully
Employees: 2,900

1994 Sales: $535.3 million
1-Yr. Sales Change: -19.1%
Exchange: OTC
Symbol: LESS

Apparel - women's & juniors' (Sassco, Leslie Fay, Nipon, Outlander, Castleberry); clothing stores

LEUCADIA NATIONAL CORPORATION

315 Park Ave. South
New York, NY 10010
Phone: 212-460-1900
Fax: 212-598-4869

CEO: Joseph S. Steinberg
CFO: Joseph A. Orlando
HR: Ruth Klindtworth
Employees: 4,374

1994 Sales: $1,384.4 mil.
1-Yr. Sales Change: -1.7%
Exchange: NYSE
Symbol: LUK

Diversified operations - insurance (Colonial Penn, Empire); trading stamps (Sperry & Hutchison); banking (American Investment Bank); manufacturing; real estate development

LEXINGTON CORPORATE PROPERTIES, INC.

355 Lexington Ave.
New York, NY 10017
Phone: 212-692-7260
Fax: 212-986-6972

Real estate investment trust

CEO: Richard J. Rouse
CFO: Antonia G. Trigiani
HR: T. Wilson Eglin
Employees: 14

1994 Sales: $26 million
1-Yr. Sales Change: 0.4%
Exchange: NYSE
Symbol: LXP

LEXINGTON PRECISION CORPORATION

767 Third Ave., 29th Fl.
New York, NY 10017-2023
Phone: 212-319-4657
Fax: 212-319-4659

CEO: Warren Delano
CFO: Dennis J. Welhouse
HR: —
Employees: 992

1994 Sales: $88.5 million
1-Yr. Sales Change: 18.0%
Exchange: OTC
Symbol: LEXP

Diversified operations - silicone & organic rubber components; close-tolerance metal components

LEXMARK INTERNATIONAL GROUP, INC.

55 Railroad Ave.
Greenwich, CT 06836
Phone: 203-629-6700
Fax: 203-629-6725

CEO: Marvin L. Mann
CFO: Achim Knust
HR: A. Richard Murphy
Employees: 5,000

1994 Sales: $1,852.3 mil.
1-Yr. Sales Change: 10.5%
Exchange: NYSE
Symbol: LXK

Computers - keyboards, laser & inkjet printers, notebook computers, electric typewriters & related supplies

LIFE RE CORPORATION

969 High Ridge Rd.
Stamford, CT 06905
Phone: 203-321-3000
Fax: 203-968-0920

Insurance - life

CEO: Jacques E. Dubois
CFO: Samuel V. Filoromo
HR: Heather Bonaparte
Employees: 99

1994 Sales: $433.4 million
1-Yr. Sales Change: 13.0%
Exchange: NYSE
Symbol: LRE

LIFETIME HOAN CORPORATION

One Merrick Ave.
Westbury, NY 11590
Phone: 516-683-6000
Fax: 516-683-6116

CEO: Milton L. Cohen
CFO: Fred Spivak
HR: Sally Mogadero
Employees: 446

1994 Sales: $77.4 million
1-Yr. Sales Change: 19.6%
Exchange: Nasdaq
Symbol: LCUT

Housewares - cutlery & kitchenware (Hoffritz, Old Homestead,Tristar)

LIGHT SAVERS U.S.A., INC.

969 3rd Ave.
New York, NY 10022
Phone: 212-755-5267
Fax: 212-755-5365

CEO: Tova Schwartz
CFO: Howard Anders
HR: —
Employees: 6

1994 Sales: $0.5 million
1-Yr. Sales Change: -79.2%
Exchange: Nasdaq (SC)
Symbol: LTSV

Building products - decorative energy-saving lighting units for hotels, including ceiling, table & floor lamps

LINCOLN CENTER FOR THE PERFORMING ARTS, INC.

70 Lincoln Center Plaza
New York, NY 10023
Phone: 212-875-5000
Fax: 212-875-5414

CEO: Nathan Leventhal
CFO: Robert A. Cappiello
HR: Jay Spivack
Employees: 500

1995 Sales: $31.5 million
1-Yr. Sales Change: —
Ownership: Privately Held

Arts center - concerts & other performances, services to visitors & patrons, educational & community outreach

LINCOLN SNACKS COMPANY

4 High Ridge Park
Stamford, CT 06905
Phone: 203-329-4545
Fax: 203-329-4555

CEO: Karen Brenner
CFO: Kristine A. Crabs
HR: Karen Catano
Employees: 96

1995 Sales: $27.1 million
1-Yr. Sales Change: —
Exchange: Nasdaq (SC)
Symbol: SNAX

Food - snacks, primarily popcorn lines (Poppycock, Fiddle Faddle, Screaming Yellow Zonkers)

LIZ CLAIBORNE, INC.

1441 Broadway
New York, NY 10018
Phone: 212-354-4900
Fax: 212-626-3416

CEO: Paul R. Charron
CFO: Samuel M. Miller
HR: Jorge L. Figueredo
Employees: 8,000

1994 Sales: $2,162.9 mil.
1-Yr. Sales Change: -1.9%
Exchange: NYSE
Symbol: LIZ

Apparel - women's & men's; cosmetics

LOEHMANN'S HOLDINGS, INC.

2500 Halsey St.
New York, NY 10463
Phone: 718-409-2000
Fax: 718-518-2766

CEO: Robert N. Friedman
CFO: Robert Glass
HR: Linda Merker
Employees: 2,406

1995 Sales: $392.6 million
1-Yr. Sales Change: 5.1%
Ownership: Privately Held

Retail - designer women's clothing & accessories

LOEWS CORPORATION

667 Madison Ave.	CEO: Laurence A. Tisch	1994 Sales: $13,515 million
New York, NY 10021-8087	CFO: Roy E. Posner	1-Yr. Sales Change: -1.3%
Phone: 212-545-2000	HR: Kenneth Abrams	Exchange: NYSE
Fax: 212-545-2498	Employees: 25,400	Symbol: LTR

Diversified operations - insurance (CNA); tobacco (Kent, Newport, True); hotels (Loews); watches (Bulova)

 See pages 158–159 for a full profile of this company.

LONE STAR INDUSTRIES, INC.

PO Box 120014	CEO: David W. Wallace	1994 Sales: $306.7 million
Stamford, CT 06912-0014	CFO: William E. Roberts	1-Yr. Sales Change: 12.9%
Phone: 203-969-8600	HR: Gerald F. Hyde Jr.	Exchange: NYSE
Fax: 203-969-8546	Employees: 1,500	Symbol: LCE

Building products - cement, construction aggregates & ready-mixed concrete

LONG ISLAND BANCORP

201 Old Country Rd.	CEO: John J. Conefry Jr.	1994 Sales: $295 million
Melville, NY 11747-2724	CFO: Mark Fuster	1-Yr. Sales Change: -29.4%
Phone: 516-547-2000	HR: —	Exchange: Nasdaq
Fax: 516-547-2567	Employees: 1,188	Symbol: LISB

Financial - savings and loans

LONG ISLAND LIGHTING COMPANY

175 E. Old Country Rd.	CEO: William J. Catacosinos	1994 Sales: $3,067.3 mil.
Hicksville, NY 11801	CFO: Anthony Nozzolillo	1-Yr. Sales Change: 6.5%
Phone: 516-755-6650	HR: Robert X. Kelleher	Exchange: NYSE
Fax: 516-931-3165	Employees: 5,950	Symbol: LIL

Utility - electric power

 See pages 160–161 for a full profile of this company.

LORAL CORPORATION

600 Third Ave.	CEO: Bernard L. Schwartz	1995 Sales: $5,484.4 mil.
New York, NY 10016	CFO: Michael P. DeBlasio	1-Yr. Sales Change: 36.8%
Phone: 212-697-1105	HR: Stephen L. Jackson	Exchange: NYSE
Fax: 212-661-8988	Employees: 28,900	Symbol: LOR

Electronics - advanced electronic systems, components & service for the military, US government & foreign governments

See pages 162–163 for a full profile of this company.

LOUIS BERGER INTERNATIONAL, INC.

100 Halsted St.
East Orange, NJ 07019
Phone: 201-678-1960
Fax: 201-672-4284

CEO: Derish M. Wolff
CFO: Leon Marantz
HR: Richard Bergailo
Employees: 2,036

1994 Sales: $170 million
1-Yr. Sales Change: 0.0%
Ownership: Privately Held

Consulting - engineers, economists, scientists & planners

LUCILLE FARMS, INC.

150 River Rd., PO Box 517
Montville, NJ 07045
Phone: 201-334-6030
Fax: 201-402-6361

CEO: Alfonso Falivene
CFO: Stephen M. Katz
HR: —
Employees: 59

1995 Sales: $35.2 million
1-Yr. Sales Change: 9.7%
Exchange: Nasdaq (SC)
Symbol: LUCY

Food - mozzarella cheese & other Italian variety cheeses

LUMEX, INC.

81 Spence St.
Bay Shore, NY 11706
Phone: 516-273-2200
Fax: 516-273-1706

CEO: J. Raymond Elliott
CFO: Robert McNally
HR: Sophie Cardone
Employees: 1,215

1994 Sales: $131.2 million
1-Yr. Sales Change: 20.4%
Exchange: AMEX
Symbol: LUM

Medical products - testing & rehabilitation equipment, cardiovascular equipment, mobility &
therapeutic support systems for rehab, geriatric & home health care, sports medicine & fitness markets

LUNN INDUSTRIES, INC.

One Garvies Point Rd.
Glen Cove, NY 11542-2828
Phone: 516-671-9000
Fax: 516-671-9005

CEO: Alan W. Baldwin
CFO: Lawrence Schwartz
HR: Lana Defelice
Employees: 140

1994 Sales: $15.2 million
1-Yr. Sales Change: -7.3%
Exchange: Nasdaq (SC)
Symbol: LUNN

Metal products - metal bonding, bonding panels, composite assemblies utilizing honeycomb fiber &
resin laminates & wound-filament assemblies

LYNCH CORPORATION

8 Sound Shore Dr., Ste. 290
Greenwich, CT 06830
Phone: 203-629-3333
Fax: 203-629-3718

CEO: Mario J. Gabelli
CFO: Robert E. Dolan
HR: Robert Hurwich
Employees: 1,173

1994 Sales: $188.7 million
1-Yr. Sales Change: 48.6%
Exchange: AMEX
Symbol: LGL

Transportation - trucking services (#1 in US: the Morgan Group) for manufactured housing &
recreational vehicle industries; adhesive-coated papers; telecommunications services & television
stations

LYNTON GROUP, INC.

Morristown Municipal Airport
Morristown, NJ 07960
Phone: 201-292-9000
Fax: 201-292-1497

CEO: Christopher Tennant
CFO: Manus O'Donnell
HR: Sue Hubbard
Employees: 156

1994 Sales: $33.1 million
1-Yr. Sales Change: 28.3%
Exchange: Nasdaq (SC)
Symbol: LYNG

Transportation services - sales & service of corporate helicopters & fixed-wing aircraft

M FABRIKANT & SONS

One Rockefeller Plaza
New York, NY 10020
Phone: 212-757-0790
Fax: 212-262-9757

CEO: Charles Fortgang
CFO: Michael Shaffet
HR: Cheryl Brinker
Employees: 850

1995 Sales: $650 million
1-Yr. Sales Change: 8.3%
Ownership: Privately Held

Wholesale distribution - diamonds & jewelry

MACANDREWS & FORBES HOLDINGS, INC.

35 E. 62nd St.
New York, NY 10021
Phone: 212-688-9000
Fax: 212-572-8400

CEO: Ronald O. Perelman
CFO: Erwin Engelman
HR: Christine Castari
Employees: 22,328

1994 Est. Sales: $3,030 mil.
1-Yr. Sales Change: 10.3%
Ownership: Privately Held

Diversified operations - cosmetics (Revlon); banking; publishing (Marvel); outdoor equipment (Coleman); boats (Boston Whaler); cigars

 See pages 164–165 for a full profile of this company.

MACROMEDIA INC.

150 River St.
Hackensack, NJ 07601
Phone: 201-646-4000
Fax: 201-646-4782

CEO: Malcolm Borg
CFO: Charles Gibney
HR: —
Employees: 1,899

1994 Sales: $186 million
1-Yr. Sales Change: 2.2%
Ownership: Privately Held

Publishing - newspapers (The [Hackensack] Record); TV stations

MAFCO CONSOLIDATED GROUP INC.

35 E. 62nd St.
New York, NY 10021
Phone: 212-572-8600
Fax: 212-572-5965

CEO: James Maher
CFO: Irwin Engelman
HR: —
Employees: 310

1994 Sales: $180.3 million
1-Yr. Sales Change: -27.4%
Exchange: NYSE
Symbol: MFO

Tobacco - cigars & smoking tobaccos; licorice extract; military & commercial aircraft flight & engine control systems, pumps, motors & related subsystems

MAGELLAN PETROLEUM CORPORATION

149 Durham Rd.
Madison, CT 06443-
Phone: 203-245-8380
Fax: —

CEO: James R. Joyce
CFO: James R. Joyce
HR: —
Employees: 36

1995 Sales: $15.4 million
1-Yr. Sales Change: 15.8%
Exchange: Nasdaq (SC)
Symbol: MPET

Oil & gas - exploration in Australia, Canada & US

MAGIC RESTAURANTS, INC.

One Executive Blvd.
Yonkers, NY 10701
Phone: 914-969-0600
Fax: 914-969-1040

CEO: Gary Rogers
CFO: Gary Rogers
HR: —
Employees: 1,600

1994 Sales: $24.7 million
1-Yr. Sales Change: 57.3%
Exchange: Nasdaq (SC)
Symbol: MGIKQ

Retail - restaurants (Red Robin Burger, Spirit Emporium, Carmella's Cafe) in the New York & Washington, DC metropolitan areas

MAGNA-LAB INC.

950 S. Oyster Bay Rd.
Hicksville, NY 11801
Phone: 516-575-2111
Fax: 516-575-6222

CEO: Lawrence A. Minkoff
CFO: Kenneth C. Riscica
HR: Isabel Schaefer
Employees: 26

1995 Sales: $0
1-Yr. Sales Change: —
Exchange: Nasdaq (SC)
Symbol: MAGLA

Medical instruments - anatomy-specific MRI products (MAGNA-SL)

MAGRUDER COLOR COMPANY

1029 Newark Ave.
Elizabeth, NJ 07208
Phone: 201-242-1300
Fax: 201-642-3632

CEO: John Cook
CFO: Marvin Weissglass
HR: Jay Weissglass
Employees: 300

1994 Sales: $100 million
1-Yr. Sales Change: -22.5%
Ownership: Privately Held

Chemicals - cyclic crudes & intermediates

MAIDENFORM, INC.

90 Park Ave.
New York, NY 10016
Phone: 212-953-1400
Fax: 212-983-5834

CEO: Elizabeth J. Coleman
CFO: Ira Glazer
HR: Hope Sunshine
Employees: 10,000

1994 Sales: $400 million
1-Yr. Sales Change: 42.9%
Ownership: Privately Held

Apparel - lingerie

MAJOR AUTOMOTIVE GROUP

43-40 Northern Blvd.
Long Island City, NY 11101
Phone: 718-937-3700
Fax: 718-937-9770

Retail - new & used cars

CEO: Bruce Bendell
CFO: Patrick Gawrysiak
HR: —
Employees: 131

1995 Sales: $138 million
1-Yr. Sales Change: 5.3%
Ownership: Privately Held

MAJOR LEAGUE BASEBALL

350 Park Ave.
New York, NY 10022
Phone: 212-339-7800
Fax: 212-355-0007

Leisure & recreational services - professional baseball leagues

CEO: Alan H. "Bud" Selig
CFO: Jeff White
HR: Wendy Lewis
Employees: 150

1994 Sales: $1,134 million
1-Yr. Sales Change: -36.1%
Ownership: Privately Held

MALCOLM PIRNIE, INC.

PO Box 751
White Plains, NY 10602
Phone: 914-694-2100
Fax: 914-694-2986

Pollution control - environmental engineers, scientists & planners

CEO: Paul L. Busch
CFO: Craig Alfson
HR: Jack O'Neill
Employees: 1,050

1994 Sales: $131 million
1-Yr. Sales Change: 3.1%
Ownership: Privately Held

MANCHESTER EQUIPMENT CO. INC.

50 Market Blvd.
New York, NY 11788
Phone: 516-435-1199
Fax: 516-434-3548

Computers - retail PCs, peripherals & software

CEO: Barry Steinberg
CFO: Michael Bivona
HR: Joel G. Stemple
Employees: 240

1995 Sales: $170 million
1-Yr. Sales Change: 21.4%
Ownership: Privately Held

MAN-DELL FOOD STORES, INC.

241-10 Hillside Ave.
Bellrose, NY 11426
Phone: 718-470-1930
Fax: 718-470-1988

Retail - supermarkets

CEO: Lawrence Mandell
CFO: Ronald Schubert
HR: Bob Leo
Employees: 1,000

1994 Sales: $150 million
1-Yr. Sales Change: 0.0%
Ownership: Privately Held

MANHATTAN BAGEL COMPANY, INC.

15 Meridian Rd.
Eatontown, NJ 07724
Phone: 908-544-0155
Fax: 908-544-1315

CEO: Jack Grumet
CFO: Daniel D. Levy
HR: —
Employees: 108

1994 Sales: $6.2 million
1-Yr. Sales Change: —
Exchange: Nasdaq
Symbol: BGLS

Food - franchising & operation of bagel bakeries/delicatessens

MANHATTAN SCHOOL OF MUSIC

120 Claremont Ave.
New York, NY 10027
Phone: 212-749-2802
Fax: 212-749-5571

CEO: Marta Istomin
CFO: Wendy Mercer
HR: —
Employees: 100

1995 Est. Sales: $31 mil.
1-Yr. Sales Change: 100.0%
Ownership: Privately Held

School of music

MANHATTAN THEATRE CLUB, INC.

453 W. 16th St.
New York, NY 10011
Phone: 212-645-5590
Fax: 212-691-9106

CEO: Lynne Meadow
CFO: Barry Grove
HR: —
Employees: 50

1995 Sales: $8.1 million
1-Yr. Sales Change: 47.3%
Ownership: Privately Held

Not-for-profit theatrical production company

MARCAL PAPER MILLS, INC.

One Market St.
Elmwood Park, NJ 07407
Phone: 201-796-4000
Fax: 201-703-6451

CEO: N.R. Marcalus
CFO: Michael Mazzarino
HR: Jim Nelson
Employees: 1,000

1994 Sales: $160 million
1-Yr. Sales Change: 0.0%
Ownership: Privately Held

Paper & paper products - paper mills

MARCH OF DIMES BIRTH DEFECTS FOUNDATION

1275 Mamaroneck Ave.
White Plains, NY 10605
Phone: 914-428-7100
Fax: 914-997-4587

CEO: Jennifer L. Howse
CFO: Edward L. Hennessy Jr.
HR: Anne Casey
Employees: 1,500

1994 Sales: $129.1 million
1-Yr. Sales Change: 6.6%
Ownership: Privately Held

Foundation supporting programs of research, community services, education & advocacy for the prevention of birth defects & infant mortality

MARCHON EYEWEAR, INC.

35 Hub Dr.
New York, NY 11747
Phone: 516-755-2020
Fax: 516-755-2045

CEO: Al Berg
CFO: Bob Gentile
HR: Tina Omberellino
Employees: 240

1994 Sales: $152 million
1-Yr. Sales Change: 16.9%
Ownership: Privately Held

Metal & plastic eyeglass frames

MARINE TRANSPORT LINES, INC.

150 Meadowland Pkwy.
Secaucus, NJ 07096
Phone: 201-330-0200
Fax: 201-330-9860

CEO: Richard duMoulin
CFO: Mark Filanowski
HR: Joe Kelly
Employees: 1,800

1994 Sales: $120 million
1-Yr. Sales Change: 0.0%
Ownership: Privately Held

Transportation - deep sea foreign transportation of freight

MARISA CHRISTINA, INCORPORATED

415 Second Ave.
New Hyde Park, NY 11040
Phone: 516-352-5050
Fax: 516-358-9369

CEO: Michael H. Lerner
CFO: S.E. Melvin Hecht
HR: Melvin Hecht
Employees: 299

1994 Sales: $76.2 million
1-Yr. Sales Change: 33.9%
Exchange: Nasdaq
Symbol: MRSA

Apparel - women's (Marisa Christina) & children's (Flapdoodles) sweaters with holiday & nautical themes

MARK SOLUTIONS, INC.

87 Rte. 17 North
Maywood, NJ 07607
Phone: 201-368-8118
Fax: 201-368-8831

CEO: Carl C. Coppola
CFO: Joseph L. Ferraro
HR: Frederick Bolio
Employees: 60

1995 Sales: $7 million
1-Yr. Sales Change: 75.0%
Exchange: Nasdaq (SC)
Symbol: MCSI

Protection - modular steel cells for housing prisoners & for use as infectious disease isolation units for correctional & health care facilities; communicable disease treatment booths; archiving computer systems; cosmetics

MARKET GUIDE INC.

2001 Marcus Ave., PO Box 7200
Lake Success, NY 11042-1011
Phone: 516-327-2400
Fax: 516-327-2425

CEO: Homi Byramji
CFO: Lewis Leonardi
HR: Angela Dimaggio
Employees: 60

1995 Sales: $2.7 million
1-Yr. Sales Change: 35.0%
Exchange: OTC
Symbol: MAGE

Computers - financial database software, which includes company reports & financial statements for over 7,300 publicly traded companies

MARKS-ROILAND COMMUNICATIONS, INC.

26 Jericho Tnpk.
Jericho, NY 11753
Phone: 516-333-7400
Fax: 516-393-9304

CEO: Steven R. Ferber
CFO: —
HR: —
Employees: 700

1994 Sales: $75 million
1-Yr. Sales Change: —
Ownership: Privately Held

Publishing - periodicals & printing

MARSH & MCLENNAN COMPANIES, INC.

1166 Avenue of the Americas
New York, NY 10036-2774
Phone: 212-345-5000
Fax: 212-345-4838

CEO: A. J. C. Smith
CFO: Frank J. Borelli
HR: Francis N. Bonsignore
Employees: 26,000

1994 Sales: $3,435 million
1-Yr. Sales Change: 8.6%
Exchange: NYSE
Symbol: MMC

Insurance - brokerage, consulting, investment management

 See pages 166–167 for a full profile of this company.

MARVEL ENTERTAINMENT GROUP, INC.

387 Park Ave. South
New York, NY 10016
Phone: 212-696-0808
Fax: 212-576-8598

CEO: William C. Bevins Jr.
CFO: Bobby G. Jenkins
HR: Jacquelyn Green
Employees: 1,600

1994 Sales: $514.8 million
1-Yr. Sales Change: 24.0%
Exchange: NYSE
Symbol: MRV

Publishing - comic books & sports picture cards; theme restaurants

 See page 277 for a full profile of this company.

MASCOTT CORPORATION

304 Regent St.
Livingston, NJ 07039
Phone: 201-535-1000
Fax: 201-535-0911

CEO: Scott M. Gillman
CFO: Scott M. Gillman
HR: Scott M. Gillman
Employees: —

1994 Sales: $9.8 million
1-Yr. Sales Change: 4.3%
Ownership: Privately Held

Retail - restaurants (Markers Restaurant & Bar, Markers Italian Grille)

MASTER GLAZIER'S KARATE INTERNATIONAL, INC.

570 N. Broad St., Ste. 16
Elizabeth, NJ 07028
Phone: 908-354-2349
Fax: 908-289-5519

CEO: Mark Glazier
CFO: Larry Kaufman
HR: —
Employees: 30

1994 Sales: $1 million
1-Yr. Sales Change: 0.0%
Exchange: Nasdaq (SC)
Symbol: KICK

Leisure & recreational services - karate centers

MASTERCARD INTERNATIONAL INCORPORATED

2000 Purchase St.
Purchase, NY 10577
Phone: 914-249-4600
Fax: 914-249-4141

Financial - business services

CEO: H. Eugene Lockhart
CFO: Edward H. Brode
HR: Philip M. Thawley
Employees: 1,975

1994 Sales: $664.9 million
1-Yr. Sales Change: 23.2%
Ownership: Privately Held

MAX KAHAN, INC.

200 W. 47th St.
New York, NY 10036
Phone: 212-575-4646
Fax: 212-575-0888

Precious metals & refining

CEO: Max Kahan
CFO: Max Kahan
HR: —
Employees: 11

1994 Sales: $226 million
1-Yr. Sales Change: 1.3%
Ownership: Privately Held

MAYFAIR SUPERMARKETS INC.

681 Newark Ave.
Elizabeth, NJ 07208
Phone: 908-352-6400
Fax: 908-352-0103

Retail - supermarkets

CEO: Stanley P. Kaufelt
CFO: Frank Curci
HR: John Kovaleski
Employees: 4,200

1994 Sales: $591 million
1-Yr. Sales Change: —
Ownership: Privately Held

MBIA CORPORATION

113 King St.
Armonk, NY 10504
Phone: 914-273-4545
Fax: 914-765-3163

CEO: David H. Elliott
CFO: Julliette S. Tehrani
HR: Hilda Boas
Employees: 319

1994 Sales: $439.5 million
1-Yr. Sales Change: 2.4%
Exchange: NYSE
Symbol: MBI

Insurance - financial guarantee insurance for municipal bonds & asset-backed securities

MCCRORY CORPORATION

667 Madison Ave.
New York, NY 10021
Phone: 212-735-9500
Fax: 212-735-9450

Retail - discount & variety stores

CEO: Meshulam Ricklis
CFO: Paul Weiner
HR: Tom Russell
Employees: 11,300

1995 Sales: $840 million
1-Yr. Sales Change: -17.9%
Ownership: Privately Held

THE MCGRAW-HILL COMPANIES, INC.

1221 Avenue of the Americas	CEO: Joseph L. Dionne	1994 Sales: $2,760.9 mil.
New York, NY 10020	CFO: Robert J. Bahash	1-Yr. Sales Change: 25.8%
Phone: 212-512-2000	HR: Patrick Pavelski	Exchange: NYSE
Fax: 212-512-4871	Employees: 15,339	Symbol: MHP

Publishing - books, periodicals & electronic (Business Week, BYTE, Standard & Poor's); financial services; radio & TV broadcasting

 See pages 168–169 for a full profile of this company.

MCKINSEY & COMPANY

55 E. 52nd St.	CEO: Rajat Gupta	1994 Est. Sales: $1,500 mil.
New York, NY 10022	CFO: James Rogers	1-Yr. Sales Change: 15.4%
Phone: 212-446-7000	HR: Jerome Vascellaro	Ownership: Privately Held
Fax: 212-688-8575	Employees: 6,000	

Consulting - management

MDY ADVANCED TECHNOLOGIES INC.

21-00 Rte. 208 South	CEO: Galina Datskovsky	1995 Sales: $6 million
Fair Lawn, NJ 07410-2605	CFO: David Stott	1-Yr. Sales Change: 50.0%
Phone: 201-797-6676	HR: Roy Strunin	Ownership: Privately Held
Fax: 201-797-6852	Employees: 30	

Computers - consulting, development & network integration

MEARL CORPORATION

217 N. Highland Ave.	CEO: Dominic A. Pinciaro	1994 Sales: $110 million
Ossining, NY 10562	CFO: Anthony Venuto	1-Yr. Sales Change: 0.0%
Phone: 914-941-7450	HR: —	Ownership: Privately Held
Fax: 914-941-2311	Employees: 700	

Chemicals - inorganic pigments

MEASUREMENT SPECIALTIES, INC.

80 Little Falls Rd.	CEO: Joseph R. Mallon Jr.	1995 Sales: $17 million
Fairfield, NJ 07004-1615	CFO: Mark A. Shornick	1-Yr. Sales Change: 60.4%
Phone: 201-808-1819	HR: Pete Sentowski	Exchange: AMEX
Fax: 201-808-1787	Employees: 95	Symbol: MSS

Digital electronic measurement devices

MECKLERMEDIA CORPORATION

20 Ketchum St.	CEO: Alan M. Meckler	1995 Sales: $14.5 million
Westport, CT 06880	CFO: Joseph G. Cohen	1-Yr. Sales Change: 74.7%
Phone: 203-226-6967	HR: —	Exchange: Nasdaq (SC)
Fax: 203-454-5840	Employees: 49	Symbol: MECK

Publishing - CD-ROMs, magazines (Internet World, VR World, Web Week), professional journals & books, directories & Internet-related trade shows

MEDAREX, INC.

1545 Rte. 22 East, PO Box 953	CEO: Donald L. Drakeman	1994 Sales: $0.4 million
Annandale, NJ 08801-0953	CFO: Michael A. Appelbaum	1-Yr. Sales Change: 0.0%
Phone: 908-713-6001	HR: Rebecca Hollins	Exchange: Nasdaq
Fax: 908-713-6002	Employees: 31	Symbol: MEDX

Drugs - immune system enhancement therapeutics

MEDICAL ACTION INDUSTRIES INC.

150 Motor Pkwy., Ste. 205	CEO: Joseph R. Meringola	1995 Sales: $35.1 million
Hauppauge, NY 11788	CFO: Victor Bacchioni	1-Yr. Sales Change: -3.8%
Phone: 516-231-4600	HR: —	Exchange: Nasdaq
Fax: 516-231-3075	Employees: 162	Symbol: MDCI

Medical products - disposable surgical products, including sponges, towels & dressings

MEDICAL MANAGEMENT, INC.

254 W. 31st St.	CEO: Steven Rabinovici	1994 Sales: $6 million
New York, NY 10001-3854	CFO: Joseph M. Scotti	1-Yr. Sales Change: 81.8%
Phone: 212-868-1188	HR: Maria Russo	Exchange: Nasdaq
Fax: 212-868-6631	Employees: 43	Symbol: MMGT

Medical services - financing, installation & management of magnetic resonance imaging facilities

MEDICAL RESOURCES, INC.

1339 Broad St.	CEO: Robert J. Adamson	1994 Sales: $36 million
Clifton, NJ 07013	CFO: Robert J. Adamson	1-Yr. Sales Change: 33.8%
Phone: 201-773-0318	HR: —	Exchange: Nasdaq (SC)
Fax: 201-773-9092	Employees: 199	Symbol: MRII

Medical services - diagnostic imaging

MEDICAL STERILIZATION, INC.

225 Underhill Blvd.	CEO: Kennard H. Morganstern	1994 Sales: $8.2 million
Syosset, NY 11791	CFO: Paul V. Rossi	1-Yr. Sales Change: -3.5%
Phone: 516-496-8822	HR: Debbie Lampitok	Exchange: OTC
Fax: 516-496-8328	Employees: —	Symbol: MSTI

Medical services - off-site processing & sterilization services for hospitals, ambulatory care facilities & manufacturers of disposable medical devices

MEDIWARE INFORMATION SYSTEMS, INC.

1121 Old Walt Whitman Rd.	CEO: Les Dace	1995 Sales: $8.1 million
Melville, NY 11747-3005	CFO: Patty Schwartz	1-Yr. Sales Change: -2.4%
Phone: 516-423-7800	HR: —	Exchange: Nasdaq (SC)
Fax: 516-423-0161	Employees: —	Symbol: MEDW

Computers - computer-based management information systems for use in various clinical departments of hospitals

MEEHAN-TOOKER INC.

55 Madison Circle Dr.	CEO: Michael D. Voss	1994 Sales: $98.9 million
East Rutherford, NJ 07073	CFO: Thomas Morely	1-Yr. Sales Change: -1.1%
Phone: 201-933-9600	HR: Diane Caivano	Ownership: Privately Held
Fax: 201-933-8322	Employees: 325	

Printing - commercial

MEENAN OIL CO.

6800 Jericho Tnpk.	CEO: Stanley Orczyk	1994 Sales: $160 million
New York, NY 11791	CFO: Paul Vermylen	1-Yr. Sales Change: -15.8%
Phone: 516-364-9030	HR: —	Ownership: Privately Held
Fax: 516-364-9171	Employees: 800	

Oil marketing

MELLON CORPORATION

351 W. 35th St.	CEO: A. Sharkey	1994 Sales: $170 million
New York, NY 10001	CFO: —	1-Yr. Sales Change: 6.3%
Phone: 212-563-5278	HR: —	Ownership: Privately Held
Fax: 212-967-5875	Employees: 450	

Paper used to make patterns for the garment district

MELVILLE CORPORATION

One Theall Rd.	CEO: Stanley P. Goldstein	1994 Sales: $11,285.6 mil.
Rye, NY 10580	CFO: Gary L. Crittenden	1-Yr. Sales Change: 8.1%
Phone: 914-925-4000	HR: Jerald L. Maurer	Exchange: NYSE
Fax: 914-925-4026	Employees: 117,000	Symbol: MES

Retail - shoes (Thom McAn, Footaction), apparel (Marshalls, Bob's), drugs (CVS), home furnishings (Linens 'n Things), health & beauty aids & toys (Kay-Bee)

 See pages 170–171 for a full profile of this company.

MEM COMPANY, INC.

Union Street Extension	CEO: Gay A. Mayer	1994 Sales: $53.1 million
Northvale, NJ 07647	CFO: Michael G. Kazimir Jr.	1-Yr. Sales Change: 37.9%
Phone: 201-767-0100	HR: Margaret A. Powers	Exchange: AMEX
Fax: 201-767-0698	Employees: 411	Symbol: MEM

Cosmetics & toiletries manufacturer & distributor (English Leather, Heaven Sent, British Sterling, Generation X, Acqua di Selva, Tinkerbell)

MEMORIAL SLOAN-KETTERING CANCER CENTER

1275 York Ave.	CEO: Paul A. Marks	1994 Sales: $637.4 million
New York, NY 10021	CFO: Michael Gutnick	1-Yr. Sales Change: 5.0%
Phone: 212-639-2000	HR: Michael Browne	Ownership: Privately Held
Fax: 212-639-3508	Employees: 6,050	

Hospitals - not-for-profit cancer center

MENDIK COMPANY

330 Madison Ave.	CEO: Bernard H. Mendik	1994 Sales: $328 million
New York, NY 10017	CFO: Christopher Bonk	1-Yr. Sales Change: 1.5%
Phone: 212-557-1100	HR: Pearl Weinstock	Ownership: Privately Held
Fax: 212-370-7863	Employees: 1,200	

Real estate operations - investing & management

MERCHANTS BANK OF NEW YORK

434 Broadway	CEO: James G. Lawrence	1994 Sales: $64.6 million
New York, NY 10013	CFO: William J. Cardew	1-Yr. Sales Change: -6.0%
Phone: 212-973-6600	HR: Ruth Aimetti	Exchange: Nasdaq
Fax: 212-973-6634	Employees: 240	Symbol: MBNY

Banks - Northeast

MERCK & CO., INC.

One Merck Dr., PO Box 100
Whitehouse Station, NJ 08889-0100
Phone: 908-423-1000
Fax: 908-594-4662

CEO: Raymond V. Gilmartin
CFO: Judy C. Lewent
HR: Steven M. Darien
Employees: 47,500

1994 Sales: $14,969.8 mil.
1-Yr. Sales Change: 42.6%
Exchange: NYSE
Symbol: MRK

Drugs - cardiovasculars, antibiotics, anti-ulcerants (acquired Medco Containment Services Co.)

 See pages 172–173 for a full profile of this company.

MERIDIAN SPORTS INCORPORATED

625 Madison Ave.
New York, NY 10022
Phone: 212-527-6300
Fax: 212-527-4094

CEO: George Napier
CFO: Mark L. Wilson
HR: —
Employees: 1,537

1994 Sales: $187.6 million
1-Yr. Sales Change: 53.3%
Exchange: Nasdaq
Symbol: MSPO

Leisure & recreational products - boats & water sports equipment

MERRILL LYNCH & CO., INC.

World Financial Center, 250 Vesey St.
New York, NY 10281-1332
Phone: 212-449-1000
Fax: 212-236-4384

CEO: Daniel P. Tully
CFO: Joseph T. Willett
HR: Patrick J. Walsh
Employees: 44,000

1994 Sales: $18,233.1 mil.
1-Yr. Sales Change: 9.9%
Exchange: NYSE
Symbol: MER

Financial - securities brokerage, investment banking, asset management & insurance

 See pages 174–175 for a full profile of this company.

MERRIMAC INDUSTRIES, INC.

41 Fairfield Place
West Caldwell, NJ 07006
Phone: 201-575-1300
Fax: 201-575-0531

CEO: Eugene W. Niemiec
CFO: Eugene W. Niemiec
HR: David Palumbo
Employees: 122

1994 Sales: $13.6 million
1-Yr. Sales Change: -4.9%
Exchange: AMEX
Symbol: MRM

Electronics - military

MESABI TRUST

PO Box 318, Church Street Station
New York, NY 10015
Phone: 212-250-6696
Fax: 212-250-6392

CEO: Mark Woodward
CFO: —
HR: —
Employees: —

1995 Sales: $3.5 million
1-Yr. Sales Change: -2.8%
Exchange: NYSE
Symbol: MSB

Oil & gas - US royalty trust

METALLURG, INC.

25 E. 39th St.
New York, NY 10016
Phone: 212-686-4010
Fax: 212-697-2874

CEO: Michael A. Standen
CFO: Barry C. Nuss
HR: Michael Banks
Employees: 1,700

1994 Sales: $700 million
1-Yr. Sales Change: 35.9%
Ownership: Privately Held

Metal products - fabrication, alloys

METRO-TEL CORP.

500 N. Broadway, Ste. 240
Jericho, NY 11753-2111
Phone: 516-937-3420
Fax: 516-937-3426

CEO: Venerando J. Indelicato
CFO: Venerando J. Indelicato
HR: Millie Pino
Employees: 32

1995 Sales: $4.2 million
1-Yr. Sales Change: 2.4%
Exchange: Nasdaq (SC)
Symbol: MTRO

Telecommunications equipment - telephone test & telephone station equipment

METROMEDIA COMPANY

One Meadowlands Plaza
East Rutherford, NJ 07073
Phone: 201-531-8000
Fax: 201-833-1349

CEO: John W. Kluge
CFO: Robert A. Maresca
HR: Arnold L. Wadler
Employees: 20,000

1994 Est. Sales: $1,700 mil.
1-Yr. Sales Change: -15.0%
Ownership: Privately Held

Diversified operations - restaurants (Bennigan's, Bonanza, Ponderosa, Steak and Ale); entertainment
(Orion Pictures); telecommunications (WorldCom)

METROPOLITAN BASEBALL CLUB INC.

126th St. & Roosevelt Ave.
Flushing, NY 11368
Phone: 718-507-6387
Fax: 718-565-4382

CEO: Fred Wilpon
CFO: Harry O'Shaughnessy
HR: Russell Richardson
Employees: 85

1994 Sales: $45 million
1-Yr. Sales Change: -44.3%
Ownership: Privately Held

Leisure & recreational services - professional baseball team (New York Mets)

METROPOLITAN LIFE INSURANCE COMPANY

One Madison Ave.
New York, NY 10010-3690
Phone: 212-578-2211
Fax: 212-578-3320

CEO: Harry R. Kamen
CFO: Stewart G. Nagler
HR: Anne E. Hayden
Employees: 53,000

1994 Sales: $29,983 million
1-Yr. Sales Change: 4.5%
Ownership: Privately Held

Insurance - life; real estate brokerage franchise (Century 21)

 See pages 176–177 for a full profile of this company.

THE METROPOLITAN MUSEUM OF ART

1000 Fifth Ave.
New York, NY 10028
Phone: 212-535-7710
Fax: 212-570-3979

Museum

CEO: William H. Luers
CFO: William H. Luers
HR: Carol S. Cantrell
Employees: 2,500

1994 Sales: $181 million
1-Yr. Sales Change: -0.3%
Ownership: Privately Held

METROPOLITAN OPERA ASSOCIATION, INC.

Lincoln Center
New York, NY 10023
Phone: 212-799-3100
Fax: 212-870-4524

CEO: Bruce Crawford
CFO: Ray J. Groves
HR: —
Employees: 820

1994 Sales: $73.4 million
1-Yr. Sales Change: -4.1%
Ownership: Privately Held

Foundation supporting the Metropolitan Opera

M. H. MEYERSON & CO., INC.

30 Montgomery St.
Jersey City, NJ 07302
Phone: 201-332-3380
Fax: 201-332-1562

CEO: Martin H. Meyerson
CFO: Martin H. Meyerson
HR: Gene Whitehouse
Employees: 120

1995 Sales: $20.6 million
1-Yr. Sales Change: -4.6%
Exchange: Nasdaq
Symbol: MHMY

Financial - securities brokerage

MICHAEL ANTHONY JEWELERS, INC.

115 S. MacQuesten Pkwy.
Mt. Vernon, NY 10550
Phone: 914-699-0000
Fax: 914-699-9869

CEO: Michael Paolercio
CFO: Allan Corn
HR: Roseanne Boscoe
Employees: 602

1995 Sales: $93.3 million
1-Yr. Sales Change: -34.7%
Exchange: AMEX
Symbol: MAJ

Precious metals & jewelry - charms, pendants, rings, rope chain, bracelets, earrings & watches; items
with diamonds & semiprecious stones

MICHAEL WOLFF & COMPANY, INC.

1633 Broadway, 27th Fl.
New York, NY 10019
Phone: 212-841-1572
Fax: 212-841-1539

CEO: Michael Wolff
CFO: Alison Anthoine
HR: Shaun Witten
Employees: 21

1994 Est. Sales: $2.2 mil.
1-Yr. Sales Change: 57.1%
Ownership: Privately Held

Publishing consultancy & book packager (Net Chat, Net Games, Net Guide, Net Money, Net Trek)

MICKELBERRY COMMUNICATIONS, INCORPORATED

405 Park Ave.	CEO: James C. Marlas	1994 Sales: $127.6 million
New York, NY 10022	CFO: George Kane	1-Yr. Sales Change: 7.3%
Phone: 212-832-0303	HR: —	Exchange: NYSE
Fax: 212-832-0554	Employees: 657	Symbol: MBC

Advertising - promotions & printing

MICRO WAREHOUSE, INC.

535 Connecticut Ave.	CEO: Peter Godfrey	1994 Sales: $776.4 million
Norwalk, CT 06854	CFO: Steven Purcell	1-Yr. Sales Change: 72.4%
Phone: 203-899-4000	HR: Michael Kurtz	Exchange: Nasdaq
Fax: 203-899-4203	Employees: 2,300	Symbol: MWHS

Retail - mail-order marketing of peripheral equipment & software (MacWAREHOUSE & MicroWAREHOUSE)

 See page 278 for a full profile of this company.

MICROBIZ CORPORATION

300 Corporate Dr.	CEO: Craig L. Aberle	1994 Sales: $8.9 million
Mahwah, NJ 07430	CFO: Virginia Baker	1-Yr. Sales Change: 2.3%
Phone: 201-512-0900	HR: Patricia Baker	Ownership: Privately Held
Fax: 201-512-1919	Employees: 50	

Computers - business automation software & systems; mail-order peripherals

THE MICROCAP FUND, INC.

733 Third Ave., 11th Fl.	CEO: Kamal Mustafa	1995 Sales: $1.1 million
New York, NY 10017	CFO: Mark T. Behrman	1-Yr. Sales Change: 57.1%
Phone: 800-888-6534	HR: —	Exchange: Nasdaq (SC)
Fax: 212-297-5695	Employees: 2	Symbol: MCAP

Financial - investment management & nondiversified, closed-end operations

MICROS-TO-MAINFRAMES, INC.

614 Corporate Way	CEO: Steven H. Rothman	1995 Sales: $43 million
Valley Cottage, NY 10989	CFO: Frank Wong	1-Yr. Sales Change: 48.3%
Phone: 914-268-5000	HR: Dottie Sloaman	Exchange: Nasdaq (SC)
Fax: 914-268-9695	Employees: 62	Symbol: MTMC

Computer services - microcomputers, microcomputer products, supplies, accessories & custom-designed microcomputer systems, network analysis & design, systems configuration

MICROWAVE POWER DEVICES, INC.

49 Wireless Blvd.	CEO: Edward J. Shubel	1994 Sales: $25.1 million
Hauppauge, NY 11788-3935	CFO: Paul E. Donofrio	1-Yr. Sales Change: 5.5%
Phone: 516-231-1400	HR: Polly Winters	Exchange: Nasdaq
Fax: 516-231-4084	Employees: 250	Symbol: MPDI

Telecommunications equipment - power amplifiers & related subsystems for cellular base stations

MIDDLESEX WATER COMPANY

1500 Ronson Rd.	CEO: J. Richard Tompkins	1994 Sales: $36.1 million
Iselin, NJ 08830-3020	CFO: Ernest C. Gere	1-Yr. Sales Change: 1.7%
Phone: 908-634-1500	HR: Carolyn Stuart	Exchange: Nasdaq
Fax: 908-750-5981	Employees: 151	Symbol: MSEX

Utility - water collection, treatment & distribution for domestic, commercial, industrial & fire protection purposes primarily in eastern Middlesex County, NJ

MIDLANTIC CORPORATION

Metro Park Plaza, PO Box 600	CEO: Garry J. Scheuring	1994 Sales: $1,084.4 mil.
Edison, NJ 08818	CFO: Howard I. Atkins	1-Yr. Sales Change: 7.2%
Phone: 908-321-8000	HR: Eugene J. McNamara	Exchange: Nasdaq
Fax: 908-321-2271	Employees: 6,174	Symbol: MIDL

Banks - Northeast

MID-WEST SPRING MANUFACTURING COMPANY

17 Camptown Rd.	CEO: C. Stephen Clegg	1994 Sales: $32.6 million
Irvington, NJ 07111	CFO: Richard G. Reece	1-Yr. Sales Change: 16.0%
Phone: 201-372-1112	HR: Miriam Kenyon	Exchange: Nasdaq (SC)
Fax: 201-372-7723	Employees: 532	Symbol: PATH

Metal products - non-bedding springs, specialty springs, wire forms & metal stamping products

MIKRON INSTRUMENT COMPANY, INC.

445 W. Main St.	CEO: K. Irani	1994 Sales: $5.5 million
Wyckoff, NJ 07481	CFO: Alex Wu	1-Yr. Sales Change: 7.8%
Phone: 201-891-7330	HR: Alex Wu	Exchange: Nasdaq (SC)
Fax: 201-891-1205	Employees: 58	Symbol: MIKR

Instruments - hand-held infrared thermometers for industrial applications

MILBANK, TWEED, HADLEY & MCCLOY

One Chase Manhattan Plaza
New York, NY 10005
Phone: 212-530-5000
Fax: 212-530-5219

Law firm

CEO: Francis D. Logan
CFO: Steven M. Gamcsik
HR: Jane L. MacLennan
Employees: 900

1995 Sales: $180 million
1-Yr. Sales Change: 4.3%
Ownership: Privately Held

MILGRAY ELECTRONICS, INC.

77 Schmitt Blvd.
Farmingdale, NY 11735
Phone: 516-420-9800
Fax: 516-752-9221

Electrical components - distribution

CEO: Herbert S. Davidson
CFO: John R. Tortorici
HR: Gerry Reagen
Employees: 450

1995 Sales: $239.5 million
1-Yr. Sales Change: 31.7%
Exchange: Nasdaq (SC)
Symbol: MGRY

MINERALS TECHNOLOGIES INC.

405 Lexington Ave.
New York, NY 10174-1901
Phone: 212-878-1800
Fax: 212-878-1801

CEO: Jean-Paul Valles
CFO: John R. Stack
HR: Howard R. Crabtree
Employees: 2,200

1994 Sales: $472.6 million
1-Yr. Sales Change: 10.3%
Exchange: NYSE
Symbol: MTX

Chemicals - specialty minerals, mineral-based & synthetic mineral products for paper producers, steel, cement & glass industries

MISONIX, INC.

1938 New Hwy.
Farmingdale, NY 11735
Phone: 516-694-9555
Fax: 516-694-9412

CEO: Joseph Librizzi
CFO: Peter Gerstheimer
HR: Carol Hlavac
Employees: 80

1995 Sales: $8.6 million
1-Yr. Sales Change: 7.5%
Exchange: Nasdaq (SC)
Symbol: MSON

Instruments - ultrasonic equipment for scientific & industrial purposes; ductless fume enclosures

MISTER JAY FASHIONS INTERNATIONAL, INC.

448 W. 16th St.
New York, NY 10011
Phone: 212-391-2272
Fax: 212-691-4129

CEO: Ilan Arbel
CFO: Allean Goode
HR: Allean Goode
Employees: 327

1995 Sales: $16.1 million
1-Yr. Sales Change: -38.5%
Exchange: Nasdaq (SC)
Symbol: MRJY

Apparel - lower-priced women's dresses, gowns & separates for formal events

MOBILEMEDIA CORPORATION

65 Challenger Rd.	CEO: Gregory M. Rorke	1994 Sales: $78 million
Ridgefield Park, NJ 07660	CFO: Santo J. Pittsman	1-Yr. Sales Change: 20.2%
Phone: 201-440-8400	HR: Tracey Zimmerman	Exchange: Nasdaq
Fax: 201-440-2491	Employees: 1,284	Symbol: MBLM

Telecommunications services - paging & wireless messaging services in 19 states & the District of Columbia (#2 in US)

MODELL'S SPORTING GOODS, INC.

34-24 Vernon Blvd.	CEO: William Modell	1994 Sales: $238 million
New York, NY 11106	CFO: Larry Brustein	1-Yr. Sales Change: 19.0%
Phone: 718-956-8600	HR: Phyllis Siegel	Ownership: Privately Held
Fax: 718-956-3175	Employees: 2,300	

Retail - sporting goods, athletic footwear & activewear

MODERN MEDICAL MODALITIES CORPORATION

95 Madison Ave., Ste. 301	CEO: Roger Findlay	1994 Sales: $7.8 million
Morristown, NJ 07960	CFO: Jan Goldberg	1-Yr. Sales Change: 143.8%
Phone: 201-538-9955	HR: —	Exchange: Nasdaq (SC)
Fax: 201-267-7359	Employees: 33	Symbol: MODM

Leasing - MRI & computerized axial tomography equipment to hospitals & physicians; medical imaging center management

THE MONEY STORE INC.

2840 Morris Ave.	CEO: Marc Turtletaub	1994 Sales: $330.5 million
Union, NJ 07083	CFO: Morton Dear	1-Yr. Sales Change: 50.4%
Phone: 908-686-2000	HR: Charlotte L. Moffett	Exchange: Nasdaq
Fax: 908-686-6907	Employees: 2,035	Symbol: MONE

Financial - consumer & commercial loans, including home equity, Small Business Administration & government-guaranteed student loans

 See page 279 for a full profile of this company.

MONMOUTH REAL ESTATE INVESTMENT CORPORATION

125 Wycoff Rd., PO Box 335	CEO: Eugene W. Landy	1994 Sales: $3.9 million
Eatontown, NJ 07724	CFO: Ann A. Chen	1-Yr. Sales Change: 14.7%
Phone: 908-542-4927	HR: —	Exchange: Nasdaq
Fax: 908-544-8541	Employees: 5	Symbol: MNRTA

Real estate investment trust

MONTEFIORE MEDICAL CENTER

111 E. 210th St.
New York, NY 10467
Phone: 718-920-4321
Fax: 718-920-6321

Hospitals

CEO: Spencer Foreman
CFO: Joel A. Perlman
HR: Donald G. Revelle
Employees: 8,223

1994 Sales: $700.3 million
1-Yr. Sales Change: -24.5%
Ownership: Privately Held

MORGAN STANLEY GROUP INC.

1251 Avenue of the Americas
New York, NY 10020
Phone: 212-703-4000
Fax: 212-761-0086

CEO: John J. Mack
CFO: Philip N. Duff
HR: William Higgins
Employees: 9,685

1995 Sales: $9,376 million
1-Yr. Sales Change: 2.2%
Exchange: NYSE
Symbol: MS

Financial - investment banking & merchant banking stock brokerage

 See pages 178–179 for a full profile of this company.

MORSE DIESEL INTERNATIONAL, INC.

1633 Broadway, 24th Fl.
New York, NY 10019
Phone: 212-484-0300
Fax: 212-484-0585

Construction & consulting

CEO: Donald H. Piser
CFO: Norman G. Fornella
HR: Irwin Wicker
Employees: 450

1994 Est. Sales: $500 mil.
1-Yr. Sales Change: 0.0%
Ownership: Privately Held

MOTOR CLUB OF AMERICA

484 Central Ave.
Newark, NJ 07107
Phone: 201-733-1234
Fax: 201-596-8132

CEO: Archer McWhorter
CFO: Patrick J. Haveron
HR: George B. Patterson
Employees: 125

1994 Sales: $33.7 million
1-Yr. Sales Change: -4.8%
Exchange: Nasdaq
Symbol: MOTR

Insurance - property & casualty & personal automobile insurance

MOVIE STAR, INC.

136 Madison Ave.
New York, NY 10016
Phone: 212-679-7260
Fax: 212-684-3295

Apparel - women's underwear

CEO: Mark M. David
CFO: Saul Pomerantz
HR: Yolaine Goldberg
Employees: 2,300

1995 Sales: $101.9 million
1-Yr. Sales Change: -1.2%
Exchange: AMEX
Symbol: MSI

MOVIEFONE, INC.

4 World Trade Center, Ste. 5290
New York, NY 10048
Phone: 212-504-7442
Fax: 212-504-7567

CEO: Andrew R. Jarecki
CFO: Adam H. Slutsky
HR: Sandy Hughes
Employees: 59

1994 Sales: $22.6 million
1-Yr. Sales Change: 67.4%
Exchange: Nasdaq
Symbol: MOFN

Business services - interactive telephone advertising, information & ticketing services to the motion picture industry

MSB BANCORP, INC.

35 Matthews St
Goshen, NY 10924-0908
Phone: 914-294-8100
Fax: 914-294-1124

CEO: William C. Myers
CFO: Anthony J. Fabiano
HR: Jane Matheson
Employees: 217

1994 Sales: $27 million
1-Yr. Sales Change: -11.5%
Exchange: Nasdaq
Symbol: MSBB

Banks - Northeast

MSI ELECTRONICS INC.

31-00 47th Ave.
Long Island City, NY 11101
Phone: 718-937-3330
Fax: 718-937-3499

CEO: Albert Lederman
CFO: Albert Lederman
HR: —
Employees: 16

1994 Sales: $1.1 million
1-Yr. Sales Change: -15.4%
Exchange: OTC
Symbol: MSIE

Electrical components - semiconductor diodes & electronic instruments designed to measure the properties of semiconductors; hardware & software for telephone switching systems

MTA NEW YORK CITY TRANSIT

370 Jay St.
New York, NY 11201
Phone: 718-330-3000
Fax: 718-243-8501

CEO: Alan F. Kiepper
CFO: Harvey Spector
HR: Liz Lowe
Employees: 44,000

1994 Sales: $5,322.8 mil.
1-Yr. Sales Change: —
Ownership: Privately Held

Transportation - buses & subways in the Bronx, Brooklyn, Manhattan, Queens & Staten Island boroughs of New York City

 See pages 180–181 for a full profile of this company.

MUDGE ROSE GUTHRIE ALEXANDER & FERDON

180 Maiden Ln.
New York, NY 10038
Phone: 212-510-7000
Fax: 212-248-2655

CEO: Donald J. Zoeller
CFO: Emmett Ward
HR: —
Employees: —

1994 Sales: $93 million
1-Yr. Sales Change: -15.1%
Ownership: Privately Held

Law firm

THE MULTICARE COMPANIES, INC.

411 Hackensack Ave.
Hackensack, NJ 07601-6328
Phone: 201-488-8818
Fax: 201-525-5954

CEO: Daniel E. Straus
CFO: Stephen R. Baker
HR: Ronald G. Clarendon
Employees: 7,000

1994 Sales: $262.4 million
1-Yr. Sales Change: 61.6%
Exchange: NYSE
Symbol: MUL

Medical services - long-term care, Alzheimer's care & related support services

 See page 280 for a full profile of this company.

MULTI-MARKET RADIO, INC.

150 E. 58th St., 19th Fl.
New York, NY 10155
Phone: 212-407-9150
Fax: 212-753-3188

CEO: Bruce Morrow
CFO: Jerry D. Emlet
HR: —
Employees: 200

1994 Sales: $7.1 million
1-Yr. Sales Change: 222.7%
Exchange: Nasdaq
Symbol: RDIOA

Broadcasting - ownership & operation of radio stations in small & medium-sized markets in the eastern US

THE MUSEUM OF MODERN ART

11 W. 53rd St.
New York, NY 10019
Phone: 212-708-9480
Fax: 212-708-9691

CEO: Glenn Lowry
CFO: James Gara
HR: Nancy Dill
Employees: 530

1995 Sales: $51.9 million
1-Yr. Sales Change: -11.3%
Ownership: Privately Held

Art museum

THE MUTUAL LIFE INSURANCE COMPANY OF NEW YORK

1740 Broadway
New York, NY 10019
Phone: 212-708-2000
Fax: 212-708-2056

CEO: Michael I. Roth
CFO: Richard D'addario
HR: Catherine Gushue
Employees: 6,400

1994 Sales: $2,839.4 mil.
1-Yr. Sales Change: -18.7%
Ownership: Privately Held

Insurance - individual life & disability; annuities, mutual funds & investment securities

 See pages 182–183 for a full profile of this company.

NABISCO HOLDINGS CORP.

7 Campus Dr.
Parsippany, NJ 07054
Phone: 201-682-5000
Fax: 201-503-2153

CEO: H. John Greeniaus
CFO: H. F. "Jake" Powell
HR: C. Michael Sayeau
Employees: 45,000

1994 Sales: $7,699 million
1-Yr. Sales Change: 9.6%
Exchange: NYSE
Symbol: NA

Food - cookies (Oreos, Chips Ahoy!), snacks (SnackWells, Ritz, Wheat Thins), condiments (A.1., Grey Poupon) & gum & candy (Bubble Yum, Care-Free, Life Savers, Breath Savers)

NAC RE CORP.

One Greenwich Plaza, PO Box 2568	CEO: Ronald L. Bornhuetter	1994 Sales: $478.4 million
Greenwich, CT 06836-2568	CFO: John Adimari	1-Yr. Sales Change: 19.0%
Phone: 203-622-5200	HR: Celia Brown	Exchange: NYSE
Fax: 203-622-1494	Employees: 233	Symbol: NRC

Insurance - treaty & facultative reinsurance (Greenwich Insurance Company, Indian Harbor Insurance Company, NAC Re International Holdings Limited)

NAI TECHNOLOGIES, INC.

1000 Woodbury Rd.	CEO: Robert A. Carlson	1994 Sales: $54.5 million
Woodbury, NY 11797-2530	CFO: Richard A. Schneider	1-Yr. Sales Change: -32.7%
Phone: 516-364-4433	HR: Len Stanton	Exchange: Nasdaq
Fax: 516-364-8855	Employees: 393	Symbol: NATL

Computers - rugged computers & peripheral equipment

NANTUCKET INDUSTRIES, INC.

105 Madison Ave.	CEO: Stephen M. Samberg	1995 Sales: $37 million
New York, NY 10016	CFO: Ronald Hoffman	1-Yr. Sales Change: -11.1%
Phone: 212-889-5656	HR: —	Exchange: AMEX
Fax: 212-532-3217	Employees: 620	Symbol: NAN

Apparel - high-fashion men's (Brut, McGregor, Brittania, Arrow, Botany 500, Guess?) & women's undergarments (Brittania, Mary Duffy)

NAPCO SECURITY SYSTEMS, INC.

333 Bayview Ave.	CEO: Richard Soloway	1995 Sales: $48.1 million
Amityville, NY 11701	CFO: Kevin Buchel	1-Yr. Sales Change: 2.6%
Phone: 516-842-9400	HR: Sally Beebe	Exchange: Nasdaq
Fax: 516-842-9137	Employees: 1,150	Symbol: NSSC

Protection - electronic security equipment, including alarm control panels, sensor devices & door security hardware used in residential, commercial, institutional & industrial installations

NAPORANO IRON & METAL CO.

PO Box 5158	CEO: Joseph Naporano	1994 Est. Sales: $220 mil.
Newark, NJ 07105	CFO: Joseph Naporano	1-Yr. Sales Change: 0.0%
Phone: 201-344-4570	HR: Lin Griffin	Ownership: Privately Held
Fax: 201-344-8155	Employees: 350	

Pollution control - scrap metal recycling

NASSAU SUFFOLK FROZEN FOOD, INC.

286 Northern Blvd.
Great Neck, NY 11201
Phone: 516-466-8500
Fax: 516-466-8540

Frozen foods, bakeries

CEO: Victor Bahar
CFO: Merick Bahar
HR: Karyn Goldman
Employees: 200

1994 Sales: $190 million
1-Yr. Sales Change: 0.0%
Ownership: Privately Held

NASTECH PHARMACEUTICAL COMPANY, INC.

45 Davids Dr.
Hauppauge, NY 11788
Phone: 516-273-0101
Fax: 516-273-0252

Drugs - antihistamines, analgesic agents & sleep-aid products

CEO: Vincent D. Romeo
CFO: Joel Girsky
HR: Carol Wenig
Employees: 13

1995 Sales: $2.9 million
1-Yr. Sales Change: 31.8%
Exchange: Nasdaq (SC)
Symbol: NSTK

NATHAN'S FAMOUS, INC.

1400 Old Country Rd., Ste. 400
Westbury, NY 11590
Phone: 516-338-8500
Fax: 516-338-7220

Retail - hot dog restaurants, carts & kiosks

CEO: Howard M. Lorber
CFO: Ronald G. DeVos
HR: Karen C. Brown
Employees: 573

1995 Sales: $26.2 million
1-Yr. Sales Change: 4.4%
Exchange: Nasdaq
Symbol: NATH

 See page 281 for a full profile of this company.

NATIONAL BASKETBALL ASSOCIATION

645 Fifth Ave., 15th Fl.
New York, NY 10022
Phone: 212-826-7000
Fax: 212-754-6414

Leisure & recreational services - international professional basketball league

CEO: David J. Stern
CFO: Robert Criqui
HR: Leroy D. Nunery
Employees: 550

1994 Sales: $1,259 million
1-Yr. Sales Change: 22.2%
Ownership: Privately Held

NATIONAL ENVELOPE CORPORATION

29-10 Hunters Point Ave.
Long Island City, NY 11101-718
Phone: 718-786-0300
Fax: 718-361-3127

Paper & paper products - envelopes

CEO: William Ungar
CFO: Don Cifu
HR: Zalina Borukhovich
Employees: 2,800

1994 Sales: $300 million
1-Yr. Sales Change: 20.0%
Ownership: Privately Held

NATIONAL FOOTBALL LEAGUE

410 Park Ave.
New York, NY 10022
Phone: 212-758-1500
Fax: 212-758-1742

CEO: Paul Tagliabue
CFO: Tom Spock
HR: John Buzzeo
Employees: 150

1994 Sales: $1,729.5 mil.
1-Yr. Sales Change: -1.3%
Ownership: Privately Held

Leisure & recreational services - professional football league

NATIONAL GAMING CORPORATION

339 Jefferson Rd.
Parsippany, NJ 07054-0278
Phone: 201-952-8599
Fax: 201-428-9757

CEO: Henry R. Silverman
CFO: Stephen P. Holmes
HR: —
Employees: 5

1994 Sales: $2.4 million
1-Yr. Sales Change: 2,300%
Exchange: Nasdaq
Symbol: NAGC

Casinos & entertainment facilities (spinoff of Hospitality Franchise Systems, Inc.)

NATIONAL HOCKEY LEAGUE

1251 Avenue of the Americas, 47th Fl.
New York, NY 10020
Phone: 212-789-2000
Fax: 212-789-2020

CEO: Gary Bettman
CFO: Craig Harnett
HR: —
Employees: 150

1995 Sales: $455 million
1-Yr. Sales Change: -40.4%
Ownership: Privately Held

Leisure & recreational services - professional hockey league

NATIONAL HOME HEALTH CARE CORPORATION

700 White Plains Rd., Ste. 363
Scarsdale, NY 10583
Phone: 914-722-9000
Fax: 914-722-9199

CEO: Frederick H. Fialkow
CFO: Robert P. Heller
HR: —
Employees: 855

1995 Sales: $24.6 million
1-Yr. Sales Change: 22.4%
Exchange: Nasdaq
Symbol: NHHC

Health care - outpatient & home

NATIONAL MULTIPLE SCLEROSIS SOCIETY

733 Third Ave.
New York, NY 10017-3288
Phone: 212-986-3240
Fax: 212-986-7981

CEO: Michael J. Dugan
CFO: Joseph C. DeSapio
HR: Lisa Sersoglia
Employees: 121

1995 Sales: $37.8 million
1-Yr. Sales Change: 11.8%
Ownership: Privately Held

Voluntary membership organization with 430,000 members dedicated to the cure, prevention & treatment of MS & to improving the lives of those affected by the disease

NATIONAL PATENT DEVELOPMENT CORPORATION

9 W. 57th St.
New York, NY 10019
Phone: 212-826-8500
Fax: 212-230-9545

CEO: Jerome I. Feldman
CFO: Scott N. Greenberg
HR: —
Employees: 2,368

1994 Sales: $204.8 million
1-Yr. Sales Change: 6.1%
Exchange: AMEX
Symbol: NPD

Medical & dental supplies

NATIONAL RE CORPORATION

777 Long Ridge Rd., PO Box 10167
Stamford, CT 06904-2167
Phone: 203-329-7700
Fax: 203-329-5220

CEO: William D. Warren
CFO: Peter A. Cheney
HR: William J. Hunt
Employees: 263

1994 Sales: $377.8 million
1-Yr. Sales Change: -5.9%
Exchange: NYSE
Symbol: NRE

Insurance - property & casualty

NATIONAL SPINNING COMPANY

183 Madison Ave.
New York, NY 10016
Phone: 212-889-3800
Fax: 212-889-9712

CEO: Joseph Leff
CFO: Jeff Koch
HR: —
Employees: 2,500

1994 Sales: $215 million
1-Yr. Sales Change: -17.3%
Ownership: Privately Held

Textiles - yarn mills & craft manufacturing

NATIONWIDE CELLULAR SERVICE, INC.

20 E. Sunrise Hwy.
Valley Stream, NY 11581-1252
Phone: 516-568-2000
Fax: 516-568-0554

CEO: Stephen Katz
CFO: Edward Seidenberg
HR: Miny Durando
Employees: 629

1994 Sales: $213.2 million
1-Yr. Sales Change: 16.7%
Exchange: Nasdaq
Symbol: NCEL

Telecommunications services

NATURE'S ELEMENTS HOLDING CORPORATION

115 River Rd.
Edgewater, NJ 07020-1009
Phone: 201-945-2640
Fax: 201-945-2247

CEO: Bernard R. Kossar
CFO: Rocky J. Smith
HR: —
Employees: —

1995 Sales: $13 million
1-Yr. Sales Change: 38.3%
Exchange: OTC
Symbol: NELMQ

Retail - cosmetics & personal-care stores, offering a complete line of cosmetics, skincare products, haircare items & fragrances

NAUTICA ENTERPRISES, INC.

40 W. 57th St., Third Fl.
New York, NY 10019
Phone: 212-541-5990
Fax: 212-956-3373

CEO: Harvey Sanders
CFO: Neal Nackman
HR: Laura Crespo
Employees: 760

1995 Sales: $247.6 million
1-Yr. Sales Change: 28.4%
Exchange: Nasdaq
Symbol: NAUT

Apparel - men's & boys'

 See page 282 for a full profile of this company.

THE NAVIGATORS GROUP, INC.

123 William St.
New York, NY 10038
Phone: 212-406-2900
Fax: 212-406-3042

CEO: Terence N. Deeks
CFO: W. Allen Barnett
HR: Joan Pentek
Employees: 160

1994 Sales: $113.9 million
1-Yr. Sales Change: 5.5%
Exchange: Nasdaq
Symbol: NAVG

Insurance - property & casualty

NBTY, INC.

90 Orville Dr.
Bohemia, NY 11716
Phone: 516-567-9500
Fax: 516-563-1180

CEO: Arthur Rudolph
CFO: Arthur Rudolph
HR: —
Employees: 850

1995 Sales: $178.8 million
1-Yr. Sales Change: 14.5%
Exchange: Nasdaq
Symbol: NBTY

Vitamins & nutritional products (Nature's Bounty)

NEDERLANDER ORGANIZATION, INC.

810 7th Ave.
New York, NY 10019
Phone: 212-262-2400
Fax: 212-262-5558

CEO: Robert Nederlander
CFO: James Nederlander Jr.
HR: —
Employees: 50

1994 Est. Sales: $5 million
1-Yr. Sales Change: —
Ownership: Privately Held

Theater production

NEUMAN DISTRIBUTORS, INC.

175 Railroad Ave.
Ridgefield, NJ 07657
Phone: 201-941-2000
Fax: 201-941-6328

CEO: Samuel Toscano Jr.
CFO: Philip A. Piscopo
HR: Barbara Toscano
Employees: 625

1995 Sales: $1,050 million
1-Yr. Sales Change: 8.9%
Ownership: Privately Held

Drugs & sundries - wholesale

NEUROGEN CORPORATION

35 NE Industrial Rd.
Branford, CT 06405
Phone: 203-488-8201
Fax: 203-481-8683

CEO: Harry H. Penner Jr.
CFO: Stephen R. Davis
HR: Vivienne Formichella
Employees: 47

1994 Sales: $5.8 million
1-Yr. Sales Change: 26.1%
Exchange: Nasdaq
Symbol: NRGN

Psychotherapeutics & drugs to treat central nervous system disorders, including anxiety, depression, dementia & psychosis

NEW BRUNSWICK SCIENTIFIC CO., INC.

44 Talmadge Rd., PO Box 4005
Edison, NJ 08818-4005
Phone: 908-287-1200
Fax: 908-287-4089

CEO: Ezra Weisman
CFO: Samuel Eichenbaum
HR: —
Employees: 360

1994 Sales: $38.8 million
1-Yr. Sales Change: 7.8%
Exchange: Nasdaq
Symbol: NBSC

Instruments - high-technology equipment & instruments used to produce therapeutic drugs, enzymes, biochemicals, antibiotics, vaccines & other biological products

NEW DAY BEVERAGE, INC.

134 Morgan Ave.
New York, NY 11237
Phone: 718-894-4300
Fax: 718-894-8950

CEO: Robert Sipper
CFO: Joseph Vigliarolo
HR: —
Employees: 70

1994 Sales: $9.8 million
1-Yr. Sales Change: 12.6%
Exchange: Nasdaq (SC)
Symbol: SUNS

Beverages - all-natural fruit drinks

NEW JERSEY DEVILS

PO Box 504
East Rutherford, NJ 07073
Phone: 201-935-6050
Fax: 201-935-2127

CEO: Lou Lamoriello
CFO: Chris Modrzynski
HR: —
Employees: 110

1994 Sales: $26.7 million
1-Yr. Sales Change: —
Ownership: Privately Held

Leisure & recreational services - professional hockey team

NEW JERSEY NETS

Meadowlands Arena
East Rutherford, NJ 07073
Phone: 201-935-8888
Fax: 201-935-1088

CEO: Michael Rowe
CFO: Ray Schaetzle
HR: —
Employees: 60

1994 Sales: $41.8 million
1-Yr. Sales Change: —
Ownership: Privately Held

Leisure & recreational services - professional basketball team

NEW JERSEY RESOURCES CORPORATION

1415 Wyckoff Rd., PO Box 1468	CEO: Laurence M. Downes	1995 Sales: $454.6 million
Wall, NJ 07719	CFO: Glenn C. Lockwood	1-Yr. Sales Change: -8.8%
Phone: 908-938-1480	HR: Hugo C. Bottino	Exchange: NYSE
Fax: 908-938-2620	Employees: 864	Symbol: NJR

Utility - natural gas distribution & energy-related services (New Jersey Natural Gas Company)

NEW JERSEY STEEL CORPORATION

N. Crossman Rd., PO Box 96	CEO: Robert J. Pasquarelli	1994 Sales: $128.6 million
Sayreville, NJ 08872	CFO: Paul Roik	1-Yr. Sales Change: 20.9%
Phone: 908-721-6600	HR: John Sullivan	Exchange: Nasdaq
Fax: 908-721-8784	Employees: 374	Symbol: NJST

Steel - production steel reinforcing bars for various heavy construction industries

NEW PARADIGM SOFTWARE CORPORATION

335 Madison Ave.	CEO: Mark Blundell	1995 Sales: $0.1 million
New York, NY 10017	CFO: Mark Blundell	1-Yr. Sales Change: —
Phone: 212-557-0933	HR: Lauren Gray	Exchange: Nasdaq (SC)
Fax: 212-557-0935	Employees: 18	Symbol: NPSC

Computers - enterprise-wide system integration software (Copernicus)

NEW PLAN REALTY TRUST

1120 Avenue of the Americas	CEO: William Newman	1995 Sales: $130.6 million
New York, NY 10036	CFO: Michael I. Brown	1-Yr. Sales Change: 29.3%
Phone: 212-869-3000	HR: Ann Cecio	Exchange: NYSE
Fax: 212-302-4776	Employees: 480	Symbol: NPR

Real estate investment trust - income-producing properties, shopping centers, apartment communities & factory outlet centers

NEW YORK BANCORP INC.

241-02 Northern Blvd.	CEO: Michael A. McManus Jr.	1995 Sales: $204.7 million
Douglaston, NY 11362-1061	CFO: Stan I. Cohen	1-Yr. Sales Change: 63.5%
Phone: 718-631-8100	HR: Carole L. Scialdone	Exchange: NYSE
Fax: 718-631-9848	Employees: 487	Symbol: NYB

Banks - Northeast

NEW YORK CITY HEALTH & HOSPITALS CORPORATION

125 Worth St.
New York, NY 10013
Phone: 212-730-3100
Fax: 212-788-3358

CEO: Luis Marcos
CFO: Rick Langfelder
HR: —
Employees: 41,711

1995 Sales: $4,134.2 mil.
1-Yr. Sales Change: 4.7%
Ownership: Privately Held

Hospitals - not-for-profit system serving New York City (#1 US municipal hospital system)

NEW YORK CITY OPERA, INC.

20 Lincoln Center
New York, NY 10023
Phone: 212-870-5500
Fax: 212-724-1120

CEO: Mark Weinstein
CFO: Mark Weinstein
HR: Derek Davis
Employees: 650

1995 Sales: $15.1 million
1-Yr. Sales Change: 23.8%
Ownership: Privately Held

Opera

NEW YORK GIANTS

Giants Stadium
East Rutherford, NJ 07073
Phone: 201-935-8111
Fax: 201-935-8493

CEO: Wellington Mara
CFO: John Mara
HR: John Mara
Employees: 83

1994 Sales: $66.5 million
1-Yr. Sales Change: 1.8%
Ownership: Privately Held

Leisure & recreational services - professional football team

NEW YORK ISLANDERS

Nassau Coliseum
Uniondale, NY 11553
Phone: 516-794-4100
Fax: 516-542-9348

CEO: Ralph Palleschi
CFO: Ralph Sellitti
HR: Kathleen Maloney
Employees: 125

1994 Sales: $25.8 million
1-Yr. Sales Change: 0.4%
Ownership: Privately Held

Leisure & recreational services - professional hockey team

NEW YORK JETS FOOTBALL CLUB, INC.

1000 Fulton Ave.
Hempstead, NY 11550
Phone: 516-538-6600
Fax: 516-481-7461

CEO: Steve Gutman
CFO: Michael Gerstle
HR: Michael Gerstle
Employees: 125

1994 Sales: $62 million
1-Yr. Sales Change: 3.0%
Ownership: Privately Held

Leisure & recreational services - professional football team

NEW YORK KNICKERBOCKERS

2 Penn Plaza
New York, NY 10001
Phone: 212-465-6471
Fax: 212-465-6026

CEO: David Checketts
CFO: Mickey Alper
HR: Aimee Kaye
Employees: 28

1995 Sales: $79.2 million
1-Yr. Sales Change: 1.9%
Ownership: Subsidiary

Leisure & recreational services - professional basketball team (subsidiary of ITT Corp.)

NEW YORK LIFE INSURANCE COMPANY

51 Madison Ave.
New York, NY 10010
Phone: 212-576-7000
Fax: 212-576-8145

CEO: Harry G. Hohn
CFO: Jay S. Calhoun III
HR: George J. Trapp
Employees: 15,534

1994 Sales: $15,807 million
1-Yr. Sales Change: 0.1%
Ownership: Privately Held

Insurance - life

 See pages 184–185 for a full profile of this company.

NEW YORK POWER AUTHORITY

1633 Broadway
New York, NY 10019
Phone: 212-468-6000
Fax: 212-468-6040

CEO: Clarence D. Rappleyea
CFO: Robert L. Tscherne
HR: Deborah P. Estrin
Employees: 3,500

1994 Sales: $1,460 million
1-Yr. Sales Change: 2.1%
Ownership: Privately Held

Utility - electric power (#1 nonfederal power generating company in US); nuclear, hydro & fossil fuel plants; energy control center

THE NEW YORK PUBLIC LIBRARY

476 Fifth Ave.
New York, NY 10018
Phone: 212-930-0800
Fax: 212-768-7439

CEO: Paul LeClerc
CFO: Michael Zavelle
HR: Priscilla J. Southon
Employees: 3,680

1994 Sales: $176.4 million
1-Yr. Sales Change: —
Ownership: Privately Held

Library

NEW YORK RANGERS

2 Penn Plaza
New York, NY 10001
Phone: 212-465-6000
Fax: 212-465-6026

CEO: Neil Smith
CFO: Mickey Alper
HR: Aimee Kaye
Employees: 31

1995 Sales: $49.2 million
1-Yr. Sales Change: -11.7%
Ownership: Subsidiary

Leisure & recreational services - professional hockey team (subsidiary of ITT Corp.)

NEW YORK STOCK EXCHANGE, INC.

11 Wall St.
New York, NY 10005
Phone: 212-656-3000
Fax: 212-656-2126

Stock exchange

CEO: Richard A. Grasso
CFO: Keith R. Helsby
HR: Joseph P. Johnson
Employees: 1,450

1994 Sales: $452.3 million
1-Yr. Sales Change: 1.6%
Ownership: Privately Held

THE NEW YORK TIMES COMPANY

229 W. 43rd St.
New York, NY 10036
Phone: 212-556-1234
Fax: 212-556-3722

CEO: Arthur Ochs Sulzberger
CFO: Diane P. Baker
HR: Katharine P. Darrow
Employees: 12,800

1994 Sales: $2,357.6 mil.
1-Yr. Sales Change: 16.7%
Exchange: AMEX
Symbol: NYTA

Publishing - newspapers & magazines; broadcasting; information services

 See pages 186–187 for a full profile of this company.

NEW YORK UNIVERSITY

70 Washington Sq. South
New York, NY 10012
Phone: 212-998-1212
Fax: 212-995-4040

CEO: L. Jay Oliva
CFO: Harold T. Read
HR: —
Employees: 15,300

1994 Sales: $1,408.9 mil.
1-Yr. Sales Change: 6.4%
Ownership: Privately Held

Public university offering 160 undergraduate & 155 graduate degree programs

NEW YORK YANKEES

Bronx Stadium
New York, NY 10451
Phone: 718-293-4300
Fax: 718-293-8431

CEO: George Steinbrenner
CFO: David Sussman
HR: Harvey Winston
Employees: 120

1994 Sales: $71.5 million
1-Yr. Sales Change: -33.6%
Ownership: Privately Held

Leisure & professional services - professional baseball team

THE NEWARK GROUP, INC.

20 Jackson Dr.
Cranford, NJ 07016
Phone: 908-276-4000
Fax: 908-276-2888

CEO: Fred G. vonZuben
CFO: William D. Harper
HR: Carl R. Crook
Employees: 2,700

1995 Sales: $700 million
1-Yr. Sales Change: 42.9%
Ownership: Privately Held

Paper & paper products - recycled paperboard & converted products

NEWS COMMUNICATIONS, INC.

174-15 Horace Harding Expwy.
Fresh Meadows, NY 11365
Phone: 718-357-3380
Fax: 718-357-4833

CEO: Michael Schenkler
CFO: Robert Berkowitz
HR: Evelyn Spiegel
Employees: 294

1994 Sales: $13.7 million
1-Yr. Sales Change: 53.9%
Exchange: Nasdaq (SC)
Symbol: NCOM

Advertising - community newspapers & related target audience publications

NEXTEL COMMUNICATIONS, INC.

201 Rte. 17 North
Rutherford, NJ 07070
Phone: 201-438-1400
Fax: 201-438-5540

CEO: Dennis Weibling
CFO: Louis Salamone Jr.
HR: Lane Foster
Employees: 1,600

1995 Sales: $83.7 million
1-Yr. Sales Change: 23.3%
Exchange: Nasdaq
Symbol: CALL

Telecommunications services - mobile radio wireless communication services

 See page 283 for a full profile of this company.

NFO RESEARCH, INC.

2 Pickwick Plaza, Ste. 400
Greenwich, CT 06830
Phone: 203-629-8888
Fax: 203-629-8790

CEO: William E. Lipner
CFO: Patrick G. Healy
HR: Candace S. Burch
Employees: 795

1994 Sales: $61.5 million
1-Yr. Sales Change: 18.5%
Exchange: Nasdaq
Symbol: NFOR

Business services - consumer opinion & information research

NICE-PAK PRODUCTS, INC.

2 Nice-Pak Park
Orangeburg, NJ 10962
Phone: 914-365-1700
Fax: 914-365-1717

CEO: Robert Julius
CFO: Enzo Vialardi
HR: Dennis Brody
Employees: 900

1994 Sales: $148 million
1-Yr. Sales Change: 5.7%
Ownership: Privately Held

Paper & paper products - wipes & towelettes

NINE WEST GROUP INC.

9 W. Broad St.
Stamford, CT 06902
Phone: 203-324-7567
Fax: 203-328-3550

CEO: Vincent Camuto
CFO: Richard L. White
HR: Debra Trautman
Employees: 4,021

1994 Sales: $652.2 million
1-Yr. Sales Change: 18.1%
Exchange: NYSE
Symbol: NIN

Shoes & related apparel (Nine West, 9 & Co., Calico, Enzo Angiolini)

NMR OF AMERICA, INC.

430 Mountain Ave.	CEO: Joseph G. Dasti	1995 Sales: $18 million
Murray Hill, NJ 07974-2732	CFO: John P. O'Malley III	1-Yr. Sales Change: 15.4%
Phone: 908-665-9400	HR: Leslie Cohen	Exchange: Nasdaq
Fax: 908-665-2767	Employees: 117	Symbol: NMRR

Medical services - magnetic resonance imaging

NOBODY BEATS THE WIZ

1300 Federal Blvd.	CEO: Lawrence Jemal	1995 Est. Sales: $950 mil.
Carteret, NJ 07008	CFO: Stan Berg	1-Yr. Sales Change: 26.7%
Phone: 908-602-1900	HR: Bob Brummer	Ownership: Privately Held
Fax: 908-634-6856	Employees: 4,285	

Retail - consumer electronics superstores in the New York City metro area

📖 **See page 284 for a full profile of this company.**

NOEL GROUP, INC.

667 Madison Ave.	CEO: Stanley R. Rawn Jr.	1994 Sales: $193.7 million
New York, NY 10021	CFO: Todd K. West	1-Yr. Sales Change: 29.2%
Phone: 212-371-1400	HR: —	Exchange: Nasdaq
Fax: 212-593-0188	Employees: 6,025	Symbol: NOEL

Diversified operations - managed health care services, oil & gas, medical technology & mushroom production

NOISE CANCELLATION TECHNOLOGIES, INC.

800 Summer St.	CEO: John McCloy	1994 Sales: $7.1 million
Stamford, CT 06901	CFO: Stephen J. Fogarty	1-Yr. Sales Change: 31.5%
Phone: 203-961-0500	HR: Fronnie Redd	Exchange: Nasdaq
Fax: 203-348-4100	Employees: 90	Symbol: NCTI

Engineering - noise & vibration reduction technology

NOODLE KIDOODLE, INC.

105 Price Pkwy.	CEO: Stanley Greenman	1995 Sales: $136.5 million
Farmingdale, NY 11735	CFO: William A. Johnson Jr.	1-Yr. Sales Change: -4.5%
Phone: 516-293-5300	HR: Wendy Hague	Exchange: Nasdaq
Fax: 516-420-8738	Employees: 595	Symbol: NKID

Wholesale distribution - housewares, toys & stationery; retail children's toys, books & educational products (Noodle Kidoodle)

NORLAND MEDICAL SYSTEMS, INC.

142 Temple St.
New Haven, CT 06510
Phone: 203-789-8214
Fax: 203-789-8261

CEO: Reynald G. Bonmati
CFO: John W. Buckman
HR: —
Employees: 12

1994 Sales: $10 million
1-Yr. Sales Change: —
Exchange: Nasdaq
Symbol: OSTC

Medical instruments - systems that measure bone density in order to diagnose & monitor bone disorders, including osteoporosis

NORTH AMERICAN WATCH CORPORATION

125 Chubb Ave.
Lyndhurst, NJ 07071
Phone: 201-460-4800
Fax: 201-460-4540

CEO: Gedalio Grinberg
CFO: William J. Diamond
HR: Vivian D'Elia
Employees: 543

1995 Sales: $160.9 million
1-Yr. Sales Change: 13.2%
Exchange: Nasdaq
Symbol: NAWC

Precious metals & jewelry - watches (Piaget, Corum, Movado, Concord)

NORTH EUROPEAN OIL ROYALTY TRUST

43 W. Front St., Ste. 19A
Red Bank, NJ 07701
Phone: 908-741-4008
Fax: 908-741-3140

CEO: John H. Van Kirk
CFO: John R. Van Kirk
HR: —
Employees: 2

1994 Sales: $8.8 million
1-Yr. Sales Change: -13.7%
Exchange: NYSE
Symbol: NET

Oil & gas - US royalty trust

NORTH SIDE SAVINGS BANK

170 Tulip Ave.
Floral Park, NY 11001
Phone: 516-488-6900
Fax: 516-488-6546

CEO: Thomas M. O'Brien
CFO: Donald C. Fleming
HR: George D. Carter
Employees: —

1994 Sales: $94.2 million
1-Yr. Sales Change: -6.1%
Exchange: Nasdaq
Symbol: NSBK

Financial - savings & loans

NORTON MCNAUGHTON, INC.

463 Seventh Ave., 9th Fl.
New York, NY 10018
Phone: 212-947-2960
Fax: 212-563-2766

CEO: Sanford Greenberg
CFO: Amanda J. Bokman
HR: Mary Tackmann
Employees: 240

1994 Sales: $168.6 million
1-Yr. Sales Change: 26.5%
Exchange: Nasdaq
Symbol: NRTY

Apparel - women's & juniors' outerwear

NORWALK SAVINGS SOCIETY

48 Wall St.
Norwalk, CT 06852
Phone: 203-838-4545
Fax: 203-838-7570

Banks - Northeast

CEO: Robert T. Judson
CFO: Marcus I. Braverman
HR: Jeremiah T. Dorney
Employees: 139

1994 Sales: $26.9 million
1-Yr. Sales Change: -7.6%
Exchange: Nasdaq
Symbol: NSSY

NOVADIGM, INC.

One International Blvd., Ste. 200
Mahwah, NJ 07495
Phone: 201-512-1000
Fax: 201-512-1452

CEO: Albion J. Fitzgerald
CFO: Wallace D. Ruiz
HR: —
Employees: 70

1995 Sales: $9.3 million
1-Yr. Sales Change: 745.5%
Exchange: Nasdaq
Symbol: NVDM

Computers - networking & connectivity system management software applications for medium & large organizations

NOVAMETRIX MEDICAL SYSTEMS INC.

One Barnes Industrial Park Rd.
Wallingford, CT 06492
Phone: 203-265-7701
Fax: 203-284-0753

CEO: William J. Lacourciere
CFO: Joseph A. Vincent
HR: Lorraine Tagliatela
Employees: 166

1995 Sales: $24 million
1-Yr. Sales Change: 15.4%
Exchange: Nasdaq
Symbol: NMTX

Medical instruments - noninvasive, critical-care blood gas monitors, respiratory monitors & related disposable products

NU HORIZONS ELECTRONIC CORP.

6000 New Horizons Blvd.
Amityville, NY 11701
Phone: 516-226-6000
Fax: 516-226-5505

CEO: Irving Lubman
CFO: Paul Durando
HR: Patty Englert
Employees: 307

1995 Sales: $130.3 million
1-Yr. Sales Change: 41.0%
Exchange: Nasdaq
Symbol: NUHC

Electronics - parts distribution

 See page 285 for a full profile of this company.

NUI CORPORATION

550 Rte. 202-206, PO Box 760
Bedminster, NJ 07921-0760
Phone: 908-781-0500
Fax: 908-781-0718

CEO: John Kean
CFO: David P. Vincent
HR: Thomas J. Lynch
Employees: 1,167

1995 Sales: $376.4 million
1-Yr. Sales Change: -4.2%
Exchange: NYSE
Symbol: NUI

Utility - gas distribution

NUTMEG FEDERAL SAVINGS AND LOAN ASSOCIATION

301 Main St., Wooster Plaza
Danbury, CT 06810
Phone: 203-792-3332
Fax: 203-791-2443

CEO: Henry A. Bessel Jr.
CFO: David F. Lucas
HR: Ann E. McCabe
Employees: 44

1994 Sales: $5.8 million
1-Yr. Sales Change: -6.5%
Exchange: Nasdaq (SC)
Symbol: NTMG

Financial - savings & loans (Nutmeg Federal Savings & Loan)

N W AYER INC.

825 Eighth Ave.
New York, NY 10019
Phone: 212-474-5000
Fax: 212-474-5400

CEO: MaryLou Quinlan
CFO: Anthony O'Gorman
HR: Jane Beale
Employees: 575

1994 Sales: $98.8 million
1-Yr. Sales Change: -8.9%
Ownership: Privately Held

Advertising

NYCOR, INC.

287 Childs Rd.
Basking Ridge, NJ 07920
Phone: 908-953-8200
Fax: 908-953-0100

CEO: Sal Giordano Jr.
CFO: Kent E. Hansen
HR: Kent E. Hansen
Employees: 812

1994 Sales: $75.2 million
1-Yr. Sales Change: 27.0%
Exchange: Nasdaq
Symbol: NYCO

Machinery - rotary compressors & thermoelectric modules

See page 286 for a full profile of this company.

NYMAGIC, INC.

330 Madison Ave.
New York, NY 10017
Phone: 212-551-0600
Fax: 212-986-1310

CEO: Mark W. Blackman
CFO: Thomas J. Iacopelli
HR: Laura Moreno
Employees: 123

1994 Sales: $103.6 million
1-Yr. Sales Change: 12.2%
Exchange: NYSE
Symbol: NYM

Insurance - property & casualty

NYNEX CORPORATION

1095 Avenue of the Americas
New York, NY 10036
Phone: 212-395-2121
Fax: 212-921-2684

CEO: Ivan G. Seidenberg
CFO: Alan Z. Senter
HR: Donald J. Sacco
Employees: 65,400

1994 Sales: $13,306.6 mil.
1-Yr. Sales Change: -0.8%
Exchange: NYSE
Symbol: NYN

Utility - telephone; publishing

See pages 188–189 for a full profile of this company.

NYTEST ENVIRONMENTAL INC.

60 Seaview Blvd.	CEO: John Gaspari	1994 Sales: $6 million
Port Washington, NY 11050	CFO: Elliot J. Laitman	1-Yr. Sales Change: -20.0%
Phone: 516-625-5500	HR: —	Exchange: Nasdaq (SC)
Fax: 516-625-1274	Employees: 84	Symbol: NYTS

Specialized analytical services for the accurate measurement of hazardous wastes

OAK HILL SPORTSWEAR CORPORATION

1411 Broadway	CEO: Arthur L. Asch	1994 Sales: $84.2 million
New York, NY 10018	CFO: Michael A. Asch	1-Yr. Sales Change: 0.4%
Phone: 212-789-8900	HR: —	Exchange: Nasdaq
Fax: 212-789-8924	Employees: 425	Symbol: OHSC

Apparel - women's sportswear & accessories (Victoria Jones, Victoria Sport, Casey & Max, Harmal)

OCG TECHNOLOGY, INC.

450 W. 31st St.	CEO: Edward C. Levine	1995 Sales: $0.6 million
New York, NY 10001-4608	CFO: Edward C. Levine	1-Yr. Sales Change: 20.0%
Phone: 212-967-3079	HR: —	Exchange: Nasdaq (SC)
Fax: 212-967-3217	Employees: 15	Symbol: OCGT

Medical instruments - heart diagnostic machines

ODYSSEY PARTNERS, LP

31 W. 52nd St.	CEO: Leon Levy	1995 Sales: —
New York, NY 10019	CFO: Lawrence Levitt	1-Yr. Sales Change: —
Phone: 212-708-0600	HR: Mary Parker	Ownership: Privately Held
Fax: 212-708-0770	Employees: 100	

Financial - leveraged buyouts & portfolio management

OGDEN CORPORATION

2 Pennsylvania Plaza	CEO: R. Richard Ablon	1994 Sales: $2,110.2 mil.
New York, NY 10121	CFO: Philip G. Husby	1-Yr. Sales Change: 3.5%
Phone: 212-868-6100	HR: David Belka	Exchange: NYSE
Fax: 212-868-5714	Employees: 45,000	Symbol: OG

Diversified operations - facility management & maintenance; in-flight catering; hazardous waste disposal; aviation services

OKONITE COMPANY

PO Box 340
Ramsey, NJ 07446
Phone: 201-825-0300
Fax: 201-825-2672

CEO: Alfred Coppola
CFO: David J. Sokira
HR: Thomas M. Scanlon
Employees: 1,000

1994 Sales: $150 million
1-Yr. Sales Change: 0.0%
Ownership: Privately Held

Insulated wire & cable products

OLD LYME HOLDING CORPORATION

122 E. 42nd St.
New York, NY 10168
Phone: 212-338-2100
Fax: 212-986-2808

CEO: Lawrence Greenfield
CFO: Daniel Benjamin
HR: —
Employees: 83

1994 Sales: $21.1 million
1-Yr. Sales Change: 4.5%
Exchange: Nasdaq
Symbol: OLHC

Insurance - property & casualty risks (Old Lyme Insurance Company of Rhode Island, Inc., Old Lyme
Insurance Company, Ltd.)

OLIN CORPORATION

501 Merritt 7, PO Box 4500
Norwalk, CT 06856-4500
Phone: 203-750-3000
Fax: 203-750-3292

CEO: Donald W. Griffin
CFO: Anthony W. Ruggiero
HR: Peter C. Kosche
Employees: 12,800

1994 Sales: $2,658.1 mil.
1-Yr. Sales Change: 9.7%
Exchange: NYSE
Symbol: OLN

Diversified operations - chemicals; defense products & ammunition; metals; sporting ammunition
(Winchester)

THE OLSTEN CORPORATION

175 Broad Hollow Rd.
Melville, NY 11747
Phone: 516-844-7800
Fax: 516-844-7022

CEO: Frank N. Liguori
CFO: Anthony J. Puglisi
HR: Martin Gelerman
Employees: 557,900

1994 Sales: $2,260.3 mil.
1-Yr. Sales Change: 4.8%
Exchange: NYSE
Symbol: OLS

Personnel - temporary-employment services; home health care provider

OMI CORP.

90 Park Ave.
New York, NY 10016
Phone: 212-986-1960
Fax: 212-297-2100

CEO: Jack Goldstein
CFO: Vincent J. de Sostoa
HR: Anthony Naccarato
Employees: 964

1994 Sales: $266.8 million
1-Yr. Sales Change: -1.4%
Exchange: NYSE
Symbol: OMM

Transportation - 43 charter tankers & dry bulk carriers

OMNICOM GROUP INC.

437 Madison Ave.
New York, NY 10022
Phone: 212-415-3600
Fax: 212-415-3530

CEO: Bruce Crawford
CFO: Fred J. Meyer
HR: Leslie Chiocco
Employees: 16,100

1994 Sales: $1,756.2 mil.
1-Yr. Sales Change: 15.8%
Exchange: NYSE
Symbol: OMC

Advertising agencies (BBDO Worldwide, DDB Needham, TBWA Chiat/Day)

ONCOGENE SCIENCE, INC.

106 Charles Lindbergh Blvd.
Uniondale, NY 11553-3649
Phone: 516-222-0023
Fax: 516-222-0114

CEO: Gary E. Frashier
CFO: Robert L. Van Nostrand
HR: Ann McDermott
Employees: 126

1995 Sales: $15.9 million
1-Yr. Sales Change: -2.5%
Exchange: Nasdaq
Symbol: ONCS

Biomedical & genetic products

ONCORX, INC.

4 Science Park
New Haven, CT 06511
Phone: 203-498-4210
Fax: 203-498-4211

CEO: John A. Spears
CFO: Thomas Klein
HR: —
Employees: 4

1994 Sales: $0
1-Yr. Sales Change: —
Exchange: Nasdaq
Symbol: OCRX

Biomedical - R&D of therapeutic products for the treatment of cancer

ONE LIBERTY PROPERTIES, INC.

60 Cutter Mill Rd.
Great Neck, NY 11021
Phone: 516-466-3100
Fax: 516-466-3132

CEO: Matthew Gould
CFO: David W. Kalish
HR: David W. Kalish
Employees: —

1994 Sales: $4.1 million
1-Yr. Sales Change: 24.2%
Exchange: AMEX
Symbol: OLP

Real estate investment trust to invest primarily in improved commercial real estate under long-term net lease

OPPENHEIMER CAPITAL L.P.

World Financial Center
New York, NY 10281
Phone: 212-667-7000
Fax: 212-667-5988

CEO: Joseph M. La Motta
CFO: Sheldon M. Siegel
HR: —
Employees: 350

1995 Sales: $34.3 million
1-Yr. Sales Change: -2.3%
Exchange: NYSE
Symbol: OCC

Financial - investment management

ORANGE AND ROCKLAND UTILITIES, INC.

One Blue Hill Plaza	CEO: D. Louis Peoples	1994 Sales: $1,016.9 mil.
Pearl River, NY 10965	CFO: R. Lee Haney	1-Yr. Sales Change: 5.1%
Phone: 914-352-6000	HR: Thomas A. Folchi Jr.	Exchange: NYSE
Fax: 914-577-2730	Employees: 1,640	Symbol: ORU

Utility - supplies electric power & natural gas to portions of NJ, NY & PA

ORBIT INSTRUMENT CORPORATION

80 Cabot Ct.	CEO: Dennis Sunshine	1994 Sales: $57.8 million
Hauppauge, NY 11788	CFO: Mitchell Binder	1-Yr. Sales Change: -21.4%
Phone: 516-435-8300	HR: Lynn Cooper	Exchange: Nasdaq
Fax: 516-435-8458	Employees: 478	Symbol: ORBT

Electronics - military

ORBIT INTERNATIONAL CORP.

80 Cabot Ct.	CEO: Dennis Sunshine	1994 Sales: $57.8 million
Hauppauge, NY 11788	CFO: Mitchell Binder	1-Yr. Sales Change: -21.4%
Phone: 516-435-8300	HR: Lynn Cooper	Exchange: Nasdaq
Fax: 516-435-8458	Employees: 546	Symbol: ORBT

Apparel - women's active wear & outerwear & men's outerwear; customized electronic components & subsystems for military & nonmilitary governmental applications

ORION CAPITAL CORPORATION

600 Fifth Ave.	CEO: Alan R. Gruber	1994 Sales: $780.9 million
New York, NY 10020-2302	CFO: Vincent T. Papa	1-Yr. Sales Change: 8.4%
Phone: 212-332-8080	HR: Angelica Catlan	Exchange: NYSE
Fax: 212-581-7261	Employees: 1,500	Symbol: OC

Insurance - property & casualty

OSBORN COMMUNICATIONS CORPORATION

130 Mason St.	CEO: Frank D. Osborn	1994 Sales: $34.1 million
Greenwich, CT 06830	CFO: Thomas S. Douglas	1-Yr. Sales Change: 24.5%
Phone: 203-629-0905	HR: —	Exchange: Nasdaq
Fax: 203-629-1749	Employees: 322	Symbol: OSBN

Broadcasting - radio & TV

OSTEOTECH, INC.

1151 Shrewsbury Ave.	CEO: Richard Bauer	1994 Sales: $24.6 million
Shrewsbury, NJ 07702	CFO: Michael J. Jeffries	1-Yr. Sales Change: 28.8%
Phone: 908-542-2800	HR: Tony Bello	Exchange: Nasdaq
Fax: 908-542-2906	Employees: 164	Symbol: OSTE

Medical services - bone, ligament & tendon processing

OVERSEAS SHIPHOLDING GROUP, INC.

1114 Avenue of the Americas	CEO: Morton P. Hyman	1994 Sales: $364.1 million
New York, NY 10036	CFO: Myles R. Itkin	1-Yr. Sales Change: -6.5%
Phone: 212-869-1222	HR: —	Exchange: NYSE
Fax: 212-536-3776	Employees: 2,000	Symbol: OSG

Transportation - fleet of oceangoing dry bulk vessels & tankers

OVID TECHNOLOGIES, INC.

333 Seventh Ave.	CEO: Mark L. Nelson	1994 Sales: $22.2 million
New York, NY 10001	CFO: Jerry P. McAuliffe	1-Yr. Sales Change: 100.0%
Phone: 212-563-3006	HR: Beatriz Abreu	Exchange: Nasdaq
Fax: 212-563-3784	Employees: 143	Symbol: OVID

Business services - electronic information retrieval services to major medical centers in the US & Canada

OXFORD HEALTH PLANS, INC.

800 Connecticut Ave.	CEO: Stephen F. Wiggins	1994 Sales: $720.7 million
Norwalk, CT 06854	CFO: Andrew B. Cassidy	1-Yr. Sales Change: 131.1%
Phone: 203-852-1442	HR: Jeanne D. Wisniewski	Exchange: Nasdaq
Fax: 203-851-2464	Employees: 1,770	Symbol: OXHP

Health maintenance organization serving the New York City metropolitan area

 See page 287 for a full profile of this company.

OXFORD RESOURCES CORPORATION

270 S. Service Rd.	CEO: Michael C. Pascucci	1995 Sales: $243.1 million
Melville, NY 11747	CFO: Christopher S. Pascucci	1-Yr. Sales Change: 22.6%
Phone: 516-777-8000	HR: Patricia Folan	Exchange: Nasdaq
Fax: 516-777-8440	Employees: 334	Symbol: OXFD

Leasing - new & used autos, primarily Honda Accords & Civics & other mid–price range vehicles

OXIGENE, INC.

110 E. 59th St.	CEO: Bjorn Nordenvall	1994 Sales: $0.3 million
New York, NY 10022	CFO: Bjorn Nordenvall	1-Yr. Sales Change: 200.0%
Phone: 212-421-0001	HR: —	Exchange: Nasdaq (SC)
Fax: 212-421-0475	Employees: 2	Symbol: OXGN

Medical products - blood test that predicts HIV survival

P & F INDUSTRIES, INC.

300 Smith St.	CEO: Richard A. Horowitz	1994 Sales: $45.1 million
Farmingdale, NY 11735-1114	CFO: Leon D. Feldman	1-Yr. Sales Change: 11.6%
Phone: 516-694-1800	HR: —	Exchange: Nasdaq
Fax: 516-694-1836	Employees: 172	Symbol: PFINA

Metal products - fabrication, pneumatic hand tools, pipe cutting & threading tools; baseboard & radiant hot-water heating products

PACE UNIVERSITY

One Pace Plaza	CEO: Patricia Ewers	1994 Sales: $146 million
New York, NY 10038	CFO: Paul Magali	1-Yr. Sales Change: —
Phone: 212-346-1996	HR: Elizabeth H. Valentino	Ownership: Privately Held
Fax: 212-346-1036	Employees: 1,904	

University offering 105 undergraduate & 48 graduate degree programs

PAGE AMERICA GROUP, INC.

125 State St., Ste. 100	CEO: Kathleen Parramore	1994 Sales: $37.3 million
Hackensack, NJ 07601	CFO: Martin Katz	1-Yr. Sales Change: 23.1%
Phone: 201-342-6676	HR: —	Exchange: AMEX
Fax: 201-342-0046	Employees: 269	Symbol: PGG

Paging, messaging & information products & services

PAGING PARTNERS CORPORATION

4249 Rte. 9 North, Bldg. 2	CEO: Richard J. Giacchi	1994 Sales: $4 million
Freehold, NJ 07728	CFO: Jeffrey M. Bachrach	1-Yr. Sales Change: —
Phone: 908-409-7088	HR: —	Exchange: Nasdaq (SC)
Fax: 908-409-7366	Employees: 23	Symbol: PPAR

Telecommunications services - wireless data system (Corridor Network) linking customers between the Washington, DC & Boston markets

PAINE WEBBER GROUP INC.

1285 Avenue of the Americas	CEO: Donald B. Marron	1994 Sales: $3,964.1 mil.
New York, NY 10019	CFO: Regina A. Dolan	1-Yr. Sales Change: -1.0%
Phone: 212-713-2000	HR: Ronald M. Schwartz	Exchange: NYSE
Fax: 212-713-4924	Employees: 16,300	Symbol: PWJ

Financial - investment banking, retail sales, asset management & capital markets (acquired Kidder, Peabody)

 See pages 190–191 for a full profile of this company.

PALL CORPORATION

2200 Northern Blvd.	CEO: Eric Krasnoff	1995 Sales: $829.3 million
East Hills, NY 11548-1289	CFO: Jeremy Hayward-Surry	1-Yr. Sales Change: 18.3%
Phone: 516-484-5400	HR: Geri Schwalb	Exchange: NYSE
Fax: 516-484-3529	Employees: 6,500	Symbol: PLL

Filtration products for the health care, aerospace & defense & fluid processing industries

PAMRAPO BANCORP, INC.

611 Avenue C	CEO: William J. Campbell	1994 Sales: $30.5 million
Bayonne, NJ 07002	CFO: Gary J. Thomas	1-Yr. Sales Change: -5.0%
Phone: 201-339-4600	HR: Anthony Massarelli	Exchange: Nasdaq
Fax: 201-339-7375	Employees: 128	Symbol: PBCI

Banks - Northeast (Pamrapo Savings Bank, S.L.A.)

PANAMSAT CORPORATION

One Pickwick Plaza	CEO: Frederick A. Landman	1994 Sales: $63.7 million
Greenwich, CT 06830	CFO: Patrick J. Costello	1-Yr. Sales Change: 25.4%
Phone: 203-622-6664	HR: Maria Frankeo	Exchange: Nasdaq
Fax: 203-622-9163	Employees: 150	Symbol: SPOT

Telecommunications equipment - first private global satellite system for general communications

PANAX PHARMACEUTICAL COMPANY LTD.

425 Park Ave., 27th Fl.	CEO: Taffy J. Williams	1995 Sales: $0.1 million
New York, NY 10022	CFO: Norman Eisner	1-Yr. Sales Change: —
Phone: 212-319-8300	HR: —	Exchange: Nasdaq (SC)
Fax: 212-751-4131	Employees: 27	Symbol: PANX

Drugs - pharmaceutical compounds identified in & isolated from plants

PAPETTI'S HYGRADE EGG PRODUCTS, INC.

One Papetti Plaza	CEO: Arthur Papetti	1994 Sales: $200 million
Elizabeth, NJ 07206	CFO: Joe Vagnuolo	1-Yr. Sales Change: 34.2%
Phone: 908-354-4844	HR: —	Ownership: Privately Held
Fax: 908-354-8660	Employees: 500	

Food - poultry slaughtering & processing

PARK ELECTROCHEMICAL CORP.

5 Dakota Dr.	CEO: Jerry Shore	1995 Sales: $253 million
Lake Success, NY 11042	CFO: Paul R. Shackford	1-Yr. Sales Change: 21.4%
Phone: 516-354-4100	HR: —	Exchange: NYSE
Fax: 516-354-4128	Employees: 1,830	Symbol: PKE

Electrical components - advanced laminates & other circuit board materials; bathtub spouts, shower heads & faucet housings; specialty resins for aerospace, military, recreational & telecommunications products

PARSONS & WHITTEMORE, INC.

4 International Dr.	CEO: George F. Landegger	1994 Sales: $1,181 million
Rye Brook, NY 10573	CFO: Robert Masson	1-Yr. Sales Change: 35.7%
Phone: 914-937-9009	HR: Richard Martin	Ownership: Privately Held
Fax: 914-937-2259	Employees: 1,800	

Diversified operations - pulp & paper, industrial machinery

PARSONS BRINCKERHOFF, INC.

One Penn Plaza	CEO: James L. Lammie	1994 Sales: $470 million
New York, NY 10119	CFO: Nicholas Davy	1-Yr. Sales Change: 19.6%
Phone: 212-465-5000	HR: John Ryan	Ownership: Privately Held
Fax: 212-465-5591	Employees: 4,800	

Consulting - engineering

PATHMARK STORES, INC.

301 Blair Rd., PO Box 5301	CEO: Jack Futterman	1995 Sales: $4,182 million
Woodbridge, NJ 07095-0915	CFO: Ron Marshall	1-Yr. Sales Change: -0.6%
Phone: 908-499-3000	HR: Maureen McGurl	Ownership: Privately Held
Fax: 908-499-3072	Employees: 29,000	

Retail - supermarkets, drugstores & home improvement centers

See pages 192–193 for a full profile of this company.

PATRICOF & CO. VENTURES, INC.

445 Park Ave.	CEO: Alan J. Patricof	1995 Sales: —
New York, NY 10022	CFO: Arthur Burach	1-Yr. Sales Change: —
Phone: 212-753-6300	HR: Sue Smith	Ownership: Privately Held
Fax: 212-319-6155	Employees: 75	

Financial - investors

PATRIOT NATIONAL BANK

900 Bedford St.	CEO: Philip Wolford	1995 Sales: $0.3 million
Stamford, CT 06901	CFO: Philip Wolford	1-Yr. Sales Change: —
Phone: 203-324-7500	HR: —	Exchange: Nasdaq (SC)
Fax: 203-324-8877	Employees: 25	Symbol: PNBK

Banks - Northeast

PAUL, WEISS, RIFKIND, WHARTON & GARRISON

1285 Avenue of the Americas	CEO: Burton J. Cohen	1994 Sales: $175.5 million
New York, NY 10019	CFO: Emil Sommer	1-Yr. Sales Change: 4.2%
Phone: 212-373-3000	HR: —	Ownership: Privately Held
Fax: 212-373-2268	Employees: 850	

Law firm

PAXAR CORPORATION

105 Corporate Park Dr.	CEO: Arthur Hershaft	1994 Sales: $166.6 million
White Plains, NY 10604	CFO: Jack R. Plaxe	1-Yr. Sales Change: 20.0%
Phone: 914-697-6800	HR: Todd Barnett	Exchange: NYSE
Fax: 914-696-4128	Employees: 1,891	Symbol: PXR

Printed labels, woven labels & merchandise tags; bar-code tag & labeling systems for the apparel & textile industries

P.C. RICHARD & SON

2095 Express Dr. North	CEO: Gary H. Richard	1994 Sales: $400 million
New York, NY 11788	CFO: Tom Pohmer	1-Yr. Sales Change: 0.0%
Phone: 516-582-3800	HR: —	Ownership: Privately Held
Fax: 516-843-4469	Employees: 1,500	

Retail - appliances, electronics & home office products

PC WAREHOUSE INVESTMENT, INC.

174 State Rte. 17 North
Rochelle Park, NJ 07662
Phone: 201-587-9600
Fax: 201-587-1734

Computers - software stores

CEO: Robin Lu
CFO: Sean Chen
HR: Suzanne Tseng
Employees: 350

1994 Sales: $321 million
1-Yr. Sales Change: 8.8%
Ownership: Privately Held

PDK LABS, INC.

145 Ricefield Ln.
Hauppauge, NY 11788
Phone: 516-273-2630
Fax: 516-273-1582

Vitamins & nutritional products & nonprescription pharmaceuticals

CEO: Michael B. Krasnoff
CFO: Michael B. Krasnoff
HR: —
Employees: 88

1994 Sales: $21.2 million
1-Yr. Sales Change: 13.4%
Exchange: Nasdaq (SC)
Symbol: PDKL

PEC ISRAEL ECONOMIC CORPORATION

511 Fifth Ave.
New York, NY 10017
Phone: 212-687-2400
Fax: 212-599-6281

Financial - investment management of companies related to or located in Israel

CEO: Frank J. Klein
CFO: William Gold
HR: —
Employees: —

1994 Sales: $47.7 million
1-Yr. Sales Change: -26.8%
Exchange: AMEX
Symbol: IEC

PEERLESS IMPORTERS, INC.

16 Bridgewater St.
New York, NY 11222
Phone: 718-383-5500
Fax: 718-383-5500

Beverages - wine & liquor distribution

CEO: John Magliocco
CFO: —
HR: —
Employees: 1,200

1994 Sales: $585 million
1-Yr. Sales Change: 9.3%
Ownership: Privately Held

PEERLESS TUBE COMPANY

58-76 Locust Ave.
Bloomfield, NJ 07003
Phone: 201-743-5100
Fax: 201-743-6169

Containers - collapsible metal tubes & seamless extruded aluminum aerosol containers for the pharmaceutical, drug, cosmetic toiletries & household product industries

CEO: Frederic Remington Jr.
CFO: Paul Peterik
HR: Paul Peterik
Employees: 260

1994 Sales: $33.1 million
1-Yr. Sales Change: -3.2%
Exchange: OTC
Symbol: PLSU

PENNCORP FINANCIAL GROUP, INC.

745 Fifth Ave., Ste. 500
New York, NY 10151
Phone: 212-832-0700
Fax: 212-758-5442

CEO: David J. Stone
CFO: Steven W. Fickes
HR: Pam Hutton
Employees: 806

1994 Sales: $293.8 million
1-Yr. Sales Change: 17.4%
Exchange: NYSE
Symbol: PFG

Insurance - accident & life insurance (American-Amicable Life Insurance Co. of Texas, Occidental Life Insurance Co. of North Carolina, Professional Insurance Corp., Pennsylvania Life Insurance Co.)

PENNFED FINANCIAL SERVICES, INC.

622 Eagle Rock Ave.
West Orange, NJ 07052-2989
Phone: 201-669-7366
Fax: 201-669-7574

CEO: Joseph L. LaMonica
CFO: Jeffrey J. Carfora
HR: —
Employees: 197

1995 Sales: $54.8 million
1-Yr. Sales Change: 22.6%
Exchange: Nasdaq
Symbol: PFSB

Banks - Northeast (Penn Federal Savings Bank)

PENTECH INTERNATIONAL, INC.

195 Carter Dr.
Edison, NJ 08817
Phone: 908-287-6640
Fax: 908-287-6610

CEO: Norman Melnick
CFO: David Melnick
HR: Libby Melnick
Employees: 163

1995 Sales: $54.9 million
1-Yr. Sales Change: -11.6%
Exchange: Nasdaq
Symbol: PNTK

Office & art materials - pens, markers & other writing instruments (Pentech)

PEOPLE'S BANK

850 Main St.
Bridgeport, CT 06604-4913
Phone: 203-579-7171
Fax: 203-338-3600

CEO: David E. A. Carson
CFO: George W. Morriss
HR: Bryan J. Huebner
Employees: 2,700

1994 Sales: $530.5 million
1-Yr. Sales Change: 5.4%
Exchange: Nasdaq
Symbol: PBCT

Banks - Northeast (People's Bank)

PEOPLE'S CHOICE TV CORP.

2 Corporate Dr.
Shelton, CT 06484
Phone: 203-925-7900
Fax: 203-929-1454

CEO: Matthew Oristano
CFO: Charles F. Schwartz
HR: Pamela Yager
Employees: 521

1994 Sales: $12.6 million
1-Yr. Sales Change: 117.2%
Exchange: Nasdaq
Symbol: PCTV

Broadcasting - radio & TV

PEPSICO, INC.

Purchase, NY 10577-1444	CEO: D. Wayne Calloway	1994 Sales: $28,472.4 mil.
Phone: 914-253-2000	CFO: Robert G. Dettmer	1-Yr. Sales Change: 13.8%
Fax: 914-253-2070	HR: William Bensyl	Exchange: NYSE
	Employees: 471,000	Symbol: PEP

Beverages - soft drinks (Pepsi, Mountain Dew, Slice); snack foods (Frito-Lay); restaurants (KFC, Pizza Hut, Taco Bell)

 See pages 194–195 for a full profile of this company.

PEPSI-COLA BOTTLING COMPANY OF LONG ISLAND CITY

4600 Fifth Ave.	CEO: Marvin Goldstein	1994 Est. Sales: $210 mil.
Long Island City, NY 11101	CFO: Richard Sanzari	1-Yr. Sales Change: 0.0%
Phone: 718-392-1000	HR: Terry Noschese	Ownership: Privately Held
Fax: 718-392-1118	Employees: 940	

Beverages - soft drink bottling

PERGAMENT HOME CENTERS, INC.

101 Marcus Dr.	CEO: Robert Tammero	1994 Sales: $450 million
New York, NY 11747	CFO: Steve Coleman	1-Yr. Sales Change: 0.0%
Phone: 516-694-9300	HR: Robert Kramer	Ownership: Privately Held
Fax: 516-694-2411	Employees: 2,500	

Building products - home improvement & decorating products retail chain

PERIPHONICS CORPORATION

4000 Veterans Memorial Hwy.	CEO: Peter J. Cohen	1995 Sales: $64.8 million
Bohemia, NY 11716-1024	CFO: Kevin J. O'Brien	1-Yr. Sales Change: 25.8%
Phone: 516-467-0500	HR: Janet Anderson	Exchange: Nasdaq
Fax: 516-737-8520	Employees: 421	Symbol: PERI

Telecommunications equipment - interactive voice-response systems for accessing computer databases from a touch-tone phone

PERKIN-ELMER CORPORATION

761 Main Ave.	CEO: Tony L. White	1995 Sales: $1,063.5 mil.
Norwalk, CT 06859-0001	CFO: Stephen O. Jaeger	1-Yr. Sales Change: 3.8%
Phone: 203-762-1000	HR: Michael J. McPartland	Exchange: NYSE
Fax: 203-762-6000	Employees: 5,890	Symbol: PKN

Instruments - scientific biochemical analytical instrument systems used for synthesis, amplification, purification, isolation, analysis & sequencing of nucleic acids, proteins & biological molecules

PERRY H. KOPLIK & SONS INC.

505 Park Ave.	CEO: Michael R. Koplik	1994 Sales: $462 million
New York, NY 10022	CFO: Edward Stein	1-Yr. Sales Change: 12.7%
Phone: 212-752-2288	HR: Alvin Siegel	Ownership: Privately Held
Fax: 212-838-8790	Employees: 105	

Paper & paper products - forest products

PERSONAL DIAGNOSTICS, INC.

3 Entin Rd.	CEO: John H. Ichael	1994 Sales: $6.3 million
Parsippany, NJ 07054	CFO: Alan R. Shandler	1-Yr. Sales Change: -58.6%
Phone: 201-952-9000	HR: —	Exchange: Nasdaq (SC)
Fax: 201-428-9832	Employees: 34	Symbol: PERS

Medical services - contract precision machining services to the orthopedic market; components for artificial knees, hips, elbows & wrists; bone screws

PETRIE RETAIL, INC.

70 Enterprise Ave.	CEO: Verna Gibson	1994 Sales: $1,480.1 mil.
Secaucus, NJ 07094	CFO: Max Roberts	1-Yr. Sales Change: 2.9%
Phone: 201-866-3600	HR: —	Ownership: Privately Held
Fax: 201-864-9167	Employees: 19,500	

Retail - women's apparel (1,300 units: Petrie, Marianne, Stuarts, Jean Nicole, G&G, Winkelman's)

PETROLEUM HEAT AND POWER CO., INC.

2187 Atlantic St.	CEO: Irik P. Sevin	1994 Sales: $546.7 million
Stamford, CT 06902	CFO: Irik P. Sevin	1-Yr. Sales Change: 1.5%
Phone: 203-325-5400	HR: Michael Gleave	Exchange: Nasdaq
Fax: 203-328-7422	Employees: 2,574	Symbol: HEAT

Oil refining & marketing

PFIZER INC.

235 E. 42nd St.	CEO: William C. Steere Jr.	1994 Sales: $8,281.3 mil.
New York, NY 10017-5755	CFO: David Shedlarz	1-Yr. Sales Change: 10.7%
Phone: 212-573-2323	HR: Bruce R. Ellig	Exchange: NYSE
Fax: 212-573-7851	Employees: 40,800	Symbol: PFE

Diversified operations - drugs; surgical, orthopedic & cardiac devices; animal-health products; specialty chemicals & minerals; consumer products

 See pages 196–197 for a full profile of this company.

PHARMACEUTICAL RESOURCES, INC.

One Ram Ridge Rd.
Spring Valley, NY 10977
Phone: 914-425-7100
Fax: 914-425-7907

Drugs - generic

CEO: Kenneth I. Sawyer
CFO: Robert I. Edinger
HR: Steven Israel
Employees: 430

1995 Sales: $66.5 million
1-Yr. Sales Change: -5.1%
Exchange: NYSE
Symbol: PRX

PHARMHOUSE CORPORATION

860 Broadway
New York, NY 10003
Phone: 212-477-9400
Fax: 212-477-2900

Retail - deep discount drug & general merchandise stores

CEO: Kenneth Davis
CFO: Marcie Davis
HR: —
Employees: 2,000

1995 Sales: $89.6 million
1-Yr. Sales Change: -8.8%
Exchange: Nasdaq (SC)
Symbol: PHSE

PHARMOS CORPORATION

101 E. 52nd St., 36th Fl.
New York, NY 10022-6030
Phone: 212-838-0087
Fax: 212-223-4669

Drugs - eye & brain disease pharmaceuticals

CEO: Haim Aviv
CFO: S. Colin Neill
HR: S. Colin Neill
Employees: 60

1994 Sales: $0
1-Yr. Sales Change: —
Exchange: Nasdaq (SC)
Symbol: PARS

PHILIPP BROTHERS CHEMICALS, INC.

One Park Plaza
Fort Lee, NJ 07024
Phone: 201-944-6020
Fax: 201-944-6245

Chemicals - organic chemicals for pesticides

CEO: Jack Bendheim
CFO: Nathan Bistricer
HR: Maria Engel
Employees: 600

1994 Sales: $225 million
1-Yr. Sales Change: 18.4%
Ownership: Privately Held

PHILIP MORRIS COMPANIES INC.

120 Park Ave.
New York, NY 10017
Phone: 212-880-5000
Fax: 212-878-2167

Tobacco (Marlboro); food (Kraft); beer (Miller)

CEO: Geoffrey C. Bible
CFO: Hans G. Storr
HR: Larry A. Gates
Employees: 165,000

1994 Sales: $65,125 million
1-Yr. Sales Change: 6.9%
Exchange: NYSE
Symbol: MO

 See pages 198–199 for a full profile of this company.

PHILLIPS-VAN HEUSEN CORPORATION

1290 Avenue of the Americas	CEO: Bruce J. Klatsky	1995 Sales: $1,255.5 mil.
New York, NY 10104	CFO: Irwin W. Winter	1-Yr. Sales Change: 8.9%
Phone: 212-541-5200	HR: Barbara Burkepile	Exchange: NYSE
Fax: 212-247-5309	Employees: 13,800	Symbol: PVH

Apparel - men's & boys' shirts (#1 US dress shirts: Van Heusen; #1 US designer dress shirts: Geoffrey Beene), sweaters, shoes (#1 US casual shoe brand: Bass) & outerwear (Jantzen, Izod, Gant)

PHONEXPRESS INC.

14 Industrial Rd.	CEO: John Negri	1994 Sales: $13.6 million
Fairfield, NJ 07004	CFO: Joyce Cmielewski	1-Yr. Sales Change: —
Phone: 201-808-7000	HR: Joyce Cmielewski	Ownership: Privately Held
Fax: 201-227-2888	Employees: 50	

Telecommunications services - distribution & installation of telephone equipment

PHOTOCIRCUITS CORPORATION

31 Sea Cliff Ave.	CEO: John Endee	1994 Sales: $270 million
New York, NY 11542	CFO: James Zerby	1-Yr. Sales Change: 12.5%
Phone: 516-674-1000	HR: Judy Conord	Ownership: Privately Held
Fax: 516-674-1383	Employees: 2,000	

Electrical components - printed circuit boards

PHOTRONICS, INC.

15 Secor Rd., PO Box 5226	CEO: Constantine S. Macricostas	1995 Sales: $125.3 million
Brookfield, CT 06804	CFO: Robert Bollo	1-Yr. Sales Change: 53.2%
Phone: 203-775-9000	HR: Jeffrey Moonan	Exchange: Nasdaq
Fax: 203-775-5944	Employees: 425	Symbol: PLAB

Electrical components - photomasks (photographic glass plates) used to expose semiconductor wafers

PHYSICIAN COMPUTER NETWORK, INC.

1200 The American Rd.	CEO: Henry Green	1994 Sales: $20.5 million
Morris Plains, NJ 07950	CFO: Thomas Wraback	1-Yr. Sales Change: 236.1%
Phone: 201-490-3100	HR: —	Exchange: Nasdaq
Fax: 201-490-3101	Employees: 132	Symbol: PCNI

Computers - physician practice-management software

PHYSICIANS HEALTH SERVICES, INC.

120 Hawley Ln.
Trumbull, CT 06611-5343
Phone: 203-381-6400
Fax: 203-381-6690

CEO: Michael E. Herbert
CFO: James L. Elrod Jr.
HR: Regina M. Campbell
Employees: 487

1994 Sales: $294 million
1-Yr. Sales Change: 4.9%
Exchange: Nasdaq
Symbol: PHSV

Health maintenance organization, operating primarily in Connecticut & New York

THE PIERPONT MORGAN LIBRARY

Madison Ave. & 36th St.
New York, NY 10016
Phone: 212-685-0610
Fax: 212-481-3484

CEO: Charles E. Pierce Jr.
CFO: Brian Regan
HR: Nancy Shoflan
Employees: 70

1995 Sales: $10.9 million
1-Yr. Sales Change: 28.2%
Ownership: Privately Held

Museum & research library

PITNEY BOWES INC.

One Elmcroft Rd.
Stamford, CT 06926-0700
Phone: 203-356-5000
Fax: 203-351-6303

CEO: George B. Harvey
CFO: Carmine F. Adimando
HR: Johnna G. Torsone
Employees: 32,792

1995 Sales: $3,271 million
1-Yr. Sales Change: -7.7%
Exchange: NYSE
Symbol: PBI

Office equipment & supplies - mailing & copier systems & facsimile machines

 See pages 200–201 for a full profile of this company.

PITTSTON MINERALS GROUP

PO Box 120070
Stamford, CT 06912-0070
Phone: 203-978-5200
Fax: 203-978-5315

CEO: Joseph C. Farrell
CFO: James B. Hartough
HR: Frank T. Lennon
Employees: 360

1994 Sales: $795 million
1-Yr. Sales Change: 15.7%
Exchange: NYSE
Symbol: PZM

Coal; gold production & exploration

PITTSTON SERVICES GROUP

PO Box 120070
Stamford, CT 06912-0070
Phone: 203-978-5200
Fax: 203-978-5315

CEO: Joseph C. Farrell
CFO: James B. Hartough
HR: Frank T. Lennon
Employees: 15,100

1994 Sales: $1,872 million
1-Yr. Sales Change: 19.3%
Exchange: NYSE
Symbol: PZS

Diversified operations - air freight (Burlington); logistics; security services (Brink's)

P/KAUFMAN, INC.

51 Madison Ave.
New York, NY 10010
Phone: 212-292-2200
Fax: 212-292-2280

CEO: Peter Kaufman
CFO: Bruce Manberg
HR: Bruce Manberg
Employees: 210

1994 Sales: $130 million
1-Yr. Sales Change: 30.0%
Ownership: Privately Held

Textiles - decorative fabrics (P/Kaufman, Braemore, Bloomcraft, Joseph Woods)

PLAID CLOTHING GROUP, INC.

730 Fifth Ave.
New York, NY 10019
Phone: 212-830-5500
Fax: 212-315-0936

CEO: Richard C. Marcus
CFO: Robert J. Keuppers
HR: —
Employees: 2,000

1994 Sales: $210 million
1-Yr. Sales Change: -25.0%
Ownership: Privately Held

Apparel

PLANNED PARENTHOOD OF NEW YORK CITY, INC.

26 Bleecker St.
New York, NY 10012
Phone: 212-274-7200
Fax: 212-274-7218

CEO: Alexander Sanger
CFO: Andrew Kussoy
HR: —
Employees: 250

1994 Sales: $320 million
1-Yr. Sales Change: —
Ownership: Privately Held

Family-planning counseling services

PLASTIC SPECIALTIES AND TECHNOLOGIES, INC.

101 Railroad Ave.
Ridgefield, NJ 07657-2312
Phone: 201-941-2900
Fax: 201-941-0308

CEO: Fred W. Broling
CFO: Thomas Stuckey
HR: Manuel Aneiros
Employees: 1,420

1994 Sales: $203.6 million
1-Yr. Sales Change: 13.2%
Ownership: Privately Held

Chemicals - plastic products & chemicals, including polyvinyl chloride compounds, static seals, rubber & thermoplastic seals & vinyl garden hose

PLAYTEX PRODUCTS, INC.

300 Nyala Farms
Westport, CT 06880
Phone: 203-341-4000
Fax: 203-341-4260

CEO: Michael Gallagher
CFO: Michael F. Goss
HR: Frank M. Sanchez
Employees: 1,600

1994 Sales: $473.3 million
1-Yr. Sales Change: 15.5%
Exchange: NYSE
Symbol: PYX

Cosmetics & toiletries - tampons (Playtex, Ultimate), toothbrushes (Tek), baby bottles (Playtex), baby products (Cherubs, SmileTote), household & industrial gloves (Playtex Living), hair care products (Jhirmak)

PLENUM PUBLISHING CORPORATION

233 Spring St.
New York, NY 10013
Phone: 212-620-8000
Fax: 212-463-0742

CEO: Martin E. Tash
CFO: Ghanshyam A. Patel
HR: —
Employees: 300

1994 Sales: $52.5 million
1-Yr. Sales Change: -3.0%
Exchange: Nasdaq
Symbol: PLEN

Publishing - books, journals & periodicals in scientific, medical & technical fields; English translations of foreign journals; database of chemical patents

PLY GEM INDUSTRIES, INC.

777 Third Ave.
New York, NY 10017
Phone: 212-832-1550
Fax: 212-888-0472

CEO: Jeffrey S. Silverman
CFO: Herbert P. Dooskin
HR: Neil Bogus
Employees: 4,200

1994 Sales: $796.4 million
1-Yr. Sales Change: 10.2%
Exchange: NYSE
Symbol: PGI

Building products - specialty products for the home improvement industry; wood windows, vinyl siding & vinyl windows

PNY ELECTRONICS, INC.

200 Anderson Ave.
Moonachie, NJ 07074
Phone: 201-438-6300
Fax: 201-438-9144

CEO: Gadi Cohen
CFO: Steven Halpern
HR: Miriam Brilleman
Employees: 120

1994 Sales: $293 million
1-Yr. Sales Change: 51.0%
Ownership: Privately Held

Computers - memory boards

POLAROME MANUFACTURING, INC.

200 Theodore Conrad Dr.
Jersey City, NJ 07305
Phone: 201-309-4500
Fax: 201-433-0638

CEO: Pierre Bruell
CFO: Pierre Bruell
HR: —
Employees: 92

1994 Sales: $115 million
1-Yr. Sales Change: 0.9%
Ownership: Privately Held

Chemicals - flavors & fragrances, oils & chemicals

POLO/RALPH LAUREN CORPORATION

650 Madison Ave.
New York, NY 10022
Phone: 212-318-7000
Fax: 212-888-5780

CEO: Ralph Lauren
CFO: Joanne Mandry
HR: Karen Rosenback
Employees: 3,000

1995 Est. Sales: $2,000 mil.
1-Yr. Sales Change: 25.0%
Ownership: Privately Held

Apparel, home furnishings & accessories

POLYMER RESEARCH CORP. OF AMERICA

2186 Mill Ave.
New York, NY 11234
Phone: 718-444-4300
Fax: 718-241-3930

CEO: Carl Horowitz
CFO: Anna Dichter
HR: Irene Horowitz
Employees: 45

1994 Sales: $4.8 million
1-Yr. Sales Change: 4.3%
Exchange: Nasdaq (SC)
Symbol: PROA

Specialty chemicals for grafting & coating formulations

THE PORT AUTHORITY OF NEW YORK AND NEW JERSEY

One World Trade Center
New York, NY 10048
Phone: 212-435-7000
Fax: 212-435-4660

CEO: George J. Marlin
CFO: Barry Weintrob
HR: Louis J. LaCapra
Employees: 9,200

1994 Sales: $1,979.7 mil.
1-Yr. Sales Change: 3.1%
Ownership: Privately Held

Diversified operations - airport, rail passenger, bus terminal & marine terminal operations; real estate operations; cargo handling

 See pages 202–203 for a full profile of this company.

PORTA SYSTEMS CORPORATION

575 Underhill Blvd.
Syosset, NY 11791
Phone: 516-364-9300
Fax: 516-682-4674

CEO: Vincent F. Santulli
CFO: Ed Kornfeld
HR: Joan Newlin
Employees: 889

1994 Sales: $69 million
1-Yr. Sales Change: 1.3%
Exchange: AMEX
Symbol: PSI

Telecommunications equipment - connection, protection, testing & administration systems for private lines & networks

PORTFOLIO ACQUISITION CORPORATION

1500 Broadway
New York, NY 10036
Phone: 212-302-4000
Fax: 212-302-0393

CEO: Jose E. Rodriguez
CFO: Jose E. Rodriguez
HR: Jose E. Rodriguez
Employees: 22

1994 Sales: $89.3 million
1-Yr. Sales Change: 8.0%
Ownership: Privately Held

Leasing - computers

POTAMKIN MANHATTAN CORP.

787 11th Ave.
New York, NY 10019
Phone: 212-603-7231
Fax: 212-603-7034

CEO: Victor Potamkin
CFO: Peter Paris
HR: Jack Calumusa
Employees: 2,000

1994 Sales: $1,400 million
1-Yr. Sales Change: 18.1%
Ownership: Privately Held

Retail - new & used cars; communications

PRAXAIR, INC.

39 Old Ridgebury Rd.
Danbury, CT 06810-5113
Phone: 203-837-2000
Fax: 203-837-2454

CEO: H. William Lichtenberger
CFO: John A. Clerico
HR: Barbara R. Harris
Employees: 17,780

1994 Sales: $2,711 million
1-Yr. Sales Change: 11.2%
Exchange: NYSE
Symbol: PX

Chemicals - industrial gases

 See pages 204–205 for a full profile of this company.

PRESIDENTIAL LIFE CORPORATION

69 Lydecker St.
Nyack, NY 10960
Phone: 914-358-2300
Fax: 914-353-0273

CEO: Herbert Kurz
CFO: Michael V. Oporto
HR: Maria Kramer
Employees: —

1994 Sales: $173.8 million
1-Yr. Sales Change: -15.8%
Exchange: Nasdaq
Symbol: PLFE

Insurance - individual annuities & individual life policies in 46 states & the District of Columbia

PRESIDENTIAL REALTY CORPORATION

180 S. Broadway
White Plains, NY 10605
Phone: 914-948-1300
Fax: 914-948-1327

CEO: Jeffrey F. Joseph
CFO: Thomas Viertel
HR: Roz Lacative
Employees: 11

1994 Sales: $10.5 million
1-Yr. Sales Change: 1.9%
Exchange: AMEX
Symbol: PDLB

Real estate investment trust

PRESTIGE FINANCIAL CORP.

One Royal Rd., PO Box 2480
Flemington, NJ 08822
Phone: 908-806-6200
Fax: 908-806-4446

CEO: Robert J. Jablonski
CFO: Lorraine A. Cook
HR: Annette M. Dalley
Employees: 35

1994 Sales: $8.8 million
1-Yr. Sales Change: 22.2%
Exchange: Nasdaq (SC)
Symbol: PRFN

Banks - Northeast

PRESTONE PRODUCTS COMPANY

39 Old Ridgebury Rd.
Danbury, CT 06810-5109
Phone: 203-830-7800
Fax: 203-830-7884

CEO: Dave Lundstedt
CFO: Leonard DeCecchis
HR: Doug Bobay
Employees: 240

1994 Est. Sales: $200 mil.
1-Yr. Sales Change: 14.3%
Ownership: Privately Held

Auto parts - antifreeze & car care products

PRICE COMMUNICATIONS CORPORATION

45 Rockefeller Plaza
New York, NY 10020
Phone: 212-757-5600
Fax: 212-397-3755
Broadcasting - radio & TV

CEO: Robert Price
CFO: Kim I. Pressman
HR: Jim Kreps
Employees: 222

1994 Sales: $24 million
1-Yr. Sales Change: 5.3%
Exchange: AMEX
Symbol: PR

PRICE WATERHOUSE LLP

1251 Avenue of the Americas
New York, NY 10020
Phone: 212-596-7000
Fax: 212-790-6620

CEO: James J. Schiro
CFO: Thomas Chamberlain
HR: Richard P. Kearns
Employees: 53,000

1995 Sales: $4,460 million
1-Yr. Sales Change: 12.1%
Ownership: Privately Held

Business services - accounting & consulting

 See pages 206–207 for a full profile of this company.

PRICELLULAR CORPORATION

45 Rockefeller Plaza
New York, NY 10020
Phone: 212-459-0800
Fax: 212-245-3058
Telecommunications services - cellular telephone systems

CEO: Robert Price
CFO: Stuart B. Rosenstein
HR: Kim Pressman
Employees: 130

1994 Sales: $5.2 million
1-Yr. Sales Change: 36.8%
Exchange: AMEX
Symbol: PC

PRIME CELLULAR, INC.

100 First Stamford Pl., 3rd Fl.
Stamford, CT 06902-6732
Phone: 203-327-3620
Fax: 203-359-0880

CEO: Joseph K. Pagano
CFO: Joseph K. Pagano
HR: —
Employees: 1

1995 Sales: $0.4 million
1-Yr. Sales Change: 33.3%
Exchange: Nasdaq (SC)
Symbol: PCEL

Business services - business planning, marketing, engineering, design & construction consulting services to rural service area cellular telephone licensees

PRIME HOSPITALITY CORP.

700 Rte. 46 East
Fairfield, NJ 07004
Phone: 201-882-1010
Fax: 201-882-8577

CEO: David A. Simon
CFO: John M. Elwood
HR: Denis W. Driscoll
Employees: 5,000

1994 Sales: $134.3 million
1-Yr. Sales Change: 23.3%
Exchange: NYSE
Symbol: PDQ

Hotels - Wellesley Inns & AmeriSuites; Marriott, Radisson, Sheraton, Holiday Inn, Ramada & Howard Johnson licensee

PRIMEENERGY CORPORATION

One Landmark Sq., 11th Fl.
Stamford, CT 06901
Phone: 203-358-5700
Fax: 203-358-5786

Oil & gas - exploration & production

CEO: Charles E. Drimal Jr.
CFO: Beverly A. Cummings
HR: —
Employees: 168

1994 Sales: $17 million
1-Yr. Sales Change: -1.7%
Exchange: Nasdaq (SC)
Symbol: PNRG

PRINS RECYCLING CORPORATION

400 Kelby St., 6th Fl.
Fort Lee, NJ 07024
Phone: 201-886-1600
Fax: 201-886-1601

CEO: Fred L. Prins
CFO: Noel J. Prins
HR: Barbara Aubin
Employees: 165

1994 Sales: $31.3 million
1-Yr. Sales Change: 43.6%
Exchange: Nasdaq
Symbol: PRNS

Pollution control - wastepaper & other secondary paper fibers to paper & building product mills; paper recycling

PRODIGY SERVICES COMPANY

445 Hamilton Ave.
White Plains, NY 10601
Phone: 914-448-8000
Fax: 914-648-0278

CEO: Edward A. Bennett
CFO: Gerry Mueller
HR: Jill Ibarguen
Employees: 600

1994 Sales: $230 million
1-Yr. Sales Change: 15%
Ownership: Joint Venture

Computers - online information service & Internet access (joint venture between IBM & Sears)

PROFESSIONAL SPORTS CARE MANAGEMENT, INC.

550 Mamaroneck Ave., Ste. 308
Harrison, NY 10528
Phone: 914-777-2400
Fax: 914-777-2420

CEO: Russell F. Warren Jr.
CFO: Michael P. Neuscheler
HR: Melanie Johnson
Employees: 323

1994 Sales: $16.4 million
1-Yr. Sales Change: 187.7%
Exchange: Nasdaq
Symbol: PSCM

Health care - outpatient physical therapy clinics in New York, New Jersey & Connecticut providing services to patients with orthopedic injuries & postoperative impairments

PROGRAMMER'S PARADISE, INC.

1163 Shrewsbury Ave.
Shrewsbury, NJ 07702
Phone: 908-389-8950
Fax: 908-389-9227

CEO: Roger Paradis
CFO: Rick Schmidt
HR: Claudia Corbalis
Employees: 116

1994 Sales: $71.3 million
1-Yr. Sales Change: 58.4%
Exchange: Nasdaq
Symbol: PROG

Computers - direct marketing of equipment & software through catalogs, corporate reselling & wholesale distribution

PROJECTAVISION, INC.

2 Penn Plaza
New York, NY 10121
Phone: 212-971-3000
Fax: 212-971-6016

CEO: Marvin Maslow
CFO: Jules Zimmerman
HR: —
Employees: 8

1994 Sales: $0
1-Yr. Sales Change: —
Exchange: Nasdaq (SC)
Symbol: PJTV

Audio & video home products - solid-state TV projectors

PROSKAUER ROSE GOETZ & MENDELSOHN

1585 Broadway
New York, NY 10036
Phone: 212-969-3000
Fax: 212-969-2900

CEO: Henry C. Beinstein
CFO: Elly Rosenthal
HR: —
Employees: —

1994 Sales: $169 million
1-Yr. Sales Change: 8.3%
Ownership: Privately Held

Law firm

PRT CORPORATION OF AMERICA

342 Madison Ave., Ste. 1104
New York, NY 10173
Phone: 212-922-0800
Fax: 212-922-0806

CEO: Douglas Mellinger
CFO: Barbara Davis
HR: —
Employees: 160

1994 Sales: $13.9 million
1-Yr. Sales Change: —
Ownership: Privately Held

Computers - software planning, training & development services

THE PRUDENTIAL INSURANCE COMPANY OF AMERICA

751 Broad St.
Newark, NJ 07102-3777
Phone: 201-802-6000
Fax: 201-802-6092

CEO: Arthur F. Ryan
CFO: Mark Grier
HR: Donald C. Mann
Employees: 99,386

1994 Sales: $43,557 million
1-Yr. Sales Change: -5.3%
Ownership: Privately Held

Insurance - health & life

 See pages 208–209 for a full profile of this company.

PRUDENTIAL REINSURANCE HOLDINGS, INC.

3 Gateway Center
Newark, NJ 07102-4077
Phone: 201-802-6000
Fax: 201-643-8886

CEO: Joseph V. Taranto
CFO: Robert P. Jacobson
HR: —
Employees: 453

1994 Sales: $997 million
1-Yr. Sales Change: -9.6%
Exchange: NYSE
Symbol: RE

Insurance - treaty & facultative reinsurance to property & casualty companies

PTI HOLDING INC.

One River St., Bldg. 52
Hastings on Hudson, NY 10706
Phone: 914-478-8200
Fax: 914-478-8298

CEO: Meredith W. Birrittella
CFO: Meredith W. Birrittella
HR: —
Employees: 90

1994 Sales: $4.8 million
1-Yr. Sales Change: —
Exchange: Nasdaq (SC)
Symbol: PTII

Leisure & recreational - produces & markets bicycle helmets

PUBLIC SERVICE ENTERPRISE GROUP INCORPORATED

80 Park Plaza, PO Box 1171
Newark, NJ 07101-1171
Phone: 201-430-7000
Fax: 201-430-5983

CEO: E. James Ferland
CFO: Robert C. Murray
HR: Martin P. Mellett
Employees: 12,390

1994 Sales: $5,915.8 mil.
1-Yr. Sales Change: 3.7%
Exchange: NYSE
Symbol: PEG

Utility - electric & gas power

 See pages 210–211 for a full profile of this company.

PUBLICKER INDUSTRIES INC.

1445 E. Putnam Ave.
Old Greenwich, CT 06870
Phone: 203-637-4500
Fax: 203-637-4807

CEO: James J. Weis
CFO: Antonio L. DeLise
HR: —
Employees: 950

1994 Sales: $76.3 million
1-Yr. Sales Change: 5.1%
Exchange: NYSE
Symbol: PUL

Diversified operations - aluminum windows & doors; coin handling equipment; electronic components; flashlights, lanterns & batteries; engineering services

PUDGIE'S CHICKEN, INC.

333 Earle Ovington Blvd.
Uniondale, NY 11553
Phone: 516-222-8833
Fax: 516-222-8044

CEO: Steven Wasserman
CFO: Helen Papa
HR: Mark Hanna
Employees: 345

1994 Sales: $7.7 million
1-Yr. Sales Change: 450.0%
Exchange: Nasdaq (SC)
Symbol: PUDG

Retail - fast-food restaurants featuring fried chicken

PULLMAN COMPANY

3 Werner Way, Ste. 200
Lebanon, NJ 08833
Phone: 908-236-9234
Fax: 908-236-6653

CEO: Roger Pollazzi
CFO: Ted Vogtman
HR: Michael Farrell
Employees: 6,000

1994 Sales: $381 million
1-Yr. Sales Change: —
Ownership: Privately Held

Automotive & trucking - suspension bushings, high-pressure hoses & fittings, specialty wear-resistant components & multipurpose storage tanks

PULSE BANCORP, INC.

6 Jackson St.
South River, NJ 08882
Phone: 908-257-2400
Fax: 908-257-1603

Financial - savings & loans

CEO: Benjamin S. Konopacki
CFO: George T. Hornyak Jr.
HR: Jeff Gostkowski
Employees: 60

1994 Sales: $30.7 million
1-Yr. Sales Change: -4.1%
Exchange: Nasdaq
Symbol: PULS

PURE TECH INTERNATIONAL, INC.

65 Railroad Ave.
Ridgefield, NJ 07657
Phone: 201-941-6550
Fax: 201-941-0602

Recycling - plastic

CEO: Fred Broling
CFO: Terence Brennan
HR: —
Employees: 428

1995 Sales: $54 million
1-Yr. Sales Change: 11.1%
Exchange: Nasdaq
Symbol: PURT

PUREPAC, INC.

200 Elmora Ave.
Elizabeth, NJ 07207
Phone: 908-527-9100
Fax: 908-527-9639

Drugs - generic

CEO: Michael R. D. Ashton
CFO: Russell J. Reardon
HR: Douglas DiSalle
Employees: 301

1995 Sales: $61.1 million
1-Yr. Sales Change: -12.7%
Exchange: Nasdaq
Symbol: PURE

PVC CONTAINER CORPORATION

401 Industrial Way West
Eatontown, NJ 07724
Phone: 908-542-0060
Fax: 908-542-7706

CEO: Phillip L. Friedman
CFO: Bertram D. Berkowitz
HR: Diane Murphy
Employees: —

1995 Sales: $54 million
1-Yr. Sales Change: 40.6%
Exchange: Nasdaq (SC)
Symbol: PVCC

Chemicals - design & manufacture of plastic bottles & polyvinyl chloride compounds

PXRE CORPORATION

399 Thornall St.
Edison, NJ 08837
Phone: 908-906-8100
Fax: 908-906-9157

Insurance - property & casualty

CEO: Gerald L. Radke
CFO: Sanford M. Kimmel
HR: —
Employees: 42

1994 Sales: $130.2 million
1-Yr. Sales Change: 31.4%
Exchange: Nasdaq
Symbol: PXRE

Q-MED, INC.

100 Metro Park South, 3rd Fl.
Laurence Harbor, NJ 08878
Phone: 908-566-2666
Fax: 908-566-0912

Medical diagnostic devices

CEO: Michael W. Cox
CFO: Debra A. Fenton
HR: Debra A. Fenton
Employees: 76

1994 Sales: $8.9 million
1-Yr. Sales Change: -13.6%
Exchange: Nasdaq (SC)
Symbol: QEKG

QUALITY KING DISTRIBUTORS INC.

2060 Ninth Ave.
Ronkonkoma, NY 11779
Phone: 516-737-5555
Fax: 516-439-2222

Drugs & sundries - wholesale

CEO: Bernard Nussdorf
CFO: Mike Katz
HR: Glenn Satur
Employees: 660

1994 Sales: $850 million
1-Yr. Sales Change: -1.2%
Ownership: Privately Held

QUANTUM RESTAURANT GROUP, INC.

3333 New Hyde Park Rd., Ste. 210
New Hyde Park, NY 11042
Phone: 516-627-1515
Fax: 516-627-1898

Retail - restaurants (Morton's of Chicago & Dallas, Mick's, Peasant, Bertolini's)

CEO: Allen J. Bernstein
CFO: Thomas J. Baldwin
HR: Agnes Longarzo
Employees: 3,143

1994 Sales: $156.3 million
1-Yr. Sales Change: 30.9%
Exchange: NYSE
Symbol: KRG

QUEENS COUNTY BANCORP, INC.

38-25 Main St.
Flushing, NY 11354
Phone: 718-359-6400
Fax: 718-762-6000

Financial - savings & loans

CEO: Joseph R. Ficalora
CFO: Robert Wann
HR: Donald J. Powell
Employees: 311

1994 Sales: $85 million
1-Yr. Sales Change: 10.4%
Exchange: Nasdaq
Symbol: QCSB

QUEENS GROUP, INC.

52-35 Barnett Ave.
Long Island City, NY 11104
Phone: 718-457-7700
Fax: 718-457-9285

Printing - specialty

CEO: Eric Kaltman
CFO: Erwin Moskowitz
HR: Patricia Kern
Employees: 1,050

1994 Sales: $188 million
1-Yr. Sales Change: 19.0%
Ownership: Privately Held

R & R MARKETING, L.L.C.

10 Patton Dr.
West Caldwell, NJ 07006
Phone: 201-228-5100
Fax: 201-403-8679

CEO: Alvin M. Hutchinson Jr.
CFO: Howard Jacobs
HR: Joan Speer
Employees: 310

1995 Sales: $165.5 million
1-Yr. Sales Change: -2.6%
Ownership: Privately Held

Beverages - wine & liquor distribution throughout New Jersey

RAD OIL, INC.

287 Bowman Ave.
Purchase, NY 10577
Phone: 914-253-8945
Fax: 914-253-8188

CEO: Stephen Draizin
CFO: Garry Maughan
HR: Deborah Freed
Employees: 180

1994 Sales: $350 million
1-Yr. Sales Change: 0.0%
Ownership: Privately Held

Oil & gas   petroleum bulk stations & terminals

RAG SHOPS, INC.

111 Wagaraw Rd.
Hawthorne, NJ 07506-2711
Phone: 201-423-1303
Fax: 201-427-6568

CEO: Stanley Berenzweig
CFO: Steven B. Barnett
HR: Michael Aaronson
Employees: 1,280

1995 Sales: $86.1 million
1-Yr. Sales Change: -3.8%
Exchange: Nasdaq
Symbol: RAGS

Retail - fabric & craft merchandise (70 units)

RAINBOW APPAREL COMPANY

1000 Pennsylvania Ave.
New York, NY 11207
Phone: 718-485-3000
Fax: 718-485-3807

CEO: Joseph Chehebar
CFO: Nathan Hoffman
HR: Louis Laiken
Employees: 8,000

1994 Sales: $150 million
1-Yr. Sales Change: 0.0%
Ownership: Privately Held

Retail - women's clothing stores

RAMAPO FINANCIAL CORPORATION

64 Mountain View Blvd.
Wayne, NJ 07470
Phone: 201-696-6100
Fax: 201-305-4089

CEO: Mortimer J. O'Shea
CFO: Walter A. Wojcik Jr.
HR: Debra Cipoletti
Employees: 115

1994 Sales: $18.2 million
1-Yr. Sales Change: -35.5%
Exchange: Nasdaq
Symbol: RMPO

Banks - Northeast

RARITAN BANCORP INC.

9 W. Somerset St.
Raritan, NJ 08869
Phone: 908-725-0080
Fax: 908-707-9351

CEO: Arlyn D. Rus
CFO: Thomas F. Tansey
HR: Barbara A. Perry
Employees: 78

1994 Sales: $21.6 million
1-Yr. Sales Change: -8.9%
Exchange: Nasdaq
Symbol: RARB

Banks - Northeast (The Raritan Savings Bank)

THE RATTLESNAKE HOLDING COMPANY, INC.

3 Stamford Landing, Ste. 130
Stamford, CT 06902
Phone: 203-975-9455
Fax: 203-975-7973

CEO: William J. Opper
CFO: David C. Sederholt
HR: —
Employees: 4

1995 Sales: $5.3 million
1-Yr. Sales Change: —
Exchange: Nasdaq (SC)
Symbol: RTTL

Retail - casual-dining restaurants featuring a southwestern theme (Rattlesnake Southwestern Grill)

RAYONIER INC.

1177 Summer St.
Stamford, CT 06905-5529
Phone: 203-348-7000
Fax: 203-964-4528

CEO: Ronald M. Gross
CFO: Gerald J. Pollack
HR: John P. O'Grady
Employees: 2,700

1994 Sales: $1,069.5 mil.
1-Yr. Sales Change: 14.2%
Exchange: NYSE
Symbol: RYN

Paper & paper products

RAYONIER TIMBERLANDS, L.P.

1177 Summer St.
Stamford, CT 06905-5529
Phone: 203-348-7000
Fax: 203-964-4333

CEO: Ronald M. Gross
CFO: Gerald J. Pollack
HR: Ann Sheppard
Employees: 2,700

1994 Sales: $166.5 million
1-Yr. Sales Change: 43.5%
Exchange: NYSE
Symbol: LOG

Building products - wood, timberland management & marketing

RAYTECH CORPORATION

One Corporate Dr., Ste. 512
Shelton, CT 06484
Phone: 203-925-8000
Fax: 203-925-8088

CEO: Craig R. Smith
CFO: Albert A. Canosa
HR: Albert A. Canosa
Employees: 1,310

1994 Sales: $167.6 million
1-Yr. Sales Change: 20.3%
Exchange: NYSE
Symbol: RAY

Automotive & trucking - polymer matrix composite products for the automobile, heavy-duty construction & military industries

THE READER'S DIGEST ASSOCIATION, INC.

Reader's Digest Rd.
Pleasantville, NY 10570-7000
Phone: 914-238-1000
Fax: 914-238-4559

CEO: James P. Schadt
CFO: Stephen R. Wilson
HR: Joseph M. Grecky
Employees: 6,200

1995 Sales: $3,068.5 mil.
1-Yr. Sales Change: 9.3%
Exchange: NYSE
Symbol: RDA

Publishing - periodicals, books, records & videos

 See pages 212–213 for a full profile of this company.

RED APPLE GROUP

823 11th Ave.
New York, NY 10019
Phone: 212-956-5803
Fax: 212-262-4979

CEO: John Andreas Catsimatidis
CFO: Stuart Spivak
HR: Ben Focarinio
Employees: 2,425

1995 Sales: $2,250 million
1-Yr. Sales Change: -10.0%
Ownership: Privately Held

Diversified operations supermarkets & convenience stores; oil; real estate

REFAC TECHNOLOGY DEVELOPMENT CORPORATION

122 E. 42nd St.
New York, NY 10168
Phone: 212-687-4741
Fax: 212-949-8716

CEO: Eugene M. Lang
CFO: Robert L. Tuchman
HR: —
Employees: 12

1994 Sales: $6.9 million
1-Yr. Sales Change: -14.8%
Exchange: AMEX
Symbol: REF

Business services - international licensing & technology transfer, negotiation & manufacturing licenses & joint ventures involving patents & trademarks

REFINED SUGARS, INC.

One Federal St.
New York, NY 10702
Phone: 914-963-2400
Fax: 914-963-4652

CEO: Gregory J. Hoskins
CFO: John Cautillo
HR: Donald Brainard
Employees: 300

1994 Est. Sales: $250 mil.
1-Yr. Sales Change: —
Ownership: Privately Held

Food - cane sugar refining

REGENERON PHARMACEUTICALS, INC.

777 Old Saw Mill River Rd.
Tarrytown, NY 10591-6707
Phone: 914-347-7000
Fax: 914-347-2113

CEO: Leonard S. Schleifer
CFO: Murray A. Goldberg
HR: Vicki Gaddy
Employees: 193

1994 Sales: $23.2 million
1-Yr. Sales Change: 118.9%
Exchange: Nasdaq
Symbol: REGN

Biomedical & genetic products - biotechnology-based compounds for treatment of neurodegenerative diseases, peripheral neuropathies & nerve injury

RELIANCE BANCORP, INC.

585 Stewart Ave.
Garden City, NY 11530
Phone: 516-741-2323
Fax: 516-222-9254

Financial - savings & loans

CEO: Raymond L. Nielsen
CFO: John F. Traxler
HR: Dorothy Brown
Employees: —

1995 Sales: $62.5 million
1-Yr. Sales Change: 29.4%
Exchange: Nasdaq
Symbol: RELY

RELIANCE GROUP HOLDINGS, INC.

55 E. 52nd St.
New York, NY 10055
Phone: 212-909-1100
Fax: 212-909-1864

Insurance - property & casualty & title

CEO: Saul P. Steinberg
CFO: Lowell C. Freiberg
HR: Joel H. Rothwax
Employees: 9,675

1994 Sales: $3,047 million
1-Yr. Sales Change: 2.8%
Exchange: NYSE
Symbol: REL

 See pages 214–215 for a full profile of this company.

REMINGTON PRODUCTS, INC.

60 Main St.
Bridgeport, CT 06604
Phone: 203-367-4400
Fax: 203-366-6039

Electrical products - shavers & razors

CEO: Peter Cuneo
CFO: Joe Cioni
HR: Allen Lipson
Employees: 1,500

1994 Est. Sales: $210 mil.
1-Yr. Sales Change: —
Ownership: Privately Held

RENAISSANCE COMMUNICATIONS CORP.

One Fawcett Place, Ste. 120
Greenwich, CT 06830
Phone: 203-629-1888
Fax: 203-629-9821

Broadcasting - 6 TV stations (5 are affiliated with Fox Broadcasting)

CEO: Michael Finkelstein
CFO: John C. Ferrara
HR: —
Employees: 513

1994 Sales: $161.2 million
1-Yr. Sales Change: 27.3%
Exchange: NYSE
Symbol: RRR

RENCO GROUP INC.

45 Rockefeller Plaza
New York, NY 10111
Phone: 212-541-6000
Fax: 212-541-6197

Diversified operations - steel; furniture; cages; all-terrain vehicles (Hummer)

CEO: Ira L. Rennert
CFO: Roger L. Fay
HR: Marvin Koenig
Employees: 7,000

1994 Sales: $1,650 million
1-Yr. Sales Change: 10.0%
Ownership: Privately Held

REPUBLIC NEW YORK CORPORATION

452 Fifth Ave.
New York, NY 10018
Phone: 212-525-6100
Fax: 212-525-5678

Banks - Northeast

CEO: Walter H. Weiner
CFO: John D. Kaberle Jr.
HR: Hillel Davis
Employees: 5,500

1994 Sales: $2,560 million
1-Yr. Sales Change: 9.9%
Exchange: NYSE
Symbol: RNB

RESEARCH FRONTIERS INCORPORATED

240 Crossways Park Dr.
Woodbury, NY 11797-2033
Phone: 516-364-1902
Fax: 516-364-3798

CEO: Robert L. Saxe
CFO: Robert L. Saxe
HR: Juliette Madden
Employees: 11

1994 Sales: $0.6 million
1-Yr. Sales Change: 200.0%
Exchange: Nasdaq (SC)
Symbol: REFR

Suspended particle technology & devices used to control the transmission of light

RESOURCE, INC.

123 Varick Ave.
New York, NY 11237
Phone: 718-386-7900
Fax: 718-417-1128

CEO: Anthony Lomangino
CFO: William Kaiser
HR: —
Employees: 900

1995 Est. Sales: $135 mil.
1-Yr. Sales Change: -3.6%
Ownership: Privately Held

Pollution control - waste management & recycling services (#1 private waste management company in New York City)

RF MANAGEMENT CORPORATION

95 Madison Ave., Ste. 301
Morristown, NJ 07960
Phone: 201-538-9955
Fax: 201-267-7359

CEO: Roger Findlay
CFO: Jan Goldberg
HR: Jan Goldberg
Employees: —

1995 Sales: —
1-Yr. Sales Change:
Exchange: Nasdaq (SC)
Symbol: RFMC

Health care - outpatient centers which perform ambulatory surgery

RHEOMETRIC SCIENTIFIC, INC.

One Possumtown Rd.
Piscataway, NJ 08854
Phone: 908-560-8550
Fax: 908-560-7451

CEO: Robert E. Davis
CFO: John C. Fuhrmeister
HR: Matthew Bilt
Employees: 249

1994 Sales: $34.6 million
1-Yr. Sales Change: 28.6%
Exchange: Nasdaq
Symbol: RHEM

Computer-controlled materials test systems used to make physical property measurements on various materials including plastics, composites, petrochemicals, rubber, paints & cosmetics

RICHTON INTERNATIONAL CORPORATION

340 Main St.
Madison, NJ 07940-2363
Phone: 201-966-0104
Fax: 201-966-0105

Financial - investments

CEO: Fred R. Sullivan
CFO: Cornelius F. Griffin
HR: —
Employees: 4

1994 Sales: $50.3 million
1-Yr. Sales Change: —
Exchange: AMEX
Symbol: RHT

RIDDELL SPORTS INC.

900 3rd Ave.
New York, NY 10022
Phone: 212-826-4300
Fax: 800-848-9917

CEO: David M. Mauer
CFO: Lawrence F. Simon
HR: Belinda Jackson
Employees: 573

1994 Sales: $55.4 million
1-Yr. Sales Change: 13.5%
Exchange: Nasdaq
Symbol: RIDL

Leisure & recreational products - football helmets & protective equipment, athletic products for baseball, hockey, biking & other sports (Riddell, MacGregor, Maxpro)

THE RIESE ORGANIZATION

162 W. 34th St.
New York, NY 10001
Phone: 212-536-7400
Fax: 212-737-0492

CEO: Dennis Riese
CFO: Shari Moss
HR: Andrew Johnson
Employees: 5,000

1994 Sales: $225 million
1-Yr. Sales Change: 3.7%
Ownership: Privately Held

Retail - fast-food & casual-theme franchised restaurants (TGI Fridays, Houlihan's, Dunkin' Donuts)

RJR NABISCO HOLDINGS CORP.

1301 Avenue of the Americas
New York, NY 10019
Phone: 212-258-5600
Fax: 212-969-9173

CEO: Steven F. Goldstone
CFO: Robert S. Roath
HR: Gerald I. Angowitz
Employees: 70,600

1994 Sales: $15,366 million
1-Yr. Sales Change: 1.7%
Exchange: NYSE
Symbol: RN

Tobacco (Camel, Doral, Salem & Winston)

 See pages 216–217 for a full profile of this company.

ROBERTS PHARMACEUTICAL CORPORATION

4 Industrial Way West
Eatontown, NJ 07724
Phone: 908-389-1182
Fax: 908-389-1014

CEO: Robert A. Vukovich
CFO: Anthony P. Maris
HR: Laura J. DiMichele
Employees: 568

1994 Sales: $112.2 million
1-Yr. Sales Change: 25.1%
Exchange: Nasdaq
Symbol: RPCX

Drugs

 See page 288 for a full profile of this company.

ROBOTIC VISION SYSTEMS, INC.

425 Rabro Dr. East
Hauppauge, NY 11788
Phone: 516-273-9700
Fax: 516-273-1167

CEO: Pat V. Costa
CFO: Robert H. Walker
HR: Pat Jennison
Employees: 128

1995 Sales: $63.6 million
1-Yr. Sales Change: 158.5%
Exchange: Nasdaq
Symbol: ROBV

Machine vision products used in quality control & measurement applications

 See page 289 for a full profile of this company.

ROCKBOTTOM STORES, INC.

83 Harbor Rd.
New York, NY 11050
Phone: 516-944-9000
Fax: 516-944-9409

CEO: Jonathan Otto
CFO: Bruce Respler
HR: —
Employees: 1,000

1994 Sales: $311 million
1-Yr. Sales Change: 24.4%
Ownership: Privately Held

Retail - drugstores

ROCKEFELLER CENTER PROPERTIES, INC.

1270 Avenue of the Americas
New York, NY 10020
Phone: 212-698-1440
Fax: 212-698-1453

CEO: Richard M. Scarlata
CFO: Janet P. King
HR: Janet P. King
Employees: —

1994 Sales: $109.3 million
1-Yr. Sales Change: -3.8%
Exchange: NYSE
Symbol: RCP

Real estate investment trust - the 12 buildings comprising Rockefeller Center, including the GE Building housing NBC & Radio City Music Hall

THE ROCKEFELLER FOUNDATION

420 Fifth Ave.
New York, NY 10018-2702
Phone: 212-869-8500
Fax: 212-398-1858

CEO: Peter C. Goldmark Jr.
CFO: Rosalie J. Wolf
HR: Charlotte N. Church
Employees: 137

1994 Sales: $21 million
1-Yr. Sales Change: -89.9%
Ownership: Privately Held

Charitable foundation

THE ROCKEFELLER UNIVERSITY

1230 York Ave.
New York , NY 10021
Phone: 212-327-8000
Fax: 212-327-7876

CEO: Torsten N. Wiesel
CFO: David J. Lyons
HR: Virginia Huffman
Employees: 1,600

1995 Sales: $115.5 million
1-Yr. Sales Change: 5.3%
Ownership: Privately Held

Private university offering 52 graduate degree programs in the natural & physical sciences

ROGER GIMBEL ACCESSORIES, INC.

4 W. 33rd St.
New York, NY 10001
Phone: 212-594-1480
Fax: 212-736-2307

Wholesale distribution - leather goods

CEO: Roger Gimbel
CFO: Geoffrey Gimbel
HR: —
Employees: 200

1994 Sales: $140 million
1-Yr. Sales Change: 0.0%
Ownership: Privately Held

ROGERS & WELLS

200 Park Ave.
New York, NY 10166
Phone: 212-878-8000
Fax: 212-878-8375

Law firm

CEO: James M. Ashar
CFO: Ed O'Sullivan
HR: —
Employees: —

1994 Sales: $158 million
1-Yr. Sales Change: 32.8%
Ownership: Privately Held

ROSE ART INDUSTRIES

6 Regent St.
Livingston, NJ 07039
Phone: 201-414-1313
Fax: 201-533-9447

Toys - dolls, jigsaw puzzles, markers & bulletin boards

CEO: Geoffrey Rosen
CFO: Randy Tarino
HR: Nora Gonzales
Employees: 1,100

1994 Sales: $130 million
1-Yr. Sales Change: 0.0%
Ownership: Privately Held

ROSENMAN & COLIN

575 Madison Ave., Ste. 11
New York, NY 10022
Phone: 212-940-8800
Fax: 212-940-8776

Law firm

CEO: Robert Smith
CFO: Ric DiBartolo
HR: Elizabeth Hahm
Employees: 600

1994 Est. Sales: $75 mil.
1-Yr. Sales Change: 7.1%
Ownership: Privately Held

ROSENTHAL AND ROSENTHAL, INC.

1370 Broadway
New York, NY 10018
Phone: 212-356-1400
Fax: 212-356-0900

Financial - lending & factoring

CEO: Imre J. Rosenthal
CFO: Brent Baumgardt
HR: Phyllis Wilson
Employees: 250

1995 Est. Sales: $125 mil.
1-Yr. Sales Change: —
Ownership: Privately Held

ROTARY POWER INTERNATIONAL, INC.

PO Box 128	CEO: Richard M. H. Thompson	1994 Sales: $7.8 million
Wood-Ridge, NJ 07075-0128	CFO: Gerald Horowitz	1-Yr. Sales Change: -27.1%
Phone: 201-777-7373	HR: —	Exchange: Nasdaq (SC)
Fax: 201-779-5595	Employees: 63	Symbol: RPII

Engines - rotary engines for military & commercial use

RPS REALTY TRUST

747 Third Ave.	CEO: Joel M. Pashcow	1994 Sales: $26.4 million
New York, NY 10017	CFO: Edwin R. Frankel	1-Yr. Sales Change: -2.2%
Phone: 212-355-1255	HR: —	Exchange: NYSE
Fax: 212-355-2522	Employees: —	Symbol: RPS

Real estate investment trust - holding & acquisition of mortgage loans

RUSH COMMUNICATIONS

652 Broadway	CEO: Russell Simmons	1994 Sales: $65 million
New York, NY 10036	CFO: —	1-Yr. Sales Change: 109.7%
Phone: 212-388-0012	HR: —	Ownership: Privately Held
Fax: 212-388-0312	Employees: 65	

Music production & publishing; TV, radio & film production; apparel

RUSS BERRIE & COMPANY INC.

111 Bauer Dr.	CEO: Russell Berrie	1994 Sales: $278.1 million
Oakland, NJ 07436	CFO: Paul Cargotch	1-Yr. Sales Change: -0.4%
Phone: 201-337-9000	HR: —	Exchange: NYSE
Fax: 201-405-7399	Employees: 2,400	Symbol: RUS

Sundries - wholesale

RYAN, BECK & CO., INC.

80 Main St.	CEO: Allen S. Greene	1994 Sales: $29.7 million
West Orange, NJ 07052-5414	CFO: Leonard J. Stanley	1-Yr. Sales Change: 3.8%
Phone: 201-325-3000	HR: Millie Santillo	Exchange: Nasdaq
Fax: 201-325-2089	Employees: 155	Symbol: RBCO

Financial - tax-exempt bank equity & debt securities, capital finance & merger-related services

S2 GOLF INC.

18 Gloria Ln.	CEO: Douglas A. Buffington	1994 Sales: $8.8 million
Fairfield, NJ 07004	CFO: Douglas A. Buffington	1-Yr. Sales Change: -1.1%
Phone: 201-227-7783	HR: —	Exchange: Nasdaq (SC)
Fax: 201-227-7018	Employees: 38	Symbol: GOLF

Leisure & recreational products - golf clubs, bags, balls & accessories

SAKS HOLDINGS, INC.

12 Eighth St.	CEO: Philip B. Miller	1995 Sales: $1,600 million
New York, NY 10017	CFO: Brian Kendrick	1-Yr. Sales Change: 33.3%
Phone: 212-753-4000	HR: Owen Dorsey	Ownership: Privately Held
Fax: 212-940-4299	Employees: 11,000	

Retail - department stores (46 units: Saks Fifth Avenue); off-price clearance centers (Off 5th); mail-order catalogs (Off 5th, Folio)

SALANT CORPORATION

1114 Avenue of the Americas	CEO: Nicholas P. DiPaolo	1994 Sales: $419.3 million
New York, NY 10036	CFO: Richard P. Randall	1-Yr. Sales Change: 4.3%
Phone: 212-221-7500	HR: Gloria Adams	Exchange: NYSE
Fax: 212-221-5363	Employees: 4,200	Symbol: SLT

Apparel - men's, women's & children's apparel & accessories, principally under internationally recognized brand names owned by the company or licensed from others

SALOMON INC

7 World Trade Center	CEO: Robert E. Denham	1994 Sales: $6,278 million
New York, NY 10048	CFO: Jerome H. Bailey	1-Yr. Sales Change: -28.7%
Phone: 212-783-7000	HR: Ed Weihenmayer	Exchange: NYSE
Fax: 212-783-2110	Employees: 9,077	Symbol: SB

Financial - investment banking & securities trading; oil refining & marketing

 See pages 218–219 for a full profile of this company.

SAM & LIBBY, INC.

58 W. 40th St.	CEO: Samuel L. Edelman	1994 Sales: $36.5 million
New York, NY 10018	CFO: Robert W. Schultz	1-Yr. Sales Change: 9.9%
Phone: 212-944-4830	HR: Joanne Lime	Exchange: Nasdaq
Fax: 212-944-4837	Employees: 39	Symbol: SAML

Shoes & related apparel

SAM ASH MUSIC CORPORATION

PO Box 9047	CEO: Jerome Ash	1995 Sales: $178 million
New York, NY 11802	CFO: David Ash	1-Yr. Sales Change: 17.1%
Phone: 516-932-6400	HR: Sam Ash	Ownership: Privately Held
Fax: 516-938-1437	Employees: 600	

Retail - musical instruments, sheet music, sound systems & recording equipment; wholesale microphones, bass amplifiers, mixing boards & sound sampling & modifying devices

SANDATA, INC.

26 Harbor Park Dr.	CEO: Bert E. Brodsky	1995 Sales: $7.5 million
Port Washington, NY 11050-4626	CFO: Larry Bobroff	1-Yr. Sales Change: 15.4%
Phone: 516-484-9060	HR: Lorraine Leshiekh	Exchange: Nasdaq (SC)
Fax: 516-484-4400	Employees: 101	Symbol: SAND

Data collection & systems - computerized data processing services, primarily to health care industries; turnkey computer systems based on standard & customized software

SARATOGA BRANDS, INC.

1835 Swarthmore Ave.	CEO: Scott G. Halperin	1994 Sales: $5.1 million
Lakewood, NJ 08701	CFO: John W. Kuhlman	1-Yr. Sales Change: 96.2%
Phone: 908-363-3800	HR: —	Exchange: Nasdaq (SC)
Fax: 908-363-1019	Employees: 197	Symbol: STGA

Food - branded products such as specialty Italian cheeses & rices; food catering & distribution (JR's Delis)

SAVOY PICTURES ENTERTAINMENT, INC.

152 W. 57th St.	CEO: Victor A. Kaufman	1994 Sales: $85.8 million
New York, NY 10019	CFO: Howard K. Bass	1-Yr. Sales Change: 1,108%
Phone: 212-247-5810	HR: Courtney Carmack	Exchange: Nasdaq
Fax: 212-247-5811	Employees: 130	Symbol: SPEI

Motion pictures - independent film distributor; TV station owner

SBARRO, INC.

763 Larkfield Rd.	CEO: Mario Sbarro	1994 Sales: $296 million
Commack, NY 11725	CFO: Robert S. Koebele	1-Yr. Sales Change: 11.4%
Phone: 516-864-0200	HR: James M. O'Shea	Exchange: AMEX
Fax: 516-462-9058	Employees: 9,100	Symbol: SBA

Retail - specialty pizza & pasta restaurants in airports, malls, universities & large chain stores

SBM INDUSTRIES, INC.

2 Madison Ave., Ste. 201	CEO: Peter Nisselson	1994 Sales: $13.9 million
Larchmont, NY 10538	CFO: Lawrence J. Goldstein	1-Yr. Sales Change: 75.9%
Phone: 914-833-0649	HR: —	Exchange: AMEX
Fax: 914-833-1068	Employees: 125	Symbol: SBM

Electrical components - watch batteries & related products; book publishing

SCHEIN PHARMACEUTICAL, INC.

100 Campus Dr.	CEO: Martin Sperber	1994 Sales: $420 million
Florham Park, NJ 07932	CFO: Dari Ashrafi	1-Yr. Sales Change: 12.0%
Phone: 201-593-5500	HR: Oliver Esman	Ownership: Privately Held
Fax: 201-593-5840	Employees: 1,800	

Drugs & sundries - wholesale

SCHERING-PLOUGH CORPORATION

One Giralda Farms	CEO: Richard J. Kogan	1994 Sales: $4,657.1 mil.
Madison, NJ 07940-1000	CFO: Jack L. Wyszomierski	1-Yr. Sales Change: 7.3%
Phone: 201-822-7000	HR: Gordon C. O'Brien	Exchange: NYSE
Fax: 201-822-7447	Employees: 21,200	Symbol: SGP

Drugs & consumer health care products (Dr. Scholl's, Coppertone)

 See pages 220–221 for a full profile of this company.

SCHLUMBERGER N.V.

277 Park Ave.	CEO: D. Euan Baird	1994 Sales: $6,696.8 mil.
New York, NY 10172-0266	CFO: Arthur Lindenauer	1-Yr. Sales Change: -0.1%
Phone: 212-350-9400	HR: Pierre E. Bismuth	Exchange: NYSE
Fax: 212-350-9564	Employees: 48,000	Symbol: SLB

Oil & gas - field services; measurement systems

 See pages 222–223 for a full profile of this company.

SCHOLASTIC CORPORATION

555 Broadway	CEO: Richard Robinson	1995 Sales: $749.9 million
New York, NY 10012-3999	CFO: Kevin J. McEnery	1-Yr. Sales Change: 18.7%
Phone: 212-343-6100	HR: Larry V. Holland	Exchange: Nasdaq
Fax: 212-343-6928	Employees: 5,636	Symbol: SCHL

Publishing - books (The Baby-Sitters Club, The Magic School Bus) & periodicals; online services for schools (Scholastic Network)

SCHOTT CORPORATION

3 Odell Plaza	CEO: Gary De Coninck	1994 Sales: $300 million
New York, NY 10701	CFO: George Giatras	1-Yr. Sales Change: 0.0%
Phone: 914-968-8900	HR: Alec Myers	Ownership: Privately Held
Fax: 914-378-3891	Employees: 2,500	

Glass products - specialty

SDI TECHNOLOGIES, INC.

1299 Main St.	CEO: Morris Franco	1994 Sales: $202 million
Rahway, NJ 07311	CFO: Chabetaye Chraime	1-Yr. Sales Change: 0.0%
Phone: 908-574-9000	HR: Leslie Switzer	Ownership: Privately Held
Fax: 908-574-1634	Employees: 900	

Audio & video home products - clock radios & other audio products (Timex)

SEALED AIR CORPORATION

Park 80 East	CEO: T. J. Dermot Dunphy	1994 Sales: $519.2 million
Saddle Brook, NJ 07663	CFO: Warren H. McCandless	1-Yr. Sales Change: 14.9%
Phone: 201-791-7600	HR: Heidi Calcagno	Exchange: NYSE
Fax: 201-703-4205	Employees: 3,000	Symbol: SEE

Containers - packaging & cushioning materials including padded mailing envelopes (Jiffy) & food packaging products

SEAMAN FURNITURE COMPANY, INC.

300 Crossways Park Dr.	CEO: Alan Rosenberg	1995 Sales: $228.2 million
Woodbury, NY 11797	CFO: Peter McGeough	1-Yr. Sales Change: 28.1%
Phone: 516-496-9560	HR: Maria Infante	Exchange: Nasdaq
Fax: 516-682-1610	Employees: 972	Symbol: SEAM

Retail - home furnishings, specializing in furniture packages

SECURITAS LOCK GROUP, INC.

103-00 Foster Ave.	CEO: Carl-Hendrick Svanberg	1994 Sales: $1,000 million
New York, NY 11236	CFO: Martin Hoffman	1-Yr. Sales Change: 0.0%
Phone: 718-257-4700	HR: Evelyn Steinfeld	Ownership: Privately Held
Fax: 718-649-9097	Employees: 5,000	

Building products - locks

SEL-LEB MARKETING, INC.

1435 51st St.	CEO: Jorge Lazaro	1994 Sales: $11 million
North Bergen, NJ 07047	CFO: Jan Mirsky	1-Yr. Sales Change: 23.6%
Phone: 201-864-3316	HR: —	Exchange: Nasdaq (SC)
Fax: 201-864-3586	Employees: 25	Symbol: SELB

Wholesale distribution - consumer merchandise such as health & beauty aids, cosmetics, fragrances, telephones & kitchen items to mass merchandisers, discount chain stores & the Home Shopping Network

SEMICONDUCTOR PACKAGING MATERIALS CO., INC.

431 Fayette Ave.	CEO: Gilbert D. Raker	1994 Sales: $16.5 million
Mamaroneck, NY 10543	CFO: Andrew A. Lozyniak	1-Yr. Sales Change: 63.4%
Phone: 914-698-5353	HR: Charles Italiano	Exchange: AMEX
Fax: 914-381-1436	Employees: 223	Symbol: SEM

Fine wire & metal ribbon, precision metal stampings, seal frames & powdered metal copper tungsten heat sinks for use in electronic components

SENTEX SENSING TECHNOLOGY, INC.

375 Sylvan Ave.	CEO: Joanne Bianco	1994 Sales: $1.6 million
Englewood Cliffs, NJ 07632	CFO: Joanne Bianco	1-Yr. Sales Change: -20.0%
Phone: 201-568-7079	HR: —	Exchange: Nasdaq (SC)
Fax: 201-568-7081	Employees: 10	Symbol: SENS

Electronics - analysis equipment & automated gas chromatography devices

SEQUA CORPORATION

200 Park Ave.	CEO: Norman E. Alexander	1994 Sales: $1,419.6 mil.
New York, NY 10166	CFO: Gerald S. Gutterman	1-Yr. Sales Change: -16.3%
Phone: 212-986-5500	HR: Michael F. Robilotto	Exchange: NYSE
Fax: 212-370-1969	Employees: 9,200	Symbol: SQAA

Diversified operations - aerospace; machinery; metal coatings & special chemicals

SFX BROADCASTING, INC.

150 E. 58th St., 19th Fl.	CEO: Robert F. X. Sillerman	1994 Sales: $55.6 million
New York, NY 10155-5749	CFO: D. Geoffrey Armstrong	1-Yr. Sales Change: 62.6%
Phone: 212-407-9191	HR: —	Exchange: Nasdaq
Fax: 212-832-5121	Employees: 357	Symbol: SFXBA

Broadcasting - radio stations

SGA SALES & MARKETING, INC.

108 Corporate Park Dr.	CEO: Don Schaevitz	1994 Sales: $120 million
White Plains, NY 10604	CFO: Don Schaevitz	1-Yr. Sales Change: -20.0%
Phone: 914-694-4090	HR: Susan Satz	Ownership: Privately Held
Fax: 914-694-4319	Employees: 70	

Food - general line grocery distrubution

SHEARMAN & STERLING

599 Lexington Ave.	CEO: Steven Volk	1994 Sales: $268 million
New York, NY 10022	CFO: Anthony Cassino	1-Yr. Sales Change: 4.7%
Phone: 212-848-4000	HR: —	Ownership: Privately Held
Fax: 212-848-7179	Employees: —	

Law firm

SHEFFIELD MEDICAL TECHNOLOGIES INC.

666 Fifth Ave., 13th Fl.	CEO: Douglas R. Eger	1994 Sales: $0
New York, NY 10103-2546	CFO: George Lombardi	1-Yr. Sales Change: —
Phone: 212-957-6600	HR: —	Exchange: AMEX
Fax: 212-957-6608	Employees: 6	Symbol: SHM

Medical services - commercialization of university-developed biomedical technologies

THE SHERWOOD GROUP, INC.

10 Exchange Place Center, 15th Fl.	CEO: Arthur Kontos	1995 Sales: $103 million
Jersey City, NJ 07032	CFO: William Karsh	1-Yr. Sales Change: 15.0%
Phone: 212-294-8000	HR: —	Exchange: NYSE
Fax: 212-946-4445	Employees: 425	Symbol: SHD

Financial - wholesale securities brokerage of Nasdaq and small-cap companies & retail deep-discount securities brokerage (National Discount Brokers)

SHERWOOD LUMBER COMPANY

300 Corporate Plaza	CEO: Andrew Goodman	1994 Sales: $100 million
Islandia, NY 11722	CFO: —	1-Yr. Sales Change: 11.1%
Phone: 516-232-9191	HR: —	Ownership: Privately Held
Fax: 516-232-1976	Employees: 21	

Building products - lumber

SHOPCO LAUREL CENTER, L.P.

388 Greenwich St., 28th Fl.
New York, NY 10013
Phone: 212-526-3237
Fax: 212-497-9619

CEO: Paul L. Abbott
CFO: Robert J. Hellman
HR: —
Employees: —

1994 Sales: $11.1 million
1-Yr. Sales Change: 4.7%
Exchange: AMEX
Symbol: LSC

Real estate operations - enclosed regional shopping mall management

SHOREWOOD PACKAGING CORPORATION

55 Engineers Ln.
Farmingdale, NY 11735
Phone: 516-694-2900
Fax: 516-752-9369

CEO: Paul B. Shore
CFO: Howard M. Liebman
HR: —
Employees: 2,200

1995 Sales: $357 million
1-Yr. Sales Change: 64.9%
Exchange: Nasdaq
Symbol: SHOR

Paper & paper products- packaging for consumer goods

SID TOOL COMPANY

151 Sunnyside Blvd.
Plainview, NY 11803
Phone: 516-349-7100
Fax: 516-349-7096

CEO: Mitchell Jacobson
CFO: —
HR: —
Employees: 700

1994 Sales: $248 million
1-Yr. Sales Change: 106.7%
Ownership: Privately Held

Wholesale distribution - industrial tools & equipment

SIGMA PLASTICS GROUP

PO Box 433
Lyndhurst, NJ 07071
Phone: 201-933-6000
Fax: 201-933-6429

CEO: Alfred Teo
CFO: John Reier
HR: —
Employees: 1,800

1995 Sales: $325 million
1-Yr. Sales Change: 22.6%
Ownership: Privately Held

Chemicals - polyethylene bags

SILGAN HOLDINGS INC.

4 Landmark Square
Stamford, CT 06901
Phone: 203-975-7110
Fax: 203-975-7902

CEO: R. Philip Silver
CFO: Harley Rankin Jr.
HR: Sharon Budds
Employees: 4,000

1994 Sales: $861 million
1-Yr. Sales Change: 33.4%
Ownership: Privately Held

Containers - plastic, steel & aluminum

SIMPSON THACHER & BARTLETT

425 Lexington Ave.
New York, NY 10017
Phone: 212-455-2000
Fax: 212-455-2502
Law firm

CEO: Cyrus Vance
CFO: Chris Conroy
HR: Eric Edelson
Employees: —

1994 Sales: $216 million
1-Yr. Sales Change: 3.3%
Ownership: Privately Held

SIRCO INTERNATIONAL CORP.

10 W. 33rd St., Ste. 606
New York, NY 10001-3306
Phone: 212-564-0114
Fax: 212-564-3618

CEO: Takeshi Yamaguchi
CFO: Tsuguya Saeki
HR: —
Employees: 140

1994 Sales: $27.6 million
1-Yr. Sales Change: -1.4%
Exchange: Nasdaq (SC)
Symbol: SIRC

Wholesale distribution - handbags, children's bags, soft luggage, purses, wallets, personal accessories & other related products

SITE HOLDINGS, INC.

369 Lexington Ave.
New York, NY 10017
Phone: 212-697-7580
Fax: 212-697-5910

CEO: Eugene L. Lewis
CFO: Eugene L. Lewis
HR: —
Employees: —

1994 Sales: $0.8 million
1-Yr. Sales Change: 166.7%
Exchange: Nasdaq (SC)
Symbol: SITE

Broadcasting - point-of-purchase video advertisements

SITHE ENERGIES INC.

450 Lexington Ave.
New York, NY 10017
Phone: 212-450-9000
Fax: 212-450-9005
Energy - cogeneration

CEO: William Kriegel
CFO: Richard J. Cronin III
HR: Karen Sands
Employees: 217

1994 Sales: $298.9 million
1-Yr. Sales Change: 13.6%
Exchange: NYSE
Symbol: SYT

SKADDEN, ARPS, SLATE, MEAGHER & FLOM

919 Third Ave.
New York, NY 10022
Phone: 212-735-3000
Fax: 212-735-2000
Law firm

CEO: Robert C. Sheehan
CFO: Karl Duchek
HR: Laurel Henschel
Employees: 3,200

1994 Sales: $582 million
1-Yr. Sales Change: 21.8%
Ownership: Privately Held

SKYLINE MULTIMEDIA ENTERTAINMENT, INC.

350 Fifth Ave.	CEO: Zalman Silber	1995 Sales: $2.2 million
New York, NY 10118	CFO: Steven Schwartz	1-Yr. Sales Change: —
Phone: 212-564-2224	HR: Mark Messersmith	Exchange: Nasdaq (SC)
Fax: 212-564-0652	Employees: 95	Symbol: SKYL

Leisure & recreational services - tourist attraction utilizing flight simulators to take aerial tours of New York & the Empire State Building

SKYSAT COMMUNICATIONS NETWORK CORPORATION

405 Lexington Ave., 33rd Fl.	CEO: Howard A. Foote	1994 Sales: $0
New York, NY 10174	CFO: Paul Wasserman	1-Yr. Sales Change: —
Phone: 212-972-0070	HR: —	Exchange: Nasdaq (SC)
Fax: 212-972-0093	Employees: 5	Symbol: SKATA

Aerospace - development of microwave-powered unmanned aircraft systems, which will carry communications payloads for use with cellular, personal & long-distance communications

SLIM-FAST NUTRITIONAL FOODS INTERNATIONAL, INC.

919 Third Ave., 26th Fl.	CEO: Daniel Abraham	1994 Sales: $625 million
New York, NY 10022	CFO: Carl Tfang	1-Yr. Sales Change: -7.4%
Phone: 212-415-7100	HR: Jack Portlock	Ownership: Privately Held
Fax: 212-415-7171	Employees: 500	

Food - diet foods & beverages

SLM INTERNATIONAL, INC.

30 Rockefeller Plaza, Ste. 4314	CEO: Howard J. Zunenshine	1994 Sales: $180.8 million
New York, NY 10112	CFO: John A. Sarto	1-Yr. Sales Change: -42.5%
Phone: 212-332-1620	HR: Benita Charles	Exchange: Pink Sheets
Fax: 212-332-1601	Employees: 1,800	Symbol: SLMI

Leisure & recreational products - hockey & related sporting goods products & licensed sports apparel

SLOAN'S SUPERMARKETS, INC.

823 11th Ave.	CEO: John A. Catsimatidis	1995 Sales: $48.4 million
New York, NY 10019-3535	CFO: Mark S. Kassner	1-Yr. Sales Change: 7.6%
Phone: 212-541-5534	HR: Benedict Focarino	Exchange: AMEX
Fax: 212-333-7418	Employees: 355	Symbol: SLO

Retail - supermarkets in Manhattan & Brooklyn

SMITH AND WOLLENSKY

305 E. 63rd St.	CEO: Michael Byrne	1994 Est. Sales: $5 million
New York, NY 10021	CFO: Michael Byrne	1-Yr. Sales Change: —
Phone: 212-753-1530	HR: —	Ownership: Privately Held
Fax: 212-751-5446	Employees: 180	
Retail - steak house		

SMITH CORONA CORPORATION

65 Locust Ave.	CEO: Robert Van Buren	1995 Sales: $196.3 million
New Canaan, CT 06840	CFO: John A. Piontkowski	1-Yr. Sales Change: -29.5%
Phone: 203-972-1471	HR: David Vorostko	Exchange: NYSE
Fax: 203-972-4220	Employees: 3,000	Symbol: SCO
Office equipment & supplies		

THE SOLOMON R. GUGGENHEIM FOUNDATION

1071 Fifth Ave.	CEO: Thomas Krens	1994 Sales: $34.4 million
New York, NY 10128	CFO: Bob Gebbie	1-Yr. Sales Change: -3.6%
Phone: 212-423-3600	HR: Laurie Price	Ownership: Privately Held
Fax: 212-423-3650	Employees: 300	
Foundation		

SONIC ENVIRONMENTAL SYSTEMS, INC.

141 New Rd.	CEO: Richard H. Hurd	1995 Sales: $7.3 million
Parsippany, NJ 07054	CFO: Richard H. Hurd	1-Yr. Sales Change: 160.7%
Phone: 201-882-9288	HR: —	Exchange: Nasdaq (SC)
Fax: 201-882-1486	Employees: 46	Symbol: SONA
Pollution control & heat exchanger systems for industrial applications		

SOROS FUND MANAGEMENT COMPANY

888 Seventh Ave.	CEO: George Soros	1995 Sales: —
New York, NY 10106	CFO: George Soros	1-Yr. Sales Change:
Phone: 212-262-6300	HR: —	Ownership: Privately Held
Fax: 212-245-5154	Employees: —	
Financial - investment management		

SOUTHERN CONTAINER CORPORATION

115 Engineers Rd.	CEO: Steven Grossman	1994 Sales: $260 million
Hauppauge, NY 11788	CFO: Todd Blatterman	1-Yr. Sales Change: 81.8%
Phone: 516-231-0444	HR: —	Ownership: Privately Held
Fax: 516-231-0618	Employees: 1,000	

Paper - corrugated, solid-fiber & recycled paper products

SOUTHERN NEW ENGLAND TELECOMMUNICATIONS

227 Church St.	CEO: Daniel J. Miglio	1994 Sales: $1,717 million
New Haven, CT 06510	CFO: Donald R. Shassian	1-Yr. Sales Change: 3.8%
Phone: 203-771-5200	HR: Jean LaVecchia	Exchange: NYSE
Fax: 203-865-0246	Employees: 9,797	Symbol: SNG

Utility - telephone

SPANISH BROADCASTING SYSTEMS INC.

26 W. 56th St.	CEO: Raul Alarcon Jr.	1994 Sales: $46 million
New York, NY 10019	CFO: Jose Antonio Garcia	1-Yr. Sales Change: 9.5%
Phone: 212-541-9200	HR: Albert Riera	Ownership: Privately Held
Fax: 212-541-8535	Employees: 150	

Broadcasting - radio stations

SPECIALTY RETAIL GROUP, INC.

1720 Post Rd. East, Ste. 112	CEO: Kevin R. Greene	1995 Sales: $5.6 million
Westport, CT 06880	CFO: Russell S. Fein	1-Yr. Sales Change: 51.4%
Phone: 203-256-4380	HR: —	Exchange: Nasdaq (SC)
Fax: 203-256-4375	Employees: 87	Symbol: SRGC

Retail - specialty & developmental toys (Building Blocks)

SPECTRUM INFORMATION TECHNOLOGIES, INC.

2700 Westchester Ave.	CEO: Donald J. Amoruso	1995 Sales: $11.6 million
Purchase, NY 10577	CFO: Salvatore T. Marino	1-Yr. Sales Change: 81.3%
Phone: 914-251-1800	HR: Kent Kessler	Exchange: OTC
Fax: 914-251-1811	Employees: 29	Symbol: SPCL

Telecommunications services - wireless-data technology

SPORTS MEDIA, INC.

101 E. 52nd St., Ninth Fl.	CEO: James Mason	1995 Sales: $2.3 million
New York, NY 10022	CFO: Michael Puccini	1-Yr. Sales Change: 76.9%
Phone: 212-308-6666	HR: —	Exchange: Nasdaq (SC)
Fax: 212-826-9033	Employees: 21	Symbol: SPTS

Publishing - professional sports team yearbooks

SQUARE INDUSTRIES, INC.

921 Bergen Ave.	CEO: Lowell Harwood	1994 Sales: $64.1 million
Jersey City, NJ 07306	CFO: Marvin Fruchtman	1-Yr. Sales Change: -5.5%
Phone: 201-798-0090	HR: John Kowl	Exchange: Nasdaq
Fax: 201-798-3179	Employees: 1,139	Symbol: SQAI

Parking lots & garage operations

ST. JOHN'S UNIVERSITY

800 Utopia Pkwy.	CEO: Donald Harrington	1995 Est. Sales: $100 mil.
Jamaica, NY 11439	CFO: Pat Breen	1-Yr. Sales Change: —
Phone: 718-990-6161	HR: Irene Kouril	Ownership: Privately Held
Fax: 718-380-0339	Employees: 2,230	

Jesuit-run Catholic university offering 70 undergraduate & 51 graduate degree programs

STAFF BUILDERS, INC.

1983 Marcus Ave.	CEO: Stephen Savitsky	1995 Sales: $325.1 million
Lake Success, NY 11042	CFO: Gary Tighe	1-Yr. Sales Change: 32.1%
Phone: 516-358-1000	HR: Don Ramsey	Exchange: Nasdaq
Fax: 516-358-1036	Employees: 2,200	Symbol: SBLI

Personnel - temporary office staff

STAGE II APPAREL CORP.

350 Fifth Ave.	CEO: Stuart Goldman	1994 Sales: $65.2 million
New York, NY 10118	CFO: Philip London	1-Yr. Sales Change: -1.8%
Phone: 212-564-5865	HR: Tom Hammell	Exchange: AMEX
Fax: 212-239-0377	Employees: 99	Symbol: SA

Apparel - men's & boys' casualwear & activewear

STANDARD MICROSYSTEMS CORPORATION

80 Arkay Dr.
Hauppauge, NY 11788
Phone: 516-435-6000
Fax: 516-273-5550

CEO: Victor F. Trizzino
CFO: Anthony M. D'Agostino
HR: Ernest W. Sern
Employees: 861

1995 Sales: $378.7 million
1-Yr. Sales Change: 17.4%
Exchange: Nasdaq
Symbol: SMSC

Computers - local area network interface hardware; VLSI circuitry

 See page 290 for a full profile of this company.

STANDARD MOTOR PRODUCTS, INC.

37-18 Northern Blvd.
Long Island City, NY 11101
Phone: 718-392-0200
Fax: 718-729-4549

CEO: Lawrence I. Sills
CFO: Michael J. Bailey
HR: Sanford Kay
Employees: 3,300

1994 Sales: $640.8 million
1-Yr. Sales Change: 9.9%
Exchange: NYSE
Symbol: SMP

Automotive & trucking - replacement parts & accessories & supplies for auto repair shops

STAR MULTI CARE SERVICES, INC.

99 Railroad Station Plaza, Ste. 208
Hicksville, NY 11801
Phone: 718-488-7300
Fax: 718-802-1455

CEO: Stephen Sternbach
CFO: William Fellerman
HR: Dawn Stillwell
Employees: —

1995 Sales: $27.1 million
1-Yr. Sales Change: 22.1%
Exchange: Nasdaq (SC)
Symbol: SMCS

Health care - home health care & services; temporary health care personnel to hospitals, nursing homes & medical facilities

STARRETT CORPORATION

909 Third Ave.
New York, NY 10022
Phone: 212-751-3100
Fax: 212-759-7699

CEO: Paul M. Milstein
CFO: Lewis A. Weinfeld
HR: Evelyn F. Betlesky
Employees: 1,100

1994 Sales: $141.3 million
1-Yr. Sales Change: 15.6%
Exchange: NYSE
Symbol: SHO

Building - single-family homes & garden apartments

STARTER CORPORATION

370 James St.
New Haven, CT 06513
Phone: 203-781-4000
Fax: 203-777-8820

CEO: David A. Beckerman
CFO: Lawrence C. Longo Jr.
HR: Juli Wilhelm
Employees: 800

1994 Sales: $379.5 million
1-Yr. Sales Change: 5.4%
Exchange: NYSE
Symbol: STA

Apparel

STATE BANCORP, INC.

699 Hillside Ave.	CEO: Thomas F. Goldrick Jr.	1994 Sales: $32.5 million
New Hyde Park, NY 11040	CFO: Daniel T. Rowe	1-Yr. Sales Change: 0.3%
Phone: 516-437-1000	HR: Mary Durkin	Exchange: Nasdaq (SC)
Fax: 516-437-1032	Employees: 166	Symbol: STBC

Banks - Northeast

STERLING BANCORP

540 Madison Ave.	CEO: Louis J. Cappelli	1994 Sales: $50 million
New York, NY 10022-3299	CFO: John W. Tietjen	1-Yr. Sales Change: 37.4%
Phone: 212-826-8000	HR: Roger Maglio	Exchange: NYSE
Fax: 212-490-8852	Employees: 189	Symbol: STL

Banks - Northeast

STERLING VISION, INC.

10 Peninsula Blvd.	CEO: Robert Cohen	1994 Sales: $38.7 mil.
Lynbrook, NY 11563	CFO: Sebastian Giordano	1-Yr. Sales Change: 20.9%
Phone: 516-887-2100	HR: Donna Landeck	Exchange: Nasdaq
Fax: 516-887-2246	Employees: —	Symbol: ISEE

Retail - optical stores; laser centers offering photorefractive keratectomy for the correction of nearsightedness

STEVEN MADDEN, LTD.

52-16 Barnett Ave.	CEO: Steven Madden	1994 Sales: $8.4 million
Long Island City, NY 11104	CFO: Arvino Dharia	1-Yr. Sales Change: 223.1%
Phone: 718-446-1800	HR: —	Exchange: Nasdaq (SC)
Fax: 718-446-5599	Employees: 20	Symbol: SHOO

Retail - shoe stores

STONE & WEBSTER, INCORPORATED

250 W. 34th St.	CEO: Bruce C. Coles	1994 Sales: $818.2 million
New York, NY 10119	CFO: William M. Egan	1-Yr. Sales Change: -22.3%
Phone: 212-290-7500	HR: Darlene Lucas	Exchange: NYSE
Fax: 212-290-7507	Employees: 5,000	Symbol: SW

Construction - engineering & consulting services; construction & full environmental services for power, industrial, governmental, transportation & civil works projects

THE STROBER ORGANIZATION, INC.

550 Hamilton Ave.
New York, NY 11232
Phone: 718-832-1212
Fax: 718-788-3614

CEO: Robert J. Gaites
CFO: David J. Polishook
HR: Susan Plaza
Employees: 344

1994 Sales: $125.4 million
1-Yr. Sales Change: 5.4%
Exchange: Nasdaq
Symbol: STRB

Building products - wholesale building materials for professional contractors & do-it-yourselfers

STROOCK & STROOCK & LAVAN

7 Hanover Square
New York, NY 10004
Phone: 212-806-5400
Fax: 212-806-6006

CEO: Lewis Cole
CFO: R. Ronald Maselli
HR: Jackie Weiss
Employees: 900

1994 Sales: $148 million
1-Yr. Sales Change: 5.0%
Ownership: Privately Held

Law firm

STURM, RUGER & COMPANY, INC.

Lacey Place
Southport, CT 06490
Phone: 203-259-7843
Fax: 203-254-2195

CEO: William B. Ruger
CFO: John M. Kingsley Jr.
HR: Carol Markland
Employees: 1,910

1994 Sales: $196.4 million
1-Yr. Sales Change: 1.1%
Exchange: NYSE
Symbol: RGR

Ordnance - guns

SUBWAY SANDWICH SHOPS, INC.

325 Bic Dr.
Milford, CT 06460
Phone: 203-877-4281
Fax: 203-876-6688

CEO: Peter Buck
CFO: Haydee Buck
HR: —
Employees: 500

1994 Est. Sales: $2,700 mil.
1-Yr. Sales Change: 22.7%
Ownership: Privately Held

Retail - restaurants (oversees the Subway Sandwiches & Salads chain)

SUGAR FOODS CORPORATION

950 Third Ave.
New York, NY 10022
Phone: 212-753-6900
Fax: 212-753-6988

CEO: Donald G. Tober
CFO: Jim Walsh
HR: George Reichel
Employees: 300

1994 Sales: $165 million
1-Yr. Sales Change: 0.0%
Ownership: Privately Held

Food - sugar substitutes

SULLIVAN & CROMWELL

125 Broad St.
New York, NY 10004
Phone: 212-558-4000
Fax: 212-558-3588

CEO: Ricardo Mestres Jr.
CFO: Larry Tsaousis
HR: Walter Kehoe
Employees: —

1994 Sales: $298 million
1-Yr. Sales Change: -0.3%
Ownership: Privately Held

Law firm with offices in Hong Kong, London, Los Angeles, Melbourne, New York, Paris, Tokyo & Washington, DC

THE SUMMIT BANCORPORATION

One Main St.
Chatham, NJ 07928
Phone: 201-701-6200
Fax: 201-701-0464

Banks - Northeast

CEO: Robert G. Cox
CFO: John R. Feeney
HR: J. Page Stiger Jr.
Employees: 1,623

1994 Sales: $393.8 million
1-Yr. Sales Change: 3.5%
Exchange: Nasdaq
Symbol: SUBN

SUNNYDALE FARMS, INC.

400 Stanley Ave.
New York, NY 11207
Phone: 718-257-7600
Fax: 718-257-7466

Food - milk

CEO: Gerald Rosen
CFO: Sharad Mathur
HR: Sarah Macy
Employees: 390

1994 Sales: $140 million
1-Yr. Sales Change: 0.0%
Ownership: Privately Held

SUNRISE BANCORP, INC.

375 Fulton St.
Farmingdale, NY 11735-2680
Phone: 516-249-8025
Fax: 516-249-2173

CEO: Joseph A. Melillo
CFO: John G. Lombardo
HR: —
Employees: 241

1994 Sales: $40.6 million
1-Yr. Sales Change: 0.0%
Exchange: Nasdaq
Symbol: SUNY

Financial - savings & loans (Sunrise Federal Savings Bank)

SUPREMA SPECIALTIES, INC.

510 E. 35th St.
Paterson, NJ 07543
Phone: 201-684-2900
Fax: 201-684-8680

Food - dairy products

CEO: Mark Cocchiola
CFO: Stuart D. Schwartz
HR: Anna Cocchiola
Employees: 86

1995 Sales: $52.1 million
1-Yr. Sales Change: 62.8%
Exchange: Nasdaq
Symbol: CHEZ

SYMBOL TECHNOLOGIES, INC.

116 Wilbur Place
Bohemia, NY 11716
Phone: 516-563-2400
Fax: 516-244-1403

CEO: Jerome Swartz
CFO: Thomas G. Amato
HR: Allen C. Creveling
Employees: 2,387

1994 Sales: $465.3 million
1-Yr. Sales Change: 29.3%
Exchange: NYSE
Symbol: SBL

Optical character recognition - bar code-based data capture transaction systems

SYMS CORP.

Syms Way
Secaucus, NJ 07094
Phone: 201-902-9600
Fax: 201-902-9278

CEO: Sy Syms
CFO: Arthur Weber
HR: Maryjane Lauria
Employees: 2,364

1994 Sales: $326.7 million
1-Yr. Sales Change: 2.4%
Exchange: NYSE
Symbol: SYM

Retail - apparel stores offering off-price merchandise consisting primarily of men's tailored clothing, women's dresses, suits & separates & children's apparel (39 units)

SYNETIC, INC.

669 River Dr.
Elmwood Park, NJ 07407
Phone: 201-703-3400
Fax: 201-703-3401

CEO: Martin J. Wygod
CFO: James V. Manning
HR: —
Employees: 1,090

1995 Sales: $39.2 million
1-Yr. Sales Change: -64.9%
Exchange: Nasdaq
Symbol: SNTC

Plastic products

TAMBRANDS INC.

777 Westchester Ave.
White Plains, NY 10604
Phone: 914-696-6000
Fax: 914-696-6161

CEO: Edward T. Fogarty
CFO: Raymond F. Wright
HR: Thomas Soper III
Employees: 3,400

1994 Sales: $644.5 million
1-Yr. Sales Change: 5.4%
Exchange: NYSE
Symbol: TMB

Medical products - personal-care products & sanitary napkins (TAMPAX)

TANDLER TEXTILE, INC.

104 W. 40th St.
New York, NY 10018
Phone: 212-869-9800
Fax: 212-575-8714

CEO: Martin Tandler
CFO: Ezra Berkowitz
HR: Ezra Berkowitz
Employees: 95

1994 Sales: $180 million
1-Yr. Sales Change: 68.2%
Ownership: Privately Held

Textiles - piece-dyed, yarn-dyed & printed fabrics

TEACHERS INSURANCE AND ANNUITY ASSOCIATION-COLLEGE RETIREMENT EQUITIES FUND

730 Third Ave.
New York, NY 10017-3206
Phone: 212-490-9000
Fax: 212-916-6231

CEO: John H. Biggs
CFO: Richard L. Gibbs
HR: Matina S. Horner
Employees: 4,000

1994 Sales: $10,412.6 mil.
1-Yr. Sales Change: 2.6%
Ownership: Privately Held

Financial - retirement annuities; insurance

 See pages 224–225 for a full profile of this company.

TBWA CHIAT/DAY

180 Maiden Ln.
New York, NY 10038
Phone: 212-804-1000
Fax: 212-804-1200

CEO: Ira Matathia
CFO: Colette Chestnut
HR: —
Employees: 656

1994 Sales: $122.9 million
1-Yr. Sales Change: 4%
Ownership: Privately held

Advertising

TECHKNITS, INC.

10 Grand Ave.
New York, NY 11205
Phone: 718-875-3299
Fax: 718-852-3944

CEO: Simon Taub
CFO: Simon Taub
HR: Simon Taub
Employees: 350

1995 Sales: $19.3 million
1-Yr. Sales Change: 26.1%
Exchange: Nasdaq (SC)
Symbol: KNIT

Apparel - women's, children's & men's knitted apparel for national retail chains

TELEOS COMMUNICATIONS, INC.

2 Meridian Rd.
Eatontown, NJ 07724
Phone: 908-389-5700
Fax: 908-544-9890

CEO: Michael Caglarcan
CFO: Thomas Aiken
HR: Phyllis Lockwood
Employees: 115

1994 Sales: $19 million
1-Yr. Sales Change: 46.2%
Ownership: Privately Held

Computers - global bandwidth on-demand network access solutions for integrated video, data & voice communications

TELEWAY, INC.

1600 Stewart Ave.
Westbury, NY 11590
Phone: 516-237-6000
Fax: 516-237-6112

CEO: James McCann
CFO: Glenn Reed
HR: Harriet Abrams
Employees: —

1994 Est. Sales: $140 mil.
1-Yr. Sales Change: 40.0%
Ownership: Privately Held

Retail - express flowers (800-Flowers) & gifts (800-Baskets, 800-Gifthouse)

TENNEY ENGINEERING, INC.

1090 Springfield Rd.
Union, NJ 07083
Phone: 908-686-7870
Fax: 908-686-9205

CEO: Robert S. Schiffman
CFO: Martin Pelman
HR: Frank C. Gosztyla
Employees: 66

1994 Sales: $7.2 million
1-Yr. Sales Change: -5.3%
Exchange: OTC
Symbol: TNGI

Pollution control equipment & services - environmental test & vacuum equipment

TEREX CORPORATION

500 Post Rd. East, Ste. 320
Westport, CT 06880
Phone: 203-222-7170
Fax: 203-222-7976

CEO: Ronald M. DeFeo
CFO: Ralph T. Brandifino
HR: Steve Hooper
Employees: 2,850

1994 Sales: $786.8 million
1-Yr. Sales Change: 17.4%
Exchange: NYSE
Symbol: TEX

Machinery - heavy-duty construction, mining, maintenance & related equipment

TEXACO INC.

2000 Westchester Ave.
White Plains, NY 10650
Phone: 914-253-4000
Fax: 914-253-7753

CEO: Alfred C. DeCrane Jr.
CFO: William C. Bousquette
HR: John D. Ambler
Employees: 29,713

1994 Sales: $33,353 million
1-Yr. Sales Change: -2.1%
Exchange: NYSE
Symbol: TX

Oil & gas - international integrated

 See pages 226–227 for a full profile of this company.

TEXAS PACIFIC LAND TRUST

80 Broad St., Ste. 2700
New York, NY 10004
Phone: 212-269-2266
Fax: 212-269-2267

CEO: George C. Fraser III
CFO: Roy Thomas
HR: —
Employees: 9

1994 Sales: $9.1 million
1-Yr. Sales Change: 71.7%
Exchange: NYSE
Symbol: TPL

Real estate operations

THACKERAY CORPORATION

400 Madison Ave., Ste. 1508
New York, NY 10017-1909
Phone: 212-759-3695
Fax: 212-759-4481

CEO: Martin J. Rabinowitz
CFO: Jules Ross
HR: —
Employees: 62

1994 Sales: $19.1 million
1-Yr. Sales Change: 41.5%
Exchange: NYSE
Symbol: THK

Door hardware, doors & frames, mechanical & electrical hardware, including locks, door knobs, hinges (Atlantic Hardware & Supply Corp.); mortgage loans & real estate investments (Thackeray)

THIRTEEN/WNET

356 W. 58th St.
New York, NY 10019
Phone: 212-560-2000
Fax: 212-582-3297

Broadcasting - PBS TV station

CEO: William F. Baker
CFO: Tom Conway
HR: Mark Morales
Employees: 365

1994 Sales: $102.2 million
1-Yr. Sales Change: -25.8%
Ownership: Privately Held

THOMAS PUBLISHING COMPANY

5 Penn Plaza
New York, NY 10001
Phone: 212-695-0500
Fax: 212-290-7311

CEO: Carl T. Holst-Knudsen
CFO: Donald Macpherson
HR: Ivy Molofsky
Employees: 400

1994 Est. Sales: $50 mil.
1-Yr. Sales Change: —
Ownership: Privately Held

Publishing - industrial directories (Thomas Register); online information retrieval systems

THT INC.

33 Riverside Ave.
Westport, Ct 06880
Phone: 203-226-6408
Fax: 203-226-8022

CEO: Frederick A. Rossetti
CFO: Frederick A. Rossetti
HR: —
Employees: 153

1995 Sales: $18.5 million
1-Yr. Sales Change: 8.2%
Exchange: Nasdaq (SC)
Symbol: TXHI

Rolled paper products for the confectionery & health-related industries; stove-top grills, fabricated steel parts & wire forming products

THYPIN STEEL COMPANY

49-49 30th St.
Long Island City, NY 11101
Phone: 718-937-2700
Fax: 718-706-4501

CEO: David Thypin
CFO: Alan Aronovitz
HR: Rita Herman
Employees: 200

1994 Est. Sales: $250 mil.
1-Yr. Sales Change: 25.0%
Ownership: Privately Held

Metal products - service centers

TIFFANY & CO.

727 5th Ave.
New York, NY 10022
Phone: 212-755-8000
Fax: 212-605-4465

CEO: William R. Chaney
CFO: James N. Fernandez
HR: Michael H. Mitchell
Employees: 3,306

1995 Sales: $682.8 million
1-Yr. Sales Change: 20.5%
Exchange: NYSE
Symbol: TIF

Retail - fine jewelry, timepieces, sterling silverware, china, crystal, stationery, writing instruments, fragrance, leather goods, scarves & ties

 See page 291 for a full profile of this company.

TIG HOLDINGS, INC.

65 E. 55th St., 28th Fl.
New York, NY 10022
Phone: 212-446-2700
Fax: 212-371-8360

CEO: Jon W. Rotenstreich
CFO: Edwin G. Pickett
HR: Lon McClimon
Employees: 2,550

1994 Sales: $1,778 million
1-Yr. Sales Change: -5.5%
Exchange: NYSE
Symbol: TIG

Insurance - multiline, including property & casualty & reinsurance

TIGERA GROUP, INC.

730 Fifth Ave.
New York, NY 10019
Phone: 212-644-6211
Fax: 212-644-5498

CEO: Donald T. Pascal
CFO: Robert E. Kelly
HR: —
Employees: 2

1994 Sales: $0.2 million
1-Yr. Sales Change: -75.0%
Exchange: OTC
Symbol: TYGR

Financial - investments in other businesses

TII INDUSTRIES, INC.

1385 Akron St.
Copiague, NY 11726
Phone: 516-789-5000
Fax: 516-789-5063

CEO: Alfred J. Roach
CFO: —
HR: Angie Kane
Employees: 1,006

1995 Sales: $4.8 million
1-Yr. Sales Change: -88.0%
Exchange: Nasdaq
Symbol: TIII

Electrical products - gas tube overvoltage protectors

TIME WARNER INC.

75 Rockefeller Plaza
New York, NY 10019
Phone: 212-484-8000
Fax: 212-484-8734

CEO: Gerald M. Levin
CFO: Richard J. Bressler
HR: Carolyn McCandless
Employees: 53,000

1994 Sales: $7,396 million
1-Yr. Sales Change: 12.4%
Exchange: NYSE
Symbol: TWX

Publishing - periodicals (Time, FORTUNE, Money, People, Sports Illustrated) & books (Little Brown, Warner, Book-of-the-Month); filmed entertainment (Warner Brothers); cable TV systems (#2 in US)

 See pages 228–229 for a full profile of this company.

TINGUE BROWN & CO.

535 N. Midland Ave.
Saddle Brook, NJ 07662
Phone: 201-796-4490
Fax: 201-796-5820

CEO: William J. Tingue
CFO: Ron Midili
HR: John Hurst
Employees: 200

1994 Sales: $380 million
1-Yr. Sales Change: 0.0%
Ownership: Privately Held

Apparel - piece goods, notions & other dry goods

TISHMAN REALTY & CONSTRUCTION CO. INC.

666 Fifth Ave.
New York, NY 10103
Phone: 212-399-3600
Fax: 212-957-9791

CEO: John Tishman
CFO: Larry Schwarzwalder
HR: Gina Perrone
Employees: 575

1995 Sales: $572 million
1-Yr. Sales Change: 5.9%
Ownership: Privately Held

Building - management services; hotel management; real estate development

TITAN INDUSTRIAL CORPORATION

555 Madison Ave.
New York, NY 10022
Phone: 212-421-6700
Fax: 212-421-6708

CEO: Michael S. Levin
CFO: George Cady
HR: —
Employees: 200

1994 Sales: $425 million
1-Yr. Sales Change: 6.3%
Ownership: Privately Held

Steel - manufacturing & marketing

TLC BEATRICE INTERNATIONAL HOLDINGS, INC.

9 W. 57th St.
New York, NY 10019
Phone: 212-756-8900
Fax: 212-888-3093

CEO: Loida N. Lewis
CFO: Peter Offerman
HR: Rene S. Meilly
Employees: 4,300

1994 Sales: $1,821.7 mil.
1-Yr. Sales Change: 10.0%
Ownership: Privately Held

Food - wholesale & retail distribution, grocery product marketing & manufacturing, primarily in Europe

TMP WORLDWIDE

1633 Broadway
New York, NY 10019
Phone: 212-977-4200
Fax: 212-247-0015

CEO: Andrew McKelvey
CFO: Roxane Previty
HR: Lynn Harris
Employees: 970

1994 Sales: $117.7 million
1-Yr. Sales Change: 28.6%
Ownership: Privately Held

Advertising

TOFUTTI BRANDS INC.

50 Jackson Dr.
Cranford, NJ 07016
Phone: 908-272-2400
Fax: 908-272-9492

CEO: David Mintz
CFO: Steven Kass
HR: Steven Kass
Employees: 8

1994 Sales: $5.2 million
1-Yr. Sales Change: 26.8%
Exchange: AMEX
Symbol: TOF

Food - nondairy frozen desserts

TOLLMAN HUNDLEY HOTELS

100 Summit Lake Dr.
Valhalla, NY 10595
Phone: 914-747-3636
Fax: 914-747-1938

Hotels & motels

CEO: Monty Hundley
CFO: Rusty Zuckerman
HR: Tom Damewood
Employees: 7,000

1994 Sales: $270 million
1-Yr. Sales Change: 0.0%
Ownership: Privately Held

THE TOPPS COMPANY, INC.

One Whitehall St.
New York, NY 10004-2109
Phone: 212-376-0300
Fax: 212-376-0573

CEO: Arthur T. Shorin
CFO: Catherine K. Jessup
HR: William G. O'Connor
Employees: 1,100

1995 Sales: $265.4 million
1-Yr. Sales Change: -1.0%
Exchange: Nasdaq
Symbol: TOPP

Leisure - entertainment products, picture trading cards (Topps), confections (Bazooka, Ring Pop, Push Pop) & comic books

TOPS APPLIANCE CITY, INC.

45 Brunswick Ave.
Edison, NJ 08818
Phone: 908-248-2850
Fax: 908-248-2719

CEO: Leslie S. Turchin
CFO: William J. Tennant
HR: Charles Rosenberg
Employees: 2,200

1994 Sales: $461.5 million
1-Yr. Sales Change: 12.2%
Exchange: Nasdaq
Symbol: TOPS

Retail - consumer electronics & appliances in New York City metropolitan area

TORESCO ENTERPRISES INC.

170 Route 22
Springfield, NJ 07081
Phone: 201-467-2900
Fax: 201-467-1824

Retail - new & used cars

CEO: Donald Toresco
CFO: Donald Toresco
HR: —
Employees: 585

1994 Est. Sales: $412 mil.
1-Yr. Sales Change: 3.0%
Ownership: Privately Held

TOSCO CORPORATION

72 Cummings Point Rd.
Stamford, CT 06902
Phone: 203-977-1000
Fax: 203-964-3187

Oil refining & marketing

CEO: Thomas D. O'Malley
CFO: Jefferson F. Allen
HR: Timothy J. McGarvey
Employees: 3,613

1994 Sales: $6,365.7 mil.
1-Yr. Sales Change: 78.9%
Exchange: NYSE
Symbol: TOS

 See pages 230–231 for a full profile of this company.

TOTAL-TEL USA COMMUNICATIONS, INC.

150 Clove Rd., Eighth Fl., Box 449
Little Falls, NJ 07424
Phone: 201-773-7000
Fax: 201-812-8302

CEO: Warren H. Feldman
CFO: Thomas P. Gunning
HR: Karen Singer
Employees: 100

1995 Sales: $29.8 million
1-Yr. Sales Change: 56.8%
Exchange: Nasdaq
Symbol: TELU

Telecommunications services - long distance

TOUCHSTONE APPLIED SCIENCE ASSOCIATES, INC.

Fields Lane, PO Box 382
Brewster, NY 10509-0382
Phone: 914-277-8100
Fax: 914-277-3548

CEO: Andrew L. Simon
CFO: Andrew L. Simon
HR: —
Employees: 23

1994 Sales: $2 million
1-Yr. Sales Change: -13.0%
Exchange: Nasdaq (SC)
Symbol: TASA

Publishing - reading comprehension tests, instructional materials & software for elementary &
secondary schools, colleges & universities

TOWER AIR, INC.

John F. Kennedy International Airport
Jamaica, NY 11430-2478
Phone: 718-553-4300
Fax: 718-553-4312

CEO: Morris K. Nachtomi
CFO: Josefina M. Essex
HR: Pamela Marett
Employees: 1,367

1994 Sales: $368 million
1-Yr. Sales Change: 7.7%
Exchange: Nasdaq
Symbol: TOWR

Transportation - low-fare, no-frills airline serving Israel & other international destinations from New
York City

 See page 292 for a full profile of this company.

TOWERS PERRIN

245 Park Ave.
New York, NY 10167
Phone: 212-309-3400
Fax: 212-309-3760

CEO: John T. Lynch
CFO: Patrick Gonnelli
HR: Ken Ranftle
Employees: 5,000

1994 Sales: $766.8 million
1-Yr. Sales Change: 8.2%
Ownership: Privately Held

Consulting & reinsurance

TOY BIZ, INC.

333 E. 38th St.
New York, NY 10016
Phone: 212-682-4700
Fax: 212-682-5317

CEO: Joseph M. Ahearn
CFO: Bobby G. Jenkins
HR: David Fremed
Employees: 55

1994 Sales: $155.7 million
1-Yr. Sales Change: 73.6%
Exchange: NYSE
Symbol: TBZ

Toys - exclusive licensee of toys for Marvel Entertainment Group

TOYS "R" US, INC.

461 From Rd.
Paramus, NJ 07652
Phone: 201-262-7800
Fax: 201-262-7606

CEO: Michael Goldstein
CFO: Louis Lipschitz
HR: Jeffrey S. Wells
Employees: 58,000

1995 Sales: $8,745.6 mil.
1-Yr. Sales Change: 10.1%
Exchange: NYSE
Symbol: TOY

Retail - toys & children's clothing

 See pages 232–233 for a full profile of this company.

T R FINANCIAL CORP.

1122 Franklin Ave.
Garden City, NY 11530
Phone: 516-742-9300
Fax: 516-742-6145

CEO: John M. Tsimbinos
CFO: Dennis E. Henchy
HR: Elaine E. Cordiello
Employees: 477

1994 Sales: $155.3 million
1-Yr. Sales Change: 17.2%
Exchange: Nasdaq
Symbol: ROSE

Financial - savings & loans (Roosevelt Savings Bank)

TRANSAMMONIA, INC.

350 Park Ave.
New York, NY 10022
Phone: 212-223-3200
Fax: 212-759-1410

CEO: Ronald P. Stanton
CFO: Edward G. Weiner
HR: Marguerite Harrington
Employees: 200

1995 Sales: $2,320 million
1-Yr. Sales Change: 74.4%
Ownership: Privately Held

Fertilizers; petroleum products; methanol; commodities trading

TRANSATLANTIC HOLDINGS, INC.

80 Pine St.
New York, NY 10005
Phone: 212-770-2000
Fax: 212-785-7230

CEO: Robert F. Orlich
CFO: Steven S. Skalicky
HR: Maria McGlockin
Employees: 245

1994 Sales: $1,004.8 mil.
1-Yr. Sales Change: 39.6%
Exchange: NYSE
Symbol: TRH

Insurance - property & casualty

TRANS-LUX CORPORATION

110 Richards Ave.
Norwalk, CT 06856-5090
Phone: 203-853-4321
Fax: 203-866-9496

CEO: Victor Liss
CFO: Angela D. Toppi
HR: Richard K. Kramer
Employees: 478

1994 Sales: $33.7 million
1-Yr. Sales Change: -5.9%
Exchange: AMEX
Symbol: TLX

Electrical products - large-scale monochrome & multicolor real-time electronic information displays; motion picture theater chain

TRANSNATIONAL RE CORPORATION

399 Thornall St., 14th Fl.
Edison, NJ 08837
Phone: 908-906-8100
Fax: 908-906-9157

CEO: Gerald L. Radke
CFO: Sanford M. Kimmel
HR: Linda Clauser
Employees: 42

1994 Sales: $71.5 million
1-Yr. Sales Change: 5,007%
Exchange: Nasdaq
Symbol: TREX

Insurance - brokered property, marine & aviation retrocessional reinsurance

TRANSNET CORPORATION

45 Columbia Rd.
Somerville, NJ 08876-3576
Phone: 908-253-0500
Fax: 908-688-7813

CEO: Steven J. Wilk
CFO: John J. Wilk
HR: Susan Wilk
Employees: 101

1995 Sales: $56.2 million
1-Yr. Sales Change: 39.5%
Exchange: Nasdaq
Symbol: TRNT

Computers - wholesale hardware & software

TRANS-RESOURCES, INC.

9 W. 57th St.
New York, NY 10019
Phone: 212-888-3044
Fax: 212-888-3708

CEO: Arie Genger
CFO: Lester Youner
HR: —
Employees: 1,600

1994 Sales: $325 million
1-Yr. Sales Change: 0.0%
Ownership: Privately Held

Chemicals - specialty plant nutrients & industrial chemicals

TRANSTECHNOLOGY CORPORATION

700 Liberty Ave.
Union, NJ 07083-8198
Phone: 908-964-5666
Fax: 908-688-8518

CEO: Michael J. Berthelot
CFO: Chandler J. Moisen
HR: Monica Lazorchak
Employees: 1,014

1995 Sales: $102.7 million
1-Yr. Sales Change: -15.5%
Exchange: NYSE
Symbol: TT

Metal products - fasteners; helicopter rescue hoist & cargo-hook equipment

TRANSWITCH CORPORATION

8 Progress Dr.
Shelton, CT 06484
Phone: 203-929-8810
Fax: 203-926-9453

CEO: Santanu Das
CFO: Michael F. Stauff
HR: Michael McCoy
Employees: 80

1994 Sales: $12.1 million
1-Yr. Sales Change: 0.8%
Exchange: Nasdaq
Symbol: TXCC

Telecommunications equipment - VLSI products & related technology

TRANSWORLD HOME HEALTHCARE, INC.

11 Skyline Dr.
Hawthorne, NY 10532
Phone: 914-345-8880
Fax: 914-345-8935

CEO: Joseph J. Raymond
CFO: Wayne A. Palladino
HR: Tina Zarillo
Employees: 375

1995 Sales: $71.6 million
1-Yr. Sales Change: 80.4%
Exchange: Nasdaq
Symbol: TWHH

Health care - in-home intravenous, respiratory & nursing services

THE TRAVELERS INC.

388 Greenwich St.
New York, NY 10013
Phone: 212-816-8000
Fax: 212-816-8913

CEO: Sanford I. Weill
CFO: Heidi G. Miller
HR: Barry L. Mannes
Employees: 52,000

1994 Sales: $18,464.7 mil.
1-Yr. Sales Change: 171.7%
Exchange: NYSE
Symbol: TRV

Insurance - property & casualty; retail brokerage (Smith Barney Shearson)

See pages 234–235 for a full profile of this company.

TRENWICK GROUP INC.

Metro Ctr., One Station Place
Stamford, CT 06902
Phone: 203-353-5500
Fax: 203-353-5559

CEO: James F. Billett Jr.
CFO: Alan L. Hunte
HR: Joyce Haske
Employees: 73

1994 Sales: $166.4 million
1-Yr. Sales Change: 28.0%
Exchange: Nasdaq
Symbol: TREN

Insurance - reinsurance for property & casualty risks

TRIARC COMPANIES, INC.

900 Third Ave.
New York, NY 10022
Phone: 212-230-3000
Fax: 212-230-3216

CEO: Nelson Peltz
CFO: Joseph A. Levato
HR: —
Employees: 11,250

1994 Sales: $1,062.5 mil.
1-Yr. Sales Change: 0.4%
Exchange: NYSE
Symbol: TRY

Diversified operations - textiles; soft drinks (Royal Crown Cola); restaurants (Arby's); gas distribution

TRIDEX CORPORATION

61 Wilton Rd.
Westport, CT 06880
Phone: 203-226-1144
Fax: 203-226-8806

CEO: Seth M. Lukash
CFO: Richard L. Cote
HR: Thomas F. Curtin Jr.
Employees: 422

1995 Sales: $54.7 million
1-Yr. Sales Change: 62.3%
Exchange: Nasdaq
Symbol: TRDX

Computers - printers, printer mechanisms & data processing terminals

TRIGEN ENERGY CORPORATION

One Water St.
White Plains, NY 10601
Phone: 914-948-9150
Fax: 914-948-9157

CEO: Thomas R. Casten
CFO: David H. Kelly
HR: Bertrand Henderson
Employees: 560

1994 Sales: $182.2 million
1-Yr. Sales Change: 101.1%
Exchange: NYSE
Symbol: TGN

Energy - community energy systems, including heating, cooling & electricity-generating facilities

TRINITECH SYSTEMS, INC.

333 Ludlow St.
Stamford, CT 06902
Phone: 203-425-8000
Fax: 203-425-8100

CEO: Peter K. Hansen
CFO: William E. Alvarez Jr.
HR: —
Employees: 28

1994 Sales: $3.3 million
1-Yr. Sales Change: 57.1%
Exchange: AMEX
Symbol: TSI

Computers - ticketless trading systems & related equipment for the financial industry (Trinitech TouchPad)

TROPIC TEX INTERNATIONAL, INC.

111 Port Jersey Blvd.
Jersey City, NJ 07305
Phone: 201-435-2022
Fax: 201-435-0639

CEO: Marc Setton
CFO: —
HR: —
Employees: 185

1994 Sales: $195 million
1-Yr. Sales Change: 34.5%
Ownership: Privately Held

Women's & children's clothing

TRUMP ORGANIZATION

725 Fifth Ave.
New York, NY 10022-2519
Phone: 212-832-2000
Fax: 212-935-0141

CEO: Donald J. Trump
CFO: Francis X. McCarthy Jr.
HR: —
Employees: 19,000

1994 Est. Sales: $1,450 mil.
1-Yr. Sales Change: -15.8%
Ownership: Privately Held

Diversified operations - hotels (Plaza), casinos (Trump Taj Mahal) & real estate (Trump Tower, Empire State Building)

 See pages 236–237 for a full profile of this company.

THE TRUST COMPANY OF NEW JERSEY

35 Journal Square
Jersey City, NJ 07306
Phone: 201-420-2500
Fax: 201-420-2674

CEO: Siggi B. Wilzig
CFO: Michael A. Marinelli
HR: Robert McCarthy
Employees: 858

1994 Sales: $145.6 million
1-Yr. Sales Change: 1.7%
Exchange: Nasdaq
Symbol: TCNJ

Banks - Northeast (The Trust Company of New Jersey)

TSR, INC.

400 Oser Ave.
Hauppauge, NY 11788
Phone: 516-231-0333
Fax: 516-435-1428

CEO: Joseph F. Hughes
CFO: John G. Sharkey
HR: —
Employees: 139

1995 Sales: $26.7 million
1-Yr. Sales Change: 21.9%
Exchange: Nasdaq
Symbol: TSRI

Computers - programming services & database management

TURBOCHEF, INC.

126 E. 56th St.
New York, NY 10022
Phone: 212-244-5553
Fax: 212-244-6044

CEO: Philip R. McKee
CFO: George W. Minette
HR: —
Employees: 14

1994 Sales: $0.3 million
1-Yr. Sales Change: —
Exchange: Nasdaq (SC)
Symbol: TRBO

Appliances - high-speed commercial ovens (Turbochef)

THE TURNER CORPORATION

375 Hudson St.
New York, NY 10014
Phone: 212-229-6000
Fax: 212-229-6390

CEO: Harold J. Parmelee
CFO: David J. Smith
HR: Richard H. Esau Jr
Employees: 2,499

1994 Sales: $2,639 million
1-Yr. Sales Change: -4.7%
Exchange: AMEX
Symbol: TUR

Construction - heavy

TURTLES & HUGHES, INCORPORATED

1900 Lower Rd.
Linden, NJ 07036
Phone: 908-574-3600
Fax: 908-388-4471

CEO: Suzanne T. Millard
CFO: Trevor Barnett
HR. —
Employees: 300

1994 Sales: $125 million
1-Yr. Sales Change: 9.6%
Ownership: Privately Held

Wholesale - electrical & industrial supplies

TWIN COUNTY GROCERS INC.

145 Talmadge Rd.
Edison, NJ 08817
Phone: 908-287-4600
Fax: 908-287-6027

CEO: Martin Vitale
CFO: George Farley
HR: Joseph Casemento
Employees: 900

1994 Est. Sales: $1,200 mil.
1-Yr. Sales Change: 0.0%
Ownership: Privately Held

Retail - cooperative of supermarkets in New York & New Jersey (over 150 units: Foodtown, D'Agostino)

TWIN LABORATORIES, INC.

2120 Smithtown Ave.
Ronkonkoma, NY 11779
Phone: 516-467-3140
Fax: 516-471-2375

CEO: David Blechman
CFO: Dom Bonanno
HR: Nestor Nazario
Employees: 400

1994 Est. Sales: $100 mil.
1-Yr. Sales Change: —
Ownership: Privately Held

Dietary supplements (Slippery Elm Bark, Oyster Shell Calcium capsules, Devil's Claw)

UCAR INTERNATIONAL INC.

39 Old Ridgebury Rd.
Danbury, CT 06817
Phone: 203-794-2000
Fax: 203-794-3180

CEO: Robert P. Krass
CFO: William P. Wiemels
HR: Malcolm Kessinger
Employees: 4,074

1994 Sales: $758 million
1-Yr. Sales Change: 2.4%
Exchange: NYSE
Symbol: UCR

Electrical connectors - graphite & carbon electrodes for the steel manufacturing industry

UIS, INC.

600 Fifth Ave., 27th Fl.
New York, NY 10020
Phone: 212-581-7660
Fax: 212-581-7517

CEO: Andrew E. Pietrini
CFO: Joseph F. Arrigo
HR: Joseph F. Arrigo
Employees: 8,100

1994 Sales: $830 million
1-Yr. Sales Change: 11.4%
Ownership: Privately Held

Diversified - auto parts; candy (Necco wafers)

ULTRAMAR CORPORATION

2 Pickwick Plaza, Ste. 300
Greenwich, CT 06830
Phone: 203-622-7000
Fax: 203-622-7007

CEO: Jean Gaulin
CFO: H. Pete Smith
HR: Patrick Guarino
Employees: 3,000

1994 Sales: $2,475.4 mil.
1-Yr. Sales Change: 1.5%
Exchange: NYSE
Symbol: ULR

Oil & gas - refining & marketing

UNAPIX ENTERTAINMENT, INC.

550 Fifth Ave.
New York, NY 10110
Phone: 212-575-7070
Fax: 212-575-6869

CEO: David M. Fox
CFO: Steven Low
HR: —
Employees: 38

1994 Sales: $13.2 million
1-Yr. Sales Change: 594.7%
Exchange: AMEX
Symbol: UPX

Motion pictures - licensing of movies, TV programs, home video & educational products

UNET 2 CORPORATION

80 E. 11th St.
New York, NY 10003
Phone: 212-777-5463
Fax: 212-777-5534

CEO: James Monaco
CFO: Harlan Levinson
HR: —
Employees: 15

1994 Sales: $5 million
1-Yr. Sales Change: —
Ownership: Privately Held

Computers - private online network

UNIFLEX INC.

383 W. John St.
Hicksville, NY 11802
Phone: 516-932-2000
Fax: 516-932-3129

CEO: Herbert Barry
CFO: Robert Gugliotta
HR: Robert Gugliotta
Employees: 300

1995 Sales: $30.1 million
1-Yr. Sales Change: 17.1%
Exchange: AMEX
Symbol: UFX

Containers - plastic packaging products

UNIFORCE SERVICES, INC.

1335 Jericho Tnpk.
New Hyde Park, NY 11040
Phone: 516-437-3300
Fax: 516-437-3392

CEO: John Fanning
CFO: Harry V. Maccarrone
HR: —
Employees: 215

1994 Sales: $115.2 million
1-Yr. Sales Change: 33.8%
Exchange: Nasdaq
Symbol: UNFR

Financial - licensor of personnel staffing services companies

UNIGENE LABORATORIES, INC.

110 Little Falls Rd.
Fairfield, NJ 07004-2193
Phone: 201-882-0860
Fax: 201-227-6088

CEO: Warren P. Levy
CFO: Jay Levy
HR: Linda Roloff
Employees: 55

1994 Sales: $0.2 million
1-Yr. Sales Change: -75.0%
Exchange: Nasdaq
Symbol: UGNE

Biomedical & genetic products - amidated peptide hormones to treat osteoporosis

UNIHOLDING CORP.

96 Spring St.
New York, NY 10012
Phone: 212-219-9496
Fax: —

CEO: Edgard Zwirn
CFO: Bruno Adam
HR: —
Employees: 809

1995 Sales: $82.5 million
1-Yr. Sales Change: 28.9%
Exchange: Nasdaq (SC)
Symbol: UHLD

Medical services - clinical laboratory testing in Europe, primarily in hospitals & labs

UNION CAMP CORPORATION

1600 Valley Rd.	CEO: W. Craig McClelland	1994 Sales: $3,395.8 mil.
Wayne, NJ 07470	CFO: James M. Reed	1-Yr. Sales Change: 8.8%
Phone: 201-628-2000	HR: Russell W. Boekenheide	Exchange: NYSE
Fax: 201-628-2722	Employees: 18,894	Symbol: UCC

Paper & paperboard, packaging products & wood products; chemicals, flavors & fragrances

UNION CARBIDE CORPORATION

39 Old Ridgebury Rd.	CEO: William H. Joyce	1994 Sales: $4,865 million
Danbury, CT 06817	CFO: Gilbert E. Playford	1-Yr. Sales Change: 4.8%
Phone: 203-794-2000	HR: Malcolm A. Kessinger	Exchange: NYSE
Fax: 203-794-4336	Employees: 12,004	Symbol: UK

Chemicals - diversified

See pages 238–239 for a full profile of this company.

THE UNION CORPORATION

145 Mason St.	CEO: Melvin L. Cooper	1995 Sales: $97.6 million
Greenwich, CT 06830	CFO: Nicholas P. Gill	1-Yr. Sales Change: 6.0%
Phone: 203-629-0505	HR: Sue Roer	Exchange: NYSE
Fax: 203-629-1046	Employees: 1,315	Symbol: UCO

Financial - accounts-receivable management & debt-collection services

UNITED AUTO GROUP, INC.

375 Park Ave.	CEO: Carl Spielvogel	1994 Sales: $1,200 million
New York, NY 10152	CFO: Arthur Rawl	1-Yr. Sales Change: 84.6%
Phone: 212-223-3300	HR: —	Ownership: Privately Held
Fax: 212-223-5148	Employees: 1,700	

Retail - multifranchise auto dealership

UNITED CAPITAL CORP.

9 Park Place Rd., 4th Fl.	CEO: Attilio F. Petrocelli	1994 Sales: $106.9 million
Great Neck, NY 11021	CFO: Dennis S. Rosatelli	1-Yr. Sales Change: 53.6%
Phone: 516-466-6464	HR: Susan DeThomasis	Exchange: AMEX
Fax: 516-829-4301	Employees: 900	Symbol: AFP

Real estate operations

UNITED COUNTIES BANCORPORATION

4 Commerce Dr.
Cranford, NJ 07016-3564
Phone: 908-931-6600
Fax: 908-709-1583

Banks - Northeast

CEO: Eugene H. Bauer
CFO: Nicholas A. Frungillo Jr.
HR: Paul Laveque
Employees: 606

1994 Sales: $107.9 million
1-Yr. Sales Change: -2.3%
Exchange: Nasdaq (SC)
Symbol: UCTC

UNITED CREDIT CORPORATION

15 W. 44th St.
New York, NY 10036
Phone: 212-843-0808
Fax: 212-843-0817

Financial - asset-based lending & factoring

CEO: Leonard Landis
CFO: Henry Wells
HR: —
Employees: 20

1994 Sales: $215 million
1-Yr. Sales Change: 21.5%
Ownership: Privately Held

THE UNITED ILLUMINATING COMPANY

157 Church St., PO Box 1564
New Haven, CT 06506-0901
Phone: 203-499-2000
Fax: 203-499-5906

Utility - electric power

CEO: Richard J. Grossi
CFO: Robert L. Fiscus
HR: Karen Desiderio
Employees: 1,377

1994 Sales: $656.7 million
1-Yr. Sales Change: 0.6%
Exchange: NYSE
Symbol: UIL

UNITED INDUSTRIAL CORPORATION

18 E. 48th St.
New York, NY 10017
Phone: 212-752-8787
Fax: 212-838-4629

CEO: Bernard Fein
CFO: Thomas J. Carmody
HR: Susan Zawel
Employees: 1,900

1994 Sales: $209.7 million
1-Yr. Sales Change: -17.1%
Exchange: NYSE
Symbol: UIC

Electronics - electronic training & simulations systems; aircraft test & maintenance equipment; combat vehicles; ordnance systems

UNITED JEWISH APPEAL, INC.

99 Park Ave., Ste. 300
New York, NY 10016-1599
Phone: 212-818-9100
Fax: 212-818-9509

Religious & charitable organization

CEO: Joel Tauber
CFO: Leon Cwersky
HR: —
Employees: 200

1994 Sales: $382.4 million
1-Yr. Sales Change: -6.3%
Ownership: Privately Held

UNITED MERCHANTS AND MANUFACTURERS, INC.

1650 Palisade Ave.
Teaneck, NJ 07666
Phone: 201-837-1700
Fax: 201-837-9015

Textile - mill products

CEO: Usi Ruskin
CFO: Judith A. Nadzick
HR: Stanley Siegel
Employees: 2,400

1995 Sales: $59.5 million
1-Yr. Sales Change: -39.5%
Exchange: NYSE
Symbol: UMM

UNITED MOBILE HOMES, INC.

125 Wyckoff Rd.
Eatontown, NJ 07724
Phone: 908-389-3890
Fax: 908-542-1106

Real estate investment trust - manufactured-housing communities

CEO: Samuel A. Landy
CFO: Anna T. Chew
HR: Jean Hering
Employees: 80

1994 Sales: $12.3 million
1-Yr. Sales Change: 7.0%
Exchange: AMEX
Symbol: UMH

UNITED NATIONAL BANCORP

65 Readington Rd.
Branchburg, NJ 08876
Phone: 908-756-5000
Fax: 908-707-4463

Banks - Northeast

CEO: Thomas C. Gregor
CFO: Donald W. Malwitz
HR: Grace K. Barrett
Employees: 464

1994 Sales: $58.2 million
1-Yr. Sales Change: 2.6%
Exchange: Nasdaq
Symbol: UNBJ

UNITED RETAIL GROUP, INC.

365 W. Passaic St.
Rochelle Park, NJ 07662
Phone: 201-845-0880
Fax: 201-909-2162

Retail - women's large-size apparel & accessories

CEO: Raphael Benaroya
CFO: George R. Remeta
HR: Charles R. Wilkerson
Employees: 4,400

1995 Sales: $357.7 million
1-Yr. Sales Change: 4.0%
Exchange: Nasdaq
Symbol: URGI

UNITED STATES SURGICAL CORPORATION

150 Glover Ave.
Norwalk, CT 06856
Phone: 203-845-1000
Fax: 203-845-4478

Medical products - surgical staplers, sutures & clamps

CEO: Leon C. Hirsch
CFO: Howard M. Rosenkrantz
HR: David A. Renker
Employees: 5,922

1994 Sales: $918.7 million
1-Yr. Sales Change: -11.4%
Exchange: NYSE
Symbol: USS

UNITED WASTE SYSTEMS, INC.

4 Greenwich Office Park
Greenwich, CT 06830
Phone: 203-622-3131
Fax: 203-622-6080

CEO: Bradley S. Jacobs
CFO: Michael J. Nolan
HR: Anna Petersen
Employees: 1,507

1994 Sales: $106.6 million
1-Yr. Sales Change: 37.5%
Exchange: Nasdaq
Symbol: UWST

Pollution control equipment & services - trash disposal

 See page 293 for a full profile of this company.

UNITED WATER RESOURCES INC.

200 Old Hook Rd.
Harrington Park, NJ 07640-1799
Phone: 201-784-9434
Fax: 201-767-7142

CEO: Donald L. Correll
CFO: John J. Turner
HR: James Vaeth
Employees: 1,282

1994 Sales: $293 million
1-Yr. Sales Change: 46.2%
Exchange: NYSE
Symbol: UWR

Utility - water supply

UNITED WAY OF NEW YORK CITY

99 Park Ave.
New York, NY 10016
Phone: 212-973-3800
Fax: 212-490-9477

CEO: Ralph Dickerson Jr.
CFO: Guy Benson
HR: Margaret Carter
Employees: 140

1994 Sales: $84.3 million
1-Yr. Sales Change: -3.7%
Ownership: Privately Held

Charitable organization

UNITED-GUARDIAN, INC.

230 Marcus Blvd.
Hauppauge, NY 11787
Phone: 516-273-0900
Fax: 516-273-0858

CEO: Alfred R. Globus
CFO: Kenneth H. Globus
HR: Robert S. Rubinger
Employees: 46

1994 Sales: $6.7 million
1-Yr. Sales Change: -4.3%
Exchange: AMEX
Symbol: UG

Drugs - pharmaceuticals, health care products, medical devices & cosmetic bases; research chemicals,
test solutions, dyes & reagents

UNITEL VIDEO, INC.

510 W. 57th St.
New York, NY 10019
Phone: 212-265-3600
Fax: 212-986-9791

CEO: David Micciulla
CFO: Barry Knepper
HR: —
Employees: 475

1995 Sales: $83.3 million
1-Yr. Sales Change: 3.2%
Exchange: AMEX
Symbol: UNV

Motion pictures & services - studio & mobile production & video editing

UNIVERSAL HOLDING CORP.

Mt. Ebo Corporate Park
Brewster, NY 10509
Phone: 914-278-4094
Fax: 914-278-4283

CEO: Marvin Barasch
CFO: Robert A. Waegelein
HR: Susan Bach
Employees: 250

1994 Sales: $48 million
1-Yr. Sales Change: 70.8%
Exchange: Nasdaq
Symbol: UHCO

Insurance - insurance holding company (American Progressive Life and Health Insurance Company of New York, American Pioneer Life Insurance, WorldNet Services Corp.)

UNIVISION HOLDINGS

603 Third Ave.
New York, NY 10158
Phone: 212-445-5200
Fax: 212-445-5068

CEO: Jaime Davila
CFO: —
HR: Felipa Bernard
Employees: 500

1994 Sales: $271.7 million
1-Yr. Sales Change: 27.0%
Ownership: Privately Held

Broadcasting - Spanish-language TV network

US BRIDGE OF NEW YORK, INC.

5309 97th Place
Corona, NY 11368
Phone: 718-699-0100
Fax: 718-760-5696

CEO: Joseph Polito
CFO: John Bauer
HR: —
Employees: 12

1995 Sales: $6.6 million
1-Yr. Sales Change: -25.8%
Exchange: Nasdaq
Symbol: USBR

Construction - steel erection services for building, roadway & bridge repair contractors

U.S. HOMECARE CORPORATION

141 S. Central Ave.
Hartsdale, NY 10530
Phone: 914-946-9601
Fax: 914-946-1005

CEO: G. Robert O'Brien
CFO: Stephen H. Matheson
HR: Elaine Arbizo
Employees: 4,000

1994 Sales: $79.1 million
1-Yr. Sales Change: -12.2%
Exchange: Nasdaq
Symbol: USHO

Comprehensive home health care services, including nursing care, personal care, infusion therapy & other specialized therapies in New York, New Jersey, Connecticut & Pennsylvania

U.S. INDUSTRIES, INC.

101 Wood Ave. South
Iselin, NJ 08830
Phone: 908-767-0700
Fax: 908-767-2222

CEO: David H. Clarke
CFO: Frank R. Reilly
HR: —
Employees: 23,230

1995 Sales: $2,284 million
1-Yr. Sales Change: -23.7%
Exchange: NYSE
Symbol: USN

Diversified operations - whirlpool baths & spas (Jacuzzi); lighting fixtures; golf clubs (Tommy Armour); cookware (Farberware); automotive components; toys (Ertl); garden tools (Ames); footwear

 See pages 240–241 for a full profile of this company.

US SERVIS, INC.

414 Eagle Rock Ave.	CEO: Graham O. King	1995 Sales: $16 million
West Orange, NJ 07052	CFO: Walter R. Cruickshank	1-Yr. Sales Change: -25.2%
Phone: 201-731-9252	HR: Daniel Beards	Exchange: Nasdaq
Fax: 201-731-9810	Employees: 262	Symbol: USRV

Computers - turnkey software management systems for health care

U.S. TRUST CORPORATION

114 W. 47th St.	CEO: H. Marshall Schwarz	1994 Sales: $457.3 million
New York, NY 10036	CFO: Donald M. Roberts	1-Yr. Sales Change: 2.6%
Phone: 212-852-1000	HR: Patricia W. McGuire	Exchange: Nasdaq
Fax: 212-852-1140	Employees: 2,500	Symbol: USTC

Banks - Northeast (United States Trust Company of New York)

USLIFE CORPORATION

125 Maiden Ln.	CEO: William A. Simpson	1994 Sales: $1,651.1 mil.
New York, NY 10038-4992	CFO: Greer F. Henderson	1-Yr. Sales Change: 3.2%
Phone: 212-709-6000	HR: John G. Kelly	Exchange: NYSE
Fax: 212-425-8006	Employees: 2,100	Symbol: USH

Insurance - life

UST INC.

100 W. Putnam Ave.	CEO: Vincent A. Gierer Jr.	1994 Sales: $1,223 million
Greenwich, CT 06830-5316	CFO: John J. Bucchignano	1-Yr. Sales Change: 10.1%
Phone: 203-661-1100	HR: Richard Kohlberger	Exchange: NYSE
Fax: 203-622-3626	Employees: 3,817	Symbol: UST

Smokeless tobacco (Copenhagen, Skoal); wine (Stimson Lane, Chateau Ste. Michelle, Columbia Crest); home video distribution

UVG, INC.

34 State St.	CEO: Preston Moon	1994 Sales: $28 million
Ossining, NY 10562-4610	CFO: Michael Sommer	1-Yr. Sales Change: 27.3%
Phone: 914-762-5934	HR: Susan Bouachri	Ownership: Privately Held
Fax: 914-762-5961	Employees: 600	

Housewares - wooden-inlay gifts & furniture

V BAND CORPORATION

565 Taxter Rd.	CEO: Thomas E. Feil	1995 Sales: $29.4 million
Elmsford, NY 10523	CFO: Mark R. Hahn	1-Yr. Sales Change: -5.5%
Phone: 914-789-5000	HR: Ray Irizarry	Exchange: Nasdaq
Fax: 914-347-3432	Employees: 288	Symbol: VBAN

Telecommunications equipment - voice trading telephone systems that support common equipment for switching & access to telephone network facilities for financial services firms

VALLEY NATIONAL BANCORP

1445 Valley Rd.	CEO: Gerald H. Lipkin	1994 Sales: $265.4 million
Wayne, NJ 07470	CFO: Alan D. Eskow	1-Yr. Sales Change: 0.5%
Phone: 201-305-8800	HR: Peter Verbout	Exchange: NYSE
Fax: 201-633-0098	Employees: 1,168	Symbol: VLY

Banks - Northeast

VALUE LINE, INC.

220 E. 42nd St.	CEO: Jean B. Buttner	1995 Sales: $79.1 million
New York, NY 10017-5891	CFO: Paul Ehrenstein	1-Yr. Sales Change: -3.7%
Phone: 212-907-1500	HR: Elizabeth Denlea	Exchange: Nasdaq
Fax: 212-818-9747	Employees: 372	Symbol: VALU

Publishing - investment analysis newsletters; investment management

VASOMEDICAL, INC.

180 Linden Ave.	CEO: Anthony Viscusi	1994 Sales: $1.4 million
Westbury, NY 11590	CFO: Joseph A. Giacalone	1-Yr. Sales Change: —
Phone: 516-997-4600	HR: —	Exchange: Nasdaq (SC)
Fax: 516-997-2299	Employees: 12	Symbol: VASO

Medical instruments - noninvasive counterpulsation devices that treat cardiac patients suffering from angina pectoris & acute myocardial & cardiogenic shock

VEECO INSTRUMENTS INC.

Terminal Dr.	CEO: Edward H. Braun	1994 Sales: $49.4 million
Plainview, NY 11803	CFO: John F. Rein Jr.	1-Yr. Sales Change: 14.6%
Phone: 516-349-8300	HR: JoAnne Mancini	Exchange: Nasdaq
Fax: 516-349-9079	Employees: 245	Symbol: VECO

Electronics - precision ion beam etching & surface measurement systems used to make microelectronic products

VERNITRON CORPORATION

645 Madison Ave.
New York, NY 10022
Phone: 212-593-7900
Fax: 212-754-6348

CEO: Stephen W. Bershad
CFO: Raymond Kunzmann
HR: Irene Fabin
Employees: 700

1994 Sales: $62.1 million
1-Yr. Sales Change: -8.3%
Exchange: Nasdaq (SC)
Symbol: VRNT

Precision components, electromagnetic subsystems, specialty AC & DC motors & other equipment

VERONIS SUHLER & ASSOCIATES, INC.

350 Park Ave.
New York, NY 10022
Phone: 212-935-4990
Fax: 212-935-0877

CEO: John S. Suhler
CFO: Martin I. Visconti
HR: —
Employees: 55

1995 Sales: —
1-Yr. Sales Change:
Ownership: Privately Held

Financial - investment bankers to the communications, media, broadcasting, publishing, interactive digital media & information industries

VERTEX INDUSTRIES INC.

23 Carol St., PO Box 996
Clifton, NJ 07014-0996
Phone: 201-777-3500
Fax: 201-472-0814

CEO: James Q. Maloy
CFO: Ronald Byer
HR: Eleanor L. Morris
Employees: 37

1995 Sales: $3.5 million
1-Yr. Sales Change: -19.6%
Exchange: OTC
Symbol: VTXL

Computers - data collection systems, automated card readers, encoders & decoders for credit & debit cards & badges

VERTEX TECHNOLOGIES, INC.

61 Executive Blvd.
Farmingdale, NY 11735
Phone: 516-293-9880
Fax: 516-293-9650

CEO: Donald W. Rowley
CFO: Nicholas T. Hutzel
HR: Elena Ferraro
Employees: 212

1995 Sales: $34.5 million
1-Yr. Sales Change: -19.6%
Exchange: AMEX
Symbol: VTX

Wire & cable products

VIACOM INC.

1515 Broadway
New York, NY 10036
Phone: 212-258-6000
Fax: 212-258-6597

CEO: Frank J. Biondi Jr.
CFO: George S. Smith Jr.
HR: William A. Roskin
Employees: 70,000

1994 Sales: $7,363.2 mil.
1-Yr. Sales Change: 267.2%
Exchange: NYSE
Symbol: VIA

Diversified operations - information & entertainment operations, including broadcasting, film, cable TV, publishing, video rentals (Blockbuster) & theme parks

 See pages 242-243 for a full profile of this company.

VICON INDUSTRIES, INC.

525 Broad Hollow Rd.	CEO: Kenneth M. Darby	1995 Sales: $43.8 million
Melville, NY 11747-0112	CFO: Arthur D. Roche	1-Yr. Sales Change: -8.2%
Phone: 516-293-2200	HR: Marie Rossi	Exchange: AMEX
Fax: 516-293-2627	Employees: 185	Symbol: VII
Video equipment		

VILLAGE BANCORP, INC.

25 Prospect St.	CEO: Robert V. Macklin	1994 Sales: $10.6 million
Ridgefield, CT 06877	CFO: James R. Umbarger	1-Yr. Sales Change: 0.0%
Phone: 203-438-9551	HR: Lisa Campanaro	Exchange: Nasdaq (SC)
Fax: 203-438-4233	Employees: 79	Symbol: VBNK

Banks - Northeast (The Village Bank & Trust Company, Liberty National Bank)

VILLAGE SUPER MARKET, INC.

733 Mountain Ave.	CEO: Perry Sumas	1995 Sales: $677.3 million
Springfield, NJ 07081-3298	CFO: Kevin Begley	1-Yr. Sales Change: -2.6%
Phone: 201-467-2200	HR: Vic D'Anna	Exchange: Nasdaq
Fax: 201-467-6582	Employees: 3,800	Symbol: VLGEA

Retail - supermarkets (ShopRite: 21 units in New Jersey & Pennsylvania)

VIMRX PHARMACEUTICALS INC.

1177 High Ridge Rd.	CEO: M. S. Koly	1994 Sales: $3.2 million
Stamford, CT 06905	CFO: Francis M. O'Connell	1-Yr. Sales Change: 18.5%
Phone: 203-329-0811	HR: Mary Mancuso	Exchange: Nasdaq (SC)
Fax: 203-329-0557	Employees: 5	Symbol: VMRX
Drugs for viral-induced diseases		

VISTA BANCORP, INC.

305 Roseberry St., PO Box 5360	CEO: Barbara Harding	1994 Sales: $28.2 million
Phillipsburg, NJ 08865-5360	CFO: William F. Keefe	1-Yr. Sales Change: 4.8%
Phone: 908-859-9500	HR: Gayle F. Gunderman	Exchange: Nasdaq (SC)
Fax: 908-859-0855	Employees: 33	Symbol: VBNJ
Banks - Northeast		

VITAL SIGNS, INC.

20 Campus Rd.	CEO: Terence D. Wall	1995 Sales: $89.6 million
Totowa, NJ 07512	CFO: Anthony J. Dimun	1-Yr. Sales Change: 5.3%
Phone: 201-790-1330	HR: Elizabeth Greenberg	Exchange: Nasdaq
Fax: 201-790-3307	Employees: 730	Symbol: VITL

Medical products - anesthesia, respiratory & critical-care products

VITT MEDIA INTERNATIONAL, INC.

114 Sixth Ave.	CEO: John Power	1994 Est. Sales: $450 mil.
New York , NY 10036	CFO: Ron Shapiro	1-Yr. Sales Change: -1.7%
Phone: 212-921-0500	HR: Ron Shapiro	Ownership: Privately Held
Fax: 212-455-0519	Employees: 130	

Business services - media planning, buying & syndication

VOLT INFORMATION SCIENCES, INC.

1221 Avenue of the Americas	CEO: William Shaw	1995 Sales: $907.4 million
New York, NY 10020	CFO: James J. Groberg	1-Yr. Sales Change: 23.5%
Phone: 212-704-2400	HR: Norma Kraus	Exchange: Nasdaq
Fax: 212-704-2424	Employees: 23,000	Symbol: VOLT

Personnel - engineering, design, data processing, scientific & technical support personnel; computerized image-setting & publishing equipment & software

VORNADO REALTY TRUST

Park 80 West, Plaza II	CEO: Steven Roth	1994 Sales: $94 million
Saddle Brook, NJ 07663	CFO: Joseph Macnow	1-Yr. Sales Change: 5.9%
Phone: 201-587-1000	HR: —	Exchange: NYSE
Fax: 201 587 0600	Employees: 64	Symbol: VNO

Real estate investment trust - 56 retail shopping centers in 7 states, 8 New Jersey warehouse/industrial properties & one New Jersey office building

THE VOYAGER COMPANY

578 Broadway, Ste. 406	CEO: Robert Stein	1994 Sales: $12 million
New York, NY 10012	CFO: Jonathan B. Turell	1-Yr. Sales Change: 9.1%
Phone: 212-431-5199	HR: —	Ownership: Privately Held
Fax: 212-431-5799	Employees: 100	

Publishing - laserdisc movies (Exotic Japan), CD-ROMs (The Complete Maus, A Hard Day's Night) & interactive books (The Complete Hitchhiker's Guide to the Galaxy, Jurassic Park)

W. GAMBY & COMPANY

1071 Sixth Ave., 3rd Fl.	CEO: Werner Gamby	1994 Sales: $130 million
New York, NY 10018	CFO: Herb Ehrlich	1-Yr. Sales Change: -13.3%
Phone: 212-354-4040	HR: Herb Ehrlich	Ownership: Privately Held
Fax: 212-354-5388	Employees: 40	

Wholesale distribution - snowboarding outerwear (Below Zero)

WACHTELL, LIPTON, ROSEN & KATZ

51 W. 52nd St.	CEO: Herbert Wachtell	1994 Sales: $108 million
New York, NY 10019	CFO: —	1-Yr. Sales Change: 6.9%
Phone: 212-403-1000	HR: Bridin Conaghan	Ownership: Privately Held
Fax: 212-403-2000	Employees: —	

Law firm

WAKEFERN FOOD CORPORATION

600 York St.	CEO: Thomas P. Infusino	1994 Sales: $3,740 million
Elizabeth, NJ 07207	CFO: Dominick V. Romano	1-Yr. Sales Change: 0.0%
Phone: 908-527-3300	HR: Marty Glass	Ownership: Privately Held
Fax: 908-906-5215	Employees: 3,000	

Food - wholesale

THE WARNACO GROUP, INC.

90 Park Ave.	CEO: Linda J. Wachner	1995 Sales: $788.8 million
New York, NY 10016	CFO: William S. Finkelstein	1-Yr. Sales Change: 12.1%
Phone: 212-661-1300	HR: Lissa Law	Exchange: NYSE
Fax: 212-370-0832	Employees: 14,800	Symbol: WAC

Apparel - women's intimate apparel (Warner's, Calvin Klein, Olga, Valentino Intimo) & men's apparel (Chaps by Ralph Lauren, Christian Dior, Hathaway) & accessories (Calvin Klein)

WARNER INSURANCE SERVICES, INC.

17-01 Pollitt Dr.	CEO: Alfred J. Moccia	1994 Sales: $34.8 million
Fair Lawn, NJ 07410	CFO: Bradley J. Hughes	1-Yr. Sales Change: -55.7%
Phone: 201-794-4800	HR: Sue Southgate	Exchange: NYSE
Fax: 201-791-9113	Employees: 432	Symbol: WCP

Business services - insurance advisory services

WARNER-LAMBERT COMPANY

201 Tabor Rd.
Morris Plains, NJ 07950-2693
Phone: 201-540-2000
Fax: 201-540-3761

CEO: Melvin R. Goodes
CFO: Ernest J. Larini
HR: Raymond M. Fino
Employees: 36,000

1994 Sales: $6,416.8 mil.
1-Yr. Sales Change: 10.8%
Exchange: NYSE
Symbol: WLA

Drugs; consumer & health care products; confectionery

 See pages 244–245 for a full profile of this company.

WARRANTECH CORPORATION

300 Atlantic St.
Stamford, CT 06901
Phone: 203-975-1100
Fax: 203-357-0449

CEO: Joel San Antonio
CFO: Bernard White
HR: Kim Caban
Employees: 240

1995 Sales: $70.5 million
1-Yr. Sales Change: 45.1%
Exchange: Nasdaq
Symbol: WTEC

Financial - extended warranty services

WARREN EQUITIES INC.

375 Park Ave., Ste. 2502
New York, NY 10152
Phone: 212-751-8100
Fax: 212-758-1798

CEO: Warren Alpert
CFO: John Dziedzic
HR: Thomas Palumbo
Employees: 1,600

1995 Sales: $701 million
1-Yr. Sales Change: 7.8%
Ownership: Privately Held

Oil refining & marketing; convenience stores; wholesale consumer products

WATCHTOWER BIBLE & TRACT SOCIETY OF NEW YORK INC.

25 Columbia Heights
New York, NY 11201-1300
Phone: 718-625-3600
Fax: 718-625-3066

CEO: Milton G. Henschel
CFO: Lyman A. Swingle
HR: Max Larson
Employees: 1,000

1994 Est. Sales: $680 mil.
1-Yr. Sales Change: —
Ownership: Privately Held

Publishing - religious periodicals (publishing arm of the Jehovah's Witnesses)

WATERHOUSE INVESTOR SERVICES, INC.

100 Wall St.
New York, NY 10005
Phone: 212-806-3500
Fax: 212-809-0274

CEO: Lawrence M. Waterhouse Jr.
CFO: M. Bernard Siegel
HR: Karen Buck
Employees: 756

1995 Sales: $143 million
1-Yr. Sales Change: 32.9%
Exchange: NYSE
Symbol: WHO

Financial - discount securities brokerage

 See page 294 for a full profile of this company.

WATER-JEL TECHNOLOGIES, INC.

243 Veterans Blvd.	CEO: Peter D. Cohen	1995 Sales: $5 million
Carlstadt, NJ 07072	CFO: Alex Alaminos	1-Yr. Sales Change: -10.7%
Phone: 201-507-8300	HR: —	Exchange: Nasdaq (SC)
Fax: 201-507-8325	Employees: 20	Symbol: BURN

Medical - products for first aid treatment of burns (Water-Jel, Burn Jel, UV/OD)

WAVE SYSTEMS CORP.

540 Madison Ave., 38th Fl.	CEO: Peter J. Sprague	1994 Sales: $0
New York, NY 10022	CFO: Thomas R. Dilk	1-Yr. Sales Change: —
Phone: 212-755-3282	HR: Thomas R. Dilk	Exchange: Nasdaq
Fax: 212-755-3436	Employees: 41	Symbol: WAVX

Computers - encryption systems & electronic information metering (WaveMeter)

WEBCRAFT TECHNOLOGIES, INC.

Rte. One & Adams Ave.	CEO: Thomas R. Cochill	1994 Sales: $260 million
North Brunswick, NJ 08902	CFO: Thomas J. Gardner	1-Yr. Sales Change: 5.3%
Phone: 908-297-5100	HR: Jordan Vargas	Ownership: Privately Held
Fax: 908-821-3666	Employees: 1,516	

Printing - commercial

WEDCO TECHNOLOGY, INC.

PO Box 397	CEO: William E. Willoughby	1995 Sales: $43.6 million
Bloomsbury, NJ 08804-0397	CFO: Robert F. Bush	1-Yr. Sales Change: 13.8%
Phone: 908-479-4181	HR: Timothy Kita	Exchange: Nasdaq
Fax: 908-479-4876	Employees: 490	Symbol: WEDC

Machinery - size reduction, custom processing & grinding for the plastics industry

WEIL, GOTSHAL & MANGES

767 Fifth Ave.	CEO: Stephen J. Dannhauser	1994 Sales: $311 million
New York, NY 10153	CFO: John W. Neary	1-Yr. Sales Change: -1.3%
Phone: 212-310-8000	HR: Pat Bowers	Ownership: Privately Held
Fax: 212-310-8007	Employees: —	

Law firm

WELDOTRON CORPORATION

1532 S. Washington Ave.	CEO: William L. Remley	1995 Sales: $19.7 million
Piscataway, NJ 08855	CFO: Varghese Reju	1-Yr. Sales Change: -35.2%
Phone: 908-752-6700	HR: —	Exchange: AMEX
Fax: 908-752-6062	Employees: 188	Symbol: WLD

Packaging machinery & electronic systems for personnel safety & controls for high-speed automatic production machinery

WELLMAN, INC.

1040 Broad St., Ste. 302	CEO: Thomas M. Duff	1994 Sales: $936.1 million
Shrewsbury, NJ 07702	CFO: Keith R. Phillips	1-Yr. Sales Change: 11.2%
Phone: 908-542-7300	HR: Steve Lefevre	Exchange: NYSE
Fax: 908-542-9344	Employees: 3,600	Symbol: WLM

Chemicals - polyethylene terephthalate (PET) products including polyester & nylon fibers & polyester partially oriented yarn; amorphous & solid-state PET resins; materials recovery facilities

WELLSFORD RESIDENTIAL PROPERTY TRUST

610 Fifth Ave., 7th Fl.	CEO: Edward Lowenthal	1994 Sales: $82.8 million
New York, NY 10020	CFO: Gregory F. Hughes	1-Yr. Sales Change: 97.1%
Phone: 212-333-2300	HR: —	Exchange: NYSE
Fax: 212-333-2323	Employees: —	Symbol: WRP

Real estate investment trust - multifamily properties in the Southwest & Pacific Northwest

WENNER MEDIA

1290 Sixth Ave.	CEO: Jann Wenner	1994 Sales: $190.9 million
New York, NY 10104	CFO: John Lagana	1-Yr. Sales Change: 17.9%
Phone: 212-484-1616	HR: Pam Fox	Ownership: Privately Held
Fax: 212-767-8209	Employees: —	

Publishing - periodicals (Rolling Stone, US, Men's Journal, Family Life)

WESTERN BEEF, INC.

47-05 Metropolitan Ave.	CEO: Peter Castellana Jr.	1994 Sales: $291.9 million
Ridgewood, NY 11385	CFO: Robert C. Ludlow	1-Yr. Sales Change: 6.5%
Phone: 718-821-0011	HR: —	Exchange: Nasdaq
Fax: 718-497-4462	Employees: 1,660	Symbol: BEEF

Food - wholesale warehouse grocery chain in the New York City metropolitan area

WESTERN PUBLISHING GROUP, INC.

444 Madison Ave.
New York, NY 10022
Phone: 212-688-4500
Fax: 212-888-5025

Publishing - books

CEO: Richard A. Bernstein
CFO: Steven M. Grossman
HR: Ira A. Gomberg
Employees: 3,800

1995 Sales: $402.6 million
1-Yr. Sales Change: -34.7%
Exchange: Nasdaq
Symbol: WPGI

WESTPORT BANCORP, INC.

87 Post Rd. East
Westport, CT 06880
Phone: 203-222-6911
Fax: 203-222-7404

Banks - Northeast

CEO: Michael H. Flynn
CFO: William B. Laudano Jr.
HR: Richard E. Brown III
Employees: 124

1994 Sales: $21.3 million
1-Yr. Sales Change: 0.9%
Exchange: Nasdaq
Symbol: WBAT

WESTVACO CORPORATION

299 Park Ave.
New York, NY 10171
Phone: 212-688-5000
Fax: 212-318-5050

Paper, building products, chemicals, corrugated boxes, envelopes & other packaging

CEO: John A. Luke Jr.
CFO: George E. Cruser
HR: Jack Furnas
Employees: 14,170

1995 Sales: $3,272.4 mil.
1-Yr. Sales Change: 25.5%
Exchange: NYSE
Symbol: W

WHITE & CASE

1155 Avenue of the Americas
New York, NY 10036
Phone: 212-819-8200
Fax: 212-819-7604

Law firm

CEO: James B. Hurlock
CFO: James Lotchford
HR: Fran Verdele
Employees: —

1994 Sales: $232.5 million
1-Yr. Sales Change: 10.7%
Ownership: Privately Held

WHITE RIVER CORPORATION

777 Westchester Ave., Ste. 201
White Plains, NY 10604-4506
Phone: 914-251-0237
Fax: 914-251-0313

Financial - investments

CEO: Robert T. Marto
CFO: Brian P. Zwarych
HR: Bonnie B. Stewart
Employees: 860

1994 Sales: $62.5 million
1-Yr. Sales Change: 3,372%
Exchange: Nasdaq
Symbol: WHRC

WHITMAN MEDICAL CORP.

485 Bldg. E, US Hwy. One South
Iselin, NJ 08830-3005
Phone: 908-636-3640
Fax: 908-636-2359

CEO: Randy S. Proto
CFO: Joseph Lichtenstein
HR: Bob Sloop
Employees: 479

1995 Sales: $11.8 million
1-Yr. Sales Change: 90.3%
Exchange: AMEX
Symbol: WIX

School - sonography & medical diagnostic ultrasound training (#1 in US: Ultrasound Diagnostic School)

WHITNEY MUSEUM OF AMERICAN ART

945 Madison Ave.
New York, NY 10021
Phone: 212-570-3600
Fax: 212-570-1807

CEO: David A. Ross
CFO: Michael Wolfe
HR: Mary McGoldrick
Employees: 204

1995 Sales: $14.6 million
1-Yr. Sales Change: 9.0%
Ownership: Privately Held

Museum

WHX CORPORATION

110 E. 59th St.
New York, NY 10022
Phone: 212-355-5200
Fax: 212-355-5336

CEO: Ronald LaBow
CFO: Frederick G. Chbosky
HR: Kathy Beerf
Employees: 5,684

1994 Sales: $1,193.9 mil.
1-Yr. Sales Change: 14.1%
Exchange: NYSE
Symbol: WHX

Steel - production

WILDLIFE CONSERVATION SOCIETY

185th St. & Southern Blvd.
New York, NY 10460
Phone: 718-220-5100
Fax: 718-220-2685

CEO: William Conway
CFO: John G. Hoare
HR: Charles Vasser
Employees: 1,200

1995 Sales: $74.3 million
1-Yr. Sales Change: 9.6%
Ownership: Privately Held

Not-for-profit conservation society that runs 5 zoos (Bronx Zoo, Central Park Wildlife Center, Queens Wildlife Center, Prospect Park Wildlife Center, St. Catherines Wildlife Survival Center) & the Aquarium for Wildlife Conservation

WILLIAM GREENBERG JR. DESSERTS & CAFES, INC.

533 W. 47th St.
New York, NY 10036
Phone: 212-586-7600
Fax: 212-586-2418

CEO: Maria M. Marfuggi
CFO: Willa R. Abramson
HR: —
Employees: 48

1994 Sales: $0
1-Yr. Sales Change: —
Exchange: Nasdaq (SC)
Symbol: BAKE

Food - pastries, cakes, pies, cookies & other desserts; wholesale bakery products to restaurants, hotels & corporate dining facilities

WILLIAM H. SADLIER, INC.

9 Pine St.	CEO: William Sadlier Dinger	1994 Sales: $22.2 million
New York, NY 10005-1002	CFO: Henry E. Christel	1-Yr. Sales Change: 11.6%
Phone: 212-227-2120	HR: —	Exchange: Nasdaq (SC)
Fax: 212-267-8696	Employees: 130	Symbol: SADL

Publishing - textbooks & related workbooks, teacher's guides & other supplementary materials

WILLKIE FARR & GALLAGHER

153 E. 53rd St.	CEO: Robert B. Hodes	1994 Sales: $172 million
New York, NY 10022	CFO: —	1-Yr. Sales Change: 4.2%
Phone: 212-821-8000	HR: Ruth McFadden	Ownership: Privately Held
Fax: 212-821-8111	Employees: —	
Law firm		

WILSHIRE OIL COMPANY OF TEXAS

921 Bergen Ave.	CEO: S. Wilzig Izak	1994 Sales: $15.8 million
Jersey City, NJ 07306	CFO: William Goldberg	1-Yr. Sales Change: 5.3%
Phone: 201-420-2796	HR: —	Exchange: NYSE
Fax: 201-420-2804	Employees: 17	Symbol: WOC

Oil & gas - US exploration & production

WILSON, ELSER, MOSKOWITZ, EDELMAN & DICKER

150 E. 42nd St.	CEO: Albert J. Caro	1995 Sales: $110 million
New York, NY 10017	CFO: Hal Stewart	1-Yr. Sales Change: 10.0%
Phone: 212-490-3000	HR: —	Ownership: Privately Held
Fax: 212-490-3038	Employees: 900	

Law firm specializing in insurance, corporate & regulatory services with offices in New York, Baltimore, Chicago, Dallas, Los Angeles, Miami, Philadelphia, San Francisco, Washington, DC, London & Tokyo

WILTEK, INC.

542 Westport Ave.	CEO: David Teitelman	1994 Sales: $4.6 million
Norwalk, CT 06851-4492	CFO: Cindy Elwood	1-Yr. Sales Change: 0.0%
Phone: 203-853-7400	HR: —	Exchange: OTC
Fax: 203-846-3177	Employees: 40	Symbol: WLTK

Telecommunications services - worldwide message & data communications services allowing otherwise incompatible terminals, computers & communications networks to send & receive information

WINSTAR COMMUNICATIONS, INC.

230 Park Ave., 31st Fl.
New York, NY 10169
Phone: 212-687-7577
Fax: 212-687-1565

CEO: William J. Rouhana Jr.
CFO: Fredric E. von Stange
HR: Fredric E. von Stange
Employees: 92

1995 Sales: $25.6 million
1-Yr. Sales Change: 60.0%
Exchange: Nasdaq (SC)
Symbol: WCII

Telecommunications services - long-distance services; wireless network

WINSTON RESOURCES, INC.

535 Fifth Ave.
New York, NY 10017-3663
Phone: 212-557-5000
Fax: 212-972-3364

CEO: Seymour Kugler
CFO: David Frankel
HR: David Silver
Employees: 92

1994 Sales: $24.3 million
1-Yr. Sales Change: 32.8%
Exchange: AMEX
Symbol: WRS

Personnel - recruiting services

WINTHROP, STIMSON, PUTNAM & ROBERTS

One Battery Park Plaza, 31st Fl.
New York, NY 10004
Phone: 212-858-1000
Fax: 212-858-1500

CEO: Arthur H. Fredston
CFO: Carl Culler
HR: —
Employees: 595

1994 Sales: $88 million
1-Yr. Sales Change: -15.0%
Ownership: Privately Held

Law firm

WIRELESS TELECOM GROUP, INC.

E. 49 Midland Ave.
Paramus, NJ 07652
Phone: 201-261-8797
Fax: 201-261-8339

CEO: Karabet "Gary" Simonyan
CFO: Eugene Ferrara
HR: —
Employees: 34

1994 Sales: $8.6 million
1-Yr. Sales Change: 72.0%
Exchange: AMEX
Symbol: WTT

Electronic noise-sources & instruments to test performance & capability of satellite, cellular & personal communications, radio, radar, wireless local area network, digital TV & other communications systems

WITCO CORPORATION

One American Ln.
Greenwich, CT 06831-2559
Phone: 203-552-2000
Fax: 203-552-2870

CEO: William R. Toller
CFO: Michael D. Fullwood
HR: Clark E. Tucker
Employees: 7,955

1994 Sales: $2,234.7 mil.
1-Yr. Sales Change: 3.9%
Exchange: NYSE
Symbol: WIT

Chemicals - specialty chemical & petroleum additives & intermediates

WOOLWORTH CORPORATION

233 Broadway
New York, NY 10279-0003
Phone: 212-553-2000
Fax: 212-553-2042

CEO: Roger N. Farah
CFO: Andrew P. Hines
HR: Patricia A. Peck
Employees: 119,000

1995 Sales: $8,293 million
1-Yr. Sales Change: -13.8%
Exchange: NYSE
Symbol: Z

Retail - discount & variety, athletic footwear

 See pages 246–247 for a full profile of this company.

WORLD COLOR

101 Park Ave.
New York, NY 10178
Phone: 212-986-2440
Fax: 212-455-9266

CEO: Robert G. Burton
CFO: Marc Reisch
HR: Jennifer Adams
Employees: 8,100

1995 Est. Sales: $1,300 mil.
1-Yr. Sales Change: 33.7%
Ownership: Privately Held

Printing - consumer magazines & catalogs

W.P. CAREY & CO.

50 Rockefeller Plaza
New York, NY 10020
Phone: 212-492-1100
Fax: 212-977-3022

CEO: William P. Carey
CFO: Claude Fernando
HR: Sheila Murphy
Employees: 60

1994 Sales: $300 million
1-Yr. Sales Change: 33.3%
Ownership: Privately Held

Investment banking

WR ACQUISITION, INC.

28 W. 23rd St.
New York, NY 10010
Phone: 212-691-2000
Fax: 212-645-8917

CEO: Martin R. Lewis
CFO: Frank Ginolfi
HR: Michael Callahan
Employees: 4,000

1994 Sales: $368.1 million
1-Yr. Sales Change: 25.1%
Ownership: Privately Held

Paper & paper products - envelopes & wedding & other social event announcements
(WilliamhouseRegency)

W. R. BERKLEY CORPORATION

165 Mason St., PO Box 2518
Greenwich, CT 06836-2518
Phone: 203-629-2880
Fax: 203-629-3492

CEO: William R. Berkley
CFO: Anthony J. Del Tufo
HR: Joseph M. Pennachio
Employees: 2,607

1994 Sales: $830.8 million
1-Yr. Sales Change: 42.8%
Exchange: Nasdaq
Symbol: BKLY

Insurance - property & casualty

W.W. NORTON & CO.

500 Fifth Ave.	CEO: W. Drake McFeely	1994 Est. Sales: $500 mil.
New York, NY 10110	CFO: Victor Schmalcer	1-Yr. Sales Change: 0.0%
Phone: 212-354-5500	HR: Lisa Geath	Ownership: Privately Held
Fax: 212-869-0856	Employees: 400	

Publishing - employee-owned publisher of trade, college, professional & medical books

XECHEM INTERNATIONAL, INC.

100 Jersey Ave., Bldg. B, Ste. 310	CEO: Ramesh C. Pandey	1994 Sales: $0
New Brunswick, NJ 08901	CFO: Leonard A. Mudry	1-Yr. Sales Change: —
Phone: 908-247-3300	HR: —	Exchange: Nasdaq (SC)
Fax: 908-247-4090	Employees: 19	Symbol: ZKEM

Biomedical - bio-pharmaceutical production of generic & proprietary drugs from natural sources, primarily anticancer compound (Taxol)

XEROX CORPORATION

800 Long Ridge Rd., PO Box 1600	CEO: Paul A. Allaire	1994 Sales: $17,837 million
Stamford, CT 06904	CFO: Barry D. Romeril	1-Yr. Sales Change: 22.2%
Phone: 203-968-3000	HR: Anne M. Mulcahy	Exchange: NYSE
Fax: 203-968-4312	Employees: 87,600	Symbol: XRX

Office equipment & supplies - business machines; insurance

 See pages 248–249 for a full profile of this company.

XPEDITE SYSTEMS, INC.

446 State Hwy. 35	CEO: Roy B. Andersen Jr.	1994 Sales: $41.4 million
Eatontown, NJ 07724	CFO: Stuart S. Levy	1-Yr. Sales Change: 42.3%
Phone: 908-389-3900	HR: Jayne Droge	Exchange: Nasdaq
Fax: 908-389-8823	Employees: 247	Symbol: XPED

Telecommunications services - electronic document (fax) distribution service; Windows software to access service

 See page 295 for a full profile of this company.

YALE UNIVERSITY

451 College St.	CEO: Richard C. Levin	1994 Sales: $1,576.2 mil.
New Haven, CT 06520	CFO: Joseph Mullinix	1-Yr. Sales Change: 7.1%
Phone: 203-432-4771	HR: Peter Vallone	Ownership: Privately Held
Fax: 203-432-7891	Employees: 10,000	

Private university offering 60 undergraduate degree programs & 61 graduate degree programs

YANKEE ENERGY SYSTEM, INC.

599 Research Pkwy.
Meriden, CT 06450-1030
Phone: 203-639-4000
Fax: 203-639-4143
Utility - gas distribution

CEO: Bronco Terzic
CFO: Michael E. Bielonko
HR: Doris Rosado
Employees: 670

1995 Sales: $294 million
1-Yr. Sales Change: -7.3%
Exchange: NYSE
Symbol: YES

YAR COMMUNICATIONS, INC.

220 Fifth Ave.
New York, NY 10001
Phone: 212-447-4000
Fax: 212-447-4020
Multicultural advertising & marketing

CEO: Yuri Radzievsky
CFO: —
HR: —
Employees: 120

1994 Sales: $120 million
1-Yr. Sales Change: 4.3%
Ownership: Privately Held

YORK RESEARCH CORPORATION

280 Park Ave., Ste. 2700 West
New York, NY 10017
Phone: 212-557-6200
Fax: 212-557-5678

CEO: Robert M. Beningson
CFO: Michael Trachtenberg
HR: —
Employees: 31

1995 Sales: $7.5 million
1-Yr. Sales Change: 15.4%
Exchange: Nasdaq
Symbol: YORK

Energy - cogeneration development, electric power brokering & marketing & alternative energy

YOUNG & RUBICAM INC.

285 Madison Ave.
New York, NY 10017-6486
Phone: 212-210-3000
Fax: 212-370-3796
Advertising & communications

CEO: Peter A. Georgescu
CFO: Dave Greene
HR: Raquel Suarez
Employees: 9,932

1994 Sales: $1,060 million
1-Yr. Sales Change: 5.1%
Ownership: Privately Held

YOUNG BROADCASTING INC.

599 Lexington Ave.
New York, NY 10022
Phone: 212-754-7070
Fax: 212-758-1229
Broadcasting - network-affiliated TV stations

CEO: Vincent J. Young
CFO: James A. Morgan
HR: Alfred A. Porzio
Employees: 820

1994 Sales: $78.8 million
1-Yr. Sales Change: 27.5%
Exchange: Nasdaq
Symbol: YBTVA

THE YOUNG WOMEN'S CHRISTIAN ASSOCIATION OF THE UNITED STATES OF AMERICA

726 Broadway, 5th Fl.
New York, NY 10003
Phone: 212-614-2700
Fax: 212-614-2703

CEO: Prema Mathai-Davis
CFO: Kathryn A. Dessonville
HR: —
Employees: 75

1995 Sales: $12.3 million
1-Yr. Sales Change: 0.0%
Ownership: Privately Held

Women's not-for-profit membership organization with more than 350 member associations offering transitional housing, child care, counseling & educational services

ZIFF-DAVIS PUBLISHING COMPANY

One Park Ave.
New York, NY 10016-5801
Phone: 212-503-3500
Fax: 212-503-4599

CEO: Eric Hippeau
CFO: Bruce Barnes
HR: Fred Staudmyer
Employees: 3,300

1994 Est. Sales: $852 mil.
1-Yr. Sales Change: 18.7%
Ownership: Subsidiary

Publishing - computer magazine publisher (#1 in US: PC Magazine, PC Week, Computer Shopper); TV programming; online services (ZiffNet) & CD-ROMs (subsidiary of Softbank)

ZING TECHNOLOGIES, INC.

115 Stevens Ave.
Valhalla, NY 10595
Phone: 914-747-7474
Fax: 914-747-2316

CEO: Robert E. Schrader
CFO: Martin S. Fawer
HR: Michelle Mastrapolo
Employees: 198

1995 Sales: $22.6 million
1-Yr. Sales Change: 96.5%
Exchange: Nasdaq
Symbol: ZING

Electronics - parts distribution

ZURICH REINSURANCE CENTRE HOLDINGS, INC.

One Chase Manhattan Plaza, 43rd Fl.
New York, NY 10005
Phone: 212-898-5000
Fax: 212-898-5005

CEO: Steven M. Gluckstern
CFO: Peter R. Porrino
HR: Mary Rauscher
Employees: 184

1994 Sales: $243.2 million
1-Yr. Sales Change: 76.4%
Exchange: NYSE
Symbol: ZRC

Insurance - property & casualty underwriting

ZYGO CORPORATION

Laurel Brook Rd.
Middlefield, CT 06455
Phone: 860-347-8506
Fax: 860-347-8372

CEO: Gary K. Willis
CFO: Mark J. Bonney
HR: Andrea Media
Employees: 210

1995 Sales: $32.2 million
1-Yr. Sales Change: 33.6%
Exchange: Nasdaq
Symbol: ZIGO

Electronics - electro-optical products that use light to make precise but noncontact measurements for laser fusion research, semiconductor manufacturing equipment & aerospace optical systems

The Indexes

CONNECTICUT

A

Ansonia
Birmingham Utilities, Inc.
329
Farrel Corporation 390

B

Bethel
Duracell International Inc.
377
Branford
Branford Savings Bank
334
Echlin Inc. **108–109**, 379
Neurogen Corporation 478
Bridgeport
Aquarion Company 315
Bridgeport Machines, Inc.
334
Connecticut Energy
Corporation 357
Lafayette American Bank
and Trust Company 443
People's Bank 498
Remington Products, Inc.
517
Brookfield
Photronics, Inc. 502

C

Clinton
Connecticut Water Service,
Inc. 358

D

Danbury
Advanced Technology
Materials, Inc. 300
Cognitronics Corporation
352
Energy Research
Corporation 383
Ethan Allen Interiors Inc.
386
First Brands Corporation
392
Nutmeg Federal Savings
and Loan Association 487
Praxair, Inc. **204–205**, 507
Prestone Products
Company 507
UCAR International Inc.
552
Union Carbide Corporation
238–239, 554

Darien
Air Express International
Corporation 302
Hometown
Bancorporation, Inc. 418
Derby
DS Bancor, Inc. 377

F

Fairfield
Acme United Corporation
299
General Electric Company
116–117, 400

G

Georgetown
Cannondale Corporation
260, 340
Greenwich
Blyth Industries, Inc. 331
Coca-Cola Bottling Co. of
351
Dynamics Corporation of
America 378
Helm Resources, Inc. 414
HRE Properties 419
Interlaken Investment
Partners L.P. 427
Lexmark International
Group, Inc. 448
Lynch Corporation 451
NAC Re Corp. 473
NFO Research, Inc. 483
Osborn Communications
Corporation 491
PanAmSat Corporation
494
Renaissance
Communications Corp.
517
Ultramar Corporation 552
The Union Corporation
554
United Waste Systems, Inc.
293, 557
UST Inc. 559
Witco Corporation 571
W. R. Berkley Corporation
572

M

Madison
Magellan Petroleum
Corporation 453
Meriden
Yankee Energy System,
Inc. 574

Middlefield
Zygo Corporation 575
Middletown
Farmers & Mechanics Bank
389
Milford
BIC Corporation 328
EXECUTONE Information
Systems, Inc. 388
Subway Sandwich Shops,
Inc. 537

N

New Canaan
Avalon Properties, Inc. 320
Centennial Cellular Corp.
261, 345
Century Communications
Corp. 346
Smith Corona Corporation
532
New Haven
Aristotle Corporation 316
BNH Bancshares, Inc. 332
Norland Medical Systems,
Inc. 485
OncoRx, Inc. 490
Southern New England
Telecommunications 533
Starter Corporation 535
The United Illuminating
Company 555
Yale University 573
North Haven
Avitar, Inc. 321
Norwalk
Alcide Corporation 303
The Caldor Corporation
72–73, 339
EMCOR Group, Inc. 382
Micro Warehouse, Inc.
278, 466
Norwalk Savings Society
486
Olin Corporation 489
Oxford Health Plans, Inc.
287, 492
Perkin-Elmer Corporation
499
Trans-Lux Corporation
547
United States Surgical
Corporation 556
Wiltek, Inc. 570

INTRODUCING HOOVER'S COMPANY PROFILES ON DEMAND

A new fax delivery service that puts detailed company profiles from the

Hoover's Company Database at your fingertips

WHY WAIT? Get invaluable information immediately on more than 1,000 public and private companies.

The information is arranged in the same easy-to-use format as the company profiles found in *Hoover's Handbooks* and includes company overviews and histories, up to 10 years of key financial and employment data, lists of products and key competitors, names of key officers, addresses, and phone and fax numbers.

IT'S SIMPLE.

1. Choose any number of companies from the index on the following pages.

2. Then call **415-598-4335**, 24 hours a day, 7 days a week, to receive a detailed profile for only $2.95* for each company you choose. Have your fax number and the five-digit company code number ready.

3. A voice-automated system will guide you through your order, and you'll receive your company profiles via fax within minutes.

*American Express, MasterCard, and Visa accepted.

Company	Code	Company	Code	Company	Code
3Com Corporation	12475	Benetton Group S.p.A.	41756	CS Holding	40794
AAON, Inc.	16562	Benson Eyecare Corporation	11905	Daewoo Group	40802
AB Volvo	41854	Bertelsmann AG	40661	The Dai-Ichi Kangyo Bank, Limited	41864
ABB Asea Brown Boveri Ltd	40615	BET Holdings, Inc.	10916	The Daiei, Inc.	50022
Acclaim Entertainment, Inc.	10544	Biogen, Inc.	12776	Daimler-Benz Aktiengesellschaft	41231
Accor SA	40552	The BISYS Group, Inc.	14874	DAKA International, Inc.	13165
Acordia, Inc.	12336	Bloomberg L.P.	40671	Del Webb Corporation	10445
ACT Manufacturing, Inc.	43463	The Body Shop International PLC	41856	Dentsu Inc.	40829
Active Voice Corporation	16684	Bombardier Inc.	42381	Deutsche Bank AG	40833
Adaptec, Inc.	12515	Books-A-Million, Inc.	14665	Deutsche Lufthansa AG	41803
Adobe Systems Incorporated	12518	The Boots Company PLC	42397	Dial-A-Mattress Franchise Corporation	42092
ADTRAN, Inc.	40558	The Boston Beer Company, Inc.	40674	Dialogic Corporation	42073
Advance Ross Corporation	12522	Boston Chicken, Inc.	16244	Digi International Inc.	14110
Advanta Corp.	12489	Boston Technology, Inc.	14031	DOVatron International Inc.	11577
Airbus Industrie	40566	Breed Technologies, Inc.	11296	Dreyer's Grand Ice Cream, Inc.	13233
Akzo Nobel N.V.	41855	Bridgestone Corporation	41861	DSC Communications Corporation	13159
Alcan Aluminum Limited	42408	Brinker International, Inc.	10330	EIS International, Inc.	15796
Alcatel Alsthom Compagnie		Brite Voice Systems, Inc.	12584	Aktiebolaget Electrolux	41778
Generale d'Electricite	41751	British Aerospace Public Limited Company	40681	Electronics for Imaging, Inc.	15872
All Nippon Airways Co., Ltd.	41752	British Airways PLC	41761	Elf Aquitaine	41775
Alliance Semiconductor Corporation	16807	The British Petroleum Company PLC	41759	Ente Nazionale Idrocarburi S.p.A.	40875
Allianz AG Holding	40572	British Telecommunications PLC	41763	Evergreen Marine Corporation, Ltd.	42001
Allied Domecq PLC	50001	The Broken Hill Proprietary Company Limited	41757	Express Scripts, Inc.	15773
Altera Corporation	12568	BTR PLC	42398	Fair, Isaac and Company, Incorporated	13357
Alternative Resources Corporation	20015	Buffets, Inc.	12815	Ferolito, Vultaggio & Sons	42106
America Online, Inc.	15558	Cable and Wireless Public Limited Company	41766	Fiat S.p.A.	41777
American Business Information, Inc.	15513	Cabletron Systems, Inc.	10276	First Alert, Inc.	17196
American Classic Voyages Co.	15544	Cadbury Schweppes PLC	41767	First USA, Inc.	15687
American Freightways Corporation	12657	Callaway Golf Company	15521	Fletcher Challenge Limited	42413
American HomePatient, Inc.	13121	Cambridge Technology Partners, Inc.	13621	FORE Systems, Inc.	42045
American Homestar Corporation	20161	Cameron Ashley Inc.	17198	Formosa Plastics Corporation	40934
American Medical Response, Inc.	15818	Canadian Imperial Bank of Commerce	40707	Forschner Group, Inc.	13503
American Medical Security Group, Inc.	40587	Canadian Pacific Limited	41851	Fossil, Inc.	16093
American Power Conversion Corporation	12609	Canal +	41802	Foster's Brewing Group Ltd.	42414
American United Global, Inc.	15518	Canandaigua Wine Company, Inc.	11800	Fried. Krupp AG Hoesch-Krupp	41144
AmeriData Technologies, Inc.	16433	Canon Inc.	41862	FTP Software, Inc.	16553
Anglo American Corporation of		Carlsberg A/S	40715	Fuji Photo Film Co., Ltd.	41760
South Africa Limited	41809	Carmike Cinemas, Inc.	12900	Fujitsu Limited	41865
Apple South, Inc.	15463	Carrefour SA	40719	The General Electric Company P.L.C.	41750
Applebee's International, Inc.	13585	Cascade Communications Corp.	42090	General Nutrition Companies, Inc.	15942
Arctco, Inc.	13346	Casio Computer Co., Ltd.	41863	George Weston Limited	41280
Argosy Gaming Company	14601	Catalina Marketing Corporation	15571	Glaxo Wellcome PLC	41781
Ascend Communications, Inc.	41997	CDW Computer Centers, Inc.	16199	Glenayre Technologies, Inc.	14179
Aspect Telecommunications Corporation	14113	CellStar Corporation	41895	Global Village Communication, Inc.	16980
Atmel Corporation	14420	Checkpoint Systems, Inc.	12955	The Good Guys, Inc.	14910
Authentic Fitness Corporation	15727	The Cheesecake Factory Incorporated	15835	Grand Casinos, Inc.	15382
Avid Technology, Inc.	15999	Cheyenne Software, Inc.	12967	Grand Metropolitan PLC	41782
Baby Superstore, Inc.	42110	Chiron Corporation	12972	Green Tree Financial Corporation	10679
Banco Espirito Santo e Comercial		Ciba-Geigy Limited	41771	Groupe Danone	41774
de Lisboa, S.A.	42907	CIDCO Incorporated	17123	Guinness PLC	41783
Bank of Montreal	42380	Cifra, S.A. de C.V.	42411	The Gymboree Corporation	16057
Barclays PLC	41754	Cirrus Logic, Inc.	12986	HA-LO Industries, Inc.	10660
Barefoot Inc.	15449	Clear Channel Communications, Inc.	11824	Hanson PLC	41784
BASF Group	41755	Club Mediterranee S.A.	42391	Havas S.A.	42387
Bass PLC	41788	Cognex Corporation	13017	Healthsource, Inc.	13876
B.A.T. Industries	41762	Coles Myer Ltd.	42412	Healthwise of America, Inc.	16990
Bayer AG	41808	CommNet Cellular Inc.	15401	Heartland Express, Inc.	13665
Bayerische Motoren Werke AG	41758	CONMED Corporation	12850	Heilig-Meyers Co.	10717
BCE, Inc.	43059	The Continuum Company, Inc.	11847	Heineken N.V.	41852
Beazer Homes USA, Inc.	16951	Cornerstone Imaging, Inc.	16506	Henkel KGaA	41028
Bed Bath & Beyond, Inc.	14933	Cracker Barrel Old Country Store, Inc.	13128	Herbalife International, Inc.	15594
Bell Microproducts Inc.	16410	Credit Acceptance Corporation	15713	HFS Inc.	10003
Benchmark Electronics, Inc.	13094	Credit Lyonnais	40792	Hirsch International Corporation	16992

CALL TODAY FOR A FREE CATALOG FEATURING OVER 140 BUSINESS SOURCES